HAMMOND

Ambassador
World Atlas

Happy Birthday Guy. 2003.
"all of my Best Wishes.
and all my Love"
Mom.

HAMMOND World Atlas
Part of the Langenscheidt Publishing Group

Hammond Publications Advisory Board

ENTIRE CONTENTS © COPYRIGHT 2000
BY HAMMOND WORLD ATLAS CORPORATION

PRINTED IN THE UNITED STATES OF AMERICA

Library of Congress Cataloging-in-Publication Data
Hammond World Atlas Corporation.
    Citation world atlas. -- Rev.
        p.   cm.
    At head of title: Hammond
    Includes indexes.
    ISBN 0-8437-1295-3 (softcover)
    ISBN 0-8437-1382-8 (hardcover)
    1. Atlases. I. Title. II. Title: Hammond citiation world atlas.
G1021. H2446   1998   <G&M>
912--DC21   98-12358
                                                    CIP
                                                    MAP

HAMMOND

Ambassador World Atlas

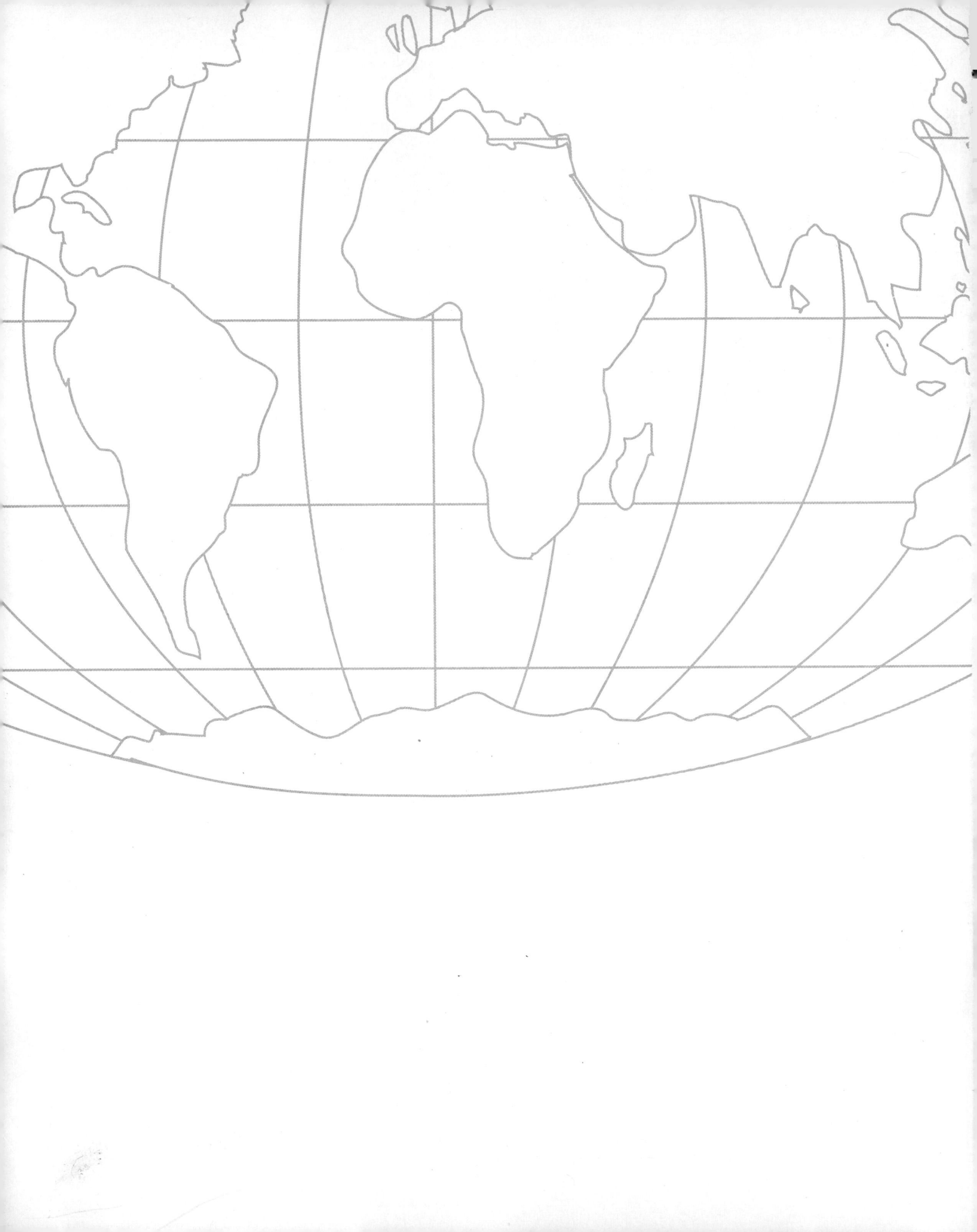

Contents

Part I—Terrain Maps of Land Forms and Ocean Floors

Part II—Modern Maps and Indexes

WORLD and POLAR REGIONS

EUROPE

ASIA

PACIFIC OCEAN and AUSTRALIA

AFRICA

SOUTH AMERICA

NORTH AMERICA

CANADA

UNITED STATES

METROPOLITAN AREAS

WORLD TABLES

Introduction

This unique Hammond World Atlas is organized to make the retrieval of information as pleasant and quick as possible. Our guiding principle is to present individual subjects on separate maps. In this manner, each map topic is shown with the greatest degree of clarity, unencumbered by extraneous information. Equally important is the use of separate atlas units to present all information on a given country or state. Thus, the basic reference map of an area is accompanied on adjacent pages by all supplementary information relating to that area. For example, the detailed index for any map always appears on the same page as, or on the pages immediately following, the reference map. This index provides population data for many cities, towns, and villages shown on the map. Pertinent statistics on the area, i.e. the total population and area, the capital, and the highest point, are found in the summary fact listing accompanying each unit. An adjacent locator map relates the subject area to the larger world, and a "three-dimensional" picture of the area is provided by a full-color topographic map. A separate economic map defines vital agricultural, industrial, and mineral resources. The flag of each independent nation or state also appears on the appropriate page. Finally, certain country units contain special subject maps dealing with the history, climate, demography, and vegetation of the area.

Another section features The Physical World - an outstanding series of terrain maps of land forms and ocean floors. These physical maps were originally produced as sculptured terrain models, thus simulating the earth's surface in a highly realistic manner. The three-dimensional effect is both informative and pleasing to the eye.

Of course, the maps have been thoroughly updated. These revisions reflect the new nations, and shifting international boundaries, and internal divisions of many countries. Even new communities generated by the tapping of resources in developing nations are recorded. Thorough research and worldwide contacts provide the most up-to-date geographical and demographic information available.

Uniquely designed, comprehensive, and easy-to-use, this World Atlas is the ideal reference for families, executives, students, travelers, or anyone who wants to be geographically informed about today's fast-changing world. Enjoy the adventure as you explore the pages of one of the world's finest atlases.

The Publisher

Introduction to the Maps and Indexes

The following notes have been added to aid the reader in making the best use of this atlas. Though the reader may be familiar with maps and map indexes, the publisher believes that a quick review of the material below will add to his enjoyment of this reference work.

Arrangement—*The Plan of the Atlas.* The atlas has been designed with maximum convenience for the user as its objective. Part I of the atlas is devoted to the physical world—terrain maps of land forms and the sea floor. Part II contains the general political reference maps, area by area. All geographically related information pertaining to a country or region appears on adjacent pages, eliminating the task of searching throughout the entire volume for data on a given area. Thus, the reader will find, conveniently assembled, political, topographic, economic and special maps of a political area or region, accompanied by detailed map indexes, statistical data, and illustrations of the national flags of the area.

The sequence of country units in this American-designed atlas is international in arrangement. Units on the world as a whole are followed by a section on the polar regions which, in turn, is followed by pages devoted to Europe and its countries. Every continent map is accompanied by special population distribution, climatic and vegetation maps of that continent. Following the maps of the European continent and its countries, the geographic sequence plan proceeds as follows: Asia, the Pacific and Australia, Africa, South America, North America, and ends with detailed coverage on the United States.

Political Maps—*The Primary Reference Tool.* The most detailed maps in each country unit are the *political maps.* It is our feeling that the reader is likely to refer to these maps more often than to any other in the book when confronted by such questions as—Where? How big? What is it near? Answering these common queries is the function of the political maps. Each political map stresses *political* phenomena—countries, internal political divisions, boundaries, cities and towns. The major political unit or units, shown on the map, are banded in distinctive colors for easy identification and delineation. First-order political subdivisions (states, provinces, counties on the state maps) are shown, scale permitting.

The reader is advised to make use of the *legend* appearing under the title on each political map. Map *symbols,* the special "language" of maps, are explained in the legend. Each variety of dot, circle, star or interrupted line has a special meaning which should be clearly understood by the user so that he may interpret the map data correctly.

Each country has been portrayed at a *scale* commensurate with its political, areal, economic or tourist importance. In certain cases, a whole map unit may be devoted to a single nation if that nation is considered to be of prime interest to most atlas users. In other cases, several nations will be shown on a single map if, as separate entities, they are of lesser relative importance. Areas of dense settlement and important significance within a country have been enlarged and portrayed in inset maps inserted on the margins of the main map. The scale of each map is indicated as a fractional representation (1:1,000,000). The reader is advised to refer to the linear or "bar" scale appearing on each map or map inset in order to determine the distance between points.

The *projection* system used for each map is noted near the title of the map. Map projections are the special graphic systems used by cartographers to render the curved three-dimensional surface of the globe on a flat surface. Optimum map projections determined by the attributes of the area have been used by the publishers for each map in the atlas.

A word here as to the choice of place names on the maps. Throughout the atlas names appear, with a few exceptions, in their local official spellings. However, conventional Anglicized spellings are used for major geographical divisions and for towns and topographic features for which English forms exist; i.e., "Spain" instead of "España" or "Munich" instead of "München." Names of this type are normally followed by the local official spelling in parentheses. As an aid to the user the indexes are cross-referenced for all current and most former spellings of such names.

Names of cities and towns in the United States follow the forms listed in the *Post Office Directory* of the United States Postal Service. Domestic physical names follow the decisions of the Board on Geographic Names, U.S. Department of the Interior, and of various state geographic name boards. It is the belief of the publishers that the boundaries shown in a general reference atlas should reflect current geographic and political realities. This policy has been followed consistently in the atlas. The presentation of *de facto* boundaries in cases of territorial dispute between various nations does not imply the political endorsement of such boundaries by the publisher, but simply the honest representation of boundaries as they exist at the time of the printing of the atlas maps.

Indexes—*Pinpointing a Location.* Each political map is accompanied by a comprehensive index of the place names appearing on the map. If you are unfamiliar with the location of a particular geographical place and wish to find its position within the confines of the subject area of the map, consult the map index as your first step. The name of the feature sought will be found in its proper alphabetical sequence with a key reference letter-number combination corresponding to its location on the map. After noting the key reference letter-number combination for the place name, turn to the map. The place name will be found within the square formed by the two lines of latitude and the two lines of longitude which enclose the coordinates—i.e., the marginal letters and numbers. The diagram below illustrates the system of indexing.

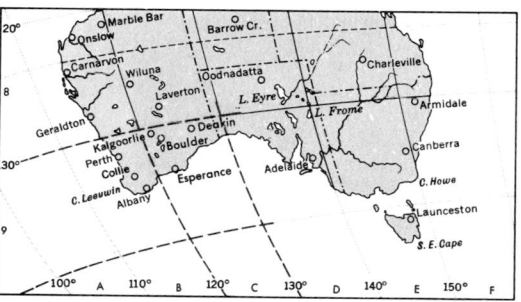

In the case of maps consisting entirely of insets, the place name is found near the intersection point of the imaginary lines connecting the coordinates at right angles. See below.

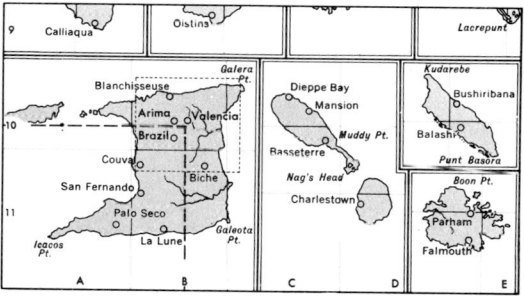

Where space on the map has not permitted giving the complete form of the place name, the complete form is shown in the index. Where a place is known by more than one name or by various spellings of the same name, the different forms have been included in the index. Physical features are listed under their proper names and not according to their generic terms; that is to say, Rio Negro will be found under Negro and not under Rio Negro. On the other hand, Rio Grande will be found under Rio Grande. Accompanying most index entries for cities and towns, and for other political units, are *population figures* for the particular entries. The large number of population figures in the atlas makes this work one of the most comprehensive statistical sources available to the public today. The population figures have been taken from the latest official censuses and estimates of the various nations.

Population and area figures for countries and major political units are listed in bold type *fact lists* on the margins of the index. In addition, the capital, largest city, highest point, monetary unit, principal languages and the prevailing religions of the country concerned are also listed. The Gazetteer-Index of the World on the following pages provides a quick reference index for countries and other important areas. Though population and area figures for each major unit are also found in the map section, the Gazetteer-Index provides a conveniently arranged statistical comparison contained in five pages.

Relief Maps. Accompanying each political map is a relief map of the area. The purpose of the relief map is to illustrate the surface configuration (TOPOGRAPHY) of the region. A shading technique in color simulates the relative ruggedness of the terrain — plains, plateaus, valleys, hills and mountains. Graded colors, ranging from greens for lowlands, yellows for intermediate elevations to brown in the highlands, indicate the height above sea level of each part of the land. A vertical scale at the margin of the map shows the approximate height in meters and feet represented by each color.

Economic Maps—*Agriculture, Industry and Resources.* One of the most interesting features that will be found in each country unit is the economic map. From this map one can determine the basic activities of a nation as expressed through its economy. A perusal of the map yields a full understanding of the area's economic geography and natural resources.

The agricultural economy is manifested in two ways: color bands and commodity names. The color bands express broad categories of dominant land use, such as cereal belts, forest lands, livestock range lands or nonagricultural wastes. The red commodity names, on the other hand, pinpoint the areas of production of *specific* crops, i.e., wheat, cotton, sugar beets, etc.

Major mineral occurrences are denoted by standard letter symbols appearing in blue. The relative size of the letter symbols signifies the relative importance of the deposit.

The manufacturing sector of the economy is presented by means of diagonal line patterns expressing the various *industrial* areas of consequence within a country.

The fishing industry is represented by names of commercial fish species appearing offshore in blue letters. Major waterpower sites are designated by blue symbols.

The publishers have tried to make this work the most comprehensive and useful atlas available, and it is hoped that it will prove a valuable reference work. Any constructive suggestions from the reader will be welcomed.

Sources and Acknowledgements

A multitude of sources goes into the making of a large-scale reference work such as this. To list them all would take many pages and would consume space better devoted to the maps and reference materials themselves. However, certain general sources were very useful in preparing this work and are listed below.

STATISTICAL OFFICE OF THE UNITED NATIONS.
Demographic Yearbook. New York. Issued annually.

STATISTICAL OFFICE OF THE UNITED NATIONS.
Statistical Yearbook. New York. Issued annually.

THE GEOGRAPHER, U.S. DEPARTMENT OF STATE.
International Boundary Study papers. Washington. Various dates.

THE GEOGRAPHER, U.S. DEPARTMENT OF STATE.
Geographic Notes. Washington. Various dates.

UNITED STATES BOARD ON GEOGRAPHIC NAMES.
Decisions on Geographic Names in the United States. Washington. Various dates.

UNITED STATES BOARD ON GEOGRAPHIC NAMES.
Official Standard Names Gazetteers. Washington. Various dates.

CANADIAN PERMANENT COMMITTEE ON GEOGRAPHICAL NAMES.
Gazetteer of Canada series. Ottawa. Various dates.

UNITED STATES POSTAL SERVICE.
National Five Digit ZIP Code and Post Office Directory. Washington. Issued annually.

UNITED STATES POSTAL SERVICE.
Postal Bulletin. Washington. Issued weekly.

UNITED STATES DEPARTMENT OF THE INTERIOR, BUREAU OF MINES.
Minerals Yearbook. 4 vols. Washington. Various dates.

UNITED STATES GEOLOGICAL SURVEY.
Elevations and distances in the United States. Reston, Va. 1990.

CARTACTUAL.
Cartactual — Topical Map Service. Budapest. Issues bi-monthly.

AMERICAN GEOGRAPHICAL SOCIETY.
Focus. New York. Issued ten times a year.

THE AMERICAN UNIVERSITY.
Foreign Area Studies. Washington. Various dates.

CENTRAL INTELLIGENCE AGENCY.
General reference maps. Washington. Various dates.

A sample list of sources used for specific countries follows:

Afghanistan
CENTRAL STATISTICS OFFICE.
Preliminary Results of the First Afghan Population Census 1979. Kabul.

Albania
DREJTORIA E STATISTIKES.
1979 Census. Tiranë.

Argentina
INSTITUTO NACIONAL DE ESTADISTICA Y CENSOS.
Censo Nacional de Población y Vivienda 1980. Buenos Aires.

Australia
AUSTRALIAN BUREAU OF STATISTICS.
Census of Population and Housing 1986. Canberra.

Brazil
FUNDACAO INSTITUTO BRASILEIRO DE GEOGRAFIA E ESTATISTICA.
IX Recenseamento Geral do Brasil 1980. Rio de Janeiro.

Canada
STATISTICS CANADA.
1986 Census of Canada. Ottawa.

Cuba
COMITE ESTATAL DE ESTADISTICAS.
Censo de Población y Viviendas 1981. Havana.

Hungary
HUNGARIAN CENTRAL STATISTICAL OFFICE.
1990 Census. Budapest.

Indonesia
BIRO PUSAT STATISTIK.
Sensus Penduduk 1980. Jakarta.

Kuwait
CENTRAL OFFICE OF STATISTICS.
1985 Census. Al Kuwait.

New Zealand
DEPARTMENT OF STATISTICS.
New Zealand Census of Population and Dwellings 1986. Wellington.

Panama
DIRECCION DE ESTADISTICA Y CENSO.
Censos Nacionales de 1990. Panamá.

Papua New Guinea
BUREAU OF STATISTICS.
National Population Census 1980. Port Moresby.

Philippines
NATIONAL CENSUS AND STATISTICS OFFICE.
1980 Census of Population. Manila.

Saint Lucia
CENSUS OFFICE.
1980 Population Census. Castries.

Singapore
DEPARTMENT OF STATISTICS.
Census of Population 1980. Singapore.

Russia
CENTRAL STATISTICAL ADMINISTRATION.
1989 Census. Moscow.

United States
BUREAU OF THE CENSUS.
1990 Census of Population. Washington.

Vanuatu
CENSUS OFFICE.
1979 Population Census. Port Vila.

Zambia
CENTRAL STATISTICAL OFFICE.
1980 Census of Population and Housing. Lusaka.

Gazetteer-Index of the World

This alphabetical list of continents, countries, states, possessions and other major geographical areas provides a quick reference to their area in square miles and square kilometers, population, capital or chief town, map page number and an alpha-numeric index reference. The index reference indicates the square on the respective page in which the name may be found. The population figures used in each case are the latest reliable figures obtainable. The government listings are based primarily on the nomenclature contained in the World Factbook published by the CIA of the United States Government. Those governments currently unsettled or in transition are indicated with a † symbol.

Country	Square Miles	Area Square Kilometers	Population	Capital or Chief Town	Page and Index Ref.	Government or Ownership
*Afghanistan	250,775	649,507	16,450,000	Kabul	68/A 2	authoritarian†
Africa	11,707,000	30,321,130	648,000,000	....	102/....	
Alabama, U.S.	51,705	133,916	4,040,587	Montgomery	195/....	state of the U.S.
Alaska, U.S.	591,004	1,530,700	550,043	Juneau	196/....	state of the U.S.
*Albania	11,100	28,749	3,335,000	Tiranë	45/E 5	emerging democracy†
Alberta, Canada	255,285	661,185	2,545,553	Edmonton	182/....	province of Canada
*Algeria	919,591	2,381,740	26,022,000	Algiers	106/D 3	republic
American Samoa	77	199	46,773	Pago Pago	87/J 7; 86/....	unincorporated, unorganized territory of the U.S.
*Andorra	188	487	53,000	Andorra la Vella	33/G 1	parliamentary democracy
*Angola	481,351	1,246,700	8,668,000	Luanda	114/C 6	Marxist people's republic†
Anguilla, U.K.	35	91	7,000	The Valley	156/F 3	dependent territory of the U.K.
Antarctica	5,500,000	14,245,000	....	....	5/....	
*Antigua and Barbuda	171	443	64,000	St. John's	161/E11; 156/G 3	parliamentary democracy
*Argentina	1,072,070	2,776,661	32,664,000	Buenos Aires	143/....	republic
Arizona, U.S.	114,000	295,260	3,665,228	Phoenix	198/....	state of the U.S.
Arkansas, U.S.	53,187	137,754	2,350,725	Little Rock	202/....	state of the U.S.
*Armenia	11,506	29,800	3,283,000	Yerevan	52/F 6	republic
Aruba, Netherlands	75	193	64,000	Oranjestad	161/E 9	autonomous member of the Netherlands realm
Ascension Island, St. Helena	34	88	719	Georgetown	102/A 5	part of St. Helena
Ashmore & Cartier Islands, Australia	61	159	....	(Canberra, Austr.)	88/C 2	territory of Australia
Asia	17,128,500	44,362,815	3,176,000,000	....	54/....	
*Australia	2,966,136	7,682,300	17,288,000	Canberra	88/....	federal parliamentary state
Australian Capital Territory	927	2,400	221,609	Canberra	96/E 4	territory of Australia
*Austria	32,375	83,851	7,666,000	Vienna	40/B 3	federal republic
*Azerbaijan	33,436	86,600	7,029,000	Baku	52/G 6	republic
Azores, Portugal	902	2,335	275,900	Ponta Delgada	32/....	autonomous region of Portugal
*Bahamas	5,382	13,939	252,000	Nassau	156/C 1	independent commmonwealth
*Bahrain	240	622	537,000	Manama	58/F 4	traditional monarchy
Baker Island, U.S.	1	2.6	....	....	87/J 5	unincorporated territory of the U.S.
Balearic Islands, Spain	1,936	5,014	655,909	Palma	33/H 3	autonomous community of Spain
*Bangladesh	55,126	142,776	116,601,000	Dhaka	68/G 4	republic
*Barbados	166	430	255,000	Bridgetown	161/B 8	parliamentary democracy
*Belarus	80,154	207,600	10,200,000	Minsk	52/C 4	republic
*Belgium	11,781	30,513	9,922,000	Brussels	27/E 7	constitutional monarchy
*Belize	8,867	22,966	228,000	Belmopan	154/C 2	parliamentary democracy
*Benin	43,483	112,620	4,832,000	Porto-Novo	106/E 6	democratic reform†
Bermuda, U.K.	21	54	58,000	Hamilton	156/H 3	dependent territory of the U.K.
*Bhutan	18,147	47,000	1,598,000	Thimphu	68/G 3	monarchy
*Bolivia	424,163	1,098,582	7,157,000	La Paz; Sucre	136/.....	republic
Bonaire, Neth. Antilles	112	291	8,087	Kralendijk	161/E 9	part of Netherland Antilles
*Bosnia & Herzegovina	19,940	51,129	4,124,256	Sarajevo	45/C 3	emerging democracy†
*Botswana	224,764	582,139	1,258,000	Gaborone	119/C 4	parliamentary republic
Bouvet Island, Norway	22	57	....	....	5/D 1	territory of Norway
*Brazil	3,284,426	8,506,663	155,356,000	Brasília	132/.....	federal republic
British Columbia, Canada	366,253	948,596	3,282,061	Victoria	184/.....	province of Canada
British Indian Ocean Terr., U.K.	29	75	2,000	(London, U.K.)	54/L10	dependent territory of the U.K.
British Virgin Islands	59	153	12,000	Road Town	157/H 1	dependent territory of the U.K.
*Brunei	2,226	5,765	398,000	Bandar Seri Begawan	85/E 4	constitutional sultanate
*Bulgaria	42,823	110,912	8,911,000	Sofia	45/F 4	democratic reform†
*Burkina Faso	105,869	274,200	9,360,000	Ouagadougou	106/D 6	parliamentary
*Burma (Myanmar)	261,789	678,034	42,112,000	Rangoon	72/B 2	military
*Burundi	10,747	27,835	5,831,000	Bujumbura	114/E 4	republic
California, U.S.	158,706	411,049	29,760,021	Sacramento	204/.....	state of the U.S.
*Cambodia	69,898	181,036	7,146,000	Phnom Penh	72/E 4	constitutional monarchy†
*Cameroon	183,568	475,441	11,390,000	Yaoundé	114/B 2	one-party republic
*Canada	3,851,787	9,976,139	29,123,194	Ottawa	162/.....	confederation with parliamentary democracy
Canary Islands, Spain	2,808	7,273	1,367,646	Las Palmas; Santa Cruz	32/B 4	autonomous community of Spain
*Cape Verde	1,557	4,033	387,000	Praia	106/B 8	republic
Cayman Islands, U.K.	100	259	27,000	Georgetown	156/B 3	dependent territory of the U.K.
Celebes, Indonesia	72,986	189,034	7,732,383	Ujung Pandang	85/G 6	part of Indonesia
*Central African Republic	242,000	626,780	2,952,000	Bangui	114/C 2	republic
Central America	197,480	511,475	28,296,000	....	154/.....	
*Chad	495,752	1,283,998	5,122,000	N'Djamena	111/C 4	republic
Channel Islands, U.K.	75	194	133,000	St. Helier; St. Peter Port	13/E 8	part of the United Kingdom
*Chile	292,257	756,946	13,287,000	Santiago	138/.....	republic
*China, People's Rep. of	3,705,386	9,596,960	1,221,591,778	Beijing	77/.....	communist party-led state
China, Republic of (Taiwan)	13,971	36,185	21,665,515	T'aipei	77/K 7	multiparty democratic
Christmas Island, Australia	52	135	3,184	Flying Fish Cove	54/M11	territory of Australia
Clipperton Island, France	2	5.2	....	....	146/H 8	possession of France
Cocos (Keeling) Islands, Australia	5.4	14	555	West Island	54/N11	territory of Australia

*Member of the United Nations

Gazetteer-Index of the World

Country	Square Miles	Area Square Kilometers	Population	Capital or Chief Town	Page and Index Ref.	Government or Ownership
*Colombia	439,513	1,138,339	40,036,927	Bogotá	126/.....	republic
Colorado, U.S.	104,091	269,596	3,294,394	Denver	208/.....	state of the U.S.
*Comoros	719	1,862	580,509	Moroni	119/G 2	republic
*Congo, Dem. Rep. of the	905,063	2,344,113	51,987,773	Kinshasa	114/D 4	republic
*Congo, Rep. of the	132,046	342,000	2,775,659	Brazzaville	114/B 4	republic
Connecticut, U.S.	5,018	12,997	3,287,116	Hartford	210/.....	state of the U.S.
Cook Islands, New Zealand	91	236	20,407	Avarua	87/K 7	self-governing in free association with New Zealand
Coral Sea Islands, Australia	8.5	22	....	....	88/J 3	territory of Australia
Corsica, France	3,352	8,682	249,737	Ajaccio; Bastia	28/B 6	part of France
*Costa Rica	19,575	50,700	3,743,677	San José	154/E 5	democratic republic
Côte d'Ivoire, see Ivory Coast						
*Croatia	22,050	56,538	4,681,015	Zagreb	45/B 3	parliamentary democracy
*Cuba	44,206	114,494	11,139,412	Havana	158/.....	communist state
Curaçao, Neth. Antilles	178	462	145,430	Willemstad	161/G 7	part of Netherlands Antilles
*Cyprus	3,473	8,995	759,048	Nicosia	62/E 5	republic
*Czech Republic	30,449	78,863	10,283,762	Prague	41/C 2	parliamentary democracy
Delaware, U.S.	2,044	5,294	666,168	Dover	245/R 3	state of the U.S.
*Denmark	16,629	43,069	5,374,554	Copenhagen	21/.....	constitutional monarchy
District of Columbia, U.S.	69	179	606,900	Washington	244/F 5	district of the United States
*Djibouti	8,880	23,000	454,294	Djibouti	111/H 5	republic
*Dominica	290	751	63,944	Roseau	161/E 7	parliamentary democracy
*Dominican Republic	18,704	48,443	8,261,536	Santo Domingo	158/D 6	republic
*Ecuador	109,483	283,561	12,782,161	Quito	128/C 3	republic
*Egypt	386,659	1,001,447	68,494,584	Cairo	110/E 2	republic
*El Salvador	8,260	21,393	5,925,374	San Salvador	154/C 4	republic
England, U.K.	50,516	130,836	49,089,100	London	13/.....	part of the United Kingdom
*Equatorial Guinea	10,831	28,052	477,763	Malabo	114/A 3	republic
*Eritrea	45,410	117,600	4,142,481	Asmara	110/G 4	transitional government†
*Estonia	17,413	45,100	1,398,140	Tallinn	53/.....	republic
*Ethiopia	426,366	1,104,300	60,967,436	Addis Ababa	110/G5.	federal republic
Europe	4,057,000	10,507,630	732,653,000	....	7/......	
Falkland Islands & Dependencies, U.K.	6,198	16,053	1,813	Stanley	120/E 8; 143/D 7	dependent territory of the U.K.
Faroe Islands, Denmark	540	1,399	40,172	Tórshavn	21/B 2	self-governing overseas administrative division of Denmark
*Fiji	7,055	18,272	823,376	Suva	87/H 8; 86/.....	republic
*Finland	130,128	337,032	5,164,825	Helsinki	18/O 6	republic
Florida, U.S.	58,664	151,940	12,937,926	Tallahassee	212/.....	state of the U.S.
*France	210,038	543,998	59,128,187	Paris	28/.....	republic
French Guiana	35,135	91,000	173,246	Cayenne	131/E 3	overseas department of France
French Polynesia	1,544	4,000	246,171	Papeete	87/L 8	overseas territory of France
*Gabon	103,346	267,666	1,244,192	Libreville	114/B 4	republic
*Gambia	4,127	10,689	1,381,496	Banjul	106/A 6	republic
Gaza Strip	139	360	1,162,777	Gaza	65/A 4	occupied by Israel
*Georgia	26,911	69,700	5,034,051	T'bilisi	52/F 6	republic
Georgia, U.S.	58,910	152,577	6,478,216	Atlanta	217/.....	state of the U.S.
*Germany	137,753	356,780	82,081,365	Berlin	22/.....	republic
*Ghana	92,099	238,536	19,271,744	Accra	106/D 7	constitutional democracy
Gibraltar, U.K.	2.28	5.91	29,272	Gibraltar	33/D 4	dependent territory of the U.K.
*Great Britain & Northern Ireland (United Kingdom)	94,399	244,493	57,236,000	London	10/.....	see United Kingdom
*Greece	50,944	131,945	10,750,705	Athens	45/F 6	presidential parliamentary republic
Greenland, Denmark	840,000	2,175,600	60,324	Nuuk (Godthåb)	4/B12	self-governing overseas administrative division of Denmark
*Grenada	133	344	97,913	St. George's	161/D 9; 156/G 4	parliamentary democracy
Guadeloupe & Dependencies, France	687	1,779	425,317	Basse-Terre	161/A 5; 156/F 4	overseas department of France
Guam, U.S.	209	541	154,623	Hagåtña	87/E 4; 86/.....	organized, unincorporated territory of the U.S.
*Guatemala	42,042	108,889	12,669,576	Guatemala	154/B 3	republic
*Guinea	94,925	245,856	7,610,869	Conakry	106/B 6	republic
*Guinea-Bissau	13,948	36,125	1,263,341	Bissau	106/A 6	republic
*Guyana	83,000	214,970	703,399	Georgetown	131/B 3	republic
*Haiti	10,694	27,697	6,991,589	Port-au-Prince	158/C 5	republic
Hawaii, U.S.	6,471	16,760	1,108,229	Honolulu	218/.....	state of the U.S.
Heard & McDonald Islands, Australia	113	293	....	....	2/N 8	territory of Australia
Holland, see Netherlands						
*Honduras	43,277	112,087	6,130,135	Tegucigalpa	154/D 3	republic
Hong Kong	422	1,092	6,966,929	Victoria	77/H 7; 78/.....	special administrative region of China
Howland Island, U.S.	1	2.6	....	....	87/J 5	unincorporated territory of the U.S.
*Hungary	35,919	93,030	10,167,182	Budapest	41/D 3	republic
*Iceland	39,768	103,000	274,141	Reykjavík	21/B 1	republic
Idaho, U.S.	83,564	216,431	1,006,749	Boise	220/.....	state of the U.S.
Illinois, U.S.	56,345	145,934	11,430,602	Springfield	222/.....	state of the U.S.
*India	1,269,339	3,287,588	1,017,645,163	New Delhi	68/D 4	federal republic
Indiana, U.S.	36,185	93,719	5,544,159	Indianapolis	227/.....	state of the U.S.
*Indonesia	788,430	2,042,034	219,266,557	Jakarta	85/D 7	republic
Iowa, U.S.	56,275	145,752	2,776,755	Des Moines	229/.....	state of the U.S.

Gazetteer-Index of the World

Country	Area Square Miles	Area Square Kilometers	Population	Capital or Chief Town	Page and Index Ref.	Government or Ownership
*Iran	636,293	1,648,000	59,051,000	Tehran	66/F 4	theocratic republic
*Iraq	172,476	446,713	19,525,000	Baghdad	66/C 4	republic
*Ireland	27,136	70,282	3,489,000	Dublin	17/.....	republic
Ireland, Northern, U.K.	5,452	14,121	1,543,000	Belfast	17/F 2	part of the United Kingdom
Isle of Man, U.K.	227	588	64,000	Douglas	13/C 3	part of the United Kingdom
*Israel	7,847	20,324	4,558,000	Jerusalem	65/B 4	republic
*Italy	116,303	301,225	57,772,000	Rome	34/.....	republic
*Ivory Coast (Côte d'Ivoire)	124,504	322,465	12,978,000	Yamoussoukro	106/C 7	republic
*Jamaica	4,411	11,424	2,489,000	Kingston	158/.....	parliamentary democracy
Jan Mayen, Norway	144	373	....		6/D 1	territory of Norway
*Japan	145,730	377,441	124,017,000	Tokyo	81/.....	constitutional monarchy
Jarvis Island, U.S.	1	2.6	....	....	87/K 6	unincorporated territory of the U.S.
Java, Indonesia	48,842	126,500	73,712,411	Jakarta	85/J 2	part of Indonesia
Johnston Atoll, U.S.	0.91	2.4	327	....	87/K 4	unincorporated territory of the U.S.
*Jordan	35,000	90,650	3,413,000	Amman	65/D 3	constitutional monarchy
Kansas, U.S.	82,277	213,097	2,477,574	Topeka	232/.....	state of the U.S.
*Kazakhstan	1,048,300	2,715,100	16,538,000	Astana	48/G 5	republic
Kentucky, U.S.	40,409	104,659	3,685,296	Frankfort	237/.....	state of the U.S.
*Kenya	224,960	582,646	25,242,000	Nairobi	115/G 3	republic
Kermadec Islands, New Zealand	13	33	5	....	87/J 9	part of New Zealand
Kingman Reef, U.S.	0.1	0.26	....	....	87/K 5	unincorporated territory of the U.S.
Kiribati	277	717	82,449	Tarawa	87/J 6	republic
*Korea, North	46,540	120,539	21,815,000	P'yŏngyang	80/D 3	communist
*Korea, South	38,175	98,873	43,134,000	Seoul	80/D 5	republic
*Kuwait	6,532	16,918	2,048,000	Kuwait	58/E 4	constitutional monarchy
*Kyrgyzstan	76,641	198,500	4,291,000	Bishkek	48/H 5	republic
*Laos	91,428	236,800	4,113,000	Vientiane	72/D 3	communist
*Latvia	24,595	63,700	2,681,000	Riga	53/.....	republic
*Lebanon	4,015	10,399	3,385,000	Beirut	62/F 6	republic
*Lesotho	11,720	30,355	1,801,000	Maseru	119/D 5	constitutional monarchy
*Liberia	43,000	111,370	2,730,000	Monrovia	106/C 7	republic
*Libya	679,358	1,759,537	4,353,000	Tripoli	110/B 2	socialist people's (masses) state
*Liechtenstein	61	158	28,000	Vaduz	39/J 2	hereditary constitutional monarchy
*Lithuania	25,174	65,200	3,690,000	Vilnius	53/.....	republic
Louisiana, U.S.	47,752	123,678	4,219,973	Baton Rouge	238/.....	state of the U.S.
*Luxembourg	999	2,587	388,000	Luxembourg	27/J 9	constitutional monarchy
Macau, Portugal	8	21	429,152	Macau	77/H 7	overseas territory of Portugal
*Macedonia	9,889	25,713	1,909,136	Skopje	45/E 5	emerging democracy
*Madagascar	226,657	587,041	12,185,000	Antananarivo	119/H 3	republic
Madeira Islands, Portugal	307	796	262,800	Funchal	32/A 2	autonomous region of Portugal
Maine, U.S.	33,265	86,156	1,227,928	Augusta	243/.....	state of the U.S.
*Malawi	45,747	118,485	9,438,000	Lilongwe	114/F 6	multiparty democracy
Malaya, Malaysia	50,806	131,588	11,138,227	Kuala Lumpur	72/D 6	part of Malaysia
*Malaysia	128,308	332,318	17,982,000	Kuala Lumpur	72/D 6; 85/E 4	constitutional monarchy
*Maldives	115	298	226,000	Male	54/L 9	republic
*Mali	464,873	1,204,021	8,339,000	Bamako	106/C 6	republic
*Malta	122	316	356,000	Valletta	34/E 7	parliamentary democracy
Manitoba, Canada	250,999	650,087	1,091,942	Winnipeg	179/.....	province of Canada
Marquesas Islands, French Polynesia	492	1,274	5,419	Atuona	87/N 6	part of French Polynesia
*Marshall Islands	70	181	60,652	Majuro	87/G 4	constitutional; free association with the U.S.
Martinique, France	425	1,101	359,572	Fort-de-France	161/D 5	overseas department of France
Maryland, U.S.	10,460	27,091	4,781,468	Annapolis	245/.....	state of the U.S.
Massachusetts, U.S.	8,284	21,456	6,016,425	Boston	249/.....	state of the U.S.
*Mauritania	419,229	1,085,803	1,996,000	Nouakchott	106/B 5	republic
*Mauritius	790	2,046	1,081,000	Port Louis	119/G 5	parliamentary democracy
Mayotte, France	144	373	75,000	Mamoutzou	119/G 2	territorial collectivity of France
*Mexico	761,601	1,972,546	90,007,000	Mexico City	150/.....	federal republic
Michigan, U.S.	58,527	151,585	9,295,297	Lansing	250/.....	state of the U.S.
*Micronesia, Federated States of	271	702	122,950	Palikir	87/E 5	constitutional; free association with the U.S.
Midway Islands, U.S.	1.9	4.9	453	....	87/J 3	unincorporated territory of the U.S.
Minnesota, U.S.	84,402	218,601	4,375,099	St. Paul	255/.....	state of the U.S.
Mississippi, U.S.	47,689	123,515	2,573,216	Jackson	256/.....	state of the U.S.
Missouri, U.S.	69,697	180,515	5,117,073	Jefferson City	261/.....	state of the U.S.
*Moldova	13,012	33,700	4,341,000	Chişinău	52/C 5	republic
*Monaco	368 acres	149 hectares	30,000	....	28/G 6	constitutional monarchy
*Mongolia	606,163	1,569,962	2,538,211	Ulaanbaatar	77/E 2	republic
Montana, U.S.	147,046	380,849	799,065	Helena	262/.....	state of the U.S.
Montserrat, U.K.	40	104	13,000	Plymouth	157/G 3	dependent territory of the U.K.
*Morocco	172,414	446,550	26,182,000	Rabat	106/C 2	constitutional monarchy
*Mozambique	303,769	786,762	15,113,000	Maputo	119/E 4	republic
Myanmar, see Burma						
*Namibia	317,827	823,172	1,521,000	Windhoek	118/B 3	republic
Nauru	7.7	20	10,390	Yaren (district)	87/G 6	republic
Navassa Island, U.S.	2	5	....	....	156/C 3	unincorporated territory of the U.S.
Nebraska, U.S.	77,355	200,349	1,578,385	Lincoln	264/.....	state of the U.S.
*Nepal	54,663	141,577	19,612,000	Kathmandu	68/E 3	parliamentary democracy
*Netherlands	15,892	41,160	15,022,000	The Hague; Amsterdam	27/F 5	constitutional monarchy
Netherlands Antilles	320	817	184,000	Willemstad	156/E 4	autonomous member of the Netherlands realm
Nevada, U.S.	110,561	286,353	1,201,833	Carson City	266/.....	state of the U.S.

Gazetteer-Index of the World

Country	Square Miles	Area Square Kilometers	Population	Capital or Chief Town	Page and Index Ref.	Government or Ownership
New Brunswick, Canada	28,354	73,437	738,133	Fredericton	170/.....	province of Canada
New Caledonia & Dependencies, France	7,335	18,998	200,481	Nouméa	87/G 8	overseas territory of France
Newfoundland, Canada	156,184	404,517	551,792	St. John's	166/.....	province of Canada
New Hampshire, U.S.	9,279	24,033	1,109,252	Concord	268/.....	state of the U.S.
New Jersey, U.S.	7,787	20,168	7,730,188	Trenton	273/.....	state of the U.S.
New Mexico, U.S.	121,593	314,926	1,515,069	Santa Fe	274/.....	state of the U.S.
New South Wales, Australia	309,498	801,600	6,428,700	Sydney	96/B 2	state of Australia
New York, U.S.	49,108	127,190	17,990,455	Albany	276/.....	state of the U.S.
*New Zealand	103,736	268,676	3,697,850	Wellington	100/.....	parliamentary democracy
*Nicaragua	45,698	118,358	4,850,976	Managua	154/D 4	republic
*Niger	489,189	1,267,000	10,260,316	Niamey	106/F 5	republic
*Nigeria	357,000	924,630	117,170,948	Abuja	106/F 6	military
Niue, New Zealand	100	259	3,578	Alofi	87/K 7	self-governing territory in free association with New Zealand
Norfolk Island, Australia	13.4	34.6	2,175	Kingston	88/L 5	territory of Australia
North America	9,363,000	24,250,170	443,438,000	....	146/.....	
North Carolina, U.S.	52,669	136,413	6,628,637	Raleigh	281/.....	state of the U.S.
North Dakota, U.S.	70,702	183,118	638,800	Bismarck	282/.....	state of the U.S.
Northern Ireland, U.K.	5,452	14,121	1,663,300	Belfast	17/F 2	part of the United Kingdom
Northern Marianas, U.S.	184	477	71,912	Saipan	87/E 4	commonwealth associated with the U.S.
Northern Territory, Australia	519,768	1,346,200	193,400	Darwin	93/.....	territory of Australia
*North Korea	46,540	120,539	21,687,550	P'yŏngyang	80/D 3	communist state
Northwest Territories, Canada	589,315	1,526,328	39,672	Yellowknife	187/F 3	territory of Canada
*Norway	125,053	323,887	4,455,707	Oslo	18/F 7	constitutional monarchy
Nova Scotia, Canada	21,425	55,491	909,282	Halifax	168/.....	province of Canada
Nunavut, Canada	733,590	1,900,000	24,730	Iqaluit	187/J 3	territory of Canada
Oceania	3,292,000	8,526,280	23,000,000	....	87/.....	
Ohio, U.S.	41,330	107,045	10,847,115	Columbus	284/.....	state of the U.S.
Oklahoma, U.S.	69,956	181,186	3,145,585	Oklahoma City	288/.....	state of the U.S.
*Oman	120,000	310,800	2,532,556	Muscat	58/G 6	absolute monarchy
Ontario, Canada	412,580	1,068,582	10,753,573	Toronto	175,177/	province of Canada
Oregon, U.S.	97,073	251,419	2,842,321	Salem	291/.....	state of the U.S.
Orkney Islands, Scotland	376	974	17,675	Kirkwall	15/E 1	part of the United Kingdom
*Pakistan	310,403	803,943	141,145,344	Islamabad	68/B 3	federal republic
*Palau	188	487	18,827	Koror	86/D 5	constitutional; free association with the U.S.
Palmyra Atoll, U.S.	12	31	....	....	87/K 5	unincorporated territory of the U.S.
*Panama	29,761	77,082	2,821,085	Panamá	154/G 6	constitutional republic
*Papua New Guinea	183,540	475,369	4,811,939	Port Moresby	85/B 7; 87/E 6	parliamentary democracy
Paracel Islands, China	....	....	....	....	85/E 2	occupied by China; claimed by Taiwan and Vietnam
*Paraguay	157,047	406,752	5,579,503	Asunción	144/.....	republic
Pennsylvania, U.S.	45,308	117,348	11,881,643	Harrisburg	294/.....	state of the U.S.
*Peru	496,222	1,285,215	27,135,689	Lima	128/.....	republic
*Philippines	115,707	299,681	80,961,430	Manila	82/.....	republic
Pitcairn Islands, U.K.	18	47	54	Adamstown	87/O 8	dependent territory of the U.K.
*Poland	120,725	312,678	38,644,184	Warsaw	47/.....	democratic
*Portugal	35,549	92,072	9,902,147	Lisbon	32/B 3	parliamentary democracy
Prince Edward Island, Canada	2,184	5,657	134,557	Charlottetown	168/E 2	province of Canada
Puerto Rico, U.S.	3,515	9,104	3,522,037	San Juan	161/.....	commonwealth associated with the U.S.
*Qatar	4,247	11,000	749,542	Doha	58/F 4	traditional monarchy
Québec, Canada	594,857	1,540,680	7,138,795	Québec	172,174/	province of Canada
Queensland, Australia	666,872	1,727,200	3,525,600	Brisbane	95/.....	state of Australia
Réunion, France	969	2,510	730,201	St-Denis	119/F 5	overseas department of France
Rhode Island, U.S.	1,212	3,139	1,003,464	Providence	249/H 5	state of the U.S.
*Romania	91,699	237,500	22,291,200	Bucharest	45/F 3	republic
*Russia	6,592,812	17,075,400	145,904,542	Moscow	48/D 4	federation
*Rwanda	10,169	26,337	8,336,995	Kigali	114/E 4	republic
Sabah, Malaysia	29,300	75,887	1,002,608	Kota Kinabalu	85/F 4	state of Malaysia
Saint Helena & Dependencies, U.K.	162	420	7,197	Jamestown	102/B 6	dependent territory of the U.K.
*Saint Kitts and Nevis	104	269	43,441	Basseterre	156/F 3; 161/C11	constitutional monarchy
*Saint Lucia	238	616	155,678	Castries	161/G 6	parliamentary democracy
Saint Pierre & Miquelon, France	93.5	242	7,018	Saint-Pierre	166/C 4	territorial collectivity of France
*Saint Vincent & the Grenadines	150	388	121,188	Kingstown	161/A 8; 157/G 4	constitutional monarchy
Sakhalin, Russia	29,500	76,405	655,000	Yuzhno-Sakhalinsk	48/P 4	part of Russia
*Samoa	1,133	2,934	235,302	Apia	87/J 7	constitutional monarchy
*San Marino	23.4	60.6	25,215	San Marino	34/D 3	republic
*São Tomé and Príncipe	372	963	159,832	São Tomé	106/F 8	republic
Sarawak, Malaysia	48,202	124,843	1,294,753	Kuching	85/E 5	state of Malaysia
Sardinia, Italy	9,301	24,090	1,450,483	Cagliari	34/B 4	region of Italy
Saskatchewan, Canada	251,699	651,900	990,237	Regina	181/.....	province of Canada
*Saudi Arabia	829,995	2,149,687	22,245,751	Riyadh	58/D 4	monarchy
Scotland, U.K.	30,414	78,772	5,128,000	Edinburgh	15/.....	part of the United Kingdom
*Senegal	75,954	196,720	10,390,296	Dakar	106/A 5	republic
*Seychelles	145	375	79,672	Victoria	119/H 5	republic
Shetland Islands, Scotland	552	1,430	18,494	Lerwick	15/G 2	part of the United Kingdom
Siam, see Thailand						
Sicily, Italy	9,926	25,708	4,628,918	Palermo	34/D 6	region of Italy
*Sierra Leone	27,925	72,325	5,509,263	Freetown	106/B 7	constitutional democracy
*Singapore	226	585	3,571,710	Singapore	72/F 6	republic
*Slovakia	18,924	49,014	5,401,134	Bratislava	41/E 2	parliamentary democracy

Gazetteer-Index of the World

Country	Area Square Miles	Area Square Kilometers	Population	Capital or Chief Town	Page and Index Ref.	Government or Ownership
*Slovenia	7,898	20,251	1,970,056	Ljubljana	45/A 3	emerging democracy
Society Islands, French Polynesia	677	1,753	117,703	Papeete	87/L 7	part of French Polynesia
*Solomon Islands	11,500	29,785	470,000	Honiara	87/G 6; 86/.....	parliamentary democracy
*Somalia	246,200	637,658	7,433,922	Mogadishu	115/H 3	no functioning government
*South Africa	455,318	1,179,274	43,981,758	Cape Town; Pretoria	118/C 5	republic
South America	6,875,000	17,806,250	314,335,000	....	120/.....	
South Australia, Australia	379,922	984,000	1,494,800	Adelaide	94/.....	state of Australia
South Carolina, U.S.	31,113	80,583	3,486,703	Columbia	296/.....	state of the U.S.
South Dakota, U.S.	77,116	199,730	696,004	Pierre	298/.....	state of the U.S.
*South Korea	38,175	98,873	47,350,529	Seoul	80/D 5	republic
*Spain	194,881	504,742	39,208,236	Madrid	33/.....	parliamentary monarchy
Spratly Islands	....	....	....	....	85/E 4	in dispute; claims by China, Malaysia, Philippines, Taiwan, Vietnam
*Sri Lanka	25,332	65,610	19,355,053	Colombo	68/E 7	republic
*Sudan	967,494	2,505,809	35,530,371	Khartoum	110/E 4	transitional†
Sumatra, Indonesia	164,000	424,760	19,360,400	Medan	84/B 5	see Indonesia
*Suriname	55,144	142,823	434,093	Paramaribo	131/C 3	republic
Svalbard, Norway	23,957	62,049	3,431	Longyearbyen	18/C 2	territory of Norway
*Swaziland	6,705	17,366	1,004,072	Mbabane	119/E 5	monarchy
*Sweden	173,665	449,792	8,938,559	Stockholm	18/J 8	constitutional monarchy
Switzerland	15,943	41,292	7,288,715	Bern	39/.....	federal republic
*Syria	71,498	185,180	17,758,925	Damascus	62/G 5	military republic
Tahiti, French Polynesia	402	1,041	95,604	Papeete	87/L 7	see French Polynesia
Taiwan	13,971	36,185	22,319,222	T'aipei	77/K /	multiparty democratic
*Tajikistan	55,251	143,100	6,194,373	Dushanbe	48/G 6	republic
*Tanzania	363,708	942,003	31,962,769	Dar es Salaam	114/F 5	republic
Tasmania, Australia	26,178	67,800	470,100	Hobart	99/.....	state of Australia
Tennessee, U.S.	42,144	109,153	4,877,185	Nashville	237/.....	state of the U.S.
Texas, U.S.	266,807	691,030	16,986,510	Austin	303/.....	state of the U.S.
*Thailand	198,455	513,998	61,163,833	Bangkok	72/D 3	constitutional monarchy
Tibet, China	463,320	1,200,000	1,790,000	Lhasa	76/C 5	part of China
*Togo	21,622	56,000	5,262,611	Lomé	106/E 7	republic†
Tokelau, New Zealand	3.9	10	1,575	Fakaofo	87/J 6	territory of New Zealand
Tonga	270	699	109,959	Nuku'alofa	87/J 8	hereditary constitutional monarchy
*Trinidad and Tobago	1,980	5,128	1,086,908	Port-of-Spain	157/G 5; 161/A10	parliamentary democracy
Tristan da Cunha, St. Helena	38	98	251	Edinburgh	2/J 7	see St. Helena
Tuamotu Archipelago, French Polynesia	341	883	9,052	Apataki	87/M 7	see French Polynesia
*Tunisia	63,378	164,149	9,645,499	Tunis	106/F 1	republic
*Turkey	300,946	779,450	66,620,120	Ankara	62/D 3	republican parliamentary democracy
*Turkmenistan	188,455	488,100	4,435,507	Ashgabat	48/F 6	republic
Turks and Caicos Islands, U.K.	166	430	17,480	Cockburn Town, Grand Turk	156/D 2	dependent territory of the U.K.
Tuvalu	9.78	25.33	10,730	Funafuti	87/H 6	democracy
*Uganda	91,076	235,887	23,451,687	Kampala	114/F 3	republic
*Ukraine	233,089	603,700	49,506,779	Kiev	52/D 5	republic
*United Arab Emirates	32,278	83,600	2,386,472	Abu Dhabi	58/F 5	federation of sheikdoms
*United Kingdom	94,399	244,493	59,247,439	London	10/.....	constitutional monarchy
*United States	3,623,420	9,384,658	274,943,496	Washington, D.C.	188/.....	federal republic
*Uruguay	72,172	186,925	3,332,782	Montevideo	145/.....	republic
Utah, U.S.	84,899	219,888	1,722,850	Salt Lake City	304/.....	state of the U.S.
*Uzbekistan	173,591	449,600	24,422,518	Tashkent	48/G 5	republic
*Vanuatu	5,700	14,763	192,848	Port-Vila	87/G 7	republic
Vatican City	108.7 acres	44 hectares	1,000	....	34/B 6	sacerdotal (priest-related) monarchy
*Venezuela	352,143	912,050	23,595,822	Caracas	124/.....	republic
Vermont, U.S.	9,614	24,900	562,758	Montpelier	268/.....	state of the U.S.
Victoria, Australia	87,876	227,600	4,726,600	Melbourne	96/B 5	state of Australia
*Vietnam	128,405	332,569	78,349,503	Hanoi	72/E 3	communist state
Virginia, U.S.	40,767	105,587	6,187,358	Richmond	307/.....	state of the U.S.
Virgin Islands, British	59	153	19,610	Road Town	157/H 1	dependent territory of the U.K.
Virgin Islands, U.S.	132	342	101,809	Charlotte Amalie	161/A 4	organized, unincorporated territory of the U.S.
Wake Island, U.S.	2.5	6.5	302	Wake Islet	87/G 4	unincorporated territory of the U.S.
Wales, U.K.	8,017	20,764	2,921,100	Cardiff	13/D 5	part of the United Kingdom
Wallis and Futuna, France	106	275	15,283	Mata Utu	87/J 7	overseas territory of France
Washington, U.S.	68,139	176,480	4,866,692	Olympia	310/.....	state of the U.S.
West Bank	2,100	5,439	1,661,749	....	65/C 3	occupied by Israel
Western Australia, Australia	975,096	2,525,500	1,868,200	Perth	92/.....	state of Australia
Western Sahara	102,703	266,000	244,943	....	106/B 3	occupied by Morocco
West Virginia, U.S.	24,231	62,758	1,793,477	Charleston	312/.....	state of the U.S.
Wisconsin, U.S.	56,153	145,436	4,891,769	Madison	317/.....	state of the U.S.
World (land)	57,970,000	150,142,300	5,292,000,000	....	1,2/.....	
Wyoming, U.S.	97,809	253,325	453,588	Cheyenne	319/.....	state of the U.S.
*Yemen	188,321	487,752	17,521,085	Sanaa	58/D 7	republic
*Yugoslavia	38,989	102,173	11,210,243	Belgrade	45/C 3	republic
Yukon Territory, Canada	207,075	536,324	30,766	Whitehorse	186/E 3	territory of Canada
*Zambia	290,586	752,618	9,872,007	Lusaka	114/E 7	republic
*Zimbabwe	150,803	390,580	11,272,013	Harare	119/D 3	parliamentary democracy

Glossary of Abbreviations

A

A.A.F. — Army Air Field
Acad. — Academy
A.C.T. — Australian Capital Territory
adm. — administration; administrative
A.F.B. — Air Force Base
Afgh., Afghan. — Afghanistan
Afr. — Africa
Ala. — Alabama
Alb. — Albania
Alg. — Algeria
Alta. — Alberta
Amer. — American
Amer. Samoa — American Samoa
And. — Andorra
Ant., Antarc. — Antarctica
Ant. & Bar. — Antigua and Barbuda
Ar. — Arabia
arch. — archipelago
Arg. — Argentina
Ariz. — Arizona
Ark. — Arkansas
Arm. — Armenia
Aust. — Austria
Aust. Cap. Terr. — Australian Capital
    Territory
Austr., Austral. — Australian, Australia
aut. — autonomous
Aut. Obl. — Autonomous Oblast
Aut. Rep. — Autonomous
    Republic
Azer. — Azerbaijan

B

B. — Bay
Bah. — Bahamas
Barb. — Barbados
Battlef. — Battlefield
Bch. — Beach
Bel. — Belarus
Belg. — Belgium
Berm. — Bermuda
Bol. — Bolivia
Bos. — Bosnia & Hercegovina
Bots. — Botswana
Br. — Branch
Br. — British
Braz. — Brazil
Br. Col. — British Columbia
Br. Ind. Oc. Terr. — British Indian
    Ocean Territory
Bulg. — Bulgaria

C

C. — Cape
Calif. — California
Can. — Canada
can. — canal
cap. — capital
Cent. Afr. Rep. — Central African
    Republic
Cent. Amer. — Central America
C.G. Sta. — Coast Guard Station
C.H. — Court House
chan. — channel
Chan. Is. — Channel Islands
Chem. Ctr. — Chemical Center
co. — county
Col. — Colombia
Colo. — Colorado
comm. — commissary
Conn. — Connecticut
cont. — continent
cord. — cordillera (mountain range)
C. Rica — Costa Rica
Cro. — Croatia
C.S. — County Seat
C. Verde — Cape Verde
Czech. — Czech Republic

D

D.C. — District of Columbia
Del. — Delaware
Dem. — Democratic
Den. — Denmark
depr. — depression
dept. — department
des. — desert
dist., dist's — district, districts
div. — division
Dom. Rep. — Dominican Republic

E

E. — East
Ec., Ecua. — Ecuador
elec. div. — electoral division
El Salv. — El Salvador
Eng. — England

Equat. Guinea, Eq. Guin. — Equatorial
    Guinea
Erit. — Eritrea
escarp. — escarpment
est. — estuary
Est. — Estonia
Eth. — Ethiopia

F

Falk. Is. — Falkland Islands
Fin. — Finland
Fk., Fks. — Fork, Forks
Fla. — Florida
for. — forest
Fr. — France, French
Fr. Gui. — French Guiana
Fr. Poly. — French Polynesia
Ft. — Fort

G

G. — Gulf
Ga. — Georgia (state)
Game Res. — Game Reserve
Geo. — Georgia (nation)
Ger. — Germany
geys. — geyser
Gibr. — Gibraltar
glac. — glacier
gov. — governorate
Gr. — Group
Greenl. — Greenland
Gren. — Grenada
Gt. Brit. — Great Britain
Guad. — Guadeloupe
Guat. — Guatemala
Guinea-Biss. — Guinea-Bissau
Guy. — Guyana

H

har., harb., hbr. — harbor
hd. — head
highl. — highland, highlands
Hist. — Historic, Historical
Hond. — Honduras
Hts. — Heights
Hung. — Hungary

I

I., isl. — island, isle
I.C. — independent city
Ice., Icel. — Iceland
Ida. — Idaho
Ill. — Illinois
Ind. — Indiana
ind. city — independent city
Indon. — Indonesia
Ind. Res. — Indian Reservation
int. div. — internal division
inten. — intendency
Int'l — International
Ire. — Ireland
Is., isls. — islands
Isr. — Israel
isth. — isthmus
Iv. Coast — Ivory Coast

J

Jam. — Jamaica
Jct. — Junction

K

Kans. — Kansas
Kaz., Kazakh. — Kazakhstan
Ky. — Kentucky
Kyr. — Kyrgyzstan

L

L. — Lake, Loch, Lough
La. — Louisiana
Lab. — Laboratory
lag. — lagoon
Lat. — Latvia
ld. — land
Leb. — Lebanon
Les. — Lesotho
Liecht. — Liechtenstein
Lith. — Lithuania
Lux. — Luxembourg

M

Mac. — Macedonia
Mad., Madag. — Madagascar
Man. — Manitoba
Mart. — Martinique
Mass. — Massachusetts
Maur. — Mauritania
Md. — Maryland
met. area — metropolitan area

Mex. — Mexico
Mich. — Michigan
Minn. — Minnesota
Miss. — Mississippi
Mo. — Missouri
Mold. — Moldova
Mon. — Monument
Mong. — Mongolia
Mont. — Montana
Mor. — Morocco
Moz., Mozamb. — Mozambique
mt. — mount
mtn. — mountain

N

N., No. — North
N. Amer. — North America
Nam., Namib. — Namibia
N.A.S. — Naval Air Station
Nat'l — National
Nat'l Cem. — National Cemetery
Nat'l Mem. Park — National Memorial
    Park
Nat'l Mil. Park — National Military
    Park
Nat'l Pkwy. — National Parkway
Nav. Base — Naval Base
Nav. Sta. — Naval Station
N.B., N. Br. — New Brunswick
N.C. — North Carolina
N. Dak. — North Dakota
Nebr. — Nebraska
Neth. — Netherlands
Neth. Ant. — Netherlands Antilles
Nev. — Nevada
New Bruns. — New Brunswick
New Cal., New Caled. — New Caledonia
Newf. — Newfoundland
New Hebr. — New Hebrides
N.H. — New Hampshire
Nic. — Nicaragua
N. Ire. — Northern Ireland
N.J. — New Jersey
N. Mex. — New Mexico
Nor. — Norway, Norwegian
North. — Northern
North. Terr., No. Terr. — Northern
    Territory
    (Australia)
N.S. — Nova Scotia
N.S.W., N.S. Wales — New South Wales
N.W.T., N.W. Terrs. — Northwest
    Territories
    (Canada)
N.Y. — New York
N.Z., N. Zealand — New Zealand

O

Obl. — Oblast
Okla. — Oklahoma
Okr. — Okrug
Ont. — Ontario
Ord. Depot — Ordnance Depot
Oreg. — Oregon

P

Pa. — Pennsylvania
Pak. — Pakistan
Pan. — Panama
Papua N.G. — Papua New Guinea
Par. — Paraguay
par. — parish
passg. — passage
P.E.I. — Prince Edward Island
pen. — peninsula
Phil., Phil. Is. — Philippines
Pk. — Park
pk. — peak
plat. — plateau
P.N.G. — Papua New Guinea
Pol. — Poland
Port. — Portugal, Portuguese
Pr. Edward I. — Prince
    Edward Island
pref. — prefecture
P. Rico — Puerto Rico
prom. — promontory
prov. — province, provincial
pt. — point

Q

Que. — Québec
Queens. — Queensland

R

R. — River

ra. — range
Rec., Recr. — Recreation, Recreational
reg. — region
Rep. — Republic
res. — reservoir
Res. — Reservation, Reserve
R.I. — Rhode Island
riv. — river
Rom. — Romania

S

S. — South
sa. — sierra, serra
S. Afr., S. Africa — South Africa
salt dep. — salt deposit
salt des. — salt desert
S. Amer. — South America
São T. & Pr. — São Tomé
    and Príncipe
Sask. — Saskatchewan
Saudi Ar. — Saudi Arabia
S. Aust., S. Austral. — South Australia
S.C. — South Carolina
Scot. — Scotland
Sd. — Sound
S. Dak. — South Dakota
Sen. — Senegal
Seych. — Seychelles
Sing. — Singapore
S. Leone — Sierra Leone
Slvk. — Slovakia
Slvn. — Slovenia
S. Marino — San Marino
Sol. Is. — Solomon Islands
Sp. — Spanish
Spr., Sprs. — Spring, Springs
St., Ste. — Saint, Sainte
Sta. — Station
St. P.& M. — Saint Pierre and
    Miquelon
St. Vin. & Grens. — St. Vincent & The
    Grenadines
str., strs. — strait, straits
Sur. — Suriname
Swaz. — Swaziland
Switz. — Switzerland

T

Taj. — Tajikistan
Tanz. — Tanzania
Tas. — Tasmania
Tenn. — Tennessee
terr., terrs. — territory, territories
Tex. — Texas
Thai. — Thailand
trad. — traditional
Trin. & Tob. — Trinidad and Tobago
Tun. — Tunisia
Turk. — Turkmenistan
twp. — township

U

U.A.E. — United Arab Emirates
U.K. — United Kingdom
Ukr. — Ukraine
urb. area — urban area
Urug. — Uruguay
U.S. — United States
Uzb. — Uzbekistan

V

Va. — Virginia
Ven., Venez. — Venezuela
V.I. (U.K.) — Virgin Islands (U.K.)
V.I. (U.S.) — Virgin Islands (U.S.)
Vic. — Victoria
Viet. — Vietnam
Vill. — Village
vol. — volcano
Vt. — Vermont

W

W. — West, Western
Wash. — Washington
W. Aust., W. Austral. — Western
    Australia
W. Indies — West
    Indies
Wis. — Wisconsin
W. Va. — West Virginia
Wyo. — Wyoming

Y

Yugo. — Yugoslavia
Yukon — Yukon Territory

Z

Zim. — Zimbabwe

Index to Terrain Maps

on pages X through XXXII

This index contains only names of land and ocean physical features. Names of towns, internal divisions and countries are not included. The entry name is followed by a letter-number combination which refers to the area on the map in which the name will be found. The number following the map reference for the entry refers, not to the page on which the entry will be found, but to the map plate number.

Index Continued

THE PHYSICAL WORLD
Terrain Maps of Land Forms and Ocean Floors

CONTENTS

RELIEF MODELS BY ERNST G. HOFMANN, ASSISTED BY RAFAEL MARTINEZ

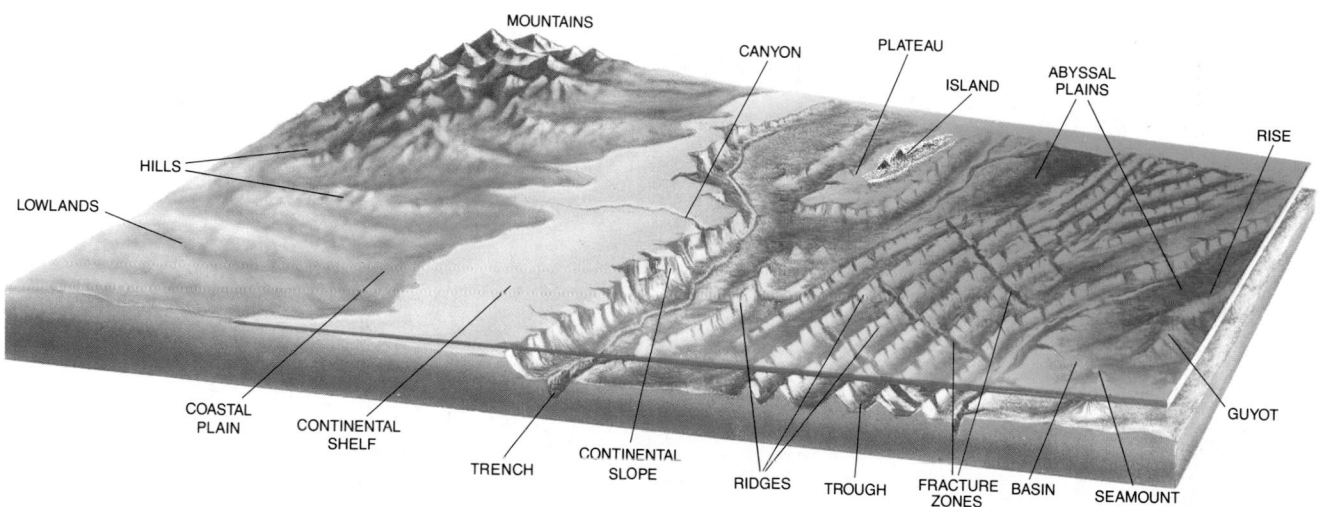

The oblique view diagram above is designed to provide a detailed view of the ocean floor as if seen through the depth of the sea. Graduating blue tones are used to contrast ocean floor depths: from light blue to represent shallow continental shelves to dark blues in the greater depths. Land relief is shown in conventional hypsometric tints.

In this dramatic collection of topographic maps of continents, oceans and major regions of the world, Hammond introduces a revolutionary new technique in cartography.

While most maps depicting terrain are created from painted artwork that is then photographed, Hammond now premiers the use of a remarkable sculptured model mapping technique created by one of our master cartographers.

The process begins with the sculpting of large scale three-dimensional models. Once physical details have been etched on the models and refinements completed, relief work is checked for accurate elevation based on a vertical scale exaggerated for visual effect.

Finished models are airbrushed and painted, then photographed using a single northwesterly light source to achieve a striking three-dimensional effect. The result is the dynamic presentation of mountain ranges and peaks on land, and canyons, trenches and seamounts on the ocean floor. Never before have maps conveyed such rich beauty while providing a realistic representation of the world as we know it.

ARCTIC OCEAN

QUEEN ELIZABETH
ISLANDS

Ellesmere I.

GREENLAND

CANADA
BASIN

Devon I.

Greenland
Sea

Beaufort Sea

Banks I.

Baffin

Baffin
Island

Bay

Arctic Circle

Norwegian
Sea

Wrangel
I.

Pt. Barrow

Victoria
I.

NORTH
BASIN

Chukchi
Sea

Yukon

Great Bear
L.

Iceland

Mt. McKinley

ROCKY

Great Slave
L.

LABRADOR
BASIN

IRMINGER BASIN

Great
Britain

Bering Sea

Gulf of Alaska

NORTH

Hudson
Bay

ICELAND BASIN

North
Sea

ALEUTIAN
BASIN

Peace

Bay

Ireland

ALEUTIAN ISLANDS

Mountains

AMERICA

CHARLIE GIBBS
FRACTURE ZONE

ALEUTIAN TRENCH

Great
Lakes

Newfoundland

MENDOCINO FRACTURE ZONE

Great Plains

Missouri

C. Race

HAWAIIAN

C. Mendocino

Ohio

ATLANTIC

C. Hatteras

Mt.

RIDGE

Appalachian Mts.

Mid

HAWAIIAN ISLANDS

MOLOKAI FRACTURE ZONE

Colorado

Mississippi

ATLANTIC

RIDGE

Tropic of Cancer

Rio Grande

L. Chad

California

Gulf of
Mexico

WEST

Sah

CENTRAL

CLIPPERTON FRACTURE ZONE

Cuba

Equator

Caribbean
Sea

INDIES

C. Verde

A F

PACIFIC

PACIFIC

GUATEMALA
BASIN

Orinoco

Niger

BASIN

Negro

Amazon

ROMANCHE FRACTURE ZONE

C. de São Roque

Andes

Madeira

BRAZIL

OCEAN

TONGA
TRENCH

Tropic of Capricorn

PERU
BASIN

PERU CHILE TRENCH

SOUTH

AMERICA

São Francisco

MID

BASIN

Parana

KERMADEC
TRENCH

Mountains

CHILE
BASIN

SOUTHWEST

PACIFIC

Cerro
Aconcagua

ARGENTINE

BASIN

ATLANTIC

BASIN

Falkland Is.

RIDGE

Tierra del Fuego

SOUTH
SANDWICH
TRENCH

C. Horn

Drake Passage

PACIFIC ANTARCTIC RIDGE

AMUNDSEN ABYSSAL PLAIN

Antarctic
Peninsula

WEDDELL

Antarctic Circle

ABYSSAL PLAIN

Bellingshausen
Sea

Weddell

Sea

ANTARCTICA

0 500 1000 1500 2000 2500   3000 MILES at Equator

0 500 1000 1500 2000 2500 3000 KILOMETERS at Equator

A R C T I C   O C E A N

FRANZ JOSEF LAND

SEVERNAYA
ZEMLYA

NEW SIBERIAN IS.

SVALBARD

Novaya
Zemlya

*Laptev
Sea*

Wrangel
I.

Nordkapp

Kjölen

*Barents
Sea*

*Kara
Sea*

S   i   b   e   r   i   a

L. Ladoga

Baltic Sea

Ob

Yenisey

Lena

Ural Mountains

Angara

Kamchatka
Pen.

*Bering
Sea*

ALEUTIAN
BASIN

E U R O P E

A   S   I   A

Irtysh

Dnieper

Volga

Balkhash

L. Baykal

Aldan

Amur

Sea
of
Okhotsk

ALEUTIAN ISLANDS

ALPS

Danube

Black Sea

Caspian Sea

Aral
Sea

Gobi

Sakhalin

KURIL-KAMCHATKA TRENCH

ALEUTIAN TRENCH

Mediterranean Sea

Euphrates

Kunlun

Huang

Honshu

Sea of
Japan

JAPAN
TRENCH

NORTHWEST
PACIFIC
BASIN

P A C I F I C

A F R I C A

Nile

Red Sea

Indus

Himalaya

Mt. Everest

Ganges

Lhasa

East
China
Sea

Tropic of Cancer

*Arabian
Sea*

ARABIAN
BASIN

Taiwan

MARIANA
IS.

MARIANA
TRENCH

MARSHALL IS.

CENTRAL
PACIFIC
BASIN

*Bay of
Bengal*

C. Comorin

South
China
Sea

Luzon

PHILIPPINE
BASIN

Challenger
Deep

Ceylon

CEYLON

Mekong

Borneo

Mindanao

CAROLINE IS.

CARLSBERG RIDGE

SOMALI
BASIN

CENTRAL

PLAIN

MELANESIAN
BASIN

Equator

Congo

Victoria

Kilimanjaro

INDIAN
RIDGE

Sumatra

Java

Celebes

New Guinea

O C E A N

NINETYEAST RIDGE

JAVA TRENCH

*Coral
Sea*

Fiji Is.

GOLA

Zambezi

I N D I A N

Madagascar

Broken
Plateau

A U S T R A L I A

Tropic of Capricorn

SIN

WALVIS RIDGE

Orange

O C E A N

C. Leeuwin

Great Barrier Reef

*Tasman
Sea*

North Cape

CAPE
BASIN

C. of Good Hope

S. AUSTRALIA BASIN

North I.

AGULHAS RIDGE

SOUTHWEST INDIAN RIDGE

SOUTHEAST INDIAN RIDGE

KERGUELEN

South I.

Tasmania

SOUTHEAST INDIAN RIDGE

PLATEAU

ENDERBY ABYSSAL PLAIN

AUSTRALIAN-ANTARCTIC BASIN

Antarctic Circle

*Amery
Ice Shelf*

C. Adare

A N T A R C T I C A

*Ross
Sea*

LEGEND FOR TERRAIN MAPS

International Boundaries —··—	Mountain Peaks ▲
State and Provincial Boundaries —·—·	National Capitals ⊛
Other Boundaries ——	Other Capitals ⊙
Boundaries Along Rivers	Canals —

World | Plate 1

XII

Plate 2 | **Europe**

0   100   200   300   400   500 MILES

0   100   200   300   400   500 KILOMETERS

Western Europe | Plate 3

XIV

Plate 4 | **Asia**

© Copyright by HAMMOND INCORPORATED, Maplewood, N.J.

| 0 | 300 | 600 | 900 | 1200 | 1500 MILES |
| 0 | 300 | 600 | 900 | 1200 | 1500 KILOMETERS |

Southwest Asia | Plate 5

0   100   200   300   400   500 MILES

0   100   200   300   400   500 KILOMETERS

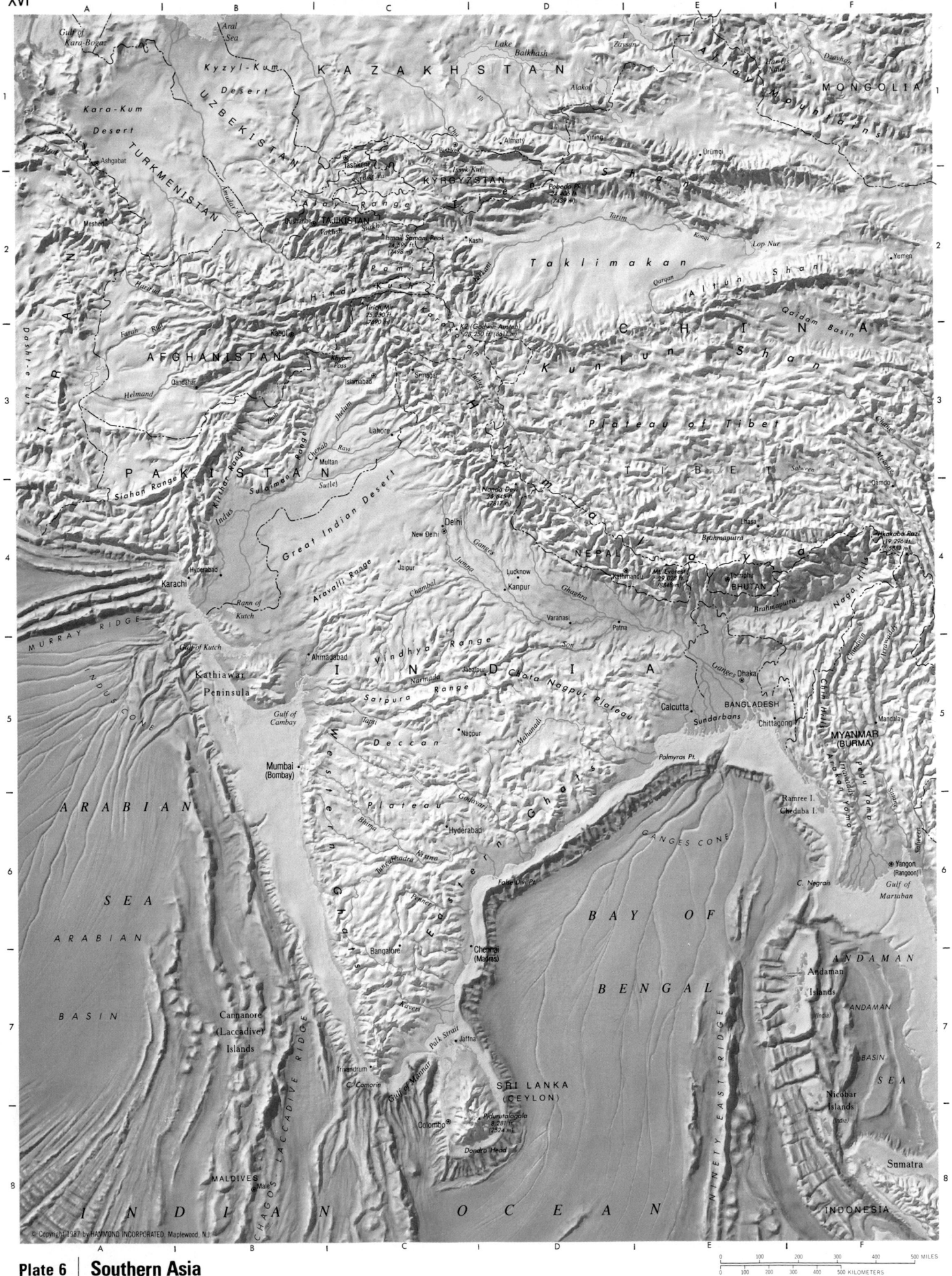

Plate 6 | **Southern Asia**

East Asia | Plate 7

© Copyright 1987 by HAMMOND INCORPORATED, Maplewood, N.J.

0   100   200   300   400   500   600 MILES
0   100   200   300   400   500   600 KILOMETERS

Plate 8 | Southeast Asia

PACIFIC OCEAN

KYUSHU PALAU RIDGE

PARECE VELA BASIN

PHILIPPINE SEA BASIN

PHILIPPINE

RYUKYU TRENCH

PALAU TRENCH

WEST CAROLINE BASIN

PAPUA NEW GUINEA

IRIAN JAYA

Maoke Mts. Puncak Jaya (5,030 m) (16,500 ft.)

ARAFURA SEA

ARAFURA SHELF

AUSTRALIA

Gulf of Carpentaria

Darwin

C. Wessel

Melville I.

Bathurst I.

Cobourg Pen.

Groote Eylandt

Kolepom

Schouten Is.

Dolak

Aru Is.

Kai Is.

Tanimbar Is.

Ceram

Misool

Banda Is.

Alor

Wetar

Timor

TIMOR SEA

FLORES SEA

BANDA SEA

MOLUCCA SEA

CERAM SEA

CELEBES SEA

CELEBES BASIN

Sangihe Is.

Talaud Is.

Celebes

Mindanao

Apo Vol. 9,692 ft. (2,954 m)

PHILIPPINES

Luzon

Manila

Bataan

Batan Is.

Babuyan Is.

Mindoro

Panay

Cebu

Negros

Samar

Leyte

Bohol

Jolo

Sulu Archipelago

SULU SEA

SULU BASIN

SOUTH CHINA SEA BASIN

SOUTH CHINA SEA

TAIWAN

Taipei

Kao-hsiung

Taichung

EAST CHINA SEA

RYUKYU TRENCH

Ryukyu Islands

Okinawa

Naha

Amami

Yaku

Tanega

C. Balinao

CHINA

Guangzhou

Guilin

HONG KONG

Macau

Shantou

Xiamen

Fuzhou

Nanchang

Changsha

Poyang Hu

Leizhou Bandao

Hainan

Haikou

VIETNAM

Hanoi

Haiphong

Gulf of Tonkin

Da Nang

Ho Chi Minh City

CONTINENTAL SHELF

Mekong

Annam Cordillera

LAOS

Vientiane

CAMBODIA

Phnom Penh

Tonle Sap

Mekong

Mui Bai Bung

THAILAND

Bangkok

Chao Phraya

Korat Plateau

Mun

Gulf of Thailand

Isthmus of Kra

Mekong

MYANMAR (BURMA)

Yangon (Rangoon)

Pegu Yoma

Arakan Yoma

Irrawaddy

Shan Plateau

Hkakabo Razi 19,296 ft. (5,881 m)

Brahmaputra

BHUTAN

BANGLADESH

Dhaka

Chittagong

INDIA

Calcutta

Ganges

Sundarbans

BAY OF BENGAL

ANDAMAN SEA

ANDAMAN BASIN

Andaman Islands

Nicobar Islands

C. Negrais

Mergui Arch.

Malay Peninsula

Georgetown

Kuala Lumpur

MALAYA

MALAYSIA

SINGAPORE

Str. of Malacca

Medan

Padang

Mt. Kerinci 12,467 ft. (3,800 m)

SUMATRA

Palembang

Bangka

Billiton

Karimata Str.

SUNDA SHELF

Natuna Is.

Anambas Is.

Riau Arch.

Lingga Arch.

BORNEO

Kuching

Pontianak

Kapuas

BRUNEI

Bandar Seri Begawan

Mt. Kinabalu 13,455 ft. (4,104 m)

Mt. Raya 7,474 ft. (2,278 m)

Balikpapan

Banjarmasin

Barito

Makassar Strait

Ujung Pandang

Gulf of Bone

Gulf of Tomini

Manado

INDONESIA

JAVA SEA

Jakarta

Bandung

Surabaya

Madura

JAVA

Semeru 12,060 ft. (3,676 m)

Bali

Lombok

Sumbawa

Flores

Sunda Str.

JAVA TRENCH

SUNDA TRENCH

COCOS BASIN

INDIAN OCEAN

Sunda

Mentawai Is.

Nias

Siberut

Enggano

© Copyright 1987 by HAMMOND INCORPORATED Maplewood, N.J.

| 0 | 100 | 200 | 300 | 400 | 500 | 600 MILES |

| 0 | 100 | 200 | 300 | 400 | 500 | 600 KILOMETERS |

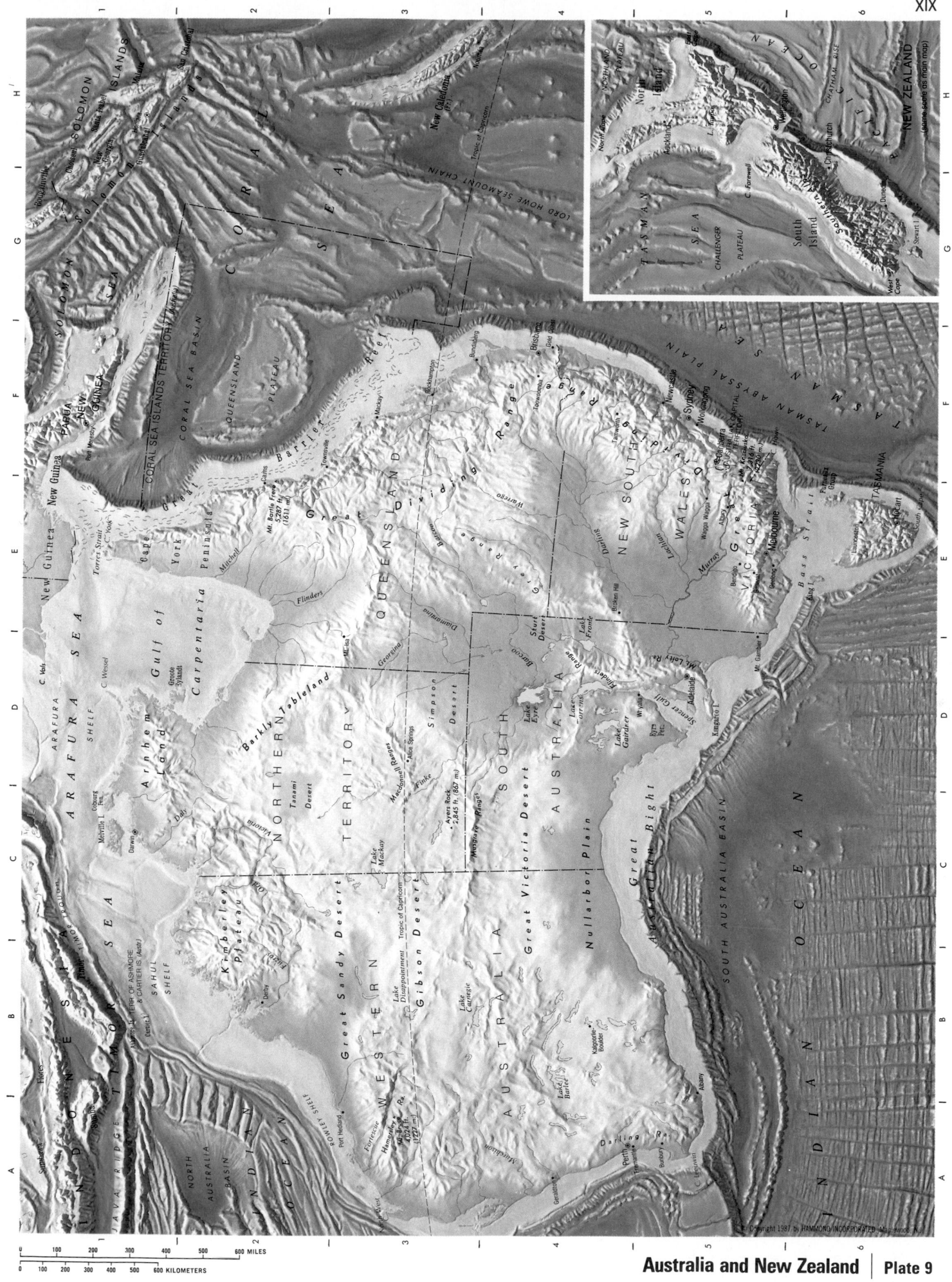

Australia and New Zealand | Plate 9

INDONESIA

SOLOMON ISLANDS

SOLOMON SEA

Bougainville
Choiseul
New Georgia
Malaita
San Cristobal
Guadalcanal

PAPUA NEW GUINEA

New Guinea

Port Moresby

C O R A L   S E A

New Caledonia (Fr.)

LORD HOWE SEAMOUNT CHAIN

Tropic of Capricorn

CORAL SEA BASIN

CORAL SEA ISLANDS TERRITORY (Austl.)

QUEENSLAND PLATEAU

Great Barrier Reef

Cairns
Townsville
Mackay

Mt. Bartle Frere
5287 ft.
(1611 m.)

Rockhampton
Bundaberg
Gympie
Gold Coast
Brisbane
Toowoomba
Warrego

Q U E E N S L A N D

Great Dividing Range

Mitchell

Flinders

C. York
Torres Strait
Cape York Peninsula

Barcoo
Diamantina

Grey Range

N E W   S O U T H   W A L E S

Darling
Newcastle
Sydney
Wollongong
Canberra
AUSTRALIAN CAPITAL TERRITORY
Mt. Kosciusko
7316 ft.
(2230 m.)
Albury
Wagga Wagga

Warrego

Lachlan
Murrumbidgee
Murray

Tasman
Bendigo
Geelong
Ballarat
V I C T O R I A
Melbourne

Bass Strait
King I.
Furneaux Group

T A S M A N I A
Launceston
Hobart
South Cape

TASMAN SEA

ARAFURA SEA

C. Van Diemen
ARAFURA SHELF

Gulf of Carpentaria

C. Wessel
Groote Eylandt

Arnhem Land

Melville I.
Coburg Pen.

Darwin

N O R T H E R N

T E R R I T O R Y

Barkly Tableland

Tanami Desert

Macdonnell Ranges
Alice Springs

Finke

Ayers Rock
2,845 ft. (867 m.)
Musgrave Ranges

S O U T H

A U S T R A L I A

Lake Eyre
Lake Frome
Sturt Desert
Simpson Desert
Georgina

Lake Torrens
Flinders Range

Lake Gairdner
Eyre Pen.
Mt. Loftv Ra.
Mt. Gambier
Adelaide
Spencer Gulf
Kangaroo I.
Wyalla

Broken Hill

TIMOR SEA

Timor

Bathurst I.

Daly
Victoria

Kimberley Plateau

Derby

Ord

Lake Mackay

Lake Disappointment

W E S T E R N

Gibson Desert

Great Sandy Desert

Tropic of Capricorn

Lake Carnegie

Great Victoria Desert

A U S T R A L I A

Nullarbor Plain

Great Australian Bight

TERR. OF ASHMORE & CARTIER IS. (Austl.)

SAHUL SHELF

BROWSE SHELF

NORTH AUSTRALIA BASIN

INDIAN

OCEAN

JAVA RIDGE

TIMOR TROUGH

Port Hedland
Fortescue
Hamersley
Mt. Bruce
4,024 ft.
(1227 m.)

Lake Barlee

Kalgoorlie-Boulder

Lake
Lefroy

Albany

Murchison
Darling Ra.
Perth
Geraldton

C. Leeuwin

SOUTH AUSTRALIA BASIN

I N D I A N

O C E A N

PACIFIC OCEAN

NORTHLAND PLATEAU

North Cape
North Island
Auckland
L. Taupo
Wellington

CHATHAM RISE

Christchurch
Dunedin
South Island
Southern Alps
C. Farewell
West Cape
Stewart I.

TASMAN SEA

CHALLENGER PLATEAU

S O U T H   A U S T R A L I A   B A S I N

TASMAN ABYSSAL PLAIN

T A S M A N   S E A

0 100 200 300 400 500 600 MILES
0 100 200 300 400 500 600 KILOMETERS

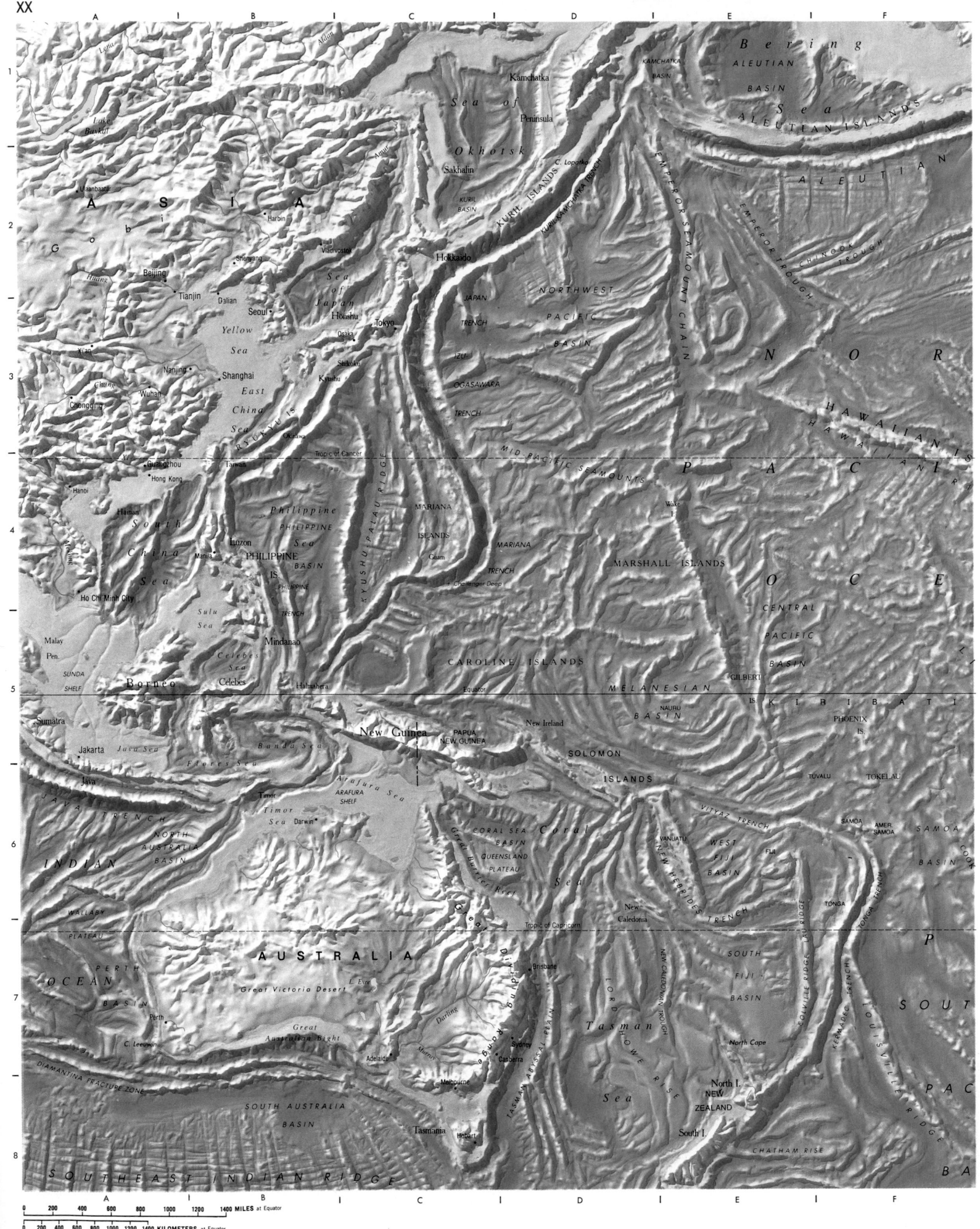

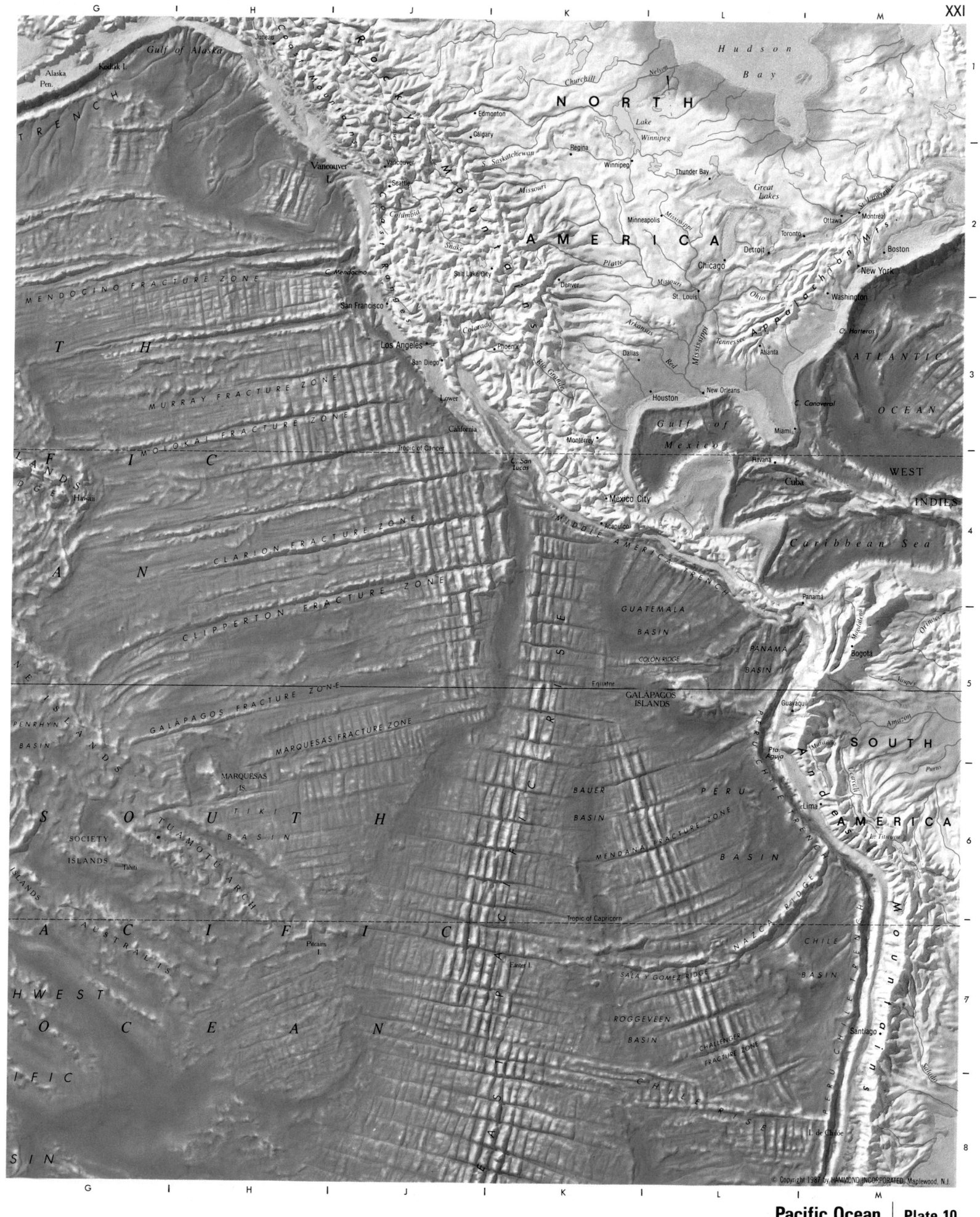

Pacific Ocean | Plate 10

© Copyright 1997 by HAMMOND INCORPORATED, Maplewood, N.J.

A | B | C | D | E | F

1

2

3

4

5

6

7

8

Plate 11 | **Africa**

© Copyright by HAMMOND INCORPORATED, Maplewood, N.J.

| 0 | 200 | 400 | 600 | 800 | 1000 MILES |
| 0 | 200 | 400 | 600 | 800 | 1000 KILOMETERS |

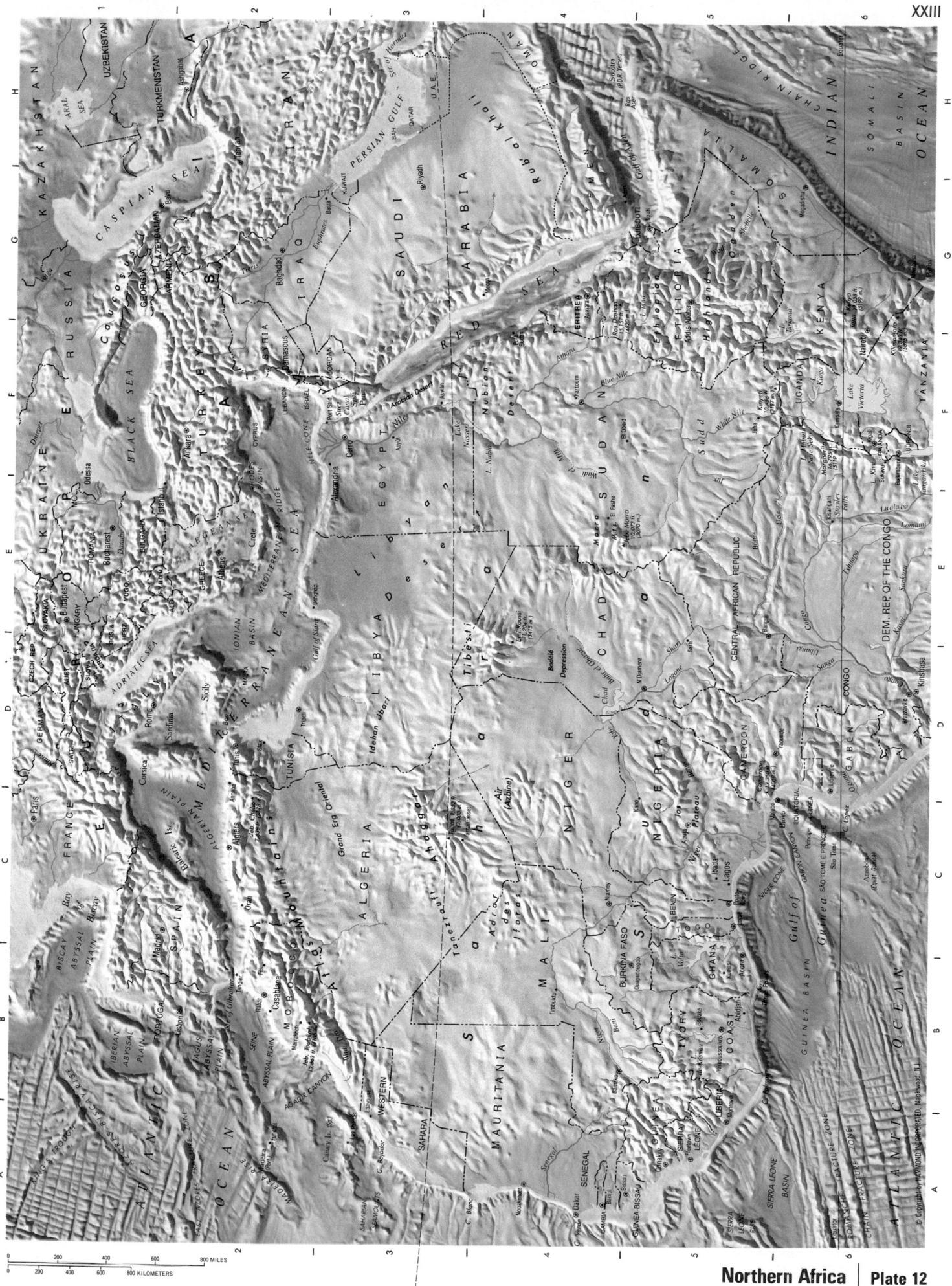

Northern Africa | Plate 12

0   200   400   600   800 MILES

0   200   400   600   800 KILOMETERS

© Copyright HAMMOND INCORPORATED, Maplewood, NJ

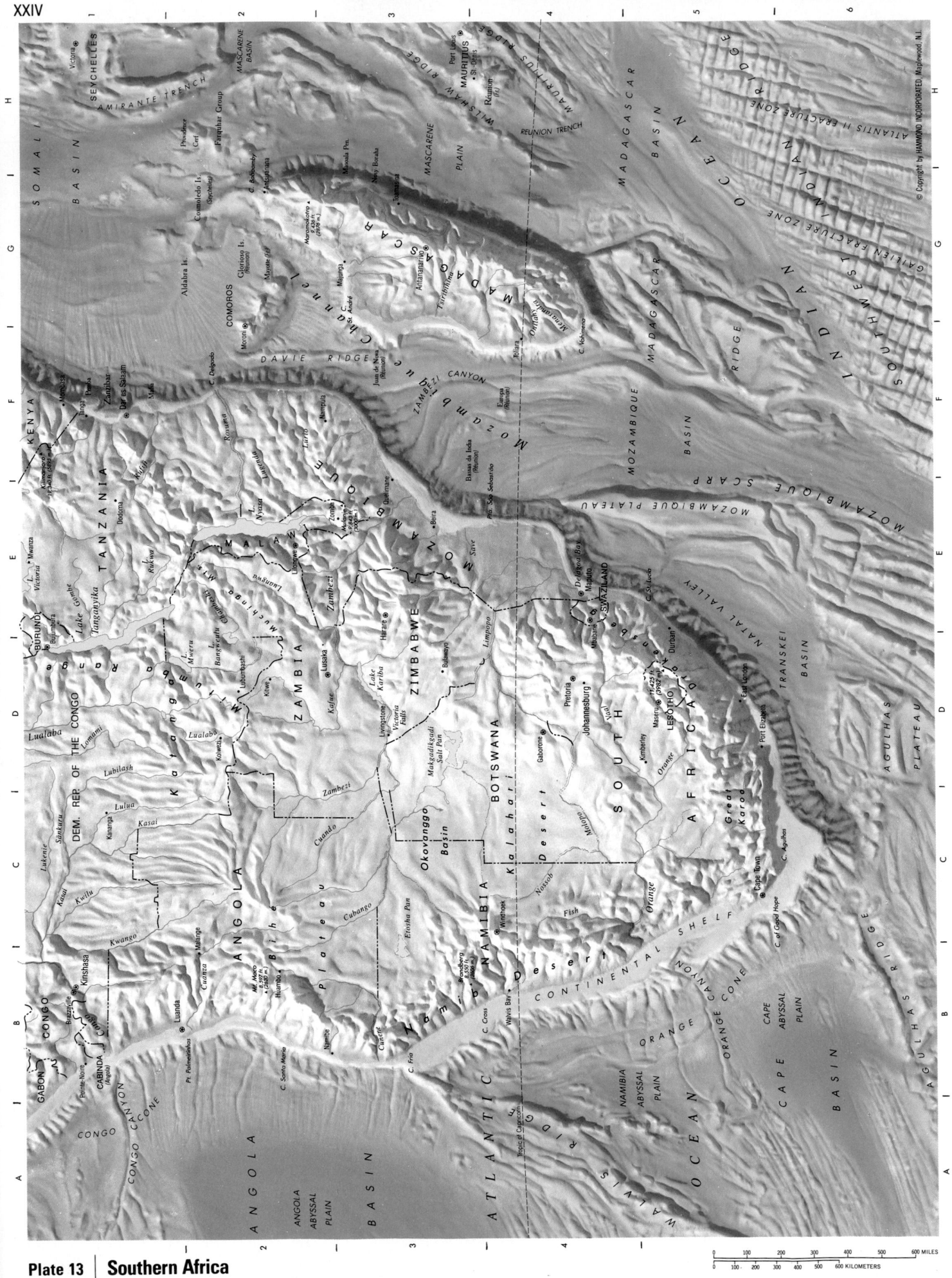

Plate 13 | **Southern Africa**

SEYCHELLES

Victoria ⊛

AMIRANTE TRENCH

SOMALI BASIN

Providence Cert

Cosmoledo Is. (Seychelles)

Farquhar Group

MASCARENE BASIN

Port Louis ⊛ MAURITIUS St.-Denis

Reunion (Fra)

WILSHAM RIDGE

MAURITIUS RIDGE

REUNION TRENCH

© Copyright by HAMMOND INCORPORATED Maplewood, N.I.

MADAGASCAR BASIN

SOUTHWEST INDIAN RIDGE

GALIEN FRACTURE ZONE

ATLANTIS II FRACTURE ZONE

INDIAN OCEAN

Aldabra Is.

C. Bobaomby

St-Grégoire

Cosaid Pen.

Nosy Boraha

MASCARENE PLAIN

Glorioso Is. (France)

Mayotte (Fra)

St. André

COMOROS

Moroni ⊛

Maromokotro 9,436 ft. (2876 m.)

Maunga

Antananarivo ⊛

MADAGASCAR

Tsiribihina

C. Kohmena

Toamasina

DAVIE RIDGE

C. Delgado

Onilaly

Menabizoari (Reunion)

C. Kohmena

Toliara

MADAGASCAR BASIN

MADAGASCAR RIDGE

KENYA

Mombasa ●

Tanga ●

Pemba

Zanzibar

Dar es Salaam ⊛

Mafia

MOZAMBIQUE

ZAMBEZI CANYON

Juan de Nova (Reunion)

Bassas da India (Reunion)

Ilha São Sebastião

Europa (Reunion)

MOZAMBIQUE BASIN

MOZAMBIQUE SCARP

Pemba

C. Delgado

Nampula

MOZAMBIQUE CHANNEL

MOZAMBIQUE PLATEAU

TANZANIA

Kilimanjaro 19,340 ft. (5895 m.)

Mwanza ●

L. Victoria

Dodoma

L. Kukwa

Rovuma

Lurio

Lichinga

MALAWI

L. Nyasa

Mulanje 9,843 ft. (3000 m.)

Lilongwe ⊛

Blantyre

Zomba

Quelimane

Beira

Save

Delagoa Bay

Maputo ⊛

SWAZILAND

Mbabane ⊛

NATAL VALLEY

BURUNDI

Bujumbura ⊛

L. Tanganyika

Kigoma

Range

L. Mweru

Banweulu

Chambeshi

Luangwa

Muchinga Mts.

Zambezi

Lake Kariba

Harare ⊛

ZIMBABWE

Bulawayo ●

Limpopo

C. St. Lucia

Drakensberg

Durban ●

TRANSKEI BASIN

DEM. REP. OF THE CONGO

Lualaba

Lomami

Lubumbashi ●

Kolwezi

Kitwe ●

ZAMBIA

Lusaka ⊛

Kafue

Livingstone

Victoria Falls

Makgadikgadi Salt Pan

BOTSWANA

Gaborone ⊛

Pretoria ⊛

Johannesburg ●

Vaal

Kimberley ●

Maseru ⊛ 11,425 ft. (3482 m.)

LESOTHO

Orange

East London ●

Port Elizabeth ●

AGULHAS PLATEAU

Lualaba

Lubilash

Sankuru

Lulua

Kasai

Kananga

Katanga

Plateau

Zambezi

Okovango Basin

Kalahari

Desert

Molopo

SOUTH AFRICA

Great Karoo

AGULHAS RIDGE

Lukenie

Kwilu

Kasai

Kwango

ANGOLA

Bié

Plateau

Cuando

Cubango

Nossob

Fish

Orange

NAMIB Desert

Cape Town ●

C. Agulhas

C. of Good Hope

CAPE ABYSSAL PLAIN

CAPE BASIN

Kinshasa ⊛

Brazzaville ⊛

CONGO

GABON

Pointe-Noire ●

CABINDA (Angola)

Pt. Palmeirinhas

Luanda ⊛

Malange ●

Mt. Moco 8,597 ft. (2620 m.)

Huambo ●

Cuanza

Cunene

Namibe ●

C. Santa Maria

C. Frio

Zambie

C. Cross

Walvis Bay ●

Brandberg 8,550 ft.

Etosha Pan

Windhoek ⊛

NAMIBIA

CONTINENTAL SHELF

ORANGE CANYON

ORANGE CONE

NAMIBIA ABYSSAL PLAIN

Tropic of Capricorn

ATLANTIC OCEAN

WALVIS RIDGE

CONGO CANYON

CONGO CONE

ANGOLA

ANGOLA ABYSSAL PLAIN

BASIN

0	100	200	300	400	500	600 MILES
0 100 200	300	400	500	600 KILOMETERS

0   200   400   600   800 MILES

0   200   400   600   800 KILOMETERS

South America | Plate 14

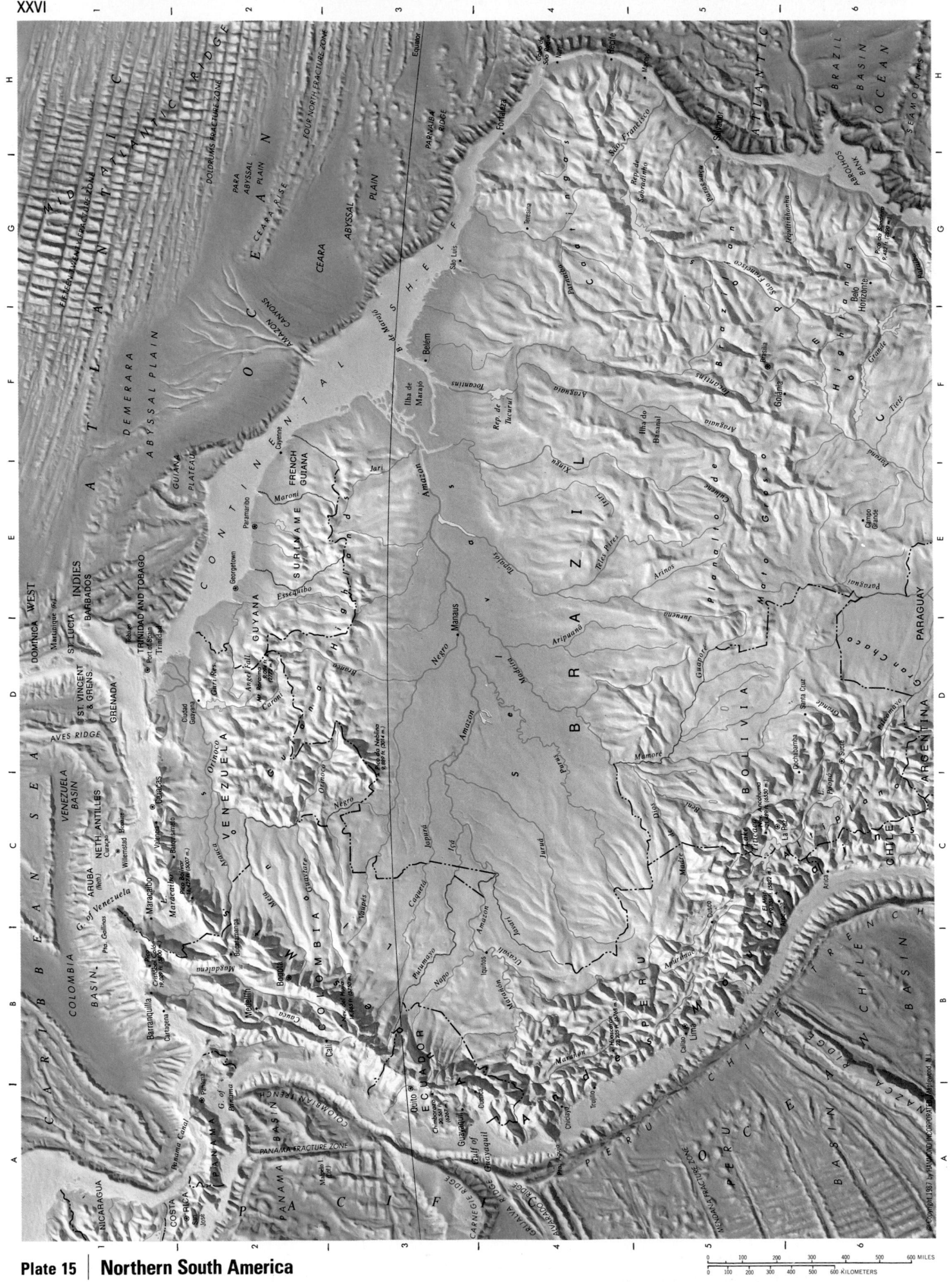

Plate 15 | **Northern South America**

5   100   200   300   400   500   600 MILES
0   100   200   300   400   500   600 KILOMETERS

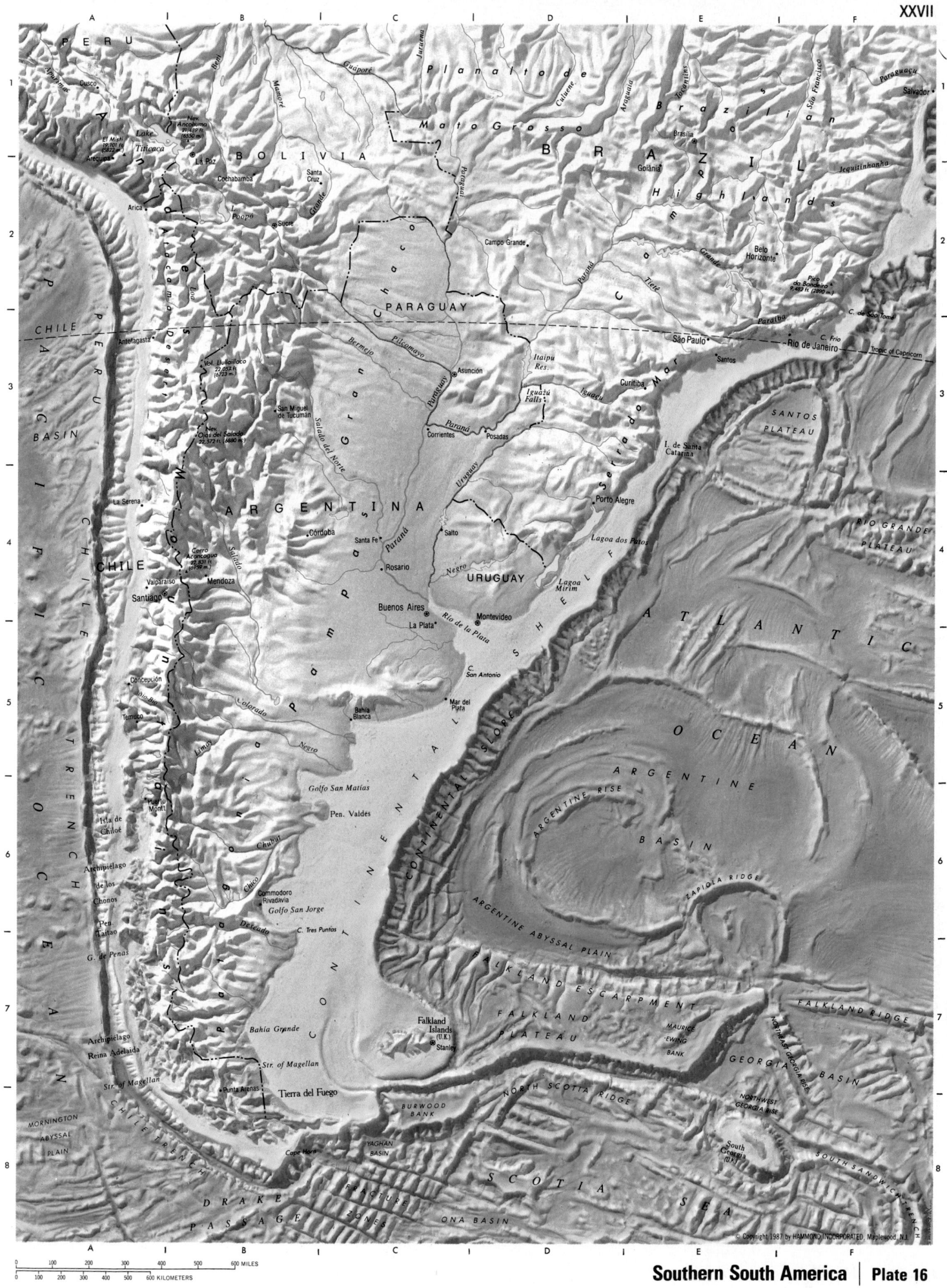

PERU

BOLIVIA

BRAZIL

Planalto de

Mato Grosso

Brazilian Highlands

PARAGUAY

Chaco

ARGENTINA

URUGUAY

CHILE

PACIFIC OCEAN

ATLANTIC OCEAN

Cusco
El Misti 19,101 ft (5822 m)
Arequipa
Lake Titicaca
La Paz
Cochabamba
Santa Cruz
Arica
L. Poopó
Sucre
Nev. Ancohuma 21,489 ft (6550 m)

Antofagasta
Vol. Llullaillaco 22,053 ft (6723 m.)
San Miguel de Tucumán
Nev. Ojos del Salado 22,572 ft (6880 m.)
La Serena
Córdoba
Santa Fe
Cerro Aconcagua 22,831 ft (6959 m.)
Valparaíso
Mendoza
Santiago
Rosario
Buenos Aires
La Plata
Concepción
Río Bío
Temuco
Colorado
Negro
Bahía Blanca
Isla de Chiloé
Puerto Montt
Limay
Archipiélago de los Chonos
Pen. Taitao
Golfo San Matías
Pen. Valdés
Chubut
Chico
Commodoro Rivadavia
Golfo San Jorge
C. Tres Puntas
Deseado
G. de Penas
Bahía Grande
Archipiélago Reina Adelaida
Str. of Magellan
Punta Arenas
Tierra del Fuego
Cape Horn

Campo Grande
Asunción
Paraguay
Pilcomayo
Bermejo
Grand Chaco
Salado del Norte
Paraná
Corrientes
Posadas
Iguazú Falls
Itaipú Res.
Salto
Negro
Lagoa Mirim
Montevideo
Río de la Plata
C. San Antonio
Mar del Plata

Goiânia
Brasília
Belo Horizonte
Pico da Bandeira 9,483 ft (2890 m.)
Jequitinhonha
Paraguaçu
Salvador
C. de São Tomé
São Paulo
Santos
Rio de Janeiro
Tropic of Capricorn
C. Frio
Curitiba
Porto Alegre
I. de Santa Catarina
Lagoa dos Patos

Serra do Mar

SANTOS PLATEAU
RIO GRANDE PLATEAU

ARGENTINE RISE
ARGENTINE BASIN
ZAPIOLA RIDGE
ARGENTINE ABYSSAL PLAIN

CONTINENTAL SLOPE
CONTINENTAL SHELF

FALKLAND ESCARPMENT
FALKLAND PLATEAU
FALKLAND RIDGE
Falkland Islands (U.K.)
Stanley
MAURICE EWING BANK

BURWOOD BANK
YAGHAN BASIN
NORTH SCOTIA RIDGE
SCOTIA SEA
SOUTH SANDWICH TRENCH
SOUTH GEORGIA RIDGE
GEORGIA BASIN
NORTHWEST GEORGIA RISE
South Georgia (U.K.)

DRAKE PASSAGE
FRACTURE ZONES
ONA BASIN

MORNINGTON ABYSSAL PLAIN
CHILE TRENCH
Str. of Magellan

PERU-CHILE TRENCH
Atacama Desert
CHILE BASIN
PERU BASIN

0 100 200 300 400 500 600 MILES
0 100 200 300 400 500 600 KILOMETERS

Plate 17 | **North America**

0   200   400   600   800   1000 MILES

0   200   400   600   800   1000 KILOMETERS

C. Copyright 1987 by HAMMOND INCORPORATED Maplewood, N.J.

Canada | **Plate 18**

0   100   200   300   400   500   600 MILES
0   100   200   300   400   500   600 KILOMETERS

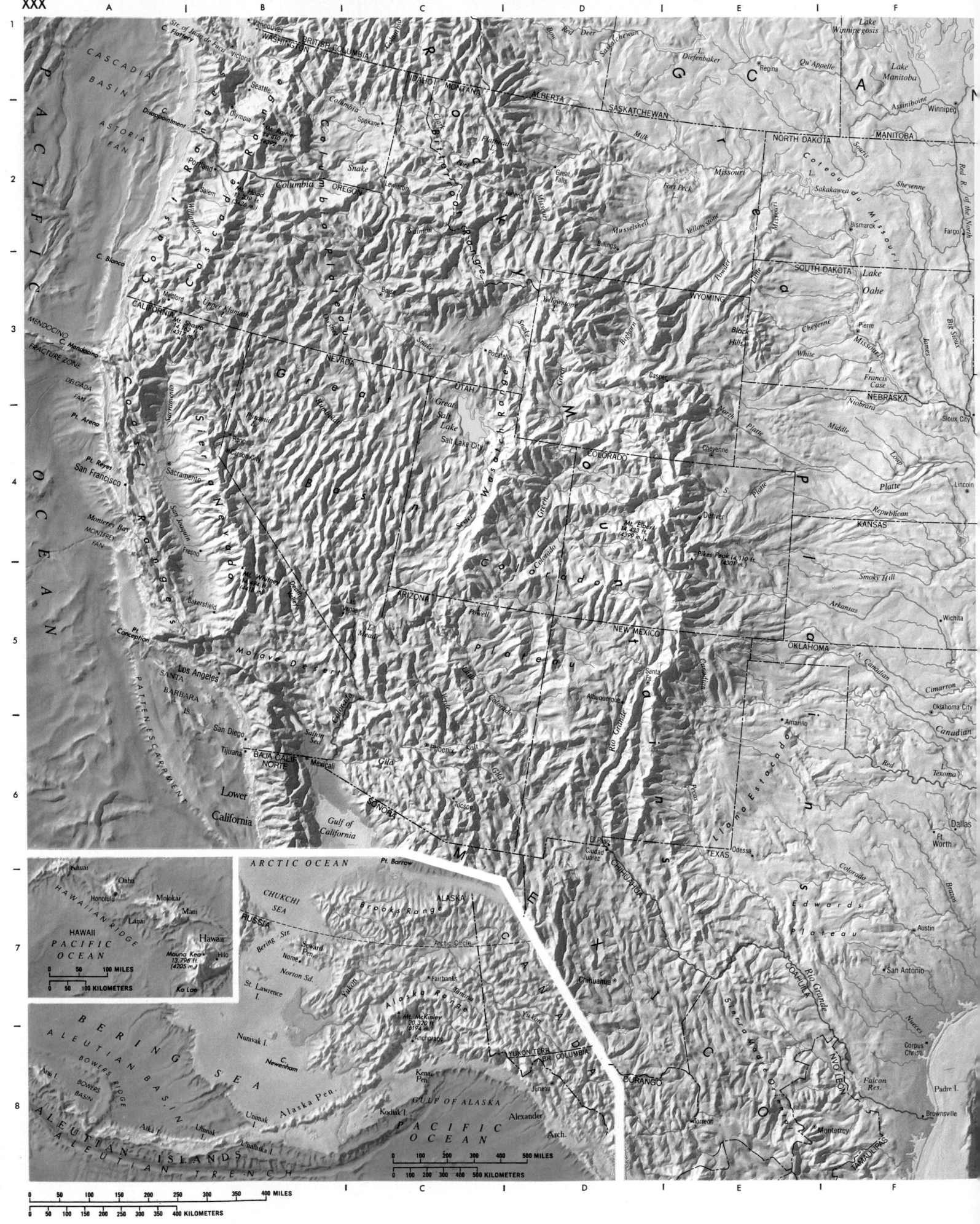

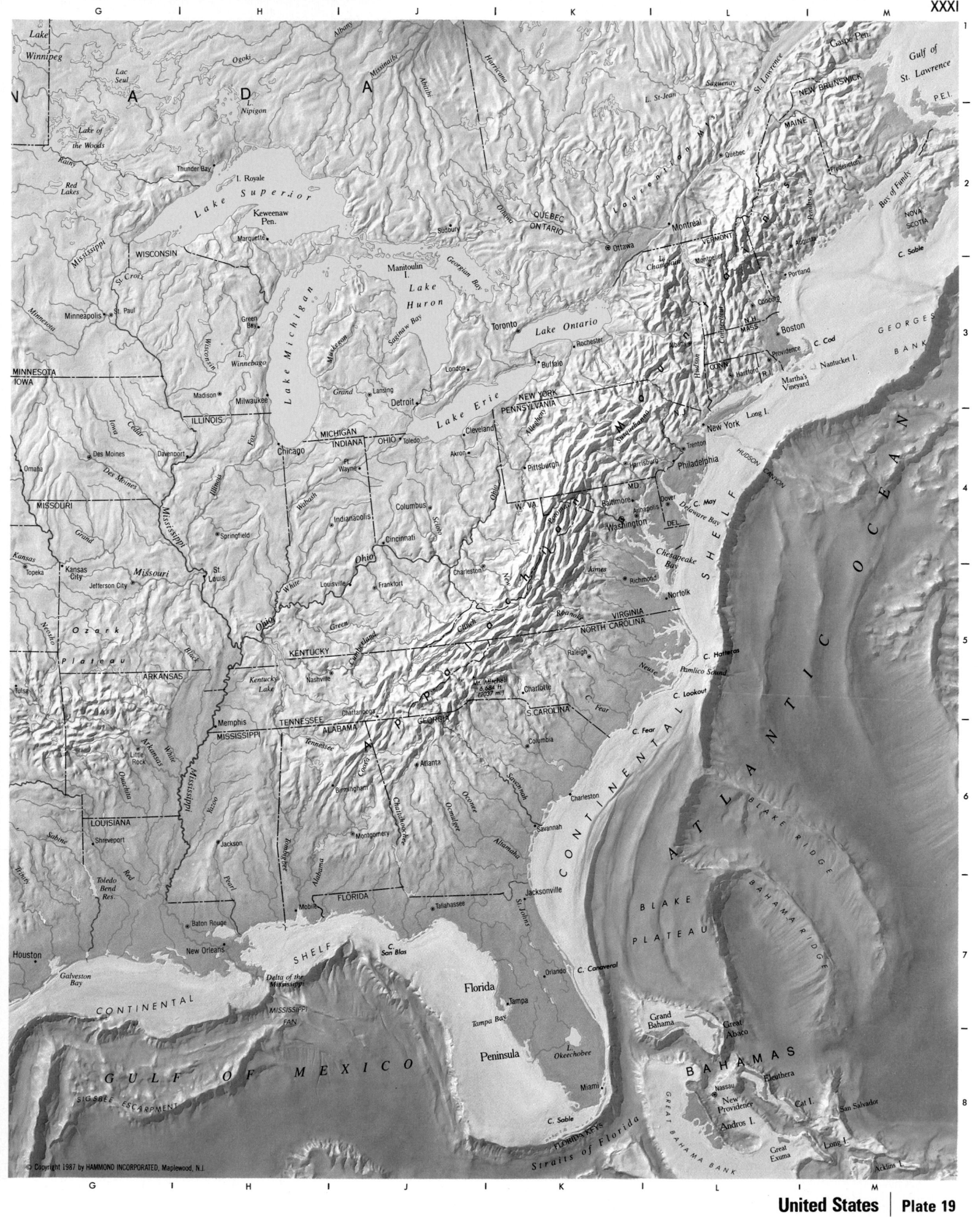

Lake Winnipeg

N

C A N A D A

Lac Seul

Ogoki

Missinaibi

Abitibi

Harricana

L. St-Jean

Saguenay

St. Lawrence

NEW BRUNSWICK

Gaspé Pen.

Gulf of St. Lawrence

P.E.I.

Lake of the Woods

L. Nipigon

Thunder Bay

Lake Superior

Keweenaw Pen.

Marquette

Sudbury

Ottawa

QUEBEC ONTARIO

Laurentian Mts.

Québec

Montréal

MAINE

Fredericton

NOVA SCOTIA

Augusta

C. Sable

Rainy

Red Lakes

I. Royale

WISCONSIN

St. Croix

Minnesota

Minneapolis

St. Paul

Green Bay

Manitoulin I.

Georgian Bay

Lake Huron

Saginaw Bay

Toronto

Lake Ontario

Rochester

VERMONT

L. Champlain

Montpelier

Concord

N.H.

Portland

Bay of Fundy

MINNESOTA

IOWA

Madison

Milwaukee

L. Winnebago

Fox

Grand

Muskegon

Lansing

Buffalo

London

Albany

Hudson

Boston

MASS.

Providence

C. Cod

GEORGES BANK

Des Moines

Davenport

ILLINOIS

Chicago

MICHIGAN

Ft. Wayne

INDIANA

OHIO

Toledo

Detroit

Lake Erie

Cleveland

Akron

NEW YORK PENNSYLVANIA

Allegheny

Pittsburgh

CONN.

Hartford

Nantucket I.

Martha's Vineyard

New York

Long I.

Omaha

MISSOURI

Iowa

Cedar

Wabash

Springfield

Indianapolis

Columbus

Scioto

Cincinnati

Harrisburg

Susquehanna

Trenton

Philadelphia

N.J.

HUDSON CANYON

Kansas

Topeka

Kansas City

Jefferson City

Missouri

Grand

St. Louis

Ohio

White

Louisville

Frankfort

Charleston

New

W. VA.

MD.

Baltimore

Washington

Annapolis

Dover

DEL.

Delaware Bay

C. May

CONTINENTAL SHELF

Neosho

Ozark Plateau

Black

KENTUCKY

Cumberland

Green

James

Richmond

Chesapeake Bay

ATLANTIC OCEAN

Tulsa

ARKANSAS

Kentucky Lake

Nashville

Clinch

VIRGINIA

NORTH CAROLINA

Roanoke

Norfolk

C. Hatteras

Little Rock

Ouachita

Arkansas

White

Memphis

TENNESSEE

Tennessee

Chattanooga

Mt. Mitchell 6,684 ft. (2037 m.)

Charlotte

Raleigh

Neuse

Pamlico Sound

C. Lookout

BLAKE RIDGE

MISSISSIPPI

ALABAMA

GEORGIA

Coosa

S. CAROLINA

Columbia

C. Fear

Roanoke

Atlanta

Birmingham

Montgomery

Alabama

Chattahoochee

Ocmulgee

Oconee

Savannah

Altamaha

Charleston

Savannah

C. Fear

BLAKE PLATEAU

ATLANTIC

LOUISIANA

Shreveport

Jackson

Pearl

Tombigbee

Yazoo

FLORIDA

Mobile

Tallahassee

Jacksonville

St. Johns

BAHAMA RIDGE

Toledo Bend Res.

Red

Sabine

Baton Rouge

New Orleans

SHELF

C. San Blas

Orlando

C. Canaveral

Grand Bahama

Great Abaco

Trinity

Houston

Galveston Bay

CONTINENTAL

Delta of the Mississippi

MISSISSIPPI FAN

Florida

Tampa

Tampa Bay

Florida Peninsula

L. Okeechobee

Miami

Blake

BAHAMAS

Nassau

New Providence

Eleuthera

Cat I.

San Salvador

GULF OF MEXICO

SIGSBEE ESCARPMENT

C. Sable

FLORIDA KEYS

Straits of Florida

GREAT BAHAMA BANK

Andros I.

Great Exuma

Long I.

Acklins I.

United States | **Plate 19**

Plate 20 | Middle America

0 100 200 300 400 500 600 MILES

0 100 200 300 400 500 600 KILOMETERS

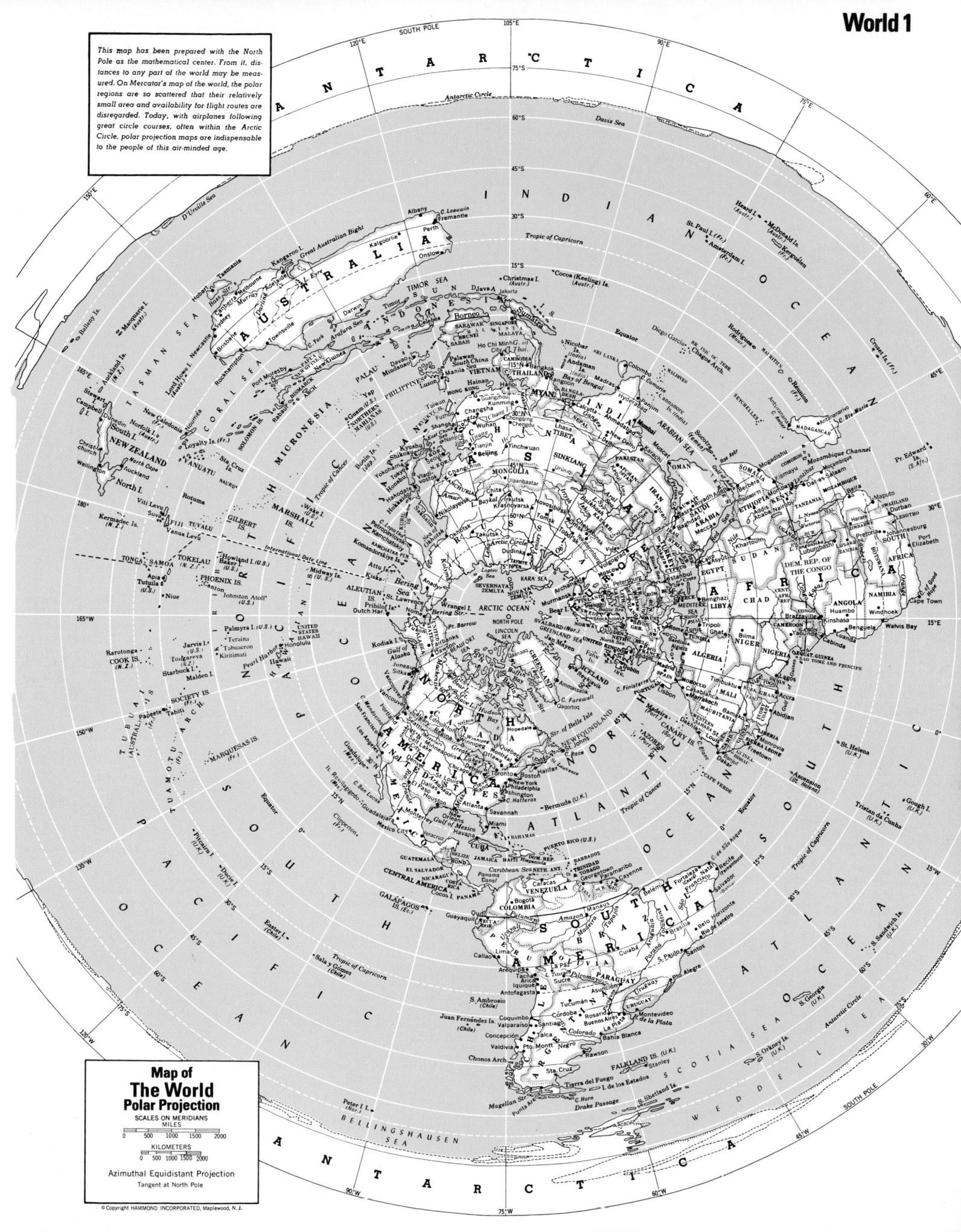

World 1

This map has been prepared with the North Pole as the mathematical center. From it, distances to any part of the world may be measured. On Mercator's map of the world, the polar regions are so scattered that their relatively small area and availability for flight routes are disregarded. Today, with airplanes following great circle courses, often within the Arctic Circle, polar projection maps are indispensable to the people of this air-minded age.

Map of
The World
Polar Projection
SCALES ON MERIDIANS
MILES

0   500   1000   1500   2000

KILOMETERS

0   500 1000 1500 2000

Azimuthal Equidistant Projection
Tangent at North Pole

© Copyright HAMMOND INCORPORATED, Maplewood, N.J.

The World

BRIESEMEISTER ELLIPTICAL
EQUAL-AREA PROJECTION

Capitals of Countries ....⊛
Other Capitals...........................⊛
International Boundaries......– – –

Scale 1:80,000,000

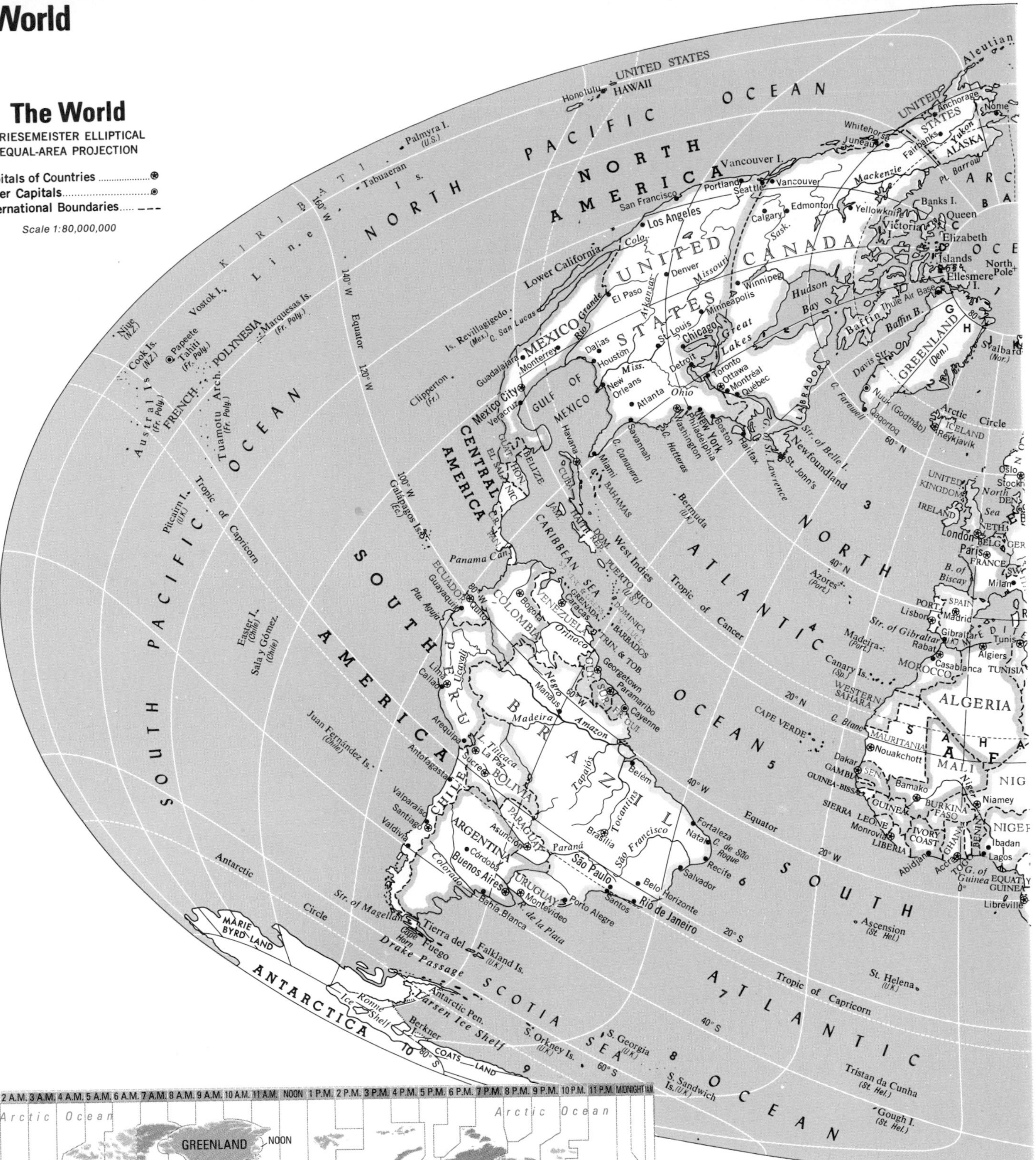

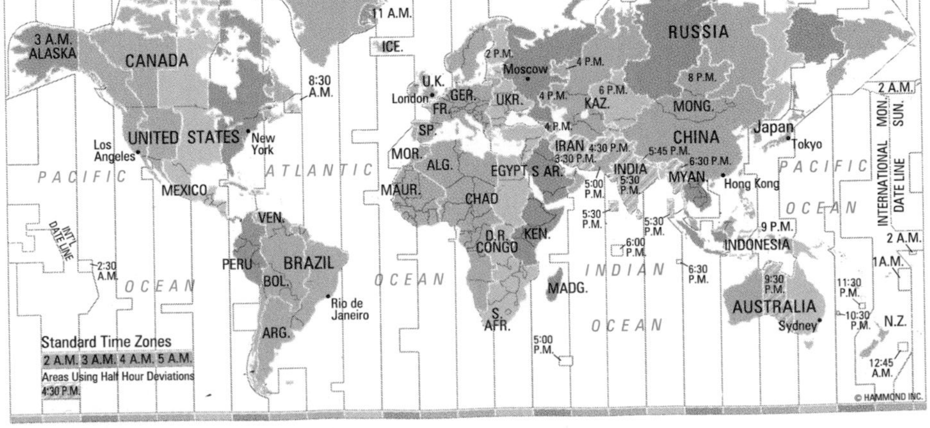

NORTH PACIFIC OCEAN

NORTH AMERICA

UNITED STATES

CANADA

SOUTH PACIFIC OCEAN

SOUTH AMERICA

CENTRAL AMERICA

CARIBBEAN SEA

BRAZIL

NORTH ATLANTIC OCEAN

SOUTH ATLANTIC OCEAN

GREENLAND (Den.)

ICELAND

UNITED KINGDOM

IRELAND

ALGERIA

SAHARA

MAURITANIA

MALI

ANTARCTICA

MARIE BYRD LAND

SCOTIA SEA

Drake Passage

Tierra del Fuego

Tropic of Cancer

Tropic of Capricorn

Equator

Standard Time Zones

| 1 A.M. | 2 A.M. | 3 A.M. | 4 A.M. | 5 A.M. | 6 A.M. | 7 A.M. | 8 A.M. | 9 A.M. | 10 A.M. | 11 A.M. | NOON | 1 P.M. | 2 P.M. | 3 P.M. | 4 P.M. | 5 P.M. | 6 P.M. | 7 P.M. | 8 P.M. | 9 P.M. | 10 P.M. | 11 P.M. | MIDNIGHT |

Arctic Ocean

GREENLAND — NOON

11 A.M.

ICE.

3 A.M. ALASKA

CANADA

RUSSIA

8:30 A.M.

U.K. London

GER. FR.

UKR.

KAZ.

MONG.

CHINA

Japan Tokyo

2 P.M. Moscow

4 P.M.

6 P.M.

8 P.M.

UNITED STATES — New York

SP.

MOR.

ALG.

MAUR.

CHAD

EGYPT

S. AR.

IRAN 4:30 P.M. 3:30 P.M.

INDIA 5:45 P.M.

5:30 P.M.

6:30 P.M.

Hong Kong

Los Angeles

MEXICO

VEN.

PERU

BRAZIL

BOL.

ARG.

D.R. CONGO

KEN.

MADG.

S. AFR.

INDONESIA

AUSTRALIA

Sydney

N.Z.

Rio de Janeiro

INTERNATIONAL DATE LINE

INT. DATE LINE

2 A.M. MON. SUN.

2 A.M.

1 A.M.

9 P.M.

9:30 P.M.

10:30 P.M.

11:30 P.M.

12:45 A.M.

5:00 P.M.

5:30 P.M.

6:00 P.M.

6:30 P.M.

2 A.M. 3 A.M. 4 A.M. 5 A.M.

Areas Using Half Hour Deviations
4:30 P.M.

© HAMMOND INC.

LAND AREA 57,970,000 sq. mi.
(150,142,300 sq. km.)
WATER AREA 139,781,000 sq. mi.
(362,032,790 sq. km.)
TOTAL SURFACE AREA 197,751,000 sq.mi.
(512,175,090 sq. km.)
POPULATION 5,292,000,000

Antarctica

AZIMUTHAL EQUIDISTANT PROJECTION

ANTARCTICA
+ SOUTH POLE

© Copyright HAMMOND INCORPORATED, Maplewood, N.J.

4 Arctic Ocean

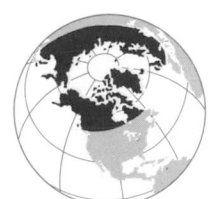

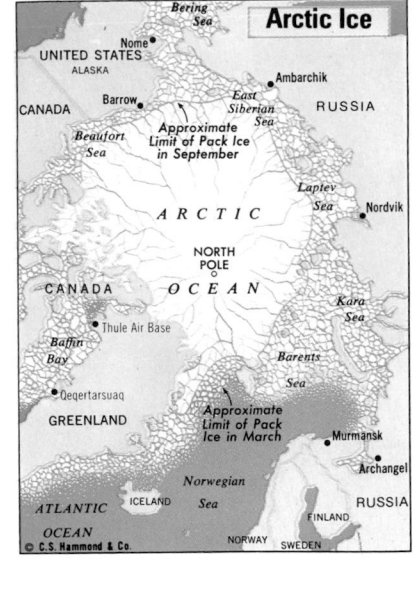

Arctic Ice

Approximate Limit of Pack Ice in September

Approximate Limit of Pack Ice in March

© C.S. Hammond & Co.

Arctic Ocean

AZIMUTHAL EQUIDISTANT PROJECTION

SCALE OF MILES
0 100 200 400 600

SCALE OF KILOMETERS
0 200 400 600 800 1000

Scale 1: 41,000,000

EXPLORERS' ROUTES

Peary 1909 ————
Byrd 1926 ————
Amundsen, Ellsworth & Nobile 1926 ••••••••
Anderson in U.S.S. Nautilus 1958 —·—·—

By ship · By sledge
By airplane · By dirigible
By nuclear submarine

© Copyright HAMMOND INCORPORATED, Maplewood, N.J.

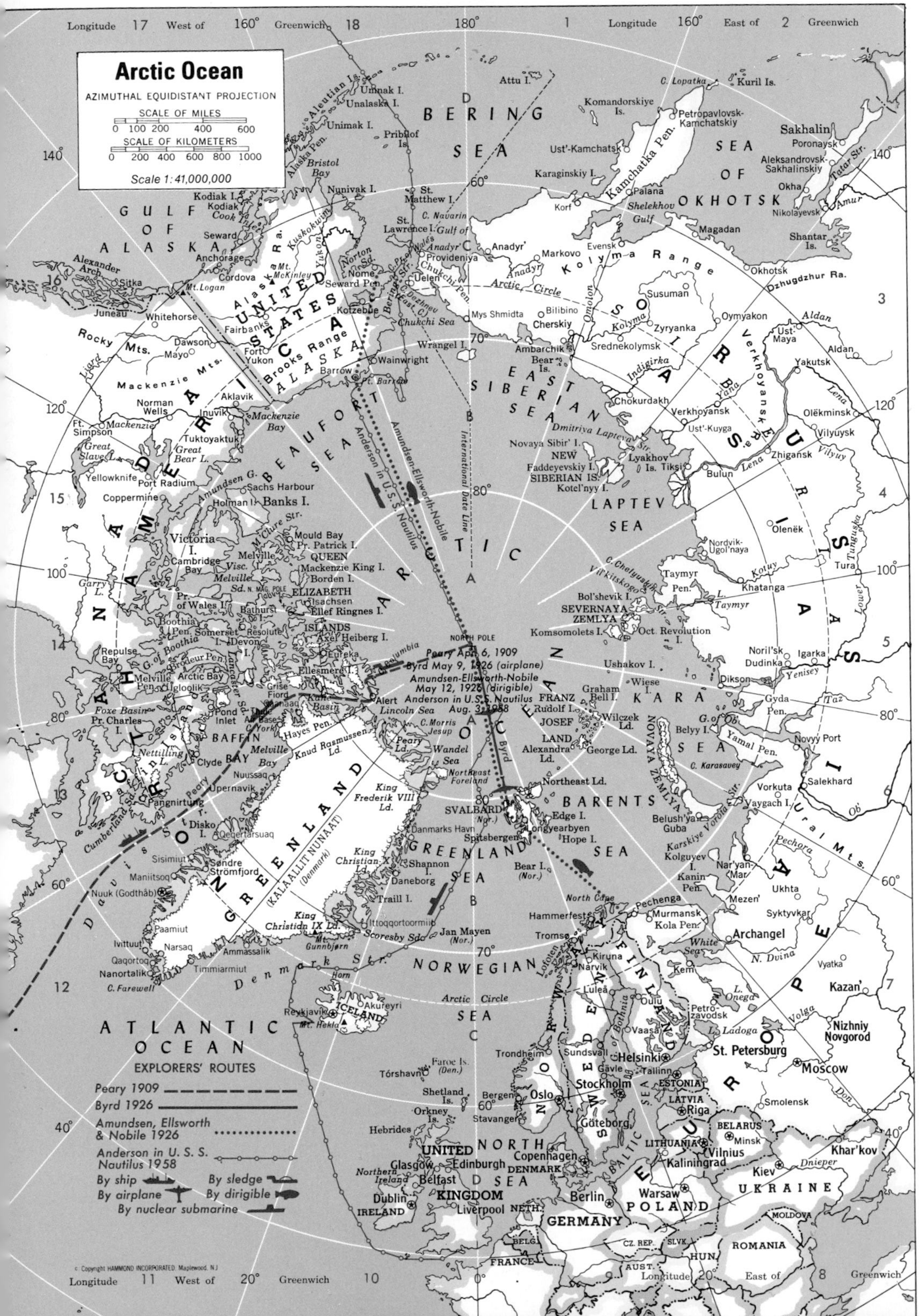

Antarctica
AZIMUTHAL EQUIDISTANT PROJECTION

SCALE OF MILES
0 200 400 600 800
KILOMETERS
0 200 400 600 800 1000

© Copyright HAMMOND INCORPORATED, Maplewood, N. J.

Explorers' Routes

- Palmer 1820
- Amundsen 1910-12
- Scott 1910-13
- Byrd 1928-30
- Fuchs 1957-58

By ship   By sledge   By airplane
By snow tractor

Amundsen Dec. 14, 1911
Scott Jan. 18, 1912
Byrd Nov. 29, 1929 (airplane)
Fuchs Jan. 19, 1958

Weddell Sea — Traverse of Cross Section Shown Below — SOUTH POLE — ANTARCTICA — Ross Sea

Antarctic Cross Section: Weddell Sea to Ross Sea

Meters — 3000 — 2000 — 1000 — Sea Level — -1000 — -2000

Whichaway Nunataks — Recovery Glacier — SOUTH POLE — Beardmore Glacier — Queen Alexandra Range — Ross Island

Weddell Sea — Filchner Ice Shelf — ICE — ROCK — ROCK — Ross Ice Shelf — Ross Sea

VERTICAL EXAGGERATION 95 TIMES

Information Based on American Geographical Society's "Antarctic Map Folio Series"

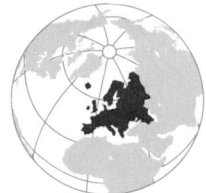

AREA 4,057,000 sq. mi.
(10,507,630 sq. km.)
POPULATION 689,000,000
LARGEST CITY Paris
HIGHEST POINT El'brus 18,510 ft.
(5,642 m.)
LOWEST POINT Caspian Sea -92 ft.
(-28 m.)

Population Distribution

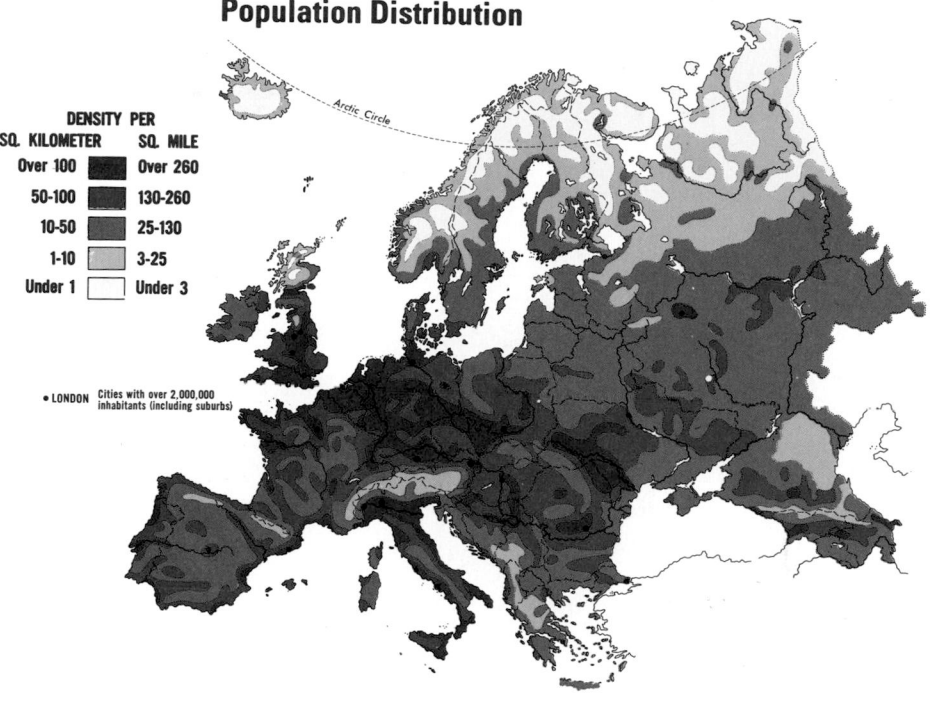

DENSITY PER

SQ. KILOMETER	SQ. MILE
Over 100	Over 260
50-100	130-260
10-50	25-130
1-10	3-25
Under 1	Under 3

• LONDON Cities with over 2,000,000
inhabitants (including suburbs)

Vegetation

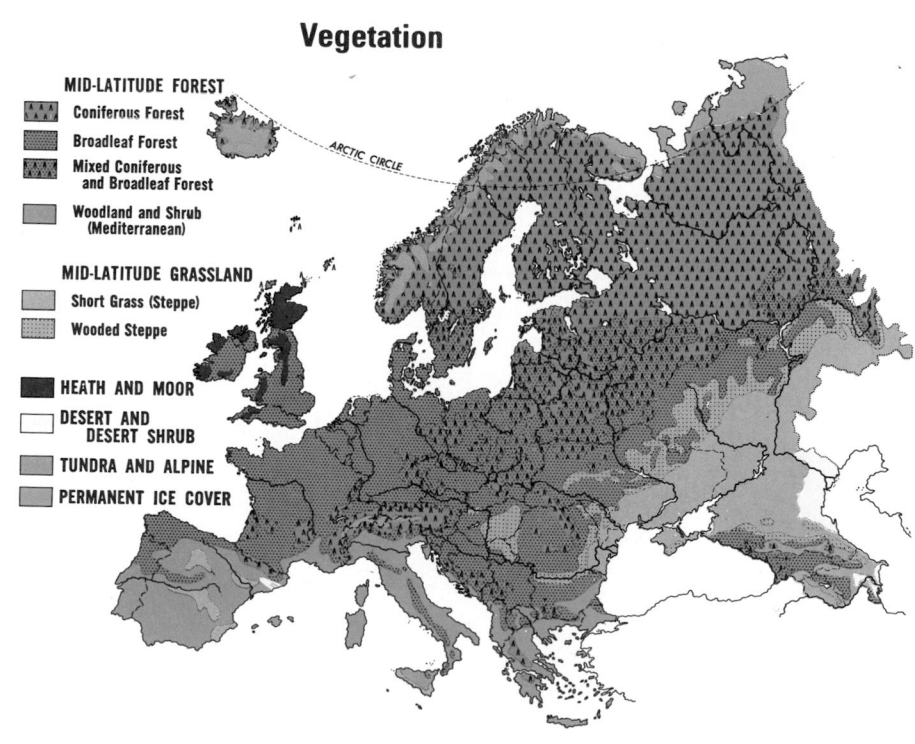

MID-LATITUDE FOREST

Coniferous Forest

Broadleaf Forest

Mixed Coniferous
and Broadleaf Forest

Woodland and Shrub
(Mediterranean)

MID-LATITUDE GRASSLAND

Short Grass (Steppe)

Wooded Steppe

HEATH AND MOOR

DESERT AND
DESERT SHRUB

TUNDRA AND ALPINE

PERMANENT ICE COVER

© Copyright HAMMOND INCORPORATED, Maplewood, N.J.

Vegetation/Relief

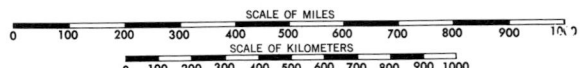

SCALE OF MILES

0 100 200 300 400 500 600 700 800 900 1000

SCALE OF KILOMETERS

0 100 200 300 400 500 600 700 800 900 1000

Capitals of Countries.......................⊛
International Boundaries............ —·—·—
Canals....................................

Depths in Fathoms

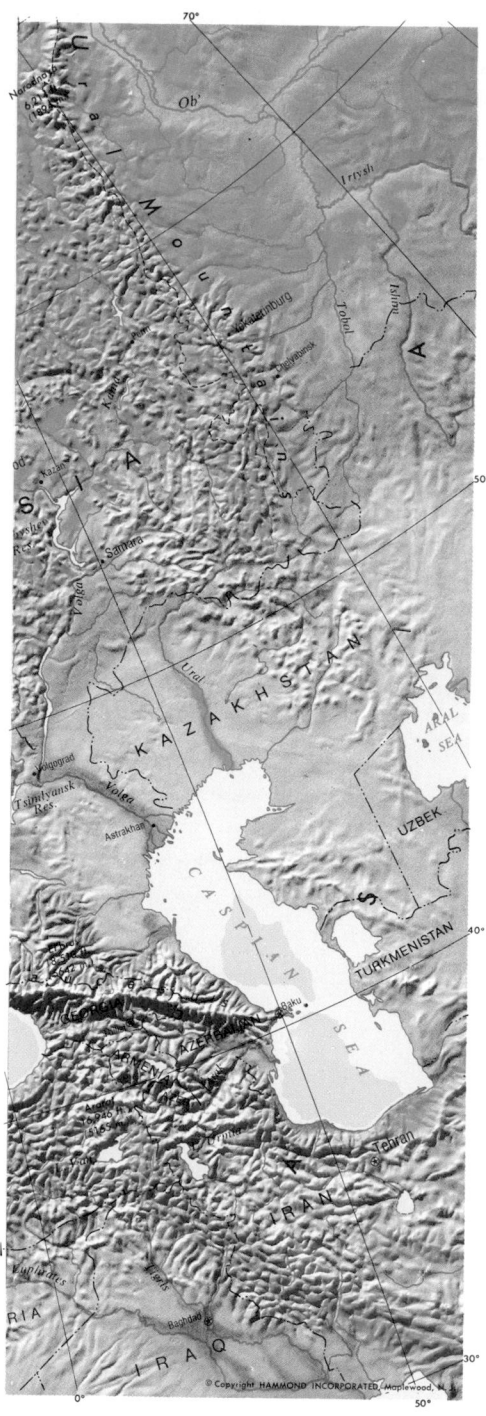

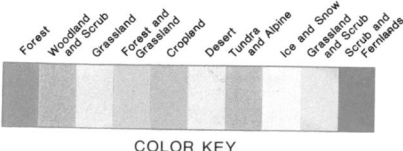

COLOR KEY

Forest / Woodland and Scrub / Grassland / Forest and Grassland / Cropland / Desert / Tundra and Alpine / Ice and Snow / Grassland and Scrub / Scrub and Farmlands

Rainfall

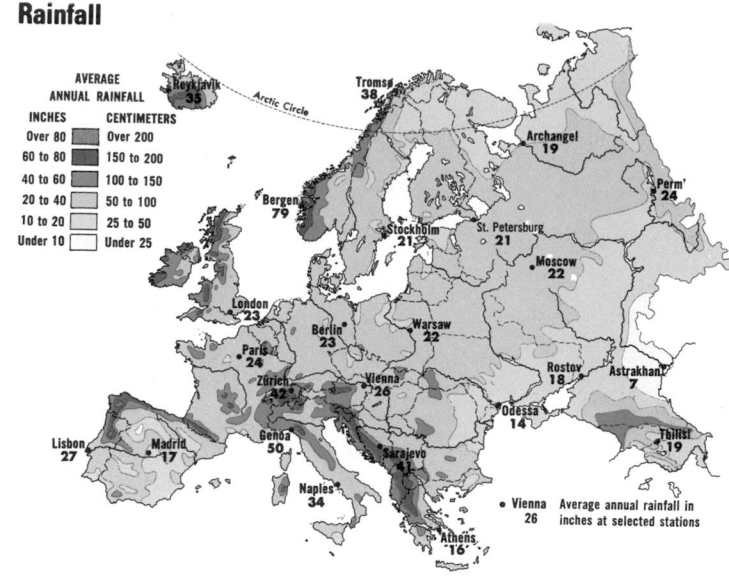

AVERAGE ANNUAL RAINFALL

INCHES	CENTIMETERS
Over 80	Over 200
60 to 80	150 to 200
40 to 60	100 to 150
20 to 40	50 to 100
10 to 20	25 to 50
Under 10	Under 25

• Vienna Average annual rainfall in
  26   inches at selected stations

Average January Temperature

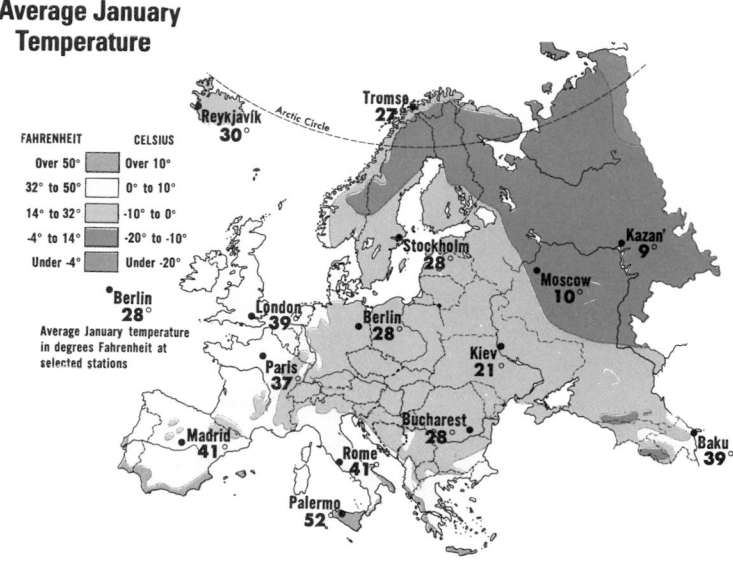

FAHRENHEIT	CELSIUS
Over 50°	Over 10°
32° to 50°	0° to 10°
14° to 32°	-10° to 0°
-4° to 14°	-20° to -10°
Under -4°	Under -20°

Average January temperature
in degrees Fahrenheit at
selected stations

Average July Temperature

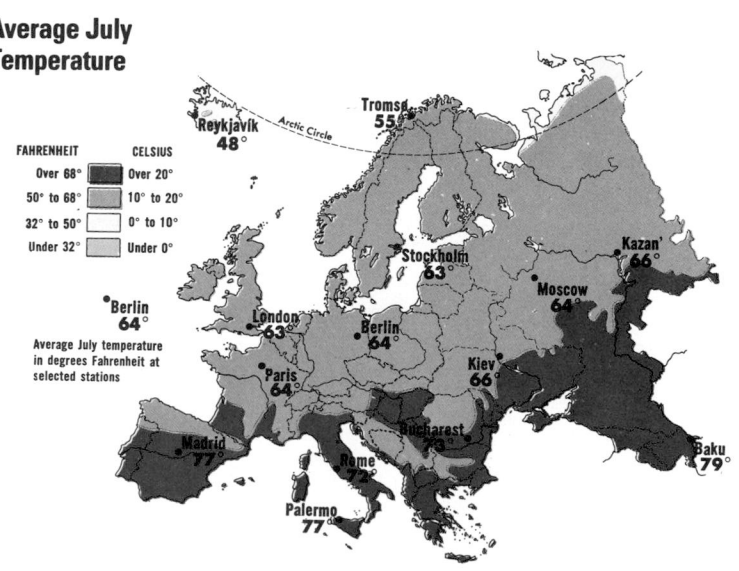

FAHRENHEIT	CELSIUS
Over 68°	Over 20°
50° to 68°	10° to 20°
32° to 50°	0° to 10°
Under 32°	Under 0°

Average July temperature
in degrees Fahrenheit at
selected stations

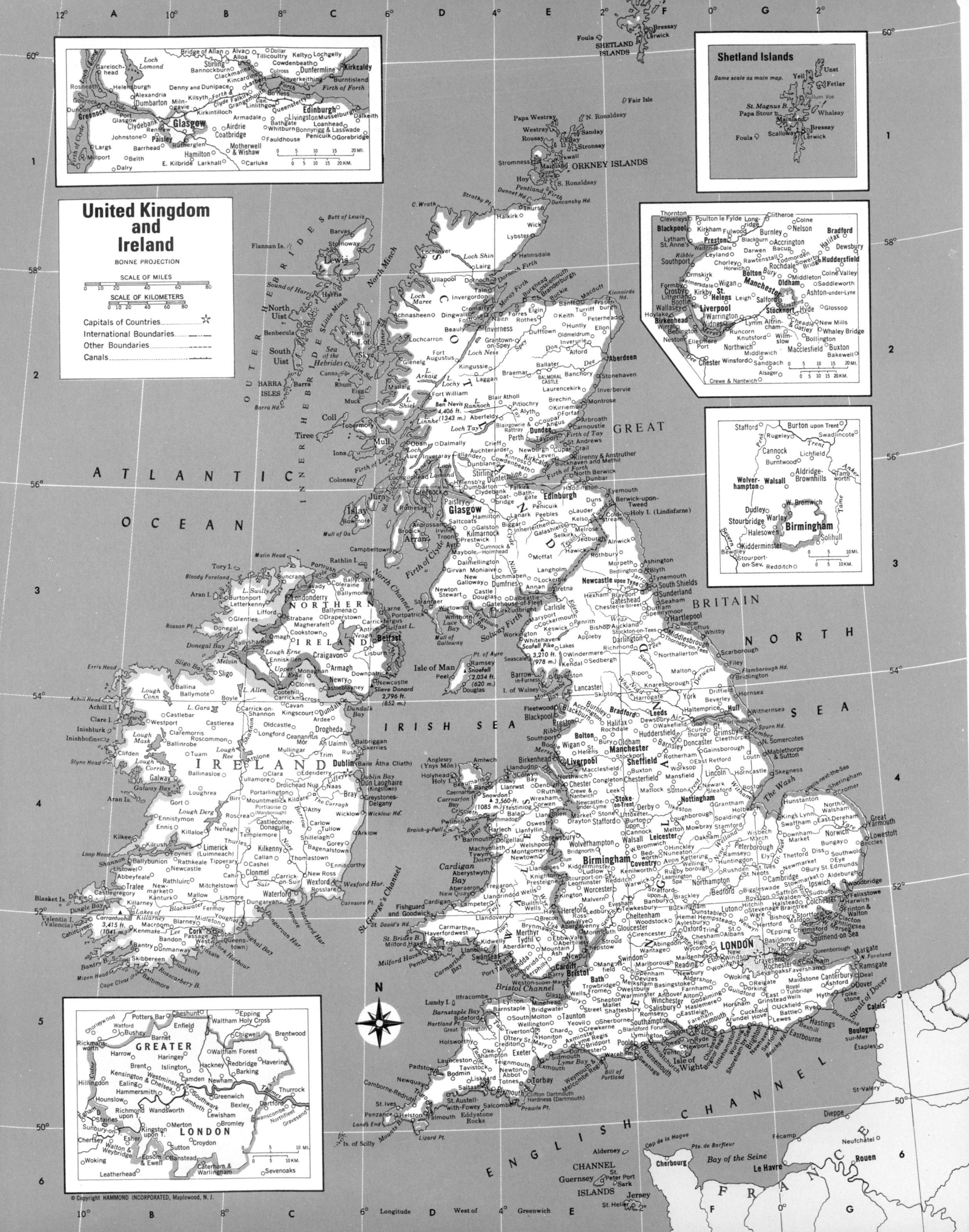

United Kingdom and Ireland

BONNE PROJECTION

SCALE OF MILES

SCALE OF KILOMETERS

Capitals of Countries.............☆
International Boundaries.........
Other Boundaries...................
Canals...................................

Shetland Islands

Same scale as main map.

© Copyright HAMMOND INCORPORATED, Maplewood, N.J.

UNITED KINGDOM

AREA 94,399 sq. mi. (244,493 sq. km.)
POPULATION 57,236,000
CAPITAL London
LARGEST CITY London
HIGHEST POINT Ben Nevis 4,406 ft. (1,343 m.)
MONETARY UNIT pound sterling
MAJOR LANGUAGES English, Gaelic, Welsh
MAJOR RELIGIONS Protestantism, Roman Catholicism

IRELAND

AREA 27,136 sq. mi. (70,282 sq. km.)
POPULATION 3,540,643
CAPITAL Dublin
LARGEST CITY Dublin
HIGHEST POINT Carrantuohill 3,415 ft. (1,041 m.)
MONETARY UNIT Irish pound
MAJOR LANGUAGES English, Gaelic (Irish)
MAJOR RELIGION Roman Catholicism

UNITED KINGDOM

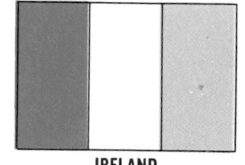

IRELAND

ENGLAND
(map on page 13)

COUNTIES

Avon 900,947..........E6
Bedfordshire 502,164..........G5
Berkshire 670,859..........F6
Buckinghamshire 562,221..........G6
Cambridgeshire 569,893..........G5
Cheshire 921,623..........E4
Cleveland 565,845..........F3
Cornwall 418,631..........C7
Cumbria 471,696..........D3
Derbyshire 901,831..........F5
Devon 930,112..........D7
Dorset 578,993..........E7
Durham 598,881..........F3
East Sussex 641,016..........H7
Essex 1,416,890..........H6
Gloucestershire 493,166..........E6
Hampshire 1,442,598..........F6
Hereford and Worcester 624,393..........E5
Hertfordshire 950,760..........G6
Humberside 843,282..........G4
Isle of Wight 114,879..........F7
Isles of Scilly..........A7
Kent 1,448,393..........H6
Lanoashire 1,362,801..........E4
Leicestershire 835,647..........F5
Lincolnshire 542,944..........G4
London 6,608,598..........H8
Manchester 2,575,407..........H2
Merseyside 1,503,120..........G2
Norfolk 685,232..........H5
North Yorkshire 653,456..........F3
Northamptonshire 524,967..........G5
Northumberland 295,451..........E2
Nottinghamshire 976,748..........F4
Oxfordshire 507,230..........F6
Shropshire 370,355..........E5
Somerset 417,457..........E6
South Yorkshire 1,292,029..........F4
Staffordshire 1,005,641..........E5
Suffolk 590,133..........H5
Surrey 992,489..........G6
Tyne and Wear 1,135,492..........H3
Warwickshire 469,801..........F5
West Midlands 2,628,419..........F5
West Sussex 650,124..........G7
West Yorkshire 2,021,707..........J1
Wiltshire 512,635..........E6
Yorkshire, North 653,456..........F3
Yorkshire, South 1,292,029..........F4
Yorkshire, West 2,021,707..........J1

CITIES and TOWNS

Abingdon 29,130..........F6
Accrington 36,459..........H1
Adwickle Street 10,293..........K2
Aldershot 53,665..........G8
Aldridge 17,549..........H6
Alfreton 21,284..........F4
Alsager 12,944..........E4
Alton 14,163..........G6
Altrincham 39,528..........H2
Amersham⊚ 21,326..........G7
Andover 30,632..........F6
Arnold 37,721..........F4
Ashford 45,198..........H6
Ashington 27,786..........F2
Ashton-under-Lyne 43,605..........H2
Aylesbury 51,999..........G7
Aylesford 21,017..........J8
Bacup 14,082..........H1
Banbury 37,463..........F5
Banstead 35,360..........H8
Barking 149,132..........H8
Barnet 289,277..........H7
Barnoldswick 10,125..........H1
Barnsley 76,783..........J2
Barnstaple 24,490..........D6
Barrow-in-Furness 50,174..........D3
Basildon 94,800..........J8
Basingstoke 73,027..........F6
Bath 84,283..........E6
Batley 45,582..........J1
Beaconsfield 13,397..........G8
Bebington 62,618..........G2
Beccles 10,677..........J5
Bedford 75,632..........G5
Bedlington 15,074..........F2
Bedworth 29,192..........F5
Beeston and Stapleford 64,785..........F5
Benfleet 50,783..........J8
Bentley with Arksey 34,273..........F4
Berkhamsted 16,874..........G7
Berwick-upon-Tweed 12,772..........F2
Beverley 19,368..........G4
Bexhill 34,625..........H7
Bexley 213,215..........H8
Bicester 15,946..........F6
Biddulph 16,697..........H2
Bideford 13,826..........C6
Biggleswade 10,905..........G5
Birkenhead 99,075..........G2
Birmingham 1,013,995..........F5
Bishop Auckland 23,560..........E3
Bishop's Stortford 22,535..........H6
Blackburn 109,564..........H1
Blackpool 146,297..........G1
Blaydon 16,719..........H3
Blyth 35,101..........F2
Bodmin 11,992..........C7
Bognor Regis 50,323..........G7
Boldon 11,639..........J3
Bolsover 11,497..........J2
Bolton 143,960..........H2
Bootle 70,860..........G2
Boston 33,908..........G5
Bournemouth 142,829..........F7
Bracknell 52,257..........G8
Bradford 293,336..........J1
Braintree 30,975..........H6
Brent 251,238..........H8
Brentwood 51,212..........J8
Bridgnorth 10,332..........E5
Bridgwater 30,782..........E6
Bridlington 28,426..........G3
Bridport 10,615..........E7
Brighouse 32,597..........J1
Brighton 134,581..........G7
Bristol 413,861..........E6
Broadstairs 21,551..........J6
Bromley 280,525..........H8
Bromsgrove 24,576..........E5
Brownhills 18,200..........E5
Buckingham 6,439..........G6
Burgess Hill 23,577..........G7
Burnham-on-Sea 17,022..........D6
Burnley 76,365..........H1
Burntwood 28,938..........F5
Burton upon Trent 59,040..........F5
Bury 61,785..........H2
Bury Saint Edmunds 30,563..........H5
Bushey 15,759..........H7
Buxton 19,502..........J2
Calne 10,235..........F6
Camborne-Redruth 34,262..........B7
Cambridge 87,111..........G5
Camden 161,098..........H8
Cannock 54,503..........E5
Canterbury 34,546..........H6
Canvey Island 35,243..........J8
Carlisle 72,206..........D3
Carlton 46,053..........F5
Carterton 10,876..........F6
Caterham and Warlingham 30,331..........H8
Charlton Kings 10,786..........F6
Chatham 65,835..........J8
Cheadle 10,470..........E5
Cheadle and Gatley 59,478..........H2
Chelmsford 91,109..........J7
Cheltenham 87,188..........E6
Chertsey 10,195..........G8
Chesham 20,883..........G7
Cheshunt 49,616..........H7
Chester 80,154..........G2
Chester-le-Street 34,776..........J3
Chesterfield 73,352..........J2
Chichester 26,050..........G7
Chippenham 21,325..........E6
Chorley 33,465..........G2
Christchurch 32,854..........F7
Cirencester 13,491..........E6
Clacton 39,618..........J6
Clay Cross 22,635..........J2
Cleethorpes 33,238..........H4
Clevedon 17,875..........D6
Clitheroe 13,671..........H1
Coalville 28,831..........F5
Colchester 87,476..........H6
Colne 19,094..........H1
Congleton 23,482..........H2
Consett 22,409..........H3
Corby 48,704..........G5
Corsham 11,259..........E6
Coventry 318,718..........F5
Cowes 16,134..........F7
Cranleigh 10,334..........G6
Crawley 80,113..........G6
Crewe 59,097..........E4
Crosby 54,103..........G2
Crowborough 17,008..........H6
Croydon 298,794..........H8
Darlington 85,519..........F3
Dartford 62,032..........J8
Darton 13,743..........J2
Darwen 30,883..........H1
Daventry 16,096..........F5
Deal 26,311..........J6
Dearne 13,391..........K2
Denton 37,784..........H2
Derby 218,026..........F5
Devizes 12,430..........F6
Dewsbury 49,612..........J1
Didcot⊚ 15,147..........F6
Doncaster 74,727..........F4
Dorchester 13,734..........E7
Dorking 14,602..........G8
Dover 33,461..........J6
Droitwich 18,025..........E5
Dronfield 22,641..........J2
Dudley 186,513..........E5
Dunstable 48,436..........G6
Durham 38,105..........J3
Ealing 278,677..........H8
East Dereham 11,798..........H5
East Grinstead 23,867..........G6
East Retford 19,308..........G4
Eastbourne 86,715..........H7
Eastleigh 58,585..........F7
Egham 21,810..........G8
Ellesmere Port 65,829..........G2
Enfield 257,154..........H7
Epping 10,148..........H7
Epsom and Ewell 65,830..........G8
Esher 46,688..........H8
Eston⊚ 37,694..........F3
Eton..........G8
Evesham 15,069..........F5
Exeter 88,235..........D7
Exmouth 28,037..........D7
Falmouth 17,810..........B7
Fareham 55,563..........F7
Farnborough 48,063..........G8
Farnham 34,541..........G8
Farnworth 25,591..........H2
Faversham 15,914..........H6
Felixstowe 24,207..........J6
Felling 36,377..........J3
Fleet 27,406..........G8
Fleetwood 27,899..........D4
Folkestone 42,949..........J6
Formby 26,852..........G2
Frinton and Walton 12,689..........J6
Frome 19,678..........E6
Gainsborough 20,326..........G4
Gateshead 91,421..........J3
Gillingham 92,531..........J8
Glastonbury 6,751..........E6
Glossop 29,923..........J2
Gloucester 106,526..........E6
Godalming 18,758..........G8
Golborne 20,633..........G2
Goole 19,394..........G4
Gosport 69,664..........F7
Grantham 30,700..........G5
Gravesend 53,450..........J8
Great Grimsby 91,532..........G4
Great Harwood 10,968..........H1
Great Malvern (Malvern) 30,153..........E5
Great Yarmouth 54,777..........J5
Greenwich 211,013..........H8
Guildford 61,509..........G8
Guisborough 19,242..........F3
Hackney 179,529..........H8
Hailsham 16,367..........H7
Hale 21,863..........H2
Halesowen 57,533..........E5
Halifax 76,675..........J1
Hammersmith 144,616..........H8
Haringey 202,650..........H8
Harlow 79,150..........H7
Harrogate 63,637..........J1
Harrow 195,292..........G8
Hartlepool 91,749..........F3
Harwich 17,245..........J6
Haslemere 10,544..........G6
Haslingden 14,347..........H1
Hastings 74,979..........H7
Hatfield 33,174..........H7
Havant 50,098..........G7
Haverhill 16,970..........H5
Havering 238,335..........J8
Haxby 11,415..........F3
Hazel Grove and Bramhall 40,819..........H2
Heanor 21,863..........F4
Hebburn 20,098..........J3
Hemel Hempstead 80,110..........G7
Henley-on-Thames 10,910..........G8
Hereford 48,277..........E5
Hertford 21,350..........H7
Hetton 14,529..........J3
Heywood 29,639..........H2
High Wycombe 69,575..........G8
Hillingdon 226,659..........G8
Hinckley 35,510..........F5
Hitchin 33,480..........G6
Hoddesdon 37,960..........H7
Holmfirth 21,138..........J2
Horley 17,700..........G8
Horsham 38,356..........G6
Horwich 16,758..........G2
Houghton-le-Spring 35,337..........J3
Hounslow 198,938..........G8
Hove 65,587..........G7
Hoylake 24,815..........G2
Hoyland Nether 15,845..........J2
Hucknall 27,463..........F4

(continued on following page)

ENGLAND

AREA 50,516 sq. mi. (130,836 sq. km.)
POPULATION 46,220,955
CAPITAL London
LARGEST CITY London
HIGHEST POINT Scafell Pike 3,210 ft. (978 m.)

WALES

AREA 8,017 sq. mi. (20,764 sq. km.)
POPULATION 2,749,640
CAPITAL Cardiff
LARGEST CITY Cardiff
HIGHEST POINT Snowdon 3,560 ft. (1,085 m.)

SCOTLAND

AREA 30,414 sq. mi. (78,772 sq. km.)
POPULATION 5,130,735
CAPITAL Edinburgh
LARGEST CITY Glasgow
HIGHEST POINT Ben Nevis 4,406 ft. (1,343 m.)

NORTHERN IRELAND

AREA 5,452 sq. mi. (14,121 sq. km.)
POPULATION 1,543,000
CAPITAL Belfast
LARGEST CITY Belfast
HIGHEST POINT Slieve Donard 2,796 ft. (852 m.)

Topography

0   75   150 MI.
0   75   150 KM.

5,000 m. 16,404 ft. | 2,000 m. 6,562 ft. | 1,000 m. 3,281 ft. | 500 m. 1,640 ft. | 200 m. 656 ft. | 100 m. 328 ft. | Sea Level | Below

(continued)

Huddersfield 147,825 ... J2
Hugh Town⊙ ... A8
Hull 322,144 ... G4
Huntingdon 14,395 ... G5
Huyton-with-Roby 62,011 ... G2
Hyde 30,461 ... H2
Hythe 13,118 ... H6
Ilkeston 34,683 ... F5
Immingham⊙ 11,480 ... G4
Ipswich 129,661 ... J5
Islington 157,522 ... H8
Jarrow 31,345 ... J3
Kempston 15,454 ... G5
Kendal 23,710 ... E3
Kenilworth 18,782 ... F5
Kensington and Chelsea 125,892 ... G8
Kettering 44,758 ... G5
Kidderminster 50,385 ... E5
Kidsgrove 27,999 ... E4
King's Lynn 37,323 ... H5
Kingston upon Thames 130,829 ... H8
Kingswood 54,736 ... E6
Kirkby 52,825 ... G2
Knaresborough 12,910 ... F4
Knutsford 13,628 ... H2
Lambeth 244,143 ... H8
Lancaster 43,902 ... E3
Leamington Spa 56,552 ... F5
Leatherhead 42,399 ... G8
Leeds 451,841 ... J1
Leek 18,495 ... H2
Leicester 324,394 ... F5
Leigh 42,627 ... H2
Letchworth 31,146 ... G6
Lewes 14,499 ... H7
Lewisham 230,488 ... H8
Leyland 36,694 ... G1
Lichfield 25,408 ... F5
Lincoln 79,980 ... G4
Litherland 21,989 ... G2
Littlehampton 46,028 ... G7
Liverpool 538,809 ... G2
London (cap.) 7,566,620 ... H8
Long Eaton 42,285 ... F5
Longbenton 36,780 ... J3
Loughborough 44,895 ... F5
Louth 13,019 ... H4
Lowestoft 59,430 ... J5
Luton 163,209 ... G6
Lymington 11,614 ... F7
Lymm 10,036 ... H2
Lytham Saint Anne's 39,559 ... G1
Macclesfield 47,525 ... H2
Maidenhead 59,809 ... G8
Maidstone 86,067 ... J8
Maldon 14,638 ... H6
Malvern 30,153 ... E5
Manchester 448,604 ... H2
Mangotsfield 28,664 ... E6
Mansfield 71,325 ... K2
Mansfield Woodhouse 17,564 F4
March 14,155 ... H5
Margate 53,137 ... J6
Market Harborough 15,852 ... G5
Marlow 18,584 ... G8
Matlock 13,706 ... J2
Melksham 13,248 ... E6
Melton Mowbray 23,379 ... G5
Merton 165,102 ... H8
Middlesbrough 158,516 ... F3
Middleton 51,373 ... H2
Milton Keynes 93,305 ... G5
Morpeth 14,301 ... F2
Nantwich 11,867 ... E4
Nelson 30,449 ... H1
Neston 14,902 ... G2
New Romney 6,559 ... J7
Newark 33,143 ... G4
Newbury 31,488 ... F6
Newcastle upon Tyne 199,064 ... H3
Newcastle-under-Lyme 73,208 ... E4
Newham 209,128 ... H8
Newhaven 10,697 ... H7
Newmarket 15,861 ... H5
Newport, Isle of Wight 19,758 F7
Newport, Shropshire 10,339 ... E5
Newport Pagnell 10,733 ... G5
Newquay 13,905 ... B7
Newton Abbot 20,567 ... D7
Newton-le-Willows 19,466 ... H2
Northallerton 13,566 ... F3
Northampton 154,172 ... F5
Northfleet 21,400 ... J8
Northwich 32,664 ... H2
Norton-Radstock 17,668 ... E6
Norwich 169,814 ... J5
Nottingham 273,300 ... F5
Nuneaton 60,337 ... F5
Oadby 18,331 ... F5
Oldham 107,095 ... H2
Ormskirk 22,308 ... G2
Oswaldtwistle 11,188 ... H1
Oswestry 13,200 ... E5
Oxford 113,847 ... F6
Padiham 13,856 ... H1
Penrith 12,086 ... E3
Penzance 18,501 ... B7
Peterborough 113,404 ... G5
Peterlee⊙ 31,405 ... J3
Petersfield 10,078 ... F6
Plymouth 238,583 ... C7
Ponteland 10,215 ... H3
Poole 122,815 ... E7
Portishead 13,684 ... E6
Portslade 17,831 ... G7
Portsmouth 174,218 ... F7
Potters Bar 22,610 ... H7
Poulton-le-Fylde 18,477 ... G1
Preston 166,675 ... G1
Prestwich 31,854 ... H2
Prudhoe 11,140 ... H3
Radcliffe 27,664 ... H2
Ramsbottom 16,334 ... H2
Ramsgate 36,678 ... J6
Rawtenstall 21,247 ... H1
Rayleigh 28,574 ... J8
Reading 194,727 ... G8
Redbridge 226,977 ... H8
Redcar⊙ 35,373 ... F3
Redditch 61,639 ... E5
Reigate 48,241 ... H8
Richmond upon Thames 157,304 ... H8
Rickmansworth 15,960 ... G8
Ringwood 10,941 ... F7
Ripley 17,548 ... F4
Ripon 13,036 ... F3
Rochdale 97,292 ... H2
Rochester 23,840 ... J8
Romney (New Romney) 6,559 ... J7
Romsey 14,818 ... F6
Rotherham 122,374 ... K2
Royal Leamington Spa 56,552 ... F5
Royal Tunbridge Wells 57,699 ... H6
Royston 12,904 ... G5
Rugby 59,039 ... F5
Rugeley 23,751 ... E5
Runcorn 63,995 ... G2
Rushden 22,394 ... G5
Ryde 19,384 ... F7
Ryton 15,138 ... H3
Saffron Walden 11,879 ... H5
Saint Albans 76,709 ... H7
Saint Austell 20,267 ... C7
Saint Helens 114,397 ... G2
Saint Ives, Cambridgeshire 13,431 ... G5
Saint Ives, Cornwall 9,439 ... B7
Saint Neots 12,468 ... G5
Sale 57,872 ... H2
Salford 96,525 ... H2
Salisbury 36,890 ... F6
Saltash 12,486 ... C7
Sandbach 13,734 ... H2
Sandhurst 13,539 ... G8
Sandown-Shanklin 15,252 ... F7
Scarborough 36,665 ... G3
Scunthorpe 79,043 ... G4
Seaford 16,367 ... H7
Seaham 21,807 ... J3
Selby 12,224 ... F4
Sevenoaks 24,493 ... J8
Sheffield 470,685 ... J2
Shepshed 10,479 ... F5
Shildon 11,583 ... F3
Shoreham 20,562 ... G7
Shrewsbury 57,731 ... E5
Sidmouth 10,808 ... D7
Sittingbourne 35,893 ... H6
Skegness 12,645 ... H4
Skelmersdale 42,611 ... G2
Skipton 13,009 ... H1
Slough 106,341 ... G8
Solihull 93,940 ... F5
South Shields 86,488 ... J3
Southampton 211,321 ... F7
Southend-on-Sea 155,720 ... H6
Southport 88,596 ... G1
Southwark 209,735 ... H8
Southwick 11,364 ... G7
Sowerby Bridge 11,280 ... H1
Spalding 18,182 ... G5
Spennymoor 18,563 ... F3
Stafford 60,915 ... E5
Staines 51,949 ... G8
Stamford 16,127 ... G5
Standish 11,504 ... G2
Stanley 20,058 ... H3
Staveley 24,457 ... K2
Stevenage 74,757 ... G6
Stockport 135,489 ... H2
Stocksbridge 13,394 ... J2
Stockton-on-Tees 86,699 ... F3
Stoke-on-Trent 272,446 ... E4
Stone 12,119 ... E5
Stourbridge 55,136 ... E5
Stourport-on-Severn 17,880 ... E5
Stowmarket 10,913 ... J5
Stratford-upon-Avon 20,941 ... F5
Stretford 47,522 ... H2
Stroud 37,791 ... E6
Sudbury 17,723 ... H5
Sunbury 28,240 ... G8
Sunderland 195,064 ... J3
Sutton 165,323 ... H8
Sutton in Ashfield 39,536 ... K2
Swadlincote 33,667 ... F5
Swindon 127,348 ... F6
Tadley 13,668 ... F6
Tamworth 63,260 ... F5
Taunton 47,793 ... D6
Teignmouth 11,995 ... D7
Telford⊙ 28,645 ... E5
Tewkesbury 9,454 ... E6
Thatcham 14,940 ... F6
Thetford 19,529 ... H5
Thornaby⊙ 26,319 ... F3
Thornbury 11,948 ... E6
Thorne⊙ 16,662 ... F4
Thornton Cleveleys 26,697 ... G1
Tiverton 14,745 ... D7
Todmorden 11,936 ... H1
Tonbridge 34,407 ... H8
Torbay 93,995 ... D7
Tower Hamlets 139,996 ... H8
Tring 10,610 ... G7
Trowbridge 27,299 ... E6
Truro 17,852 ... B7
Tynemouth 17,877 ... J3
Uckfield 10,749 ... H7
Ulverston 11,976 ... D3
Urmston 43,706 ... H2
Uttoxeter 10,008 ... E5
Wakefield 74,764 ... J2
Wallasey 62,465 ... G2
Wallsend 44,542 ... J3
Walsall 177,923 ... E5
Waltham Forest 214,595 ... H8
Waltham Holy Cross 16,498 ... H7
Walton and Weybridge 50,031 ... G8
Wandsworth 252,240 ... H8
Ware 15,344 ... H7
Warminster 14,826 ... E6
Warrington 81,366 ... G2
Warsop 10,294 ... F4
Warwick 21,701 ... F5
Washington 48,856 ... J3
Waterloo 57,296 ... G7
Watford 109,503 ... H7
Wellingborough 38,598 ... G5
Wellington 8,980 ... D7
Welwyn 40,665 ... H7
West Bridgford 27,463 ... F5
West Bromwich 153,725 ... F5
Westminster 163,892 ... H8
Weston-super-Mare 60,821 ... D6
Weymouth 38,384 ... E7
Whickham 17,882 ... J3
Whitby 12,982 ... G3
Whitehaven 27,512 ... D3
Whitley Bay 36,040 ... J3
Widnes 55,973 ... G2
Wigan 88,725 ... G2
Wigston 32,373 ... F5
Wilmslow 28,827 ... H2
Wilton 4,002 ... F6
Wimborne Minster 14,193 ... E7
Winchester 34,127 ... F6
Windermere 6,835 ... E3
Windsor 30,832 ... G8
Winsford 26,548 ... G2
Wisbech 22,932 ... H5
Witham 21,875 ... H6
Witney 14,215 ... F6
Woking 92,667 ... G8
Wokingham 30,344 ... G8
Wolverhampton 263,501 ... E5
Wombwell 17,143 ... K2
Worcester 75,466 ... E5
Workington 25,978 ... D3
Worksop 34,551 ... F4
Worsbrough 10,821 ... J2
Worthing 90,687 ... G7
Yateley⊙ 14,121 ... G8
Yeovil 36,114 ... E7
York 123,126 ... F4

OTHER FEATURES

Aire (riv.) ... F4
Avon (riv.) ... F5
Barnstaple (bay) ... C6
Beachy (head) ... H7
Blackwater (riv.) ... H6
Bristol (chan.) ... C6
Cheviot (hills) ... E2
Chiltern (hills) ... G6
Cleveland (hills) ... F3
Colne (riv.) ... G8
Cotswold (hills) ... E6
Cross Fell (mt.) ... E3
Cumbrian (mts.) ... D3
Dart (riv.) ... D7
Dartmoor National Park ... C7
Dee (riv.) ... D4
Derwent (riv.) ... G3
Derwent (riv.) ... H3
Don (riv.) ... F4
Dove (riv.) ... J2
Dover (strait) ... J7
Dungeness (prom.) ... J7
Eddyston (rocks) ... C7
Eden (riv.) ... E3
English (chan.) ... D8
Esk (riv.) ... D2
Exe (riv.) ... D7
Exmoor National Park ... D6
Fens, The (reg.) ... G5
Flamborough (head) ... G3
Foulness Island (pen.) ... J6
Great Ouse (riv.) ... H5
Hartland (pt.) ... C6
Holderness (pen.) ... G4
Holy (isl.) ... F2
Humber (riv.) ... G4
Irish (sea) ... B4
Kennet (riv.) ... F6
Lake District National Park ... D3
Land's End (prom.) ... B7
Lea (riv.) ... G6
Lincoln Wolds (hills) ... G4
Lindisfarne (Holy) (isl.) ... F2
Lizard (pt.) ... B8
Lundy (isl.) ... C6
Lyme (bay) ... D7
Medway (riv.) ... H6
Mendip (hills) ... E6
Mersey (riv.) ... G2
Morecambe (bay) ... D3
Mounts (bay) ... B7
Naze, The (prom.) ... J6
Nene (riv.) ... H5
New (for.) ... F6
North (sea) ... J4
North Downs (hills) ... G6
North Foreland (prom.) ... J6
Northumberland National Park ... E2
North York Moors National Park ... G3
Ouse (riv.) ... G6
Ouse (riv.) ... G4
Peak District National Park ... F4
Peak, The (mt.) ... J2
Pennine Chain (range) ... E3
Portland, Bill of (pt.) ... E7
Purbeck, Isle of (pen.) ... F7
Ribble (riv.) ... E4
Saint Bees (head) ... D3
Saint Mary's (isl.) ... A8
Scafell Pike (mt.) ... D3
Scilly (isls.) ... A7
Severn (riv.) ... E6
Sheppey (isl.) ... J6
Sherwood (for.) ... F4
Solent (chan.) ... F7
Solway (firth) ... D3
South Downs (hills) ... G7
South Foreland (prom.) ... J6
Spithead (chan.) ... F7
Stonehenge (ruin) ... F6
Stour (riv.) ... H6
Stour (riv.) ... E7
Stour (riv.) ... J6
Swale (riv.) ... F3
Tees (riv.) ... F3
Thames (riv.) ... H6
Tintagel (head) ... C7
Trent (riv.) ... G4
Tweed (riv.) ... E2
Tyne (riv.) ... F3
Ure (riv.) ... F3
Walney, Isle of (isl.) ... D3
Wash, The (bay) ... H5
Weald, The (reg.) ... H6
Wear (riv.) ... F3
Welland (riv.) ... G5
Wey (riv.) ... G6
Wharfe (riv.) ... E3
Wight (isl.) 114,879 ... F7
Wirral (pen.) ... G2
Wolds, The (hills) ... G4
Wye (riv.) ... D5
Yare (riv.) ... J5
Yorkshire Dales National Park ... E3

CHANNEL ISLANDS

CITIES and TOWNS

Saint Helier (cap.), Jersey⊙ 27,549 ... E8
Saint Peter Port (cap.), Guernsey⊙ 16,085 ... E8
Saint Sampson's⊙ 7,475 ... E8

OTHER FEATURES

Alderney (isl.) 2,130 ... E8
Guernsey (isl.) 55,421 ... E8
Herm (isl.) 59 ... E8
Jersey (isl.) 82,809 ... E8
Sark (isl.) 560 ... E8

ISLE of MAN

CITIES and TOWNS

Castletown 2,788 ... C3
Douglas (cap.) 19,897 ... C3
Laxey 1,242 ... C3
Onchan 6,395 ... C3
Peel 3,295 ... C3
Port Erin 2,356 ... C3
Port Saint Mary 1,525 ... C3
Ramsey 5,372 ... C3

OTHER FEATURES

Ayre (pt.) ... C3
Calf of Man (isl.) ... C3
Langness (prom.) ... C3
Snaefell (mt.) ... C3

WALES

COUNTIES

Clwyd 385,581 ... D4
Dyfed 323,040 ... C6
Gwent 436,500 ... D6
Gwynedd 222,291 ... C4
Mid Glamorgan 533,770 ... D6
Powys 108,121 ... D5
South Glamorgan 376,718 ... A7
West Glamorgan 363,619 ... D6

CITIES and TOWNS

Abercarn 16,811 ... B6
Aberdare 31,617 ... A6
Abergavenny 13,880 ... B6
Abergele 12,264 ... D4
Abertillery and Brynmawr 28,239 ... B6
Aberystwyth 10,290 ... C5
Ammanford 10,735 ... C6
Bangor 12,244 ... C4
Barry 44,443 ... B7
Bethesda 3,558 ... D4
Brecknock (Brecon) 7,166 ... D6
Bridgend 31,008 ... A7
Brynmawr and Abertillery 28,239 ... B6
Buckley 16,693 ... G2
Caernarfon 9,271 ... C4
Caerphilly 28,681 ... B6
Caldicot 12,310 ... E6
Cardiff (cap.) 262,313 ... B7
Cardigan 3,815 ... C5
Carmarthen 13,860 ... C6
Chepstow 9,039 ... E6
Colwyn Bay 27,002 ... D4
Connah's Quay 14,785 ... G2
Cwmbran 44,592 ... B6
Denbigh 7,710 ... D4
Ebbw Vale 21,048 ... B6
Ffestiniog 4,507 ... D5
Flint 11,411 ... G2
Gelligaer 16,812 ... A6
Gwersyllt 13,374 ... E4
Harlech⊙ 1,292 ... C5
Haverfordwest 13,572 ... B6
Hawarden⊙ 22,361 ... G2
Holyhead 12,569 ... C4
Holywell 11,101 ... G2
Llandeilo 1,598 ... C6
Llandovery 1,676 ... D5
Llandrindod Wells 4,232 ... D5
Llandudno 13,202 ... D4
Llanelli 45,336 ... C6
Llanfairfechan 3,173 ... D4
Llangollen 2,546 ... D5
Llanidloes 2,392 ... D5
Llantrisant⊙ 8,317 ... A7
Llantwit Major 13,375 ... A7
Maesteg 21,821 ... D6
Menai Bridge 2,942 ... C4
Merthyr Tydfil 38,893 ... A6
Milford Haven 13,883 ... B6
Mold 8,487 ... G2
Monmouth 7,379 ... E6
Montgomery ... D5
Mountain Ash 23,520 ... A6
Narberth ... C6
Neath 48,687 ... D6
Nefyn⊙ 2,086 ... C5
Newport 115,896 ... B6
Newtown 8,906 ... D5
Neyland 3,095 ... B6
Ogmore 7,092 ... A6
Pembroke 8,235 ... C6
Penarth 22,467 ... B7
Pontypool 36,064 ... B6
Pontypridd 29,465 ... A6
Port Talbot 40,078 ... D6
Porthcawl 15,162 ... D6
Prestatyn 16,246 ... D4
Pwllheli 3,978 ... C5
Rhondda 70,980 ... A6
Rhosllanerchrugog 11,080 ... D4
Rhyl 23,130 ... D4
Risca 16,627 ... B6
Ruthin 4,417 ... D4
Saint David's⊙ 1,428 ... B6
Swansea 172,433 ... C6
Tenby 5,226 ... C6
Tredegar 16,188 ... B6
Welshpool 4,869 ... D5
Wrexham 39,929 ... E4
Ystradgynlais 10,406 ... D6

OTHER FEATURES

Anglesey (isl.) ... C4
Bardsey (isl.) ... C5
Brecon Beacons National Park ... D6
Bristol (chan.) ... C6
Caldy (isl.) ... C6
Cambrian (mts.) ... D5
Cardigan (bay) ... C5
Carmarthen (bay) ... C6
Conwy (bay) ... C4
Dee (riv.) ... D4
Gower (pen.) ... C6
Great Ormes (head) ... C4
Holy (isl.) ... C4
Irish (sea) ... B4
Lleyn (pen.) ... C5
Menai (strait) ... C4
Milford Haven (inlet) ... B6
Pembrokeshire Coast National Park ... C6
Radnor (for.) ... D5
Saint Brides (bay) ... B6
Saint George's (chan.) ... B5
Severn (riv.) ... E6
Snowdon (mt.) ... C4
Snowdonia National Park ... D4
Taff (riv.) ... B7
Teifi (riv.) ... C5
Towy (riv.) ... D6
Tremadoc (prom.) ... C5
Usk (riv.) ... B6
Wye (riv.) ... D5
Ynys Môn (Anglesey) (isl.) ... C4

⊙ Population of parish.

SCOTLAND

(map on page 15)

REGIONS

Borders 99,784 ... E5
Central 273,391 ... D4
Dumfries and Galloway 145,139 ... E5
Fife 327,362 ... E4
Grampian 471,942 ... F3
Highland 200,150 ... D3
Lothian 738,372 ... E5
Orkney (islands area) 19,056 ... E1
Shetland (islands area) 27,277 ... F2
Strathclyde 2,404,532 ... C4
Tayside 391,846 ... E4
Western Isles (islands area) 31,884 ... A3

CITIES and TOWNS

Aberchirder 1,021 ... F3
Aberdeen 190,465 ... F3
Aberfeldy 1,613 ... E4
Aberfoyle 793 ... D4
Abernethy 776 ... E4
Aboyne 1,529 ... F3
Achiltibuie⊙ 1,564 ... C3
Achnasheen⊙ 1,078 ... C3
Airdrie 45,747 ... C2
Alexandria 26,329 ... A1
Alford 764 ... F3
Alloa 26,428 ... C1
Alness 6,289 ... D3
Altnaharra⊙ 1,227 ... D2
Alva 4,874 ... C1
Alyth 2,289 ... E4
Annan 8,314 ... E6
Annbank Station 3,223 ... D5
Arbroath 24,119 ... F4
Ardrishaig 1,325 ... C4
Ardrossan 11,421 ... D5
Armadale 9,527 ... C2
Auchinleck 4,463 ... D5
Auchterarder 2,904 ... E4
Auchtermuchty 1,646 ... E4
Aviemore 1,224 ... E3
Ayr 49,522 ... D5
Baillieston 7,671 ... B2
Balerno 3,576 ... D2
Balfron 1,127 ... B1
Ballantrae 262 ... C5
Ballater 1,218 ... F3
Ballingry 7,021 ... D1
Balloch 1,484 ... B1
Banchory 4,890 ... F3
Banff 3,938 ... F3
Bankhead 1,492 ... F3
Bannockburn 5,889 ... C1
Barrhead 18,418 ... B2
Bathgate 14,477 ... C2
Bearsden 27,183 ... B2
Beauly 1,148 ... D3
Beith 5,742 ... D5
Bellsbank 2,482 ... D5
Bellshill 39,676 ... C2
Berriedale⊙ 1,927 ... E2
Bieldside 1,137 ... F3
Biggar 1,938 ... E5
Bishopbriggs 23,501 ... B2
Bishopton 5,283 ... B2
Blackburn 5,785 ... C2
Blair Atholl 437 ... E4
Blairgowrie and Rattray 7,184 E4
Blantyre 19,948 ... B2
Bo'ness 14,641 ... C1
Boddam 1,367 ... G3
Bonhill 4,385 ... B1
Bonnybridge 5,701 ... C1
Bonnyrigg and Lasswade 14,399 ... D2
Brechin 7,692 ... F4
Bridge of Allan 4,694 ... C1
Bridge of Don 4,086 ... F3
Bridge of Weir 4,724 ... A2
Brightons 3,106 ... C1
Brora 1,736 ... E2
Broxburn 12,032 ... D1
Buckhaven and Methil 18,265 F4
Buckie 7,839 ... E3
Bucksburn 6,567 ... F3
Burghead 1,380 ... E3
Burntisland 5,865 ... D1
Callander 2,520 ... D4
Cambuslang 14,607 ... B2
Campbeltown 6,098 ... C5
Caol 3,719 ... C4
Cardenden 5,898 ... D1
Carluke 11,674 ... E5
Carnoustie 9,225 ... F4
Carnwath 1,374 ... E5
Carron 2,626 ... C1
Castle Douglas 3,521 ... E6
Catrine 2,790 ... D5
Cawdor 111 ... E3
Chirnside 1,263 ... F5
Chryston 11,067 ... C2
Clackmannan 3,258 ... C1
Clarkston 8,404 ... B2
Clydebank 51,854 ... B2
Coalburn 1,241 ... E5
Coatbridge 50,957 ... C2
Cockenzie and Port Seton 3,760 ... D1
Coldstream 1,645 ... F5
Comrie 1,477 ... E4
Cononbridge 2 187 ... D3
Corpach 1,296 ... C4
Coupar Angus 2,186 ... E4
Cove and Kilcreggan 1,220 ... A1
Cove Bay 2,840 ... F3
Cowdenbeath 12,272 ... D1
Cowie 2,513 ... C1
Crail 1,181 ... F4
Creetown 769 ... D6
Crieff 5,477 ... E4
Crimond 1,002 ... G3
Cromarty 492 ... E3
Cruden Bay 1,453 ... G3
Cullen 1,414 ... F3
Culross 504 ... C1
Cults 3,336 ... F3
Cumbernauld 47,901 ... C1
Cumnock and Holmhead 9,650 ... D5
Cupar 6,637 ... E4
Currie 6,764 ... D2
Dailly 1,098 ... D5
Dalbeattie 3,917 ... E6
Dalkeith 11,255 ... D2
Dalmellington 1,425 ... D5
Dalry 5,856 ... D5
Dalrymple 1,237 ... D5
Darvel 3,461 ... D5
Denny and Dunipace 23,158 ... C1
Dervaig⊙ 1,081 ... B4
Dingwall 4,842 ... D3
Dollar 2,486 ... E4
Dornoch 880 ... D3
Douglas 1,727 ... E5
Doune 1,046 ... D4
Drongan 3,129 ... D5
Dufftown 1,643 ... E3
Dumbarton 23,430 ... B1
Dumfries 32,100 ... E5
Dunbar 6,035 ... F4
Dunblane 6,855 ... E4
Dundee 174,345 ... F4
Dundonald 2,669 ... D5
Dunfermline 52,227 ... D1
Dunoon 9,369 ... A2
Duns 2,253 ... F5
Duntocher 3,532 ... B2
Dyce 7,039 ... F3
Eaglesham 3,166 ... D5
Earlston 1,610 ... F5
East Calder 5,112 ... D2
East Kilbride 70,676 ... B2
East Linton 1,206 ... F5
Eastriggs 1,845 ... E5
East Wemyss 1,782 ... D1
Edinburgh (cap.) 420,169 ... D1
Elderslie 5,204 ... B2
Elgin 18,908 ... E3
Ellon 6,319 ... F3
Errol 762 ... E4
Eyemouth 3,398 ... F5
Fairlie 1,326 ... D5
Falkirk 36,880 ... C1
Falkland 998 ... E4
Fallin 2,663 ... C1
Fauldhouse 5,036 ... C2
Findhorn 664 ... E3
Findochty 1,019 ... E3
Fochabers 1,483 ... E3
Forfar 12,770 ... F4
Forres 8,354 ... E3
Forth 2,890 ... C2
Fortrose 1,332 ... D3
Fort William 11,061 ... C4
Fraserburgh 12,512 ... G3
Gairloch 125 ... C3
Galashiels 12,244 ... F5
Galston 5,311 ... D5
Garelochhead 2,072 ... A1
Gatehouse-of-Fleet 835 ... D6
Giffnock 33,634 ... B2
Girvan 7,795 ... D5
Glamis 190 ... F4
Glasgow 765,030 ... B2
Glenbarr⊙ 691 ... C5
Glencoe 195 ... C4
Glenelg⊙ 1,468 ... C3
Glenrothes 32,971 ... E4
Golspie 1,491 ... E3
Gorebridge 6,036 ... D2
Gourock 11,203 ... A1
Grangemouth 21,599 ... C1
Grantown-on-Spey 2,034 ... E3
Greenock 59,016 ... A2
Gretna 2,811 ... E5
Gullane 2,232 ... F4
Haddington 8,139 ... F5
Halkirk 679 ... E2
Hamilton 51,718 ... C2
Harthill 4,161 ... C2
Hawick 16,364 ... F5
Heathhall 1,365 ... E5
Helensburgh 16,621 ... A1
Helmsdale 727 ... E2
Hillside 1,233 ... F4
Hillswick⊙ 696 ... G2
Hopeman 1,398 ... E3
Huntly 3,952 ... F3
Hurlford 4,294 ... D5
Inchnadamph⊙ 833 ... D2
Innerleithen 2,468 ... E5
Insch 1,256 ... F3
Inveraray 473 ... C4
Inverbervie 1,799 ... F4
Invercassley⊙ 1,067 ... D3
Invergordon 4,067 ... D3
Invergowrie 1,389 ... E4
Inverie⊙ 1,468 ... C3
Inverkeithing 5,770 ... D1
Inverness 40,010 ... D3
Inverurie 7,680 ... F3
Irvine 32,968 ... D5
Jedburgh 4,069 ... F5
John O'Groats 195 ... E2
Johnstone 42,669 ... B2
Keith 4,407 ... F3
Kelso 5,648 ... F5
Kelty 5,623 ... D1
Kemnay 3,034 ... F3
Kilbarchan 2,669 ... A2
Kilbirnie 8,710 ... A2
Kilchoan⊙ 764 ... B4
Kildonan⊙ 1,105 ... E2
Killearn 1,771 ... B1
Kilmacolm 3,676 ... A2
Kilmarnock 52,083 ... D5
Kilmaurs 2,738 ... D5
Kilrenny and Anstruther 2,951 F4
Kilsyth 10,538 ... B1
Kilwinning 16,266 ... D5
Kinbrace⊙ 1,105 ... E2
Kincardine 3,166 ... C1
Kinghorn 2,698 ... D1
Kingussie 1,229 ... D3
Kinlochewe⊙ 1,794 ... C3
Kinlochleven 1,047 ... D4
Kinloss 2,813 ... E3
Kinross 3,496 ... E4
Kintore 1,644 ... F3
Kirkcaldy 46,522 ... D1
Kirkconnel 2,656 ... E5
Kirkcudbright 3,427 ... E6
Kirkintilloch 33,148 ... B2
Kirkmuirhill 3,624 ... E5
Kirkwall 5,995 ... E2
Kirriemuir 5,326 ... E4
Kyle of Lochalsh 687 ... C3
Kylestrome⊙ 745 ... D2
Ladybank 1,355 ... E4
Lairg 572 ... D2
Lanark 9,806 ... E5
Langholm 2,615 ... E5
Larbert 4,922 ... C1
Largs 9,905 ... A2
Larkhall 16,216 ... E5
Lauder 639 ... F5
Laurencekirk 1,329 ... F4
Lennoxtown 4,829 ... B1
Lerwick 7,561 ... G2
Leslie 3,551 ... E4
Lesmahagow 3,408 ... E5
Letham 804 ... F4
Leuchars 2,244 ... F4
Leven 8,624 ... F4
Lhanbryde 1,811 ... E3
Limekilns 1,444 ... D1
Linlithgow 9,582 ... C1
Linwood 10,510 ... B2
Livingston 38,954 ... C2
Loanhead 6,159 ... D2
Lochailort⊙ 673 ... C4
Locharbriggs 4,230 ... E5
Lochgelly 7,334 ... D1
Lochgilphead 2,461 ... C4
Lochinver 283 ... C2
Lochmaben 1,713 ... E5
Lochore 2,994 ... D1
Lochwinnoch 2,273 ... A2
Lockerbie 3,561 ... E5

(continued)

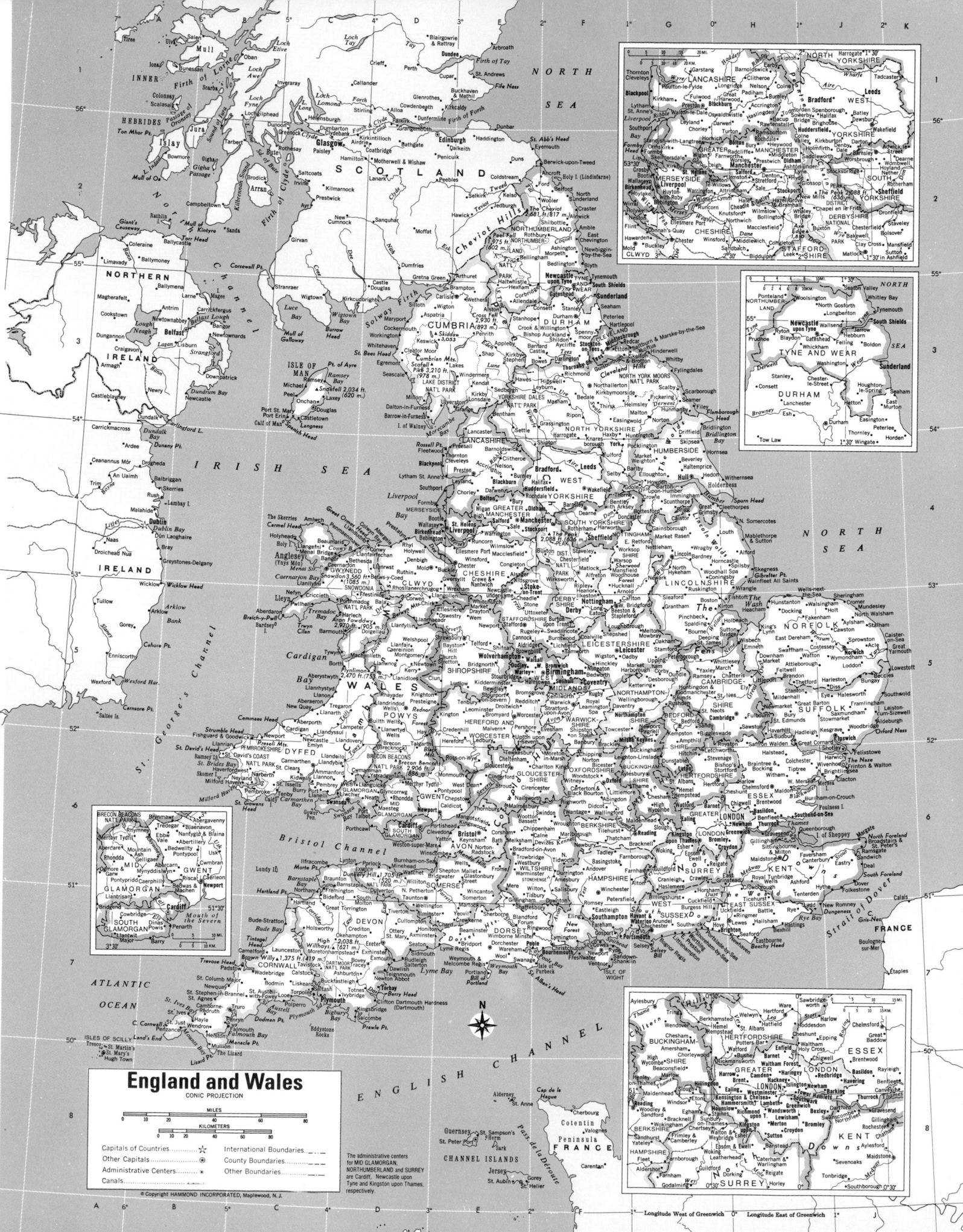

England and Wales

CONIC PROJECTION

MILES
0 20 40 60 80

KILOMETERS
0 20 40 60 80

Capitals of Countries............☆
Other Capitals..................⊛
Administrative Centers...........•
Canals.........................

International Boundaries.........
County Boundaries...............
Other Boundaries................

The administrative centers
for MID GLAMORGAN,
NORTHUMBERLAND and SURREY
are Cardiff, Newcastle upon
Tyne and Kingston upon Thames,
respectively.

© Copyright HAMMOND INCORPORATED, Maplewood, N.J.

Longitude West of Greenwich 0° Longitude East of Greenwich 1°

(continued)

Lossiemouth and
  Branderburgh 6,847 .... E3
Macduff 3,887 .... F3
Mallaig 903 .... C4
Markinch 2,078 .... E4
Mauchline 3,663 .... D5
Maud 634 .... F3
Maybole 4,798 .... D5
Mayfield 1,333 .... D2
Melrose 2,345 .... F5
Melvaig⊙ 1,794 .... C3
Millport 1,472 .... A2
Milnathort 1,118 .... E4
Milngavie 12,067 .... B1
Mintlaw 2,299 .... F3
Moffat 2,051 .... E5
Monifieth 7,100 .... F4
Montrose 12,325 .... F4
Motherwell 30,676 .... C2
Muir of Ord 1,714 .... D3
Muirkirk 2,356 .... E5
Musselburgh 19,081 .... D2
Nairn 7,705 .... E3
Neilston 4,678 .... B2
Newarthill 7,003 .... C2
Newburgh 2,002 .... E4
Newcastleton 903 .... F5
New Cumnock 4,484 .... D5
New Galloway 337 .... D5
Newmains 6,847 .... C2
Newmilns and Greenholm
  3,339 .... D5
New Pitsligo 1,125 .... F3
Newport-on-Tay 3,652 .... F4
New Scone 4,173 .... E4
Newtongrange 4,555 .... D2
Newton Mearns 15,543 .... B2
Newton Stewart 3,246 .... D6
Newtown Saint Boswells
  1,095 .... F5
North Berwick 5,162 .... F4
Oakley 4,157 .... C1
Oban 8,111 .... C4
Old Kilpatrick 3,256 .... B2
Oldmeldrum 1,356 .... F3
Paisley 84,954 .... B2
Patna 2,490 .... D5
Peebles 6,692 .... E5
Penicuik 17,607 .... D2
Perth 43,010 .... E4
Peterculter 3,226 .... F3
Peterhead 17,085 .... G3
Pitlochry 12,621 .... E4
Pitmedden 1,103 .... F3
Pittenweem 1,544 .... F4
Poolewe⊙ 1,794 .... C3
Port Appin⊙ 2,172 .... C4
Port Askaig⊙ 1,795 .... B5
Port Bannatyne 1,414 .... A2
Port Ellen 1,020 .... B5
Port Glasgow 22,580 .... A2
Portknockie 1,239 .... F3
Portree 1,505 .... B3
Portsoy 1,784 .... F3
Prestonpans 7,621 .... D1
Prestwick 13,599 .... D5
Queensferry 7,540 .... D1
Renfrew 21,458 .... B2
Renton 3,443 .... A1
Rhu 1,540 .... A1
Rigside 1,066 .... E5
Rosehearty 1,243 .... F3
Rosneath 1,439 .... A1
Rothes 1,425 .... E3
Rothesay 5,455 .... A2
Rutherglen 24,091 .... B2
Saint Andrews 11,369 .... F4
Saint Monance 1,244 .... F4
Saline 1,192 .... C1
Saltcoats 12,834 .... D5
Sandbank 1,435 .... A1
Sanquhar 2,082 .... D5
Sauchie 6,082 .... C1
Selkirk 5,437 .... F5
Shotts 9,427 .... C2
Skelmorlie 1,689 .... A2
Slamannan 1,578 .... C2
Stanley 1,170 .... E4
Stenhousemuir 19,771 .... C1
Stevenston 11,337 .... D5
Stewarton 6,330 .... D5
Stirling 38,842 .... C1
Stonehaven 7,922 .... F4
Stonehouse 5,308 .... D5
Stornoway 8,638 .... B2
Stranraer 10,873 .... C6
Strathaven 6,152 .... D5
Stromeferry⊙ 1,724 .... C3
Stromness 1,832 .... E2
Sullam Voe G2
Tain 3,486 .... D3
Tarbert 1,403 .... C5
Tarbolton 2,012 .... D5
Tayport 3,029 .... F4
Thornhill, Central 443 .... D4
Thornhill, Dumfries and
  Galloway 1,473 .... E5
Thurso 8,896 .... E2
Tillicoultry 6,161 .... C1
Tobermory 652 .... B4
Tolob⊙ 2,033 .... G2
Tranent 8,079 .... F5
Troon 14,233 .... D5
Tullibody 6,082 .... C1
Turriff 3,683 .... F3
Tweedsmuir⊙ 105 .... E5
Tyndrum⊙ 1,153 .... D4
Uddingston 10,678 .... B2
Uig, Highland 103 .... B3
Uig, Western Isles⊙ 1,948 .... A2
Ullapool 1,146 .... C3
Uphall 3,035 .... C1
Viewpark 15,343 .... C2
Walkerburn 842 .... F5
Wemyss Bay 1,322 .... A2
West Calder 2,281 .... C2
West Kilbride 4,241 .... D5
West Linton 705 .... D2
Whitburn 12,010 .... C2
Whitehills 875 .... F3
Whithorn 990 .... D6
Wick 7,900 .... E2
Wigtown 1,015 .... D6
Winchburgh 2,398 .... D1
Wishaw 37,783 .... C2

OTHER FEATURES

A'Chralaig (mt.) C3
Annan (riv.) E5
Appin (dist.) 2,006 .... C4
Ardgour (dist.) 315 .... C4
Ardnamurchan (pt.) B4
Ardnamurchan (pen.) 764 .... B4
Argyll (dist.) 4,940 .... C4
Arisaig (sound) C4
Arkaig, Loch (lake) C4
Arran (isl.) 3,564 .... C5
Askival (mt.) B4
Assynt (dist.) 833 .... C2
Athol (dist.) 1,082 .... D4
Atlantic Ocean B2
Awe, Loch (lake) C4
Ayr (riv.) D5
Badenoch (dist.) 2,717 .... D4
Baleshare (isl.) 64 .... A3
Balmoral Castle (site) E3
Barra (head) A4
Barra (isl.) 1,005 .... A4
Barra Isles (isls.) 1,092 .... A4
Beauly (riv.) D3
Beinn a Ghlo (mt.) E4
Beinn Bheigeir (mt.) B5
Beinn Dearg (mt.) D3
Beinn Dhorain (mt.) E2
Beinn Eighe (mt.) C3
Ben Alder (mt.) D4
Ben Barvas (mt.) B2
Benbecula (isl.) 1,355 .... A3
Ben Cruachan (mt.) C4
Ben Hope (mt.) D2
Ben Kilbreck (mt.) D2
Ben Lawers (mt.) D4
Ben Lomond (mt.) D4
Ben Macdhui (mt.) E3
Ben Mhor (mt.) A3
Ben More (mt.) D4
Ben More Assynt (mt.) D2
Ben Nevis (mt.) D4
Bernera (isl.) 276 .... B2
Berneray (isl.) 131 .... A3
Berneray (isl.) 6 .... A4
Bidean nam Bian (mt.) D4
Black Isle (pen.) 7,209 .... D3
Blackwater (res.) D4
Bracadale, Loch (inlet) B3
Braemar (dist.) 7,624 .... E3
Bran (riv.) D3
Breadalbane (dist.) 3,649 .... D4
Bressay (isl.) 248 .... G2
Broad (bay) B2
Broad Law (mt.) E5
Broom, Loch (inlet) C3
Brough Ness (prom.) F2
Buchan (dist.) 40,089 .... F3
Buchan Ness (prom.) G3
Burray (isl.) 209 .... F2
Burrow (head) D6
Bute (isl.) 8,423 .... C5
Butt of Lewis (prom.) B2
Cairn Gorm (mt.) E3
Cairngorm (mts.) E3
Cairnsmore (mt.) D5
Caledonian (canal) D3
Canna (isl.) 22 .... B3
Carn Eige (mt.) C3
Carrick (dist.) 21,425 .... D5
Carron (riv.) C1
Cheviot (hills) F5
Cheviot, The (mt.) F5
Clisham (mt.) B3
Clyde (firth) D5
Clyde (riv.) D5
Coll (isl.) 144 .... B4
Colonsay (isl.) 137 .... B4
Corserine (mt.) D5
Corsewall (pt.) C5
Cowal (dist.) 15,548 .... C4
Cromarty (firth) D3
Cuillin (hills) B3
Cuillin (sound) B3
Dee (riv.) F3
Dennis (head) F1
Deveron (riv.) F3
Don (riv.) F3
Doon (riv.) D5
Dornoch (firth) D3
Duirinish (dist.) 1,085 .... B3
Duncansby (head) F2
Dunnet (head) E2
Dunnet (bay) E2
Earn (riv.) E4
Earn, Loch (lake) D4
East Loch Tarbert (inlet) B3
Eday (isl.) 179 .... F1
Eddrachillis (bay) C2
Eigg (isl.) 69 .... B4
Eishort, Loch (inlet) B3
Enard (bay) C2
Eriboll, Loch (inlet) D2
Ericht, Loch (lake) D4
Eriskay (isl.) 219 .... A3
Erisort, Loch (inlet) B2
Esk (riv.) F5
Etive, Loch (inlet) C4
Ewe, Loch (inlet) C3
Eye (pen.) 850 .... B2
Eynhallow (sound) E1
Eynort, Loch (inlet) A3
Fair Isle (isl.) 65 .... F3
Fannich, Loch (lake) D3
Fetlar (isl.) 88 .... G2
Fife Ness (prom.) F4
Findhorn (riv.) E3
Fionn Loch (lake) C3
Flannan (isls.) 3 .... A2
Fleet, Loch (inlet) D3
Formartine (dist.) 10,768 .... F3
Forth (firth) F4
Forth (riv.) B1
Forth and Clyde (canal) B2
Foula (isl.) 33 .... F2
Fyne, Loch (inlet) C5
Gairloch, Loch (inlet) C3
Gallan (head) A2
Galloway (dist.) 54,972 .... D5
Galloway, Mull of (prom.) D6
Garioch (dist.) 6,863 .... F3
Garry, Loch (lake) D3
Gigha (isl.) 174 .... C5
Glen More (dist.) 55,035 .... D3
Goat Fell (mt.) C5
Grampian (mts.) D4
Great Cumbrae (isl.) 1,296 .... A2
Green Lowther (mt.) E5
Greenstone (pt.) C3
Gruinard (bay) C3
Harris (dist.) 2,175 .... B3
Heads of Ayr (cape) D5
Hebrides (sea) B3
Hebrides, Inner (isls.) 14,881 .... B4
Hebrides, Outer (isls.) 29,615 .... A3
Helmsdale (riv.) E2
Herma Ness (prom.) G2
Hope, Loch (lake) D2
Hourn, Loch (inlet) C3
Hoy (isl.) 419 .... E2
Indaal, Loch (inlet) B5
Inner (sound) C3
Inner Hebrides (isls.) 14,881 .... B4
Iona (isl.) 145 .... B4
Islay (isl.) 3,816 .... B5
Jura (isl.) 210 .... C5
Katrine, Loch (lake) D4
Kerrera (isl.) 27 .... C4
Kilbrannan (sound) C5
Kinnairds (head) G3
Kintyre (pen.) 10,077 .... C5
Kintyre, Mull of (prom.) C5
Knapdale (dist.) 4,082 .... C5
Kyle of Tongue (inlet) D2
Ladder (hills) E3
Lammermuir (hills) F5
Langavat (lake) B2
Laxford, Loch (inlet) C2
Lennox (hills) B1
Leven (lake) E4
Leven, Loch (inlet) D4
Lewis (dist.) 20,047 .... B2
Lewis, Butt of (prom.) B2
Liddel Water (riv.) F5
Linnhe, Loch (inlet) C4
Lismore (isl.) 166 .... C4
Little Minch (sound) B3
Lochaber (dist.) 13,813 .... D4
Lochnagar (mt.) E4
Lochy, Loch (lake) D3
Lomond, Loch (lake) D4
Long, Loch (inlet) D4
Lorne (dist.) 12,162 .... C4
Lorne (firth) C4
Loyal, Loch (lake) D2
Loyne, Loch (lake) C3
Luce (bay) D6
Luing (isl.) 151 .... C4
Machers, The (pen.) 6,192 .... D6
Maddy, Loch (inlet) A3
Mainland (isl.) 12,747 .... E1
Mainland (isl.) 12,944 .... G2
Mar (dist.) 23,931 .... F3
Maree, Loch (lake) C3
May, Isle of (isl.) 10 .... F4
Merrick (mt.) D5
Minginish (dist.) 772 .... B3
Mingulay (isl.) A4
Moidart (dist.) 155 .... C4
Monach (isls.) A3
Monadhliath (mts.) D3
Monar, Loch (lake) C3
Moorfoot (hills) E5
Morar, Loch (lake) C4
Moray (firth) E3
Morven (mt.) E2
Morven (dist.) 398 .... C4
Muck (isl.) 24 .... B4
Muckle Flugga (isl.) 3 .... G2
Mull (isl.) 2,024 .... C4
Mull (head) F2
Mullardoch, Loch (lake) C3
Mull of Galloway (prom.) D6
Mull of Kintyre (prom.) C5
Mull of Oa (prom.) B5
Nairn (riv.) D3
Naver (riv.) D2
Ness (riv.) D3
Ness, Loch (lake) D3
Nevis, Loch (inlet) C3
Nith (riv.) E5
North (chan.) C5
North (sea) G4
North (sound) F1
North Esk (riv.) F4
North Minch (sound) B3
North Ronaldsay (isl.) 134 .... F1
North Uist (isl.) 1,469 .... A3
Noss (head) F2
Noup (head) E1
Oa, Mull of (prom.) B5
Ochil (hills) E4
Oich (riv.) D3
Oich, Loch (lake) D3
Orkney (isls.) 17,675 .... F1
Oronsay (isl.) 2 .... B4
Outer Hebrides (isls.) 29,615 .... A3
Oykel (riv.) D3
Pabbay (isl.) 4 .... A3
Papa Stour (isl.) 24 .... F2
Papa Westray (isl.) 106 .... F1
Paps of Jura (mt.) C5
Park (dist.) 210 .... B2
Peel Fell (mt.) F5
Pentland (firth) E2
Pentland (hills) D2
Quoich, Loch (lake) C3
Raasay (isl.) 163 .... C3
Rannoch (dist.) 1,177 .... D4
Rannoch, Loch (lake) D4
Renish (pt.) B3
Resort, Loch (inlet) A2
Rhinns (pt.) B5
Rhinns, The (pen.) 8,295 .... C6
Rhum (sound) B4
Riddon, Loch (inlet) C5
Roag, Loch (inlet) B2
Rona (isl.) 3 .... B3
Ronay (isl.) A3
Rora (head) E2
Ross of Mull (pen.) 585 .... B4
Rousay (isl.) 181 .... E1
Rudha Hunish (cape) B3
Rum (sound) B4
Rum (isl.) 40 .... B3
Ryan, Loch (inlet) C5
Saint Abbs (head) F5
Saint Kilda (isl.) 65 .... A2
Saint Magnus (bay) F2
Sanday (isl.) 592 .... F1
Sandray (isl.) A4
Scalpay (isl.) 483 .... B3
Scalpay (isl.) 5 .... C3
Scapa Flow (chan.) E2
Scarba (isl.) C4
Scarp (isl.) 12 .... A2
Scridain, Loch (inlet) B4
Seaforth, Loch (inlet) B3
Seil (isl.) 326 .... C4
Sgurr Alasdair (mt.) B3
Sgurr Mor (mt.) C3
Sgurr na Ciche (mt.) C3
Sgurr na Lapaich (mt.) C3
Shapinsay (isl.) 346 .... F1
Shetland (isls.) 18,494 .... G2
Shiant (isls.) B3
Shiel, Loch (lake) C4
Shin, Loch (lake) D2
Sidlaw (hills) E4
Sinclair's (bay) E2
Skye, Isle of (isl.) 7,183 .... B3
Sleat (dist.) 449 .... C3
Sleat (pt.) B4
Sleat (sound) C3
Small Isles (isls.) 171 .... B4
Snizort, Loch (inlet) B3
Soay (isl.) 5 .... B3
Solway (firth) E6
South Esk (riv.) F4
South Ronaldsay (isl.) 776 .... F2
South Uist (isl.) 2,281 .... A3
Spean (riv.) D4
Spey (riv.) E3
Staffa (isl.) B4
Start (pt.) F1
Stoer (pt.) C2
Storr, The (mt.) B3
Strathbogie (dist.) 7,959 .... F3
Strathmore (valley) E4
Strathspey (dist.) 6,668 .... E3
Striven Loch (inlet) A2
Stroma (isl.) 8 .... E2
Stronsay (isl.) 436 .... F1
Sumburgh (head) G2
Summer Isles (isls.) C2
Sunart Loch (inlet) C4
Taransay (isl.) 5 .... A3
Tarbat Ness (prom.) E3
Tarbert, East Loch (inlet) B3
Tarbert, Loch (inlet) B5
Tarbert, West Loch (inlet) A3
Tarbert, West Loch (inlet) C5
Tay (firth) F4
Tay (riv.) E4
Tay, Loch (lake) D4
Teith (riv.) D4
Teviot (riv.) F5
Thurso (riv.) E2
Tiree (isl.) 875 .... B4
Tiumpan (head) B2
Toe (head) A3
Tolsta (head) B2
Tor Ness (prom.) E2
Torridon, Loch (inlet) C3
Trossachs, The (valley) D4
Trotternish (dist.) 1,948 .... B3
Troup (head) F3
Tummel (lake) E4
Tweed (riv.) F5
Tyne (riv.) F5
Ulva (isl.) 23 .... B4
Unst (isl.) 1,124 .... G2
Vaternish (pt.) B3
Vaternish (dist.) 162 .... B3
Vatersay (isl.) 77 .... A4
Watten, Loch (lake) E2
West Loch Tarbert (inlet) C5
West Loch Tarbert (inlet) A3
Westray (isl.) 735 .... E1
Whalsay (isl.) 870 .... G2
White Coomb (mt.) E5
Wiay (isl.) A3
Wigtown (bay) D6
Wrath (cape) C2
Yarrow (riv.) E5
Yell (isl.) 1,143 .... G2
Yell (sound) G2

⊙ Population of parish.

Agriculture, Industry and Resources

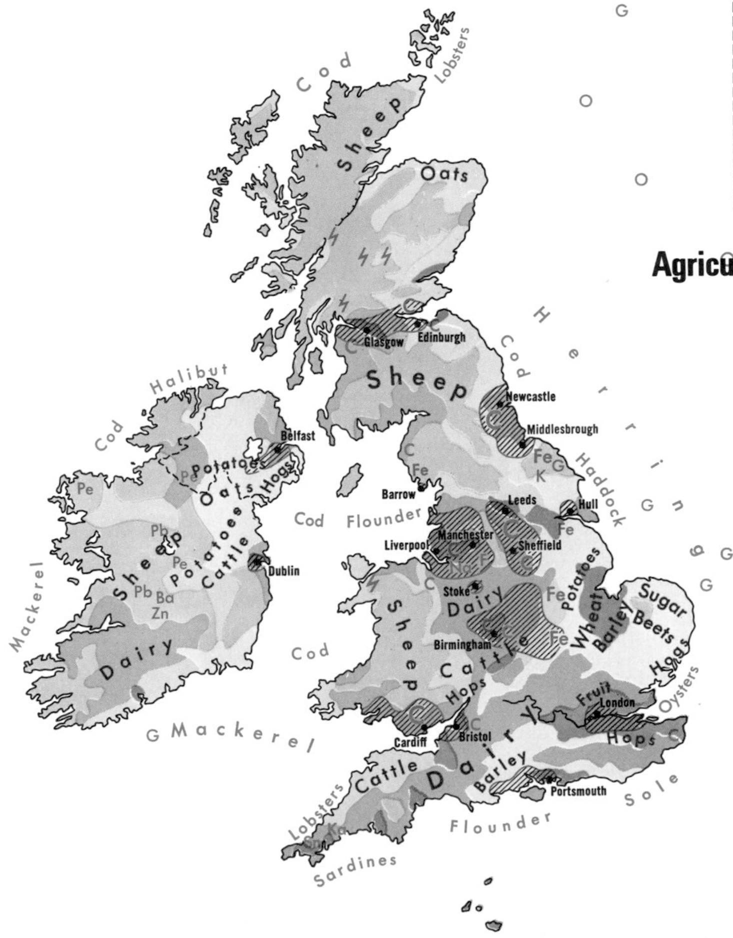

DOMINANT LAND USE

- Cereals (chiefly oats, barley)
- Truck Farming, Horticulture
- Dairy, Mixed Farming
- Livestock, Mixed Farming
- Pasture Livestock

MAJOR MINERAL OCCURRENCES

Ba	Barite	Na	Salt
C	Coal	O	Petroleum
F	Fluorspar	Pb	Lead
Fe	Iron Ore	Pe	Peat
G	Natural Gas	Sn	Tin
K	Potash	Zn	Zinc
Ka	Kaolin (china clay)		

Water Power

Major Industrial Areas

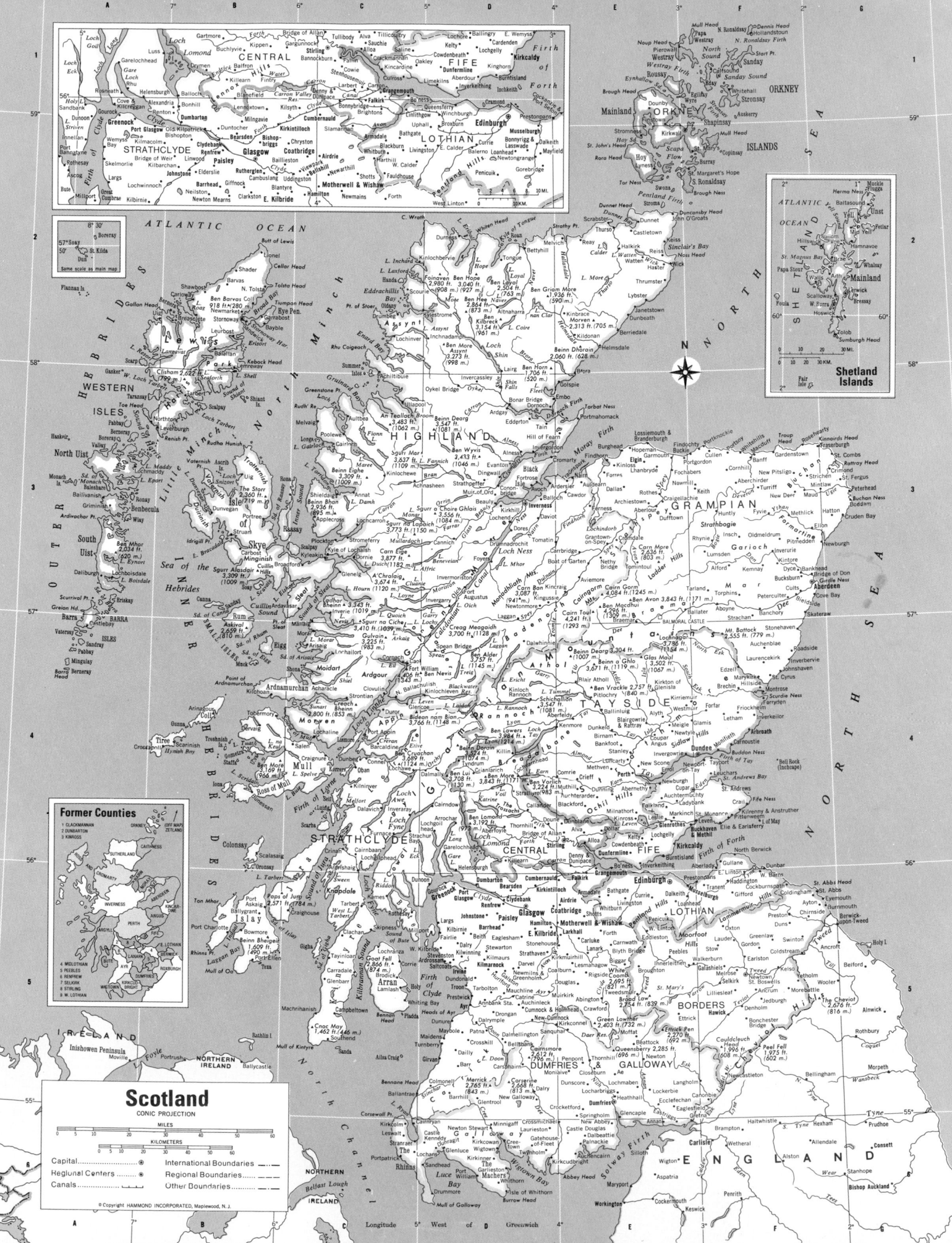

Scotland

CONIC PROJECTION

MILES

KILOMETERS

Capital.........................⊛
Regional Centers........⊙
Canals..........................

International Boundaries ———
Regional Boundaries.... — — —
Other Boundaries........ ·····

© Copyright HAMMOND INCORPORATED, Maplewood, N.J.

Former Counties

1 CLACKMANNAN
2 DUNBARTON
3 KINROSS
4 MIDLOTHIAN
5 PEEBLES
6 RENFREW
7 SELKIRK
8 STIRLING
9 W. LOTHIAN

Shetland Islands

IRELAND

COUNTIES

Carlow 40,988 H6
Cavan 53,965 G4
Clare 91,344 D6
Cork 412,735 D7
Donegal 129,664 F2
Dublin 1,021,449 J5
Galway 178,552 D5
Kerry 124,159 B7
Kildare 116,247 H5
Kilkenny 73,186 G6
Laois 53,284 G6
Leitrim 27,035 E3
Leix (Laois) 53,284 G6
Limerick 164,569 D7
Longford 31,496 F4
Louth 91,810 J4
Mayo 115,184 C4
Meath 103,881 H4
Monaghan 52,379 H3
Offaly 59,835 F5
Roscommon 54,592 E4
Sligo 56,046 D3
Tipperary 136,619 F6
Waterford 91,151 F7
Westmeath 63,379 G5
Wexford 102,552 H7
Wicklow 94,542 J6

CITIES and TOWNS

Abbeyfeale 1,483 C7
Abbeyleix 1,468 G6
Adare 792 D6
Aghada-Farsid-Rostellan 818 E8
An Uaimh 3,660 H4
Ardee 3,253 H4
Ardfinnan 827 F7
Ardmore 343 F8
Arklow 8,388 J6
Ashford 782 J5
Askeaton 951 D6
Athboy 1,055 H4
Athenry 1,642 D5
Athlone 8,815 F5
Athy 4,734 H6
Aughrim 756 J6
Avoca 490 J6
Bagenalstown (Muinebeag) 2,653 H6
Baile Atha Cliath (Dublin) (cap.) 502,749 K5
Bailieborough 1,645 G4
Balbriggan 5,680 J4
Ballaghaderreen 1,366 E4
Ballina, Mayo 6,714 C3
Ballina, Tipperary 507 E6
Ballinamore 810 F3
Ballinasloe 6,125 E5
Ballincollig-Carrigrohane 7,231 D8
Ballineen 592 D8
Ballinrobe 1,270 C4
Ballybofey-Stranorlar 2,964 F2
Ballybunion 1,452 B7
Ballycastle 219 C3
Ballyconnell 466 F3
Ballygar 472 E4
Ballygeary 891 J7
Ballyhaunis 1,338 D4
Ballyheigue 660 B7
Ballyjamesduff 842 G4
Ballylanders 343 E7
Ballylongford 523 B6
Ballymahon 859 F4
Ballymore Eustace 575 J5
Ballymote 1,064 D3
Ballyragget 833 G6
Ballyshannon 2,573 E3
Baltinglass 1,089 H6
Banagher 1,465 F5
Bandon 1,943 D8
Bantry 2,811 C8
Belmullet 1,033 B3
Belturbet 1,228 G3
Bennettsbridge 601 G6
Birr 3,417 F5
Blanchardstown H5
Blarney 1,952 D8
Blessington 1,322 J5
Borrisokane 837 E6
Borrisoleigh 624 E6
Boyle 1,859 E4
Bray 24,686 K5
Bri Chualann (Bray) 24,686 K5
Bruff 819 D7
Bunbeg-Derrybeg 1,469 E1
Bunclody-Carrickduff 1,423 H6
Buncrana 3,106 G1
Bundoran 1,535 E3
Buttevant 1,133 D7
Cahir 2,118 F7
Cahirciveen 1,310 A8
Callan 1,266 G7
Cappamore 765 E6
Cappoquin 920 F7
Carlingford 635 J3
Carlow 11,509 H6
Carndonagh 1,600 G1
Carnew 723 H6
Carrickmacross 1,815 H4
Carrick-on-Shannon 1,984 F4
Carrick-on-Suir 5,353 F7
Carrigaline 5,893 E8
Carrigtwohill 1,272 E8
Cashel 2,458 F7
Castlebar 6,349 C4
Castlebellingham 848 J4
Castleblayney 2,157 H3
Castlebridge 655 J7
Castlecomer-Donaguile 1,490 G6
Castledermot 792 H6
Castlefin 694 F2
Castleisland 2,281 B7
Castlemartyr 585 E8
Castlepollard 803 G4
Castlerea 1,840 D4
Castletown 303 F6
Castletownbere 905 B8
Castletownroche 474 D7
Cavan 3,381 G3
Ceanannus Mór 2,413 G4
Celbridge 7,135 H5
Charlestown-Bellahy 754 D4
Charleville (Rathluirc) 2,814 D7
Clara 2,736 F5
Claremorris 1,992 C4
Clifden 896 B5
Cloghan 496 F5
Clogh-Chatsworth 319 G6
Clogheen 502 F7
Clogherhead 765 J4
Clonakilty 2,567 D8
Clones 2,280 G3
Clonfert E5
Clonmel 11,759 F7
Cloughjordan 499 E6
Cloyne 721 E8
Cóbh 6,369 E8
Coill Dubh 772 H5
Collooney 705 E3
Convoy 891 F2
Coolgreany 352 J6
Cootehill 1,487 G3
Cork 133,271 E8
Corofin 391 C6
Courtown Harbour 317 J6
Creeslough 340 F1
Croom 1,024 D6
Crosshaven 1,362 E8
Crossmolina 1,250 C3
Daingean 659 G5
Delvin 309 G4
Dingle 1,253 A7
Donabate 599 J5
Donegal 2,242 F2
Doneraile 846 D7
Dooagh-Keel 650 A4
Doon 308 E6
Drimoleague 381 C8
Drogheda 24,086 J4
Droichead Nua 5,983 H5
Dromahair 353 E3
Drumconrath 334 H4
Drumshanbo 622 E3
Dublin (cap.) 502,749 K5
Duleek 1,679 J4
Duncannon 388 H7
Dundalk 26,669 H3
Dunfanaghy 314 F1
Dungarvan 6,849 F7
Dungloe 940 E2
Dún Laoghaire 54,715 K5
Dunkineely 442 E2
Dunlavin 734 H5
Dunleer 1,184 J4
Dunmanway 1,382 C8
Dunmore 445 D4
Dunmore East 1,041 G7
Dunshaughlin 878 H5
Durrow 707 G6
Edenderry 3,539 G5
Elphin 513 E4
Emyvale 464 G3
Ennis 5,917 D6
Enniscorthy 4,483 J7
Enniskerry 1,229 J5
Ennistymon 1,039 C6
Eyrecourt 351 E5
Fahan 367 G1
Falcarragh 996 E1
Fenit 401 B7
Ferbane 1,374 F5
Fermoy 2,872 E7
Ferns 811 J6
Fethard 982 F7
Foxford 1,033 C4
Foynes 707 C6
Frankford (Kilcormac) 1,118 F5
Freshford 700 G6
Galbally 248 E7
Galway 47,104 C5
Geashill 339 G5
Glanworth 379 E7
Glenamaddy 369 D4
Glenties 914 E2
Glin 569 C6
Golden 295 F7
Gorey 2,445 J6
Gormanston 870 J4
Gort 1,021 D5
Gowran 517 G6
Graiguenamanagh-Tinnahinch 1,485 H6
Granard 1,338 F4
Greencastle 584 H1
Greystones 8,455 K5
Hacketstown 710 H6
Headford 675 C5
Holycross 274 F6
Hospital 751 E7
Inniscrone 633 C3
Johnstown 408 G6
Kanturk 1,870 D7
Keel-Dooagh 650 A4
Kells (Ceanannus Mór) 2,413 G4
Kenmare 1,130 B8
Kilbeggan 603 G5
Kilcar 345 D2
Kilcock 1,414 H5
Kilcoole 2,335 K5
Kilcormac 1,118 F5
Kilcullen 1,693 H5
Kildare 4,268 H5
Kildysart 347 C6
Kilfinane 788 D7
Kilkee 1,448 B6
Kilkenny 8,969 G6
Killala 674 C3
Killaloe 1,033 D6
Killarney 7,837 C7
Killenaule 717 F6
Killeshandra 455 F3
Killorglin 1,304 B7
Killucan-Rathwire 353 G4
Killybegs 1,632 E2
Kilmacrennan 412 F1
Kilmacthomas 648 G7
Kilmallock 1,424 D7
Kilmihill 338 C6
Kilmore Quay 458 H7
Kilnaleck 321 G4
Kilronan 282 B5
Kilrush 2,961 C6
Kiltimagh 982 C4
Kilworth 411 E7
Kingscourt 1,242 H4
Kingstown (Dún Laoghaire) 54,715 K5
Kinnegad 433 G5
Kinnitty 261 F5
Kinsale 1,811 D8
Kinvara 425 D5
Knightstown 204 A8
Knock 332 D4
Knocklong 273 D7
Lahinch 511 C6
Lanesborough-Ballyleague 1,058 E4
Laytown-Bettystown-Mornington 3,321 J4
Leighlinbridge 540 H6
Leitrim F3
Leixlip 11,938 H5
Letterkenny 6,691 F2
Lifford 1,478 F2
Limerick 56,279 D6
Lisdoonvarna 648 C5
Lismore 703 F7
Listowel 3,494 C7
Littleton 566 F6
Longford 6,457 F4
Loughrea 3,360 E5
Louisburgh 209 B4
Louth 435 J4
Lucan 12,259 J5
Luimneach (Limerick) 56,279 D6
Lusk 1,831 J4
Macroom 2,449 C8
Malahide 9,940 J5
Mallow 6,488 D7
Manorhamilton 1,031 E3
Maryborough (Portlaoise) 3,773 G5
Maynooth 4,768 H5
Meathas Truim 806 G4
Midleton 3,111 E8
Milford 981 F1
Millstreet 1,330 D7
Milltown 347 A7
Miltownmalbay 719 C6
Mitchelstown 3,210 E7
Moate 1,659 F5
Mohill 930 F4
Monaghan 6,075 G3
Monasterevan 2,143 H5
Moneygall 346 F6
Mooncoin 868 G7
Mount Bellew 519 D5
Mountcharles 480 E2
Mountmellick 2,789 G5
Mountrath 1,402 F5
Moville 1,331 G1
Moycullen 366 C5
Muinebeag 2,653 H6
Mullagh 462 H4
Mullinahone 385 F7
Mullinavat 355 G7
Mullingar 8,077 G4
Naas 10,017 H5
Navan (An Uaimh) 3,660 H4
Nenagh 5,483 E6
Newbliss 293 G3
Newbridge (Droichead Nua) 5,983 H5
Newcastle 3,370 C7
Newmarket 1,022 C7
Newmarket-on-Fergus 1,678 D6
Newport, Mayo 492 C4
Newport, Tipperary 857 E6
New Ross 5,343 H7
Newtown Forbes 393 F4
Newtownmountkennedy 2,183 J5
Newtownsandes 357 C6
O'Briensbridge-Montpelier 385 D6
Oldcastle 869 G4
Oola 451 E6
Oranmore 1,064 D5
Oughterard 682 C5
Passage East 563 G7
Passage West 3,511 E8
Patrickswell 905 D6
Piltown 691 G7
Portarlington 3,295 G5
Portlaoise 3,773 G5
Portlaw 1,260 G7
Portmarnock 9,055 J5
Portumna 1,062 E5
Queenstown (Cóbh) 6,369 E8
Ramelton 989 F1
Raphoe 1,027 F2
Rathangan 1,270 G5
Rathcoole 2,991 J5
Rathdowney 1,095 F6
Rathdrum 1,307 J6
Rathkeale 1,815 D7
Rathluirc 2,814 D7
Rathmore 548 J5
Rathmullen 554 F1
Rathnew 1,389 J6
Rathvilly 512 H6
Ratoath 551 J5
Riverstown 1,416 E8
Roscommon 1,363 E4
Roscrea 4,378 F6
Rosscarbery 425 C8
Rosses Point 598 D3
Rosslare 704 J7
Rosslare Harbour (Ballygeary) 891 J7
Roundwood 371 J5
Rush 4,513 J4
Saint Johnston 468 F2
Scarriff 847 E6
Schull 509 B8
Shanagolden 402 C6
Shannon 8,005 D6
Shannon Bridge 310 F5
Shercock 406 G4
Shillelagh 334 J6
Shinrone 479 F5
Sixmilebridge 1,182 D6
Skerries 6,864 J4
Skibbereen 1,999 C8
Slane 689 H4
Sligo 17,259 E3
Sneem 309 B8
Stepaside 748 J5
Stradbally, Laois 1,046 G5
Stradbally, Waterford 255 F7
Strokestown 620 E4
Swinford 1,197 C4
Swords 15,312 J5
Taghmon 607 H7
Tallow 867 F7
Tarbert 683 C6
Templemore 2,258 F6
Templetuohy 242 F6
Termonfeckin 741 J4
Thomastown 1,465 G7
Thurles 7,049 F6
Timoleague 330 D8
Tinahely 594 H6
Tipperary 5,033 E7
Toomevara 428 E6
Tralee 17,109 B7
Tramore 5,999 G7
Trim 1,967 H4
Tuam 4,109 D4
Tubbercurry 1,250 D3
Tulla 403 D6
Tullamore 8,484 G5
Tullow 2,324 H6
Tyrrellspass 328 G5
Urlingford 676 F6
Virginia 699 G4
Waterford 39,529 G7
Waterville-Spunkane 475 A8
Westport 3,456 C4
Wexford 10,336 H7
Wicklow 5,304 K6
Woodford 242 E5
Youghal 5,706 F8

OTHER FEATURES

Achill (head) A4
Achill (isl.) A4
Allen (lake) E3
Allen, Bog of (marsh) H5
Annalee (riv.) G3
Aran (isls.) B5
Aran (isl.) D2
Arrow (lake) E3
Ballinskelligs (bay) A8
Ballyhoura (hills) E7
Ballyteige (bay) H7
Bandon (riv.) D8
Bantry (bay) B8
Barrow (riv.) H7
Baurtregaum (mt.) A7
Bear (isl.) B8
Ben Dash (hill) C6
Bertraghboy (bay) A5
Black (head) C5
Blacksod (bay) A3
Blackstairs (mt.) H6
Blackwater (riv.) H4
Blackwater (riv.) D7
Blasket (isls.) A7
Bloody Foreland (prom.) E1
Blue Stack (mts.) E2
Boderg (lake) E4
Boggeragh (mts.) D7
Bolus (head) A8
Boyne (riv.) J4
Brandon (bay) A7
Brandon (head) A7
Brandon (mt.) A7
Bray (head) A8
Bride (riv.) E7
Broad Haven (harb.) B3
Brosna (riv.) F5
Bull, The (isl.) A8
Caha (mts.) B8
Cahore (pt.) J6
Cark (mt.) F2
Carlingford (inlet) J3
Carnsore (pt.) J7
Carra (lake) C4
Carrantuohill (mt.) B7
Carrowmore (lake) B3
Clare (isls.) A4
Clare (riv.) D5
Clear (cape) B9
Clear (isl.) C9
Clew (bay) B4
Clonakilty (bay) D8
Comeragh (mts.) F7
Conn (lake) C3
Connacht (prov.) 431,409 C4
Connemara (dist.) B5
Cork (harb.) E8
Corrib (lake) C5
Croagh Patrick (mt.) C4
Cuilcagh (mt.) F3
Cullin (lake) C4
Curragh, The (plain) H5
Dash, Ben (hill) C6
Dee (riv.) H4
Deel (riv.) C3
Deel (riv.) C7
Deel (riv.) G4
Deele (riv.) F2
Derg (lake) F2
Derg (lake) E6
Derravaragh (lake) G4
Derryveagh (mts.) E2
Devilsbit (mt.) E6
Dingle (bay) A7
Donegal (bay) D3
Donegal (pt.) B6
Doulus (head) A8
Downpatrick (head) C3
Drum (hills) F7
Dublin (bay) J5
Dunany (pt.) J4
Dundalk (bay) J4
Dungarvan (harb.) G7
Dunkellin (riv.) D5
Dunmanus (bay) B8
Dursey (isl.) A8
Eask (lake) E2
Ennell (lake) G5
Erne (riv.) E3
Errigal (mt.) E1
Erris (head) A3
Fanad (head) F1
Fastnet Rock (isl.) B9
Feale (riv.) C7
Feeagh (lake) B4
Fergus (riv.) D6
Finn (riv.) F2
Finn (riv.) G3
Foul (sound) B5
Foyle (inlet) G1
Foyle (riv.) G2
Galley (head) D9
Galtee (mts.) E7
Galtymore (mt.) E7
Galway (bay) C5
Gara (lake) D4
Garadice (lake) F3
Gill (lake) E3
Gola (isl.) E1
Golden Vale (plain) E7
Gorumna (isl.) B5
Gowna (lake) G4
Grand (canal) G5
Great Blasket (isl.) A7
Gregory's (sound) B5
Gweebarra (bay) D2
Hags (head) B6
Hook (head) H7
Horn (head) E1
Iar Connacht (dist.) C5
Inishbofin (isl.) A4
Inisheer (isl.) B5
Inishmaan (isl.) C5
Inishmore (isl.) B5
Inishmurray (isl.) D3
Inishowen (head) H1
Inishowen (pen.) G1
Inishshark (isl.) A4
Inishtrahull (isl.) G1
Inishtrahull (sound) G1
Inishturk (isls.) A4
Inny (riv.) F4
Ireland's Eye (isl.) K5
Irish (sea) K4
Joyce's Country (dist.) B4
Keeper (hill) E6
Kenmare (riv.) A8
Kerry (head) A7
Key (lake) E3
Kilkieran (bay) B5
Killala (bay) C3
Killary (harb.) A4
Kinsale (harb.) E8
Kinsale, Old Head of (head) E8
Kippure (mt.) J5
Knockanefune (mt.) C7
Knockboy (mt.) B8
Knockmealdown (mts.) F7
Lambay (hill) K4
Laune (riv.) B7
Leane (lake) G4
Lee (riv.) D8
Leinster (mt.) H6
Leinster (prov.) 1,852,649 G5
Lettermullan (isl.) B5
Liffey (riv.) H5
Liscannor (bay) B6
Loop (head) A6
Loughros More (bay) D2
Lugnaquillia (mt.) J5
Lung (riv.) D4
Macgillicuddy's Reeks (mts.) B7
Macnean (lake) F3
Maigue (riv.) D6
Malin (head) F1
Mangerton (mt.) C8
Mask (lake) C4
Maumakeogh (mt.) C3
Maumturk (mts.) B5
Melvin (lake) E3
Mine (head) F8
Mizen (head) B9
Mizen (head) K6
Moher (cliff) B6
Monavullagh (mts.) F7
Moy (riv.) C3
Mullaghareirk (mts.) C7
Mulroy (bay) F1
Munster (prov.) 1,020,577 D7
Mutton (isl.) B6
Mweelrea (mt.) B4
Nagles (mts.) E7
Nephin (mt.) C3
Nephin Beg (mt.) B3
Nore (riv.) G7
North (sound) B5
North Inishkea (isl.) A3
Oughter (lake) G3
Ovoca (riv.) J6
Owenmore (riv.) B3
Owenmore (riv.) D3
Paps, The (mt.) C7
Partry (mts.) C4
Pollaphuca (res.) J5
Puffin (isl.) A8
Punchestown H5
Ramor (lake) G4
Rathlin O'Birne (isl.) C2
Ree (lake) F5
Rinn (lake) F4
Roaringwater (bay) B9
Rosscarbery (bay) D9
Rosskeeragh (pt.) D3
Royal (canal) G4
Saint Finan's (bay) A8
Saint George's (chan.) K7
Saint John's (pt.) D2
Saltee (isls.) H7
Scarriff (isl.) A8
Seven Hogs, The (isls.) A7
Shannon (riv.) E6
Shannon, Mouth of the (delta) B6
Sheeffry (hills) B4
Sheelin (lake) G4
Sheep Haven (harb.) F1
Sheeps (head) B8
Shehy (mts.) C8
Sherkin (isl.) C9
Silvermine (mts.) E6
Slaney (riv.) H7
Slieve Anierin (mt.) F3
Slieve Aughty (mts.) D5
Slieve Bernagh (mt.) D6
Slieve Bloom (mts.) F5
Slieve Callan (mt.) C6
Slieve Car (mt.) B3
Slieve Elva (mt.) C5
Slieve Gamph (Ox) (mts.) D3
Slievefelim (mts.) E6
Slievenaman (mt.) F7
Sligo (bay) D3
Slyne (head) A5
Smerwick (harb.) A7
South (sound) C5
Stacks (mts.) B7
Suck (riv.) E5
Sugarloaf (mt.) B8
Suir (riv.) G7
Swilly (inlet) F1
Tara (hill) H4
Toe (head) C9
Tory (isl.) E1
Tory (sound) E1
Tralee (bay) B7
Tramore (bay) G7
Truskmore (mt.) E3
Twelve Pins (mt.) B4
Ulster (part) (prov.) 236,008 G2
Valencia (Valentia) (isl.) A8
Valentia (isl.) A8
Waterford (harb.) G7
Wexford (harb.) J7
Wexford (bay) J7
Wicklow (mts.) J6
Youghal (bay) F8

NORTHERN IRELAND

DISTRICTS

Antrim 44,384 J2
Ards 57,626 K2
Armagh 47,618 H3
Ballymena 54,426 J2
Ballymoney 22,873 J1
Banbridge 29,885 J3
Belfast 295,223 J2
Carrickfergus 28,458 K2
Castlereagh 60,757 K2
Coleraine 46,272 H1
Cookstown 26,624 H2
Craigavon 71,202 J3
Down 52,869 K3
Dungannon 41,073 H3
Fermanagh 51,008 F3
Larne 28,929 K2
Limavady 26,270 H1
Lisburn 82,091 J2
Londonderry 83,384 G2
Magherafelt 30,825 H2
Mourne (Newry and Mourne) 72,243 J3
Moyle 14,252 J1
Newtownabbey 71,631 J2
North Down 65,849 K2
Omagh 41,159 G2
Strabane 35,028 G2

CITIES and TOWNS

Annalong 1,823 K3
Antrim 22,342 J2
Armagh 12,700 H3
Augher 1,874 G3
Aughnacloy 1,659 H3
Ballycarry 1,652 K2
Ballycastle 3,284 J1
Ballyclare 6,159 J2
Ballygawley 2,099 G3
Ballymena 28,166 J2
Ballymoney 5,679 J1
Ballynahinch 3,721 J3
Banbridge 9,650 J3
Bangor 46,585 K2
Belfast (cap.) 295,223 J2
Bellaghy 1,854 H2
Belleek and Boa 2,469 E3
Beragh 2,028 G2
Bessbrook 2,756 J3
Brookeborough 2,250 G3
Broughshane 1,503 J2
Bushmills 1,381 J1
Caledon 1,633 H3
Carnlough 1,462 K2
Carrickfergus 17,633 K2
Carrowdore 3,019 K2
Carryduff 2,666 K2
Castledawson 1,460 H2
Castlederg 1,730 F2
Castlewellan 2,105 K3
Claudy 2,516 G2
Clogher 1,792 G3
Cloughmills 1,558 J2
Coalisland 3,324 H2
Coleraine 15,967 H1
Comber 7,600 K2
Cookstown 7,649 H2
Craigavon 10,195 J3
Crumlin 1,708 J2
Cullybackey 2,098 J2
Derrygonnelly 2,627 F3
Donaghadee 3,874 K2
Downpatrick 8,245 K3
Dromore, Banbridge 3,089 J3
Dromore, Omagh 2,286 G3
Drumquin 1,865 F2
Dundrum 2,295 K3
Dungannon 8,295 H3
Dungiven 2,249 H2
Dunloy 1,593 J1
Dunnamanagh 2,191 G2
Ederney, Kesh and Lark 2,607 F2
Enniskillen 10,429 F3
Feeny 1,402 H2
Fintona 1,353 G3
Fivemiletown 1,758 G3
Garvagh 2,222 H2
Gilford 1,512 J3
Glenarm 1,533 J2
Glenavy 2,402 J2
Glynn 1,689 K2
Gortin 1,877 G2
Greenisland 5,103 K2
Grey Abbey 2,945 K2
Groomsport 3,870 K2
Holywood 9,462 K2
Irvinestown 1,827 F3
Keady 2,561 H3
Kells 2,564 J2
Kesh, Ederney and Lark 2,607 F3
Kilkeel 6,036 K3
Killough 3,104 K3
Killyclogher 5,557 G2
Killyleagh 2,094 K3
Kilrea 1,320 H2
Lambeg J2
Larne 18,224 K2
Limavady 8,015 H1
Lisbellaw 2,395 K2
Lisburn 40,391 J2
Lisnaskea 1,568 G3
Londonderry (Derry) 62,692 G2
Loughbrickland 2,244 J3
Lurgan 20,991 J3
Macosquin 2,267 H1
Maghera 1,953 H2
Magherafelt 5,044 H2
Millisle 1,373 K2
Moy 2,163 H3
Newcastle 6,246 J3
Newry 19,426 J3
Newtownabbey 56,149 K2
Newtownards 20,531 K2
Newtownbutler 2,632 G3
Newtownhamilton 1,654 H3
Newtownstewart 1,425 G2
Omagh 14,627 G2
Pomeroy 1,638 H2
Portadown 21,333 H3
Portaferry 2,148 K3
Portglenone 2,017 H2
Portrush 5,114 H1
Portstewart 5,312 H1
Randalstown 3,591 J2
Rathfriland 2,243 J3
Richhill 1,728 H3
Rostrevor 1,852 J3
Sion Mills 1,771 G2
Sixmilecross 1,613 G2
Stewartstown 1,554 H2
Strabane 9,413 G2
Strangford 2,062 K3
Strathfoyle 2,050 G1
Tandragee 2,224 J3
Tempo 2,149 G3
Trillick 2,017 G3
Warrenpoint 4,798 J3
Whitehead 3,546 K2

OTHER FEATURES

Arney (riv.) F3
Bann (riv.) H2
Beg (lake) J2
Belfast (inlet) K2
Blackwater (riv.) H3
Bush (riv.) H1
Copeland (isl.) K2
Derg (riv.) F2
Divis (mt.) J2
Dundrum (bay) K3
Erne, Lough (lake) F3
Fair (head) J1
Foyle (riv.) G2
Foyle (inlet) G1
Garron (pt.) K1
Giant's Causeway H1
Lagan (riv.) K2
Larne (inlet) K2
Macnean (lake) F3
Magee, Island (pen.) K2
Main (riv.) J2
Mourne (riv.) G2
Mourne (mts.) J3
Neagh (lake) J2
North (chan.) K1
Owenkillew (riv.) G2
Rathlin (sound) J1
Rathlin (isl.) J1
Red (bay) K1
Roe (riv.) H1
Saint John's (pt.) K3
Slieve Beagh (mt.) G3
Slieve Donard (mt.) K3
Sperrin (mts.) G2
Strangford (inlet) K3
Trostan (mt.) J1
Ulster (part) (prov.) G2
Upper Lough Erne (lake) F3

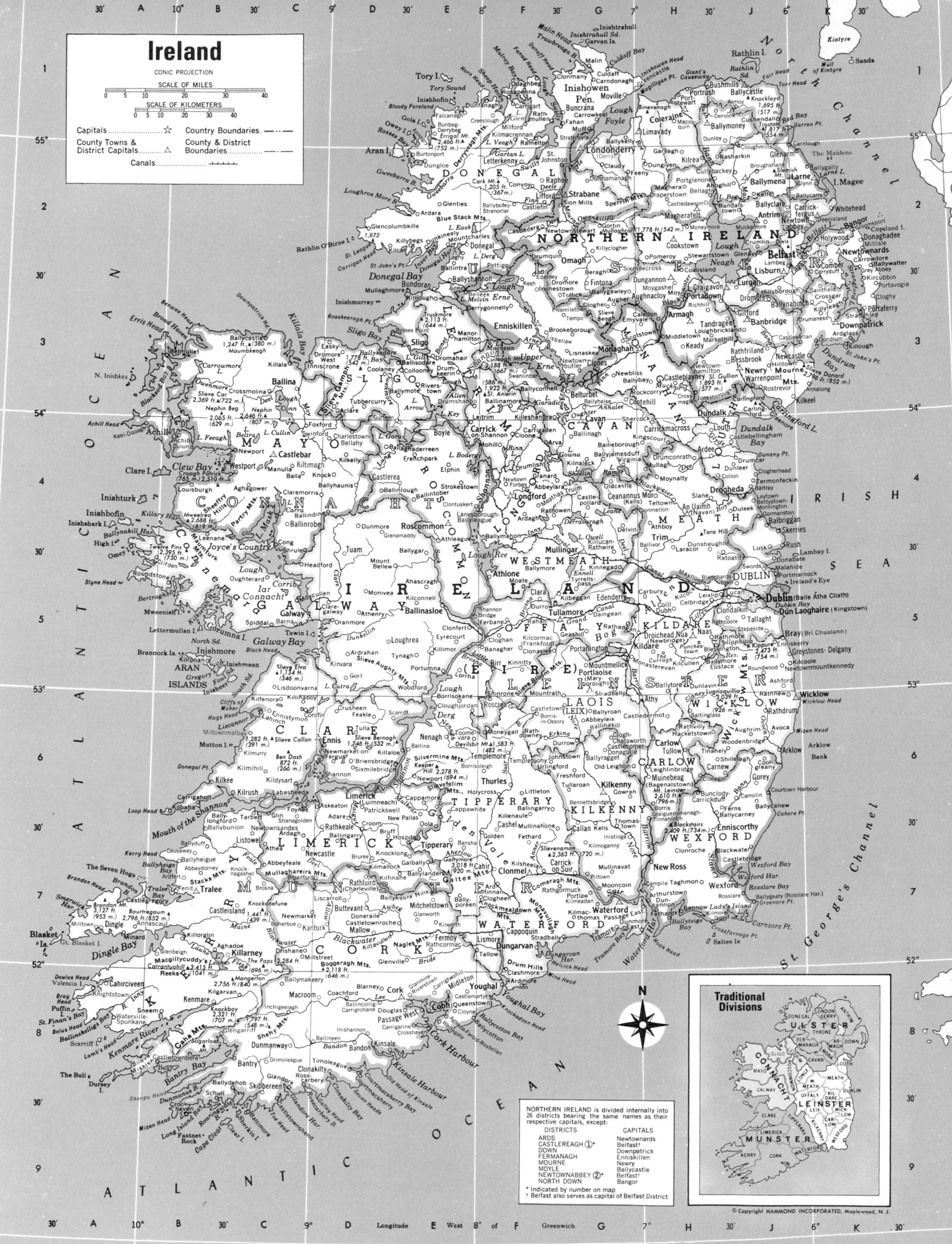

Ireland

CONIC PROJECTION

SCALE OF MILES

SCALE OF KILOMETERS

Capitals .... ☆
County Towns &
District Capitals .... △
Canals ....

Country Boundaries. —··—··—
County & District
Boundaries ....

Traditional Divisions

NORTHERN IRELAND is divided internally into
26 districts bearing the same names as their
respective capitals, except:

DISTRICTS	CAPITALS
ARDS	Newtownards
CASTLEREAGH ① *	Belfast†
DOWN	Downpatrick
FERMANAGH	Enniskillen
MOURNE	Newry
MOYLE	Ballycastle
NEWTOWNABBEY ② *	Belfast†
NORTH DOWN	Bangor

* Indicated by number on map
† Belfast also serves as capital of Belfast District

© Copyright HAMMOND INCORPORATED, Maplewood, N.J.

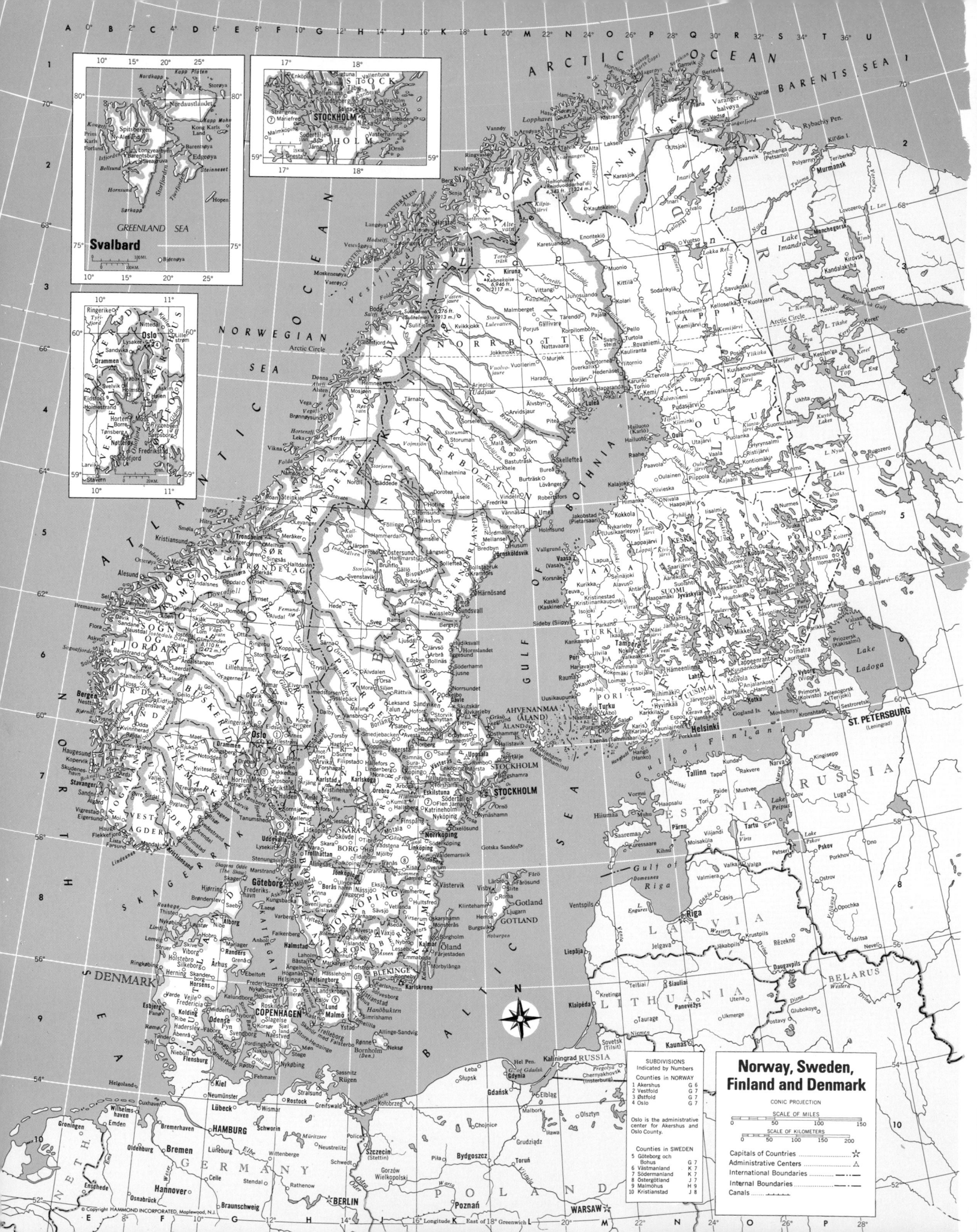

Norway, Sweden, Finland and Denmark

CONIC PROJECTION

SUBDIVISIONS
Indicated by Numbers

Counties in NORWAY
1 Akershus .... G 6
2 Vestfold .... G 7
3 Østfold .... G 7
4 Oslo .... G 7

Oslo is the administrative
center for Akershus and
Oslo County.

Counties in SWEDEN
5 Göteborg och
  Bohus .... G 7
6 Västmanland .... K 7
7 Södermanland .... K 7
8 Östergötland .... H 7
9 Malmöhus .... H 9
10 Kristianstad .... J 8

SCALE OF MILES
0   50   100   150

SCALE OF KILOMETERS
0   50   100   150   200

Capitals of Countries .... ☆
Administrative Centers .... △
International Boundaries .... ━ ━ ━
Internal Boundaries .... ━━━━
Canals ....

AREA 125,053 sq. mi.
(323,887 sq. km.)
POPULATION 4,242,000
CAPITAL Oslo
LARGEST CITY Oslo
HIGHEST POINT Glittertinden
8,110 ft. (2,472 m.)
MONETARY UNIT krone
MAJOR LANGUAGE Norwegian
MAJOR RELIGION Protestantism

AREA 173,665 sq. mi.
(449,792 sq. km.)
POPULATION 8,541,000
CAPITAL Stockholm
LARGEST CITY Stockholm
HIGHEST POINT Kebnekaise 6,946 ft.
(2,117 m.)
MONETARY UNIT krona
MAJOR LANGUAGE Swedish
MAJOR RELIGION Protestantism

AREA 130,128 sq. mi.
(337,032 sq. km.)
POPULATION 4,973,000
CAPITAL Helsinki
LARGEST CITY Helsinki
HIGHEST POINT Haltiatunturi
4,343 ft. (1,324 m.)
MONETARY UNIT markka
MAJOR LANGUAGES Finnish, Swedish
MAJOR RELIGION Protestantism

NORWAY

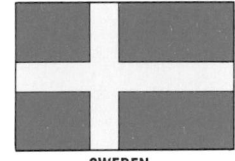

SWEDEN

FINLAND

FINLAND

PROVINCES

Ahvenanmaa 23,591	L6
Åland (Ahvenanmaa) 23,591	L6
Häme 677,567	O6
Keski-Suomi 247,693	O5
Kuopio 256,036	P3
Kymi 340,665	Q6
Lappi 200,943	P3
Mikkeli 239,029	P6
Oulu 432,141	P4
Pohjois-Karjala 177,567	Q5
Turku ja Pori 713,050	N6
Uusimaa 1,187,851	O6
Vaasa 444,348	N5

CITIES and TOWNS

Abo (Turku) 161,398	N6
Alavus 10,701	N5
Äänekoski 11,447	O5
Anjalamkoski 19,703	P6
Borga 19,513	O6
Espoo 156,778	O6
Forssa 20,074	N6
Haapajärvi 8,454	O5
Hämeenlinna 42,382	O6
Hamina 10,313	P6
Hangö 12,071	N7
Hanko (Hangö) 12,071	N7
Harjavalta 8,955	M6
Heinola 16,112	O6
Helsinki (cap.) 485,795	O6
Hyvinkää 38,742	O6
Iisalmi 23,612	P5
Ikaalinen 8,184	N6
Imatra 35,085	Q6
Jakobstad 20,458	N5
Jämsä 12,498	O6
Järvenpää 27,220	O6
Joensuu 46,850	R5
Jyväskylä 65,282	O5
Kajaani 36,020	P4
Kankaanpää 13,652	M6
Karis (Karjaa)	N6
Karkkila 8,355	N6
Kauniainen 7,746	O6
Kemi 26,421	O4
Kemijärvi 12,762	P3
Kerava 26,207	O6
Kokemäki 9,741	N6
Kokkola 34,489	N5
Kotka 58,956	P6
Kouvola 31,829	P6
Kristiinankaupunki (Kristinestad) 9,081	N5
Kristinestad 9,081	N5
Kuopio 78,124	O5
Kurikka 11,512	M5
Kuusankoski 22,089	P6
Lahti 94,447	O6
Lappeenranta 54,102	P6
Lapua 14,644	N5
Lieksa 18,588	R5
Loimaa 7,053	N6
Lovisa 8,697	P6
Maarianhamina (Mariehamn) 9,829	M7
Mänttä 8,092	O6
Mariehamn 9,829	M7
Mikkeli 31,636	P6
Naantali 10,246	M6
Nokia 24,325	N6
Nurmes 11,410	Q5
Nykarleby 7,768	N5
Oulainen 8,225	O4
Oulu 97,297	O4
Outokumpu 9,678	Q5
Parainen 11,618	M6
Parkano 8,692	N6
Pieksämäki 14,372	P5
Pietarsaari (Jakobstad) 20,458	N5
Pori 78,376	M6
Pudasjärvi 11,453	P4
Raahe 18,932	O4
Raisio 19,671	M6
Rauma 30,921	M6
Riihimäki 24,366	O6
Rovaniemi 32,782	O3
Salo 20,495	N6
Savonlinna 28,667	Q6
Seinäjoki 26,257	N5
Suonenjoki 8,981	P5
Tampere 169,026	N6
Toijala 8,046	N6
Tornio 22,328	O4
Turku 161,398	N6
Utsjoki 1,548	P2
Uusikaarlepyy (Nykarleby) 7,768	N5
Uusikaupunki 14,026	M6
Vaasa 54,333	M5
Valkeakoski 22,582	N6
Vammala 16,024	N6
Vantaa 143,844	O6
Varkaus 24,856	Q5
Vasa (Vaasa) 54,333	M5
Virrat 9,391	N5
Ylivieska 12,559	O4

OTHER FEATURES

Åland (isls.)	L6
Baltic (sea)	K9
Bothnia (gulf)	M5
Finland (gulf)	P7
Hailuoto (isl.)	O4
Haltiatunturi (mt.)	M2
Haukivesi (lake)	Q5
Iijoki (riv.)	O4
Inari (lake)	P2
Ivalojoki (riv.)	P2
Kallavesi (lake)	P5
Karlö (Hailuoto) (isl.)	O4
Keitele (lake)	O5
Kemijärvi (lake)	Q3
Kemijoki (riv.)	O3
Lapland (reg.)	O2
Lappajärvi (lake)	O5
Lapuanjoki (riv.)	N5
Lokka (reg.)	Q3
Muojärvi (lake)	R4
Muonio (riv.)	M2
Näsijärvi (lake)	O6
Orihvesi (lake)	Q5
Oulujärvi (lake)	P4
Oulujoki (riv.)	O4
Ounasjoki (riv.)	O3
Päijänne (lake)	O6
Pielinen (lake)	Q5
Porkkala (pen.)	O7
Puruvesi (lake)	Q6
Saimaa (lake)	Q6
Tana (riv.)	P2
Tornionjoki (riv.)	O3
Ylikitka (lake)	Q3

NORWAY

COUNTIES

Akershus 399,797	G6
Aust-Agder 95,475	E7
Buskerud 221,384	F6
Finnmark 74,690	O2
Hedmark 186,305	G6
Hordaland 402,343	E6
Møre og Romsdal 237,489	E5
Nordland 241,048	J3
Nord-Trøndelag 126,648	H4
Oppland 181,620	F6
Oslo (city) 449,220	D3
Østfold 235,813	G7
Rogaland 326,611	D7
Sogn og Fjordane 105,466	E6
Sør-Trøndelag 247,354	G5
Telemark 162,595	F7
Troms 146,595	L2
Vest-Agder 141,284	E7
Vestfold 192,934	G7

CITIES and TOWNS

Ålesund 40,868	D5
Ålgård 2,322	D7
Alta 5,582	N2
Åndalsnes 2,574	F5
Årdalstangen 2,360	F6
Arendal 11,701	F7
Ärnes 2,267	G6
Askim 8,413	E4
Bamble† 7,031	F7
Bergen 213,434	E6
Bodø 31,077	J3
Borge† 3,294	G7
Brate 2,107	G7
Brønnøysund 3,130	G4
Drammen 50,777	C4
Drøbak 4,538	D4
Eidsvoll 2,906	G6
Eigersund 11,379	D7
Elverum 7,391	G6
Farsund 8,908	E7
Flekkefjord 8,750	E7
Flora 8,822	D6
Fredrikstad 29,024	D4
Gjøvik 25,963	G6
Grimstad 13,091	F7
Halden 27,087	G7
Hamar 16,418	G6
Hammerfest 7,610	N1
Harstad 21,125	K2
Hauge 2,079	E7
Haugesund 27,386	D7
Holmestrand 8,246	C4
Honningsvag 3,780	O1
Horten 13,746	D4
Kirkenes 4,466	Q2
Kongsberg 19,854	F7
Kongsvinger 16,146	H6
Kopervik 4,221	D7
Kornsjøt 6,079	G7
Kragerø 5,249	F7
Kristiansand 59,488	F8
Kristiansund 18,847	E5
Kvinnherad† 2,898	E6
Larvik 9,097	C4
Lenvik† 11,098	L2
Levanger 5,066	G5
Lillehammer 21,248	F6
Lillesand 3,028	F7
Lillestrøm† 11,550	E3
Lodingen 1,840	J2
Longyearbyen	D2
Lysaker† 81,612	D3
Mandal 11,579	E7
Meråker† 2,907	G7
Mo 21,033	J3
Molde 20,334	E5
Mosjøen 9,341	H4
Moss 25,786	D4
Mysen 3,760	G7
Namsos 11,452	G4
Narvik 19,582	K2
Nesttun† 11,519	D6
Nittedal† 8,889	D3
Notodden 12,970	F7
Nøtterøy 11,944	D4
Odda 7,401	E6
Oppdal 2,173	F5
Orkanger 3,685	F5
Oslo (cap.) 462,732	D3
Oslo* 645,413	D3
Porsgrunn 31,709	G7
Rakkestad 2,392	G7
Ringerike 30,156	C3
Risør 6,560	F7
Rjukan 5,334	F7
Røros 3,041	G5
Saetermoen 2,114	L2
Sandefjord 33,350	C4
Sandnes 33,934	D7
Sandvika† 34,337	C3
Sarpsborg 12,889	D4
Seljet 3,386	D5
Ski 5,081	D4
Skien 47,105	F7
Skudeneshavn 2,206	D7
Stavanger 86,639	D7
Staven 2,604	D7
Steinkjer 20,553	G4
Stor-Elvdal† 2,993	G6
Sunndalsøra 5,114	F5
Svelvik 2,256	D4
Svolvaer 3,942	J2
Tana 1,893	Q1
Tønsberg 9,964	D4
Tromsø 43,830	L2
Trondheim 134,910	F5
Tvedestrand 1,689	F7
Ullensvang† 2,326	E6
Vadsø 6,019	Q1
Vanylven 1,966	E5
Vardø 3,875	R1
Vik 1,019	E6
Volda 3,511	E5
Voss 5,944	E6

OTHER FEATURES

Andøya (isl.)	J2
Barentsøya (isl.)	D2
Bjørnøya (isl.)	D3
Boknafjord (fjord)	D7
Dovrefjell (hills)	F5
Edgeøya (isl.)	E2
Femundsjø (lake)	G5
Folda (fjord)	G4
Folda (fjord)	J3
Frohavet (bay)	F5
Frøya (isl.)	F5
Glittertinden (mt.)	F6
Greenland (sea)	C3
Hadselfjorden (fjord)	J2
Haltiatunturi (mt.)	M2
Hardangerfjord (fjord)	D7
Hardangervidda (plat.)	E6
Hinlopenstreten (strait)	C1
Hinnøya (isl.)	K2
Hitra (isl.)	F5
Hortensfjord (fjord)	G4
Istjorden (fjord)	C2
Kjølen (mts.)	K3
Kvaenangen (fjord)	N2
Kvaløy (isl.)	K2
Kvaløya (isl.)	O1
Laksefjorden (fjord)	P1
Langøya (isl.)	J2
Lapland (reg.)	K2
Lindesnes (cape)	E8
Lofoten (isls.)	H2
Lopphavet (bay)	M1
Magerøya (isl.)	P1
Moskenesøya (isl.)	H3
Namsen (riv.)	H4
Nordaustlandet (isl.)	U1
Nordfjord (fjord)	E6
Nordkapp (pt.)	C1
North Cape (Nordkapp) (cape)	P1
Norwegian (sea)	F3
Ofotfjorden (fjord)	K2
Oslofjord (fjord)	D4
Otra (riv.)	E7
Pasvikelv (riv.)	Q2
Porsanger (fjord)	O1
Prins Karls Forland (isl.)	B2
Rana (fjord)	H3
Rauma (riv.)	F5
Ringvassøy (isl.)	L2
Romsdalsfjorden (fjord)	E5
Saltfjorden (fjord)	J3
Seiland (isl.)	N1
Senja (isl.)	K2
Skagerrak (strait)	F8
Sognafjorden (fjord)	D6
Sørkapp (pt.)	C2
Sorøya (isl.)	N1
Spitsbergen (isl.)	C2
Steinneset (cape)	E2
Storfjorden (fjord)	D2
Sulitjelma (mt.)	J3
Svalbard (isls.)	C3
Tana (riv.)	P1
Tanafjord (fjord)	Q1
Trondheimsfjorden (fjord)	G5
Tyrifjord (lake)	C3
Vannøy (isl.)	L1
Varangerfjord (fjord)	Q2
Varangerhalvøya (pen.)	Q1
Vegafjorden (fjord)	G4
Vesterålen (isls.)	J2
Vestfjord (fjord)	H3
Vestvågøya (isl.)	H3
Vikna (isls.)	G4

(continued on following page)

Topography

Iceland — Reykjavík, Faxaflói, VATNA-JÖKULL, Hvannadalshnúkur 6,946 ft. (2117 m.), Horn, Fontur

Nordkapp (North Cape), Varangerfjord, VESTER-ÅLEN, LOFOTEN, Haltiatunturi 4,343 ft. (1324 m.), Inari

Nordfjord, Sognafjorden, Bergen, Hardanger fjord, Glittertinden 8,110 ft. (2,472 m.), Oslo, Mjøsa, GULF OF BOTHNIA, Oulujärvi, Helsinki, Ståckholm, Vänern, Göteborg, Vättern, Gøta Canal, Gotland, ÅLAND IS., Skagerrak, Lindesnes, Kattegat, Öland, Copenhagen, Bornholm, Lolland, Ydinge Skovhoj 568 ft. 173 m.

Below Sea Level	100 m. 328 ft.	200 m. 656 ft.	500 m. 1,640 ft.	1,000 m. 3,281 ft.	2,000 m. 6,562 ft.	5,000 m. 16,404 ft.

Scale: 0 — 100 — 200 MI. / 0 — 100 — 200 KM.

Agriculture, Industry and Resources

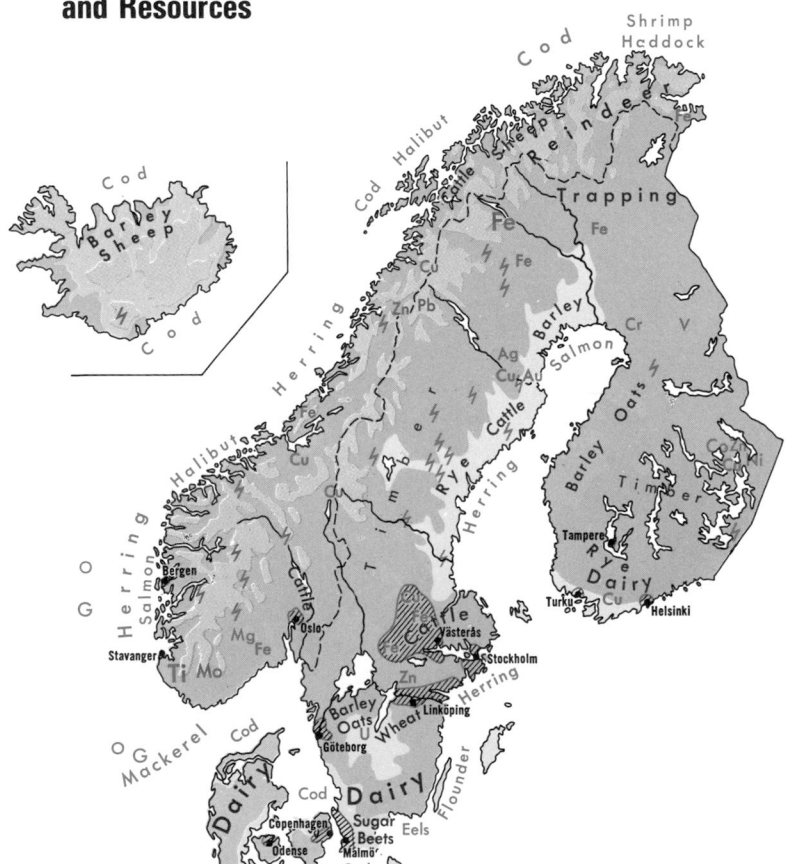

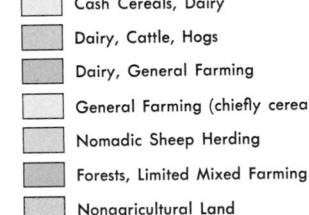

DOMINANT LAND USE

- Cash Cereals, Dairy
- Dairy, Cattle, Hogs
- Dairy, General Farming
- General Farming (chiefly cereals)
- Nomadic Sheep Herding
- Forests, Limited Mixed Farming
- Nonagricultural Land

MAJOR MINERAL OCCURRENCES

Ag	Silver	Ni	Nickel
Au	Gold	O	Petroleum
Co	Cobalt	Pb	Lead
Cr	Chromium	Ti	Titanium
Cu	Copper	U	Uranium
Fe	Iron Ore	V	Vanadium
Mg	Magnesium	Zn	Zinc
Mo	Molybdenum		

⚡ Water Power

▨ Major Industrial Areas

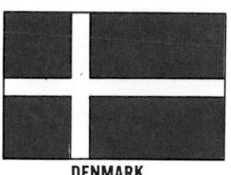

DENMARK

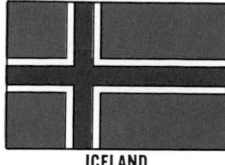

ICELAND

DENMARK

AREA 16,629 sq. mi. (43,069 sq. km.)
POPULATION 5,135,000
CAPITAL Copenhagen
LARGEST CITY Copenhagen
HIGHEST POINT Yding Skovhøj
 568 ft. (173 m.)
MONETARY UNIT krone
MAJOR LANGUAGE Danish
MAJOR RELIGION Protestantism

ICELAND

AREA 39,768 sq. mi. (103,000 sq. km.)
POPULATION 250,000
CAPITAL Reykjavík
LARGEST CITY Reykjavík
HIGHEST POINT Hvannadalshnúkur
 6,952 ft. (2,119 m.)
MONETARY UNIT króna
MAJOR LANGUAGE Icelandic
MAJOR RELIGION Protestantism

Ringe 4,440	D7
Ringkøbing 7,907	A5
Ringsted 16,564	E7
Rødby 2,572	E8
Rødding 2,291	B7
Rødekro 4,195	C7
Rønde 1,745	D5
Ronne 14,143	F9
Roskilde 39,659	E6
Rudkøbing 4,667	D8
Ry 3,648	C5
Ryomgård 1,578	D5
Saeby 7,464	D3
Sakskøbing 7,518	E8
Silkeborg 33,304	C5
Sindal 2,665	C3
Skaelskør 5,574	E7
Skaerbaek 2,946	B7
Skagen 11,743	D2
Skals 1,410	C4
Skanderborg 11,094	D5
Skibby 2,259	C7
Skive 19,034	B4
Skjern 6,351	B5
Skørping 2,016	C4
Slagelse 28,539	E7
Slangerup 5,218	E6
Søllested 1,431	E8
Sønderborg 25,885	C8
Sønder Omne 1,751	B5
Sondersø 2,667	D7
Sora 6,067	E7
Stege 3,906	F8
Stenlille 1,370	E7
Stenstrup 1,501	D7
Stoholm 1,830	C5
Store Heddinge 2,881	F7
Støvring 4,615	C4
Strandby 2,264	D3
Struer 10,973	B4
Stubbekøbing 2,255	F8
Svendborg 23,847	D7
Svinninge 2,281	E6
Tarm 4,008	B6
Tårnby 41,517	F6
Them 1,382	C5
Thisted 12,469	B4
Thyborøn 2,766	A4
Tinglev 2,508	C8
Toftlund 3,388	B7
Tølløse 2,703	E6
Tommerup 1,890	D7
Tønder 7,914	B8
Tørring 1,922	C6
Ulfborg 1,781	B5
Vamdrup 3,960	C7
Varde 10,888	B6
Vejen 7,412	C7
Vejle 43,300	C6
Vemb 1,261	B5
Viborg 28,659	C5
Viby 2,942	F6
Videbaek 3,440	B5
Vildbjerg 2,703	B5
Vinderup 2,865	B5
Vojens 6,792	C7
Vordingborg 8,706	E7
Vrå 2,312	C3

OTHER FEATURES

AEro (isl.)	D8
Alborg (bay)	D4
Als (isl.)	C8
Amager (isl.)	F6
Anholt (isl.)	E4
Baltic (sea)	E9
Blavands Huk (pt.)	A6
Bornholm (isl.)	F9
Dovns Klint (cliff)	D8
Endelave (isl.)	D6
Fakse (bay)	F7
Falster (isl.)	F8
Fanø (isl.)	B7
Fejø (isl.)	E8
Femø (isl.)	E8
Fehmarn (strait)	D8
Frisian, North (isls.)	B7
Fyn (isl.)	D7
Fyns Hoved (pt.)	D6
Gedser Odde (pt.)	E8
Gelså (riv.)	C7
Gudenå (riv.)	C5
Isefjord (fjord)	E6
Jammerbugt (bay)	C3
Jutland (pen.)	C5
Jylland (Jutland) (pen.)	C5
Kattegat (strait)	E4
Knosen (mt.)	D3
Koge (bay)	F7

Laesä (isl.)	D3
Langeland (isl.)	D8
Langelands Baelt (chan.)	D8
Lille Baelt (chan.)	C7
Lillea (riv.)	B5
Limfjorden (fjord)	A4
Limfjorden (fjord)	D4
Lolland (isl.)	E8
Løgstør Bredning (fjord)	C4
Mariager (fjord)	D4
Møn (isl.)	F8
Mons Klint (cliff)	F8
Mors (isl.)	B4
Nissum (fjord)	A5
North (sea)	B9
North Frisian (isls.)	B7
Omme (riv.)	B6
Omø (isl.)	E7
Oresund (sound)	F6
Ringkobing (fjord)	B6
Rømø (isl.)	B7
Rosnaes (pen.)	D6
Sams Baolt (chan.)	D6
Samsø (isl.)	D6
Sejerø (isl.)	E6
Sjaelland (isl.)	E6
Sjaellands Odde (pen.)	E5
Skagens Odde (cape)	D2
Skagerrak (strait)	C2
Skaw, The (Skagens Odde) (cape)	D2
Skive (riv.)	C5
Stevns Klint (cliff)	F7
Storå (riv.)	B5
Store Baelt (chan.)	D6
The Skaw (Skagens Odde) (cape)	D2
Varde (riv.)	B6
Vejle (fjord)	C6
Vorgod (riv.)	B6
Yding Skovhøj (mt.)	C6

FAROE ISLANDS

CITIES and TOWNS

Klaksvík 4,536	B2
Tórshavn (cap.)	
Faroe Is. 11,618	A3

OTHER FEATURES

Faroe (isls.)	B2
Sandoy (isl.)	B3
Streymoy (isl.)	B3
Sudhuroy (isl.)	B3

ICELAND

CITIES and TOWNS

Akranes 5,404	B1
Akureyri 13,972	C1
Hafnarfjórdhur 14,199	B2
Húsavík 2,499	C1
Ísafjördhur 3,458	B1
Keflavík 7,305	B1
Kópavogur 15,551	B1
Ólafsfjórdhur 1,179	C1
Reykjavík (cap.) 95,811	B1
Saudhárkrokur 2,478	B1
Vestmannaeyjar 4,743	B2

OTHER FEATURES

Bjargtangar (pt.)	A1
Breidhafjördhur (fjord)	B1
Faxaflói (bay)	B1
Fontur (pt.)	D1
Gerpir (cape)	D1
Grímsey (isl.)	C1
Hekla (vol.)	C1
Hofsjökull (glacier)	C1
Horn (cape)	B1
Húnaflói (bay)	B1
Hvannadalshnúkur (mt.)	C1
Jökulsá (riv.)	C1
Lagarfljót (stream)	D1
Langjökull (glacier)	B1
North (Horn) (cape)	B1
Reykjanesta (cape)	A2
Rifstangi (cape)	C1
Skagata (cape)	C1
Skjálfandafljót (stream)	C1
Surtsey (isl.)	B2
Thjórsá (riv.)	C1
Vatnajökull (glacier)	C1
Vopnafjördhur (fjord)	D1

Denmark and Iceland

CONIC PROJECTION

SCALE OF MILES
0 10 20 30 40 50

SCALE OF KILOMETERS
0 10 20 30 40 50

Capitals of Countries ......☆
Capitals of Counties (amter) ......△
International Boundaries ------
Internal Boundaries --- ---

Denmark is divided into fourteen Counties plus
Copenhagen and Frederiksberg communes.

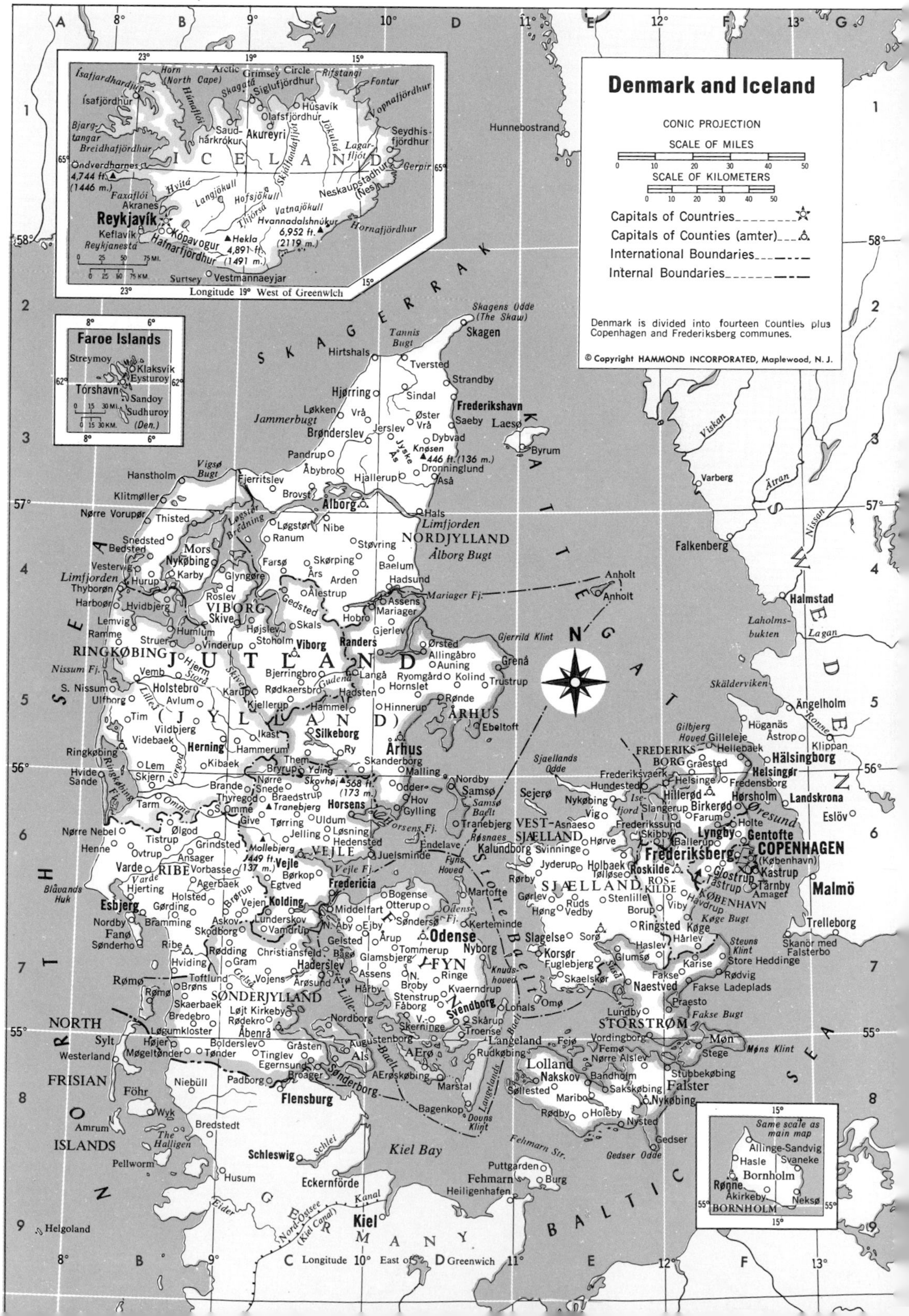

Germany

CONIC PROJECTION
SCALE OF MILES

SCALE OF KILOMETERS

Capitals of Countries .... ☆
State Capitals .... ◉
International Boundaries ....
State Boundaries ....
Canals ....

Scale 1:3,040,000

Berlin

© Copyright HAMMOND INCORPORATED, Maplewood, N.J.

AREA 137,753 sq. mi. (356,780 sq. km.)
POPULATION 78,890,000
CAPITAL Berlin
LARGEST CITY Berlin
HIGHEST POINT Zugspitze 9,718 ft. (2,962 m.)
MONETARY UNIT Deutsche mark
MAJOR LANGUAGE German
MAJOR RELIGIONS Protestantism, Roman
    Catholicism

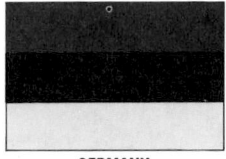

GERMANY

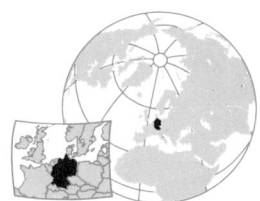

Topography

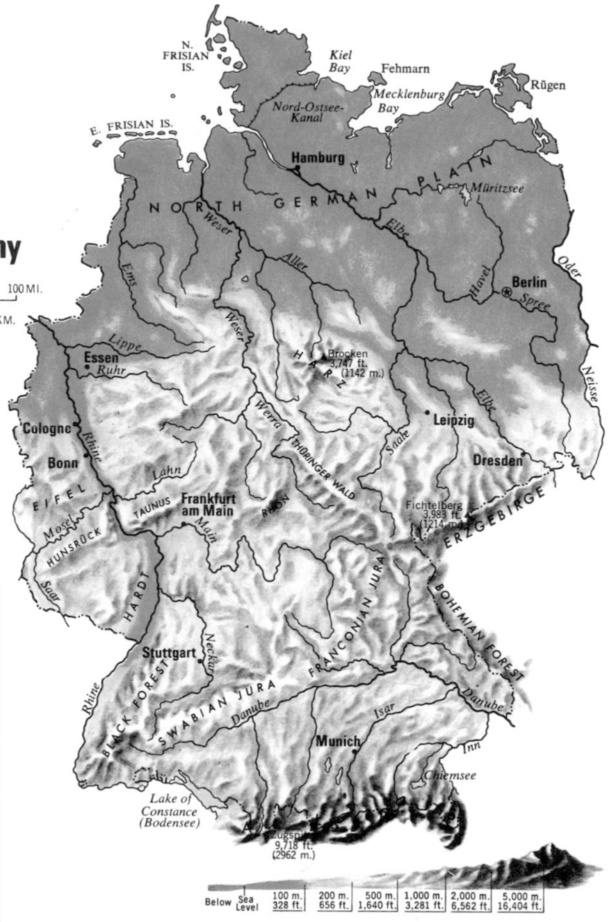

0   50   100 MI.

0   50   100 KM.

| Below Sea Level | 100 m. 328 ft. | 200 m. 656 ft. | 500 m. 1,640 ft. | 1,000 m. 3,281 ft. | 2,000 m. 6,562 ft. | 5,000 m. 16,404 ft. |

Zugspitze 9,718 ft. (2962 m.)

GERMANY

STATES

Baden-Württemberg
    9,432,709 ....C4
Bavaria 11,049,263.......D4
Berlin 3,304,561 ....E4
Brandenberg* E2
Bremen 661,992 ....C2
Hamburg 1,603,070 ......D2
Hesse 5,568,892 ....C3
Lower Saxony 7,184,943 ...C2
Mecklenburg-Western
    Pomerania* E2
North Rhine-Westphalia
    16,874,059 ....B3
Rhineland-Palatinate
    3,653,155 ....B4
Saarland 1,054,142 ......B4
Saxony* E3
Saxony-Anhalt* D3
Schleswig-Holstein
    2,564,565 ....C1
Thuringia* D3

*East German States
    15,611,488 ....D-E 2-3

CITIES and TOWNS

Aachen 233,255 ....B3
Aalen 62,812 ....D4
Ahaus 30,180 ....B2
Ahlen 52,836 ....B3
Ahrensburg 27,174 ....D2
Alfeld 21,986 ....C2
Alsdorf 46,328 ....B3
Alsfeld 16,686 ....C3
Altena 23,301 ....B3
Altenburg 53,602 ....E3
Amberg 42,246 ....D4
Andernach 27,171 ....B3
Anklam 19,946 ....E2
Annaberg-Buchholz 26,002 ...E3
Ansbach 36,912 ....D4
Apolda 28,230 ....D3
Arnsberg 73,912 ....C3
Arnstadt 30,207 ....D3
Aschaffenburg 62,048 ....C4
Aschersleben 34,166 .....D3
Aue 27,935 ....E3
Auerbach 22,324 ....E3
Augsburg 247,731 ....D4
Aurich 36,063 ....B2
Backnang 30,583 ....C4
Bad Berleburg 20,080 ....C3
Bad Driburg 16,698 ......C3
Bad Dürkheim 16,670 .....C4
Baden-Baden 50,761 ......C4
Bad Harzburg 23,079 .....D3
Bad Hersfeld 28,214 .....C3
Bad Homburg vor der Höhe
    51,035 ....C3
Bad Honnef 21,812 ....B3
Bad Kissingen 20,237 ....D3
Bad Kreuznach 39,400 ....B4
Bad Langensalza 17,027 ..D3
Bad Mergentheim 19,801 ..C4
Bad Münstereifel 15,232 ..B3
Bad Nauheim 27,561 ......C3
Bad Neuenahr-Ahrweiler
    24,610 ....B3
Bad Oldesloe 20,473 .....D2
Bad Pyrmont 20,437 ......C3
Bad Reichenhall 16,365 ..E5
Bad Salzuflen 50,875 ....C2
Bad Salzungen 21,387 ....C3
Bad Schwartau 19,960 ....D2
Bad Vilbel 24,567 ....C4
Bad Zwischenahn 23,348 ..B2
Balingen 30,615 ....C4
Bamberg 69,809 ....D4
Barsinghausen 37,792 ....C2
Bautzen 52,354 ....F3
Bayreuth 70,933 ....D4
Bensheim 34,241 ....C4
Berchtesgaden 7,644 .....E5
Bergen 16,713 ....E1
Bergisch Gladbach 101,983 ...B3
Berleburg
    (Bad Berleburg) 20,080 ...C3

Berlin (cap.) 3,304,561 ....E4
Bernau bei Berlin 19,919 ...E2
Bernburg 40,834 ....D3
Biberach an der Riss 28,319 ...C4
Bielefeld 311,946 ....C2
Bietigheim-Bissingen 37,573 ...C4
Bingen 23,141 ....B4
Bitburg 10,758 ....B4
Bitterfeld 20,869 ....D3
Blankenburg am Harz 19,279 ..D3
Böblingen 43,400 ....C4
Bocholt 67,565 ....B3
Bochum 389,087 ....B3
Bonn 282,190 ....B3
Borghorst 17,238 ....B2
Borken 34,710 ....B3
Borna 24,397 ....E3
Bornheim 34,536 ....B3
Bottrop 116,363 ....B3
Brake 16,069 ....C2
Bramsche 28,653 ....B2
Brandenburg 94,755 .....D2
Braunschweig 253,794 ....D2
Bremen 535,058 ....C2
Bremerhaven 126,934 ....C2
Bremervörde 17,629 .....C2
Bretten 23,894 ....C4
Brilon 24,341 ....C3
Bruchsal 36,831 ....C4
Brühl 40,710 ....B3
Buchholz in der Nordheide
    30,523 ....C2
Bückeburg 19,758 ....C2
Büdingen 17,013 ....C3
Bühl 23,470 ....C4
Bünde 39,103 ....C2
Burg bei Magdeburg 28,359 ..D2
Burghausen 16,761 ......E4
Burgsteinfurt 31,367 ....B2
Butzbach 21,095 ....C3
Buxtehude 31,132 ....C2
Castrop-Rauxel 77,660 ...B3
Celle 71,050 ....D2
Cham 16,641 ....E4
Chemnitz 313,799 ....E3
Clausthal-Zellerfeld 16,069 ...D3
Cloppenburg 22,536 .....C2
Coburg 43,233 ....D3
Coesfeld 31,979 ....B3
Cologne 937,482 ....B3
Coswig 27,590 ....E3
Cottbus 123,894 ....F3
Crailsheim 26,678 ......C4
Crimmitschau 24,440 ....E3
Cuxhaven 55,249 ....C2
Dachau 34,353 ....D4
Darmstadt 136,067 ......C4
Deggendorf 28,680 ......E4
Delitzsch 27,636 ....D3
Delmenhorst 72,901 .....C2
Demmin 16,992 ....E2
Dessau 103,538 ....E3
Detmold 66,809 ....C3
Dillenburg 23,672 ......C3
Dillingen 21,358 ....D4
Döbeln 27,706 ....E3
Donaueschingen 18,296 ..C5
Donauwörth 17,420 ......D4
Dorsten 75,518 ....B3
Dortmund 587,328 ....B3
Dresden 519,810 ....E3
Duderstadt 22,265 ......D3
Duisburg 527,447 ....B3
Dülmen 39,344 ....B3
Düren 83,120 ....B3
Düsseldorf 569,641 .....B3
Eberswalde-Finow 54,566 ..E2
Eckernförde 22,197 .....C1
Ehingen 22,580 ....C4
Eilenburg 21,931 ....E3
Einbeck 25,813 ....C3
Eisenach 49,534 ....D3
Eisenhüttenstadt 51,729 ..F2
Eisleben 26,484 ....D3
Ellwangen 21,857 ....D4
Elmshorn 42,784 ....C2
Emden 49,803 ....B2
Emmendingen 22,959 .....B4
Emmerich 27,906 ....B3
Emsdetten 31,063 ....B2
Erfurt 217,134 ....D3

Erkelenz 36,525 ....B3
Erlangen 100,583 ....D4
Eschwege 21,527 ....C3
Eschweiler 53,516 ......B3
Espelkamp 23,868 ....C2
Essen 620,594 ....B3
Esslingen am Neckar 90,537 ..C4
Ettlingen 37,269 ....C4
Euskirchen 47,756 ......B3
Eutin 16,567 ....D1
Falkensee 23,024 ....E3
Fellbach 39,612 ....C4
Finsterwalde 23,857 ....E3
Flensburg 85,830 ....C1
Forchheim 28,784 ....D4
Forst 26,501 ....F3
Frankenberg-Eder 16,283 ..C3
Frankenthal 45,408 .....C4
Frankfurt am Main 625,258 ..C3
Frankfurt an der Oder 86,441 ..F2
Frechen 42,516 ....B3
Freiberg 50,415 ....E3
Freiburg im Breisgau
    183,979 ....B5
Freising 35,201 ....D4
Freital 43,092 ....E3
Freudenstadt 21,355 ....C4
Friedberg 24,279 ....C3
Friedrichshafen 52,295 ..C5
Fulda 54,320 ....C3
Fürstenfeldbruck 30,313 ..D4
Fürstenwalde 35,282 ....F2
Fürth 98,832 ....D4
Füssen 13,173 ....D5
Gaggenau 28,182 ....C4
Garbsen 59,225 ....C2
Garmisch-Partenkirchen
    25,908 ....D5
Geesthacht 25,054 ......D2
Geislingen an der Steige
    26,176 ....C4
Geldern 28,465 ....B3
Gelnhausen 18,866 ......C3
Gelsenkirchen 287,255 ..B3
Genthin 17,347 ....D2
Georgsmarienhütte 30,880 ..B2
Gera 123,319 ....E3
Geretsried 21,081 ......D5
Gifhorn 35,697 ....D2
Glauchau 28,309 ....E3
Goch 29,592 ....B3
Göppingen 52,873 ....C4
Görlitz 78,856 ....F3
Goslar 45,614 ....D3
Gotha 57,423 ....D3
Göttingen 118,073 ......D3
Greifswald 67,298 ......E1
Greiz 34,858 ....E3
Greven 29,671 ....B2
Grevenbroich 59,204 ....B3
Griesheim 20,531 ....C4
Grimma 17,812 ....E3
Gronau 39,397 ....B2
Guben 34,665 ....F3
Gummersbach 49,017 .....B3
Günzburg 18,303 ....D4
Güstrow 38,971 ....E2
Gütersloh 83,407 ....C3
Haar 16,553 ....D4
Hagen 210,640 ....B3
Halberstadt 47,017 .....D3
Haldensleben 20,369 ....D2
Halle 236,148 ....D3
Halle-Neustadt 93,477 ..D3
Haltern 33,093 ....B3
Hamburg 1,603,070 ......D2
Hameln 57,642 ....C2
Hamm 173,611 ....B3
Hanau 84,300 ....C3
Hannover 498,495 ....C2
Hasslach 18,646 ....C4
Heide 20,640 ....C1
Heidelberg 131,429 .....C4
Heidenau 19,133 ....E3
Heidenheim an der Brenz
    48,497 ....D4
Heilbronn 112,279 ......C4
Helmstedt 26,554 ....D2
Hennef 30,516 ....B3
Hennigsdorf bei Berlin
    26,574 ....E3
Herborn 20,409 ....C3

Herford 61,700 ....C2
Herne 174,664 ....B3
Hettstedt 21,861 ....D3
Hildesheim 103,512 .....D2
Hof 50,938 ....D3
Holzminden 20,877 ......C3
Homburg 41,888 ....B4
Höxter 31,925 ....C3
Hoyerswerda 69,113 .....F3
Hückelhoven 33,841 .....B3
Hürth 49,094 ....B3
Husum 20,649 ....C1
Ibbenbüren 43,424 ......B2
Idar-Oberstein 33,227 ..B4
Ilmenau 29,338 ....D3
Ingolstadt 97,702 ......D4
Iserlohn 93,337 ....B3
Itzehoe 32,342 ....C2
Jena 107,610 ....D3
Jülich 30,496 ....B3
Kaiserslautern 96,990 ..B4
Kamenz 18,323 ....F3
Karlsruhe 265,100 ......C4
Kassel 189,156 ....C3
Kaufbeuren 39,192 ......D5
Kehl 28,902 ....B4
Kempten 60,052 ....D5
Kevelaer 22,633 ....B3
Kiel 240,675 ....D1
Kirchheim unter Teck 34,534 ..C4
Kitzingen 19,085 ....C4
Koblenz 107,286 ....B3
Königs Wusterhausen 19,085 ..E2
Königswinter 34,136 ....B3
Konstanz 72,862 ....C5
Köpenick 118,059 ....F2
Korbach 21,406 ....C3
Kornwestheim 28,519 ....C4
Köthen 34,617 ....E3
Krefeld 235,423 ....B3
Kreuztal 29,716 ....C3
Kronach 18,246 ....D3
Kulmbach 27,116 ....D3
Lage 32,612 ....C3
Lahnstein 17,972 ....B3
Lahr 33,369 ....B4
Lampertheim 30,263 .....C4
Landau in der Pfalz 36,297 ..C4
Landsberg am Lech 19,808 ..D4
Landshut 57,194 ....D4
Langen 31,206 ....C4
Langenhagen 46,298 .....C2
Lauchhammer 24,391 .....E3
Lauenburg an der Elbe
    10,786 ....D2
Lauf an der Pegnitz
    22,593 ....D4
Leer 31,292 ....B2
Lehrte 39,600 ....D2
Leipzig 550,641 ....E3
Lemgo 38,351 ....C2
Lengerich 20,235 ....B2
Leverkusen 157,358 .....B3
Lichtenberg 95,426 .....F2
Lichtenfels 20,252 .....D3
Limbach-Oberfrohna 22,059 ..E3

Lindau 23,699 ....C5
Lingen 47,837 ....B2
Lippstadt 60,396 ....C3
Löhne 36,882 ....C2
Lörrach 41,087 ....B5
Lübbenau 20,815 ....F3
Lübeck 210,681 ....D2
Luckenwalde 26,761 .....F2
Lüdenscheid 76,118 .....B3
Ludwigsburg 79,342 .....C4
Ludwigshafen am Rhein
    158,478 ....C4
Lüneburg 60,053 ....D2
Lünen 85,584 ....B3
Magdeburg 288,975 .....D2
Mainz 174,828 ....C4
Mannheim 300,468 ......C4
Marburg 70,905 ....C3
Markkleeberg 19,240 ....E3
Marktredwitz 18,605 ....E4
Marl 89,601 ....B3
Mayen 18,427 ....B3
Mechernich 21,986 ......B3
Meerane 21,879 ....E3
Meiningen 25,352 ....D3
Meissen 37,757 ....E3
Melle 40,490 ....C2
Memmingen 37,942 ....D5
Meppen 29,900 ....B2
Merseburg 46,188 ....D3
Merzig 29,237 ....B4
Meschede 30,853 ....C3
Metzingen 19,875 ....C4
Minden 75,169 ....C2
Mittenwald 7,998 ....D5
Mittweida 18,469 ....E3
Mönchengladbach 252,910 ..B3
Mosbach 23,897 ....C4
Mülhausen 43,046 ....D3

Mülheim an der Ruhr
    175,454 ....B3
München (Munich)
    1,211,617 ....D4
Munich 1,211,617 ....D4
Münden 24,794 ....C3
Münster 248,919 ....B3
Nagold 20,405 ....C4
Naumburg 32,100 ....D3
Neckarsulm 21,785 ......C4
Neubrandenburg 87,235 ..E2
Neuburg an der Donau
    24,502 ....D4
Neu-Isenburg 34,896 ....C3
Neumarkt in der Oberpfalz
    33,603 ....D4
Neumünster 79,574 ......C1
Neunkirchen 50,784 .....B4
Neuruppin 26,934 ....E2
Neuss 143,976 ....B3
Neustadt an der Weinstrasse
    50,453 ....C4
Neustadt bei Coburg 16,211 ..D3
Neustrelitz 27,300 .....E2
Neu-Ulm 45,116 ....D4
Neuwied 60,665 ....B3
Nienburg 29,545 ....C2
Norden 23,655 ....B2
Nordenham 28,393 ....C2
Norderstedt 66,747 .....D2
Nordhausen 47,681 ......D3
Nordhorn 48,556 ....B2
Nördlingen 18,278 ......D4
Northeim 30,349 ....C3
Nuremberg 480,078 .....D4
Nürnberg (Nuremberg)
    480,078 ....D4
Nürtingen 36,807 ....C4
Oberammergau 4,980 .....D5
Oberhausen 221,017 .....B3

Oberursel 39,105 ....C3
Offenbach am Main 112,450 ..C3
Offenburg 51,730 ....B4
Oldenburg 140,785 ......C2
Oranienburg 28,667 .....E2
Oschatz 19,100 ....E3
Oschersleben 16,976 ....D2
Osnabrück 154,594 ......C2
Osterholz-Scharmbeck
    24,205 ....C2
Osterode am Harz 26,631 ..D3
Paderborn 114,148 ......C3
Pankow 62,847 ....F3
Papenburg 29,237 ....B2
Parchim 23,454 ....D2
Passau 49,137 ....E4
Peenemünde E1
Peine 45,522 ....D2
Pfaffenhofen an der Ilm
    18,335 ....D4
Pforzheim 108,887 ......C4
Pinneberg 36,583 ....C2
Pirmasens 47,102 ....B4
Pirna 46,991 ....E3
Plauen 77,514 ....E3
Plettenberg 28,113 .....C3
Pössneck 17,895 ....D3
Potsdam 141,231 ....E2
Prenzlau 23,642 ....E2
Quedlinburg 29,166 .....D3
Radeberg 15,702 ....E3
Radebeul 33,757 ....E3
Radolfzell 25,712 ......C5
Rastatt 40,909 ....C4
Rastede 18,191 ....C2
Rathenow 31,302 ....E2
Ratingen 89,880 ....B3
Ravensburg 44,146 ......C5
Recklinghausen 121,666 ..B3
Regensburg 119,078 .....E4

(continued on following page)

Germany Before World War I 1871-1914

Germany Between Wars 1919-1937

Occupied Germany 1945-1949

Reichenbach 24,749 ....E3
Remagen 14,375 ....B3
Remscheid 120,979 ....B3
Rendsburg 30,752 ....C1
Reutlingen 100,400 ....C4
Rheda-Wiedenbrück 30,990 ....C3
Rheine 69,324 ....B2
Rheinfelden 27,711 ....B5
Ribnitz-Damgarten 17,512 .....E1
Riesa 49,108 ....E3
Rietberg 23,058 ....C3
Rinteln 26,120 ....C2
Rosenheim 54,304 ....D5
Rostock 249,349 ....E1
Rotenburg 18,392 ....C2
Roth bei Nürnberg 20,288 .....D4
Rothenburg ob der Tauber
  11,071 ....D4
Rottenburg am Neckar
  33,907 ....C4
Rottweil 23,080 ....C4
Rudolstadt 32,264 ....D3
Rüsselsheim 58,426 ....C4
Saalfeld 33,453 ....D3
Saarbrücken 188,467 ....B4
Saarlouis 37,662 ....B4
Salzgitter 111,674 ....C2
Salzwedel 23,163 ....D2
Sangerhausen 33,604 ....D2
Sankt Ingbert 40,527 ....B4
Sankt Wendel 26,649 ....B4
Saulgau 14,864 ....C5
Schleswig 26,648 ....C1
Schmalkalden 17,409 ....D3
Schneeberg 22,105 ....E3
Schönebeck 45,155 ....D2
Schramberg 18,208 ....C4
Schwabach 34,217 ....D4
Schwäbisch Gmünd 57,861 ....C4
Schwäbisch Hall 31,375 ....C4

Schwalmstadt 17,371 ....C3
Schwandorf im Bayern
  25,874 ....E4
Schwedt 51,753 ....F2
Schweinfurt 52,818 ....D3
Schwelm 29,564 ....B3
Schwerin 128,328 ....D2
Schwetzingen 18,029 ....C4
Seesen 21,604 ....C3
Selb 19,275 ....E3
Senftenberg 32,428 ....F3
Siegburg 34,402 ....B3
Siegen 106,160 ....C3
Sigmaringen 15,270 ....C4
Sindelfingen 57,524 ....C4
Singen 42,605 ....C5
Soest 40,775 ....C3
Solingen 160,824 ....B3
Soltau 19,115 ....C2
Sömmerda 23,398 ....D3
Sondershausen 24,178 ....D3
Sonneberg 28,512 ....D3
Sonthofen 20,037 ....C5
Spandau E3
Speyer 45,089 ....C4
Spremberg 24,815 ....F3
Springe 29,209 ....C2
Stade 41,223 ....C2
Stadthagen 22,218 ....C2
Starnberg 19,845 ....D4
Stassfurt 27,372 ....D3
Stendal 47,880 ....D2
Stolberg 56,182 ....B3
Stralsund 75,857 ....E1
Straubing 40,612 ....E4
Strausberg 27,527 ....F2
Stuttgart 562,658 ....C4
Suhl 55,295 ....D3
Sulzbach 19,753 ....B4
Sulzbach-Rosenberg 18,134 ..D4

Telgte 16,834 ....B3
Tempelhof F4
Thale 16,605 ....D3
Torgau 22,749 ....E3
Traunstein 17,145 ....E5
Treptow 58,938 ....F4
Treuchtlingen 12,314 ....D4
Triberg im Schwarzwald
  5,697 ....C4
Trier 95,692 ....B4
Troisdorf 62,011 ....B3
Tübingen 76,046 ....C4
Tuttlingen 31,752 ....C5
Übach-Palenberg 23,005 ......B3
Überlingen 18,043 ....C5
Ueckermünde 12,304 ....F2
Uelzen 34,891 ....D2
Uetersen 17,218 ....C2
Ulm 106,508 ....C4
Varel 23,718 ....C2
Vechta 22,759 ....C2
Verden 26,211 ....C2
Viersen 76,163 ....B3
Villingen-Schwenningen
  76,258 ....C4
Völklingen 42,916 ....B4
Waldheim 10,316 ....E3
Waldkirch 18,893 ....B4
Waldkraiburg 23,177 ....E4
Waldshut-Tiengen 21,372 .....C5
Walsrode 22,232 ....C2
Waltershausen 14,127 ....D3
Wangen im Allgäu 23,822 .....C5
Warburg 21,802 ....C3
Waren 24,318 ....E2
Warendorf 33,891 ....B3
Wedel 30,158 ....C2
Weida 10,602 ....D3
Weiden in der Oberpfalz
  41,539 ....D4

Weilheim im Oberbayern
  17,602 ....D5
Weimar 63,910 ....D3
Weingarten 21,522 ....C5
Weinheim 41,876 ....C4
Weissenburg im Bayern
  17,318 ....D4
Weissenfels 38,763 ....D3
Weissensee 31,858 ....F3
Weisswasser 36,472 ....F3
Werdau 19,451 ....D3
Wernigerode 36,499 ....D3
Wertheim 20,457 ....C4
Wesel 57,986 ....B3
Westerstede 18,184 ....C2
Wiehl 21,897 ....B3
Wiesbaden 254,209 ....B4
Wiesmoor 10,827 ....B2
Wilhelmshaven 89,892 ....B2
Winsen 26,139 ....D2
Wismar 58,066 ....D2
Witten 103,637 ....B3
Wittenberg 53,670 ....D3
Wittenberge 30,389 ....D2
Wolfen 43,606 ....D3
Wolfenbüttel 50,960 ....D2
Wolfsburg 125,831 ....D2
Worms 74,809 ....C4
Wunstorf 37,115 ....C2
Wuppertal 371,283 ....B3
Würzburg 125,589 ....C4
Wurzen 19,330 ....E3
Xanten 16,097 ....B3
Zeitz 42,985 ....E3
Zerbst 18,717 ....D3
Zeulenroda 14,409 ....D3
Zirndorf 21,608 ....D4
Zittau 39,305 ....F3
Zweibrücken 33,377 ....B4
Zwickau 120,923 ....E3

OTHER FEATURES

Aller (riv.) C2
Allgäu (reg.) D5
Altmark (reg.) D2
Ammersee (lake) D4
Amrum (isl.) C1
Arkona (cape) E1
Baltic (sea) E1
Bavarian (forest) E4
Bavarian Alps (range) D5
Bayerischer Wald Nat'l Park ..E4
Black (forest) C4
Black Elster (riv.) E3
Bodensee (Constance) (lake) .C5
Bohemian (forest) E4
Borkum (isl.) B2
Breisgau (reg.) B5
Brocken (mt.) D3
Chiemsee (lake) E5
Constance (lake) C5
Danube (riv.) C4
Donau (Danube) (riv.) C4
East Friesland (reg.) B2
Eder (riv.) C3
Elbe (riv.) D2
Elde (riv.) D2
Ems (riv.) B2
Erzgebirge (mts.) E3
Fehmarn (isl.) D1
Feldberg (mt.) C5
Fichtelberg (mt.) E3
Fichtelgebirge (range) D3
Föhr (isl.) C1
Franconian Jura (range) D4
Frisian, East (isls.) B2
Frisian, North (isls.) B1
Fulda (riv.) C3
Grosser Arber (mt.) E4
Harz (mts.) D3

Havel (riv.) E2
Hegau (reg.) C5
Helgoland (bay) C1
Helgoland (isl.) B1
Hunsrück (mts.) B4
Iller (riv.) C5
Ilmenau (riv.) D2
Inn (riv.) E4
Isar (riv.) E4
Jade (bay) B2
Juist (isl.) B2
Kaiserstuhl (mt.) B4
Kiel (bay) D1
Kiel (Nord-Ostsee) (canal) C1
Königssee (lake) E5
Lahn (riv.) C3
Langeoog (isl.) B2
Lech (riv.) D4
Leine (riv.) C2
Lippe (riv.) C3
Lüneburger Heide (dist.) C2
Lusatia (reg.) F3
Main (riv.) C4
Mecklenburg (bay) D1
Mosel (riv.) B3
Mulde (riv.) D3
Müritzsee (lake) E2
Naab (riv.) E4
Neckar (riv.) C4
Neisse (riv.) F3
Norderney (isl.) B2
Nord-Ostsee (canal) C1
Nordstrand (isl.) C1
North (sea) B1
North Friesland (reg.) C1
Odenwald (forest) C4
Oder (riv.) F2
Oder-Haff (lag.) F2
Our (riv.) B3
Peene (riv.) E2

Pellworm (isl.) C1
Plauersee (lake) E2
Pomeranian (bay) F1
Regnitz (riv.) D4
Rhine (riv.) B3
Rhön (mts.) D3
Rügen (isl.) E1
Ruhr (riv.) B3
Saale (riv.) D3
Saar (riv.) B4
Salzach (riv.) E5
Sauer (riv.) B4
Sauerland (reg.) B3
Schwarzwald (Black) (forest) .C4
Schwerinersee (lake) D2
Spessart (range) C4
Spiekeroog (isl.) B2
Spree (riv.) F3
Spreewald (forest) F3
Starnbergsee (lake) D5
Swabian Jura (range) C4
Sylt (isl.) C1
Taunus (range) C4
Tegernsee (lake) D5
Teutoburger Wald (forest) B2
Thüringer Wald (forest) D3
Unstrut (riv.) D3
Usedom (isl.) F1
Vechte (riv.) B2
Vogelsberg (mts.) C3
Walchensee (lake) D5
Wasserkuppe (mt.) C3
Watzmann (mt.) E5
Werra (riv.) D3
Weser (riv.) C2
Westerwald (forest) B3
White Elster (riv.) E3
Würmsee (Starnbergersee)
  (lake) D5
Zugspitze (mt.) D5

Agriculture, Industry and Resources

DOMINANT LAND USE

Wheat, Sugar Beets

Cereals (chiefly rye, oats, barley)

Potatoes, Rye

Dairy, Livestock

Mixed Cereals, Dairy

Truck Farming

Grapes, Fruit

Forests

MAJOR MINERAL OCCURRENCES

Ag Silver
Ba Barite
C   Coal
Cu Copper
Fe Iron Ore
G   Natural Gas
Gr Graphite

K   Potash
Lg Lignite
Na Salt
O   Petroleum
Pb Lead
U   Uranium
Zn Zinc

⚡ Water Power

▨ Major Industrial Areas

AREA 15,892 sq. mi. (41,160 sq. km.)
POPULATION 14,906,000
CAPITALS The Hague, Amsterdam
LARGEST CITY Amsterdam
HIGHEST POINT Vaalserberg 1,056 ft. (322 m.)
MONETARY UNIT guilder (florin)
MAJOR LANGUAGE Dutch
MAJOR RELIGIONS Protestantism, Roman Catholicism

AREA 11,781 sq. mi. (30,513 sq. km.)
POPULATION 9,883,000
CAPITAL Brussels
LARGEST CITY Brussels (greater)
HIGHEST POINT Botrange 2,277 ft. (694 m.)
MONETARY UNIT Belgian franc
MAJOR LANGUAGES French (Walloon), Flemish
MAJOR RELIGION Roman Catholicism

AREA 999 sq. mi. (2,587 sq. km.)
POPULATION 378,000
CAPITAL Luxembourg
LARGEST CITY Luxembourg
HIGHEST POINT Ardennes Plateau 1,825 ft. (556 m.)
MONETARY UNIT Luxembourg franc
MAJOR LANGUAGES Luxembourgeois (Letzeburgisch), French, German
MAJOR RELIGION Roman Catholicism

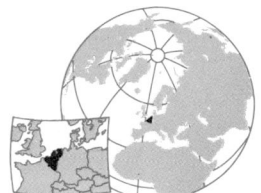

NETHERLANDS

BELGIUM

LUXEMBOURG

BELGIUM

PROVINCES

Antwerp 1,569,876	F6
Brabant 2,221,222	F7
East Flanders 1,331,192	D7
Hainaut 1,301,477	D7
Liège 999,413	H7
Limburg 716,888	G7
Luxembourg 221,926	G9
Namur 407,400	F8
West Flanders 1,079,253	B7

CITIES and TOWNS

Aalst 78,938	D7
Aalter 15,554	C6
Aarlen (Arlon) 22,279	H9
Aarschot 25,168	G7
Alken 9,563	G7
Amay 12,725	G7
Andenne 22,341	G8
Anderlecht 94,764	B9
Anderlues 11,700	E8
Ans 26,016	H7
Antoing 7,970	C7
Antwerp 185,897	E6
Antwerp* 918,144	E6
Antwerpen (Antwerp) 185,897	E6
Ardooie 9,458	C7
Arendonk 10,561	G6
Arlon 22,279	H9
Asse 26,425	E7
Assenede 13,353	D6
Aubange 14,696	H9
Auderghem 30,435	C9
Audenarge (Oudenarde) 26,615	D7
Aywaille 8,194	H8
Baerle-Hertog 2,111	F6
Balen 18,162	G6
Bastenaken (Bastogne) 11,386	H9
Bastogne 11,386	H9
Beauraing 7,641	F8
Beernem 13,526	C6
Beloeil 13,553	D7
Berchem 45,423	F6
Berchem-Sainte-Agathe 18,719	B9
Bergen (Mons) 94,417	E8
Beringen 34,254	G6
Bertrix 7,244	G9
Beveren 40,857	E6
Bilzen 25,683	G7
Binche 33,651	E8
Blankenberge 14,832	C6
Bocholt 10,142	H6
Boom 14,827	E6
Borgerhout 43,521	E6
Borgworm (Waremme) 11,907	G7
Bourg-Léopold (Leopoldsburg) 9,593	G6
Boussu 21,558	D8
Braine-l'Alleud 30,028	E7
Braine-le-Comte 16,475	D7
Brecht 16,391	F6
Bredene 10,538	B6
Bree 13,345	H6
Bruges 118,020	C6
Brugge (Bruges) 118,020	C6
Brussels (cap.)* 997,293	C9
Bruxelles (Brussels) (cap.)* 997,293	C9
Charleroi 222,343	E8
Charleroi* 443,832	E8
Châtelet 38,506	F8
Chimay 9,273	E8
Ciney 13,330	G8
Comines 18,034	B7
Courcelles 29,757	E8
Courtrai (Kortrijk) 75,917	C7
Couvin 12,909	F8
Damme 9,881	C6
De Haan 8,655	C6
Deinze 24,871	C7
Denderleeuw 16,497	D7
Dendermonde 22,119	E6
De Panne 9,507	B6
Dessel 8,074	G6
Destelbergen 15,741	D6
Deurne 77,635	F6
Diest 20,491	F7
Diksmuide 15,347	B6
Dilbeek 35,050	B9
Dilsen 15,910	H6
Dinant 12,105	G8
Dison 14,225	H7
Dixmude (Diksmuide) 15,347	B6
Doornik (Tournai) 67,906	C7
Dour 17,737	D8
Duffel 14,684	F6
Durbuy 7,729	H8
Ecaussinnes 9,739	E7
Edingen (Enghien) 10,095	D7
Eeklo 19,637	D6
Éghezée 10,683	F7
Eigenbrakel (Braine-l'Alleud) 30,028	E7
Ekeren 30,294	E6
Enghien 10,095	D7
Erquelinnes 10,029	E8
Esneux 11,559	H7
Essen 12,505	F6
Estampuis 9,601	C7
Etterbeek 44,218	B9
Eupen 16,847	J7
Evere 30,520	C9
Evergem 28,974	D6
Farciennes 12,205	E8
Flémalle 28,217	G7
Fleurus 22,574	E8
Florennes 10,537	F8
Forest 50,607	B9
Fosses-La-Ville 7,678	F8
Frameries 21,470	D8
Frasnes-lez Anvaing 10,751	D7
Furnes (Veurne) 11,253	B6
Ganshoren 21,445	B9
Geel 31,463	F6
Geldenaken (Jodoigne) 8,983	F7
Gembloux-sur-Orneau 17,636	F7
Genk 61,502	H7
Gent (Ghent) 239,256	D6
Geraardsbergen 17,533	D7
Gerpinnes 10,808	F8
Ghent 239,256	D6
Ghent* 485,565	D6
Gistel 9,531	B6
Grammont (Geraardsbergen) 17,533	D7
Grez-Doiceau 8,795	F7
Grimbergen 32,038	E7
Haacht 11,285	F7
Hal (Halle) 15,293	E7
Halen 7,865	G7
Halle 15,293	E7
Hamme 22,790	E6
Hamont-Achel 11,939	H6
Hannuit (Hannut) 11,527	G7
Hannut 11,527	G7
Harelbeke 25,214	C7
Hasselt 64,613	G7
Heist-op-den-Berg 34,617	F6
Hensies 6,806	D8
Herentals 23,797	F6
Herselt 11,340	F6
Herstal 38,592	H7
Herve 14,276	H7
Heuvelland 8,540	B7
Hoboken 34,563	E6
Hoei (Huy) 17,331	G8
Hoeselt 8,497	G7
Hoogstraten 14,368	F6
Huy 17,331	G8
Ichtegem 12,259	C6
Ieper 34,425	B7
Ingelmunster 10,434	C7
Ixelles 75,723	C9
Izegem 26,410	C7
Jabbeke 10,629	C6
Jemappes 18,632	D8
Jemeppe-sur-Sambre 17,120	F8
Jette 40,109	B9
Jodoigne 8,983	F7
Kalmthout 14,960	F6
Kapellen 14,536	E6
Kasterlee 14,612	F6
Kinrooi 10,138	H6
Knokke-Heist 28,868	C6
Koekelare 7,606	B6
Koekelberg 16,643	B9
Koksijde 13,679	B6
Kontich 17,878	F6
Kortemark 12,580	C6
Kortrijk 75,917	C7
Kraainem 11,780	C9
La Louvière 77,326	D8
Lanaken 20,272	H7
Landen 14,081	G7
Langemark-Poelkapelle 7,097	B7
Lasne 10,919	F7
Lede 17,249	D7
Lens 3,726	D7
Leopoldsburg 9,593	G6
Le Roeulx 7,754	E8
Lessen (Lessines) 16,553	D7
Lessines 16,553	D7
Leuven 85,076	F7
Leuze-en-Hainaut 12,863	D7
Libramont-Chevigny 7,859	G9
Lichtervelde 7,459	C6
Liedekerke 11,609	D7
Liège 214,119	H7
Liège* 605,123	H7
Lier 31,261	F6
Lierre (Lier) 31,261	F6
Limbourg 5,350	J7
Limburg (Limbourg) 5,350	J7
Linter 6,568	G7
Lochristi 16,125	D6
Lokeren 33,369	D6
Lommel 25,412	G6
Louvain (Leuven) 85,076	F7
Luik (Liège) 214,119	H7
Lummen 11,793	G7
Maaseik 20,056	H6
Maasmechelen 33,618	H7
Machelen 11,273	C9
Maldegem 42,694	C6
Malines (Mechelen) 77,269	F6
Malmédy 10,036	J8
Marche-en-Famenne 14,115	G8
Mechelen 77,269	F6
Meerhout 8,613	G6
Meise 15,170	E7
Menen 33,542	C7
Menin (Menen) 33,542	C7
Merchtem 12,972	D7
Merelbeke 19,773	D7
Merksem 41,600	E6
Merksplas 6,136	F6
Mettet 9,958	F8
Meulebeke 10,471	C7
Middelkerke 14,168	B6
Moeskroen (Mouscron) 54,590	C7
Mol 29,798	G6
Molenbeek-Saint-Jean 70,850	B9
Mons 94,417	E8
Montigny-le-Tilleul 9,726	E8
Moorslede 10,974	B7
Mortsel 26,746	E6
Mouscron 54,590	C7
Namen (Namur) 102,321	F8
Namur 102,321	F8
Nazareth 9,248	D7
Neerpelt 12,779	G6
Neufchâteau 6,039	G9
Nevele 10,471	D6
Nieuport (Nieuwpoort) 8,195	B6
Nieuwpoort 8,195	B6
Nijvel (Nivelles) 21,580	E7
Ninove 33,333	D7
Nivelles 21,580	E7
Oostende (Ostend) 68,915	B6
Oostkamp 19,747	C6
Opwijk 11,451	E7
Ostend 68,915	B6
Oudenaarde 26,615	D7
Oudenburg 8,138	B6
Oud-Turnhout 10,733	F6
Oupeye 22,453	H7
Overijse 21,428	F7
Overpelt 11,233	G6
Peer 12,099	G6
Péruwelz 16,664	D8
Philippeville 6,916	F8
Poelkapelle-Langemark 7,097	B7
Pont-à-Celles 15,444	E8
Poperinge 19,886	B7
Profondeville 8,724	F8
Putte 14,017	F6
Quaregnon 20,071	D8
Quévy 7,391	D8
Quiévrain 6,945	D8
Raeren 8,046	J7
Ravels 10,328	G6
Rebecq 8,891	E7
Renaix (Ronse) 25,056	D7
Retie 8,359	G6
Rochefort 4,357	G8
Roeselare 51,984	C7
Ronse (Renaix) 25,056	C7
Roulers (Roeselare) 51,984	C7
Saint-Gilles 46,076	B9
Saint-Josse-ten-Noode 20,381	C9
Saint-Nicolas 25,755	D7
Saint-Trond (Sint-Truiden) 36,374	G7
Saint-Vith (Sankt Vith) 8,434	J8

(continued on following page)

Agriculture, Industry and Resources

DOMINANT LAND USE

- Dairy, Truck Farming
- Cash Crops, Livestock
- Mixed Cereals, Dairy
- Specialized Horticulture
- Grapes, Wine
- Forests
- Sand Dunes

MAJOR MINERAL OCCURRENCES

C	Coal	Na	Salt
Fe	Iron Ore	O	Petroleum
G	Natural Gas		

Major Industrial Areas

(continued)

Sankt Vith 8,434 .... J8
Schaerbeek 106,754 .... C9
Schoten 31,128 .... F6
Seraing 64,543 .... G7
's-Gravenbrakel
(Braine-le-Comte) 16,475 .... D7
Sint-Laureins 6,620 .... D6
Sint-Niklaas 67,992 .... E6
Sint-Pieters-Leeuw 27,968 .... B9
Sint-Truiden 36,374 .... G7
Soignies 23,352 .... D7
Spa 9,619 .... H8
Sprimont 9,660 .... H8
Staden 11,135 .... B7
Steenokkerzeel 9,638 .... C9
Stekene 14,125 .... E6
Tamise (Temse) 23,525 .... E6
Temse 23,525 .... E6
Termonde
(Dendermonde) 22,119 .... E6
Tessenderlo 13,800 .... G6
Theux 9,167 .... H8
Thuin 13,757 .... E8
Tielt 19,103 .... C7
Tielt-Winge 8,237 .... F7
Tienen 32,620 .... F7
Tirlemont 32,620 .... F7
Tongeren 29,603 .... G7
Tongres (Tongeren) 29,603 .... G7
Torhout 17,165 .... C6
Tournai 67,906 .... C7
Tubeke (Tubize) 19,827 .... E7
Tubize 19,827 .... E7
Turnhout 37,453 .... F6
Uccle 76,004 .... B9
Ukkel (Uccle) 76,004 .... B9
Verviers 55,371 .... H7
Veurne 11,253 .... B6
Vielsalm 6,731 .... H8
Vilvoorde 33,264 .... F7
Vilvorde (Vilvoorde) 33,264 .... F7
Viroinval 5,589 .... F8
Virton 10,490 .... H9
Visé 16,469 .... H7
Vorst (Forest) 50,607 .... B9
Waarschoot 7,574 .... D6
Wachtebeke 6,951 .... D6
Waimes (Weismes) 5,713 .... J8
Walcourt 14,866 .... F8
Waregem 32,810 .... C7
Waremme 11,907 .... G7
Waterloo 24,755 .... E7
Watermael-Boitsfort 24,880 .... C9
Watermael-Bosvoorde
(Watermael-Boitsfort)
24,880 .... C9
Waver (Wavre) 25,153 .... F7
Wavre 25,153 .... F7
Wemmel 13,547 .... B9
Wervik 18,086 .... B7
Westerlo 19,459 .... F6
Wetteren 23,460 .... D7
Wezembeek-Oppem 12,006 .... D9
Wezet (Visé) 16,469 .... H7
Willebroek 22,265 .... E6
Wilrijk 42,328 .... E6
Wingene 12,188 .... C6
Woluwe-Saint-Lambert
48,801 .... C9
Woluwe-Saint-Pierre 40,686 .... C9
Ypres (Ieper) 34,425 .... B7
Yvoir 6,527 .... F8
Zaventem 25,393 .... C9
Zedelgem 19,198 .... C6
Zele 19,631 .... E6
Zelzate 12,934 .... D6
Zemst 17,167 .... E7
Zinnik (Soignies) 23,352 .... D7
Zonhoven 15,965 .... G6
Zottegem 25,109 .... D7

OTHER FEATURES

Albert (canal) F6
Ardennes (forest) F9
Botrange (mt.) J8
Dender (riv.) D7
Deûle (riv.) B7
Dyle (riv.) F7
Hohe Venn (plat.) H8
Lys (riv.) B7
Mark (riv.) F6
Meuse (riv.) F8
Nethe (riv.) F6
North (sea) D4
Ourthe (riv.) G8
Rupel (riv.) F7
Sambre (riv.) D8
Schelde (Scheldt) (riv.) C7
Scheldt (riv.) C7
Semois (riv.) G9
Senne (riv.) E7
Vaalserberg (mt.) J7
Vesdre (riv.) H7
Yser (riv.) B7

LUXEMBOURG

CITIES and TOWNS

Bascharage 4,870 .... H9
Diekirch† 5,470 .... J9
Differdange 15,940 .... H9
Dudelange† 14,070 .... J1
Echternach† 4,290 .... J9
Esch-sur-Alzette† 23,800 .... H9
Ettelbruck† 6,600 .... J9
Grevenmacher† 2,940 .... J9
Hesperange 9,470 .... J9
Luxembourg (cap.) 75,540 .... J9
Mamer 6,090 .... H9
Mersch 5,560 .... J9
Mertert 3,000 .... J9
Pétange 11,800 .... H9
Remich 2,430 .... J9
Troisvierges 1,890 .... J9
Vianden† 1,510 .... J9
Wasserbillig 2,097 .... J9
Wiltz 3,850 .... H9

OTHER FEATURES

Alzette (riv.) J9
Clerf (riv.) J8
Mosel (riv.) J9
Our (riv.) J9
Sauer (riv.) J9

NETHERLANDS

PROVINCES

Drenthe 439,066 .... K3
Flevoland 202,678 .... G4
Friesland 599,190 .... H2
Gelderland 1,794,678 .... H4
Groningen 555,200 .... K2
Limburg 1,099,622 .... H6
North Brabant 2,172,604 .... F5
North Holland 2,365,160 .... F3
Overijssel 1,014,949 .... J4
South Holland 3,200,408 .... E5
Utrecht 1,004,632 .... G4
Zeeland 355,585 .... D6

CITIES and TOWNS

Aalsmeer 21,984 .... F4
Aalten 18,202 .... K5
Alkmaar 88,571 .... F3
Almelo 62,008 .... K4
Almere 63,785 .... G4
Alphen aan de Rijn 59,586 .... F4
Amersfoort 96,072 .... G4
Amstelveen 69,505 .... B5
Amsterdam (cap.) 694,680 .... B4
Apeldoorn 147,270 .... H4
Appingedam 12,668 .... K2
Arnhem 128,946 .... H4
Assen 49,398 .... K3
Asten 14,965 .... H6
Axel 12,219 .... D6
Baarn 24,897 .... G4
Barneveld 41,649 .... H4
Beilen 14,057 .... K3
Bemmel 15,842 .... H5
Bergen 14,075 .... F3
Bergen op Zoom 46,842 .... E5
Berkel 15,690 .... F5
Beverwijk 35,126 .... F4
Bloemendaal 8,977 .... E4
Bodegraven 17,720 .... F4
Bolsward 9,799 .... H2
Borculo 10,057 .... J4
Borger 12,730 .... K3
Borne 21,261 .... K4
Boskoop 14,524 .... F4
Boxmeer 14,363 .... H5
Boxtel 24,951 .... G5
Breda 121,362 .... F5
Brielle 14,973 .... E5
Brummen 20,802 .... J4
Brunssum 29,799 .... J7
Bussum 31,988 .... G4
Capelle 57,423 .... F5
Castricum 22,433 .... F3
Coevorden 14,344 .... K3
Culemborg 21,116 .... G5
De Bilt 31,729 .... G4
Delft 88,135 .... E4
Delfzijl 23,472 .... K2
Denekamp 12,206 .... L4
Den Helder 62,094 .... F3
Deurne 29,308 .... H6
Deventer 66,398 .... J4
Didam 16,036 .... J5
Diemen 18,083 .... C5
Dinxperlo 8,133 .... K5
Dirksland 7,341 .... E5
Doesburg 10,578 .... J4
Doetinchem 41,260 .... J5
Dongen 21,124 .... F5
Doorn 10,419 .... G4
Dordrecht 108,519 .... F5
Driebergen 18,294 .... G4
Dronten 24,281 .... H3
Druten 14,630 .... H5
Echt 16,927 .... H6
Edam-Volendam 24,572 .... G4
Ede 92,293 .... H4
Egmond aan Zee 11,163 .... E3
Eindhoven 190,736 .... G6
Elst 17,654 .... H5
Emmen 92,422 .... K3
Enkhuizen 15,939 .... G3
Enschede 145,223 .... K4
Epe 33,872 .... H4
Ermelo 25,644 .... H4
Etten-Leur 32,010 .... F5
Flushing 44,022 .... C6
Geertruidenberg 6,645 .... F5
Geldermalsen 22,017 .... G5
Geldrop 25,817 .... H6
Geleen 33,756 .... H7
Gemert 17,613 .... H5
Gendringen 20,186 .... J5
Genemuiden 7,545 .... H3
Gennep 16,264 .... H5
Giessendam 16,722 .... F5
Gilze 22,577 .... F5
Goes 31,815 .... D6
Goirle 18,852 .... G5
Goor 11,804 .... K4
Gorinchem 28,222 .... G5
Gouda 63,232 .... F4
Gramsbergen 6,080 .... K3
Grave 10,447 .... H5
Groenlo 8,895 .... K4
Groesbeek 18,221 .... H5
Groningen 167,788 .... K2
Haaksbergen 22 690 .... K4
Haarlem 149,198 .... F4
Haarlemmermeer
(Hoofddorp) 93,427 .... F4
Hague, The (cap.) 443,845 .... E4
Hardenberg 32,065 .... J3
Harderwijk 34,600 .... H4
Hardinxveld-Giessendam
16,722 .... G5
Harlingen 15,727 .... G2
Hasselt 6,871 .... J3
Hattem 11,571 .... H4
Heemskerk 32,910 .... F3
Heemstede 26,308 .... F4
Heerde 18,171 .... H4
Heerenveen 37,700 .... H3
Heerhugowaard 35,522 .... F3
Heerlen 94,149 .... J7
Heesch 11,309 .... G5
Heiloo 20,467 .... F3
Hellendoorn 34,287 .... J4
Hellevoetsluis 34,276 .... E5
Helmond 66,791 .... H6
Hengelo 76,175 .... J4
's Hertogenbosch 90,584 .... G5
Heusden 5,761 .... G5
Hillegom 20,001 .... E4
Hilvarenbeek 9,975 .... G6
Hilversum 84,983 .... G4
Hoek van Holland
(Hook of Holland) D4
Hoofddorp
(Haarlemmermeer) 93,427 .... F4
Hoogeveen 45,601 .... J3
Hoogezand-Sappemeer
34,618 .... K2
Hook of Holland D4
Hoorn 56,474 .... G3
Horst 17,614 .... H6
Huissen 15,544 .... H5
Huizen 20,501 .... G4
Hulst 18,575 .... E6
IJsselstein 19,516 .... F4
Kampen 32,769 .... H3
Katwijk aan Zee 39,441 .... E4
Kerkrade 52,994 .... J7
Kesteren 9,389 .... G5
Krimpen aan den IJssel
27,638 .... F5
Landsmeer 9,121 .... C4
Laren 11,643 .... G4
Leek 17,743 .... J2
Leerdam 19,015 .... G5
Leeuwarden 85,296 .... H2
Leiden 109,254 .... E4
Lelystad 58,125 .... H3
Lisse 20,826 .... F4
Lith 6,115 .... G5
Lochem 18,295 .... J4
Loon op Zand 21,372 .... G5
Losser 22,526 .... L4
Maarssen 37,629 .... F4
Maasbree 11,752 .... H6
Maassluis 33,155 .... E5
Maastricht 116,380 .... H7
Margraten 13,365 .... H7
Medemblik 6,876 .... G3
Meerssen 20,462 .... H7
Meppel 23,492 .... J3
Middelburg 39,462 .... C6
Middelharnis 15,480 .... E5
Millingen aan den Rijn 5,287 .... J5
Monnickendam 9,953 .... C4
Montfoort 12,397 .... G4
Muiden 6,772 .... G4
Muntendam 5,022 .... K2
Naaldwijk 27,683 .... E4
Naarden 16,101 .... G4
Neede 10,982 .... K4
Nieuwegein 58,316 .... G4
Nieuwkoop 10,723 .... F4
Nijkerk 25,613 .... H4
Nijmegen 145,405 .... H5
Noordwijk 24,996 .... E4
Norg 6,595 .... J2
Nunspeet 24,573 .... H4
Odoorn 12,225 .... K3
Oisterwijk 18,177 .... G5
Oldenzaal 29,680 .... K4
Olst 9,039 .... J4
Ommen 17,957 .... J3
Oostburg 18,145 .... C6
Oosterhout 48,157 .... F5
Oostzaan 7,292 .... C4
Oss 50,987 .... H5
Oud-Beijerland 20,385 .... E5
Oude-Pekela 8,028 .... K2
Oudenbosch 12,576 .... E5
Oudewater 9,410 .... F4
Purmerend 56,233 .... F4
Putten 20,898 .... H4
Raalte 26,883 .... J4
Renkum 33,841 .... H5
Reusel 7,813 .... G6
Rheden 46,088 .... J4
Rhenen 16,613 .... H5
Ridderkerk 46,163 .... F5
Rijnsburg 13,412 .... F4
Rijssen 23,927 .... J4
Rijswijk 48,189 .... E4
Roden 18,331 .... J2
Roermond 38,486 .... J6
Roosendaal 59,237 .... F5
Rotterdam 576,232 .... E5
Ruurlo 7,418 .... J4
Sappemeer-Hoogezand
34,618 .... K2
Schagen 16,759 .... F3
Schiedam 69,438 .... E5
Schijndel 21,397 .... G5
Schoonebeek 7,740 .... K3
Schoonhoven 11,231 .... F5
's Gravendeel 8,424 .... E5
's Gravenhage (The Hague)
(cap.) 443,845 .... E4
's Gravenzande 18,453 .... E4
Simpelveld 11,882 .... J7
Sittard 44,894 .... H6
Sliedrecht 22,833 .... F5
Slochteren 13,958 .... K2
Sloten H3
Sluis 2,882 .... C6
Smilde 9,212 .... K3
Sneek 29,408 .... H2
Soest 41,598 .... G4
Stadskanaal 33,047 .... L3
Staphorst 13,580 .... J3
Staveren G3
Steenbergen 13,826 .... E5
Steenwijk 20,907 .... J3
Stiens H2
Tegelen 18,991 .... J6
Ter Apel L3
Termunten 4,378 .... K2
Terneuzen 35,043 .... D6
The Hague (cap.) 443,845 .... E4
Tholen 19,019 .... E5
Tiel 31,394 .... G5
Tilburg 155,110 .... G5
Twello J4
Uden 35,057 .... H5
Uithoorn 22,205 .... F4
Uithuizen K2
Ulrum 3,657 .... J2
Urk 12,728 .... H3
Utrecht 230,634 .... G4
Vaals 10,639 .... H7
Valkenswaard 29,811 .... H6
Veendam 28,234 .... K2
Veenendaal 47,258 .... G4
Veere 4,836 .... D5
Veghel 25,701 .... H5
Veldhoven 38,644 .... G6
Velsen 57,608 .... F4
Venlo 63,607 .... J6
Venraij 34,172 .... H6
Vianen 18,704 .... G5
Vlaardingen 74,480 .... E5
Vlagtwedde 16,181 .... L3
Vlijmen 15,655 .... G5
Vlissingen (Flushing) 44,022 .... C6
Volendam-Edam 24,572 .... G4
Voorburg 40,455 .... E4
Voorst 23,678 .... J4
Vorden 8,282 .... J4
Vriezenveen 18,601 .... K4
Vught 23,718 .... G5
Waalre 15,126 .... G6
Waalwijk 28,674 .... F5
Wageningen 32,370 .... H5
Warmenhuizen 4,765 .... F3
Weert 40,068 .... H6
Weesp 18,362 .... C5
Westkapelle 2,666 .... C5
Wierden 22,200 .... K4
Wijhe 7,155 .... J4
Wijk bij Duurstede 15,401 .... G5
Willemstad 3,357 .... F5
Winschoten 19,680 .... L2
Winsum 6,583 .... K2
Winterswijk 28,024 .... K5
Woensdrecht 10,077 .... E6
Woerden 34,166 .... F4
Wolvega J3
Workum G3
Zaandam (Zaanstad) 129,653 .... B4
Zaltbommel 9,534 .... G5
Zandvoort 15,428 .... E4
Zeewolde 5,930 .... G4
Zeist 59,431 .... G4
Zevenaar 26,848 .... J5
Zevenbergen 15,562 .... E5
Zierikzee 9,804 .... D5
Zundert 13,385 .... F6
Zutphen 31,144 .... J4
Zwartsluis 4,465 .... H3
Zwijndrecht 41,357 .... E5
Zwolle 92,517 .... J3

OTHER FEATURES

Alkmaardermeer (lake) F3
Ameland (isl.) H2
Beulaker Wijde (lake) H3
Borndiep (chan.) H2
De Fluessen (lake) G3
De Honte (bay) D6
De Peel (reg.) H6
De Twente (reg.) K4
De Zaan (riv.) B4
Dollard (bay) L2
Dommel (riv.) H6
Duiveland (isl.) D5
Eems (riv.) K2
Eijerlandsche Gat (strait) F2
Flevoland Polders G4
Frisian, West (isls.) G2
Goeree (isl.) D5
Grevelingen (strait) E5
Griend (isl.) G2
Groninger Wad (sound) J2
Groote IJ Polder B4
Haarlemmermeer Polder B5
Haringvliet (strait) E5
Het IJ (est.) C4
Hoek van Holland (cape) D5
Houtrak Polder A4
Hunse (riv.) K3
IJmeer (bay) C4
IJssel (riv.) J4
IJsselmeer (lake) G3
Lauwers (chan.) J1
Lauwers Zee (bay) J2
Lek (riv.) F5
Lower Rhine (riv.) H5
Maas (riv.) G5
Marken (isl.) G4
Markerwaard Polder G3
Marsdiep (chan.) F3
North (sea) E3
North Beveland (isl.) D5
North East Polder H3
North Holland (canal) C4
North Sea (canal) F4
Old Rhine (riv.) E4
Oostzaan Polder B4
Orange (canal) K3
Overflakkee (isl.) E5
Rhine (riv.) J5
Roer (riv.) J6
Scheldt, Eastern (est.) D5
Scheldt, Western
(De Honte) (bay) D6
Schiermonnikoog (isl.) J1
Schouwen (isl.) D5
Slotermeer (lake) H3
Sneekermeer (lake) H2
South Beveland (isl.) D6
Terschelling (isl.) G2
Texel (isl.) F2
Tjeukemeer (lake) H3
Vaalserberg (mt.) J7
Vecht (riv.) F4
Vechte (riv.) J3
Veersche Meer (lake) D5
Veluwe (reg.) H4
Vlieland (isl.) F2
Vliestroom (strait) G2
Voorne (isl.) D5
Waal (riv.) G5
Waddenzee (sound) G2
Walcheren (isl.) C5
West Frisian (isls.) F2
Wester Eems (chan.) K1
Western Scheldt
(De Honte) (bay) D6
Wieringermeer Polder G3
Wilhelmina (canal) G6
Willems (canal) G5

* City and suburbs.
† Population of urban area.

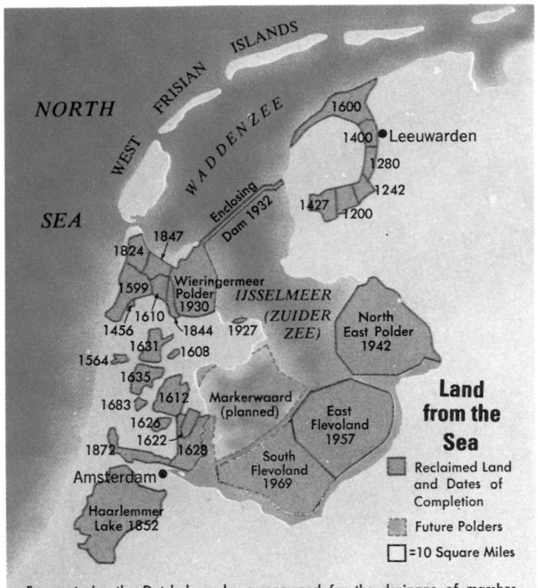

For centuries the Dutch have been renowned for the drainage of marshes and the construction of polders, i.e., arable land reclaimed from the sea. Future projects will convert much of the present IJsselmeer to agricultural land.

Topography

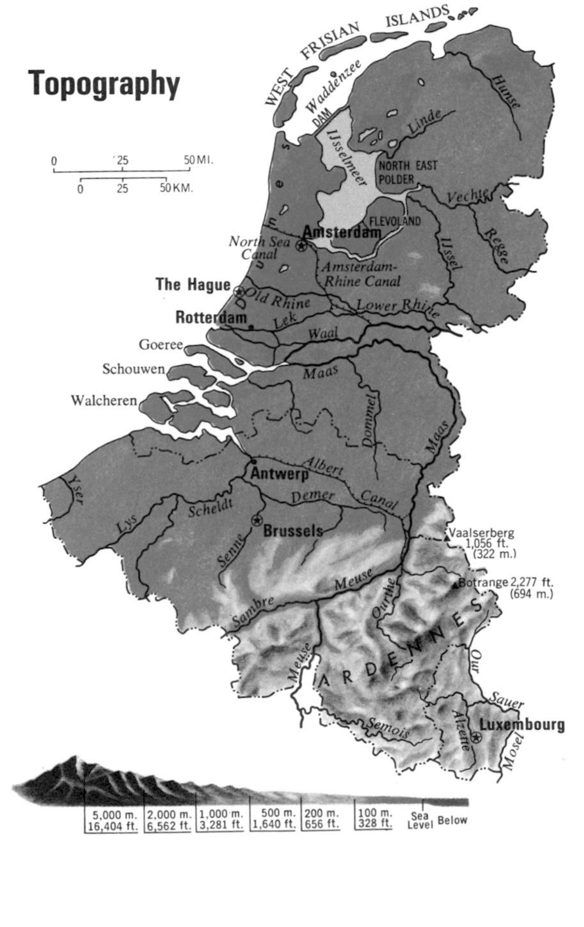

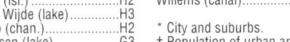

Netherlands, Belgium and Luxembourg

CONIC PROJECTION

SCALE OF MILES

0 5 10 20 30 40

SCALE OF KILOMETRES

0 5 10 20 30 40 50

Capitals of Countries .... ★

Provincial Capitals .... △

International Boundaries .... — ·· —

Provincial Boundaries .... — · —

Canals ....

© Copyright HAMMOND INCORPORATED, Maplewood, N.J.

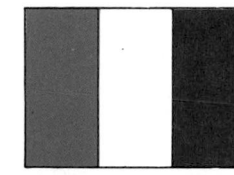

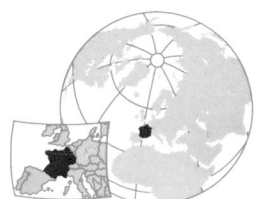

AREA 210,038 sq. mi. (543,998 sq. km.)
POPULATION 56,160,000
CAPITAL Paris
LARGEST CITY Paris
HIGHEST POINT Mont Blanc 15,771 ft. (4,807 m.)
MONETARY UNIT franc
MAJOR LANGUAGE French
MAJOR RELIGION Roman Catholicism

DEPARTMENTS

Ain 418,516	F 4
Aisne 533,970	E 3
Allier 369,580	E 4
Alpes-de-Haute-Provence 119,068	G 5
Alpes-Maritimes 881,198	G 6
Ardèche 267,970	F 5
Ardennes 302,338	F 3
Ariège 135,725	D 6
Aube 289,300	E 3
Aude 280,686	E 6
Aveyron 278,654	E 5
Bas-Rhin 915,676	G 3
Belfort 131,999	G 4
Bouches-du-Rhône 1,724,199	F 6
Calvados 589,559	C 3
Cantal 162,838	E 5
Charente 340,770	D 5
Charente-Maritime 513,220	C 5
Cher 320,174	E 4
Corrèze 241,448	D 5
Corse du Sud 108,604	B 6
Côte-d'Or 473,548	F 4
Côtes-du-Nord 538,869	B 3
Creuse 139,968	D 4
Deux-Sèvres 342,812	C 4
Dordogne 377,356	D 5
Doubs 477,163	G 4
Drôme 389,781	F 5
Essonne 988,000	E 3
Eure 462,323	D 3
Eure-et-Loir 362,813	D 3
Finistère 828,364	A 3
Gard 530,478	F 6
Gers 174,154	D 6
Gironde 1,127,546	C 5
Haute-Corse 131,574	B 6
Haute-Garonne 824,501	D 6
Haute-Loire 205,895	E 5
Haute-Marne 210,670	F 3
Hautes-Alpes 105,070	G 5
Haute-Saône 231,962	G 4
Haute-Savoie 494,505	G 5
Hautes-Pyrénées 227,922	D 6
Haute-Vienne 355,737	D 5
Haut-Rhin 650,372	G 4
Hauts-de-Seine 1,387,039	A 2
Hérault 706,499	E 6
Ille-et-Vilaine 749,764	C 3
Indre 243,191	D 4
Indre-et-Loire 506,097	D 4
Isère 936,771	F 5
Jura 242,925	F 4
Landes 297,424	C 5
Loire 739,521	F 5
Loire-Atlantique 995,498	C 4
Loiret 535,669	E 3
Loir-et-Cher 296,220	D 4
Lot 154,533	D 5
Lot-et-Garonne 298,522	D 5
Lozère 74,294	E 5
Maine-et-Loire 675,321	C 4
Manche 465,948	C 3
Marne 543,627	F 3
Mayenne 271,784	C 3
Meurthe-et-Moselle 716,846	G 3
Meuse 200,101	F 3
Morbihan 590,889	B 4
Moselle 1,007,189	G 3
Nièvre 239,635	E 4
Nord 2,520,526	E 2
Oise 661,781	E 3
Orne 295,472	C 3
Paris 2,188,918	B 2
Pas-de-Calais 1,412,413	E 2
Puy-de-Dôme 594,365	E 5
Pyrénées-Atlantiques 555,696	C 6
Pyrénées-Orientales 334,557	E 6
Rhône 1,445,208	F 5
Saône-et-Loire 571,852	F 4
Sarthe 504,768	D 3
Savoie 323,675	G 5
Seine-et-Marne 887,112	E 3
Seine-Maritime 1,324,301	D 3
Seine-Saint-Denis 1,324,301	C 1
Somme 544,570	E 2
Tarn 339,345	E 6
Tarn-et-Garonne 190,485	D 5
Val-de-Marne 1,193,655	C 1
Val-d'Oise 920,598	E 3
Var 708,331	G 6
Vaucluse 427,343	F 6
Vendée 483,027	C 4
Vienne 371,428	D 4
Vosges 395,769	G 3
Yonne 311,019	E 4
Yvelines 1,196,111	D 3

CITIES and TOWNS

Aigues-Mortes 4,106	F 6
Aix-en-Provence 100,221	F 6
Aix-les-Bains 22,331	G 5
Ajaccio 48,324	B 7
Alençon 30,952	D 3
Amboise 10,823	D 4
Amiens 130,302	E 3
Angers 135,293	C 4
Angoulême 45,495	D 5
Annecy 49,753	G 5
Antibes 62,427	G 6
Argenteuil 94,826	A 1
Arles 37,554	F 6
Armentières 22,849	E 2
Arras 41,376	E 2
Asnières-sur-Seine 71,058	A 1
Aubervilliers 67,684	B 1
Aubusson 5,326	E 4
Aulnay-sous-Bois 75,543	B 1
Aurignac 772	D 6
Avignon 75,178	F 6
Ax-les-Thermes 1,283	D 6
Bagnolet 32,556	B 2
Barbizon 478	E 3
Barcelonnette 2,674	G 5
Barfleur 617	C 3
Bastia 43,502	B 6
Bayeux 14,568	C 3
Bayonne 40,088	C 6
Beaucaire 10,622	F 6
Beaune 19,110	F 4
Beauvais 51,542	E 3
Belfort 51,034	G 4
Bergerac 24,604	D 5
Besançon 112,023	G 4
Bessèges 4,352	F 5
Béziers 74,114	E 6
Biarritz 26,579	C 6
Blois 46,925	D 4
Bobigny 42,630	B 1
Bonifacio 1,727	B 7
Bordeaux 201,965	C 5
Boulogne-Billancourt 102,582	A 2
Boulogne-sur-Mer 47,482	D 2
Bourg-en-Bresse 37,582	F 4
Bourges 74,622	E 4
Brest 154,110	A 3
Brignoles 8,529	G 6
Brive-la-Gaillarde 50,898	D 5
Bruay-en-Artois 22,502	E 2
Caen 112,332	C 3
Cahors 16,206	D 2
Caluire-et-Cuire 41,864	F 5
Cambrai 35,070	E 2
Cannes 71,888	G 6
Carcassonne 38,379	E 6
Castres 39,216	E 6
Chalons-sur-Marne 49,941	F 3
Chalon-sur-Saône 53,893	F 4
Chambéry 49,465	F 5
Chambord 159	D 4
Chamonix-Mont-Blanc 7,406	G 5
Champigny-sur-Marne 76,039	C 2
Chantilly 10,065	E 3
Charleville-Mézières 7,814	F 3
Chartres 36,706	D 3
Chateaudun 15,905	D 3
Chateauneuf-sur-Loire 5,630	E 4
Chateauroux 51,744	D 4
Chateau-Thierry 14,457	E 3
Chatou 28,435	A 1
Cherbourg 28,324	C 3
Chinon 6,030	D 4
Choisy-le-Roi 35,443	B 2
Cholet 51,620	C 4
Clamart 48,210	A 2
Clermont-Ferrand 145,901	E 5
Clichy 46,830	B 1
Cluny 4,133	F 4
Cognac 20,247	C 5
Colmar 61,560	G 3
Colombes 78,485	A 1
Compiègne 39,909	E 3
Courbevoie 59,821	A 1
Creil 34,332	E 3
Créteil 71,559	B 2
Deauville 4,682	C 3
Dieppe 35,659	D 3
Digne 12,540	G 5
Dijon 139,188	F 4
Dinard 9,562	B 3
Domrémy-la-Pucelle 162	F 3
Douai 41,576	E 2
Drancy 60,122	B 1
Dunkirk 71,756	E 2
Ernée 5,253	C 3
Évreux 45,215	D 3
Falaise 8,424	C 3
Fécamp 21,212	D 3
Foix 9,212	D 6
Fontainebleau 14,687	E 3
Fontenay-sous-Bois 52,397	C 2
Gex 4,776	G 4
Grasse 24,257	G 6
Grenoble 156,437	F 5
Guise 6,179	E 2
Harfleur 9,470	D 3
Hazebrouck 19,266	E 2
Hendaye 10,492	C 6
Héricourt 9,239	G 4
Honfleur 8,125	D 3
Issy-les-Moulineaux 45,702	A 2
Istres 21,286	F 6
Ivry-sur-Seine 55,682	B 2
La Baule-Escoublac 13,151	B 4
La Courneuve 33,525	B 1
Langres 9,718	F 4
Lapalisse 3,173	E 4
La Rochelle 74,728	C 4
La Roche-sur-Yon 42,026	C 4
Laval 53,582	C 3
Le Bourget 11,020	B 1
Le Creusot 32,013	F 4
Le Havre 198,700	C 3
Le Mans 145,976	C 3
Le Puy 22,806	F 5
Le Tréport 6,330	D 2
Levallois-Perret 53,485	B 1
Lille 167,791	E 2
Limoges 137,809	D 5
Lisieux 24,454	D 3
Lorient 62,207	B 4
Lourdes 17,252	C 6
Lunéville 21,200	G 3
Lyon 410,455	F 5
Maisons-Alfort 51,041	B 2
Maisons-Laffitte 22,565	A 1
Mantes-la-Jolie 43,551	D 3
Marmande 14,264	D 5
Marseille 868,435	F 6
Maubeuge 35,424	F 2
Mayenne 12,156	C 3
Meaux 44,386	E 3
Melun 34,379	E 3
Mende 10,520	E 5
Menton 22,234	G 6
Metz 113,236	G 3
Meudon 29,356	A 2
Montauban 36,122	D 5
Montbéliard 31,174	G 4
Montceau-les-Mines 26,877	F 4
Mont-de-Marsan 25,896	C 6
Mont-Dore 2,091	E 5
Montfort 4,029	C 3
Montluçon 49,737	E 4
Montmédy 1,880	F 3
Montpellier 190,423	E 6
Montreuil 96,441	B 2
Mont-Saint-Michel 65	C 3
Mulhouse 111,742	G 4
Nancy 95,654	G 3
Nanterre 88,567	A 1
Nantes 237,789	C 4
Narbonne 38,222	E 6
Nemours 11,624	E 3
Neufchatel-en-Bray 5,452	D 3
Neuilly-sur-Seine 64,093	A 1
Nice 331,165	G 6
Nîmes 120,515	F 6
Niort 56,256	C 4
Nogent-le-Rotrou 11,963	D 3
Noisy-le-Sec 36,821	B 1
Nontron 3,407	D 5
Noyon 13,949	E 3
Nyons 5,219	F 5
Orléans 81,615	D 3
Orly 23,729	B 2
Oyonnax 22,516	F 4
Paris (cap.) 2,165,892	B 2
Paris *10,073,059	B 2
Pau 82,186	C 6
Périgueux 32,632	D 5
Perpignan 107,812	E 6
Pessac 49,019	C 5
Poitiers 76,793	D 4
Pontoise 27,885	E 3
Port-Vendres 4,871	E 6
Privas 9,253	F 5
Quimper 52,335	A 4
Rambouillet 21,136	D 3
Redon 9,071	C 4
Reims 176,419	F 3
Rennes 190,861	C 3
Roanne 48,574	F 4
Rochefort 25,392	C 4
Roubaix 101,488	E 2
Rouen 100,696	D 3
Rueil-Malmaison 63,310	A 2
Saint-Brieuc 48,259	B 3
Saint-Cloud 28,561	A 2
Saint-Denis 90,686	B 1
Saint-Dizier 34,074	F 3
Sainte-Mère-Église 1,205	C 3
Saint-Étienne 193,938	F 5
Saint-Germain-en-Laye 36,585	D 3
Saint-Jean-d'Angély 9,268	C 4

Topography

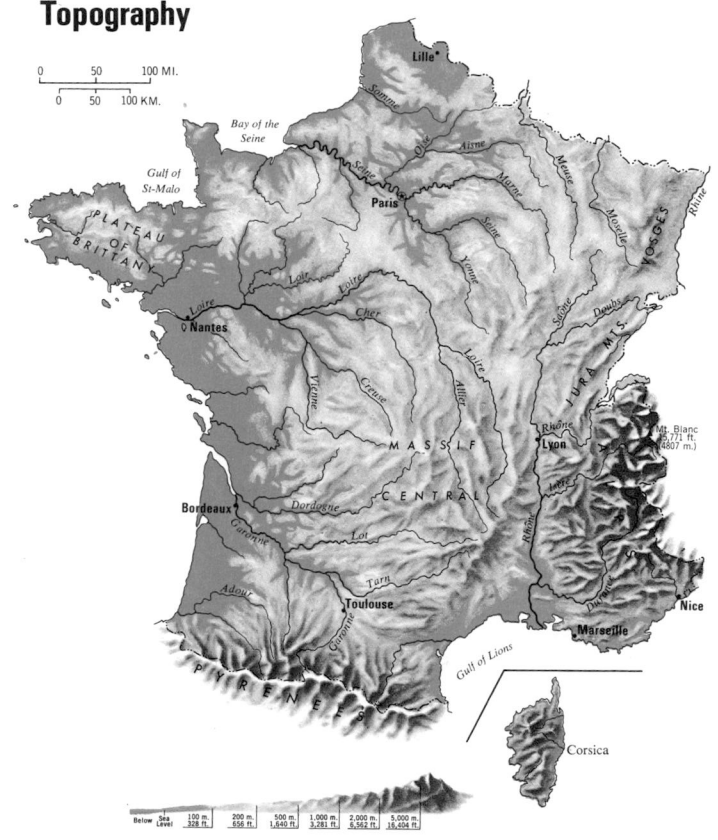

Historic Provinces

A resident of the city of Caen thinks of himself as a Norman rather than as a citizen of the modern department of Calvados. In spite of the passing of nearly two centuries, the historic provinces which existed before 1790 command the local patriotism of most Frenchmen.

(continued on following page)

(continued)

Saint-Jean-de-Luz 12,124 C 6
Saint-Lô 21,790 C 3
Saint-Malo 44,030 B 3
Saint-Maur-des-Fossés 80,686 B 2
Saint-Nazaire 68,040 B 4
Saint-Ouen 43,589 B 1
Saint-Quentin 63,010 E 3
Saint-Raphaël 22,221 G 6
Saint-Tropez 4,956 G 6
Salon-de-Provence 31,185 F 6
Sarreguemines 23,699 G 3
Sartrouville 46,018 A 1
Saumur 30,037 D 4
Sedan 23,357 F 3
Senlis 14,345 E 3
Sens 25,793 E 3
Sète 39,258 E 6
Sèvres 20,184 A 2
Soissons 29,871 E 3
Sotteville-les-Rouen 29,335 D 3
Stiring-Wendel 13,563 G 3
Strasbourg 247,068 H 3
Tarascon 8,968 F 6
Tarbes 50,306 D 6
Thiers 13,492 E 5
Thionville 34,758 G 3
Thiviers 3,047 D 5
Thonon-les-Bains 26,421 G 4
Tonneins 7,162 D 5
Tonnerre 5,744 E 4
Toulon 177,443 F 6
Toulouse 344,917 D 6
Tourcoing 96,536 E 2
Tours 131,265 D 4
Trouville D 3
Troyes 62,946 F 3
Uckange 9,524 G 3
Uzès 5,975 F 5
Valence 66,143 F 5
Valenciennes 39,979 E 2
Vannes 39,214 B 4
Vendôme 16,949 D 4
Vénissieux 64,621 F 5
Verdun-sur-Meuse 21,170 F 3
Vernon 21,271 D 3
Versailles 91,014 A 2
Vesoul 18,257 F 4
Vichy 30,522 E 4
Vienne 25,414 F 5
Villefranche 6,627 G 6
Villefranche-sur-Saône 28,858 F 4
Villejuif 50,970 B 2
Villeneuve-Saint-Georges 27,839 E 3
Villeurbanne 115,378 F 5
Vincennes 42,852 B 2
Vitry-sur-Seine 84,956 B 2
Voiron 16,383 F 5
Yssingeaux 4,393 F 5
Yvetot 10,574 D 3

OTHER FEATURES

Adour (riv.) C 6
Ain (riv.) F 4
Aisne (riv.) E 3
Ajaccio (gulf) B 7
Allier (riv.) E 5
Aube (riv.) F 3
Auvergne (mt.) E 5
Belle-Île (isl.) B 4
Biscay (bay) B 5
Blanc (mt.) G 5
Bonifacio (strait) B 7
Calais, Pas de (Dover) (strait) D 2
Causses (reg.) D 5
Cévennes (mt.) E 5
Charente (riv.) C 5
Cher (riv.) D 4
Corse (cape) B 6
Corsica (isl.) 240,178 B 6
Côte-d'Or (mt.) F 4
Cotentin (pen.) C 3
Cottian Alps (range) G 5
Creuse (riv.) D 4
Dordogne (riv.) D 5
Dore Alps (mt.) E 5
Doubs (riv.) G 4
Dover (strait) D 2
Drôme (riv.) F 5
Dronne (riv.) D 5
Durance (riv.) F 6
English (chan.) B 3
Eure (riv.) D 3
Faucilles (mt.) G 3
Forez (mt.) E 5
Fréjus (pass) G 5
Gard (riv.) F 5
Garonne (riv.) C 5
Gave de Pau (riv.) C 6
Geneva (lake) G 4
Gers (riv.) D 6
Gironde (riv.) C 5
Graian Alps (range) G 5
Groix (isl.) 2,605 B 4
Hague (cape) C 3
Hérault (riv.) E 6
Hyères (isl.) G 6
Indre (riv.) D 4
Isère (riv.) F 5
Isle (riv.) D 5
Jura (mt.) F 4
Langres (plat.) F 4
Limousin (reg.) D 5
Lions (gulf) F 6
Little Saint Bernard (pass) G 5
Loir (riv.) D 4
Loire (riv.) C 4
Lot (riv.) D 5
Maritime Alps (range) G 5
Marne (riv.) C 2
Mayenne (riv.) C 4
Mediterranean (sea) E 7
Médoc (reg.) C 5
Meuse (riv.) F 3
Mézenc (mt.) E 5
Mont Cenis (tunnel) G 5
Morvan (plat.) E 4
Moselle (riv.) G 3
Noirmoutier (isl.) B 4
North (sea) E 1
Oise (riv.) E 3
Oléron (isl.) C 5
Omaha (beach) C 3
Orb (riv.) E 6
Orne (riv.) C 3
Penmarch (pt.) A 4
Perche (reg.) D 3
Puy-de-Dôme (mt.) E 5
Pyrenees (range) C 6
Ré (isl.) C 4
Rhine (riv.) G 3
Rhône (riv.) F 5
Risle (riv.) D 3
Riviera (reg.) G 6
Saar (riv.) G 3
Saint-Florent (gulf) B 6
Saint-Malo (gulf) B 3
Saône (riv.) F 4
Sarthe (riv.) D 4
Sein (isl.) 504 A 3
Seine (bay) C 3
Seine (riv.) D 3
Sologne (reg.) E 4
Somme (riv.) D 2
Tarn (riv.) E 6
Ushant (isl.) 1,255 A 3
Utah (beach) C 3
Vaccarès (lag.) F 6
Vienne (riv.) D 4
Vilaine (riv.) C 4
Vosges (mt.) G 3
Yonne (riv.) E 3

Monaco

CITIES and TOWNS

Monte Carlo (cap.) 13,154 G 6

* City and Suburbs.

MONACO
368 acres
(149 hectares)
27,063

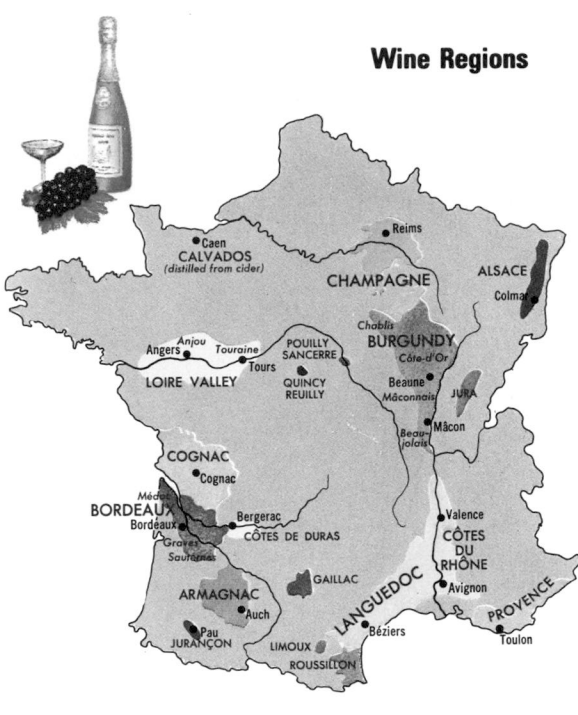

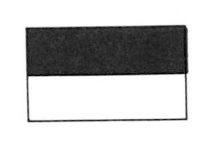

Wine Regions

Climate, soil and variety of grape planted determine the quality of wine. Long, hot and fairly dry summers with cool, humid nights constitute an ideal climate. The nature of the soil is such a determining influence that identical grapes planted in Bordeaux, Burgundy and Champagne, will yield wines of widely different types.

Agriculture, Industry and Resources

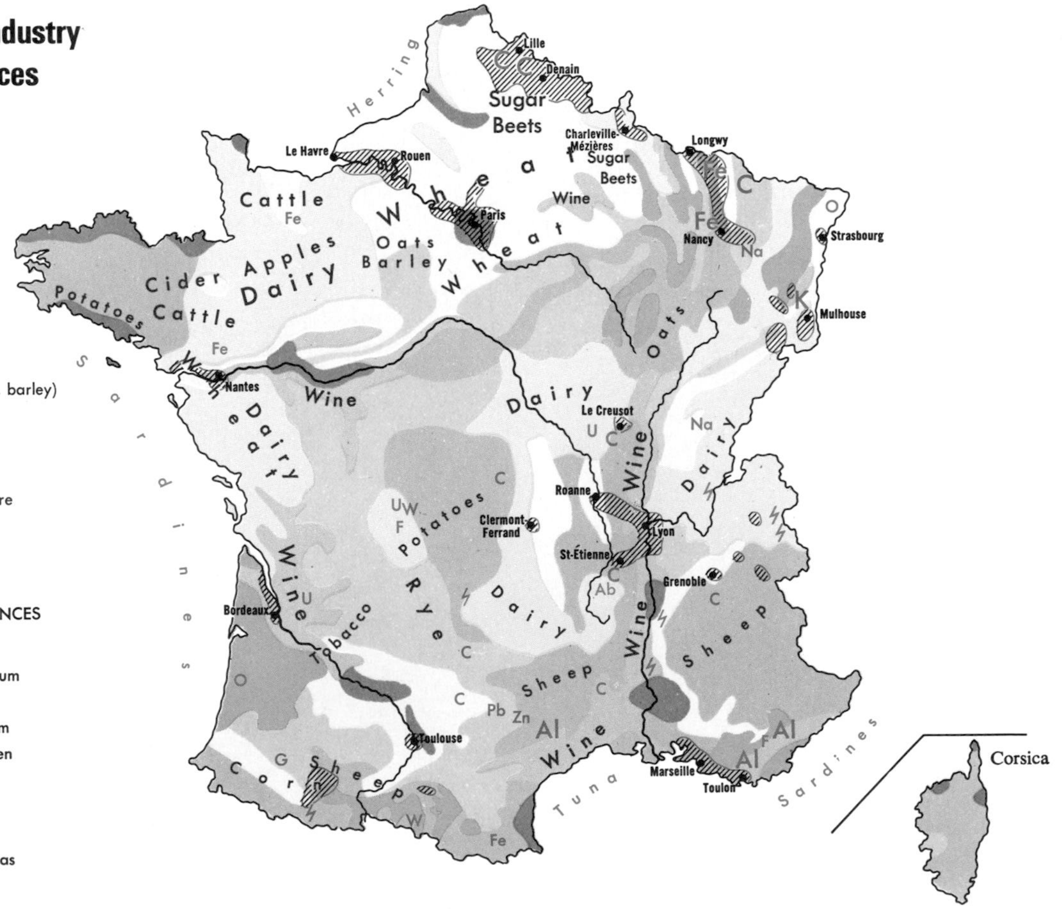

DOMINANT LAND USE

- Cereals (chiefly wheat)
- Cereals (chiefly rye, oats, barley)
- Dairy
- Pasture Livestock
- Truck Farming, Horticulture
- Grapes, Wine
- Forests

MAJOR MINERAL OCCURRENCES

Ab	Asbestos	Na	Salt
Al	Bauxite	O	Petroleum
C	Coal	Pb	Lead
F	Fluorspar	U	Uranium
Fe	Iron Ore	W	Tungsten
G	Natural Gas	Zn	Zinc
K	Potash		

Water Power
Major Industrial Areas

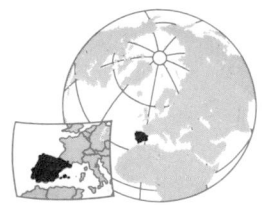

ANDORRA   **SPAIN**   **PORTUGAL**

(continued on following page)

Agriculture, Industry and Resources

DOMINANT LAND USE

- Cereals (chiefly wheat)
- Livestock (chiefly sheep, goats)
- Mixed Cereals, Livestock
- Olives, Fruit
- Grapes, Fruit, Nuts, Mixed Cereals
- Forests
- Nonagricultural Land

MAJOR MINERAL OCCURRENCES

Ag	Silver		Na	Salt
C	Coal		O	Petroleum
Cu	Copper		Pb	Lead
Fe	Iron Ore		Py	Pyrites
G	Natural Gas		Sb	Antimony
Hg	Mercury		Sn	Tin
K	Potash		U	Uranium
Lg	Lignite		W	Tungsten
Mg	Magnesium		Zn	Zinc

⚡ Water Power

▨ Major Industrial Areas

(continued on following page)

Topography

0   50   100 MI.

0   50   100 KM.

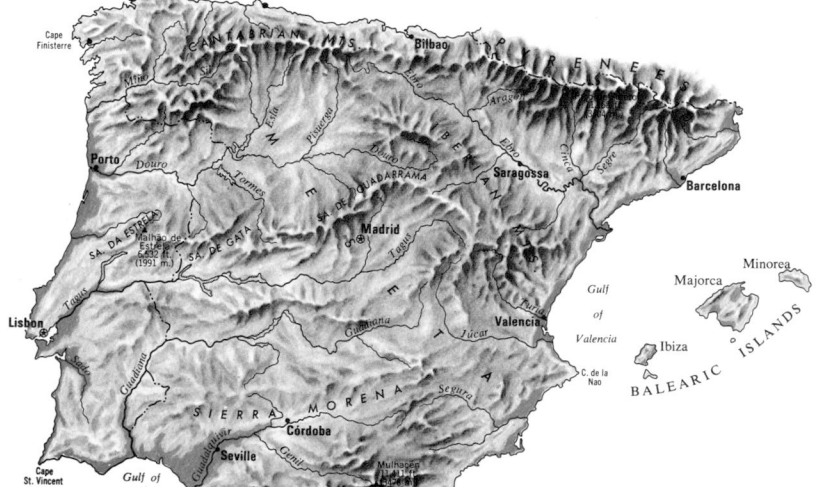

Below Sea Level | 100 m. 328 ft. | 200 m. 656 ft. | 500 m. 1,640 ft. | 1,000 m. 3,281 ft. | 2,000 m. 6,562 ft. | 5,000 m. 16,404 ft.

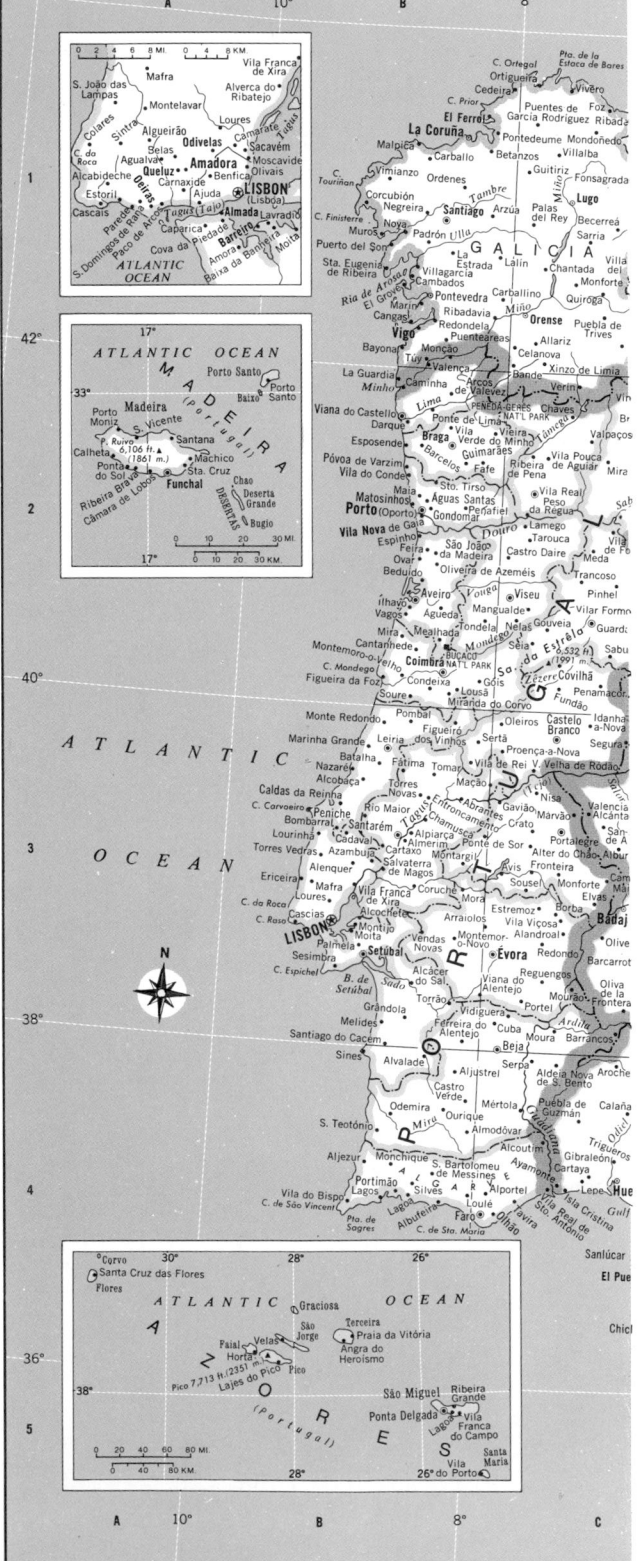

Baixa da Banheira 18,550 ....A1
Barreiro 53,690 ....A1
Beja 14,760 ....C3
Belas 12,001 ....A1
Benfica 39,459 ....A1
Braga 48,735 ....B2
Bragança 9,310 ....C2
Caldas da Rainha 13,070 ....B3
Câmara de Lobos 14,068 ....A2
Caparica 13,315 ....A1
Carnaxide 38,309 ....A1
Cascais 14,925 ....A1
Castelo Branco 18,740 ....C3
Chaves 11,465 ....C2
Coimbra 55,985 ....B2
Coruche 17,461 ....B3
Cova da Piedade 21,000 ....A1
Covilhã 26,530 ....C2
Elvas 10,305 ....C3
Espinho 11,745 ....B2
Estoril 15,740 ....A1

Évora 23,665 ....C3
Fafe 8,142 ....B2
Faro 20,470 ....B4
Figueira da Foz 10,485 ....B2
Funchal 38,340 ....A2
Gondomar 14,105 ....B2
Grândola 9,698 ....B3
Guarda 9,735 ....C2
Guimarães 24,280 ....B2
Ilhavo 11,083 ....B2
Lagos 10,359 ....B4
Lamego 10,350 ....C2
Lisbon (Lisboa) (cap.)
    769,410 ....A1
Lisbon‡ 1,100,000 ....A1
Loulé 12,777 ....B4
Machico 10,905 ....A2
Marinha Grande 18,548 ....B3
Matosinhos 22,505 ....B2
Mira 12,740 ....B2
Monchique 8,155 ....B4

Montemor-o-Novo 9,284 ....B3
Montijo 26,730 ....B3
Moscavide 21,765 ....A1
Moura 9,351 ....C3
Nazaré 8,553 ....B3
Odivelas 26,020 ....A1
Oeiras 14,880 ....A1
Olhão 11,155 ....C4
Olivais 55,138 ....A1
Oporto (Porto) 300,925 ....B2
Ovar 16,004 ....B2
Paço de Arcos 11,791 ....A1
Peniche 12,555 ....B3
Pombal 12,508 ....B3
Ponta Delgada 20,195 ....B5
Ponte de Sor 9,951 ....B3
Portalegre 10,970 ....C3
Portimão 10,300 ....B4
Porto 300,925 ....B2
Póvoa de Varzim 17,415 ....B2
Queluz 25,845 ....A1

Rio Maior 10,206 ....B3
Sacavém 12,625 ....A1
Santarém 16,850 ....B3
São Brás de Alportel (Alportel)
    7,632 ....B4
São João da Madeira 14,225 ....B2
Sesimbra 16,614 ....B3
Setúbal 49,670 ....B3
Silves 9,493 ....B4
Sintra 15,994 ....A1
Tavira 10,263 ....C4
Tomar 10,905 ....B3
Torres Novas 13,806 ....B3
Torres Vedras 14,833 ....B3
Vendas Novas 8,979 ....B3
Viana do Castelo 12,510 ....B2
Vila do Conde 16,485 ....B2
Vila do Porto 4,149 ....B5
Vila Franca de Xira 13,070 ....B3
Vila Nova de Foz Côa 2,439 ....C2
Vila Nova de Gaia 50,805 ....B2

Vila Real 10,050 ....C2
Vila Real de Santo António
    10,320 ....C4
Vila Velha de Ródão
    2,658 ....C3
Viseu 16,140 ....C2

OTHER FEATURES

Algarve (reg.) B4
Atlantic Ocean A3
Azores (isls.) B5
Baixo (isl.) A2
Bugio (isl.) A1
Carvoeiro (cape) B3
Chao (isl.) A2
Corvo (isl.) A4
Deserta Grande (isl.) A2
Desertas (isls.) A2
Douro (riv.) B2
Espichel (cape) B3

Estrela, Serra da (mts.) C2
Faial (isl.) B4
Flores (isl.) A4
Graciosa (isl.) B4
Guadiana (riv.) C4
Lima (riv.) B2
Madeira (isl.) A2
Minho (riv.) B2
Mira (riv.) B4
Mondego (riv.) B2
Mondego (cape) B2
Pico (isl.) B4
Porto Santo (isl.) B3
Roca (cape) A3
Sado (riv.) B3
Santa Maria (cape) C4
Santa Maria (isl.) C5
São Jorge (isl.) B4
São Miguel (isl.) B5
São Vincent (cape) B4
Setúbal (bay) B3

Tagus (riv.) B3
Tâmega (riv.) C2
Terceira (isl.) B4

ANDORRA

CITIES and TOWNS

Andorra la Vella (cap.) 12,000 G1

GIBRALTAR

CITIES and TOWNS

Gibraltar 31,000 ....D4

OTHER FEATURES

Europa (pt.) D4

‡Population of metropolitan area

VATICAN CITY

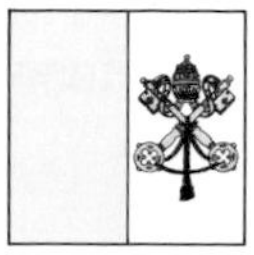

AREA 108.7 acres (44 hectares)
POPULATION 1,000

SAN MARINO

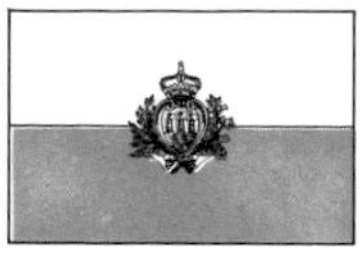

AREA 23.4 sq. mi. (60.6 sq. km.)
POPULATION 23,000

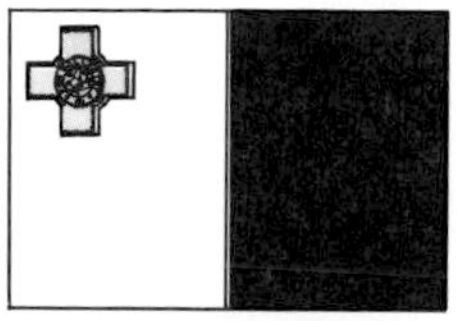

MALTA

AREA 122 sq. mi. (316 sq. km.)
POPULATION 353,000
CAPITAL Valletta
LARGEST CITY Sliema
HIGHEST POINT 787 ft. (240 m.)
MONETARY UNIT Maltese lira
MAJOR LANGUAGES Maltese, English
MAJOR RELIGION Roman Catholicism

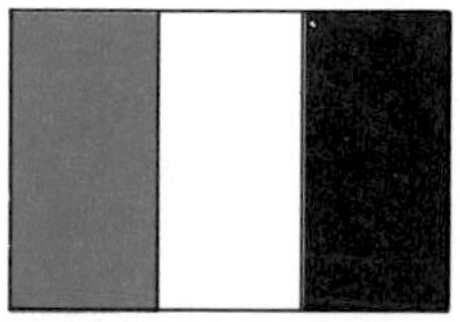

ITALY

AREA 116,303 sq. mi. (301,225 sq. km.)
POPULATION 57,574,000
CAPITAL Rome
LARGEST CITY Rome
HIGHEST POINT Dufourspitze (Mte. Rosa) 15,203 ft. (4,634 m.)
MONETARY UNIT lira
MAJOR LANGUAGE Italian
MAJOR RELIGION Roman Catholicism

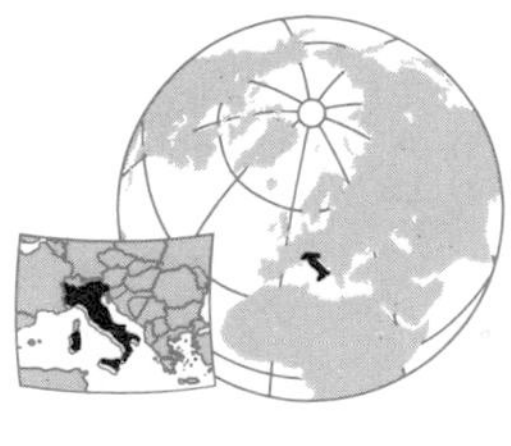

ITALY

REGIONS

Abruzzi 1,217,791 ... D3
Aosta 112,353 ... A2
Apulia (Puglia) 3,871,617 ... F4
Basilicata 610,186 ... F4
Calabria 2,061,182 ... F5
Campania 5,463,134 ... E4
Emilia-Romagna 3,957,513 ... C2
Friuli-Venezia Giulia 1,233,984 ... D1
Latium (Lazio) 5,001,684 ... D3
Liguria 1,807,893 ... B2
Lombardy 8,891,652 ... B2
Marche 1,412,404 ... D3
Molise 328,371 ... E4
Piedmont 4,479,031 ... A2
Sardinia 1,594,175 ... B4
Sicily 4,906,878 ... D6
Trentino-Alto Adige 873,413 ... C1
Tuscany 3,581,051 ... C3
Umbria 807,552 ... D3
Veneto 4,345,047 ... C2

PROVINCES

Agrigento 466,495 ... D6
Alessandria 466,102 ... B2
Ancona 433,417 ... D3
Arezzo 313,157 ... C3
Ascoli Piceno 352,567 ... D3
Asti 215,382 ... B2
Avellino 434,021 ... E4
Bari 1,464,627 ... F4
Belluno 220,335 ... D1
Benevento 289,143 ... E4
Bergamo 896,117 ... B2
Bologna 930,284 ... C2
Bolzano-Bozen 430,568 ... C1
Brescia 1,017,093 ... C2
Brindisi 391,064 ... G4
Cagliari 730,473 ... B5
Caltanissetta 285,829 ... D6
Campobasso 235,847 ... E4
Caserta 755,628 ... E4
Catania 1,005,577 ... E6
Catanzaro 744,834 ... F5
Chieti 370,534 ... E3
Como 755,979 ... B2
Cosenza 743,255 ... F5
Cremona 332,236 ... B2
Cuneo 548,452 ... A2
Enna 190,939 ... E6
Ferrara 381,118 ... C2
Florence 1,202,013 ... C3
Foggia 681,595 ... E4
Forlì 599,420 ... D2
Frosinone 460,395 ... D4
Genoa 1,045,109 ... B2
Gorizia 144,726 ... D2
Grosseto 220,905 ... C3
Imperia 223,738 ... B3
Isernia 92,524 ... E4
L'Aquila 291,742 ... D3
La Spezia 241,371 ... B2
Latina 434,086 ... D4
Lecce 762,017 ... G4
Livorno (Leghorn) 346,657 ... C3
Lucca 385,876 ... C3
Macerata 292,932 ... D3
Mantua 377,158 ... C2
Massa-Carrara 203,530 ... C2
Matera 203,570 ... F4
Messina 669,323 ... E5
Milan 4,018,108 ... B2
Modena 596,025 ... C2
Naples 2,970,563 ... E4
Novara 507,367 ... B2
Nuoro 274,817 ... B4
Padua 809,667 ... C2
Palermo 1,198,575 ... D5
Parma 400,192 ... C2
Pavia 512,895 ... B2
Perugia 580,988 ... D3
Pesaro e Urbino 333,488 ... D3
Pescara 286,240 ... E3
Piacenza 278,424 ... B2
Pisa 388,800 ... C3
Pistoia 264,995 ... C3
Pordenone 275,888 ... D2
Potenza 406,616 ... E4
Ragusa 274,583 ... E6
Ravenna 358,654 ... D2
Reggio di Calabria 573,093 ... E5
Reggio nell'Emilia 413,396 ... C2
Rieti 142,794 ... D3
Rome 3,695,961 ... F6
Rovigo 253,508 ... C2
Salerno 1,013,779 ... E4
Sassari 433,842 ... B4
Savona 297,675 ... B2
Siena 255,118 ... C3
Sondrio 174,009 ... B1
Syracuse 394,692 ... E6
Taranto 572,314 ... F4
Teramo 269,275 ... D3
Terni 807,552 ... D3
Trapani 420,865 ... D5
Trento 442,845 ... C1
Treviso 720,580 ... D2
Trieste 283,641 ... D2
Turin 2,345,771 ... A2
Udine 529,729 ... D1
Varese 788,057 ... B2
Venice 838,794 ... D2
Vercelli 395,957 ... B2
Verona 775,745 ... C2
Vicenza 726,418 ... C2
Viterbo 268,448 ... C3

CITIES and TOWNS

Acireale 46,711 ... E6
Acqui Terme 20,951 ... B2
Adrano 32,865 ... E6
Agrigento 38,681 ... D6
Alba 25,853 ... B2
Albano Laziale 27,796 ... F7
Alcamo 41,626 ... D6
Alessandria 79,552 ... B2
Alghero 32,519 ... B4
Altamura 50,539 ... F4
Amalfi 4,423 ... E4
Ancona 97,118 ... D3
Andria 84,070 ... F4
Anzio 25,932 ... D4
Aosta 36,649 ... A2
Aprilia 31,604 ... D4
Arezzo 74,477 ... C3
Ascoli Piceno 44,411 ... D3
Assisi 4,683 ... D3
Asti 65,483 ... B2
Augusta 37,162 ... E6
Avellino 50,894 ... E4
Aversa 55,788 ... E4
Avezzano 30,227 ... D3
Avola 30,360 ... E6
Bagheria 39,869 ... D5
Barcellona Pozzo di Gotto 33,404 ... E5
Bari 369,444 ... F4
Barletta 82,290 ... F4
Bassano del Grappa 33,724 ... C2
Belluno 28,468 ... D1
Benevento 51,831 ... E4
Bergamo 121,389 ... B2
Biancavilla 20,047 ... E6
Biella 52,587 ... B2
Bisceglie 46,209 ... F4
Bitonto 46,538 ... F4
Bologna 454,897 ... C2
Bolzano (Bolzen) 103,241 ... C1
Borgomanero 18,701 ... B2
Bra 21,304 ... A2
Brescia 202,539 ... C2
Brindisi 84,887 ... G4
Bronte 17,477 ... E6
Busto Arsizio 79,321 ... B2
Cagliari 219,423 ... B5
Caltagirone 32,860 ... E6
Caltanissetta 57,704 ... D6
Camaiore 24,284 ... C3
Campobasso 41,687 ... E4
Canicatti 31,726 ... D6
Canosa di Puglia 30,555 ... E4
Cantù 35,644 ... B2
Capannori 39,717 ... C3
Carbonia 25,140 ... B5
Carmagnola 19,581 ... A2
Carpi 49,370 ... C2
Carrara 61,709 ... C2
Casale Monferrato 37,157 ... B2
Cascina-Navacchio 32,570 ... C3
Caserta 59,185 ... E4
Cassino 22,406 ... D4
Castel Gandolfo 6,176 ... F7
Castelfranco Veneto 20,196 ... D2
Castellammare di Stabia 70,507 ... E4
Castelvetrano 29,503 ... D6
Castrovillari 18,648 ... F5
Catania 379,754 ... E6
Catanzaro 96,930 ... F5
Cava de'Tirreni 47,007 ... E4
Cecina 22,264 ... C3
Ceglie Messapico 17,915 ... F4
Cerignola 48,105 ... E4
Cesena 72,145 ... D2
Cesenatico 15,634 ... D2
Chiavari 29,171 ... B2
Chieri 28,296 ... A2
Chieti 49,267 ... E3
Chioggia 46,728 ... D2
Chivasso 22,230 ... A2
Ciampino 31,981 ... F7
Città di Castello 21,492 ... C3
Civitavecchia 46,465 ... C3
Comiso 25,469 ... E6
Como 94,167 ... B2
Conegliano 32,406 ... D2
Conversano 18,518 ... F4
Corato 41,078 ... F4
Cosenza 101,144 ... F5
Crema 33,901 ... B2
Cremona 74,341 ... B2
Crotone 51,204 ... F5
Cuneo 47,836 ... A2
Desenzano del Garda 17,296 ... C2
Domodossola 19,825 ... A1
Eboli 24,152 ... E4
Empoli 34,066 ... C3
Enna 26,760 ... E6
Fabriano 21,155 ... D3
Faenza 40,635 ... D2
Fano 42,440 ... D3
Fasano 22,918 ... F4
Favara 30,031 ... D6
Fermo 17,603 ... D3
Ferrara 117,590 ... C2
Fidenza 19,482 ... B2
Fiesole 3,711 ... C3
Firenze (Florence) 442,721 ... C3
Fiumicino 21,167 ... F7
Florence 442,721 ... C3
Floridia 17,790 ... E6
Foggia 150,480 ... E4
Foligno 41,696 ... D3
Fondi 19,580 ... D4
Forlì 91,366 ... D2
Formia 29,147 ... D4
Fossano 17,116 ... A2
Francavilla Fontana 31,371 ... F4
Frascati 18,356 ... F7
Frosinone 42,626 ... D4
Gaeta 23,190 ... D4
Galatina 22,611 ... G4
Gallarate 47,259 ... B2
Gela 74,077 ... E6
Genoa 755,389 ... B2
Genova (Genoa) 787,011 ... B2
Giarre 23,377 ... E6
Gioia del Colle 23,868 ... F4
Giovinazzo 18,832 ... F4
Giulianova 20,189 ... E3
Gorizia 40,679 ... D2
Gravina in Puglia 35,891 ... F4
Grosseto 55,569 ... C3
Grottaglie 27,140 ... F4
Iglesias 26,313 ... B5
Imola 47,365 ... C2
Imperia 39,151 ... B3
Isernia 16,919 ... E4
Ivrea 26,446 ... B2
Jesi 37,075 ... D3
L'Aquila 40,467 ... D3
La Spezia 110,632 ... B2
Lanciano 25,828 ... E3
Latina 64,529 ... D4
Lecce 80,127 ... G4
Lecco 51,160 ... B2
Leghorn (Livorno) 171,811 ... C3
Legnago 23,232 ... C2
Lentini 30,950 ... E6
Leonforte 15,745 ... E6
Licata 40,309 ... D6
Lido di Ostia 85,043 ... F7
Lido di Venezia 20,863 ... D2
Livorno 171,811 ... C3
Lodi 41,338 ... B2
Lucca 84,836 ... C3
Lucera 31,252 ... E4
Lugo 21,593 ... D2
Macerata 34,409 ... D3
Manduria 28,112 ... F4
Manfredonia 52,162 ... F4
Mantua 52,477 ... C2
Marino 30,261 ... F7
Marsala 76,843 ... D6
Martina Franca 34,911 ... F4
Massa 60,810 ... C2
Massafra 26,172 ... F4
Matera 48,226 ... F4
Mazara del Vallo 42,320 ... D6
Merano 31,854 ... C1
Mesagne 29,770 ... G4
Messina 240,121 ... E5
Mestre 197,952 ... D2
Milan 1,601,797 ... B2
Milazzo 29,868 ... E5
Minturno 15,795 ... D4
Mira Taglio 26,031 ... D2
Modena 164,529 ... C2
Modica 34,488 ... E6
Mola di Bari 25,744 ... F4
Molfetta 64,738 ... F4
Moncalieri 59,344 ... A2
Monfalcone 29,960 ... D2
Monopoli 33,928 ... F4
Monreale 18,168 ... D5
Monte Sant'Angelo 16,491 ... F4
Montebelluna 19,708 ... D2
Monterotondo 25,383 ... F6
Montevarchi 17,110 ... C3
Monza 122,541 ... B2
Naples 1,210,365 ... E4
Nardò 27,384 ... F4
Nettuno 27,929 ... D4
Nicastro-Sambiase 49,325 ... F5
Niscemi 25,677 ... E6
Nocera Inferiore 43,879 ... E4
Noto 20,609 ... E6
Novara 94,477 ... B2
Novi Ligure 28,756 ... B2
Nuoro 35,491 ... B4
Olbia 26,702 ... B4
Oristano 23,938 ... B5
Orvieto 7,509 ... D3
Ostia Antica 3,939 ... F7
Ostuni 27,948 ... F4
Otranto 4,334 ... G4
Pachino 20,631 ... E6
Padua 228,333 ... C2
Palermo 698,481 ... D5
Palma di Montechiaro 23,918 ... D6
Palmi 16,394 ... E5
Pantelleria 3,454 ... C6
Parma 160,374 ... C2
Partinico 27,479 ... D6
Paterno 42,916 ... E6
Pavia 82,629 ... B2
Perugia 103,542 ... D3
Pesaro 78,550 ... D3
Pescara 131,016 ... E3
Piacenza 103,584 ... B2
Piazza Armerina 20,119 ... E6
Pietrasanta 20,404 ... B3
Pinerolo 33,176 ... A2
Piombino 35,312 ... C3
Pisa 95,015 ... C3
Pistoia 78,105 ... C3
Poggibonsi 22,644 ... C3
Pomezia 19,453 ... F7
Pordenone 51,270 ... D2
Porto Empedocle 16,126 ... D6
Porto Torres 20,233 ... B4
Portocivitanova 28,155 ... D3
Portoferraio 8,108 ... C3
Portofino 615 ... B2
Potenza 55,175 ... E4
Pozzuoli 61,856 ... D4
Prato 156,894 ... C3
Putignano 22,361 ... F4
Quartu Sant'Elena 40,506 ... B5
Ragusa 60,871 ... E6
Rapallo 26,457 ... B2
Ravenna 87,582 ... D2
Reggio di Calabria 159,416 ... E5
Reggio nell'Emilia 107,484 ... C2
Rho 50,373 ... B2
Rieti 33,614 ... D3
Rimini 111,991 ... D2
Rome (cap.) 2,605,441 ... F6
Rovereto 31,286 ... C2
Rovigo 41,050 ... C2
Ruvo di Puglia 23,510 ... F4
Salerno 150,252 ... E4
Saluzzo 13,078 ... A2
San Benedetto del Tronto 43,189 ... E3
San Cataldo 20,694 ... D6
San Giovanni in Fiore 19,391 ... F5
Sannicandro Garganico 18,652 ... E4
San Remo 59,872 ... A3
San Severo 53,948 ... E4
Santa Maria Capua Vetere 32,129 ... E4
Santeramo in Colle 21,154 ... F4
San Vito dei Normanni 18,366 ... F4
Saronno 36,732 ... B2
Sassari 104,334 ... B4
Sassuolo 37,515 ... C2
Savona 65,040 ... B2
Schio 30,738 ... C2
Sciacca 35,063 ... D6
Scicli 18,419 ... E6
Senigallia 27,474 ... D3
Sesto Fiorentino 43,307 ... C3
Sestri Levante 19,672 ... B2
Siena 54,982 ... C3
Siracusa (Syracuse) 109,038 ... E6
Sondrio 19,955 ... B1
Sora 20,380 ... D4
Sorrento 15,747 ... E4
Spoleto 21,625 ... D3
Stresa 4,290 ... B2
Sulmona 21,504 ... D3
Syracuse 109,038 ... E6
Taranto 231,441 ... F4
Teramo 35,142 ... D3
Termini Imerese 24,252 ... D6

(continued on following page)

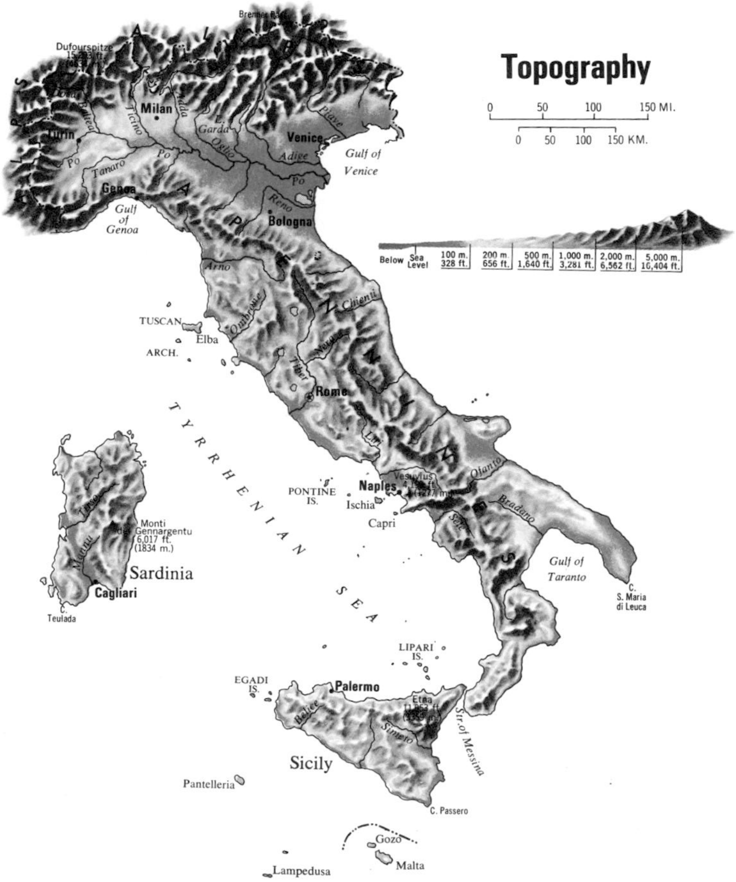
Topography
0 50 100 150 MI.
0 50 100 150 KM.
Below Sea Level
100 m. 328 ft.
200 m. 656 ft.
500 m. 1,640 ft.
1,000 m. 3,281 ft.
2,000 m. 6,562 ft.
5,000 m. 16,404 ft.
Dufourspitze
Milan
Turin
Venice
Gulf of Venice
Genoa
Gulf of Genoa
Bologna
Po
Adige
Piave
Ticino
Tanaro
Reno
Arno
Garda
TUSCAN ARCH.
Elba
Rome
T Y R R H E N I A N S E A
PONTINE IS.
Ischia
Capri
Naples
Vesuvius
Gulf of Taranto
C. S. Maria di Leuca
Sardinia
Monti Gennargentu 6,017 ft. (1834 m.)
Cagliari
Teulada
LIPARI IS.
EGADI IS.
Palermo
Etna
Str. of Messina
Sicily
C. Passero
Pantelleria
Gozo
Malta
Lampedusa

Agriculture, Industry and Resources

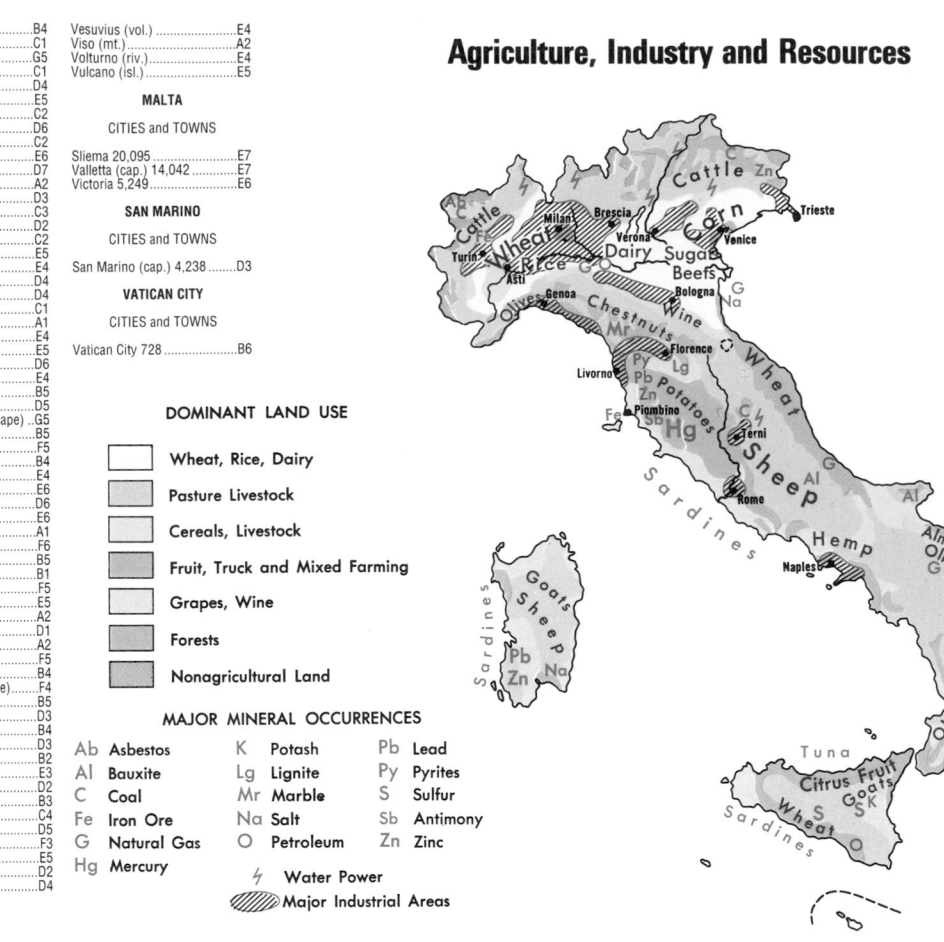

DOMINANT LAND USE

- Wheat, Rice, Dairy
- Pasture Livestock
- Cereals, Livestock
- Fruit, Truck and Mixed Farming
- Grapes, Wine
- Forests
- Nonagricultural Land

MAJOR MINERAL OCCURRENCES

Ab Asbestos
Al Bauxite
C   Coal
Fe Iron Ore
G   Natural Gas
Hg Mercury
K   Potash
Lg Lignite
Mr Marble
Na Salt
O   Petroleum
Pb Lead
Py Pyrites
S   Sulfur
Sb Antimony
Zn Zinc

⚡ Water Power
▨ Major Industrial Areas

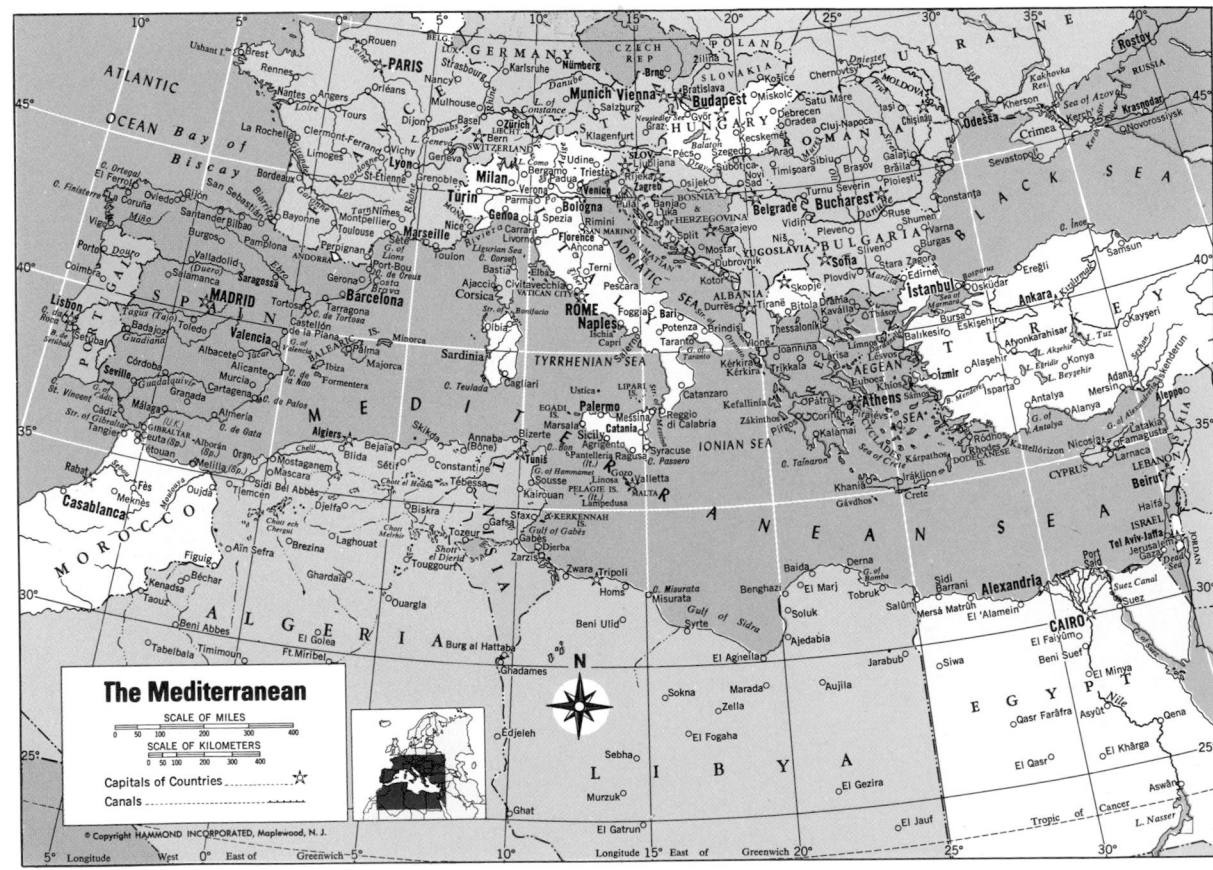

The Mediterranean

SCALE OF MILES
0 50 100   200   300   400

SCALE OF KILOMETERS
0 50 100   200   300   400

Capitals of Countries .... ☆
Canals ....

© Copyright HAMMOND INCORPORATED, Maplewood, N.J.

SWITZERLAND
AREA 15,943 sq. mi. (41,292 sq. km.)
POPULATION 6,647,000
CAPITAL Bern
LARGEST CITY Zürich
HIGHEST POINT Dufourspitze
    (Mte. Rosa) 15,203 ft. (4,634 m.)
MONETARY UNIT Swiss franc
MAJOR LANGUAGES German, French,
    Italian, Romansch
MAJOR RELIGIONS Protestantism,
    Roman Catholicism

LIECHTENSTEIN
AREA 61 sq. mi. (158 sq. km.)
POPULATION 28,000
CAPITAL Vaduz
LARGEST CITY Vaduz
HIGHEST POINT Grauspitze 8,527 ft.
    (2,599 m.)
MONETARY UNIT Swiss franc
MAJOR LANGUAGE German
MAJOR RELIGION Roman Catholicism

SWITZERLAND

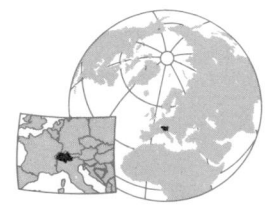

LIECHTENSTEIN

Languages

Basel
Zürich
St. Gallen
Biel
Lucerne
Chur
★ Bern
Fribourg
Lausanne
St. Moritz
Geneva
Sion
Bellinzona

- German
- French
- Italian
- Romansch

Switzerland is a multilingual nation with four official languages. 70% of the people speak German, 19% French, 10% Italian and 1% Romansch.

Agriculture, Industry and Resources

DOMINANT LAND USE
- Cereals, Dairy
- Pasture Livestock
- General Farming, Livestock
- Fruit, Truck, Mixed Farming
- Forests
- Nonagricultural Land

⚡ Water Power
▨ Major Industrial Areas

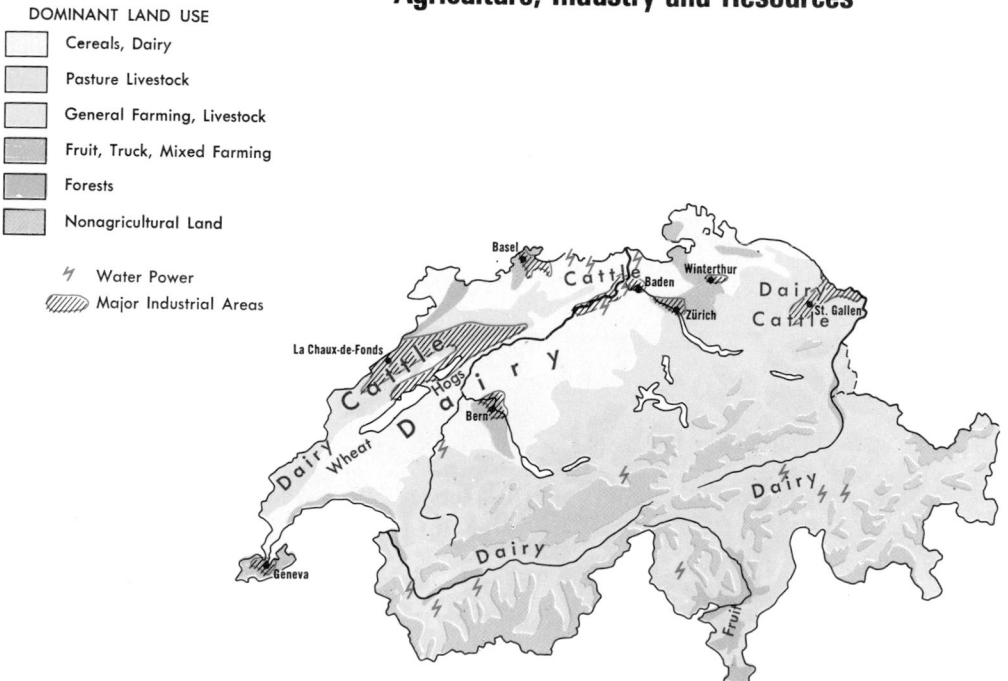

Basel
Winterthur
Baden
Cattle
Zürich
Dairy
Cattle
St. Gallen
La Chaux-de-Fonds
Cattle
Dairy
Hogs
Wheat
Bern
Dairy
Dairy
Dairy
Fruit
Geneva

SWITZERLAND

CANTONS

Aargau 453,442	F2
Appenzell, Ausser Rhoden 47,611	H2
Appenzell, Inner Rhoden 12,844	H2
Baselland 219,822	E2
Baselstadt 203,915	E1
Bern 912,022	D2
Fribourg 185,246	D3
Geneva (Genève) 349,040	B4
Glarus 36,718	H3
Graubünden (Grisons) 164,641	H3
Jura 64,986	D2
Lucerne (Luzern) 296,159	F2
Luzern 296,159	F2
Neuchâtel 158,368	C3
Nidwalden 28,617	F3
Obwalden 25,865	F3
Sankt Gallen 391,995	H2
Schaffhausen 69,413	G1
Schwyz 97,354	G2
Soleure (Solothurn) 218,102	E2
Solothurn 218,102	E2
Thurgau 183,795	H1
Ticino 265,899	G4
Uri 33,883	G3
Valais 218,707	D4
Vaud 520,747	B3

Zug 75,930	G2
Zürich 1,122,839	G2

CITIES and TOWNS

Aadorf 3,257	G2
Aarau 15,788	F2
Aarberg 3,212	D2
Aarburg 5,354	E2
Adelboden 3,276	C3
Adliswil 16,418	F2
Affoltern am Albis 8,064	F2
Aigle 6,233	C4
Allschwil 17,952	D1
Alpnach 3,556	F3
Altdorf 8,230	G3
Altstätten 9,260	J2
Amriswil 8,790	H1
Appenzell 4,781	H2
Arbedo-Castione 3,058	G4
Arbon 11,333	H1
Arosa 2,782	J3
Arth 7,795	F2
Ascona 4,722	G4
Au 5,434	J2
Avenches 2,177	D3
Baar 15,196	F2
Bad Ragaz 3,721	H2
Baden 13,870	F2
Balerna 3,455	G5
Balsthal 5,090	E2
Bäretswil 3,145	G2
Basel 182,143	E1

Basel 364,813	E1
Bassecourt 2,942	D2
Bauma 3,010	G2
Bellinzona 16,743	H4
Belp 7,578	D3
Bern (cap.) 145,254	D3
Bettlach 3,851	D2
Bex 4,843	D4
Biasca 5,447	H4
Biberist 7,519	D2
Biel 53,793	D2
Binningen 14,195	D1
Bischofszell 3,390	H1
Bolligen 32,312	E3
Boudry 4,488	C3
Breitenbach 2,518	E2
Bremgarten 4,815	F2
Brienz 2,759	F3
Brig 9,608	F4
Brittnau 2,822	E2
Brugg 5,911	F2
Bubikon 3,601	G2
Buchs 9,066	H2
Bülach 12,292	G1
Bulle 7,595	D3
Buochs 3,742	F3
Büren an der Aare 2,761	D2
Burgdorf 15,379	E2
Bürglen 3,456	G3
Bussigny-près-Lausanne 4,909	B3
Bütschwil 3,423	H2
Carouge 13,100	B4
Castagnola 4,430	G4
Cham 9,275	F2
Château-d'Oex 2,872	D4
Châtel-Saint-Denis 3,141	C3
Chêne-Bougeries 9,068	B4
Chiasso 8,583	G5
Chur 32,037	J3
Collombey-Muraz 2,982	C4
Collonge-Bellerive 4,531	B4
Conthey 4,828	D4
Courrendlin 2,435	D2
Couvet 2,627	C3
Davos 10,468	J3
Degersheim 3,269	H2
Delémont 11,682	D2
Derendingen 4,675	E2
Dielsdorf 3,767	F1
Diepoldsau 3,562	J2
Diessenhofen 2,535	G1
Dietikon 21,765	F2
Disentis-Mustér 2,320	G3
Domat-Ems 6,266	H3
Dornach 5,442	E2
Döttingen 3,264	F1
Dübendorf 20,683	G2
Düdingen 5,572	D3
Dürnten 4,927	G2
Ebnat-Kappel 4,950	H2
Echallens 2,163	C3
Ecublens 7,615	B3
Effretikon 14,788	G2
Egg 6,074	G2
Eggiwil 2,323	E3
Egnach 3,397	H1
Einsiedeln 9,629	G2
Elgg 3,041	G2
Emmen 22,392	F2
Engelberg 2,963	F3
Ennenda 2,512	H2
Entlebuch 3,238	F3
Erstfeld 4,158	G3
Eschenbach 3,661	G2
Escholzmatt 3,033	E3
Estavayer-le-Lac 3,662	C3
Feuerthalen 2,920	G1
Flawil 8,575	H2
Fleurier 3,573	C3
Flims 2,136	H3
Flums 4,228	H2
Frauenfeld 18,607	G1
Freienbach 9,912	G2
Fribourg 37,400	D3
Frick 3,116	E1
Frutigen 5,779	E3
Fully 3,926	D4
Gais 2,388	H2
Gelterkinden 4,954	E2

(continued on following page)

Topography

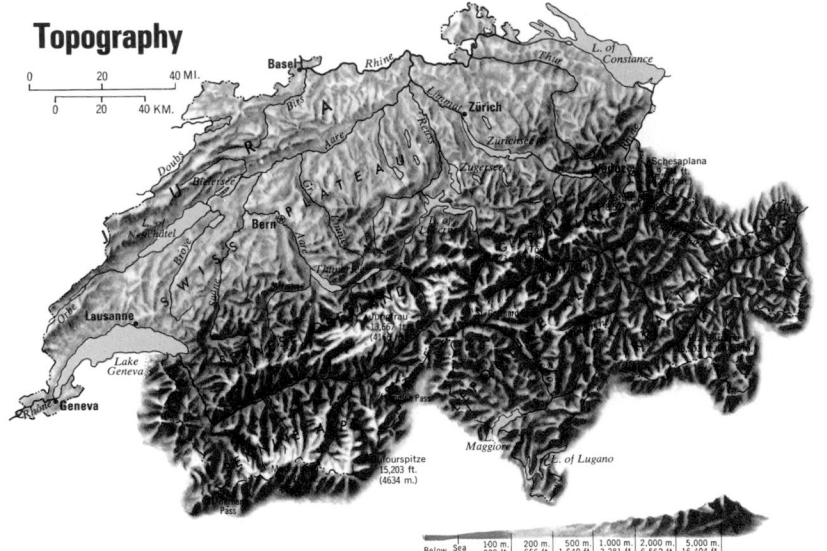

0   20   40 MI.

0   20   40 KM.

Below Sea Level | 100 m. 328 ft. | 200 m. 656 ft. | 500 m. 1,640 ft. | 1,000 m. 3,281 ft. | 2,000 m. 6,562 ft. | 5,000 m. 16,404 ft.

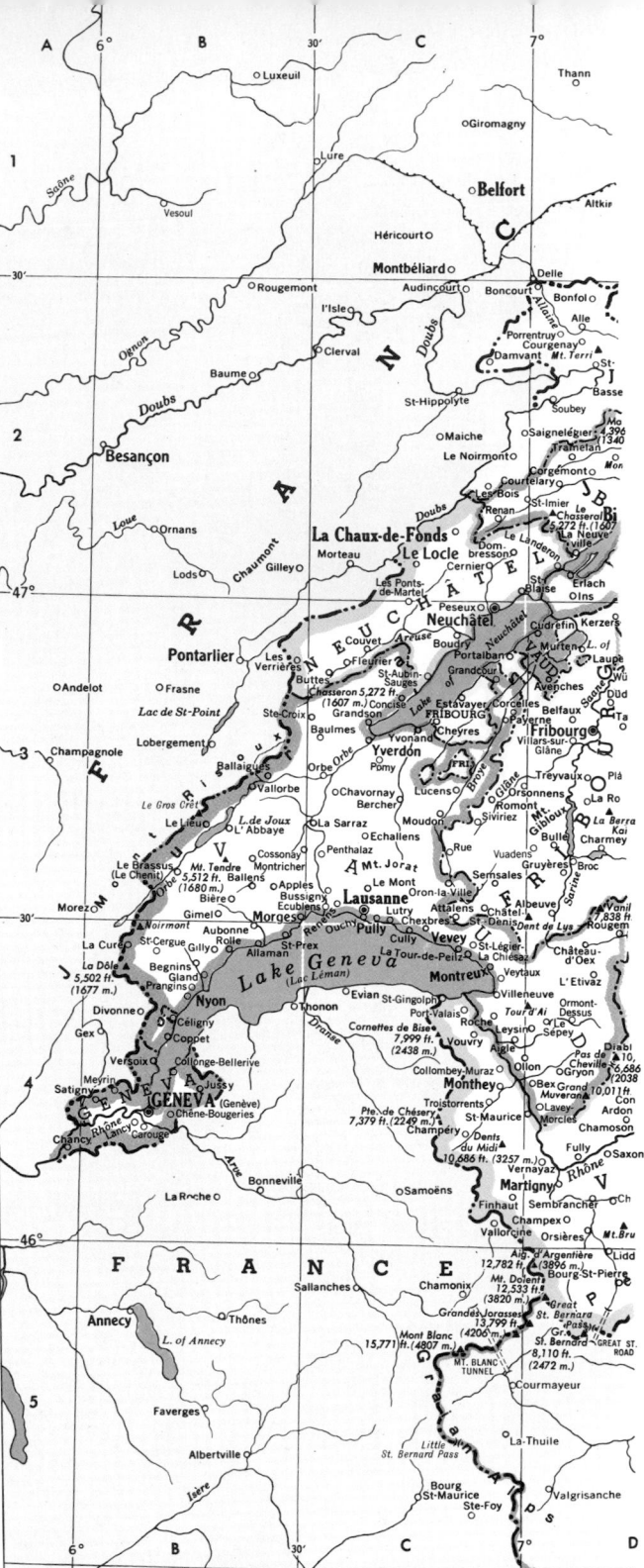

Geneva (Genève) 156,505......B4
Giswil 2,595 ....F3
Giubiasco 6,585.................H4
Gland 4,906 ....B4
Glarus 5,969....................H2
Glattfelden 2,753...............F1
Glis 3,389 ....E4
Gordola 2,956...................G4
Gossau 14,584 ....H2
Grabs 4,844 ....H2
Grenchen 16,800.................D2
Grindelwald 3,555 ....E3
Grosswangen 2,235..............F2
Gstaad D4
Heiden 3,620 ....H2
Heimberg 4,107..................E3
Hergiswil 4,254.................F3
Herisau 14,160 ....H2
Herzogenbuchsee 5,107..........E2
Hilterfingen 3,600..............E3
Hinwil 7,554....................G2
Hochdorf 6,034..................F2
Horgen 16,577...................G2
Huttwil 4,612...................F2
Igis 5,392......................J3
Ingenbohl 6,232.................F3
Ins 2,608.......................D2
Interlaken 4,852................E3
Jegenstorf 3,541................D2
Jona 12,156.....................G2
Kaltbrunn 2,735.................H2
Kerns 4,200.....................F3
Kerzers 4,053...................D3
Kirchberg, Bern 3,966...........E2
Kirchberg, St. Gallen 6,398.....G2
Klingnau 2,433..................F1
Klosters-Serneus 3,487..........J3
Kloten 15,845...................G2
Kölliken 3,080..................F2
Köniz 33,441....................D3
Konolfingen 4,360...............E3
Kreuzlingen 16,101..............H1
Kriens 21,097...................F2
Küsnacht 12,766.................G2
Küssnacht am Rigi 8,091.........F2
Küttigen 4,356..................F2
La Chaux-de-Fonds 37,234........C2
Lachen 5,352....................G2
Lancy 23,527....................B4
La Neuveville 3,519.............D2
Langenthal 13,408...............E2
Langnau am Albis 6,694..........G2
Langnau in Emmental 8,821.......E3
La Tour-de-Peilz 9,411..........C4
Laufen 4,444....................D2
Laupen 2,261....................D3
Lauperswil 2,482................E3
Lausanne 127,349................C4
Lauterbrunnen 3,077.............E3
Le Brassus 4,359................B3
Le Châble 4,541.................D4
Le Chenit (Le Brassus) 4,359....B3
Le Landeron 3,287...............C2
Le Locle 12,039.................C2
Le Mont-sur-Lausanne 3,664......C3
Lengnau 4,317...................D2
Lenk 2,089......................D4
Lens 2,412......................D4
Lenzburg 7,585..................F2
Leuk 2,983......................E4
Leukerbad 1,070.................E4
Liestal 12,158..................E2
Liestal-Sissach 40,800..........E2
Littau 14,996...................F2
Locarno 14,103..................G4
Lucerne 63,278..................F2
Lugano 27,815...................G4
Lutry 5,884.....................C3
Lützelflüh 3,770................E3
Luzern (Lucerne) 63,278.........F2
Lyss 8,723......................D2
Malters 4,900...................F2
Männedorf 7,833.................G2
Martigny 11,309.................C4

Meilen 10,430...................G2
Meiringen 4,072.................F3
Mellingen 3,285.................F2
Mels 6,235......................H2
Mendrisio 6,590.................G5
Menzingen 3,564.................G2
Menznau 2,248...................F2
Meyrin 18,808...................B4
Minusio 5,602...................G4
Möhlin 6,360....................E1
Mollis 2,621....................H2
Monthey 11,285..................C4
Montreux 19,685.................C4
Morges 13,057...................B3
Moudon 3,805....................C3
Moutier 7,959...................D2
Mümliswil-Ramiswil 2,386........E2
Münchenbuchsee 8,395............E2
Münsingen 9,340.................E3
Muotathal 2,896.................G3
Muri 5,399......................F2
Muri bei Bern 12,285............E3
Murten 4,558....................D3
Muttenz 16,911..................E1
Näfels 3,766....................H2
Naters 6,662....................E4
Nendaz 4,372....................D4
Netstal 2,642...................H2
Neuchâtel 34,428................C3
Neuenegg 3,727..................D3
Neuhausen am Rheinfall
   10,662........................G1
Niederbipp 3,165................E2
Niederurnen 3,438...............G2
Nyon 12,842.....................B4
Oberägeri 3,563.................G2
Oberburg 2,869..................E2
Oberdiessbach 2,319.............E3
Oberriet 6,222..................J2
Obersiggenthal 7,442............F1
Oberuzwil 4,616.................H2
Oensingen 3,543.................E2
Oftringen 9,006.................F2
Ollon 4,429.....................D4
Olten 18,991....................E2
Opfikon 11,444..................G2
Orbe 3,985......................C3
Orsières 2,357..................D4
Paradiso 3,261..................G5
Payerne 6,713...................C3
Peseux 5,212....................C3
Pfäffikon 8,306.................G2
Pfaffnau 2,453..................F2
Pieterlen 3,127.................D2
Porrentruy 7,039................C2
Poschiavo 3,294.................J4
Prangins 2,028..................B4
Pratteln 15,751.................E1
Pully 14,988....................C4
Rafz 2,325......................G1
Rapperswil 7,826................G2
Regensdorf 12,300...............F2
Reichenbach im Kandertal
   2,948.........................E3
Reiden 3,363....................F2
Reinach in Aargau 5,696.........F2
Reinach in Baselland 17,813.....E2
Renens 16,977...................C3
Rheineck 3,037..................J2
Rheinfelden 9,456...............E1
Richterswil 8,672...............G2
Riehen 20,611...................E1
Riggisberg 2,196................D3
Roggwil 3,333...................E2
Rolle 3,409.....................B4
Romanshorn 7,893................H1
Romont 3,495....................C3
Rorschach 9,878.................H2
Rothrist 5,619..................E2
Rüti, Zürich 9,331..............G2
Rumlang 5,055...................G2
Ruswil 4,870....................F2
Saanen 5,522....................D4
Sachseln 3,406..................F3

Saint-Blaise 2,788..............D2
Sainte-Croix 4,543..............B3
Saint-Imier 5,430...............D2
Saint-Légier-La Chiésaz 2,787...C4
Saint-Maurice 3,458.............C4
Saint Moritz 5,900..............J3
Saint Niklaus 2,036.............E4
Saint-Prex 2,937................B4
Samedan 2,553...................J3
Sankt Gallen 75,847.............H2
Sankt Margrethen 4,935..........J2
Sargans 4,267...................H2
Sarnen 7,372....................F3
Savièse 4,097...................D4
Saxon 2,394.....................D4
Schänis 2,426...................H2
Schaffhausen 34,250.............G1
Schattdorf 4,516................G3
Schiers 2,253...................J3
Schlieren 12,891................F2
Schönenwerd 4,746...............E2
Schübelbach 4,720...............G2
Schüpfheim 3,537................F3
Schwanden 2,519.................H2
Schwyz 12,100...................G2
Seon 3,826......................F2
Sempach 2,237...................F2
Seuzach 4,659...................G1
Sevelen 2,839...................H2
Sierre 13,050...................D4
Signau 2,606....................E3
Sigriswil 3,536.................E3
Silenen 2,115...................G3
Simplon 328.....................F4
Sins 2,625......................F2
Sion 22,877.....................D4
Sirnach 4,170...................G2
Sissach 4,564...................E2
Solothurn (Soleure) 15,778......E2
Spiez 9,800.....................E3
Stäfa 10,558....................G2
Stans 5,681.....................F3
Steckborn 3,232.................G1
Steffisburg 12,539..............E3
Stein am Rhein 2,507............G1
Suhr 7,366......................F2
Sumiswald 5,070.................E2
Sursee 7,645....................F2
Tafers 2,263....................D3
Tavannes 3,336..................D2
Teufen 5,027....................H2
Thal 4,725......................J2
Thalwil 15,412..................G2
Thayngen 3,751..................G1
Therwil 7,311...................E1
Thun 36,891.....................E3
Thunstetten 2,567...............E2
Thusis 2,525....................H3
Tramelan 4,733..................D2
Turbenthal 2,975................G2
Uetendorf 4,538.................E3
Unterägeri 5,371................G2
Unterkulm 2,558.................F2
Unterseen 4,568.................E3
Uster 23,702....................G2
Utzenstorf 3,141................E2
Uznach 4,269....................H2
Uzwil 9,614.....................H2
Vallorbe 3,375..................B3
Vechigen 4,036..................E3
Versoix 7,483...................B4
Vevey 16,139....................C4
Vevey-Montreux 60,558...........C4
Villars-sur-Glâne 5,788.........D3
Villeneuve 3,573................C4
Visp 6,383......................E4
Wädenswil 18,485................G2
Wahlern 5,104...................D3
Wald 7,447......................G2
Waldkirch 2,827.................H2
Walenstadt 3,605................H2
Wallisellen 10,887..............G2
Wartau 3,692....................H2

Wattwil 7,874...................H2
Weinfelden 8,793................H1
Wettingen 18,377................F2
Wetzikon 15,859.................G2
Wil 16,245......................H2
Willisau 2,639..................F2
Windisch 7,598..................F1
Winterthur 86,758...............G1
Wohlen 12,024...................F2
Wohlen 15,746...................D3
Wohlen bei Bern 7,666...........D3
Wohlusen 3,670..................F2
Worb 11,080.....................E3
Wünnewil 3,774..................D3
Yverdon 20,802..................C3
Zell 4,138......................G2
Zermatt 3,548...................E4
Zofingen 8,643..................E2
Zollikofen 8,717................D3
Zollikon 12,134.................G2
Zug 21,609......................G2
Zürich 369,522..................F2
Zurzach 3,068...................F1
Zweisimmen 2,852................D3

OTHER FEATURES

Aa (riv.).......................F3
Aare (riv.).....................E3
Ägerisee (lake).................G2
Aiguille d'Argentière (mt.).....C5
Albristhorn (mt.)...............D4
Aletschhorn (mt.)...............F4
Allaine (riv.)..................D2
Areuse (riv.)...................C3
Aroser Rothorn (mt.)............J3
Ault (peak).....................H3
Baldeggersee (lake).............F2
Balmhorn (mt.)..................E4
Bärenhorn (mt.).................H3
Basodino (peak).................G4
Bernese Oberland (reg.).........E3
Bernina (mts.)..................J4
Bernina (pass)..................K4
Bernina (peak)..................J4
Bernina (riv.)..................J4
Beverin (peak)..................H3
Bielersee (lake)................D2
Bietschhorn (mt.)...............E4
Birs (riv.).....................D2
Blas (peak).....................G3
Blinnenhorn (mt.)...............F4
Blümlisalp (mt.)................E4
Bodensee (Constance) (lake).....H1
Borgne (riv.)...................D4
Breithorn (mt.).................E5
Breithorn (mt.).................E4
Brienzer Rothorn (mt.)..........F3
Brienzersee (lake)..............F3
Broye (riv.)....................C3
Brule (riv.)....................D4
Buchegg (mts.)..................D2
Buin (peak).....................K3
Bürkelkopf (mt.)................K3
Bütschelegg (mt.)...............D3
Calancasca (riv.)...............G4
Campo Tencia (peak).............G4
Ceneri (pass)...................G4
Chasseron (mt.).................C3
Chéserg, Pointe de (mt.)........C4
Cheville (pass).................D4
Churfirsten (mts.)..............H2
Clariden (mt.)..................G3
Collon (mt.)....................D5
Constance (Bodensee) (lake).....H1
Cornettes de Bise (mts.)........C4
Dammastock (mt.)................F3
Davos (valley)..................J3
Dent Blanche (mt.)..............E4
Dent de Lys (mt.)...............D4
Dent de Morcles (mt.)...........D3
Dent de Ruth (mt.)..............D3
Dent d'Hérens (mt.).............D4
Dents du Midi (mt.).............C4
Diablerets (mt.)................D4

Doldenhorn (mt.)........E4
Dolent (mt.)............C5
Dom (mt.)...............E4
Doubs (riv.)............C2
Drance (riv.)...........D4
Dufourspitze (mt.)......E5
Emmental (riv.).........E3
Engadine (valley).......K3
Err (peak)..............J3
Finsteraarhorn (mt.)....F3
Finstermünz (pass)......K3
Fletschhorn (mt.).......F4
Fluchthorn (mt.)........K3
Flüela (pass)...........J3
Fluhberg (mt.)..........G2
Fort (mt.)..............D4
Frienisberg (mt.).......D2
Furka (pass)............F3
Gelgia (riv.)...........J3
Generoso (mt.)..........H5
Geneva (lake)...........G4
Giacomo (pass)..........G4

Gibloux (mt.)...........D3
Gläne (riv.)............D3
Glärnisch (mt.).........H2
Glarus Alps (mts.)......H3
Glatt (riv.)............G2
Goms (valley)...........F4
Grand Combin (mt.)......D4
Grand Muveran (mt.).....D4
Grande Dixence (dam)....D4
Grauehörner (mts.)......H3
Great Saint Bernard (mt.)....D5
Great Saint Bernard (pass)...D5
Great Saint Bernard (tunnel).D5
Greifensee (lake).......G2
Greina (pass)...........G4
Gridone (mt.)...........G4
Grimsel (pass)..........F3
Gross Emme (riv.).......E3
Gross Litzner (mt.).....K3
Hallwilersee (lake).....F2
Hausstock (mt.).........H3
Helsenhorn (mt.)........F4

Hinterrhein (riv.)......H3
Hochwang (mt.)..........J3
Hohenstollen (mt.)......F3
Honegg (mt.)............E3
Hörnli (mt.)............H2
Ilfis (riv.)............E3
Inn (riv.)..............K3
Joch (pass).............F3
Jorat (mt.).............C3
Joux (lake).............B3
Joux (pass).............B3
Jungfrau (mt.)..........E3
Jura (mts.).............B3
Kaiseregg (mt.).........D3
Kesch (peak)............J3
Kisten (pass)...........H3
Klausen (pass)..........G3
Kleine Emme (riv.)......F3
La Berra (mt.)..........D3
La Dôle (mt.)...........B4
Landquart (riv.)........J3
Le Chasseral (mt.)......D2
Le Gros Crêt (mt.)......B3

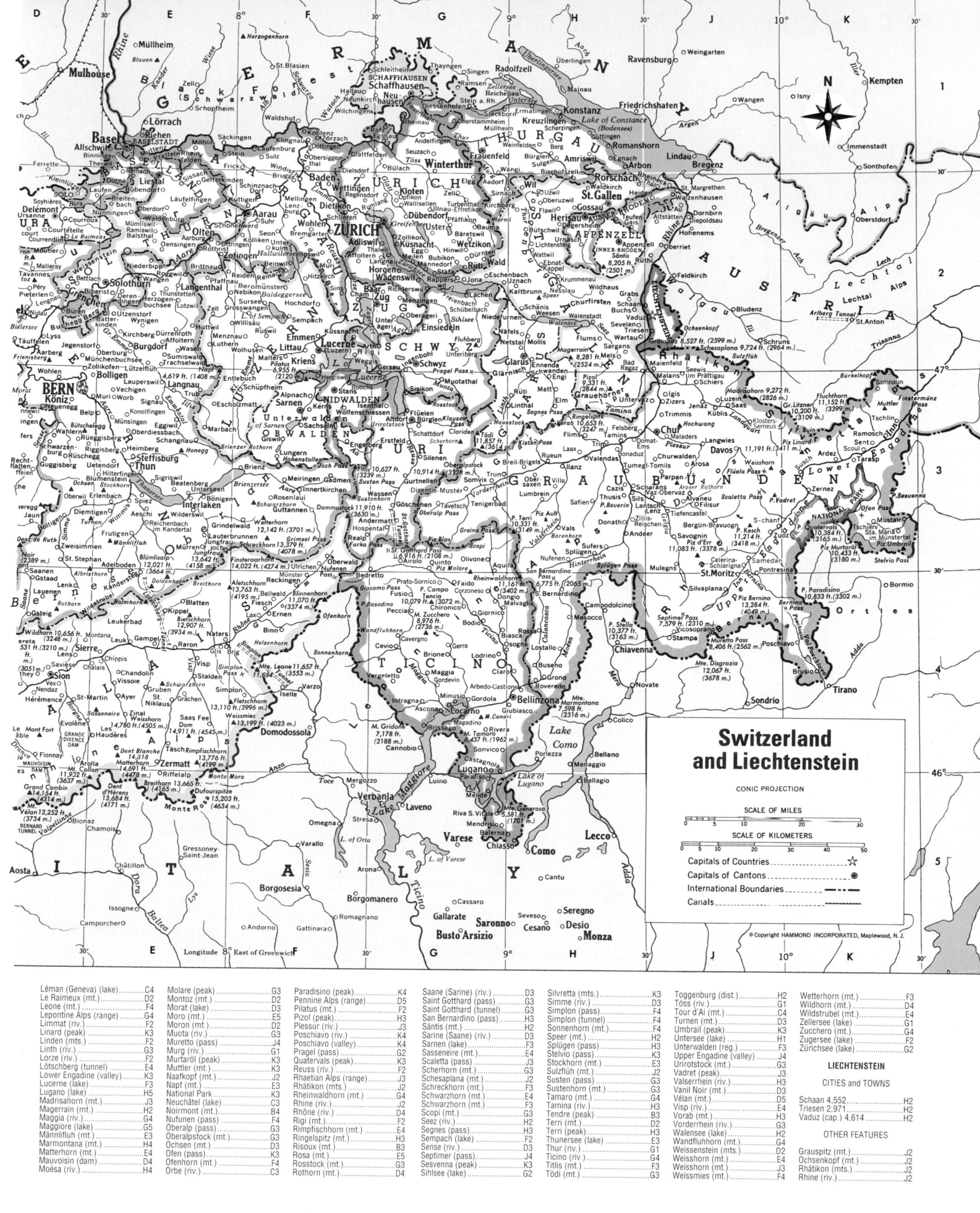

Switzerland and Liechtenstein

CONIC PROJECTION

SCALE OF MILES

SCALE OF KILOMETERS

Capitals of Countries .... ☆
Capitals of Cantons .... ◉
International Boundaries .... — · — · —
Canals ....

© Copyright HAMMOND INCORPORATED, Maplewood, N.J.

Léman (Geneva) (lake)..........C4	Molare (peak) G3	Paradisino (peak)..........K4	Saane (Sarine) (riv.)..........D3	Silvretta (mts.) K3	Toggenburg (dist.)..........H2	Wetterhorn (mt.)..........F3
Le Raimeux (mt.)..........D2	Montoz (mt.)..........D2	Pennine Alps (range)..........D5	Saint Gotthard (pass)..........G3	Simme (riv.)..........D3	Töss (riv.)..........G1	Wildhorn (mt.)..........D4
Leone (mt.)..........F4	Morat (lake)..........D3	Pilatus (mt.)..........F2	Saint Gotthard (tunnel)..........G3	Simplon (pass)..........F4	Tour d'Ai (mt.)..........C4	Wildstrubel (mt.)..........E4
Lepontine Alps (range)..........G3	Moro (mt.)..........E5	Pizol (peak)..........H3	San Bernardino (pass)..........H3	Simplon (tunnel)..........F4	Turnen (mt.)..........D3	Zellersee (lake)..........G1
Limmat (riv.)..........F2	Moron (mt.)..........D2	Plessur (riv.)..........J3	Säntis (mt.)..........H2	Sonnenhorn (mt.)..........F4	Umbrail (peak)..........K3	Zuccherо (mt.)..........G4
Linard (peak)..........K3	Muota (riv.)..........G3	Poschiavo (riv.)..........K4	Sarine (Saane) (riv.)..........D3	Speer (mt.)..........H2	Untersee (lake)..........H1	Zugersee (lake)..........F2
Linden (mts.)..........F2	Murg (riv.)..........G1	Poschiavo (valley)..........K4	Sarnen (mt.)..........E4	Splügen (pass)..........H3	Unterwalden (reg.)..........F3	Zürichsee (lake)..........G2
Linth (riv.)..........G2	Muretto (pass)..........J4	Pragel (pass)..........G2	Sasseneire (mt.)..........E4	Stelvio (pass)..........K3	Upper Engadine (valley)..........J4	
Lorze (riv.)..........F2	Murtaröl (peak)..........K3	Quatervals (peak)..........K3	Scaletta (pass)..........J3	Stockhorn (mt.)..........E3	Urirotstock (mt.)..........G3	**LIECHTENSTEIN**
Lötschberg (tunnel)..........E4	Muttler (mt.)..........K3	Reuss (riv.)..........F2	Scherhorn (mt.)..........G3	Sulzfluh (mt.)..........J2	Vadret (peak)..........J3	
Lower Engadine (valley)..........K3	Naafkopf (mt.)..........J2	Rhaetian Alps (range)..........J3	Schesaplana (mt.)..........J2	Susten (pass)..........G3	Valserrhein (riv.)..........H3	**CITIES and TOWNS**
Lucerne (lake)..........F3	Napf (mt.)..........E3	Rhätikon (mts.)..........J2	Schreckhorn (mt.)..........F3	Sustenhorn (mt.)..........G3	Vanil Noir (mt.)..........D3	
Lugano (lake)..........H5	National Park..........K3	Rheinwaldhorn (mt.)..........H3	Schwarzhorn (mt.)..........E4	Tamaro (mt.)..........G4	Vélan (mt.)..........D5	Schaan 4,552..........H2
Madrisahorn (mt.)..........J3	Neuchâtel (lake)..........C3	Rhine (riv.)..........G2	Schwarzhorn (mt.)..........F3	Tamina (riv.)..........H3	Visp (riv.)..........E4	Triesen 2,971..........H2
Magerrain (mt.)..........H2	Noirmont (mt.)..........B4	Rhône (riv.)..........D4	Scopi (mt.)..........G3	Tendre (peak)..........B3	Vorab (mt.)..........H3	Vaduz (cap.) 4,614..........H2
Maggia (riv.)..........G4	Nufenen (pass)..........F4	Rigi (mt.)..........F2	Seez (riv.)..........H2	Terri (mt.)..........H3	Vorderrhein (riv.)..........G3	
Maggiore (lake)..........G5	Oberalp (pass)..........G3	Rimpfischhorn (mt.)..........E4	Segnes (pass)..........H3	Terri (mt.)..........G3	Walensee (lake)..........H2	**OTHER FEATURES**
Männlifluh (mt.)..........E3	Oberalpstock (mt.)..........G3	Ringelspitz (mt.)..........H3	Sempach (lake)..........F2	Thunersee (lake)..........E3	Wandfluhhorn (mt.)..........G4	
Marmontana (mt.)..........H4	Ochsen (mt.)..........D3	Risoux (mt.)..........B3	Sense (riv.)..........E3	Thur (riv.)..........G1	Weissenstein (mts.)..........D2	Grauspitz..........J2
Matterhorn (mt.)..........E5	Ofen (pass)..........K3	Rosa (mt.)..........E5	Septimer (pass)..........J3	Ticino (riv.)..........G4	Weisshorn (mt.)..........E4	Ochsenkopf (mt.)..........J2
Mauvoisin (dam)..........D4	Ofenhorn (mt.)..........F4	Rosstock (mt.)..........G3	Sesvenna (peak)..........K3	Titlis (mt.)..........F3	Weisshorn (mt.)..........J3	Rhätikon (mts.)..........J2
Moësa (riv.)..........H4	Orbe (riv.)..........C3	Rothorn (mt.)..........D4	Sihlsee (lake)..........G2	Tödi (mt.)..........G3	Weissmies (mt.)..........F4	Rhine (riv.)..........J2

AUSTRIA

PROVINCES

Burgenland 272,274 ....D3
Carinthia 536,727 ....B3
Lower Austria 1,439,137 ....C2
Salzburg 441,842 ....B3
Styria 1,187,512 ....B3
Tirol 586,139 ....A3
Upper Austria 1,270,426 ....B2
Vienna (city) 1,515,666 ....D2
Vorarlberg 305,615 ....A3

CITIES and TOWNS†

Altheim 4,702 ....B2
Althofen 4,274 ....C3
Amstetten 22,015 ....C2
Arnoldstein 6,641 ....B3
Attnang-Puchheim 8,058 .....B3
Bad Aussee 5,047 ....B3
Bad Goisern 6,500 ....B3
Bad Hofgastein 5,960 ....B3
Bad Ischl 13,027 ....B3
Bad Sankt-Leonhard im
  Lavanttal 5,008 ....D2
Baden 23,235 ....D2
Badgastein 5,600 ....B3
Berndorf 8,189 ....C3
Bischofshofen 9,520 ....B3
Bludenz 12,893 ....A3
Bramberg am Wildkogel
  3,410 ....B3
Brandau am Inn 16,192 ......B2
Bregenz 24,683 ....A3
Bruck an der Leitha 7,170 ..D2
Bruck an der Mur 15,086 ....C3
Deutsch Feistritz 3,719 ....C3
Deutschkreutz 3,563 ....D3
Deutsch Landsberg 7,623 ....C3

Hermagor-Preseggersee
  7,116 ....B3
Herzogenburg 7,313 ....C2
Hohenems 12,669 ....A3
Hollabrunn 10,254 ....D2
Hopfgarten in Nordtirol
  4,956 ....B3
Horn 6,319 ....C2
Imst 6,691 ....A3
Innsbruck 116,110 ....A3
Jenbach 5,725 ....A3
Jennersdorf 4,131 ....D3
Judenburg 11,199 ....C3
Kapfenberg 25,719 ....C3
Kaprun 2,764 ....B3
Kindberg 6,269 ....C3
Kirchdorf an der Krems
  3,708 ....C3
Kitzbühel 7,872 ....B3
Klagenfurt 86,303 ....C3
Klosterneuburg 23,307 .....D2
Knittelfeld 14,153 ....C3
Köflach 12,009 ....C3
Korneuburg 9,132 ....C2
Kötschach-Mauthen 3,633 ...B3
Krems an der Donau 23,123 ..C2
Kufstein 13,125 ....A3
Laa an der Thaya 6,485 ....D2
Laakirchen 7,670 ....B3
Landeck 7,325 ....A3
Landskron 10,429 ....B3
Langenlois 6,474 ....C2
Langenwang 4,187 ....C3
Lavamünd 3,824 ....C3
Leibnitz 6,659 ....C3
Lenzing 5,079 ....B3
Leoben 32,006 ....C3
Lienz 11,699 ....B3
Liezen 7,021 ....C3
Lilienfeld 3,030 ....C3
Linz 197,962 ....C2

Salzburg 138,213 ....B3
Sankt Johann in Tirol 6,495 .B3
Sankt Michael im Lungau
  3,246 ....B3
Sankt Michael in
  Obersteiermark 3,604 .....C3
Sankt Paul im Lavanttal
  5,770 ....C3
Sankt Pölten 51,102 ....C2
Sankt Valentin 8,759 ......C2
Sankt Veit an der Glan 12,021 .C3
Schärding 5,784 ....B2
Scheibbs 4,537 ....C2
Schladming 3,930 ....B3
Schrems 6,010 ....C2
Schwarzach im Pongau
  3,607 ....B3
Schwaz 10,936 ....A3
Schwechat 14,844 ....D2
Schwertberg 4,385 ....C2
Sierning 7,891 ....C2
Solbad Hall in Tirol 12,622 .A3
Spittal an der Drau 14,769 ..B3
Steyr 38,967 ....C2
Stockerau 12,692 ....D2
Tamsweg 5,256 ....B3
Telfs 7,749 ....A3
Ternitz 16,154 ....C3
Traiskirchen 14,102 ....D2
Traun 21,524 ....C2
Trieben 4,471 ....C3
Trofaiach 8,959 ....C3
Tulln 11,287 ....D2
Velden am Wörthersee 7,458 ..C3
Vienna (cap.) 1,515,666 ...D2
Villach 52,744 ....B3
Vöcklabruck 11,039 ....B2
Voitsberg 110,951 ....C3
Völkermarkt 10,900 ....C3
Waidhofen an der Thaya
  5,401 ....C2

Waidhofen an der Ybbs
  11,339 ....C2
Weitensfeld-Flattnitz 5,158 .C3
Weiz 8,418 ....C3
Wels 51,024 ....C2
Wien (Vienna) (cap.)
  1,515,666 ....D2
Wiener Neustadt 35,050 ....D3
Wilhelmsburg 6,339 ....C2
Wolfsberg 28,182 ....C3
Wörgl 8,644 ....B3
Ybbs an der Donau 5,983 ...C2
Zell am See 7,959 ....B3
Zeltweg 8,722 ....C3
Zistersdorf 5,814 ....D2
Zwettl-Niederösterreich
  11,579 ....C2

OTHER FEATURES

Allgäu Alps (mts.) A3
Atter See (lake) B3
Bavarian Alps (mts.) A3
Bodensee (Constance) (lake) .A3
Brenner (pass) A3
Carnic Alps (mts.) B3
Coglians (mt.) B3
Constance (lake) A3
Danube (riv.) C2
Donau (Danube) (riv.) D2
Drau (riv.) C3
Enns (riv.) C3
Greiner Wald (mts.) C2
Grosser Peilstein (mt.) C2
Grossglockner (mt.) B3
Hochgolling (mt.) B3
Hohe Tauern (range) B3
Hohe Warte (Coglians) (mt.) .B3
Inn (riv.) A3
Kamp (riv.) C2
Karawanken (range) C3

Lafnitz (riv.) D3
March (riv.) D2
Mühlviertel (reg.) C2
Mur (riv.) C3
Mürz (riv.) C3
Neusiedler See (lake) D3
Niedere Tauern (range) B3
Olsa (riv.) C3
Ötztal Alps (mts.) A3
Parseierspitze (mt.) A3
Raab (riv.) C3
Rhine (riv.) A3
Salzach (riv.) B3
Salzkammergut (reg.) B3
Semmering (pass) C3
Thaya (riv.) C2
Traun (riv.) B3
Traun See (lake) B3
Wildspitze (mt.) A3
Zugspitze (mt.) A3

CZECH REPUBLIC

REGIONS

Jihočeský 689,229 ....C2
Jihomoravský 2,040,903 ....D2

Praha (city) 1,182,186 ....C1
Severočeský 1,167,231 .....C1
Severomoravský 1,932,722 ..D2
Středočeský 1,151,265 .....C2
Východočeský 1,248,466 ....C1
Západočeský 879,925 ....B2

CITIES and TOWNS

Aš 13,551 ....B1
Austerlitz (Slavkov) 6,316 .D2
Benešov 15,172 ....C2
Beroun 23,580 ....B2
Bílina 18,836 ....B1
Blansko 19,508 ....D2
Blatná 7,264 ....C2
Boskovice 12,025 ....D2
Brandýs nad Labem-Stará
  Boleslav 15,071 ....C1
Břeclav 23,978 ....D2
Brno 371,463 ....D2
Broumov 7,834 ....D1
Bruntál 17,062 ....D2
Bystřice nad Pernštejnem
  10,044 ....D2
Bystřice pod Hostýnem
  10,359 ....D2

Čáslav 9,950 ....C2
Česká Kamenice 7,272 .....C1
Česká Lípa 24,924 ....C1
Česká Třebová 17,136 .....C2
České Budějovice 90,415 ..C2
Český Krumlov 13,776 .....C2
Český Těšín 23,389 ....E2
Cheb 31,039 ....B1
Chodov 14,704 ....B1
Chomutov 51,769 ....B1
Chotěbor 8,744 ....C2
Chrastava 7,022 ....C1
Chrudim 20,517 ....C2
Dačice 7,443 ....C2
Děčín 49,682 ....C1
Dobříš 7,466 ....C2
Domažlice 11,461 ....B2
Duchcov 10,554 ....B1
Dvůr Králové nad Labem
  17,270 ....C1
Falknov (Sokolov) 28,523 .B1
Frenštát pod Radhoštěm
  10,434 ....E2
Frýdek-Místek 59,430 ....E2
Frýdlant nad
  Ostravicí 14,065 ......E2
Frýdlant v. Čechách 7,418 .C1
(continued)

CITIES and TOWNS (second index block)

Deutsch Wagram 5,111 ......D2
Dornbirn 38,663 ....A3
Ebensee 9,005 ....B3
Eggenburg 3,729 ....C2
Eisenerz 10,074 ....C3
Eisenkappel-Vellach 3,520 .C3
Eisenstadt 10,150 ....D3
Enns 9,731 ....C2
Feldbach 4,073 ....C3
Feldkirch 23,876 ....A3
Feldkirchen in Kärnten
  12,181 ....B3
Ferlach 7,658 ....C3
Fieberbrunn 3,926 ....B3
Fohnsdorf 10,360 ....C3
Frankenmarkt 3,166 ....B3
Friesach 7,074 ....C3
Freistadt 6,289 ....C2
Frohnleiten 5,061 ....C3
Fürstenfeld 6,040 ....C3
Gaming 4,099 ....C3
Gänserndorf 4,948 ....D2
Gleisdorf 5,078 ....C3
Gloggnitz 6,290 ....D3
Gmünd 6,457 ....C2
Gmunden 12,720 ....B3
Golling an der Salzach 3,409 .B3
Götzis 8,740 ....A3
Graz 243,405 ....C3
Grieskirchen 4,813 ....B2
Grosssieghars 3,374 ......C2
Grünburg 3,630 ....C3
Güssing 3,895 ....D3
Haag 5,095 ....C2
Hainburg an der Donau
  5,749 ....D2
Hainfeld 3,735 ....C2
Hallein 15,404 ....B3
Hartberg 6,048 ....C3
Heidenreichstein 5,351 ...C2
Heiligenblut 1,334 ....B3

Lustenau 17,404 ....A3
Mannersdorf am
  Leithagebirge 3,878 .....D3
Marchegg 2,676 ....D2
Matrei in Osttirol 4,298 ..B3
Mattersburg 5,682 ....C3
Mattighofen 1,566 ....B2
Mauthausen 4,353 ....C2
Mauthen-Kötschach 3,633 ..B3
Mayrhofen 3,274 ....A3
Melk 5,074 ....C2
Mistelbach an der Zaya
  10,300 ....D2
Mittersill 5,033 ....C3
Mödling 19,333 ....D2
Mürzzuschlag 10,774 .....C3
Neumarkt am Wallersee
  3,703 ....B3
Neunkirchen 10,780 ......D3
Neusiedl am See 4,154 ...D3
Ober Grafendorf 4,475 ...C2
Oberndorf bei Salzburg 3,838 .B3
Oberwart 5,973 ....C3
Oberwölz 9,510 ....C3
Paternion 5,914 ....B3
Perg 5,079 ....C2
Pinkafeld 4,802 ....D3
Pöchlarn 3,637 ....C2
Poysdorf 5,658 ....D2
Pregarten 3,823 ....C2
Raabs an der Thaya 3,839 .C2
Radenthein 7,083 ....B3
Radstadt 3,994 ....B3
Rankweil 9,929 ....A3
Reichenau an der Rax 3,601 .D3
Retz 4,373 ....C2
Reutte 5,145 ....A3
Ried im Innkreis 10,952 ..B2
Rottenmann 5,425 ....C3
Saalfelden am Steinernen
  Meer 11,436 ....B3

AUSTRIA

AREA 32,375 sq. mi. (83,851 sq. km.)
POPULATION 7,666,000
CAPITAL Vienna
LARGEST CITY Vienna
HIGHEST POINT Grossglockner 12,457 ft. (3,797 m.)
MONETARY UNIT schilling
MAJOR LANGUAGE German
MAJOR RELIGION Roman Catholicism

CZECH REPUBLIC

AREA 30,449 sq. mi. (78,863 sq. km.)
POPULATION 10,291,927
CAPITAL Prague
LARGEST CITY Prague
HIGHEST POINT Sněžka 5,256 ft. (1,602 m.)
MONETARY UNIT Czech koruna
MAJOR LANGUAGE Czech
MAJOR RELIGIONS Roman Catholicism, Protestantism

HUNGARY

AREA 35,919 sq. mi. (93,030 sq. km.)
POPULATION 10,558,000
CAPITAL Budapest
LARGEST CITY Budapest
HIGHEST POINT Kékes 3,330 ft. (1,015 m.)
MONETARY UNIT forint
MAJOR LANGUAGE Hungarian
MAJOR RELIGIONS Roman Catholicism, Protestantism

SLOVAKIA

AREA 18,924 sq. mi. (49,014 sq. km.)
POPULATION 4,991,168
CAPITAL Bratislava
LARGEST CITY Bratislava
HIGHEST POINT Gerlachovky Štít 8,707 ft. (2,654 m.)
MONETARY UNIT Slovak koruna
MAJOR LANGUAGE Slovak
MAJOR RELIGIONS Roman Catholicism, Protestantism

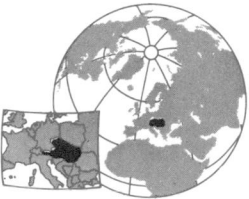

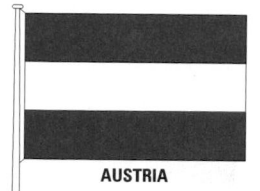

AUSTRIA

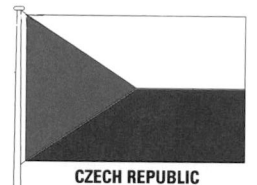

CZECH REPUBLIC

HUNGARY

SLOVAKIA

Austria, Czech Republic Slovakia and Hungary

CONIC PROJECTION

SCALE OF MILES
0 10 20 40 60 80

SCALE OF KILOMETERS
0 10 20 40 60 80

Capitals of Countries ☆	International Boundaries
Administrative Centers △	Internal Boundaries
	Canals

Longitude East of Greenwich

(continued)

Fulnek 8,214...D2
Havířov 89,920...E2
Havlíčkuv Brod 24,550...C2
Hlinsko 10,635...C2
Hlučín 22,581...E2
Hodonín 25,485...D2
Holešov 13,323...D2
Hořice v Podkrkonoší 9,251...C1
Hradec Králové 95,588...C1
Hranice 18,099...D2
Hronov 9,609...D1
Humpolec 10,042...C2
Ivančice 9,746...D2
Jablonec nad Nisou 42,179...C1
Jablunkov 15,962...E2
Jaroměř 11,562...C1
Jeseník 14,314...D1
Jičín 16,440...C1
Jihlava 51,144...C2
Jindřichuv Hradec 20,096...C2
Jiřkov 11,980...B1
Kadăn 18,420...B1
Karlovy Vary 60,950...B1
Karviná 78,334...E2
Kladno 71,141...B1
Klatovy 21,782...B2
Kojetín 8,881...D2
Kolín 30,921...C1
Kralupy nad Vltavou 17,528...C1
Kraslice 7,371...B1
Krnov 25,678...D1
Kroměříž 25,887...D2
Krupka 9,336...B1
Kutná Hora 20,927...C2
Kyjov 12,632...D2
Lanškroun 10,620...D2
Liberec 97,474...C1
Lidice...C1
Lipník nad Bečvou 9,961...D2
Litoměřice 23,835...C1
Litomyšl 10,079...D2
Prague (Praha) (cap.) 1,182,186...C1
Přelouč 8,561...C1
Přerov 50,265...D2
Příbor 12,711...E2
Příbram 37,854...C2
Prostějov 49,599...D2
Rakovník 16,233...B1
Říčany u Prahy 10,703...C2
Rokycany 15,041...B2
Roudnice nad Labem 13,956...C1
Rožnov pod Radhoštěm 15,468...E2
Rumburk 10,255...C1
Rychnov nad Kněžnou 8,955...D1
Rýmařov 9,927...D2
Sedlčany 7,453...C2
Semily 8,464...C1
Slaný 14,705...C1
Slavkov 6,316...D2
Soběslav 8,406...C2
Sokolov 28,523...B1
Staré Město 6,293...D2
Šternberk 16,342...D2
Strakonice 22,611...B2
Stříbro 8,169...B2
Studénka 12,497...E2
Šumperk 31,873...D2
Sušice 11,400...B2
Svitavy 19,075...D2
Tábor 31,867...C2
Tachov 12,798...B2
Teplice 53,964...B1
Tišnov 12,179...D2
Třebíč 30,246...C2
Třeboň 8,878...C2
Třinec 44,739...E2
Trutnov 27,648...C1
Turnov 13,906...C1
Ústí nad Labem 87,909...C1
Jihlava (riv.)...D2
Jizera (riv.)...C1
Krušné Hory (Erzgebirge) (mts.)...B1
Labe (riv.)...C1
Lipno (res.)...C2
Lužnice (riv.)...C2
Moldau (Vltava) (riv.)...C2
Morava (riv.)...D2
Mže (riv.)...B2
Oder (Odra) (riv.)...D2
Ohře (riv.)...B1
Ondava (riv.)...F2
Orlice (riv.)...D1
Orlickă (res.)...C2
Otava (riv.)...B2
Radbuza (riv.)...B2
Sázava (riv.)...C2
Sudeten (mts.)...C1
Svitava (riv.)...D2
Svratka (riv.)...D2
Úhlava (riv.)...B2
Vltava (riv.)...C2

HUNGARY

COUNTIES

Bács-Kiskun 553,000...E3
Baranya 434,000...E4
Békés 416,000...F3
Borsod-Abaúj-Zemplén 779,000...F2
Budapest (city) 2,104,000...E3
Csongrád 457,000...F3
Fejér 426,000...E3
Győr-Sopron 426,000...D3
Hajdú-Bihar 549,000...F3
Heves 338,000...F3
Komárom 320,000...E3
Nógrád 229,000...E3
Pest 988,000...E3
Csorna 13,000...D3
Dabas 13,075...E3
Debrecen 217,000...F3
Derecske 9,579...F3
Dévaványa 11,208...F3
Dombóvár 21,000...E3
Dorog 13,000...E3
Dunaföldvár 10,318...E3
Dunaharaszti 15,788...E3
Dunakeszi 29,000...E3
Dunaújváros 62,000...E3
Edelény 12,000...F2
Eger 67,000...F3
Egyek 7,956...F3
Endrőd 8,136...F3
Enying 7,518...E3
Érd 44,904...E3
Esztergom 30,476...E3
Fegyvernek 8,421...F3
Fehérgyarmat 9,000...G3
Füzesgyarmat 7,097...F3
Gödöllő 30,000...E3
Gyöngyös 36,000...E3
Gyoma 10,392...F3
Győr 131,000...D3
Gyula 36,000...F3
Hadházteglás 13,626...F3
Hajdúboszormény 31,000...F3
Hajdúdorog 10,118...F3
Hajdúnánás 18,000...F3
Hajdúsámson 7,492...F3
Hajdúszoboszló 24,000...F3
Hatvan 25,000...E3
Heves 11,000...F3
Hódmezővásárhely 54,000...F3
Izsák 7,686...E3
Jánoshalma 12,534...E3
Jászapáti 10,424...F3
Jászárokszállás 10,139...E3
Jászberény 30,000...E3
Jászladány 7,823...F3
Kalocsa 20,000...E3
Mezőtúr 21,000...F3
Mindszent 8,730...F3
Miskolc 210,000...F2
Mohács 21,000...E4
Monor 16,838...E3
Mór 12,066...E3
Mosonmagyaróvár 30,000...D3
Nádudvar 9,447...F3
Nagyatád 15,000...D3
Nagyecsed 8,225...G3
Nagykálló 11,282...F3
Nagykanizsa 55,000...D3
Nagykáta 11,922...E3
Nagykőrös 27,000...E3
Nagyszénás 7,124...F3
Nyíradony 7,146...F3
Nyírbátor 14,000...G3
Nyíregyháza 119,000...F3
Orosháza 36,000...F3
Oroszlány 22,000...E3
Ózd 45,000...F2
Paks 26,000...E3
Pápa 35,000...D3
Pásztó 12,000...E3
Pécs 182,000...E3
Pilis 9,055...E3
Pilisvörösvár 10,217...E3
Polgár 9,429...F3
Püspökladány 16,000...F3
Putnok 7,103...F2
Ráckeve 7,534...E3
Rákospalota 60,983...E3
Sajószentpéter 13,992...F2
Salgótarján 49,000...E2
Sárbogárd 13,000...E3
Sarkad 11,937...F3
Sárospatak 15,000...F2
Sárvár 16,000...D3
Sátoraljaújhely 20,000...F2
Siklós 11,000...E4
Siófok 24,000...E3
Soltvadkert 7,934...E3

OTHER FEATURES

Bakony (mts.)...D3
Balaton (lake)...D3
Berettyó (riv.)...F3
Börzsöny (mts.)...E3
Bükk (mts.)...F2
Csepelsziget (isl.)...E3
Danube (riv.)...E3
Dráva (riv.)...D3
Duna (Danube) (riv.)...E3
Fertő tó (Neusiedler See) (lake)...D3
Great Alföld (plain)...F3
Hernád (riv.)...F2
Ipoly (riv.)...E2
Kapos (riv.)...D3
Kékes (mt.)...E3
Korishegy (mt.)...D3
Körös (riv.)...F3
Little Alfold (plain)...D3
Maros (riv.)...F3
Mátra (mts.)...E3
Mecsek (mts.)...D3
Mura (riv.)...D3
Rába (riv.)...D3
Sajó (riv.)...F2
Sárviz csatorna (canal)...E3
Sebes Körös (riv.)...F3
Sió csatorna (canal)...E3
Szentendreisziget (isl.)...E3
Tarna (riv.)...F3
Tisza (riv.)...F3
Zagyva (riv.)...F3
Zala (riv.)...D3

SLOVAKIA

REGIONS

Bratislava (city) 380,259...D2
Středoslovenský
Liptovský Mikuláš 24,520...E2
Lučenec 26,399...E2
Malacky 15,218...D2
Martin 56,208...E2
Michalovce 29,765...F2
Modra 7,679...D2
Myjava 11,668...D2
Nitra 76,663...E2
Nová Baňa 8,321...E2
Nové Město nad Váhom 18,170...D2
Nové Zámky 34,147...D3
Partizánske 23,266...E2
Pezinok 17,116...D2
Piešťany 30,487...D2
Poprad 38,077...F2
Považská Bystrica 30,444...E2
Prešov 71,500...F2
Prievidza 40,813...E2
Púchov 17,554...E2
Revúca 11,881...F2
Rimavská Sobota 19,699...E2
Rožňava 18,039...F2
Ružomberok 26,396...E2
Sabinov 7,008...F2
Šafárikovo 7,021...F2
Šahy 8,034...E2
Šal'a 19,167...D2
Samorín 9,677...D2
Senec 10,772...D2
Senica 15,515...D2
Sered' 16,071...D2
Skalica 13,833...D2
Snina 13,347...G2
Spišská Nová Ves 31,917...F2
Stropkov 7,405...F2
Štúrovo 12,807...E3
Šurany 11,320...E2
Svidník 7,538...F2
Topol'čany 31,340...E2
Trebišov 14,961...F2
Trenčín 47,887...E2

Agriculture, Industry and Resources

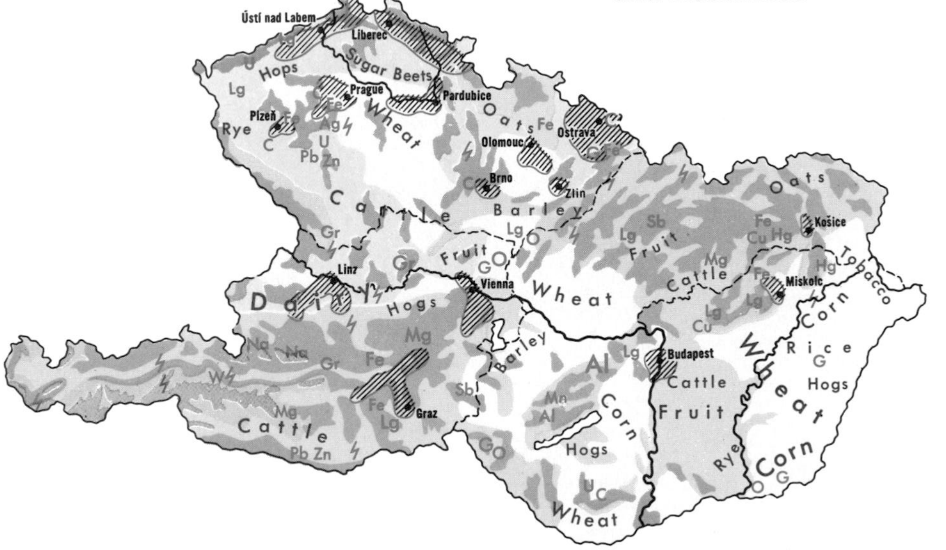

Ústí nad Labem
Liberec
Hops
Sugar Beets
Prague
Pardubice
Plzeň
Rye
Wheat
Oats
Ostrava
Olomouc
Brno
Zlín
Cattle
Barley
Košice
Linz
Vienna
Fruit
Miskolc
Tobacco
Dairy
Hogs
Corn
Budapest
Rice
Graz

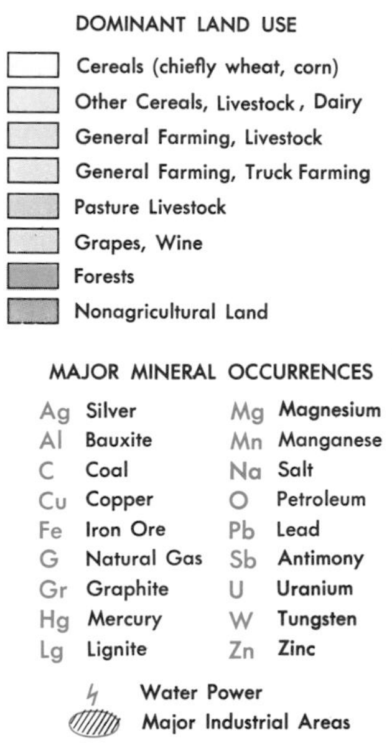

DOMINANT LAND USE
Cereals (chiefly wheat, corn)
Other Cereals, Livestock, Dairy
General Farming, Livestock
General Farming, Truck Farming
Pasture Livestock
Grapes, Wine
Forests
Nonagricultural Land
MAJOR MINERAL OCCURRENCES
Ag Silver
Al Bauxite
C Coal
Cu Copper
Fe Iron Ore
G Natural Gas
Gr Graphite
Hg Mercury
Lg Lignite
Mg Magnesium
Mn Manganese
Na Salt
O Petroleum
Pb Lead
Sb Antimony
U Uranium
W Tungsten
Zn Zinc
Water Power
Major Industrial Areas

Litovel 12,454...D2
Litvínov 22,624...B1
Louny 20,436...B1
Lovosice 11,456...C1
Lysá nad Labem 9,113...C1
Mariánské Lázně 17,932...B2
Mělník 18,941...C1
Mikulov 8,472...D2
Milevsko 8,852...C2
Mimoň 7,437...C1
Mladá Boleslav 45,896...C1
Mnichovo Hradiště 7,340...C1
Mohelnice 9,405...D2
Moravská Třebová 11,543...D2
Moravské Budějovice 8,943...C2
Most 60,119...B1
Náchod 19,892...D1
Nejdek 9,768...B1
Nové Město na Moravě 11,330...D2
Nový Bohumín 16,700...E2
Nový Bor 10,493...C1
Nový Bydžov 9,317...C1
Nový Jičín 31,506...D2
Nymburk 14,033...C1
Odry 10,032...D2
Olomouc 102,112...D2
Opava 59,384...D2
Orlová 31,190...E2
Ostrava 322,073...E2
Ostrov 19,618...B1
Pardubice 91,855...C1
Písek 28,104...C2
Plzeň 170,701...B2
Poděbrady 13,782...C1
Pohořelice 5,125...D2
Polička 8,972...D2
Prachatice 10,354...B2
Ustí nad Orlicí 15,945...D2
Uherské Hradiště 36,756...D2
Uherský Brod 17,459...D2
Uničov 12,507...D2
Valašské Meziříčí 26,531...D2
Varnsdorf 16,356...C1
Velké Meziřičí 14,073...D2
Veselí nad Moravou 12,464...D2
Vimperk 7,257...B2
Vítkov 7,543...D2
Vlašim 13,284...C2
Vodňany 6,989...C2
Vrbno pod Pradědem 6,912...D1
Vrchlabí 12,419...C1
Vsetín 29,927...D2
Vyškov 18,330...D2
Vysoké Mýto 10,887...D2
Zábřeh 15,184...D2
Žatec 19,529...B1
Žd'ár nad Sázavou 25,015...C2
Zlin 83,983...D2
Znojmo 39,271...D2

OTHER FEATURES

Bečva (riv.)...E2
Berounka (riv.)...C2
Bohemian (for.)...B2
Bohemian-Moravian Heights (hills)...C2
Chrudimka (riv.)...C2
Cidlina (riv.)...C1
Danube (riv.)...C2
Dyje (riv.)...D2
Erzgebirge (mts.)...B1
Jablunka (pass)...E2
Jeseniky (mts.)...D1
Somogy 349,000...D3
Szabolcs-Szatmár 570,000...G3
Szolnok 428,000...F3
Tolna 263,000...E3
Vas 277,000...D3
Veszprém 387,000...D3
Zala 311,000...D3

CITIES and TOWNS

Abádszalók 6,386...F3
Abaújszántó 4,209...F2
Abony 15,624...E3
Ács 8,423...E3
Ajka 34,000...D3
Albertirsa 11,252...E3
Alsózsolca 5,045...F2
Bácsalmás 8,000...E3
Baja 41,000...E3
Balassagyarmat 20,000...E2
Balatonfüred 15,000...D3
Balkány 7,667...F3
Balmazújváros 17,371...F3
Barcs 12,000...D4
Bátaszék 7,274...E3
Battonya 9,324...F3
Békés 22,000...F3
Békéscsaba 71,000...F3
Berettyóújfalu 18,000...F3
Bicske 13,000...E3
Bonyhád 15,000...E3
Budafok 40,623...E3
Budakeszi 10,429...E3
Budaörs 22,000...E3
Budapest (cap.) 2,104,000...E3
Cegléd 40,000...E3
Celldömölk 12,000...D3
Csepel 71,693...E3
Csongrád 21,000...F3
Kaposvár 74,000...D3
Kapuvár 11,000...D3
Karcag 25,000...F3
Kazincbarcika 39,000...F2
Kecel 10,493...E3
Kecskemét 105,000...E3
Keszthely 23,000...D3
Kisbér 8,000...D3
Kiskőrös 15,000...E3
Kiskunfélegyháza 35,000...E3
Kiskunhalas 32,000...E3
Kiskunmajsa 14,439...E3
Kispest 65,106...E3
Kistelek 8,544...E3
Kisújszállás 13,000...F3
Kisvarda 17,828...G2
Komádi 8,765...F3
Komárom 19,955...E3
Komló 30,301...E3
Kondoros 7,319...F3
Körmend 12,000...D3
Kőszeg 14,000...D3
Kunhegyes 10,116...F3
Kunmadaras 7,343...F3
Kunszentmárton 12,000...F3
Kunszentmiklós 7,952...E3
Lajosmizse 12,872...E3
Leninváros 19,000...F3
Lenti 9,000...D3
Létavértes 9,106...F3
Lőrinci 10,679...E3
Makó 29,000...F3
Marcali 13,000...D3
Mátészalka 20,000...G3
Mélykút 7,640...E3
Mezőberény 12,702...F3
Mezőhegyes 8,631...F3
Mezőkovácsháza 7,000...F3
Mezőkövesd 18,000...F3
Sopron 57,000...D3
Szabadszállás 8,223...E3
Szarvas 19,000...F3
Százhalombatta 18,000...E3
Szeged 188,000...F3
Szeghalom 10,000...F3
Székesfehérvár 113,000...E3
Szekszárd 39,000...E3
Szentendre 20,000...E3
Szentes 35,000...F3
Szentgotthárd 8,000...D3
Szerencs 10,000...F2
Szigetvár 13,000...D3
Szolnok 81,000...F3
Szombathely 87,000...D3
Tamási 10,000...E3
Tapolca 18,000...D3
Tata 26,000...E3
Tatabánya 76,000...E3
Tiszaföldvár 12,560...F3
Tiszafüred 14,000...F3
Tiszakécske 12,000...F3
Tiszavasvári 14,000...F3
Tolna 8,997...E3
Törökszentmiklós 24,000...F3
Tótkomlós 8,803...F3
Tura 8,235...E3
Túrkeve 11,000...F3
Újfehértó 14,412...F3
Újpest 80,384...E3
Vác 36,000...E3
Várpalota 28,000...E3
Vásárosnamény 9,000...G2
Vecsés 19,193...E3
Veszprém 66,000...D3
Vészto 9,815...F3
Zalaegerszeg 63,000...D3
Zalaszentgrót 8,000...D3
Zirc 11,000...D3
1,524,766...E2
Východoslovenský 1,402,252...F2
Západoslovenský 1,683,891...D2

CITIES and TOWNS

Bánovce nad Bebravou 15,342...E2
Banská Bystrica 66,412...E2
Banská Štiavnica 9,180...E2
Bardejov 23,741...F2
Bratislava (cap.) 380,259...D2
Brezno 17,872...E2
Bytča 11,789...E2
Čadca 19,319...E2
Čalovo 8,063...D3
Detva 14,261...E2
Dolný Kubín 13,971...E2
Dubnica nad Váhom 15,580...E2
Dunajská Streda 18,715...D3
Fil'akovo 10,497...E2
Galanta 15,477...D2
Handlová 17,777...E2
Hlohovec 21,148...D2
Holíč 8,741...D2
Hriňová 8,485...E2
Humenné 27,285...F2
Hurbanovo 7,613...E3
Kežmarok 17,570...F2
Kolárovo 11,295...D3
Komárno 32,520...D3
Košice 202,368...F2
Kremnica 7,168...E2
Krupina 7,337...E2
Kysucké Nové Mesto 14,083...E2
Levice 26,132...E2
Levoča 11,025...F2
Liptovský Hrádok 9,197...E2
Trnava 64,062...D2
Turzovka 6,962...E2
Vel'ké Kapušany 8,459...G2
Vráble 7,586...E2
Vranov nad Teplou 18,423...F2
Žiar nad Hronom 19,098...E2
Žilina 83,016...E2
Zlaté Moravce 14,119...E2
Zvolen 36,538...E2

OTHER FEATURES

Beskids, East (mts.)...F2
Beskids, West (mts.)...E2
Dudvá (riv.)...D2
Dukla (pass)...F2
Dunajec (riv.)...F2
Gerlachovka (mt.)...F2
Hornád (riv.)...F2
Hron (riv.)...E2
Ipel' (riv.)...E2
Laborec (riv.)...F2
Latorica (riv.)...F2
Nitra (riv.)...E2
Orava (riv.)...E2
Poprad (riv.)...F2
Slaná (riv.)...F2
Slovenské Rudohorie (mts.)...E2
Tatra, High (riv.)...E2
Topl'a (riv.)...F2
Torysa (riv.)...F2
Už (riv.)...G2
Váh (riv.)...D2
White Carpathians (mts.)...E2

†Population of Austrian cities are communes.

Balkan States 43

ALBANIA

AREA 11,100 sq. mi. (28,749 sq. km.)
POPULATION 3,401,126
CAPITAL Tiranë
LARGEST CITY Tiranë
HIGHEST POINT Korab 9,026 ft. (2,751 m.)
MONETARY UNIT lek
MAJOR LANGUAGE Albanian
MAJOR RELIGIONS Islam, Eastern Orthodoxy, Roman Catholicism

BOSNIA AND HERZEGOVINA

AREA 19,940 sq. mi. (51,129 sq. km.)
POPULATION 3,591,618
CAPITAL Sarajevo
LARGEST CITY Sarajevo
HIGHEST POINT Pločna 7,310 ft. (2,228 m.)
MONETARY UNIT dinar
MAJOR LANGUAGE Serbo-Croatian
MAJOR RELIGIONS Islam, Roman Catholicism, Eastern Orthodoxy,

BULGARIA

AREA 42,823 sq. mi. (110,912 sq. km.)
POPULATION 8,155,828
CAPITAL Sofia
LARGEST CITY Sofia
HIGHEST POINT Musala 9,597 ft. (2,925 m.)
MONETARY UNIT lev
MAJOR LANGUAGE Bulgarian
MAJOR RELIGION Eastern Orthodoxy

CROATIA

AREA 22,050 sq. mi. (56,538 sq. km.)
POPULATION 4,681,015
CAPITAL Zagreb
LARGEST CITY Zagreb
HIGHEST POINT Mali Rajinac 5,574 ft. (1,699 m.)
MONETARY UNIT Croatian kuna
MAJOR LANGUAGE Serbo-Croatian
MAJOR RELIGIONS Roman Catholicism, Eastern Orthodoxy

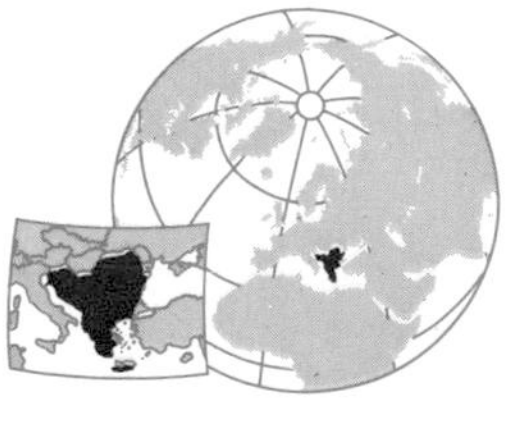

FORMER YUGOSLAV REP. OF MACEDONIA

AREA 9,889 sq. mi. (25,713 sq. km.)
POPULATION 2,035,044
CAPITAL Skopje
LARGEST CITY Skopje
HIGHEST POINT Solunska Glava 8,333 ft. (2,540 m.)
MONETARY UNIT denar
MAJOR LANGUAGES Macedonian, Serbo-Croatian, Albanian
MAJOR RELIGIONS Eastern Orthodoxy, Islam, Roman Catholicism

GREECE

AREA 50,944 sq. mi. (131,945 sq. km.)
POPULATION 10,750,705
CAPITAL Athens
LARGEST CITY Athens
HIGHEST POINT Olympus 9,570 ft. (2,917 m.)
MONETARY UNIT drachma
MAJOR LANGUAGE Greek
MAJOR RELIGION Eastern (Greek) Orthodoxy

ROMANIA

AREA 91,699 sq. mi. (237,500 sq. km.)
POPULATION 22,291,200
CAPITAL Bucharest
LARGEST CITY Bucharest
HIGHEST POINT Moldoveanul 8,343 ft. (2,543 m.)
MONETARY UNIT leu
MAJOR LANGUAGES Romanian, Hungarian
MAJOR RELIGION Eastern Orthodoxy

SLOVENIA

AREA 7,898 sq. mi. (20,251 sq. km.)
POPULATION 1,970,056
CAPITAL Ljubljana
LARGEST CITY Ljubljana
HIGHEST POINT Triglav 9,393 ft. (2,863 m.)
MONETARY UNIT tolar
MAJOR LANGUAGES Slovenian, Serbo-Croatian
MAJOR RELIGIONS Roman Catholicism, Eastern Orthodoxy

YUGOSLAVIA

AREA 38,989 sq. mi. (102,173 sq. km.)
POPULATION 11,210,243
CAPITAL Belgrade
LARGEST CITY Belgrade
HIGHEST POINT Daravica 8,714 ft. (2,656 m.)
MONETARY UNIT Yugoslav new dinar
MAJOR LANGUAGES Serbo-Croatian, Slovenian, Montenegrin, Albanian
MAJOR RELIGIONS Eastern Orthodoxy, Roman Catholicism

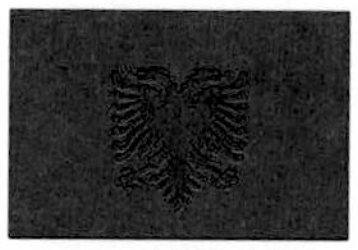
ALBANIA

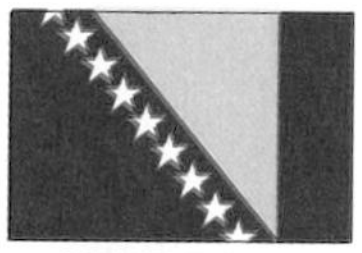
BOSNIA AND HERZEGOVINA

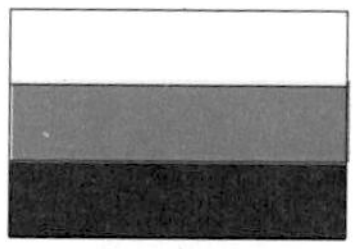
BULGARIA

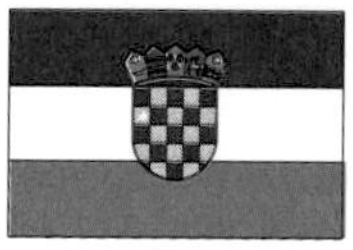
CROATIA

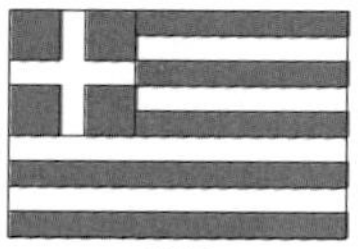
GREECE

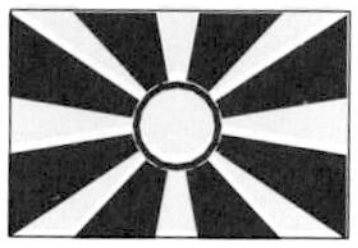
MACEDONIA

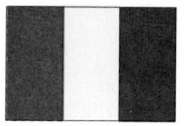

ROMANIA

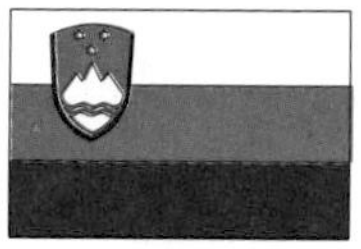
SLOVENIA

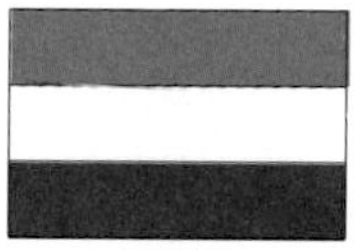
YUGOSLAVIA

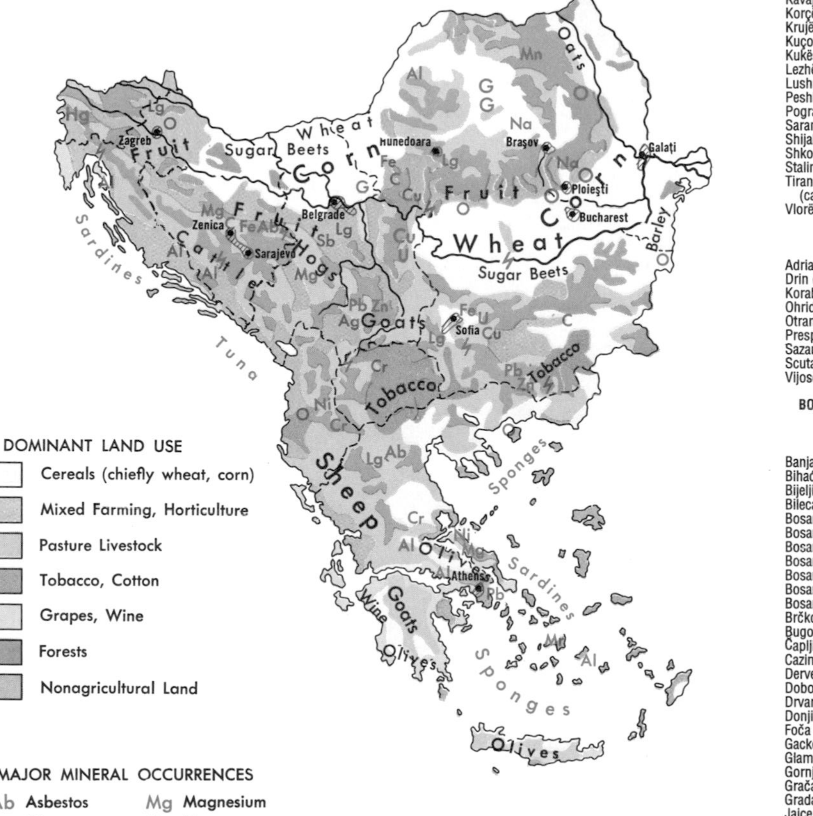

DOMINANT LAND USE

- Cereals (chiefly wheat, corn)
- Mixed Farming, Horticulture
- Pasture Livestock
- Tobacco, Cotton
- Grapes, Wine
- Forests
- Nonagricultural Land

MAJOR MINERAL OCCURRENCES

Ab	Asbestos	Mg	Magnesium
Ag	Silver	Mn	Manganese
Al	Bauxite	Mr	Marble
C	Coal	Na	Salt
Cr	Chromium	Ni	Nickel
Cu	Copper	O	Petroleum
Fe	Iron Ore	Pb	Lead
G	Natural Gas	Sb	Antimony
Hg	Mercury	U	Uranium
Lg	Lignite	Zn	Zinc

Agriculture, Industry and Resources

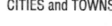

Water Power
Major Industrial Areas

ALBANIA

CITIES and TOWNS

Berat 40,500 .... D5
Delvinë 6,000 .... D6
Durrës (Durazzo) 78,700 .... D5
Elbasan 78,300 .... E5
Fier 40,300 .... D5
Gjirokastër 23,800 .... E5
Kavajë 24,200 .... D5
Korçë 61,500 .... E5
Krujë 9,600 .... D5
Kuçovë (Stalin) 20,600 .... D5
Kukës 9,500 .... E4
Lezhë 6,900 .... D5
Lushnjë 26,900 .... D5
Peshkopi 7,600 .... E5
Pogradec 13,100 .... E5
Sarandë 10,800 .... E6
Shijak 6,200 .... D5
Shkodër 76,300 .... D4
Stalin 20,600 .... D5
Tiranë (Tirana) (cap.) 225,700 .... E5
Vlorë 67,700 .... D5

OTHER FEATURES

Adriatic (sea) B4
Drin (riv.) E4
Korab (mt.) E4
Ohrid (lake) E5
Otranto (str.) D5
Prespa (lake) E5
Sazan (isl.) D5
Scutari (lake) D4
Vijosë (riv.) D5

BOSNIA and HERZEGOVINA

CITIES and TOWNS

Banja Luka 183,618 .... C3
Bihać 65,544 .... B3
Bijeljina 92,808 .... D3
Bileca 13,199 .... D4
Bosanska Dubica 30,867 .... C3
Bosanska Gradiška 58,095 .... C3
Bosanska Krupa 55,229 .... C3
Bosanski Brod 32,286 .... D3
Bosanski Novi 42,142 .... C3
Bosanski Petrovac 16,095 .... C3
Bosanski Šamac 32,320 .... D3
Brčko 82,768 .... D3
Bugojno 39,969 .... C3
Čapljina 26,032 .... C4
Cazin 57,110 .... B3
Derventa 57,010 .... C3
Doboj 99,548 .... C3
Drvar 17,983 .... C3
Donji Vakuf 22,606 .... C3
Foča 44,661 .... D4
Gacko 10,729 .... D4
Glamoč 14,120 .... C3
Gornji Vakuf 22,432 .... C4
Gračanica 54,311 .... D3
Gradačac 54,281 .... D3
Jajce 41,197 .... C3
Kladanj 15,641 .... D3
Ključ 40,008 .... C3
Konjic 43,677 .... C4
Livno 40,438 .... C4
Ljubinje 4,516 .... D4
Ljubuški 27,603 .... C4
Maglaj 42,160 .... D3
Modriča 34,541 .... D3
Mostar 110,377 .... C4
Nevesinje 16,326 .... D4
Prijedor 108,868 .... C3
Prozor 19,108 .... C4
Rogatica 23,578 .... D4
Sanski Most 62,467 .... C3
Sarajevo (cap.) 448,500 .... D4
Srebrenica 36,292 .... D3
Stolac 18,910 .... C4
Teslić 60,434 .... C3
Travnik 64,100 .... C3
Trebinje 30,372 .... D4
Tuzla 121,717 .... D3
Vareš 22,822 .... D3
Višegrad 23,201 .... D4
Visoko 40,901 .... D4
Vlasenica 30,498 .... D3
Zenica 132,733 .... C3
Žepče 19,754 .... D3
Zvornik 73,845 .... D3

OTHER FEATURES

Adriatic (sea) B4
Bosna (riv.) D3
Dinaric Alps (mts.) B3
Drina (riv.) D3
Neretva (riv.) D4
Tara (riv.) D4
Una (riv.) C3
Vrbas (riv.) C3

BULGARIA

CITIES and TOWNS

Asenovgrad 47,159 .... G5
Aytos 23,124 .... H4
Balchik 12,764 .... J4
Bansko 10,025 .... F5
Berkovitsa 16,340 .... F4
Blagoevgrad 65,481 .... F5
Botevgrad 22,659 .... F4
Burgas 182,856 .... H4
Byala 11,017 .... G4
Byala Slatina 16,034 .... F4
Chirpan 20,440 .... G4
Dimitrovgrad 54,056 .... G4
Dobrich (Tolbukhin) 109,170 .... H4
Dryanovo 10,306 .... G4
Elkhovo 13,655 .... H4
Gabrovo 81,629 .... G4
Gorna Oryakhovitsa 40,895 .... G4
Gotse Delchev 19,836 .... F5
Grudovo 10,736 .... H4
Ikhtiman 13,001 .... F4
Isperikh 11,235 .... H4
Karlovo 28,403 .... G4
Karnobat 22,536 .... H4
Kavarna 12,024 .... J4
Kazanlŭk 61,396 .... G4
Kharmanli 21,050 .... G5
Khaskovo 87,847 .... G5
Kubrat 10,758 .... H4
Kŭrdzhali 55,201 .... G5
Kyustendil 53,498 .... F4
Lom 32,307 .... F4
Lovech 48,992 .... G4
Lukovit 10,645 .... G4
Mikhaylovgrad 51,714 .... F4
Momchilgrad 10,189 .... G5
Nesebŭr 8,130 .... H4
Nova Zagora 25,327 .... H4
Novi Pazar 16,314 .... H4
Omurtag 9,505 .... H4
Oryakhovo 14,012 .... F4
Panagyurishte 22,034 .... G4
Pazardzhik 77,603 .... G4
Pernik 94,460 .... F4
Peshtera 18,763 .... G4
Petrich 26,451 .... F5
Pirdop 8,248 .... G4
Pleven 129,863 .... G4
Plovdiv 343,064 .... G4
Pomorie 13,507 .... H4
Popovo 21,236 .... H4
Provadiya 15,762 .... H4
Radomir 16,733 .... F4
Razgrad 49,582 .... H4
Razlog 14,010 .... F5
Rositsa 185,485 .... H4
Ruse 185,485 .... H4
Samokov 27,485 .... F4
Sandanski 24,629 .... F5
Sevlievo 26,560 .... G4
Shumen 100,125 .... H4
Silistra 53,537 .... H3
Sliven 9,037 .... H4
Smolyan 31,456 .... G5
Sofia (cap.) 1,121,763 .... F4
Stanke Dimitrov 41,897 .... F4
Stara Zagora 151,163 .... G4
Svilengrad 17,472 .... H5
Svishtov 30,555 .... G4
Teteven 12,784 .... G4
Tolbukhin 109,170 .... H4
Troyan 26,179 .... G4
Tŭrgovishte 46,043 .... H4
Tutrakan 12,153 .... H4
Varna 302,816 .... H4
Veliko Tŭrnovo 69,173 .... G4
Vidin 62,541 .... F4
Vratsa 75,180 .... F4
Yambol 90,019 .... H4
Zlatograd 8,780 .... G5

OTHER FEATURES

Arda (riv.) G5
Balkan (mts.) G4
Black (sea) J4
Danube (riv.) H4
Dunav (Danube) (riv.) H4
Emine (cape) J4
Iskŭr (riv.) G4
Kaliakra (cape) J4
Maritsa (riv.) G4
Mesta (riv.) F5
Midzhur (mt.) F4
Musala (mt.) F4
Osŭm (riv.) G4
Rhodope (mts.) G5
Rujen (mt.) F4
Struma (riv.) F5
Timok (riv.) F3
Tundzha (riv.) G4
Vit (riv.) G4

CROATIA

CITIES and TOWNS

Beli Manastir 53,409 .... D3
Biograd 15,865 .... B4
Bjelovar 66,553 .... C3
Čakovec 116,825 .... C2
Daruvar 31,424 .... C3
Djakovo 52,349 .... D3
Dubrovnik 66,131 .... D4
Fiume (Rijeka) 193,044 .... B3
Gospić 31,263 .... B3
Gračac 11,863 .... B3
Karlovac 78,363 .... B3
Knin 43,731 .... C3
Koprivnica 61,166 .... C2
Kostajnica 15,548 .... C3
Križevci 41,316 .... C2
Krk 13,334 .... B3
Kutina 38,597 .... C3
Makarska 17,819 .... C4
Našice 38,938 .... D3
Nova Gradiška 61,267 .... C3
Novska 24,530 .... C3
Ogulin 31,076 .... B3
Omiš 24,082 .... C4
Opatija 29,274 .... B3
Osijek 158,790 .... D3
Pag 7,076 .... B3
Petrinja 33,570 .... C3
Plŏce (Kardeljevŏ) 11,328 .... C4
Pola (Pula) 77,278 .... A3

(continued on following page)

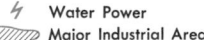

(continued)

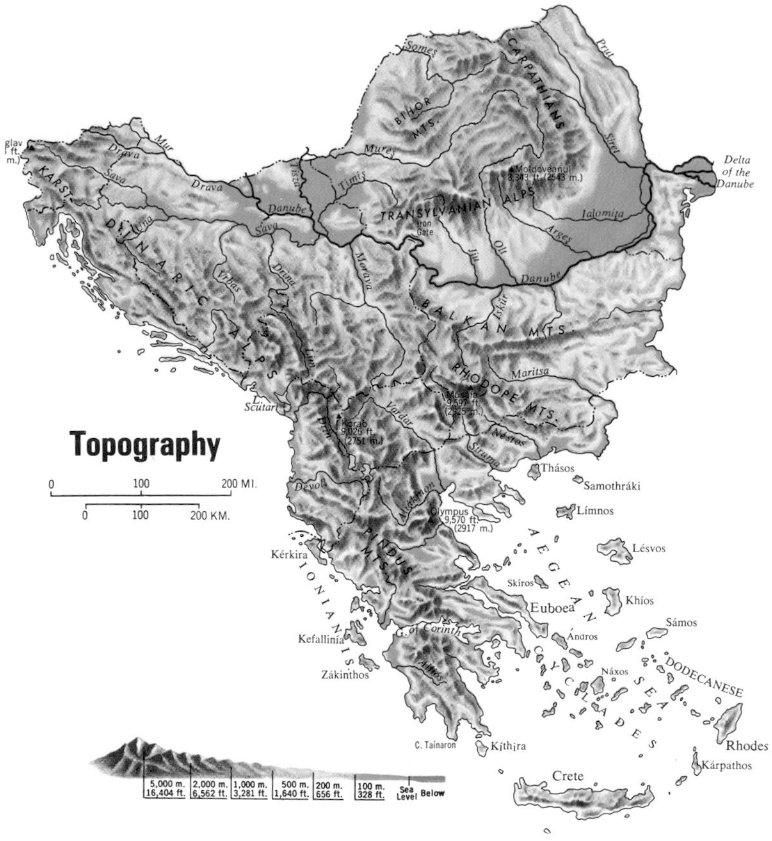
Topography
0 100 200 MI.
0 100 200 KM.
CARPATHIANS
BIHOR MTS.
TRANSYLVANIAN ALPS
Moldoveanul 8,343 ft. (2543 m.)
Delta of the Danube
Danube
Drava
Sava
Mureş
Timiş
Olt
Jiu
Argeş
Ialomiţa
Prut
Siret
Someş
Mur
Iron Gate
BALKAN MTS.
RHODOPE MTS.
Maritsa
Vardar
Struma
Néstos
DINARIC ALPS
Scutari
Thásos
Samothráki
Límnos
Lésvos
Khíos
Sámos
Olympus 9,570 ft. (2917 m.)
PINDUS MTS.
Kérkira
IONIAN SEA
AEGEAN SEA
Skíros
Euboea
Ándros
Kefallinía
Zákinthos
Corinth
CYCLADES
Náxos
DODECANESE
C. Tainaron
Kíthira
Rhodes
Kárpathos
Crete
5,000 m. 16,404 ft.
2,000 m. 6,562 ft.
1,000 m. 3,281 ft.
500 m. 1,640 ft.
200 m. 656 ft.
100 m. 328 ft.
Sea Level
Below

Poreč 19,946 ....A3
Pula 77,278 ....A3
Rab 8,877 ....B3
Ragusa (Dubrovnik) 66,131....C4
Rijeka 193,044 ....B3
Rovinj 18,277 ....A3
Samobor 43,855 ....B3
Senj 9,582 ....B3
Šibenik 80,148 ....C4
Sinj 59,298 ....C4
Sisak 84,756 ....C3
Slavonska Požega 71,286....C3
Slavonski Brod 106,400 ....D3
Split 235,922 ....C4
Trogir 19,856 ....C4
Varaždin 90,729 ....C2
Vinkovci 95,245 ....D3
Virovitica 47,417 ....C3
Vukovar 81,203 ....D3
Zadar 116,174 ....B3
Zagreb (cap.) 681,173 ....C3
Zara (Zadar) 116,174 ....B3

OTHER FEATURES

Adriatic (sea) B4
Brač (isl.) C4
Cazma (riv.) C3
Cres (isl.) B3
Dalmatia (reg.) C4
Danube (riv.) E3
Dinaric Alps (mts.) B3
Drava (riv.) C3
Dugi Otok (isl.) B3
Hvar (isl.) C4
Istria (pen.) A3
Kamenjak (cape) A3
Korčula (isl.) C4
Kornat (isl.) B4
Krk (isl.) B3
Kupa (riv.) B3
Kvarner (gulf) B3
Lastovo (Lagosta) (isl.) C4
Lošinj (isl.) B3
Mljet (isl.) C4
Pag (isl.) B3
Palagruža (Pelagosa) (isl.) C4
Rab (isl.) B3
Sava (riv.) D3
Slavonia (reg.) C3
Šolta (isl.) C4
Una (riv.) C3
Vis (isl.) C4
Žirje (isl.) B4

FORMER YUGOSLAV REP. OF MACEDONIA

CITIES and TOWNS

Berovo 20,226 ....F5
Bitola 137,835 ....E5
Debar 22,506 ....E5
Gevgelija 32,023 ....F5
Gostivar 101,188 ....E5
Kavadarci 39,738 ....F5
Kičevo 51,452 ....E5
Kočani 47,976 ....F5
Kumanovo 126,368 ....E4
Ohrid 64,316 ....E5
Prilep 99,941 ....E5
Radoviš 28,574 ....F5
Skopje (cap.) 506,547 ....E5
Štip 46,651 ....F5
Struga 54,489 ....E5
Strumica 87,446 ....F5
Tetovo 162,414 ....E5
Titov Veles 64,901 ....E5

OTHER FEATURES

Korab (mt.) E5
Ohrid (lake) E5
Prespa (lake) E5
Rujen (mt.) F4
Vardar (riv.) E5

GREECE

REGIONS

Aegean Islands 417,813 ....G6
Athens, Greater 3,027,331 ....F7
Áyion Óros (aut. dist.) 1,732 ....G5
Central Greece and Euboea 1,099,841 ....F6
Crete 502,165 ....G8
Epirus 324,541 ....E6
Ionian Islands 182,651 ....D6
Macedonia 2,121,953 ....F5
Pelopónnisos 1,012,528 ....F7
Thessaly 695,654 ....F6
Thrace 345,220 ....G5

CITIES and TOWNS

Agrínion 34,328 ....E6
Aíyion 20,824 ....F6
Alexandroúpolis 34,535 ....G5
Amaliás 14,698 ....E7
Árgos 20,702 ....F7
Árta 18,283 ....E6
Atalándi 5,456 ....F6
Athens (cap.) 885,737 ....F7
Áyios Nikólaos 8,130 ....G8
Candia (Iráklion) 101,634 ....G8
Canea (Khaniá) 40,564 ....G8
Corinth 22,658 ....F7
Dhidhimótikhon 8,374 ....H5
Dráma 36,109 ....G5
Édhessa 16,054 ....F5
Ermoúpolis 13,876 ....G7
Flórina 12,562 ....E5
Grevená 7,433 ....E5
Ierápetra 8,575 ....G8
Ioánnina 44,829 ....E6
Iráklion 101,634 ....G8
Itháki 2,037 ....E6
Kalámai 41,911 ....F7
Kálimnos 10,118 ....H7
Kardhítsa 27,291 ....E6
Kastoría 17,133 ....E5
Kateríni 38,016 ....F5
Kaválla 56,375 ....G5
Kérkira 33,561 ....D6
Khalkís 44,867 ....F6
Khaniá 40,564 ....G8
Khíos 24,070 ....G6
Kiáton 7,392 ....F6
Kilkís 11,148 ....F5
Komotiní 34,051 ....G5
Koropí 11,214 ....G7
Kos 11,851 ....H7
Kozáni 30,994 ....F5
Lamía 41,667 ....F6
Lárisa 102,048 ....F6
Lávrion 8,921 ....G7
Levádhia 16,864 ....F6
Marathón 2,052 ....G6
Mégara 17,719 ....F6
Mesolóngion 10,164 ....E6
Mitilíni 24,115 ....H6
Náousa 19,383 ....F5
Návpaktos 9,012 ....F6
Návplion 10,609 ....F7
Náxos 3,735 ....G7
Orestías 12,685 ....H5
Pátrai 141,529 ....E6
Piraiévs (Piraeus) 196,389 ....F7
Pírgos 21,958 ....E7
Préveza 12,662 ....E6
Psakhná 5,320 ....F6
Ptolemaís 22,109 ....E5
Réthimnon 17,736 ....G8
Rhodes (Ródhos) 40,392 ....J7
Salamís 20,437 ....F6
Salonika (Thessaloníki) 406,413 ....F5
Sámos 5,575 ....H7
Samothráki 941 ....G5
Sérrai 45,213 ....F5
Sparta 11,911 ....F7
Thásos 2,300 ....G5
Thessaloníki 406,413 ....F5
Thívai 18,712 ....F6
Tirnávos 10,965 ....F6
Trikkála 40,857 ....E6
Trípolis 21,311 ....F7
Vérria 37,087 ....F5
Vólos 71,378 ....F6
Vónitsani 3,627 ....E6
Xánthi 31,541 ....G5
Yiannitsá 21,082 ....F5
Zante (Zákinthos) 9,764 ....E7

OTHER FEATURES

Aegean (sea) G6
Akrí (cape) E7
Aktí (pen.) G5
Amorgós (isl.) G7
Anáfi (isl.) G7
Andikíthira (isl.) F8
Ándros (isl.) G7
Arda (riv.) G5
Argolís (gulf) F7
Astipálaia (isl.) H7
Áthos (mt.) G5
Áyios Evstrátios (isl.) G6
Áyios Yeóryios (cape) G5
Cephalonia (Kefalliníia) (isl.) E6
Corfu (Kérkira) (isl.) D6
Corinth (gulf) F6
Crete (isl.) G8
Crete (sea) G7
Cyclades (isls.) G7
Día (isl.) G8
Dodecanese (isls.) H8
Euboea (Évvoia) (isl.) G6
Évros (riv.) H5
Gávdhos (isl.) F8
Ídhi (mt.) G8
Ikaría (isl.) G7
Ionian (sea) D7
Íos (isl.) G7
Itháki (Ithaca) (isl.) E6
Kafirévs (cape) G6
Kálimnos (isl.) H7
Kárpathos (isl.) H8
Kásos (isl.) H8
Kassándra (pen.) F6
Kéa (isl.) G7
Kefalliníia (isl.) E6
Kérkira (isl.) D6
Khálki (isl.) H7
Khaniá (gulf) G8
Khíos (isl.) G6
Kímilos (isl.) G7
Kiparissía (gulf) E7
Kíthira (isl.) F7
Kíthnos (isl.) G7
Kos (isl.) H7
Kriós (cape) F8
Kriti (Crete) (isl.) G8
Lakonía (gulf) F7
Léros (isl.) H7
Lésvos (isl.) G6
Levítha (isl.) H7
Levkás (isl.) E6
Límnos (isl.) G6
Maléa (cape) F7
Matapan (Taínaron) (cape) F7
Merabéllou (gulf) H8
Mesará (gulf) G8
Messíni (gulf) E7
Míkinos (isl.) G7
Mílos (isl.) G7
Mirtóön (sea) F7
Náxos (isl.) G7
Néstos (riv.) G5
Nísiros (isl.) H7
Northern Sporades (isls.) F6
Olympia (isls.) E7
Olympus (mt.) F5
Parnassus (mt.) F6
Páros (isl.) G7
Pátmos (isl.) H7
Paxoí (isl.) D6
Pindus (mts.) E6
Pinió (riv.) E6
Prespa (lake) E5
Psará (isl.) G6
Psevdhókavos (cape) G6
Rhodes (isl.) H7
Rhodope (mts.) G5
Salonika (Thermaic) (gulf) F6
Sámos (isl.) H7
Samothráki (isl.) G5
Saría (isl.) H8
Saronic (gulf) F7
Sérifos (isl.) G7
Sídheros (cape) H8
Sífnos (isl.) G7
Sími (isl.) H7
Síros (isl.) G7
Sithoniá (pen.) F5
Skíros (isl.) G6
Spátha (cape) F8
Strimón (gulf) G5
Strofádhes (isls.) E7
Taínaron (cape) F7
Thásos (isls.) G5
Thermaic (gulf) F5
Thíra (isl.) G7
Tílos (isl.) H7
Tínos (isl.) G7
Toronaic (gulf) F5
Vardar (riv.) E5
Vólvi (lake) F5
Voïviis (lake) F6
Voúxa (cape) F8
Zákinthos (Zante) (isl.) E7

ROMANIA

CITIES and TOWNS

Aiud 27,600 ....F2
Alba Iulia 53,000 ....F2
Alexandria 43,700 ....G3
Anina 11,300 ....E3
Arad 182,000 ....E2
Babadag 9,000 ....J3
Bacău 156,200 ....H2
Baia Mare 123,300 ....F2
Băileşti 21,500 ....F3
Balş 17,300 ....G3
Beiuş 10,100 ....F2
Bicaz 9,300 ....G2
Bîrlad 63,800 ....H2
Bistrita 59,800 ....G2
Blaj 22,200 ....F2
Borşa 25,287 ....F2
Botoşani 84,900 ....H2
Brad 18,600 ....F2
Brăila 219,200 ....H3
Braşov 320,200 ....G3
Bucharest (Bucureşti) (cap.) 1,929,400 ....G3
Buhuşi 20,300 ....H2
Buzău 116,300 ....H3
Buziaş 8,700 ....E3
Calafat 17,100 ....F3
Călăraşi 58,000 ....H3
Caracal 33,600 ....G3
Caransebeş 28,800 ....F3
Carei 25,500 ....F2
Cernavodă 15,000 ....J3
Chişineu Criş 9,600 ....E2
Cîmpia Turzii 25,300 ....F2
Cîmpina 35,300 ....G3
Cîmpulung 37,400 ....G3
Cîmpulung Moldovenesc 20,500 ....G2
Cisnădie 21,100 ....G3
Cluj-Napoca 289,800 ....F2
Comaneşti 18,500 ....H2
Constanta 293,900 ....J3
Corabia 20,300 ....G4
Costeşti 10,900 ....G3
Craiova 239,700 ....F3
Curtea de Argeş 26,900 ....G3
Darabani 11,500 ....H1
Dej 36,500 ....F2
Deva 73,300 ....F3
Dorohoi 25,700 ....H2
Drăgăneşti Olt 11,800 ....G3
Drăgăşani 17,300 ....G3
Drobeta-Turnu Severin 86,600 ....F3
Făgăraş 37,200 ....G3
Fălticeni 24,000 ....H2
Feteşti 29,600 ....H3
Focşani 70,700 ....H3
Găeşti 14,000 ....G3
Galati 268,000 ....H3
Gheorghe Gheorghiu-Dej 46,100 ....H2
Gheorghieni 21,800 ....G2
Gherla 20,700 ....G2
Giurgiu 57,000 ....G4
Hateg 10,200 ....F3
Hîrlău 8,900 ....H2
Hîrşova 9,000 ....J3
Huedin 8,700 ....F2
Hunedoara 85,700 ....F3
Huşi 26,000 ....J2
Iaşi 279,800 ....H2
Ineu 10,800 ....E2
Jimbolia 14,600 ....E3
Lipova 12,900 ....E2
Luduş 16,000 ....G2
Lugoj 50,000 ....E3
Lupeni 29,100 ....F3
Mangalia 31,100 ....J4
Medgidia 45,300 ....J3
Mediaş 69,000 ....G2
Miercurea Ciuc 40,400 ....G2
Mizil 15,200 ....H3
Moineşti 21,200 ....H2
Moldova Nouă 17,800 ....E3
Moreni 18,900 ....G3
Ocna Mureş 16,200 ....G2
Odorheiu Secuiesc 36,200 ....G2
Oltenita 26,800 ....H3
Oradea 192,600 ....E2
Orăştie 19,900 ....F3
Oravita 114,300 ....E3
Orşova 115,800 ....F3
Panciu 77,900 ....H3
Paşcani 229,500 ....H2
Petrila 25,900 ....F3
Petroşeni 45,600 ....F3
Piatra Neamt 93,300 ....H2
Piteşti 143,600 ....G3
Ploieşti 219,900 ....H3
Pucioasa 14,100 ....G3
Rădăuti 26,000 ....G2
Reghin 33,600 ....G2
Reşita 96,800 ....E3
Rîmnicu Sărat 32,400 ....H3
Rîmnicu Vîlcea 78,900 ....G3
Roman 62,700 ....H2
Roşiori de Vede 31,700 ....G3
Săcele 33,900 ....G3
Salonta 20,400 ....E2
Satu Mare 115,600 ....F2
Sebeş 29,500 ....F3
Segarcea 8,700 ....F3
Sfîntu Gheorghe 57,900 ....G3
Sibiu 164,200 ....G3
Sighetu Marmaţiei 40,500 ....F2
Sighişoara 33,000 ....G2
Şimleul Silvaniei 15,100 ....F2
Sinaia 14,700 ....G3
Sînnicolaul Mare 13,600 ....E2
Slatina 62,800 ....G3
Slobozia 39,400 ....H3
Sovata 11,200 ....G2
Strehaia 11,800 ....F3
Suceava 76,500 ....H2
Tăşnad 10,400 ....F2
Techirghiol 11,800 ....J3
Tecuci 40,300 ....H3
Timişoara 288,200 ....E3
Tîrgovişte 77,500 ....G3
Tîrgu Jiu 75,200 ....F3
Tîrgu Mureş 141,300 ....G2
Tîrgu Neamt 16,600 ....H2
Tîrgu Ocna 12,800 ....H2
Tîrgu Secuiesc 19,800 ....H2
Tîrnăveni 27,900 ....G2
Toplita 15,200 ....G2
Tulcea 73,600 ....J3
Turda 58,700 ....F2
Turnu Măgurele 33,000 ....G4
Urlata 11,200 ....H3
Urziceni 14,300 ....H3
Vaslui 50,100 ....H2
Vatra Dornei 17,800 ....G2
Videle 11,500 ....G3
Vişeul de Sus 20,800 ....G2
Zalău 43,300 ....F2
Zărneşti 25,000 ....G3
Zimnicea 16,400 ....G4

OTHER FEATURES

Argeş (riv.) G3
Bîrlad (riv.) H2
Black (sea) J4
Brăila (marshes) H3
Buzău (riv.) H3
Carpathian (mts.) G2
Crişul Alb (riv.) F2
Crişul Repede (riv.) F2
Danube (delta) J3
Danube (riv.) H4
Ialomiţa (marshes) J3
Ialomiţa (riv.) H3
Jijia (riv.) H2
Jiu (riv.) F3
Moldoveanul (mt.) G3
Mureş (riv.) E2
Olt (riv.) G3
Peleaga (mt.) F3
Pietrosul (mt.) G2
Prut (riv.) J2
Siret (riv.) H2
Someş (riv.) F2
Timiş (riv.) E3
Tîrnava Mare (riv.) G2
Transylvanian Alps (mts.) G3

SLOVENIA

CITIES and TOWNS

Bled 4,710 ....A2
Brežice 25,238 ....C3
Celje 63,877 ....B2
Jesenice 31,094 ....A2
Kočevje 18,139 ....B3
Koper 41,843 ....A3
Kranj 66,879 ....B2
Krško 27,774 ....B3
Ljubljana (cap.) 305,211 ....B3
Maribor 185,699 ....B2
Murska Sobota 64,299 ....C2
Nova Gorizia 56,758 ....A3
Novo Mesto 55,584 ....B3
Piran 15,235 ....A3
Postojna 19,892 ....B3
Ptuj 67,754 ....B2
Ravne na Koroškem 25,907 ....B2
Škofja Loka 35,276 ....B2
Trbovlje 18,786 ....B2
Tržič 14,014 ....B2
Velenje 38,041 ....B2

OTHER FEATURES

Adriatic (sea) B4
Drava (riv.) C3
Kupa (riv.) B3
Mur (riv.) B2
Triglav (mt.) A2

YUGOSLAVIA

INTERNAL DIVISIONS

Kosovo (aut. reg.) 1,240,919 ....E4
Montenegro (rep.) 527,207 ....D4
Serbia (rep.) 8,401,673 ....E3
Vojvodina (aut. prov.) 1,953,980 ....D3

CITIES and TOWNS

Aleksinac 67,286 ....E4
Apatin 33,843 ....D3
Arendjelovac 46,803 ....E3
Bačka Topola 41,889 ....D3
Bar 32,535 ....D4
Bečej 44,243 ....E3
Bela Crkva 25,690 ....E3
Belgrade (cap.) 1,470,073 ....E3
Beograde (Belgrade) (cap.) 1,470,073 ....E3
Bijelo Polje 55,634 ....D4
Bor 56,486 ....E3
Čačak 110,676 E4
Caribrod (Dimitrovgrad) 15,158 ....F4
Cetinje 20,213 ....D4
Ćuprija 38,841 ....E4
Dimitrovgrad 15,158 ....F4
Djakovica 92,203 ....E4
Gnjilane 84,085 ....E4
Gornji Milanovac 50,651 ....E3
Herceg Novi 23,258 ....D4
Ivangrad 49,772 ....D4
Kanjiža 32,709 ....D2
Kikinda 69,854 ....E3
Knjaževac 48,789 ....F4
Kosovska Mitrovica 105,353 ....E4
Kotor 20,455 ....D4
Kragujevac 164,823 ....E3
Kraljevo 121,622 ....E4
Kruševac 132,972 ....E4
Leskovac 159,001 ....E4
Loznica 84,180 ....D3
Negotin 63,973 ....F3
Nikšić 72,299 ....D4
Niš 230,711 ....E4
Novi Pazar 74,000 ....E4
Novi Sad 257,685 ....D3
Pančevo 123,791 ....E3
Paraćin 64,718 ....E4
Peć 111,071 ....E4
Pirot 69,653 ....F4
Plav 19,560 ....D4
Pljevlja 43,316 ....D4
Podgorica 132,290 ....D4
Požarevac 81,123 ....E3
Preševo 33,948 ....E4
Priboj 35,200 ....D4
Prijedor 108,868 ....C3
Prijepolje 46,902 ....D4
Priština 210,040 ....E4
Prizren 134,526 ....E4
Prokuplje 56,256 ....E4
Ruma 55,083 ....D3
Šabac 119,668 ....D3
Senta 30,519 ....D3
Šid 37,459 ....D3
Sjenica 35,570 ....E4
Smederevo 107,366 ....E3
Smederevska Palanka 60,945 ....E3
Sombor 99,168 ....D3
Sremska Mitrovica 85,129 ....D3
Subotica 154,611 ....D2
Surdulica 27,029 ....F4
Svetozarevo 76,460 ....E4
Svilajnac 34,888 ....E3
Titovo Užice 77,049 ....D4
Trstenik 53,695 ....E4
Ub 36,259 ....E3
Ulcinj 21,575 ....D5
Uroševac 113,680 ....E4
Valjevo 95,449 ....D3
Velika Plana 52,619 ....E3
Veliki Bečkerek (Zrenjanin) 139,000 ....E3
Vranje 82,527 ....E4
Vrbas 45,755 ....D3
Vršac 61,005 ....E3
Vučitrn 65,512 ....E4
Zaječar 76,681 ....F4
Zrenjanin 139,000 ....E3

OTHER FEATURES

Adriatic (sea) B4
Bobotov Kuk (mt.) D4
Danube (riv.) E3
Drina (riv.) D3
Ibar (riv.) E4
Lim (riv.) D4
Midzhur (mt.) F4
Morava (riv.) E3
Sava (riv.) D3
Scutari (lake) D4
Timok (riv.) F3
Tisa (riv.) E3

The Balkan States

CONIC PROJECTION

SCALE OF MILES

0 25 50 75 100 125 150 175

SCALE OF KILOMETERS

Capitals of Countries	☆
Administrative Centers	△
International Boundaries	
Major Internal Boundaries	
Minor Internal Boundaries	
Canals	

* Former Yugoslav Republic of Macedonia

BULGARIA and GREECE are divided into regions and departments, respectively. Because of the scale no attempt has been made to delimit and name these sub-divisions; their administrative centers have, however, been designated.

The larger divisions named in Greece are well-known geographical regions, without administrative function.

ROMANIA consists of thirty-nine counties and three cities of regional status, Bucharest, Constanța and Petroșeni. Scale does not permit delimiting these counties.

ALBANIA is divided into twenty-seven districts. Scale does not permit the delimitation of these divisions.

© Copyright HAMMOND INCORPORATED, Maplewood, N.J.

Topography

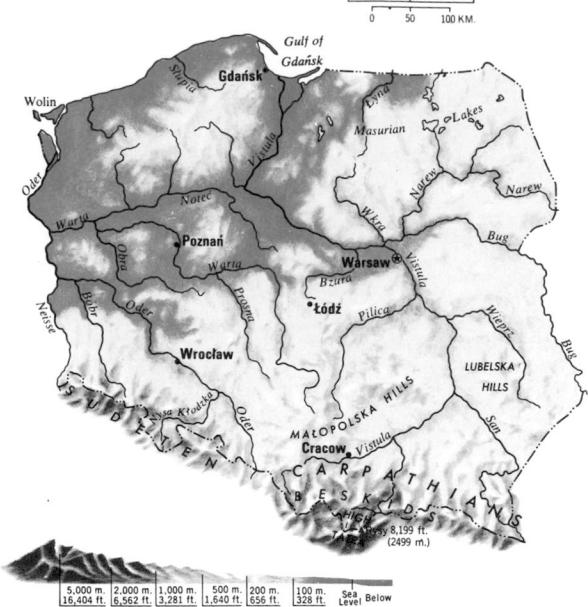

100 MI.
0 50
0 50 100 KM.

Gulf of Gdańsk

Wolin
Gdańsk
Słupia
Lakes
Masurian
Oder
Warta
Noteć
Poznań
Warta
Wkra
Narew
Bug
Warsaw
Bzura
Łódź
Pilica
Wieprz
Bug
Wrocław
LUBELSKA HILLS
MAŁOPOLSKA HILLS
Vistula
Cracow
CARPATHIANS
BESKIDS
HIGH TATRA 8,199 ft. (2499 m.)

5,000 m.	2,000 m.	1,000 m.	500 m.	200 m.	100 m.	Sea
16,404 ft.	6,562 ft.	3,281 ft.	1,640 ft.	656 ft.	328 ft.	Level Below

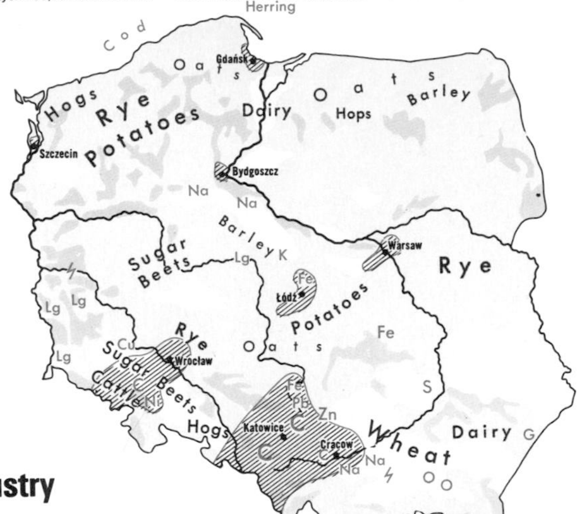

MAJOR MINERAL OCCURRENCES

Ag Silver
C Coal
Cu Copper
Fe Iron Ore
G Natural Gas
K Potash
Lg Lignite

Na Salt
Ni Nickel
O Petroleum
Pb Lead
S Sulfur
Zn Zinc

 Water Power
Major Industrial Areas

DOMINANT LAND USE

☐ Cereals (chiefly wheat)

☐ Rye, Oats, Barley, Potatoes

☐ General Farming, Livestock

▨ Forests

Agriculture, Industry and Resources

PROVINCES

Biała Podlaska 304,028	F3
Białystok 687,806	F2
Bielsko 895,357	D4
Bydgoszcz 1,104,048	C2
Chełm 245,484	F3
Ciechanów 425,608	E2
Cracow (Kraków) 1,223,137	E3
Cracow (city) 651,300	E3
Częstochowa 773,365	D3
Elbląg 475,862	D1
Gdańsk 1,417,801	D1
Gorzów 497,342	B2
Jelenia Góra 514,947	B3
Kalisz 706,514	D3
Katowice 3,953,769	D3
Kielce 1,123,691	E3
Konin 465,928	D2
Koszalin 502,750	C1
Krosno 491,471	E4
Legnica 510,000	C3
Leszno 383,315	C3
Łódź 777,800	D3

Łódź (city) 1,139,379	D3
Łomza 344,518	F2
Lublin 1,010,641	F3
Nowy Sącz 690,737	E4
Olsztyn 746,185	E2
Opole 1,010,416	C3
Ostrołęka 393,427	E2
Piła 475,953	C2
Piotrków 638,948	D3
Płock 512,626	D2
Poznań 1,323,368	C2
Przemyśl 404,200	F4
Radom 745,374	E3
Rzeszów 716,317	F4
Siedlce 648,111	F3
Sieradz 408,082	D3
Skierniewice 416,690	E3
Słupsk 410,049	C1
Suwałki 467,048	F1
Szczecin 964,298	B2
Tarnobrzeg 594,255	E3
Tarnów 664,953	E4
Toruń 656,421	D2
Wałbrzych 738,092	C3

Warsaw 2,415,950	E2
Warsaw (city) 1,377,100	E2
Włocławek 427,418	D2
Wrocław 1,122,806	C3
Zamość 488,193	F3
Zielona Góra 655,146	B3

CITIES and TOWNS

Aleksandrów Łódzki 19,711	D3
Allenstein (Olsztyn) 160,956	E2
Andrychów 22,387	D4
Augustów 28,307	F2
Auschwitz (Oświęcim) 45,402	D3
Bartoszyce 25,195	E1
Bedzin 76,883	B3
Belchatów 55,632	D3
Beuthen (Bytom) 229,991	A3
Biała Podlaska 52,119	F3
Bialogard 23,973	C1
Bialystok 267,670	F2
Bielawa 34,224	C3
Bielsk Podlaski 26,145	F2

Bielsko-Biala 181,072	D4
Bilgoraj 25,542	F3
Bochnia 28,846	E4
Bogatynia 18,616	B3
Boguszów-Gorce 19,452	B3
Boleslawiec 43,076	B3
Braniewo 17,594	D1
Breslau (Wrocław) 640,557	C3
Brieg (Brzeg) 38,504	C3
Brodnica 26,056	D2
Brzeg 38,504	C3
Busko Zdrój 17,675	E3
Bydgoszcz 380,426	C2
Bytom 229,991	A3
Bytów 16,720	C1
Chelm 64,683	F3
Chelmno 21,506	D2
Chodziez 19,831	C2
Chojnice 37,733	C2
Chorzów 131,850	B4
Chrzanów 42,195	B4
Ciechanów 43,068	E2
Cieszyn 36,682	D4
Cracow 745,568	E3

Herring
Cod
Hogs
Oats
Rye
Potatoes
Gdańsk
Dairy
Hops
Oats
Barley
Szczecin
Bydgoszcz
Na
Sugar Beets
Barley
K
Lg
Fe
Warsaw
Rye
Lg
Lg
Rye
Łódź
Potatoes
Fe
Sugar Beets
Wrocław
Oats
S
Hogs
Katowice
Zn
Cracow
Wheat
Dairy G
Na
O O

Former Republics of Yugoslavia

CONIC PROJECTION
MILES
0 25 50 75 100
KILOMETERS
0 25 50 75 100

Capitals
⊛ National
★ Federal Republics
⊙ Autonomous Provinces

Boundaries
National
Federal Republics
Autonomous Provinces
Canals

© Copyright HAMMOND INCORPORATED, Maplewood, N.J.

AUSTRIA
Carnic Alps
ITALY
Villach
Klagenfurt
Belluno
Drau
Mur
Murska Sobota
Zalaegerszeg
Kecskemét
Dunaújváros
Lake Balaton
HUNGARY
Szeged
Békéscsaba
Arad
Timișoara
Maribor
SLOVENIA
Ljubljana
Triglav 9,393 ft. (2863 m.)
Zagreb
VOJVODINA
Novi Sad
Belgrade (Beograd)
ROMANIA
Reșita
Trieste
Venice (Venezia)
Gulf of Venice
Rijeka (Fiume)
Istria
BOSNIA AND HERZEGOVINA
Banja Luka
Tuzla
Zenica
Sarajevo
Ploča 7,310 ft. (2228 m.)
Split
ADRIATIC SEA
ITALY
San Marino
Ancona
Pescara
MONTENEGRO
KOSOVO
Priština
BULGARIA
Sofia
Pernik
FYROM
Skopje
ALBANIA
Tirane (Tirana)
Korab 9,026 ft. (2751 m.)
GREECE
Thessaloniki

Longitude 18° East of Greenwich

* Former Yugoslav Republic of Macedonia

Czechowice-Dziedzice 35,194 ... D4
Czeladź 37,569 ... B4
Czestochowa 256,578 ... D3
Dabrowa Górnicza 134,934 ... B3
Danzig (Gdańsk) 462,076 ... D1
Debica 44,966 ... E3
Deblin 18,763 ... E3
Dzialdowo 19,295 ... E2
Dzierzoniów 37,908 ... C3
Elbing (Elblag) 125,778 ... D1
Elblag 125,778 ... D1
Elk 51,274 ... F2
Gdańsk 462,076 ... D1
Gdynia 251,303 ... D1
Gizycko 28,918 ... E1
Gleiwitz (Gliwice) 212,481 ... A4
Gliwice 212,481 ... A4
Głogów (Glogau) 71,854 ... C3
Gniezno 69,646 ... C2
Goleniów 21,756 ... B2
Gorlice 29,019 ... E4
Gorzów Wielkopolski 123,222 ... B2
Gostyń 19,344 ... C3
Gostynin 18,738 ... D2
Grajewo 20,635 ... F2
Grodzisk Mazowiecki 24,648 ... E2
Grudziadz 101,571 ... D2
Grünberg (Zielona Góra) 113,108 ... B3
Gryfice 17,294 ... B2
Gryfino 20,783 ... B2
Guben (Gubin) 17,779 ... B3
Hajnowka 23,390 ... F2
Hindenburg (Zabrze) 202,824 ... A4
Hirschberg (Jelenia Góra) 93,205 ... B3
Ilawa 31,312 ... D2
Inowrocław 76,497 ... D2
Jarocin 24,692 ... C3
Jaroslaw 41,267 ... F4
Jaslo 37,046 ... E4
Jastrzebie Zdroj 102,312 ... D3
Jawor 24,079 ... C3
Jaworzno 98,480 ... B4
Jedrzejów 18,109 ... E3
Jelenia Góra 93,205 ... B3
Kamienna Góra 21,000 ... B3
Katowice 366,077 ... B4
Kedzierzyn-Koźle 71,012 ... D3
Ketrzyn 29,987 ... E1
Kety 18,731 ... D4
Kielce 213,012 ... E3
Klodzko 30,261 ... C3
Kluczbork 25,988 ... D3
Knurów 44,468 ... A4
Kolberg (Kołobrzeg) 44,426 ... B1
Kolo 22,807 ... D2
Kołobrzeg 44,426 ... B1
Konin 79,315 ... D2
Końskie 21,548 ... E3
Kościan 23,554 ... C2
Kościerzyna 22,287 ... C1
Köslin (Koszalin) 107,592 ... C1
Koszalin 107,592 ... C1
Kozienice 20,557 ... E3
Kraków (Cracow) 745,568 ... E3
Krapkowice 19,452 ... D3
Kraśnik Fabryczny 36,202 ... F3
Krasnystaw 19,832 ... F3
Krosno 49,094 ... E4
Krotoszyn 27,807 ... C3
Kutno 49,753 ... D2
Kwidzin 36,409 ... D2
Landsberg (Gorzów Wielkopolski) 123,222 ... B2
Lask 19,569 ... D3
Laziska Górne 19,569 ... A4
Lebork 33,981 ... C1
Leczyca 16,491 ... D2
Legionowo 50,577 ... E2
Legnica 103,949 ... C3
Leszcyny 29,746 ... A4
Leszno 57,673 ... C3
Liegnitz (Legnica) 103,949 ... C3
Lódź 849,204 ... D3
Lomza 57,976 ... F2
Lowicz 30,322 ... D2
Lubań 23,708 ... B3
Lubartów 22,117 ... F3
Lubin 80,757 ... C3
Lublin 348,881 ... F3
Lubliniec 33,084 ... D3
Luboń 20,255 ... C2
Luków 30,356 ... F3
Malbork (Marienburg) 39,018 ... D1
Miedzyrzecz 19,805 ... B2
Mielec 60,187 ... E3
Mikolow 37,022 ... B4
Mińsk Mazowiecki 33,913 ... E2
Mlawa 28,743 ... E2
Mragowo 21,674 ... E2
Myslowice 92,009 ... B4
Myszków 33,084 ... D3
Naklo nad Notecia 20,056 ... C2
Neissa (Nysa) 46,686 ... C3
Nowa Ruda 27,507 ... C3
Nowa Sól 43,053 ... B3
Nowy Dwór Mazowiecki 26,842 ... E2
Nowy Sacz 76,658 ... E4
Nowy Targ 32,143 ... E4
Nysa 46,686 ... C3
Olawa 31,188 ... C3
Oleśnica 37,767 ... C3
Olkusz 40,571 ... D3
Olsztyn 160,956 ... E2
Opoczno 20,670 ... E3
Opole (Oppeln) 126,962 ... C3
Orzesze 18,100 ... A4
Ostróda 33,641 ... E2
Ostroleka 49,032 ... E2
Ostrów Mazowiecka 20,367 ... E2
Ostrów Wielkopolski 72,085 ... C3
Ostrowiec Świetokrzyski 77,466 ... E3
Oświecim 45,402 ... D3
Otwock 44,488 ... E2
Ozorków 21,676 ... D3
Pabianice 74,755 ... D3
Piaseczno 24,359 ... D2
Plekary Ślaskie 68,274 ... B4
Pila 71,109 ... C2
Pionki 20,701 ... E3
Piotrków Trybunalski 80,598 ... D3
Pisz 18,286 ... E2
Pleszew 17,712 ... C3
Plock 120,933 ... D2
Plońsk 20,956 ... E2
Police 33,478 ... B2
Polkowice 20,823 ... C3
Poznań 586,908 ... C2
Prudnik 24,598 ... C3
Pruszcz Gdanski 20,575 ... D1
Pruszków 53,889 ... E2
Przemyśl 68,121 ... F4
Pulawy 52,624 ... F3
Pultusk 17,619 ... E2
Racibórz 62,733 ... D3
Radom 226,025 ... E3
Radomsko 50,059 ... D3
Ratibor (Racibórz) 62,733 ... D3
Rawa Mazowiecka 17,428 ... E3
Rawicz 20,548 ... C3
Ruda Ślaska 169,017 ... B4
Rumia 36,762 ... D1
Rybnik 142,059 ... D3
Rzeszów 150,702 ... F4
Sandomierz 23,815 ... E3
Sanok 39,163 ... F4
Schneidemühl (Piła) 71,109 ... C2
Schweidnitz (Świdnica) 62,424 ... C3
Siedlce 70,529 ... F2
Siemianowice Ślaskie 80,412 ... B4
Sieradz 42,041 ... D3
Sierpc 18,956 ... D2
Skarzysko-Kamienna 50,455 ... E3
Skawina 23,487 ... D4
Skierniewice 43,963 ... E3
Słupsk 100,127 ... C1
Sochaczew 38,170 ... E2
Sokólka 19,059 ... F2
Sopot 46,874 ... D1
Sosnowiec 259,318 ... B4
Śrem 27,719 ... C2
Środa Wielkopolska 20,053 ... C2
Stalowa Wola 68,856 ... F3
Starachowice 55,996 ... E3
Stargard Szczeciński 69,852 ... B2
Starogard Gdański 47,142 ... D2
Stettin (Szczecin) 411,275 ... B2
Stolp (Słupsk) 100,127 ... C1
Strzegom 17,185 ... C3
Strzelce Opolskie 21,238 ... D3
Suwalki 59,684 ... F1
Swarzedz 22,022 ... C2
Świdnica 62,424 ... C3
Świdnik 39,651 ... F3
Świebodzice 24,392 ... C3
Świebodzin 21,617 ... B2
Świecie 25,415 ... D2
Świetochlowice 58,770 ... A4
Świnoujście (Swinemünde) 42,932 ... B1
Szamotuly 17,970 ... C2
Szczecin 411,275 ... B2
Szczecinek 40,428 ... C2
Szczytno 26,878 ... E2
Tarnobrzeg 45,702 ... E3
Tarnów 120,639 ... E4
Tarnowskie Góry 73,460 ... A3
Tczew 58,887 ... D1
Tomaszów Lubelski 20,011 ... F3
Tomaszów Mazowiecki 69,579 ... E3
Toruń 200,860 ... D2
Trzebinia-Siersza 20,376 ... C4
Turek 28,559 ... D2
Tychy 189,816 ... B4
Wadowice 18,691 ... D4
Wagrowiec 22,736 ... C2
Wałbrzych 141,504 ... C3
Walcz 26,367 ... C2
Waldenburg (Wałbrzych) 141,504 ... C3
Warsaw (Warszawa) (cap.) 1,651,225 ... E2
Wejherowo 46,465 ... D1
Wieliczka 17,775 ... E3
Wieluń 24,061 ... D3
Włocławek 120,680 ... D2
Wodzislaw Ślaski 111,099 ... D4
Wolomin 36,762 ... E2
Wrocław 640,557 ... C3
Września 27,449 ... C2
Wyszków 23,411 ... E2
Zabrze 202,824 ... A4
Zagań 27,333 ... B3
Zakopane 28,417 ... D4
Zambrów 22,175 ... F2
Zamość 60,565 ... F3
Zary 39,172 ... B3
Zawiercie 56,017 ... D3
Zduńska Wola 44,686 ... D3
Zgierz 58,836 ... D3
Zgorzelec 36,008 ... B3
Zielona Góra 113,108 ... B3
Zlotów 17,533 ... C2
Zyrardów 33,196 ... E2
Zywiec 30,572 ... D4

OTHER FEATURES

Baltic (sea) ... B1
Beskids (range) ... D4
Biebrza (riv.) ... F2
Bobr (riv.) ... B3
Brda (riv.) ... C2
Brynica (riv.) ... B4
Bug (riv.) ... F2
Danzig (Gdańsk) (gulf) ... D1
Dukla (pass) ... E4
Dunajec (riv.) ... E4
Frisches Haff (lag.) ... D1
Gwda (riv.) ... C2
Hel (pen.) ... D1
High Tatra (range) ... D4
Jezioro Śniardwy (lake) ... E2
Kłodnica (riv.) ... A4
Łyna (riv.) ... E1
Mamry, Jezioro (lake) ... E1
Masurian (lakes) ... E2
Narew (riv.) ... E2
Neisse (riv.) ... B3
Noteć (riv.) ... B2
Nysa Łuzycka (Neisse) (riv.) ... B3
Nysa Kłodzka (riv.) ... C3
Oder (riv.) ... B2
Oder-Haff (lag.) ... B2
Orava (res.) ... D4
Pilica (riv.) ... D3
Plonia (riv.) ... B2
Pomeranian (bay) ... B1
Prosna (riv.) ... C3
Przemsza (riv.) ... B4
Rega (riv.) ... B2
Rysy (mt.) ... D4
San (riv.) ... F3
Słupia (riv.) ... C1
Sudeten (range) ... B3
Uznam (Usedom) (isl.) ... B1
Vistula (riv.) ... D2
Vistula (spit) ... D1
Warmia (reg.) ... D1
Warta (riv.) ... B2
Wieprz (riv.) ... F3
Wisła (Vistula) (riv.) ... D2
Wkra (riv.) ... E2
Włocławskie (lake) ... D2
Wolin (Wollin) (isl.) ... B2
Zegrzýnskie (lake) ... E2

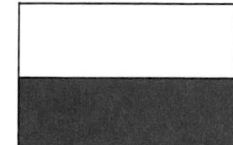

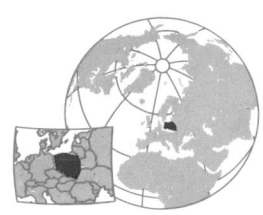

AREA 120,725 sq. mi. (312,678 sq. km.)
POPULATION 37,931,000
CAPITAL Warsaw
LARGEST CITY Warsaw
HIGHEST POINT Rysy 8,199 ft. (2,499 m.)
MONETARY UNIT zloty
MAJOR LANGUAGE Polish
MAJOR RELIGION Roman Catholicism

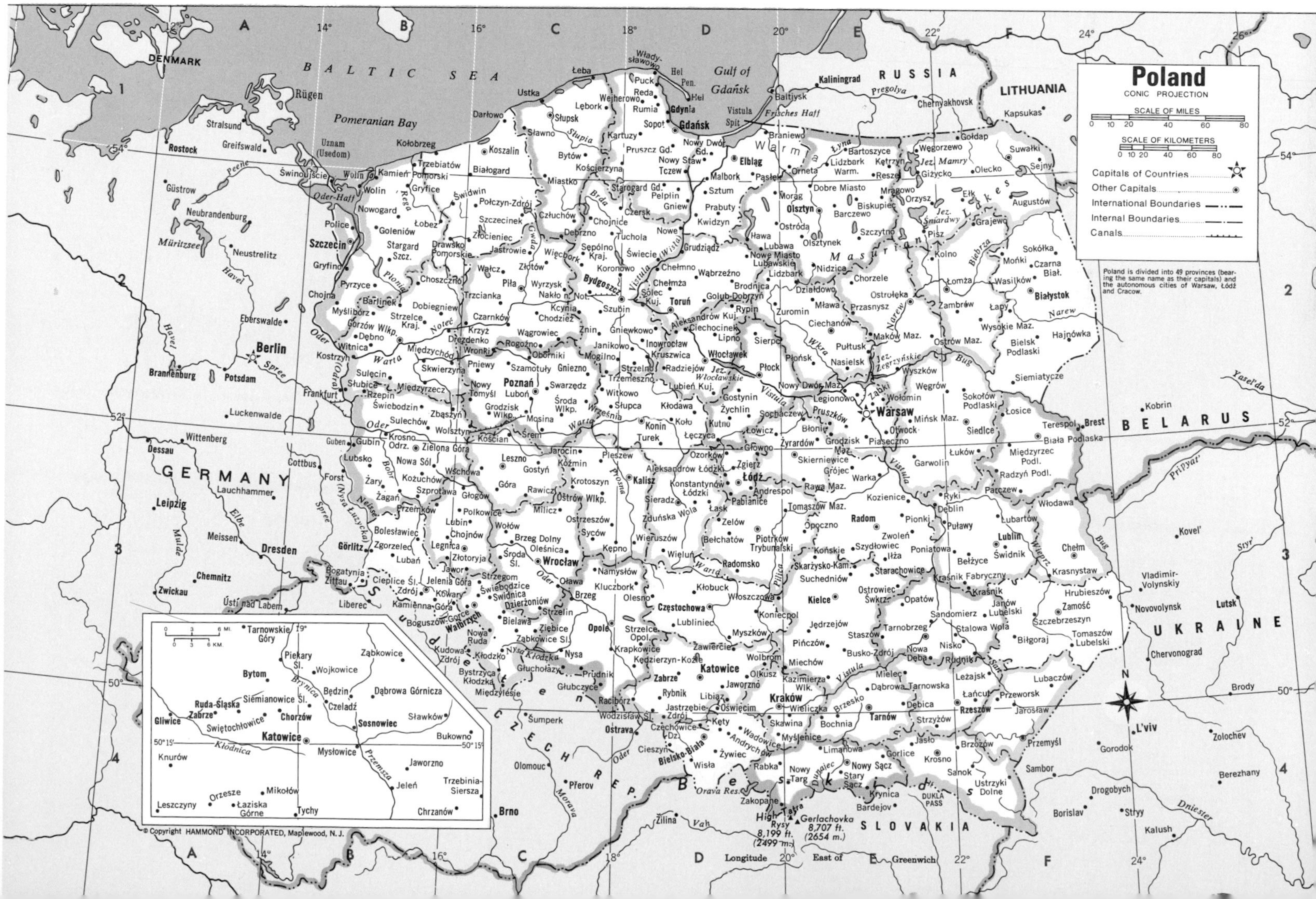

Poland
CONIC PROJECTION
SCALE OF MILES
0 10 20 40 60 80
SCALE OF KILOMETERS
0 10 20 40 60 80
Capitals of Countries
Other Capitals
International Boundaries
Internal Boundaries
Canals
Poland is divided into 49 provinces (bearing the same name as their capitals) and the autonomous cities of Warsaw, Łódź and Cracow.
BALTIC SEA
Gulf of Gdańsk
Pomeranian Bay
DENMARK
RUSSIA
LITHUANIA
BELARUS
UKRAINE
SLOVAKIA
CZECH REP.
GERMANY
Warsaw
Berlin
Kraków
Łódź
Poznań
Wrocław
Gdańsk
Szczecin
Katowice
Lublin
Białystok
Rysy 8,199 ft. (2499 m.)
Gerlachovka 8,707 ft. (2654 m.)
Longitude 20° East of Greenwich
© Copyright HAMMOND INCORPORATED, Maplewood, N. J.

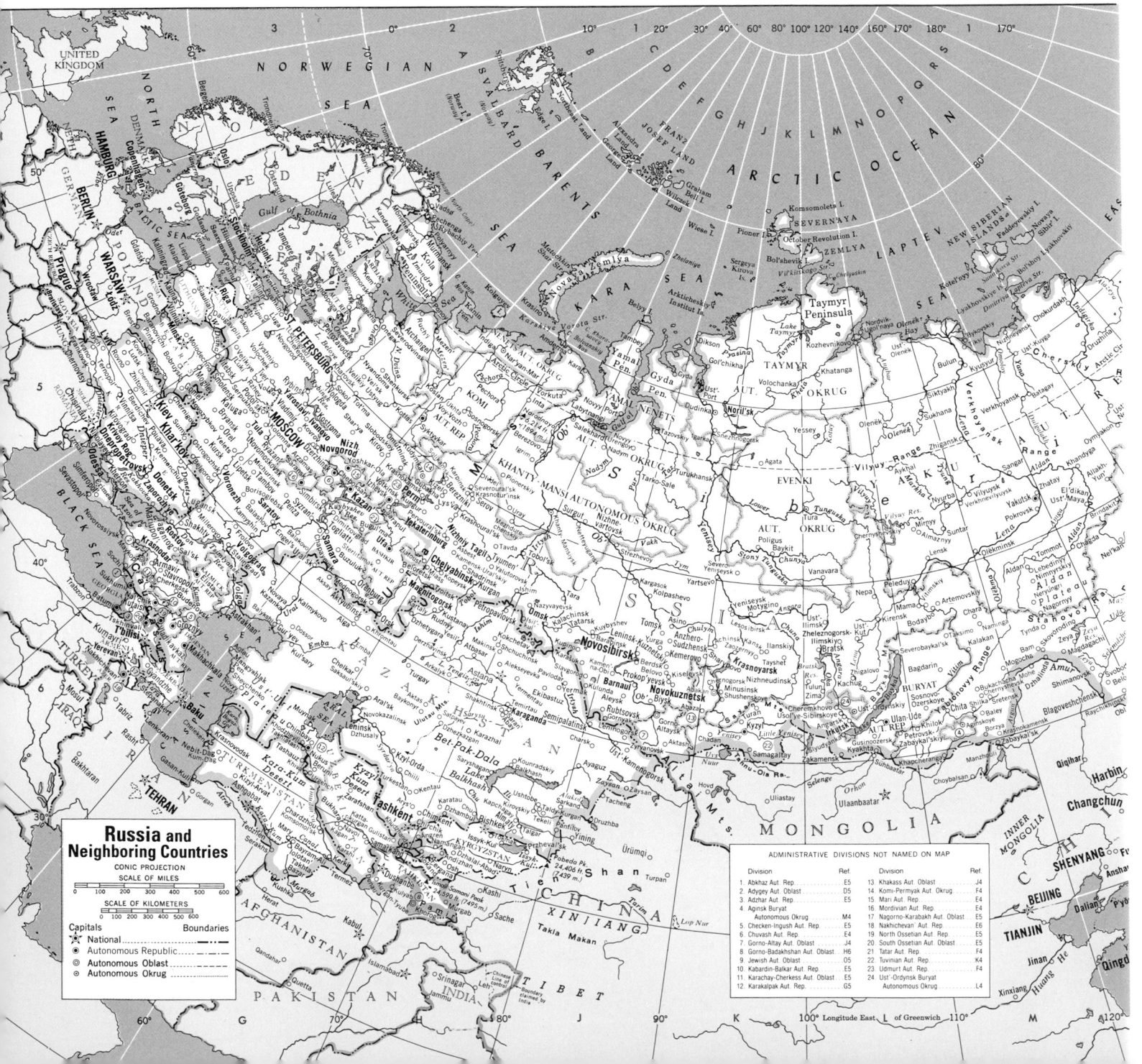

Russia and Neighboring Countries

CONIC PROJECTION

SCALE OF MILES

0 100 200 300 400 500 600

SCALE OF KILOMETERS

0 100 200 300 400 500 600

Capitals   Boundaries

★ National
★ Autonomous Republic
⊚ Autonomous Oblast
⊙ Autonomous Okrug

ADMINISTRATIVE DIVISIONS NOT NAMED ON MAP			
Division	Ref.	Division	Ref.
1. Abkhaz Aut. Rep.	E5	13. Khakass Aut. Oblast	J4
2. Adygey Aut. Oblast	D5	14. Komi-Permyak Aut. Okrug	F4
3. Adzhar Aut. Rep.	E5	15. Mari Aut. Rep.	E4
4. Aginsk Buryat		16. Mordivian Aut. Rep.	E4
Autonomous Okrug	M4	17. Nagorno-Karabakh Aut. Oblast	E5
5. Checken-Ingush Aut. Rep.	E5	18. Nakhichevan' Aut. Rep.	E6
6. Chuvash Aut. Rep.	E4	19. North Ossetian Aut. Rep.	E5
7. Gorno-Altay Aut. Oblast	J4	20. South Ossetian Aut. Oblast	E5
8. Gorno-Badakhshan Aut. Oblast	H6	21. Tatar Aut. Rep.	F4
9. Jewish Aut. Oblast	O5	22. Tuvinian Aut. Rep.	K4
10. Kabardin-Balkar Aut. Rep.	E5	23. Udmurt Aut. Rep.	F4
11. Karachay-Cherkess Aut. Oblast	E5	24. Ust'-Ordynsk Buryat	
12. Karakalpak Aut. Rep.	G5	Autonomous Okrug	L4

100° Longitude East L of Greenwich 110°

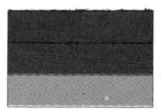
ARMENIA

AZERBAIJAN

BELARUS

GEORGIA

KAZAKHSTAN

KYRGYZSTAN

MOLDOVA

RUSSIA

TAJIKISTAN

TURKMENISTAN

UKRAINE

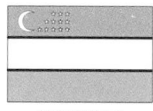
UZBEKISTAN

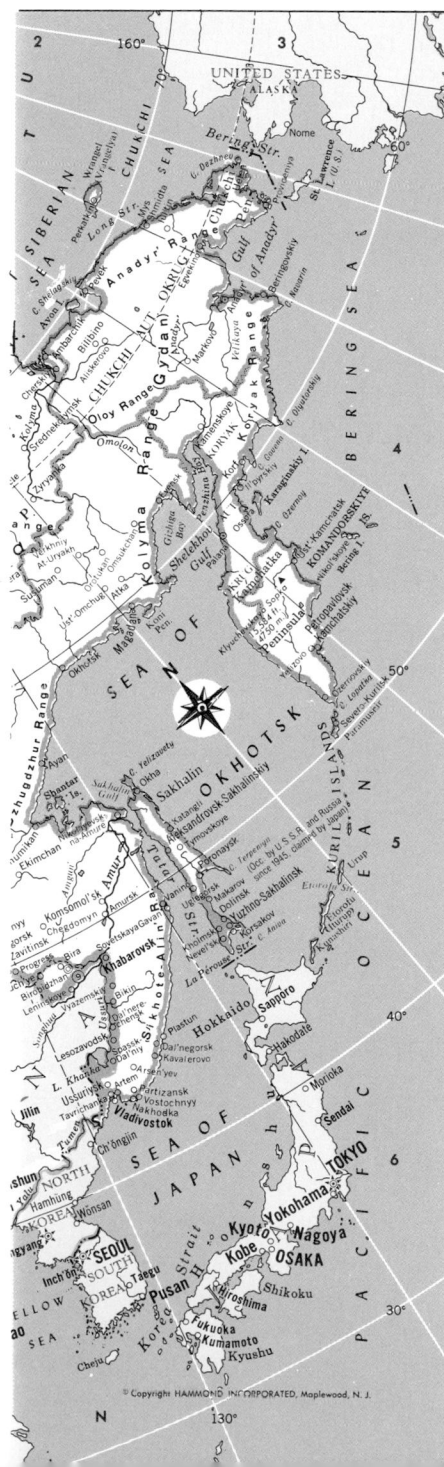

ARMENIA
AREA 11,506 sq. mi. (29,800 sq. km.)
POPULATION 3,283,000
CAPITAL Yerevan
LARGEST CITY Yerevan
HIGHEST POINT Alagez 13,435 ft. (4,095 m.)
MAJOR LANGUAGES Armenian, Azerbaijani, Kurdish, Russian
MAJOR RELIGIONS Eastern (Armenian Apostolic) Orthodoxy, Islam

AZERBAIJAN
AREA 33,436 sq. mi. (86,600 sq. km.)
POPULATION 7,029,000
CAPITAL Baku
LARGEST CITY Baku
HIGHEST POINT Bazardyuzyu 14,653 ft. (4,466 m.)
MAJOR LANGUAGES Azerbaijani, Russian, Armenian
MAJOR RELIGIONS Islam, Eastern (Russian) Orthodoxy

BELARUS
AREA 80,154 sq. mi. (207,600 sq. km.)
POPULATION 10,200,000
CAPITAL Minsk
LARGEST CITY Minsk
HIGHEST POINT Dzerzhinskaya 1,135 ft. (346 m.)
MAJOR LANGUAGES Belorussian, Russian, Polish, Ukrainian, Yiddish
MAJOR RELIGIONS Eastern (Russian) Orthodoxy, Roman Catholicism, Judaism

GEORGIA
AREA 26,911 sq. mi. (69,700 sq. km.)
POPULATION 5,449,000
CAPITAL T'bilisi
LARGEST CITY T'bilisi
HIGHEST POINT Kazbek 16,558 ft. (5,047 m.)
MAJOR LANGUAGES Georgian, Armenian, Russian, Azerbaijani, Abkhazian, Ossetian
MAJOR RELIGIONS Eastern (Georgian) Orthodoxy, Islam

KAZAKHSTAN
AREA 1,048,300 sq. mi. (2,715,100 sq. km.)
POPULATION 16,538,000
CAPITAL Astana
LARGEST CITY Almaty
HIGHEST POINT Khan-Tengri 22,951 ft. (6,995 m.)
MAJOR LANGUAGES Kazakh, Russian, German, Ukrainian, Uzbek, Tatar
MAJOR RELIGIONS Islam, Eastern (Russian) Orthodoxy

KYRGYZSTAN
AREA 76,641 sq. mi. (198,500 sq. km.)
POPULATION 4,291,000
CAPITAL Bishkek (Frunze)
LARGEST CITY Bishkek (Frunze)
HIGHEST POINT Pobeda Peak 24,406 ft. (7,439 m.)
MAJOR LANGUAGES Kirgiz, Russian, Uzbek, Ukrainian, German, Tatar
MAJOR RELIGIONS Islam, Eastern (Russian) Orthodoxy

MOLDOVA
AREA 13,012 sq. mi. (33,700 sq. km.)
POPULATION 4,341,000
CAPITAL Chişinău
LARGEST CITY Chişinău
HIGHEST POINT 1,408 ft. (429 m.)
MAJOR LANGUAGES Moldavian (Romanian), Ukrainian, Russian, Gagauzi, Yiddish
MAJOR RELIGIONS Eastern (Romanian) Orthodoxy, Judaism

RUSSIA
AREA 6,592,812 sq. mi. (17,075,400 sq. km.)
POPULATION 147,386,000
CAPITAL Moscow
LARGEST CITY Moscow
HIGHEST POINT El'brus 18,510 ft. (5,642 m.)
MONETARY UNIT ruble
MAJOR LANGUAGES Russian, Tatar, Ukrainian, Chuvash, Bashkir, Belorussian, Mordvinian, German, Kazakh, Yiddish, Chechen, Udmurt, Ossetian, Buryat, Yakut, Ingush, Tuvan
MAJOR RELIGIONS Eastern (Russian) Orthodoxy, Roman Catholicism, Islam, Judaism, Lamaism, Buddhism, Animism

TAJIKISTAN
AREA 55,251 sq. mi. (143,100 sq. km.)
POPULATION 5,112,000
CAPITAL Dushanbe
LARGEST CITY Dushanbe
HIGHEST POINT Ismail Samani Peak 24,590 ft. (7,495 m.)
MAJOR LANGUAGES Tajik, Uzbek, Russian, Tatar, Kirgiz
MAJOR RELIGIONS Islam, Eastern (Russian) Orthodoxy

TURKMENISTAN
AREA 188,455 sq. mi. (488,100 sq. km.)
POPULATION 3,534,000
CAPITAL Ashgabat
LARGEST CITY Ashgabat
HIGHEST POINT Rize 9,653 ft. (2,942 m.)
MAJOR LANGUAGES Turkmenian, Russian, Uzbek, Kazakh, Tatar
MAJOR RELIGIONS Islam, Eastern (Russian) Orthodoxy

UKRAINE
AREA 233,089 sq. mi. (603,700 sq. km.)
POPULATION 51,704,000
CAPITAL Kiev
LARGEST CITY Kiev
HIGHEST POINT Goverla 6,762 ft. (2,061 m.)
MAJOR LANGUAGES Ukrainian, Russian, Yiddish, Belorussian, Moldavian (Romanian), Polish, Tatar
MAJOR RELIGIONS Eastern (Ukrainian) Orthodoxy, Roman (Ukrainian Uniate) Catholicism, Judaism

UZBEKISTAN
AREA 173,591 sq. mi. (449,600 sq. km.)
POPULATION 19,906,000
CAPITAL Tashkent
LARGEST CITY Tashkent
HIGHEST POINT Khodzha-Pir'yakh 14,515 ft. (4,424 m.)
MAJOR LANGUAGES Uzbek, Russian, Tajik, Kazakh, Tatar, Karakalpak, Kirgiz, Ukrainian, Turkmenian
MAJOR RELIGIONS Islam, Eastern (Russian) Orthodoxy

Topography

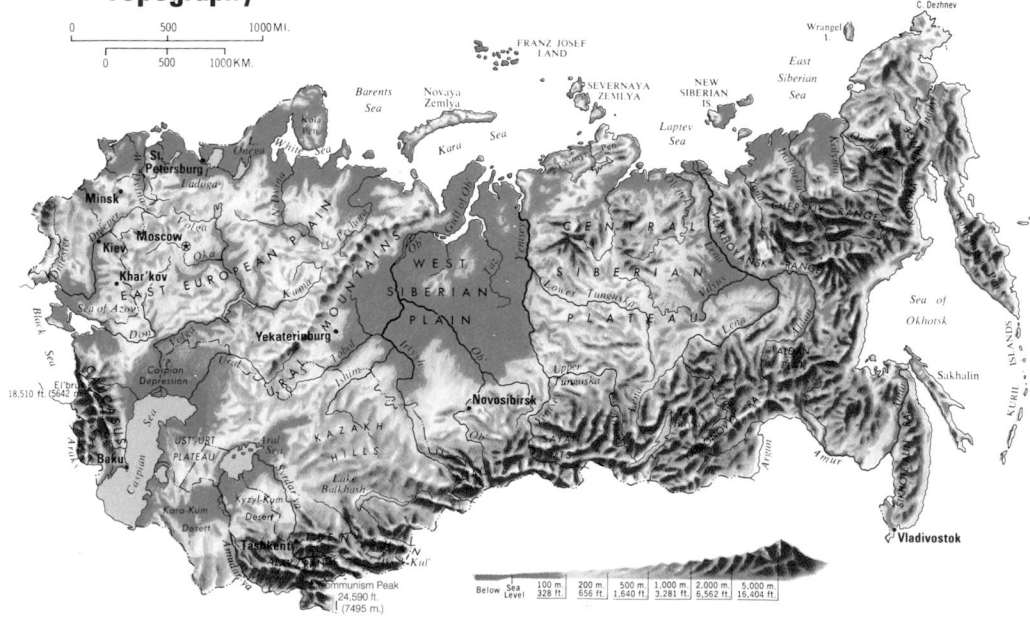

(continued)

OTHER FEATURES

Chu (riv.) H5
Issyk-Kul' (lake) H5
Pobeda (peak) J5

MOLDOVA (MOLDAVIA)

CITIES and TOWNS

Chişinău (cap.) 665,000 C5

OTHER FEATURES

Black (sea) D5
Dniester (riv.) C5

RUSSIA

INTERNAL DIVISIONS

Adygey Aut. Obl. 432,000 D5
Aginsk Buryat Aut. Okr. 77,000 M4
Bashkir Aut. Rep. 3,952,000 F4
Buryat Aut. Rep. 1,042,000 M4
Chechen-Ingush Aut. Rep. 1,277,000 E5
Chukchi Aut. Okr. 158,000 R3
Chuvash Aut. Rep. 1,336,000 E4
Dagestan Aut. Rep. 1,792,000 E5
Evenki Aut. Okr. 24,000 K3
Gorno-Altay Aut. Obl. 192,000 J4
Kabardin-Balkar Aut. Rep. 760,000 E5
Kalmuck Aut. Rep. 322,000 E5
Karachay-Cherkess Aut. Obl. 418,000 E5
Karelian Aut. Rep. 792,000 D3
Khakass Aut. Obl. 569,000 J4
Khanty-Mansi Aut. Okr. 1,269,000 G3
Komi Aut. Rep. 1,263,000 F3
Komi-Permyak Aut. Okr. 159,000 F4
Koryak Aut. Okr. 39,000 R3
Mari Aut. Rep. 750,000 E4
Mordvinian Aut. Rep. 964,000 E4
Nenets Aut. Okr. 55,000 F3
North Ossetian Aut. Rep. 634,000 E5
Tatar Aut. Rep. 3,640,000 F4
Taymyr Aut. Okr. 55,000 K2
Tuvinian Aut. Rep. 309,000 K4
Udmurt Aut. Rep. 1,609,000 F4
Ust'-Ordynskiy Buryat Aut. Okr. 136,000 L4
Yakut Aut. Rep. 1,081,000 N3
Yamal-Nenets Aut. Okr. 487,000 H3
Yevrey Aut. Obl. 216,000 O5

CITIES and TOWNS

Abakan 154,000 K4
Abaza 15,202 K4
Achinsk 122,000 K4
Aginskoye 7,922 M4
Aldan 17,689 N4
Aleksandrovsk-Sakhalinskiy 20,342 P4
Aleysk 32,487 J4
Amursk 24,010 O4
Anadyr' 7,703 S3
Angarsk 266,000 L4
Anzhero-Sudzhensk 108,000 J4
Archangel (Arkhangel'sk) 416,000 E3
Armavir 161,000 E5
Arsen'yev 60,000 O5
Artem 69,000 O5
Arzamas 109,000 E4
Asbest 79,000 G4
Asino 29,395 J4
Astrakhan' 509,000 E5
Balakovo 198,000 E4
Balashov 93,000 E4
Baley 27,215 M4
Barabinsk 37,274 H4
Barnaul 602,000 J4
Belgorod 300,000 D4
Belogorsk 63,000 N4
Belomorsk 16,595 D3
Beloretsk 71,000 F4
Belovo 112,000 J4
Berdsk 67,000 J4
Berezniki 201,000 F4
Berezovo 6,000 G3
Bikin 17,473 O5
Bilibino 10,000 S3
Birobidzhan 69,000 O5
Biysk 233,000 J4
Blagoveshchensk 206,000 N4
Bodaybo 19,000 M4
Borisoglebsk 68,000 E4
Borzya 27,815 M4
Bratsk 255,000 L4
Bryansk 452,000 D4
Bugul'ma 80,000 F4
Bukachacha 10,000 M4
Buzuluk 76,000 F4
Chapayevsk 85,000 F4
Cheboksary 420,000 E4
Chegdomyn 16,499 O4
Chelyabinsk 1,143,000 G4
Cheremkhovo 77,000 L4
Cherepovets 310,000 D4
Cherkessk 113,000 E5
Chernenko (Sharypovo) 54,000 K4
Chernogorsk 71,000 K4
Chernyshevsk 10,000 M4
Chernyshevskiy 10,000 M3
Chita 366,000 M4
Dal'negorsk 33,506 O5
Dal'nerechensk 28,224 O5
Dimitrovgrad 124,000 F4
Dudinka 19,701 J3
Dzerzhinsk 285,000 E4
Elista 70,000 E5
Engel's 182,000 E4
Frolovo 33,398 E5
Gorno-Altaysk 34,413 J4
Gornyak 16,643 J4
Groznyy 401,000 E5
Gubakha 33,243 F4
Gusinoozersk 10,000 L4
Igarka 15,624 J3
Ilanskiy 22,852 K4
Inta 51,000 G3
Irkutsk 626,000 L4
Ishim 63,000 H4
Isil'kul' 25,958 H4
Ivanovo 481,000 E4
Ivdel' 15,308 G3
Izhevsk 635,000 F4
Kalachinsk 20,809 H4
Kalinin (Tver') 451,000 D4
Kaliningrad 401,000 B4
Kaluga 312,000 D4
Kamen'-na-Obi 35,604 H4
Kamenskoye R3
Kamensk-Ural'skiy 209,000 G4
Kamyshin 122,000 E4
Kandalaksha 42,656 C3
Kansk 110,000 K4
Karasuk 22,637 H4
Kartaly 42,801 G4
Kavalerovo 16,415 O5
Kazan' 1,094,000 F4
Kem' 21,025 D3
Kemerovo 520,000 J4
Khabarovsk 601,000 O5
Khanty-Mansiysk 24,754 H3
Khilok 17,000 M4
Kholmsk 37,412 P5
Kirov 441,000 E4
Kiselevsk 128,000 J4
Kizel 46,264 F4
Kolomna 162,000 D4
Kolpashevo 24,911 J4
Komsomol'sk-na-Amure 315,000 O4
Kondopoga 27,908 D3
Kopeysk 146,000 G4
Korsakov 38,210 P5
Kostroma 278,000 E4
Kotlas 61,000 E3
Kovrov 160,000 E4
Krasnodar 620,000 E5
Krasnokamensk 51,000 M4
Krasnokamsk 56,000 F4
Krasnotur'insk 61,000 G3
Krasnoural'sk 39,743 G4
Krasnoyarsk 912,000 K4
Kudymkar 26,350 F4
Kulunda 15,264 H4
Kungur 80,000 F4
Kupino 20,799 H4
Kurgan 356,000 G4
Kursk 424,000 D4
Kuybyshev 40,166 H4
Kuybyshev (Samara) 1,257,000 F4
Kyakhta 15,316 L4
Kyzyl 66,000 K4
Leningrad (St. Petersburg) 4,456,000 D4
Leninsk-Kuznetskiy 165,000 J4
Lensk 16,758 M3
Lesozavodsk 34,957 O5
Lipetsk 450,000 E4
Luga 31,905 D4
Lys'va 75,000 F4
Magadan 152,000 P4
Magdagachi 15,059 N4
Magnitogorsk 440,000 G4
Makarov 10,000 P5
Makhachkala 315,000 E5
Maykop 149,000 D5
Mednogorsk 38,024 F4
Medvezh'yegorsk 17,465 D3
Mezen' E3
Miass 168,000 G4
Michurinsk 109,000 E4
Millerovo 34,627 E5
Minusinsk 56,000 K4
Mirnyy 23,826 M3
Mogocha 17,884 M4
Monchegorsk 51,000 C3
Moscow (cap.) 8,769,000 D4
Motygino 10,000 K4
Murmansk 468,000 D3
Mys Shmidta T3
Nakhodka 165,000 O5
Nal'chik 235,000 E5
Nar'yan-Mar 16,864 F3
Nazyvayevsk 15,792 H4
Nefteyugansk 52,000 H3
Nevel'sk 20,726 P5
Nikolayevsk-na-Amure 30,082 P4
Nizhneudinsk 39,743 K4
Nizhnevartovsk 242,000 H3
Nizhniy Novgorod (Gor'kiy) 1,438,000 E4
Nizhniy Tagil 440,000 G4
Nordvik-Ugol'naya M2
Noril'sk 174,000 J3
Novgorod 229,000 D4
Novokuznetsk 600,000 J4
Novomoskovsk 146,000 E4
Novorossiysk 186,000 D5
Novosibirsk 1,436,000 J4
Novozybkov 34,433 D4
Novyy Port G3
Novyy Urengoy H3
Nyandoma 23,366 E3

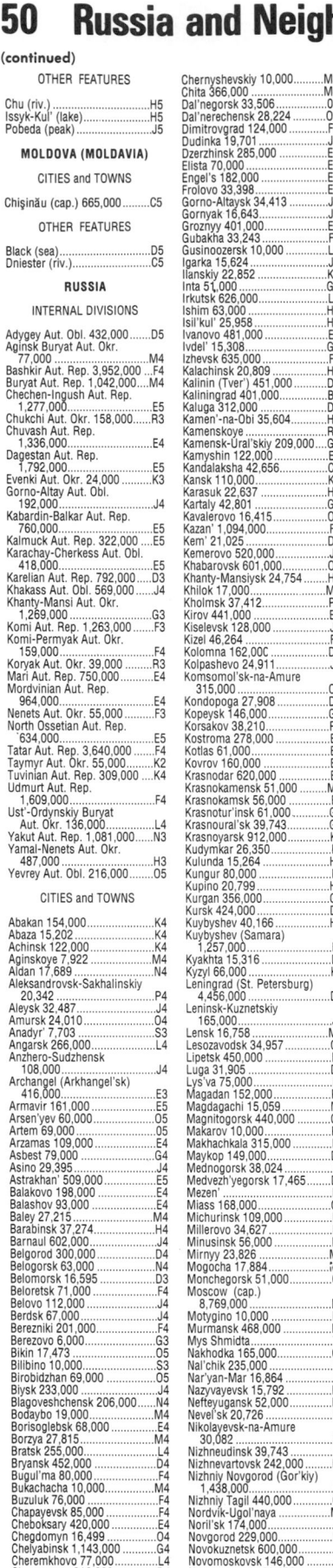

Agriculture, Industry and Resources
(Eastern Europe)

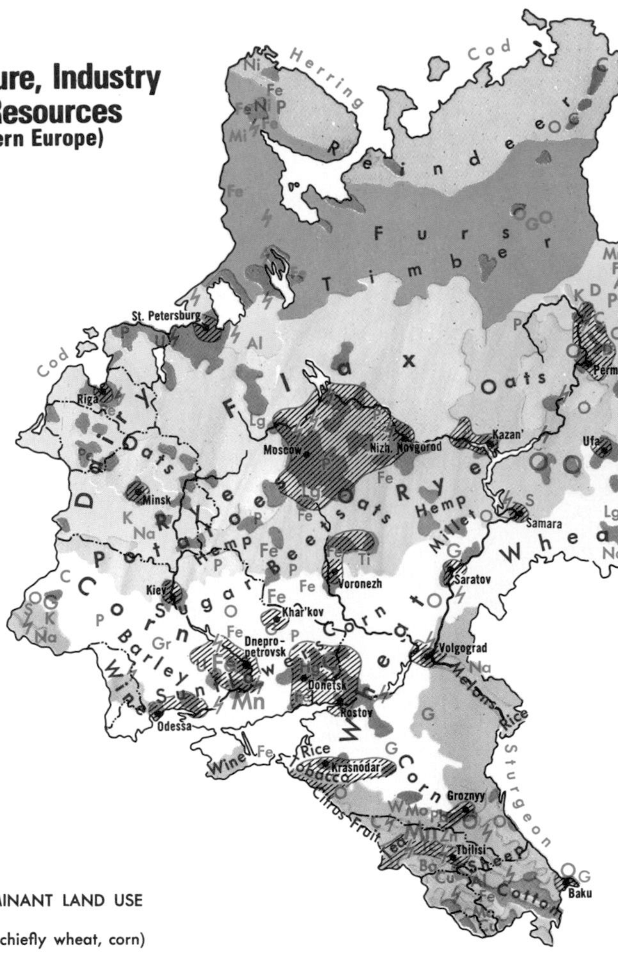

DOMINANT LAND USE

- Cereals (chiefly wheat, corn)
- Cereals (chiefly wheat, rye, oats)
- Dairy, Hogs, Livestock
- Livestock, Dairy
- Pasture Livestock
- Truck Farming, Potatoes, Vegetables, Dairy
- Flax, Dairy, Potatoes
- Cotton
- Vineyards, Orchards, Horticulture
- Sheep Herding, Limited Agriculture
- Forests
- Nonagricultural Land

MAJOR MINERAL OCCURRENCES

Ab	Asbestos	Hg	Mercury	Pb	Lead
Al	Bauxite	K	Potash	Pe	Peat
Au	Gold	Lg	Lignite	Pt	Platinum
Ba	Barite	Mg	Magnesium	S	Sulfur, Pyrites
C	Coal	Mi	Mica	Tc	Talc
Cr	Chromium	Mn	Manganese	Ti	Titanium
Cu	Copper	Mo	Molybdenum	U	Uranium
D	Diamonds	Na	Salt	V	Vanadium
Fe	Iron Ore	Ni	Nickel	W	Tungsten
G	Natural Gas	O	Petroleum	Zn	Zinc
Gr	Graphite	P	Phosphates		

Water Power
Major Industrial Areas

Obluch'ye 17,000 O5
Okha 30,890 P4
Okhotsk P4
Omsk 1,148,000 H4
Omutninsk 28,777 F4
Onega 25,047 D3
Ordzhonikidze (Vladikavkaz) 300,000 E5
Orel 337,000 D4
Orenburg 547,000 F4
Orsk 271,000 F4
Ostrogozhsk 29,921 D4
Partizansk 48,345 O5
Pechenga D2
Pechora 56,000 F3
Penza 483,000 E4
Perm' 1,091,000 F4
Pervoural'sk 142,000 F4
Petropavlovsk-Kamchatskiy 269,000 R4
Petrovsk-Zabaykal'skiy 28,313 L4
Petrozavodsk 270,000 D3
Pionerskiy 10,000 G3
Podol'sk 210,000 D4
Polyarnyy 15,321 D3
Poronaysk 23,610 P5
Prikumsk 35,768 E5
Prokop'yevsk 274,000 J4
Pskov 204,000 C4
Pushkin 90,000 C4
Raychikhinsk 25,157 N5
Rostov 1,020,000 E5
Rubtsovsk 172,000 J4
Ryazan' 515,000 E4
Rybinsk 252,000 D4
Rzhev 69,000 D4
St. Petersburg 4,456,000 D4
Salekhard 21,929 G3
Sal'sk 61,000 E5
Samara 1,257,000 F4
Saransk 312,000 E4
Sarapul 111,000 F4
Saratov 905,000 E4
Segezha 28,810 D3
Serov 104,000 G4
Serpukhov 144,000 D4
Severodvinsk 249,000 E3
Severo-Kuril'sk 8,000 Q4
Severoural'sk 29,880 G3
Severo-Yeniseyskiy K3
Shadrinsk 82,000 G4
Shakhty 224,000 E5
Shar'ya 25,788 E4
Sharypovo 54,000 K4
Shilka 16,065 M4
Shimanovsk 16,880 N4
Shushenskoye 10,000 K4
Simbirsk 625,000 E4
Skovorodino 10,000 N4
Slavgorod 32,908 H4
Slobodskoy 34,374 E4
Slyudyanka 20,639 L4
Smolensk 341,000 D4
Sochi 337,000 D5
Sokol 48,243 E4
Solikamsk 110,000 F3
Sortavala 22,188 C3
Sosnogorsk 24,688 F3
Sovetskaya Gavan' 28,455 O5
Spassk-Dal'niy 53,000 O5
Sretensk 16,000 M4
Stalingrad (Volgograd) 999,000 E5
Stavropol' 318,000 E5
Sterlitamak 248,000 F4
Surgut 248,000 H3
Susuman 12,000 P3
Sverdlovsk (Yekaterinburg) 1,367,000 F4
Svobodnyy 75,000 N4
Syktyvkar 233,000 F3
Syzran' 174,000 E4
Taganrog 291,000 D5
Tambov 305,000 E4
Tara 22,358 H4
Tatarsk 29,589 H4
Tayshet 34,232 K4
Tobol'sk 62,000 G4
Togliatti (Tol'yatti) 630,000 F4
Tommot 8,000 N4
Tomsk 502,000 J4
Troitsk 88,000 G4
Tula 540,000 D4
Tulun 52,000 L4
Tura 3,528 L3
Tver' 451,000 D4
Tyumen' 477,000 G4
Uelen T3
Ufa 1,083,000 F4
Uglegorsk 17,921 P5
Ukhta 111,000 F3
Ulan-Ude 353,000 L4
Ul'yanovsk (Simbirsk) 625,000 E4
Uray 17,385 G3
Usol'ye-Sibirskoye 107,000 L4
Ussuriysk 162,000 O5
Ust'-Ilimsk 109,000 L4
Ust'-Kamchatsk 10,000 R4
Ust'-Kut 50,000 L4
Ust'-Olenëk M2
Ust'-Ordynskiy 10,693 L4
Vanino 15,401 P5
Velikiye Luki 114,000 D4
Velikiy Ustyug 36,737 E3
Vel'sk 21,899 E3
Verkhoyansk 2,000 N3
Vladikavkaz 300,000 E5
Vladimir 350,000 D4
Vladivostok 648,000 O5
Volgograd 999,000 E5
Vologda 283,000 E4
Vorkuta 116,000 G3
Voronezh 887,000 E4
Votkinsk 103,000 F4
Voy-Vozh 10,000 F3
Vyazemskiy 18,365 O5

Agriculture, Industry and Resources
(Northern Asia)

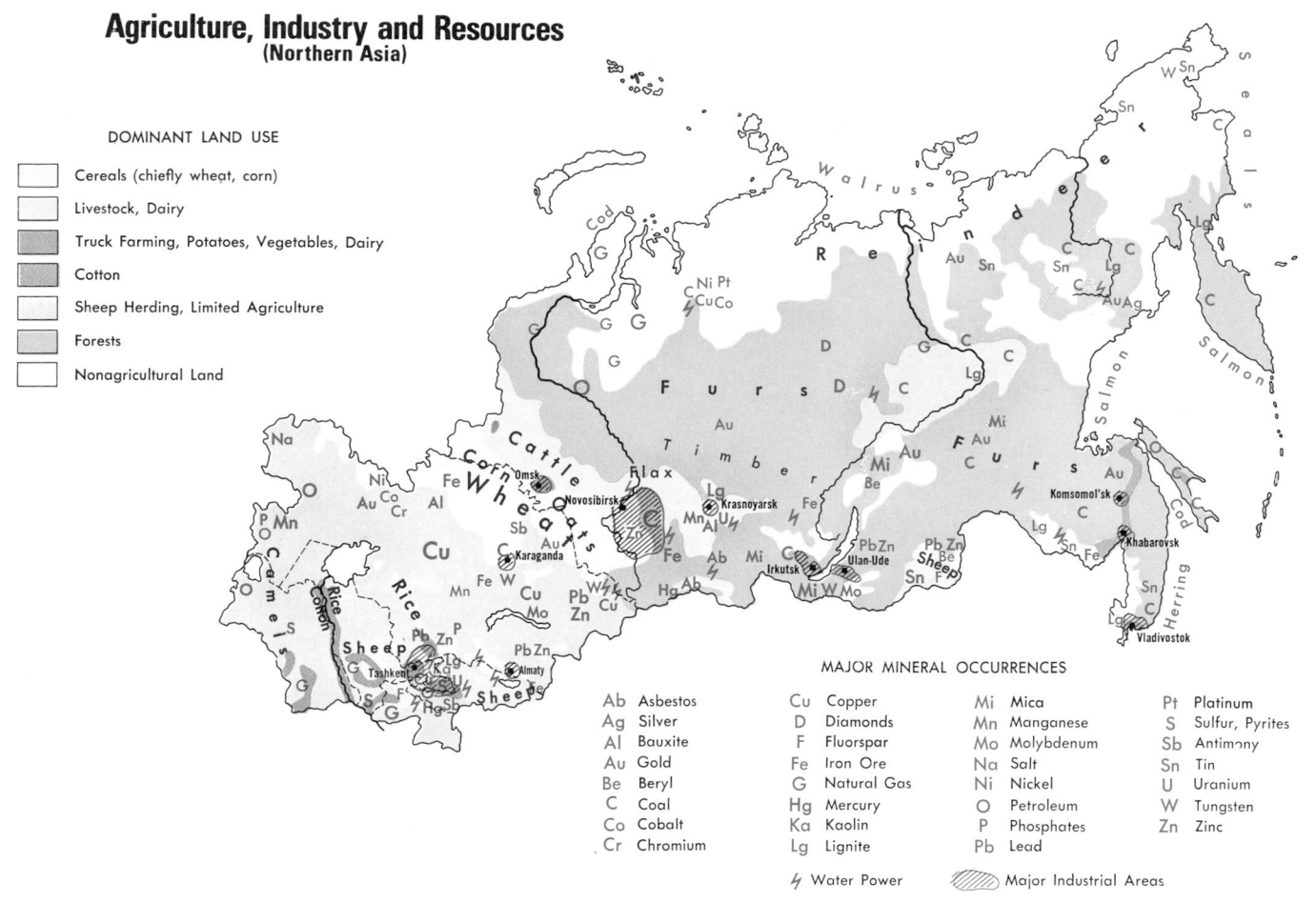

DOMINANT LAND USE

- Cereals (chiefly wheat, corn)
- Livestock, Dairy
- Truck Farming, Potatoes, Vegetables, Dairy
- Cotton
- Sheep Herding, Limited Agriculture
- Forests
- Nonagricultural Land

MAJOR MINERAL OCCURRENCES

Ab	Asbestos	Cu	Copper	Mi	Mica	Pt	Platinum
Ag	Silver	D	Diamonds	Mn	Manganese	S	Sulfur, Pyrites
Al	Bauxite	F	Fluorspar	Mo	Molybdenum	Sb	Antimony
Au	Gold	Fe	Iron Ore	Na	Salt	Sn	Tin
Be	Beryl	G	Natural Gas	Ni	Nickel	U	Uranium
C	Coal	Hg	Mercury	O	Petroleum	W	Tungsten
Co	Cobalt	Ka	Kaolin	P	Phosphates	Zn	Zinc
Cr	Chromium	Lg	Lignite	Pb	Lead		

⚡ Water Power   ▨ Major Industrial Areas

Russia and Neighboring Countries
European Part

CONIC PROJECTION

SCALE OF MILES

0   50   100   200   300

SCALE OF KILOMETERS

0   50   100   200   300

National Capitals .... ★
Administrative Centers .... △
International boundaries ....
Aut. Rep., Oblast, Kray boundaries ....
Autonomous Oblast boundaries ....
Autonomous Okrug boundaries ....

© Copyright HAMMOND INCORPORATED, Maplewood, N.J.

Administrative Divisions bear same names as their respective Capitals or Centers, except:

Abkhaz Aut. Rep.	Sukhumi	F6
Adygey Aut. Oblast	Maykop	F6
Adzhar Aut. Rep.	Batumi	F6
Bashkir Aut. Rep.	Ufa	J4
Chechen-Ingush Aut. Rep.	Groznyy	G6
Chuvash Aut. Rep.	Cheboksary	G3
Crimean Oblast	Simferopol'	D6
Dagestan Aut. Rep.	Makhachkala	G6
Kabardin-Balkar Aut. Rep.	Nal'chik	F6
Kalmuck Aut. Rep.	Elista	F5
Karachay-Cherkess Aut. Obl.	Cherkessk	F6
Karelian Aut. Rep.	Petrozavodsk	D2
Komi Aut. Rep.	Syktyvkar	H2
Komi-Permyak Aut. Okrug	Kudymkar	H3
Mari Aut. Rep.	Yoshkar-Ola	G3
Mordvinian Aut. Rep.	Saransk	G4
Nagorno-Karabakh Aut. Obl.	Stepanakert	G7
Nenets Aut. Okrug	Nar'yan-Mar	H1
North Ossetian Aut. Rep.	Vladikavkaz	F6
South Ossetian Aut. Obl.	Tskhinvali	F6
Tatar Aut. Rep.	Kazan	G3
Trans-Carpathian Oblast	Uzhgorod	B5
Udmurt Aut. Rep.	Izhevsk	H3
Volyn Oblast	Lutsk	C4

(continued)

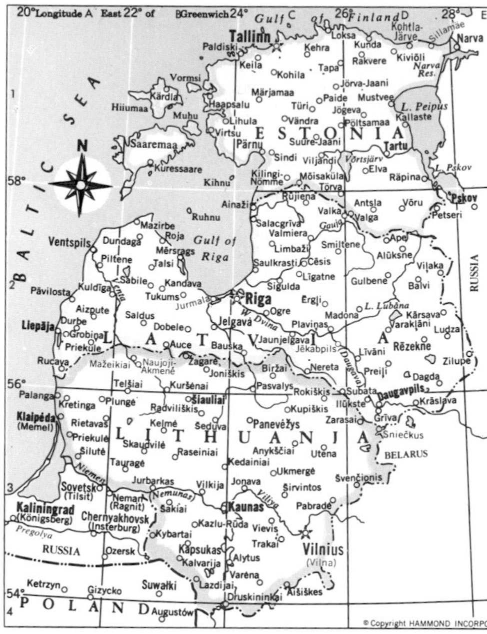

Gulf of Finland
BALTIC SEA
Gulf of Riga
ESTONIA
LATVIA
LITHUANIA
RUSSIA
POLAND
BELARUS
Tallinn
Riga
Vilnius
Kaunas
Kaliningrad (Königsberg)
Narva
Tartu
Pärnu
Liepāja
Ventspils
Klaipėda (Memel)
Daugavpils
Šiauliai
Panevėžys

© Copyright HAMMOND INCORPORATED, Maplewood, N. J.

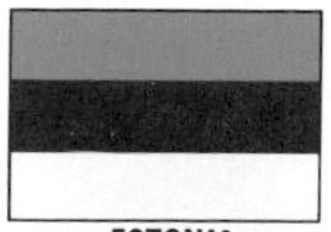
ESTONIA

LATVIA

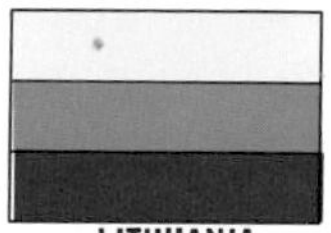
LITHUANIA

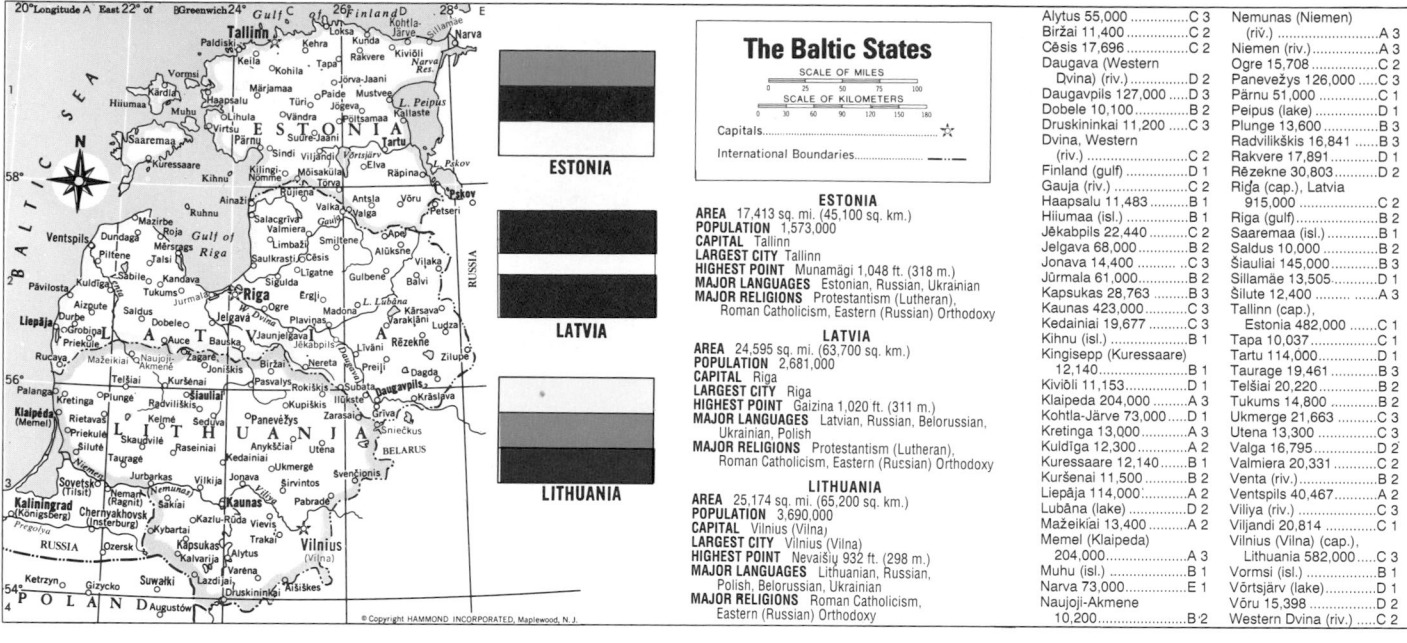

The Baltic States

SCALE OF MILES: 0 25 50 75 100
SCALE OF KILOMETERS: 0 30 60 90 120 150 180

Capitals ☆

International Boundaries —·—

ESTONIA

AREA 17,413 sq. mi. (45,100 sq. km.)
POPULATION 1,573,000
CAPITAL Tallinn
LARGEST CITY Tallinn
HIGHEST POINT Munamägi 1,048 ft. (318 m.)
MAJOR LANGUAGES Estonian, Russian, Ukrainian
MAJOR RELIGIONS Protestantism (Lutheran), Roman Catholicism, Eastern (Russian) Orthodoxy

LATVIA

AREA 24,595 sq. mi. (63,700 sq. km.)
POPULATION 2,681,000
CAPITAL Riga
LARGEST CITY Riga
HIGHEST POINT Gaizina 1,020 ft. (311 m.)
MAJOR LANGUAGES Latvian, Russian, Belorussian, Ukrainian, Polish
MAJOR RELIGIONS Protestantism (Lutheran), Roman Catholicism, Eastern (Russian) Orthodoxy

LITHUANIA

AREA 25,174 sq. mi. (65,200 sq. km.)
POPULATION 3,690,000
CAPITAL Vilnius (Vilna)
LARGEST CITY Vilnius (Vilna)
HIGHEST POINT Nevaišių 932 ft. (298 m.)
MAJOR LANGUAGES Lithuanian, Russian, Polish, Belorussian, Ukrainian
MAJOR RELIGIONS Roman Catholicism, Eastern (Russian) Orthodoxy

Alytus 55,000 ....C 3
Biržai 11,400 ....C 2
Cēsis 17,696 ....C 2
Daugava (Western Dvina) (riv.) ....D 2
Daugavpils 127,000 ....D 3
Dobele 10,100 ....B 2
Druskininkai 11,200 ....C 3
Dvina, Western (riv.) ....C 2
Finland (gulf) ....D 1
Gauja (riv.) ....C 2
Haapsalu 11,483 ....B 1
Hiiumaa (isl.) ....B 1
Jēkabpils 22,440 ....C 2
Jelgava 68,000 ....B 2
Jonava 14,400 ....C 3
Jūrmala 61,000 ....B 2
Kapsukas 28,763 ....B 3
Kaunas 423,000 ....C 3
Kedainiai 19,677 ....C 3
Kihnu (isl.) ....B 1
Kingisepp (Kuressaare) 12,140 ....B 1
Kiviõli 11,153 ....D 1
Klaipeda 204,000 ....A 3
Kohtla-Järve 73,000 ....D 1
Kretinga 13,000 ....A 3
Kuldīga 12,300 ....A 2
Kuressaare 12,140 ....B 1
Kuršenai 11,500 ....B 2
Liepāja 114,000 ....A 2
Lubāna (lake) ....D 2
Mažeikiai 13,400 ....A 2
Memel (Klaipeda) 204,000 ....A 3
Muhu (isl.) ....B 1
Narva 73,000 ....E 1
Naujoji-Akmene 10,200 ....B 2
Nemunas (Niemen) (riv.) ....A 3
Niemen (riv.) ....A 3
Ogre 15,708 ....C 2
Panevežys 126,000 ....C 3
Pärnu 51,000 ....C 1
Peipus (lake) ....D 1
Plunge 13,600 ....B 3
Radvilikškis 16,841 ....B 3
Rakvere 17,891 ....D 1
Rēzekne 30,803 ....D 2
Riga (cap.), Latvia 915,000 ....C 2
Riga (gulf) ....B 2
Saaremaa (isl.) ....B 1
Saldus 10,000 ....B 2
Šiauliai 145,000 ....B 3
Sillamäe 13,505 ....D 1
Šilute 12,400 ....A 3
Tallinn (cap.), Estonia 482,000 ....C 1
Tapa 10,037 ....C 1
Tartu 114,000 ....D 1
Taurage 19,461 ....B 3
Telšiai 20,220 ....B 2
Tukums 14,800 ....B 2
Ukmerge 21,663 ....C 3
Utena 13,300 ....C 3
Valga 16,795 ....D 2
Valmiera 20,331 ....C 2
Venta (riv.) ....B 2
Ventspils 40,467 ....A 2
Viliya (riv.) ....C 3
Viljandi 20,814 ....C 1
Vilnius (Vilna) (cap.), Lithuania 582,000 ....C 3
Vormsi (isl.) ....B 1
Võrtsjärv (lake) ....D 1
Võru 15,398 ....D 2
Western Dvina (riv.) ....C 2

ARMENIA

CITIES and TOWNS

Kirovakan 162,000 ....F6
Kumayri 120,000 ....F6
Leninakan (Kumayri) 120,000 ....F6
Yerevan (cap.) 1,199,000 ....F6

OTHER FEATURES

Alagez (mt.) F6
Araks (riv.) G7
Caucasus (mts.) F6
Kapydzhik (mt.) G7
Sevan (lake) G6

AZERBAIJAN

INTERNAL DIVISIONS

Nagorno-Karabakh Aut. Obl. 188,000 ....G7
Nakhichevan' Aut. Rep. 295,000 ....F7

CITIES and TOWNS

Baku (cap.) 1,150,000 ....H6
Gyandzhe 278,000 ....G6
Kirovabad (Gyandzhe) 278,000 ....G6
Mingechaur 60,000 ....G6
Nakhichevan' 33,279 ....G7
Stepanakert 30,293 ....G7
Sumgait 231,000 ....G6

OTHER FEATURES

Apsheron (pen.) H6
Araks (riv.) G7
Caspian (sea) G6
Caucasus (mts.) F6
Kura (riv.) G6

BELARUS (BELORUSSIA)

CITIES and TOWNS

Baranovichi 159,000 ....C4
Bobruysk 223,000 ....C4
Borisov 144,000 ....C4
Brest 258,000 ....B4
Gomel' 500,000 ....D4
Grodno 270,000 ....B4
Lida 73,000 ....C4
Minsk (cap.) 1,589,000 ....C4
Mogilev 356,000 ....C4
Molodechno 82,000 ....C4
Mozyr' 101,000 ....C4
Orsha 123,000 ....D4
Pinsk 119,000 ....C4
Polotsk 71,000 ....C3
Rechitsa 67,000 ....C4
Soligorsk 82,000 ....C4
Vitebsk 350,000 ....C3

OTHER FEATURES

Berezina (riv.) C4
Bug (riv.) B4
Dnieper (riv.) D5
Dvina, Western (riv.) C3
Goryn' (riv.) C4
Niemen (riv.) B4
Pripet (marshes) C4
Pripyat' (riv.) C4
Western Dvina (riv.) C3

GEORGIA

INTERNAL DIVISIONS

Abkhaz Aut. Rep. 537,000 ....F6
Adzhar Aut. Rep. 393,000 ....F6
South Ossetian Aut. Obl. 99,000 ....F6

CITIES and TOWNS

Batumi 136,000 ....F6
Gori 60,000 ....F6
Kutaisi 235,000 ....F6
Makaradzhe (Ozurgeti) 21,679 ....F6
Ozurgeti 21,679 ....F6
Poti 45,979 ....F6
Rustavi 159,000 ....G6
Sukhumi 121,000 ....F6
T'bilisi (cap.) 1,260,000 ....F6
Tiflis (T'bilisi) 1,260,000 ....F6
Tskhinvali 30,311 ....F6

OTHER FEATURES

Black (sea) D6
Caucasus (mts.) F6

MOLDOVA (MOLDAVIA)

CITIES and TOWNS

Bel'tsy 159,000 ....C5
Bendery 130,000 ....C5
Kishinev (cap.) 665,000 ....C5
Tighina (Bendery) 130,000 ....C5
Tiraspol' 182,000 ....D5

OTHER FEATURES

Black (sea) D6
Dniester (riv.) C5
Prut (riv.) C5

RUSSIA

INTERNAL DIVISIONS

Adygey Aut. Obl. 432,000 ....F6
Bashkir Aut. Rep. 3,952,000 ....J4
Chechen-Ingush Aut. Rep. 1,277,000 ....G6
Chuvash Aut. Rep. 1,336,000 ....G3
Dagestan Aut. Rep. 1,792,000 ....G6
Kabardin-Balkar Aut. Rep. 760,000 ....F6
Kalmuck Aut. Rep. 322,000 ....F5
Karachay-Cherkess Aut. Obl. 418,000 ....F6
Karelian Aut. Rep. 792,000 ....D2
Komi Aut. Rep. 1,263,000 ....H2
Komi-Permyak Aut. Okr. 159,000 ....H3
Mari Aut. Rep. 750,000 ....G3
Mordvinian Aut. Rep. 964,000 ....G4
Nenets Aut. Okr. 55,000 ....H1
North Ossetian Aut. Rep. 634,000 ....F6
Tatar Aut. Rep. 3,640,000 ....G3
Udmurt Aut. Rep. 1,609,000 ....H3

CITIES and TOWNS

Akhtubinsk 51,000 ....G5
Al'met'yevsk 129,000 ....H3
Archangel (Arkhangel'sk) 416,000 ....F2
Armavir 161,000 ....F5
Arzamas 109,000 ....F3
Astrakhan' 509,000 ....G5
Azov 79,000 ....E5
Balakovo 198,000 ....G4
Balashov 97,000 ....F4
Bataysk 95,000 ....E5
Belgorod 300,000 ....E4
Berezniki 201,000 ....J3
Borisoglebsk 63,000 ....F4
Borovichi 63,000 ....D3
Bryansk 452,000 ....D4
Bugul'ma 85,000 ....H4
Buzuluk 76,000 ....H4
Chapayevsk 86,000 ....G4
Chaykovskiy 76,000 ....H3
Cheboksary 420,000 ....G3
Cherepovets 310,000 ....E3
Cherkessk 113,000 ....F6
Chistopol' 65,000 ....H3
Derbent 78,000 ....G6
Dimitrovgrad 124,000 ....G4
Dzerzhinsk 285,000 ....F3
Elektrostal' 153,000 ....E3
Elista 80,000 ....F5
Engel's 182,000 ....G4
Gatchina 78,000 ....D3
Glazov 104,000 ....H3
Groznyy 401,000 ....G6
Gubkin 70,000 ....E4
Gukovo 71,000 ....F5
Gus'-Khrustal'nyy 74,000 ....F3
Ishimbay 63,000 ....J4
Ivanovo 481,000 ....E3
Izhevsk 635,000 ....H3
Kaliningrad, Kaliningrad 401,000 ....B4
Kaliningrad, Moscow Oblast 160,000 ....E3
Kaluga 312,000 ....E4
Kamensk-Shakhtinskiy 75,000 ....F5
Kamyshin 122,000 ....F4
Kazan' 1,094,000 ....G3
Khasavyurt 72,000 ....G6
Kimry 60,000 ....E3
Kineshma 105,000 ....F3
Kirov 441,000 ....G3
Kirovo-Chepetsk 83,000 ....H3
Kislovodsk 114,000 ....F6
Klintsy 71,000 ....D4
Kolomna 162,000 ....E4
Kolpino 142,000 ....D3
Königsberg (Kaliningrad) 410,000 ....B4
Kostroma 278,000 ....F3
Kotlas 66,000 ....G2
Kovrov 160,000 ....F3
Krasnodar 620,000 ....E6
Kropotkin 73,000 ....F5
Kungur 82,000 ....J3
Kursk 424,000 ....E4
Kuznetsk 97,000 ....G4
Leningrad (St. Petersburg) 4,456,000 ....C3
Lipetsk 450,000 ....E4
Lys'va 76,000 ....J3
Lyubertsy 165,000 ....E3
Makhachkala 315,000 ....G6
Maykop 149,000 ....F6
Michurinsk 109,000 ....F4
Mineral'nye Vody 72,000 ....F6
Moscow (Moskva) (cap.) 8,769,000 ....E3
Murmansk 468,000 ....D1
Murom 124,000 ....F3
Mytishchi 154,000 ....E3
Naberezhnye Chelny 501,000 ....H3
Nal'chik 235,000 ....F6
Neftekamsk 107,000 ....H3
Nevinnomyssk 121,000 ....F6
Nizhnekamsk 191,000 ....H3
Nizhniy Novgorod (Gor'kiy) 1,438,000 ....F3
Novgorod 229,000 ....D3
Novocherkassk 187,000 ....F5
Novokuybyshevsk 113,000 ....G4
Novomoskovsk 146,000 ....E4
Novorossiysk 186,000 ....E6
Novoshakhtinsk 106,000 ....E5
Novotroitsk 106,000 ....J4
Obninsk 100,000 ....E3
Oktyabr'skiy 105,000 ....H4
Ordzhonikidze (Vladikavkaz) 300,000 ....F6
Orekhovo-Zuyevo 137,000 ....D3
Orel 337,000 ....E4
Orenburg 547,000 ....J4
Orsk 271,000 ....J4
Penza 483,000 ....G4
Perm' (Molotov) 1,091,000 ....J3
Petrozavodsk 270,000 ....D2
Podol'sk 210,000 ....E3
Pskov 204,000 ....C3
Pyatigorsk 129,000 ....F6
Rostov 1,020,000 ....F5
Ryazan' 515,000 ....E4
Rybinsk 252,000 ....E3
Rzhev 70,000 ....D3
St. Petersburg 4,456,000 ....C3
Salavat 150,000 ....H4
Samara (Kuybyshev) 1,257,000 ....H4
Saransk 312,000 ....G4
Sarapul 111,000 ....H3
Saratov 905,000 ....G4
Sergiyev Posad 115,000 ....E3
Serpukhov 144,000 ....E4
Sevastopol' 356,000 ....D6
Severodvinsk 249,000 ....E2
Shakhty 224,000 ....F5
Shchekino 70,000 ....E4
Shuya 72,000 ....F3
Simbirsk 625,000 ....G4
Smolensk 341,000 ....D4
Sochi 337,000 ....E6
Solikamsk 110,000 ....J3
Stalingrad (Volgograd) 999,000 ....F5
Staryy Oskol 174,000 ....E4
Stavropol' 318,000 ....F5
Sterlitamak 248,000 ....J4
Stupino 72,000 ....E4
Syktyvkar 233,000 ....H2
Syzran' 174,000 ....G4
Taganrog 291,000 ....E5
Tambov 305,000 ....F4
Togliatti (Tol'yatti) 630,000 ....G4
Tula 540,000 ....E4
Tver' (Kalinin) 451,000 ....E3
Ufa 1,083,000 ....J4
Ukhta 111,000 ....H2
Ul'yanovsk (Simbirsk) 625,000 ....G4
Velikiye Luki 114,000 ....D3
Viipuri (Vyborg) 79,000 ....C2
Vladikavkaz 300,000 ....F6
Vladimir 350,000 ....F3
Volgodonsk 176,000 ....F5
Volgograd 999,000 ....F5
Vologda 283,000 ....F3
Volzhskiy 269,000 ....G5
Vorkuta 116,000 ....K1
Voronezh 887,000 ....E4
Voskresensk 79,000 ....E3
Votkinsk 103,000 ....H3
Vyborg 79,000 ....C2
Vyshniy Volochek 71,000 ....D3
Yaroslavl' 633,000 ....E3
Yelets 120,000 ....E4
Yessentuki 82,000 ....F6
Yeysk 75,000 ....E5
Yoshkar-Ola 242,000 ....G3
Zagorsk (Sergiyev Posad) 115,000 ....E3
Zelenodol'sk 88,000 ....G3
Zheleznodorozhnyy 76,000 ....H2
Zheleznogorsk 74,000 ....E4

OTHER FEATURES

Azov (sea) E5
Baltic (sea) B3
Barents (sea) E1
Baydarata (bay) L1
Belaya (riv.) H3
Beloye (lake) E2
Black (sea) D6
Bolvanskiy Nos (cape) K1
Caspian (sea) G6
Caucasus (mts.) F6
Central Ural (mts.) J2
Cheshskaya (bay) G1
Chir (riv.) F5
Denezhkin Kamen' (mt.) J2
Desna (riv.) D4
Dnieper (riv.) D5
Dolgiy (isl.) J1
Don (riv.) F5
Dvina (bay) E2
Dvina (riv.) F2
Dykhtau (mt.) F6
El'brus (mt.) F6
Finland (gulf) C3
Ilek (riv.) J4
Il'men' (lake) D3
Imandra (lake) D1
Izhma (riv.) H2
Kama (res.) J3
Kama (riv.) H2
Kandalaksha (gulf) D1
Kanin (pen.) G1
Kanin Nos (cape) F1
Kara (sea) K1
Karskiye Vorota (str.) J1
Kazbek (mt.) F6
Khoper (riv.) F4
Kil'din (isl.) D1
Kinel' (riv.) H4
Kola (pen.) E1
Kolguyev (isl.) G1
Kolva (riv.) J1
Kuban' (riv.) E5
Kubeno (lake) E3
Kuma (riv.) G5
Kuybyshev (res.) G4
Kuyto (lake) D2
Lacha (lake) E2
Ladoga (lake) D2
Lapland (reg.) D1
Lovat' (riv.) D3
Mansel'ka (mts.) C1
Manych-Gudilo (lake) F5
Matveyev (isl.) J1
Medveditsa (riv.) F4
Mezen' (bay) F1
Mezen' (riv.) G1
Mezhdusharskiy (isl.) H1
Moksha (riv.) F4
Moskva (riv.) E3
Msta (riv.) D3
Narodnaya (mt.) J1
Northern Dvina (riv.) F2
North Ural (mts.) K1
Novaya Zemlya (isls.) H1
Oka (riv.) F4
Onega (bay) E2
Onega (lake) E2
Onega (riv.) E2
Payyer (mt.) K1
Pechora (bay) H1
Pechora (riv.) H1
Pechora (sea) H1
Peipus (lake) C3
Pinega (riv.) G2
Ponoy (riv.) E1
Russkiy Zavorot (cape) H1
Rybachiy (pen.) D1
Rybinsk (res.) E3
Samara (riv.) H4
Seg (lake) D2
Solovetskiye (isls.) E1
South Ural (mts.) J4
Suda (riv.) E3
Sukhona (riv.) F2
Sura (riv.) G4
Svir' (riv.) D2
Sysola (riv.) H2
Tel'pos-Iz (mt.) K2
Timan (ridge) G1
Top (lake) D1
Tsil'ma (riv.) H1
Tsimlyansk (res.) F5
Tuloma (riv.) D1
Ufa (riv.) J3
Unzha (riv.) F3
Ural (mts.) J2
Ural (riv.) J4
Usa (riv.) K1
Vaga (riv.) F2
Valday (hills) D3
Vashka (riv.) G2
Vaygach (isl.) K1
Velikaya (riv.) C3
Vetluga (riv.) G3
Vishera (riv.) J2
Vodl (lake) E2
Volga (riv.) G5
Volga-Don (canal) F5
Volgograd (res.) G5
Volkhov (riv.) D3
Vorona (riv.) F4
Vorskla (riv.) E4
Vozhe (lake) F2
Vyatka (riv.) H3
Vychegda (riv.) G2
Vyg (lake) E2
Vym' (riv.) H2
Western Dvina (riv.) C3
White (sea) E1
Yamantau (mt.) J4
Yug (riv.) G2
Yugorskiy (pen.) K1

UKRAINE

INTERNAL DIVISIONS

Crimean Oblast 2,456,000 ....D6
Trans-Carpathian Obl. 1,252,000 ....B5
Volyn Oblast 1,062,000 ....C4

CITIES and TOWNS

Aleksandriya 103,000 ....D5
Balaklava D6
Belaya Tserkov' 197,000 ....C5
Belgorod-Dnestrovskiy 51,000 ....D5
Berdichev 85,000 ....C5
Berdyansk 132,000 ....E5
Cherkassy 290,000 ....D5
Chernigov 296,000 ....D4
Chernovtsy 257,000 ....C5
Dneprodzerzhinsk 282,000 ....D5
Dnepropetrovsk 1,179,000 ....D5
Donetsk 1,110,000 ....E5
Drogobych 73,000 ....B5
Feodosiya 81,000 ....D5
Gorlovka 337,000 ....E5
Ivano-Frankovsk 214,000 ....B5
Izmail 87,000 ....C5
Kadiyevka (Stakhanov) 112,000 ....E5
Kalush 64,000 ....B5
Kamenets-Podol'skiy 102,000 ....C5
Kerch' 174,000 ....E5
Khar'kov 1,611,000 ....E5
Kherson 355,000 ....D5
Khmel'nitskiy 237,000 ....C5
Kiev (cap.) 2,587,000 ....D4
Kirovograd 269,000 ....D5
Lugansk 497,000 ....E5
Lutsk 198,000 ....B4
Lviv (L'vov) (Lwów) 790,000 ....B5
Makeyevka 430,000 ....E5
Mariupol' 517,000 ....E5
Melitopol' 174,000 ....D5
Mukachevo 82,000 ....B5
Nikolayev 503,000 ....D5
Nikopol' 158,000 ....D5
Odessa 1,115,000 ....D5
Osipenko (Berdyansk) 132,000 ....E5
Pavlograd 131,000 ....E5
Pervomaysk 76,000 ....D5
Poltava 315,000 ....D5
Priluki 70,000 ....D4
Rovno 228,000 ....C4
Rubezhnoye 68,000 ....E5
Sevastopol' 356,000 ....D6
Severodonetsk 131,000 ....E5
Shostka 82,000 ....D4
Simferopol' 344,000 ....D6
Slavyansk 135,000 ....E5
Smela 70,000 ....D5
Stakhanov 112,000 ....E5
Sumy 291,000 ....E4
Ternopol' 205,000 ....C5
Uman' 85,000 ....D5
Uzhgorod 117,000 ....B5
Vinnitsa 374,000 ....C5
Voroshilovgrad (Lugansk) 497,000 ....E5
Yalta 85,000 ....D6
Yenakiyevo 121,000 ....E5
Yevpatoriya 108,000 ....D5
Zaporozh'ye 884,000 ....E5
Zhitomir 292,000 ....C4

OTHER FEATURES

Azov (sea) E5
Berezina (riv.) C4
Black (sea) D6
Bug (riv.) B4
Crimea (pen.) D5
Desna (riv.) D4
Dnieper (riv.) D5
Dniester (riv.) C5
Donets (riv.) E5
Goryn' (riv.) C4
Kakhovka (res.) D5
Kiev (res.) C4
Pripet (marshes) C4
Pripyat' (riv.) C4
Prut (riv.) C5
Psel (riv.) D4
Seym (riv.) D4
Vorskla (riv.) E4

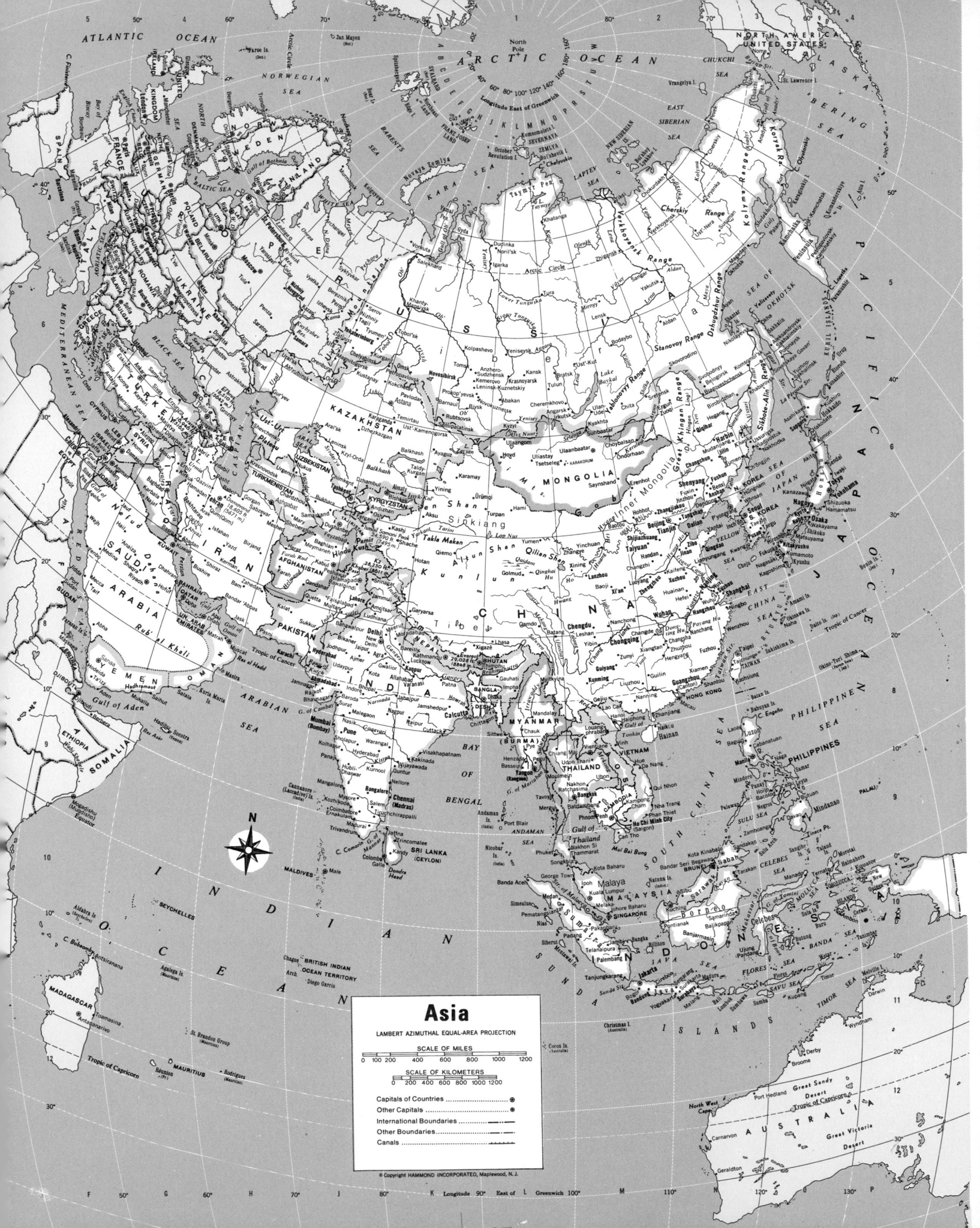

Asia

LAMBERT AZIMUTHAL EQUAL-AREA PROJECTION

SCALE OF MILES

0 100 200 400 600 800 1000 1200

SCALE OF KILOMETERS

0 200 400 600 800 1000 1200

Capitals of Countries .... ⊛

Other Capitals .... ⊙

International Boundaries ....

Other Boundaries.......................

Canals ....

© Copyright HAMMOND INCORPORATED, Maplewood, N.J.

Population Distribution

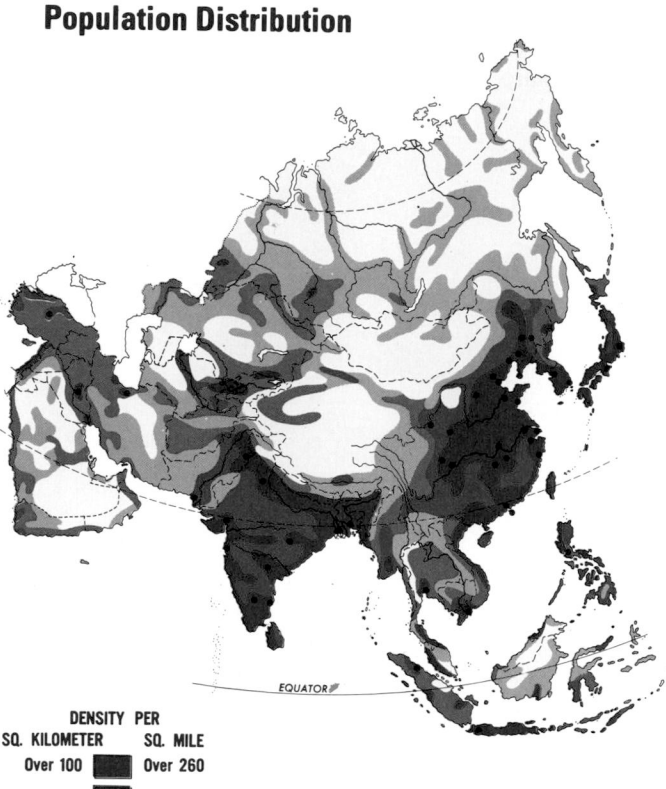

AREA 17,128,500 sq. mi.
(44,362,815 sq. km.)
POPULATION 3,176,000,000
LARGEST CITY Tokyo
HIGHEST POINT Mt. Everest 29,028 ft.
(8,848 m.)
LOWEST POINT Dead Sea -1,296 ft.
(-395 m.)

Vegetation

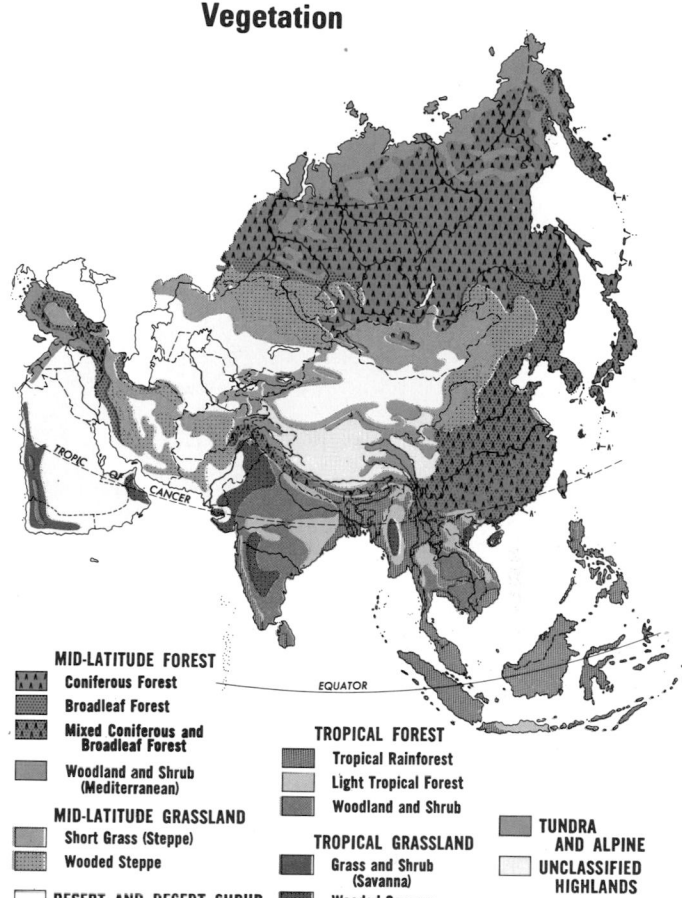

DENSITY PER

SQ. KILOMETER	SQ. MILE
Over 100	Over 260
50-100	130-260
10-50	25-130
1-10	3-25
Under 1	Under 3

• Cities with over 3,000,000 inhabitants (including suburbs)

MID-LATITUDE FOREST
- Coniferous Forest
- Broadleaf Forest
- Mixed Coniferous and Broadleaf Forest
- Woodland and Shrub (Mediterranean)

MID-LATITUDE GRASSLAND
- Short Grass (Steppe)
- Wooded Steppe

DESERT AND DESERT SHRUB

TROPICAL FOREST
- Tropical Rainforest
- Light Tropical Forest
- Woodland and Shrub

TROPICAL GRASSLAND
- Grass and Shrub (Savanna)
- Wooded Savanna

TUNDRA AND ALPINE

UNCLASSIFIED HIGHLANDS

Average January Temperature

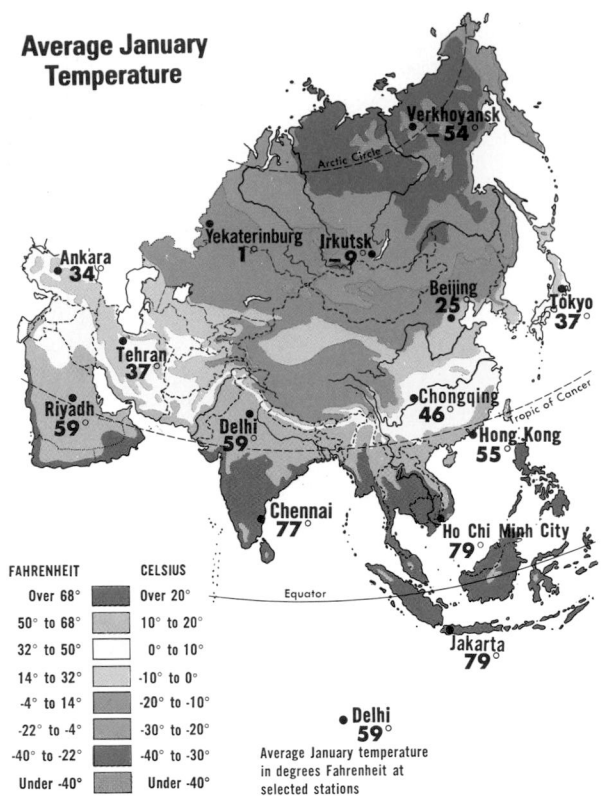

Verkhoyansk
−54°

Yekaterinburg
1°

Irkutsk
−9°

Ankara
34°

Beijing
25°

Tokyo
37°

Tehran
37°

Chongqing
46°

Riyadh
59°

Delhi
59°

Hong Kong
55°

Chennai
77°

Ho Chi Minh City
79°

Jakarta
79°

Arctic Circle

Tropic of Cancer

Equator

FAHRENHEIT	CELSIUS
Over 68°	Over 20°
50° to 68°	10° to 20°
32° to 50°	0° to 10°
14° to 32°	-10° to 0°
-4° to 14°	-20° to -10°
-22° to -4°	-30° to -20°
-40° to -22°	-40° to -30°
Under -40°	Under -40°

● Delhi
59°
Average January temperature in degrees Fahrenheit at selected stations

Average July Temperature

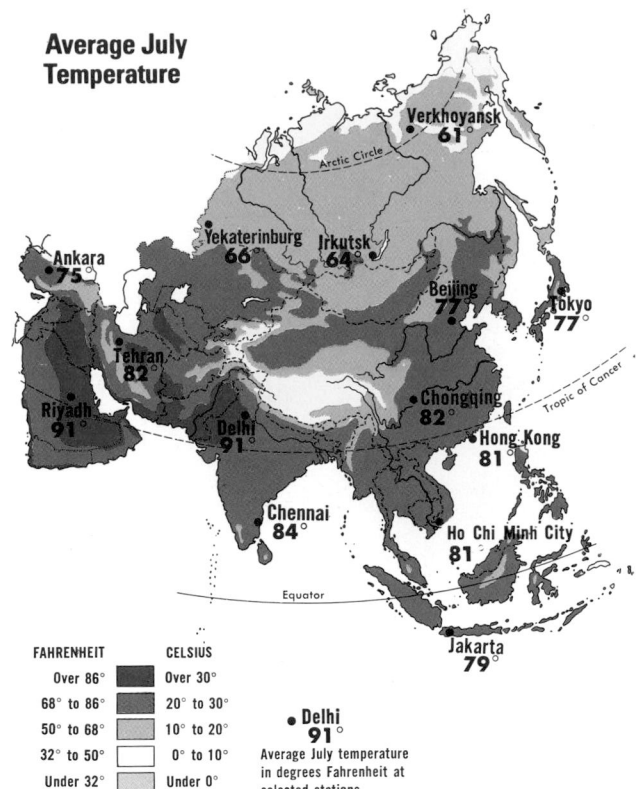

Verkhoyansk
61°

Yekaterinburg
66°

Irkutsk
64°

Ankara
75°

Beijing
77°

Tokyo
77°

Tehran
82°

Chongqing
82°

Riyadh
91°

Delhi
91°

Hong Kong
81°

Chennai
84°

Ho Chi Minh City
81°

Jakarta
79°

Arctic Circle

Tropic of Cancer

Equator

FAHRENHEIT	CELSIUS
Over 86°	Over 30°
68° to 86°	20° to 30°
50° to 68°	10° to 20°
32° to 50°	0° to 10°
Under 32°	Under 0°

● Delhi
91°
Average July temperature in degrees Fahrenheit at selected stations

Rainfall

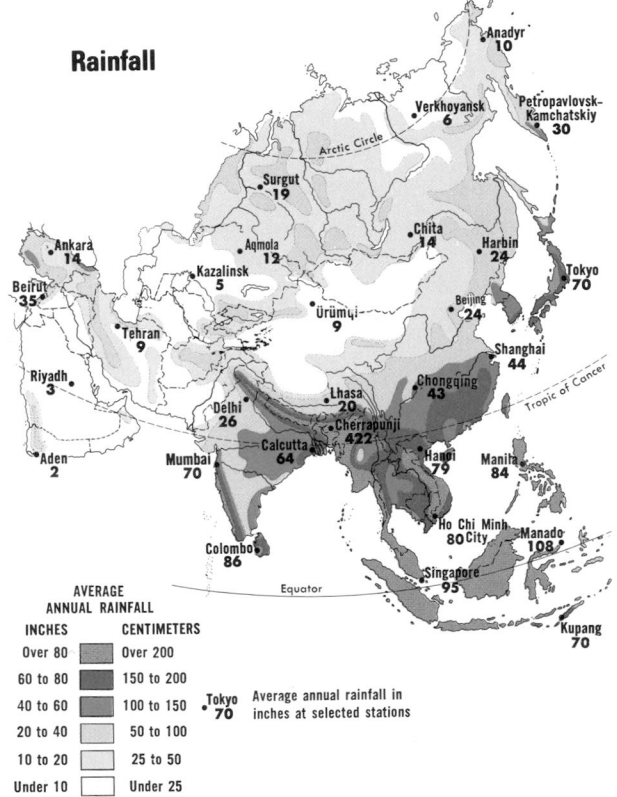

Anadyr
10

Verkhoyansk
6

Petropavlovsk-Kamchatskiy
30

Surgut
19

Chita
14

Harbin
24

Ankara
14

Aqmola
12

Kazalinsk
5

Tokyo
70

Beirut
35

Ürümqi
9

Beijing
24

Tehran
9

Shanghai
44

Riyadh
3

Lhasa
20

Chongqing
43

Delhi
26

Cherrapunji
422

Aden
2

Calcutta
64

Hanoi
79

Manila
84

Mumbai
70

Ho Chi Minh City
80

Manado
108

Colombo
86

Singapore
95

Kupang
70

Arctic Circle

Tropic of Cancer

Equator

AVERAGE ANNUAL RAINFALL

INCHES	CENTIMETERS
Over 80	Over 200
60 to 80	150 to 200
40 to 60	100 to 150
20 to 40	50 to 100
10 to 20	25 to 50
Under 10	Under 25

● Tokyo
70
Average annual rainfall in inches at selected stations

Vegetation/Relief

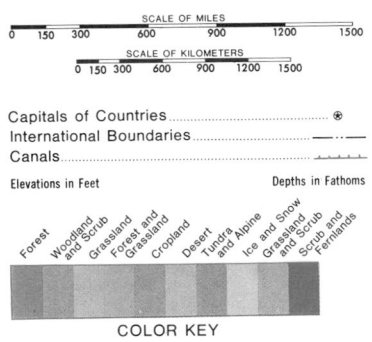

SCALE OF MILES
0 150 300   600   900   1200   1500

SCALE OF KILOMETERS
0 150 300   600   900   1200   1500

Capitals of Countries .... ⊛
International Boundaries ....
Canals ....

Elevations in Feet   Depths in Fathoms

Forest | Woodland and Scrub | Grassland | Forest and Grassland | Cropland | Desert | Tundra and Alpine | Ice and Snow | Grassland and Scrub | Scrub and Fernlands

COLOR KEY

ATLANTIC OCEAN

ICELAND

GREENLAND

North Pole

ARCTIC OCEAN

EAST SIBERIAN SEA

BERING SEA

Alaska
UNITED STATES

NORWEGIAN SEA

Arctic Circle

BARENTS SEA

LAPTEV SEA

KARA SEA

Novaya Zemlya

Severnaya Zemlya

New Siberian Is.

Dezhnev Bering Str.

Aleutian Islands

NORTH SEA

IRELAND
UNITED KINGDOM
London

Bay of Biscay

FINLAND
SWEDEN
NORWAY

BALTIC SEA

DENMARK

POLAND

Moscow

R U S S I A

S i b e r i a

Kamchatka Peninsula

Kolyma

SEA OF OKHOTSK

Sakhalin

Kuril Is.

Hokkaido

PACIFIC OCEAN

MEDITERRANEAN SEA

Rome

UKRAINE
Volga

Chelyabinsk

Omsk

Tobol

Irtysh

Ob

Novosibirsk

Krasnoyarsk

Angara

L. Baykal

Ulan Bator

Harbin

Shenyang

N. KOREA

Seoul

S. KOREA

SEA OF JAPAN

JAPAN

Honshu

Tokyo

Osaka

Nagoya

Shikoku

Kyushu

BLACK SEA

CYPRUS
LEBANON
ISRAEL

Cairo
EGYPT

JORDAN

SAUDI ARABIA

Riyadh

CASPIAN SEA

ARAL SEA

KAZAKHSTAN

Karaganda

Astana

L. Balkhash

Almaty

MONGOLIA

G o b i

Beijing

Tianjin

Dalian

YELLOW SEA

Taiyuan

C H I N A

Nanjing

Shanghai

EAST CHINA SEA

RED SEA

IRAQ

KUWAIT

BAHRAIN
QATAR
U.A.E.

Persian Gulf

IRAN

Tehran

TURKMENISTAN

UZBEKISTAN

Syr Darya

Amu Darya

-STAN

Tarim

Taklimakan

K2 (Godwin Austen)
28,250
Everest
29,028

T i b e t

Kunlun

Lanzhou

Xian

Chengdu

Chongqing

Wuhan

YEMEN

Aden
Gulf of Aden

OMAN

Muscat

Gulf of Oman

AFGHANISTAN

Helmand

PAKISTAN

Indus

Karachi

Delhi

New Delhi

Kanpur

Ganges

Brahmaputra

BANGLADESH

Dhaka

Guangzhou

HONG KONG

Taipei

Taiwan

Tropic of Cancer

RYUKYU Is.

ETHIOPIA
SOMALIA

Ras Asér

ARABIAN SEA

Mumbai (Bombay)

I N D I A

Ahmadabad

Narbada

Godavari

Hyderabad

Krishna

Calcutta

MYANMAR (BURMA)

Yangon (Rangoon)

Hanoi

Haikou

C. Engaño

Luzon

PHILIPPINES

BAY OF BENGAL

Chennai (Madras)

Bangalore

Western Ghats

Eastern Ghats

Andaman Is.

THAILAND

Bangkok

CAMBODIA

VIETNAM

Ho Chi Minh City

SOUTH CHINA SEA

Manila

Mindanao

COMOROS

SEYCHELLES

C. Comorin

SRI LANKA (CEYLON)

Colombo

Dondra Head

MALDIVES

ANDAMAN SEA

Nicobar Is.

Gulf of Siam

Palawan

SULU SEA

CELEBES SEA

New Guinea

MADAGASCAR

BRITISH INDIAN OCEAN TERR.

Equator

INDIAN OCEAN

S u n d a   I s l a n d s

Kuala Lumpur

SINGAPORE

Sumatra

MALAYSIA

BRUNEI

Borneo

Celebes

I N D O N E S I A

BANDA SEA

Réunion (Fr.)

MAURITIUS

Jakarta

Java

JAVA SEA

Surabaya

FLORES SEA

Timor

TIMOR SEA

Tropic of Capricorn

AUSTRALIA

© Copyright HAMMOND INCORPORATED, Maplewood, N.J.

Longitude 70° East of Greenwich

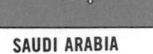
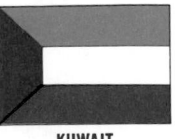

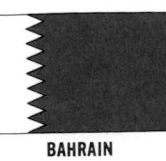
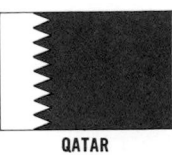
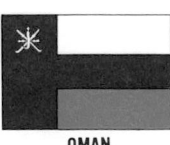

SAUDI ARABIA	KUWAIT	YEMEN	BAHRAIN	QATAR	OMAN

AFGHANISTAN

CITIES and TOWNS

Andkhvoy 13,137..............H2
Aybak 33,016..................J2
Baghlan 75,130...............J2
Bamian 7,355..................J3
Chaghcharan 2,974.........J3

Charikar 25,093...............J2
Farah 18,797..................H3
Feyzabad 10,142.............K2
Gardez 11,415................J3
Ghazni 30,425................J3
Ghurian 12,404..............H3
Herat 163,960.................H3
Jalalabad 56,384............K3
Kabul (cap.) 905,108.......J3

Kalat (Qalat) 5,946..........J3
Kandahar (Qandahar)
 178,409.......................J3
Khanabad 26,803............J2
Kholm 28,078.................J2
Khowst.........................J3
Kuhestan.......................H3
Landay...........................H3
Lashkar Gah 26,646.........H3

Mazar-e Sharif 122,567.....J2
Meymaneh 54,954...........H2
Pol-e Khomri 31,101.........J2
Qalat 5,946.....................J3
Qal'eh-ye Now 5,340........H2
Qandahar 178,409............J3
Qonduz 107,191..............J2
Sar-e Pol 15,699.............J2
Sheberghan 54,870.........H2

Taloqan 46,202...............J2
Zaranj 6,477...................H3

OTHER FEATURES

Farah Rud (riv.)...............H3
Gowd-e Zerreh (depr.)......H4
Harirud (riv.)...................H3
Helmand (riv.)..................J3

Hindu Kush (mts.).............J2
Kabul (riv.).......................K3
Konar (riv.)......................K2
Lurah (riv.).......................J3
Margow, Dasht-e (des.)....H3
Murghab (riv.)..................H2
Namaksar (salt lake).........H3
Nurestan (reg.).................K2
Paropamisus (mts.)...........H3

Qonduz (riv.)....................J2
Rigestan (reg.).................H3
Vakhan (reg.)...................K2

BAHRAIN

CITIES and TOWNS

Manama (cap.) 88,785.......F4

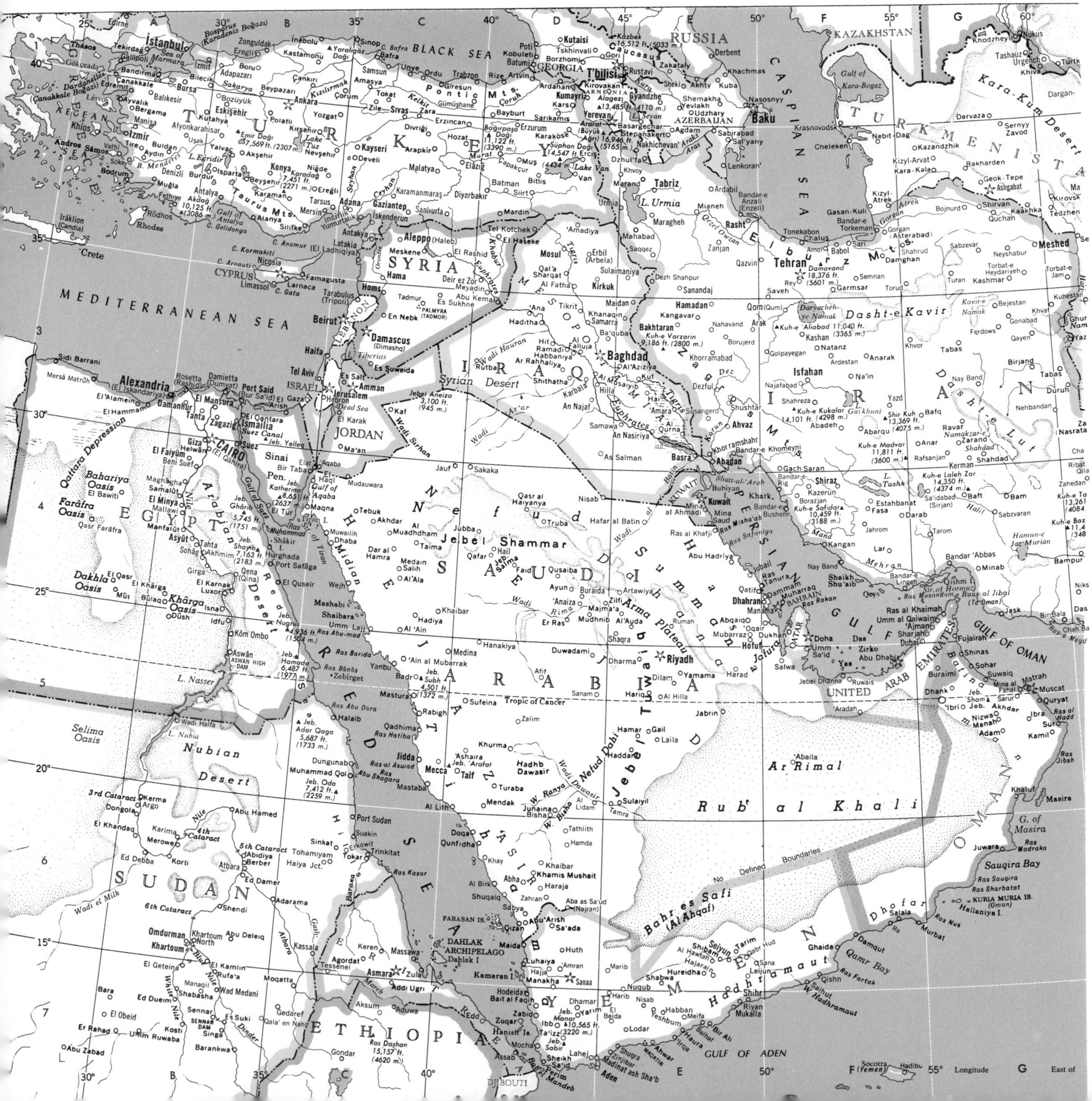

UNITED ARAB EMIRATES

Muharraq 37,732 ....F4

GAZA STRIP

CITIES and TOWNS

Gaza*
118,272 ....B3

IRAN

CITIES and TOWNS

Abadan 296,081 ....E3
Abadeh 16,000 ....F3
Abarqu 8,000 ....F3
Bafq 5,000 ....G3
Ahvaz 329,006 ....E3
Amol 68,782 ....F2

Anarak 2,038 ....F3
Arak 114,507 ....E3
Ardabil 147,404 ....E2
Ardestan 5,868 ....F3
  55,978 ....E2
Asterabad (Gorgan) 88,348...F2
Babol 67,790 ....F2
Bakhtaran 290,861 ....E3

Bam 22.000 ....G4
Bandar 'Abbas 89,103 ....G4
Bandar-e Anzali (Enzeli)
  55.978 ....E2
Bandar-e Bushehr 57,681 ....F4
Bandar-e Khomeyni 6,000....E3
Bandar-e Lengeh 4,920 ......F4
Bandar-e Rig 1,889 ....F4
Bandar-e Torkeman 13,000...F2

Bejestan 3,823 ....G3
Birjand 25,854 ....G3
Bojnurd 31,248 ....G2
Borazjan 20,000 ....F4
Borujerd 100,103 ....E3
Chalus 15,000 ....F2
Damghan 13,000 ....F2
Darab 13,000 ....G4
Dezful 110,287 ....E3

(continued on following page)

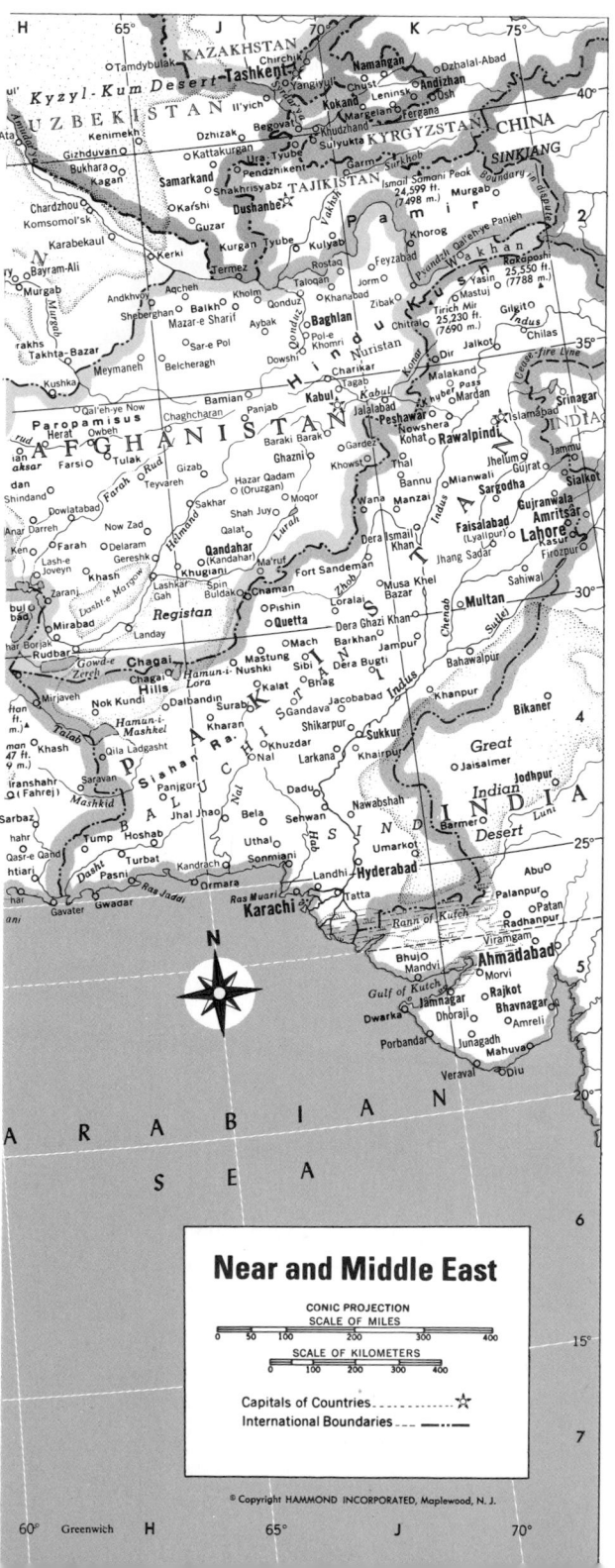

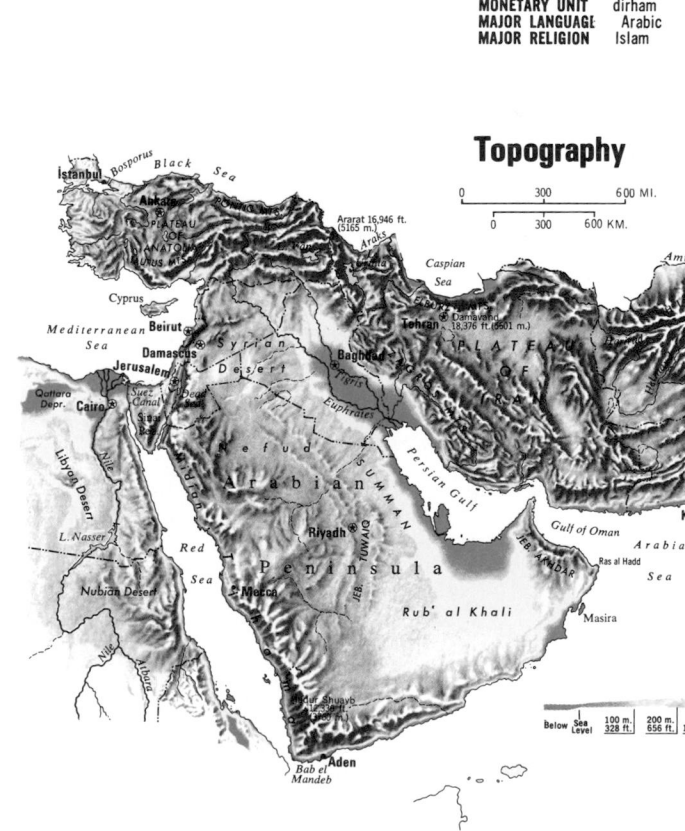

SAUDI ARABIA
AREA 829,995 sq. mi. (2,149,687 sq. km.)
POPULATION 14,435,000
CAPITAL Riyadh
MONETARY UNIT Saudi riyal
MAJOR LANGUAGE Arabic
MAJOR RELIGION Islam

YEMEN
AREA 188,321 sq. mi. (487,792 sq. km.)
POPULATION 10,183,000
CAPITAL Sanaa
MONETARY UNIT Yemeni rial
MAJOR LANGUAGE Arabic
MAJOR RELIGION Islam

QATAR
AREA 4,247 sq. mi. (11,000 sq. km.)
POPULATION 422,000
CAPITAL Doha
MONETARY UNIT Qatari riyal
MAJOR LANGUAGE Arabic
MAJOR RELIGION Islam

KUWAIT
AREA 6,532 sq. mi. (16,918 sq. km.)
POPULATION 2,048,000
CAPITAL Kuwait
MONETARY UNIT Kuwaiti dinar
MAJOR LANGUAGE Arabic
MAJOR RELIGION Islam

BAHRAIN
AREA 240 sq. mi. (622 sq. km.)
POPULATION 489,000
CAPITAL Manama
MONETARY UNIT Bahraini dinar
MAJOR LANGUAGE Arabic
MAJOR RELIGION Islam

OMAN
AREA 120,000 sq. mi. (310,800 sq. km.)
POPULATION 2,000,000
CAPITAL Muscat
MONETARY UNIT Omani rial
MAJOR LANGUAGE Arabic
MAJOR RELIGION Islam

UNITED ARAB EMIRATES
AREA 32,278 sq. mi. (83,600 sq. km.)
POPULATION 1,206,000
CAPITAL Abu Dhabi
MONETARY UNIT dirham
MAJOR LANGUAGE Arabic
MAJOR RELIGION Islam

Topography

Near and Middle East
CONIC PROJECTION
SCALE OF MILES
SCALE OF KILOMETERS

Capitals of Countries ....☆
International Boundaries ----

© Copyright HAMMOND INCORPORATED, Maplewood, N.J.

Dezh Shahpur 1,384 ......E2
Enzeli 55,978 ......E2
Estahbanat 18,187 ......F4
Fahrej (Iranshahr) 5,000...H4
Fasa 19,000 ......F4
Ferdows 11,000 ......G3
Garmsar 4,723 ......F2
Gogpayegan 20,515 ......F3
Gonabad 8,000 ......G3
Gorgan 88,348 ......F2
Hamadan 155,846 ......E3
Iranshahr 5,000 ......H4
Isfahan 671,825 ......F4
Jahrom 38,236 ......F4
Jask 1,078 ......G4
Kangan 2,682 ......F4
Kangavar 9,414 ......E3
Kashan 84,545 ......F3
Kashmar 17,000 ......G3
Kazerun 51,309 ......F4
Kerman 140,309 ......H3
Khash 7,439 ......H4
Khorramabad 104,928 ......E3
Khorramshahr 146,709 ......E3
Khvaf 5,000 ......G3
Khvor 2,912 ......G3
Khvoy 70,040 ......E2
Lar 22,000 ......F4
Mahabad 28,610 ......E2
Maragheh 60,820 ......E2
Marand 24,000 ......E2
Meshed 670,180 ......H2
Mianeh 28,447 ......E2
Minab 4,228 ......G4
Mirjaveh 11,000 ......H4
Nahavand 24,000 ......E3
Na'in 5,925 ......F3
Najafabad 76,236 ......F3
Nasratabad (Zabol) 20,000...H3
Natanz 4,370 ......F3
Nehbandan 2,130 ......G3
Neyshabr 59,101 ......G2
Nikshahr 1,879 ......H4
Qasr-e Qand 1,879 ......H4
Qayen 6,000 ......G3
Qazvin 138,527 ......E2
Qom 246,831 ......F3
Quchan 29,133 ......G2
Qum (Qom) 246,831 ......F3
Rafsanjan 21,000 ......G3
Rasht 187,203 ......E2
Ravar 5,074 ......G3
Rey 102,825 ......F2
Reza'iyeh (Urmia) 163,991 ...D2
Sabzevar 69,174 ......G2
Sabzvaran 7,000 ......G4
Sa'idabad 20,000 ......G4
Sanandaj 95,834 ......E2
Saqqez 17,000 ......E2
Saravan 4,012 ......H4
Sari 70,936 ......F2
Saveh 17,565 ......F3
Semnan 31,058 ......F2
Shahdad 2,777 ......G3
Shahreza 34,220 ......F3
Shahrud 30,767 ......G2

Shiraz 416,408 ......F4
Shirvan 11,000 ......G2
Shushtar 24,000 ......E3
Sirjan (Sa'idabad) 20,000...G4
Susangerd 21,000 ......E3
Tabas 10,000 ......G3
Tabriz 598,576 ......E2
Tehran (cap.) 4,496,159...F2
Tonekabon 12,000 ......F2
Torbat-e Heydariyeh 30,106...G2
Torbat-e Jam 13,000 ......H2
Torud 721 ......G2
Urmia 163,991 ......D2
Yazd 135,978 ......F3
Zabol 20,000 ......H3
Zahedan 92,628 ......H4
Zanjan 99,967 ......E2
Zarand 5,000 ......G3

OTHER FEATURES

'Aliabad, Kuh-e (mt.) F3
Aras (riv.) E1
Bazman, Kuh-e (mt.) H4
Damavand (mt.) F2
Dez (riv.) E3
Elburz (mts.) F2
Euphrates (riv.) E3
Gavkhuni (lake) F3
Gorgan (riv.) F2
Halil (riv.) G4
Hormuz (str.) G4
Jaz Murian, Hamun-e
  (marsh) G4
Karun (riv.) E3
Kavir, Dasht-e (salt des.) ...G3
Kavir-e Namak (salt des.) ...G3
Khark (isl.) F4
Kukalar, Kuh-e (mt.) H3
Laleh Zar, Kuh-e (mt.) G4
Lut, Dasht-e (salt des.) G3
Madvar, Kuh-e (mt.) F3
Maidani, Ras (cape) F4
Mand Rud (riv.) F4
Mashkid (riv.) H4
Mehran (riv.) F4
Namak, Daryacheh-ye
  (salt lake) F3
Namakzar-e Shahdad
  (salt lake) G3
Oman (gulf) G5
Persian (gulf) F4
Qeshm (isl.) G4
Qeys (isl.) F4
Qezel Owzan (riv.) E2
Safidar, Kuh-e (mt.) F4
Shaikh Shu'aib (isl.) F4
Shatt-al-'Arab (riv.) E4
Shir Kuh (mt.) F3
Taftan, Kuh-e (mt.) H4
Talab (riv.) H4
Tashk (lake) F4
Tigris (riv.) E3
Urmia (lake) E2
Varzarin, Kuh-e (mt.) E3
Zagros (mts.) E3

IRAQ

CITIES and TOWNS

Al 'Aziziya 7,450 ......E3
Al Falluja 38,072 ......D3
Al Fatha 15,329 ......D2
Al Musaiyib 15,955 ......D3
Al Qurna 5,638 ......E4
'Amara 64,847 ......E3
'Ana 15,729 ......D3
An Najaf 128,096 ......D3
An Nasiriya 60,405 ......E3
Arbela (Erbil) 90,320 ......D2
Ar Rahhaliya 1,579 ......D3
As Salman 1,789 ......D4
Baghdad (cap.) 502,503 ...E3
Baghdad* 1,745,328 ......E3
Baq'uba 34,575 ......E3
Basra 313,327 ......E4
Erbil 90,320 ......D2
Habbaniya 14,405 ......D3
Haditha 6,870 ......D3
Hai 16,988 ......E3
Hilla 84,717 ......D3
Hit 9,131 ......D3
Karbal'a 83,301 ......D3
Khanaqin 23,522 ......E3
Kirkuk 167,413 ......D2
Kirkuk* 176,794 ......D2
Kut 42,116 ......E3
Mosul 315,157 ......D2
Qal'a Sharqat 2,434 ......D2
Ramadi 28,723 ......D3
Rutba 5,091 ......D3
Samarra 24,746 ......D3
Samawa 33,473 ......D3
Shithatha 2,326 ......D3
Sulaimaniya 86,822 ......E2
Tikrit 9,921 ......D3

OTHER FEATURES

'Ar'ar, Wadi (dry riv.) D3
'Aneiza, Jebel (mt.) C3
Batin, Wadi al (dry riv.) ...E4
Euphrates (riv.) E3
Hauran, Wadi (dry riv.) ...D3
Mesopotamia (reg.) D3
Persian (gulf) F4
Shatt-al-'Arab (riv.) E4
Syrian (El Hamad)(des.) ...D3
Tigris (riv.) E3

KUWAIT

CITIES and TOWNS

Kuwait (cap.) 181,774 ......E4
Mina al Ahmadi E4
Mina Sa'ud E4

OTHER FEATURES

Bubiyan (isl.) E4
Persian (gulf) F4

OMAN

CITIES and TOWNS

'Ibri G5
Matrah 15,000 ......G5
Muscat (cap.) 7,500 ......G5
Quryat G5
Raysut (Risut) F6
Salala 4,000 ......F6
Sohar G5
Suwaiq G5

OTHER FEATURES

Akhdar, Jebel (range) G5
Batina (reg.) G5
Dhofar (reg.) F6
Hadd, Ras al (cape) G5
Hallaniya (isl.) G6
Hormuz (str.) G4
Jibsh, Ras (cape) G5
Kuria Muria (isls.) G6
Madraka, Ras (cape) G6
Masira (gulf) G6
Masira (isl.) G6
Musandam, Ras (cape) G4
Nus, Ras (cape) G6
Oman (gulf) G5
Oman (reg.) G5
Ruus al Jibal (dist.) G4
Sauqira (bay) G5
Sauqira, Ras (cape) G5
Sham, Jebel (mt.) G5
Sharbatat, Ras (cape) G6

QATAR

CITIES and TOWNS

Doha (cap.) 150,000 ......F4
Dukhan F4
Umm Sa'id F5

OTHER FEATURES

Persian (gulf) F4
Rakan, Ras (cape) F4

SAUDI ARABIA

CITIES and TOWNS

Aba as Sa'ud 47,501 ......D6
Abha 30,150 ......D6
Abu 'Arish D6
Abu Hadriya E4
'Ain al Mubarrak C5
Al 'Ain D6
Al Birk D6
Al Hilla E5
Al Lidam D5
Al Muaddham C4
'Anaiza D4
Artawiya E4
Ayun D4

Badr C5
Bisha D5
Buraida 69,940 ......D4
Dammam 127,844 ......F4
Dhaba C4
Dhahran E5
Dilam E5
El Haql C4
Er Ras D4
Hadiya C4
Hafar al Batin E4
Hail 40,502 ......D4
Hofuf 101,271 ......E4
Jauf C4
Jidda 561,104 ......C5
Jizan (Qizan) 32,812 ......D6
Jubail E4
Jubba D4
Kaf C3
Khaibar, Hejaz C4
Khamis Mushait 49,581 ...D6
Mastaba C5
Mastura C4
Mecca 366,801 ......C5
Medina 198,186 ......C5
Mubarraz 54,325 ......E4
Najran (Aba as'Sa'ud) 47,501..D6
Nisab D4
'Oqair E4
Qadhima C5
Qatif E4
Qizan 32,812 ......D6
Ra's al Khafji E4
Ras Tanura F4
Riyadh (cap.) 666,840 ...E5
Rumah E4
Sakaka D4
Shaqra E4
Sufeina D5
Taif 204,857 ......D5
Tebuk (Tabuk) 74,825 ......C4
Turaba D5
Umm Lajj C4
Wejh C4
Yenbo C5
Zahran D6
Zalim D5

OTHER FEATURES

Abu-Mad, Ras (cape) C5
'Aneiza, Jebel (mt.) C3
Aqaba (gulf) C4
Arafat, Jebel (mt.) D5
'Ar'ar, Wadi (dry riv.) D3
Arma (plat.) E4
'Asir (reg.) D6
Aswad, Ras al (cape) C5
Bab el Mandeb (str.) D7
Bahr es Safi (des.) E6
Barida, Ras (cape) C5
Batin, Wadi al (dry riv.) ...E4
Bisha, Wadi (dry riv.) D5
Dahana (des.) E4
Dawasir, Hadhb (range) ...D5
Dawasir, Wadi (dry riv.) ...D5

Farasan (isls.) D6
Hatiba, Ras (cape) C5
Hejaz (reg.) C4
Jafura (des.) F5
Mashabi (isl.) C4
Midian (dist.) C4
Misha'ab, Ras (cape) E4
Nefud (des.) D4
Nefud Dahi (des.) D5
Nejd (reg.) D4
Persian (gulf) E6
Ranya, Wadi (dry riv.) D5
Red (sea) C5
Rima, Wadi (dry riv.) D4
Rimal, Ar (des.) F5
Rub al Khali (des.) F5
Safaniya, Ras (cape) E4
Salma, Jebel (mts.) D4
Shaibara (isl.) C4
Shammar, Jebel (plat.) D4
Sirhan, Wadi (dry riv.) C3
Subh, Jebel (mt.) C4
Summan (plat.) E4
Tihama (reg.) C5
Tiran (isl.) C4
Tiran (str.) C4
Tuwaiq, Jebel (range) E5

UNITED ARAB EMIRATES

CITIES and TOWNS

Abu Dhabi (cap.) 347,000 ...F5
'Ajman G4
Buraimi F5
Dubai F4
Fujairah G4
Jebel Dhanna F5
Ras al Khaimah F4
Ruwais F5
Sharjah G4
Umm al Qaiwain G4

OTHER FEATURES

Das (isl.) F4
Oman (gulf) G4
Yas (isl.) F5
Zirko (isl.) F5

WEST BANK

CITIES and TOWNS

Hebron 38,309 ......C3

OTHER FEATURES

Dead (sea) C3

YEMEN

CITIES and TOWNS

Aden 240,370 ......E7
Al Hawtah E6

'Amran D6
Bait al Faqih D7
Balhaf E7
Bir 'Ali E7
Damqut F7
Dhamar 19,467 ......D7
El Beida 5,975 ......E7
Hadibu F7
Hajja 5,814 ......D6
Hodeida 80,314 ......D7
Hureidha E6
Ibb 19,066 ......D7
Lodar E7
Luhaiya D6
Madinat ash Sha'b E6
Marib 292 ......E6
Meifa E7
Mocha D7
Mukalla 45,000 ......E7
Nisab E7
Qabr Hud F6
Qishn F6
Riyan F6
Sa'ada 4,252 ......D6
Saihut F6
Sanaa (cap.) 134,588 ......D7
Sana E6
Seiyun 20,000 ......E6
Shabwa E6
Sheikh Sa'id D7
Shibam E6
Shihr F7
Shuqra E7
Ta'izz 78,642 ......D7
Tarim E6
Yarim D7
Yeshbum E7
Zabid D7

OTHER FEATURES

Bab el Mandeb (str.) D7
Fartak, Ras (cape) F6
Hadhramaut (dist.) E7
Hadhramaut, Wadi (dry riv.)...F7
Hanish (isls.) D7
Jebel Manar (mt.) D7
Jebel Sabir (mt.) D7
Kamaran (isl.) D6
Manar, Jebel (mt.) D7
Mandeb, Bab el (str.) D7
Maqatin (ruins) E7
Perim (isl.) D7
Qamr (bay) F6
Ras Fartak (cape) F6
Red (sea) C5
Sabir, Jebel (mt.) D7
Socotra (isl.) F7
Tihama (reg.) C5
Wadi Hadhramaut (dry riv.)...F7
Zuqar (isl.) D7

† Population of commune.
* City and suburbs.

Agriculture, Industry and Resources

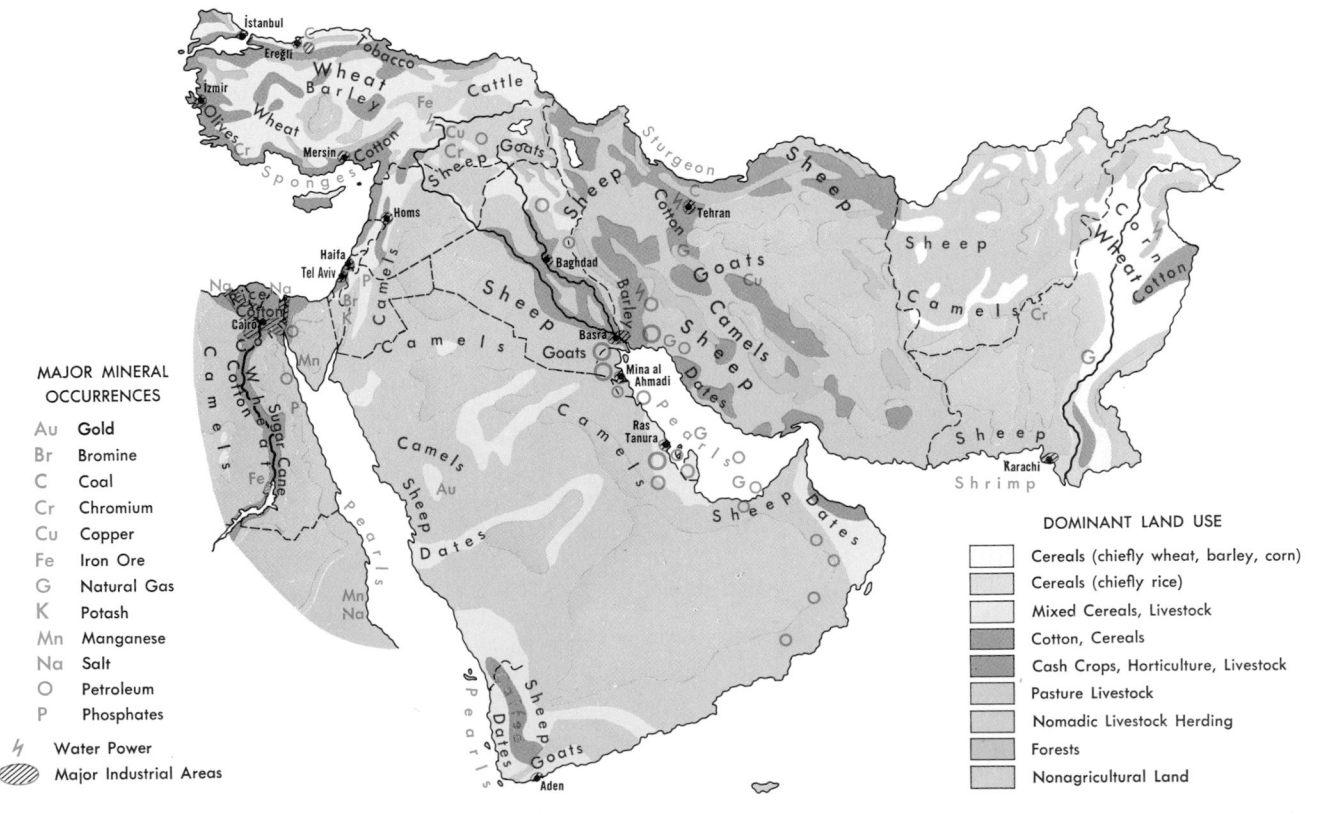

MAJOR MINERAL OCCURRENCES

Au Gold
Br Bromine
C   Coal
Cr Chromium
Cu Copper
Fe Iron Ore
G   Natural Gas
K   Potash
Mn Manganese
Na Salt
O   Petroleum
P   Phosphates
⚡ Water Power
▨ Major Industrial Areas

DOMINANT LAND USE

Cereals (chiefly wheat, barley, corn)
Cereals (chiefly rice)
Mixed Cereals, Livestock
Cotton, Cereals
Cash Crops, Horticulture, Livestock
Pasture Livestock
Nomadic Livestock Herding
Forests
Nonagricultural Land

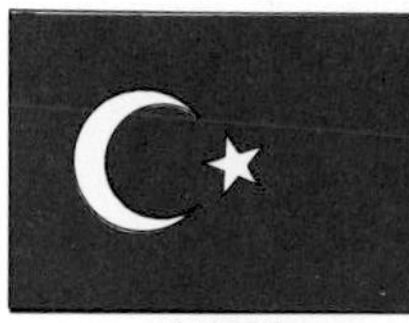

TURKEY

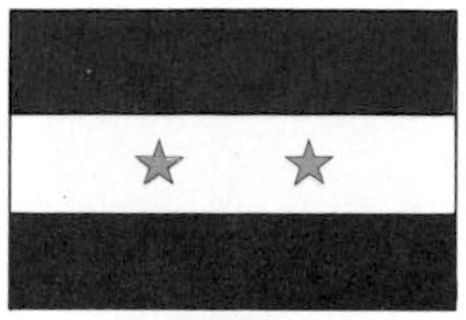

SYRIA

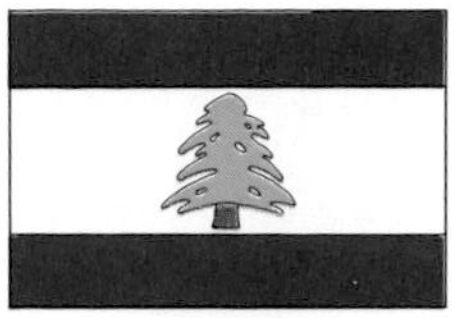

LEBANON

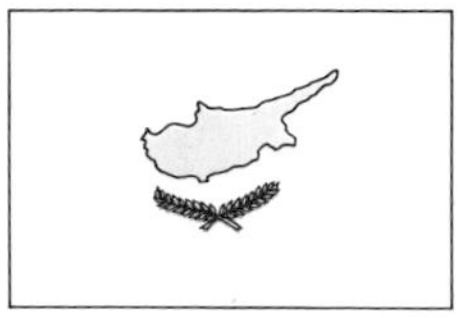

CYPRUS

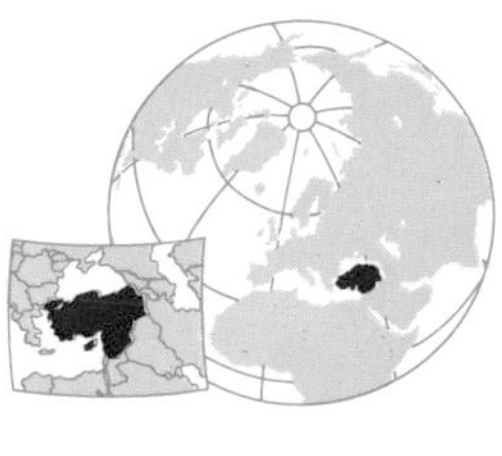

TURKEY

AREA 300,946 sq. mi. (779,450 sq. km.)
POPULATION 56,741,000
CAPITAL Ankara
LARGEST CITY Istanbul
HIGHEST POINT Ararat 16,946 ft. (5,165 m.)
MONETARY UNIT Turkish lira
MAJOR LANGUAGE Turkish
MAJOR RELIGION Islam

SYRIA

AREA 71,498 sq. mi. (185,180 sq. km.)
POPULATION 11,719,000
CAPITAL Damascus
LARGEST CITY Damascus
HIGHEST POINT Hermon 9,232 ft. (2,814 m.)
MONETARY UNIT Syrian pound
MAJOR LANGUAGES Arabic, French, Kurdish, Armenian
MAJOR RELIGIONS Islam, Christianity

LEBANON

AREA 4,015 sq. mi. (10,399 sq. km.)
POPULATION 2,897,000
CAPITAL Beirut
LARGEST CITY Beirut
HIGHEST POINT Qurnet es Sauda 10,131 ft. (3,088 m.)
MONETARY UNIT Lebanese pound
MAJOR LANGUAGES Arabic, French
MAJOR RELIGIONS Christianity, Islam

CYPRUS

AREA 3,473 sq. mi. (8,995 sq. km.)
POPULATION 699,000
CAPITAL Nicosia
LARGEST CITY Nicosia
HIGHEST POINT Troödos 6,406 ft. (1,953 m.)
MONETARY UNIT Cypriot pound
MAJOR LANGUAGES Greek, Turkish, English
MAJOR RELIGIONS Eastern (Greek) Orthodoxy,

CYPRUS

CITIES and TOWNS

Famagusta 38,960 F5
Kyrenia 3,892 E5
Kythrea 3,400 E5
Lapithos 3,600 E5
Larnaca 19,608 E5
Lefka 3,650 E5
Limassol 79,641 E5
Morphou 9,040 E5
Nicosia (cap.) 115,718 E5
Paphos 8,984 E5
Polis 2,200 E5
Rizokarpasso 3,600 F5
Yialousa 2,750 E5

OTHER FEATURES

Andreas (cape) F5
Arnauti (cape) E5
Famagusta (bay) F5
Gata (cape) E5
Greco (cape) F5
Klides (isls.) F5
Kormakiti (cape) E5
Larnaca (bay) E5
Morphou (bay) E5
Pomos (pt.) E5
Troodos (mt.) E5

LEBANON

CITIES and TOWNS

'Aleih 18,630 F6
Amyun 7,926 F5
Ba'albek 15,560 G5
Beirut (cap.) 474,870 F6
Beirut* 938,940 F6
Merj 'Uyun 9,318 F6
Rasheiya 6,731 F6
Saida 32,200 F6
Sidon (Saida) 32,200 F6
Sur 16,483 F6
Tarabulus 127,611 F5
Tripoli (Tarabulus) 127,611 F5
Tyre (Sur) 16,483 F6
Zahle 53,121 F6
Zegharta 18,210 G5

OTHER FEATURES

Lebanon (mts.) F6
Leontes (Litani) (riv.) F6
Litani (riv.) F6
Sauda, Qurnet es (mt.) G5

SYRIA

PROVINCES

Aleppo 1,316,872 G4
Damascus 1,457,934 G6
Deir ez Zor 292,780 H5
Der'a 230,481 G6
El Quneitra 16,490 F6
Es Suweida 139,650 G6
Hama 514,748 G5
Haseke 468,506 J4
Homs 546,176 G5
Idlib 383,695 G5
Latakia 389,552 G5
Rashid 243,736 H5
Tartus 302,065 G5

CITIES and TOWNS

Abu Kemal 6,907 J5
'Ain el 'Arab 4,529 H4
Aleppo 639,428 G4
Azaz 13,923 G4
Baniyas 8,537 F5
Damascus (cap.) 836,668 G6
Damascus* 923,253 G6
Deir ez Zor 66,164 H5
Der'a 27,651 G6
Dimashq (Damascus) (cap.) 836,668 G6
Duma 30,050 G6
El Bab 27,366 G4
El Haseke 32,746 J4
El Ladhiqya (Latakia) 125,716 F5
El Qaryatein G5
El Quneitra 17,752 F6
El Rashid 37,151 H5
En Nebk 16,334 G5
Es Suweida 29,524 G6
Et Tell el Abyad H4
Haffe 4,656 G5
Haleb (Aleppo) 639,428 G4
Hama 137,421 G5
Harim 6,837 G4
Homs 215,423 G5
Idlib 34,515 G5
Izra 3,226 G6
Jeble 15,715 F5
Jerablus 8,610 G4
Jisr esh Shughur 13,131 G5
Khan Sheikhun G5
Latakia 125,716 F5
Masyaf 7,058 G5
Membij 13,796 G4
Meskene H5
Meyadin 12,515 J5
Qal'at es Salihiye J5
Qamishliye 31,448 J4
Quteife 4,993 G6
Raqqa (El Rashid) 37,151 H5
Safita 9,650 G5
Selemiya 21,677 G5
Tadmur 10,670 H5
Tartus 29,842 F5
Telkalakh 6,242 F5
Zebdani 10,010 G6

OTHER FEATURES

Abdul 'Aziz, Jebel (mts.) J4
'Amrit (ruins) F5
Arwad (Ruad) (isl.) F5
'Asi (Orontes) (riv.) G5
Bahrat Assad (lake) H4
Druz, Jebel ed (mts.) G6
El Furat (riv.) H4
Euphrates (El Furat) (riv.) H4
Hermon (mt.) F6
Khabur (riv.) J5
Orontes (riv.) G5
Palmyra (Tadmor) (ruins) H5
Tigris (riv.) K4

TURKEY

PROVINCES

Adana 1,485,743 F4
Adıyaman 367,595 H4
Afyonkarahisar 597,516 D3
Ağri 368,009 K3
Amasya 341,287 F2
Ankara 2,854,689 E3
Antalya 748,706 D4
Artvin 228,997 J2
Aydın 652,488 B4
Balıkesir 853,177 B3
Bilecik 147,001 D2
Bingöl 228,702 J3
Bitlis 257,908 J3
Bolu 471,751 D2
Burdur 235,009 D4
Bursa 1,148,492 C2
Çanakkale 338,091 B2
Çankırı 258,436 E2
Çorum 571,831 F2
Denizli 603,338 C4
Diyarbakır 778,150 H4
Edirne 363,286 B2
Elâzig 440,800 H3
Erzincan 282,022 H3
Erzurum 801,809 J3
Eskişehir 543,802 D3
Gaziantep 808,697 G4
Giresun 480,083 H2
Gümüşhane 275,191 H2
Hakkâri 155,463 K4
Hatay 856,271 G4
İçel 842,817 F4
İsparta 301,166 D4
İstanbul 3,264,393 C2
İzmir 1,976,763 B3
Kahramanmaraş 738,032 G4
Kars 700,238 K2
Kastamonu 450,946 E2
Kayseri 778,383 F3
Kırklareli 283,408 B2
Kırşehir 240,497 F3
Kocaeli 596,899 C2
Konya 1,562,139 E4
Kütahya 497,089 C3
Malatya 669,962 H3
Manisa 941,941 B3
Mardin 564,967 J4
Muğla 438,145 C4
Muş 302,406 J3
Nevşehir 256,933 F3
Niğde 512,071 F4
Ordu 713,535 G2
Rize 361,258 J2
Sakarya 548,747 D2
Samsun 1,008,113 F2
Siirt 445,483 J4
Sinop 276,242 F2
Sivas 750,144 G3
Tekirdağ 360,742 B2
Tokat 624,508 G2
Trabzon 731,045 H2
Tunceli 157,974 H3
Urfa 602,736 H4
Uşak 247,224 C3
Van 468,646 K3
Yozgat 504,433 F3
Zonguldak 972,856 D2

CITIES and TOWNS

Adalia (Antalya) 176,446 D4
Adana 842,845 F4
Adapazarı 131,400 D2
Adilcevaz 10,342 K3
Adıyaman 116,986 H4
Afşin 20,084 G3
Afyonkarahisar 597,516 D3
Ağri (Karaköse) 41,103 K3
Ahlat 10,422 K3
Akçaabat 13,384 H2
Akçadağ 8,015 G3
Akçakale 11,184 H4
Akçakoca 9,639 D2
Akdağmadeni 10,192 F3
Akhisar 61,491 B3
Aksaray 62,927 F3
Akşehir 40,312 D3
Akseki 6,815 D4
Akyazı 14,795 D2
Alaca 15,649 F2
Alaçam 11,402 F2
Alanya 22,190 D4
Alaşehir 25,611 C3
Alexandretta (İskenderun) 120,985 G4
Alibeyköyü 33,387 D6
Altındağ 608,689 E2
Altınova 6,980 B3
Alucra 8,795 H2
Amasya 48,010 F2
Anamur 23,025 E4
Andırın 6,045 G4
Ankara (cap.) 2,203,729 E3
Antakya 99,551 F4
Antalya 176,446 D4
Antioch (Antakya) 99,551 F4
Arapkir 8,816 H3
Ardahan 14,912 K2
Ardeşen 9,582 J2
Arhavi 6,801 J2
Arsin 6,892 H2
Artvin 14,203 J2
Aşkale 12,045 J3
Avanos 8,927 F3
Ayancık 8,257 F1
Aybastı 13,517 G2
Aydın 37,696 B4
Aydıncık 19,371 E4
Ayvalık 19,371 B3
Babaeski 18,145 B2
Bafra 50,213 F2
Bahçe 12,366 G4
Bakırköy 234,226 D6
Balıkesir 124,122 B3
Banaz 8,356 C3
Bandırma 53,497 B2
Bartin 20,728 E2
Başkale 9,770 K3
Batman 86,172 J4
Bayat 5,366 F2
Bayburt 22,578 J2
Bayındır 12,440 B3
Bayramiç 7,854 B3
Bergama 34,716 B3
Beşiktaş 188,117 D6
Besni 15,833 G4
Beykoz 94,101 D5
Beyoğlu 223,360 D6
Beypazarı 16,971 D2
Beyşehir 15,845 D4
Biga 16,359 B2
Bigadiç 8,955 C3
Bilecik 15,108 D2
Bingöl (Çapakçur) 27,904 J3
Birecik 20,412 H4
Bismil 19,059 J4
Bitlis 27,114 J3
Bodrum 32,517 B4
Boğazlıyan 10,827 F3
Bolu 38,400 D2
Bolvadin 30,599 D3
Bor 45,480 F4
Bornova 60,397 B3
Boyabat 14,397 F2
Bozdoğan 7,682 C4
Bozova 5,510 H4
Bozüyük 18,052 C3
Bucak 18,852 D4
Bulancak 16,089 H2
Bulanık 9,140 K3
Buldan 10,939 C3

(continued on following page)

Agriculture, Industry and Resources

DOMINANT LAND USE

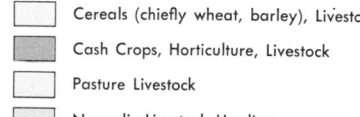

- Cereals (chiefly wheat, barley), Livestock
- Cash Crops, Horticulture, Livestock
- Pasture Livestock
- Nomadic Livestock Herding
- Forests
- Nonagricultural Land

MAJOR MINERAL OCCURRENCES

Ab	Asbestos	Na	Salt
Al	Bauxite	O	Petroleum
C	Coal	P	Phosphates
Cr	Chromium	Pb	Lead
Cu	Copper	Py	Pyrites
Fe	Iron Ore	Sb	Antimony
Hg	Mercury	Zn	Zinc
Mg	Magnesium		

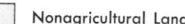

Water Power
Major Industrial Areas

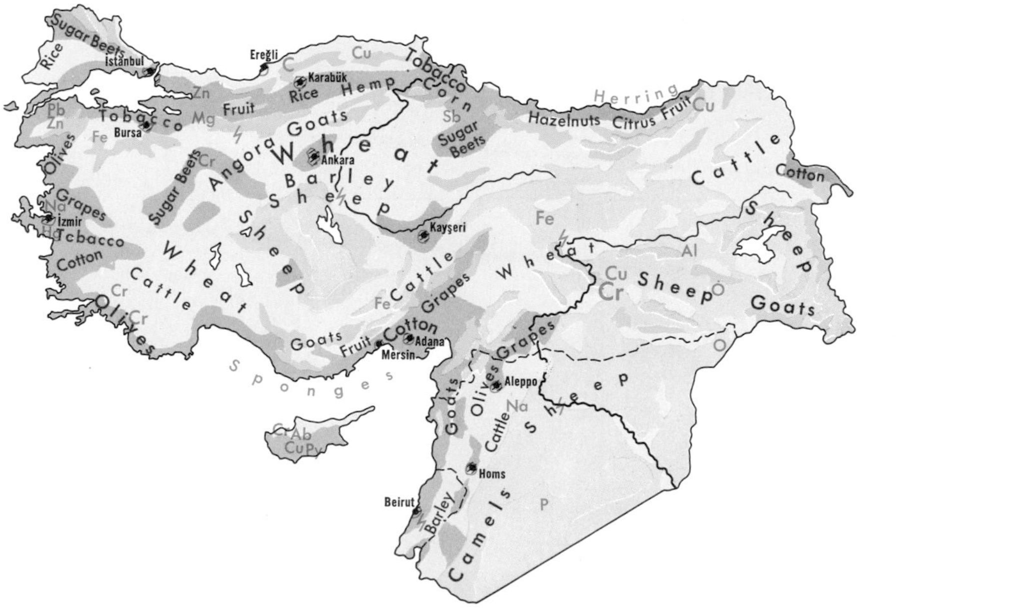

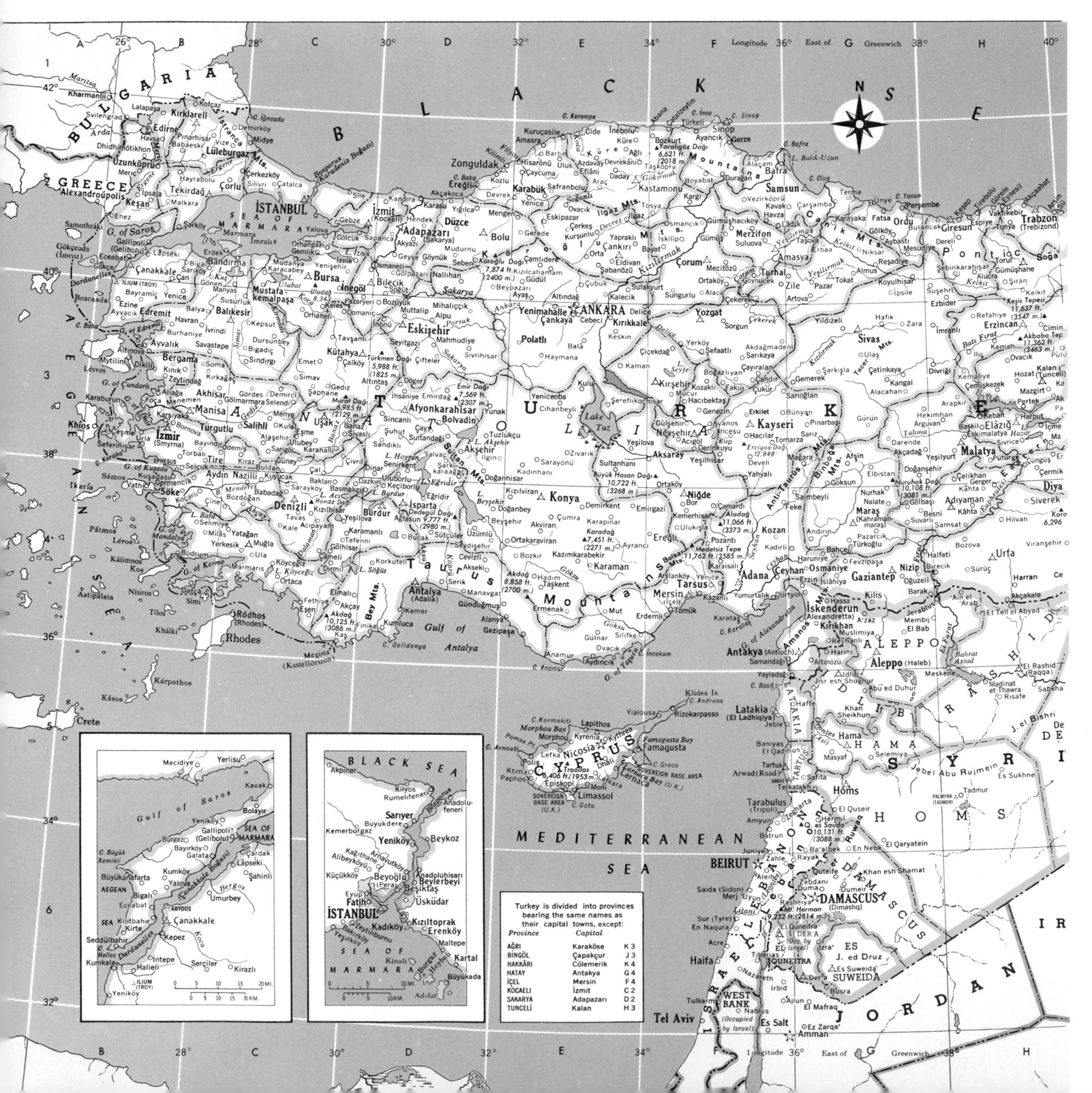

Kaman 19,997	E3	Kemalpaşa 10,032	J2
Kandıra 8,142	D2	Kemerburgaz 7,234	D5
Kangal 6,644	G3	Kemirhisar 6,205	F4
Karabük 84,975	E2	Kepsut 5,136	C3
Karacabey 23,600	C2	Keşan 28,428	B2
Karaköse (Ağrı) 41,103	K3	Keşap 5,821	H2
Karakoçan 6,462	H3	Keskin 14,595	E3
Karaman 51,868	E4	Kiğı 6,046	J3
Karamanlı 5,904	C4	Kilimli 26,649	D2
Karapınar 24,558	E4	Kilis 58,686	G4
Karasu 10,025	D2	Kınık 12,034	B3
Karataş 5,700	F4	Kiraz 5,569	C3
Kargı 5,232	F2	Kınık 47,688	G4
Karlıova 5,750	J3	Kırıkkale 175,235	E3
Kars 58,651	K2	Kırkağaç 18,475	B3
Karşıyaka 226,982	B3	Kırklareli 36,183	B2
Kartal 67,627	D6	Kırşehir 50,063	F3
Kastamonu 35,636	E2	Kızılcahamam 9,604	E2
Kayseri 273,362	F3	Kızılhisar 11,119	C4
Keban 5,172	H3	Kızıltepe 30,530	J4
Keçiborlu 7,843	D4	Koçarlı 5,721	B4
Kelkit 7,002	H2	Kocaeli (İzmit) 19,140	D2

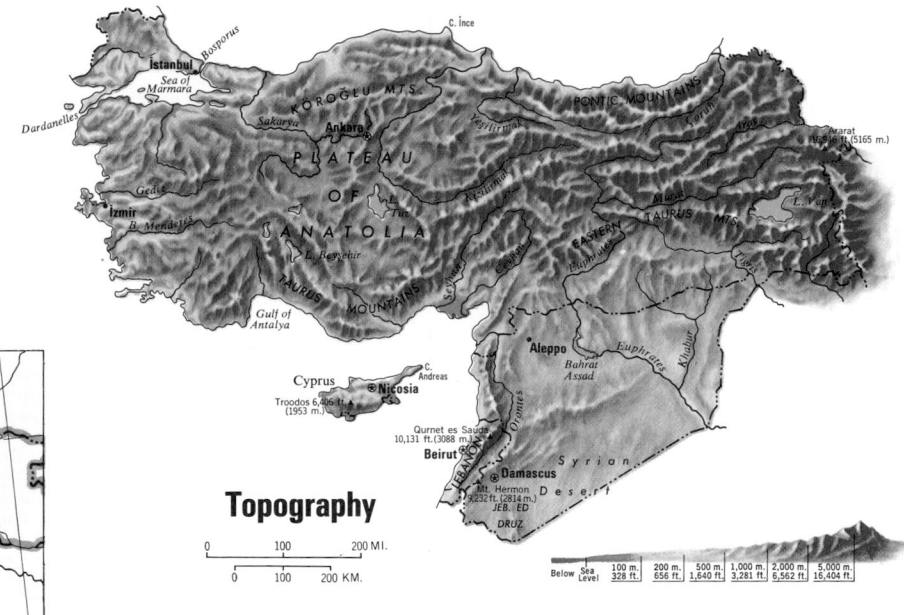

Topography

0   100   200 MI.

0   100   200 KM.

Below Sea Level   100 m. 328 ft.   200 m. 656 ft.   500 m. 1,640 ft.   1,000 m. 3,281 ft.   2,000 m. 6,562 ft.   5,000 m. 16,404 ft.

Turkey, Syria, Lebanon and Cyprus

® Copyright HAMMOND INCORPORATED, Maplewood, N.J.

SCALE OF MILES

0   25   50   75   100   125   150

SCALE OF KILOMETERS

0   25   50   75   100   125   150

Capitals of Countries ....☆   Capitals of Provinces ....△

Provincial Boundaries ....

Konya 325,850	E4	Safranbolu 19,155	E2
Korkuteli 10,774	D4	Sakarya (Adapazarı) 131,400	D2
Köyceğiz 5,347	C4	Salihli 51,638	C3
Kozaklı 6,764	F3	Samandağı 25,349	F4
Kozan 42,410	F4	Samsun 198,266	F2
Kozlu 27,322	D2	Sandıklı 15,966	D3
Kozluk 10,215	J3	Sapanca 10,228	D2
Küçükköy 56,411	C6	Sarayköy 11,009	C4
Kula 12,763	C3	Sarayönü 8,643	E3
Kulp 5,577	J3	Sarıgöl 7,880	C3
Kulu 12,183	E3	Sarıkamış 23,331	K2
Kumluca 7,977	D4	Sarıkaya 7,297	F3
Kurşunlu 6,678	E2	Sarıköy 4,695	B2
Kütahya 101,087	C3	Sarıyer 110,555	D5
Kurtalan 9,748	J3	Şarkikaraağaç 5,905	D3
Kuşadası 14,299	B4	Şarkışla 12,611	G3
Kuyucak 6,532	C4	Şarköy 6,755	B2
Lâdik 7,200	G2	Savaştepe 7,110	B3
Lice 8,486	J3	Savur 6,169	J4
Lüleburgaz 35,643	B2	Şebinkarahisar 12,550	H2
Mağara 5,037	G3	Şefaatlı 7,513	F3
Mahmudiye 5,352	D3	Şeferihisar 6,506	B3
Malatya 184,390	H3	Selçuk 12,819	B3
Malazgirt 14,150	K3	Selendi 5,012	C3
Malkara 15,570	B2	Şemdinli 19,677	L4
Maltepe 66,343	D6	Senirkent 8,382	D3
Manavgat 14,392	E4	Şereflikoçhisar 22,208	E3
Manisa 93,970	B3	Şerik 15,662	D4
Maraş (Kahramanmaraş) 177,919	G4	Seydişehir 30,394	D4
		Siirt 42,692	J4
Mardin 37,750	J4	Şile 4,870	C2
Marmaris 7,710	C4	Silifke 22,045	E4
Mazıdağı 7,941	J4	Silivri 13,922	C2
Mecitözü 5,874	F2	Silopi 6,832	K4
Menemen 22,080	B3	Silvan 44,412	J3
Mersin 215,300	F4	Simav 10,775	C3
Merzifon 32,031	F2	Sındırgı 8,992	C3
Mesudiye 5,013	G2	Sinop 18,381	F2
Midyat 20,112	J4	Şiran 6,088	H2
Milâs 20,333	B4	Şırnak 10,947	K4
Mucur 9,386	F3	Sivas 173,831	G3
Mudanya 10,556	C2	Sivaslı 4,627	C3
Mudurnu 5,307	D2	Siverek 30,000	H4
Muğla 27,162	C4	Sivrihisar 9,608	D3
Muradiye 10,036	K3	Smyrna (İzmir) 753,749	B3
Muş 40,297	J3	Söğüt 6,353	D2
Mustafakemalpaşa 30,099	C2	Söke 37,362	B4
Mut 14,029	E4	Solhan 7,170	J3
Nallıhan 9,791	D2	Soma 30,219	B3
Nazilli 64,015	C4	Sorgun 19,623	F3
Nevşehir 37,106	F3	Şuhut 8,154	D3
Niğde 39,972	F4	Sulakyurt 4,712	E2
Niksar 23,570	G2	Sultandağı 5,115	D3
Nizip 39,267	G4	Sultanhanı 5,112	E3
Nurhak 5,330	G4	Suluova 25,682	F2
Nusaybin 32,620	J4	Sungurlu 24,170	F2
Ödemiş 40,652	C3	Sürmene 10,152	J2
Oğuzeli 7,826	G4	Sürüç 19,000	H4
Oltu 12,288	J2	Suşehri 11,442	H2
Ordu 52,080	G2	Susurluk 16,113	C3
Orhangazi 18,537	C2	Tarsus 120,270	F4
Ortaca 8,604	C4	Taşkent 7,098	E4
Ortaköy 8,848	F3	Taşköprü 8,659	F2
Osmancık 15,304	F2	Taşova 6,208	G2
Osmaneli 6,664	D2	Tatvan 40,324	K3
Osmaniye 84,338	G4	Tavas 10,335	C4
Palu 6,842	H3	Tavşanlı 23,325	C3
Pasinler 20,039	J3	Tekirdağ 51,327	B2
Patnos 18,040	K3	Tercan 5,506	J3
Pazarcık 19,821	G4	Terme 15,530	G2
Pazaryeri 6,005	C2	Tire 32,242	B3
Pera (Beyoğlu) 94,101	D5	Tirebolu 9,274	H2
Perşembe 7,190	G2	Tokat 60,369	G2
Pervari 5,021	K4	Tomarza 7,733	F3
Pınarbaşı 10,578	G3	Tömük 7,660	F4
Pınarhisar 10,649	B2	Tonya 11,010	H2
Polatlı 43,514	E3	Tortum 4,280	J2
Pozantı 5,588	F4	Torbalı 15,504	B3
Refahiye 7,505	H3	Tosya 18,544	F2
Reşadiye 5,922	G2	Trebizond (Trabzon) 107,412	H2
Reyhanlı 30,843	G4	Tunceli (Kalan) 12,859	H3
Rize 41,740	J2	Türkoğlu 8,528	G4
		Turgutlu 55,575	B3
		Turhal 47,364	F2
		Tuzluca 6,716	K3
		Tuzlukçu 6,716	D3
		Ula 5,119	C4
		Uluborlu 6,002	D3
		Uludere 4,989	K4
		Ulukışla 7,841	F4
		Ünye 27,946	G2
		Urfa 148,434	H4
		Ürgüp 6,955	F3
		Urla 14,347	B3
		Uşak 70,822	C3
		Üsküdar 255,899	D6
		Uzunköprü 27,706	B2
		Vakfıkebir 13,814	H2
		Van 93,823	K3
		Varto 7,360	J3
		Vezirköprü 13,547	F2
		Viranşehir 41,934	H4
		Vize 9,528	B2
		Yahyalı 15,585	F3
		Yalova 41,869	C2
		Yalvaç 19,986	D3
		Yatağan 7,350	C4
		Yayladağı 5,300	F5
		Yenice, Çanakkale 4,016	B3
		Yenice, İçel 4,106	F4
		Yenice, Zonguldak 5,791	E2
		Yeniceoba 5,740	E3
		Yenimahalle 265,752	E3
		Yenişehir 17,013	C2
		Yerköy 20,623	F3
		Yeşilhisar 11,132	F3
		Yeşilova, Burdur 4,393	C4
		Yeşilova, Niğde 5,237	E3
		Yeşilyurt 7,040	H3
		Yıldızeli 11,124	G3
		Yozgat 36,220	F3
		Yüksekova 11,867	L4
		Yunak 7,144	D3
		Zara 10,196	G3
		Zeytinburnu 126,899	D6
		Zile 30,066	G2
		Zonguldak 108,661	D2

OTHER FEATURES

Abydos (ruins)	B6	Ceyhan (riv.)	F4
Acı (lake)	C4	Çıldır (lake)	K2
Adalar (isl.)	D6	Cilo Dağı (mt.)	K4
Aegean (sea)	A3	Çoruh (riv.)	J2
Ağrı, Büyük (Ararat) (mt.)	L3	Çorum (riv.)	F2
Akbaba Tepesi (mt.)	H3	Dalaman (riv.)	C4
Akşehir (lake)	D3	Dardanelles (strait)	B6
Aksu (riv.)	D4	Delice (riv.)	E2
Alexandretta (gulf)	F4	Devrez (riv.)	E2
Amanos (mts.)	G4	Dicle (riv.)	J4
Anatolia (reg.)	D3	Eastern Taurus (mts.)	J3
Ankara (riv.)	E3	Edremit (gulf)	B3
Antalya (gulf)	D4	Eğridir (lake)	D4
Anti-Taurus (mts.)	G3	Emir Dağı (mt.)	D3
Araks (riv.)	K2	Ephesus (ruins)	B3
Ararat (mt.)	L3	Erciyas-Dağı (mt.)	F3
Arpa (riv.)	K2	Ergene (riv.)	B2
Baba (cape)	A3	Euphrates (Fırat) (riv.)	G4
Bafra (cape)	G2	Filyos (riv.)	D2
Banaz (riv.)	C3	Fırat (riv.)	G4
Batı Fırat (riv.)	H3	Gediz (riv.)	C3
Bey (riv.)	D4	Gelidonya (cape)	D4
Beyşehir (lake)	D4	Gökçeada (isl.)	A2
Bingöl Dağları (mts.)	J3	Gökırmak (riv.)	F2
Black (sea)	E1	Göksu (riv.)	E4
Bosporus (strait)	D6	Hakkâri (mts.)	K4
Burgaz (isl.)	D6	Helles (cape)	B6
Büyük Ağrı (Ararat) (mt.)	L3	Heybeli (isl.)	D6
Büyük Hasan Dağı (mt.)	E3	Hoyran (lake)	D3
Büyük Kemikli (cape)	B6	Ilgaz (mts.)	E2
Çanakkale Boğazı (Dardanelles) (str.)	B6	Ilium (ruins)	B6
Çandarlı (gulf)	B3	İmroz (Gökçeada) (isl.)	A2
Çekerek (riv.)	F3	İnce (cape)	F1
		İstranca (mts.)	C2
		İzmir (gulf)	B3
		İznik (lake)	C2
		Kaçkar Dağı (mt.)	J2
		Karacadağ (mt.)	H4
		Karadeniz Boğazı (Bosporus) (str.)	C2
		Karasu-Aras (mts.)	J3
		Karataş (cape)	F4
		Kelkit (riv.)	G2
		Kerme (gulf)	B4
		Keşiş Tepesi (mt.)	H3
		Kırmasti (riv.)	C3
		Kızılırmak (riv.)	F2
		Köroğlu (mts.)	E2
		Küre (mts.)	E2
		Kuş (lake)	B2
		Kuşada (gulf)	B4
		Mandalya (gulf)	B4
		Marmara (isl.)	B2
		Marmara (sea)	C2
		Medetsiz Tepe (mt.)	F4
		Menderes, Büyük (riv.)	C4
		Meriç (riv.)	B2
		Murat (riv.)	H3
		Murat Dağı (mt.)	C3
		Pontic (mts.)	H2
		Porsuk (riv.)	D3
		Prinkipo (Adalar) (isl.)	D6
		Sakarya (riv.)	D2
		Saros (gulf)	B2
		Seyhan (riv.)	F4
		Simav (riv.)	C3
		Sinop (cape)	F1
		Süphan Dağı (mt.)	K3
		Taşucu (gulf)	E4
		Taurus (mts.)	D4
		Tecer (mts.)	G3
		Tigris (Dicle) (riv.)	J4
		Troy (Ilium) (ruins)	B6
		Türkmen Dağ (mt.)	D3
		Tuz (lake)	E3
		Ulubat (lake)	C2
		Uludağ (mt.)	C2
		Van (lake)	K3
		Yaralıgöz Dağı (mt.)	E2
		Yeşilırmak (riv.)	G2

*City and suburbs

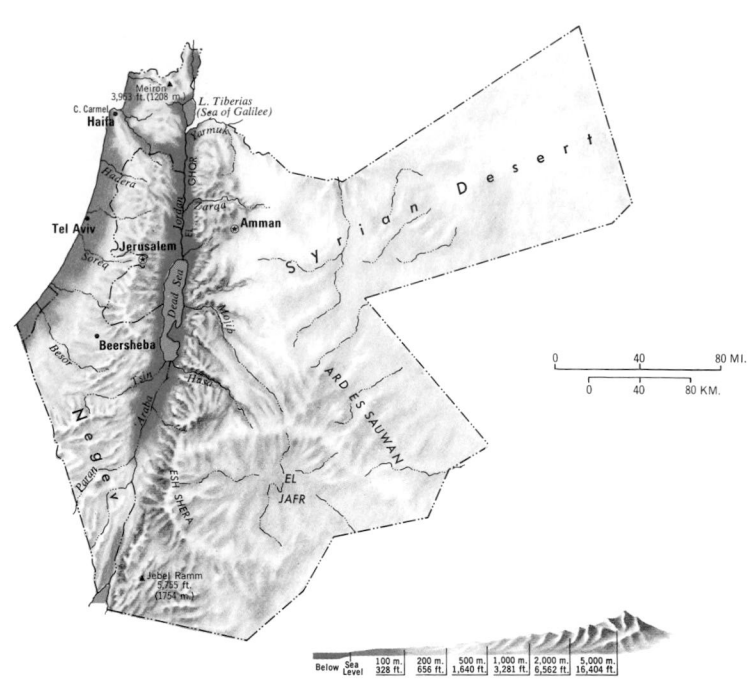

ISRAEL

DISTRICTS

Central 572,300 ....B3
Haifa 480,800 ....C2
Jerusalem 338,600 ....B4
Northern 473,700 ....C2
Southern 351,300 ....B5
Tel Aviv 905,100 ....B3

CITIES and TOWNS

Acre 34,400 ....C2
Afiqim 1,243 ....D2
'Afula 17,400 ....C2
Akko (Acre) 34,400 ....C2
Arad 5,400 ....C5
'Arrabe 6,000 ....C2
Ashdod 40,500 ....B4
Ashdot Ya'aqov 1,197 ......D2
Ashqelon 43,100 ....B4
Atlit 1,516 ....B2
Bat Yam 124,100 ....B3
Be'eri 390 ....A5
Beersheba
  (Beer Sheva) 101,000 ...B5
Bene Beraq 74,100 ....B3
Bet She'an 11,300 ....D3
Bet Shemesh 10,100 ....B4
Binyamina 2,701 ....B2
Carmiel C2
Dalyat al-Karmel 6,200 ....C2
Dan 498 ....D1
Dimona 23,700 ....D4
Dor 195 ....B2
'Ein Harod 1,372 ....C2
Elat 12,800 ....D6
Elath (Elat) 12,800 ....D6
Even Yehuda 3,464 ....B3
Gat 430 ....B4
Gedera 5,400 ....B4
Ginnosar 473 ....D2
Giv'atayim 48,500 ....B3
Giv'at Brenner 1,505 ....B4
Giv'at Hayyim 1,360 ....B3
Hadera 31,900 ....B3
Haifa 227,800 ....B2
Haifa* 367,400 ....B2
Helez 466 ....B4
Herzeliyya 41,200 ....B3
Hod Hasharon 13,500 .....B3
Hodiyya 400 ....B4
Holon 121,200 ....B3
Iksal 2,156 ....C2
Jerusalem (cap.) 376,000 ..C4
Jish 1,498 ....C1
Kafar Kanna 5,200 ....C2
Kafr Yasif 2,975 ....C2

Karkur-Pardes Hanna 13,600..C3
Kefar Blum 565 ....D1
Kefar Gil'adi 701 ....C1
Kefar Ruppin 306 ....D3
Kefar Sava 26,500 ....B3
Kefar Vitkin 808 ....B3
Kefar Zekhariya 420 ....B4
Kinneret 909 ....D2
Lod (Lydda) 30,500 ....B4
Lydda 30,500 ....B4
Magen 149 ....A5
Mash 'Abbe Sade 238 ......B6
Mavqi'im 177 ....B4
Megiddo C2
Metula 261 ....D1
Migdal 688 ....C2
Mikhmoret 608 ....B3
Mishmar Hanegev 336 .....B5
Mishmar Hayarden D1
Mivtahim 398 ....A5
Mizpe Ramon 331 ....D5
Moza Illit 219 ....C4
Mughar 4,010 ....C2
Muqeible 459 ....C2
Nahariyya 24,000 ....C1
Nazareth 33,300 ....C2
Negba 453 ....B4
Nesher 9,400 ....C2
Nes Ziyyona 11,700 ....B4
Netanya 70,700 ....B3
Nevatim 436 ....B5
Newe Yam 211 ....B2
Nizzanim 479 ....B4
Pardes Hanna-Karkur 13,600..B2
Peduyim 361 ....B5
Petah Tiqwa 112,000 ....B3
Qadima 2,937 ....B3
Qedma 157 ....B4
Qiryat Bialik 18,000 ....C2
Qiryat Gat 19,200 ....B4
Qiryat Mal'akhi B4
Qiryat Motzkin 17,600 .....C2
Qiryat Shemona 15,200 ...C1
Qiryat Tiv'on 9,800 ....C2
Qiryat Yam 19,800 ....C2
Ra'anana 14,900 ....B3
Ramat Gan 120,900 ....B3
Ramat Hasharon 20,100 ...B3
Rame 2,986 ....C2
Ramla 34,100 ....B4
Re'im 155 ....A5
Revadim 175 ....B4
Revivim 258 ....D5
Rishon Le Ziyyon 51,900 ..B4
Rosh Pinna 700 ....D2
Ruhama 497 ....B4
Sa'ad 418 ....B5
Safad (Zefat) 13,600 ....C2

Sakhnin 8,400 ....C2
Sedot Yam 511 ....B3
Shave Ziyyon 269 ....B2
Shefar'am 11,800 ....C2
Shefayim 614 ....B3
Shoval 393 ....B5
Tayibe 11,700 ....C3
Tel Aviv 343,300 ....B3
Tel Aviv* 1,219,000 ....B3
Tiberias 23,800 ....C2
Tirat Hakarmel 14,400 .....C2
Tirat Zevi 353 ....D3
Tur'an 2,304 ....C2
Umm el Fahm 13,300 ......C2
Uzza 487 ....B4
Yad Mordekhai 416 ....A4
Yagur 1,266 ....C2
Yavne 10,100 ....B4
Yavne'el 1,580 ....C2
Yehud 8,900 ....B3
Yeroham 5,800 ....B6
Yesud Hama'ala 428 ....D1
Yirka 2,715 ....C2
Zavdi'el 396 ....B4
Zefat 13,600 ....C2
Zikhron Ya'aqov 6,500 ....B2

OTHER FEATURES

Aqaba (gulf) D6
'Araba, Wadi (valley) D5
Beer Sheva (dry riv.) B5
Besor (riv.) B5
Carmel (cape) B2
Carmel (mt.) C2
Dead (sea) C4
Dimona (mt.) C5
Galilee, Sea of
  (Tiberias) (lake) D2
Galilee (reg.) C2
Gerar (dry riv.) B5
Hadera (dry riv.) B3
Haifa (bay) C2
Haniqra, Rosh (cape) C1
Hatira (mt.) B6
Jordan (riv.) D3
Judaea (reg.) B5
Lakhish (dry riv.) B4
Meiron (mt.) C1
Negev (reg.) D5
Qarn (riv.) C1
Qishon (riv.) C2
Ramon (mt.) D5
Rubin (dry riv.) B4
Shiqma (riv.) B4
Tabor (mt.) C2
Tiberias (lake) D2
Yarmuk (riv.) D2
Yarqon (riv.) B3

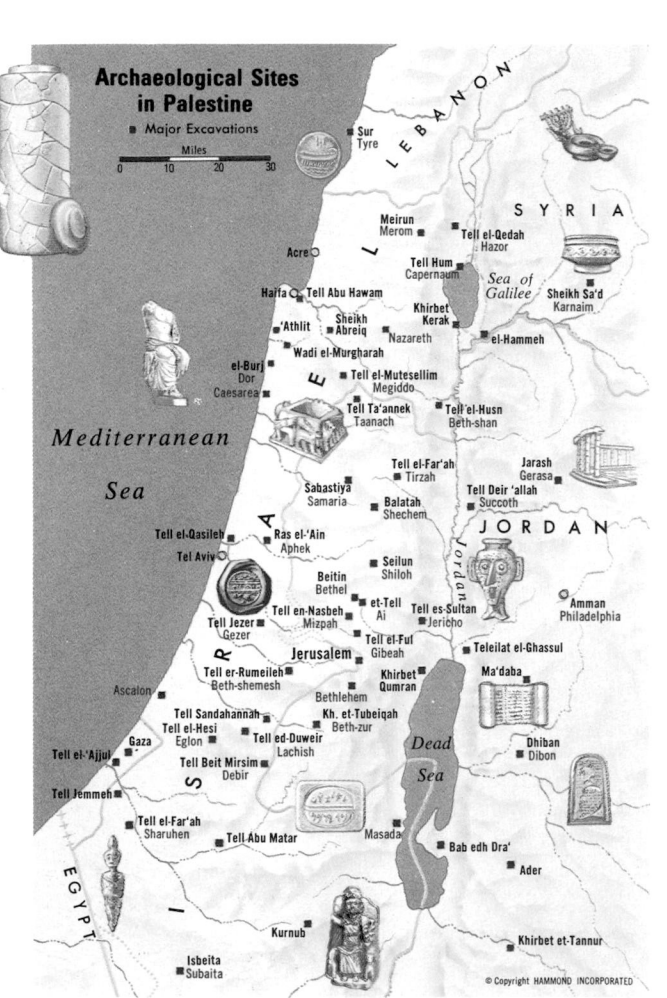

Archaeological Sites in Palestine

■ Major Excavations

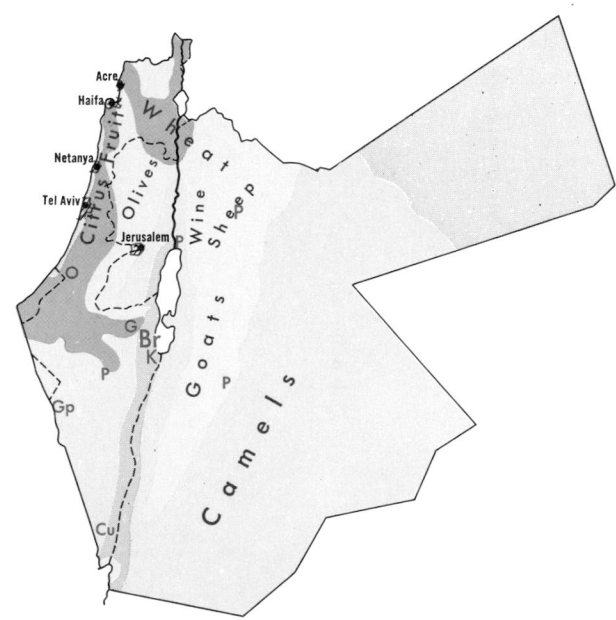

Agriculture, Industry and Resources

DOMINANT LAND USE

Cereals, Livestock
Cash Crops, Horticulture
Nomadic Livestock Herding
Nonagricultural Land

MAJOR MINERAL OCCURRENCES

Br Bromine
Cu Copper
G   Natural Gas
Gp Gypsum
K   Potash
O   Petroleum
P   Phosphates

▨ Major Industrial Areas

© Copyright HAMMOND INCORPORATED

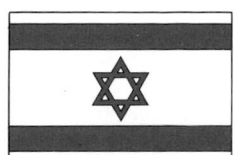

ISRAEL

JORDAN

ISRAEL

AREA 7,847 sq. mi. (20,324 sq. km.)
POPULATION 4,625,000
CAPITAL Jerusalem
LARGEST CITY Tel Aviv
HIGHEST POINT Meiran 3,963 ft.
  (1,208 m.)
MONETARY UNIT shekel
MAJOR LANGUAGES Hebrew, Arabic
MAJOR RELIGIONS Judaism, Islam,
  Christianity

JORDAN

AREA 35,000 sq. mi.
  (90,650 sq. km.)
POPULATION 2,779,000
CAPITAL Amman
LARGEST CITY Amman
HIGHEST POINT Jeb. Ramm 5,755 ft.
  (1,754 m.)
MONETARY UNIT Jordanian dinar
MAJOR LANGUAGE Arabic
MAJOR RELIGION Islam

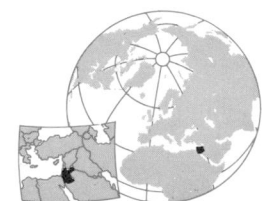

GAZA STRIP
CITIES and TOWNS

'Abasan 1,481 ....A5
Bani Suheila 7,561 ....A5
Beit Hanun 4,756 ....A4
Deir el Balah 10,854 ....A5
Deir el Balah* 18,118 ....A5
Gaza 87,793 ....A5
Gaza* 118,272 ....A5
Jabaliya 10,508 ....A4
Jabaliya* 43,604 ....A4
Khan Yunis 29,522 ....A5
Khan Yunis* 52,997 ....A5
Rafah 10,812 ....A5
Rafah* 49,812 ....A5

WEST BANK
CITIES and TOWNS

'Ajja 1,322 ....C3
'Anabta 3,426 ....C3
Anin 914 ....C2
'Anza 807 ....C3
'Aqraba 2,501 ....C3
Ariha (Jericho) 5,312 ....C4
'Arraba 4,231 ....C3
'Arura 849 ....C3
'Attil 3,808 ....C3
Beit Fajjar 2,474 ....C4
Beit Hanina 1,177 ....C4
Beit Jala 6,041 ....C4
Beit Lahm
  (Bethlehem) 14,439 ....C4
Beit Sahur 5,380 ....C4
Bethlehem 14,439 ....C4
Biddu 1,259 ....C4
Birqin 2,036 ....C3
Bir Zeit 2,311 ....C3
Burqa 2,477 ....C3
Deir Ballut 1,058 ....C3
Deir Sharaf 973 ....C3
Dhahiriya 4,875 ....B5
Dura 4,954 ....C4
El Bira 9,674 ....C4
El Bira* 13,037 ....C4
El Khalil (Hebron) 38,309 ....C4
Er Rihiya 679 ....C5
Ez Zababida 1,474 ....C3
Halhul 6,041 ....C4
Hebron 38,309 ....C4
Idna 3,713 ....B4
Jaba 2,817 ....C3
Jalama 784 ....C3
Jalbun 914 ....C3
Jenin 8,346 ....C3
Jenin* 13,365 ....C3
Jericho 5,312 ....C4
Jericho* 6,931 ....C4
Jifna 655 ....C4
Kharas 1,364 ....C4
Nablus (Nabulus) 41,799 ....C3
Nahhalin 1,109 ....C4
Ni'lin 1,227 ....C4
Qabalan 1,970 ....C3
Qabatiya 6,005 ....C3
Qaffin 2,480 ....C3
Qalqiliya 8,926 ....C3
Qibya 926 ....C4
Rafidiya 1,123 ....C3
Ramallah 12,134 ....C4
Rammun 1,198 ....C4
Rantis 897 ....C3
Salfit 3,201 ....C3
Samu 3,784 ....C5
Shu'fat 14,000 ....C4
Shuweika 2,332 ....C3
Silat Dhahr 2,104 ....C3
Sinjil 1,823 ....C3
Siris 1,285 ....C3
Tammun 2,952 ....C3
Tarqumiya 2,412 ....C4
Tubas 5,262 ....C3
Tulkarm 10,255 ....C3
Tulkarm* 15,275 ....C3
Tur 12,200 ....C4
Ya'bad 4,857 ....C3
Yamun 4,384 ....C3
Yatta 7,281 ....C5

OTHER FEATURES

Ebal (mt.) C3
Golan Heights (reg.) D1
Judaea (reg.) C4
Khirhet Qumran (site) C4
Mashash, Wadi (riv.) C4
Samaria (reg.) C3
Tell 'Asur (mt.) C4
West Bank (reg.) C3

JORDAN
GOVERNORATES

Amman 1,000,000 ....D4
El Balqa 113,000 ....D4
El Karak 93,000 ....E5
Irbid 506,000 ....D3
Ma'an 62,000 ....D5

CITIES and TOWNS

Ajlun ⊙ 42,000 ....D3
Amman (cap.) 711,850 ....D4
'Anjara 3,163 ....D3
'Aqaba 15,000 ....D6
Bal'ama 769 ....E3
Baqura 3,042 ....D2
Damiya 483 ....D3
Dana 844 ....E5
Deir Abu Sa'id 1,927 ....D3
El 'Al 492 ....D4
El Husn 3,728 ....D3
El Karak 10,000 ....E4
El Mafraq 15,500 ....E3
Er Rafid 787 ....D2
Er Ramtha 19,000 ....E3
Er Ruseifa 6,200 ....E3
Es Sahab 2,580 ....E4
Es Salt 24,000 ....D3
Es Sukhna 649 ....E3
Esh Shaubak 4,634 ....D5
Et Tafila ⊙ 17,000 ....E5
Et Taiyiba 2,606 ....D2
Ez Zarqa 263,400 ....E3
Harima 635 ....D2
Hawara 2,342 ....D2
Hisban 718 ....D4
'Ibbin 1,364 ....D3
Irbid 136,770 ....D3
Jarash 29,000 ....D3
Kitim 1,026 ....D2
Kufrinja 3,922 ....D3
Ma'ad 125 ....D2
Ma'an 9,500 ....D5
Ma'daba 22,600 ....D4
Ma'in 1,271 ....D4
Mazra' D5
Na'ur 2,382 ....D4
Qumeim 955 ....D2
Ra's en Naqb 225 ....E5
Safi E5
Safut 4,210 ....D4
Samar 716 ....D2
Sarih 3,390 ....D3
Subeihi 514 ....D4
Suweileh 3,457 ....D4
Suweima 315 ....D4
Um Jauza 582 ....D5
Wadi es Sir 4,455 ....D4
Wadi Musa 654 ....E5
Waqqas 2,321 ....D2

OTHER FEATURES

'Ajlun, Jebel (range) D3
'Aqaba (gulf) D6
'Araba, Wadi (valley) D5
Dead (sea) C4
Hasa, Wadi el (dry riv.) E5
Jordan (riv.) C3
Nebo (mt.) D4
Petra (ruins) D5
Ramm, Jebel (mt.) D6
Shallala, Wadi esh (dry riv.) D2
Shu'eib, Wadi (dry riv.) D3
Zarqa (riv.) D3

*City and suburbs
⊙ Population of subdivision.

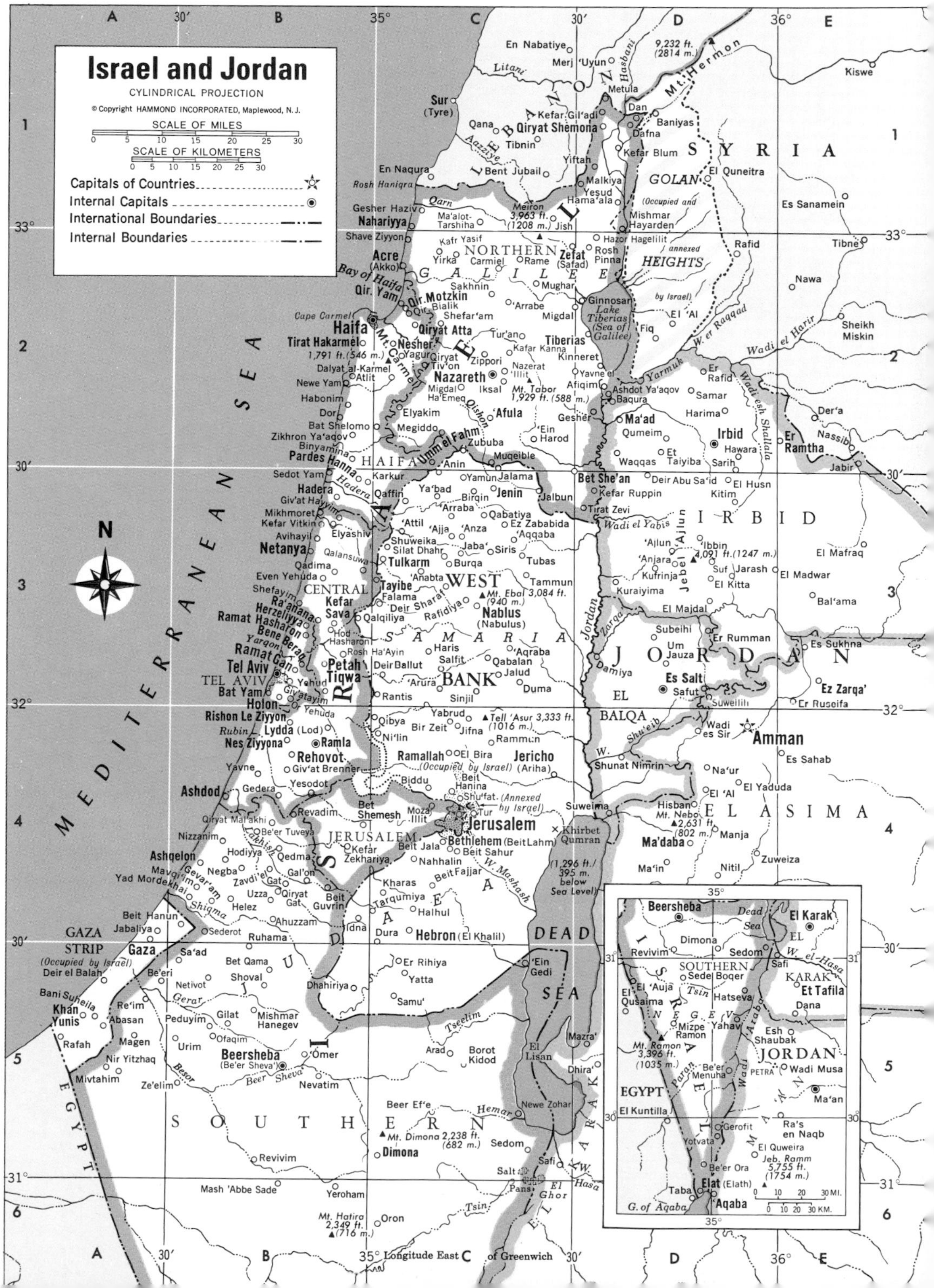

Israel and Jordan

CYLINDRICAL PROJECTION

℗ Copyright HAMMOND INCORPORATED, Maplewood, N.J.

SCALE OF MILES
0 5 10 15 20 25 30

SCALE OF KILOMETERS
0 5 10 15 20 25 30

Capitals of Countries .... ☆
Internal Capitals ------------------ ⊙
International Boundaries ━━━ ▬ ━━━
Internal Boundaries ━━ ▬ ━━

Namaksar (lake) M4
Namakzar-e Shahdad
(salt lake) L5
Oman (gulf) M8
Pasargadae (ruins) H5
Persepolis (ruins) H6
Persian (gulf) F6
Qaranqu (riv.) E2
Qareh Dagh (mts.) E1
Qareh Su (riv.) E1
Qeshm (isl.) J7
Qezel Owzam (riv.) F2
Ras al Kuh (cape) K8
Ras-e Meydani (cape) L8
Safid Rud (riv.) F2
Seistan (reg.) M5
Shatt-al-'Arab (riv.) F5
Shelagh (riv.) M5
Shirvan (riv.) E3
Shur (riv.) J7
Sirri (isl.) J8
Susa (ruins) F4
Talab (riv.) N6
Talkheh (riv.) E1
Tashk (lake) J6
Urmia (lake) D2
Zagros (mts.) E4
Zarineh (riv.) E2
Zayandeh (riv.) H4
Zilbir (riv.) D1
Zohreh (riv.) F5

IRAQ

GOVERNORATES

Anbar 535,627 ....B4
An Najaf 438,971 ....C5
Babil 680 700 ....D4
Baghdad 4,038,430 ....D4
Basra 1,184,500 ....E4
Dhi Qar 683,537 ....E5
Diyala 650,211 ....D4
Dohuk 296,339 ....C2
Erbil 657,294 ....C3
Karbala' 305,627 ....B4
Maysan 395,666 ....E5
Muthanna 239,044 ....D5
Ninawa 1,258,001 ....B3
Qadisiya 475,676 ....D4
Salahuddin 411,734 ....C3
Sulaimaniya 816,406 ....D3
Tamin 587,079 ....C3
Wasit 455,853 ....D4

CITIES and TOWNS

Ad Diwaniya 60,553 ....D5
'Afaq 5,390 ....D4
Al 'Aziziya 7,450 ....D4
Al Falluja 38,072 ....C4
Al Fatha† 15,329 ....C3
'Ali Gharbi 15,456 ....E4
'Ali Sharqi 8,398 ....E4
Al Kufa 30,862 ....D4
Al Musaiyib 15,955 ....D4
'Amara 64,847 ....E5
'Ana 15,729 ....B3
An Najaf 128,096 ....D5
An Nasiriya 60,405 ....D5
Arbela (Erbil) 90,320 ....D2
Ar Rumaila 1,439 ....E5
'Aqra 8,659 ....D2
Az Zubair 41,408 ....E5
Baghdad (cap.) 502,503 ....D4
Ba'quba 34,575 ....D4
Basra 313,327 ....E5
Dohuk 16,998 ....C2
Erbil 90,320 ....D2
Fao 15,399 ....F6
Habbaniya 14,405 ....C4
Hai 16,988 ....E4
Halabja 11,206 ....D3
Hilla 84,717 ....C4
Hindiya 16,436 ....C4
Hit 9,131 ....C4
Karbal'a 58,000 ....C4
Khanaqin 23,522 ....D3
Kifri 8,500 ....D3
Kirkuk 167,413 ....D3
Kut 42,116 ....D4
Mandali 11,262 ....D4
Mosul 315,157 ....C2
Muqdadiyah 12,181 ....D4
N'amaniya 11,943 ....D4
Qal'at Diza 6,250 ....D2
Ramadi 28,723 ....C4
Rumaitha 10,222 ....D5
Samarra 24,746 ....C3
Samawa 33,473 ....D5
Shatra 18,822 ....E5
Sinjar 7,942 ....B2
Sulaimaniya 86,822 ....D3
Tal Kaif 7,482 ....C2
Taza Khurmatu 2,681 ....D3
Tikrit 9,921 ....C3
Tuz Khurmatu 13,860 ....D3
Zakho 14,790 ....C2

OTHER FEATURES

Adhaim (riv.) D3
Al Hajara (plain) D5
'Aneiza, Jebel (mt.) A4
'Ar'ar, Wadi (dry riv.) B5
Babylon (ruins) D4
Batin, Wadi al (dry riv.) E6
Ctesiphon (ruins) D4
Dalmaj, Hor (lake) D4
Darbandikhan (dam) D3
Diyala (riv.) D4
Euphrates (riv.) D4
Great Zab (riv.) C2
Habbaniya, Hor al (lake) C4
Haji Ibraham (mt.) D2
Hammar, Hor al (lake) E5
Hamrin, Jabal (mts.) D3
Hauran, Wadi (dry riv.) B4
Little Zab (riv.) C3
Mesopotamia (reg.) B3
Nineveh (ruins) C2
Razaza (res.) C4
Sa'diya, Hor (lake) E4
Saniya, Hor (lake) E5
Sha'ib Hisb, Wadi (dry riv.) C4
Sinjar, Jebel (mts.) B2
Siyah Kuh (mt.) D2
Suwaiqiya, Hor as (lake) D4
Tharthar (res.) C3
Tharthar, Wadi (dry riv.) C3
Tigris (riv.) E4
Tubal, Wadi al (dry riv.) B4
Ubaiyidh, Wadi (dry riv.) B5
Ur (ruins) E5

† Population of commune.

IRAN

IRAQ

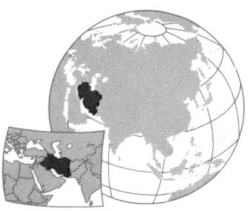

AREA 636,293 sq. mi. (1,648,000 sq. km.)
POPULATION 55,208,000
CAPITAL Tehran
LARGEST CITY Tehran
HIGHEST POINT Damavand 18,605 ft. (5,671 m.)
MONETARY UNIT Iranian rial
MAJOR LANGUAGES Persian, Azerbaijani, Kurdish
MAJOR RELIGION Islam

AREA 172,476 sq. mi. (446,713 sq. km.)
POPULATION 16,335,000
CAPITAL Baghdad
LARGEST CITY Baghdad
HIGHEST POINT Haji Ibrahim 11,811 ft. (3,600 m.)
MONETARY UNIT Iraqi dinar
MAJOR LANGUAGES Arabic, Kurdish
MAJOR RELIGION Islam

Topography

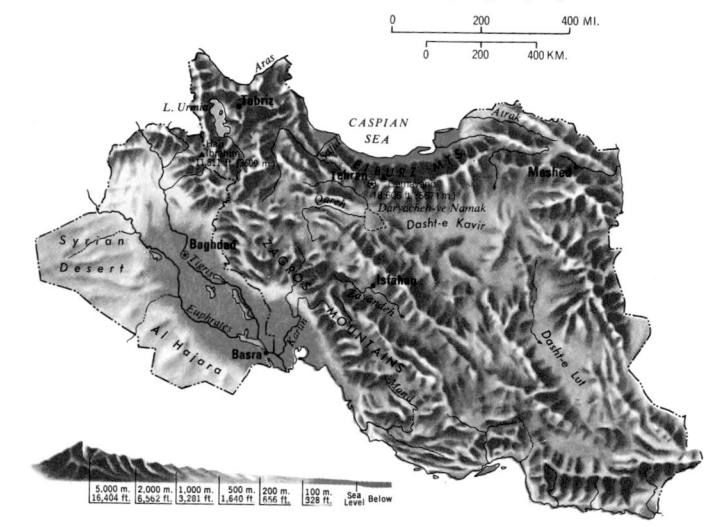

Agriculture, Industry and Resources

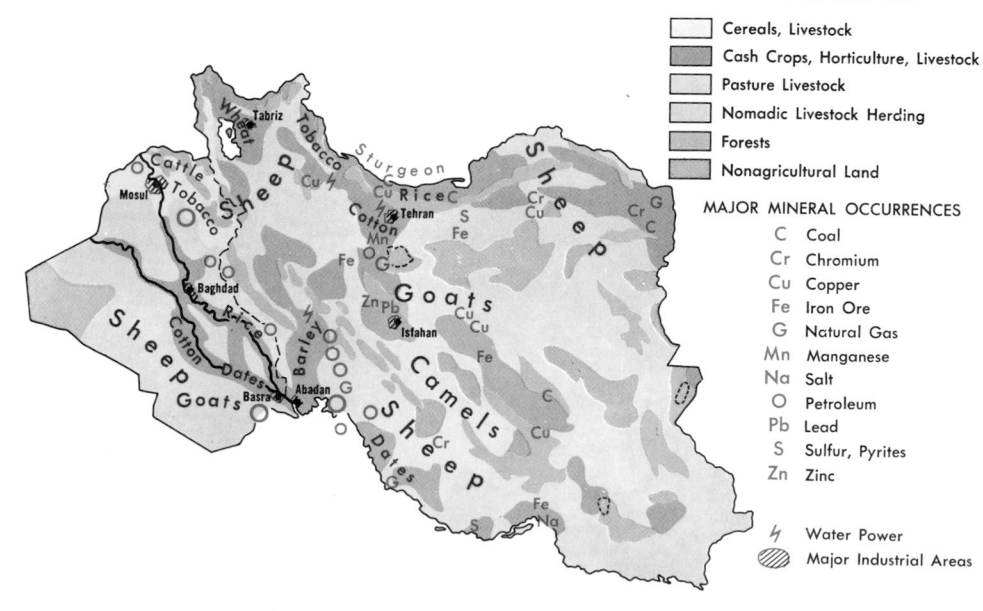

DOMINANT LAND USE

Cereals, Livestock
Cash Crops, Horticulture, Livestock
Pasture Livestock
Nomadic Livestock Herding
Forests
Nonagricultural Land

MAJOR MINERAL OCCURRENCES

C   Coal
Cr Chromium
Cu Copper
Fe Iron Ore
G   Natural Gas
Mn Manganese
Na Salt
O   Petroleum
Pb Lead
S   Sulfur, Pyrites
Zn Zinc

⚡ Water Power
▨ Major Industrial Areas

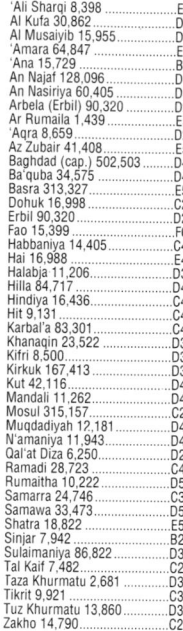

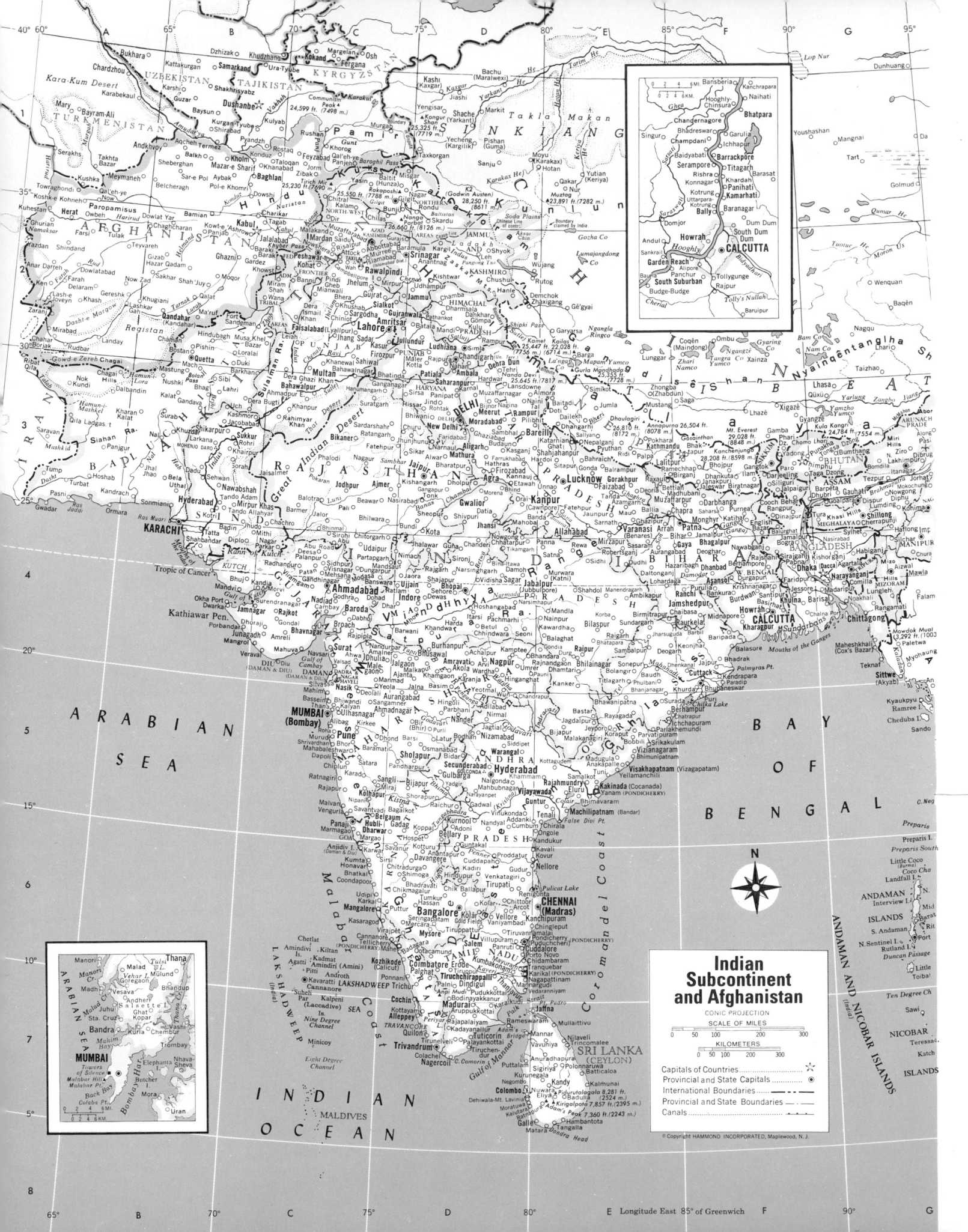

Indian Subcontinent and Afghanistan

CONIC PROJECTION

SCALE OF MILES

KILOMETERS

Capitals of Countries .... ✦
Provincial and State Capitals .... ⊙
International Boundaries ....
Provincial and State Boundaries ....
Canals ....

© Copyright HAMMOND INCORPORATED, Maplewood, N.J.

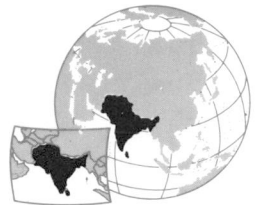

INDIA

AREA 1,269,339 sq. mi. (3,287,588 sq. km.)
POPULATION 843,930,861
CAPITAL New Delhi
LARGEST CITY Calcutta (greater)
HIGHEST POINT Nanda Devi 25,645 ft. (7,817 m.)
MONETARY UNIT Indian rupee
MAJOR LANGUAGES Hindi, English, Bengali,
Telugu, Marathi, Tamil, Urdu, Gujarati,
Malayalam, Kannada, Oriya, Punjabi,
Assamese, Kashmiri, Sindhi
MAJOR RELIGIONS Hinduism, Islam, Christianity,
Sikhism, Buddhism, Jainism, Zoroastrianism, Animism

PAKISTAN

AREA 310,403 sq. mi. (803,944 sq. km.)
POPULATION 112,050,000
CAPITAL Islamabad
LARGEST CITY Karachi
HIGHEST POINT K2 (Godwin Austen)
28,250 ft. (8,611 m.)
MONETARY UNIT Pakistani rupee
MAJOR LANGUAGES Urdu, English, Punjabi,
Pushtu, Sindhi, Baluchi, Brahui
MAJOR RELIGIONS Islam, Hinduism, Sikhism,
Christianity, Buddhism

SRI LANKA (CEYLON)

AREA 25,332 sq. mi.
(65,610 sq. km.)
POPULATION 16,806,000
CAPITAL Colombo
LARGEST CITY Colombo
HIGHEST POINT Pidurutalagala
8,281 ft. (2,524 m.)
MONETARY UNIT Sri Lanka rupee
MAJOR LANGUAGES Sinhala, Tamil,
English
MAJOR RELIGIONS Buddhism,
Hinduism, Christianity, Islam

AFGHANISTAN

AREA 250,775 sq. mi.
(649,507 sq. km.)
POPULATION 15,814,000
CAPITAL Kabul
LARGEST CITY Kabul
HIGHEST POINT Nowshak
24,557 ft. (7,485 m.)
MONETARY UNIT afghani
MAJOR LANGUAGES Pushtu, Dari,
Uzbek
MAJOR RELIGION Islam

NEPAL

AREA 54,663 sq. mi.
(141,577 sq. km.)
POPULATION 18,442,000
CAPITAL Kathmandu
LARGEST CITY Kathmandu
HIGHEST POINT Mt. Everest
29,028 ft. (8,848 m.)
MONETARY UNIT Nepalese rupee
MAJOR LANGUAGES Nepali,
Maithili, Tamang, Newari, Tharu
MAJOR RELIGIONS Hinduism,
Buddhism

MALDIVES

AREA 115 sq. mi. (298 sq. km.)
POPULATION 206,000
CAPITAL Male
LARGEST CITY Male
HIGHEST POINT 20 ft. (6 m.)
MONETARY UNIT Maldivian rufiyaa
MAJOR LANGUAGE Divehi
MAJOR RELIGION Islam

BHUTAN

AREA 18,147 sq. mi.
(47,000 sq. km.)
POPULATION 1,483,000
CAPITAL Thimphu
LARGEST CITY Thimphu
HIGHEST POINT Kula Kangri
24,784 ft. (7,554 m.)
MONETARY UNIT ngultrum
MAJOR LANGUAGES Dzongka,
Nepali
MAJOR RELIGIONS Buddhism,
Hinduism

BANGLADESH

AREA 55,126 sq. mi.
(142,776 sq. km.)
POPULATION 106,507,000
CAPITAL Dhaka
LARGEST CITY Dhaka
HIGHEST POINT Keokradong
4,034 ft. (1,230 m.)
MONETARY UNIT taka
MAJOR LANGUAGES Bengali,
English
MAJOR RELIGIONS Islam,
Hinduism Christianity

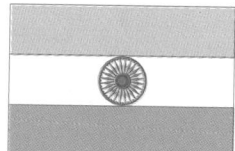

INDIA

PAKISTAN

SRI LANKA (CEYLON)

BHUTAN

AFGHANISTAN

MALDIVES

BANGLADESH

NEPAL

AFGHANISTAN

CITIES and TOWNS

Andkhvoy 13,137	A1
Aybak 33,016	B1
Baghlan 75,130	B1
Bamian 7,355	B2
Chaghcharan 2,974	B2
Charikar 25,093	B1
Farah 18,797	A2
Feyzabad 10,142	C1
Gardez 11,415	B2
Gereshk	A2
Ghazni 30,425	B2
Ghurian 12,404	A2
Hazar Qadam	B2
Herat 163,960	A2
Jalalabad 56,384	B2
Kabul (cap.) 905,108	B2
Kalat (Qalat) 5,946	B2
Kandahar (Qandahar) 178,409	B2
Khanabad 26,803	B1
Khash	A2
Kholm 28,078	B1
Khowst	B2
Konduz 107,191	B1
Kuhestan	A2
Lashkar Gah 26,646	A2
Mazar-e Sharif 122,567	B1
Meymaneh 54,954	A1
Mirabad	A2
Oruzgan (Hazar Qadam)	B2
Panjab	B2
Pol-e Khomri 31,101	B1
Qalat 5,946	B2
Qal'eh-ye Now 5,340	A1
Qandahar 178,409	B2
Qonduz (Konduz) 107,191	B1
Sakhar	B2
Sar-e Pol 15,699	B1
Sheberghan 54,870	B1
Shindand	A2
Tagab	B2
Taloqan 46,202	B1
Zaranj 6,477	A2

OTHER FEATURES

Baroghil (pass)	C1
Chagai (hills)	A3
Margow, Dasht-e (des.)	A2
Farah Rud (riv.)	A2
Gowd-e Zereh (depr.)	A2
Harirud (riv.)	A1
Helmand (riv.)	B2
Hindu Kush (mts.)	B1
Kabul (riv.)	C2
Konar (riv.)	C1
Konduz (riv.)	B1
Lurah (riv.)	B2
Namaksar (salt lake)	A2
Nuristan (reg.)	C1

Panj (riv.)	C1
Paropamisus (range)	A2
Qonduz (Konduz) (riv.)	B1
Registan (reg.)	A2
Tarnak (riv.)	B2

BANGLADESH

CITIES and TOWNS

Barisal 159,298	G4
Bogra 68,237	F4
Chalna Port 14,590	F4
Chittagong 1,388,476	G4
Comilla 126,130	G4
Cox's Bazar	G4
Dhaka (cap.) 3,458,602	G4
Dinajpur 96,348	F3
Faridpur 66,911	F4
Habiganj 16,281	G4
Jamalpur 89,847	F4
Jessore 149,426	F4
Khulna 623,184	F4
Kishorganj 52,081	G4
Madaripur 58,645	G4
Maheshkhali 29,530	G4
Mymensingh (Nasirabad) 107,863	G4
Narayanganj 196,139	G4
Nasirabad 107,863	G4
Nawabganj 65,286	F4
Noakhali 32,490	G4
Pabna 101,080	F4
Rajshahi 171,600	F4
Rangamati 36,490	G4
Rangpur 72,829	F3
Sirajganj 74,457	F4
Sylhet 59,546	G4

OTHER FEATURES

Bengal, Bay of (bay)	F5
Brahmaputra (riv.)	G3
Ganges (riv.)	F3
Ganges, Mouths of the (delta)	F3
Mowdok Mual (mt.)	G4
Sundarbans (reg.)	F4

BHUTAN

CITIES and TOWNS

Bumthang 10,000	G3
Paro 35,000	F3
Punakha 12,000	G3
Taga Dzong 18,000	G3
Thimphu (cap.) 50,000	G3
Tongsa Dzong 2,500	G3

OTHER FEATURES

Chomo Lhari (mt.)	F3
Himalaya (mts.)	E2
Kula Kangri (mt.)	G3

(continued on following page)

Topography

0 200 400 MI.
0 200 400 KM.

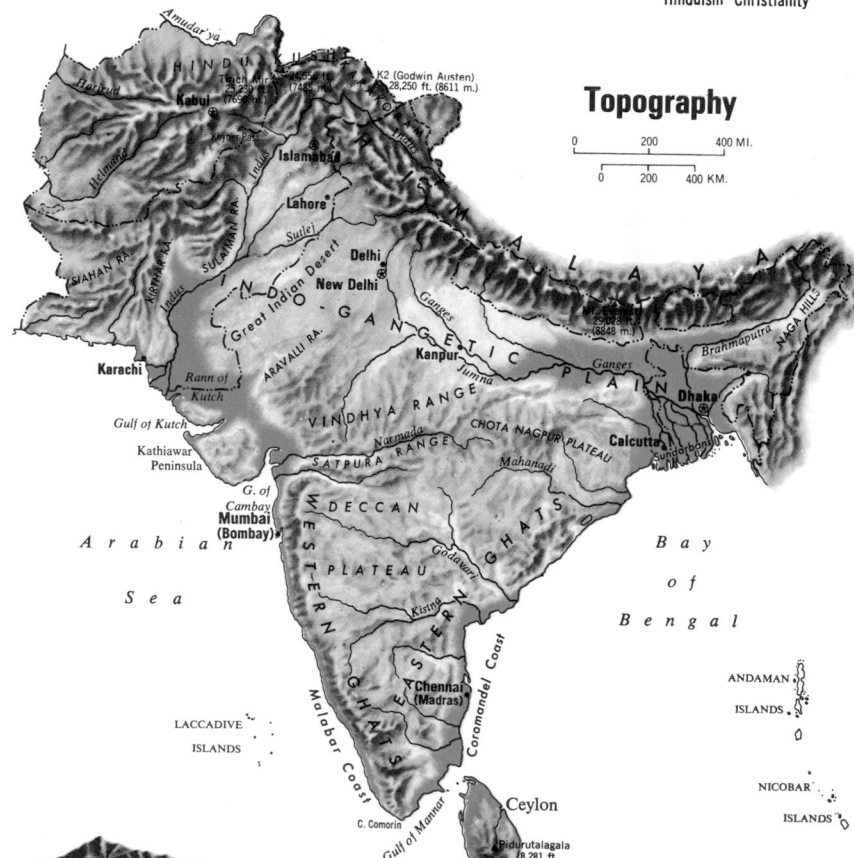

(continued)

INDIA

INTERNAL DIVISIONS

Andaman and Nicobar Isls. (terr.) 188,741 ....G6
Andhra Pradesh (state) 53,549,673 ....D5
Arunachal Pradesh (state) 631,839 ....G3
Assam (state) 19,902,826 ....G3
Bihar (state) 69,914,734 ....F4
Chandigarh (terr.) 451,610 ....D2
Dādra and Nagar Haveli (terr.) 103,676 ....C4
Daman and Diu (state) C4
Delhi (terr.) 6,220,406 ....D3
Goa (state) C4
Gujarāt (state) 34,085,799 ....C4
Haryana (state) 12,922,618 ....D3
Himachal Pradesh (state) 4,280,818 ....D2
Jammu and Kashmir (state) 5,987,389 ....D2
Karnataka (state) 37,135,714 .D6
Kerala (state) 25,453,680 ....D6
Lakshadweep (terr.) 40,249 ....C6
Madhya Pradesh (state) 52,178,844 ....D4
Mahārāshtra (state) 62,784,171 ....C5
Manipur (state) 1,420,953 ....G4
Meghalaya (state) 1,335,819 ..G3
Mizoram (state) 493,757 ....G4
Nagaland (state) 774,930 ....G3
Orissa (state) 26,370,271 ....E5
Pondicherry (terr.) 604,471 ....E6
Punjab (state) 16,788,915 ....D2
Rajasthan (state) 34,261,862 ..C3
Sikkim (state) 316,385 ....F3
Tamil Nadu (state) 48,408,077 ....D6
Tripura (state) 2,053,058 ....G4
Uttar Pradesh (state) 110,862,013 ....D3
West Bengal (state) 54,580,647 ....F4

CITIES and TOWNS

Abu 9,840 ....C4
Achalpur 42,326 ....D4
Adoni 108,905 ....D5
Agartala 131,513 ....G4
Agra 770,352 ....D3
Ahmadabad 2,515,195 ....C4
Ahmadnagar 181,239 ....C5
Ajmer 374,350 ....C3
Akola 225,402 ....D4
Alibag 11,913 ....C5
Aligarh 319,981 ....D3
Allahabad 642,420 ....E3
Alleppey-Cochin 160,166 ....D7
Almora 19,671 ....D3
Alwar 139,973 ....D3
Amalner 55,544 ....C4
Ambala 121,135 ....D2
Ambikapur 23,087 ....E4
Amravati 261,387 ....D4
Amreli 39,520 ....C4
Amritsar 589,229 ....C2
Anakapalle 57,273 ....E5
Anantapur 119,536 ....D6
Arrah 124,614 ....E3
Aruppukkottai 62,223 ....D7
Asansol 366,371 ....F4
Azamgarh 40,963 ....E3
Badagara 53,938 ....D6
Bagalkot 51,746 ....D5
Bahraich 102,580 ....E3
Baidyabati 54,130 ....F1
Balasore 46,239 ....F4
Ballia 47,101 ....E3
Bally 38,892 ....F1
Balurghat 67,088 ....F3
Banda 50,575 ....D3
Bandar (Machilipatnam) 138,525 ....E5
Bandra B7
Bangalore 4,100,000 ....D6
Bankura 79,129 ....F4
Bansberia 61,748 ....F1
Baranagar 136,842 ....F1
Barasat 42,642 ....F1
Bareilly 437,801 ....D3
Barmer 38,630 ....C3
Baroda (Vadodara) 744,043 ....C4
Barrackpore 96,889 ....F1
Barsi 62,374 ....D5
Barwani 22,099 ....D4
Basirhat 63,816 ....F4
Batala 100,790 ....D2
Beawar 66,114 ....C3
Belgaum 300,290 ....C5
Bellary 201,014 ....D5
Benares (Varanasi) 793,542 ....E3
Berhampore 100,150 ....F4
Berhampur 162,407 ....F5
Bettiah 51,018 ....E3
Bhadrak 40,487 ....F4
Bhadravati 130,459 ....D6
Bhadreswar 45,586 ....F1
Bhagalpur 221,276 ....F4
Bhandara 39,423 ....E4
Bharuch 91,589 ....C4
Bharatpur 105,239 ....D3
Bhatinda 127,450 ....C2
Bhatpara 204,750 ....F1
Bhavnagar 308,194 ....C4
Bhawanipatna 22,808 ....E5
Bhilainagar 157,173 ....E4
Bhilwara 122,338 ....C3
Bhimavaram 101,940 ....E5
Bhind 42,371 ....D3
Bhir (Bir) 49,965 ....D5
Bhiwandi 115,256 ....C5
Bhiwani 101,263 ....D3
Bhopal 672,329 ....D4
Bhubaneswar 219,419 ....F4
Bhuj 52,177 ....B4
Bhusawal 132,146 ....D4
Bidar 50,670 ....D5
Bihar 151,308 ....F3
Bijapur 146,808 ....D5
Bijnor 43,290 ....D3
Bikaner 280,356 ....C3
Bilaspur 186,885 ....E4
Bir 49,965 ....D5
Bodhan 37,589 ....D5
Bodinayakkanur 54,176 ....D6
Bolangir 35,748 ....E4
Broach (Bharuch) 91,589 ....C4
Budaun 72,204 ....D3
Budge-Budge 51,039 ....F2
Bundi 34,279 ....D3
Burdwan 143,318 ....F4
Burhanpur 141,142 ....D4
Calcutta 10,860,000 ....F2
Calicut (Kozhikode) 333,979 ...D6
Cambay 62,097 ....C4
Cannanore 157,777 ....C6
Cawnpore (Kanpur) 1,688,242 ....E3
Chaibasa 35,386 ....F4
Chamba 11,814 ....D2
Champdani 58,596 ....F1
Chanderi 10,294 ....D4
Chandernagore 75,238 ....F1
Chandigarh 421,256 ....D2
Chandrapur 115,352 ....D5
Chapra 111,461 ....F3
Chennai (Madras) 5,360,000 ....E6
Cherrapunji▲ 83,987 ....G3
Chhatarpur 32,271 ....D4
Chhindwara 53,492 ....D4
Chidambaram 48,811 ....E6
Chikmagalur 41,639 ....D6
Chinglept 38,419 ....E6
Chirala 54,487 ....E5
Chitradurga 50,254 ....D6
Chittoor 63,035 ....D6
Churachandpur 8,706 ....G4
Churu 52,502 ....D3
Cocanada (Kakinada) 226,642 ....E5
Cochin-Alleppey 439,066 ....D6
Coimbatore 917,155 ....D6
Colachel 18,819 ....D7
Cooch Behar 53,684 ....F3
Cuddalore 127,569 ....E6
Cuddapah 103,146 ....D6
Cuttack 326,468 ....F4
Dabhoi 37,892 ....C4
Damoh 59,489 ....D4
Darbhanga 175,879 ....F3
Darjeeling 42,873 ....F3
Datia 36,439 ....D3
Davangere 196,481 ....D6
Dehra Dun 293,628 ....D2
Delhi 8,380,000 ....D3
Deoghar 40,356 ....F4
Deolali 55,436 ....C5
Deoria 38,161 ....E3
Dewas 51,545 ....D4
Dhanbad 676,736 ....F4
Dhar 36,172 ....C4
Dharmsala 10,939 ....D2
Dharwar-Hubli 379,166 ....C5
Dhoraji 59,773 ....C4
Dhubri 36,503 ....G3
Dhulia 210,927 ....C4
Dibrugarh 80,348 ....G3
Dindigul 170,196 ....D6
Diphu 10,200 ....G3
Diu 6,214 ....C4
Dungarpur 19,773 ....C4
Durg 67,892 ....E4
Durg-Bhilainagar 490,158 ....E4
Durgapur 305,838 ....F4
Dwarka 17,801 ....B4
Eluru 168,148 ....E5
English Bazar 61,335 ....F3
Erode 275,103 ....D6
Etawah 112,426 ....D3
Faizabad-cum-Ayodhya 102,835 ....E3
Faridabad 326,968 ....D3
Farrukhabad-cum-Fatehgarh 160,927 ....D3
Firozabad 202,837 ....D3
Firozpur 49,545 ....C2
Gadag 116,596 ....D5
Ganganagar 121,516 ....C3
Gangtok 12,000 ....F3
Garden Reach 154,913 ....F2
Garulia 44,271 ....F1
Gauhati 123,783 ....G3
Gaya 246,778 ....F4
Ghaziabad 291,995 ....D3
Ghazipur 45,635 ....E3
Godhra 66,403 ....C4
Gonda 52,662 ....E3
Gondal 54,928 ....C4
Gondia 100,342 ....E4
Gorakhpur 306,399 ....E3
Gulbarga 218,621 ....D5
Guna 40,006 ....D4
Guntakal 66,320 ....D5
Guntur 367,219 ....D5
Gwalior 38,472 ....D3
Haflong 5,197 ....G3
Hanumangarh 30,017 ....C3
Hardoi 46,639 ....E3
Hardwar 146,186 ....D2
Hassan 51,325 ....D6
Hathras 74,349 ....D3
Hazaribagh 54,818 ....F4
Hindupur 42,959 ....D6
Hinganghat 44,349 ....D4
Hissar 137,254 ....D3
Honavar 12,444 ....C6
Hooghly-Chinsura 105,241 ....F1
Hospet 114,711 ....D5
Howrah 737,877 ....F2
Hubli-Dharwar 526,493 ....C5
Hyderabad 4,270,000 ....D5
Ichchapuram 15,850 ....F5
Imphal 155,639 ....G4
Indore 827,021 ....D4
Itanagar▲ 18,787 ....G3
Itarsi 44,191 ....D4
Jabalpur 757,726 ....D4
Jaipur 1,004,669 ....D3
Jaisalmer 16,578 ....C3
Jajpur 16,707 ....F4
Jalgaon 145,254 ....D4
Jalna 122,246 ....D4
Jalor 15,478 ....C3
Jalpaiguri 55,159 ....F3
Jamalpur 61,731 ....F3
Jammu 155,338 ....D2
Jamnagar 317,037 ....B4
Jamshedpur 669,984 ....F4
Jaora 37,235 ....D4
Jaunpur 104,994 ....E3
Jhansi 231,332 ....D3
Jind 38,161 ....D3
Jodhpur 493,604 ....C3
Jubbulpore (Jabalpur) 757,726 ....D4
Jullundur 296,106 ....D2
Junagadh 120,072 ....B4
Kadayanallur 50,295 ....D7
Kakinada 226,642 ....E5
Kalyan 99,547 ....C5
Kamarhati 169,404 ....F1
Kamptee 53,412 ....D4
Kanchipuram 145,329 ....E6
Kanchrapara 78,768 ....F1
Kandla 17,995 ....C4
Kanker 9,278 ....E4
Kanpur 1,688,242 ....E3
Karad 42,329 ....C5
Karaikudi 100,187 ....D7
Kargil 2,390 ....D2
Karnal 132,067 ....D3
Kasganj 46,467 ....D3
Katarnian Ghat E3
Katihar 121,693 ....F3
Katni (Murwara) 125,096 ....E4
Kavaratti 4,420 ....C6
Kendrapara 20,079 ....F4
Khamgaon 53,692 ....D4
Khamman 56,919 ....D5
Khandwa 114,463 ....D4
Kharagpur 234,931 ....F4
Kirkee 65,497 ....C5
Kishangarh 37,405 ....D3
Kishtwar 5,276 ....D2
Kohima 21,545 ....G3
Kolar 43,418 ....D6
Kolar Gold Fields 144,406 ....D6
Kolhapur 351,073 ....C5
Koraput 21,505 ....E5
Korba 30,963 ....E4
Kota 346,928 ....D3
Kottaguden 75,542 ....E5
Kottayam 59,714 ....D7
Kozhikode 333,979 ....D6
Krishnanagar 85,923 ....F4
Kumbakonam 141,639 ....D6
Kumta 19,112 ....C6
Kurnool 206,661 ....D5
Latur 111,961 ....D5
Leh 5,519 ....D2
Lucknow 1,006,538 ....E3
Ludhiana 606,250 ....D2
Machilipatnam 138,525 ....E5
Madugula 8,376 ....E5
Madurai 904,362 ....D7
Mahabaleshwar 7,318 ....C5
Mahbubnagar 51,756 ....D5
Mahe 8,972 ....D6
Mahuva 39,497 ....C4
Malegaon 245,769 ....C4
Maler Kotla 48,536 ....D2
Malkapur 35,476 ....D4
Malvan 17,579 ....C5
Mandi 16,849 ....D2
Mandla 24,406 ....E4
Mandsaur 52,347 ....C4
Mangalore 3,055,113 ....C6
Mannargudi 42,783 ....E6
Margao 41,655 ....C5
Marmagao 44,065 ....C5
Mathura 160,995 ....D3
Mau 64,058 ....E3
Mayuram 60,195 ....D6
Meerut 538,461 ....D3
Mehsana 51,598 ....C4
Mercara 19,357 ....D6
Mhow 59,037 ....D4
Midnapore 71,326 ....F4
Miraj 77,606 ....D5
Mirzapur-cum-Vindhyachal 128,179 ....E4
Monghyr 102,474 ....F3
Moradabad 347,983 ....D3
Morena 44,901 ....D3
Morvi 60,976 ....C4
Mumbai (Bombay) (Greater)* 8,227,332 ....B7
Murwara 125,096 ....E4
Muzaffarnagar 172,435 ....D3
Muzaffarpur 189,765 ....E3
Mysore 476,446 ....D6
Nadiad 142,279 ....C4
Nagapattinam 68,026 ....E6
Nagaur 36,448 ....C3
Nagercoil 171,641 ....D7
Nagina 37,066 ....D3
Nagpur 1,297,977 ....D4
Nahan 16,017 ....D2
Naihati 82,080 ....F1
Naini Tal 23,986 ....D3
Nander 190,819 ....D5
Nandurbar 54,070 ....C4
Nandyal 63,193 ....D5
Nasik 428,778 ....C5
Navsari 129,122 ....C4
Nellore 236,225 ....E6
New Delhi (cap.) 301,801 ....D3
Nimach 47,113 ....D4
Nipani 35,116 ....C5
Nizamabad 183,135 ....D5
Nova Goa (Panaji) 34,953 ....C5
Nowgong 56,537 ....G3
Okha Port 10,687 ....B4
Ongole 53,330 ....E5
Ootacamund 63,310 ....D6
Orai 42,513 ....D3
Pachmarhi 1,212 ....D4
Palanpur 42,114 ....C4
Palayankottai 70,070 ....D7
Palghat 117,961 ....D6
Pali 49,834 ....C3
Palni 49,575 ....D6
Panaji 34,953 ....C5
Panchur 59,021 ....F2
Pandharpur 53,638 ....D5
Panihati 148,046 ....F1
Panipat 137,953 ....D3
Panna 22,316 ....E4
Parbhani 109,328 ....D5
Pasighat 5,116 ....G3
Patan 105,191 ....C4
Pathankot 108,777 ....D2
Patiala 205,849 ....D2
Patna 916,102 ....F3
Pilibhit 68,273 ....D3
Pondicherry 251,471 ....E6
Ponnani 35,723 ....D6
Porbandar 133,545 ....B4
Port Blair 26,218 ....G6
Porto Novo 17,412 ....E6
Proddatur 107,068 ....D6
Puduchcheri (Pondicherry) 251,471 ....E6
Pudukkottai 66,384 ....D6
Pune 1,135,034 ....C5
Puri 101,089 ....F5
Purli 31,078 ....D5
Purnea 109,649 ....F3
Purulia 57,708 ....F4
Quilon 167,583 ....D7
Raichur 124,600 ....D5
Raigarh 46,745 ....E4
Raipur 338,973 ....E4
Rajahmundry 267,749 ....E5
Rajapalaiyam 101,633 ....D7
Rajapur 9,017 ....C5
Rajkot 444,156 ....C4
Rajnandgaon 41,183 ....E4
Rajpur 34,393 ....F2
Rameswaram 16,755 ....D7
Ranchi 500,593 ....F4
Ratlam 156,490 ....C4
Ratnagiri 37,551 ....C5
Raurkela 321,326 ....F4
Raxaul 12,064 ....E3
Rewa 100,519 ....E4
Rishra 63,486 ....F1
Rohtak 166,631 ....C5
Sadiya▲ 64,252 ....H3
Sagar 207,401 ....D4
Saharanpur 294,391 ....D3
Salem 515,021 ....D6
Sambalpur 162,190 ....E4
Sambhal 108,379 ....D3
Sangli 268,962 ....C5
Santipur 61,166 ....F4
Sardarshahr 37,703 ....C3
Sasaram 48,282 ....E4
Satara 66,433 ....C5
Satna 57,531 ....E4
Sehore 35,657 ....D4
Seoni 38,396 ....D4
Serampore 102,023 ....F1
Seringapatam 14,100 ....D6
Shahjahanpur 205,325 ....E3
Shillong 173,064 ....G3
Shimoga 151,562 ....D6
Shivpuri 42,120 ....D3
Sholapur 514,461 ....D5
Sidhi 8,341 ....E4
Sidhpur 40,521 ....C4
Sikar 102,946 ....D3
Silchar 52,596 ....G4
Siliguri 153,825 ....F3
Simla 55,368 ....D2
Sirohi 18,774 ....C4
Sirsa 48,808 ....D3
Sitapur 66,715 ....E3
South Dum Dum 174,538 ....F2
South Suburban 272,600 ....F2
Srikakulam 45,179 ....E5
Srinagar 403,413 ....D2
Sundargarh 17,244 ....E4
Surat 912,568 ....C4
Surendranagar 66,667 ....C4
Tanda 41,611 ....E3
Tellicherry 68,759 ....C6
Tenali 119,216 ....E5
Tezpur 39,870 ....G3
Thana 388,577 ....B6
Thanjavur 183,464 ....D6
Tinsukia 54,911 ....H3
Tiruchchirappalli 607,815 ....D6
Tiruchendur 18,126 ....D7
Tirunelveli 324,034 ....D7
Tirupati 115,244 ....D6
Tiruppattur 40,357 ....D6
Tiruppur 215,743 ....D6
Tiruvannamalai 61,370 ....D6
Titagarh 88,218 ....F1
Tonk 55,866 ....D3
Tranquebar 17,318 ....E6
Trichur 170,093 ....D6
Trivandrum 519,766 ....D7
Tumkur 109,231 ....D6
Tura 15,489 ....G3
Tuticorin 250,673 ....D7
Udaipur 229,762 ....C4
Udhampur 16,392 ....D2
Ujjain 231,878 ....D4
Ulhasnagar 648,149 ....C5
Unnao 38,195 ....E3
Uttarpara-Kotrung 67,568 ....F1
Vadodara 744,043 ....C4
Valsad 43,254 ....C4
Vaniyambadi 51,810 ....D6
Varanasi 793,542 ....E3
Vellore 246,937 ....D6
Vengurla 11,805 ....C5
Veraval 58,771 ....C4

British India

RUSSIA
AFGHANISTAN
IRAN
BALUCHISTAN
GILGIT AGENCY
KASHMIR & JAMMU
N.W. FRONTIER PROV.
PUNJAB
PUNJAB STATES
BAHAWALPUR (PUNJ. ST.)
PUNJ. ST.
RAJPUTANA
AJMER-MERWARA
SIND
Gwadar (Oman)
DELHI
RAMPUR
UNITED PROVINCES
GWALIOR
TIBET
NEPAL
CHINA
SIKKIM
BHUTAN
ASSAM
KHASI HILLS
MANIPUR
TRIPURA
BENARES
BIHAR
BENGAL
Chandernagore (Fr.)
BURMA
WESTERN INDIA
CENTRAL INDIA
EASTERN STATES
CENTRAL PROVINCES
BERAR
Arabian Sea
Diu (Port.)
Damão (Port.)
BOMBAY
EASTERN STATES
ORISSA
HYDERABAD
DECCAN STATES
Yanaon (Fr.)
Bay of Bengal
Gôa (Port.)
MYSORE
COORG
Bangalore (Br.)
MADRAS
Mahé (Fr.)
Pondichéry (Fr.)
Karikal (Fr.)
Laccadive Islands (Madras)
Cochin (Br.)
MADRAS STATES
CEYLON
Andaman Islands (Br.)
Nicobar Islands (Br.)
British India. The provinces of British India were directly administered by Britain. A few areas were leased from the Indian princes.
Indian States. The Indian States, sometimes referred to as the "Native" or "Princely States," were under the nominal control of maharajas or other hereditary princes.
Possessions of Other Countries in India
State or Provincial Boundaries
Other Internal Boundaries

Vidisha 43,212 ... D4
Vijayawada 544,958 ... D5
Villupuram 60,242 ... D6
Viramgam 43,790 ... C4
Visakhapatnam 594,259 ... E5
Visnagar 34,863 ... C4
Vizagapatam (Visakhapatnam) 594,259 ... E5
Vizianagaram 115,209 ... E5
Warangal 336,018 ... D5
Wardha 69,037 ... D4
Yadgir 32,756 ... D5
Yanam 8,291 ... E5
Yeola 24,533 ... C4

OTHER FEATURES

Abor (hills) ... G3
Adam's Bridge (sound) ... D7
Agatti (isl.) ... C6
Amindiri (isl.) ... C6
Amindivi (isls.) ... C6
Amini (Amindiri) (isl.) ... C6
Anai Mudi (mt.) ... D6
Andaman (isls.) ... G6
Andaman (sea) ... G6
Androth (isl.) ... C6
Anjidiv (Angedeva) (isl.) ... C6
Arabian (sea) ... B5
Back (bay) ... B7
Banas (riv.) ... D3
Baratang (isl.) ... G6
Barren (isl.) ... G6
Batti Malv (isl.) ... G7
Bengal, Bay of (bay) ... F5
Berar (reg.) ... D4
Betwa (riv.) ... D4
Bhima (riv.) ... D5
Bidyadhari (riv.) ... F2
Bombay (harbor) ... B7
Brahmaputra (riv.) ... G3
Butcher (isl.) ... B7
Cambay (gulf) ... C4
Camorta (isl.) ... G7
Cannanore (isls.) ... C6
Chambal (riv.) ... D3
Chenab (riv.) ... C2
Cherial (riv.) ... F2
Chetlat (isl.) ... C6
Chilka (lake) ... F5
Coco (chan.) ... G6
Colaba (pt.) ... B7
Colair (lake) ... E5
Comorin (cape) ... D7
Coromandel Coast (reg.) ... E6
Daman (dist.) ... C4
Damodar (riv.) ... F4
Deccan (plat.) ... D6
Diu (dist.) ... C4
Duncan (passage) ... G6
Eastern Ghats (mts.) ... D6
Eight Degree (chan.) ... C7
Elephanta (isl.) ... B7
False Divi (pt.) ... E5
Ganga (Ganges) (riv.) ... F3
Ganges, Mouths of the (delta) ... F4
Ganges (riv.) ... F3
Ghaghra (riv.) ... E3
Ghea (riv.) ... F1
Goa (dist.) ... C5
Godavari (riv.) ... D5
Golconda (ruins) ... D5
Great (chan.) ... G7
Great Indian (des.) ... C3
Great Nicobar (isl.) ... G7
Hagari (riv.) ... D6
Himalaya (mts.) ... D2
Hindu Kush (mts.) ... C1
Hooghly (riv.) ... F2
Indira (Pygmalion) (pt.) ... G7
Indravati (riv.) ... E5
Indus (riv.) ... B3
Interview (isl.) ... G6
Jhelum (riv.) ... C2
Jumna (riv.) ... E3
Kachchh (gulf) ... B4
Kachchh (reg.) ... B4
Kachchh, Rann of (salt marsh) ... B4
Kadmat (isl.) ... C6
Kalpeni (isl.) ... C7
Kamet (mt.) ... D2
Kanchenjunga (mt.) ... F3
Karakoram (mts.) ... D1
Katchall (isl.) ... G7
Kathiawar (pen.) ... B4
Kaveri (riv.) ... D6
Khasi (hills) ... G3
Kiltan (isl.) ... C6
Kistna (Krishna) (riv.) ... D5
Kunlun (range) ... D1
Kutch (Kachchh) (reg.) ... B4
Kutch (Kachchh), Rann of (salt marsh) ... B4
Laccadive (Cannanore) (isls.) ... C6
Ladakh (reg.) ... D2
Lakshadweep (sea) ... C6
Landfall (isl.) ... G6
Little Andaman (isl.) ... G6
Little Nicobar (isl.) ... G7
Luni (riv.) ... C3
Mahanadi (riv.) ... E4
Mahim (bay) ... B7
Malabar (hill) ... B7
Malabar (pt.) ... B7
Malabar Coast (reg.) ... C6
Malad (creek) ... B7
Mannar (gulf) ... D7
Manori (creek) ... B7
Middle Andaman (isl.) ... G6
Minicoy (isl.) ... C7
Miri (hills) ... G3
Mishmi (hills) ... H3
Mizo (hill) ... G4
Nancowry (isl.) ... G7
Nanda Devi (mt.) ... D2
Narcondam (isl.) ... G6
Narmada (riv.) ... D4
Nicobar (isls.) ... G7
Nine Degree (chan.) ... C7
North Andaman (isl.) ... G6
North Sentinel (isl.) ... G6
Palk (str.) ... D7
Palmyras (pt.) ... F4
Pangong Tso (lake) ... D2
Penganga (riv.) ... D5
Penner (riv.) ... D6
Periyar (lake) ... D7
Pitti (isl.) ... C6
Pulicat (lake) ... E6
Pygmalion (pt.) ... G7
Ritchies (arch.) ... G6
Rutland (isl.) ... G6
Salsette (isl.) ... B7
Sambhar (lake) ... C3
Saraswati (riv.) ... F1
Sarsati (riv.) ... F1
Satpura (range) ... D4
Shipki (pass) ... D2
Soda (plains) ... D1
Sombrero (chan.) ... G7
Son (riv.) ... E3
South Andaman (isl.) ... G6
Suheli Par (atoll) ... C6
Sundarbans (reg.) ... F4
Sutlej (riv.) ... C3
Tapti (riv.) ... D4
Tel (riv.) ... E4
Ten Degree (chan.) ... G7
Teressa (isl.) ... G7
Thana (creek) ... B7
Tillanchong (isl.) ... G7
Tolly's Nullah (riv.) ... F2
Towers of Silence ... B7
Travancore (reg.) ... D7
Tulsi (lake) ... B6
Tungabhadra (riv.) ... D5
Vehar (lake) ... B7
Vindhya (range) ... D4
Wardha (riv.) ... D4
Western Ghats (mts.) ... C5
Zaskar (mts.) ... D2

MALDIVES

Maldives 143,046 ... C7

NEPAL

CITIES and TOWNS

Baitadi 128,696 ... E3
Bhaktapur 40,112 ... F3
Bhaktapur▲ 110,157 ... F3
Bhojpur 194,506 ... F3
Biratnagar 45,100 ... F3
Dailekh 156,072 ... E3
Dhankuta 107,649 ... F3
Doti 166,070 ... E3
Janakpur 14,294 ... F3
Jumla▲ 122,753 ... E3
Kathmandu (cap.) 150,402 ... E3
Kathmandu▲ 353,752 ... E3
Lalitpur 59,049 ... E3
Lalitpur▲ 154,998 ... E3
Mustang▲ 26,944 ... E3
Nepalganj 23,523 ... E3
Palpa 212,633 ... E3
Pokhara 20,611 ... E3
Pyuthan▲ 137,338 ... E3
Ramechhap 157,349 ... F3
Sallyan▲ 141,457 ... E3

OTHER FEATURES

Annapurna (mt.) ... E3
Bheri (riv.) ... E3
Dhaulagiri (mt.) ... E3
Everest (mt.) ... F3
Himalaya (mts.) ... D2
Kanchenjunga (mt.) ... F3

PAKISTAN

PROVINCES

Azad Kashmir ... C2
Balochistan 4,332,376 ... B3
Federal Administrated Tribal Areas 2,198,547 ... C2
Islamabad District 340,286 ... C2
Northern Areas ... D1
North-West Frontier 11,061,328 ... C2
Punjab 47,292,441 ... C2
Sindh 19,028,666 ... B3

CITIES and TOWNS

Abbottabad 66,000 ... C2
Ahmadpur East 57,000 ... C3
Attock 40,000 ... C2
Badin 23,000 ... B4
Bahawalnagar 74,000 ... C2
Bahawalpur 178,000 ... C3
Baltit ... C1
Bannu 43,000 ... C2
Bela 11,000 ... B3
Bhera 29,000 ... C2
Bunji ... C1
Campbellpore 19,041 ... C2
Chagai▲ 41,263 ... A3
Chaman 30,000 ... B2
Chiniot 106,000 ... C2
Chitral ... C1
Dadu 39,000 ... B3
Dera Ghazi Khan 103,000 ... C3
Dera Ismail Khan 68,000 ... C2
Diplo 7,000 ... B4
Faisalabad 1,092,000 ... C2
Fort Sandeman 8,058 ... B2
Gujranwala 654,000 ... C2
Gujrat 154,000 ... C2
Gwadar 17,000 ... A4
Hunza (Baltit) ... C1
Hyderabad 795,000 ... B3
Islamabad (cap.) 201,000 ... C2
Jacobabad 80,000 ... B3
Jhang Sadar 195,000 ... C2
Jhelum 106,000 ... C2
Kalat 11,000 ... B3
Karachi 4,979,000 ... B4
Kasur 155,000 ... C2
Khairpur 62,000 ... B3
Khanewal 89,000 ... C2
Khanpur 71,000 ... C3
Kharan Kalat 10,000 ... A3
Khushab 56,000 ... C2
Kohat 78,000 ... C2
Kotri 38,000 ... B3
Lahore 3,922,000 ... C2
Larkana 123,000 ... B3
Leiah 52,000 ... C2
Loralai 14,000 ... B2
Lyallpur (Faisalabad) 1,092,000 ... C2
Mach 8,000 ... B3
Malakand ... C2
Mardan 148,000 ... C2
Mastung 17,000 ... B3
Mianwali 59,000 ... C2
Mirpur Khas 124,000 ... B3
Multan 730,000 ... C2
Muzaffarabad ... C2
Nagar ... D1
Nawabshah 102,000 ... B3
Nok Kundi 861 ... A3
Nowshera 75,000 ... C2
Nushki 11,000 ... B3
Pasni 18,000 ... A3
Peshawar 555,000 ... C2
Pindi Gheb 20,000 ... C2
Quetta 285,000 ... B2
Rahimyar Khan 119,000 ... C3
Rawalpindi 806,000 ... C2
Risalpur Cantonment 20,000 ... C2
Rohri 32,000 ... B3
Sahiwal 152,000 ... C2
Saidu 15,920 ... C2
Sargodha 294,000 ... C2
Shikarpur 88,000 ... B3
Sialkot 296,000 ... C2
Sibi 23,000 ... B3
Skardu ... D1
Sonmiani ... B3
Sukkur 193,000 ... B3
Tando Adam 63,000 ... B3
Tando Allahyar 31,000 ... B3
Tatta 12,786 ... B4
Turbat 52,000 ... A3
Uch 5,483 ... B3
Wah 122,000 ... C2
Wana ... C2
Yasin ... C1

OTHER FEATURES

Aksai Chin (reg.) ... D2
Arabian (sea) ... B5
Baltistan (reg.) ... D1
Baroghil (pass) ... C1
Bejhi (riv.) ... B3
Bolan (pass) ... B3
Chagai (hills) ... A3
Chenab (riv.) ... C2
Dasht (riv.) ... A3
Gilgit (dist.) ... C1
Hab (riv.) ... B3
Hamun-i-Lora (swamp) ... B3
Hamun-i-Mashkel (swamp) ... A3
Hindu Kush (mts.) ... B1
Indus (riv.) ... B3
Indus, Mouths of the (delta) ... B4
Jaddi, Ras (pt.) ... A4
Jhelum (riv.) ... C2
K2 (mt.) ... D1
Kabul (riv.) ... C2
Kachchh, Rann of (salt marsh) ... B4
Karakoram (mts.) ... D1
Khyber (pass) ... C2
Konar (riv.) ... C1
Kutch (Kachchh), Rann of (salt marsh) ... B4
Mashkid (riv.) ... A3
Mohenjo Daro (ruins) ... B3
Muari, Ras (cape) ... B4
Nal (riv.) ... B3
Nanga Parbat (mt.) ... D1
Rakaposhi (mt.) ... C1
Ravi (riv.) ... C2
Siahan (range) ... A3
Sulaiman (range) ... C3
Sutlej (riv.) ... C3
Talab (riv.) ... A3
Taxila (ruins) ... C2
Thar (des.) ... C3
Tirich Mir (mt.) ... C1
Zhob (riv.) ... B2

SRI LANKA (CEYLON)

CITIES and TOWNS

Anuradhapura 34,836 ... E7
Badulla 34,658 ... E7
Batticaloa 36,761 ... E7
Colombo (cap.) 618,000 ... D7
Colombo* 852,098 ... D7
Dehiwala-Mt. Lavinia 54,785 ... D7
Galle 72,720 ... D7
Hambantota 6,908 ... E7
Jaffna 112,000 ... E7
Kalmunai 19,176 ... E7
Kalutara 28,748 ... D7
Kandy 93,602 ... E7
Kurunegala 25,189 ... E7
Mannar 11,157 ... E7
Matara 36,641 ... E7
Moratuwa 96,489 ... D7
Mullaittivu 4,930 ... E7
Negombo 57,115 ... D7
Nuwara Eliya 16,347 ... E7
Polonnaruwa 9,551 ... E7
Puttalam 17,982 ... D7
Ratnapura 29,116 ... D7
Sigiriya 1,446 ... E7
Tangalla 8,748 ... E7
Trincomalee 41,780 ... E7
Vavuniya 15,639 ... E7

OTHER FEATURES

Adam's (peak) ... E7
Adam's Bridge (shoals) ... D7
Dondra (head) ... E7
Kirigalpota (mt.) ... E7
Mannar (gulf) ... D7
Palk (str.) ... D7
Pedro (pt.) ... E6
Pidurutalagala (mt.) ... E7

* City and suburbs.
▲ Population of district.

Agriculture, Industry and Resources

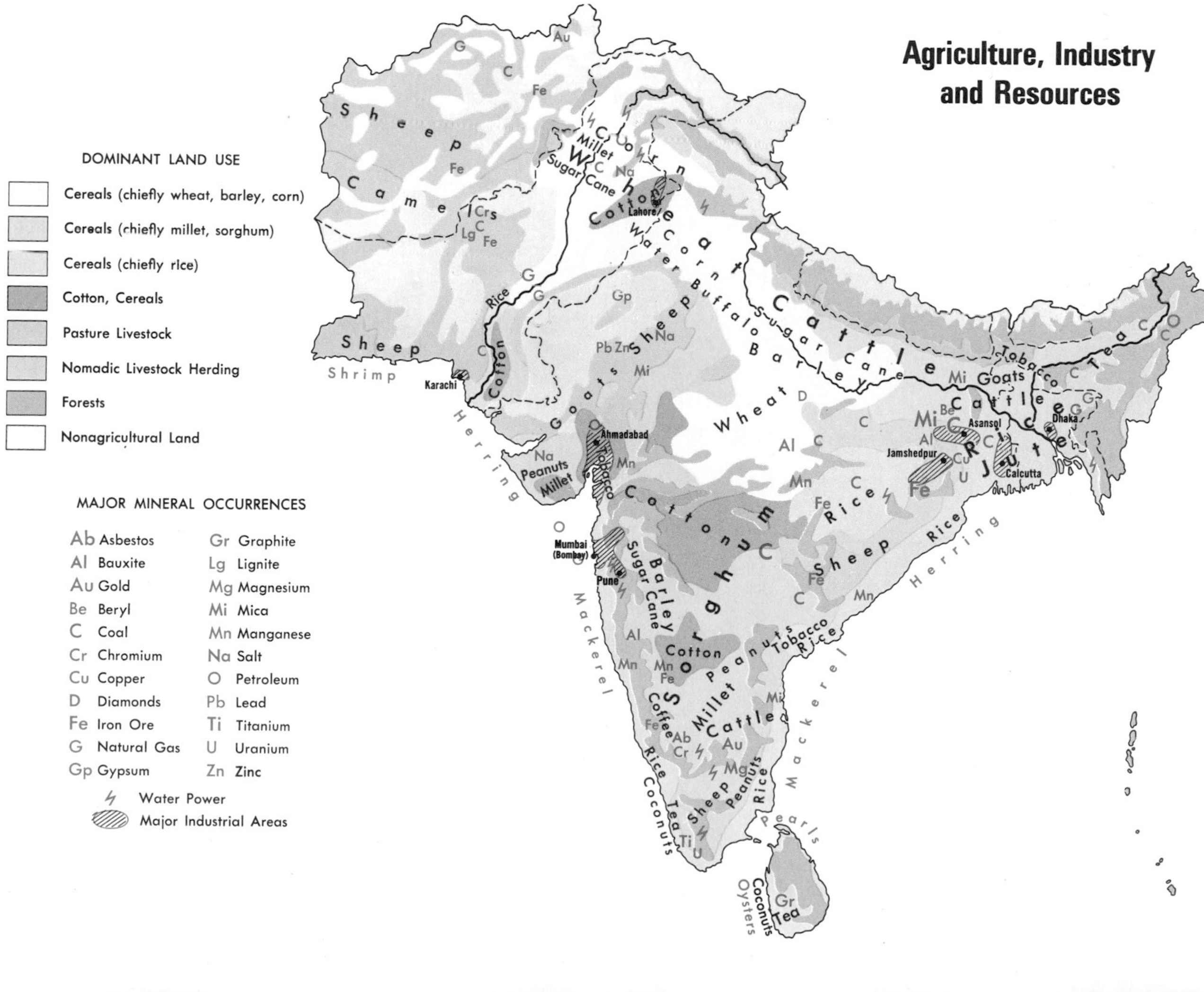

DOMINANT LAND USE
Cereals (chiefly wheat, barley, corn)
Cereals (chiefly millet, sorghum)
Cereals (chiefly rice)
Cotton, Cereals
Pasture Livestock
Nomadic Livestock Herding
Forests
Nonagricultural Land
MAJOR MINERAL OCCURRENCES
Ab Asbestos
Al Bauxite
Au Gold
Be Beryl
C Coal
Cr Chromium
Cu Copper
D Diamonds
Fe Iron Ore
G Natural Gas
Gp Gypsum
Gr Graphite
Lg Lignite
Mg Magnesium
Mi Mica
Mn Manganese
Na Salt
O Petroleum
Pb Lead
Ti Titanium
U Uranium
Zn Zinc
Water Power
Major Industrial Areas
Lahore
Karachi
Ahmadabad
Mumbai (Bombay)
Pune
Jamshedpur
Asansol
Calcutta
Dhaka
Sheep
Camels
Shrimp
Herring
Mackerel
Pearls
Oysters
Coconuts
Wheat
Corn
Barley
Millet
Sugar Cane
Cotton
Rice
Goats
Peanuts
Tobacco
Sorghum
Cattle
Jute
Tea
Coffee

Burma, Thailand, Indochina and Malaya

CONIC PROJECTION

SCALE OF MILES

SCALE OF KILOMETERS

International Boundaries
Division and State Boundaries
Capitals of Countries
Division and State Capitals

© Copyright HAMMOND INCORPORATED, Maplewood, N. J.

MYANMAR (BURMA)

THAILAND

LAOS

CAMBODIA

VIETNAM

MALAYSIA

SINGAPORE

CAMBODIA

AREA 69,898 sq. mi. (181,036 sq. km.)
POPULATION 11,918,865
CAPITAL Phnom Penh
LARGEST CITY Phnom Penh
HIGHEST POINT 5,948 ft. (1,813 m.)
MONETARY UNIT new riel
MAJOR LANGUAGE Khmer (Cambodian)
MAJOR RELIGIONS Buddhism

LAOS

AREA 91,428 sq. mi. (236,800 sq. km.)
POPULATION 5,556,821
CAPITAL Vientiane
LARGEST CITY Vientiane
HIGHEST POINT Phou Bia 9,252 ft. (2,820 m.)
MONETARY UNIT new kip
MAJOR LANGUAGE Lao
MAJOR RELIGIONS Buddhism, tribal religions

MALAYSIA

AREA 128,308 sq. mi. (332,318 sq. km.)
POPULATION 21,820,143
CAPITAL Kuala Lumpur
LARGEST CITY Kuala Lumpur
HIGHEST POINT Mt. Kinabalu 13,455 ft. (4,101 m.)
MONETARY UNIT ringgit
MAJOR LANGUAGES Malay, Chinese, English, Tamil, Dayak, Kadazan
MAJOR RELIGIONS Islam, Confucianism, Buddhism, tribal religions, Hinduism, Taoism, Christianity, Sikhism

MYANMAR (BURMA)

AREA 261,789 sq. mi. (678,034 sq. km.)
POPULATION 48,852,098
CAPITAL Yangon (Rangoon)
LARGEST CITY Yangon (Rangoon)
HIGHEST POINT Hkakabo Razi 19,296 ft. (5,881 m.)
MONETARY UNIT kyat
MAJOR LANGUAGES Burmese, Karen, Shan, Kachin, Chin, Kayah, English
MAJOR RELIGIONS Buddhism, tribal religions

SINGAPORE

AREA 226 sq. mi. (585 sq. km.)
POPULATION 3,571,710
CAPITAL Singapore
LARGEST CITY Singapore
HIGHEST POINT Bukit Timah 581 ft. (177 m.)
MONETARY UNIT Singapore dollar
MAJOR LANGUAGES Chinese, Malay, Tamil, English, Hindi
MAJOR RELIGIONS Confucianism, Buddhism, Taoism, Hinduism, Islam, Christianity

THAILAND

AREA 198,455 sq. mi. (513,998 sq. km.)
POPULATION 61,163,833
CAPITAL Bangkok
LARGEST CITY Bangkok
HIGHEST POINT Doi Inthanon 8,452 ft. (2,576 m.)
MONETARY UNIT baht
MAJOR LANGUAGES Thai, Lao, Chinese, Khmer, Malay
MAJOR RELIGIONS Buddhism, tribal religions

VIETNAM

AREA 128,405 sq. mi. (332,569 sq. km.)
POPULATION 78,349,503
CAPITAL Hanoi
LARGEST CITY Ho Chi Minh City
HIGHEST POINT Fan Si Pan 10,308 ft. (3,142 m.)
MONETARY UNIT new dong
MAJOR LANGUAGES Vietnamese, Thai, Muong, Meo, Yao, Khmer, French, Chinese, Cham
MAJOR RELIGIONS Buddhism, Taoism, Confucianism, Roman Catholicism, Cao-Dai

Topography

0   200   400 MI.
0   200   400 KM.

MYANMAR (BURMA)

INTERNAL DIVISIONS

Chin (state) 368,985	B2
Irrawaddy (div.) 4,991,057	B3
Kachin (state) 903,982	C1
Karan (state) 1,057,505	C3
Kayah (state) 100,355	C3
Magwe (div.) 3,241,103	B2
Mandalay (div.) 4,580,923	B2
Mon (state) 1,682,041	C4
Pegu (div.) 3,800,240	C3
Rakhine (state) 1,710,913	B3
Rangoon (div.) 3,973,782	C3
Sagaing (div.) 3,855,991	B1
Shan (state) 3,718,706	C2
Tenasserim (div.) 917,628	C4

CITIES and TOWNS

Akyab (Sittwe) 107,607	B2
Allanmyo 15,580	B3
Amarapura 11,268	B2
Amherst 6,000	C3
Bassein 144,092	B3
Bhamo 9,821	C1
Chauk 24,466	B2
Gyobingauk 9,922	B3
Henzada 82,531	B3
Hmawbi 23,032	C3
Insein 143,625	C3
Kanbalu 3,281	B2
Katha 7,648	C1
Kawthaung 1,520	C5
Kyaikto 13,154	C3
Kyangin 6,073	B3
Kyaukpadaung 5,480	B2
Kyaukpyu 7,335	B3
Kyaukse 8,659	C2
Labutta 12,982	B3
Lashio 69,567	C2
Letpadan 15,896	C3
Madauk 4,618	C3
Magwe 13,270	B2
Mandalay 532,895	C2
Martaban 5,661	C3
Ma-ubin 23,362	B3
Maungdaw 3,772	B2
Mawlaik 2,993	B2
Maymyo 58,059	C2
Meiktila 73,210	B2
Mergui 67,351	C4
Minbu 9,096	B2
Minhla 6,470	B3
Mogaung 2,920	C1
Mogok 8,334	C2
Monywa 106,873	B2
Moulmein 219,991	C3
Mudon 20,136	C3
Myanaung 11,155	B3
Myaungmya 24,532	B3
Myingyan 70,162	B2
Myitkyina 12,382	C1
Myohaung 6,534	B2
Okkan 14,443	B3
Pakokku 58,132	B2
Palaw 5,596	C4
Paungde 17,286	B3
Pegu 150,447	C3
Prome (Pye) 36,997	B3
Pyapon 19,174	B3
Pye 36,997	B3
Pyinmana 22,025	C3
Pyu 10,443	C3
Rathedaung 2,969	B2
Sagaing 15,382	B2
Sanduway 5,172	B3
Shwebo 17,827	B2
Singu 4,027	C2
Sittwe 107,607	B2
Syriam 15,296	C3
Taungdwingyi 16,233	B2
Taunggyi 107,907	C2
Tavoy 60,435	C4
Tharrawaddy 8,977	C3
Thaton 51,025	C3
Thayetmyo 11,649	B3
Thazi 7,531	C2
Thongwa 10,829	C3
Toungoo 31,589	C3
Wakema 20,716	B3
Yamethin 11,167	C2
Yandoon 15,245	B3
Yangon (Rangoon) (cap.) 2,458,712	C3
Ye 12,852	C4
Yenangyaung 57,652	B2
Ye-u 5,307	B2
Zalun 899	B3

OTHER FEATURES

Amya (pass)	C4
Andaman (sea)	B4
Arakan Yoma (mts.)	B3
Ataran (riv.)	C4
Bengal, Bay of (bay)	B3
Bentinck (isl.)	C5
Bilauktaung (range)	C4
Chaukan (pass)	C1
Cheduba (isl.)	B3
Chin (hills)	B2
Chindwin (riv.)	B2
Coco (chan.)	B4
Combermere (bay)	B3
Daung Kyun (isl.)	C4
Dawna (range)	C3
Great Coco (isl.)	B4
Great Tenasserim (riv.)	C4
Heinze Chaung (bay)	C4
Heywood (chan.)	B3
Hkakabo Razi (mt.)	C1
Hka, Nam (riv.)	C2
Indawgyi (lake)	C1
Inle (lake)	C2
Irrawaddy (riv.)	B3
Irrawaddy, Mouths of the (delta)	B4
Kadan Kyun (isl.)	C4
Kaladan (riv.)	B2
Kalegauk (isl.)	C4
Khao Luang (mt.)	C5
Lanbi Kyun (isl.)	C5
Launglon Bok (isls.)	C4
Letsök-aw Kyun (isl.)	C5
Little Coco (isl.)	B4

(continued on following page)

74 Myanmar, Thailand, Indochina and Malaya

(continued)

Loi Leng (mt.)....C2
Mali (riv.)....C1
Mali Kyun (isl.)....C4
Manipur (riv.)....B2
Martaban (gulf)....C4
Mekong (riv.)....D2
Mergui (arch.)....C5
Mon (riv.)....B2
Mu (riv.)....B2
Myitnge (riv.)....C2
Negrais (cape)....B3
Nmai (riv.)....C1
Pakchan (riv.)....C5
Pangsau (pass)....C1
Pawn, Nam (riv.)....C2
Pegu Yoma (mts.)....B3
Popa Hill (mt.)....B2
Preparis (isl.)....B4
Preparis North (chan.)....B4
Preparis South (chan.)....B4
Ramree (isl.)....B3
Salween (riv.)....C3
Shan (plat.)....C2
Shweli (riv.)....C2
Sittang (riv.)....C3
Taping (riv.)....C1
Taungthonton (mt.)....B1
Tavoy (pt.)....C4
Tenasserim (isl.)....C4
Teng, Nam (riv.)....C2
Thayawthadangyi Kyun (isl.)....C4
Three Pagodas (pass)....C4
Victoria (mt.)....B2
Zadetkyi Kyun (isl.)....C5

CAMBODIA (KAMPUCHEA)

CITIES and TOWNS

Batdambang (Battambang)....D4
Kampong Cham....E4
Kampong Chhnang....D4
Kampong Saom....D5
Kampong Spoe....E5
Kampong Thum....E4
Kampot....E5
Kracheh....E4
Krong Kaoh Kong....D5
Krong Keb....E5
Lumphat....E4
Paoy Pet....D4
Phnom Penh (cap.) 300,000....E5
Phnum Tbeng Meanchey....E4
Phumi Samraong....D4
Pouthisat....D4
Proy Veng....E5
Pursat (Pouthisat)....D4
Senmonoron....E4
Siemreab....D4
Stoeng Treng....E4
Svay Rieng....E5

OTHER FEATURES

Angkor Wat (ruins)....D4
Chrouy Samit (pt.)....D5
Dangrek (mts.)....D4
Drang, Ia (riv.)....E4
Joncs (plain)....E5
Kong, Kaoh (isl.)....D5
Khong, Se (riv.)....E4
Mekong (riv.)....E4
Rung, Kaoh (isl.)....D5
San, Se (riv.)....E4
Sen, Stoeng (riv.)....E4
Srepok (riv.)....E4
Tang, Kaoh (isl.)....D5
Tonle Sap (lake)....D4
Wai, Poulo (isls.)....D5

LAOS

CITIES and TOWNS

Attapu 2,750....E4
Ban Kèngkok 2,000....E3
Boun Nua 2,500....D2
Champasak 3,500....E4
Khamkeut▲ 31,206....E3
Louang Namtha 1,459....D2
Louangphrabang 7,596....D3
Mahaxai 2,000....E3
Muang Hinboun 1,750....E3
Muang Khammouan 5,500....E3
Muang Không 1,750....E4
Muang Khôngxédôn 2,000....E4
Muang Ou Tai....D2
Muang Pak-Lay 2,000....D3
Muang Pakxan 2,500....D3
Muang Xaignabouri (Sayaboury) 2,500....D3
Muang Xay 2,000....D2
Pakxé 8,000....E4
Phiafai▲ 17,216....E4
Phôngsali 2,500....D2
San Nua (Sam Neua) 3,000....E2
Saravan 2,350....E4
Savannakhét 8,500....E3
Sayaboury (Muang Xaignabouri) 2,500....D3
Thakhek (Muang Khammouan) 5,500....E3
Viangchan (Vientiane) 132,253....D3
Vientiane (cap.) 132,253....D3
Xiangkhoang 3,500....D3

OTHER FEATURES

Bolovens (plat.)....E4
Jars (plain)....D3
Mekong (riv.)....D3
Ou, Nam (riv.)....D2
Phou Bia (mt.)....D3
Phou Cô Pi (mt.)....E3
Phou Loi (mt.)....D2
Phou San (mt.)....D3
Rao Co (mt.)....E3
Se Khong (riv.)....E4
Tha, Nam (riv.)....D2
Xiangkhoang (plat.)....D3

MALAYA, MALAYSIA

(See Southeast Asia, p. 85 for other part of Malaysia.)

STATES

Federal Territory 937,875....D7
Johor (Johore) 1,601,504....D7
Kedah 1,102,200....D6
Kelantan 877,575....D6
Melaka 453,153....D7
Negeri Sembilan 563,955....D7
Pahang 770,644....D7
Penang (Pinang) 911,586....D6
Perak 1,762,288....D6
Perlis 147,726....D6
Pinang (Penang) 911,586....D6
Selangor 1,467,441....D7
Terengganu 542,280....D6

CITIES and TOWNS

Alor Gajah 2,222....D7
Alor Setar 66,260....D6
Bandar Maharani (Muar) 61,218....D7
Bandar Penggaram (Batu Pahat) 53,291....D7
Batu Gajah 10,692....D6
Batu Pahat 53,291....D7
Bentong 22,683....D7
Butterworth 61,187....D6
Chukai 12,514....D6
Gemas 5,214....D7
George Town (Pinang) 269,603....C6
Ipoh 247,953....D6
Johor Baharu (Johore Bharu) 136,234....F5
Kampar 26,591....D6
Kampong Kuala Besut 3,524....D6
Kangar 8,758....D6
Kelang 113,611....D7
Keluang 43,272....D7
Kota Baharu 55,124....D6
Kota Tinggi 8,725....F5
Kuala Dungun 17,560....D6
Kuala Lipis 9,270....D6
Kuala Lumpur (cap.) 451,977....D7
Kuala Pilah 12,508....D7
Kuala Rompin 1,384....D7
Kuala Selangor 3,132....D7
Kuala Terengganu 53,320....D6
Kuantan 43,358....D7
Kulai 11,841....F5
Lumut 3,255....D6
Malacca (Melaka) 87,160....D7
Mersing 18,246....E7
Muar 61,218....D7
Pekan 4,682....D7
Pinang (George Town) 269,603....C6
Pontian Kechil 8,349....E5
Port Dickson 10,300....D7
Port Weld 3,233....D6
Raub 18,433....D7
Segamat 17,796....D7
Seremban 80,921....D7
Sungai Petani 35,959....C6
Taiping 54,645....D6
Tanah Merah 7,012....D6
Teluk Intan 44,524....D6
Tumpat 10,673....D6

OTHER FEATURES

Aur, Pulau (isl.)....E7
Belumut, Gunong (mt.)....D7
Benom, Gunong (mt.)....D7
Gelang, Tanjong (pt.)....D6
Johore (str.)....E6
Johor, Sungai (riv.)....F5
Kelantan, Sungai (riv.)....D6
Langkawi, Pulau (isl.)....C6
Ledang, Gunong (mt.)....D7
Lima, Pulau (isl.)....F6
Malacca (str.)....D7
Malay (pen.)....D6
Malaya (West Malaysia) (reg.)....D6
Pahang, Sungai (riv.)....D7
Pangkor, Pulau (isl.)....D6
Perak, Gunong (mt.)....D6
Perhentian, Kepulauan (isls.)....D6
Piai, Tanjong (pt.)....E6
Pinang, Pulau (isl.)....C6
Pulai, Sungai (riv.)....E5
Ramunia, Tanjong (pt.)....F6
Redang, Pulau (isl.)....D6
Sedili Kechil, Tanjong (pt.)....F5
Singapore (str.)....F6
Tahan, Gunong (mt.)....D6
Temiang, Bukit (mt.)....D6
Tenggol, Pulau (isl.)....D6
Tinggi, Pulau (isl.)....E7
Tioman, Pulau (isl.)....E7

SINGAPORE

CITIES and TOWNS

Jurong 50,974....E6
Nee Soon 37,641....F6
Paya Lebar 21,636....F6
Serangoon 89,558....F6
Singapore (cap.) 2,413,945....F6

OTHER FEATURES

Keppel (harb.)....F6
Main (str.)....F6
Singapore (str.)....F6
Tekong Besar, Pulau (isl.)....F6

THAILAND (SIAM)

CITIES and TOWNS

Ang Thong 7,267....C4
Ayutthaya (Phra Nakhon Si Ayutthaya) 37,213....D4
Ban Aranyaprathet 12,276....D4
Bangkok (cap.) 1,867,297....D4
Ban Pak Phanang 13,590....D5
Buriram 16,431....D4
Chachoengsao 22,106....D4
Chainat 9,944....D4
Chaiyaphum 12,540....D4
Chanthaburi 15,479....D4
Chiang Mai 101,594....C3
Chiang Rai 13,927....C3
Chon Buri 115,350....D4
Chumphon 11,643....C5
Hat Yai 47,953....C6
Hua Hin 21,426....D4
Kalasin 14,960....D3
Kamphaeng Phet 12,378....C3
Kanchanaburi 16,397....C4
Khon Kaen 29,431....D3
Khorat (Nakhon Ratchasima) 66,071....D4
Krabi 8,764....C5
Krung Thep (Bangkok) (cap.) 1,867,297....D4
Lampang 40,100....C3
Lamphun 11,309....C3
Lang Suan 4,020....C5
Loei 10,137....D3
Lom Sak 10,597....D3
Lop Buri 23,112....D4
Mae Hong Son 3,981....C3
Maha Sarakham 19,707....D3
Nakhon Nayok 8,185....D4
Nakhon Pathom 34,300....C4
Nakhon Phanom 20,385....D3
Nakhon Ratchasima 66,071....D4
Nakhon Sawan 46,853....D4
Nakhon Si Thammarat 102,123....D5
Nan 17,738....D3
Narathiwat 21,256....D6
Nong Khai 21,150....D3
Pattani 21,938....D6
Phanat Nikhom 10,514....D4
Phangnga 5,738....C5
Phatthalung 13,336....D6
Phayao 20,346....C3
Phet Buri 27,755....C4
Phetchabun 6,240....D3
Phichit 10,814....D3
Phitsanulok 33,883....D3
Phrae 17,555....D3
Phra Nakhon Si Ayutthaya 37,213....D4
Phuket 34,362....C6
Prachin Buri 14,167....D4
Prachuap Khiri Khan 9,075....D5
Rahaeng (Tak) 16,317....C3
Ranong 10,301....C5
Rat Buri 32,271....C4
Rayong 14,846....D4
Roi Et 20,242....D4
Sakon Nakhon 18,943....E3
Samut Prakan 46,632....D4
Samut Sakhon 33,619....D4
Samut Songkhram 23,574....C4
Sara Buri 25,025....D4
Satun 7,315....C6
Sawankhalok 8,387....C3
Sing Buri 9,050....D4
Singora (Songkhla) 172,604....D6
Sisaket 13,662....E4
Songkhla 172,604....D6
Sukhothai 15,488....D3
Suphan Buri 18,768....C4
Surat Thani 24,923....C5
Surin 16,342....D4
Tak 16,317....C3
Takua Pa 7,825....C5
Thon Buri 628,015....D4
Trang 32,985....C6
Trat 7,917....D4
Ubon 40,650....E4
Udon Thani 56,218....D3
Uthai Thani 10,525....C4
Uttaradit 12,022....D3
Warin Chamrap 21,520....E4
Yala 30,051....D6
Yasothon 12,079....D4

OTHER FEATURES

Amya (pass)....C4
Bilauktaung (range)....C4
Chang, Ko (isl.)....D4
Chan, Ko (isl.)....C5
Chao Phraya, Mae Nam (riv.)....D4
Chi, Mae Nam (riv.)....D3
Dangrek (Dong Rak) (mts.)....D4
Doi Inthanon (mt.)....C3
Doi Pha Hom Pok (mt.)....C2
Doi Pia Fai (mt.)....D4
Khao Luang (mt.)....C5
Kao Prawa (mt.)....C3
Khwae Noi, Mae Nam (riv.)....C4
Kra (isth.)....C5
Kut, Ko (isl.)....D5
Laem Chong Phra (cape)....C5
Laem Pho (cape)....D6
Laem Talumphuk (cape)....D5
Lanta, Ko (isl.)....C6
Libong, Ko (isl.)....C6
Luang (mt.)....C5
Mae Klong, Mae Nam (riv.)....C4
Malay (pen.)....D6
Mekong (riv.)....E3
Mun, Mae Nam (riv.)....D4
Nan, Mae Nam (riv.)....D3
Nong Lahan (lake)....D3
Pakchan (riv.)....C5
Pa Sak, Mae Nam (riv.)....D4
Phangan, Ko (isl.)....D5
Phuket, Ko (isl.)....C5
Ping, Mae Nam (riv.)....C3
Rawi, Ko (isl.)....C6
Salween (riv.)....C3
Samui (str.)....D5
Samui, Ko (isl.)....D5
Tao, Ko (isl.)....C5
Tapi, Mae Nam (riv.)....C5
Terutao, Ko (isl.)....C6
Tha Chin, Mae Nam (riv.)....C4
Thale Luang (lag.)....D6
Thalu, Ko (isls.)....C5
Three Pagodas (pass)....C4
Wang, Mae Nam (riv.)....C3

VIETNAM

CITIES and TOWNS

An Loc (Binh Long) 15,276....E5
An Tuc (An Khe)....F4
Bac Giang....E2
Bac Lieu 53,841....E5
Bac Ninh 22,560....E2
Ban Me Thuot 68,771....F4
Bien Hoa 87,135....E5
Binh Long (An Loc) 15,276....E5
Cam Ranh 118,111....F5
Can Tho 182,424....E5
Cao Bang 565,967....E2
Cao Lanh 16,482....E5
Chau Phu 37,175....E5
Chu Lai....F4
Da Lat 105,072....F5
Da Nang 492,194....E3
Dien Bien Phu....D2
Dong Hoi....E3
Go Cong 33,191....E5
Ha Giang....E2
Haiphong* 1,447,614....E2
Hanoi (cap.) 3,056,549....E2
Ha Tinh....E3
Ho Chi Minh City (Saigon)* 3,934,326....E5
Hoa Binh....E2
Hoi An 45,059....F4
Hon Gai 100,000....E2
Hue 209,043....E3
Khanh Hung 59,015....E5
Khe Sanh....E3
Kon Tum 33,554....E4
Lac Giao (Ban Me Thuot) 68,771....F4
Lai Chau 437,983....D2
Lang Son 610,501....E2
Lao Cai....E2
Loc Ninh....E5
Long Xuyen 72,658....E5
My Tho 119,892....E5
Nam Dinh 125,000....E2
Nha Trang 216,227....F4
Ninh Binh....E2
Phan Rang 33,377....F5
Phan Thiet 80,122....F5
Phu Cuong 28,267....E5
Phu Ly....E2
Phu Tho 10,888....E2
Phu Vinh 48,485....E5
Pleiku 23,720....E4
Quang Ngai 14,119....F4
Quang Tri 15,874....E3
Quan Long 59,331....E5
Qui Nhon 213,757....F4
Rach Gia 104,161....E5
Sa Dec 51,867....E5
Saigon (Ho Chi Minh City)* 3,934,326....E5
Son La 682,385....D2
Son Tay 19,213....E2
Song Cau....F4
Tam Ky 38,532....F4
Tam Quan....F4
Tan An 38,082....E5
Tay Ninh 791,762....E5
Thai Binh 1,632,525....E2
Thai Nguyen 110,000....E2
Thanh Hoa 2,991,317....E3
Tra Vinh (Phu Vinh) 48,485....E5
Truc Giang 68,629....E5
Tuy Hoa 63,552....F4
Vinh 43,954....E3
Vinh Long 30,667....E5
Vinh Yen....E2
Vung Tau 136,225....E5
Yen Bai....E2

OTHER FEATURES

Bach Long Vi, Dao (isl.)....F2
Ba Den, Nui (mt.)....E5
Bai Bung, Mui (Ca Mau) (pt.)....E5
Ba Lang An, Mui (cape)....F4
Ben Goi (bay)....F4
Black (riv.)....D2
Ca Mau (Mui Bai Bung) (pt.)....E5
Cam Ranh, Vinh (bay)....F5
Cao Nguyen Dac Lac (plat.)....F4
Cat Ba, Dao (isl.)....E2
Chon May, Vung (bay)....F3
Con Son (isls.)....E5
Cu Lao, Hon (isls.)....F5
Da Nang, Mui (cape)....F3
Deux Frères, Les (isls.)....E5
Dinh, Mui (cape)....F5
Fan Si Pan (mt.)....D2
Gio, Hon (isl.)....E3
Hon Tho Chau (isl.)....D5
Ia Drang (riv.)....E4
Indochina (reg.)....D2
Joncs (plain)....E5
Khoai, Hon (isl.)....E5
Kontum (plat.)....E4
Lang Bian, Nui (mts.)....E4
Lay, Mui (cape)....E3
Mekong, Mouths of the (delta)....E5
Nam Tram, Mui (cape)....F4
Ngoc Linh (mt.)....E4
Nightingale (Bach Long Vi) (isl.)....F2
Panjang, Hon (Hon Tho Chau) (isl.)....D5
Phu Quoc, Dao (isl.)....D5
Quan Dao Nam Du (isls.)....D5
Rao Co (mt.)....E3
Red (riv.)....E2
Ron, Mui (cape)....E3
Se San (riv.)....E4
Sip Song Chau Thai (mts.)....D2
Song Ba (riv.)....F4
Song Ca (riv.)....E3
Song Cai (riv.)....E4
South China (sea)....F4
Tonkin (gulf)....E3
Varella, Mui (cape)....F4
Yang Sin, Chu (mt.)....F4

*City and suburbs.
▲Population of district.

Agriculture, Industry and Resources

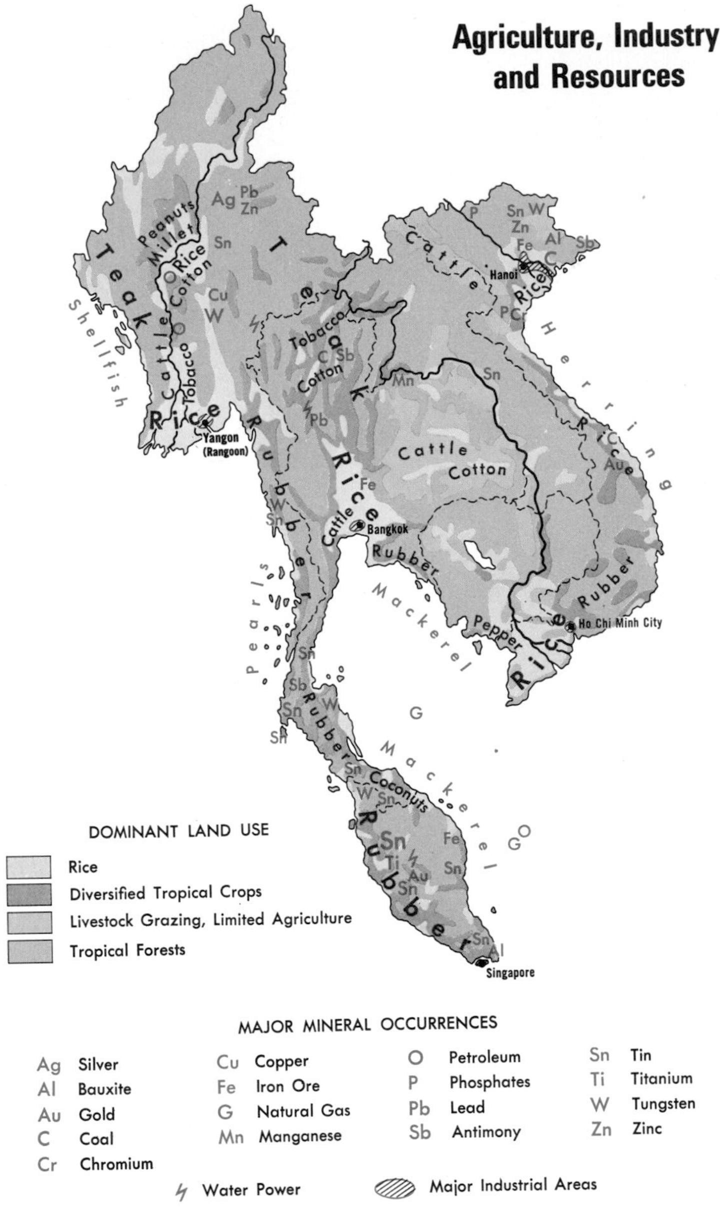

Teak
Peanuts
Millet
Rice
Cotton
Cattle
Tobacco
Shellfish
Rubber
Pearls
Mackerel
Pepper
Herring
Coconuts
Yangon (Rangoon)
Bangkok
Hanoi
Ho Chi Minh City
Singapore
DOMINANT LAND USE
Rice
Diversified Tropical Crops
Livestock Grazing, Limited Agriculture
Tropical Forests
MAJOR MINERAL OCCURRENCES
Ag Silver
Al Bauxite
Au Gold
C Coal
Cr Chromium
Cu Copper
Fe Iron Ore
G Natural Gas
Mn Manganese
O Petroleum
P Phosphates
Pb Lead
Sb Antimony
Sn Tin
Ti Titanium
W Tungsten
Zn Zinc
Water Power
Major Industrial Areas

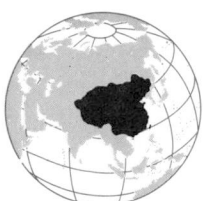

CHINA (MAINLAND)
AREA 3,705,386 sq. mi. (9,596,960 sq. km.)
POPULATION 1,256,167,701
CAPITAL Beijing
LARGEST CITY Shanghai
HIGHEST POINT Mt. Everest 29,028 ft. (8,848 m.)
MONETARY UNIT yuan
MAJOR LANGUAGES Chinese, Chuang, Uiguar, Yi, Tibetan, Maio, Mongol, Kazakh
MAJOR RELIGIONS Confucianism, Buddhism, Taoism, Islam

CHINA (TAIWAN)
AREA 13,971 sq. mi. (36,185 sq. km.)
POPULATION 22,319,222
CAPITAL T'aipei
LARGEST CITY T'aipei
HIGHEST POINT Yü Shan 13,115 ft. (3,997 m.)
MONETARY UNIT new Taiwan dollar
MAJOR LANGUAGES Chinese, Formosan
MAJOR RELIGIONS Confucianism, Buddhism, Taoism, Christianity, tribal religions

MONGOLIA
AREA 606,163 sq. mi. (1,569,962 sq. km.)
POPULATION 2,538,211
CAPITAL Ulaanbaatar
LARGEST CITY Ulaanbaatar
HIGHEST POINT Tabun Bogdo 14,288 ft. (4,355 m.)
MONETARY UNIT tughrik
MAJOR LANGUAGES Khalkha Mongolian, Kazakh (Turkic)
MAJOR RELIGION Buddhism

MONGOLIA
AREA 606,163 sq. mi. (1,569,962 sq. km.)
POPULATION 2,654,572
CAPITAL Ulaanbaatar
LARGEST CITY Ulaanbaatar
HIGHEST POINT Tabun Bogdo 14,288 ft. (4,355 m.)
MONETARY UNIT tughrik
MAJOR LANGUAGES Khalkha Mongolian, Kazakh (Turkic)
MAJOR RELIGION Buddhism

MACAU
AREA 8 sq. mi. (21 sq. km.)
POPULATION 429,152
CAPITAL Macau
MONETARY UNIT pataca
MAJOR LANGUAGES Chinese, Portuguese
MAJOR RELIGIONS Confucianism, Buddhism, Taoism, Christianity

CHINA (MAINLAND)   **CHINA (TAIWAN)**   **MONGOLIA**

CHINA
PROVINCES
Anhui (Anhwei) 49,665,724 ...J5
Chekiang (Zhejiang) 38,884,603 ....K6
Fujian (Fukien) 25,931,106 .....J6
Gansu (Kansu) 19,569,261 .....E3
Guangdong (Kwangtung) 59,299,220 ....H7
Guangxi Zhuangzu (Kwangsi Chuang Aut. Reg.) 36,420,960 ....G7
Guizhou (Kweichow) 28,552,997 ....G6
Hainan H8
Hebei (Hopei) 53,005,875 ...J4
Heilongjiang (Heilungkiang) 32,665,546 ....K2
Henan (Honan) 74,422,739 ...H5
Hubei (Hupei) 47,804,150 ....H5
Hunan 54,008,851 ....H6
Inner Mongolian Aut. Reg. (Nei Monggol) 19,274,279 ..H3
Jiangsu (Kiangsu) 60,521,114 ....K5
Jiangxi (Kiangsi) 33,184,827 ...J6
Jilin (Kirin) 22,560,053 .....L3
Kansu (Gansu) 19,569,261 ....E3
Kiangsi (Jiangxi) 33,184,827 ...J6
Kiangsu (Jiangsu) 60,521,114 ....K5
Kirin (Jilin) 22,560,053 .....L3
Kwangsi Chuang Aut. Reg. (Guangxi Zhuang) 36,420,960 ....G7
Kwangtung (Guangdong) 59,299,220 ....H7
Kweiichow (Guizhou) 28,552,997 ....G6
Liaoning 35,721,693 ....K3
Nei Monggol (Inner Mongolian Aut. Reg.) 19,274,279 ....H3
Ningxia Huizu (Ningsia Hui Aut. Reg.) 3,895,578 ....F3
Qinghai (Tsinghai) 3,895,706..E4
Shaanxi (Shensi) 28,904,423 .G5
Shandong (Shantung) 74,419,054 ....J4
Shanxi (Shansi) 25,291,389 ...H4
Sichuan (Szechwan) 99,713,310 ....F5
Sinkiang-Uigur Aut. Reg. (Xinjiang Uygur) 13,081,631 .....B3
Taiwan 21,665,515 ....K7
Tibet Aut. Reg. (Xizang) 1,892,393 ....B5
Tsinghai (Qinghai) 3,895,706..E4
Xinjian Uygur (Sinkiang-Uigur Aut. Reg.) 13,081,631 .....B3
Xizang (Tibet Aut. Reg.) 1,892,393 ....B5
Yunnan 32,553,817 ....F7
Zhejiang (Chekiang) 38,884,603 ....K6

SPECIAL ADMINISTRATIVE REGIONS
Hong Kong 6,966,929 ....H7
Macau 445,427 ....H7

CITIES and TOWNS
Aihui (Aigun) (Heihe) 73,660 ..L1
Amoy (Xiamen) 507,390 ......J7
Anqing (Anking) 449,310 ....J5
Anshan 1,195,580 ....K3
Anshun 200,680 ....G6
Anyang 501,390 ....H4
Baicheng, Jilin 276,420 ......K2
Baoding (Paoting) 495,140 ...J4
Baoji (Paoki) 341,240 ....G5
Baotou (Paotow) 1,075,920...G3
Beihai (Pakhoi) 173,740 .....G7
Beijing (Peking) (cap.) 5,715,368 ....J3
Bengbu (Pengpu) 550,360 ...J5
Canton (Guangzhou, Kwangchow) 3,181,510......H7
Changchih (Changzhi) 450,320 ....H4
Changchow (Changzhou) 533,940 ....J5
Changchow (Zhangzhou) 283,490 ....J7
Changchun 1,747,410..........K3
Changde (Changteh) 213,890.H6
Changhua 185,816 ....K7
Changsha 1,066,030............H6
Changteh (Changde) 213,890.H6
Changzhi (Changchih) 450,320 ....H4
Changzhou (Changchow) 533,940 ....K5
Chankiang (Zhanjiang) 853,970 ....H7
Chaotung (Zhaotung) 133,080 ....F6
Chaoyang, Liaoning 206,700..J3
Chefoo (Yantai) 385,180.......K4
Chengchow (Zhengzhou) 1,404,050 ....H5
Chengde (Chengteh) 326,910 .J3
Chengdu (Chengtu) 2,499,000 ....F5
Chiai 251,840 ....K7
Chifeng 293,460..................K3
Chinchow (Jinzhou) 599,490..K3
Chinkiang (Zhenjiang) 345,560 ....J5
Chinwangtao (Qinhuangdao) 374,210 ....K4
Chongqing (Chungking) 2,673,170 ....G6
Chüanchow (Quanzhou) 403,180 ....J7
Chuchow (Zhuzhou) 382,950.H6
Chumatien (Zhumadian) 150,440 ....H5
Chungking (Chongqing) 2,673,170 ....G6
Chungshan (Zhongshan) 135,000 ....H7
Conghua 280,250 ....H7
Dafang 962,470 ....G6
Dalian 1,480,240.................K4
Dandong (Tantung) 545,180..K3
Daqing 758,430 ....L2
Datong (Tatung), Shanxi 962,470 ....H3

(continued on following page)

China and Mongolia Transportation
Railroads	———
Under Construction	– – –
Connecting Roads	———
Navigable Rivers	~~~
Canals	≡≡≡
Major Seaports	⚓

© Copyright HAMMOND INCORPORATED, Maplewood, N.J.

Da Xian 193,490 ....G5
Dezhou (Tehchow) 258,860 ...J4
Dukou 497,330 ....F6
Fatshan (Foshan) 273,840 ...H7
Fengcheng 995,900 ....K3
Foochow (Fuzhou) 1,111,550..J6
Foshan (Fatshan) 273,840 ...H7
Fowyang (Fuyang) 177,850 ...J5
Fushun 1,184,940 ....K3
Fuxin 646,580 ....K3
Fuyang (Fowyang) 177,850 ...J5
Fuzhou (Foochow), Fujian
  1,111,550 ....J6
Fuzhou, Jiangxi 158,300 .....J6
Ganzhou (Kanchow) 362,880 ..H6
Gejiu (Kokiu) 352,980 ....F7
Guangzhou (Canton)
  3,181,510 ....H7
Guilin (Kweilin) 432,410 .....G6
Guiyang (Kweiyang), Guizhou
  1,350,190 ....G6
Gulja (Yining) 257,280 ....B3
Haikou (Hoihow) 263,280 ....H7
Hailar 157,490 ....J2
Hanchung (Hanzhong)
  374,270 ....G5
Handan (Hantan) 929,530 ...H4
Hangzhou (Hangchow)
  1,171,450 ....J5
Hanton (Handan) 929,530 ...H4
Hanzhong (Hanchung)
  374,270 ....G5
Harbin 2,519,120 ....L2
Hebi 336,430 ....J4
Hefei (Hofei) 795,420 ....J5
Hegang (Hokang) 592,470 ...L2
Heihe (Aigun, Aihui) 73,660 .L1
Hengshui 101,260 ....J4
Hengyang 531,720 ....H6
Hofei (Hefei) 795,420 ....J5
Hohhot (Huhehot) 754,120 ..H3
Hoihow (Haikou) 263,280 ....H7
Hokang (Hegang) 592,470 ...L2
Horqin Youyi Qianqi
  (Ulanhot) 174,050 ....K2
Houma 144,460 ....J4
Hsüchang (Xuchang)
  218,960 ....H5
Huaibei 444,820 ....J5
Huainan 1,029,220 ....J5
Huangshi 375,640 ....J5
Huhehot (Hohhot) 754,120 ..H3
Huize 158,380 ....F6
Hunjiang 694,160 ....L3
Huzhou (Wuxing) 925,900 ...K5
Hwainan (Huainan)
  1,029,220 ....J5

Hwangshih (Huangshi)
  375,640 ....J5
Ichang (Yichang) 365,000 ...H5
Ichun (Yichun) 755,830 ......L2
Ipin (Yibin) 245,240 ....F6
Jiamusi (Kiamusze) 540,190 .M2
Ji'an (Kian) 167,550 ....J6
Jiangmen (Kongmoon)
  212,450 ....H7
Jiaozuo (Tsiaotso) 484,370 .H4
Jiaxing (Kashing) 656,130 ..K5
Jilin (Kirin) 1,808,420 ....L3
Jinan (Tsinan) 1,359,130 ...J4
Jingdezhen (Kingtehchen)
  611,030 ....J6
Jinhua (Kinhwa) 869,490 ...J6
Jining (Tsining), Nei Monggol
  158,570 ....H3
Jining (Tsining), Shandong
  190,420 ....J4
Jinzhou (Chinchow) 599,490..K3
Jiujiang (Kiukiang) 350,910 .J6
Jixi (Kisi) 781,800 ....M2
Kaifeng 602,230 ....H5
Kaiyuan, Yunnan 223,420 ...F7
Kalgan (Zhangjiakou)
  617,120 ....H3
Kanchow (Ganzhou) 362,880.H6
Kaohsiung 1,227,454 ....J7
Karamay 156,970 ....B2
Kashi 256,890 ....A4
Kashing (Jiaxing) 656,130 ..K5
Keelung 347,828 ....J6
Kiamusze (Jiamusi) 540,190 .M2
Kian (Ji'an) 167,550 ....J6
Kingtehchen (Jingdezhen)
  611,030 ....J6
Kinhwa (Jinhua) 869,490 ...J6
Kirin (Jilin) 1,808,420 ....L3
Kisi (Jixi) 781,800 ....M2
Kiukiang (Jiujiang) 350,910 .J6
Kokiu (Gejiu) 352,980 ....F7
Kongmoon (Jiangmen)
  212,450 ....H7
Korla 117,690 ....C3
Kowloon 2,450,187 ....H7
Kuldja (Yining) 257,280 ......B3
Kunming 1,418,640 ....F6
Kuytun 239,870 ....C3
Kwangchow (Canton)
  3,181,510 ....H7
Kweilin (Guilin) 432,410 .....G6
Kweisui (Hohhot) 754,120 ..H3
Kweiyang (Guiyang)
  1,350,190 ....G6
Lanzhou (Lanchow)
  1,364,480 ....F4

Lengshuijiang 254,590 ....H6
Leshan (Loshan) 958,360 ...F6
Lhasa 83,540 ....D6
Lianyungang (Lienyünkang)
  397,090 ....J5
Liaoyang 646,580 ....K3
Liaoyuan 771,510 ....K3
Linfen 208,210 ....H4
Lizhou (Liuchow) 581,940 ..G7
Loho (Luohe) 157,670 ....H5
Loshan (Leshan) 958,360 ...F6
Longyan 346,700 ....J6
Loyang (Luoyang) 951,610 ..H5
Lu'an 145,880 ....J5
Luchow (Luzhou) 305,220 ..G6
Lüde (Dalian) 1,480,240 ....K4
Luohe 157,670 ....H5
Luoyang (Loyang) 951,610 ..H5
Luzhou (Luchow) 305,220 ..G6
Ma'anshan 351,880 ....J5
Macau (Macao) 238,413 ....H7
Manchouli (Manzhouli)
  104,220 ....J2
Maoming (Mowming)
  412,540 ....H7
Mianyang, Sichuan 768,500..G5
Mowming (Maoming)
  412,540 ....H7
Mudanjiang (Mutankiang)
  581,300 ....M3
Mukden (Shenyang)
  3,944,240 ....K3
Nanchang 1,075,710 ....J6
Nanchong (Nanchung)
  ....G5
Nanjing (Nanking) 2,091,400.J5
Nanning 889,790 ....G7
Nanping 407,810 ....J6
Nantong 402,990 ....K5
Nanyang 288,300 ....H5
Neijiang (Neikiang) 270,950..G6
Ningbo (Ningpo) 478,940 ...K6
Ningpo (Ningbo) 478,940 ...K6
Ningsia (Yinchuan,
  Yinchuan) 354,100 ....G4
Paicheng (Baicheng)
  276,420 ....K2
Pakhoi (Beihai) 173,740 .....G7
Paoki (Baoji) 341,240 ....G5
Paoting (Baoding) 495,140 ..J4
Paotow (Baotou) 1,075,920..G3
Peking (Beijing) (cap.)
  5,715,368 ....J4
Pengpu (Bengbu) 550,360 ..J5
Pingtung 189,347 ....K7
Pingxiang, Guangxi
  Zhuangzu 1,189,030 ......G7

Pingxiang, Jiangxi 76,260 ...H6
Qingdao (Tsingtao)
  1,172,370 ....K4
Qingjiang 234,750 ....J5
Qinhuangdao (Chinwangtao)
  374,210 ....K4
Qinzhou 981,280 ....G7
Qiqihar (Tsitsihar) 1,209,180.K2
Qitaihe 283,420 ....M2
Quanzhou (Chüanchow)
  403,810 ....J7
Sanmenxia 147,050 ....H5
Sanming 199,230 ....J6
Shanghai 7,551,236 ....K5
Shangqiu (Shangkiu)
  186,760 ....J5
Shangrao (Shangjao)
  135,160 ....J6
Shantou (Swatow) 717,620..J7
Shaoguan (Shiukwan)
  370,550 ....H7
Shaoxing (Shaohing)
  1,091,170 ....K5
Shaoyang 396,600 ....H6
Shashi 238,960 ....H5
Shenyang (Mukden)
  3,944,240 ....K3
Shenzhen 98,060 ....H7
Shihezi (Shihhotzu) 563,740..C3
Shijiazhuang (Shihkiachwang)
  1,068,720 ....J4
Shiukwan (Shaoyuan)
  370,550 ....H7
Shiyan 306,830 ....H5
Shuangyashan 400,050 .....M2
Siakwan (Xiaguan) 117,190..E6
Sian (Xi'an) 2,185,040 ....G5
Siangfan (Xiangfan) 323,000.H5
Siangtan (Xiangtan) 493,040.H6
Sienyang (Xianyang)
  501,810 ....G5
Sinchu 208,038 ....K7
Singtai (Xingtai) 334,210 ...H4
Sining (Xining) 566,650 ......F4
Sinsiang (Xinxiang) 525,280.H4
Sinyang (Xinyang) 240,000..H5
Siping (Szeping) 333,850 ...K3
Soochow (Suzhou) 191,710..K5
Süchow (Xuzhou) 776,770...J5
Suizhong 669,940 ....K3
Suzhou (Soochow) 191,710..K5
Swatow (Shantou) 717,620..J7
Szeping (Siping) 333,850 ...K3
Tai'an 1,274,770 ....J4
Taichow (Taizhou) 161,200..K5
Taichung 565,255 ....K7
Tainan 541,390 ....J7

T'aipei 2,108,193 ....K7
Taiyuan 1,745,820 ....H4
Taizhou (Taichow) 161,200..K5
Tangshan 1,407,840 ....J4
Tantung (Dandong) 545,180.K3
Taoyuan 105,841 ....K6
Tatung (Datong) 962,470 ...G5
Tehchow (Dezhou) 258,860 .J4
Tianjin (Tientsin) 4,521,266.J4
Tianshui 185,230 ....F5
Tieling 220,850 ....K3
Tientsin (Tianjin) 4,521,266.J4
Tienshui (Tianshui) 185,230.F5
Tongchuan (Tungchwan)
  353,520 ....G5
Tongliao 213,470 ....K3
Tongling 184,060 ....J5
Tsiaotso (Jiaozuo) 484,370 .H4
Tsinan (Jinan) 1,359,130 ...J4
Tsingkiang (Qingjiang)
  234,750 ....J5
Tsingtao (Qingdao)
  1,172,370 ....K4

Tsining (Jining), Nei Monggol
  158,570 ....H3
Tsining (Jining), Shandong
  190,420 ....J4
Tsitsihar (Qiqihar) 1,209,180.K2
Tsunyi (Zunyi) 250,670 ......G6
Tungchwan (Tongchuan)
  353,520 ....G5
Tunghwa (Tonghua))
  359,960 ....L3
Tungliao (Tongliao) 213,470.K3
Tunxi (Tunki) 103,560 ....J6
Tzekung (Zigong) 866,020 ..F6
Tzepo (Zibo) 2,197,668 ....J4
Ulanhot (Horqin Youyi
  Qianqi) 174,050 ....K2
Ürümqi (Urumchi)
  961,240 ....C3
Victoria 1,183,621 ....H7
Wanxian (Wanhsien)
  267,000 ....G5
Weifang 393,410 ....J4
Weihai (Weihaiwei) 205,010.K4

Wenchow (Wenzhou)
  515,650 ....J6
Wenzhou 515,650 ....J6
Wuchow (Wuzhou) 245,250.H7
  245,250
Wuhan 3,287,720 ....H5
Wuhu 449,070 ....J5
Wusih (Wuxi) 798,310 ....K5
Wuxi (Wusih) 798,310 ....K5
Wuxing 925,900 ....K5
Wuzhou (Wuchow) 245,250.H7
  245,250 ....G4
Xiaguan (Siakwan) 117,190.E6
Xiamen (Amoy) 507,390 ....J7
Xi'an (Sian) 2,185,040 ....G5
Xiangfan (Siangfan) 323,000.H5
Xiangtan (Siangtan) 493,040.H6
Xianyang (Sienyang) 501,810.G5
Xingtai (Singtai) 334,210 ...H4
Xining (Sining) 566,650 ......F4
Xinxiang (Sinsiang) 525,280.H4

Topography

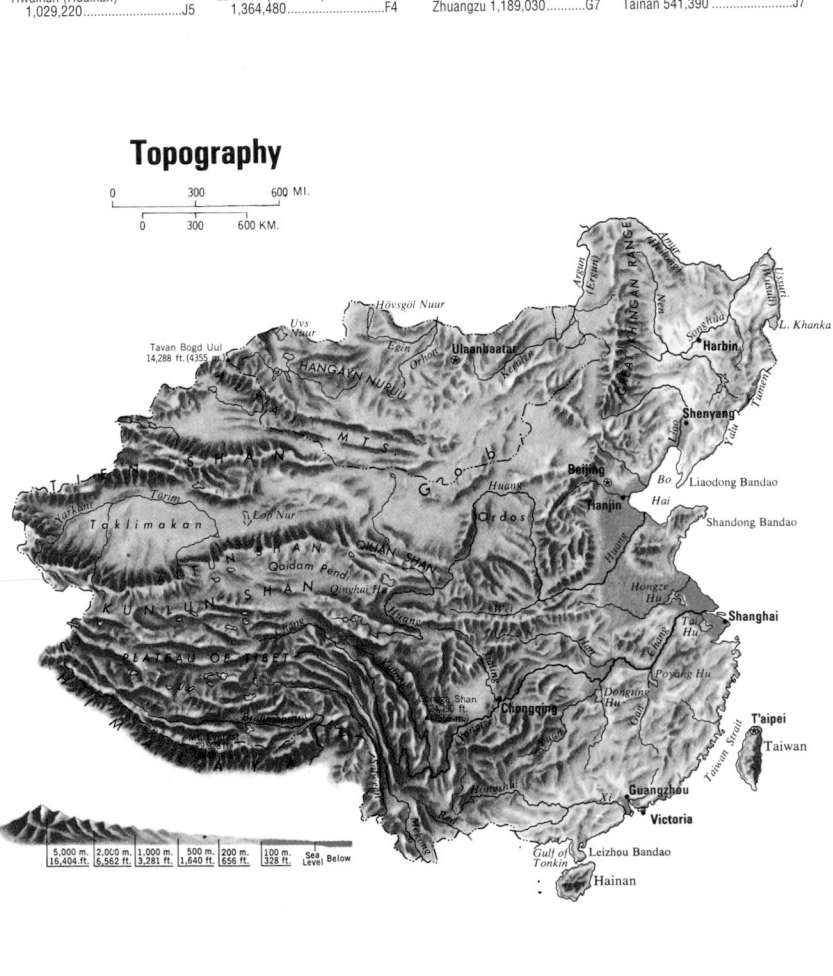

0   300   600 MI.

0   300   600 KM.

| 5,000 m. | 2,000 m. | 1,000 m. | 500 m. | 200 m. | 100 m. | Sea |
| 16,404 ft. | 6,562 ft. | 3,281 ft. | 1,640 ft. | 656 ft. | 328 ft. | Level Below |

On this map Chinese place-names have been rendered according to the Pinyin spelling system within the area controlled by the People's Republic of China. Alphabetically listed below are selected Chinese place-names spelled in the traditional manner, followed by the equivalent Pinyin form.

Amoy (Hsiamen)	Xiamen	Kirin	Jilin	Sian	Xi'an
Anhwei	Anhui	Kiukiang	Jiujiang	Siangtan	Xiangtan
Canton		Kwangsi	Guangxi	Sining	Xining
(Kwangchow)	Guangzhou	Chuang	Zhuangzu	Sinkiang	Xinjiang Uygur
Chefoo (Yentai)	Yantai	Kwangtung	Guangdong	Uighur	
Chekiang	Zhejiang	Kweichow	Guizhou	Soochow	Suzhou
Chengchow	Zhengzhou	Kweilin	Guilin	Süchow	Xuzhou
Chengtu	Chengdu	Kweiyang	Guiyang	Swatow	Shantou
Chinchow	Jinzhou	Lanchow	Lanzhou	Szechuan	Sichuan
Chungking	Chongqing	Liuchow	Liuzhou	Tachai	Dazhai
Foochow	Fuzhou	Loyang	Luoyang	Tatung	Datong
Fukien	Fujian	Lüta (Dalian)	Dalian	Tibet	Xizang
Hangchow	Hangzhou	Mutankiang	Mudanjiang	Tientsin	Tianjin
Heilungkiang	Heilongjiang	Nanking	Nanjing	Tsinan	Jinan
Hofei	Hefei	Ningpo	Ningbo	Tsinghai	Qinghai
Honan	Henan	Ningsia Hui	Ningxia Huizu	Tsingtao	Qingdao
Hopei	Hebei	Paoting	Baoding	Tsining	Jining
Hupeh	Hubei	Paotow	Baotou	Tsunyi	Zunyi
Hwainan	Huainan	Peking	Beijing	Tungchwan	Tongchuan
Inner Mongolia	Nei Monggol	Pengpu	Bengbu	Tzepo	Zibo
Kansu	Gansu	Shansi	Shanxi	Wusih	Wuxi
Kiangsi	Jiangxi	Shantung	Shandong	Yenan	Yan'an
Kiangsu	Jiangsu	Shensi	Shaanxi	Yinchuan	Yinchuan
Kingtehchen	Jingdezhen	Shihkiachwang	Shijiazhuang		

Yanji (Yenki) 176,000 ....L3
Yantai (Chefoo) 385,180 ......K4
Yenki (Yanji) 176,000 ....L3
Yibin (Ipin) 245,240 ....F6
Yichang (Ichang) 365,000 ....H5
Yichun, Heilongjiang 755,830 L2
Yichun, Jiangxi 171,720 ......H6
Yinchuan Ningsia 354,100...G4
Yingkou 422,590 ....K3
Yining 257,280 ....B3
Yiyang 165,040 ....H6
Yuci (Yütze) 270,890 ....H4
Yueyang 971,790..............H6
Yumen 195,290 ....E4
Yungkia (Wenzhou) 515,650...J6
Yütze (Yuci) 270,890 ....H4
Zaozhuang 1,244,020..........J5
Zhangjiakou (Kalgan)
617,120..........................J3
Zhangzhou (Changchow)
283,490..........................J7
Zhanjiang (Chankiang)
853,970..........................H7

Zhaoqing 172,080 ....H7
Zhaotong (Chaotung)
133,080........................F6
Zhengzhou (Chengchow)
1,404,050....................H5
Zhenjiang (Chinkiang)
345,560........................J5
Zhongshan (Chungshan)
135,000........................H7
Zhumadian (Chumatien)
150,440........................H5
Zhuzhou (Chuchow) 382,950.H6
Zibo (Tzepo) 2,197,668........J4
Zigong (Tzekung) 866,020....F6
Zunyi (Tsunyi) 350,670........G6

OTHER FEATURES

Altun Shan (range).............C4
Alxa Shamo (des.)..............F4
Amur (Heilong Jiang) (riv.)...L2
A'nyêmaqên Shan (mts.)......E5
Aqqikkol Hu (lake).............C4

Argun' (Ergun He) (riv.).......K1
Ayakkum Hu (lake)............C4
Bagrax (Bosten Hu) (lake)....C3
Bangong Co (lake).............A5
Bashi (chan.)...................K7
Bayan Har Shan (range).......E5
Bo Hai (gulf)....................J4
Bosten Hu (Bagrax) (lake)....C3
Chang Jiang (Yangtze) (riv.)..K5
Daba Shan (range)..............G5
Da Hingan Ling (range).........J3
Dian Chi (lake)..................F7
Dogai Coring (lake)............C5
Dongsha (isl.)..................J7
Dongting Hu (lake).............H6
East China (sea)................L6
Ebinur Hu (lake).................B2
Ergun He (Argun') (riv.)........K1
Er Hai (lake)....................F6
Everest (mt.)...................C6
Fen He (riv.)....................H4
Formosa (Taiwan) (isl.).......K7
Formosa (Taiwan) (str.).......J7

Gangdisê Shan (range).........B5
Gan He (riv.)....................K2
Gaoyou Hu (lake)...............J5
Ghenghis Khan Wall (ruin)....H2
Gobi (des.).....................G3
Gongga Shan (mt.).............F6
Grand (canal)...................J4
Great Wall (ruins)..............G4
Gurla Mandhata (mt.).........B5
Gyaring Co (lake)...............C5
Gyaring Hu (lake)...............E4
Hailar He (riv.).................K2
Hainan (isl.)....................H8
Hangzhou Wan (bay).........K5
Han Shui (riv.)..................H5
Har Hu (lake)...................E4
Heilong Jiang (Amur) (riv.)....L2
Hengduan Shan (mts.)........E6
Himalaya (mts.)................C6
Hoh Xil Shan (mts.)...........C4
Hongshui He (riv.)..............G7
Hongze Hu (lake)...............J5
Hotan He (riv.).................B4

Huang He (Yellow) (riv.).......F5
Hulun Nur (lake)................J2
Huma (riv.).....................K1
Inner Mongolia (reg.)..........H3
Jinmen (Quemoy) (isl.).......J7
Jinsha Jiang (Yangtze) (riv.)..E5
Junggar Pendi (desert basin)..C2
Kangrinboqê Feng (mt.).......B5
Karakax He (riv.)...............A4
Karakhoto (ruins)..............G4
Karamiran Shankou (pass)....C4
Keriya He (riv.).................B4
Keriya Shankou (pass).........B4
Khanka (lake)...................M3
Kongur Shan (mt.).............A4
Konqi He (riv.)..................C3
Künes He (riv.).................B3
Kunlun Shan (range)...........B4
Kuruktag Shan (range)........C3
Lancang Jiang (riv.).............F7
Laoha He (riv.)..................J3
Leizhou Bandao (pen.).........G7
Liao He (riv.)....................K3

Liaodong Bandao (pen.).......K3
Lop Nor (Lop Nur) (lake).......D3
Lumajangdong Co (lake)......B5
Manas He (riv.).................C3
Manas Hu (lake)...............C2
Margai Caka (lake).............C4
Mazu (Matsu) (isl.)............K6
Mekong (Lancang Jiang)
(riv.)..........................F7
Min Jiang (riv.)..................J6
Moron Us He (riv.)..............D5
Mudan Jiang (riv.)..............L3
Mu Us Shamo (des.)...........G4
Muztag (mt.)....................B4
Muztagata (mt.)................A4
Nam Co (lake)..................D5
Namzha Parwa (mt.)..........E6
Nan Ling (mts.).................H6
Nanpan Jiang (riv.).............F7
Nen Jiang (riv.).................K2
Ngangla Ringco (lake)..........B5
Ngangzê Co (lake)..............C5
Ngom Qu (riv.).................E5

Ngoring Hu (lake)..............E5
Nu Jiang (riv.)..................E6
Nyainqêntanglha Shan
(range).........................D5
Ordos (reg.)....................G4
Penghu (Pescadores) (isls.)...J7
Pingtan (isl.)....................K6
Pobeda (peak)..................A3
Poyang Hu (lake)...............J6
Pratas (Dongsha) (isl.)........J7
Qaidam Pendi (basin)..........D4
Qarqan He (riv.)................C4
Qilian Shan (range).............E4
Qinghai Hu (lake)...............E4
Qumar He (riv.)................D4
Rola Co (lake)..................C4
Salween (Nu Jiang) (riv.)......E6
Siling Co (lake).................C5
Songhua Hu (lake).............L3
Songhua Jiang (Sungari)
(riv.)...........................M2
Tai Hu (lake)....................J5
Taiwan (Formosa) (isl.).......K7
(continued on following page)

China and Mongolia

SCALE OF MILES
0 100 200 300 400 500
SCALE OF KILOMETERS
0 100 200 300 400 500

Capitals of Countries......⊛   International Boundaries ____
Provincial Capitals........●   Provincial Boundaries ____
Canals ____   Walls ~~~~~

© Copyright HAMMOND INCORPORATED, Maplewood, N.J.

(continued)

Pratas (Dongsha) (isl.)............J7
Qaidam Pendi (basin).............D4
Qarqan He (riv.).......................C4
Qilian Shan (range).................E4
Qinghai Hu (lake)....................E4
Qumar He (riv.)........................D4
Rola Co (lake)..........................C4
Salween (Nu Jiang) (riv.)........E6
Siling Co (lake)........................C5
Songhua Hu (lake)...................L3
Songhua Jiang (Sungari)
(riv.).......................................M2
Tai Hu (lake).............................J5
Taiwan (Formosa) (isl.)...........K7
Taiwan (Formosa) (str.)..........J7
Taizhou (Tachen) (isls.)..........K6
Takla Makan (Taklimakan
Shamo) (des.).........................B4
Tanggula Shan (range)...........D5
Tangra Yumco (lake)..............C5
Tarim He (riv.)........................B3
Tarim Pendi (basin)................B4
Tian Shan (range)...................C3
Tibet (reg.)..............................B5
Tongtian He (Zhi Qu) (riv.)......E5
Tonkin (gulf)............................G7
Toson Hu (lake).......................E4
Tumen (riv.).............................L3
Tuotuo He (riv.).......................D5
Ulu Muztag (mt.).....................C4
Ulungur He (riv.).....................C2
Ulungur Hu (lake)...................C2
Ussuri (Wusuli Jiang) (riv.)....M2
Wei He (riv.)...........................G5
Wu Jiang (riv.)........................G6
Wusuli Jiang (Ussuri) (riv.)....M2
Wuyi Shan (range)..................J6
Xar Moron He (riv.).................J3
Xiang Jiang (riv.)....................H6
Xi Jiang (riv.)..........................H7
Xinyi He (riv.)..........................J5
Yagradagzê Shan (mt.)...........D4
Yalong Jiang (riv.)...................F6
Yalu (riv.)................................L3
Yamzho Yumco (lake).............C6
Yangtze (Chang Jiang))
(riv.).......................................K5
Yarkant He (riv.).....................A4
Yellow (Huang He) (riv.)..........F5
Yellow (sea).............................K4
Yibug Caka (lake)....................C5
Yin Shan (mts.).......................G3
Yuan Jiang (riv.).....................H6
Yuhuan (isl.)...........................K6
Yurungkax He (riv.)................A4
Yü Shan (mt.)..........................K7
Yushan (isls.)..........................K6
Za Qu (riv.).............................E5
Zhari Namco (lake).................C5
Zhaxi Co (lake)........................C5
Zhoushan (arch.).....................K5

MONGOLIA

PROVINCES

Arhangay 90,500.....................F2
Bayamhongor 64,900..............E2
Bayan-Ölgiy 73,300................C2
Bulgan 45,700.........................F2
Dornod 51,100........................H2
Dornogovĭ 36,400...................G3
Dundgovĭ 37,800....................G2
Dzavhan 87,600......................E2
Govĭ-Altay 59,200...................E3
Hentiy 49,900.........................H2
Hovd 68,300............................D2
Hövsgöl 89,600........................E1
Ömnögovĭ 32,200....................F3
Övörhangay 84,100..................F2
Selenge 53,700........................G2
Sühbaatar 44,100....................H2
Töv 74,900..............................G2
Uvs 76,300.............................D2

CITIES and TOWNS

Altay 10,000............................E2
Arvayheer 9,100......................F2
Baatsagaan 800.......................E2
Baruun-Urt 8,200....................H2
Bayandalay 500.......................F3
Bayangovĭ 400.........................F3
Bayanhongor 11,300...............E2
Bayan-Öndör 300....................E3
Bayan-Uul 1,200......................E2
Beger 800................................E2
Bulgan, Bulgan 9,800..............F2
Bulgan, Hovd 700....................F3
Bulgan, Ömnögovĭ 3,100........D2
Bürentsogt 3,000.....................H2
Chandmanĭ 700.......................E2
Choybalsan 31,000..................J2
Dalandzadgad 6,600...............G3
Darhan (Darkhan) 56,400.......G2
Dashbalbar 1,100....................H2
Dashinchilen 600.....................F2
Dzamïn Üüd 1,500..................H3
Dzüünharaa 8,100...................G2
Dzuunmod 38,700...................G2
Erdenetsagaan 1,500...............J2
Hanh 500.................................F1
Hatgal 5,000............................E1
Hovd (Kobdo Jirgalanta)
12,400.....................................D2
Hyargas 1,600.........................D2
Jibhalanta (Uliastay) 13,000...E2
Kobdo (Hovd) 12,400.............D2
Mandalgovĭ 7,000...................G2
Mörön (Muren) 10,700...........F2
Nalayh (Nalaikha) 14,000.......G2
Ölgiy (Ulegei) 11,700..............C2
Öndörhaan (Undur Khan)
7,900.......................................G2
Onon 2,600..............................H2
Saynshand 10,000...................H3
Selenge 1,300.........................F2
Sühbaatar (Sukhe Bator)
35,000.....................................G1
Tsagaan-Ovoo 900..................H2
Tsagaannuur 2,000.................C2
Tsagaan-Uul 1,700..................E2
Tsetseg 700.............................D2
Tsetserleg 12,400....................F2
Ulaanbaatar (Ulan Bator)
(cap.) 435,400........................G2
Ulaangom (Ulangom) 14,000.D2
Ulegei (Ölgiy) 11,700..............C2
Uliastay (Jibhalanta) 13,000...E2
Urga (Ulaanbaatar) (cap.)
435,400...................................G2

OTHER FEATURES

Altai (mts.)..............................C2
Dörgön Nuur (lake).................D2
Dzavhan Gol (riv.)...................D2
Ghenghis Khan Wall (ruins)....H2
Gobi (des.)...............................G3
Hangayn Nuruu (mts.)............E2
Har Us Nuur (lake)..................D2
Herlen Gol (Kerulen) (riv.)......H2
Hovd Gol (riv.)........................D2
Hövsgöl Nuur (lake)................F1
Hyargas Nuur (lake)................D2
Ider Gol (riv.)..........................E2
Karakorum (ruins)...................F2
Kerulen (riv.)...........................H2
Munku-Sardyk (mt.)................F1
Orhon Gol (riv.)......................F2
Selenge Mörön (riv.)...............G2
Tannu-Ola (range)..................D1
Tavan Bogd Uul (mt.).............C2
Uvs Nuur (lake)......................D1

*City and suburbs.

† Populations of mainland cities, excluding Peking (Beijing), Shanghai and Tianjin (Tientsin), courtesy of Kingsley Davis, Office of Int'l Pop. and Research, Inst. of Int'l Studies Univ. of California.

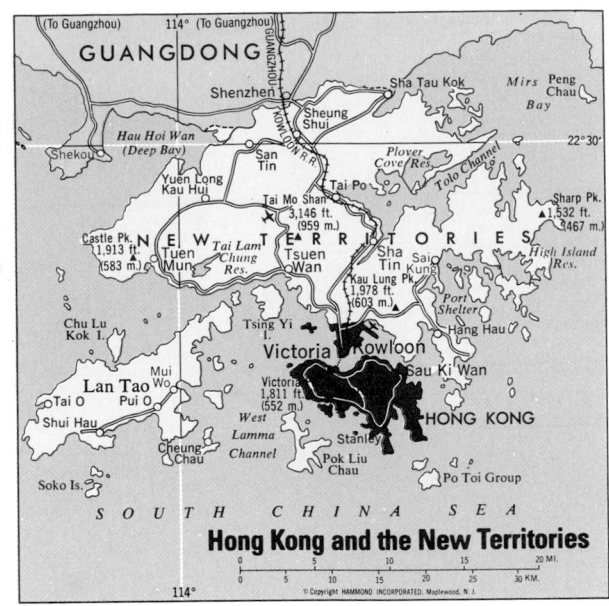

Hong Kong and the New Territories
GUANGDONG
(To Guangzhou)
Shenzhen
Sha Tau Kok
Mirs Bay
Sheung Shui
Hau Hoi Wan (Deep Bay)
San Tin
Yuen Long
Kau Hui
Tai Po
NEW TERRITORIES
Tuen Mun
Tsuen Wan
Sha Tin
Lan Tao
Victoria
Kowloon
HONG KONG
SOUTH CHINA SEA
© Copyright HAMMOND INCORPORATED, Maplewood, N. J.

Agriculture, Industry and Resources

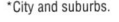

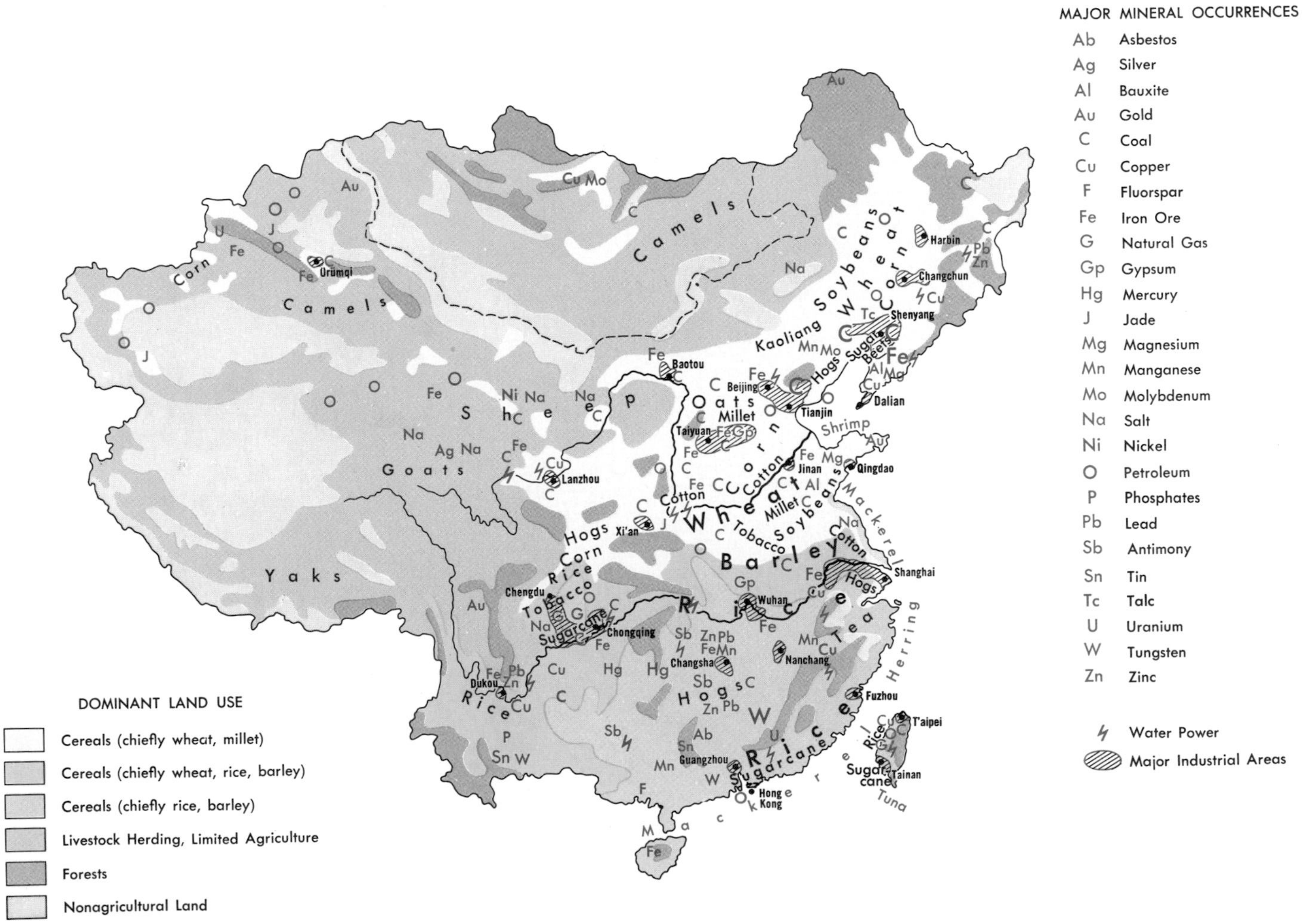

MAJOR MINERAL OCCURRENCES
Ab Asbestos
Ag Silver
Al Bauxite
Au Gold
C Coal
Cu Copper
F Fluorspar
Fe Iron Ore
G Natural Gas
Gp Gypsum
Hg Mercury
J Jade
Mg Magnesium
Mn Manganese
Mo Molybdenum
Na Salt
Ni Nickel
O Petroleum
P Phosphates
Pb Lead
Sb Antimony
Sn Tin
Tc Talc
U Uranium
W Tungsten
Zn Zinc
Water Power
Major Industrial Areas
DOMINANT LAND USE
Cereals (chiefly wheat, millet)
Cereals (chiefly wheat, rice, barley)
Cereals (chiefly rice, barley)
Livestock Herding, Limited Agriculture
Forests
Nonagricultural Land
Harbin
Changchun
Shenyang
Ürümqi
Baotou
Beijing
Tianjin
Dalian
Taiyuan
Jinan
Qingdao
Lanzhou
Xi'an
Shanghai
Chengdu
Wuhan
Chongqing
Changsha
Nanchang
Fuzhou
T'aipei
Tainan
Dukou
Guangzhou
Hong Kong

AREA 145,730 sq. mi. (377,441 sq. km.)
POPULATION 123,116,000
CAPITAL Tokyo
LARGEST CITY Tokyo
HIGHEST POINT Fuji 12,389 ft. (3,776 m.)
MONETARY UNIT yen
MAJOR LANGUAGE Japanese
MAJOR RELIGIONS Buddhism, Shintoism

AREA 46,540 sq. mi. (120,539 sq. km.)
POPULATION 22,419,000
CAPITAL P'yŏngyang
LARGEST CITY P'yŏngyang
HIGHEST POINT Paektu 9,003 ft. (2,744 m.)
MONETARY UNIT won
MAJOR LANGUAGE Korean
MAJOR RELIGIONS Confucianism, Buddhism, Ch'ondogyo

AREA 38,175 sq. mi. (98,873 sq. km.)
POPULATION 42,793,000
CAPITAL Seoul
LARGEST CITY Seoul
HIGHEST POINT Halla 6,398 ft. (1,950 m.)
MONETARY UNIT won
MAJOR LANGUAGE Korean
MAJOR RELIGIONS Confucianism, Buddhism, Ch'ondogyo, Christianity

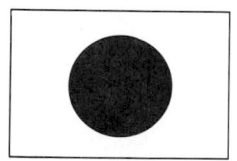

JAPAN

NORTH KOREA

SOUTH KOREA

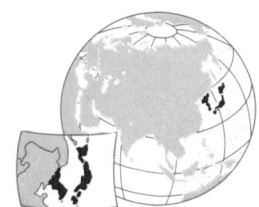

JAPAN

PREFECTURES

Aichi 6,221,638 ....H6
Akita 1,256,745 ....J4
Aomori 1,523,907 ....K3
Chiba 4,735,424 ....P2
Ehime 1,506,637 ....F7
Fukui 794,354 ....G5
Fukuoka 4,553,461 ....D7
Fukushima 2,035,272 ....K5
Gifu 1,960,107 ....H6
Gumma 1,848,562 ....J5
Hiroshima 2,739,161 ....E6
Hokkaido 5,575,989 ....K2
Hyogo 5,144,892 ....H7
Ibaraki 2,558,007 ....K5
Ishikawa 1,119,304 ....H5
Iwate 1,421,927 ....K4
Kagawa 999,864 ....G6
Kagoshima 1,784,623 ....E8
Kanagawa 6,924,348 ....O2
Kochi 831,275 ....F7
Kumamoto 1,790,327 ....E7
Kyoto 2,527,330 ....J7
Mie 1,686,936 ....H6
Miyagi 2,082,320 ....K5
Miyazaki 1,151,587 ....E8
Nagano 2,083,934 ....J5

Nagasaki 1,590,564 ....D7
Nara 1,209,365 ....J8
Niigata 2,451,357 ....J5
Oita 1,228,913 ....E7
Okayama 1,871,023 ....F6
Okinawa 1,106,559 ....N6
Osaka 8,473,446 ....J8
Saga 865,574 ....E7
Saitama 5,420,480 ....O2
Shiga 1,079,898 ....J7
Shimane 784,795 ....F6
Shizuoka 3,446,804 ....H6
Tochigi 1,792,201 ....K5
Tokushima 825,261 ....G7
Tokyo 11,618,281 ....O2
Tottori 604,221 ....G6
Toyama 1,103,459 ....H5
Wakayama 1,087,012 ....G6
Yamagata 1,251,917 ....K4
Yamaguchi 1,587,079 ....E6
Yamanashi 804,256 ....J6

CITIES and TOWNS

Abashiri 44,777 ....M1
Ageo 166,243 ....O2
Aizuwakamatsu 114,528 ....J5
Akashi 254,869 ....H8
Akita 284,863 ....J4
Amagasaki 523,650 ....H8

Amagi 42,863 ....E7
Anan 61,253 ....G7
Aomori 287,594 ....K3
Asahi 35,721 ....K6
Asahikawa 352,619 ....L2
Ashikaga 165,756 ....J5
Ashiya 81,745 ....H8
Atami 50,082 ....J6
Atsugi 145,392 ....O2
Ayabe 42,552 ....G6
Beppu 136,485 ....E7
Chiba 746,430 ....P2
Chichibu 61,285 ....O3
Chigasaki 171,016 ....O3
Chitose 66,788 ....K2
Chofu 180,548 ....O2
Choshi 89,416 ....K6
Daito 116,635 ....J8
Ebetsu 86,349 ....K2
Eniwa 42,911 ....K2
Fuji 205,761 ....J6
Fujieda 103,225 ....J6
Fujisawa 300,248 ....O3
Fukagawa 35,376 ....L2
Fukuchiyama 63,788 ....G6
Fukue 32,135 ....D7
Fukui 240,962 ....G5
Fukuoka 1,088,588 ....D7

Fukushima 262,837 ....K5
Fukuyama 346,030 ....F6
Funabashi 479,439 ....P2
Furukawa 57,060 ....K5
Gifu 410,357 ....H6
Goshogawara 50,632 ....K3
Habikino 103,181 ....J8
Hachinohe 238,179 ....K3
Hachioji 387,178 ....O2
Hadano 123,133 ....O2
Hagi 53,693 ....E6
Hakodate 320,154 ....K3
Hamada 50,799 ....E6
Hamamatsu 490,824 ....H6
Hanamaki 68,873 ....K4
Hanno 61,179 ....O2
Haramachi 46,052 ....K5
Higashiosaka 521,558 ....J8
Hikone 89,701 ....H6
Himeji 446,256 ....H7
Himi 62,413 ....H5
Hino 145,448 ....O2
Hirakata 353,358 ....J7
Hiratsuka 214,293 ....O3
Hirosaki 175,330 ....K3
Hiroshima 899,399 ....E6
Hitachi 204,596 ....K5
Hitoyoshi 42,236 ....E7
Hofu 111,468 ....E6
Hondo 42,460 ....E7

Honjo 42,962 ....J4
Hyuga 58,347 ....E7
Ichihara 216,394 ....P3
Ibaraki 234,062 ....J7
Ichikawa 364,244 ....P2
Ichinomiya 253,139 ....H6
Ichinoseki 60,214 ....K4
Iida 78,515 ....H6
Iizuka 80,288 ....E7
Ikeda 101,121 ....H7
Ikoma 70,461 ....J8
Imabari 123,234 ....F6
Imari 61,243 ....D7
Ina 56,086 ....H6
Isahaya 83,723 ....D7
Ise 105,621 ....H6
Ishinomaki 120,699 ....K4
Ishioka 47,829 ....K5
Itami 178,228 ....H7
Ito 69,638 ....J6
Itoman 42,239 ....N6
Iwaki 342,074 ....K5
Iwakuni 112,525 ....E6
Iwamizawa 78,311 ....L2
Iwata 75,810 ....H6
Iwatsuki 94,696 ....O2
Izumi 121,323 ....J8
Izumiotsu 67,474 ....J8
Izumisano 90,684 ....G6
Izumo 77,303 ....F6

Joetsu 127,842 ....H5
Joyo 74,350 ....J7
Kadoma 138,902 ....J7
Kaga 65,282 ....H5
Kagoshima 505,360 ....E8
Kaizuka 81,162 ....H8
Kakogawa 212,233 ....G6
Kamaishi 65,250 ....L4
Kamakura 172,629 ....O3
Kameoka 69,410 ....J7
Kanazawa 417,684 ....H5
Kanonji 44,927 ....F6
Kanoya 73,242 ....E8
Kanuma 85,159 ....J5
Karatsu 77,710 ....D7
Kaseda 25,392 ....D8
Kashihara 107,316 ....J8
Kashiwa 239,198 ....P2
Kashiwara 69,836 ....J8
Kashiwazaki 83,499 ....J5
Kasugai 244,119 ....H6
Kasukabe 155,555 ....O2
Katsuta 92,621 ....K5
Kawachinagano 78,572 ....J8
Kawagoe 259,314 ....O2
Kawaguchi 379,360 ....O2
Kawanishi 129,834 ....H7
Kawasaki 1,040,802 ....O2
Kesennuma 68,551 ....K4
Kimitsu 77,286 ....O3

Kiryu 132,889 ....J5
Kisarazu 110,711 ....P3
Kishiwada 180,317 ....J8
Kitaibaraki 47,670 ....K5
Kitakami 53,647 ....K4
Kitakyushu 1,065,078 ....E6
Kitami 102,915 ....L2
Kobayashi 40,033 ....E8
Kobe 1,367,390 ....H7
Kochi 300,822 ....F7
Kodaira 154,610 ....O2
Kofu 199,262 ....J6
Koga 56,657 ....J5
Koganei 102,456 ....O2
Komatsu 104,329 ....H5
Koriyama 286,451 ....K5
Koshigaya 223,241 ....P2
Kuki 54,410 ....O2
Kumagaya 136,806 ....J5
Kumamoto 525,662 ....E7
Kurashiki 403,785 ....F6
Kurayoshi 52,270 ....F6
Kure 234,549 ....F6
Kuroiso 46,574 ....K5
Kurume 216,972 ....E7
Kushiro 214,694 ....M2
Kyoto 1,473,065 ....J7
Machida 295,405 ....O2
Maebashi 265,169 ....J5
Maizuru 97,578 ....G6
Masuda 52,756 ....E6
Matsubara 135,849 ....H8
Matsudo 400,863 ....P2
Matsue 135,568 ....F6
Matsumoto 192,085 ....H5
Matsusaka 113,481 ....H6
Matsuto 43,766 ....H5
Matsuyama 401,703 ....F7
Mihara 84,450 ....F6
Miki 70,201 ....H7
Minoo 104,112 ....J7
Mitaka 164,526 ....O2
Mito 215,566 ....K5
Mitsukaido 40,435 ....P2
Miura 48,687 ....O3
Miyako 62,478 ....L4
Miyakonojo 129,009 ....E8
Miyazaki 264,855 ....E8
Mizusawa 55,226 ....K4
Mobara 71,521 ....K6
Mooka 52,764 ....K5
Moriguchi 165,630 ....J7
Morioka 229,114 ....K4
Muko 50,604 ....J7
Muroran 150,199 ....K2
Musashino 136,910 ....O2
Mutsu 47,610 ....K3
Nagahama 54,935 ....H6
Nagano 324,360 ....J5
Nagaoka 180,259 ....J5
Nagaokakyo 71,445 ....J7
Nagasaki 447,091 ....D7
Nago 45,991 ....N6
Nagoya 2,087,902 ....H6
Naha 295,778 ....N6
Nakatsu 63,941 ....E7
Nanao 50,394 ....H5
Nankoku 44,866 ....F7
Nara 297,953 ....J8
Narashino 125,155 ....P2
Naze 49,021 ....O5
Nemuro 42,880 ....M2
Neyagawa 255,859 ....J7
Nichinan 52,949 ....E8
Niigata 457,785 ....J5
Niihama 132,339 ....F6
Niitsu 62,282 ....J5
Nishinomiya 410,329 ....H8
Nobeoka 136,598 ....E7
Noboribetsu 56,503 ....K2
Noda 93,958 ....P2
Nogata 62,595 ....E7
Noshiro 60,674 ....J3
Noto 15,480 ....H5
Numata 47,150 ....J5
Numazu 203,695 ....J6
Obihiro 153,861 ....L2
Oda 38,026 ....F6

(continued on following page)

Agriculture, Industry and Resources

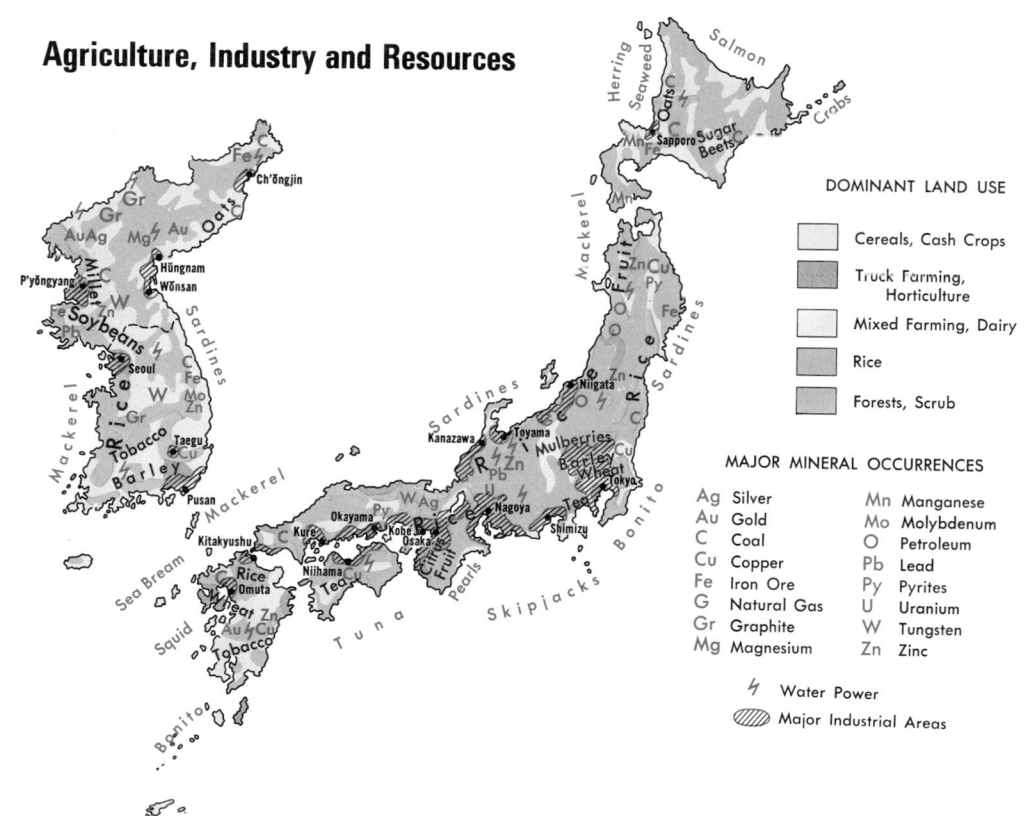

DOMINANT LAND USE

- Cereals, Cash Crops
- Truck Farming, Horticulture
- Mixed Farming, Dairy
- Rice
- Forests, Scrub

MAJOR MINERAL OCCURRENCES

Ag	Silver	Mn	Manganese
Au	Gold	Mo	Molybdenum
C	Coal	O	Petroleum
Cu	Copper	Pb	Lead
Fe	Iron Ore	Py	Pyrites
G	Natural Gas	U	Uranium
Gr	Graphite	W	Tungsten
Mg	Magnesium	Zn	Zinc

⚡ Water Power

▨ Major Industrial Areas

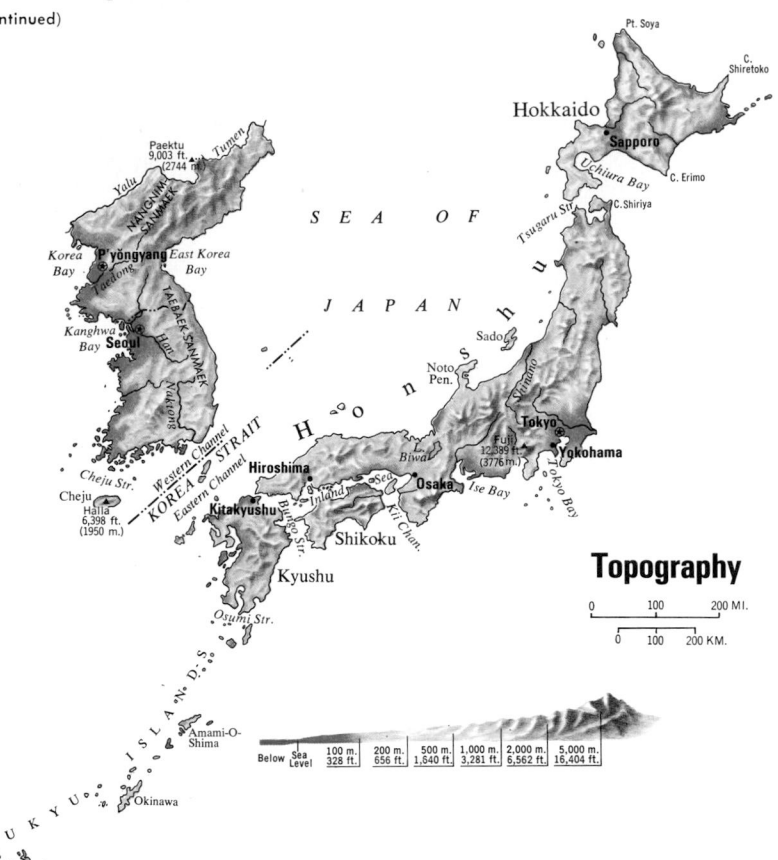

Topography

Below Sea Level | 100 m. 328 ft. | 200 m. 656 ft. | 500 m. 1,640 ft. | 1,000 m. 3,281 ft. | 2,000 m. 6,562 ft. | 5,000 m. 16,404 ft.

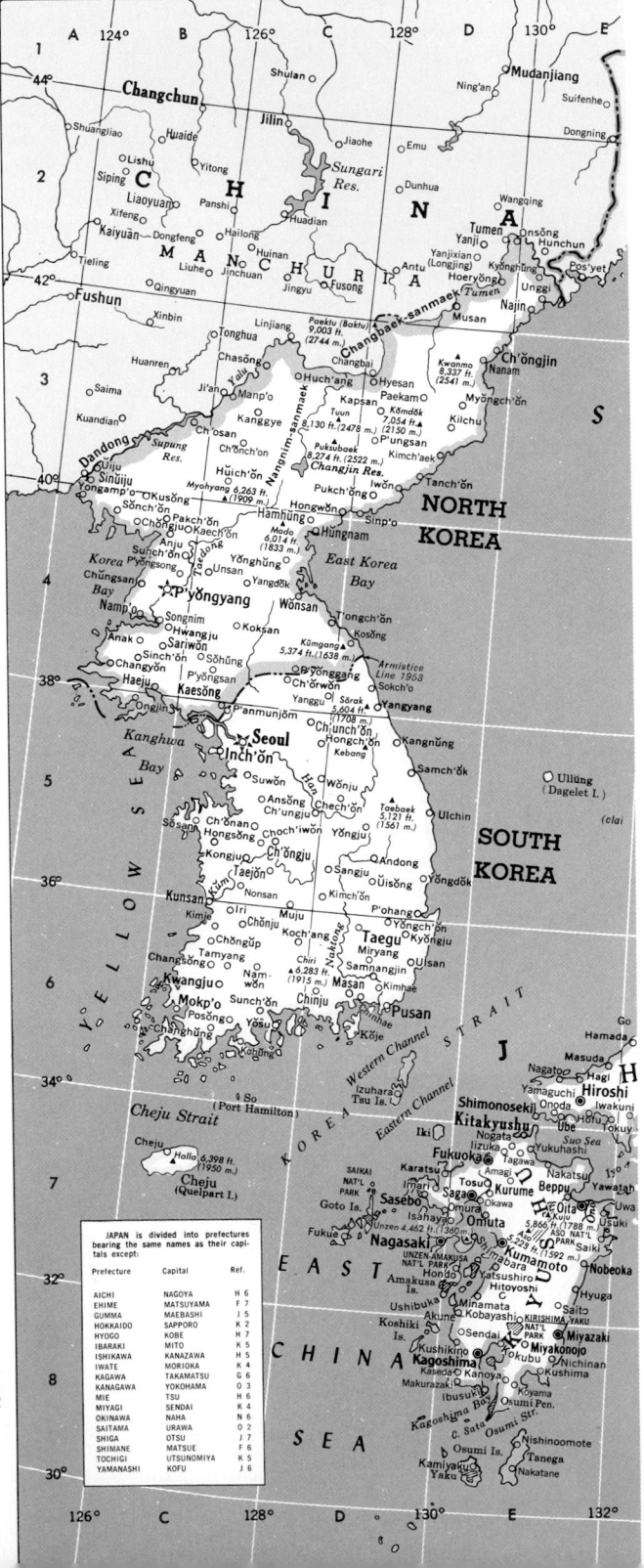

Sata (cape)....E8
Shikoku (isl.)....F7
Shikotan (isl.)....N2
Shikotsu (lake)....K2
Shimane (pen.)....F6
Shimokita (pen.)....K3
Shinano (riv.)....J5
Shiono (cape)....H7
Shiragami (cape)....J3
Shirane (mt.)....H6
Shiretoko (cape)....M1
Shiriya (cape)....K3
Soya (pt.)....L1
Suo (sea)....E7
Suruga (bay)....J6
Suzu (pt.)....H5
Takeshima (isls.)....F5
Tanega (isl.)....E8
Tappi (cape)....K3
Teshio (riv.)....L1

Tokachi (riv.)....L2
Tokachi (mt.)....L2
Tokara (isls.)....O5
Tokuno (isls.)....O5
Tokyo (bay)....O2
Tone (riv.)....K6
Tosa (bay)....F7
Towada (lake)....K3
Toya (lake)....K2
Toyama (bay)....H5
Tsu (isls.)....D6
Tsugaru (strait)....K3
Tsurugi (mt.)....G7
Uchiura (bay)....K2
Volcano (isls.)....M4
Wakasa (bay)....G6
Western Channel (strait)....D6
Yaeyama (isls.)....K7
Yaku (isl.)....E8
Yonaguni (isl.)....K7

Odate 72,478....K3
Odawara 177,467....J6
Ofunato 40,023....K4
Oga 38,940....J4
Ogaki 143,151....H6
Oita 360,478....E7
Ojiya 44,963....J5
Okawa 49,537....E7
Okaya 62,210....H5
Okayama 545,765....F6
Okazaki 262,372....H6
Omagari 41,764....K4
Omiya 354,084....O2
Omura 65,638....E7
Omuta 163,000....E7
Onagawa 16,105....H6
Ono 41,901....E6
Onoda 44,803....E6
Onomichi 102,056....F6
Osaka 2,648,180....J8
Ota 123,115....J5
Otaru 180,728....K2
Otawara 46,662....K5
Otofuke 31,134....L2
Oyabe 36,497....H5
Oyama 127,226....J5
Ozu 38,719....F7
Rumoi 36,626....K2
Ryugasaki 43,132....P2
Sabae 59,579....H5
Saga 163,765....E7
Sagamihara 439,300....O2
Saiki 54,306....E7
Saito 37,836....E7
Sakado 77,335....O2
Sakai 810,106....J8
Sakaide 66,290....G6
Sakaiminato 37,278....F6
Sakata 102,600....J4
Saku 57,361....J5
Sakurai 56,439....J8
Sanda 36,529....H7
Sanjo 85,275....J5
Sapporo 1,401,757....K2
Sasebo 251,187....D7
Satte 49,704....O1
Sawara 49,200....K6
Sayama 124,029....O2
Sendai, Kagoshima 65,645....E8
Sendai, Miyagi 664,868....K4
Shibata 76,209....J5
Shimabara 46,637....E7
Shimizu 241,576....J6
Shimonoseki 268,957....E6
Shingu 39,993....H7
Shinjo 42,911....K4
Shiogama 61,040....K4
Shirakawa 43,187....K5
Shiroishi 41,275....K4
Shizuoka 458,341....H6
Soka 186,618....O2
Suita 348,185....J8
Sukagawa 57,110....K5
Sumoto 44,131....G6

Suwa 50,558....H6
Suzuka 156,250....H6
Tachikawa 142,675....O2
Tagawa 60,077....E7
Tajimi 74,311....H6
Takaishi 66,815....H8
Takamatsu 316,661....F6
Takaoka 175,055....H5
Takarazuka 183,628....H7
Takasaki 221,429....J5
Takatsuki 340,720....J7
Takayama 63,813....H5
Takefu 67,104....G6
Takikawa 51,192....K2
Tanabe, Kyoto 39,198....J7
Tanabe, Wakayama 69,575....G7
Tateyama 56,257....K6
Tendo 52,597....K4
Tenri 64,894....J8
Teshio 6,281....K1
Togane 35,603....K6
Tokamachi 49,555....J5
Tokorozawa 236,476....O2
Tokushima 249,343....G7
Tokuyama 111,469....E6
Tokyo (cap.) 8,351,893....O2
Tokyo* 11,618,281....O2
Tomakomai 151,967....K2
Tondabayashi 97,495....J8
Tosu 54,254....E7
Tottori 131,060....G6
Towada 58,886....K3
Toyama 305,055....H5
Toyohashi 304,273....H6
Toyonaka 403,174....J7
Toyooka 47,458....G6
Toyota 281,608....H6
Tsu 144,991....H6
Tsubame 44,236....J5
Tsuchiura 112,517....K5
Tsuruga 61,844....G6
Tsuruoka 99,751....J4
Tsuyama 83,136....F6
Ube 168,958....E6
Ueda 111,540....J5
Uji 152,692....J7
Uozu 49,512....H5
Urawa 358,185....O2
Utsunomiya 377,746....K5
Uwajima 71,586....F7
Wajima 32,662....H5
Wakayama 400,802....G6
Wakkanai 53,471....K1
Warabi 70,876....O2
Yaizu 104,363....J6
Yamagata 237,041....K4
Yamaguchi 114,744....E6
Yamato 167,935....O2
Yamatokoriyama 81,266....J8
Yamatotakada 61,711....J8
Yao 272,706....J8
Yatsushiro 108,194....E7
Yawata 64,882....J7
Yawatahama 43,823....F7

Yokkaichi 255,442....H6
Yokohama 2,773,674....O3
Yokosuka 421,107....O3
Yokote 43,773....K4
Yonago 127,374....F6
Yonezawa 92,823....K5
Yono 72,326....O2
Yubari 41,715....L2
Yukuhashi 61,838....E7
Yuzawa 37,800....K4
Zushi 58,479....O3

OTHER FEATURES

Agano (riv.)....J4
Akan National Park....M2
Amakusa (isls.)....D7
Amami (isls.)....N5
Amami-O-Shima (isl.)....N5
Asahi (mt.)....J4
Asama (mt.)....J5
Ashizuri (cape)....F7
Aso (mt.)....E7
Atsumi (bay)....H6
Awaji (isl.)....H8
Bandai (mt.)....K5
Biwa (lake)....H6
Bonin (isls.)....M3
Boso (pen.)....K6
Bungo (strait)....F7
Chichi (isl.)....M3
Daio (cape)....H6
Daisetsu (mt.)....L2
Dogo (isl.)....F5
Dozen (isls.)....F5
East China (sea)....D8
Eastern Channel (strait)....D7
Erimo (cape)....L3
Etorofu (isl.)....N1
Fuji (mt.)....J6
Fuji (riv.)....J6
Fuji-Hakone-Izu Nat'l Park....J6
Gassan (mt.)....J4
Goto (isls.)....D7
Habomai (isls.)....N2
Hachijo (mts.)....J3
Haha (isl.)....M3
Hakken (isl.)....H6
Haku (mt.)....H5
Harima (bay)....F7
Hida (riv.)....H6
Hidaka (mt.)....L2
Hodaka (mt.)....H5
Hokkaido (isl.)....L2
Honshu (isl.)....J5
Ie (isl.)....N6
Iki (isl.)....D7
Inawashiro (lake)....K5
Inubo (cape)....K6
Iriomote (isl.)....K7
Iro (cape)....J6
Ise (bay)....H6
Ishigaki (isl.)....L7
Ishikari (riv.)....L2
Ishikari (bay)....K2

Iwaki (mt.)....K3
Iwate (mt.)....K4
Iwo Jima (isl.)....M4
Iwo Jima (isl.)....M4
Iyo (sea)....E7
Izu (isls.)....J6
Izu (pen.)....J6
Japan (sea)....G4
Kagoshima (bay)....E8
Kamui (cape)....K2
Kasumiga (lagoon)....K5
Kazan-retto (Volcano) (isls.)....M4
Kii (chan.)....G7
Kikai (isl.)....O5
Kita Iwo (isl.)....M4
Kitakami (riv.)....K4
Kitakami (mt.)....K2
Komaga (mt.)....K2
Kuju (mt.)....E7
Kuma (riv.)....M6
Kunashiri (isl.)....M1
Kutcharo (lake)....M2
Kyushu (isl.)....E7
Meakan (mt.)....L2
Minami Iwo (isl.)....M5
Miyako (isls.)....L7
Mogami (riv.)....K4
Muko (isl.)....M3
Muroto (pt.)....G7
Mutsu (bay)....K3
Nampo-Shoto (isls.)....M3
Nansei Shoto (Ryukyu) (isls.)....J5
Nantai (mt.)....J5
Nasu (mt.)....J5
Nemuro (strait)....M1
Nii (isl.)....J6
Nikko National Park....J5
Nojima (cape)....K6
Noto (pen.)....H5
Nyudo (cape)....J4
Oga (pen.)....J4
Ogasawara-gunto (Bonin) (isls.)....M3
Okhotsk (sea)....M1
Oki (isls.)....F5
Okinawa (isl.)....N6
Okinawa (isls.)....N6
Okinoerabu (isl.)....N5
Okushiri (isl.)....J2
Oma (cape)....K3
Omono (riv.)....J4
Ono (riv.)....E7
Ontake (mt.)....H6
Osaka (bay)....H8
O-Shima (isl.)....J6
Osumi (isls.)....E8
Osumi (strait)....E8
Otakine (mt.)....K5
Rebun (isl.)....K1
Rishiri (isl.)....K1
Ryukyu (isls.)....L7
Sado (isl.)....J4
Sagami (bay)....O3
Sagami (sea)....J6
Sakishima (isls.)....K7

JAPAN is divided into prefectures bearing the same names as their capitals except:

Prefecture	Capital	Ref.
AICHI	NAGOYA	H 6
EHIME	MATSUYAMA	F 7
GUMMA	MAEBASHI	J 5
HOKKAIDO	SAPPORO	K 2
HYOGO	KOBE	H 7
IBARAKI	MITO	K 5
ISHIKAWA	KANAZAWA	H 5
IWATE	MORIOKA	K 4
KAGAWA	TAKAMATSU	G 6
KANAGAWA	YOKOHAMA	O 3
MIE	TSU	H 6
MIYAGI	SENDAI	K 4
OKINAWA	NAHA	N 6
SAITAMA	URAWA	O 2
SHIGA	OTSU	J 7
SHIMANE	MATSUE	F 6
TOCHIGI	UTSUNOMIYA	J 5
YAMANASHI	KOFU	J 6

Yoshino (riv.)..................G6

KOREA (NORTH)

CITIES and TOWNS

Anju..................B4
Ch'ŏngjin 306,000..................E3
Ch'osan..................C3
Changyŏn..................B4
Chasŏng..................C3
Chŏngju..................B4
Haeju 140,000..................B4
Hamhŭng 484,000..................C4
Heiju (P'yŏngyang) (cap.)
1,250,000..................C4
Hongwŏn..................C3
Hŭich'ŏn..................C3
Hŭngnam..................C4
Hyesan..................D3

Kaesŏng 175,000..................C4
Kapsan..................C3
Kimch'aek 100,000..................D3
Koksan..................C4
Kosŏng..................B4
Kusŏng..................B4
Manp'o..................C3
Musan..................D2
Najin..................E2
Nampo 140,000..................B4
Nanam..................D3
Ongjin..................B5
P'anmunjŏm..................C5
P'ungsan..................D3
P'yŏngyang (cap.)
1,250,000..................C4
Pukch'ŏng..................C3
Sariwŏn..................C4
Sinp'o..................D4

Sinŭiju 300,000..................B3
Sŏhŭng..................C4
Sŏnch'ŏn..................B4
Songnim..................C4
Tanch'ŏn..................D3
T'ongch'ŏn..................D4
Ŭiju..................B3
Unggi..................E2
Unsan..................C4
Wŏnsan 275,000..................C4
Yangdŏk..................C4
Yŏnghŭng..................C4
Yongamp'o..................B4

OTHER FEATURES

Baktu (Paektu) (mt.)..................C3
Changbaek-sanmaek (mts.)..................D2
Changjin (res.)..................C3

East Korea (bay)..................D4
Japan (sea)..................G4
Kanghwa (bay)..................B5
Korea (bay)..................B4
Kwanmo (mt.)..................D3
Nangnim-sanmaek (range)..................C3
Paektu (mt.)..................C3
Puksubaek (mt.)..................C3
Supung (res.)..................B3
Taedong (riv.)..................C4
Tumen (riv.)..................D2
Yalu (riv.)..................C3
Yellow (sea)..................B6

KOREA (SOUTH)

CITIES and TOWNS

Andong 102,024..................D5
Chech'ŏn 74,239..................D5

Cheju 167,546..................C7
Chinhae 112,098..................D6
Chinju 202,753..................D6
Ch'ŏnan 120,618..................C5
Ch'ŏngju 252,985..................C5
Chŏngŭp 54,864..................C6
Chŏnju 366,997..................C6
Ch'unch'ŏn 155,247..................D5
Ch'ungju 113,138..................C5
Inch'ŏn 1,084,730..................C5
Iri 145,358..................C6
Kangnŭng 116,903..................D5
Kimch'ŏn 72,229..................C5
Kimhae 203,428..................D6
Kimje 221,414..................C6
Kohŭng 217,446..................C6
Kongju 39,756..................C5
Kunsan 165,318..................C6
Kwangju 727,627..................C6
Kyŏngju 122,038..................D6

Masan 386,773..................D6
Miryang 42,951..................D6
Mokp'o 221,856..................C6
Namwŏn 50,867..................C6
Nonsan 226,429..................C5
P'anmunjŏm..................C5
P'ohang 201,355..................D5
Pusan 3,160,276..................D6
Samch'ŏk 42,526..................D5
Sangju 52,839..................D5
Seoul (cap.) 8,366,756..................C5
Sokch'o 65,798..................D4
Sŏsan 38,081..................C5
Sunch'ŏn 114,223..................C6
Suwŏn 310,757..................C5
Taegu 1,607,458..................D6
Taejŏn 651,642..................C5
Ulsan 418,415..................D6
Wŏnju 136,961..................D5
Yanggu 277,986..................C4

Yŏngch'ŏn 50,765..................D6
Yŏngju 77,890..................D5
Yŏsu 161,009..................C6

OTHER FEATURES

Cheju (isl.)..................C7
Dagelet (Ullŭng) (isl.)..................E5
East China (sea)..................C8
Halla (mt.)..................C7
Han (riv.)..................C5
Japan (sea)..................G4
Kanghwa (bay)..................B5
Kŏje (isl.)..................D6
Korea (strait)..................D6
Naktong (riv.)..................D6
Quelpart (Cheju)..................C7
Ullŭng (isl.)..................E5
Yellow (sea)..................B6

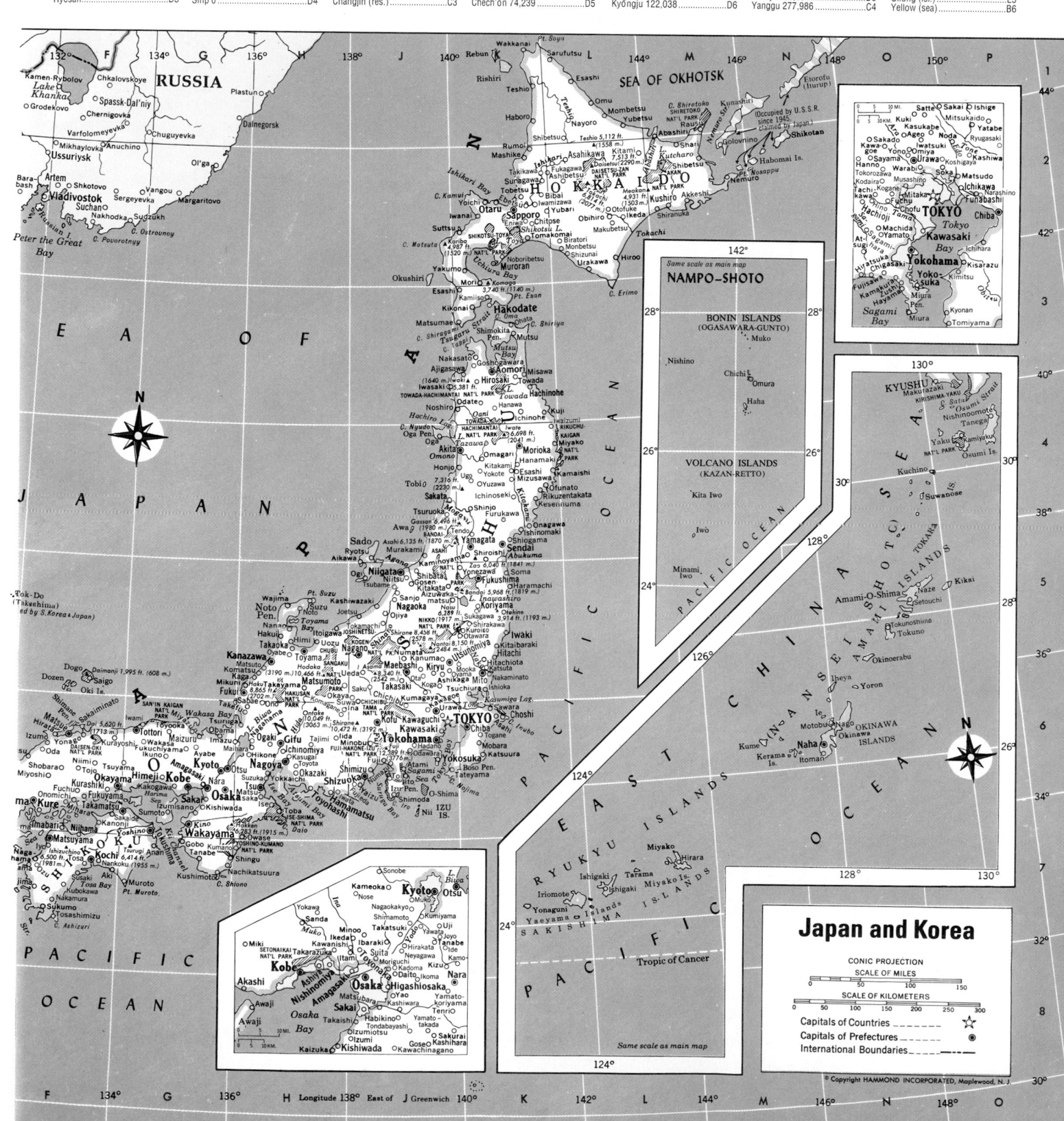

Japan and Korea — CONIC PROJECTION

Philippines

POLYCONIC PROJECTION

SCALE OF MILES
0 10 20 40 60 80 100

SCALE OF KILOMETERS
0 25 50 75 100 150

Capitals of Countries _____ ☆
Provincial Capitals _____ △
Provincial Boundaries _____·_·_

© Copyright HAMMOND INCORPORATED, Maplewood, N.J.

PROVINCES

Abra 160,198 C2
Agusan del Norte 365,421 E6
Agusan del Sur 631,634 E6
Aklan 324,563 D5
Albay 809,177 D4
Antique 344,879 D5
Aurora 107,145 C3
Basilan 201,407 D7
Bataan 323,254 C3
Batanes 12,091 A2
Batangas 1,174,201 C4
Benguet 354,751 C2
Bohol 806,031 E6
Bukidnon 631,634 E6
Bulacan 1,098,046 C3
Cagayan 711,476 C1
Camarines Norte 368,007 D3
Camarines Sur 1,099,346 D4
Camiguin 57,126 E6
Capiz 492,231 D5
Catanduanes 175,247 E4
Cavite 771,320 C3
Cebu 2,091,602 D5
Davao 725,153 E7
Davao del Sur 1,133,599 E7
Davao Oriental 339,931 F7
Eastern Samar 320,637 E5
Ifugao 111,368 C2
Ilocos Norte 390,666 C1
Ilocos Sur 443,591 C2
Iloilo 1,433,641 D5
Isabela 870,604 C2
Kalinga-Apayao 185,063 C1
Laguna 973,104 C3
Lanao del Norte 461,049 E6
Lanao del Sur 404,971 E7
La Union 452,578 C2
Leyte 1,302,648 E5
Maguindanao 536,546 E7
Manila 5,925,884 C3
Marinduque 173,715 C4
Masbate 584,526 D4
Misamis Occidental 386,328 D6
Misamis Oriental 690,032 E6
Mountain 103,052 C2
National Capital Region (Manila) 5,925,884 C3
Negros Occidental 1,930,301 D6
Negros Oriental 819,399 D6
North Cotabato 564,599 E7
Northern Samar 378,516 E4
Nueva Ecija 1,069,409 C3
Nueva Vizcaya 241,690 C2
Occidental Mindoro 222,431 C4
Oriental Mindoro 448,938 C4
Palawan 371,782 B6
Pampanga 1,181,590 C3
Pangasinan 1,636,057 C3
Quezon 1,129,277 C3
Quirino 83,230 C2
Rizal 555,533 C3
Romblon 193,174 D4
Siquijor 70,300 D6
Sorsogon 500,685 E4
South Cotabato 770,473 E7
Southern Leyte 298,294 E5
Sultan Kudarat 303,784 E7
Sulu 360,588 C7
Surigao del Norte 363,414 F5
Surigao del Sur 377,647 F6
Tarlac 638,457 C3
Tawi-Tawi 194,651 B8
Western Samar 501,439 E5
Zambales 444,037 C3
Zamboanga del Norte 588,015 D6
Zamboanga del Sur 1,183,845 D7

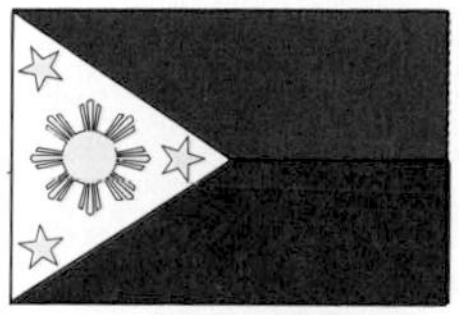

AREA 115,707 sq. mi. (299,681 sq. km.)
POPULATION 60,097,000
CAPITAL Manila
LARGEST CITY Manila
HIGHEST POINT Apo 9,692 ft. (2,954 m.)
MONETARY UNIT peso
MAJOR LANGUAGES Pilipino (Tagalog), English, Spanish, Bisayan, Ilocano, Bikol
MAJOR RELIGIONS Roman Catholicism, Islam, Protestantism, tribal religions

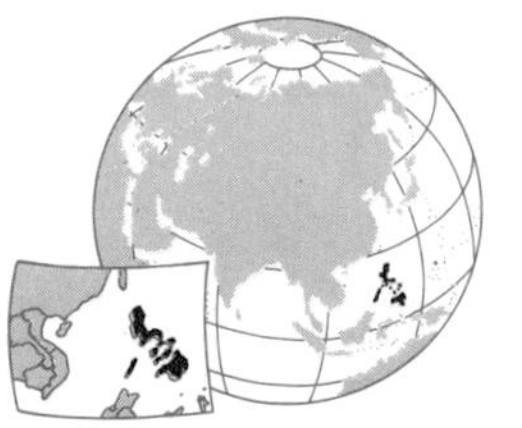

CITIES and TOWNS

Angeles 188,834 C3
Aparri 45,070 C1
Bacolod 262,415 D5
Bagac 13,109 C3
Bago 99,631 D5
Baguio 119,009 C2
Balanga 39,132 C3
Baler 18,349 C3
Balimbing (Bato-Bato) 22,189 C8
Bamban 26,072 C3
Basco 4,341 A2
Batangas 143,570 C4
Bato-Bato 22,189 C8
Baybay 74,640 E5
Bislig 81,615 F6
Boac 37,005 C4
Bontoc 17,091 C2
Burauen 48,058 E5
Butuan 172,489 E6
Cabanatuan 138,298 C3
Cabarroquis 17,450 C2
Cadiz 129,632 D5
Cagayan de Oro 227,312 E6
Calamba 121,175 C3
Calbayog 106,719 E4
Carigara 34,377 E5
Cauayan 70,017 D6
Cavite 87,666 C3
Cebu 490,281 D5
Cotabato 83,871 D7
Dagupan 98,344 C2
Davao 610,375 E7
Digos 70,065 E7
Escalante 71,293 D5
General Santos 149,396 E7
Gingoog 79,937 E6
Guihulngan 84,156 D5
Guimba 58,847 C3
Iba 22,791 B3
Ilagan 79,336 C2
Iligan 167,358 E6
Iloilo 244,827 D5
Infanta 27,914 C3
Jaro 29,739 E5
Jolo 52,429 C8
Koronadal 80,566 E7
Lagawe 15,075 C2
Lapu-Lapu 98,723 E5
Legazpi 99,766 D4
Ligao 69,860 D4
Lingayen 65,187 C2
Lipa 121,166 C4
Lucena 107,880 C4
Maganoy 45,845 E7
Mainit 18,078 E6
Malabang 18,955 D7
Malolos 95,699 C3
Mandaue 110,590 E5
Manila (cap.) 1,630,485 C3
Mariveles 48,594 C3
Mati 78,178 F7
Naga 90,712 D4
Olongapo 156,430 C3
Ormoc 104,978 E5
Ozamis 77,832 D6
Pagadian 80,861 D7
Palo 31,124 E5
Palompon 40,242 E5
Panabo 71,098 E7
Prosperidad 33,824 F6
Puerto Princesa 60,234 B6
Quezon City 1,165,865 C3
Romblon 24,251 D4
Roxas 81,183 D5
Sagay 99,118 D5
San Antonio 42,969 B3
San Carlos, Negros Occ. 91,627 D5
San Carlos Pangasinan 101,243 C3
San Fernando, La Union 68,410 C2
San Fernando, Pampanga 110,891 C3
San Jose 64,254 C3
San Jose del Monte 90,732 C3
San Pablo 131,655 C3
Santa Fe 6,338 C2
Santiago 69,877 C2
Silay 111,131 D5
Siquijor 17,533 D6
Surigao 79,745 E6
Tacloban 102,523 E5
Tagaytay 16,322 C3
Tagum 86,201 E7
Tarlac 175,691 C3
Toledo 91,668 D5
Tuguegarao 73,507 C2
Zamboanga 343,722 C7

OTHER FEATURES

Agusan (riv.) E6
Alabat (isl.) D3
Apo (vol.) E7
Babuyan (isl.) B2
Balabac (isl.) A7
Balayan (bay) C4
Balintang (chan.) A2
Baloy (mt.) D5
Bantayan (isl.) D5
Banton (isl.) D4
Bashi (chan.) A1
Basilan (isl.) D7
Batan, Albay (isl.) E4
Batan, Batanes (isl.) B2
Batan (isls.) A2
Bay, Laguna de (lake) C3
Biliran (isl.) E5
Bohol (isl.) E6
Bojeador (cape) C1
Borocay (isl.) D5
Bucas Grande (isl.) F6
Bugsuk (isl.) A6
Buliluyan (cape) A6
Bunga (pt.) E4
Burias (isl.) D4
Busuanga (isl.) B4
Cabalasan (mt.) E5
Cabulauan (isls.) C5
Cagayan (isls.) C6
Cagayan (riv.) C2
Cagayan Sulu (isl.) B7
Cagua (vol.) D1
Calagua (isls.) D3
Calamian Group (isls.) B4
Calayan (isl.) A2
Calicoan (isl.) E5
Camiguin, Cagayan (isl.) B3
Camiguin, Camiguin (isl.) E6
Camotes (isls.) E5
Camotes (sea) E5
Canigao (chan.) E5
Canlaon (peak) D5
Capotoan (mt.) E4
Carabao (isl.) D4
Catanduanes (isl.) E4
Cebu (isl.) D5
Celebes (sea) D8
Cleopatra Needle (mt.) B5
Coron (isl.) C5

Topography

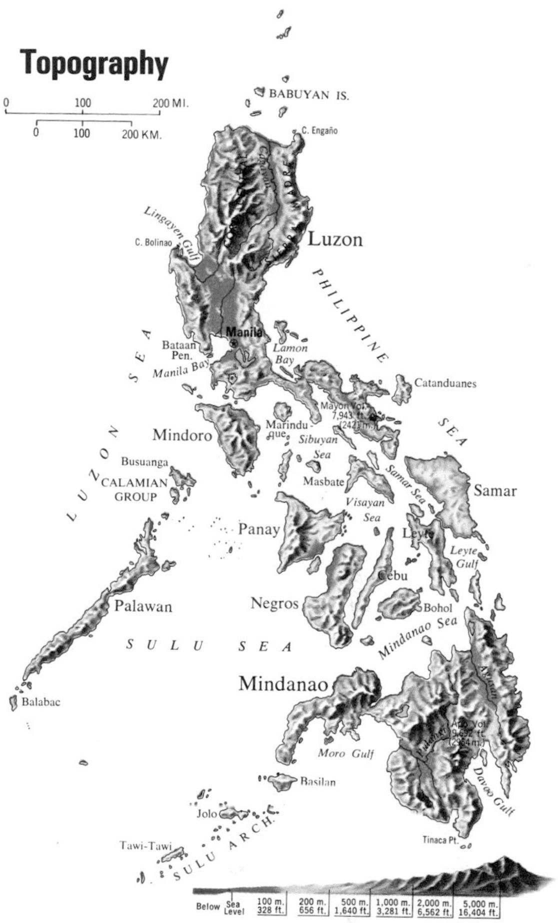

0 100 200 MI.
0 100 200 KM.
BABUYAN IS.
C. Engaño
Lingayen Gulf
C. Bolinao
Luzon
PHILIPPINE
SEA
Manila
Bataan Pen.
Manila Bay
Lamon Bay
Catanduanes
Mindoro
Marindu-que
Sibuyan Sea
Busuanga
CALAMIAN GROUP
Masbate
Samar Sea
Samar
Visayan Sea
Panay
Leyte
Leyte Gulf
Cebu
Negros
Bohol
Palawan
Mindanao Sea
SULU SEA
Mindanao
Balabac
Moro Gulf
Davao Gulf
Basilan
Jolo
Tawi-Tawi
SULU ARCH.
Tinaca Pt.
Below Sea Level
100 m. 328 ft.
200 m. 656 ft.
500 m. 1,640 ft.
1,000 m. 3,281 ft.
2,000 m. 6,562 ft.
5,000 m. 16,404 ft.

Agriculture, Industry and Resources

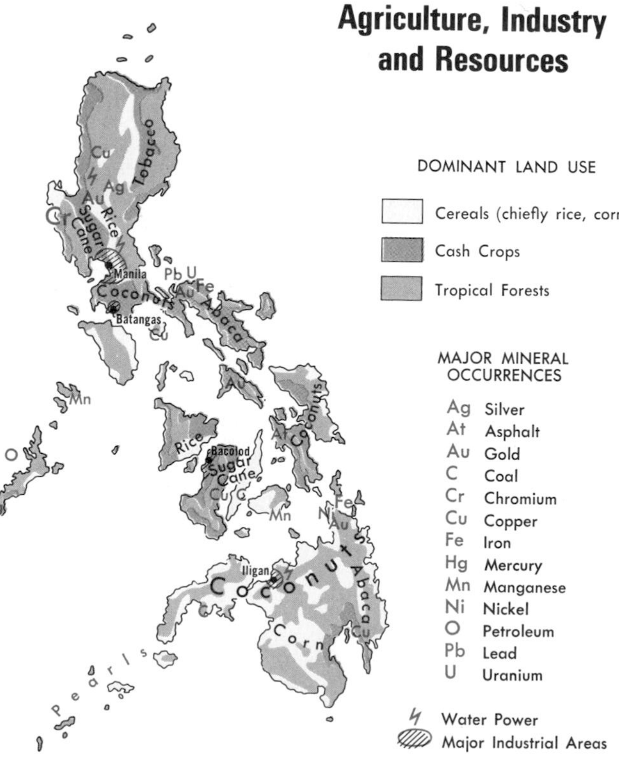

DOMINANT LAND USE
Cereals (chiefly rice, corn)
Cash Crops
Tropical Forests
MAJOR MINERAL OCCURRENCES
Ag Silver
At Asphalt
Au Gold
C Coal
Cr Chromium
Cu Copper
Fe Iron
Hg Mercury
Mn Manganese
Ni Nickel
O Petroleum
Pb Lead
U Uranium
Water Power
Major Industrial Areas
Tobacco
Rice
Sugar Cane
Manila
Coconuts
Batangas
Abaca
Bacolod
Iligan
Corn
Pearls

Corregidor (isl.) C3
Culion (isl.) B5
Cuyo (isl.) C5
Cuyo (isls.) C5
Daram (isl.) E5
Davao (gulf) E7
Dinagat (isl.) E5
Diuata (mts.) E6
Dumanquilas (bay) D7
Dumaran (isl.) C5
Engaño (cape) D1
Espiritu Santo (cape) E4
Fuga (isl.) A3
Guimaras (isl.) D5
Halcon (mt.) C4
Hibuson (isl.) E5
Homonhon (isl.) E5
Honda (bay) B6
Iligan (bay) E6
Ilin (isl.) C4
Illana (bay) D7
Imuruan (bay) B5
Island (bay) B6
Itbayat (isl.) A2
Jintotolo (chan.) D5
Jolo (isl.) C7
Jomalig (isl.) D3
Lagonoy (gulf) E4
Lamon (bay) C3
Lanao (lake) E7
Laparan (isls.) B8
Lapinin (isl.) E5
Leyte (gulf) E5
Leyte (isl.) E5
Limasawa (isl.) E6
Linapacan (isl.) B5
Lingayen (gulf) C2
Lubang (isls.) B4
Luzon (isl.) C3
Luzon (str.) A2
Macajalar (bay) E6
Malindang (mt.) D6
Mangsee (isls.) A7
Manila (bay) C3
Mantalingajan (mt.) A6
Maqueda (chan.) D3
Maraira (pt.) C1
Marinduque (isl.) C4
Masbate (isl.) D4
Mayon (vol.) D4
Maytiguid (isl.) B5
Mindanao (isl.) D7
Mindanao (riv.) E7
Mindoro (isl.) C4
Mindoro (str.) C4
Mompog (passg.) D4
Moro (gulf) D7
Mount Apo National Park E7
Naso (pt.) C5
Negros (isl.) D6
Olutanga (isl.) D7
Pacsan (mt.) C2
Palawan (isl.) B6
Palawan (passg.) A6
Panaon (isl.) E5
Panay (isl.) D5
Panglao (isl.) D6
Pangutaran (isl.) C7
Pangutaran Group (isls.) C7
Patnanongan (isl.) D3
Philippine (sea) E3
Pilas (isl.) C7
Pinatubo (mt.) C3
Polillo (isl.) C3
Pujada (bay) F7
Pulangi (riv.) E7
Ragang (vol.) E7
Ragay (gulf) D4
Rapu-Rapu (isl.) E4
Romblon (isl.) D4
Sabtang (isl.) B2
Sacol (isl.) D7
Samal (isl.) E7
Samales Group (isls.) D7
Samar (isl.) E5
Samar (sea) E4
San Agustin (cape) F7
San Bernardino (str.) E4
San Miguel (bay) D3
San Pedro (bay) E5
Santo Tomas (mt.) C2
Semirara (isls.) C5
Siargao (isl.) F6
Sibay (isl.) C5
Sibuguey (bay) D7
Sibutu Group (isls.) B8
Sibuyan (isl.) D4
Sibuyan (sea) D4
Sierra Madre (mt.) D2
Simunul (isl.) B8
Siquijor (isl.) D6
South China (sea) B3
Subic (bay) C3
Sulu (arch.) B8
Sulu (sea) B6
Suluan (isl.) F5
Surigao (str.) E6
Taal (lake) C4
Tablas (isl.) C4
Tablas (str.) C4
Tagapula (isl.) E4
Tagolo (pt.) D6
Tanon (str.) D6
Tapul (isl.) C8
Tapul Group (isls.) C8
Tara (isl.) C4
Tawi-Tawi (isl.) B8
Tayabas (bay) C4
Ticao (isl.) D4
Tinaca (pt.) E8
Tongquil (isl.) D8
Tumindao (isl.) B8
Turtle (isls.) B7
Verde Island (passg.) C4
Victoria (peaks) B6
Visayan (sea) D5

BRUNEI

CITIES and TOWNS

Bandar Seri Begawan 63,868 . . E4
Seria 23,511 . . . . E5

INDONESIA

CITIES and TOWNS

Adaut	J7
Agats	K7
Ambon (Amboina) 208,898	H6
Amuntai	F6
Amurang	G5
Atambua	G7
Aubâ	H7
Baa	G8
Bagansiapiapi	C5
Balikpapan 280,675	F6
Banda Aceh 72,090	A4
Bandanaira	H6
Bandung 1,462,637	H2
Banggai	E6
Banjarmasin 381,286	E6
Banyumas	J2
Batang	J2
Batavia (Jakarta) (cap.) 6,503,449	H1
Baukau	H2
Bekasi	H2
Belawan	B5
Bengkulu 64,783	C6
Beo	K6
Biak	K6
Binjai 76,464	B5
Bintuhan	C6
Blitar 78,503	J2
Bogor 247,409	H2
Bojonegoro	J2
Bukittinggi 70,771	B6
Bula	J6
Bulukumba	G7
Buntok	E6
Cianjur	H2
Cimahi	H2
Cirebon 223,776	H2
Demta	L6
Denpasar	E7
Dili	H7
Djambi (Jambi) 230,373	C6
Djokjakarta (Yogyakarta) 398,727	J2
Dobo	J7
Donggala	F6
Enarotali	K6
Ende	G7
Fakfak	J6
Garut	H2

Gorontalo 97,628	G5
Hollandia (Jayapura)	K6
Indramayu	H2
Jailolo	H5
Jakarta (cap.) 6,503,449	H1
Jambi 230,373	C6
Jayapura (Hollandia)	K6
Jogjakarta (Yogyakarta) 398,727	J2
Jombang	K2
Kaimana	J6
Kampung Baru (Tolitoli)	G5
Kediri 221,820	K2
Kendari	G6
Kepi	K7
Ketapang	E6
Kokonau	K6
Kolonodale	G6
Kotabaharu	E6
Kotabaru	F6
Kotawaringin	E6
Kragen	K2
Kupang	G8
Kutaraja (Banda Aceh) 72,090	A4
Labuha	H6
Labuhan	G2
Laiwui	H6
Larantuka	G7
Lekitobi	F5
Longiram	F5
Madiun 150,562	K2
Magelang 123,484	J2
Majalengka	H2
Makassar (Ujung Pandang) 709,038	F7
Malang 511,780	K2
Malili	G6
Manado 217,159	G5
Manokwari	J6
Maumere	G7
Medan 1,378,955	B5
Menggala	D6
Merauke	K7
Mindiptana	L7
Mojokerto 68,849	K2
Muarasiberut	B6
Nangatayap	E6
Pacitan	J2
Padang 480,922	B6
Padangpanjang 34,517	B6
Padangsidempuan	B5
Pakanbaru 186,262	C5
Palangkaraya 60,447	E6
Palembang 787,187	D6
Pangkalanbuun	E6
Pangkalpinang 90,096	D6
Parepare 86,450	F6
Pasangkayu	F6
Pasuruan 95,864	K2

Payakumbuh 78,836	C6
Pekalongan 132,558	J2
Pemalang	J2
Pematangsiantar 150,376	B5
Pinrang	F6
Plaju	D6
Pontianak 304,778	D6
Probolinggo 100,296	K2
Purbolinggo	J2
Raha	G6
Rantauprapat	C5
Rembang	J2
Sabang, Celebes	F5
Sabang, Weh 23,821	B4
Salatiga 85,849	J2
Samarinda 264,718	F6
Sampit	E6
Sarmi	K6
Sawahlunto 13,561	C6
Seba	G8
Semarang 1,026,671	J2
Semitau	E5
Serui	K6
Sibolga 59,897	B5
Sidli	B4
Sinabang	B5
Solo (Surakarta) 469,888	J2
Solok 31,724	C6
Sorong	J6
Sragen	J2
Subang	H2
Sukabumi 109,994	H2
Sumbawa Besar	F7
Sumedang	H2
Surabaya 2,027,913	K2
Surakarta 469,888	J2
Tanahmerah	K7
Tanjungbalai 41,894	C5
Tanjungkarang 284,275	D7
Tanjungpinang	C5
Tanjungselor	F5
Tarakan	F5
Tebingtinggi 92,087	B5
Tegal 131,728	J2
Telukbayur	C6
Tepa	H7
Teremba	D5
Tjilatjap (Cilicap)	H2
Tjirebon (Cirebon) 223,776	H2
Tolitoli	G5
Tuban	K2
Ujung Pandang 709,038	F7
Vikeke	H7
Wahai	H6
Waigama	J6
Wajabula	H5
Waren	K6
Weda	H6
Wonreli	H7

Yogyakarta 398,727	J2

OTHER FEATURES

Anambas (isls.) 29,572	D5
Arafura (sea)	J8
Aru (isls.) 34,195	K7
Babar (isl.)	H7
Bali 2,074,438	F7
Banda (sea)	H7
Banggai (arch.) 169,025	G6
Bangka (isl.) 298,017	D6
Banyak (isls.) 1,980	B5
Barisan (mts.)	C6
Barito (riv.)	E6
Batu (isls.) 16,390	B6
Bawean (isl.) 64,551	K1
Belitung (Billiton) (isl.) 128,694	D6
Berau (bay)	J6
Biak (isl.)	K6
Billiton (isl.) 128,694	D6
Binongko (isl.) 11,549	G7
Bone (gulf)	G7
Borneo (isl.)	E6
Bosch, van den (cape)	J6
Bunguran (Great Natuna) (isl.)	D5
Buru (isl.) 23,034	H6
Butung (isl.) 188,173	G6
Celebes (Sulawesi) (isl.) 7,732,383	G6
Celebes (sea)	G5
Cenderawasih (bay)	J6
Dampier (str.)	J6
Digul (riv.)	K7
Doberai (pen.)	J6
Enggano (isl.) 1,082	C7
Ewab (Kai) (isls.) 108,328	J7
Flores (isl.) 860,328	G7
Flores (sea)	F7
Frederik Hendrik (Kolepom) (isl.)	K7
Geelvink (Cenderawasih) (bay)	K6
Great Kai (isl.) 38,748	J7
Halmahera (isl.) 122,521	H5
Irian Jaya (reg.) 923,440	J6
Jambuair (cape)	B4
Jamursba (cape)	J5
Java (head)	C7
Java (isl.) 73,712,411	J2
Java (sea)	E6
Jaya, Puncak (mt.)	K6
Jayawijaya (range)	K6
Jemaja (isl.) 5,628	D5
Kabaena (isl.)	G7
Kai (isls.) 108,328	J7
Kalao (isl.)	G7
Kalaotoa (isl.)	G5

Kalimantan (reg.) 4,956,865	E5
Kangean (isl.)	F7
Kapuas (riv.)	D6
Karakelong (isl.)	H5
Karimata (arch.) 9,398	D6
Karimunjawa (isls.) 5,025	J1
Kerinci (mt.)	C6
Kisar (isl.)	H7
Komodo (isl.) 30,407	F7
Krakatau (Rakata) (isl.)	C7
Laut (isl.) 55,711	F6
Leuser (mt.)	B5
Lingga (arch.) 46,658	D5
Lingga (isl.) 18,027	D6
Lombok (isl.) 1,581,193	F7
Madura (isl.) 1,509,774	K2
Mahakam (riv.)	F6
Makassar (str.)	F6
Malacca (str.)	C5
Mamberamo (riv.)	K6
Maoke (mts.)	K6
Mapia (isls.)	J5
Mentawai (isls.) 30,107	B6
Misool (isl.)	J6
Molucca (sea)	G6
Moluccas (isls.) 944,240	H6
Morotai (isl.) 27,333	H5
Muli (str.)	K7
Müller (mts.)	E5
Muna (isl.) 156,186	G7
Musi (riv.)	C6
Natuna (isls.) 23,893	D5
Ngunju (cape)	F8
Nias (isl.) 356,093	B5
Numfoor (isl.)	J6
Obi (isls.) 12,437	H6
Ombai (str.)	H7
Pantar (isl.) 28,259	G7
Perkam (cape)	K6
Puting, Borneo (cape)	E6
Puting, Sumatra (cape)	C7
Raja Ampat Group (isls.)	H6
Rakata (isl.)	C7
Rantekombola (mt.)	F6
Raya (mt.)	E6
Riau (arch.) 483,230	C5
Rokan (riv.)	C5
Roti (isl.) 76,270	G8
Salawati (isl.)	J6
Sangihe (isl.)	H5
Sangihe (isls.) 183,000	G5
Sawu (isls.) 51,002	G8
Sawu (sea)	G7
Schouten (isls.) 110,148	K6
Schwaner (mts.)	E6
Sebuku (bay)	F5
Selatan (cape)	E6
Selayar (isl.) 92,342	G7
Semeru (mt.)	K2
Siau (isl.) 46,801	H5

Siberut (str.)	B6
Simeulue (isl.) 29,147	A5
Singkep (isl.) 28,631	D6
Sipura (isl.) 6,051	B6
South Natuna (isls.)	D5
Sorikmerapi (mt.)	B5
Sudirman (range)	K6
Sula (isls.) 36,922	H6
Sulawesi 7,732,383	G6
Sumatra (isl.) 19,360,400	B5
Sumba (isl.) 291,190	F7
Sumba (str.)	F7
Sumbawa (isl.) 621,140	F7
Sunda (str.)	C7
Tahulandang (isl.) 21,493	H5
Talaud (isls.) 46,395	H5
Taliabu (isl.) 18,303	G6
Tambelan (isls.) 4,032	D5
Tanimbar (isls.) 55,405	J7
Tariku (riv.)	K6
Tidore (isl.) 28,655	H5
Timor (reg.) 1,435,527	H7
Timor (sea)	H8
Toba (lake)	B5
Tolo (gulf)	G6
Tomini (gulf)	G6
Tukangbesi (isls.) 73,106	G7
Vals (cape)	K7
Vogelkop (Doberai) (pen.)	J6
Waigeo (isl.)	J5

Wakde (isl.)	K6
Wangiwangi (isl.) 28,469	G7
We (isl.)	B4
Wetar (isl.)	H7
Yapen (isl.) 50,888	K6

MALAYSIA

STATES

North Borneo (Sabah) 1,002,608 . . . . F3
Sarawak 1,294,753 . . . . E5

CITIES and TOWNS

Beaufort 2,709	F4
Bintulu 4,424	E5
Kabong	E5
Kampong Sibuti	E5
Kapit 1,929	E5
Keningau 2,037	F4
Kota Kinabalu 40,939	F4
Kuching 63,535	E5
Kudat 5,089	F4
Labuan 7,216	F4
Lahad Datu 5,169	F4
Lamag	F4
Marudi 4,700	E5
Miri 35,702	E5
Mukah 1,717	E5

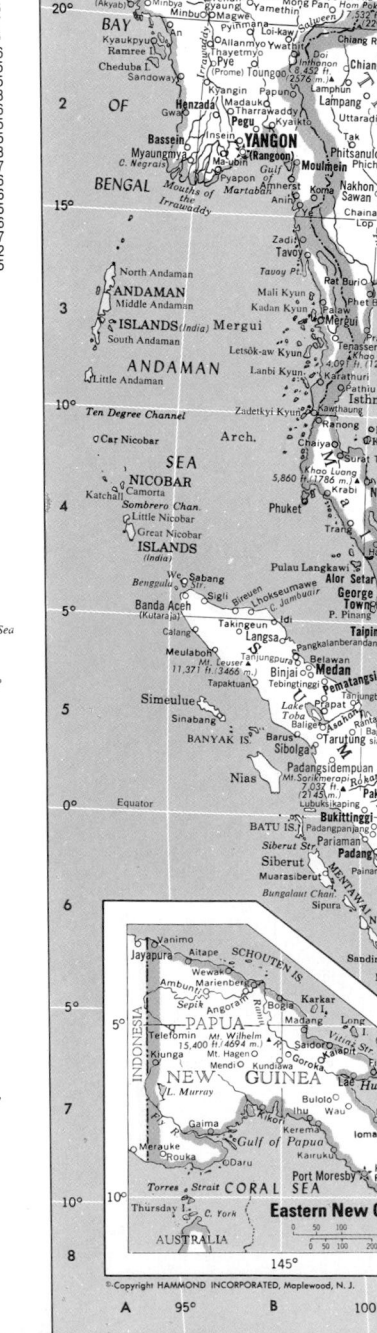

Topography

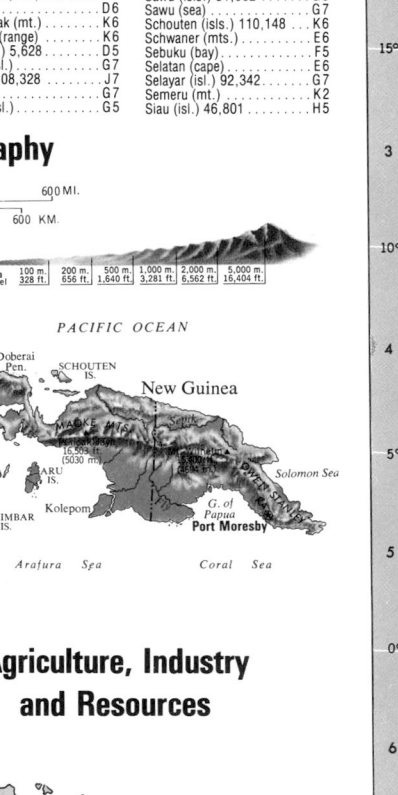

Below Sea Level	100 m. 328 ft.	200 m. 656 ft.	500 m. 1,640 ft.	1,000 m. 3,281 ft.	2,000 m. 6,562 ft.	5,000 m. 16,404 ft.

Agriculture, Industry and Resources

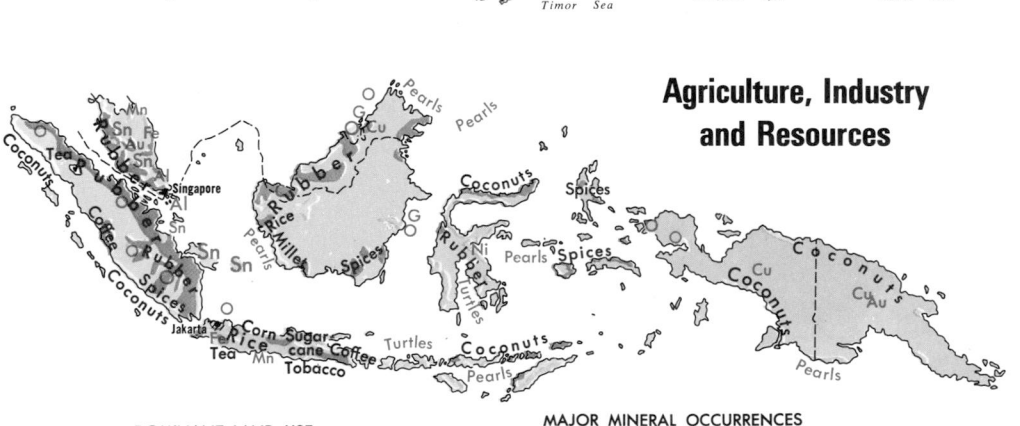

DOMINANT LAND USE

- Cereals (chiefly rice, corn)
- Diversified Tropical Crops
- Forests

MAJOR MINERAL OCCURRENCES

Al	Bauxite	Cu	Copper	Mn	Manganese
Au	Gold	Fe	Iron Ore	Ni	Nickel
C	Coal	G	Natural Gas	Sn	Tin
				O	Petroleum

Major Industrial Areas

Papar 1,855 ....F4	Baniara C7	Telefomin B7
Ranau 2,024 ....F4	Bogia 755 ....B6	Vanimo 3,071 ....B6
Sandakan 42,413 ....F4	Bulolo 6,730 ....B7	Wau 2,349 ....B7
Sematan D5	Buna C7	Wedau C7
Semporna 3,371 ....F5	Daru 7,127 ....C7	Wewak 19,890 ....B6
Serian 2,209 ....E5	Finschhafen 756 ....C7	
Sibu 50,635 ....E5	Gaima C8	OTHER FEATURES
Simanggang 8,445 ....E5	Gehua C7	
Suai E5	Gona C7	Dampier (str.) C7
Tawau 24,247 ....F5	Goroka 18,511 ....B7	D'Entrecasteaux (isls.) C7
Weston F4	Ihu 541 ....C7	Fly (riv.) A7
	Ioma C7	Huon (gulf) C7
OTHER FEATURES	Kaiapit 515 ....C7	Karkar (isl.) B6
	Kairuku C7	Kiriwina (isl.) C7
Balambangan (isl.) F4	Kerema 3,389 ....B7	Long (isl.) B7
Banggi (isl.) F4	Kikori 763 ....B7	Louisiade (arch.) D8
Iran (mts.) E5	Kiunga 1,407 ....B7	Milne (bay) C8
Kinabalu (mt.) F4	Kokoda C7	Misima (isl.) C8
Labuan (isl.) 17,189 ....F4	Kundiawa 4,299 ....B7	New Britain (isl.) 148,773 ....C7
Labuk (bay) F4	Lae 61,617 ....B7	Ramu (riv.) B7
Rajang (riv.) E5	Madang 21,335 ....B7	Rossel (isl.) D8
Sirik (cape) E5	Marienberg B6	Schouten (isls.) B6
	Mendi 4,130 ....B7	Sepik (riv.) B6
PAPUA NEW GUINEA	Morobe B7	Solomon (sea) C7
	Mount Hagen 13,441 ....B7	Tagula (isl.) C8
CITIES and TOWNS	Popondetta 6,429 ....C7	Torres (str.) A7
	Port Moresby	Trobriand (isls.) C7
Abau C7	(cap.) 123,624 ....C7	Vitiaz (str.) B7
Aitape 3,368 ....B6	Rouka B7	Woodlark (isl.) C7
Ambunti 1,035 ....B6	Saidor 500 ....B7	
Angoram 1,846 ....B6	Samarai 864 ....C8	*See page 74 for other Malaysian entries.

INDONESIA

AREA 788,430 sq. mi. (2,042,034 sq. km.)
POPULATION 179,136,000
CAPITAL Jakarta
LARGEST CITY Jakarta
HIGHEST POINT Puncak Jaya 16,503 ft.
(5,030 m.)
MONETARY UNIT rupiah
MAJOR LANGUAGES Bahasa Indonesia,
Indonesian and Papuan languages,
English
MAJOR RELIGIONS Islam, tribal religions,
Christianity, Hinduism

PAPUA NEW GUINEA

AREA 183,540 sq. mi. (475,369 sq. km.)
POPULATION 3,593,000
CAPITAL Port Moresby
LARGEST CITY Port Moresby
HIGHEST POINT Mt. Wilhelm 15,400 ft.
(4,694 m.)
MONETARY UNIT kina
MAJOR LANGUAGES pidgin English,
Hiri Motu, English
MAJOR RELIGIONS Tribal religions,
Christianity

BRUNEI

AREA 2,226 sq. mi. (5,765 sq. km.)
POPULATION 249,000
CAPITAL Bandar Seri Begawan
LARGEST CITY Bandar Seri Begawan
HIGHEST POINT Pagon 6,070 ft.
(1,850 m.)
MONETARY UNIT Brunei Dollar
MAJOR LANGUAGES Malay, English,
Chinese
MAJOR RELIGIONS Islam, Buddhism,
Christianity, tribal religions

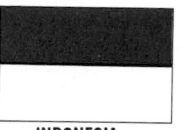

INDONESIA

PAPUA NEW GUINEA

BRUNEI

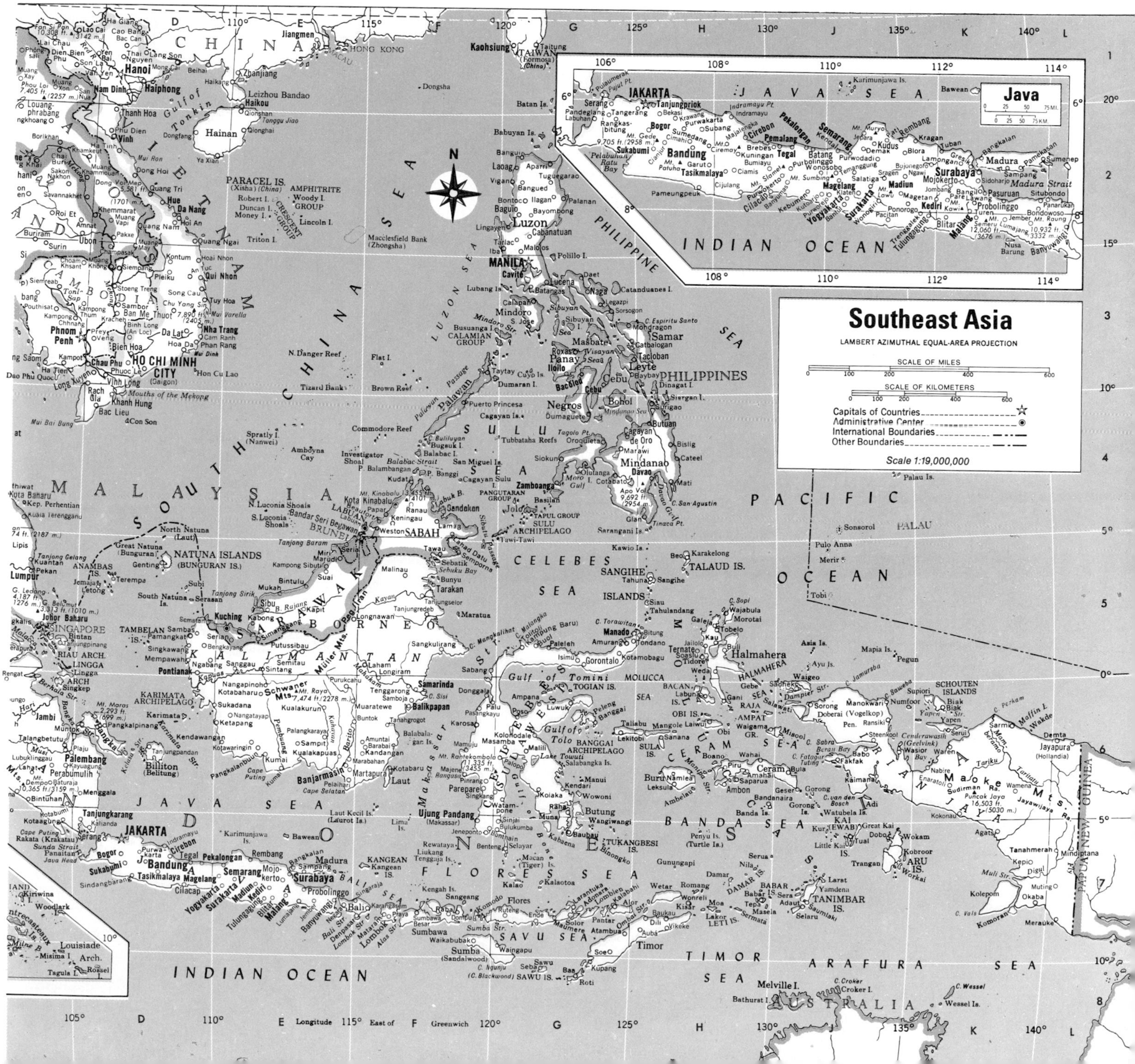

FIJI

AREA 7,055 sq. mi. (18,272 sq. km.)
POPULATION 792,441
CAPITAL Suva
LARGEST CITY Suva
HIGHEST POINT Tomaniivi 4,341 ft.
(1,323 m.)
MONETARY UNIT Fijian dollar
MAJOR LANGUAGES Fijian, Hindi, English
MAJOR RELIGIONS Protestantism, Hinduism

KIRIBATI

AREA 277 sq. mi. (717 sq. km.)
POPULATION 82,449
CAPITAL Tarawa
HIGHEST POINT (on Banaba I.) 285 ft. (87 m.)
MONETARY UNIT Australian dollar
MAJOR LANGUAGES I-Kiribati, English
MAJOR RELIGIONS Protestantism, Roman
Catholicism

NAURU

AREA 7.7 sq. mi. (20 sq. km.)
POPULATION 10,390
CAPITAL Yaren (district)
MONETARY UNIT Australian dollar
MAJOR LANGUAGES Nauruan, English
MAJOR RELIGION Protestantism

MARSHALL ISLANDS

AREA 70 sq. mi. (181 sq. km.)
POPULATION 60,652
CAPITAL Majuro
MONETARY UNIT U.S. dollar
MAJOR LANGUAGES English, Marshallese,
Japanese
MAJOR RELIGION Protestantism

SOLOMON ISLANDS

AREA 11,500 sq. mi. (29,785 sq. km.)
POPULATION 386,000
CAPITAL Honiara
LARGEST CITY Honiara
HIGHEST POINT Mount Popomanatseu
7,647 ft. (2,331 m.)
MONETARY UNIT Solomon Islands dollar
MAJOR LANGUAGES English,
pidgin English, Melanesian dialects
MAJOR RELIGIONS Tribal religions,
Protestantism, Roman Catholicism

TONGA

AREA 289 sq. mi. (748 sq. km.)
POPULATION 105,000
CAPITAL Nuku'alofa
HIGHEST POINT Kao Island 3,389 ft. (1,033 m.)
MONETARY UNIT pa'anga
MAJOR LANGUAGES Tongan, English
MAJOR RELIGION Protestantism

TUVALU

AREA 9.78 sq. mi. (25.33 sq. km.)
POPULATION 10,000
CAPITAL Funafuti
MONETARY UNIT Australian dollar
MAJOR LANGUAGES English, Tuvaluan
MAJOR RELIGION Protestantism

MICRONESIA

AREA 271 sq. mi. (702 sq. km.)
POPULATION 122,950
CAPITAL Palikir
MONETARY UNIT U.S. dollar
MAJOR LANGUAGES English, Trukese,
Pohnpeian, Yapese, Kosrean
MAJOR RELIGIONS Roman Catholicism,
Protestantism

Place	Ref
Abaiang (atoll) 3,296	H 5
Abemama (atoll) 2,300	H 5
Adamstown (cap.), Pitcairn Is. 54	N 8
Admiralty (isls.)	E 6
Agrihan (isl.)	E 4
Ailinglapalap (atoll) 1,385	G 5
Ailuk (atoll) 413	H 4
Aitutaki (atoll) 2,348	K 7
Alofi (cap.), Niue 960	K 7
Alotau 4,310	E 7
Ambrym (isl.) 6,324	G 7
American Samoa 32,297	J 7
Anaa (atoll) 444	M 7
Angaur (isl.) 243	D 5
Apataki (atoll)	M 7
Apia (cap.), Samoa 33,100	J 7
Arno (atoll) 1,487	H 5
Arorae (atoll) 1,626	H 6
Atafu (atoll) 577	J 6
Atiu (isl.) 1,225	L 8
Austral (isls.) 5,208	L 8
Avarua (cap.), Cook Is.	L 8
Babelthuap (isl.) 10,391	D 5
Baker (isl.)	J 5
Banaba (isl.) 2,314	G 6
Banks (isls.) 3,158	G 7
Belep (isls.) 624	F 7
Bellona (reefs)	G 8
Beru (atoll) 2,318	H 6
Bikini (atoll)	G 4
Bismarck (arch.) 218,339	E 6
Bonin (isls.) 1,879	E 3
Bora-Bora (isl.) 2,572	L 7
Bougainville (isl.) 71,761	F 6
Bounty (isls.)	H10
Bourail 3,149	G 8
Butaritari (atoll) 2,971	H 5
Caroline (isl.)	M 7
Caroline (isls.)	E 5
Chichi (isl.) 1,879	E 3
Choiseul (isl.) 10,349	F 6
Christmas (Kiritimati) (isl.) 674	L 5
Cook (isls.) 17,695	K 7
Coral (sea)	F 7
Danger (Pukapuka) (atoll) 797	K 7
Daru 7,127	E 6
Disappointment (isls.) 373	N 7
Ducie (isl.)	O 8
Easter (isl.) 1,598	Q 8
Ebon (atoll) 887	G 5
Efate (isl.) 18,038	G 7
Enderbury (isl.)	J 6
Enewetak (Eniwetok) (atoll) 542	G 4
Erromanga (isl.) 945	H 7
Espiritu Santo (isl.) 16,220	G 7
Fais (isl.) 207	E 5
Fakaofo (atoll) 654	J 6
Fanning (Tabuaeran) (isl.), 340	L 5
Faraulep (atoll) 132	E 5
Fatuhiva (isl.) 386	N 7
Fiji 792,441	H 8
Flint (isl.)	L 7
Fly (riv.)	F 6
Funafuti (cap.), Tuvalu	H 6
French Polynesia 137,382	L 8
Funafuti (atoll) 2,120	H 6
Futuna (Hoorn) (isls.) 3,173	J 7
Gambier (isls.) 556	N 8
Gardner (Nukumaroro) (isl.)	J 6
Gilbert (isls.) 47,711	H 6
Greenwich (Kapingamarangi) (atoll) 508	F 5
Guadalcanal (isl.) 46,619	F 7
Guam (isl.) 105,979	E 4
Hagåtña (cap.), Guam 896	E 4
Hall (isls.) 647	F 5
Hawaiian (isls.) 964,691	J 3
Henderson (isl.)	O 8
Hivaoa (isl.) 1,159	N 6
Honiara (cap.), Solomon Is. 14,942	F 6
Hoorn (isls.) 3,173	J 7
Howland (isl.)	J 5
Huahine (isl.) 3,140	L 7
Hull (Orona) (isl.)	J 6
Huon (Gulf)	E 6
Ifalik (atoll) 389	E 5
Iwo (isl.)	E 3
Jaluit (atoll) 1,450	G 5
Jarvis (isl.)	K 6
Johnston (atoll) 327	K 4
Kadavu (Kandav) (isl.) 8,699	H 7
Kanton (isl.)	J 6
Kapingamarangi (atoll) 508	F 5
Kavieng 4,633	E 6
Kermadec (isls.) 5	J 9
Kieta 3,491	F 6
Kimbe 4,662	E 6
Kingman (reef)	K 5
Kiribati 82,449	J 6
Kiritimati (isl.) 674	L 5
Koror (cap.), Palau 6,222	D 5
Kosrae (isl.) 5,491	G 5
Kwajalein (atoll) 6,624	G 5
Lae 61,617	E 6
Lau Group (isls.) 14,452	J 7
Lavongai (isl.)	E 6
Lifu (isl.) 7,585	G 8
Line (isls.)	K 5
Little Makin (atoll) 1,445	H 5
Lord Howe (Ontong Java) (isl.) 1,082	G 6
Lord Howe (isl.) 287	G 9
Lorengau 3,986	E 6
Louisiade (arch.)	F 7
Loyalty (isls.) 14,518	G 8
Luganville 4,935	G 7
Madang 21,335	E 6

Place	Ref
Majuro (atoll) (cap.), Marshall Is. 8,583	H 5
Makin (Butaritari) (atoll) 2,971	H 5
Malaita (isl.) 50,912	G 7
Malden (isl.)	L 6
Malekula (isls.) 15,931	G 7
Maloelap (atoll) 763	H 5
Mangaia (isl.) 1,364	L 8
Mangareva (isl.) 556	N 8
Manihiki (atoll) 405	K 7
Manua (isls.) 1,459	K 7
Manus (isl.) 25,844	E 6
Marcus (isl.)	F 3
Maré (isl.) 4,156	G 8
Marianas, Northern 16,780	E 4
Mariana Trench	E 4
Marquesas (isls.) 5,419	N 6
Marshall Islands 60,652	G 4
Marutea (atoll)	N 8
Mata Utu (cap.), Wallis and Futuna 558	J 7
Mauke (isl.) 684	L 8
Melanesia (reg.)	E 5
Micronesia (reg.)	F 5
Micronesia Federated States, of 122,950	F 5
Midway (isls.) 453	J 3
Mili (atoll) 763	H 5
Moen (isl.) 10,351	F 5
Moorea (isl.) 5,788	L 7
Mururoa (isl.)	M 8
Nadi 6,938	H 7
Namonuito (atoll) 783	E 5
Namorik (atoll) 617	G 5
Nanumea (atoll) 844	H 6
Nauru 10,390	G 6
Ndeni (isl.) 4,854	G 7
New Britain (isl.) 148,773	F 6
New Caledonia 133,233	G 8
New Caledonia (isl.) 118,715	G 8
New Georgia (isl.) 16,472	F 6
New Guinea (isl.)	E 6
New Ireland (isl.) 65,657	F 6
Ngatik (atoll) 560	F 5
Ngulu (atoll) 21	D 5
Niuatoputapu (isl.) 1,650	J 7
Niue (isl.) 3,578	K 7
Niutao (atoll) 866	H 6
Nomoi (isls.) 1,879	F 5
Nonouti (atoll) 2,223	H 6
Norfolk Island (terr.) 2,175	G 8
Northern Marianas 116,780	E 4
Nouméa (cap.), New Caled. 56,078	G 8
Nouméa *74,335	G 8
Nui (atoll) 603	H 6
Nuku'alofa (cap.) Tonga 18,356	J 8
Nukuhiva (isl.) 1,484	M 6

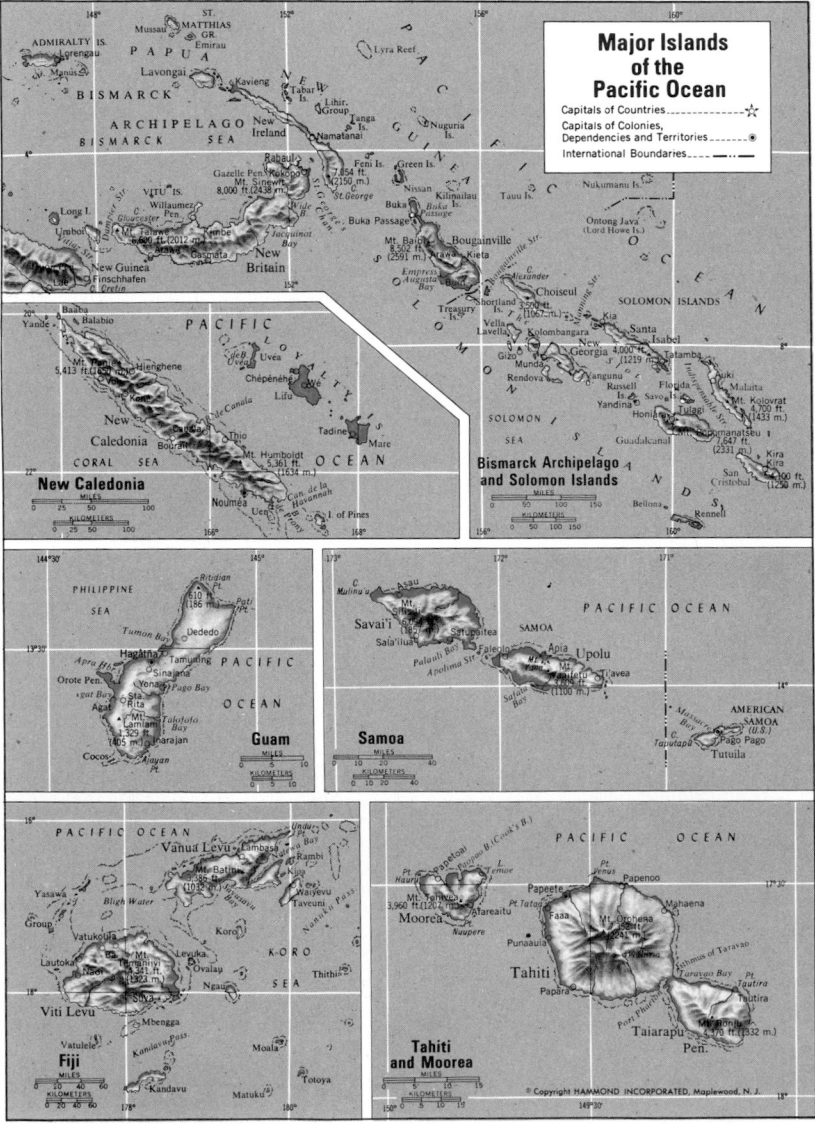

Major Islands of the Pacific Ocean

Capitals of Countries .... ☆
Capitals of Colonies, Dependencies and Territories .... ⊛
International Boundaries .... ━ ━ ━

New Caledonia

Bismarck Archipelago and Solomon Islands

Guam

Samoa

Fiji

Tahiti and Moorea

© Copyright HAMMOND INCORPORATED, Maplewood, N.J.

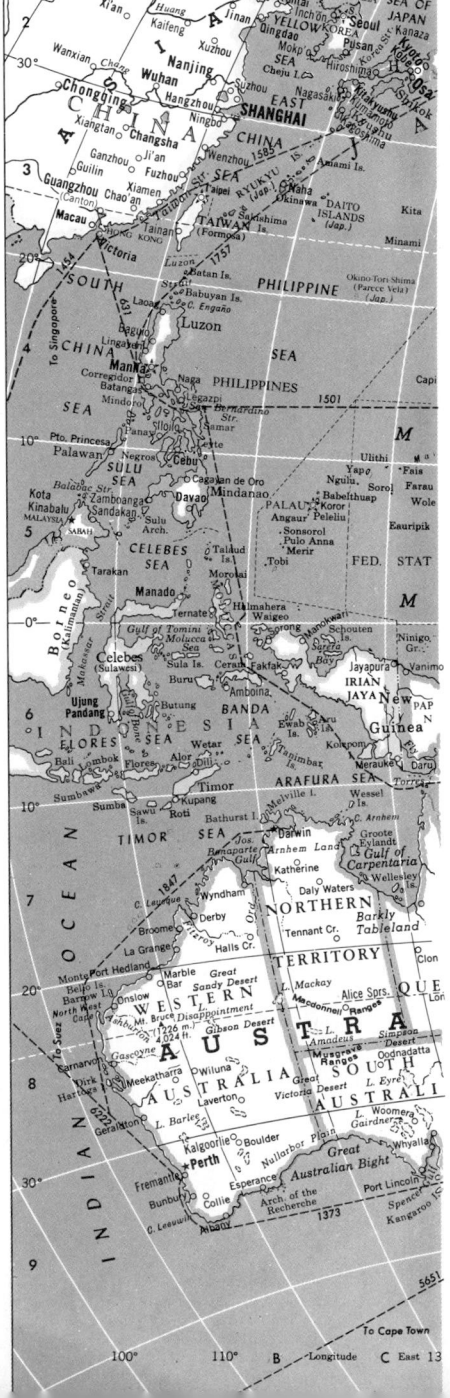

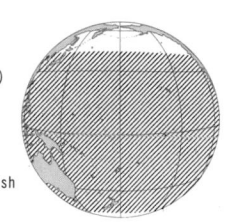

Ocean (Banaba) (isl.) 2,314 ...G 6
Oeno (isl.) ...O 8
Onotoa (atoll) 1,997 ...H 6
Onlong Java (atoll) 1,082 ...G 6
Pagan (isl.) ...E 4
Pago Pago (cap.), Amer.
  Samoa 3,075 ...J 7
Palau 12,116 ...D 5
Palikir (cap.), Micronesia
  5,549 ...F 5
Palmyra (atoll) ...K 5
Papeete (cap.), Fr. Poly.
  22,967 ...M 7
Papeete *51,987 ...M 7
Papua (gulf) ...E 6
Papua New Guinea 3,010,727 ...E 6
Peleliu (isl.) 609 ...D 5
Penrhyn (Tongareva) (atoll)
  608 ...L 6
Phoenix (isls.) ...J 6
Pines (isl.) 1,095 ...G 8
Pitcairn (isl.) 54 ...O 8
Pohnpei (isl.) 19,935 ...F 5
Polynesia (reg.) ...K 7
Popondetta 6,429 ...E 6
Port Moresby (cap.), Papua
  N.G. 123,624 ...E 6
Port-Vila (cap.), Vanuatu 4,729 .G 7
Port-Vila *14,797 ...G 7
Pukapuka (atoll) 797 ...K 7

Pulap (atoll) 427 ...E 5
Puluwat (atoll) 441 ...E 5
Rabaul 14,954 ...F 6
Raiatea (isl.) 2,517 ...L 7
Raivavae (isl.) 1,023 ...M 8
Rakahanga (atoll) 269 ...K 7
Ralik Chain (isls.) ...G 5
Rangiroa (atoll) ...M 7
Rapa (isl.) 398 ...M 8
Rarotonga (isl.) 9,477 ...K 8
Ratak Chain (isls.) ...G 5
Reao (atoll) 424 ...N 7
Rennell (isl.) 1,132 ...F 7
Rikitea ...N 8
Rimatara (isl.) 813 ...L 8
Rongelap (atoll) 235 ...G 4
Rotuma (isl.) 2,805 ...H 7
Rurutu (isl.) 1,555 ...L 8
Saipan (isl.), No. Marianas
  14,549 ...E 4
Sala y Gomez (isl.) ...P 8
Samarai 869 ...E 7
Samoa 204,000 ...J 7
Samoa (isls.) ...J 7
San Cristobal (isl.) 11,212 ...G 7
Santa Isabel (isl.) 10,420 ...G 6
Savai'i (isl.) 43,150 ...J 7
Senyavin (isls.) 20,035 ...F 5

Society (isls.) 117,703 ...L 7
Solomon (isls.) ...F 6
Solomon (sea) ...F 6
Solomon Islands 221,000 ...G 6
Starbuck (isl.) ...L 6
Suva (cap.), Fiji 63,628 ...H 7
Suva *117,827 ...H 7
Swains (isl.) 27 ...K 7
Sydney (isl.) ...K 6
Tabiteuea (atoll) 3,942 ...H 6
Tabuaeran (isl.) 340 ...L 5
Tahaa (isl.) 3,513 ...L 7
Tahiti (isl.) 95,604 ...L 7
Takaroa (atoll) 337 ...M 7
Tanna (isl.) 15,715 ...H 7
Tarawa (atoll), Kiribati 17,129 ...H 5
Tasman (sea) ...F 9
  Teraina (isl.) 458 ...L5
Tinian (isl.) 866 ...E 4
Tokelau (isls.) 1,575 ...J 6
Tonga 90,128 ...J 8
Tongareva (atoll) 608 ...L 6
Tongatapu (isl.) 57,130 ...J 8
Torres (isls.) 325 ...G 7
Torres (strait) ...D 6
Trobriand (isls.) ...F 6
Truk (isls.) 37,488 ...F 5
Tuamotu (arch.) 9,052 ...M 7
Tubuai (Austral) (isls.) 5,208 ...M 8
Tubuai (isl.) 1,419 ...M 8

Tutuila (isl.) 30,538 ...J 7
Tuvalu 7,349 ...H 6
Uapou (isl.) 1,563 ...M 6
Ujelang (atoll) 309 ...F 5
Ulithi (atoll) 710 ...D 4
Upolu (isl.) 114,620 ...J 7
Uturoa 2,517 ...L 7
Uvéa (isl.) 2,777 ...G 7
Vaitupu (atoll) 1,273 ...H 6
Vanikoro (isl.) 267 ...G 7
Vanimo 3,071 ...E 6
Vanua Levu (isl.) 103,122 ...H 7
Vanuatu 170,000 ...G 7
Viti Levu (isl.) 445,422 ...H 7

Volcano (isls.) ...E 3
Vostok (isl.) ...L 7
Wake (isl.) 302 ...G 4
Wallis (isls.) 8,973 ...J 7
Wallis and Futuna 13,705 ...J 7
Washington (Teraina) (isl.) 458 ...L 5
Wau 2,349 ...E 6
Wewak 23,224 ...E 6
Woleai (isl.) 638 ...E 5
Wotje (atoll) 535 ...H 5
Yap (isl.) 6,670 ...D 5

VANUATU

AREA 5,700 sq. mi. (14,763 sq. km.)
POPULATION 170,000
CAPITAL Port-Vila
LARGEST CITY Port-Vila
HIGHEST POINT Mt. Tabwemasana
  6,165 ft. (1,879 m.)
MONETARY UNIT Vatu
MAJOR LANGUAGES Bislama, English,
  French
MAJOR RELIGIONS Christian, animist

SAMOA

AREA 1,133 sq. mi. (2,934 sq. km.)
POPULATION 204,000
CAPITAL Apia
LARGEST CITY Apia
HIGHEST POINT Mt. Silisili 6,094 ft.
  (1,857 m.)
MONETARY UNIT tala
MAJOR LANGUAGES Samoan, English
MAJOR RELIGIONS Protestantism,
  Roman Catholicism

PALAU

AREA 177 sq. mi. (458 sq. km.)
POPULATION 15,122
CAPITAL Koror
HIGHEST POINT Mt. Makelulu 804 ft.
  (242 m.)
MONETARY UNIT U.S. dollar
MAJOR LANGUAGES English,
  Sonsorolese, Angaur, Japanese,
  Tobi, Palauan
MAJOR RELIGIONS Christian,
  Modekngei

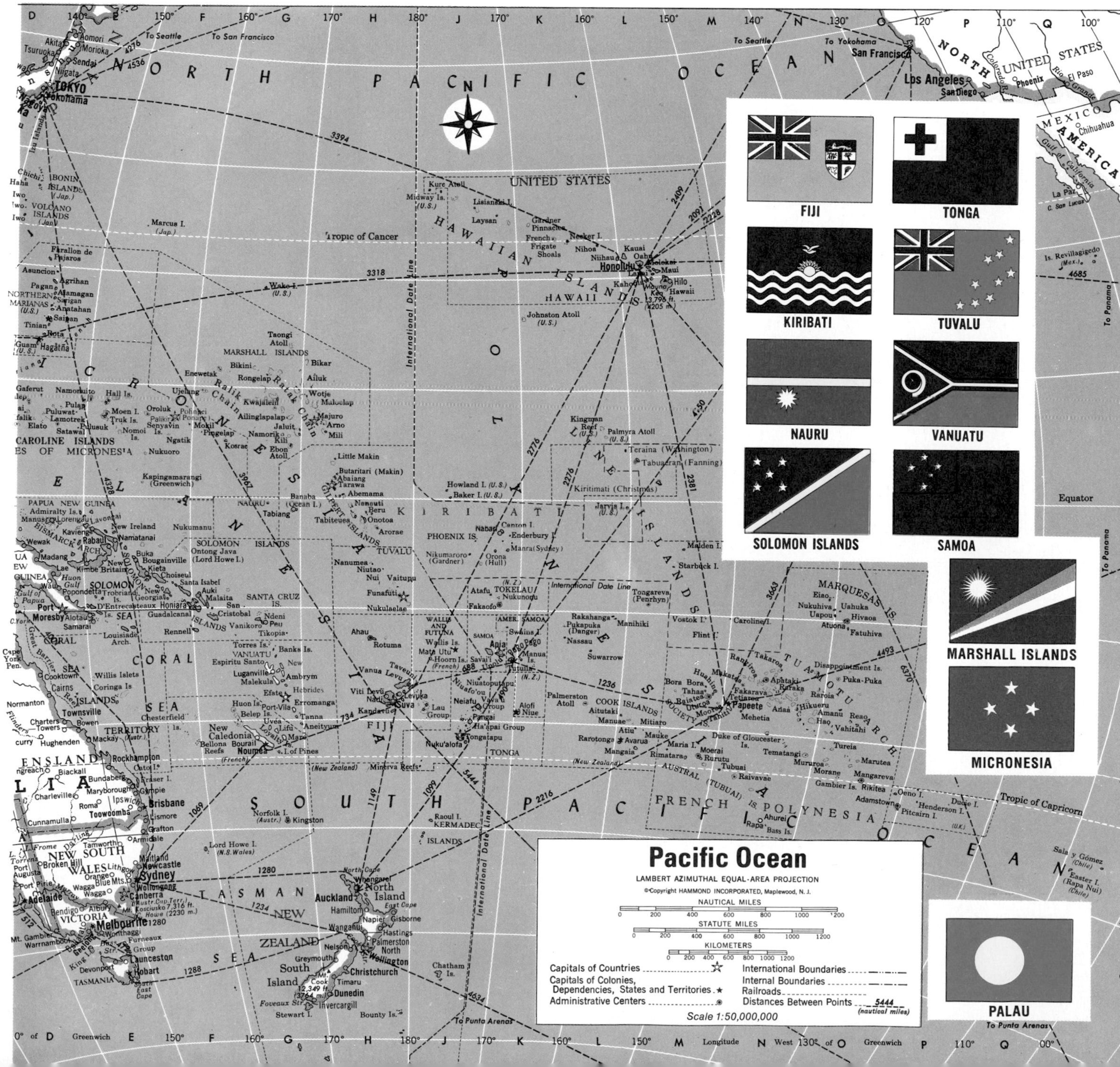

*City and suburbs.
•Population of urban area.

Australia

CONIC PROJECTION

MILES
0 50 100   200   300   400   500

KILOMETERS
0 50 100   200   300   400   500

Capital of Country .... ⊛   State & Territorial Capitals .... ⊛
International Boundaries .... — • —   State & Territorial Boundaries .... ---

© Copyright HAMMOND INCORPORATED, Maplewood, N.J.

AREA 2,966,136 sq. mi. (7,682,300 sq. km.)
POPULATION 15,602,156
CAPITAL Canberra
LARGEST CITY Sydney
HIGHEST POINT Mt. Kosciusko 7,310 ft. (2,228 m.)
LOWEST POINT Lake Eyre -39 ft. (-12 m.)
MONETARY UNIT Australian dollar
MAJOR LANGUAGE English
MAJOR RELIGIONS Protestantism, Roman Catholicism

Population Distribution

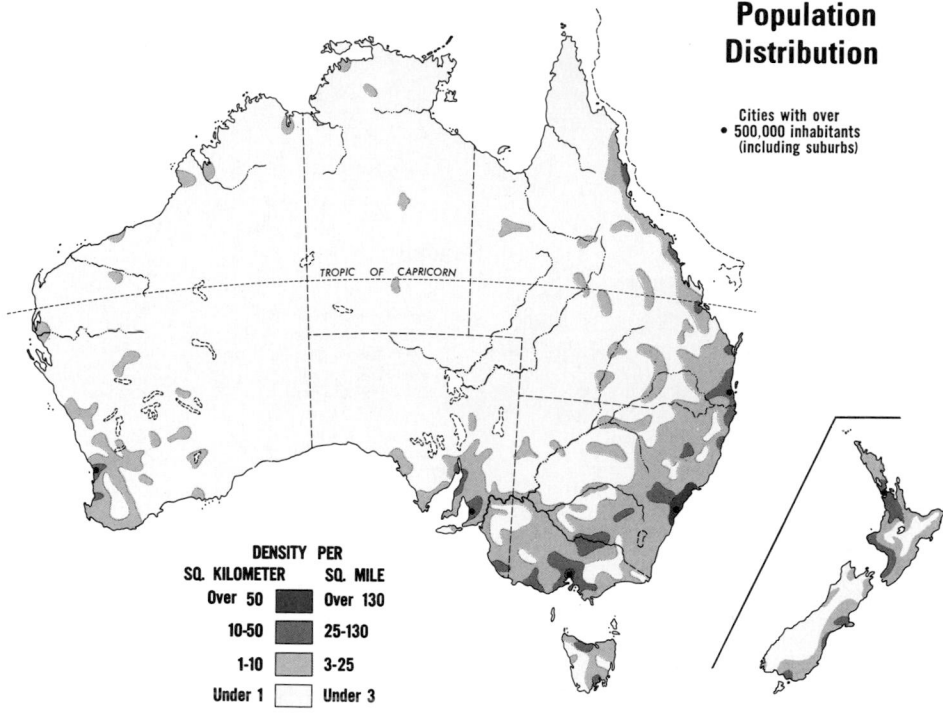

Cities with over
• 500,000 inhabitants
(including suburbs)

DENSITY PER

SQ. KILOMETER	SQ. MILE
Over 50	Over 130
10-50	25-130
1-10	3-25
Under 1	Under 3

Vegetation

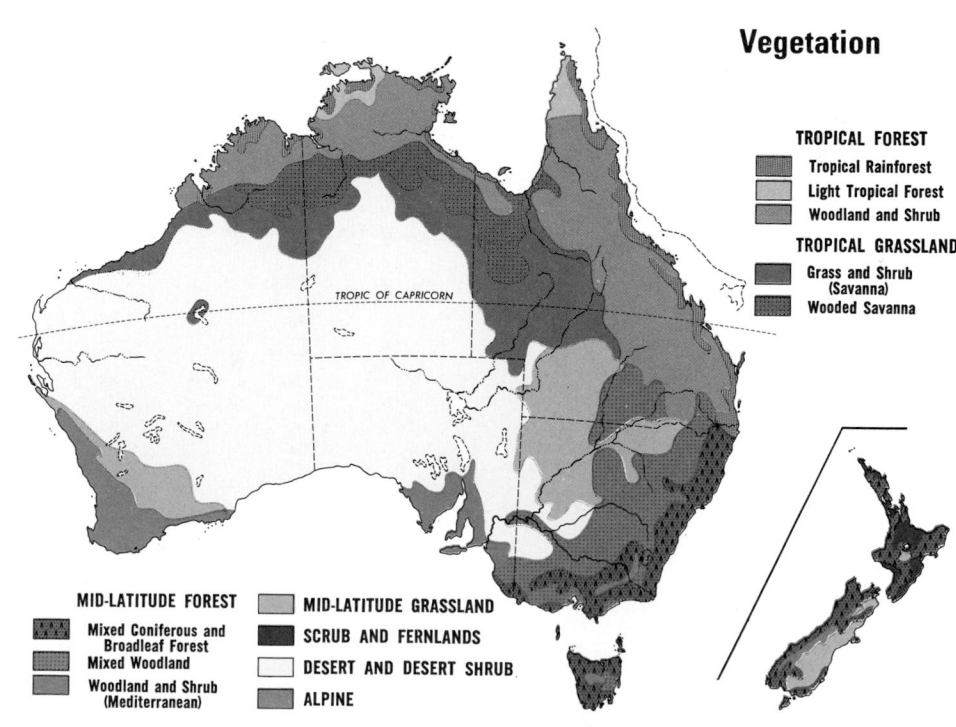

TROPICAL FOREST
Tropical Rainforest
Light Tropical Forest
Woodland and Shrub

TROPICAL GRASSLAND
Grass and Shrub (Savanna)
Wooded Savanna

MID-LATITUDE FOREST
Mixed Coniferous and Broadleaf Forest
Mixed Woodland
Woodland and Shrub (Mediterranean)

MID-LATITUDE GRASSLAND
SCRUB AND FERNLANDS
DESERT AND DESERT SHRUB
ALPINE

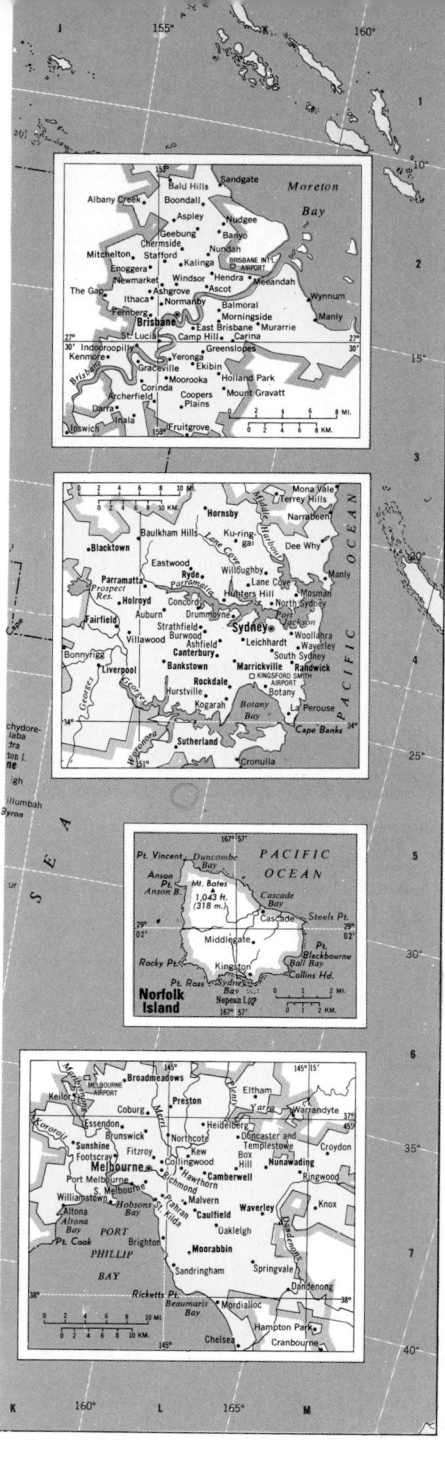

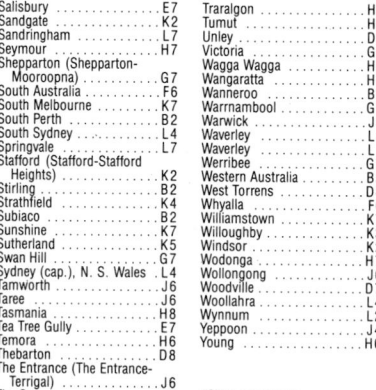

*City and suburbs.
†Population of met. area.
‡Population of urban area.

Average January Temperature

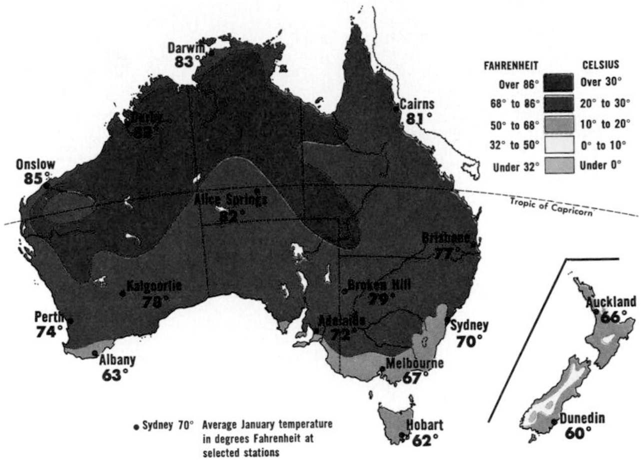
FAHRENHEIT
CELSIUS
Over 86° Over 30°
68° to 86° 20° to 30°
50° to 68° 10° to 20°
32° to 50° 0° to 10°
Under 32° Under 0°
Darwin 83°
Derby 82°
Cairns 81°
Onslow 85°
Alice Springs 82°
Tropic of Capricorn
Brisbane 77°
Kalgoorlie 78°
Broken Hill 79°
Perth 74°
Adelaide 72°
Sydney 70°
Albany 63°
Melbourne 67°
Auckland 66°
Hobart 62°
Dunedin 60°
• Sydney 70° Average January temperature in degrees Fahrenheit at selected stations

Average July Temperature

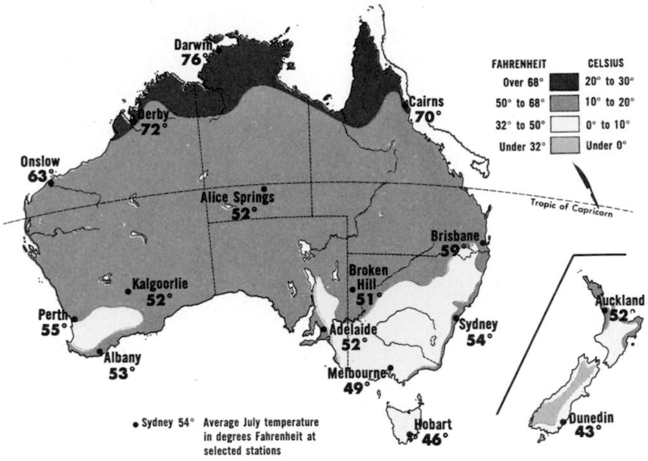
FAHRENHEIT
CELSIUS
Over 68° 20° to 30°
50° to 68° 10° to 20°
32° to 50° 0° to 10°
Under 32° Under 0°
Darwin 76°
Derby 72°
Cairns 70°
Onslow 63°
Alice Springs 52°
Tropic of Capricorn
Brisbane 59°
Kalgoorlie 52°
Broken Hill 51°
Perth 55°
Adelaide 52°
Sydney 54°
Albany 53°
Melbourne 49°
Auckland 52°
Hobart 46°
Dunedin 43°
• Sydney 54° Average July temperature in degrees Fahrenheit at selected stations

Rainfall

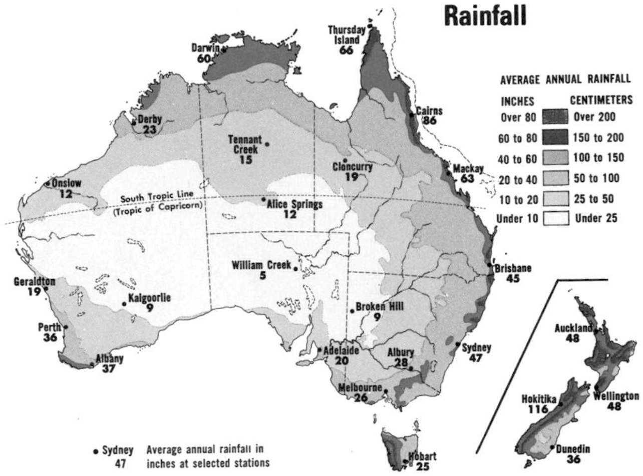
AVERAGE ANNUAL RAINFALL
INCHES
CENTIMETERS
Over 80 Over 200
60 to 80 150 to 200
40 to 60 100 to 150
20 to 40 50 to 100
10 to 20 25 to 50
Under 10 Under 25
Thursday Island 66
Darwin 60
Cairns 86
Derby 23
Tennant Creek 15
Cloncurry 19
Mackay 63
Onslow 12
South Tropic Line (Tropic of Capricorn)
Alice Springs 12
William Creek 5
Brisbane 45
Geraldton 19
Kalgoorlie 9
Broken Hill 9
Perth 36
Auckland 48
Adelaide 20
Albury 28
Sydney 47
Albany 37
Melbourne 26
Hokitika 116
Wellington 48
Dunedin 36
Hobart 25
• Sydney 47 Average annual rainfall in inches at selected stations

DOMINANT LAND USE

- Cereals (chiefly wheat), Livestock
- Dairy, Truck Farming
- Cash Crops, Horticulture, Fruit
- Pasture Livestock
- Range Livestock
- Forests
- Nonagricultural Land

MAJOR MINERAL OCCURRENCES

Ab	Asbestos	Na	Salt
Ag	Silver	Ni	Nickel
Al	Bauxite	O	Petroleum
Au	Gold	Op	Opals
C	Coal	P	Phosphates
Cu	Copper	Pb	Lead
D	Diamonds	S	Sulfur, Pyrites
Fe	Iron Ore	Sb	Antimony
G	Natural Gas	Sn	Tin
Gp	Gypsum	Ti	Titanium
Lg	Lignite	U	Uranium
Ls	Limestone	W	Tungsten
Mg	Magnesium	Zn	Zinc
Mi	Mica	Zr	Zirconium
Mn	Manganese		

- Water Power
- Major Industrial Areas

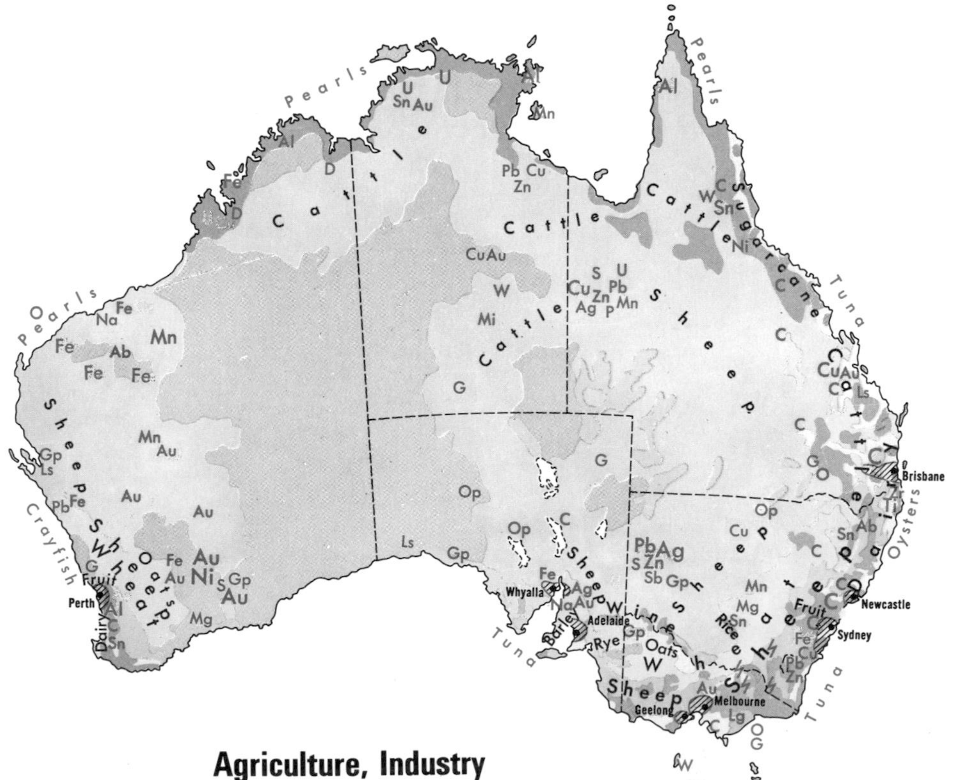
Pearls
Cattle
Sugarcane
Tuna
Sheep
Wheat
Crayfish
Oysters
Salmon
Fruit
Dairy
Barley
Rye
Oats
Rice
Perth
Whyalla
Adelaide
Geelong
Melbourne
Newcastle
Sydney
Brisbane

Agriculture, Industry and Resources

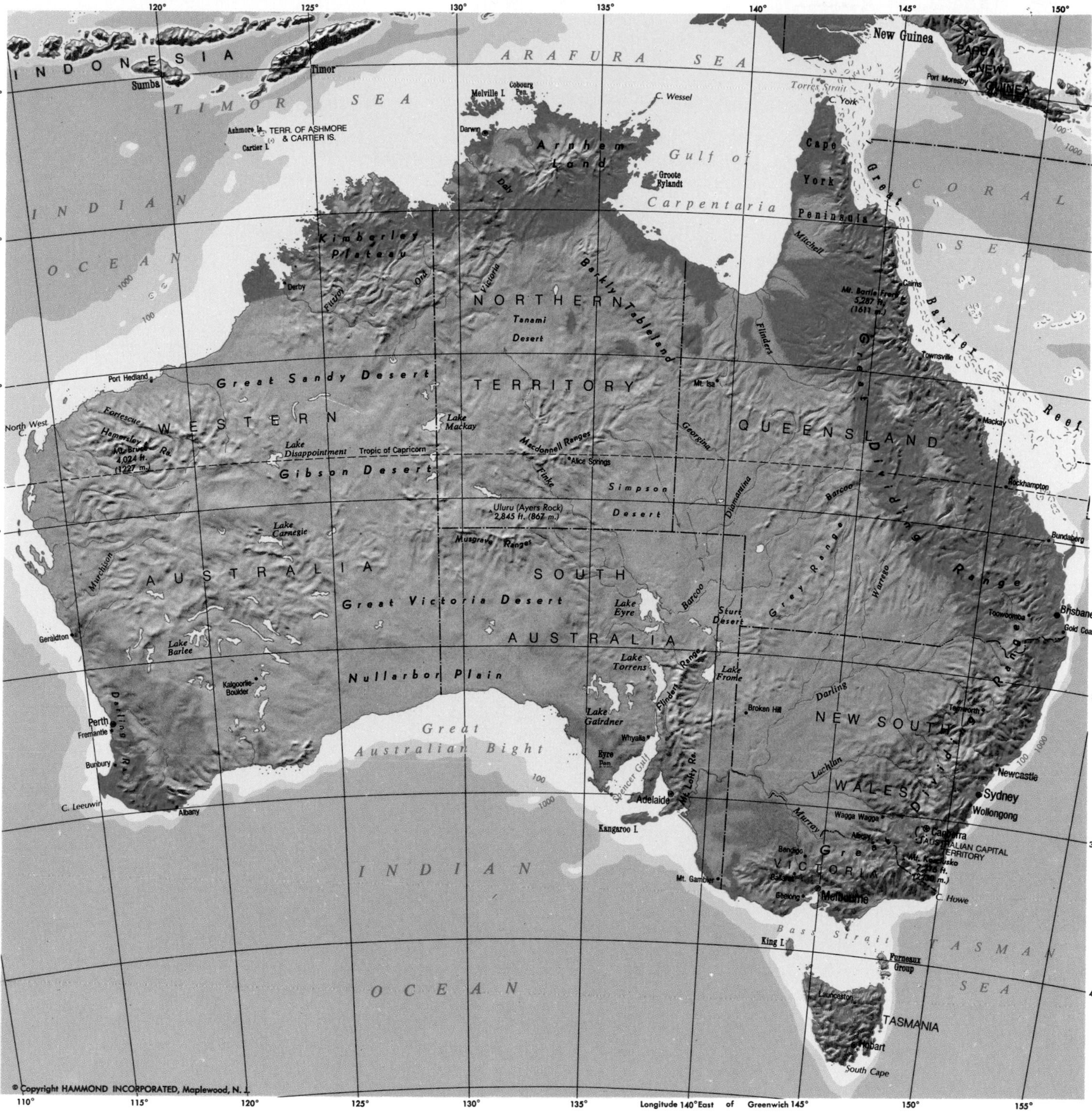

INDONESIA

ARAFURA SEA

TIMOR SEA

Sumba
Timor

Ashmore Is. TERR. OF ASHMORE & CARTIER IS.
Cartier I.

INDIAN OCEAN

Melville I.
Cobourg Pen.
Darwin
Arnhem Land
Groote Eylandt
C. Wessel

Gulf of Carpentaria

New Guinea
Port Moresby
PAPUA NEW GUINEA

Torres Strait
C. York
Cape York Peninsula

CORAL SEA

Kimberley Plateau
Derby
Ord
Victoria
Daly

NORTHERN
Tanami Desert

Barkly Tableland

Mitchell
Cairns

Great Barrier Reef

Port Hedland
Great Sandy Desert

TERRITORY
Mt. Isa

Mt. Bartle Frere 5,287 ft. (1611 m.)

Townsville

North West C.
Fortescue
Hamersley Ra.
Mt. Bruce 4,024 ft. (1227 m.)

WESTERN
Lake Disappointment
Tropic of Capricorn
Gibson Desert

Lake Mackay

Georgina

QUEENSLAND

Mackay

Macdonnell Ranges
Alice Springs
Finke
Uluru (Ayers Rock) 2,845 ft. (867 m.)
Simpson Desert

Diamantina
Barcoo
Grey Range

Rockhampton

Lake Carnegie

AUSTRALIA

SOUTH

Musgrave Ranges

Great Victoria Desert

Bundaberg

Geraldton
Lake Barlee

AUSTRALIA
Lake Eyre
Barcoo
Sturt Desert

Warrego
Great Dividing Range
Toowoomba
Brisbane
Gold Coast

Kalgoorlie-Boulder
Nullarbor Plain
Lake Torrens
Lake Gairdner
Flinders Range
Lake Frome
Broken Hill
Darling

NEW SOUTH

Perth
Fremantle
Darling Ra.
Bunbury

Great Australian Bight

Whyalla
Eyre Pen.
Spencer Gulf

Lachlan

WALES
Newcastle
Tamworth

C. Leeuwin
Albany

INDIAN

Adelaide
Mt. Lofty Ra.
Kangaroo I.

Murray
Murrumbidgee
Wagga Wagga
Sydney
Wollongong
Canberra
AUSTRALIAN CAPITAL TERRITORY

Mt. Gambier
Bendigo
Ballarat
Geelong
Mt. Kosciusko 7,316 ft. (2230 m.)
VICTORIA
Melbourne
C. Howe

OCEAN

King I.
Bass Strait
Furneaux Group
TASMAN SEA

Launceston
TASMANIA
Hobart
South Cape

© Copyright HAMMOND INCORPORATED, Maplewood, N. J.

Vegetation/Relief

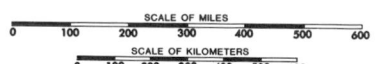

SCALE OF MILES
0   100   200   300   400   500   600

SCALE OF KILOMETERS
0   100   200   300   400   500   600

Capital of Country............................⊛
State and Territorial Capitals....................●
International Boundaries..................
State and Territorial Boundaries..............

Elevations in Feet   Depths in Fathoms

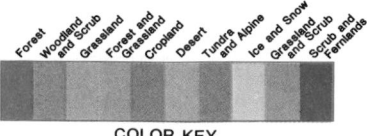

Forest
Woodland and Scrub
Grassland
Forest and Grassland
Cropland
Desert
Tundra Alpine
Ice and Snow
Grassland and Scrub
Scrub and Farmlands

COLOR KEY

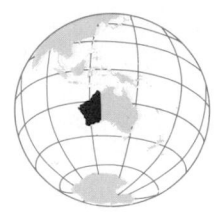

AREA 975,096 sq. mi.
(2,525,500 sq. km.)
POPULATION 1,406,929
CAPITAL Perth
LARGEST CITY Perth
HIGHEST POINT Mt. Bruce 4,024 ft.
(1,227 m.)

Topography

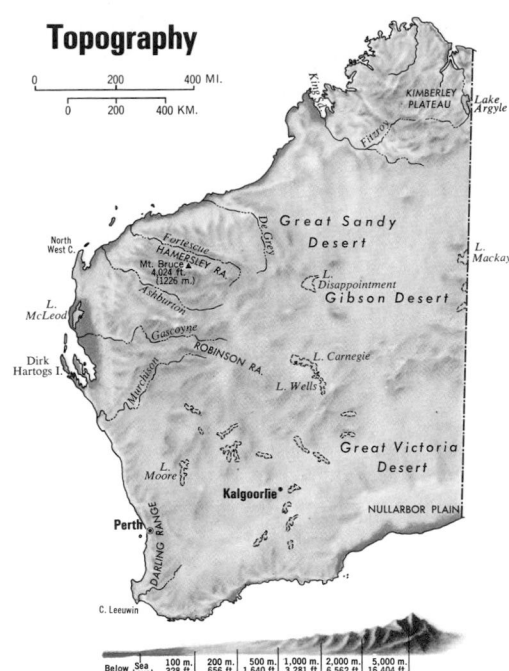

CITIES and TOWNS

Albany 15,222	B6
Augusta 588	A6
Australind 1,681	A2
Balladonia	D6
Beverley 756	B1
Boddington 367	A2
Boulder-Kalgoorlie 19,848	C5
Boyanup 365	A2
Bridgetown 1,521	B6
Brookton 595	B2
Broome 3,666	C2
Bruce Rock 565	B5
Brunswick Junction 889	A2
Bunbury 21,749	A6
Busselton 6,463	A6
Canning 52,816	A1
Capel 680	A2
Carnamah 422	A4
Carnarvon 5,053	A4
Collie 7,667	B2
Coolgardie 891	C5
Coorow 226	B5
Corrigin 841	B6
Cranbrook 316	B6
Cuballing ○647	B6
Cue 588	B4
Cunderdin 731	B5
Dalwallinu 639	B5
Dampier 2,471	B3
Dandaragan ○1,748	A5
Darkan 242	A2
Denham 402	A4
Denmark 985	B6
Derby 2,933	C2
Dongara-Port Denison 1,155	A5
Donnybrook 1,197	A2
Dwellingup 453	A2
Esperance 6,375	C6
Eucla	E5
Exmouth 2,583	A3
Fitzroy Crossing	D2
Fremantle 22,484	A1
Geraldton 20,895	A4
Gingin 382	A1
Gnowangerup 872	B6
Goldsworthy 923	B3
Goomalling 600	B1
Halls Creek 966	D2
Harvey 2,479	A2
Hopetoun	C6
Hyden	B6
Jarrahdale 315	B2
Kalbarri 820	A4
Kalgoorlie 9,145	C5
Kalgoorlie-Boulder 19,848	C5
Kambalda 4,463	C5
Karratha 8,341	B3
Katanning 4,413	B6
Kellerberrin 1,091	B5
Kojonup 544	B6
Koolyanobbing 277	B5
Kununurra 2,081	E2
Kwinana New Town 12,355.	A1
Lake Grace 575	B6
Laverton 872	C5
Learmonth	A3
Leonora 524	C5
Madura	D5
Mandurah 10,978	A2
Manjimup 4,150	B6
Marble Bar 357	C3
Margaret River 798	A6
Meekatharra 989	B4
Melville 61,211	A1
Menzies 232	C5
Merredin 3,520	B5
Mingenew 368	A5
Moora 1,677	A5
Morawa 694	A5
Mount Barker 1,519	B6
Mount Magnet 618	B5
Mukinbudin 370	B5
Mullewa 918	A5
Mundijong 356	A2
Nannup 552	B6
Narrogin 4,969	B2
Nedlands 20,257	A1
Newman 5,466	B3
New Norcia	A5
Norseman 1,895	C6
Northam 6,791	B5
Northampton 750	A5
Northcliffe	B6
Nungarin ○332	B5
Onslow 594	A3
Pannawonica 1,170	B3
Paraburdoo 2,357	B3
Pardoo	B3
Pemberton 851	A6
Perenjori 257	A5
Perth (cap.) 809,035	A1
Perth *898,918.	A1
Pingelly 937	B2
Pinjarra 1,336	A2
Port Denison-Dongara 1,155	A5
Port Hedland 12,948.	B3
Quairading 741	B1
Ravensthorpe 327	B6
Rockingham 24,932	A2
Roebourne 1,688	B3

OTHER FEATURES

Sandstone ○133	B4
Shay Gap 853	C3
Southern Cross 798	B5
South Perth 31,524	A1
Stirling 161,858	A1
Three Springs 638	A5
Tom Price 3,540	B3
Toodyay 560	B1
Turkey Creek 212	E2
Wagin 1,488	B2
Walpole 291	B6
Wandering ○470	B2
Wanneroo 6,745	A1
Waroona 1,462	A2
Wickepin 267	B2
Wickham 2,387	B3
Williams 453	B2
Wiluna 221	C4
Wittenoom 247	B3
Wongan Hills 947	B5
Wundowie 720	B1
Wyalkatchem 453	B5
Wyndham 1,509	E1
Yalgoo ○315	B5
Yampi Sound	C2
York 1,136	B1

Adele (isl.)	C1
Admiralty (gulf)	D1
Aloysius (mt.)	E4
Argyle (lake)	E2
Arid (cape)	C6
Ashburton (riv.)	A3
Augustus (mt.)	B4
Austin (lake)	B4
Australia Aboriginal Res.	E4
Bald (head)	B6
Balwina Aboriginal Res.	E3
Barlee (lake)	B5
Barrow (isl.)	A3
Beaglebay Aboriginal Res.	C2
Bluff Knoll (mt.)	B6
Bonaparte (arch.)	D1
Bougainville (cape)	D1
Brassey (range)	C4
Bruce (mt.)	B3
Brunswick Aboriginal Res.	D1
Buccaneer (arch.)	C2
Carey (lake)	C5
Carnegie (lake)	C4
Central Aboriginal Res.	E3
Churchman (mt.)	B5
Collier (bay)	C1
Cosmo Newbery Aboriginal Res.	C5
Cowan (lake)	C5
Cundeelee Aboriginal Res.	C5
Dale (mt.)	B1
Dampier (arch.)	B3
Dampier Land (reg.)	C2
Darling (range)	A1
De Grey (riv.)	B3
D'Entrecasteaux (pt.)	A6
Dirk Hartogs (isl.)	A4
Disappointment (lake)	C3
Drysdale (riv.)	D1
Dundas (lake)	C6
Egerton (mt.)	B4
Eighty Mile (beach)	C2
Enid (mt.)	B3
Esperance (bay)	C6

Exmouth (gulf)	A3
Fitzroy (riv.)	D2
Flinders (bay)	A6
Forrest River Aboriginal Res.	D1
Fortescue (riv.)	B3
Garden (isl)	A1
Gascoyne (riv.)	B4
Geelvink (chan.)	A5
Geographe (bay)	A6
Geographe (chan.)	A4
Gibson (des.)	D3
Great Australian (bight)	E6
Great Sandy (des.)	C3
Great Victoria (des.)	D5
Hamersley (range)	B3
Hann (mt.)	D1
Hopkins (lake)	E4
Houtman Abrolhos (isls.)	A5
Indian Ocean.	A5
Johnston, The (lakes)	C6
Joseph Bonaparte (gulf)	E1
Kimberley (plat.)	D2
King (sound)	C2
King Leopold (range)	D2
Koolan (isl.)	C1
Le Grand (cape)	C6
Lévêque (cape)	C2
Londonderry (cape)	D1
Lyons (riv.)	A4
Macdonald (lake)	E3
Mackay (lake)	E3
McLeod (lake)	A4
Minigwal (lake)	C5
Monte Bello (isls.)	A3
Moore (lake)	B5
Murchison (riv.)	A4
Murray (riv.)	A2
Naturaliste (cape)	A6
Naturaliste (chan.)	A4
North West (cape)	A3
North-West Aboriginal Res.	E4
Nullarbor (plain)	D5
Oakover (riv.)	C3
Ord (mt.)	D2
Ord (riv.)	E2
Percival (lakes)	C3
Peron (pen.)	A4
Petermann (ranges)	E4
Rason (lake)	D5
Rebecca (lake)	C5
Recherche (arch.)	C6
Robinson (ranges)	B4
Roebuck (bay)	C2
Rottnest (isl.)	A1
Saint George (ranges)	D2
Shark (bay)	A4
Southesk Tablelands	D3
Sturt (creek)	D2
Swan (riv.)	A1
Timor (sea)	D1
Tomkinson (ranges)	E4
Wanna (lake)	C4
Warburton Aboriginal Res.	D4
Way (lake)	C4
Weld (range)	B4
Wells (lake)	C4
Whaleback (mt.)	B3
Wooramel (riv.)	A4
York (sound)	D1

○ Population of district.
*Population of met. area.

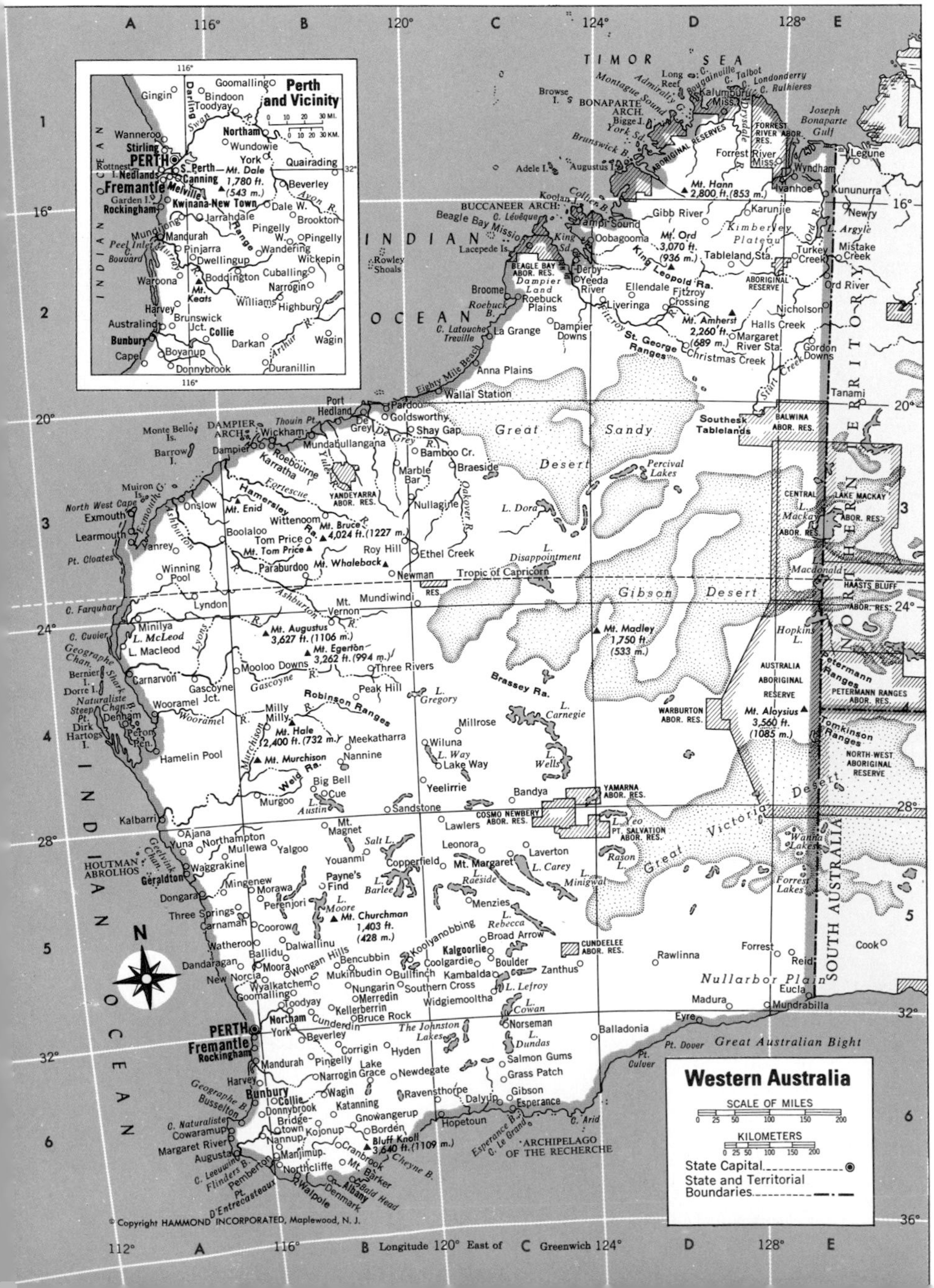

Western Australia
SCALE OF MILES

KILOMETERS
0   50   100   150   200

State Capital ....●
State and Territorial
Boundaries ------

© Copyright HAMMOND INCORPORATED, Maplewood, N.J.

CITIES and TOWNS

Adelaide River	B2
Aileron	C7
Alice Springs 18,395	D7
Alyangula 1,181	E2
Angurugu 597	E3
Anthony Lagoon	D4
Areyonga	C8
Arltunga	D7
Avon Downs	E5
Bamyili-Beswick 685	C3
Banka Banka	D5
Barrow Creek	D6
Batchelor	B2
Bathurst Island 1,032	B1
Birdum	C3
Birrimbah	C3
Birrindudu	A5
Borroloola 420	E4
Bundooma	D8
Burramurra	E6
Charlotte Waters	C8
Claravale	B3
Coniston	C7
Coolibah	B3
Creswell Downs	E4
Croker Island Mission	C1
Daly River	B2
Daly Waters	C4
Darwin (cap.) 56,482	B2
Docker River 217	A8
Elliott	C4
Epenarra	D6
Erldunda	C8
Eva Downs	D5
Ewaninga	D7
Goulburn Island 277	C1
Gove (Nhulunbuy) 3,879	E2
Harts Range	D7
Hatches Creek	D6
Helen Springs	C5
Henbury	C8
Hermannsburg 541	C7
Hooker Creek 671	B5
Humpty Doo	B2
Katherine 3,737	B3
Kildurk	A4
Koolpinyah	B2
Kulgera	C8
Kurundi	D6
Lake Nash	E6
Larrimah	C3
Legune	A3
Limbunya	B4
Lucy Creek	E7
Mainoru	C3
Maningrida 702	C2
Mataranka	C3
Milingimbi 564	D2
Mistake Creek	A4
Montejinnie	C4
Mount Cavenagh	C8
Murray Downs	D6
Napperby	C7
Newcastle Waters	C4
Nhulunbuy 3,879	E2
Numbulwar 422	D3
Oenpelli 452	C2
O. T. Downs	D4
Papunya 635	B7
Pine Creek 214	C2
Plenty River Mine	D7
Port Keats 819	A3
Powell Creek	C5
Rankine Store	E5
Robinson River	E4
Rockhampton Downs	D5
Rodinga	D7
Rum Jungle	B2
Santa Teresa 479	D8
Soudan	D6
Stirling Station	C6
Tanami	A5
Tarlton Downs	E7
Tea Tree Well	C7
Tempe Downs	C8
Tennant Creek 3,118	C5
The Granites	B6
Top Springs	C4
Ucharonidge	D4
Umbakumba 247	E3
Umbeara	C8
Urapunga	D3
Utopia	D7
Victoria River Downs	B4
Warrabri 459	D6
Warrego 991	C5
Wave Hill	B4
White Quartz Hill	D7
Willeroo	B3
Willowra	C6
Wollogorang	F4
Yambah	C7
Yirrkala 543	E2
Yuendumu 687	B7

OTHER FEATURES

Amadeus (lake)	B8
Arafura (sea)	D1
Arnhem (cape)	E2
Arnhem Land (reg.)	D2
Arnhem Land Aboriginal Res.	C2
Arnold (riv.)	D3
Barkly Tableland	E5
Bathurst (isl.)	A1
Beagle (gulf)	A1
Beatrice (cape)	E3
Bennett (lake)	B7
Beswick Aboriginal Res.	C3
Bickerton (isl.)	E2
Blaze (pt.)	A2
Carpentaria (gulf)	E3
Central Wedge (mt.)	C7
Clarence (str.)	B2
Cobourg (pen.)	C1
Conner (mt.)	C8
Croker (cape)	C1
Daly (riv.)	B2
Daly River Aboriginal Res.	A2
Davenport (mt.)	B7
Dundas (str.)	B1
East Alligator (riv.)	C2
Ehrenberg (range)	B7
Elcho (isl.)	D1
Finke (riv.)	C8
Fitzmaurice (riv.)	B3
Ford (cape)	A2
Georgina (riv.)	E6
Goulburn (isls.)	C1
Goyder (riv.)	D2
Groote Eylandt (isl.) 2,230	E3
Haasts Bluff Aboriginal Res.	B7
Hale (riv.)	D8
Hanson (riv.)	C6
Hay (dry riv.)	E7
Hogarth (mt.)	E6
Hopkins (lake)	A8
Joseph Bonaparte (gulf)	A3
Kata Tjuta (Olga) (mt.)	B8
Katherine (riv.)	C3
Lake MacKay Aboriginal Res.	A6
Lander (riv.)	C6
Leisler (mt.)	A7
Limmen Bight (riv.)	D4
Macdonald (lake)	B7
Macdonnell (ranges)	C7
MacKay (lake)	A7
Mann (riv.)	D2
Marshall (riv.)	D7
Melville (bay)	E2
Melville (isl.)	B1
Murchison (range)	D6
Napier (riv.)	A4
Neale (lake)	A8
Newcastle (creek)	C4
Nicholson (riv.)	E5
Peron (isls.)	A2
Petermann (ranges)	A8
Petermann Ranges Aboriginal Res.	A8
Port Darwin (inlet)	B2
Ranken (riv.)	E6
Robinson (riv.)	E4
Roper (riv.)	C3
Sandover (riv.)	D6
Simpson (des.)	E8
Singleton (mt.)	B6
Sir Edward Pellew Group (isls.)	E3
South Alligator (riv.)	C2
Stanley (mt.)	B7
Stewart (cape)	D1
Stirling (creek)	A4
Sturt (plain)	C4
Tanami (des.)	C5
Timor (sea)	A2
Todd (riv.)	D8
Uluru Nat'l Park	B8
Vanderlin (isl.)	E3
Van Diemen (cape)	A1
Van Diemen (gulf)	B1
Victoria (riv.)	B3
Wagait Aboriginal Res	B2
Warwick (chan.)	E3
Wessel (cape)	E1
Wessel (isls.)	E1
West Baines (riv.)	A4
White (lake)	A6
Woods (lake)	C4
Young (mt.)	D3
Ziel (mt.)	C7

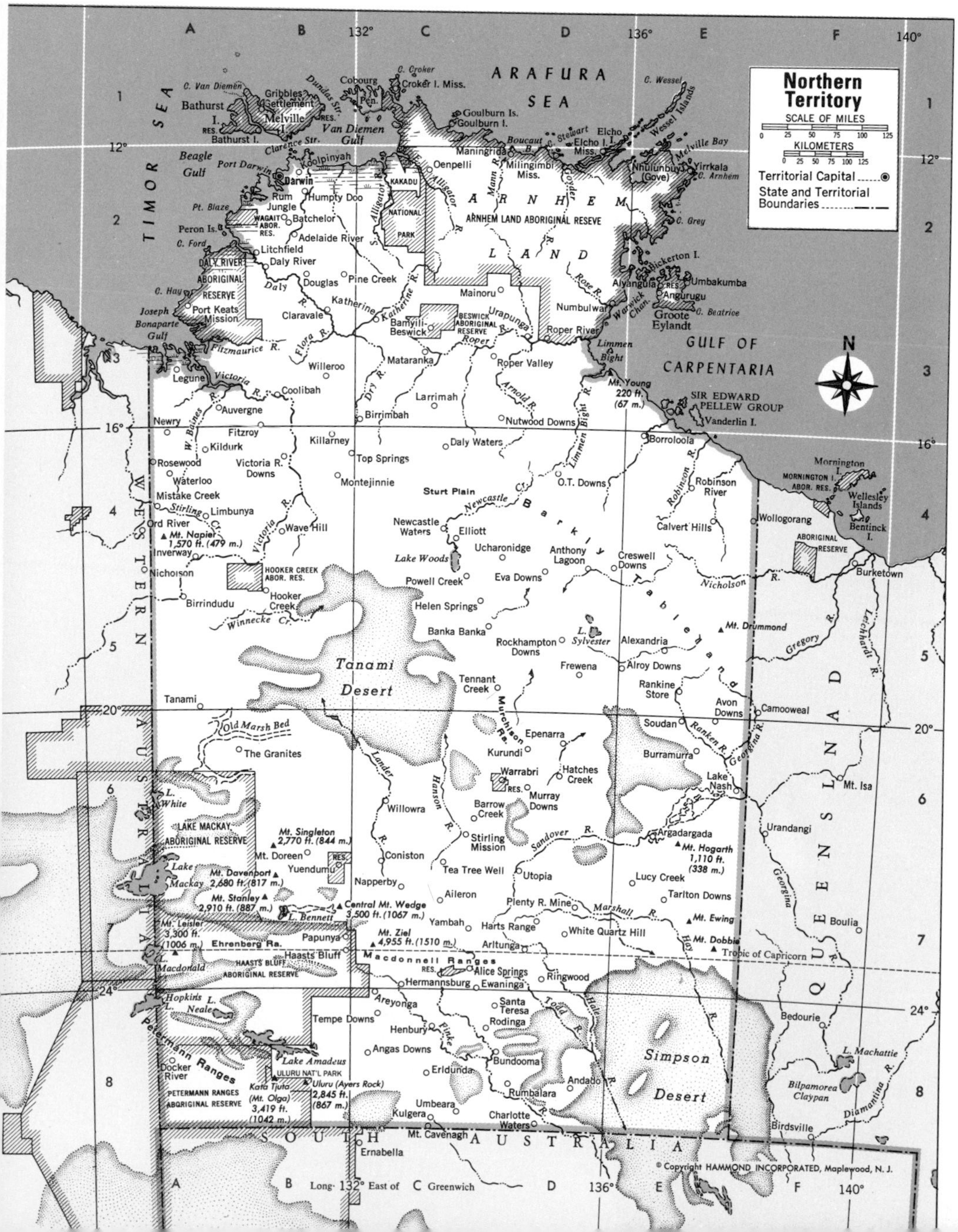

AREA 519,768 sq. mi. (1,346.200 sq. km.)
POPULATION 154,848
CAPITAL Darwin
LARGEST CITY Darwin
HIGHEST POINT Mt. Ziel 4,955 ft. (1,510 m.)

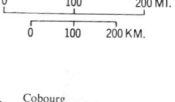

Topography

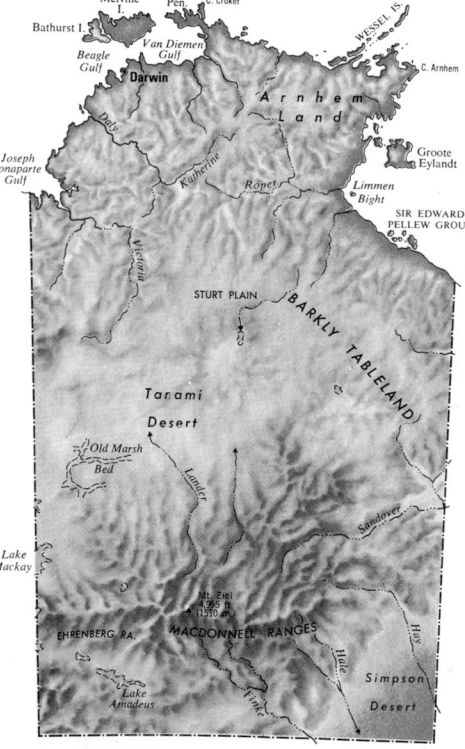

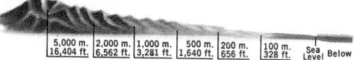

5,000 m. 16,404 ft.	2,000 m. 6,562 ft.	1,000 m. 3,281 ft.	500 m. 1,640 ft.	200 m. 656 ft.	100 m. 328 ft.	Sea Level Below

© Copyright HAMMOND INCORPORATED, Maplewood, N.J.

AREA 379,922 sq. mi. (984,000 sq. km.)
POPULATION 1,345,945
CAPITAL Adelaide
LARGEST CITY Adelaide
HIGHEST POINT Mt. Woodroffe 4,970 ft.
(1,515 m.)

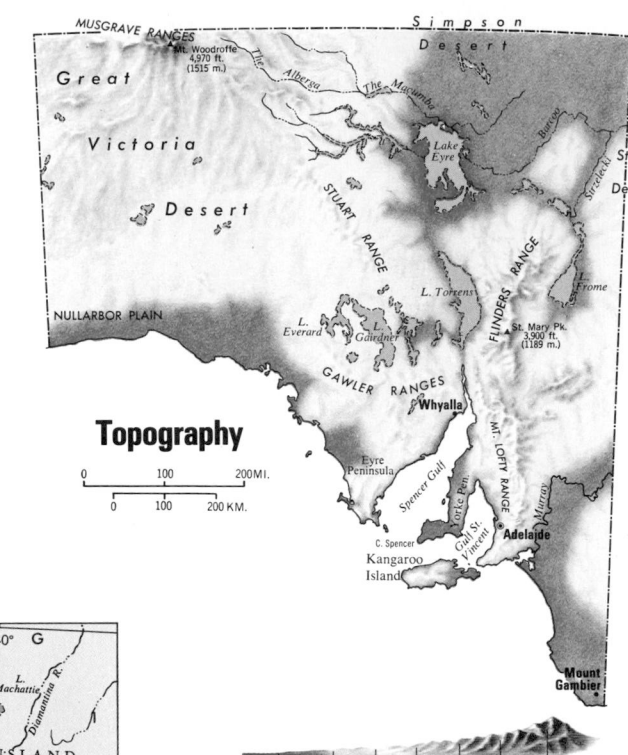

Topography

0	100	200 MI.
0	100	200 KM.

Below Sea Level	100 m. 328 ft.	200 m. 656 ft.	500 m. 1,640 ft.	1,000 m. 3,281 ft.	2,000 m. 6,562 ft.	5,000 m. 16,404 ft.

CITIES and TOWNS

Adelaide (cap.) 882,520 .... B6
Adelaide *931,886 .... B6
Andamooka 402 .... E4
Angaston 1,753 .... F6
Balaklava 1,306 .... F6
Barmera 2,014 .... G6
Beachport 357 .... F7
Berri 3,419 .... G6
Birdwood 397 .... C7
Blinman F4
Bordertown 2,138 ...... G7
Brighton 19,441 .... A8
Burnside 37,593 .... B8
Burra 1,222 .... F5
Campbelltown 43,084 ... B7
Ceduna 2,794 .... D5
Clare 2,381 .... F5
Cleve 827 .... E5
Coober Pedy 2,078 ..... D3
Cowell 626 .... E5
Crafters-Bridgewater 9,764 .. B8
Crystal Brook 1,240 .... E5
Cummins 767 .... D6
Edithburgh 359 .... E6
Elizabeth 32,608 ...... B7
Elliston ○1,345 ...... D5
Enfield 66,797 .... B7
Gawler 9,433 .... B6
Gladstone 680 .... F5
Glenelg 13,306 ...... A8
Gumeracha 387 ...... C7
Hahndorf 1,274 ...... C8
Hawker 351 .... F4
Hindmarsh 7,593 ..... A7
Iron Knob 398 ...... E5
Jamestown 1,384 .... F5
Kadina 2,943 ...... E5
Kapunda 1,340 ..... F6
Keith 1,147 .... G7
Kensington and Norwood
8,950 .... B8
Kimba 862 .... E5
Kingscote 1,236 .... E6
Kingston 1,325 ...... G7
Lameroo 599 .... G6
Laura 504 .... F5
Leigh Creek 1,635 ... F4
Lobethal 1,522 ..... C7
Lock 213 .... D5
Loxton 3,100 .... G6
Lyndoch 539 .... C6
Maitland 1,085 ..... E6
Mannum 1,984 ..... F6
Marion 66,580 ..... A8
Marree E3
Meadows 388 ..... B8
Meningie 807 ...... F6
Millicent 5,255 .... F7
Minlaton 865 ...... E6
Mitcham 60,309 ... B8
Moonta 1,751 ..... E5
Mount Barker 4,190 . C8
Mount Gambier 18,193 . G7
Murray Bridge 8,664 . F6
Nairne 706 .... C8
Nangwarry 758 .... G7

Naracoorte 4,758 .... G7
Noarlunga 60,928 ... A8
Nuriootpa 2,851 .... F6
Oodnadatta D2
Orroroo 604 .... F5
Payneham 16,502 ... B7
Penola 1,205 ...... G7
Peterborough 2,575 . F5
Pinnaroo 731 ..... G6
Port Adelaide 35,407 . A7
Port Augusta 15,566 . E5
Port Broughton 587 . F5
Port Lincoln 9,846 .. E6
Port Pirie 14,695 ... E5
Prospect 18,591 ... B7
Quorn 1,049 ...... F5
Renmark 3,475 .... G5
Robe 590 .... F7
Salisbury 86,451 ... B7
Snowtown 492 .... E5
Strathalbyn 1,756 .. F6
Streaky Bay 985 ... D5
Tailem Bend 1,677 . F6
Tanunda 2,621 .... C6
Tea Tree Gully 67,237 . B7
Thebarton 9,208 ... A7
Tumby Bay 933 .... E6
Unley 35,844 ..... B8
Uraidla 303 ...... C8
Victor Harbor 4,522 . F6
Virginia 353 ...... B7
Waikerie 1,629 .... F6
Wallaroo 2,043 .... E5
West Torrens 45,099 . A8
Whyalla 30,518 ... E5
Williamstown 495 .. C7
Willunga 667 ..... B8
Wilmington 227 ... F5
Woodside 724 .... C8
Woodville 77,634 .. A7
Woomera 1,658 ... E4
Wudinna 572 ..... D5
Yorketown 713 .... E6

OTHER FEATURES

Acraman (lake) D5
Alberga, The (riv.) .. D2
Alexandrina (lake) .. F6
Anxious (bay) D5
Arckaringa (creek) . F3
Barcoo (creek) F3
Birksgate (range) .. A2
Blanche (lake) F3
Brady (mt.) D3
Cadibarrawirracanna (lake) D3
Callabonna (lake) .. G3
Catastrophe (cape) . D6
Coffin (bay) D6
Coffin Bay (pen.) .. D6
Coorong, The (lag.) . F6
Coopers (Barcoo) (creek) F3
Dey Dey (lake) C3
Encounter (bay) ... F6
Everard (lake) D4
Everard (ranges) ... C2
Eyre (pen.) D5
Eyre North (lake) .. E3
Eyre South (lake) .. E3
Finke (riv.) C1

Flinders (range) F4
Frome (lake) G4
Gairdner (lake) D4
Gawler (ranges) E5
Gawler (riv.) B6
Gilles (lake) E5
Goyders (lag.) F2
Great Australian (bight) A5
Great Victoria (des.) . B3
Gregory (lake) F3
Hack (mt.) F4
Hamilton, The (riv.) . D2
Harris (lake) D4
Head of Bight (bay) . B4
Indian Ocean E7
Investigator (str.) .. E6
Investigator Group (isls.) D5
Island (lag.) E4
Jaffa (cape) F7
Kangaroo (isl.) 3,515 . E7
Lacepede (bay) F7
Lofty (mt.) B8
Macfarlane (lake) .. E5
Macumba, The (riv.) . E2
Maurice (lake) B3
Meramangye (lake) . C3
Morris (mt.) B2
Murray (res.) F6
Musgrave (ranges) .. B2
Neales, The (riv.) .. E3
Northumberland (cape) F8
Nukey Bluff (mt.) .. D5
Nullarbor (plain) .. A4
Nuyts (arch.) C5
Nuyts (caps.) C5
Peera Peera Poolanna (lake) F2
Saint Mary (peak) .. F4
Saint Vincent (gulf) . F6
Serpentine (lakes) .. A3
Simpson (des.) E1
Sir Joseph Banks Group
(isls.) E6
Spencer (cape) E6
Spencer (gulf) E6
Stevenson, The (riv.) . D2
Streaky (bay) C5
Strzelecki (creek) .. G3
Stuart (range) D3
Sturt (des.) G3
The Alberga (riv.) .. D2
The Coorong (lag.) . F6
The Hamilton (riv.) . D2
The Macumba (riv.) . E2
The Neales (riv.) .. E3
The Stevenson (riv.) . D2
The Warburton (riv.) . F2
Thistle (isl.) E6
Torrens (lake) E4
Torrens (riv.) C7
Warburton, The (riv.) . F2
Wilkinson (lakes) .. C3
Woodroffe (mt.) ... B2
Yalata Aboriginal Res. . B4
Yarle (lakes) B4
Yorke (pen.) E6

○ Population of district.
*Population of met. area.

Adelaide and Vicinity

South Australia

SCALE OF MILES

KILOMETERS

State Capital .... ◉
State and Territorial
Boundaries ....

© Copyright HAMMOND INCORPORATED, Maplewood, N.J.

CITIES and TOWNS

Aramac 428 .... C4
Archerfield 785 .... D3
Ascot 4,298 .... E2
Atherton 4,196 .... C3
Ayr 8,787 .... C3
Balmoral 2,915 .... E2
Barcaldine 1,432 .... C4
Beaudesert 3,780 .... E6
Biloela 4,643 .... D5
Birdsville A5
Blackall 1,609 .... C5
Blackwater 5,434 .... D4
Boulia 292 .... A4
Bowen 7,663 .... D3
Brisbane (cap.) 689,378 .... D2
Brisbane *1,028,527 .... E5
Bucasia 1,356 .... D4
Bundaberg 32,560 .... D5
Burketown 210 .... A3
Cairns 48,557 .... C3
Caloundra 16,758 .... E5
Camooweal 251 .... A3
Camp Hill 8,999 .... E3
Capella 660 .... D4
Cardwell 1,249 .... C3
Charleville 3,523 .... C5
Charters Towers 6,823 .... C4
Cherbourg 963 .... D5
Chermside 6,892 .... D2
Clermont 1,659 .... C4
Cloncurry 1,961 .... B4
Collinsville 2,756 .... C4
Coopers Plains 4,492 .... E3
Corinda 4,894 .... D3
Croydon ○255 .... B3
Cunnamulla 1,627 .... C5
Dalby 8,784 .... D5
Dirranbandi 480 .... D6
East Brisbane 4,853 .... E3
Eidsvold 613 .... D5
Emerald 4,628 .... C4
Esk 676 .... E5
Gatton 4,190 .... E5
Gayndah 1,708 .... D5
Geebung 4,850 .... E2
Georgetown 319 .... B3
Gladstone 22,083 .... D4
Gold Coast 135,437 .... E6
Goondiwindi 3,576 .... D6
Gordonvale 2,375 .... C3
Greenslopes 7,219 .... E3
Gympie 10,768 .... E5

Hervey Bay 13,569 .... E5
Holland Park 7,363 .... E3
Home Hill 3,138 .... C3
Hughenden 1,657 .... B4
Inala 17,383 .... D3
Indooroopilly 7,959 .... D3
Ingham 5,598 .... C3
Injune 407 .... D5
Innisfail 7,933 .... C3
Ipswich 68,297 .... E5
Isisford ○605 .... C5
Jandowae 781 .... D5
Jericho ○1,177 .... C4
Julia Creek 602 .... B4
Karumba 670 .... B3
Kilcoy 1,257 .... E5
Kingaroy 5,134 .... D5
Longreach 2,971 .... B4
Mackay 35,361 .... D4
Mareeba 6,309 .... C3
Marian 796 .... D4
Maroochydore-Mooloolaba 17,460 .... E5
Maryborough 20,111 .... E5
Mary Kathleen 830 .... A4
McKinlay ○1,477 .... B4
Millmerran 1,107 .... D5
Mitchell 1,171 .... C5
Mitchelton 5,810 .... D2
Monto 1,397 .... D5
Moorooka 8,740 .... D3
Moranbah 4,362 .... C9
Mossman 1,614 .... C3
Moura 2,871 .... D5
Mount Isa 23,679 .... A4
Murgon 2,327 .... D5
Nambour 7,965 .... E5
Newmarket 3,520 .... D2
Normanton 926 .... B3
Nundah 7,358 .... E2
Proserpine 3,058 .... D4
Quilpie 694 .... C5
Ravenshoe 915 .... C3
Redcliffe 42,223 .... E5
Richmond 784 .... B4
Rockhampton 50,146 .... D4
Roma 5,706 .... D5
Saint George 2,204 .... D5
Saint Lucia 6,075 .... D3
Sandgate 6,776 .... D2
Sarina 2,815 .... D4
Springsure 774 .... C5
Stafford (Stafford Heights) 13,731 .... D2
Stanthorpe 3,966 .... D6
Tara 864 .... D5

Taroom 688 .... D5
Tewantin-Noosa 9,965 .... E5
Theodore 643 .... D5
Thursday Island 2,283 .... B1
Toowoomba 63,401 .... D5
Townsville 86,112 .... C3
Tully 2,728 .... C3
Walkerston 1,277 .... D4
Warwick 8,853 .... D6
Weipa 2,433 .... B2
Windsor 6,119 .... D2
Winton 1,259 .... B4
Wynnum 10,794 .... E5

Yeppoon 6,447 .... D4
Yeronga 4,579 .... D3

OTHER FEATURES

Albatross (bay) B2
Archer (riv.) B2
Balonne (riv.) D6
Banks (isl.) B1
Barcoo (creek) C5
Barkly Tableland A4
Bartle Frere (mt.) C3
Beal (range) B5

AREA 666,872 sq. mi. (1,727,200 sq. km.)
POPULATION 2,587,315
CAPITAL Brisbane
LARGEST CITY Brisbane
HIGHEST POINT Mt. Bartle Frere 5,287 ft. (1,611 m.)

Topography

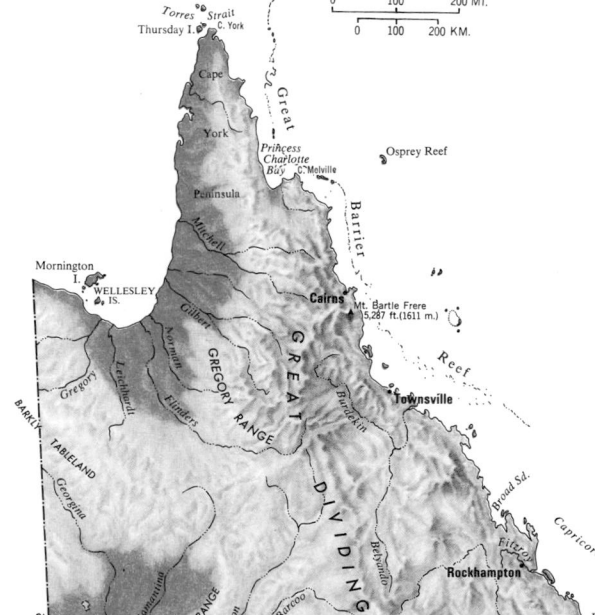

Belyando (riv.) C4
Broad (sound) D4
Bulloo (lake) B6
Bulloo (riv.) B6
Bunker Group (isls.) E4
Burdekin (riv.) C3
Cape York (pen.) B2
Capricorn (chan.) D4
Capricorn Group (isls.) E4
Carnarvon (range) D5
Carpentaria (gulf) A2
Cloncurry (riv.) B4
Coopers (Barcoo) (creek) B5
Coral (sea) C1
Culgoa (riv.) C6
Cumberland (isls.) D4
Curtis (isl.) D4
Darling Downs D5
Dawson (riv.) D5
Diamantina (riv.) B4
Drummond (range) C4
Duifken (pt.) B2
Endeavour (str.) B1

Fitzroy (riv.) D4
Flinders (riv.) B3
Fraser (isl.) E5
Georgina (riv.) A4
Gilbert (riv.) B3
Great Dividing (range) C4
Gregory (range) B3
Gregory (riv.) A3
Grey (range) B5
Hamilton (riv.) B4
Hervey (bay) E5
Hinchinbrook (isl.) C3
Hook (isl.) D4
Leichhardt (riv.) A3
Machattie (lake) B5
Macinyre (riv.) D6
Maranoa (riv.) C5
Mary (riv.) E5
Melville (cape) C2
Mitchell (riv.) B3
Moreton (bay) E5
Moreton (isl.) E5
Mornington (isl.) A3

Norman (riv.) B3
Northern Peninsula Aboriginal Res. B1
Prince of Wales (isl.) B1
Princess Charlotte (bay) C2
Sandy (cape) E5
Selwyn (range) B4
Simpson (des.) A5
Sturt (des.) B3
Suttor (riv.) C4
Swain (reefs) E4
Thompson (riv.) B5
Torres (str.) B1
Warrego (range) C5
Warrego (riv.) C5
Wellesley (isls.) A3
Whitsunday (isl.) D4
Willies (range) C6
Yamma Yamma (lake) B5
York (cape) B1

○ Population of district.
*Population of met. area.

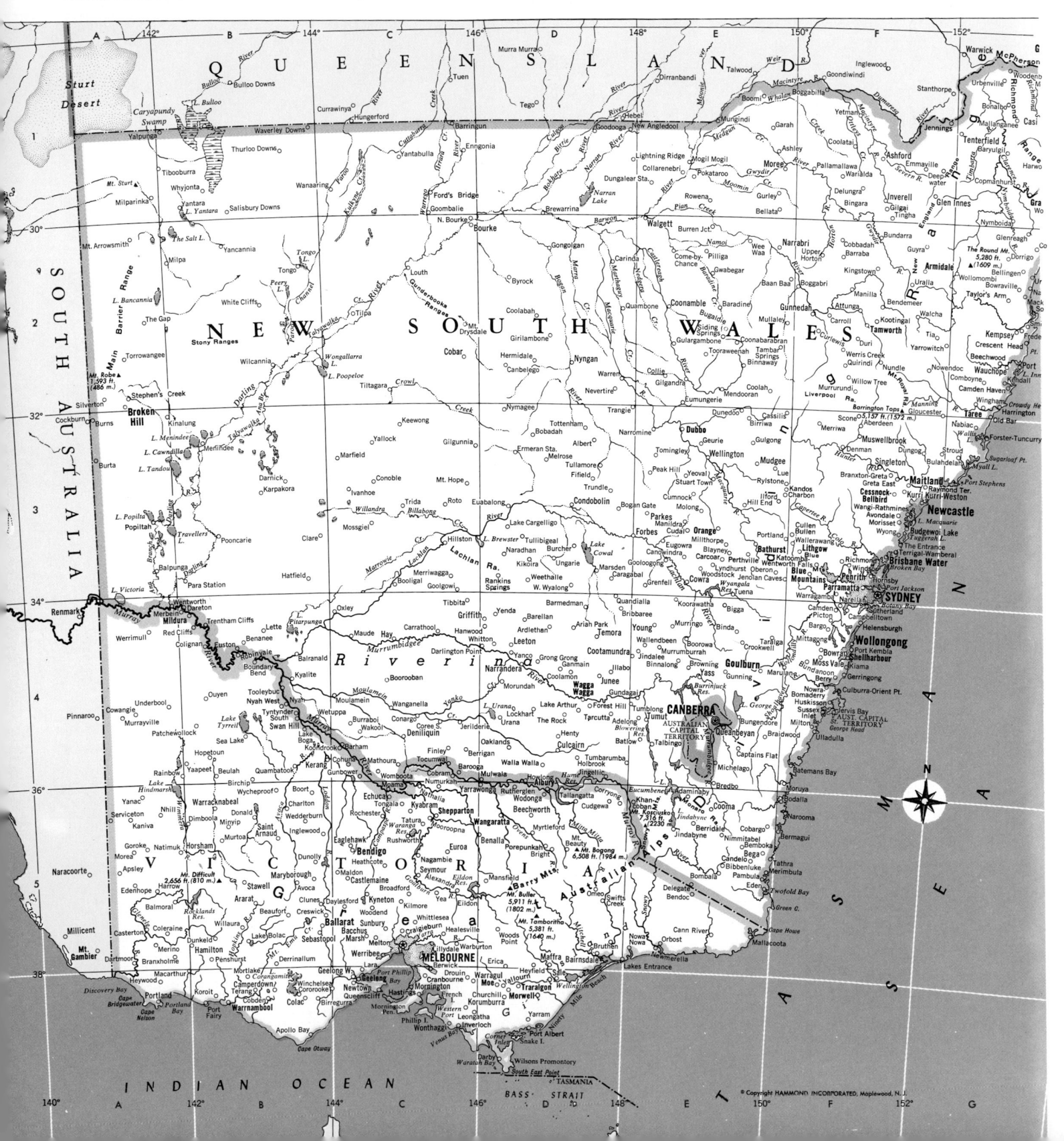

NEW SOUTH WALES

AREA 309,498 sq. mi.
(801,600 sq. km.)
POPULATION 5,401,881
CAPITAL Sydney
LARGEST CITY Sydney
HIGHEST POINT Mt. Kosciusko
7,310 ft. (2,228 m.)

VICTORIA

AREA 87,876 sq. mi.
(227,600 sq. km.)
POPULATION 4,019,478
CAPITAL Melbourne
LARGEST CITY Melbourne
HIGHEST POINT Mt. Bogong
6,508 ft. (1,984 m.)

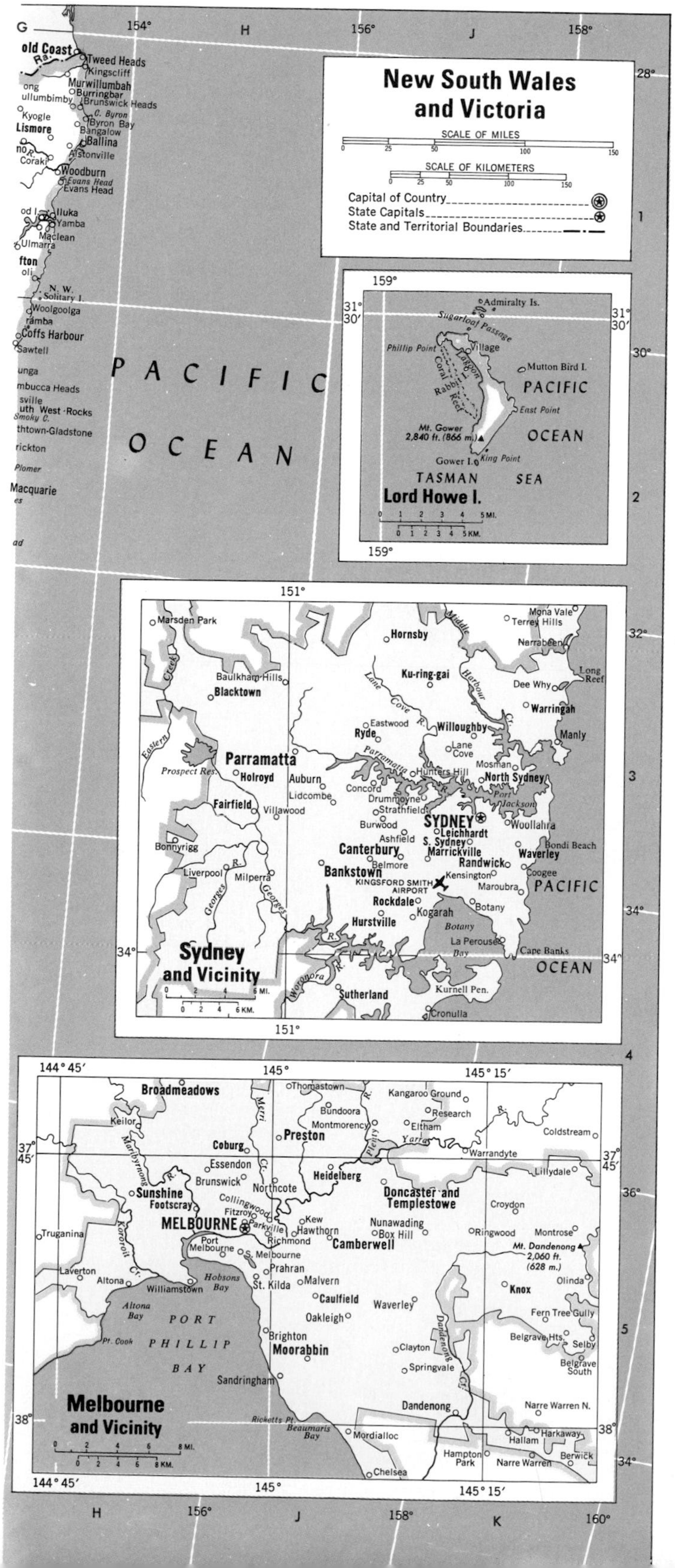

Topography

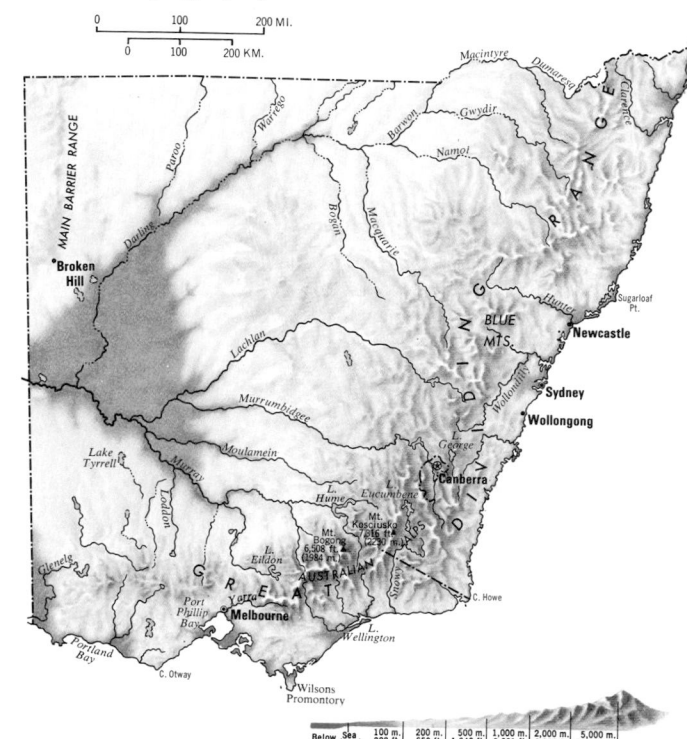

Fairfield 129,557. .... H3	Keewong C3	Moss Vale 4,415 .... F4
Finley 2,193 .... C4	Kempsey 9,037 .... G2	Mossgiel C4
Forbes 8,029 .... E3	Kendall 522. .... G2	Moulamein 396 .... C4
Forest Hill 1,977 .... D4	Khancoban 515 .... E5	Mount Arrowsmith A2
Forster-Tuncurry 9,261. ... G3	Kiama 7,717 .... F4	Mount Drysdale C2
Frederickton 616. .... G2	Kinalung B3	Mount Hope C3
Ganmain 650 .... D4	Kogarah 46,322 .... J4	Mudgee 6,015. .... E3
Geurie 290 .... E3	Koorawatha 262 .... E4	Mullumbimby 2,234 .... G1
Gilgai 257 .... F1	Kootingal 731 .... F2	Mungindi 707 .... E1
Gilgandra 2,700 .... E2	Ku-ring-gai 101,501 ...... J3	Murrumburrah 2,070 ...... E4
Gilgunnia C3	Kurri Kurri-Weston 12,795 . F3	Murrurundi 861 .... F2
Glen Innes 6,052. .... F1	Kyogle 3,070 .... G1	Murwillumbah 7,807 ...... G1
Glenreagh 233 .... G2	Lake Cargellico 1,240 ...... D3	Muswellbrook 8,548 ...... F3
Gloucester 2,488. .... F2	Lane Cove 29,113 .... J3	Nabiac 363 .... G3
Goodooga 248 .... D1	Leeton 6,498 .... D4	Nambucca Heads 4,053 .... G2
Coolgowi 245 .... C3	Leichhardt 57,332 .... J3	Narellan 2,104 .... F3
Gooloogong 221 .... E3	Lette B4	Narooma 2,758 .... F5
Goombalie C2	Lidcombe J3	Narrabeen K3
Goulburn 21,755. .... E4	Lightning Ridge 1,112 ...... E1	Narrabri 7,296 .... E2
Grafton 17,005. .... G2	Lismore 24,033 .... G1	Narrandera 5,013 .... D4
Grenfell 2,070 .... E3	Lithgow 12,793 .... F3	Narromine 2,994. .... D3
Greta-Branxton 2,849 ...... F3	Liverpool 92,715 .... H4	New Angledool E1
Greta East 398. .... F3	Lockhart 923 .... D4	Newcastle 135,207 .... F3
Griffith 13,187 .... C4	Macksville 2,352 .... G2	Newcastle †389,237 ...... F3
Gulargambone 457 ...... E2	Maclean 2,593 .... G1	Nimmitabel 257. .... E5
Gulgong 1,740 .... E3	Maitland 38,865 .... F3	North Sydney 48,500 ...... J3
Gundagai 2,308 .... D4	Manildra 520. .... E3	Nowra-Bomaderry 17,887. .. F4
Gunnedah 8,909 .... F2	Manilla 1,884 .... F2	Nundle 235 .... F2
Gunning 438 .... E4	Manly 37,080 .... K3	Nymboida ○2,044 .... G1
Guyra 1,840 .... F2	Maroubra K3	Nyngan 2,485 .... D2
Hanwood 306 .... C4	Marrickville 83,448 ...... J3	Oaklands 283 .... D4
Harrington 1,183 .... G3	Marsden D3	Oberon 1,937 .... E3
Hay 2,958 .... C4	Marsden Park 518 .... H3	Old Bar 970 .... G3
Henty 883 .... D4	Marulan 330 .... E4	Orange 27,626 .... E3
Hillston 999 .... C3	Mathoura 582 .... C4	Pallamallawa 340 .... F1
Holbrook 1,276 .... D4	Melrose D3	Pambula 604 .... E5
Holroyd 80,116. .... H3	Mendooran 325. .... E2	Parkes 9,047. .... E3
Hornsby 111,081 .... J3	Menindee 455 .... B2	Parramatta 130,943 ...... H3
Howlong 1,072 .... D4	Merimbula 2,899 .... F5	Peak Hill 1,037 .... E3
Hunters Hill 12,537 ...... J3	Merriwa 943 .... E2	Penrith 108,720 .... F3
Hurstville 64,910. .... J4	Millthorpe 607. .... E3	Perthville 639 .... E3
Huskisson 2,296 .... F4	Milpa B2	Picton 1,817 .... F4
Iluka 1,362 .... G1	Milperra H4	Pilliga 206 .... E2
Inverell 9,734 .... F1	Milton 740 .... F4	Popiltah A3
Ivanhoe 517 .... C3	Mittagong 4,266 .... F4	Portland 1,980 .... E3
Jerilderie 1,075. .... C4	Moama C5	Port Kembla F4
Jindabyne 1,602 .... E5	Mogil Mogil. E1	Port Macquarie 19,581. .... G2
Junee 3,993 .... D4	Molong 1,374 .... E3	Queanbeyan 19,383 ...... E4
Kandos 1,626 .... F3	Mona Vale K2	Quirindi 2,851 .... F2
Karpakora B3	Moree 10,459 .... E1	Randwick 116,202 .... J3
Katoomba-Wentworth Falls	Morisset 1,593 .... F3	Raymond Terrace 7,548 .... F3
13,942 .... F3	Moruya 2,003 .... F4	Richmond-Windsor 15,491. .. F3
	Mosman 26,200 .... J3	Rockdale 83,719 .... J4

(continued on following page)

(continued)

Ryde 88,948 J3
Rylstone 651 E3
Salisbury Downs B1
Sawtell 5,970 G2
Scone 3,949 F3
Shellharbour 41,790 F4
Singleton 9,572 F3
Smithtown-Gladstone 953 G2
South Sydney 30,776 J3
South West Rocks 1,314 G2
Stephen's Creek A2
Strathfield 25,882 J3
Stroud 522 G3
Sussex Inlet 1,293 F4
Sutherland 165,336 J4
Sydney (cap.) 2,876,508 J3
Sydney †3,204,696 J3
Talbingo 481 E4
Tamworth 29,657 F2
Taralga 272 E4
Tarcutta 263 D4
Taree 14,697 G2
Tathra 1,077 F5
Temora 4,350 D4
Tenterfield 3,402 G1
Terrigal-The Entrance 37,891 F3
The Rock 693 D4
Thurloo Downs B1
Tibbita C4
Tibooburra B1
Tiltagara C2
Tingha 886 F1
Tocumwal 1,174 C4
Tongo B2
Torrowangee A2
Tottenham 366 D3
Trangie 977 D3
Trundle 515 D3
Tullamore 324 D3
Tumbarumba 1,536 D4
Tumut 5,816 E4
Tweed Heads G1
Ulladulla 6,018 F4
Ulmarra 395 G1
Ungarie 428 D3
Uralla 2,090 F2
Urana 419 D4
Urbenville 282 G1
Urunga 2,045 G2
Villawood H3
Wagga Wagga 36,837 D4
Wakool 278 C4
Walcha 1,674 F2
Walgett 2,157 E2
Walla Walla 593 D4
Wallerawang 1,855 F3
Wangi-Rathmines 5,106 F3
Warialda 1,340 F1
Warragamba 1,406 F3
Warren 2,153 D2
Warringah ○172,653 K3
Wauchope 3,645 G2
Waverley 61,575 K3
Waverley Downs B1
Wee Waa 1,904 E2
Wellington 5,280 E3
Wentworth 1,180 B4
Werris Creek 1,924 F2
West Wyalong 3,778 D3
Wetuppa B4
White Cliffs B2
Whitton 344 D4
Whyjonta B1
Wilcannia 982 B2
Willoughby 52,120 J3
Willow Tree 258 F2
Wingham 3,937 G2
Wollongong 169,381 F4
Wollongong †222,539 F4
Woodburn 647 G1
Woodenbong 409 G1
Woodstock 266 E3
Woolgoolga 2,081 G2
Wooli 457 G1
Woollahra 51,659 K3
Wyong 3,902 F3
Yallock C3
Yalpunga A1
Yamba 2,528 G1
Yancannia B2
Yanco 415 D4
Yantara B1
Yass 4,283 E4
Yenda 697 D4
Yeoval 288 E3
Young 6,906 E4

OTHER FEATURES

Ana Branch, Darling (riv.) A3
Australian Alps (mts.) D5
Barrington Tops (mt.) F2
Barwon (riv.) D2
Blue (mts.) F3
Bogan (riv.) D2
Bondi (beach) K3
Botany (bay) J4
Broken (bay) F3
Burrinjuck (res.) E4
Byron (cape) G1
Caryapundy (swamp) B1
Castlereagh (riv.) E2
Cawndilla (lake) A3
Clarence (riv.) G1
Colo (riv.) F3
Cowal (lake) D3
Culgoa (riv.) D1
Cuttaburra (creek) C1
Darling (riv.) B3
Dumaresq (riv.) F1
Eucumbene (lake) E5
George (lake) E4
Georges (riv.) H4
Gower (mt.) J2
Great Dividing (range) E3
Green (cape) F5
Gunderbooka (ranges) C2
Gwydir (riv.) E1
Howe (cape) F5
Hume (res.) D4
Hunter (riv.) F3
Kosciusko (mt.) E5
Kurnell (pen.) J4
Lachlan (range) C3
Lachlan (riv.) C3
Liverpool (range) F2
Lord Howe (isl.) 287 J2
Macintyre (riv.) E1
Macquarie (lake) F3
Macquarie (riv.) D2
Main Barrier (range) A2
Manning (riv.) F2
Marthaguy (creek) D2
McPherson (range) G1
Menindee (lake) B3
Monaro (range) E5
Moonie (riv.) E1
Moulamein (creek) C4
Mount Royal (range) F2
Murray (riv.) A4
Murrumbidgee (riv.) C4
Myall (lake) G3
Namoi (riv.) E2
Narran (lake) D1
New England (range) F1
Paroo (riv.) C1
Parramatta (riv.) J3
Poopelloe (lake) C2
Port Jackson (inlet) J3
Port Stephens (inlet) G3
Richmond (range) G1
Richmond (riv.) G1
Riverina (reg.) C4
Robe (mt.) A2
Round, The (mt.) G2
Salt, The (lake) B2
Shoalhaven (riv.) E4
Smoky (cape) G2
Snowy (mts.) E5
Snowy (riv.) E5
Stony (ranges) B2
Sturt (mt.) A1
Sugarloaf (pt.) G3
Talyawalka (creek) B2
Tandou (lake) A3
Tasman (sea) F5
The Round (mts.) G2
The Salt (lake) B2
Timbarra (riv.) G1
Tuggerah (lake) F3
Victoria (lake) A3
Warrego (riv.) C1
Willandra Billabong (creek) C3
Wollondilly (riv.) F4

VICTORIA

CITIES and TOWNS

Alexandra 1,756 C5
Altona 30,909 H5
Apollo Bay 921 B6
Ararat 8,336 B5
Avoca 1,032 B5
Bacchus Marsh 6,224 C5
Bairnsdale 9,459 D5
Ballarat 35,681 C5
Ballarat †71,930 C5
Balmoral 257 A5
Beaufort 1,214 B5
Beechworth 3,154 D5
Belgrave Heights J5
Belgrave South K5
Benalla 8,151 D5
Bendigo 31,841 C5
Bendigo †58,818 C5
Berwick 36,181 K6
Beulah 290 B4
Birchip 895 B4
Birregurra 416 B6
Boort 863 B5
Box Hill 47,579 J5
Bright 1,545 D5
Brighton 33,697 J5
Broadford 1,580 C5
Broadmeadows 103,540 H4
Brunswick 44,464 H5
Bruthen 449 D5
Bundoora J4
Camberwell 85,883 J5
Camperdown 3,545 C6
Cann River 345 E5
Casterton 1,945 A5
Castlemaine 7,583 C5
Caulfield 69,922 J5
Charlton 1,377 B5
Chelsea 26,034 J6
Churchill 4,796 D6
Clunes 761 B5
Cobden 1,453 B6
Cobram 3,817 C4
Coburg 55,035 H5
Cohuna 2,178 C4
Colac 10,587 B6
Coldstream 1,395 K4
Coleraine 1,232 A5
Collingwood 15,089 J5
Corryong 1,320 D5
Craigieburn 4,296 C5
Cranbourne 9,400 C6
Creswick 2,036 B5
Croydon 36,210 K5
Dandenong 54,962 K5
Darby D6
Dartmoor 349 A5
Daylesford 2,883 C5
Derrinallum 287 B5
Dimboola 1,675 B5
Donald 1,609 B5
Doncaster and Templestowe 90,660 J5
Drouin 3,492 C6
Dunkeld 402 B5
Dunolly 621 B5
Eaglehawk 7,355 C5
Echuca 7,943 C5
Edenhope 827 A5
Eildon 737 C5
Eltham 34,648 J4
Erica 236 D5
Essendon 56,380 H5
Euroa 2,640 C5
Fitzroy 19,112 H5
Footscray 49,756 H5
Geelong 14,471 C6
Geelong †137,173 C6
Geelong West 14,823 C6
Goroke 370 A5
Gunbower 259 C4
Hamilton 9,751 B5
Hawthorn 30,689 J5
Healesville 4,526 C5
Heathcote 1,213 C5
Heidelberg 64,757 J5
Heyfield 1,635 D6
Heywood 1,266 A6
Hopetoun 1,832 B4
Horsham 12,034 B5
Inglewood 674 B5
Inverloch 1,523 C6
Kaniva 956 A5
Keilor 81,762 H5
Kerang 4,049 B4
Kew 28,870 J5
Kilmore 1,728 C5
Knox 88,902 K5
Koroit 1,988 B6
Korumburra 2,798 D6
Kyabram 5,414 C5
Kyneton 3,185 C5
Lake Boga 502 B4
Lake Bolac 211 B5
Lakes Entrance 3,414 E5
Lara 4,231 C6
Leongatha 3,736 C6
Lillydale 62,077 J4
Macarthur 322 A6
Maffra 3,822 D5
Maldon 1,009 C5
Mallacoota 726 E5
Malvern 43,211 J5
Mansfield 1,920 D5
Maryborough 7,858 B5
Melbourne (cap.) 2,578,759 H5
Melbourne †2,722,817 H5
Melton 20,599 C5
Merbein 1,735 A4
Merino 298 A5
Mildura 15,763 A4
Minyip 567 B5
Moe 16,649 D6
Montmorency J4
Montrose K5
Moorabbin 97,810 J5
Mooroopna C5
Mordialloc 27,869 J6
Morea A5
Mornington 23,512 C6
Mortlake 1,056 B6
Morwell 16,491 D5
Mount Beauty 1,509 D5
Murrayville 313 A4
Murtoa 946 B5
Myrtleford 2,815 D5
Nagambie 1,102 C5
Narre Warren North 761 K5
Nathalia 1,222 C5
Natimuk 482 A5
Newtown 10,210 C6
Nhill 1,567 A5
Northcote 51,235 J5
Numurkah 2,713 C5
Nunawading 97,052 J5
Nyah 351 B4
Nyah West 535 B4
Oakleigh 55,612 J5
Omeo 272 D5
Orbost 2,586 E5
Ouyen 1,527 B4
Penshurst 558 B5
Porepunkah 268 D5
Port Albert 267 D6
Port Fairy 2,276 B6
Portland 9,353 A6
Port Melbourne 8,585 H5
Prahran 45,018 J5
Preston 84,519 J4
Quambatook 359 B4
Queenscliff 3,420 C6
Rainbow 700 A4
Red Cliffs 2,409 B4
Richmond 24,506 J5
Ringwood 38,665 K5
Robinvale 1,751 B4
Rochester 2,399 C5
Rushworth 994 C5
Rutherglen 1,454 D5
Saint Arnaud 2,721 B5
Saint Kilda 49,366 J5
Sale 12,968 D6
Sandringham 31,175 J5
Sea Lake 943 B4
Sebastopol 6,462 B5
Seymour 6,494 C5
Shepparton-Mooroopna ‡28,373 C5
South Barwon 35,307 C6
South Melbourne 19,955 J5
Springvale 80,186 J5
Stawell 6,160 B5
Sunbury 11,085 C5
Sunshine 94,419 H5
Swan Hill 8,398 B4
Swifts Creek 288 D5
Tallangatta 950 D5
Tatura 2,697 C5
Templestowe and Doncaster 90,660 J5
Terang 2,111 B6
Tongala 994 C5
Traralgon 18,057 D6
Underbool 274 A4
Wangaratta 16,202 D5
Warburton 2,009 C5
Warracknabeal 2,735 B5
Warragul 7,712 D6
Warrnambool 21,414 B6
Waverley 122,471 J5
Wedderburn 868 B5
Werrimull A4
Whittlesea 65,657 C5
Willaura 377 B5
Williamstown 25,554 H5
Winchelsea 825 B6
Wodonga 19,208 D5
Wonthaggi 4,797 C6
Woodend 1,785 C5
Wycheproof 938 B5
Yallourn 26 D6
Yarram 2,085 D6
Yarrawonga 3,442 C5
Yea 996 C5

OTHER FEATURES

Australian Alps (mts.) D5
Avoca (riv.) B5
Barry (mts.) D5
Bogong (mt.) D5
Bridgewater (cape) A6
Buller (mt.) D5
Campaspe (riv.) C5
Corangamite (lake) B6
Corner (inlet) D6
Dandenong (mt.) K5
Difficult (mt.) B5
Discovery (bay) A6
Eildon (lake) C5
French (isl.) 123 C6
Gippsland (reg.) D6
Glenelg (riv.) A5
Goulburn (riv.) C5
Hindmarsh (lake) A5
Hobsons (bay) H5
Hopkins (riv.) B5
Hume (lake) D4
Indian Ocean B6
Loddon (riv.) B5
Mitchell (riv.) D5
Mitta Mitta (riv.) D5
Mornington (pen.) C6
Mount Emu (creek) B5
Murray (riv.) A4
Nelson (cape) A6
Ninety Mile (beach) D6
Otway (cape) B6
Ovens (riv.) D5
Phillip (isl.) 2,832 C6
Portland (bay) A6
Port Phillip (bay) C6
Rocklands (res.) B5
Snowy (riv.) E5
South East (pt.) D6
Tasman (sea) F5
Tyrrell (lake) B4
Waratah (bay) C6
Wellington (lake) D6
Western Port (inlet) C6
Wilsons (prom.) D6
Wimmera (riv.) A5
Yarra (riv.) C5

*City and suburbs.
○ Population of district.
†Population of met. area.
‡Population of urban area.

Irrigation Areas and Artesian Basins in Australia

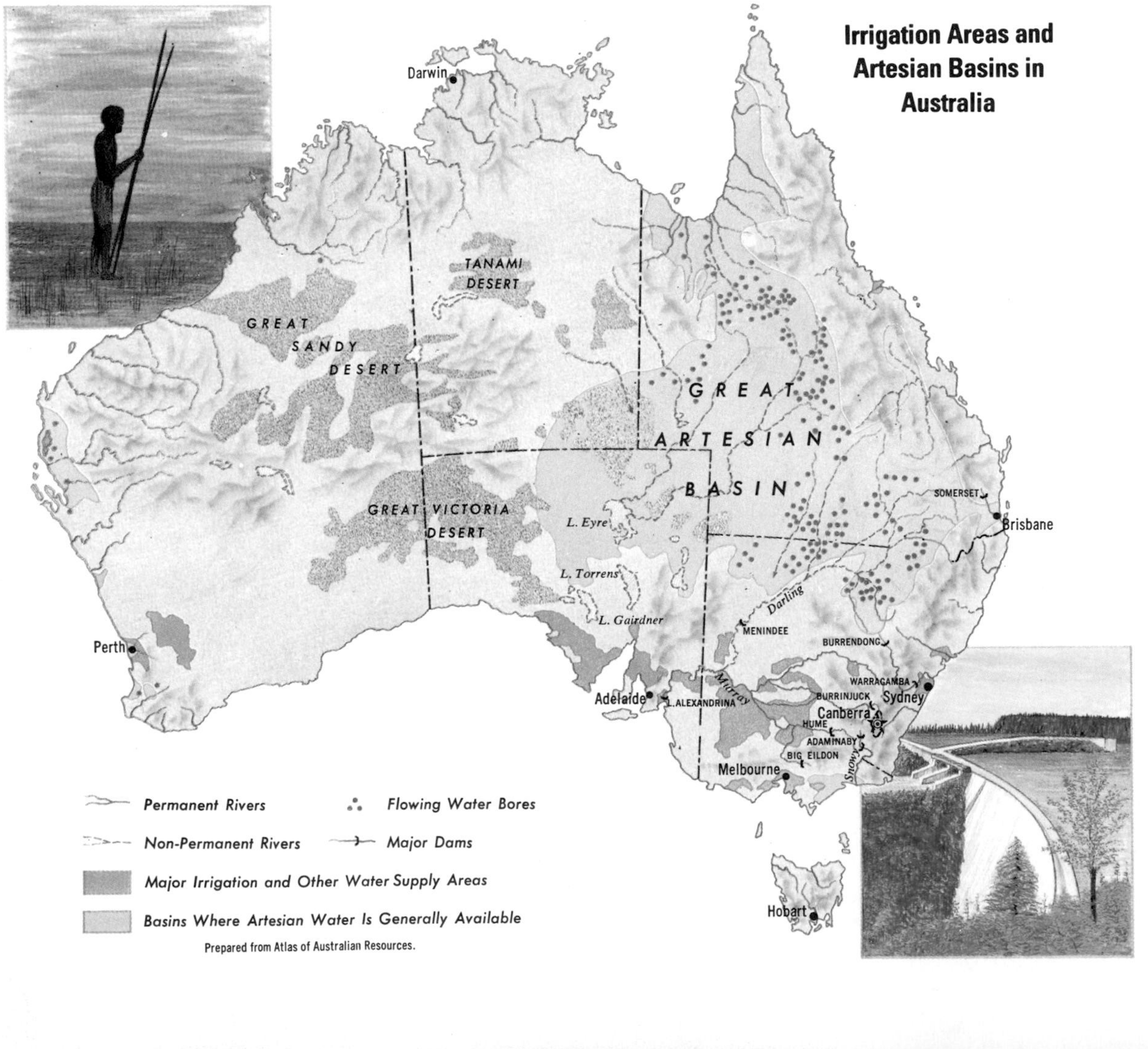
Darwin
TANAMI DESERT
GREAT SANDY DESERT
GREAT ARTESIAN BASIN
GREAT VICTORIA DESERT
L. Eyre
L. Torrens
L. Gairdner
Darling
MENINDEE
BURRENDONG
SOMERSET
Brisbane
Perth
Adelaide
L. ALEXANDRINA
Murray
WARRAGAMBA
BURRINJUCK
Sydney
Canberra
HUME
ADAMINABY
BIG EILDON
Snowy
Melbourne
Hobart
Permanent Rivers
Non-Permanent Rivers
Flowing Water Bores
Major Dams
Major Irrigation and Other Water Supply Areas
Basins Where Artesian Water Is Generally Available

Prepared from Atlas of Australian Resources.

Topography

0   30   60 MI
0   30   60 KM.

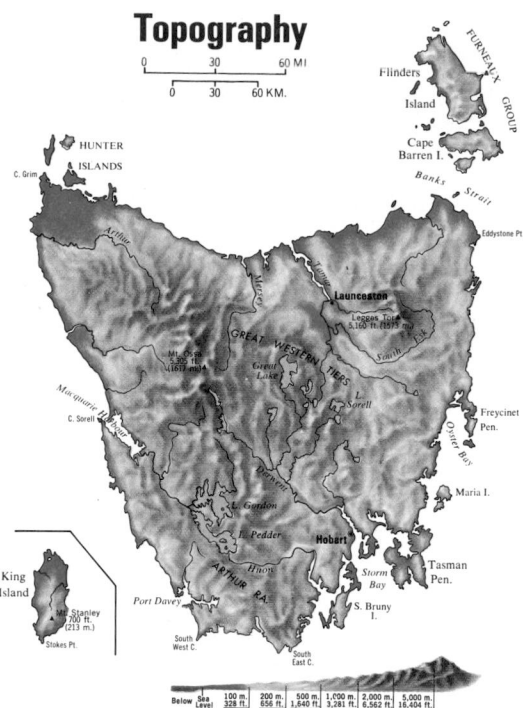

FURNEAUX GROUP

Flinders Island

Cape Barren I.

Banks Strait

HUNTER ISLANDS
C. Grim

Eddystone Pt.

Launceston
Legges Tor (5,160 ft.) (1593 m.)

GREAT WESTERN TIERS

Mt. Ossa (1617 m.)

Great Lake

L. Sorell

C. Sorell

Freycinet Pen.

Oyster Bay

Maria I.

Hobart

L. Gordon

L. Pedder

ARTHUR RA.

Huon

Port Davey

South West C.

South East C.

Storm Bay

Tasman Pen.

S. Bruny I.

King Island

Stanley 700 ft. (213 m.)

Stokes Pt.

Below Sea Level | 100 m. 328 ft. | 200 m. 656 ft. | 500 m. 1,640 ft. | 1,000 m. 3,281 ft. | 2,000 m. 6,562 ft. | 5,000 m. 16,404 ft.

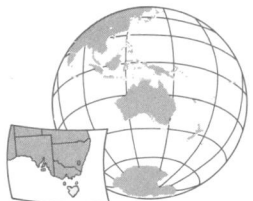

TASMANIA

AREA 26,178 sq. mi. (67,800 sq. km.)
POPULATION 436,353
CAPITAL Hobart
LARGEST CITY Hobart
HIGHEST POINT Mt. Ossa 5,305 ft. (1,617 m.)

Forth (riv.) C3
Frankland (cape) D1
Frankland (range) B4
Franklin (riv.) B4
Frenchmans Cap (mt.) B4
Freycinet (pen.) E4
Furneaux Group (isls.) 1,039 E1
Gordon (lake) B4
Gordon (riv.) B4
Great (lake) C3
Great Western Tiers (mts.) . . . C3
Grim (cape) A2
Hartz (mt.) C5
Hibbs (pt.) B4
Hogan Group (isl.) D1
Hummock (isl.) D2
Hunter (isl.) A2
Hunter (isls.) A2
Huon (riv.) C5
Indian Ocean A4
Kent Group (isls.) D1
King (isl.) 2,592 . . . . A1

King (riv.) B4
King William (lake) C4
Lake (riv.) D3
Legges Tor (mt.) D3
Leven (riv.) B3
Lofty (range) B3
Low Rocky (pt.) B4
Lyell (mt.) B4
Maatsuyker (isls.) C5
Macquarie (harb.) B4
Macquarie (riv.) D3
Maria (isl.) E4
Marion (bay) E4
Mersey (riv.) C3
Munro (mt.) E2
Naturaliste (cape) E2
Nive (riv.) C4
Norfolk (bay) D4
North (pt.) E1
North Bruny (isl.) D5
North Esk (riv.) D3
Ossa (mt.) C3

Ouse (riv.) C4
Oyster (bay) E4
Pedder (riv.) B4
Phoques (bay) A1
Picton (mt.) C5
Pieman (riv.) B3
Pillar (cape) E5
Port Davey (inlet) B5
Portland (cape) D2
Ramsey (mt.) B3
Raoul (cape) D5
Reid (rapid) B1
Ringarooma (bay) D2
Robbins (isl.) B2
Saint Clair (lake) C4
Saint Helens (pt.) E3
Saint Vincent (cape) B5
Savage (riv.) B3
Schouten (isl.) E4
Sorell (cape) B4
Sorell (lake) D4
South (cape) C5

South Bruny (isl.) D5
South East (cape) C5
South Esk (riv.) D3
South West (cape) B5
Stanley (mt.) A1
Stokes (pt.) A1
Storm (bay) D5
Strzelecki (mt.) D2
Tamar (riv.) D3
Tasman (head) D5
Tasman (pen.) E5
Tasman (sea) E4
Three Hummock (isl.) B2
Vansittart (isl.) E2
West (pt.) A2
West Sister (isl.) D1
Wickham (cape) A1

○ Population of district.
*Population of met. area.

CITIES and TOWNS

Adventure Bay D5
Avoca D3
Bagdad D4
Beaconsfield 898 . . . . C3
Beauty Point 998 . . . . C3
Bell Bay C3
Bicheno 674 . . . . E3
Boat Harbour B2
Bothwell 356 . . . . C4
Dracknell 347 . . . . C3
Branxholm 273 . . . . D3
Bridgewater 6,880 . . . . D4
Bridport 885 . . . . D3
Brighton 9,441 . . . . D4
Burnie 19,994 . . . . B3
Campbell Town 879 . . . . D3
Chudleigh C3
Colebrook D4
Cressy 640 . . . . C3
Currie 859 . . . . A1
Cygnet 715 . . . . C5
Deloraine 1,923 . . . . C3
Derwent Bridge C4
Devonport 21,424 . . . . C3
Dover 570 . . . . C5
Dunalley 203 . . . . D4
Evandale 614 . . . . D3
Exeter 353 . . . . C3
Fingal 424 . . . . E3
Forth 273 . . . . C3
Franklin 479 . . . . C5
Geeveston 860 . . . . C5
George Town 5,592 . . . . D4
Glenorchy 41,019 . . . . D4
Gormanston 126 . . . . B4
Gowrie Park C3
Grassy 780 . . . . B1
Gravelly Beach 535 . . . . C3
Hadspen 908 . . . . D3
Hagley 232 . . . . C3
Hamilton 2,488 . . . . C4
Heybridge 395 . . . . C3
Hobart (cap.) 128,603 . . . . . . D4
Hobart *168,359 . . . . D4
Huonville-Ranelagh 1,347 . . . . C5
Kettering 288 . . . . D5
Kingston 8,556 . . . . D4
Latrobe 2,401 . . . . C3
Lauderdale 2,117 . . . . D4
Launceston 31,273 . . . . C3
Launceston *64,555 . . . . C3
Legana 964 . . . . C3
Lilydale 308 . . . . C3
Longford 2,027 . . . . C3
Luina 522 . . . . B3
Margate 476 . . . . D4
Maydena 461 . . . . C4
Meander C3
Mole Creek 303 . . . . C3
New Norfolk 6,243 . . . . C4
Nubeena 225 . . . . D5
Oatlands 545 . . . . D4
Orford 378 . . . . D4
Penguin 2,616 . . . . C3
Perth 1,229 . . . . C3
Poatina C3
Port Sorell 859 . . . . C3
Queenstown 3,714 . . . . B4
Railton 857 . . . . C3
Richmond 587 . . . . D4
Ridgley 452 . . . . B3

Ringarooma 223 . . . . D3
Rosebery 2,675 . . . . B3
Ross 289 . . . . D4
Rossarden 365 . . . . D3
Saint Helens 1,005 . . . . E3
Saint Marys 653 . . . . E3
Sassafras C3
Savage River 1,141 . . . . B3
Scottsdale 2,002 . . . . D3
Sheffield 945 . . . . C3
Smithton 3,378 . . . . A2
Snug 684 . . . . D5
Sorell-Midway Point 2,544 . . . . D4
Stanley 603 . . . . B2
Storeys Creek D3
Strahan 402 . . . . B4
Strathgordon C4
Sulphur Creek 367 . . . . C3
Swansea 428 . . . . D4
Tarraleah 498 . . . . C4
Temma A3
Triabunna 924 . . . . D4
Tullah 1,894 . . . . B3
Ulverstone 9,413 . . . . C3
Waratah 342 . . . . B3
Wesley Vale C3
Westbury 1,161 . . . . C3
Whitemark D2
Woodbridge 259 . . . . D5
Wynyard 4,582 . . . . B3
Zeehan 1,750 . . . . B3

OTHER FEATURES

Anderson (bay) D2
Anne (mt.) C4
Anser Group (isls.) C1
Arthur (lake) D4
Arthur (range) C5
Arthur (riv.) B3
Babel (isl.) E1
Banks (str.) D2
Barn Bluff (mt.) B3
Barren (cape) E2
Bass (str.) C1
Bathurst (gulf) C5
Cape Barren (isl.) E2
Chappell (isls.) D2
Circular (gulf) B2
Clarke (isl.) E2
Clyde (riv.) D4
Cox (bight) C5
Cradle (mt.) B3
Cradle Mt. Lake St. Clair
  Nat'l Park B3
Crescent (lake) D4
Curtis Group (isls.) C1
D'Aguilar (range) B4
Davey (riv.) B4
Deal (isl.) D1
Dee (riv.) C4
Denison (range) C4
D'Entrecasteaux (chan.) D5
Derwent (riv.) C4
East Sister (isl.) E1
Echo (lake) C4
Eddystone (pt.) E2
Elliott (bay) B5
Fires (bay) E2
Flinders (isl.) 2,150 . . . . . . D1
Florence (lake) C4
Forestier (chan.) E4
Forestier (pen.) E4

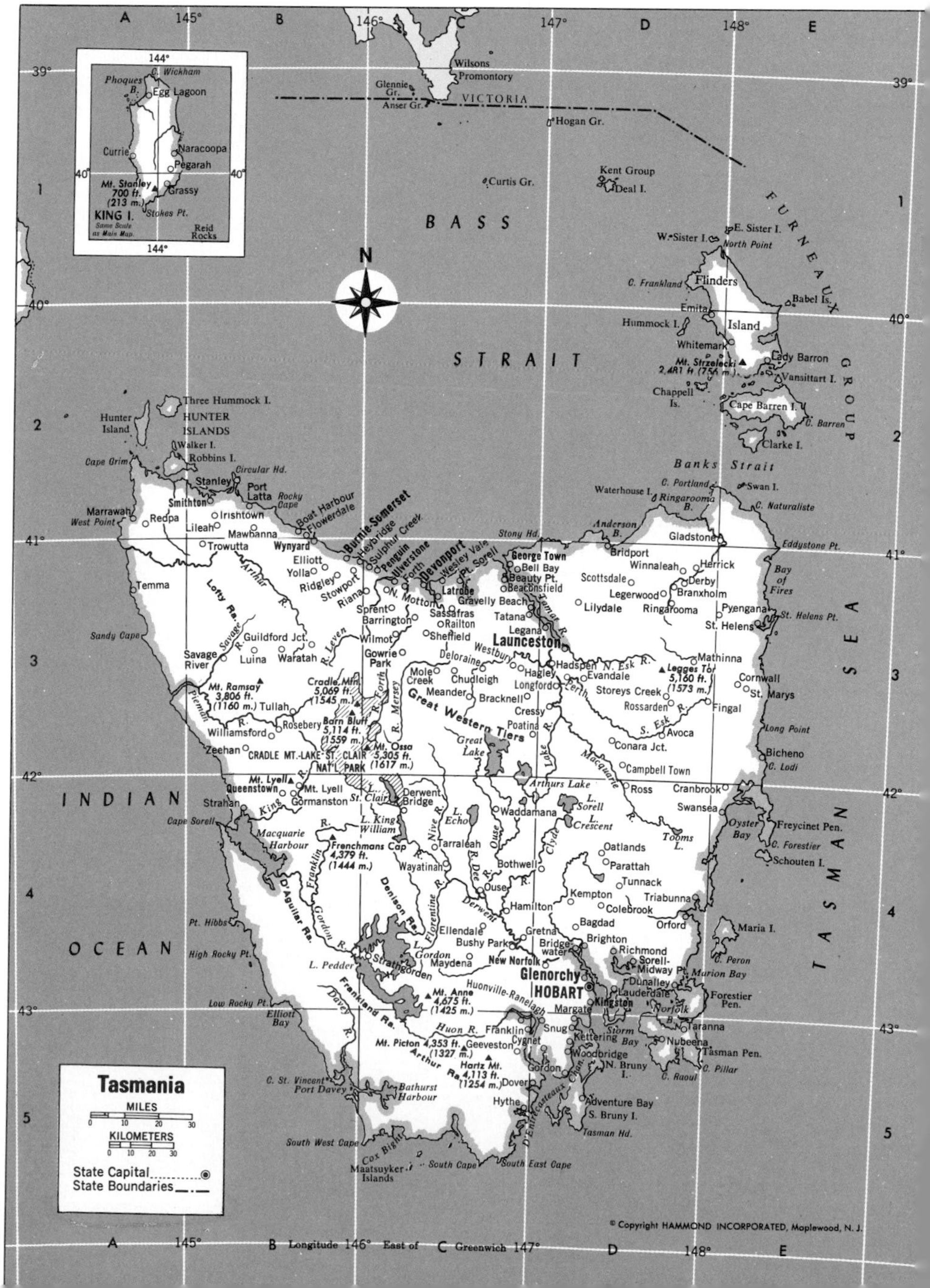

Tasmania

A 145° B 146° C 147° D 148° E

KING I. (Same Scale as Main Map)
144°
Phoques B. Wickham
Egg Lagoon
Currie Naracoopa
Pegarah
Mt. Stanley 700 ft. (213 m.) Grassy
Stokes Pt. Reid Rocks
144°

Wilsons Promontory
Glennie Gr.
Anser Gr. VICTORIA
Hogan Gr.
Curtis Gr.
Kent Group Deal I.

B A S S   S T R A I T

W. Sister I. E. Sister I.
North Point
C. Frankland Flinders Island Babel I.
Emita FURNEAUX GROUP
Hummock I. Whitemark Lady Barron
Mt. Strzelecki 2,481 ft. (756 m.) Vansittart I.
Chappell Is. Cape Barren I. C. Barren
Three Hummock I. Clarke I.
Hunter Island HUNTER ISLANDS Walker I. Banks Strait
Robbins I. C. Portland Swan I.
Cape Grim Circular Hd. Waterhouse I. Ringarooma
West Point Stanley C. Naturaliste
Marrawah Smithton Port Latta Rocky Cape Boat Harbour Anderson B. Gladstone
Redpa Irishtown Wynyard Burnie Somerset Stony Hd. Bridport Eddystone Pt.
Lileah Heybridge Devonport George Town Herrick
Trowutta Elliott Wesley Vale Bell Bay Winnaleah Derby
Yolla Ridgley Penguin Motton Beauty Pt. Scottsdale Legerwood Branxholm Bay of Fires
Temma Sorento Barrington Gravelly Beach Lilydale Ringarooma Pyengana
Sandy Cape Guildford Jct. Sassafras Legana St. Helens St. Helens Pt.
Savage River Luina Waratah Gowrie Park Sheffield Westbury Launceston Hadspen N. Esk Mathinna
Mole Creek Chudleigh Hagley Evandale Legges Tor 5,160 ft. (1573 m.) Cornwall
Meander Bracknell Cressy Storeys Creek Fingal
Mt. Ramsay 3,806 ft. (1160 m.) Cradle Mtn. 5,114 ft. (1545 m.) GREAT WESTERN TIERS Longford Rossarden S. Esk Avoca
Rosebery Tullah Barn Bluff 5,069 ft. (1559 m.) Poatina Conara Jct. Long Point
Williamsford Great Lake Bicheno
Zeehan CRADLE MT.-LAKE ST. CLAIR Ossa 5,305 ft. (1617 m.) Campbell Town C. Lodi
  NAT'L PARK Arthurs Lake
Mt. Lyell L. St. Clair Ross Cranbrook
Queenstown Gormanston Mt. Lyell Derwent Bridge L. Echo Waddamana Swansea
Strahan L. King L. Sorell Oyster Bay
Macquarie Harbour Frenchmans Cap 4,379 ft. (1444 m.) Tarraleah L. Crescent Oatlands Freycinet Pen.
Cape Sorell Wayatinah Bothwell Parattah C. Forestier
  Tunnack Triabunna Schouten I.
Pt. Hibbs New Norfolk Kempton Maria I.
High Rocky Pt. Ellendale Bushy Park Gretna Colebrook C. Peron
  Bridgewater Richmond Orford Marion Bay
  Glenorchy Sorell- Forestier Pen.
  Maydena HOBART Midway Pt.
Low Rocky Pt. L. Pedder Huonville-Ranelagh Lauderdale Norfolk C. Raoul
  Mt. Anne 4,675 ft. (1425 m.) Margate Kingston N. Bruny
  Franklin Snug Kettering Storm Nubeena Tasman Pen.
Elliott Bay Mt. Picton 4,353 ft. (1327 m.) Franklin Cygnet Woodbridge Taranna
  Hartz Mt. 4,113 ft. (1254 m.) Geeveston N. Bruny C. Pillar
C. St. Vincent Dover Adventure Bay
Port Davey Bathurst Harbour Hythe S. Bruny I. Tasman Hd.
  South West Cape Maatsuyker Islands South Cape South East Cape

I N D I A N   O C E A N

T A S M A N   S E A

N

Tasmania
MILES
0 10 20 30
KILOMETERS
0 10 20 30

State Capital ◎
State Boundaries ▬ ▪ ▬

© Copyright HAMMOND INCORPORATED, Maplewood, N.J.

A 145° B Longitude 146° East of C Greenwich 147° D 148° E

New Zealand

CONIC PROJECTION

SCALE OF MILES

0   50   100   150

SCALE OF KILOMETERS

0   50   100   150

Capital of Country .... ☆

© Copyright HAMMOND INCORPORATED, Maplewood, N.J.

NORTH ISLAND

SOUTH ISLAND

T A S M A N   S E A

P A C I F I C   O C E A N

Hauraki Gulf

AUCKLAND

Manukau Harbour

WELLINGTON

Chatham I.

Topography

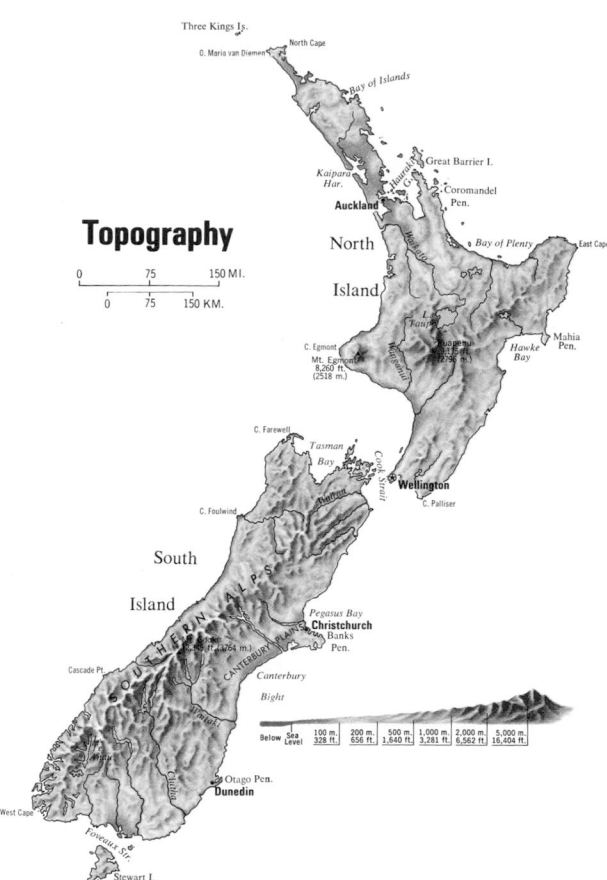

Three Kings Is.
C. Maria van Diemen — North Cape
Bay of Islands
Great Barrier I.
Kaipara Har.
Coromandel Pen.
Auckland
North Island
Bay of Plenty — East Cape
C. Egmont
Mt. Egmont 8,260 ft. (2518 m.)
Mahia Pen.
Hawke Bay
C. Farewell
Tasman Bay
Cook Strait
C. Foulwind
C. Palliser
Wellington
South Island
SOUTHERN ALPS
Pegasus Bay
Christchurch
Banks Pen.
Cascade Pt.
CANTERBURY PLAINS
Mt. Cook 12,349 ft. (3,764 m.)
Canterbury Bight
West Cape
Dunedin
Otago Pen.
Foveaux Str.
Stewart I.

0 75 150 MI.
0 75 150 KM.

| Below | Sea Level | 100 m. 328 ft. | 200 m. 656 ft. | 500 m. 1,640 ft. | 1,000 m. 3,281 ft. | 2,000 m. 6,562 ft. | 5,000 m. 16,404 ft. |

AREA 103,736 sq. mi. (268,676 sq. km.)
POPULATION 3,389,000
CAPITAL Wellington
LARGEST CITY Auckland
HIGHEST POINT Mt. Cook 12,349 ft. (3,764 m.)
MONETARY UNIT New Zealand dollar
MAJOR LANGUAGES English, Maori
MAJOR RELIGIONS Protestantism, Roman Catholicism

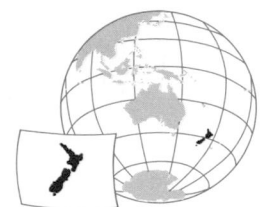

Wellington †321,004 ...... A3
Wellsford 1,621 .... E2
Westport 4,686 .... C4
Whakatane 12,286 .... F2
Whangamata 1,566 .... F2
Whangarei 36,550 .... E1
Whangarei †40,212 .... E1
Whitianga 1,960 .... E2
Winton 2,035 .... B7
Woodville 1,647 .... F4

OTHER FEATURES

Arthur's (pass) C5
Aspiring (mt.) B6
Banks (pen.) D5
Bream (bay) E1
Brett (cape) E1
Buller (riv.) D4
Campbell (cape) E4
Canterbury (bight) D6
Cascade (pt.) B6
Chatham (isls.) 751 ...... D7
Cloudy (bay) E4
Clutha (riv.) B6
Coleridge (lake) C5
Colville (cape) E2
Cook (mt.) C5
Cook (str.) E4
Coromandel (pen.) F2
Devil River (peak) D4
D'Urville (isl.) D4
Dusky (sound) A6
East (cape) G2
Egmont (cape) D3
Egmont (mt.) D3
Ellesmere (lake) D5
Farewell (cape) D4
Foulwind (cape) C4
Fournier (cape) E7
Foveaaux (str.) A7
Golden (bay) D4
Great Barrier (isl.) 572 .. E2
Haast (pass) B6
Hauraki (gulf) C1
Hawke (bay) F3
Hikurangi (mt.) G2
Hokianga (harb.) D1
Huiarau (range) F3
Hutt (riv.) C2
Islands (bay) E1
Jackson (bay) B5
Kaikoura (range) D5
Kaimanawa (range) E3
Kaipara (harb.) D2
Karamea (bight) C4
Kawhia (harb.) E3
Kidnappers (cape) F3
Mahia (pen.) G3
Manapouri (lake) A6
Manukau (harb.) B1
Maria van Diemen (cape) . D1
Mataura (riv.) B6
Mercury (isls.) F2
Milford (sound) A6
Needles (pt.) E2
Nicholson, Port (inlet) ... B3
Ninety Mile (beach) D1
North (cape) D1
North (isl.) 2,322,989 ... F1
North Taranaki (bight) ... D3
Otago (pen.) C6
Owen (mt.) D4
Palliser (cape) E4
Pegasus (bay) D5
Pitt (isl.) E7
Plenty (bay) F2
Port Nicholson (inlet) B3
Port Pegasus (inlet) B7
Pukaki (lake) B6
Puysegur (pt.) A7
Rakaia (riv.) C5
Rangitata (riv.) C5
Rangitikei (riv.) E3
Raukumara (range) F3
Reinga (cape) D1
Resolution (isl.) A6
Richmond (range) D4
Rocks (pt.) C4
Rotorua (lake) F3
Ruahine (range) F4
Ruapehu (mt.) E3
Ruapuke (isl.) B7
South (cape) A7
South (isl.) 852,748 .... B5
Southern Alps (range) ... C5
South Taranaki (bight) ... D3
Spenser (mts.) D5
Stewart (isl.) 600 .... A7
Tararua (range) E4
Tasman (bay) D4
Tasman (mts.) D4
Tasman (sea) B4
Taupo (lake) F3
Tauroa (pt.) D1

Te Anau (lake) A6
Tekapo (lake) C5
Terawhiti (cape) A3
Thames (firth) E2
Three Kings (isls.) D1
Turakirae (head) B3
Una (mt.) D5
Waiheke (isl.) 3,223 .... E2
Waikato (riv.) E2
Waimakariri (riv.) D5
Waipa (riv.) E2
Wairau (riv.) D4
Waitaki (riv.) C6
Waitemata (harb.) B1
Wakatipu (lake) B6
Wanaka (lake) B6
Wanganui (riv.) E3
West (cape) A6
Whitcombe (mt.) C5

†Population of urban area.

Agriculture, Industry and Resources

Ka — Fruit
Snapper
Dairy
Auckland
Snapper
Sheep
Dairy
Sheep
G
Sheep
Wellington
Cu
Sheep
Wheat
Christchurch
Crayfish
Sheep
Wheat
Oats
Cu
Cu
Sheep
Lg
Dunedin
Oysters
Lg
Crayfish
Soles
J

CITIES and TOWNS

Albany 2,001 .... B1
Alexandra 4,348 .... B6
Ashburton 14,151 .... C5
Ashhurst 1,906 .... E4
Auckland 144,963 .... B1
Auckland †769,558 ...... B1
Balclutha 4,495 .... B7
Belmont 2,402 .... D2
Birkenhead 21,324 ..... B1
Blenheim 17,849 .... D4
Bluff 2,720 .... B7
Bulls 1,839 .... E4
Cambridge 8,514 ...... E2
Carterton 3,971 .... E4
Christchurch 164,680 .. D5
Christchurch †289,959 .. D5
Cromwell 2,364 .... B6
Dannevirke 5,663 ..... F4
Dargaville 4,747 ...... D1
Devonport 10,410 ..... C1
Dunedin 77,176 .... C6
Dunedin †107,445 ..... C6
Eastbourne 4,561 ..... B3
East Coast Bays 28,866 . B1
Edgecumbe 1,929 .... F2
Ellerslie 5,404 .... C1
Eltham 2,411 .... E3
Fairfield 1,849 .... C6
Featherston 2,458 .... E4
Feilding 11,522 ...... E4
Foxton 2,719 .... E4
Geraldine 2,128 ..... C6
Gisborne 29,986 ..... G3
Gisborne †32,062 .... G3
Glen Eden 9,406 .... B1
Glenfield 3,691 ..... B1
Gore 9,185 .... B7
Green Bay 3,035 .... B1
Green Island 6,899 .. C7
Greymouth 8,103 ... C5
Greytown 1,797 .... E4
Half Moon Bay (Oban) 2,448 . B7
Hamilton 91,109 .... E2
Hamilton †97,907 ... E2
Hastings 36,083 .... F3
Hastings †52,563 ... F3
Havelock North 8,507 . F3
Hawera 8,400 ...... E3
Helensville 1,360 ... B1
Henderson 6,645 ... B1
Heretaunga-Pinehaven 6,171 C2
Hokitika 3,414 ..... C5
Hornby 8,215 ...... D5
Howick 13,866 .... C1
Huntly 6,534 ...... E2
Hutt (Upper and Lower) †131,257 ... B2
Inglewood 2,839 ... E3

Invercargill 49,446 ...... B7
Invercargill †53,868 .... B7
Kaiapoi 4,894 .... D5
Kaikohe 3,663 .... D1
Kaikoura 2,180 .... D5
Kaitaia 4,737 .... D1
Kawerau 8,593 .... F3
Kumeu 3,414 .... B1
Levin 14,652 .... E4
Lower Hutt 63,245 ... B2
Lyttelton 3,184 ..... D5
Manukau 159,362 ... C1
Marton 4,858 ...... E4
Masterton 18,785 .. E4
Mataura 2,345 .... B7
Milton 2,193 ..... B7
Morrinsville 5,080 . E2
Mosgiel 9,264 .... C6
Motueka 4,693 ... D4
Mount Albert 26,462 . B1
Mount Eden 18,305 .. B1
Mount Maunganui 11,391 . E2
Mount Roskill 33,577 . B1
Mount Wellington 19,528 . C1
Murupara 2,964 .... F3
Napier 48,314 ..... F3
Napier †51,330 .... F3
Nelson 33,304 .... D4
Nelson †43,121 ... D4
New Lynn 10,445 . B1
New Plymouth 36,048 . D3
New Plymouth †44,095 . D3
Ngaruawahia 4,435 . E2
Northcote 10,061 ... B1
Oamaru 13,043 .... C6
Oban (Half Moon Bay) 2,448 B7
Onehunga 15,386 .. B1
One Tree Hill 11,078 . B1
Opotiki 3,388 ..... F3
Orewa 5,552 ..... B1
Otahuhu 10,298 .. C1
Otaki 4,301 ...... E4
Otorohanga 2,574 . E2
Paeroa 3,702 .... E2
Pahiatua 2,599 ... F4
Paihia 1,740 ..... D1
Palmerston North 60,105 . E4
Palmerston North †66,691 . E4
Papakura 22,473 ... C2
Papatoetoe 21,700 . C1
Patea 1,938 ...... E3
Petone 8,113 .... B2
Picton 3,220 .... D4
Pinehaven (Heretaunga-Pinehaven) 6,171 ... C2
Porirua 41,104 ... B2
Port Chalmers 2,917 . C6
Pukekohe 9,070 .. C1
Putaruru 4,222 .. E3
Queenstown 3,367 . B6

Raetihi 1,247 .... E3
Raglan 1,414 .... E2
Rangiora 6,385 .... D5
Reefton 1,200 .... C5
Riccarton 6,709 ...... D5
Richmond 6,847 ..... D4
Riverton 1,479 ...... B7
Rotorua 38,157 ..... F3
Rotorua †48,314 .... F3
Runanga 1,264 .... C5
Russell 932 .... E1
Saint Kilda 6,147 . C7
Shannon 1,465 ... E4
Stratford 5,518 ... E3
Taihape 2,586 .... E3
Takapuna 64,844 . B1
Tapanui 1,042 ... B6
Taradale 4,681 .. F3
Taumarunui 6,541 . E3
Taupo 13,651 ... F3
Tauranga 37,099 . F2
Tauranga †53,097 . F2
Tawa 12,216 .... B2
Te Anau 2,610 .. A6
Te Aroha 3,331 . E2
Te Atatu 14,713 . B1
Te Awamutu 7,922 . E3
Te Kauwhata 842 . E2
Te Kuiti 4,795 ... E3
Temuka 3,771 ... C6
Te Puke 4,577 .. F2
Thames 6,456 .. E2
The Hermitage .. C5
Timaru 28,412 . C6
Timaru †29,225 . C6
Titirangi 8,426 . B1
Tokoroa 18,713 . F3
Tuakau 1,982 .. E2
Tuatapere 884 . A7
Turangi 5,517 . E3
Upper Hutt 31,405 . B2
Waihi 3,538 ... E2
Waikanae 4,818 . E4
Waikouaiti 858 . C6
Waimate 3,393 . C6
Wainuiomata 19,192 . B3
Waipawa 1,732 . F4
Waipukurau 3,648 . F4
Wairoa 5,439 .. F3
Waitangi D7
Waitara 6,012 . D3
Waitemata 87,452 . B1
Waiuku 3,654 .. C1
Waanaka 1,155 . B6
Wanganui 37,012 . E3
Wanganui †39,595 . E3
Warkworth 1,734 . E2
Washdyke 949 . C6
Waverley 1,239 . E3
Wellington (cap.) 135,688 . A3

DOMINANT LAND USE

Mixed Farming, Livestock
Dairy
Truck Farming, Horticulture
Pasture Livestock (chiefly sheep)
Livestock Herding
Forests
Nonagricultural Land

MAJOR MINERAL OCCURRENCES

C Coal
G Natural Gas
J Jade
Ka Kaolin
Lg Lignite
O Petroleum
U Uranium

⚡ Water Power
▨ Major Industrial Areas

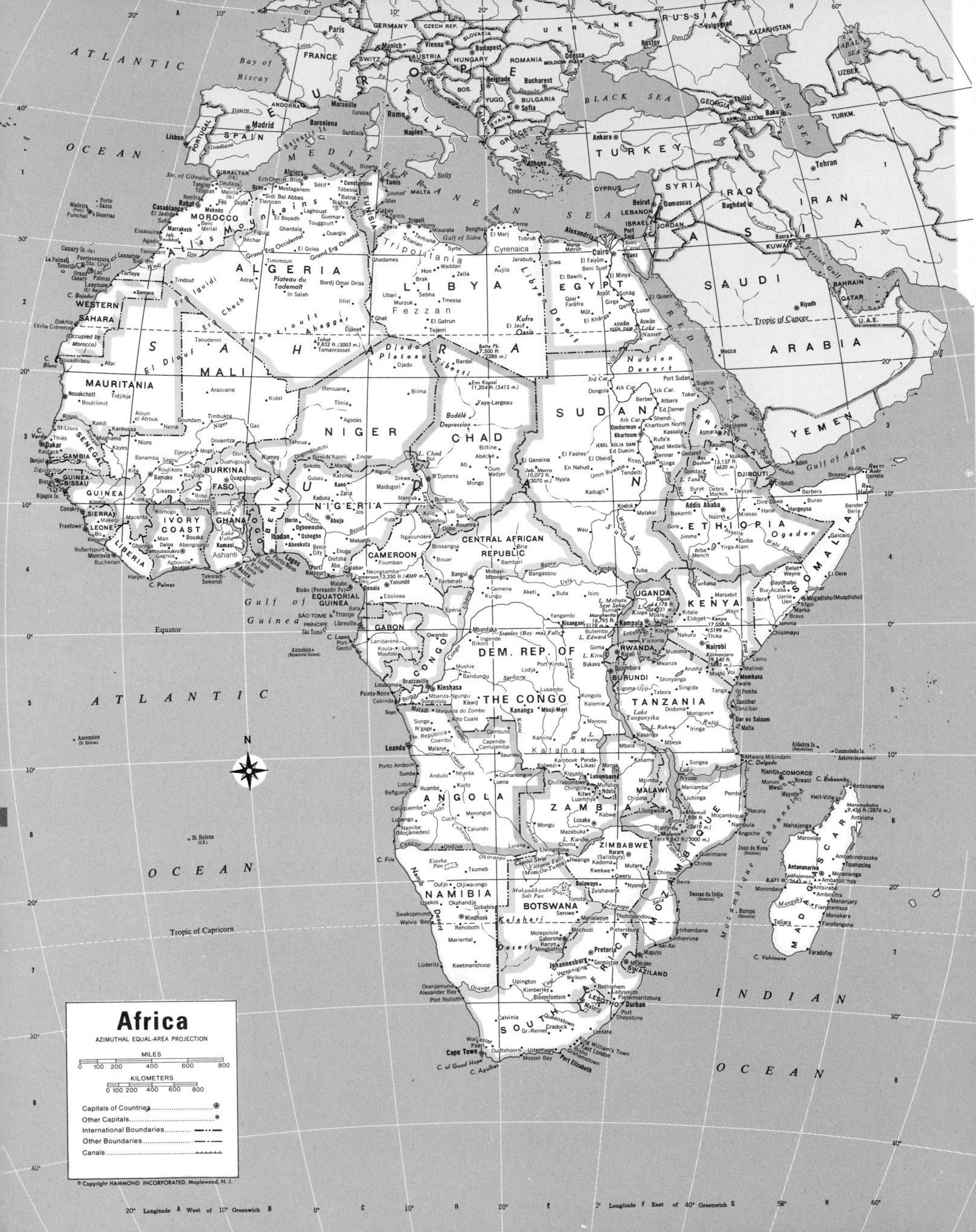

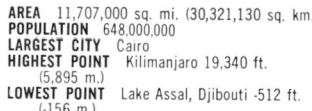

AREA 11,707,000 sq. mi. (30,321,130 sq. km.)
POPULATION 648,000,000
LARGEST CITY Cairo
HIGHEST POINT Kilimanjaro 19,340 ft.
(5,895 m.)
LOWEST POINT Lake Assal, Djibouti -512 ft.
(-156 m.)

Population Distribution

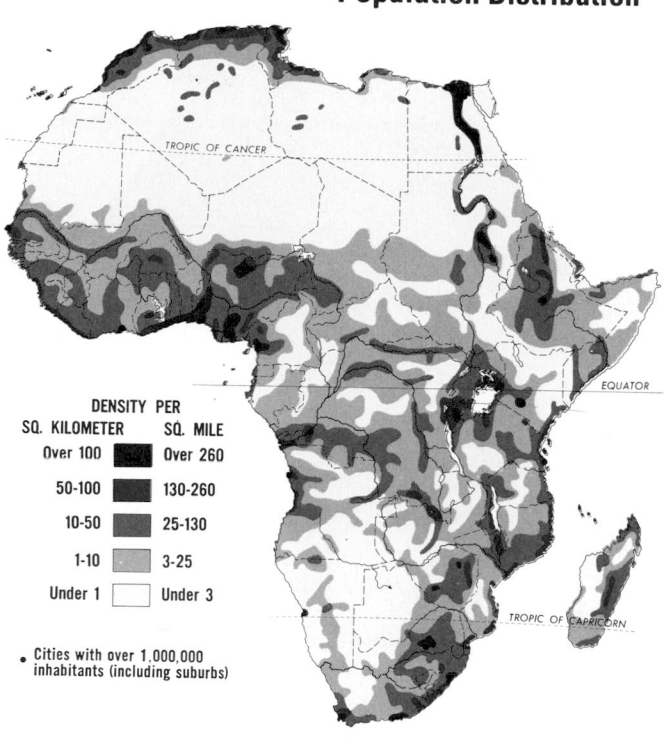

DENSITY PER

SQ. KILOMETER	SQ. MILE
Over 100	Over 260
50-100	130-260
10-50	25-130
1-10	3-25
Under 1	Under 3

• Cities with over 1,000,000
inhabitants (including suburbs)

Vegetation

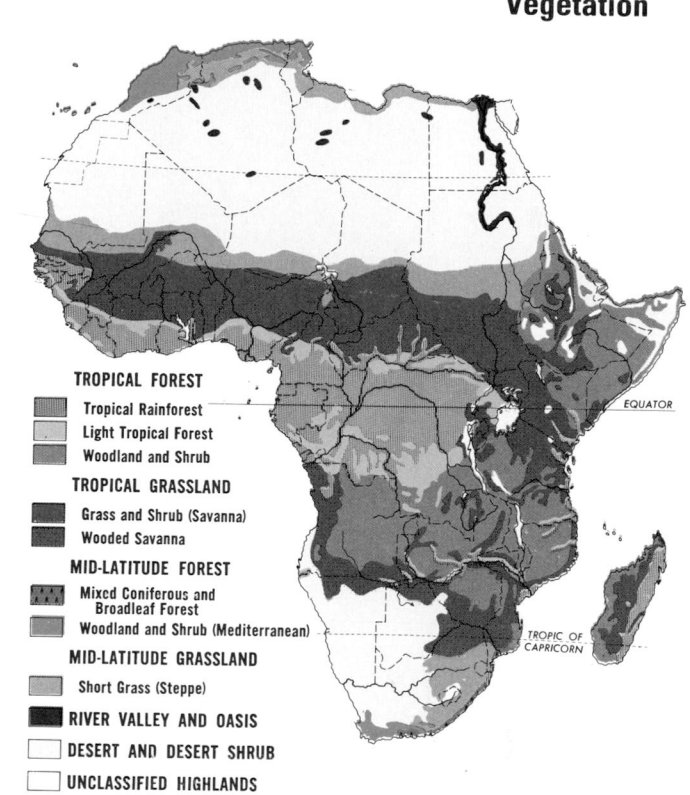

TROPICAL FOREST
Tropical Rainforest
Light Tropical Forest
Woodland and Shrub

TROPICAL GRASSLAND
Grass and Shrub (Savanna)
Wooded Savanna

MID-LATITUDE FOREST
Mixed Coniferous and Broadleaf Forest
Woodland and Shrub (Mediterranean)

MID-LATITUDE GRASSLAND
Short Grass (Steppe)

RIVER VALLEY AND OASIS

DESERT AND DESERT SHRUB

UNCLASSIFIED HIGHLANDS

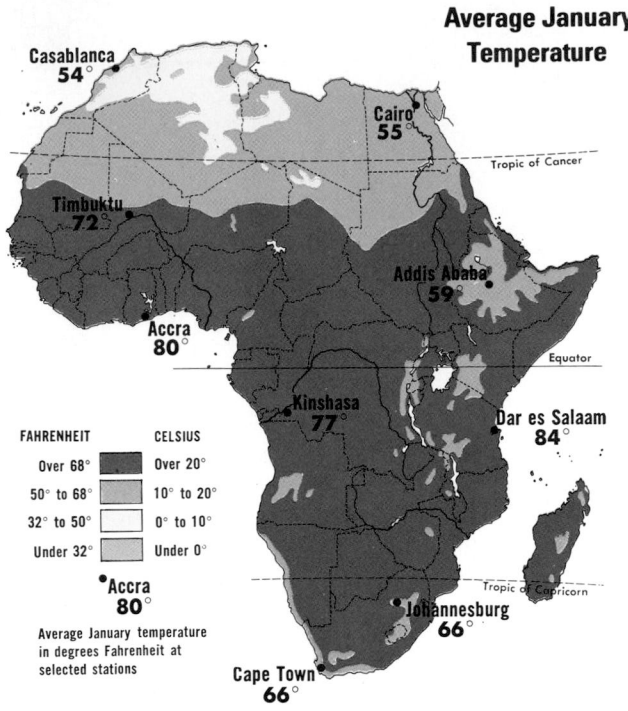

Average January Temperature

Casablanca 54°
Cairo 55°
Timbuktu 72°
Addis Ababa 59°
Accra 80°
Kinshasa 77°
Dar es Salaam 84°
Johannesburg 66°
Cape Town 66°

Tropic of Cancer
Equator
Tropic of Capricorn

FAHRENHEIT	CELSIUS
Over 68°	Over 20°
50° to 68°	10° to 20°
32° to 50°	0° to 10°
Under 32°	Under 0°

● Accra 80°

Average January temperature in degrees Fahrenheit at selected stations

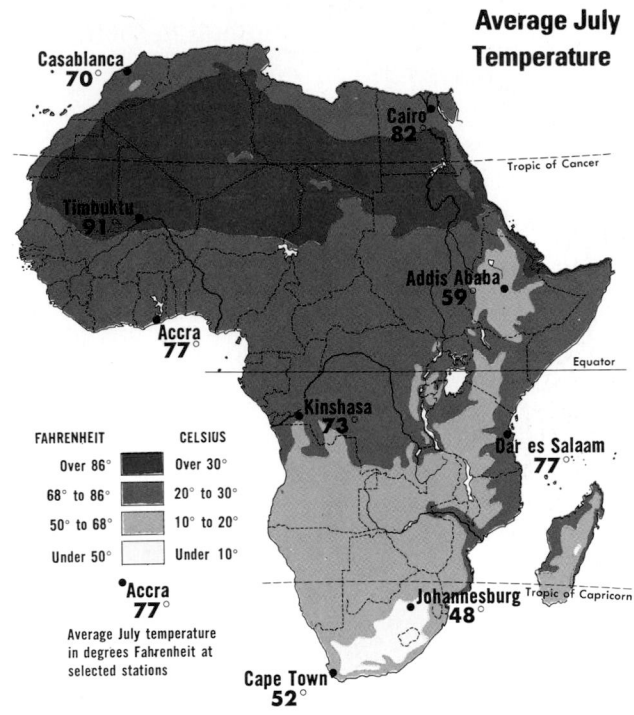

Average July Temperature

Casablanca 70°
Cairo 82°
Timbuktu 91°
Addis Ababa 59°
Accra 77°
Kinshasa 73°
Dar es Salaam 77°
Johannesburg 48°
Cape Town 52°

Tropic of Cancer
Equator
Tropic of Capricorn

FAHRENHEIT	CELSIUS
Over 86°	Over 30°
68° to 86°	20° to 30°
50° to 68°	10° to 20°
Under 50°	Under 10°

● Accra 77°

Average July temperature in degrees Fahrenheit at selected stations

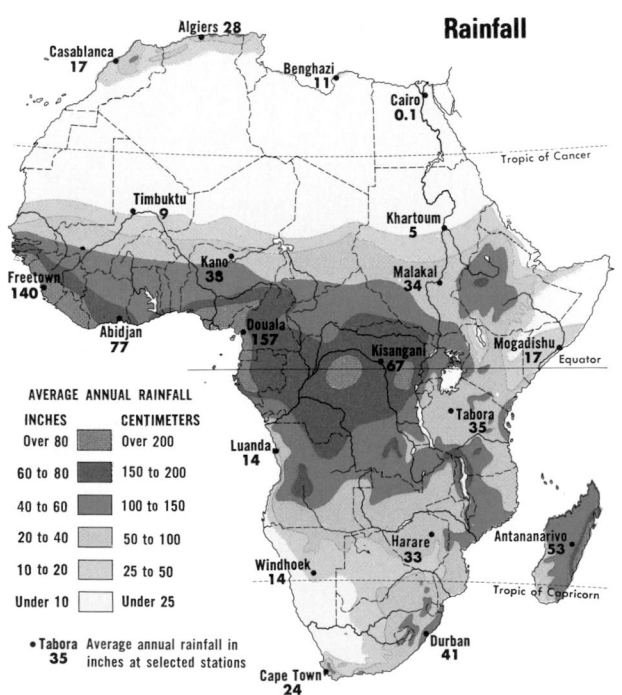

Rainfall

Algiers 28
Casablanca 17
Benghazi 11
Cairo 0.1
Timbuktu 9
Khartoum 5
Kano 35
Malakal 34
Freetown 140
Douala 157
Abidjan 77
Kisangani 67
Mogadishu 17
Tabora 35
Luanda 14
Harare 33
Antananarivo 53
Windhoek 14
Durban 41
Cape Town 24

Tropic of Cancer
Equator
Tropic of Capricorn

AVERAGE ANNUAL RAINFALL

INCHES	CENTIMETERS
Over 80	Over 200
60 to 80	150 to 200
40 to 60	100 to 150
20 to 40	50 to 100
10 to 20	25 to 50
Under 10	Under 25

● Tabora 35 Average annual rainfall in inches at selected stations

Vegetation/Relief

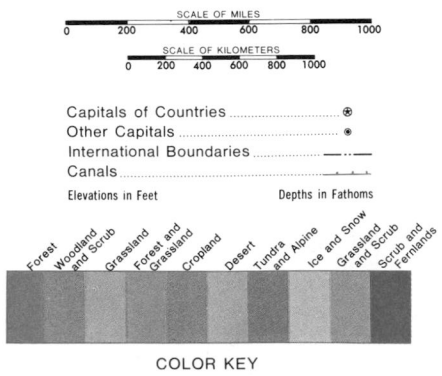

SCALE OF MILES
0 200 400 600 800 1000

SCALE OF KILOMETERS
0 200 400 600 800 1000

Capitals of Countries .... ⊛
Other Capitals .... ⊛
International Boundaries .... ——·—
Canals ....

Elevations in Feet   Depths in Fathoms

Forest
Woodland and Scrub
Grassland
Forest and Grassland
Cropland
Desert
Tundra and Alpine
Ice and Snow
Grassland and Scrub
Scrub and Farmlands

COLOR KEY

ATLANTIC OCEAN

MEDITERRANEAN SEA

Bay of Biscay

FRANCE
Paris
GERMANY
CZECH REP.
SW.
HUNGARY
ROMANIA
UKRAINE
RUSSIA
BLACK SEA
CASPIAN SEA
ARAL SEA
KAZAKH.
TURKM.

PORTUGAL
SPAIN
Madrid
Corsica
Rome
Sardinia
Balearic Is.
GREECE
ALB.
Crete
CYPRUS
Istanbul
TURKEY
GEORGIA
ARM. AZER.
IRAN
Tehran

Madeira (Port.)
Casablanca
Rabat
Tangier
Oran
Algiers
Annaba
Tunis
TUNISIA
Sfax
MALTA
Sicily
Tripoli
Benghazi
Gulf of Sidra
Alexandria
Cairo
Port Said
Suez Canal
Sinai
ISRAEL
JORDAN
LEBANON
SYRIA
IRAQ
Euphrates
Tigris
KUWAIT

Canary Is. (Sp.)
Las Palmas
Laayoune
WESTERN SAHARA
MOROCCO
Jeb. Toubkal 13,665 ft.
Atlas Mountains
Draa
ALGERIA
LIBYA
EGYPT
Libyan Desert
Asyût
Aswân
Lake Nasser
L. Nubia
Nubian Desert
Port Sudan
SAUDI ARABIA
QATAR
U.A.E.
Tropic of Cancer
Rub' al Khali

C. Blanc
MAURITANIA
Nouakchott
S a h a r a
Tahat
Ahaggar
Tamanrasset
Tibesti
Borkou Depression
RED SEA
YEMEN
Gulf of Aden
Ras Aser

Verde
Dakar
SENEGAL
GAMBIA
Banjul
GUINEA-BISSAU
Bissau
Timbuktu
MALI
Niger
Bamako
NIGER
Niamey
Kano
L. Chad
CHAD
N'Djamena
Rodélé Depression
SUDAN
El Fasher
El Obeid
Khartoum
White Nile
Blue Nile
ERITREA
Asmara
DJIBOUTI
Djibouti
Ras Dashan 15,157 ft.
ETHIOPIA

GUINEA
Conakry
Freetown
SIERRA LEONE
Monrovia
LIBERIA
C. Palmas
Bouaké
IVORY COAST
Yamoussoukro
Abidjan
BURKINA FASO
Ouagadougou
GHANA
Kumasi
TOGO
BENIN
Porto-Novo
Lomé
Accra
Volta
NIGERIA
Ibadan
Lagos
Abuja
Benue
Sarh
CENTRAL AFRICAN REPUBLIC
Bangui
Ubangi
Bomu
Uele
Juba
Wabi Shabelle
Highlands
Addis Ababa
Kenya 17,058 ft.
SOMALIA
Mogadishu (Muqdisho)

Gulf of Guinea
SÃO TOMÉ & PRÍNCIPE
EQUAT. GUINEA
Malabo
Bioko
Cameroon 13,350 ft. (4069 m.)
CAMEROON
Yaoundé
Libreville
López
GABON
Mbandaka
DEM. REP. OF THE CONGO
Congo
L. Mobutu Sese Seko
Kisangani
Margherita
Stanley Falls 16,795 ft.
L. Victoria
Kampala
UGANDA
KENYA
Nairobi
Mombasa

Equator

Annobón (Equat. Guinea)

Ascension (St. Helena)

CABINDA (Angola)
Brazzaville
Kinshasa
Kananga
RWANDA
Kigali
Bukavu
BURUNDI
Bujumbura
Kilimanjaro 19,340 ft.
Lake Victoria
TANZANIA
Zanzibar
Pemba
Dar es Salaam

ATLANTIC OCEAN

St. Helena (U.K.)

C. Fria

ANGOLA
Huambo
Malange
Luanda
Cuanza
Kasai
Katanga
Lubumbashi
Kitwe
ZAMBIA
Lusaka
Lake Mweru
Lake Tanganyika
Luapula
Ruvuma
Lake Nyasa
Lilongwe
MALAWI
C. Delgado
COMOROS
C. Bobaomby
Nampula

Cubango
Etosha Pan
NAMIBIA
Windhoek
Walvis Bay
Kalahari Desert
Makgadikgadi Salt Pan
BOTSWANA
Gaborone
Limpopo
Zambezi
Lake Kariba
Livingstone
Victoria Falls
Harare
ZIMBABWE
Bulawayo
Beira
MOZAMBIQUE
Mozambique Channel
MADAGASCAR
Antananarivo
Toamasina

Tropic of Capricorn

OCEAN

Orange
Great Karroo
Cape Town
C. of Good Hope
C. Agulhas
SOUTH AFRICA
Johannesburg
Pretoria
Gaborone
Maputo
SWAZILAND
Mbabane
LESOTHO
Maseru
Durban
East London
Port Elizabeth
Vaal
Limpopo
C. Vohimena
INDIAN OCEAN

© Copyright HAMMOND INCORPORATED, Maplewood, N.J.

Longitude 10° West of Greenwich

Longitude 10° East of Greenwich

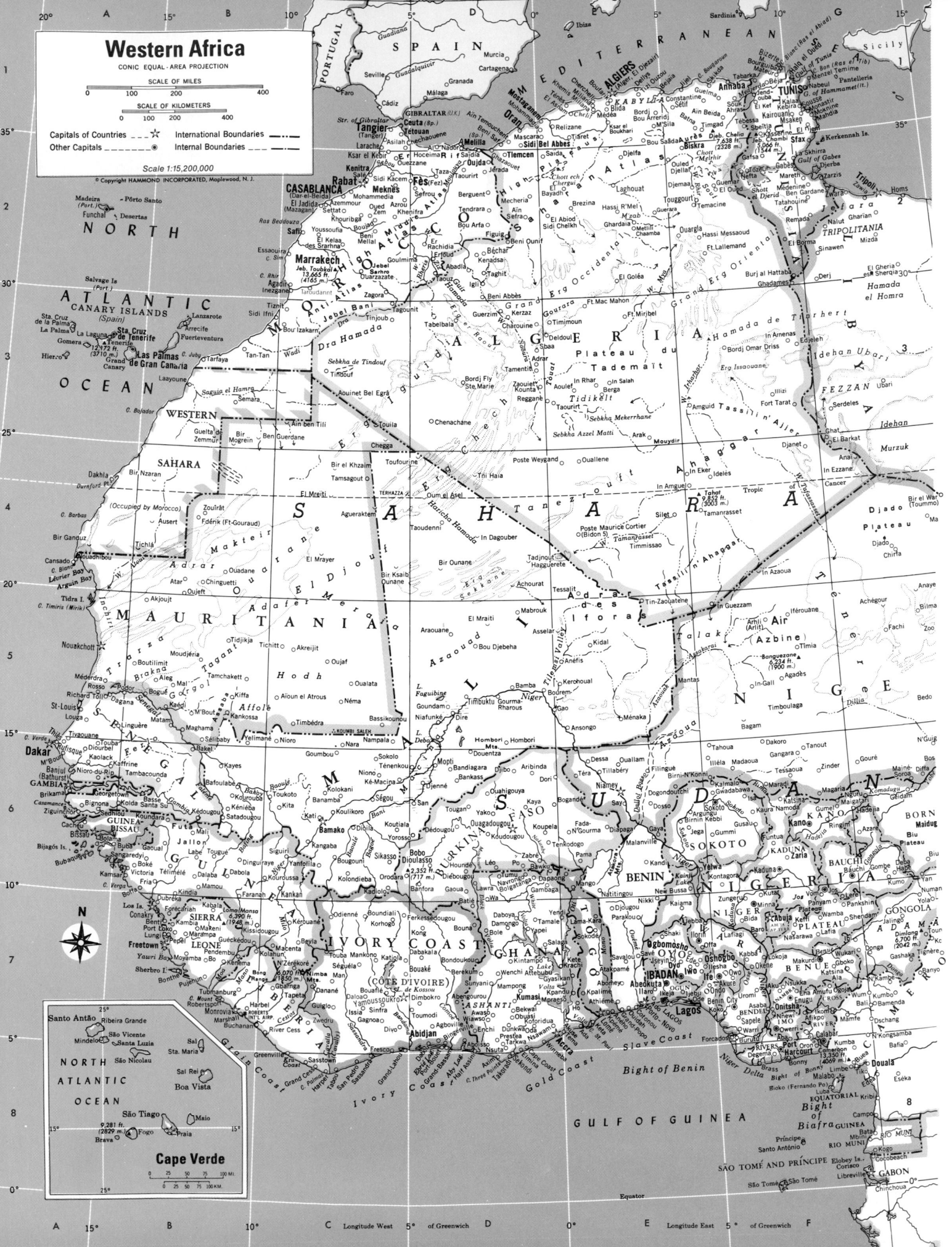

ALGERIA

AREA 919,591 sq. mi. (2,381,740 sq. km.)
POPULATION 22,971,000
CAPITAL Algiers
LARGEST CITY Algiers
HIGHEST POINT Tahat 9,852 ft. (3,003 m.)
MONETARY UNIT Algerian dinar
MAJOR LANGUAGES Arabic, Berber, French
MAJOR RELIGION Islam

BENIN

AREA 43,483 sq. mi. (112,620 sq. km.)
POPULATION 4,591,000
CAPITAL Porto-Novo
LARGEST CITY Cotonou
HIGHEST POINT Atakora Mts. 2,083 ft. (635 m.)
MONETARY UNIT CFA franc
MAJOR LANGUAGES Fon, Somba, Yoruba, Bariba, French, Mina, Dendi
MAJOR RELIGIONS Tribal religions, Islam, Roman Catholicism

CAPE VERDE

AREA 1,557 sq. mi. (4,033 sq. km.)
POPULATION 347,000
CAPITAL Praia
LARGEST CITY Praia
HIGHEST POINT 9,281 ft. (2,829 m.)
MONETARY UNIT Cape Verde escudo
MAJOR LANGUAGE Portuguese
MAJOR RELIGION Roman Catholicism

GAMBIA

AREA 4,127 sq. mi. (10,689 sq. km.)
POPULATION 688,000
CAPITAL Banjul
LARGEST CITY Banjul
HIGHEST POINT 100 ft. (30 m.)
MONETARY UNIT dalasi
MAJOR LANGUAGES Mandingo, Fulani, Wolof, English, Malinke
MAJOR RELIGIONS Islam, tribal religions, Christianity

GHANA

AREA 92,099 sq. mi. (238,536 sq. km.)
POPULATION 13,391,000
CAPITAL Accra
LARGEST CITY Accra
HIGHEST POINT Togo Hills 2,900 ft. (884 m.)
MONETARY UNIT cedi
MAJOR LANGUAGES Twi, Fante, Dagbani, Ewe, Ga, English, Hausa, Akan
MAJOR RELIGIONS Tribal religions, Christianity, Islam

GUINEA

AREA 94,925 sq. mi. (245,856 sq. km.)
POPULATION 6,706,000
CAPITAL Conakry
LARGEST CITY Conakry
HIGHEST POINT Nimba Mts. 6,070 ft. (1,850 m.)
MONETARY UNIT syli
MAJOR LANGUAGES Fulani, Mandingo, Susu, French
MAJOR RELIGIONS Islam, tribal religions

GUINEA-BISSAU

AREA 13,948 sq. mi. (36,125 sq. km.)
POPULATION 943,000
CAPITAL Bissau
LARGEST CITY Bissau
HIGHEST POINT 689 ft. (210 m.)
MONETARY UNIT Guinea-Bissau peso
MAJOR LANGUAGES Balante, Fulani, Crioulo, Mandingo, Portuguese
MAJOR RELIGIONS Islam, tribal religions, Roman Catholicism

IVORY COAST (CÔTE-D'IVOIRE)

AREA 124,504 sq. mi. (322,465 sq. km.)
POPULATION 9,300,000
CAPITAL Yamoussoukro
LARGEST CITY Abidjan
HIGHEST POINT 5,745 ft. (1,751 m.)
MONETARY UNIT CFA franc
MAJOR LANGUAGES Bale, Bete, Senufu, French, Dioula
MAJOR RELIGIONS Tribal religions, Islam

LIBERIA

AREA 43,000 sq. mi. (111,370 sq. km.)
POPULATION 2,508,000
CAPITAL Monrovia
LARGEST CITY Monrovia
HIGHEST POINT Wutivi 5,584 ft. (1,702 m.)
MONETARY UNIT Liberian dollar
MAJOR LANGUAGES Kru, Kpelle, Bassa, Vai, English
MAJOR RELIGIONS Christianity, tribal religions, Islam

MALI

AREA 464,873 sq. mi. (1,204,021 sq. km.)
POPULATION 7,960,000
CAPITAL Bamako
LARGEST CITY Bamako
HIGHEST POINT Hombori Mts. 3,789 ft. (1,155 m.)
MONETARY UNIT CFA franc
MAJOR LANGUAGES Bambara, Senufu, Fulani, Soninke, French
MAJOR RELIGIONS Islam, tribal religions

MAURITANIA

AREA 419,229 sq. mi. (1,085,803 sq. km.)
POPULATION 1,970,000
CAPITAL Nouakchott
LARGEST CITY Nouakchott
HIGHEST POINT 2,972 ft. (906 m.)
MONETARY UNIT ouguiya
MAJOR LANGUAGES Arabic, Wolof, Tukolor, French
MAJOR RELIGION Islam

MOROCCO

AREA 172,414 sq. mi. (446,550 sq. km.)
POPULATION 24,522,000
CAPITAL Rabat
LARGEST CITY Casablanca
HIGHEST POINT Jeb. Toubkal 13,665 ft. (4,165 m.)
MONETARY UNIT dirham
MAJOR LANGUAGES Arabic, Berber, French
MAJOR RELIGIONS Islam, Judaism, Christianity

NIGER

AREA 489,189 sq. mi. (1,267,000 sq. km.)
POPULATION 7,250,000
CAPITAL Niamey
LARGEST CITY Niamey
HIGHEST POINT Banguezane 6,234 ft. (1,900 m.)
MONETARY UNIT CFA franc
MAJOR LANGUAGES Hausa, Songhai, Fulani, French, Tamashek, Djerma
MAJOR RELIGIONS Islam, tribal religions

NIGERIA

AREA 357,000 sq. mi. (924,630 sq. km.)
POPULATION 104,957,000
CAPITAL Abuja
LARGEST CITY Lagos
HIGHEST POINT Dimlang 6,700 ft. (2,042 m.)
MONETARY UNIT naira
MAJOR LANGUAGES Hausa, Yoruba, Ibo, Ijaw, Fulani, Tiv, Kanuri, Ibibio, English, Edo
MAJOR RELIGIONS Islam, Christianity, tribal religions

SÃO TOMÉ AND PRÍNCIPE

AREA 372 sq. mi. (963 sq. km.)
POPULATION 116,000
CAPITAL São Tomé
LARGEST CITY São Tomé
HIGHEST POINT Pico 6,640 ft. (2,024 m.)
MONETARY UNIT dobra
MAJOR LANGUAGES Bantu languages, Portuguese
MAJOR RELIGIONS Tribal religions, Roman Catholicism

SENEGAL

AREA 75,954 sq. mi. (196,720 sq. km.)
POPULATION 7,113,000
CAPITAL Dakar
LARGEST CITY Dakar
HIGHEST POINT Futa Jallon 1,640 ft. (500 m.)
MONETARY UNIT CFA franc
MAJOR LANGUAGES Wolof, Peul (Fulani), French, Mende, Mandingo, Dida
MAJOR RELIGIONS Islam, tribal religions, Roman Catholicism

SIERRA LEONE

AREA 27,925 sq. mi. (72,325 sq. km.)
POPULATION 4,047,000
CAPITAL Freetown
LARGEST CITY Freetown
HIGHEST POINT Loma Mts. 6,390 ft. (1,947 m.)
MONETARY UNIT leone
MAJOR LANGUAGES Mende, Temne, Vai, English, Krio (pidgin)
MAJOR RELIGIONS Tribal religions, Islam, Christianity

TOGO

AREA 21,622 sq. mi. (56,000 sq. km.)
POPULATION 3,296,000
CAPITAL Lomé
LARGEST CITY Lomé
HIGHEST POINT Agou 3,445 ft. (1,050 m.)
MONETARY UNIT CFA franc
MAJOR LANGUAGES Ewe, French, Twi, Hausa
MAJOR RELIGIONS Tribal religions, Roman Catholicism, Islam

TUNISIA

AREA 63,378 sq. mi. (164,149 sq. km.)
POPULATION 7,465,000
CAPITAL Tunis
LARGEST CITY Tunis
HIGHEST POINT Jeb. Chambi 5,066 ft. (1,544 m.)
MONETARY UNIT Tunisian dinar
MAJOR LANGUAGES Arabic, French
MAJOR RELIGION Islam

BURKINA FASO

AREA 105,869 sq. mi. (274,200 sq. km.)
POPULATION 9,001,000
CAPITAL Ouagadougou
LARGEST CITY Ouagadougou
HIGHEST POINT 2,352 ft. (717 m.)
MONETARY UNIT CFA franc
MAJOR LANGUAGES Mossi, Lobi, French, Samo, Gourounsi
MAJOR RELIGIONS Islam, tribal religions, Roman Catholicism

WESTERN SAHARA

AREA 102,703 sq. mi. (266,000 sq. km.)
POPULATION 174,000
HIGHEST POINT 2,700 ft. (823 m.)
MAJOR LANGUAGE Arabic
MAJOR RELIGION Islam

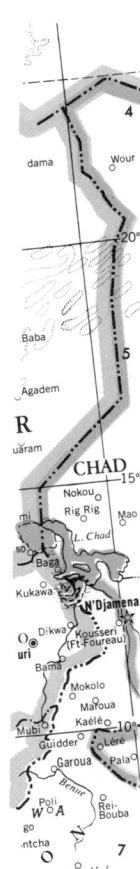

Topography

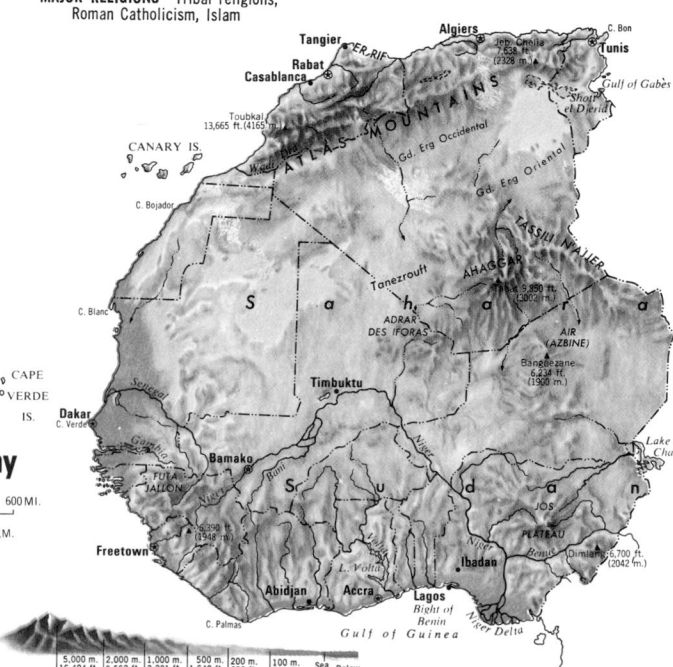

0 200 400 600 MI.

0 200 400 600 KM.

| 5,000 m. | 2,000 m. | 1,000 m. | 500 m. | 200 m. | 100 m. | Sea |
| 16,404 ft. | 6,562 ft. | 3,281 ft. | 1,640 ft. | 656 ft. | 328 ft. | Level Below |

(continued)

ALGERIA

CITIES and TOWNS

Adrar 28,495 D3
Aïn Beïda 67,281 F1
Aïn Sefra 22,400 D2
Aïn Temouchent 48,935 D1
Algiers (cap.) 1,687,579 E1
Annaba 227,795 F1
Aoulef 10,259 E3
Batna 184,833 F1
Béchar 107,042 D2
Bejaïa 118,233 F1
Beni Abbès 7,370 D2
Beni Saf 30,700 D1
Biskra 129,611 F2
Blida 131,615 E1
Bone (Annaba) 227,795 F1
Bordj Bou Arreridj 86,997 E1
Bordj Omar Driss 1,900 F3
Boufarik 54,023 E1
Bougie (Bejaïa) 118,233 F1
Bou Saâda 50,000 E1
Brezina 10,000 E2
Cherchell 32,572 E1
Constantine 449,602 F1
Dellys 29,700 E1
Djelfa 88,929 E2
Djemaa 34,600 F2
El Abiod Sidi Cheikh 15,300 E2
El Asnam 103,998 E1
El Bayadh 44,925 E2
El Djezair (Algiers) (cap.) 1,687,579 E1
El Goléa 24,400 E2
El Oued 73,093 F2
Ghardaïa 62,518 E2
Ghazaouet 29,795 D2
Guelma 84,826 F1
Guerara 22,300 E2
Hassi Messaoud F2
Hassi R'Mel 10,545 E2
In Guezzam 10,304 F5
In Salah 20,733 E3
Jijel 69,274 F1
Khemis Miliana 57,101 E1
Ksar el Boukhari 41,200 E1
Laghouat 71,808 E2
Mascara 70,885 D1
Mecheria 40,251 D2
Médéa 84,062 E1
Metlili Chaamba 21,300 E2
Miliana 36,400 E1
Mohammadia 58,967 D1
Mostaganem 115,302 D1
M'Sila 82,877 E1
Oran 598,525 D1
Orléansville (El Asnam) 103,998 E1
Ouargla 76,270 F2
Ouled Djellal 33,278 F2
Philippeville (Skikda) 128,503 F1
Reggane 10,061 D3
Relizane 83,864 E1
Saïda 84,371 E2
Sétif 185,786 F1
Sidi Bel-Abbes 154,745 D1
Skikda 128,503 F1
Souk Ahras 85,873 F1
Tamanrasset 38,146 F4
Tébessa 111,688 F1
Ténès 26,510 E1
Tiaret 105,562 E1
Timimoun 21,556 E3
Tindouf 6,500 C3
Tizi Ouzou 93,025 E1
Tlemcen 108,145 D2
Touggourt 75,600 F2
Zaouiet Kounta 10,707 D3

OTHER FEATURES

Adrar des Iforas (plat.) E5
Ahaggar (range) F4
Anaï (well) G4
Aouinet Bel Egrâ (well) C3
Atlas (mts.) E2
Aurès (lag.) F1
Azzel Mati, Sebkha (lake) E3
Bougaroun (cape) F1
Chech, Erg (des.) D3
Chelia (mt.) F1
Chelif (riv.) E1
Chergui, Chott Ech (salt lake) E2
Dra, Wadi (dry river) C3
Dra Hamada (plat.) C3
Gourara (oasis) E3
Grand Erg Occidental (des.) E2
Grand Erg Oriental (des.) F2
Guir Hamada (des.) D2
High Plateaus (ranges) D2
Iguidi, Erg (des.) C3
In Ezzane (well) G4
Irharhar, Wadi (dry river) F3
Kabylia (reg.) E1
Mediterranean (sea) E1
Medjerda (riv.) F1
Mekerrhane, Sebkha (salt lake) E3
Melrhir, Chott (salt lake) F2
Mouydir (mts.) E3
Mya, Wadi (dry river) E2
M'zab (oasis) E2
Raoui, Erg er (des.) D3
Rhir, Wadi (dry river) F2
Sahara (des.) E4
Saharan Atlas (ranges) E2
Saoura, Wadi (dry river) D3
Souf (oasis) F2
Tademaït, Plateau du (plat.) E3
Tafassasset, Wadi (dry river) F4
Tahat (mt.) F4
Tamanrasset, Wadi (dry river) E4
Tanezrouft (des.) E4
Tassili N'Ahagger (plat.) E4
Tassili N'Ajjer (plat.) F3
Tidikelt (oasis) E3
Timmissao (well) E4
Tindouf, Sebkha de (salt lake) C3
Tinrhert, Hamada de (des.) F3
Tni Haïa (well) D4
Touat (oasis) E3
Touila (well) C3

BENIN

CITIES and TOWNS

Abomey 38,000 E7
Cotonou 178,000 E7
Grand-Popo E7
Kandi E6
Natitingou 49,000 E6
Ouidah E7
Parakou 21,000 E7
Porto-Novo (cap.) 104,000 E7

OTHER FEATURES

Atakora (mts.) E6
Benin (bight) E8
Guinea (gulf) E8
Mono (riv.) E7
Niger (riv.) E6
Ouémé (riv.) E7
Slave Coast (reg.) E7
Sudan (reg.) E6

BURKINA FASO

CITIES and TOWNS

Banfora 12,358 D6
Bobo Dioulasso 115,063 D6
Bogandé E6
Dédougou D6
Diébougou D6
Djibo D6
Dori D6
Fada-N'Gourma 12,000 E6
Gaoua D6
Kaya 18,000 D6
Koudougou 36,838 D6
Koupela D6
Léo D6
Ouagadougou (cap.) 172,661 D6
Ouahigouya 25,690 D6
Po D6
Tenkodogo E6
Tougan D6
Yako D6
Zabré D6

OTHER FEATURES

Black Volta (Mouhoun) (riv.) D6
Comoé (riv.) D7
Mouhoun (riv.) D6
Nakanbe (riv.) D6
Nazinan (riv.) D6
Oti (riv.) E7
Red Volta (Nazinan) (riv.) D6
Sudan (reg.) D6
White Volta (Nakanbe) (riv.) D6

CAPE VERDE

CITIES and TOWNS

Mindelo 28,797 A7
Praia (cap.) 21,494 B8
Ribeira Grande 1,892 B7
Sal Rei 1,296 B8

OTHER FEATURES

Boa Vista (isl.) B8
Brava (isl.) B8
Fogo (isl.) B8
Maio (isl.) B8
Sal (isl.) B7
Santa Luzia (isl.) B8
Santo Antão (isl.) A7
São Nicolau (isl.) B8
São Tiago (isl.) B8
São Vicente (isl.) B7

GAMBIA

CITIES and TOWNS

Banjul (cap.) 39,476 A6
Basse Santa Su 2,899 B6
Brikama 9,483 A6
Georgetown 2,510 A6

GHANA

CITIES and TOWNS

Accra (cap.) 859,600 D7
Attebubu 9,800 D7
Axim 13,100 D8
Bawku 33,900 D6
Bekwai 11,800 D7
Berekum 21,900 D7
Bolgatanga 31,500 D6
Cape Coast 57,700 D7
Damongo 12,600 D7
Dunkwa 16,900 D7
Elmina 15,600 D8
Ho 37,200 E7
Keta 12,700 E7
Kintampo 14,100 D7
Koforidua 54,400 D7
Kpandu 15,800 E7
Kumasi 348,900 D7
Mampong 19,800 D7
Nsawam 31,900 D7
Obuasi 60,100 D7
Oda 20,957 D7
Prestea 16,300 D7
Salaga 10,600 D7
Sekondi 32,400 D8
Sunyani 36,100 D7
Takoradi 61,500 D8
Tamale 136,800 D7
Tarkwa 22,000 D7
Tema 99,600 E7
Wa 36,000 D6
Wenchi 18,400 D7
Winneba 26,200 D7
Yendi 30,700 D7

OTHER FEATURES

Ashanti (reg.) D7
Benin (bight) E8
Black Volta (riv.) D7
Gold Coast (reg.) D8
Guinea (gulf) E8
Oti (riv.) E7
Red Volta (riv.) D6
Saint Paul (cape) E7
Three Points (cape) D8
Volta (lake) D7
Volta (riv.) E7
White Volta (riv.) D7

GUINEA

CITIES and TOWNS

Boffa B6
Conakry (cap.) 525,671 B7
Dabola B6
Dubréka B7
Fria B6
Kankan 85,310 C6
Kérouané C6
Kindia 79,861 B6
Kissidougou B7
Koundara 6,000 B6
Kouroussa C6
Labé 79,670 B6
Mali B6
N'Zérékoré 23,000 C7
Siguiri C6
Télimélé 12,000 B6
Tougué B6

OTHER FEATURES

Bafing (riv.) B6
Bakoy (riv.) B6
Futa Jallon (lag.) B6
Los (isls.) B7
Milo (riv.) C6
Moa (riv.) B7
Niger (riv.) C6
Nimba (lag.) C7
Verga (cape) B6

GUINEA-BISSAU

CITIES and TOWNS

Bissau (cap.) 109,486 A6
Bolama○ 9,133 A6
Bubaque○ 8,441 A6
Cacheu○ 15,194 A6

OTHER FEATURES

Bijagós (isls.) A6

IVORY COAST

CITIES and TOWNS

Abengourou 31,239 D7
Abidjan 6 85,828 D7
Aboisso 14,272 D7
Agboville 27,192 D7
Bingerville 18,218 D7
Bondoukou 19,111 D7
Bouaflé 15,917 C7
Bouaké 1 73,248 C7
Dabou 23,870 D7
Daloa 60,958 C7
Danané 19,872 C7
Dimbokro 30,986 D7
Divo 37,896 C7
Ferkessédougou 25,307 D7
Gagnoa 42,362 C7
Grand-Bassam 25,808 D7
Grand-Lahou 4,070 C8
Guiglo 10,441 C7
Issia 11,143 C7
Katiola 21,559 C7
Korhogo 47,657 C7
Man 50,315 C7
Odienné 13,864 C7
Port-Bouet 72,616 D7
San Pedro 27,616 C8
Séguéla 12,587 C7
Sinfra 16,399 C7
Tabou 7,255 C8
Toumodi 12,983 D7
Yamoussoukro (cap.) 35,585 C7

OTHER FEATURES

Aby (lag.) D8
Bagoé (riv.) C6
Bandama (riv.) C7
Baoulé (riv.) C6
Black Volta (riv.) D6
Cavally (riv.) C7
Comoé (riv.) D7
Ebrié (lag.) D8
Guinea (gulf) D8
Ivory Coast (reg.) C8
Kossou, Lac de (lake) C7
Nimba (lag.) C7
Sassandra (riv.) C7

LIBERIA

CITIES and TOWNS

Buchanan 23,999 B7
Gbarnga 6,896 C7
Greenville 8,462 C8
Harbel 11,445 B7
Harper 10,627 C8
Monrovia (cap.) 166,507 B7
River Cess 2,041 C7
Robertsport 2,562 B7
Tapeta 3,927 C7
Tubmanburg 14,089 B7
Zwedru 6,094 C7

OTHER FEATURES

Bong (range) B7
Cavalla (riv.) C7
Cestos (riv.) C7
Grain Coast (reg.) B8
Kru Coast (reg.) C8
Mano (riv.) B7
Mount (cape) B7
Nimba (lag.) C7
Palmas (cape) C8
Roberts Field Int'l Airport C7

MALI

CITIES and TOWNS

Ansongo 3,485 E5
Bafoulabé 2,163 B6
Bamako (cap.) 404,022 C6
Banamba 6,776 C6
Bandiagara 8,920 D6
Bankass 3,229 D6
Bougouni 17,246 C6
Bourem 4,538 E5
Dioila 4,953 C6
Dire 8,941 D5
Djenné 10,251 D6
Douentza 6,746 D6
Gao 30,714 E5
Goundam 10,262 D5
Gourma-Rharous 4,671 D5
Kéniéba 4,510 B6
Kadiolo 3,991 C6
Kangaba 3,184 C6
Kati 24,991 C6
Kayes 44,736 B6
Ké-Macina 5,426 C6
Kidal 3,308 E5
Kita 17,538 C6
Kolokani 8,923 C6
Kolondiéba 5,882 C6
Koulikoro 16,376 C6
Koutiala 27,497 C6
Ménaka 3,693 E5
Mopti 53,885 D6
Nara 6,091 C5
Niafunké 6,399 D5
Niono 12,290 C6
Nioro 11,617 C5
San 22,962 D6
Ségou 64,890 C6
Sikasso 47,030 C6
Ténenkou 4,708 C6
Timbuktu (Tombouctou) 20,483 D5
Yanfolila 3,809 C6
Yélimané 1,481 B5
Yorosso 2,390 C6

OTHER FEATURES

Achourat (well) D4
Adrar des Iforas (plat.) E5
Agueraktem (well) C4
Asselar (well) D5
Azaouad (reg.) D5
Azaouak (dry riv.) E5
Bafing (riv.) B6
Bagoé (riv.) C6
Bakoy (riv.) B6
Bani (riv.) C6
Baoulé (dry riv.) C6
Baoulé (riv.) C6
Bir Ksaib Ounane (well) C4
Bir Ounane (well) D4
Chech, Erg (des.) D4
Debo (lake) D5
El Mraïti (well) D5
Faguibine (lake) D5
Faiémé (riv.) B6
Haricha Hamada (des.) D4
Hombori (mts.) D5
In Dagouber (well) D4
Macina (depr.) D6
Niger (riv.) D5
Oum el Asel (well) D4
Sahara (des.) D4
Sekkane, Erg (des.) D4
Senegal (riv.) B5
Sudan (reg.) D6
Tadjnout Hagguerete (well) D4
Terhazza (ruins) C4
Tilemsi (valley) E5
Toufourine (well) C4

MAURITANIA

CITIES and TOWNS

Aïoun el Atrous C5
Akjoujt 8,044 B5
Aleg 6,415 B5
Atar 16,326 B4
Bassikounou C5
Boutilimit 7,261 B5
Fdérik (Fort Gouraud) 2,160 B4
Kâedi 20,248 B5
Kiffa 10,629 B5
M'Bout B5
Néma 8,232 C5
Nouadhibou 21,961 A4
Nouakchott (cap.) 134,986 A5
Oualata C5
Rosso 16,466 A5
Sélibaby 5,994 B5
Tidjikja 7,870 B5
Timbédra 5,317 C5
Zouîrât 17,474 B4

OTHER FEATURES

Adafer (reg.) B5
Adrar (reg.) B4
Affolé (reg.) B5
Agueraktem (well) C4
Aïn ben Tili (well) C3
Arguin (bay) A4
Assaba (reg.) B5
Atoui, Wadi (dry riv.) B4
Ben Guerdane (well) B3
Bir el Khzaim (well) C4
Blanc (cape) A4
Brakna (reg.) B5
Chegga (well) C3
Djouf, El (des.) C4
El Mrayer (well) C4
El Mreïti (well) C4
Gorgol (reg.) B5
Hodh (reg.) C5
Iguidi, Erg (des.) C3
Inchiri (reg.) A5
Koumbi Saleh (ruins) C5

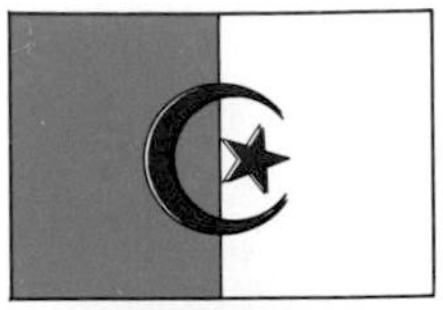
ALGERIA

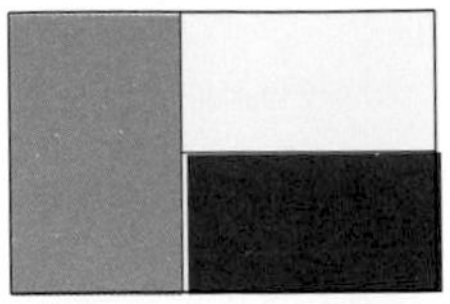
BENIN

CAPE VERDE

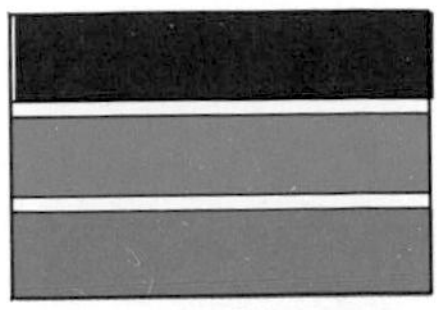
GAMBIA

GHANA

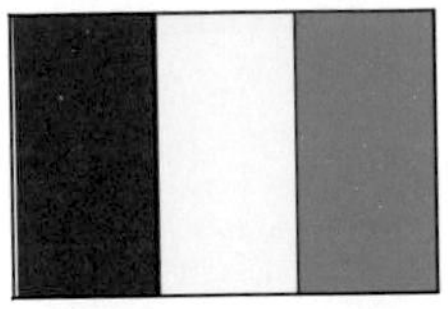
GUINEA

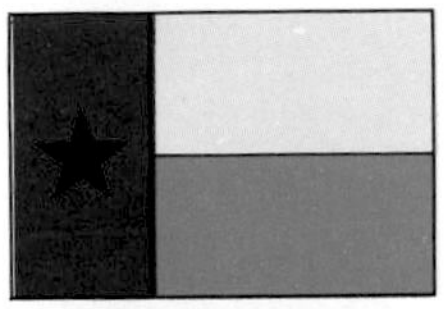
GUINEA-BISSAU

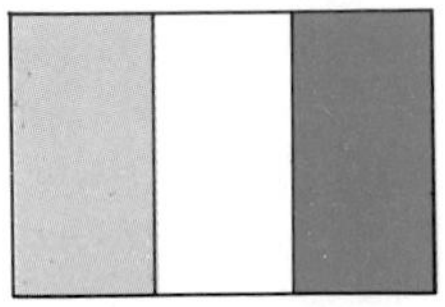
IVORY COAST

LIBERIA

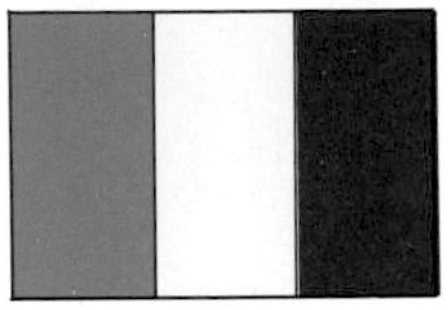
MALI

MAURITANIA

MOROCCO

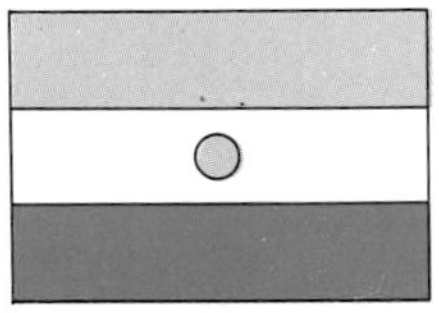
NIGER

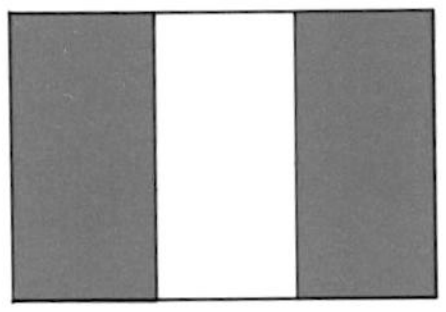
NIGERIA

SÃO TOMÉ AND PRINCIPE

SENEGAL

SIERRA LEONE

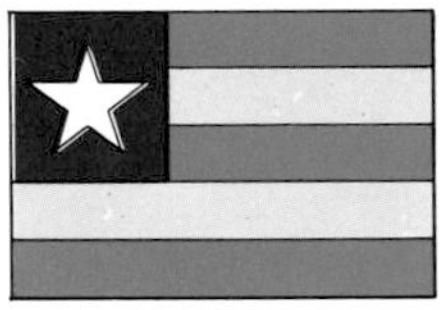
TOGO

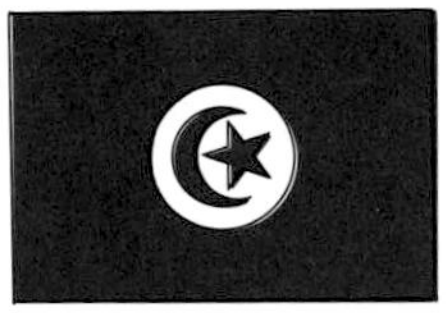
TUNISIA

BURKINA FASO

Western Africa 109

Lévrier (bay) A4
Makteïr (des.) B4
Meraia (reg.) C5
Mirik (Timiris) (cape) A5
Ouarane (reg.) B4
Sahara (des.) C4
Senegal (riv.) B5
Tagant (reg.) B5
Tidra (isl.) A5
Timiris (cape) A5
Touila (well) C3
Trarza (reg.) A5

MOROCCO

CITIES and TOWNS

Agadir 61,192 C2
Al Hoceima 18,686 D1
Azemmour 17,182 C2
Azrou 20,756 C2
Beni Mellal 53,826 C2
Boujad 18,838 C2
Casablanca 1,506,373 C2
Dar-el-Beida (Casablanca) 1,506,373 C2
El Jadida 55,501 C2
El Kelaa des Srarhna 17,163 C2
Er Rachidia 16,775 D2
Essaouira 30,061 C2
Fès (Fez) 325,327 D2
Jerada 30,633 D2
Kenitra 139,206 C2
Khenifra 25,526 C2
Khouribga 73,667 C2
Ksar el Kebir 48,262 C2
Larache 45,710 C1
Marrakech 332,741 C2
Mazagan (El Jadida) 55,501 C2
Meknès 248,369 C2
Mogador (Essaouira) 30,061 B2
Mohammedia 70,392 C2
Nador 32,490 D1
Oued Zem 33,323 C2
Ouezzane 33,267 C2
Oujda 175,532 D2
Port-Lyautey (Kénitra) 139,206 C2
Rabat (cap.) 367,620 C2
Safi 129,113 C2
Saïdia D2
Salé 155,557 C2
Sefrou 28,607 D2
Settat 42,325 C2
Sidi Ifni 13,650 B3
Sidi Kacem 26,831 C2
Tangier (Tanger) 187,894 C1
Tarfaya 1,104 B3
Taroudannt 22,272 C2
Taza 55,157 D2
Tétouan 139,105 C1
Youssoufia 22,435 C2

OTHER FEATURES

Anti-Atlas (ranges) C3
Atlas (mts.) C2
Bani, Jebel (mts.) C3
Beddouza, Ras (cape) C2
Dra, Wadi (dry riv.) C3
Gibraltar (str.) C1
High Atlas (ranges) C2
Juby (cape) B3
Mediterranean (sea) D1
Middle Atlas (ranges) C2
Moulouya (riv.) D2
Rheris, Wadi (dry riv.) D2
Rhir (cape) B2
Rif, Er (range) D2
Sarhro, Jebel (mts.) C2
Sebou (riv.) C2
Sim (cape) B2
Toubkal, Jebel (mt.) C2
Ziz, Wadi (dry riv.) D2

NIGER

CITIES and TOWNS

Agadès 11,000 F5
Arhli (Arlit) F5
Bilma G5
Birni-N'Konni 10,000 E6
Bosso G6
Dakoro F6
Diffa G6
Dosso E6
Filingué 10,000 E6
Gaya 5,000 E6
Gouré G6
Iférouane F5
In-Gall F5
Magaria F6
Mainé-Soroa G6
Maradi 45,852 F6
N'Guigmi G6
Niamey (cap.) 225,314 E6
Say E6
Tahoua 31,265 F6
Tanout F6
Tillabéry E6
Zinder 58,436 F6

OTHER FEATURES

Achégour (well) G5
Agadem (well) G5
Air (mts.) F5
Anaye (well) G5
Assakarai (dry riv.) F5
Azaoua (reg.) E5
Azbine (Air) (mts.) F5
Bagam (well) F5
Banguezane (mt.) F5
Bedouaram (well) G5
Chad (lake) G6
Dallol Bosso (dry riv.) E6
Dillia (dry riv.) G5
Djado (plat.) G4
El War (well) G4
In Azaoua (well) F4
Komadugu Yobe (riv.) G6
Mantas (well) E5
Niger (riv.) E6
Rima (riv.) F6
Sahara (des.) F4
Sudan (reg.) F6
Tafassasset, Wadi (dry riv.) F4
Talak (reg.) E5
Ténéré (des.) G5
Timboulaga (well) F5
Tummo (El War) (well) G4
Zoo Baba (well) G5

NIGERIA

STATES

Abuja Capital Territory F7
Anambra 2,300,000 F7
Bauchi 2,496,329 F6
Bendel 2,336,000 F7
Benue 2,641,496 F7
Borno 2,853,553 G6
Cross River 3,633,582 F7
Gongola 1,585,200 G7
Imo 5,000,000 F7
Kaduna 4,098,303 F6
Kano 5,775,000 F6
Kwara 5,240,600 E7
Lagos 1,100,000 E7
Niger 2,900,000 F7
Ogun 1,448,966 E7
Ondo 2,727,676 F7
Oyo 5,208,884 E7
Plateau 1,367,450 F7
Rivers 1,544,314 F8
Sokoto 1,367,450 F6

CITIES and TOWNS

Abeokuta 253,000 E7
Abuja (cap.) 1,000 F7
Ado 213,000 E7
Aku F7
Akure F7
Baga G6
Bama G6
Baro F7
Bauchi F6
Benin City 136,000 F7
Biu G6
Bonny F8
Calabar 103,000 F7
Degema F8
Dikwa G6
Ede 182,000 E7
Enugu 187,000 F7
Geidam G6
Gumel F6
Gummi F6
Gusau F6
Ibadan 847,000 E7
Ibi F7
Ife 176,000 E7
Ijebu-Ode E7
Ilesha 224,000 E7
Ilorin 282,000 E7
Iseyin 115,083 E7
Iwo 214,000 E7
Jega E6
Jos F7
Kaduna 202,000 F6
Kano 399,000 F6
Katsina 109,424 F6
Katsina Ala F7
Kontagora F6
Kumo G7
Kuta F7
Lagos 1,060,848 E7
Maiduguri 189,000 G6
Maigatari F6
Makurdi F7
Minna F7
Nnewi F7
Nsukka F7
Ogbomosho 432,000 E7
Ondo E7
Onitsha 220,000 F7
Oshogbo 282,000 F7
Owerri F7
Owo F7
Oyo 152,000 E7
Panyam F7
Port Harcourt 242,000 F8
Shaki F7
Shendam F7
Sokoto F6
Toungo G7
Wamba F7
Wukari F7
Yan G7
Yelwa E6
Yola G7
Zaria 224,000 F6

OTHER FEATURES

Adamawa (reg.) G7
Benin (bight) E8
Benue (riv.) F7
Biafra (bight) F8
Biu (plat.) G6
Bonny (bight) F8
Chad (lake) G6
Cross (riv.) F7
Dimlang (mt.) G7
Donga (riv.) G7
Gongola (riv.) G6
Guinea (gulf) E8
Hadejia (riv.) F6
Jos (plat.) F7
Kaduna (riv.) F7
Kainji (res.) E6
Komadugu Yobe (riv.) G6
Niger (delta) F8
Niger (riv.) F7
Osse (riv.) F7
Rima (riv.) F6
Slave Coast (reg.) E7
Sokoto (riv.) F6
Sudan (reg.) F6

PORTUGAL-Madeira

CITIES and TOWNS

Funchal (cap.) 38,340 A2

OTHER FEATURES

Desertas (isls.) A2
Madeira (isl.) A2
Pôrto Santo (isl.) A2

SÃO TOMÉ AND PRINCIPE

CITIES and TOWNS

São Tomé (cap.) 7,681 F8
Santo António 1,618 F8

OTHER FEATURES

Guinea (gulf) E8
Príncipe (isl.) F8
São Tomé (isl.) F8

SENEGAL

CITIES and TOWNS

Bignona 14,537 A6
Dagana 10,506 A5
Dakar (cap.) 798,792 A6
Diourbel 50,618 A6
Kaffrine 11,211 A6
Kaolack 106,899 A6
Kolda 19,302 B6
Louga 35,063 A5
Matam 10,002 B5
M'Bour 37,663 A6
Nioro-du-Rip 7,824 A6
Podor 6,914 B5
Rufisque A6
Saint-Louis 88,404 A5
Tambacounda 25,147 B6
Thiès 117,333 A5
Tivaouane 17,351 A5
Ziguinchor 72,726 A6

OTHER FEATURES

Casamance (riv.) A6
Falémé (riv.) B6
Ferlo (reg.) B6
Gambia (riv.) B6
Senegal (riv.) B5
Verde (cape) A6

SIERRA LEONE

CITIES and TOWNS

Bo 42,216 B7
Bonthe 6,230 B7
Freetown (cap.) 274,000 B7
Kabala 4,610 B7
Kenema 33,880 B7
Makeni 28,684 B7
Moyamba 4,564 B7
Pendembu 2,696 B7
Port Loko 5,809 B7
Pujehun 2,034 B7

OTHER FEATURES

Loma, Mansa (lag.) B7
Mano (riv.) B7
Moa (riv.) B7
Sherbro (isl.) B7
Yawri (bay) B7

SPAIN-Canary Islands, Ceuta and Melilla

CITIES and TOWNS

Arrecife 21,310 B3
Ceuta 60,639 C1
Las Palmas de Gran Canaria 260,368 B3
Melilla 64,942 D1
Santa Cruz de la Palma 10,393 A3
Santa Cruz de Tenerife 74,910 A3

OTHER FEATURES

Canary (isls.) A3
Fuerteventura (isl.) B3
Gomera (isl.) A3
Grand Canary (isl.) A3
Hierro (isl.) A3
Lanzarote (isl.) B3
La Palma (isl.) A3
Tenerife (isl.) A3

TOGO

CITIES and TOWNS

Aného (Anécho) 10,889 E7
Atakpamé 17,440 E7
Dapaong 10,100 E6
Kpalimé 19,801 E7
Lama-Kara 9,400 E7
Lomé (cap.) 148,443 E7
Mango 9,600 E6
Sokodé 29,623 E7

OTHER FEATURES

Benin (bight) E8
Guinea (gulf) E8
Mono (riv.) E7
Oti (riv.) E7
Slave Coast (reg.) E7

TUNISIA

CITIES and TOWNS

Béja 39,226 F1
Ben Gardane 6,593 G2
Bizerte 62,856 F1
El Djem 10,666 G1
El Kef 27,939 F1
Gabès 40,585 F2
Gafsa 42,225 F2
Halq el Oued 41,912 G1
Jendouba 18,127 F1
Kairouan 54,546 F1
Kalaa-Kebia 23,508 F1
Kasserine 22,594 F1
La Goulette (Halq el Oued) 41,912 G1
La Skhirra 4,565 G2
Mahdia 25,711 G1
Mareth 2,185 F2
Mateur 19,645 F1
Médenine 15,826 G2
Menzel Bourguiba 42,111 F1
Menzel Temime 18,857 G1
Moknine 26,035 G1
Monastir 26,759 G1
Msaken 33,559 G1
Nabeul 30,476 G1
Nefta 12,476 F2
Sfax 171,297 G2
Sousse 69,530 G1
Tatahouine 10,399 G2
Tozeur 16,772 F2
Tunis (cap.) 550,404 G1
Zarzis 14,420 G2

OTHER FEATURES

Abiad, Ras el (Blanc) (cape) G1
Blanc (cape) G1
Bon (cape) G1
Chambi, Jebel (mt.) F2
Djerba (isl.) G2
Djerid, Shott el (salt lake) F2
Gabès (gulf) G2
Grand Erg Oriental (des.) F2
Hammamet (gulf) G1
Jefara (reg.) G2
Kerkennah (isls.) G2
Mediterranean (sea) F1
Medjerda (riv.) F1
Tib, Ras el (Bon) (cape) G1
Tunis (gulf) G1

WESTERN SAHARA

CITIES and TOWNS

Dakhla 6,554 A4
El Aaiún (Laayoune) 24,519 B3
Villa Cisneros (Dakhla) 6,554 A4

OTHER FEATURES

Ausert (well) B4
Barbas (cape) A4
Bir Ganduz (well) A4
Bir Nzaran (well) B4
Blanc (cape) A4
Bojador (cape) B3
Durnford (pt.) A4
Guelta de Zemmur (well) B3
Saguia el Hamra (dry riv.) B3
Tichlá (well) B4
Atoui, Wadi (dry riv.) B4

○ Population of sub-district or division.

Agriculture, Industry and Resources

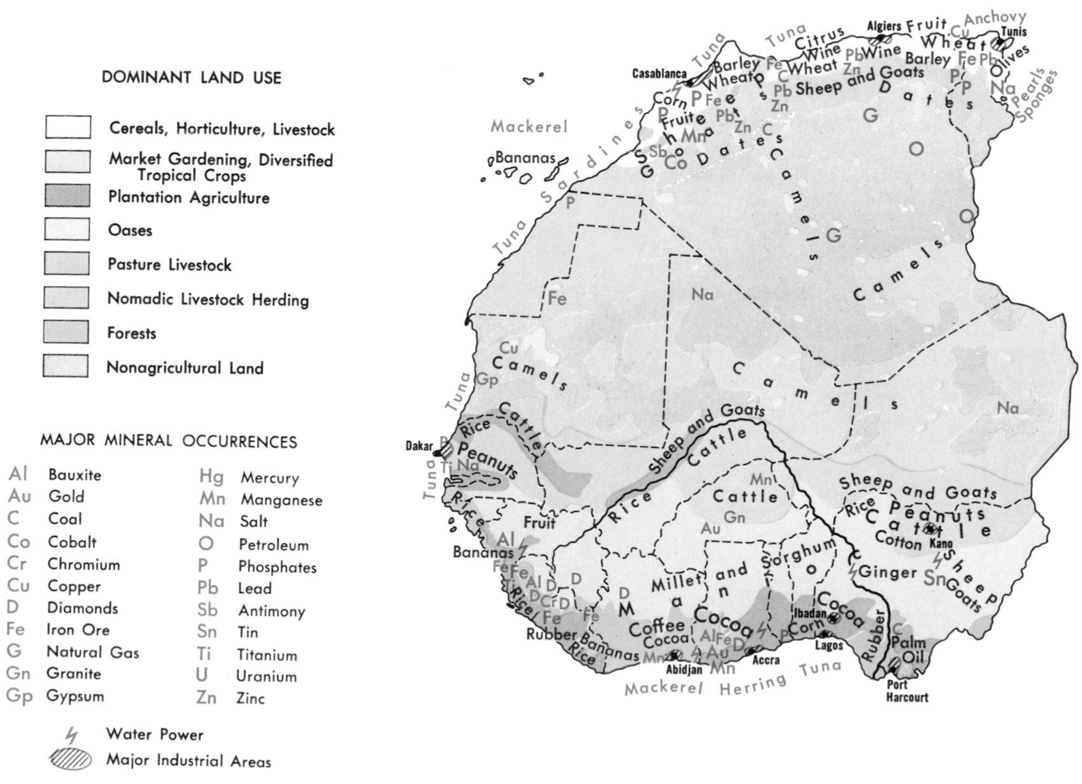

DOMINANT LAND USE
Cereals, Horticulture, Livestock
Market Gardening, Diversified Tropical Crops
Plantation Agriculture
Oases
Pasture Livestock
Nomadic Livestock Herding
Forests
Nonagricultural Land
MAJOR MINERAL OCCURRENCES
Al Bauxite
Au Gold
C Coal
Co Cobalt
Cr Chromium
Cu Copper
D Diamonds
Fe Iron Ore
G Natural Gas
Gn Granite
Gp Gypsum
Hg Mercury
Mn Manganese
Na Salt
O Petroleum
P Phosphates
Pb Lead
Sb Antimony
Sn Tin
Ti Titanium
U Uranium
Zn Zinc
Water Power
Major Industrial Areas
Algiers
Tunis
Casablanca
Dakar
Kano
Ibadan
Lagos
Abidjan
Accra
Port Harcourt
Mackerel
Sardines
Tuna
Herring
Anchovy
Pearls
Sponges
Citrus
Fruit
Wine
Wheat
Barley
Olives
Sheep and Goats
Dates
Camels
Bananas
Cattle
Rice
Peanuts
Millet and Sorghum
Cotton
Ginger
Coffee
Cocoa
Corn
Rubber
Palm Oil

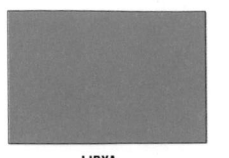

LIBYA

EGYPT

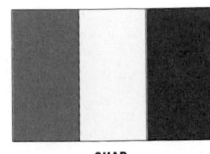

CHAD

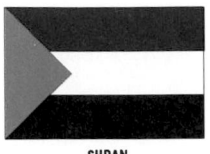

SUDAN

ETHIOPIA

ERITREA

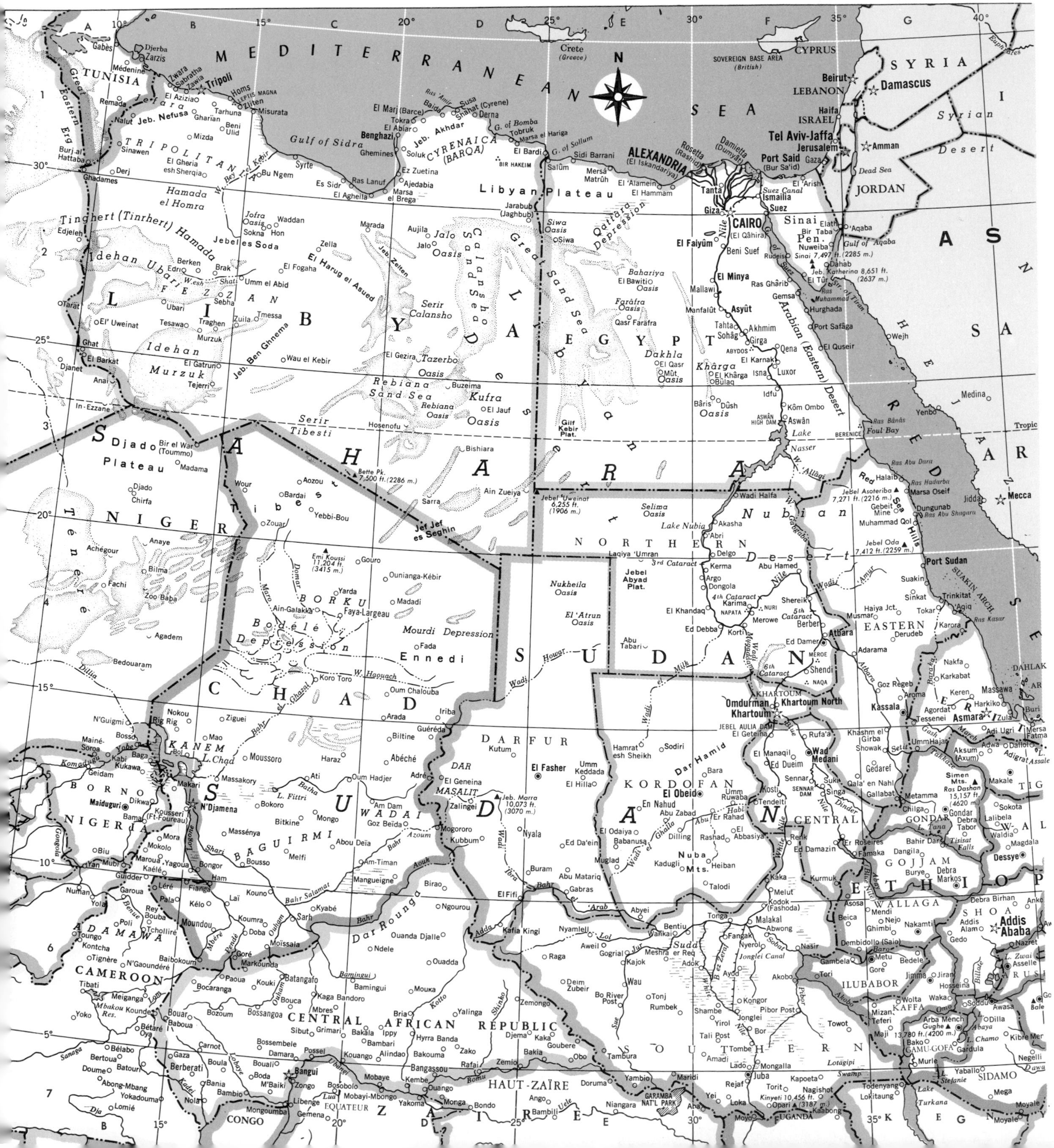

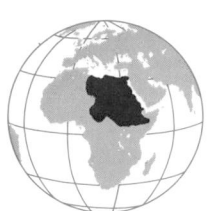

ERITREA

AREA 45,410 sq. mi. (117,600 sq. km.)
POPULATION 2,614,700
CAPITAL Asmara
LARGEST CITY Asmara
HIGHEST POINT Mount Soira 9,885 ft. (3,013 m.)
MONETARY UNIT birr
MAJOR LANGUAGES Arabic, English, Tigre, Afar
MAJOR RELIGIONS Coptic Christianity, Islam

DJIBOUTI

LIBYA

AREA 679,358 sq. mi. (1,759,537 sq. km.)
POPULATION 3,773,000
CAPITAL Tripoli
LARGEST CITY Tripoli
HIGHEST POINT Bette Pk. 7,500 ft. (2,286 m.)
MONETARY UNIT Libyan dinar
MAJOR LANGUAGES Arabic, Berber
MAJOR RELIGION Islam

EGYPT

AREA 386,659 sq. mi. (1,001,447 sq. km.)
POPULATION 53,080,000
CAPITAL Cairo
LARGEST CITY Cairo
HIGHEST POINT Jeb. Katherina 8,651 ft. (2,637 m.)
MONETARY UNIT Egyptian pound
MAJOR LANGUAGE Arabic
MAJOR RELIGIONS Islam, Coptic Christianity

CHAD

AREA 495,752 sq. mi. (1,283,998 sq. km.)
POPULATION 5,538,000
CAPITAL N'Djamena
LARGEST CITY N'Djamena
HIGHEST POINT Emi Koussi 11,204 ft. (3,415 m.)
MONETARY UNIT CFA franc
MAJOR LANGUAGES Arabic, Bagirmi, French, Sara, Massa, Moudang
MAJOR RELIGIONS Islam, tribal religions

SUDAN

AREA 967,494 sq. mi. (2,505,809 sq. km.)
POPULATION 24,485,000
CAPITAL Khartoum
LARGEST CITY Khartoum
HIGHEST POINT Jeb. Marra 10,073 ft. (3,070 m.)
MONETARY UNIT Sudanese pound
MAJOR LANGUAGES Arabic, Dinka, Nubian, Beja, Nuer
MAJOR RELIGIONS Islam, tribal religions

ETHIOPIA

AREA 426,366 sq. mi. (1,104,300 sq. km.)
POPULATION 50,576,300
CAPITAL Addis Ababa
LARGEST CITY Addis Ababa
HIGHEST POINT Ras Dashan 15,157 ft. (4,620 m.)
MONETARY UNIT birr
MAJOR LANGUAGES Amharic, Gallinya, Tigrinya, Somali, Sidamo, Arabic, Ge'ez
MAJOR RELIGIONS Coptic Christianity, Islam

DJIBOUTI

AREA 8,880 sq. mi. (23,000 sq. km.)
POPULATION 456,000
CAPITAL Djibouti
LARGEST CITY Djibouti
HIGHEST POINT Moussa Ali 6,768 ft. (2,063 m.)
MONETARY UNIT Djibouti franc
MAJOR LANGUAGES Arabic, Somali, Afar, French
MAJOR RELIGIONS Islam, Roman Catholicism

Northeastern Africa

CONIC EQUAL-AREA PROJECTION

SCALE OF MILES
0 50 100   200   300

SCALE OF KILOMETERS
0 50 100   200   300

Capitals of Countries _ _ _ _ _ _ _ ☆
Other Capitals _ _ _ _ _ _ _ _ _ _ ◉
International Boundaries _ _ _ _ _ ▬
Internal Boundaries _ _ _ _ _ _ _

Scale 1:14,300,000

© Copyright HAMMOND INCORPORATED, Maplewood, N.J.

CHAD

CITIES and TOWNS

Abéché 28,100 .... D5
Abou Deïa C5
Adré D5
Am-Timan 4,200 .... C5
Arada D4
Ati 7,500 .... D5
Baibokoum 5,500 .... C6
Biltine 3,900 .... D5
Bitkine 5,000 .... C5
Bokoro 6,500 .... C5
Bol 2,500 .... B5
Bongor 14,300 .... C5
Boussa 4,500 .... C5
Doba 13,300 .... C6
Fada D4
Faya-Largeau 6,800 .... C4
Fianga 10,000 .... C6
Goré C6
Goz Beïda D5
Guéréda D4
Iriba D4
Kélo 16,800 .... C6
Koumra 17,000 .... C6
Kouno C6
Kyabé 5,000 .... C6
Laï 10,400 .... C6
Léré B6
Mangueigne D5
Mao 4,900 .... C5
Massakory C5
Masséya C5
Melfi C5
Mogororo D5
Moissala 5,100 .... C6
Mongo 8,300 .... C5
Moundou 39,600 .... C6
Moussoro 7,700 .... C5
N'Djamena (cap.) 179,000 .... C5
Oum Hadjer 5,600 .... C5
Ounianga-Kébir D4
Pala 13,200 .... B6
Sarh 43,700 .... C6
Wour C3
Zouar C3

OTHER FEATURES

Aouk, Bahr (riv.) D5
Azoum, Bahr (riv.) D5
Baguirmi (reg.) C5
Bahr el Ghazal (dry riv.) C4
Batha (riv.) C5
Bodélé (depr.) C4
Borku (reg.) C4
Chad (lake) C5
Emi Koussi (mt.) C4
Ennedi (plat.) D4
Fittri (lake) C5
Kanem (reg.) C5
Logone (reg.) C5
Maro (riv.) C6
Mbéré (dry riv.) C6
Mourdi (riv.) D4
Ouham (depr.) C6
Pendé (riv.) C6
Sahara (riv.) C3
Salamat, Bahr (des.) C5
Shari (riv.) C5
Sudan (riv.) C5
Tibesti (mts.) C3
Wadai (reg.) D5

DJIBOUTI

CITIES and TOWNS

Ali Sabieh H5
Dikhil H5
Djibouti (cap.) 96,000 .... H5
Obock H5
Tadjoura H5

OTHER FEATURES

Abbe (lake) H5
Aden (gulf) J5
Bab el Mandeb (strait) H5

EGYPT

CITIES and TOWNS

Abnûb 39,343 .... J4
Akhmim 53,234 .... F2
Alexandria 2,318,655 .... J2
Aswân 144,377 .... F3
Asyût 213,983 .... J4
Benha 88,992 .... J3
Beni Mazar 39,373 .... J4
Beni Suef 118,148 .... J3
Biba 33,074 .... J4
Bur Sa'id
 (Port Said) 262,620 .... K2
Cairo (cap.) 5,084,463 .... J3
Dairût 31,624 .... J4
Damanhur 188,927 .... J3
Damietta 93,546 .... J3
Disûq 58,650 .... J3

(continued on following page)

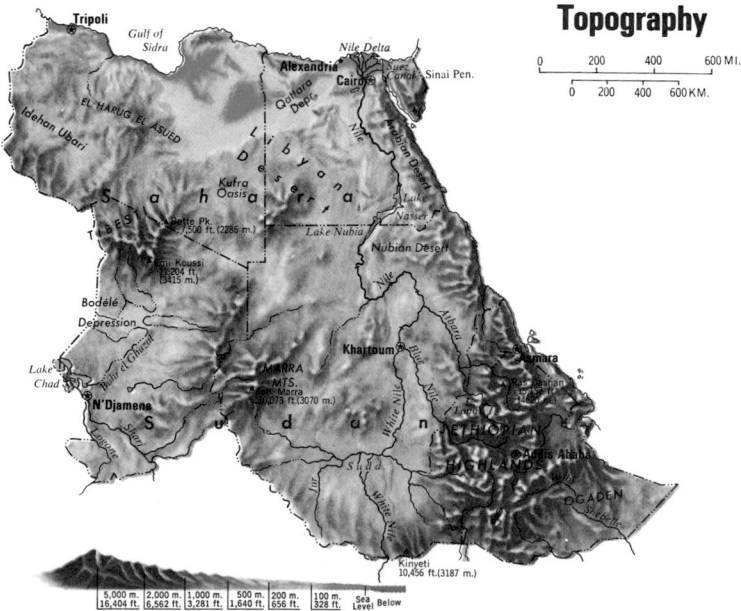

Topography

0   200   400   600 MI.
0   200   400   600 KM.

5,000 m.	2,000 m.	1,000 m.	500 m.	200 m.	100 m.	Sea
16,404 ft.	6,562 ft.	3,281 ft.	1,640 ft.	656 ft.	328 ft.	Level Below

(continued on following page)

Dumyât (Damietta) 93,546.....J3
El 'Alamein.....E1
El 'Arîsh.....F1
El Faiyûm 167,081.....J3
El Fashn 33,506.....J4
El Iskandarîya
  (Alexandria) 2,318,655.....J2
El Karnak.....F2
El Khârga 26,375.....F2
El Mahalla el Kubra 292,853.....J3
El Mansûra 257,866.....K3
El Minya 146,423.....J4
El Qâhira (Cairo)
  (cap.) 5,084,463.....J3
El Qantara 919.....K3
El Quseir 12,297.....F3
El Wasta 17,659.....J3
Girga 51,110.....F2
Giza 1,246,713.....J3
Heliopolis.....J3
Helwân.....J3
Idfu 34,858.....F3
Ismailia 145,978.....K3
Isna 34,186.....F2
Karnak (El Karnak).....F2
Kôm Ombo 44,531.....F2
Luxor 92,748.....F2
Maghâgha 40,802.....J4
Mallawi 74,256.....J4
Manfalût 41,126.....J4
Mersâ Matrûh 27,857.....E1
Minûf 55,131.....J3
Mût 8,032.....E2
Port Fuad.....K3
Port Safâga.....F2
Port Said 262,620.....K2
Port Taufiq.....K3
Qalyub 62,739.....J3
Qena 94,013.....F2
Rashid (Rosetta) 42,962.....J2
Rudeis.....F2
Salûm 4,161.....E1
Samalût 48,146.....J4
Shibin el Kom 102,844.....J3
Sidi Barrani 1,574.....E1
Sinnûris 32,022.....J3
Sohâg 101,758.....F2
Suez 194,001.....K3
Tahta 45,242.....F2
Tanta 284,636.....J3
Zagazig 202,637.....J3
Zifta 50,410.....J3

OTHER FEATURES

Abu Qir (bay).....J2
Abydos (ruins).....F2
Aqaba (gulf).....G2
Arabian (des.).....F2
Aswân (dam).....F3
Aswân High (dam).....F3
Bahariya (oasis).....E2
Bânâs, Ras (cape).....G3
Berenice (ruins).....F3

Birket Qârûn (lake).....J3
Bitter (lakes).....K3
Dakhla (oasis).....E2
Eastern (Arabian) (des.).....F2
Farâfra (oasis).....E2
Foul (bay).....G3
Gilf Kebir (plat.).....E3
Great Sand Sea (des.).....D2
Katherina, Jebel (mt.).....F2
Khârga (oasis).....F2
Libyan (des.).....E2
Libyan (plat.).....E1
Mediterranean (sea).....E1
Memphis (ruins).....J3
Muhammad, Ras (cape).....F2
Nasser (lake).....F2
Nile (riv.).....F2
Pyramids (ruins).....J3
Qattara (depr.).....E2
Sahara (des.).....E2
Sinai (des.).....F2
Sinai (pen.).....F2
Siwa (oasis).....E2
Suez (canal).....K3
Suez (gulf).....F2
Tiran (strait).....F2
'Uweinat, Jebel (mt.).....E3

ERITREA

CITIES and TOWNS

Adi Ugri 12,800.....G5
Asmara (cap.) 393,800.....G4
Assab 16,000.....H5
Karkabat.....G4
Keren.....G4
Massawa 19,800.....H5
Mersa Fatma.....G4
Nakfa.....G4
Tessenei.....G5
Thio.....H5
Umm Hajar.....G5
Zula.....G4

OTHER FEATURES

Baraka (riv.).....G4
Buri (pen.).....H4
Dahlak (arch.).....H4
Dahlak (isl.).....H4
Kasar, Ras (cape).....G4
Takkaze (riv.).....G5

ETHIOPIA

PROVINCES

Arusi 852,900.....G6
Bale 707,800.....H6
Gamu-Gofa 698,800.....G6
Gojjam 1,750,100.....G5
Gondar 1,355,800.....G5
Harar 3,359,200.....H6

Ilubabor 688,800.....F6
Kaffa 1,693,000.....G6
Shoa 5,369,500.....G6
Sidamo 2,479,800.....G7
Tigre 1,828,900.....H5
Wallaga 1,269,100.....G6
Wallo 2,459,900.....H5

CITIES and TOWNS

Addis Ababa (cap.)
  1,196,300.....G6
Adaba Alam 5,500.....G6
Adigrat 9,400.....G5
Adwa 16,400.....G5
Aksum 12,800.....G5
Ankober.....H6
Arba Mench 7,660.....G6
Asselle 19,390.....H6
Awareh.....H6
Axum (Aksum) 12,800.....G5
Bahir Dar 25,100.....G5
Dagabur.....H6
Dangila.....G5
Debra Birhan 16,700.....G6
Debra Markos 30,260.....G5
Debra Tabor 8,700.....G5
Dembidollo 7,600.....F6
Dessye 49,750.....G5
Dilla 13,800.....G6
Dire Dawa 63,700.....H6
El Carre.....H6
Gabredarre.....H6
Galadi.....J6
Gambela.....F6
Gardula 5,800.....G6
Gerlogubi.....H6
Ghimbi 8,300.....G6
Ginir.....H6
Goba 13,500.....H6
Gondar 38,600.....G5
Gore 8,500.....G6
Gorrahei.....H6
Harar 48,440.....H6
Hosseina 8,500.....G6
Jijiga 8,500.....H6
Jimma 47,360.....G6
Jiran.....G6
Kibre Mengist 8,300.....G6
Lalibela.....G5
Magdala.....G6
Maji.....G6
Makale 30,780.....H5
Metamma.....G5
Metu 6,860.....F6
Miesso.....H6
Mizan Teferi.....G6
Moyale.....G7
Murle.....G6
Mustahil.....H6
Nakamti 18,310.....G6
Nazret 42,900.....G6
Negelli 8,800.....G6
Nejo.....G6

Saio (Dembidollo) 7,600.....F6
Soddu 11,900.....G6
Sokota.....G5
Tori.....F6
Waka.....G6
Waldia 9,600.....G5
Wardere.....H6
Wolta.....G6
Yaballo.....G7

OTHER FEATURES

Abay (riv.).....G5
Abaya (lake).....G6
Abbe (lake).....H5
Akobo (riv.).....F6
Assal (lake).....H5
Assale (lake).....H5
Atbara (riv.).....G4
Awash (riv.).....H5
Axum (mt.).....G5
Blue Nile (Abay) (riv.).....G5
Chamo (lake).....G6
Danakil (reg.).....H5
Dawa (riv.).....H6
Dinder (riv.).....F5
Fafan (riv.).....H6
Ganale Dorya (riv.).....H6
Gughe (mt.).....G6
Haud (reg.).....J6
Ogaden (reg.).....H6
Omo (riv.).....G6
Ras Dashan (mt.).....G5
Red (sea).....H4
Rudolf (Turkana) (lake).....G7
Simen (mts.).....G5
Takkaze (riv.).....G5
Tana (lake).....G5
Tisisat (fall).....G5
Turkana (lake).....G7
Zwai (lake).....G6

LIBYA

CITIES and TOWNS

Ajedabia° 53,170.....D1
Aujila° 6,695.....D2
Baida° 59,765.....D1
Barce (El Marj)° 55,444.....D1
Benghazi 286,943.....C1
Beni Ulid° 19,113.....B2
Brak° 16,307.....B2
Cyrene (Shahat)° 17,157.....D1
Derj° 2,152.....B1
Derna° 44,145.....D1
El Abiar° 17,685.....D1
El Agheila 3.....C2
El Azizia° 34,077.....B1
El Barkat° 2,139.....B3
El Gatrun.....B3
El Jauf° 6,481.....D3
El Marj° 55,444.....D1
Es Sidr° 706.....C1

Ez Zuetina° 7,256.....D1
Ghadames° 6,172.....A2
Gharian° 65,224.....B1
Ghat° 6,924.....B3
Ghemines° 4,313.....C1
Homs° 66,890.....B1
Hon° 2,766.....C2
Jaghbub (Jarabub)° 1,436.....D2
Jarabub° 1,436.....D2
Marada° 3,201.....C2
Marsa el Brega° 2,618.....D1
Marsa el Hariga° 5,043.....D1
Misurata° 102,439.....C1
Mizda° 11,472.....B2
Nalut° 23,535.....B1
Ras Lanuf° 1,990.....C1
Sabrathaa° 30,836.....B1
Sebha° 35,879.....B2
Shahat° 17,157.....D1
Sinawen° 1,549.....B1
Sokna° 3,757.....C2
Soluk° 6,501.....D1
Syrte° 22,797.....C1
Tarhuna° 52,657.....B1
Tobruk° 58,384.....D1
Tokra° 10,714.....D1
Tripoli (cap.)° 550,438.....B1
Ubari° 19,132.....B2
Waddan° 5,347.....C2
Wau el Kebir.....C2
Zawia° 72,092.....B1
Zella° 72,092.....C2
Zliten° 58,981.....B1
Zwara° 15,078.....B1

OTHER FEATURES

Akhdar, Jebel (mts.).....D1
Barqa (Cyrenaica) (reg.).....D1
Ben Ghnema, Jebel (mts.).....C2
Bette (peak).....C3
Bey el Kebir, Wadi (dry riv.).....B1
Bir Hakeim (ruins).....D1
Bomba (gulf).....D1
Buzeima (well).....D3
Calansho Sand Sea (des.).....D2
Calansho, Serir (des.).....D2
Cyrenaica (reg.).....D1
Fezzan (reg.).....B2
Great Sand Sea (des.).....D2
Harug el Asued, El (mts.).....C2
Homra, Hamada el (des.).....B2
Idehan Murzuk (des.).....B2
Idehan Ubari (des.).....B2
Jalo (oasis).....D2
Jefara (reg.).....B1
Jef Jef es Seghin (plat.).....D3
Jofra (oasis).....C2
Kufra (oasis).....D3
Leptis Magna (ruins).....B1
Libyan (des.).....D2
Libyan (plat.).....D1
Mediterranean (sea).....C1

Nefusa, Jebel (mts.).....B1
Rebiana (oasis).....D3
Rebiana Sand Sea (des.).....D3
Sahara (des.).....C3
Shati, Wadi esh (dry riv.).....C1
Sidra (gulf).....C1
Soda, Jebel es (mts.).....C2
Tazerbo (oasis).....D2
Tibesti, Serir (des.).....C3
Tinghert Hamada
  (Tinrhert) (des.).....B2
Tripolitania (reg.).....B1
'Uweinat, Jebel (mt.).....E3
Zelten, Jebel (mts.).....D2

SUDAN

PROVINCES

Central.....F5
Darfur.....D5
Eastern.....G4
Khartoum.....F4
Kordofan.....E5
Northern.....E3
Southern.....E6

CITIES and TOWNS

'Abri.....F3
Abu Hamed.....F4
Adok.....F6
Akobo.....F6
Amadi.....F6
Argo.....F4
Aroma.....G4
Atbara 66,000.....F4
Babanusa.....E5
Bara.....F5
Bentiu.....E6
Berber.....F4
Bor.....F6
Buram.....D5
Damazin
  (Ed Damazin) 12,000.....F5
Deim Zubeir.....E6
Dongola 6,000.....F3
Dungunab.....G3
Ed Damazin 12,000.....F5
Ed Damer 17,000.....F4
Ed Dueim 27,000.....F5
El Fasher 52,000.....E5
El Geneina 33,000.....D5
El Obeid 90,000.....E5
El Odaiya.....E5
En Nahud 23,000.....E5
Er Roseires.....F5
Fashoda (Kodok).....F6
Gedaref 92,000.....G5
Gogrial.....E6
Goz Regeb.....G4
Haiya Junction.....G4
Halaib.....G3
Jonglei.....F6
Juba 57,000.....F7

Kadugli 18,000.....E5
Kaka.....F5
Karima.....F4
Kassala 99,000.....G4
Kerma.....F3
Khartoum (cap.) 334,000.....F4
Khartoum North 151,000.....F4
Khashm el Girba.....G5
Kodok.....F6
Kosti 57,000.....F5
Kurmuk.....F5
Kutum.....D5
Malakal 35,000.....F6
Maridi.....E7
Melut.....F5
Merowe.....F4
Meshra er Req.....F6
Mongalla.....F6
Muglad.....E5
Muhammad Qol.....G3
Nagishot.....F7
Nasir.....F6
Nyala 60,000.....D5
Nyamlell.....E6
Nyerol.....F6
Omdurman 299,000.....F4
Opari.....F7
Pibor Post.....F6
Port Sudan 133,000.....G4
Qala'en Nahl.....G5
Raga.....E6
Rashad.....F5
Rejaf.....F7
Renk.....F5
Rufa'a.....F5
Rumbek 17,000.....F6
Sennar.....F5
Shambe.....F6
Shendi.....F4
Shereik.....F4
Showak.....G5
Singa.....F5
Sinkat.....G4
Sodiri.....E5
Suakin.....G4
Suki.....F5
Tali Post.....F6
Talodi.....F5
Tambura.....E6
Tendelti.....F5
Tokar.....G4
Tombe.....F6
Tonga.....F6
Tonj.....E6
Torit.....F7
Trinkitat.....G4
Umm Keddada.....E5
Umm Ruwaba.....F5
Wadi Halfa.....F3
Wad Medani 107,000.....F5
Wankai.....E6
Wau 53,000.....E6
Yambio 7,000.....E7
Yei.....F7
Yirol.....F6
Zalingei.....D5

OTHER FEATURES

Abu Habl, Wadi (dry riv.).....F5
Abu Shagara, Ras (cape).....G3
Adda (riv.).....D6
Atbara (riv.).....G4
Bahr Azoum (riv.).....D5
Bahr el 'Arab (riv.).....E6
Bahr ez Zeraf (riv.).....F6
Blue Nile (riv.).....F5
Dar Hamid (reg.).....F5
Dar Masalit (reg.).....D5
Dinder (riv.).....F5
El 'Atrun (oasis).....E4
Fifth Cataract (falls).....F4
Fourth Cataract (falls).....F4
Gabgaba, Wadi (dry riv.).....F3
Ghalla, Wadi el (dry riv.).....E5
Hadarba, Ras (cape).....G3
Howar, Wadi (dry riv.).....E4
Ibra, Wadi (dry riv.).....D5
Jebel Aulia (dam).....F4
Jonglei (canal).....F6
Jur (riv.).....E6
Kinyeti (mt.).....F7
Libyan (des.).....E3
Lol (dry riv.).....E6
Lotagipi Swamp (plain).....F6
Marra, Jebel (mt.).....D5
Meroe (ruins).....F4
Milk, Wadi el (dry riv.).....E4
Muqaddam, Wadi (dry riv.).....F4
Napata (ruins).....F4
Naqa (ruins).....F4
Nile (riv.).....F4
Nuba (mts.).....E5
Nubia (lake).....F3
Nubian (des.).....F3
Nukheila (oasis).....E4
Nuri (ruins).....F4
Oda, Jebel (mt.).....G3
Pibor (riv.).....F6
Red (sea).....G3
Red Sea (hills).....G3
Sahara (des.).....E3
Selima (oasis).....E3
Sennar (dam).....F5
Setit (riv.).....G5
Sixth Cataract (falls).....F4
Sobat (riv.).....F6
Suakin (arch.).....G4
Sudan (reg.).....E5
Sudd (swamp).....F6
Sue (riv.).....E6
Third Cataract (falls).....E4
'Uweinat, Jebel (mt.).....E3
White Nile (riv.).....F5

Agriculture, Industry and Resources

DOMINANT LAND USE

Cereals, Horticulture, Livestock
Cash Crops, Mixed Cereals
Cotton, Cereals
Market Gardening, Diversified Tropical Crops
Plantation Agriculture
Oases
Pasture Livestock
Nomadic Livestock Herding
Forests
Nonagricultural Land

MAJOR MINERAL OCCURRENCES

Ab Asbestos
Au Gold
Cr Chromium
Fe Iron Ore
G   Natural Gas
K   Potash

Mn Manganese
Na Salt
O   Petroleum
P   Phosphates
Pt Platinum

⚡ Water Power
Major Industrial Areas

° Population of sub-district or division

ANGOLA

AREA 481,351 sq. mi. (1,246,700 sq. km.)
POPULATION 9,747,000
CAPITAL Luanda
LARGEST CITY Luanda
HIGHEST POINT Mt. Moco 8,593 ft. (2,620 m.)
MONETARY UNIT kwanza
MAJOR LANGUAGES Mbundu, Kongo, Lunda, Portuguese
MAJOR RELIGIONS Tribal religions, Roman Catholicism

BURUNDI

AREA 10,747 sq. mi. (27,835 sq. km.)
POPULATION 5,302,000
CAPITAL Bujumbura
LARGEST CITY Bujumbura
HIGHEST POINT 8,858 ft. (2,700 m.)
MONETARY UNIT Burundi franc
MAJOR LANGUAGES Kirundi, French, Swahili
MAJOR RELIGIONS Tribal religions, Roman Catholicism, Islam

CAMEROON

AREA 183,568 sq. mi. (475,441 sq. km.)
POPULATION 11,540,000
CAPITAL Yaoundé
LARGEST CITY Douala
HIGHEST POINT Cameroon 13,350 ft. (4,069 m.)
MONETARY UNIT CFA franc
MAJOR LANGUAGFS Fang, Bamileke, Fulani, Duala, French, English
MAJOR RELIGIONS Tribal religions, Christianity, Islam

CENTRAL AFRICAN REP.

AREA 242,000 sq. mi. (626,780 sq. km.)
POPULATION 2,740,000
CAPITAL Bangui
LARGEST CITY Bangui
HIGHEST POINT Gao 4,659 ft. (1,420 m.)
MONETARY UNIT CFA franc
MAJOR LANGUAGES Banda, Gbaya, Sangho, French
MAJOR RELIGIONS Tribal religions, Christianity, Islam

CONGO, REP. OF THE

AREA 132,046 sq. mi. (342,000 sq. km.)
POPULATION 1,843,000
CAPITAL Brazzaville
LARGEST CITY Brazzaville
HIGHEST POINT Leketi Mts. 3,412 ft. (1,040 m.)
MONETARY UNIT CFA franc
MAJOR LANGUAGES Kikongo, Bateke, Lingala, French
MAJOR RELIGIONS Christianity, tribal religions, Islam

EQUATORIAL GUINEA

AREA 10,831 sq. mi. (28,052 sq. km.)
POPULATION 341,000
CAPITAL Malabo
LARGEST CITY Malabo
HIGHEST POINT 9,868 ft. (3,008 m.)
MONETARY UNIT CFA franc
MAJOR LANGUAGES Fang, Bubi, Spanish
MAJOR RELIGIONS Tribal religions, Christianity

GABON

AREA 103,346 sq. mi. (267,666 sq. km.)
POPULATION 1,206,000
CAPITAL Libreville
LARGEST CITY Libreville
HIGHEST POINT Ibounzi 5,165 ft. (1,574 m.)
MONETARY UNIT CFA franc
MAJOR LANGUAGES Fang and other Bantu languages, French
MAJOR RELIGIONS Tribal religions, Christianity, Islam

KENYA

AREA 224,960 sq. mi. (582,646 sq. km.)
POPULATION 24,872,000
CAPITAL Nairobi
LARGEST CITY Nairobi
HIGHEST POINT Kenya 17,058 ft. (5,199 m.)
MONETARY UNIT Kenya shilling
MAJOR LANGUAGES Kikuyu, Luo, Kavirondo, Kamba, Swahili, English
MAJOR RELIGIONS Tribal religions, Christianity, Hinduism, Islam

MALAWI

AREA 45,747 sq. mi. (118,485 sq. km.)
POPULATION 8,022,000
CAPITAL Lilongwe
LARGEST CITY Blantyre
HIGHEST POINT Mulanje 9,843 ft. (3,000 m.)
MONETARY UNIT Malawi kwacha
MAJOR LANGUAGES Chichewa, Yao, English, Nyanja, Tumbuka, Tonga, Ngoni
MAJOR RELIGIONS Tribal religions, Islam, Christianity

RWANDA

AREA 10,169 sq. mi. (26,337 sq. km.)
POPULATION 6,274,000
CAPITAL Kigali
LARGEST CITY Kigali
HIGHEST POINT Karisimbi 14,780 ft. (4,505 m.)
MONETARY UNIT Rwanda franc
MAJOR LANGUAGES Kinyarwanda, French, Swahili
MAJOR RELIGIONS Tribal religions, Roman Catholicism, Islam

SOMALIA

AREA 246,200 sq. mi. (637,658 sq. km.)
POPULATION 7,339,000
CAPITAL Mogadishu
LARGEST CITY Mogadishu
HIGHEST POINT Surud Ad 7,900 ft. (2,408 m.)
MONETARY UNIT Somali shilling
MAJOR LANGUAGES Somali, Arabic, Italian, English
MAJOR RELIGION Islam

TANZANIA

AREA 363,708 sq. mi. (942,003 sq. km.)
POPULATION 24,802,000
CAPITAL Dar es Salaam
LARGEST CITY Dar es Salaam
HIGHEST POINT Kilimanjaro 19,340 ft. (5,895 m.)
MONETARY UNIT Tanzanian shilling
MAJOR LANGUAGES Nyamwezi-Sukuma, Swahili, English
MAJOR RELIGIONS Tribal religions, Christianity, Islam

UGANDA

AREA 91,076 sq. mi. (235,887 sq. km.)
POPULATION 17,804,000
CAPITAL Kampala
LARGEST CITY Kampala
HIGHEST POINT Margherita 16,795 ft. (5,119 m.)
MONETARY UNIT Ugandan shilling
MAJOR LANGUAGES Luganda, Acholi, Teso, Nyoro, Soga, Nkole, English, Swahili
MAJOR RELIGIONS Tribal religions, Christianity, Islam

CONGO, DEM. REP. OF THE

AREA 905,063 sq. mi. (2,344,113 sq. km.)
POPULATION 34,491,000
CAPITAL Kinshasa
LARGEST CITY Kinshasa
HIGHEST POINT Margherita 16,795 ft. (5,119 m.)
MONETARY UNIT zaire
MAJOR LANGUAGES Tshiluba, Mongo, Kikongo, Kingwana, Zande, Lingala, Swahili, French
MAJOR RELIGIONS Tribal religions, Christianity

ZAMBIA

AREA 290,586 sq. mi. (752,618 sq. km.)
POPULATION 8,073,000
CAPITAL Lusaka
LARGEST CITY Lusaka
HIGHEST POINT Sunzu 6,782 ft. (2,067 m.)
MONETARY UNIT Zambian kwacha
MAJOR LANGUAGES Bemba, Tonga, Lozi, Luvale, Nyanja, English
MAJOR RELIGIONS Tribal religions

ANGOLA

BURUNDI

CAMEROON

CENTRAL AFRICAN REP.

CONGO, REP. OF THE

EQUATORIAL GUINEA

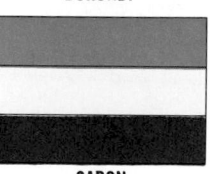
GABON

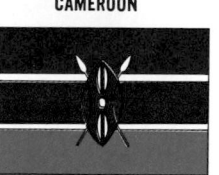
KENYA

MALAWI

R
RWANDA

SOMALIA

TANZANIA

UGANDA

CONGO, DEM. REP. OF THE

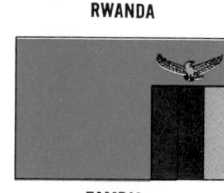
ZAMBIA

ANGOLA

PROVINCES

CITIES and TOWNS

(continued on following page)

OTHER FEATURES

Bamingui (riv.)	C2
Bomu (riv.)	D3
Dar Rounga (reg.)	D2
Gao (mt.)	C2
Kadei (riv.)	C2
Kotto (riv.)	D2
Lobaye (riv.)	C2
Mbéré (riv.)	B2
Ouham (riv.)	C2
Pendé (riv.)	C2

Sangha (riv.)	C3
Shari (riv.)	C2
Shinko (riv.)	D2
Ubangi (riv.)	C3

CONGO, REP. OF THE
CITIES and TOWNS

Abala	C4
Boundji	C4
Brazzaville (cap.) 298,967	C4

Djambala	B4
Impfondo	C3
Kinkala	B4
Loubomo 29,600	B4
Makoua	C3
Mbinda	B4
Mossaka	C4
Mossendjo	B4
Nkayi 30,600	B4
Ouesso	C3
Owando	C4
Pointe-Noire 141,700	B4

OTHER FEATURES

Alima (riv.)	B4
Congo (riv.)	B3
Crystal (mts.)	B4
Dja (riv.)	B3
Ivindo (riv.)	B3
Kadei (riv.)	C3
Kouilou (riv.)	B4
Kouiou (riv.)	B4
Likouala (riv.)	C3
N'Gounié (riv.)	B3
Niari (riv.)	B4

Ogooué (riv.)	A4
Sangha (riv.)	C3
Ubangi (riv.)	C3

EQUATORIAL GUINEA
TERRITORIES

Bioko 78,000	A3
Río Muni 203,000	B3

CITIES and TOWNS

Bata 270,241	A3
Luba 19,933	A3
Malabo (cap.) 37,237	A3
Mbini 14,503	A3

OTHER FEATURES

Biafra (bight)	A3
Corisco (isl.)	A3
Elobey (isls.)	A3
Fernando Po (Bioko) (isl.)	A3

GABON
CITIES and TOWNS

Bitam 5,936	B3
Cocobeach	A3
Fougamou	B4
Franceville 9,345	B4
Kango	B3
Koula-Moutou 8,032	B4
Lambaréné 17,770	B4
Lastoursville	B4
Libreville (cap.) 105,080	A3
Makokou 5,005	B3
Mayumba	B4
M'Bigou	B4
Médouneu	B3
Mekambo	B3
Mimongo	B4
Minvoul	B3
Moanda 10,709	B4
Mouila 15,016	B4
Mounana 4,000	B4
N'Dendé	B4
N'Djolé	B4
Okondja	B4
Omboué	A4
Owendo	A3
Oyem 12,455	B3
Port-Gentil 48,190	A4
Tchibanga 14,001	B4

OTHER FEATURES

Crystal (mts.)	B4
Ibounzi	B4
Ivindo (riv.)	B3
Lopez (cape)	A4
N'Dogo (lag.)	B4
N'Gounié (riv.)	B4
N'Komi (lag.)	A4
Ogooué (riv.)	A4
Pongara (pt.)	A3

KENYA
PROVINCES

Central 1,675,647	G4
Coast 944,082	G4
Eastern 1,907,301	G4
Nairobi 509,286	G4
North-Eastern 245,757	G3
Nyanza 2,122,045	F4
Rift Valley 2,210,289	G3
Western 1,328,298	G3

CITIES and TOWNS

Baragoi 2,383	G3
Bunyala	F3
Eldoret 18,196	G3
Embu 3,928	G4
Fort Hall 4,750	G4
Galole 3,609	G4
Garissa	G4
Gilgil 4,178	G4
Isiolo 8,201	G4
Kajiado 1,755	G4
Kakamega 6,244	F3
Kaningo 2,450	G4
Kapenguria 1,790	G3
Kericho 10,144	F4
Kiambu 2,776	G4
Kilifi 2,662	G4
Kisii 6,080	F4
Kisumu 32,431	F3
Kitale 11,573	G3
Kitui 3,071	G4
Kwale 1,092	G4
Lamu 7,403	H4
Lokitaung 4,090	G3
Machakos 6,312	G4
Mado Gashi 1,003	G3
Malindi 10,757	H4
Maralal 3,878	G3
Marsabit 6,635	G3
Migori 2,066	F4
Mombasa 247,073	G4
Nairobi (cap.) 509,286	G4
Naivasha 6,920	G4
Nakuru 47,151	G4
Nanyuki 11,624	G3
Narok 2,608	G4
Ngong 1,583	G4
Nyeri 2,436	G4
Rumuruti 1,484	G3
Thika 18,387	G4
Thomson's Falls 7,602	G4
Vanga	G4
Voi 5,313	G4
Wajir	H3
Wamba 2,650	G3

OTHER FEATURES

Daua (riv.)	H3
Elgon (mt.)	G3
Formosa (bay)	H4
Galana (riv.)	G4
Gedi (ruins)	G4
Kenya (riv.)	G4
Lak Dera (dry riv.)	H3
Lorian (swamp)	H3
Natron (lake)	G4
Nyiru (mt.)	G3
Patta (isl.)	H4
Rudolf (Turkana) (lake)	G3
Tana (riv.)	G4
Tsavo Nat'l Park	G4
Turkana (lake)	G3
Victoria (lake)	F4
Winam (bay)	F4

MALAWI
CITIES and TOWNS

Blantyre 222,153	F7
Chitipa 3,079	F6
Dedza 5,448	F6
Dowa 2,067	F6
Karonga 11,873	F5
Lilongwe (cap.) 102,924	F6
Mangochi 3,341	G6
Mchinji 1,962	F6
Mwanza 2,271	F7
Mzimba 4,962	F6

Ncheu 1,326	F6
Nkhata Bay 4,024	F6
Nkhotakota 10,312	F6
Nsanje 6,091	G7
Rumphi 3,998	F6
Salima 4,646	F6
Tiyolo 4,106	F7
Zomba 21,000	G7

OTHER FEATURES

Chilrua (lake)	G7
Malawi (Nyasa) (lake)	F6
Mulanje (mts.)	G7
Nyasa (lake)	F6
Shire (riv.)	G7

RWANDA
CITIES and TOWNS

Butare 21,691	E4
Cyangugu 7,042	E4
Gisenyi 12,436	E4
Kigali (cap.) 117,749	F4
Nyabisindu 8,587	F4

OTHER FEATURES

Kagera Nat'l Park	F4
Karisimbi (mt.)	E4
Kivu (lake)	E4
Ruzizi (riv.)	E4
Virunga (range)	E4

SOMALIA
PROVINCES

Bakool 100,000	H3
Bari 155,000	J1
Bay 302,000	H3
Galguduud 182,000	J2
Gedo 202,800	H3
Hiiraan 147,000	J3
Jubbada Hoose 246,000	H3
Mogadiscio 371,000	J3
Mudug 215,000	J2
Nugaal 85,000	J2
Sanaag 369,000	J1
Shabeellaha Dhexe 237,000	J3
Shabeellaha Hoose 398,000	H3
Togdheer 258,000	J2
Woqooyi Galbeed 440,000	H1

CITIES and TOWNS

Afgoi	J3
Afmadu 2,580	H3
Alula	K1
Ankhor	J1
Balad 1,233	J3
Barawa (Brava) 6,167	H3
Baydhabo 14,962	H3
Belet Weyne 11,426	J3
Bender Cassim	J1
Berbera 12,219	H1
Borama 3,244	H1
Bosaso	J1
Brava 6,16/	II3
Bulo Burti 5,247	J3
Bur Acaba	H3
Burao 12,617	J2
Candala	J1
Chisimayu 17,872	H4
Coriole 4,341	H3
Dante (Hafun)	K1
Dusa Mareb	J2
Eil	J2
El Athale (Itala)	J3
Erigabo 4,279	J1

(continued on following page)

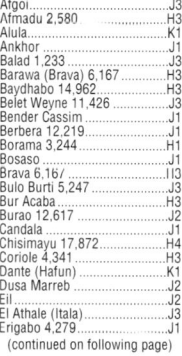

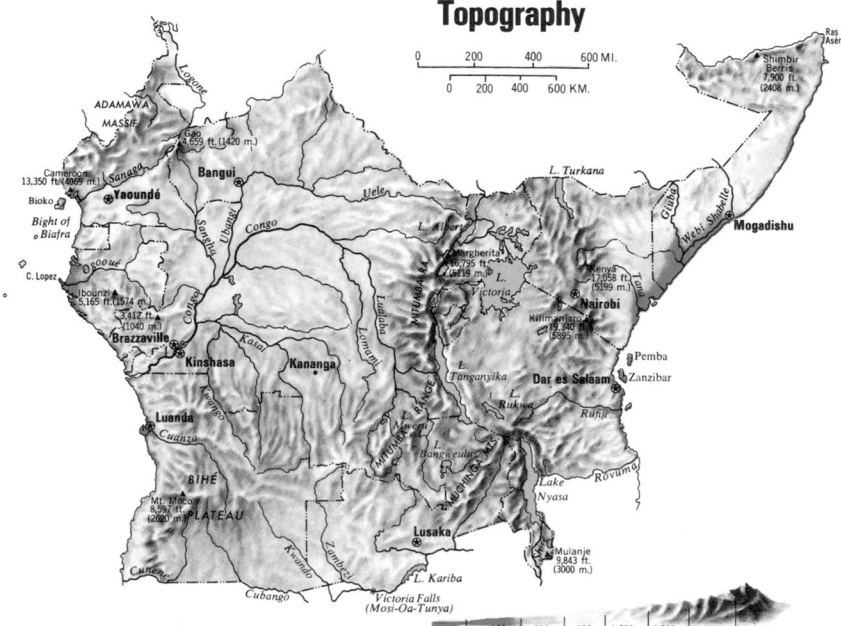

Topography

SCALE

0   200   400   600 MI.

0   200   400   600 KM.

Below Sea Level | 100 m. 328 ft. | 200 m. 656 ft. | 500 m. 1,640 ft. | 1,000 m. 3,281 ft. | 2,000 m. 6,562 ft. | 5,000 m. 16,404 ft.

Central Africa

CYLINDRICAL EQUAL-AREA PROJECTION

SCALE OF MILES

0   50   100   200   300

SCALE OF KILOMETERS

0   50 100   200   300

Capitals of Countries ─ ─ ─ ─ ─ ☆

Other Capitals ─ ─ ─ ─ ─ ⊙

International Boundaries ─ ▪ ─ ▪ ─

Internal Boundaries ─────

Scale 1:13,800,000

© Copyright HAMMOND INCORPORATED, Maplewood, N.J.

(continued)

Galcaio J2
Garbahaarrey H3
Garoe J2
Giohar 13,156 J3
Hafun K1
Hargeysa 40,254 H2
Itala J3
Jamama 5,408 H3
Jilib 3,232 H3
Kismayu (Chisimayu) 17,872 H4
Las Anod 2,441 J2
Las Khoreh 2,245 J1
Luuq H3
Margherita (Jamama) H3
Marka (Merka) 17,708 H3
Mogadishu (cap.) 371,000 J3
Muqdisho (Mogadishu) (cap.) 371,000 J3
Oddur H3
Odweina 1,422 J2
Uanle Uen H3
Villabruzzi (Johar) J3
Zeila 1,226 H1

OTHER FEATURES

Aden (gulf) J1
Asèr, Ras (cape) K1
Giuba (riv.) H3
Guban (reg.) H1
Haud (plat.) J2
Lak Dera (dry riv.) H3
Negro (bay) J2
Shimbir Berris (mt.) J1
Sura, Ras (cape) J1
Webi Shabelle (riv.) H3

TANZANIA

PROVINCES

Arusha 928,478 G4
Dar es Salaam G5
Dodoma 971,921 G5
Iringa 922,801 G5
Kagera 1,009,379 F4
Kigoma 648,950 F4
Kilimanjaro 902,394 G4
Lindi 527,902 G5
Mara 723,295 F4
Mbeya 1,080,241 F5
Morogoro 939,190 G5
Mtwara 771,726 G5
Mwanza 1,443,418 F4
Pemba 205,870 H5
Pwani (Coast) 516,949 G5
Rukwa 451,897 F5
Ruvuma 564,113 G6
Shinyanga 1,323,482 F4
Singida 614,030 F5
Tabora 818,049 F5
Tanga 1,088,592 G5
Zanzibar Mjini 143,616 G5
Zanzibar Shambani North 77,424 G5
Zanzibar Shambani South 52,325 G5

CITIES and TOWNS

Arusha 55,281 G4
Bagamoyo 5,112 G5
Biharamulo 1,011 F4
Bukene 2,288 F4
Bukoba 20,430 F4
Chake Chake 4,862 H5
Chunya 2,398 F5
Dar es Salaam (cap.) 757,346 G5
Dodoma 45,703 G5
Gelta 3,066 F4
Iringa 57,182 G5
Kahama 3,211 F4
Kasulu F4
Kibondo F4
Kigoma-Ujiji 50,044 E4
Kilosa 4,458 G5
Kilwa Kivinje 2,790 G5
Kilwa Masoko G5
Koani 1,102 G5
Kondoa 4,514 G4
Kongwa G5
Korogwe 6,675 G5
Lindi 27,308 G5
Lushoto 1,803 G4
Mahenge G5
Manyoni G5
Masasi G6
Mbeya 76,606 F5
Mbulu G4
Mchinga G5
Mkokotoni 2,220 G5
Morogoro 61,890 G5
Moshi 52,223 G4
Mpanda F5
Mpwapwa 2,429 G5
Mtwara-Mikindani 48,510 H6
Musoma 32,658 F4
Mwadui 7,383 F4
Mwanza 110,611 F4
Nachingwea 3,751 G6
Newala G6
Ngara F4
Njombe F5
Nzega 2,386 F4
Pangani 2,955 G5
Shinyanga 21,703 F4
Singida 29,252 F4
Songea 17,954 G6
Sumbawanga 28,586 F5
Tabora 67,392 F5
Tanga 103,409 G4
Tukuyu 4,089 F5
Tunduru G6
Utete G5
Wete 8,469 G4
Zanzibar 110,669 G5

OTHER FEATURES

Eyasi (lake) F4
Great Ruaha (riv.) G5
Juani (isl.) G5
Kagera Nat'l Park F4
Kalambo (falls) F5
Kilimanjaro (mt.) G4
Kilombero (riv.) G5
Mafia (isl.) H5
Manyara (lake) G4
Masai (steppe) G4
Mbarangandu (riv.) G5
Mbemkuru (riv.) G5
Meru (mt.) G4
Mikumi Nat'l Park G5
Natron (lake) G4
Ngorongoro (crater) F4
Njombe (riv.) F5
Nyasa (lake) F6
Olduvai Gorge (canyon) G4
Pangani (riv.) G4
Pemba (isl.) H5
Ras Kanzi (cape) G5
Rovuma (riv.) G6
Ruaha Nat'l Park F5
Rufiji (riv.) G5
Rukwa (lake) F5
Rungwa (riv.) F5
Rungwe (mt.) F5
Serengeti Nat'l Park F4
Tanganyika (lake) E5
Tarangire Nat'l Park G4
Victoria (lake) F4
Wami (riv.) G5
Wembere (riv.) F4
Zanzibar (isl.) G5

UGANDA

CITIES and TOWNS

Arua 10,837 F3
Butiaba 261 F3
Entebbe 21,096 F3
Fort Portal 7,947 F3
Gulu 18,170 F3
Hoima 2,339 F3
Jinja 52,509 F3
Kabale 8,234 E4
Kampala (cap.) 478,895 F3
Kasese 7,213 F3
Kitgum 3,242 F3
Lira 7,340 F3
Masaka 12,987 F4
Masindi 2,100 F3
Mbale 23,544 F3
Mbarara 16,078 F4
Moroto 5,488 F3
Moyo 266 F3
Mubende 6,004 F3
Rhino Camp 198 F3
Soroti 8,130 F3
Tororo 15,977 F3

OTHER FEATURES

Albert (Mobuto Sese Seko) (lake) F3
Edward (lake) E4
Elgon (mt.) F3
George (lake) F3
Kabalega (falls) F3
Kagalega Nat'l Park F3
Kidepo Nat'l Park F3
Kioga (lake) F3
Margherita (mt.) E3
Mobuto Sese Seko (lake) F3
Owen Falls (dam) F3
Ruwenzori (range) E3
Sese (isls.) F4
Victoria (lake) F4
Virunga (range) E4
Virunga Nat'l Park F4

CONGO, DEM. REP. OF THE

PROVINCES

Bandundu 2,600,556 C4
Bas-Zaïre 1,504,361 B5
Equateur 2,431,812 D3
Haut-Zaïre 3,356,419 E3
Kasai-Occidental 2,433,861 D4
Kasai-Oriental 1,872,231 D5
Kinshasa 1,323,039 C4
Kivu 3,361,883 E4
Shaba 2,753,714 E5

CITIES and TOWNS

Aba 7,600 F3
Aketi 17,200 D3
Bambesa E3
Banalia E3
Banana B5
Bandundu 74,467 C4
Basankusu C3
Basoko 9,100 D3
Befale D3
Beni 22,800 E3
Bikoro C4
Boende 12,800 D4
Bokungu D4
Bolobo 10,300 C4
Bolomba 7,200 C3
Boma 61,100 B5
Bomongo C3
Bondo 10,000 D3
Bongandanga 12,900 D3
Bosobolo 11,100 C3
Budjala C3
Bukama E5
Bukavu 134,861 E4
Bulungu 16,300 C4
Bumba 34,700 D3
Bunia 28,800 E3
Bunkeya 5,100 E6
Businga 11,000 D3
Busu-Djanoa D3
Buta 19,800 D3
Butembo 27,800 E3
Dekese D4
Demba 22,000 D5
Dibaya 11,400 D5
Dibaya-Lubue 7,900 C4
Dilolo 14,000 D6
Dimbelenge D5
Djolu D3
Djugu F3
Dungu 9,100 E3
Faradje 10,400 E3
Feshi C5
Fizi E4
Gandájika 60,100 D5
Gemena 37,300 D3
Goma 48,600 E4
Gungu C5
Idiofa C4
Ikela D4
Ilebo 32,200 D4
Ingende C4
Inongo 14,800 C4
Irumu 9,300 E3
Isangi D3
Isiro 49,300 E3
Kabalo 22,600 E5
Kabambare E4
Kabare 12,600 E4
Kabinda 60,500 D5
Kabongo 6,500 E5
Kahemba C5
Kalehe E4
Kalemie 62,300 E5
Kalima 27,500 E4
Kama 69,100 E4
Kambove 18,900 E6
Kamina 56,300 D5
Kampene 14,600 E4
Kananga 428,960 D5
Kaniama D5
Kapanga D5
Kasangulu 11,900 C4
Kasenga E6
Kasese E4
Kasongo 37,800 E4
Kasongo-Lunda C5
Katako-Kombe D4
Kazumba D5
Kenge 17,500 C4
Kibombo E4
Kikwit 111,960 C5
Kinshasa (cap.) 1,323,039 C4
Kipushi 32,900 E6
Kisangani 229,596 E3
Kolwezi 81,600 E6
Kongolo 14,800 E5
Kutu 10,000 C4
Libenge 13,000 C3
Lisala D3
Lodja 20,300 D4
Lomela D4
Lubefu D4
Lubudi 6,000 E5
Lubumbashi 318,000 E6
Lubutu E4
Luebo 21,800 D5
Lukula 9,400 B5
Luozi 7,000 B5
Lusambo 13,100 D4
Mambasa 7,400 E3
Mangai 41,200 C4
Manono 44,500 E5
Masi-Manimba 6,300 C4
Masisi E4
Matadi 110,436 B5
Mbandaka 107,910 C3
Mbanza-Ngungu 55,800 C5
Mbuji-Mayi 256,154 D5
Mitwaba E5
Monkoto D4
Muanda 6,400 B5
Mungbere E3
Mushie 13,700 C4
Muyumba E5
Mweka 24,900 D4
Mwene-Ditu 71,200 D5
Mwenga E4
Niangara 9,200 E3
Nyunzu 11,300 E5
Opala D4
Oshwe C4
Panda-Likasi 146,394 E6
Pangi E4
Poko E3
Popokabaka C5
Port Kindu 42,800 E4
Punia E4
Rutshuru E4
Sakania E6
Sandoa D5
Sentery 24,300 E5
Shabunda 6,900 E4
Songololo 4,600 B5
Tshela 10,700 B4
Tshikapa 38,900 D5
Ubundu 630 E4
Uvira 15,900 E4
Virunga 21,900 E5
Wamba 11,500 E3
Watsa 21,250 E3
Yangambi 22,600 D3

OTHER FEATURES

Albert (Mobuto Sese Seko) (lake) F3
Aruwimi (riv.) E3
Bomu (riv.) D3
Boyoma (Stanley) (falls) D3
Chicapa (riv.) D5
Congo (riv.) C4
Edward (lake) E4
Elila (riv.) E4
Fimi (riv.) C4
Garamba Nat'l Park E3
Giri (riv.) C3
Itimbiri (riv.) D3
Ituri (for.) E3
Karisimbi (mt.) E4
Kasai (riv.) C4
Kivu (lake) E4
Kwa (riv.) C4
Kwango (riv.) C5
Kwilu (riv.) C5
Lindi (riv.) E3
Livingstone (falls) B5
Loange (riv.) C5
Lokoro (riv.) C4
Lomami (riv.) D4
Lomela (riv.) D4
Lowa (riv.) E4
Lua (riv.) C3
Lualaba (riv.) E4
Luapula (riv.) E6
Lubilash (riv.) D5
Lufira (riv.) E5
Luilaka (riv.) C4
Lukenie (riv.) D4
Lukuga (riv.) E5
Lulua (riv.) D5
Luvua (riv.) E5
Mai-Ndombe (lake) C4
Malebo (Stanley Pool) (lake) C4
Margherita (mt.) E3
Marungu (mts.) E5
Mobuto Sese Seko (lake) F3
Mweru (lake) E5
Ruwenzori (range) E3
Ruzizi (riv.) E4
Salonga Nat'l Park D4
Sankuru (riv.) D4
Stanley (falls) D3
Stanley Pool (lake) C4
Tanganyika (lake) E5
Tshuapa (riv.) D4
Tumba (lake) C4
Ubangi (riv.) C3
Uele (riv.) E3
Ulindi (riv.) E4
Upemba (lake) E5
Upemba Nat'l Park E5
Virunga (range) E4
Virunga Nat'l Park E4

ZAMBIA

CITIES and TOWNS

Abercorn (Mbala) 11,179 F5
Bancroft (Chililabombwe) 61,928 E6
Broken Hill (Kabwe) 143,635 E6
Chilanga 12,503 E7
Chililabombwe 61,928 E6
Chingola 145,869 E6
Chipata 32,291 F6
Choma 17,943 E7
Fort Rosebery (Mansa) 34,801 E6
Isoka 6,832 F6
Kabompo 5,357 D6
Kabwe 143,635 E6
Kafue 29,794 E7
Kalabo 7,398 D6
Kalomo 5,878 E7
Kaoma 6,731 D6
Kapiri Mposhi 13,677 E6
Kasama 38,093 F6
Kawambwa 7,235 E5
Kitwe 314,794 E6
Livingstone 71,987 E7
Luanshya 132,164 E6
Lusaka (cap.) 538,469 E7
Mansa 34,801 E6
Mazabuka 29,602 E7
Mbala 11,179 F5
Mongu 24,919 D7
Monze 13,141 E7
Mpika 25,880 F6
Mporokoso 6,008 F5
Mpulungu 6,354 F5
Mufulira 149,778 E6
Mumbwa 7,570 E6
Ndola 282,439 E6
Petauke 7,531 F6
Senanga 7,204 D7
Serenje 6,008 F6
Solwezi 15,032 E6
Zambezi 8,166 D6

OTHER FEATURES

Bangweulu (lake) F6
Barotseland (reg.) D7
Chambeshi (riv.) F6
Cuando (riv.) D7
Dongwe (riv.) D6
Kabompo (riv.) D6
Kafue (riv.) E7
Kafue Nat'l Park E6
Kalambo (falls) F5
Kariba (dam) E7
Kariba (lake) E7
Luangwa (riv.) F6
Luapula (riv.) E6
Lungwebungu (riv.) D6
Mosi-Oa-Tunya (Victoria) (falls) E7
Mulungushi (dam) E6
Mweru (lake) E5
Sunzu (mt.) F5
Tanganyika (lake) E5
Victoria (falls) E7
Zambezi (riv.) D7

Agriculture, Industry and Resources

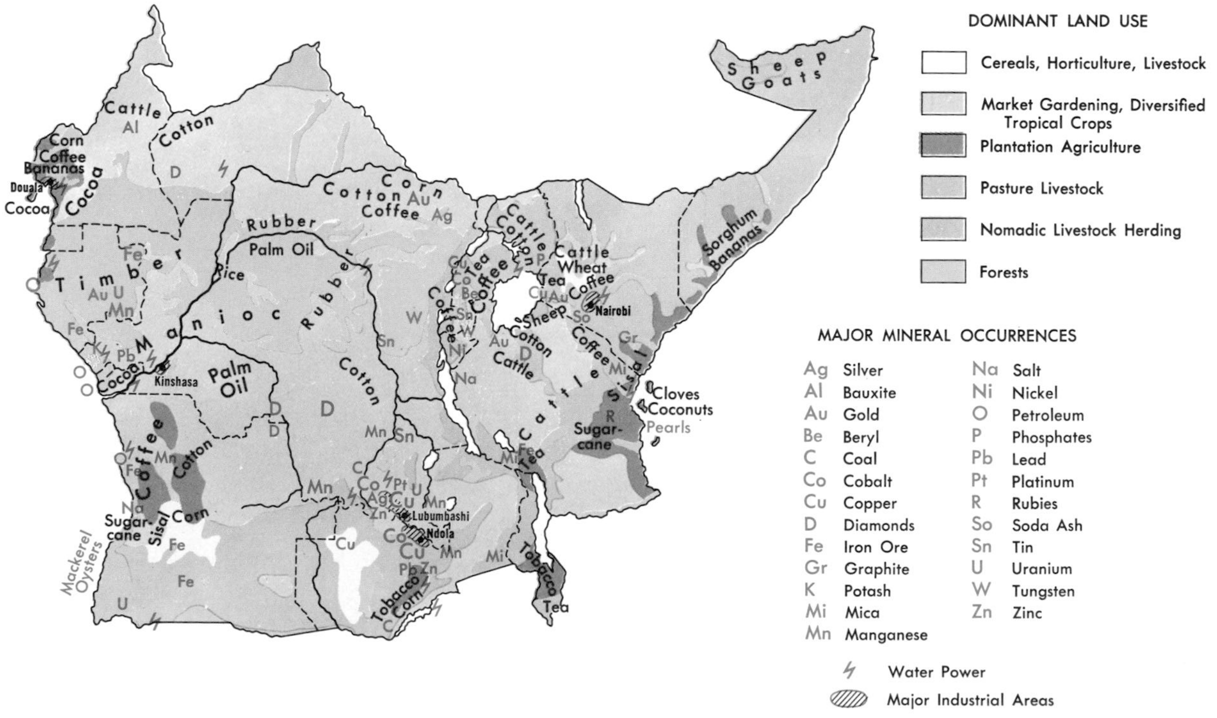

DOMINANT LAND USE
Cereals, Horticulture, Livestock
Market Gardening, Diversified Tropical Crops
Plantation Agriculture
Pasture Livestock
Nomadic Livestock Herding
Forests
MAJOR MINERAL OCCURRENCES
Ag Silver
Al Bauxite
Au Gold
Be Beryl
C Coal
Co Cobalt
Cu Copper
D Diamonds
Fe Iron Ore
Gr Graphite
K Potash
Mi Mica
Mn Manganese
Na Salt
Ni Nickel
O Petroleum
P Phosphates
Pb Lead
Pt Platinum
R Rubies
So Soda Ash
Sn Tin
U Uranium
W Tungsten
Zn Zinc
Water Power
Major Industrial Areas
Sheep
Goats
Cattle
Cotton
Corn
Coffee
Bananas
Douala
Cocoa
Rubber
Palm Oil
Timber
Manioc
Kinshasa
Sorghum
Bananas
Wheat
Tea
Nairobi
Sisal
Cloves
Coconuts
Pearls
Sugar-cane
Lubumbashi
Ndola
Tobacco
Mackerel
Oysters

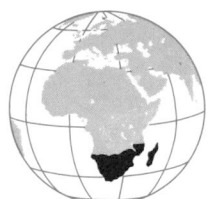

NAMIBIA

AREA 317,827 sq. mi. (823,172 sq. km.)
POPULATION 1,818,000
CAPITAL Windhoek
LARGEST CITY Windhoek
HIGHEST POINT Brandberg 8,550 ft.
(2,606 m.)
MONETARY UNIT rand
MAJOR LANGUAGES Ovambo, Hottentot,
Herero, Afrikaans, English
MAJOR RELIGIONS Tribal religions,
Protestantism

SOUTH AFRICA

AREA 455,318 sq. mi. (1,179,274 sq. km.)
POPULATION 34,492,000
CAPITALS Cape Town, Pretoria
LARGEST CITY Johannesburg
HIGHEST POINT Injasuti 11,182 ft. (3,408 m.)
MONETARY UNIT rand
MAJOR LANGUAGES Afrikaans, English,
Xhosa, Zulu, Sesotho
MAJOR RELIGIONS Protestantism,
Roman Catholicism, Islam, Hinduism,
tribal religions

LESOTHO

AREA 11,720 sq. mi. (30,355 sq. km.)
POPULATION 1,700,000
CAPITAL Maseru
LARGEST CITY Maseru
HIGHEST POINT 11,425 ft. (3,482 m.)
MONETARY UNIT loti
MAJOR LANGUAGES Sesotho, English
MAJOR RELIGIONS Tribal religions,
Christianity

BOTSWANA

AREA 224,764 sq. mi. (582,139 sq. km.)
POPULATION 1,256,000
CAPITAL Gaborone
LARGEST CITY Francistown
HIGHEST POINT Tsodilo Hill 5,922 ft.
(1,805 m.)
MONETARY UNIT pula
MAJOR LANGUAGES Setswana, Shona,
Bushman, English, Afrikaans
MAJOR RELIGIONS Tribal religions,
Protestantism

MOZAMBIQUE

AREA 303,769 sq. mi. (786,762 sq. km.)
POPULATION 15,326,000
CAPITAL Maputo
LARGEST CITY Maputo
HIGHEST POINT Mt. Binga 7,992 ft.
(2,436 m.)
MONETARY UNIT metical
MAJOR LANGUAGES Makua, Thonga,
Shona, Portuguese
MAJOR RELIGIONS Tribal religions,
Roman Catholicism, Islam

SWAZILAND

AREA 6,705 sq. mi. (17,366 sq. km.)
POPULATION 681,000
CAPITAL Mbabane
LARGEST CITY Manzini
HIGHEST POINT Emlembe 6,109 ft.
(1,862 m.)
MONETARY UNIT lilangeni
MAJOR LANGUAGES siSwati, English
MAJOR RELIGIONS Tribal religions,
Christianity

ZIMBABWE

AREA 150,803 sq. mi. (390,580 sq. km.)
POPULATION 9,122,000
CAPITAL Harare
LARGEST CITY Harare
HIGHEST POINT Mt. Inyangani 8,517 ft.
(2,596 m.)
MONETARY UNIT Zimbabwe dollar
MAJOR LANGUAGES English, Shona,
Ndebele
MAJOR RELIGIONS Tribal religions,
Protestantism

MADAGASCAR

AREA 226,657 sq. mi. (587,041 sq. km.)
POPULATION 9,985,000
CAPITAL Antananarivo
LARGEST CITY Antananarivo
HIGHEST POINT Maromokotro 9,436 ft.
(2,876 m.)
MONETARY UNIT Madagascar franc
MAJOR LANGUAGES Malagasy, French
MAJOR RELIGIONS Tribal religions,
Roman Catholicism, Protestantism

COMOROS

AREA 719 sq. mi. (1,862 sq. km.)
POPULATION 484,000
CAPITAL Moroni
LARGEST CITY Moroni
HIGHEST POINT Karthala 7,746 ft.
(2,361 m.)
MONETARY UNIT CFA franc
MAJOR LANGUAGES Arabic, French,
Swahili
MAJOR RELIGION Islam

MAURITIUS

AREA 790 sq. mi. (2,046 sq. km.)
POPULATION 1,068,000
CAPITAL Port Louis
LARGEST CITY Port Louis
HIGHEST POINT 2,711 ft. (826 m.)
MONETARY UNIT Mauritian rupee
MAJOR LANGUAGES English, French,
French Creole, Hindi, Urdu
MAJOR RELIGIONS Hinduism, Christianity,
Islam

SEYCHELLES

AREA 145 sq. mi. (375 sq. km.)
POPULATION 67,000
CAPITAL Victoria
LARGEST CITY Victoria
HIGHEST POINT Morne Seychellois
2,993 ft. (912 m.)
MONETARY UNIT Seychellois rupee
MAJOR LANGUAGES English, French,
Creole
MAJOR RELIGION Roman Catholicism

REUNION

AREA 969 sq. mi. (2,510 sq. km.)
POPULATION 570,000
CAPITAL St-Denis

MAYOTTE

AREA 144 sq. mi. (373 sq. km.)
POPULATION 47,300
CAPITAL Mamoutzou

ZIMBABWE · **BOTSWANA** · **SOUTH AFRICA** · **LESOTHO** · **SWAZILAND**

MOZAMBIQUE · **COMOROS** · **MADAGASCAR** · **MAURITIUS** · **SEYCHELLES**

NAMIBIA

Agriculture, Industry and Resources

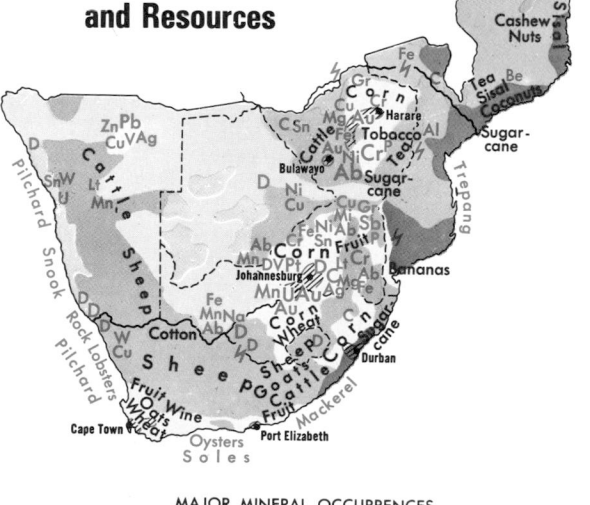

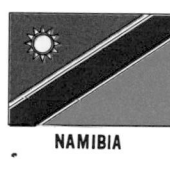

DOMINANT LAND USE

	Cereals, Horticulture, Livestock
	Market Gardening, Diversified Tropical Crops
	Plantation Agriculture
	Pasture Livestock
	Nomadic Livestock Herding
	Forests
	Nonagricultural Land

MAJOR MINERAL OCCURRENCES

Ab	Asbestos	Cu	Copper	Mn	Manganese	Sb	Antimony
Ag	Silver	D	Diamonds	Na	Salt	Sn	Tin
Al	Bauxite	Fe	Iron Ore	Ni	Nickel	U	Uranium
Au	Gold	Gr	Graphite	P	Phosphates	V	Vanadium
Be	Beryl	Lt	Lithium	Pb	Lead	W	Tungsten
C	Coal	Mg	Magnesium	Pt	Platinum	Zn	Zinc
Cr	Chromium	Mi	Mica				

 Water Power

Major Industrial Areas

BOTSWANA

CITIES and TOWNS

Dinokwe 560	D4
Francistown 22,000	D4
Gaborone (cap.) 21,000	D4
Ghanzi 1,198	C4
Kanye 10,664	D5
Kasane 1,476	C4
Lobatse 11,936	D5
Mahalapye 12,056	D4
Maun 9,614	C4
Mochudi 6,945	D4
Molepolole 9,448	D4
Palapye 5,217	D4
Ramotswa 7,991	D4
Selebi-Pikwe 20,572	D4
Serowe 15.723	D4

OTHER FEATURES

Chobe (riv.)	C3
Chobe Nat'l Park	D3
Dau (lake)	C4
Kalahari (des.)	C4
Kaukauveld (mts.)	C3
Limpopo (riv.)	D4
Mababe (depr.)	C3
Makgadikgadi (salt pan)	D3
Molopo (riv.)	C5
Ngami (lake)	C4
Ngamiland (reg.)	C3
Nossob (riv.)	B4
Okavango (riv.)	C3
Okovango (swamps)	C3
Orange (riv.)	B5
Shashe (riv.)	D4
Tati (riv.)	D4
Tsodilo Hill (mt.)	C3
Xau (Dau) (lake)	C4

COMOROS

CITIES and TOWNS

Fomboni 3,229	G2
Mitsamiouli 3,196	G2
Moroni (cap.) 12,000	G2
Mutsamudu 7,652	G2

OTHER FEATURES

Mwali (Mohéli) (isl.)	G2
Njazidja (Grand Comoro) (isl.)	G2
Nzwani (Anjouan) (isl.)	G2

LESOTHO

CITIES and TOWNS

Leribe 5,200	D5
Mafeteng 4,600	D5
Maseru (cap.) 71,500	D5
Mohaleshoek 3,600	D6

MADAGASCAR

PROVINCES

Antananarivo 2,167,973	H3
Antsiranana 597,982	H2
Fianarantsoa 1,804,365	H4
Mahajanga 819,750	H3
Toamasina 1,179,660	H3
Toliara 1,034,114	G4

CITIES and TOWNS

Ambalavao 6,988	H4
Ambanja 12,258	H2
Ambatolampy 11,539	H3
Ambatondrazaka 18,044	H3
Ambilobe 9,415	H2
Ambodifototra 1,112	J3
Ambositra 16,780	H4
Andapa 6,275	H2
Antalaha 17,541	J2
Antananarivo (cap.) 451,808	H3
Antsirabe 32,979	H3
Antsiranana 40,443	H2
Antsohihy 8,721	H2
Arivonimamo 8,497	H3
Belo-Tsiribihina 4,403	G3
Brickaville (Vohibinany) 1,741	H3
Diégo-Suarez (Antsiranana) 40,443	H2
Faradofay 19,605	H5
Farafangana 10,817	H4
Fenoarivo, Toamasina 7,696	H3
Fianarantsoa 68,054	H4
Fort-Dauphin (Faradofay) 19,605	H5
Foulpointe	H3
Hell-Ville 6,183	H2
Ihosy 4,521	H4
Maevatanana 7,197	H3
Maintirano 6,375	G3
Majunga 65,864	H3
Manakara 19,768	H4
Mananjary 14,638	H4
Mandritsara 6,826	H3
Maroantsetra 6,645	J3
Marovoay 20,253	H3
Moramanga 10,806	H3
Morombe 6,967	G4
Morondava 19,061	G4
Port-Bergé 4,734	H3
Sambava 6,215	J2
Sosumav 10,946	H2
Tamatave (Toamasina) 77,395	H3

(continued on following page)

Topography

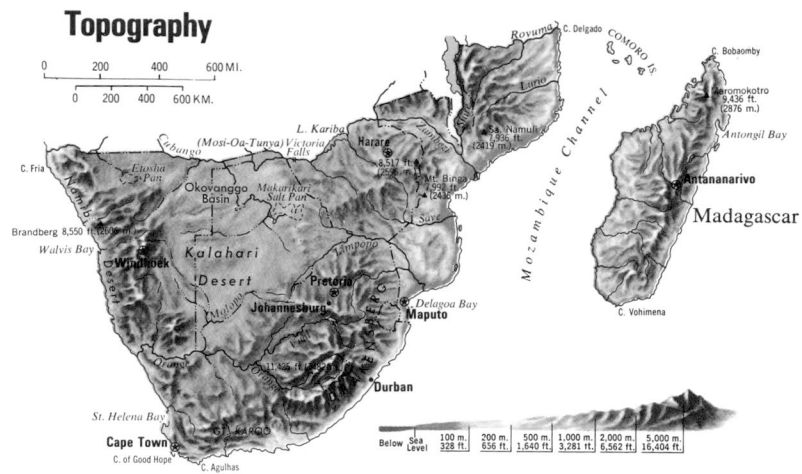

0   200   400   600 MI.
0   200   400   600 KM.

	Below Sea Level	100 m. 328 ft.	200 m. 656 ft.	500 m. 1,640 ft.	1,000 m. 3,281 ft.	2,000 m. 6,562 ft.	5,000 m. 16,404 ft.

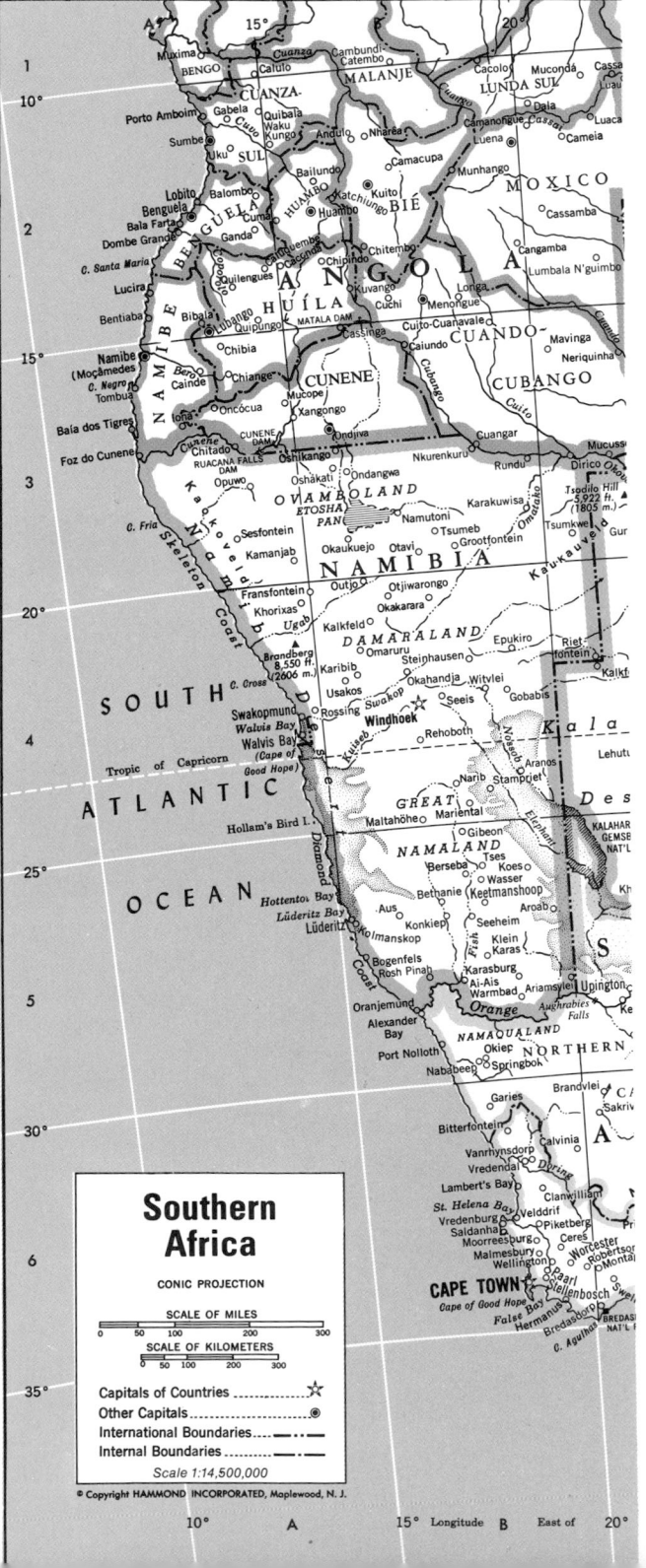

South America

AZIMUTHAL EQUAL-AREA PROJECTION

MILES
0   100   200   400   600

KILOMETERS
0 100 200   400   600

Capitals of Countries .... ⊛
Other Capitals .... ⊙
International Boundaries .... –··–··–
Canals ....

© Copyright HAMMOND INCORPORATED, Maplewood, N.J.

CARIBBEAN SEA
ATLANTIC OCEAN
PACIFIC OCEAN

VENEZUELA
COLOMBIA
ECUADOR
PERU
BRAZIL
BOLIVIA
PARAGUAY
CHILE
ARGENTINA
URUGUAY
GUYANA
SURINAME
FRENCH GUIANA

Bogotá
Quito
Lima
La Paz
Asunción
Santiago
Buenos Aires
Montevideo
Brasília
Caracas

FALKLAND ISLANDS (U.K.)

Tropic of Capricorn

Equator

Population Distribution

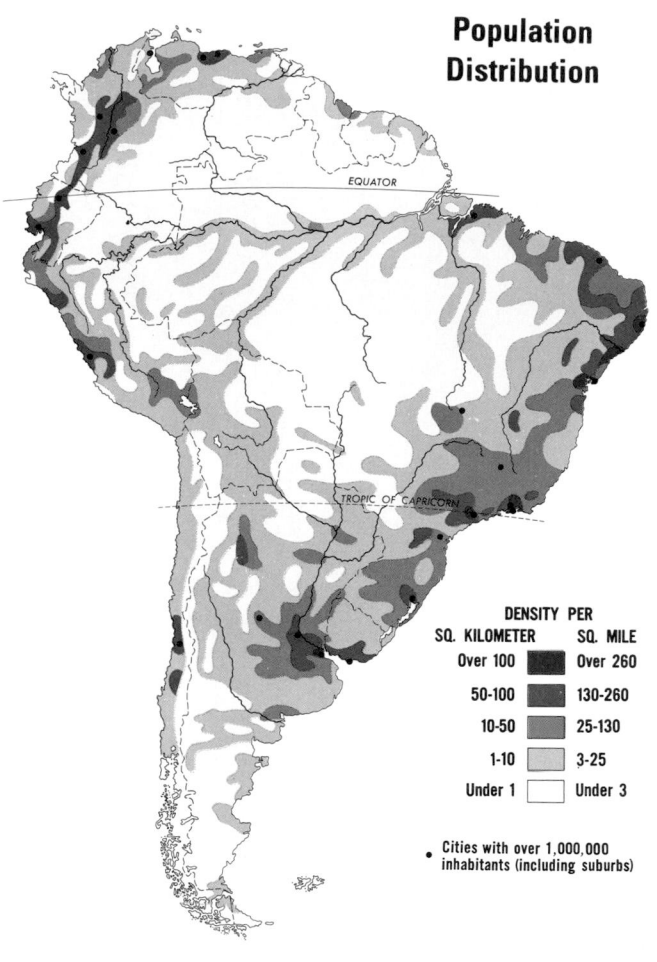

AREA 6,875,000 sq. mi. (17,806,250 sq. km.)
POPULATION 297,000,000
LARGEST CITY São Paulo
HIGHEST POINT Cerro Aconcagua 22,831 ft. (6,959 m.)
LOWEST POINT Salina Grande -131 ft. (-40 m.)

DENSITY PER	
SQ. KILOMETER	SQ. MILE
Over 100	Over 260
50-100	130-260
10-50	25-130
1-10	3-25
Under 1	Under 3

• Cities with over 1,000,000 inhabitants (including suburbs)

Vegetation

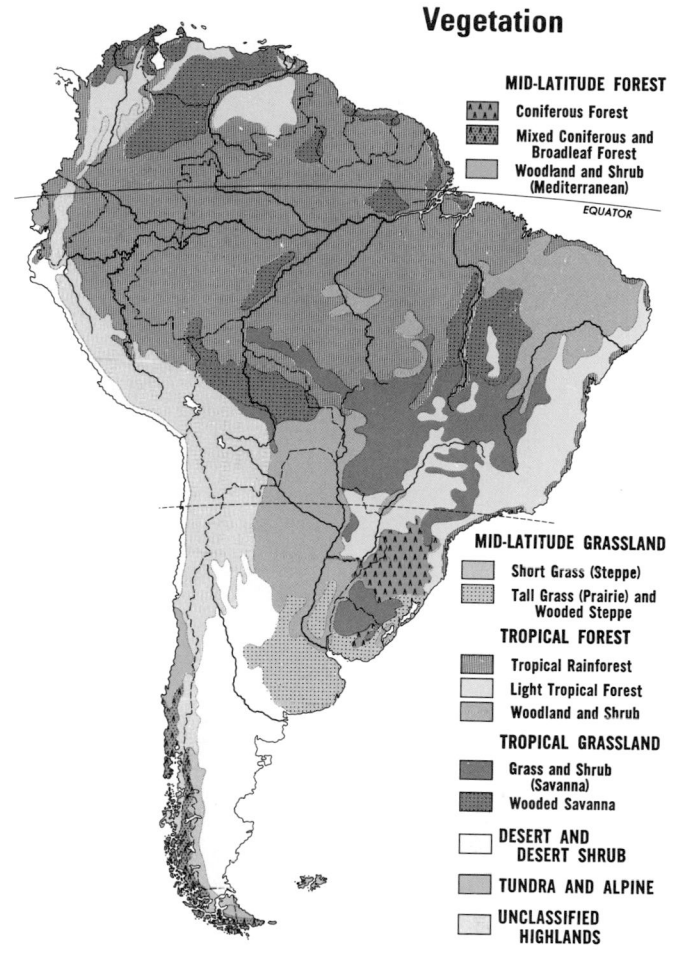

MID-LATITUDE FOREST
- Coniferous Forest
- Mixed Coniferous and Broadleaf Forest
- Woodland and Shrub (Mediterranean)

MID-LATITUDE GRASSLAND
- Short Grass (Steppe)
- Tall Grass (Prairie) and Wooded Steppe

TROPICAL FOREST
- Tropical Rainforest
- Light Tropical Forest
- Woodland and Shrub

TROPICAL GRASSLAND
- Grass and Shrub (Savanna)
- Wooded Savanna

DESERT AND DESERT SHRUB

TUNDRA AND ALPINE

UNCLASSIFIED HIGHLANDS

Average January Temperature

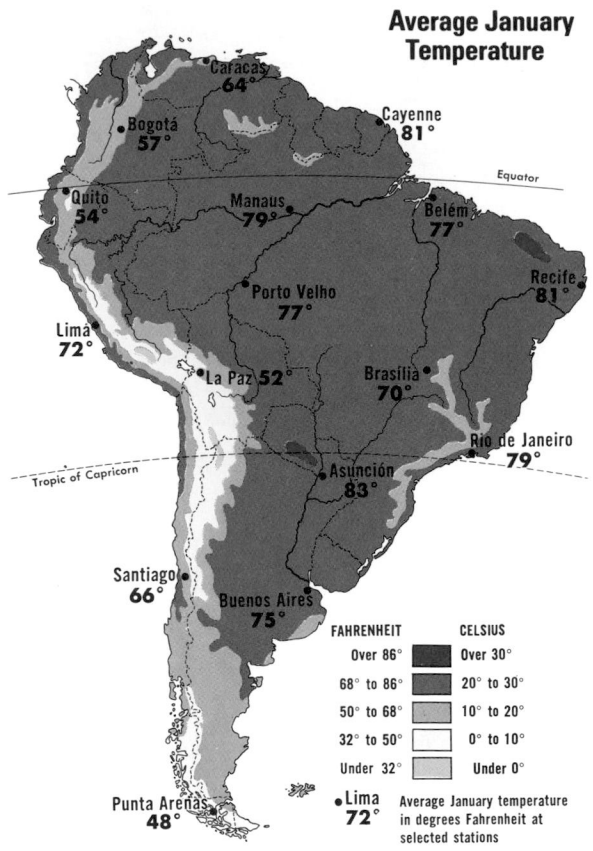

Caracas 64°
Cayenne 81°
Bogotá 57°
Quito 54°
Manaus 79°
Belém 77°
Equator
Porto Velho 77°
Recife 81°
Lima 72°
La Paz 52°
Brasília 70°
Rio de Janeiro 79°
Tropic of Capricorn
Asunción 83°
Santiago 66°
Buenos Aires 75°
Punta Arenas 48°

FAHRENHEIT	CELSIUS
Over 86°	Over 30°
68° to 86°	20° to 30°
50° to 68°	10° to 20°
32° to 50°	0° to 10°
Under 32°	Under 0°

• Lima 72°   Average January temperature in degrees Fahrenheit at selected stations

Average July Temperature

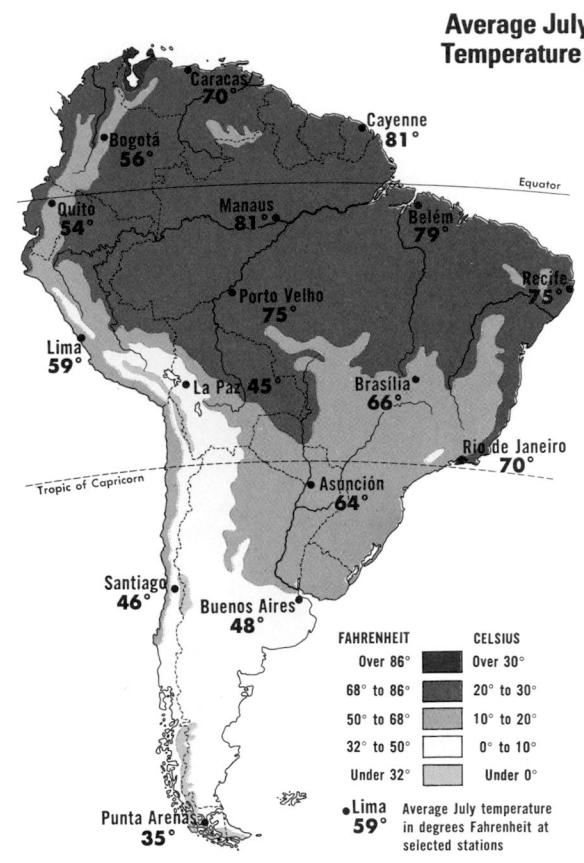

Caracas 70°
Cayenne 81°
Bogotá 56°
Quito 54°
Manaus 81°
Belém 79°
Equator
Porto Velho 75°
Recife 75°
Lima 59°
La Paz 45°
Brasília 66°
Rio de Janeiro 70°
Asunción 64°
Santiago 46°
Buenos Aires 48°
Punta Arenas 35°

FAHRENHEIT	CELSIUS
Over 86°	Over 30°
68° to 86°	20° to 30°
50° to 68°	10° to 20°
32° to 50°	0° to 10°
Under 32°	Under 0°

• Lima 59°   Average July temperature in degrees Fahrenheit at selected stations

Rainfall

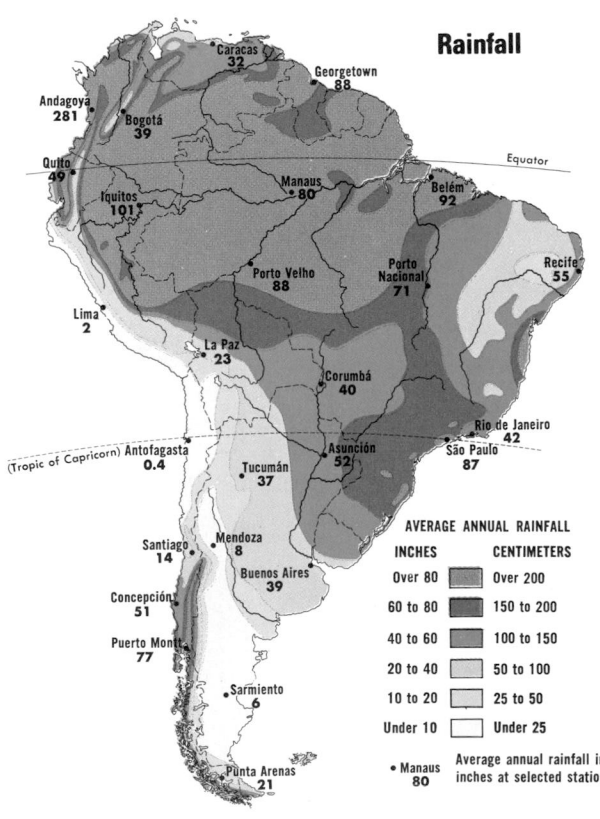

Caracas 32
Georgetown 88
Andagoya 281
Bogotá 39
Quito 49
Iquitos 101
Manaus 80
Belém 92
Equator
Porto Velho 88
Porto Nacional 71
Recife 55
Lima 2
La Paz 23
Corumbá 40
Rio de Janeiro 42
(Tropic of Capricorn) Antofagasta 0.4
Tucumán 37
Asunción 52
São Paulo 87
Santiago 14
Mendoza 8
Buenos Aires 39
Concepción 51
Puerto Montt 77
Sarmiento 6
Punta Arenas 21

AVERAGE ANNUAL RAINFALL

INCHES	CENTIMETERS
Over 80	Over 200
60 to 80	150 to 200
40 to 60	100 to 150
20 to 40	50 to 100
10 to 20	25 to 50
Under 10	Under 25

• Manaus 80   Average annual rainfall in inches at selected stations

Vegetation/Relief

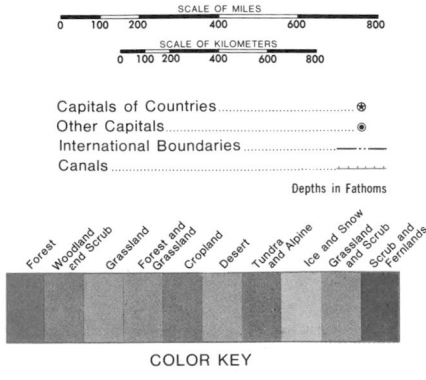

SCALE OF MILES
0   100   200   400   600   800

SCALE OF KILOMETERS
0   100 200   400   600   800

Capitals of Countries .... ⊛
Other Capitals .... ⊛
International Boundaries ....
Canals ....

Depths in Fathoms

Forest
Woodland and Scrub
Grassland
Forest and Grassland
Cropland
Desert
Tundra and Alpine
Ice and Snow
Grassland and Scrub
Scrub and Ferniands

COLOR KEY

CARIBBEAN SEA
G. of Venezuela
Pta. Gallinas
ARUBA (Neth.)
Curaçao
Bonaire
Willemstad
NETH. ANTILLES
BARBADOS
GRENADA
West Indies
Tobago
TRINIDAD & TOBAGO
Port of Spain
Trinidad
Barranquilla
Maracaibo
L. Maracaibo
Caracas
Panamá Canal
Panamá
G. of Panamá
PANAMÁ
Medellín
Bogotá
Cali
COLOMBIA
VENEZUELA
Orinoco
Ciudad Guayana
Guri Res.
Angel Fall
Mt. Roraima
GUYANA
Georgetown
Paramaribo
Cayenne
SURINAME
FRENCH GUIANA
Pico Phelps (Pico da Neblina) 9,889 ft. (3014 m.)
Vaupés
Negro
Japurá
Içá
Putumayo
Quito
Chimborazo 20,561 ft. (6267 m.)
ECUADOR
Guayaquil
Gulf of Guayaquil
Iquitos
Amazon
Yavari
Juruá
Purus
Madeira
Manaus
Tapajós
Xingu
Tocantins
Selvas
Equator
B. de Marajó
I. de Marajó
Belém
São Luís
Teresina
Fortaleza
Cabo de São Roque
Natal
Recife
Maceió
Caatingas
Parnaíba
Pta. Aguja
Trujillo
Huascarán 22,205 ft. (6768 m.)
Ucayali
Callao
Lima
PERU
BRAZIL
Aripuanã
Teles Pires
Araguaia
Tocantins
Mamoré
Guaporé
Juruena
Beni
Planalto de Mato Grosso
Brazilian Highlands
Brasília
Goiânia
São Francisco
Jequitinhonha
Paraguaçu
Salvador
BOLIVIA
Lake Titicaca
La Paz
Cochabamba
Lake Poopó
Sucre
Grande
Arica
Chaco
Paraguai
Campo Grande
Belo Horizonte
Pico da Bandeira 9,482 ft. (2890 m.)
Grande
Paraná
Tietê
C. de São Tomé
C. Frio
Rio de Janeiro
São Paulo
Santos
Paraíba
PARAGUAY
Tropic of Capricorn
Antofagasta
Volcán Llullaillaco 22,057 ft. (6723 m.)
Pilcomayo
Bermejo
Asunción
ITAIPU DAM
Curitiba
Iguaçu Falls
Iguaçu
I. de San Félix (Chile)
I. San Ambrosio (Chile)
CHILE
Salado del Norte
I. de Santa Catarina
Uruguay
Porto Alegre
Lagoa dos Patos
Lagoa Mirim
Córdoba
Santa Fe
Rosario
Cerro Aconcagua 22,831 ft. (6959 m.)
Valparaíso
Santiago
Mendoza
Salado
Pampas
Buenos Aires
La Plata
Río de la Plata
Montevideo
URUGUAY
Negro
C. San Antonio
I. Robinson Crusoe
I. Alejandro Selkirk
Juan Fernández Is. (Chile)
Concepción
Colorado
Bahía Blanca
Negro
ARGENTINA
Golfo San Matías
Pen. Valdés
Puerto Montt
Isla de Chiloé
Chubut
Archipiélago de los Chonos
Golfo San Jorge
C. Tres Puntas
Pen. Taitao
Deseado
G. de Penas
Patagonia
Bahía Grande
Falkland Islands (U.K.)
Stanley
Archipiélago Reina Adelaida
Str. of Magellan
Tierra del Fuego
Cape Horn
PACIFIC OCEAN
ATLANTIC OCEAN
Longitude West of Greenwich

STATES

Amazonas (terr.) 21,696 ......E5
Anzoátegui 683,717 ......F3
Apure 188,717 ......D4
Aragua 891,623 ......E2
Barinas 326,166 ......C3
Bolívar 668,340 ......F4
Carabobo 1,062,268 ......D2
Cojedes 133,991 ......D3
Delta Amacuro (terr.) 48,139..H3
Dependencias Federales
(terr.) 463 ......E2
Distrito Federal 1,860,637 ......E2
Falcón 503,896 ......D2
Guárico 393,467 ......E3
Lara 945,064 ......C2
Mérida 459,361 ......C3
Miranda 1,421,442 ......E2
Monagas 388,536 ......G3
Nueva Esparta 197,198 ......G2
Portuguesa 424,984 ......D3
Sucre 585,698 ......G2
Táchira 660,234 ......B3
Trujillo 433,735 ......C3

Yaracuy 300,597 ......D2
Zulia 1,674,252 ......B2

CITIES and TOWNS

Acarigua 56,743 ......D3
Achaguas 4,633 ......D4
Aguada Grande 2,901 ......D2
Agua Fría E5
Agua Linda D5
Altagracia 11,116 ......B2
Altagracia de Orituco 18,717..E3
Amuay C2
Anaco 29,487 ......F3
Aparurén G5
Apurito 740 ......D4
Arabopó H5
Aragua de Barcelona 9,107 ......F3
Aragua de Maturín 4,051 ......G3
Araure 22,466 ......D3
Aroa 5,418 ......D2
Bachaquero B2
Barbacoas 2,513 ......E3
Barcelona 78,201 ......F2
Barinas 56,329 ......C3

Barinitas 9,644 ......C3
Barquisimeto 330,815 ......D2
Barrancas, Barinas 4,489 ......C3
Barrancas, Monagas 5,738 ......G3
Betijoque 5,851 ......C3
Biruaca 2,266 ......E4
Biscucuy 6,114 ......D3
Bobures 2,468 ......C3
Boca de Aroa 2,756 ......D2
Boca del Mangle D2
Borbón F4
Buena Vista, Anzoátegui F3
Buena Vista, Apure D4
Cabimas 118,037 ......C2
Cabruta 1,927 ......E4
Cabudare 14,593 ......D3
Cachipo G3
Cagua 29,601 ......E2
Caicara 6,092 ......E3
Caicara de Orinoco 6,867 ......E4
Calabozo 37,282 ......E3
Camaguán 4,143 ......E3
Camatagua 3,335 ......E3

Candelaria F4
Cantaura 15,839 ......F3
Capatárida 1,375 ......C2
Carabobo, Bolívar H4
Carabobo, Carabobo C3
Caracas (cap.) 1,035,499 ......E2
Carache 3,966 ......C3
Cariaco 6,549 ......G2
Caribén F5
Caripe 4,729 ......G2
Caripito 19,053 ......G2
Carirubana 15,701 ......C2
Carmelo 2,556 ......C2
Carora 36,115 ......C2
Carrasquero 2,193 ......B2
Casanay 4,985 ......G2
Casigua 3,665 ......B3
Cáua 9,953 ......G3
Caucagua 6,218 ......E2
Chaguaramas 2,748 ......E3
Chichiriviche 3,236 ......D2
Chivacoa 19,210 ......D2
Churuguara 6,636 ......C2
Ciudad Bolívar 103,728 ......G3
Ciudad Bolivia 4,864 ......C3

Ciudad Guayana 143,540 ......G3
Ciudad Ojeda 83,083 ......C2
Ciudad Piar 3,965 ......G4
Clarines 2,099 ......F3
Cojoro C6
Colón E6
Comunidad E6
Coporito H3
Coro 68,701 ......D2
Corozo Pando E3
Cuchivero F4
Cumanacoa 9,179 ......F2
Curiapo H3
Dabajuro 4,515 ......C2
Democracia E6
Ejido 11,170 ......C3
El Almacén G4
El Amparo de Apure 2,015 ......C4
El Callao 6,218 ......G4
El Chaparro 3,768 ......F3
El Cristo G4
Elorza 3,184 ......D4
El Palmar 2,758 ......G3
El Pao 1,259 ......G3
El Perú H4

El Pilar 3,278 ......G2
El Roque E2
El Socorro E3
El Sombrero 8,373 ......E3
El Tigre 49,801 ......F3
El Tocuyo 19,351 ......D3
El Toro H3
El Vigía 20,970 ......B3
El Vínculo D1
Encontrados 5,607 ......B3
Esperanza E6
Garcitas C3
Guacara 35,111 ......D2
Guaina G5
Guanare 34,148 ......D3
Guanarito 3,150 ......D3
Guanoco G2
Guanta 9,017 ......F2
Guarero B2
Guarico 3,259 ......D3
Guasdualito 7,793 ......C4
Guasimal 582 ......D4
Guasipati 4,807 ......H4
Guayabal E6

Güiria 13,905 ......G2
Guri G4
Guzmán Blanco E6
Higuerote 5,008 ......F2
Icabarú H5
Independencia 4,897 ......B4
Irapa 4,470 ......H3
Juangriego 6,062 ......G2
Judibana C2
Jusepín G3
Kavanayen H5
La Aduana D3
La Canoa G3
La Ceiba C4
La Concepción B2
La Concepción 13,885 ......C2
La Esmeralda F6
La Esperanza H3
La Fría 8,134 ......B3
La Grita 9,954 ......C3
La Guaira 20,344 ......E2
Lagunetas C2
Lagunillas C2
La Horqueta G3
La Inglesa G3

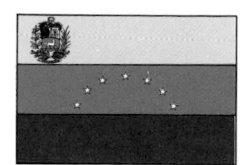

AREA 352,143 sq. mi. (912,050 sq. km.)
POPULATION 19,246,000
CAPITAL Caracas
LARGEST CITY Caracas
HIGHEST POINT Pico Bolívar 16,427 ft.
(5,007 m.)
MONETARY UNIT Bolívar
MAJOR LANGUAGE Spanish
MAJOR RELIGION Roman Catholicism

La Leona G3
La Margarita H3
Las Lajitas F4
Las Mercedes 6,739 ....E3
Las Piedras, Falcón C2
Las Piedras, Zulia 4,583 .....B2
Las Trincheras F4
Las Vegas 3,212 ....D3
La Tigra H4
La Trinidad de Arauca D4
La Vela de Coro 7,172 ....D2
La Victoria, Apure C4
La Victoria, Aragua 40,731 ...E2
Libertad 2,072 ....D3
Los Castillos G3
Los Teques 63,106 ....E2
Macareo Santo Niño H3
Machiques 18,898 ....B3
Macuro 1,122 ....H2
Macuto 11,704 ....E2
Maiquetía 59,238 ....E2
Mantecal F4
Maracaibo 651,574 ....C2
Maracay 255,134 ....E2
Marigüitar 5,645 ....G2

Mene de Mauroa 4,336 ....C2
Mene Grande 11,498 ....C3
Mesa Bolívar 956 ....C3
Mirimire 3,424 ....D2
Morganito E5
Morón 19,451 ....D2
Narical 1,047 ....F2
Nirgua 11,918 ....D2
Nuevo Mamo ....
Ocumare de la Costa 2,840 ...E2
Ocumare del Tuy 24,229 ......E2
Ospino 3,544 ....D3
Palmarejo C2
Palmarito, Apure 926 ....D4
Palmarito, Guárico F3
Paraguaipoa 3,850 ....C2
Paraíso de Chabasquén
  2,094 ....D3
Pariaguán 8,173 ....F3
Parmana F4
Pedernales G3
Peraitepuí H5
Piacoa H3
Pimichín E6
Píritu, Anzoátegui 2,479 .....F2
Píritu, Portuguesa 8,128 .....D3
Platanal F6
Porlamar 31,985 ....G2
Pozuelos 45,391 ....F2
Pregonero 3,598 ....C3
Pueblo Hondo B3
Pueblo Nuevo 3,426 ....D1
Puerto Ayacucho 10,417 .....E5
Puerto Cabello 72,103 ....E2
Puerto Cumarebo 10,064 .....C2
Puerto Hierro H2
Puerto La Cruz 63,276 ....F2
Puerto Miranda E4
Puerto Píritu 3,495 ....F2
Punta Cardón 18,182 ....C2
Punta de Mata 7,777 ....G3
Punta de Piedras 2,826 ....F2
Punto Fijo 5,548 ....D2
Puruey F4
Puruname E6
Quibor 12,216 ....D3
Quiriquire 7,304 ....G3
Río Claro 2,460 ....D3
Rosario B2
Rubio 19,156 ....B4
Sabaneta 4,680 ....D3
Samariapo E5
San Antonio, Amazonas E6
San Antonio, Monagas
  4,235 ....G2
San Antonio, Zulia C3
San Antonio del Táchira
  20,342 ....B4
San Antonio de Tabasca G3
Sanare 6,717 ....D3
San Carlos 21,029 ....D3
San Carlos del Zulia 26,762 ..C3
San Casimiro 4,843 ....E3
San Felipe, Yaracuy 43,801 ..D2
San Felipe, Zulia B3
San Félix 379 ....C2
San Fernando 38,960 ....E4
San Ignacio B2
San José, Amazonas E5
San José, Zulia 4,498 ....B3
San José de Amacuro ....
San José de Guanipa 22,530 ..G3
San José de la Costa D2
San José de Río Chico 3,600 ..F2

San Juan de Colón B3
San Juan de los Morros
  38,265 ....E3
San Juan de Manapiare E5
San Juan de Payara 1,018 ....E4
San Lorenzo C3
San Mateo 2,424 ....F3
San Mauricio E3
San Pedro de las Bocas G4
San Rafael 10,910 ....E2
San Sebastián 5,582 ....E2
San Simón del Cocuy ....
Santa Ana, Anzoátegui 3,558 .F3
Santa Ana, Táchira 5,116 .....B4
Santa Bárbara, Amazonas E6
Santa Bárbara, Barinas 6,155 .C4
Santa Bárbara, Monagas
  2,034 ....G3
Santa Bárbara, Zulia C3
Santa Cruz D4
Santa Cruz de Bucaral 2,904 ..D2
Santa Cruz de Mara 5,773 ....C2
Santa Cruz del Zulia 4,221 ...B3
Santa Elena 608 ....H5
Santa Isabel F7
Santa María, Bolívar G3
Santa María de Erebató F5
Santa María de Ipire 3,307 ...F3
Santa María del Orinoco E4
Santa Rita, Guárico E3
Santa Rita, Zulia 15,668 .....C2
Santa Rosa D4
Santa Rosa de Amanadona E7
Santa Teresa 10,220 ....F2
Santo Tomé F3
San Vicente E3
Sarare 4,236 ....D3
Seboruco 2,616 ....B3
Simaraña G5
Sinamaica B2
Siquisique 3,821 ....D2
Solano E6
Soledad 7,108 ....G3
Suripa D4
Tamatama F6
Táriba 15,683 ....B4
Temblador 5,380 ....G3
Tía Juana C2
Timotes 3,229 ....C3
Tinaco 7,263 ....D3
Tinaquillo 12,015 ....D3
Tocuyo de la Costa 4,023 ....D2

Tovar 12,814 ....C3
Trujillo 25,921 ....C3
Tucacas 4,780 ....D2
Tucupido 9,522 ....F3
Tucupita 21,417 ....H3
Tumeremo 5,036 ....H4
Turén D3
Turiamo E2
Turmero 43,832 ....E2
Upata 22,793 ....G3
Urachiche 4,759 ....D2
Urica 1,881 ....F3
Urimán G5
Uruyén G5

Uverito 468 ....F3
Valencia 367,171 ....E2
Valera 76,740 ....C3
Valle de Guanape 3,468 ......F3
Valle de la Pascua 36,809 ...F3
Villa Bruzual 14,003 ....D3
Villa de Cura 27,832 ....E2
Yaguaraparo 3,931 ....G2
Yaritagua 21,363 ....D2
Yavita E6
Yerichaña E6
Yoco 2,196 ....G2
Zanja de Lira E3
Zaraza 15,480 ....F3

OTHER FEATURES

Amacuro (riv.) H4
Angel (fall) G5
Aponguao (riv.) H5
Apure (riv.) E4
Arauca (riv.) E4
Arichuna (riv.) D4
Aro (riv.) F4
Atabapo (riv.) E6
Auyantepui (mt.) G5
Baria (riv.) E7
Boca Grande (gulf) H3
Bolívar, Pico (peak) C3
Canagua (riv.) C3
Caño Capure (riv.) H3
Caño Macareo (riv.) H3
Caño Mánamo (riv.) G3
Capanaparo (riv.) E4
Caparo (riv.) C4
Carrao (riv.) G5
Caruai (riv.) H5
Casiquiare, Brazo (riv.) E6
Catatumbo (riv.) B3
Caura (riv.) F5
Chicanán (riv.) H4
Chimantá-tepuí (mt.) G5
Chivapure (riv.) E4
Cinaruco (riv.) D4
Coche (isl.) F2
Codera (cape) F2
Cojedes (riv.) D3
Cuao (riv.) E5
Cubagua (isl.) F2
Cuchivero (riv.) F4
Cuquenán (riv.) H5
Curutú (riv.) G5
Cuyuni (riv.) H4
Delgado Chalbaud, Cerro
  (mt.) G6
Dragons Mouth (str.) H2
Duida, Cerro (mt.) F6
Erebato (riv.) F5
Guainía (riv.) E6
Guampí, Sierra de (mts.) F4
Guanare (riv.) D3
Guanare Viejo (riv.) D3
Guárico (res.) E3
Guárico (riv.) E3
Guayapo, Serranía (mts.) E5
Güere (riv.) F3
Guri (res.) G4
Imataca, Serranía (mts.) H4
Imeri, Sierra (mts.) F7
La Blanquilla (isl.) F2
La Cerbatana, Serranía de
  (mts.) E4
La Gran Sabana (plain) G5
La Orchila (isl.) F2

Las Aves (isls.) E2
La Tortuga (isl.) F2
Los Hermanos (isls.) F2
Los Monjes (isls.) C1
Los Roques (isls.) E2
Los Testigos (isls.) G2
Macanao (pen.) F2
Maigualida, Sierra (range) ...H4
Manapire (riv.) F4
Maracaibo (lake) C3
Margarita (isl.) F2
Mavaca (riv.) F6
Médanos (isth.) C2
Merevari (riv.) F5
Mérida, Cordillera de (range) .C3
Meta (riv.) E4
Morichal Largo (riv.) G3
Neblina (Phelps) (peak) E7
Negro (riv.) E7
Nuria, Sierra de (mts.) H4
Orinoco (delta) H3
Orinoco (riv.) G3
Orituco (riv.) E3
Pacaraima, Sierra (mts.) G5
Pao (riv.) D3
Paragua (riv.) G4
Paria (gulf) H2
Paria (pen.) G2
Parima, Sierra (mts.) F6
Perijá, Sierra de (mts.) B2
Phelps (peak) E7
Portuguesa (riv.) D3
Raul Leoni (dam) G4
Roraima (mt.) H5
Salto Angel (fall) G5
Sarare (riv.) C4
Serpents Mouth (passage) ...H3
Siapa (riv.) E7
Suapure (riv.) E4
Suripá (riv.) C4
Tapirapecó, Sierra (mts.) F7
Tigre (riv.) G3
Tocuco (riv.) B3
Tocuyo (riv.) D2
Tramán-tepui (mt.) G5
Triste (gulf) D2
Turagua, Serranía (mts.) F4
Tuy (riv.) E2
Unare (riv.) F3
Valencia (lake) E2
Venamo (riv.) H4
Venamo, Cerro (mt.) H4
Venezuela (gulf) C2
Ventuari (riv.) E5
Votamo (riv.) F6
Yatua (riv.) E7
Yuruari (riv.) H4
Zuata (riv.) F3
Zulia (riv.) B3

Topography

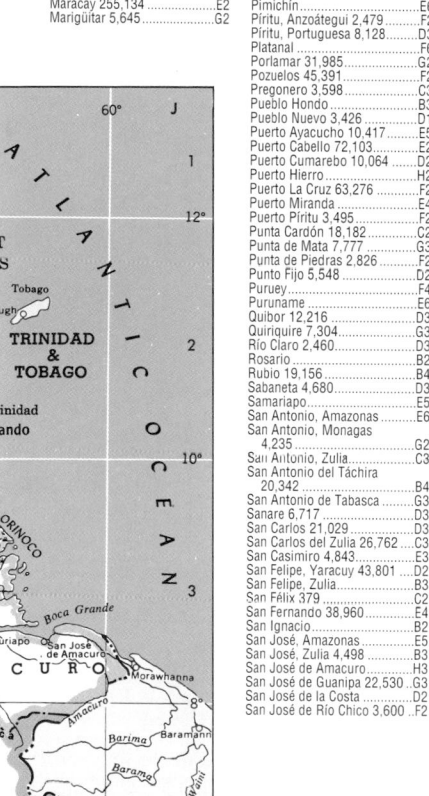

0 100 200 MI.

0 100 200 KM.

5,000 m. 2,000 m. 1,000 m. 500 m. 200 m. 100 m. Sea
16,404 ft. 6,562 ft. 3,281 ft. 1,640 ft. 656 ft. 328 ft. Level Below

Agriculture, Industry and Resources

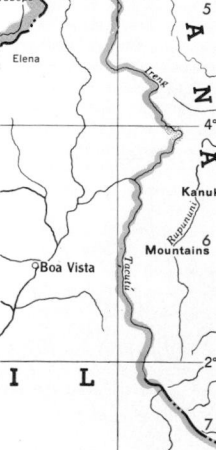

MAJOR MINERAL OCCURRENCES

Al Bauxite
Au Gold
C Coal
D Diamonds
Fe Iron Ore
G Natural Gas
Mn Manganese
Na Salt
O Petroleum

⚡ Water Power
▨ Major Industrial Areas

DOMINANT LAND USE

■ Diversified Tropical Crops (chiefly plantation agriculture)
□ Upland Cultivated Areas
▨ Upland Livestock Grazing, Limited Agriculture
▨ Extensive Livestock Ranching
▨ Forests

ght HAMMOND INCORPORATED, Maplewood, N. J.

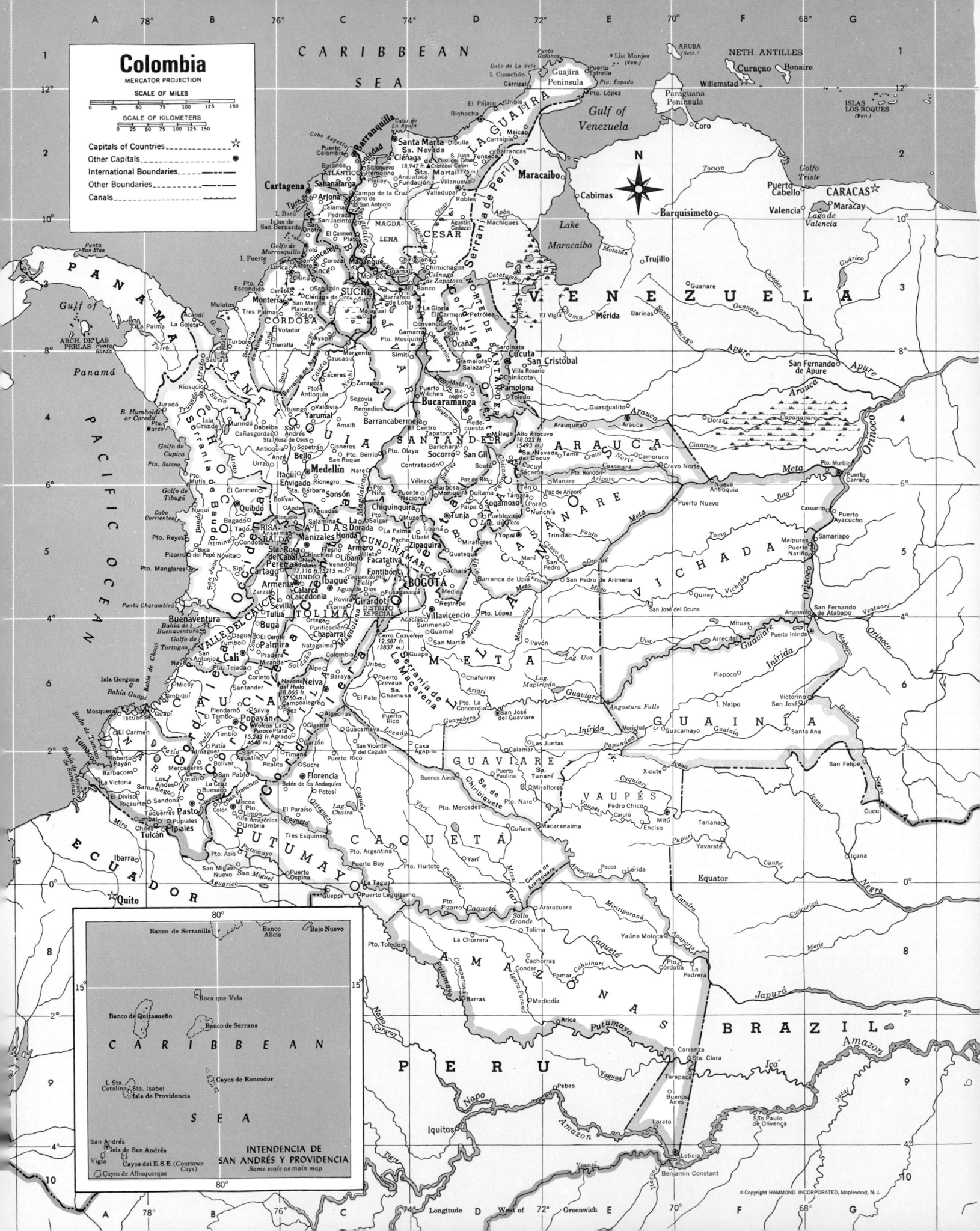

Colombia

MERCATOR PROJECTION

SCALE OF MILES

0 25 50 75 100 125 150

SCALE OF KILOMETERS

0 25 50 75 100 125 150

Capitals of Countries _____ ☆
Other Capitals _____ ◉
International Boundaries _____
Other Boundaries _____
Canals _____

INTENDENCIA DE
SAN ANDRÉS Y PROVIDENCIA
Same scale as main map

© Copyright HAMMOND INCORPORATED, Maplewood, N.J.

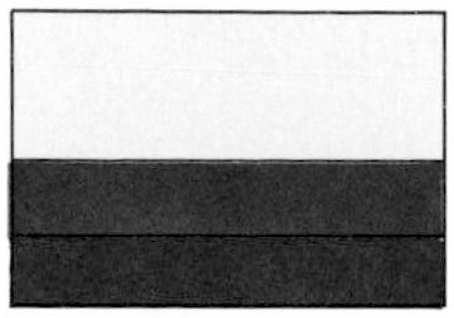

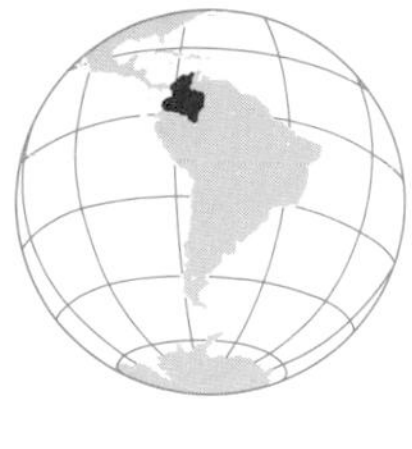

AREA 439,513 sq. mi. (1,138,339 sq. km.)
POPULATION 30,241,000
CAPITAL Bogotá
LARGEST CITY Bogotá
HIGHEST POINT Pico Cristóbal Colón 18,947 ft. (5,775 m.)
MONETARY UNIT Colombian peso
MAJOR LANGUAGE Spanish
MAJOR RELIGION Roman Catholicism

INTERNAL DIVISIONS

Amazonas (comm.) 6,825 ...... D8
Antioquia (dept.) 3,888,067 ... B4
Arauca (inten.) 19,884 ... E4
Atlántico (dept.) 958,560 ... C2
Bolívar (dept.) 802,407 ... C3
Boyacá (dept.) 1,084,766 ... D5
Caldas (dept.) 700,954 ... C5
Caquetá (inten.) 57,103 ... C7
Casanare (inten.) ... E5
Cauca (dept.) 603,894 ... B6
Cesar (dept.) 339,843 ... D3
Chocó (dept.) 201,915 ... B4
Córdoba (dept.) 645,478 ... C3
Cundinamarca (dept.) 1,106,626 ... C5
Distrito Especial 2,855,065 ... C5
Guainía (comm.) 1,792 ... F6
Huila (dept.) 469,834 ... C6
La Guajira (dept.) 180,520 ... D2
Magdalena (dept.) 536,122 ... C3
Meta (dept.) 245,176 ... D6
Nariño (dept.) 807,112 ... B7
Norte de Santander (dept.) 693,298 ... D3
Putumayo (inten.) 22,916 ... C7
Quindío (dept.) 321,677 ... C5
Risaralda (dept.) 452,626 ... B5
San Andrés y Providencia (inten.) 22,719 ... B1
Santander (dept.) 1,130,977 .. D4
Sucre (dept.) 354,412 ... C3
Tolima (dept.) 903,520 ... C5
Valle del Cauca (dept.) 2,204,722 ... B6
Vaupés (comm.) 6,923 ... E7
Vichada (comm.) 2,172 ... F5

CITIES and TOWNS

Acacías 9,230 ... D6
Acandí 2,358 ... B3
Agrado 2,771 ... C6
Aguachica 16,771 ... D3
Aguadas 9,995 ... C5
Agua de Dios 9,689 ... C5
Agustín Codazzi 28,194 ... D3
Aipe 3,794 ... C6
Algeciras 5,022 ... C6
Amalfi 6,494 ... C4
Andes 14,957 ... C5
Anserma 15,559 ... B5
Antioquia 6,841 ... B4
Aracataca 7,511 ... D2
Arauca 7,613 ... E4
Arjona 29,465 ... C2
Armenia 180,221 ... B5
Armero 19,567 ... C5
Ayapel 7,475 ... C3
Baranoa 27,394 ... C2
Baraya 2,581 ... C6
Barbacoas 4,653 ... A7
Barbosa 7,960 ... D5
Barichara 2,548 ... D4
Barrancabermeja 137,406 ... C4
Barrancas 2,979 ... D2
Barranco de Loba 2,215 ... C3
Barranquilla 896,649 ... C2
Belén de los Andaquíes 2,190 C7
Bello 206,297 ... C4
Bogotá (cap.) 3,974,813 ... D5
Bolívar 13,259 ... C5
Bucaramanga 341,513 ... D4
Buenaventura 160,342 ... B6
Buesaco 2,763 ... B7
Buga 82,992 ... B6
Cáceres 7,154 ... C4
Caicedonia 21,959 ... C5
Calamar 5,867 ... C2
Calarcá 29,349 ... C5
Cali 1,323,944 ... B6
Campo de la Cruz 13,137 ... C2
Campoalegre 11,799 ... C6
Cañasgordas 3,900 ... B4
Cartagena 491,368 ... C2
Cartago 92,524 ... B5
Caucasia 24,138 ... C4
Cereté 25,890 ... C3
Cerro de San Antonio 3,394 ... C2
Chaparral 14,546 ... C6
Chimichaqua 6,382 ... D3
Chinácota 4,478 ... D4
Chinchiná 33,441 ... C5
Chinú 10,023 ... C3
Chiquinquirá 21,727 ... C5
Chiriguaná 6,611 ... D3
Ciénaga 56,860 ... C2
Ciénaga de Oro 10,607 ... C3
Cisneros 7,226 ... C4
Colombia 2,903 ... C6
Condoto 4,798 ... B5
Contratación 3,057 ... D4
Convención 7,545 ... D3
Corinto 6,933 ... B6
Corozal 29,471 ... C3
Cúcuta 357,026 ... D4
Cumbal 2,891 ... B7
Dabeiba 7,600 ... B4
Dagua 5,392 ... B6
Duitama 56,390 ... D5
El Banco 20,756 ... D3
El Carmen 2,362 ... D3
El Carmen de Bolívar 30,778 .. C3
El Cerrito 23,575 ... B6
El Cocuy 2,740 ... D4
El Tambo 2,179 ... B6
Envigado 85,539 ... C4
Espinal 37,563 ... C5
Facatativá 44,331 ... C5
Florencia 66,430 ... C7
Fonseca 9,988 ... D2
Fontibon ... C5
Fresno 8,141 ... C5
Fundación 29,002 ... C2
Fusagasugá 41,033 ... C5
Gamarra 5,071 ... D3
Garzón 13,783 ... C6
Gigante 4,880 ... C6
Girardot 66,385 ... C5
Gramalote 2,880 ... D4
Guamal, Meta 2,854 ... D6
Guamal, Magdalena 4,986 ... C3
Guapí 5,005 ... B6
Guateque 6,032 ... D5
Honda 25,040 ... C5
Ibagué 269,495 ... C5
Ipiales 45,419 ... B7
Istmina 5,575 ... B5
Itagüí 135,797 ... C4
Ituango 5,561 ... C4
La Cruz 4,353 ... B7
La Dorada 48,572 ... C5
La Gloria 2,632 ... D3
La Palma 5,430 ... C5
La Plata 8,047 ... C6
La Unión 5,392 ... B7
Líbano 23,703 ... C5
Lorica 24,264 ... C3
Magangué 49,160 ... C3
Maicao 46,033 ... D2
Majagual 2,329 ... C3
Málaga 10,645 ... D4
Manizales 275,067 ... C5
Medellín 1,418,554 ... C4
Mercaderes 3,877 ... B7
Miraflores 3,584 ... D5
Miranda 6,430 ... B6
Mitú 1,637 ... E7
Mocoa 6,221 ... B7
Mompós 14,076 ... C3
Moniquirá 5,711 ... D5
Montería 157,466 ... B3
Natagaima 7,772 ... C6
Neiva 178,130 ... C6
Ocaña 51,443 ... D3
Ortega 5,150 ... C6
Pacho 6,786 ... C5
Páez 2,098 ... C6
Paipa 4,260 ... D5
Palmira 175,186 ... B6
Pamplona 34,213 ... D4
Pasto 197,407 ... B7
Patía 5,306 ... B6
Paz de Ariporo 2,584 ... E5
Paz de Río 3,464 ... D4
Pereira 233,271 ... C5
Piedecuesta 34,646 ... D4
Piendamó 5,046 ... B6
Pitalito 27,104 ... B7
Pivijay 10,172 ... C2
Planeta Rica 24,238 ... C3
Plato 24,895 ... C3
Popayán 141,964 ... B6
Pradera 27,152 ... B6
Puente Nacional 4,317 ... D5
Puerto Asís 6,364 ... B7
Puerto Berrío 21,414 ... C4
Puerto Carreño 2,172 ... G4
Puerto Colombia 9,255 ... C2
Puerto Escondido 1,368 ... B3
Puerto Inírida 1,792 ... F6
Puerto Leguízamo 3,179 ... C8
Puerto López 4,948 ... D5
Puerto Rico 4,853 ... C7
Puerto Rondón 1,010 ... E4
Puerto Salgar 6,396 ... C5
Puerto Tejada 26,573 ... B6
Puerto Wilches 5,282 ... D4
Pupiales 2,723 ... B7
Purificación 8,164 ... C6
Quibdó 47,950 ... B5
Remedios 4,681 ... C4
Remolino 3,408 ... C2
Restrepo 2,704 ... D5
Río de Oro 2,985 ... D3
Riohacha 46,667 ... D2
Rionegro, Antioquia 22,654 ... C4
Rionegro, Santander 3,491 ... D4
Riosucio, Caldas 11,619 ... C5
Riosucio, Chocó 2,184 ... B4
Robles 5,422 ... D2
Rovira 5,105 ... C5
Sabanalarga 35,786 ... C2
Sahagún 28,686 ... C3
Salamina 12,136 ... C5
Salazar 2,791 ... D4
Samaniego 4,790 ... B7
San Agustín 4,532 ... B7
San Andrés, Antioquia 2,003 .. C4
San Andrés, San Andrés y Providencia 23,325 ... A9
San Antero 7,129 ... C3
Sandoná 7,222 ... B7
San Gil 24,599 ... D4
San Jacinto 13,459 ... C3
San José del Guaviare 4,138 .. D6
San Juan del César 9,468 ... D2
San Marcos 26,542 ... C3
San Martín 8,281 ... D6
San Onofre 7,899 ... C3
San Pablo 3,662 ... B7
San Roque 4,972 ... C4
San Vicente del Caguán 3,182 C6
Santa Bárbara 11,848 ... C5
Santa Marta 177,922 ... D2
Santa Rosa de Cabal 37,112 ... C5
Santa Rosa de Osos 8,593 ... C4
Santander 22,644 ... B6
Sardinata 3,726 ... D3
Segovia 10,000 ... C4
Sevilla 31,309 ... C5
Sibundoy-Las Casas 2,853 ... B7
Silvia 3,045 ... B6
Simití 3,062 ... C4
Sincé 11,909 ... C3
Sincelejo 120,537 ... C3
Sitionuevo 5,919 ... C2
Soatá 4,294 ... D4
Socorro 15,596 ... D4
Sogamoso 64,437 ... D5
Soledad 164,494 ... C2
Sonsón 15,990 ... C5
Sopetrán 5,223 ... C4
Tadó 3,102 ... B5
Tame 4,811 ... E4
Tibaná 1,100 ... D5
Tierralta 7,950 ... C3
Timaná 4,262 ... C7
Timbío 4,755 ... B6
Timbiquí 1,048 ... B6
Toledo 2,942 ... D4
Tolú 9,118 ... C3
Trinidad 729 ... E5
Tuluá 99,721 ... B5
Tumaco 45,456 ... A7
Tunjá 87,851 ... D5
Túquerres 12,058 ... B7
Turbaco 28,161 ... C2
Turbo 25,992 ... B3
Ubaté 7,716 ... D5
Uribia 2,193 ... D2
Urrao 8,577 ... B4
Valdivia 4,318 ... C4
Valledupar 142,771 ... D2
Vélez 8,241 ... D4
Venadillo 8,383 ... C5
Villa Rosario 8,668 ... D4
Villanueva 9,836 ... D2
Villavicencio 82,869 ... D5
Villeta 6,507 ... C5
Yarumal 21,333 ... C4
Yopal 5,851 ... D5
Yumbo 43,508 ... B6
Zapatoca 6,258 ... D4
Zaragoza 9,660 ... C4
Zarzal 22,014 ... B5
Zipaquirá 45,676 ... D5

OTHER FEATURES

Aguarico (riv.) ... B7
Aguja, La (cape) ... C2
Alto Ritacuva (mt.) ... D4
Amazon (riv.) ... E9
Ancón de Sardinas (bay) ... A7
Angostura (falls) ... E6
Apaporis (riv.) ... F8
Arauca (riv.) ... E4
Ariari (riv.) ... D6
Ariguaní (riv.) ... D3
Ariporo (riv.) ... E4
Atabapo (riv.) ... G6
Atrato (riv.) ... B4
Baudó, Serranía de (mts.) ... B5
Caguán (riv.) ... C7
Cahuinari (riv.) ... E8
Caquetá (riv.) ... E8
Caraparaná (riv.) ... D8
Casanare (riv.) ... E4
Catatumbo (riv.) ... D3
Cauca (riv.) ... B3
Cazueleja, Cerro (mt.) ... C6
César (riv.) ... D2
Central, Cordillera (range) ... C5
Charambirá (pt.) ... B5
Chicamocha (riv.) ... D4
Chocó (bay) ... B6
Corrientes (cape) ... B5
Cristóbal Colón, Pico (peak) ... D2
Cuemaní (riv.) ... D7
Cupica (gulf) ... B4
Cusachón (isl.) ... D1
Espada (pt.) ... E1
Gallinas (pt.) ... E1
Grande (isl.) ... B4
Grande, Salto (falls) ... D8
Guainía (riv.) ... F6
Guajira (pen.) ... E1
Guaviare (riv.) ... F6
Guayabero (riv.) ... D6
Huila, Nevado del (mt.) ... C6
Igara-Paraná (riv.) ... D8
Inírida (riv.) ... F6
Isana (riv.) ... F7
La Aguja (cape) ... C2
La Macarena, Serranía de (mts.) ... D6
Llanos (plain) ... D5
Macarena, Serranía de La (mts.) ... D6
Magdalena (riv.) ... C3
Manacacías (riv.) ... D6
Meta (riv.) ... E5
Metica (riv.) ... D6
Mira (riv.) ... A7
Miritiparaná (riv.) ... E8
Morrosquillo (gulf) ... C3
Nechí (riv.) ... C4
Negro (riv.) ... G7
Occidental, Cordillera (range) . B5
Oriental, Cordillera (range) ... D5
Orinoco (riv.) ... G5
Orteguaza (riv.) ... C7
Papurí (riv.) ... F7
Patía (riv.) ... B6
Pauto (riv.) ... E5
Perijá, Serranía de (mts.) ... D2
Providencia (isl.) ... B9
Puracé (vol.) ... B6
Putumayo (riv.) ... E9
Quitasueño (bank) ... A8
Roncador (cays) ... B9
Saldaña (riv.) ... C6
Salto Grande (falls) ... D8
San Andrés (isl.) ... A10
San Jorge (riv.) ... C3
San Juan (riv.) ... B5
Santa Marta, Sierra Nevada de (range) ... D2
Serrana (bank) ... B9
Serranilla (bank) ... B8
Sinú (riv.) ... B3
Sogamoso (riv.) ... D4
Suárez (riv.) ... D4
Taraíra (riv.) ... F8
Tequendama (falls) ... C5
Tibugá (gulf) ... B5
Tolima (vol.) ... C5
Tomo (riv.) ... F5
Tortugas (gulf) ... B6
Tunahí, Sierra (mts.) ... E7
Urabá (gulf) ... B3
Uva (riv.) ... E6
Vaupés (riv.) ... E7
Vela, La (cape) ... D1
Vichada (riv.) ... F5
Yarí (riv.) ... D8
Zapatosa, Ciénaga de (swamp) ... D3

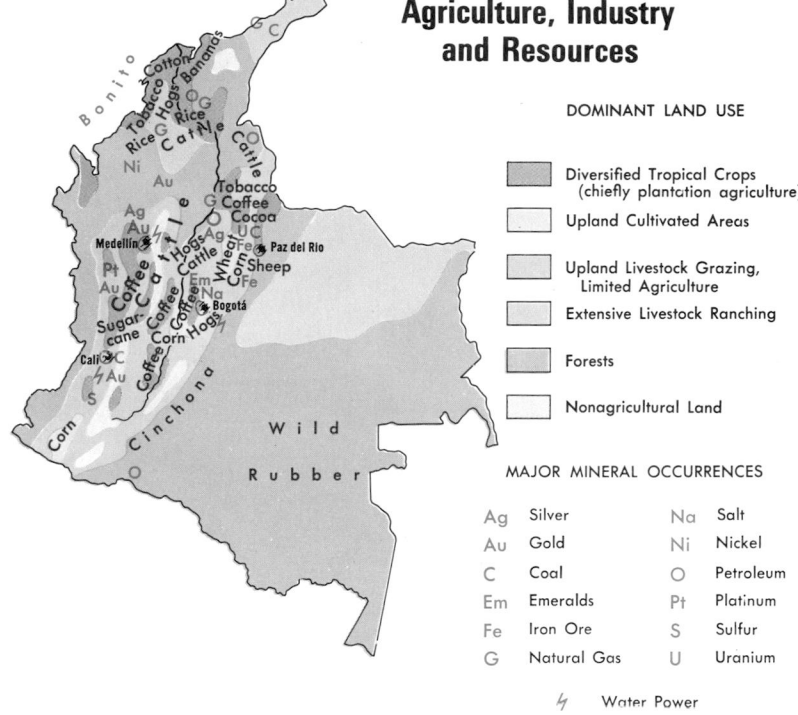

Agriculture, Industry and Resources

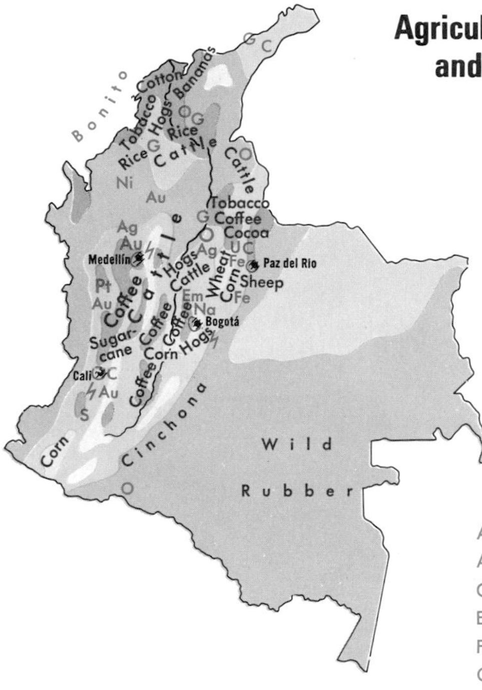

Bonito
Cotton
Tobacco
Hogs
Bananas
Rice
Cattle
Coffee
Cocoa
Medellín
Paz del Rio
Sheep
Wheat
Corn
Bogotá
Sugar-cane
Cali
Cinchona
Wild
Rubber

DOMINANT LAND USE

- Diversified Tropical Crops (chiefly plantation agriculture)
- Upland Cultivated Areas
- Upland Livestock Grazing, Limited Agriculture
- Extensive Livestock Ranching
- Forests
- Nonagricultural Land

MAJOR MINERAL OCCURRENCES

Ag	Silver	Na	Salt
Au	Gold	Ni	Nickel
C	Coal	O	Petroleum
Em	Emeralds	Pt	Platinum
Fe	Iron Ore	S	Sulfur
G	Natural Gas	U	Uranium

Water Power

Major Industrial Areas

Topography

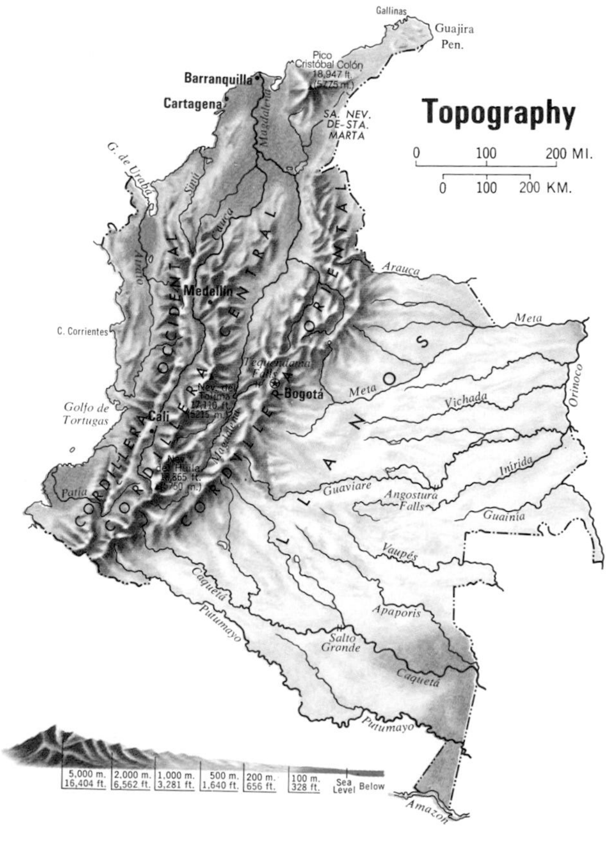

Gallinas
Guajira Pen.
Pico Cristóbal Colón 18,947 ft. (5,775 m)
Barranquilla
Cartagena
SA. NEV. DE STA. MARTA
0 100 200 MI.
0 100 200 KM.
G. de Urabá
Magdalena
Medellín
Arauca
Meta
C. Corrientes
Bogotá
Cali
Golfo de Tortugas
Vichada
Orinoco
LLANOS
Guaviare
Angostura Falls
Inírida
Guainía
Vaupés
Apaporis
Caquetá
Salto Grande
Putumayo
Amazon
5,000 m. 16,404 ft.
2,000 m. 6,562 ft.
1,000 m. 3,281 ft.
500 m. 1,640 ft.
200 m. 656 ft.
100 m. 328 ft.
Sea Level
Below

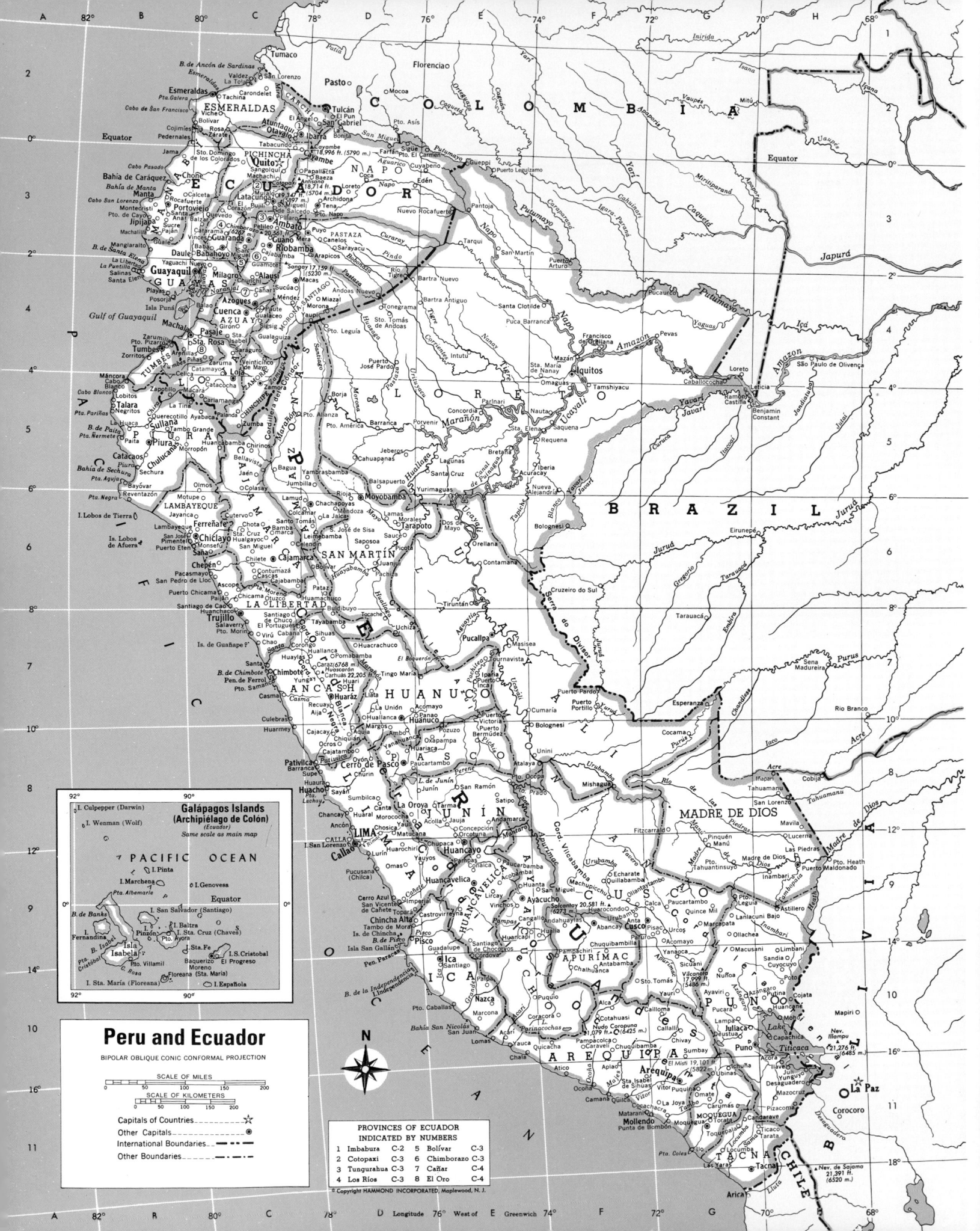

Peru and Ecuador

BIPOLAR OBLIQUE CONIC CONFORMAL PROJECTION

SCALE OF MILES
0   50   100   150   200

SCALE OF KILOMETERS
0   50   100   150   200

Capitals of Countries .... ☆
Other Capitals .... ◉
International Boundaries .... ▬ ▬ ▬
Other Boundaries .... ▬ ·· ▬ ··

PROVINCES OF ECUADOR
INDICATED BY NUMBERS

1	Imbabura	C-2	5 Bolívar C-3
2	Cotopaxi	C-3	6 Chimborazo C-3
3	Tungurahua	C-3	7 Cañar C-4
4	Los Ríos	C-3	8 El Oro C-4

© Copyright HAMMOND INCORPORATED, Maplewood, N.J.

Galápagos Islands
(Archipiélago de Colón)
(Ecuador)
Same scale as main map

PACIFIC OCEAN

I. Culpepper (Darwin)
I. Wenman (Wolf)
I. Pinta
I. Marchena
Pta. Albemarle
I. Genovesa
Equator
I. San Salvador (Santiago)
B. de Banks
I. Fernandina
Pinzón
I. Baltra
Pto. Ayora
I. Sta. Cruz (Chaves)
Isla Isabela
Sta. Fe
Pta. Cristóbal
I.S. Cristóbal
Pto. Villamil
Baquerizo
El Progreso
Moreno
Floreana (Sta. María)
I. Sta. María (Floreana)
I. Española

COLOMBIA

ECUADOR

BRAZIL

BOLIVIA

CHILE

PACIFIC OCEAN

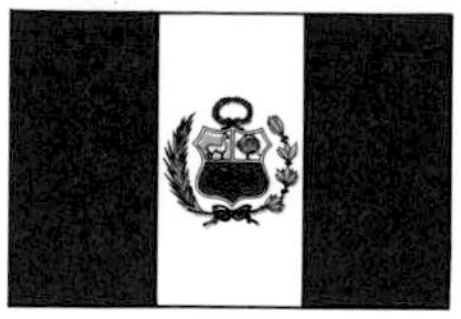

PERU

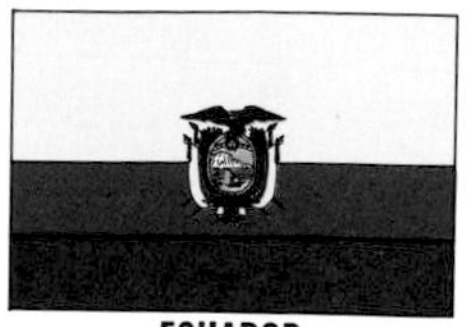

ECUADOR

PERU

AREA 496,222 sq. mi. (1,285,215 sq. km.)
POPULATION 22,332,000
CAPITAL Lima
LARGEST CITY Lima
HIGHEST POINT Huascarán 22,205 ft. (6,768 m.)
MONETARY UNIT inti
MAJOR LANGUAGES Spanish, Quechua, Aymara
MAJOR RELIGION Roman Catholicism

ECUADOR

AREA 109,483 sq. mi. (283,561 sq. km.)
POPULATION 10,490,000
CAPITAL Quito
LARGEST CITY Guayaquil
HIGHEST POINT Chimborazo 20,561 ft. (6,267 m.)
MONETARY UNIT sucre
MAJOR LANGUAGES Spanish, Quechua
MAJOR RELIGION Roman Catholicism

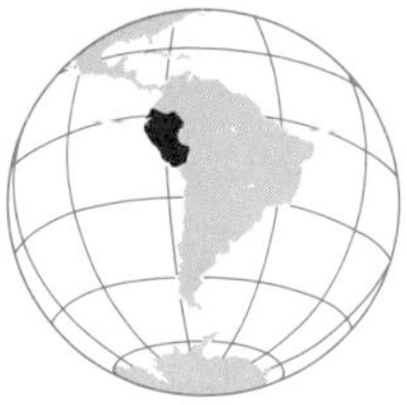

PERU

DEPARTMENTS

Amazonas 256,460 ..... C5
Ancash 815,646 ..... D7
Apurímac 321,936 ..... F10
Arequipa 702,308 ..... F10
Ayacucho 500,732 ..... E9
Cajamarca 1,044,689 ..... C6
Callao (prov.) 446,730 ..... D9
Cusco 829,294 ..... F9
Huánuco 481,924 ..... D7
Huancavelica 346,460 ..... E9
Ica 431,442 ..... E10
Junín 848,993 ..... E8
La Libertad 960,537 ..... C6
Lambayeque 683,425 ..... B6
Lima 4,738,266 ..... D8
Loreto 446,316 ..... E5
Madre de Dios 36,555 ..... G8
Moquegua 99,287 ..... G11
Pasco 221,219 ..... E8
Piura 1,168,442 ..... B5
Puno 893,586 ..... G10
San Martín 319,670 ..... D6
Tacna 133,240 ..... G11
Tumbes 103,979 ..... B4
Ucayali 200,085 ..... E6

CITIES and TOWNS

Abancay 19,807 ..... F9
Acarí 4,907 ..... E10
Acobamba 2,156 ..... E9
Acolla 5,717 ..... E8
Acomayo, Cusco 1,419 ..... G9
Acomayo, Huánuco 2,883 ..... E7
Acora 1,910 ..... H11
Acuracay 1,282 ..... F5
Aija 1,843 ..... D7
Alca 755 ..... F10
Ambo 3,060 ..... D8
Ananea 668 ..... H10
Ancón 8,610 ..... D8
Andahuaylas 7,654 ..... F9
Anta 3,703 ..... F9
Antabamba 2,223 ..... F10
Aplao 1,941 ..... F11
Aquia 970 ..... D8
Arequipa 107,858 ..... G11
Arequipa* 447,431 ..... G11
Ascope 12,070 ..... C6
Atalaya 2,132 ..... E8
Atico 2,316 ..... F11
Ayabaca 4,543 ..... C5
Ayacucho 68,535 ..... F9
Ayaviri 11,067 ..... G10
Azángaro 7,658 ..... H10
Bagua 9,735 ..... C5
Bambamarca 6,867 ..... C6
Barranca, Lima 21,312 ..... C8
Barranca, Loreto 1,351 ..... D5
Bellavista 4,906 ..... C5
Bolívar 1,106 ..... D6
Bretaña 1,035 ..... E5
Buldibuyo 582 ..... D7
Cabana 1,804 ..... C7
Cailloma 1,187 ..... G10
Cajabamba 7,282 ..... C6
Cajamarca 60,280 ..... C6
Cajatambo 1,721 ..... D8
Calca 6,112 ..... G9
Callalli 819 ..... G10
Callao 260,581 ..... D9
Callao* 441,374 ..... D9
Camaná 11,386 ..... F11
Candarave 1,207 ..... G11
Cangallo 1,584 ..... E9
Canta 3,431 ..... D8
Capachica 307 ..... H10
Caravelí 1,827 ..... F10
Caraz 6,376 ..... D7
Carhuás 3,147 ..... D7
Carumás 1,031 ..... G11
Cascas 2,638 ..... C6
Casma 12,725 ..... C7
Castrovirreyna 1,749 ..... E9
Catacaos 30,927 ..... B5
Celendín 8,538 ..... D6
Cerro Azul 2,314 ..... D9
Cerro de Pasco 71,558 ..... D8
Chachapoyas 11,919 ..... D6
Chala 1,646 ..... E10
Chalhuanca 3,071 ..... F10
Chancay 18,993 ..... D8
Chepén 29,919 ..... C6
Chicama 11,160 ..... C6
Chiclayo 280,244 ..... C6
Chilca (Pucusana) 3,329 ..... D9
Chilete 2,537 ..... C6
Chimbote 216,406 ..... C7
Chincha Alta 37,475 ..... D9
Chiquián 3,521 ..... D8
Chirinos 1,061 ..... C5
Chivay 3,296 ..... G10
Chota 8,299 ..... C6
Chulucanas 34,977 ..... B5
Chupaca 5,422 ..... E9
Chuquibamba 2,630 ..... F10
Chuquibambilla 2,147 ..... F9
Churín 1,801 ..... D8
Cocachacra 5,985 ..... G11
Cojata 888 ..... H10
Colasay 721 ..... C5
Colcamar 1,216 ..... D6
Conaica 1,154 ..... E9
Concepción 7,129 ..... E8
Concordia 1,372 ..... E5
Contamana 5,718 ..... E6
Contumazá 2,491 ..... C6
Coracora 4,598 ..... F10
Córdova 453 ..... E10
Corongo 1,762 ..... D7
Cotahuasi 1,301 ..... F10
Cusco (Cuzco) 85,044 ..... F9
Cusco* 171,604 ..... F9
Cutervo 6,890 ..... C6
Cuyocuyo 1,101 ..... H10
Desaguadero 2,682 ..... H11
Deustua 544 ..... G10
Dos de Mayo 574 ..... E6
Echarate 1,071 ..... F9
El Portugués C7
Esperanza 375 ..... G7
Espinar 6,381 ..... G10
Ferreñafe 22,200 ..... C6
Fitzcarrald G8
Francisco de Orellana 445 ..... F4
Guadalupe 7,613 ..... E9
Huacho 43,402 ..... D8
Huacrachuco 1,210 ..... D7
Hualgayoc 1,691 ..... C6
Hualla 4,042 ..... F9
Huallanca, Ancash 930 ..... D7
Huallanca, Huánuco 4,806 ..... D7
Huamachuco 8,273 ..... D6
Huancabamba 4,393 ..... C5
Huancané 5,227 ..... H10
Huancapi 2,539 ..... E9
Huancavelica 20,889 ..... E9
Huancayo 165,132 ..... E9
Hunchaco 6,005 ..... C7
Huanta 11,213 ..... E9
Huánuco 52,628 ..... E7
Huaral 34,235 ..... D8
Huaráz 45,116 ..... D7
Huari 2,344 ..... D7
Huariaca 2,671 ..... E8
Huarmey 11,094 ..... C8
Huarochirí 1,828 ..... D9
Huarocondo 2,498 ..... F9
Huaura 9,338 ..... D8
Huaylas 1,344 ..... C7
Iberia 2,307 ..... F5
Ica 111,087 ..... E10
Ichuña 277 ..... G11
Ilave 9,891 ..... H11
Ilo 31,549 ..... G11
Imperial 20,894 ..... D9
Inambari H9
Iñapari 188 ..... H8
Intutu 746 ..... E4
Iparia 278 ..... E7
Iquitos 173,629 ..... F4
Jaén 24,356 ..... C5
Jauja 14,630 ..... E8
Jayanca 6,401 ..... B6
Jeberos 1,493 ..... D5
Juanjuí 9,324 ..... D6
Juli 5,575 ..... H11
Juliaca 77,976 ..... G10
Jumbilla 1,035 ..... C5
Junín 8,988 ..... E8
Lagunas 4,601 ..... E5
La Huaca 5,161 ..... B5
La Jalca 1,769 ..... D6
La Joya 5,000 ..... G11
Lamas 8,937 ..... D6
Lambayeque 23,746 ..... B6
Lampa 4,319 ..... G10
Lamud 2,405 ..... C6
Lanlacuni Bajo 405 ..... G9
La Oroya 33,305 ..... D8
Las Piedras H9
Las Yaras 759 ..... G11
La Tina B5
La Unión 2,828 ..... D7
Leimebamba 1,957 ..... D6
Lima (cap.) 375,957 ..... D8
Lima* 3,968,972 ..... D8
Limbani 728 ..... H10
Lircay 5,213 ..... E9
Llata 2,922 ..... D7
Lobitos 2,975 ..... B5
Lurín 14,405 ..... D9
Machupicchu 544 ..... F9
Macusani 3,389 ..... G10
Madre de Dios 660 ..... G9
Manú 234 ..... G9
Máncora 5,358 ..... B5
Marcapata 369 ..... G9
Marcona 25,962 ..... E10
Margos 1,622 ..... D8
Masisea 1,586 ..... E7
Matarani F11
Matucana 4,196 ..... D8
Mazocruz 1,580 ..... H11
Mendoza 1,902 ..... D6
Moho 2,560 ..... H10
Mollendo 21,206 ..... F11
Monsefú 17,186 ..... C6
Moquegua 21,488 ..... G11
Morales 4,370 ..... D6
Morococha 11,234 ..... D8
Morropón 7,611 ..... C5
Motupe 3,411 ..... C6
Moyobamba 14,319 ..... D6
Nauta 4,083 ..... F5
Nazca 22,756 ..... E10
Negritos 12,476 ..... B5
Nuñoa 3,613 ..... G10
Ocoña 1,062 ..... F11
Ocros 1,037 ..... D8
Ollachea 1,308 ..... G9
Ollantaytambo 1,500 ..... F9
Olmos 7,946 ..... C5
Omate 1,131 ..... G11
Orcotuna 3,359 ..... E8
Orellana 1,550 ..... E6
Otuzco 5,765 ..... C6
Oxapampa 5,233 ..... E8
Oyón 6,279 ..... D8
Pacasmayo 17,588 ..... C6
Pachiza 889 ..... D6
Paiján 12,699 ..... C6
Paita 18,749 ..... B5
Palpa 3,393 ..... E10
Pampacolca 2,010 ..... F10
Pampas 3,850 ..... E9
Panao 1,363 ..... E7
Paruro 1,727 ..... F9
Paucarbamba 534 ..... E9
Paucartambo, Cusco 1,620 ..... G9
Paucartambo, Pasco 3,497 ..... E8
Pevas 1,347 ..... G4
Picota 2,288 ..... D6
Pimentel 9,129 ..... B6
Pisac 1,566 ..... G9
Pisco 53,414 ..... D9
Piura 186,354 ..... B5
Pomabamba 2,489 ..... D7
Pucallpa 91,953 ..... E7
Pucará 2,268 ..... G10
Pucaurco 628 ..... G4
Pucusana 3,329 ..... D9
Puerto Bermúdez 1,133 ..... E8
Puerto Chicama 3,630 ..... C6
Puerto Eten 2,575 ..... B6
Puerto Inca 1,286 ..... E7
Puerto Maldonado 12,609 ..... H9
Puerto Ocopa 1,088 ..... E8
Puerto Samanco 1,435 ..... C7
Puno 66,477 ..... G10
Punta de Bombón 4,647 ..... F11
Puquina 1,026 ..... G11
Putina 5,414 ..... H10
Querecotillo 10,637 ..... B5
Quillabamba 16,837 ..... F9
Ramón Castilla 1,811 ..... G5
Recuay 2,764 ..... D7
Requena 8,270 ..... F5
Rioja 9,876 ..... D6
Salaverry 5,539 ..... C7
Saña 40,144 ..... C6
Sandia 1,682 ..... H10
San José 4,070 ..... B6
San José de Sisa 3,782 ..... D6
San Miguel, Ayacucho 1,440 ..... F9
San Miguel, Cajamarca 1,798 ..... C6
San Pedro de Lloc 11,463 ..... C6
San Ramón 7,145 ..... E8
Santa 20,490 ..... C7
Santa Clotilde 1,068 ..... E4
Santa Cruz, Cajamarca 2,739 ..... C6
Santa Cruz, Loreto 449 ..... E5
Santiago 5,092 ..... E10
Santiago de Cao 22,119 ..... C6
Santiago de Chuco 5,189 ..... C7
Santo Tomás, Amazonas 1,093 ..... C6
Santo Tomás, Cusco 2,755 ..... G10
San Vicente de Cañete 15,277 ..... D9
Saposoa 4,541 ..... D6
Saquena 2,755 ..... F5
Satipo 9,208 ..... E8
Sauce 2,263 ..... D6
Sayán 5,129 ..... D8
Sechura 11,724 ..... B5
Sicuani 21,176 ..... G10
Sihuas 2,178 ..... D7
Sullana 80,947 ..... B5
Sumbilca 1,155 ..... D8
Supe 10,061 ..... D8
Tacna 92,862 ..... G11
Tahuamanu 2,619 ..... H8
Talara 55,722 ..... B5
Tambo de Mora 2,790 ..... D9
Tambo Grande 10,087 ..... B5
Tamshiyacu 2,040 ..... F5
Tarapoto 33,429 ..... D6
Tarata 2,624 ..... H11
Tarma 34,369 ..... E8
Tayabamba 1,649 ..... D7
Tingo María 25,030 ..... D7
Tocache 5,940 ..... D7
Torata 6,320 ..... G11
Trujillo 354,557 ..... C7
Tumbes 48,187 ..... B4
Uchiza 2,471 ..... D7
Urcos 4,155 ..... G9
Urubamba 4,686 ..... F9
Virú 6,587 ..... C7
Yambrasbamba 277 ..... D5
Yanahuanca 5,109 ..... D8
Yanaoca 1,152 ..... G10
Yauca 1,805 ..... E10
Yauli 1,020 ..... D8
Yauri (Espinar) 6,381 ..... G10
Yauyos 1,296 ..... E9
Yunguyo 7,253 ..... H11
Yurimaguas 22,858 ..... E5
Zarumilla 9,713 ..... B4
Zorritos 4,497 ..... B4

OTHER FEATURES

Acarí (riv.) E10
Aguaytía (riv.) E7
Aguja (pt.) B5
Amazon (riv.) F4
Andes, Cordillera de los (mts.) F10
Apurímac (riv.) F9
Azángaro (riv.) G10
Azul, Cordillera (range) E7
Blanca, Cordillera (range) D7
Blanco (cape) B5
Boquerón, El (pass) E7
Cañete (riv.) D9
Chimbote (bay) C7
Chincha (isls.) D9
Chira (riv.) B5
Cóndor, Cordillera del (range) C5
Coropuna, Nudo (mt.) F10
Corrientes (riv.) E4
Ene (riv.) E8
Ferrol (pt.) C7
Grande (riv.) E10
Guañape (isls.) C7
Heath (riv.) H9
Huallaga (riv.) D5
Huasaga (riv.) D4
Huascarán (mt.) D7
Huayabamba (riv.) D6
Ica (riv.) E10
Inambari (riv.) H9
Independencia (bay) D10
Independencia (isl.) D10
Junín (lake) E8
Juruá (riv.) F7
Lobos de Afuera (isls.) B6
Lobos de Tierra (isl.) B6
Locumba (riv.) G11
Madre de Dios (riv.) G9
Majes (riv.) F1
Mantaro (riv.) E8
Manú (riv.) G8
Marañón (riv.) E5
Mayo (riv.) D6
Misti, El (mt.) G11
Montaña, La (reg.) F8
Morona (riv.) D5
Nanay (riv.) E4
Napo (riv.) F4
Negra, Cordillera (range) D7
Negra (pt.) B6
Nermete (pt.) B5
Occidental, Cordillera (range) F10
Ocoña (riv.) F11
Oriental, Cordillera (range) H10
Pachitea (riv.) E7
Paita (bay) B5
Pampas (riv.) E9
Paracas (pt.) D9
Pariñas (pt.) B5
Parinacochas (lake) F10
Pastaza (riv.) D5
Pativilca (riv.) D8
Perené (riv.) E8
Piedras, Las (riv.) G8
Pisco (bay) D9
Pisco (riv.) D9
Piura (riv.) B5
Purús (riv.) G8
Putumayo (riv.) G4
Rimac (riv.) D9
Salcantay (mt.) F9
Sama (riv.) G11
San Gallán (isl.) D9
San Lorenzo (isl.) D9
San Nicolás (bay) E10
Santa (riv.) C7
Santiago (riv.) D4
Sechura (bay) B5
Tambo (riv.) G11
Tapiche (riv.) E6
Tigre (riv.) E4
Titicaca (lake) H10
Tumbes (riv.) B4
Ucayali (riv.) F5
Urubamba (riv.) F8

(continued on following page)

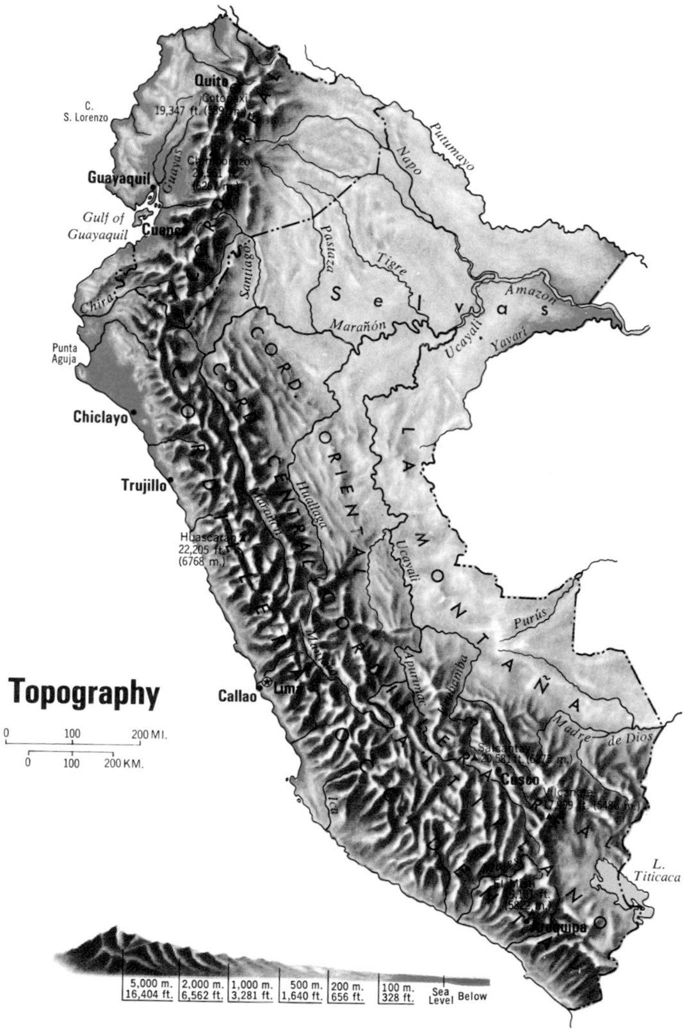

Topography
Quito
Guayaquil
Gulf of Guayaquil
Cuenca
C. S. Lorenzo
Punta Aguja
Chiclayo
Trujillo
Callao
Lima
Cusco
Arequipa
L. Titicaca
Napo
Putumayo
Pastaza
Tigre
Marañón
Amazonas
Ucayali
Yavarí
Purús
Madre de Dios
S e l v a s
L A M O N T A Ñ A
Chira
Santiago
Huallaga
Apurímac
Urubamba
Ica
0 100 200 MI.
0 100 200 KM.
5,000 m. 16,404 ft.
2,000 m. 6,562 ft.
1,000 m. 3,281 ft.
500 m. 1,640 ft.
200 m. 656 ft.
100 m. 328 ft.
Sea Level
Below

Vilcabamba, Cordillera (range) F9	Bolívar 144,593 ....C3	Manabí 817,966 ....B3	Atuntaqui 9,907 ....C2
Vilcanota (mt.) G10	Cañar 146,570 ....C4	Mera 631 ....C3	Azogues 10,953 ....C4
Vitor (riv.) F11	Carchi 120,857 ....C2	Morona-Santiago 53,325 ....C4	Baba 953 ....C3
Yaguas (riv.) G4	Chimborazo 304,316 ....C3	Napo 65,186 ....D3	Babahoyo 28,914 ....C3
Yavarí (riv.) G5	Colón, Archipiélago de (terr.) 4,037 ....C8	Pastaza 23,465 ....D3	Baeza 253 ....C3
Yavero (riv.) F9	Cotopaxi 236,313 ....C3	Pichincha 988,306 ....C3	Bahía de Caráquez 11,258 ....B3
Yuruá (riv.) F7	El Oro 262,564 ....C4	Tungurahua 279,920 ....C3	Balzar 10,924 ....C3
	Esmeraldas 203,151 ....C2	Zamora-Chinchipe 34,493 ....C5	Baquerizo Moreno 1,311 ....C9
ECUADOR	Guayas 1,512,333 ....B4		Bolívar C2
	Imbabura 216,027 ....C2	**CITIES and TOWNS**	Cajabamba 2,318 ....C4
PROVINCES	La Bonita 184 ....D2		Calceta 7,152 ....C3
	Loja 342,339 ....C4	Alausí 7,137 ....C4	Cañar 6,727 ....C4
Azuay 367,324 ....C4	Los Ríos 383,432 ....C3	Ambato 77,955 ....C3	Cariamanga 6,682 ....C5
		Arenillas 5,862 ....B4	Catacocha 3,280 ....C5

Catarama 2,868 ....C3	Gualaquiza 1,679 ....C4	**FRENCH GUIANA**
Cayambe 11,199 ....D3	Guamote 2,438 ....C4	
Guano 5,389 ....B4	Guano 5,389 ....B4	**DISTRICTS**
Chone 23,627 ....B3	Guaranda 11,364 ....C3	
Chunchi 2,802 ....C4	Guayaquil 823,219 ....B4	Cayenne 61,587 ....E3
Coca 1,211 ....D3	Ibarra 41,335 ....C2	Saint-Laurent du Maroni 11,435 ....E4
Cuenca 104,470 ....C4	Jipijapa 19,996 ....B3	
Dayle 13,170 ....B3	La Bonita 184 ....D2	**CITIES and TOWNS**
El Ángel 3,660 ....C2	La Libertad 26,078 ....B4	
El Corazón 1,073 ....C3	Latacunga 21,921 ....C3	Camopi 228 ....E4
El Pun D2	Loja 47,697 ....C4	Cayenne (cap.) 37,097 ....E3
Esmeraldas 60,364 ....B2	Loreto D3	Grand Santi 305 ....D3
Girón 2,361 ....C4	Macará 8,063 ....C5	Guisanbourg F3
Gualaceo 4,575 ....C4	Macas 1,934 ....D4	Inini E4
	Machachi 4,745 ....C3	Iracoubo 483 ....E3
	Machala 69,170 ....B4	Kourou 6,465 ....E3
	Machalilla B3	Macouria 94 ....E3
	Manglaralto B3	Malmanoury E3
	Manta 64,519 ....B3	Mana 623 ....E3
	Méndez 1,043 ....C4	Maripasoula 556 ....D4
	Mera 631 ....C3	Matoury 586 ....E3
	Milagro 53,106 ....C4	Montsinéry 94 ....E3
	Montecristi 6,386 ....B3	Ouanary 61 ....F3
	Nuevo Rocafuerte 198 ....E3	Paul Isnard D3
	Otavalo 13,605 ....C2	Régina 258 ....E3
	Paján 2,610 ....B3	Rémire 5,921 ....E3
	Pasaje 20,790 ....C4	Roura 160 ....E3
	Paute 1,998 ....C4	Saint-Élie 57 ....E3
	Pelileo 3,754 ....C3	Saint-Georges 921 ....F4
	Píllaro 4,052 ....C3	Saint-Laurent du Maroni 5,042 ....E3
	Piñas 5,770 ....C4	Saül 60 ....E4
	Portoviejo 59,550 ....B3	Saut-Tigre E4
	Puerto Ayora 900 ....B9	Sinnamary 1,669 ....E3
	Puerto El Carmen 308 ....E3	
	Pujilí 2,510 ....C3	**OTHER FEATURES**
	Puyo 4,730 ....D3	
	Quevedo 43,101 ....C3	Approuague (riv.) E4
	Quito (cap.) 599,828 ....C3	Béhague (mts.) F3
	Riobamba 58,087 ....C3	Camopi (riv.) E4
	Rocafuerte 5,519 ....B3	Devil's (isl.) E3
	Rosa Zárate 4,847 ....C2	Inini (riv.) E4
	Salinas 12,409 ....B4	Lawa (riv.) D4
	San Gabriel 10,036 ....D2	Litani (riv.) D4
	Sangolquí 10,554 ....C3	Mana (riv.) E3
	San Lorenzo C2	Maroni (riv.) D3
	San Miguel 2,743 ....C3	Marouini (riv.) D4
	San Miguel de Salcedo 4,159 ....C3	Oyapock (riv.) E4
	Santa Ana 5,004 ....B3	Rémire (isls.) F3
	Santa Elena 7,687 ....B4	Salut (isls.) E3
	Santa Isabel 2,068 ....C4	Sinnamary (riv.) E3
	Santa Rosa 19,696 ....C4	Tampoc (riv.) E4
	Santo Domingo de los Colorados 30,523 ....C3	Tumuc-Humac (mts.) D3
	Saraguro 1,739 ....C4	
	Sarayacu D3	**GUYANA**
	Sigsig 2,021 ....C4	
	Sucre 2,929 ....B3	**DISTRICTS**
	Sucúa 9,694 ....C4	
	Tabacundo 1,942 ....C2	East Berbice-Courantyne C3
	Tachina C2	East Demerara-West Coast Berbice C2
	Tulcán 24,398 ....D2	Mazaruni-Potaro A2
	Valdez 3,837 ....C2	North West A2
	Venticinco de Mayo 266 ....C4	Rupununi B4
	Vinces 10,126 ....C3	West Demerara-Essequibo Coast B2
	Yaguachi Nuevo 3,816 ....B4	
	Zamora 2,667 ....C5	**CITIES and TOWNS**
	Zumba 905 ....C5	
		Adventure ○ 645 ....B2
	OTHER FEATURES	Annai ○ 569 ....B4
		Anna Regina 1,124 ....B2
	Aguarico (riv.) D3	Apoteri ○ 74 ....B3
	Albemarle (pt.) B9	Baramanni ○ 231 ....B2
	Ancón de Sardinas (bay) C2	Bartica ○ 4,087 ....B2
	Antisana (mt.) D3	Biloku ○ 290 ....B5
	Baltra (isl.) B9	Charity ○ 1,175 ....B2
	Banks (bay) B9	Corriverton 10,502 ....C3
	Bobonaza (riv.) D3	Danielstown 861 ....B2
	Cayambe (mt.) D2	Epira ○ 230 ....C3
	Chaves (Santa Cruz) (isl.) C9	Georgetown (cap.) 63,184 ....C2
	Chimborazo (mt.) C3	Georgetown * 164,039 ....C2
	Chira (riv.) B5	Imbaimadai ○ 270 ....A3
	Cóndor, Cordillera del (range) C5	Issano ○ 207 ....B3
	Cotopaxi (mt.) C3	Issineru ○ 124 ....A3
	Cristóbal (pt.) B9	Kamakusa ○ 211 ....A3
	Culpepper (isl.) B8	Kamarang ○ 308 ....A3
	Curaray (riv.) D3	Kurupukari ○ 284 ....B3
	Darwin (Culpepper) (isl.) B8	Lethem ○ 645 ....B4
	Esmeraldas (riv.) C2	Linden 23,956 ....B2
	Española (isl.) C10	Mabaruma ○ 391 ....B1
	Fernandina (isl.) B9	Mahaica ○ 6,967 ....C2
	Floreana (Santa María) (isl.) B10	Mahaicony Village ○ 4,665 ....C2
	Galápagos (isls.) C8	Mahdia ○ 147 ....B3
	Genovesa (isl.) B9	Mara ○ 203 ....C3
	Guayaquil (gulf) B4	Morawhanna ○ 292 ....B1
	Guayas (riv.) C4	Mount Everard ○ 369 ....B2
	Isabela (isl.) B9	New Amsterdam 17,782 ....B2
	La Puntilla (cape) B4	Orealla ○ 674 ....C3
	Manta (bay) B3	Parika ○ 1,101 ....B2
	Marchena (isl.) B9	Pickersgill ○ 508 ....B2
	Mira (riv.) C2	Queenstown ○ 1,211 ....B2
	Napo (riv.) D3	Rockstone ○ 728 ....B2
	Naranjal (riv.) B4	Rosignol ○ 2,001 ....C2
	Pastaza (riv.) D4	Suddie ○ 705 ....B2
	Pinta (isl.) B9	Tumatumari ○ 353 ....B3
	Pinzón (isl.) B9	Tumereng ○ 238 ....B2
	Puná (isl.) B4	Vreed-en-Hoop ○ 3,054 ....B2
	Putumayo (riv.) E2	Wichabai ○ 216 ....B4
	Rosa (cape) B10	
	San Cristóbal (isl.) C9	**OTHER FEATURES**
	San Francisco (cape) B2	
	San Lorenzo (cape) B3	Acarai (mts.) B5
	San Miguel (riv.) D2	Amakura (riv.) A2
	San Salvador (isl.) B9	Amuku (mts.) B4
	Santa Cruz (isl.) C9	Barama (riv.) A2
	Santa Fe (isl.) C9	Barima (riv.) B2
	Santa María (isl.) B10	Berbice (riv.) B3
	Santiago (San Salvador) (isl.) B9	Burro-Burro (riv.) B3
	Sangay (mt.) C4	Courantyne (riv.) C3
	Tumbes (riv.) B4	Cuyuni (riv.) B2
	Wenman (isl.) B8	Demerara (riv.) B3
	Wolf (Wenman) (isl.) B8	Essequibo (riv.) B3
	Zamora (riv.) C4	Great (fall) B3
		Ireng (riv.) B3
	*City and suburbs	Kaieteur (fall) B3

Agriculture, Industry and Resources

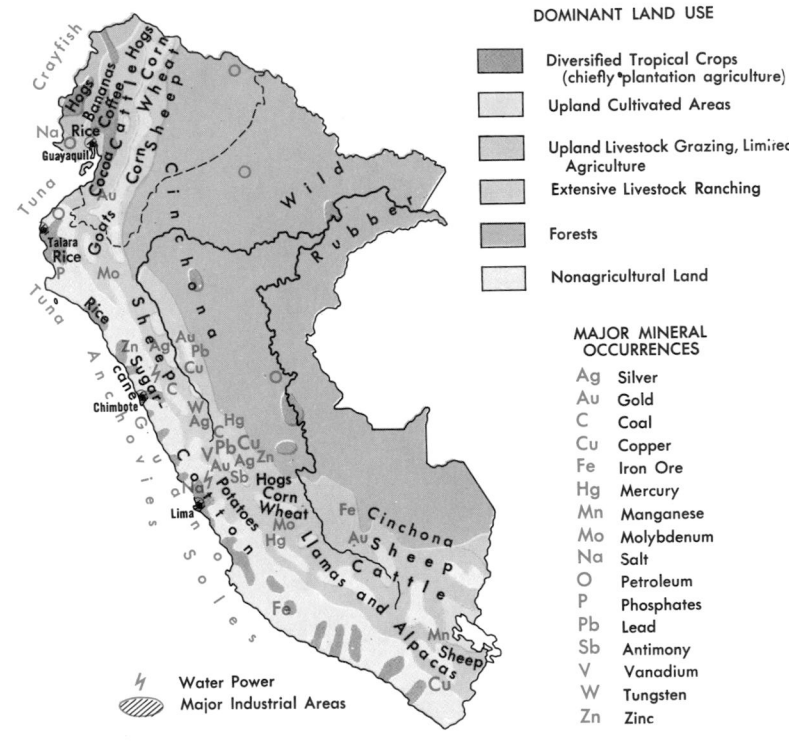

DOMINANT LAND USE

- Diversified Tropical Crops (chiefly plantation agriculture)
- Upland Cultivated Areas
- Upland Livestock Grazing, Limited Agriculture
- Extensive Livestock Ranching
- Forests
- Nonagricultural Land

MAJOR MINERAL OCCURRENCES

Ag	Silver
Au	Gold
C	Coal
Cu	Copper
Fe	Iron Ore
Hg	Mercury
Mn	Manganese
Mo	Molybdenum
Na	Salt
O	Petroleum
P	Phosphates
Pb	Lead
Sb	Antimony
V	Vanadium
W	Tungsten
Zn	Zinc

⚡ Water Power

▨ Major Industrial Areas

DOMINANT LAND USE

- Diversified Tropical Crops (chiefly plantation agriculture)
- Extensive Livestock Ranching
- Forests

Agriculture, Industry and Resources

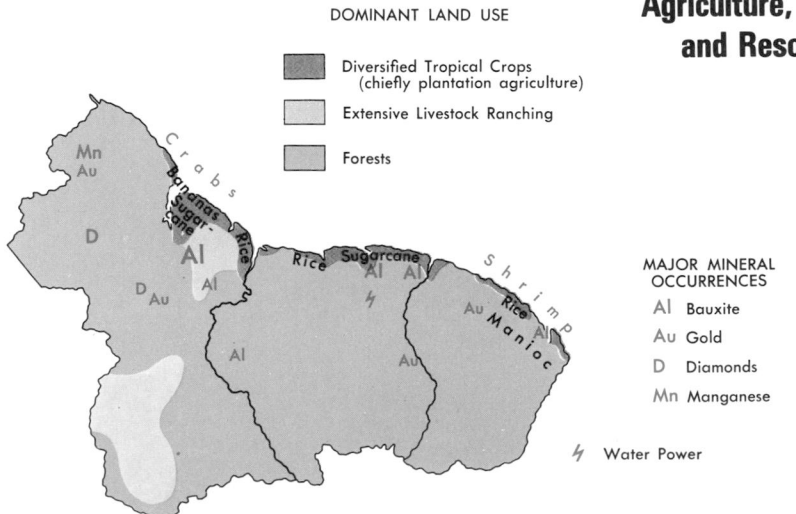

MAJOR MINERAL OCCURRENCES

Al	Bauxite
Au	Gold
D	Diamonds
Mn	Manganese

⚡ Water Power

GUYANA

AREA 83,000 sq. mi. (214,970 sq. km.)
POPULATION 1,024,000
CAPITAL Georgetown
LARGEST CITY Georgetown
HIGHEST POINT Mt. Roraima 9,094 ft. (2,772 m.)
MONETARY UNIT Guyana dollar
MAJOR LANGUAGES English, Hindi
MAJOR RELIGIONS Christianity, Hinduism, Islam

SURINAME

AREA 55,144 sq. mi. (142,823 sq. km.)
POPULATION 400,000
CAPITAL Paramaribo
LARGEST CITY Paramaribo
HIGHEST POINT Julianatop 4,200 ft. (1,280 m.)
MONETARY UNIT Suriname guilder
MAJOR LANGUAGES Dutch, Hindi, Indonesian
MAJOR RELIGIONS Christianity, Islam, Hinduism

FRENCH GUIANA

AREA 35,135 sq. mi. (91,000 sq. km.)
POPULATION 90,000
CAPITAL Cayenne
LARGEST CITY Cayenne
HIGHEST POINT 2,723 ft. (830 m.)
MONETARY UNIT French franc
MAJOR LANGUAGE French
MAJOR RELIGIONS Roman Catholicism, Protestantism

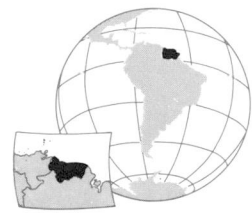

GUYANA

Kamaria (falls)	B2
Kuyuwini (riv.)	B4
Kwitaro (riv.)	B4
Leguan (isl.)	B2
Mazaruni (riv.)	A2
Moruka (riv.)	B2
New (riv.)	C4
Pakaraima (mts.)	A3
Pomeroon (riv.)	B2
Potaro (riv.)	B3
Puruni (riv.)	B2
Roraima (mt.)	A3
Rupununi (riv.)	B4
Takutu (riv.)	B4
Venamo (mt.)	A3
Waini (riv.)	B2
Wenamu (riv.)	A2

Lelydorp 300	D3
Mariënburg 3,500	D2
Moengo 2,100	D3
Nieuw-Amsterdam 1,400	D2
Nieuw-Nickerie 34,480	C2
Paramaribo (cap.) ⓞ 67,905	D3
Paranam	D3
Totness 1,300	C3
Uitkijk	D3
Wageningen 800	C3
Zanderij	D3

SURINAME

DISTRICTS

Brokopondo 17,763	D4
Commewijne 18,740	D3
Coronie 3,251	C3
Marowijne 25,911	D4
Nickerie 35,178	C3
Para 16,635	D3
Paramaribo 102,297	D2
Saramacca 13,554	C3
Suriname 151,585	D3

CITIES and TOWNS

Albina 1,000	D3
Brokopondo	D3
Calcutta 1,100	C3
Domburg 1,200	D3
Groningen 600	D2

OTHER FEATURES

Bakhuys (mts.)	C3
Coeroeni (riv.)	C4
Commewijne (riv.)	D3
Coppename (riv.)	C3
Corantijn (riv.)	C3
Cottica (riv.)	D3
Eilerts de Haan (mts.)	C4
Frederik Willem IV (falls)	C4
Julianatop (mt.)	C4
Kutari (riv.)	C4
Lely (mts.)	D3
Litani (riv.)	D4
Marowijne (riv.)	D4
Nickerie (riv.)	C3
Orange (mts.)	D4
Saramacca (riv.)	D3
Sipaliwini (riv.)	C4
Suriname (riv.)	D3
Tapanahoni (riv.)	D4

*City and suburbs
ⓞ Population of sub-district or division.
ⓞ Population of district

Topography

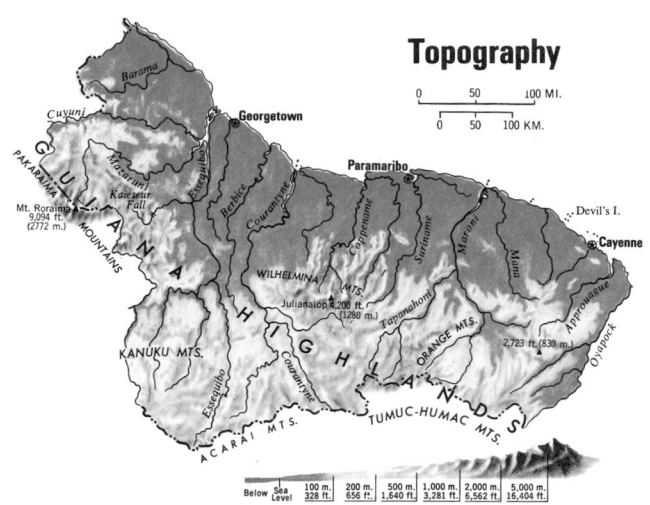

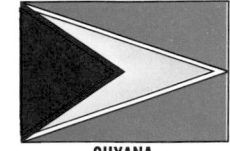

GUYANA

SURINAME

FRENCH GUIANA

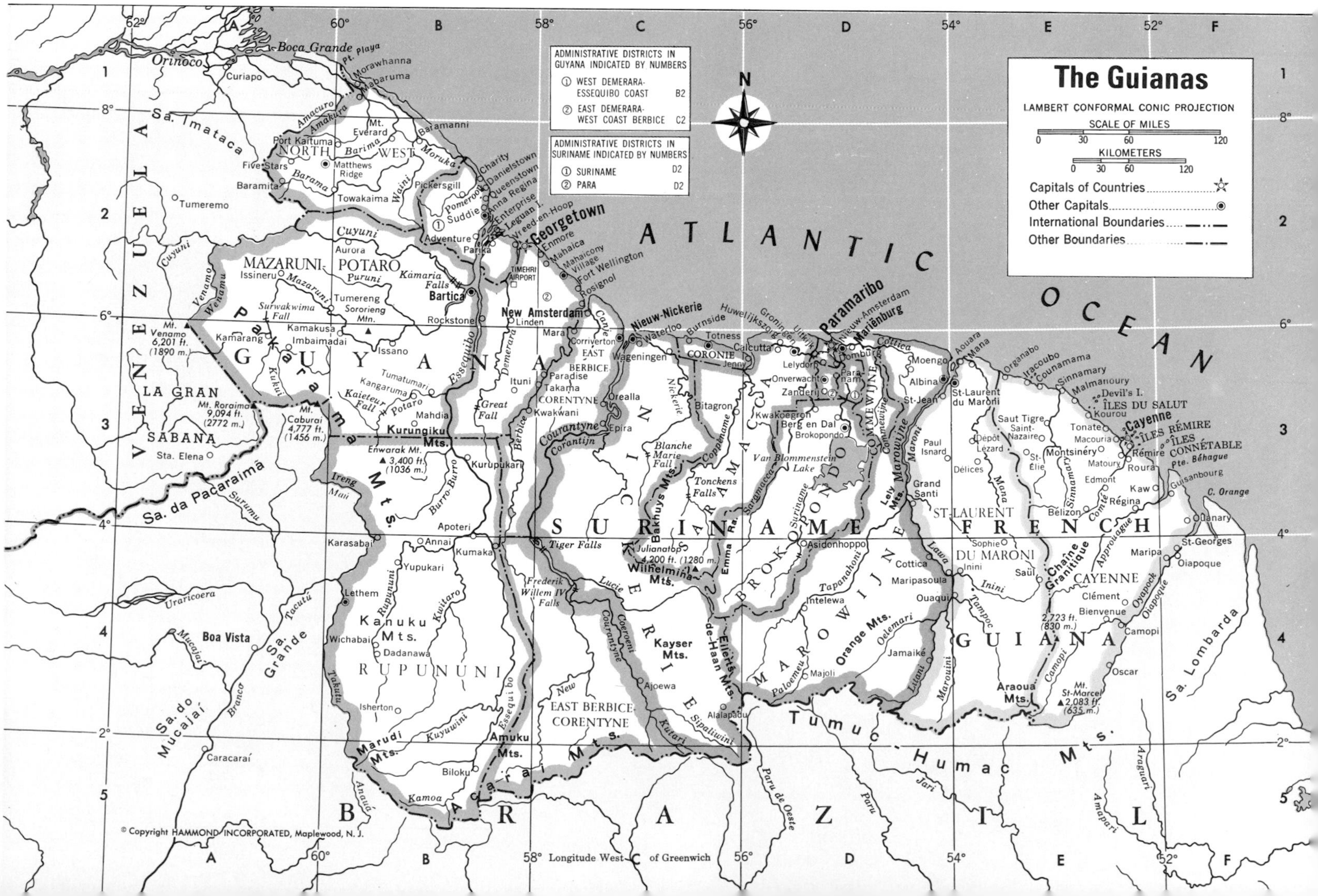

The Guianas

LAMBERT CONFORMAL CONIC PROJECTION

SCALE OF MILES
0   30   60   120

KILOMETERS
0   30   60   120

Capitals of Countries .... ☆
Other Capitals .... ⊙
International Boundaries ___ __ ___
Other Boundaries ___ __ ___

ADMINISTRATIVE DISTRICTS IN GUYANA INDICATED BY NUMBERS
① WEST DEMERARA-ESSEQUIBO COAST ... B2
② EAST DEMERARA-WEST COAST BERBICE ... C2

ADMINISTRATIVE DISTRICTS IN SURINAME INDICATED BY NUMBERS
① SURINAME ... D2
② PARA ... D2

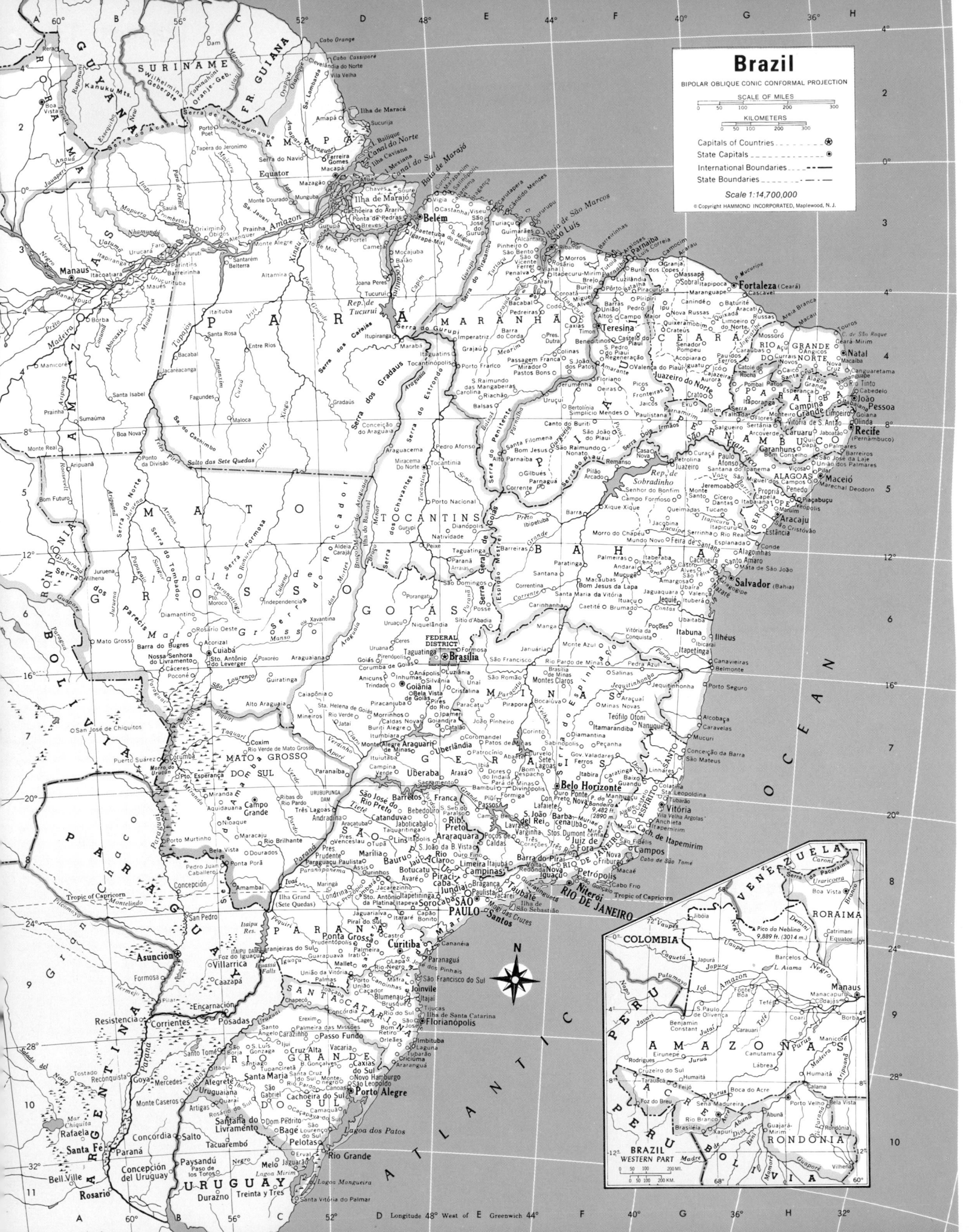

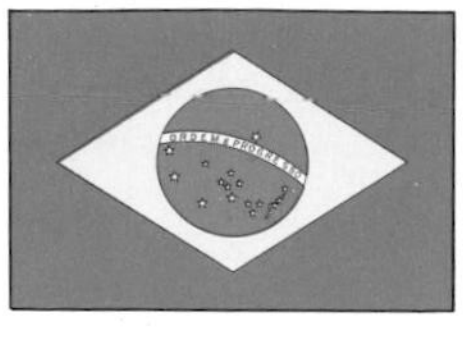

AREA 3,284,426 sq. mi. (8,506,663 sq. km.)
POPULATION 150,368,000
CAPITAL Brasília
LARGEST CITY São Paulo (greater)
HIGHEST POINT Pico da Neblina 9,889 ft. (3,014 m.)
MONETARY UNIT cruzado
MAJOR LANGUAGE Portuguese
MAJOR RELIGION Roman Catholicism

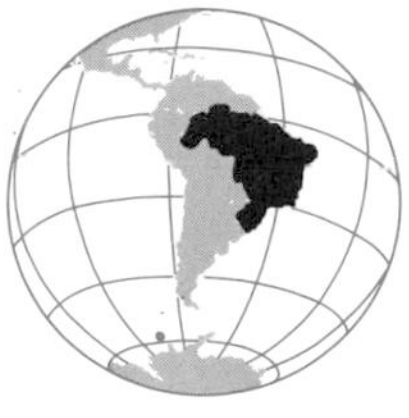

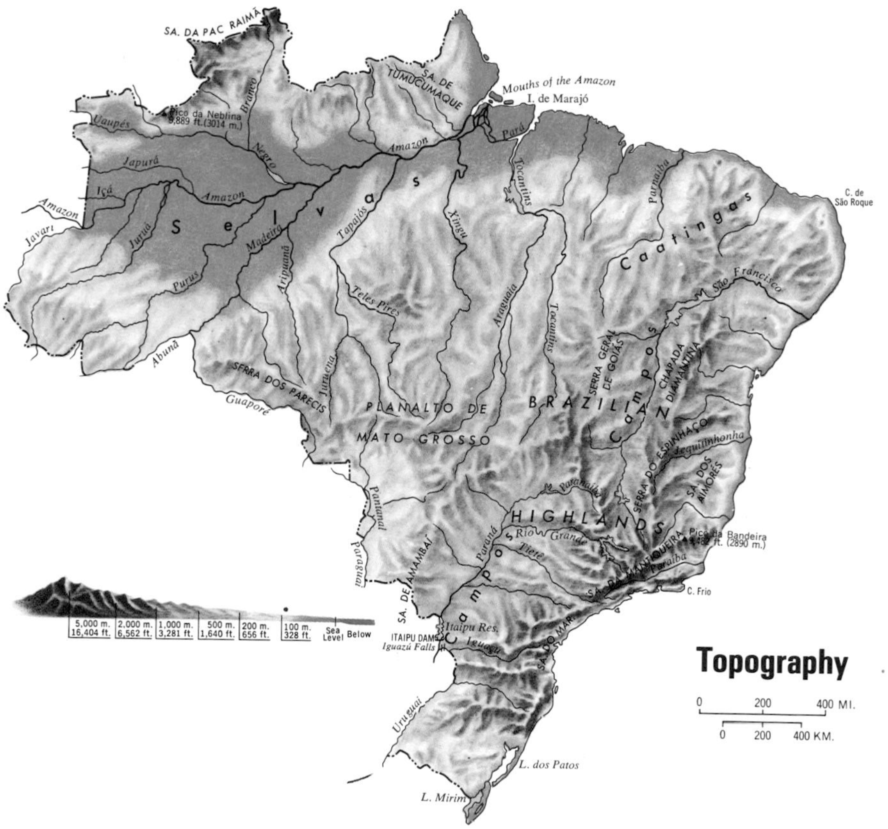

Topography

STATES and TERRITORIES

Acre 301,605 ... G10
Alagoas 1,987,581 ... G5
Amapá (terr.) 175,634 ... D2
Amazonas 1,432,066 ... G9
Bahia 9,474,263 ... F6
Ceará 5,294,876 ... G4
Espirito Santo 2,023,821 ... F7
Federal District 1,177,393 ... E6
Goiás 3,865,482 ... D6
Maranhão 4,002,599 ... E4
Mato Grosso 1,141,661 ... B6
Mato Grosso do Sul 1,370,333 ... C7
Minas Gerais 13,390,805 ... E7
Pará 3,411,868 ... C4
Paralba 2,772,600 ... G4
Paraná 7,630,466 ... D9
Pernambuco 6,147,102 ... G5
Piaul 2,140,066 ... F4
Rio de Janeiro 11,297,327 ... F8
Rio Grande do Norte 1,899,720 ... G4
Rio Grande do Sul 7,777,212 ... C10
Rondônia 492,810 ... H10
Roraima (terr.) 79,153 ... H8
Santa Catarina 3,628,751 ... D9
São Paulo 25,040,698 ... D8
Sergipe 1,141,834 ... G5
Tocantins ... D5

CITIES and TOWNS

Abaeté 12,861 ... E7
Abaetetuba 33,031 ... D3
Acaraú 7,144 ... F3
Acopiara 10,747 ... G4
Açu 20,544 ... G4
Agudos 18,790 ... *B3
Alagoa Grande 14,204 ... H4
Alagoinhas 76,377 ... G6
Alcobaça 3,430 ... G7
Alegre 9,441 ... *F2
Alegrete 54,786 ... B10
Além Paralba 23,028 ... *E2
Alenquer 16,477 ... C3
Alfenas 31,815 ... *D2
Altamira 24,846 ... C3
Altos 13,621 ... F4
Amambal 12,507 ... C8
Amapá 2,676 ... D2
Amarante 6,848 ... F4
Amargosa 11,118 ... F6
Americana 121,794 ... *C3
Amparo 26,970 ... *C3
Anápolis 160,520 ... D7
Anchieta 5,741 ... F8
Andaral 2,476 ... F6
Andradina 42,036 ... D8
Andrelândia 8,737 ... *D2
Angra dos Reis 24,894 ... *D3
Antonina 11,950 ... *B4
Aparecida 27,265 ... *D3
Apiai 7,809 ... *B4
Aquidauana 21,514 ... C8
Aracaju 288,106 ... G5
Aracati 20,282 ... G4
Araçatuba 113,486 ... *A2
Araçuaí 12,292 ... F7
Araquari 73,302 ... D7
Araranquá 22,468 ... D10
Araraquara 77,202 ... *B2
Araras 54,323 ... *C3
Araxá 51,339 ... E7
Arcoverde 40,646 ... G5
Areia Branca 12,979 ... G4
Assis 57,217 ... *A3
Avaré 40,716 ... *B3
Bacabai 43,229 ... E4
Bagé 66,743 ... C10
Bahia (Salvador) 1,496,276 ... G6
Baixo Guandu 13,714 ... F7
Balsas 13,566 ... E4
Bambui 14,172 ... *C2
Barão de Cocais 11,950 ... *E1
Barbacena 69,675 ... *E2
Bariri 15,372 ... *B3
Barra 10,809 ... F5
Barra do Corda 19,280 ... E4
Barra do Piraí 51,214 ... *E3
Barra Mansa 123,421 ... *D3
Barras 8,904 ... F4
Barreiras 30,355 ... E6
Barreiros 19,419 ... H5
Barretos 65,294 ... *B2
Batatais 30,478 ... *C2
Baturité 12,388 ... G4
Bauru 178,861 ... *B3
Bebedouro 39,070 ... *B2
Bela Vista 11,936 ... C8
Belém 758,117 ... E3
Belém †1,000,349 ... E3
Belo Horizonte 1,442,483 ... *D1
Belo Horizonte †2,541,788 ... *D1
Benjamin Constant 6,563 ... G9
Bento Gonçalves 40,323 ... C10
Betim 71,599 ... *D2
Bicas 8,611 ... *E2
Birigui 45,348 ... *A2
Blumenau 144,819 ... D9
Boa Esperanca 17,394 ... *D2
Boa Vista 43,131 ... H8
Bocaiúva 16,616 ... E7
Bom Conselho 13,196 ... G5
Bom Despacho 22,941 ... *D1
Bom Jesus da Lapa 19,978 ... F6
Bom Sucesso 10,331 ... *D2
Borba 5,366 ... H9
Bragança Paulista 61,021 ... *C3
Brasiléia 4,835 ... G10
Brasília (cap.) 411,305 ... E6
Brasilia de Minas 10,171 ... F7
Brejo 5,859 ... F3
Breves 31,452 ... D3
Brumado 24,663 ... F6
Brusque 37,898 ... D9
Cabedolo 18,581 ... H4
Cabo Frio 40,668 ... *F3
Caçador 25,287 ... D9
Caçapava 45,258 ... *D3
Caçapava do Sul 15,180 ... C10
Cáceres 33,472 ... B7
Cachoeira 11,520 ... G6
Cachoeira do Sul 59,967 ... C10
Cachoeiro de Itapemirim 84,994 ... G8
Caeté 23,331 ... *E1
Caetité 8,823 ... F6
Caiaponia 9,358 ... C7
Caicó 30,777 ... G4
Cajazeiras 30,834 ... G4
Cajuru 9,670 ... *C2
Camaquá 28,078 ... C10
Cambará 13,218 ... *A3
Cambui 8,552 ... *C3
Cametá 15,539 ... D3
Camocim 19,921 ... F3
Campina Grande 222,229 ... G4
Campinas 566,517 ... *C3
Campo Belo 30,392 ... *D2
Campo Formoso 10,324 ... F5
Campo Grand 282,844 ... C8
Campo Largo 34,506 ... *B4
Campo Major 24,009 ... F4
Campos 174,218 ... *F2
Cananéia 5,581 ... *C4
Canavieiras 14,076 ... G6
Canindé 18,573 ... G4
Canoas 214,115 ... D10
Canoinhas 25,880 ... D9
Capanema 28,272 ... E3
Capão Bonito 24,081 ... *B4
Caraguatatuba 22,932 ... *D3
Carangola 15,621 ... *E2
Caratinga 39,621 ... *E1
Caravelas 3,704 ... G7
Carazinho 41,913 ... C10
Carolina 10,136 ... E4
Caruaru 137,636 ... G5
Casa Banca 13,739 ... *C2
Cascavel 16,238 ... G4
Cássia 10,701 ... *C2
Castanhal 51,797 ... E3
Castelo 9,162 ... F8
Castro 21,079 ... *B4
Castro Alves 11,286 ... G6
Cataguases 40,659 ... *F2
Catalão 30,516 ... E7
Catanduva 64,813 ... *B2
Catolé do Rocha 12,165 ... G4
Caxambu 16,221 ... *D2
Caxias 56,755 ... F4
Caxlas do Sul 198,824 ... D10
Ceará (Fortaleza) 648,815 ... G3
Ceará-Mirim 17,097 ... H4
Ceres 13,671 ... D6
Chapecó 53,198 ... C9
Coari 14,841 ... H9
Codajás 4,923 ... H9
Codó 11,593 ... E4
Colatina 61,057 ... F7
Conceição do Araguaia 18,143 ... D5
Concórdia 17,973 ... D9
Conselheiro Lafaiete 66,262 ... E2
Corinto 17,056 ... E7
Cornélio Procópio 31,201 ... D8
Coroatá 16,070 ... F3
coromandel 11,604 ... F7
Corumbá 66,014 ... B7
Coxim 14,876 ... C7
Crateús 29,905 ... F4
Crato 49,244 ... G4
Criciúma 74,003 ... D10
Cristalina 10,521 ... E7
Cruz Alta 53,315 ... C10
Cruzeiro 55,175 ... *D3
Cruzeiro do Sul 11,189 ... G10
Cubatão 78,327 ... *C3
Cuiabá 167,894 ... C6
Curitiba 843,733 ... *B4
Curitiba †1,441,743 ... *B4
Currais Novos 25,663 ... G4
Cururupu 10,358 ... E3
Curvelo 37,734 ... E7
Diamantina 20,197 ... F7
Divinópolis 108,344 ... *D2
Dois Córregos 11,811 ... *B3
Dom Pedrito 25,773 ... C10
Dores do Indaiá 13,058 ... E7
Dourados 76,838 ... C8
Duque de Caxias 306,057 ... *E3
Erexim 46,927 ... C9
Esperanca 12,964 ... G4
Esplanada 9,822 ... G5
Estancia 28,250 ... G5
Feira de Santana 225,003 ... G5
Fernandópolis 39,737 ... *A2
Floriano 35,761 ... F4
Florianópolis 153,547 ... E9
Fonte Boa 3,278 ... G9
Formiga 36,681 ... *D2
Formosa 29,304 ... E6
Fortaleza 648,815 ... G3
Fortaleza †1,581,588 ... G3
Foz do Iguacu 93,619 ... C9
Franca 143,630 ... *C2
Frutal 22,955 ... *B2
Garanhuns 64,854 ... G5
Garca 26,527 ... *B3
Goiana 30,108 ... H4
Goiânia 703,263 ... D7
Goiás 15,768 ... D6
Governador Valadares 173,699 ... F7
Grajaú 11,147 ... E4
Guacul 12,715 ... *F2
Guajará-Mirim 19,992 ... H10
Guarapuava 17,189 ... C9
Guarantiguetá 68,370 ... *D3
Guarujá 67,730 ... *C4
Guarulhos 395,117 ... *C3
Guaxupé 23,637 ... *C2
Guirantinga 8,981 ... C7
Gurupi 27,39 ... D5
Humaitá 10,004 ... H10
Ibaiti 11,352 ... *A3
Ibiá 11,161 ... E7
Ibicaraí 18,202 ... G6
Ibitinga 23,359 ... *B2
Icó 13,007 ... G4
Igarapava 15,342 ... C2
Igarapé-Miri 12,172 ... D3
Iguape 16,827 ... *C4
Iguatu 39,611 ... G4
Ijui 51,925 ... C10
Ilhéus 71,240 ... G6
Imbituba 9,998 ... D10
Imperatiz 111,818 ... E4
Inhumas 23,455 ... D7
Ipameri 14,163 ... E7
Ipu 12,787 ... F4
Irati 21,956 ... *A4
Itabaiana, Paralba 17,843 ... H4
Itabaiana, Sergipe 26,055 ... G5
Itaberaba 27,590 ... F6
Itabira 57,691 ... F7
Itabirito 22,978 ... *E2
Itabuna 129,938 ... G6
Itacoatiara 26,737 ... B3
Itaituba 19,644 ... C4
Itajai 78,867 ... D9
Itajubá 53,506 ... *D3
Itanhaem 26,181 ... C4
Itapecerica 10,234 ... *D2
Itapecuru-Mirim 12,216 ... F3
Itapemirim 16,829 ... F8
Itaperuna 34,644 ... *F2
Itapetinga 36,897 ... G6
Itapetininga 61,344 ... *B3
Itapeva 36,551 ... *B3
Itapipoca 19,463 ... G3
Itapira 36,308 ... *C3
Itápolis 13,750 ... *B2
Itaporanga 8,988 ... G4
Itaqui 23,136 ... B10
Itararé 24,368 ... *B4
Itatiba 35,537 ... *C3
Itaúna 49,372 ... *D2
Itu 62,211 ... *C3
Ituacu 1,749 ... F6
Ituiutaba 65,178 ... D7
Itumbiara 56,602 ... D7
Iturama 12,363 ... *A1
Ituverava 21,323 ... *C2
Jaboatao 67,129 ... H5
Jaboticabal 40,276 ... *B2
Jacarel 103,652 ... *D3
Jacarezinho 23,684 ... *A3
Jacobina 26,723 ... F5
Jacupiranga 7,044 ... B4
Jaguaquara 11,336 ... F6
Jaguarao 18,165 ... C11
Jaguariaiva 8,566 ... *B4
Januária 20,484 ... E6
Jatai 40,957 ... D7
Jaú 59,522 ... *B3
Jequié 84,792 ... F6
Jequitinhonha 10,900 ... F7
Ji-Paraná 31,724 ... H10
Joacaba 16,195 ... D9
Joao Pessoa 290,424 ... H4
Joao Pinheiro 17,013 ... E7
Joinvile 217,074 ... D9
Juazeiro 60,940 ... G5
Juazeiro do Norte 125,248 ... F4
Juiz de Fora 299,728 ... *E2
Jundiai 210,015 ... *C3
Lages 108,768 ... D9
Laguna 27,743 ... D10
Lambari 9,722 ... *D2
Lapa 13,314 ... D9
Laranjeiras do Sul 19,329 ... C9
Lavras 35,345 ... *D2
Leme 40,155 ... *C3
Leopoldina 28,554 ... *E2
Limeira 137,812 ... *C3
Limoeiro 36,088 ... H4
Limoeiro do Norte 13,112 ... G4
Linhares 51,575 ... F7
Lins 44,633 ... *B2
Londrina 258,054 ... D8
Lorena 51,276 ... *D3
Luis Correia 3,576 ... F3
Luz 10,068 ... *D1
Luziania 67,284 ... E7
Macaé 39,644 ... *F3
Macalba 17,036 ... H4
Macapá 89,081 ... D2
Macau 17,543 ... G4
Maceio 376,479 ... H5
Machado 16,164 ... *C2
Mafra 26,226 ... D9
Magé 37,597 ... *E3
Mamanguape 16,321 ... H4
Manacapuru 17,016 ... H9
Manaus 613,068 ... H9
Manhuacu 22,678 ... *E2
Manhumirim 11,085 ... *E2
Manicoré 9,532 ... H9
Marabá 41,564 ... D4
Maracaju 9,699 ... C8
Maragogipe 13,512 ... G6
Maranguape 20,098 ... G3
Marechal Deodoro 9,400 ... H5
Mariana 11,785 ... *E2
Marilla 103,904 ... *A3
Maringá 158,047 ... D8
Mata de São João 23,741 ... G6
Mato Grosso (Vila Bela da Santissima Trindade) 1,401 ... B6
Maués 10,846 ... B3
Mineiros 16,844 ... C7
Miracema 15,545 ... *E2
Miracema do Norte ... D5
Mirassol 25,173 ... *B2
Mococa 33,682 ... *C2
Mogi das Cruzes 122,265 ... *C3
Mogi-Mirim 41,827 ... *C3
Monte Alegre 10,646 ... C3
Monte Aprazivel 9,767 ... *A2
Monteiro 11,051 ... G4
Montenegro 27,246 ... D10
Montes Claros 151,881 ... E7
Morrinhos 20,154 ... D7
Mossoró 118,007 ... G4
Muriaé 50,040 ... *E2
Muzambinho 8,803 ... *C2
Nanuque 34,445 ... F7
Natal 376,552 ... H4
Nazaré 18,068 ... G6
Niquelandia 8,828 ... D6
Niterói 386,185 ... *E3
Nova Cruz 12,824 ... H4
Nova Era 11,126 ... *E1
Nova Friburgo 88,943 ... *E3
Nova Iguaçu 491,802 ... *E3
Nova Lima 35,035 ... *E2
Nova Russas 10,021 ... F4
Novo Hamburgo 132,066 ... D10
Novo Horizonte 18,439 ... *B2
Óbidos 17,143 ... C3
Oeiras 12,406 ... F4
Olimpia 24,376 ... *B2
Olinda 266.392 ... H4
Oliveira 22,642 ... *D2
Oriximiná 12,078 ... C3
Orlândia 22,924 ... *C2
Osasco 376,689 ... *C3
Ourinhos 52,698 ... *B3
Ouro Preto 27,821 ... *E2
Palmares 40,624 ... H5
Palmas 15,823 ... C9
Palmeira 11,521 ... *B4
Palmeira das Missões 23,943 ... C9
Pará (Belém) 758,117 ... E3
Paracatu 29,911 ... E7
Pará de Minas 37,127 ... *D1
Paraguaçu Paulista 17,399 ... D8
Paralba do Sul 13,510 ... *E3
Paranalba 21,305 ... D7
Paranaguá 68,366 ... *B4
Parati 8,684 ... *D3
Parintins 29,369 ... B3
Parnalba 78,718 ... F3
Passo Fundo 103,121 ... D10
Passos 56,998 ... *C2
Patos 58,735 ... G4
Patos de Minas 59,896 ... E7
Patrocínio 29,520 ... E7
Pau dos Ferros 12,985 ... G4
Paulo Afonso 62,066 ... G5
Pederneiras 18,864 ... *B3
Pedra Azul 13,615 ... F6
Pedreiras 30,843 ... E4
Pedro Segundo 9,693 ... F4
Pelotas 197,092 ... C10
Penápolis 32,168 ... *A2
Penedo 27,064 ... G5
Pernambuco (Recife) 1,184,215 ... H5
Petrolina 73,436 ... G5
Petrópolis 149,427 ... *E3
Picos 33,098 ... F4
Piedade 13,054 ... *C3
Pilar 14,778 ... H5
Pindamonhangaba 51,174 ... *D3

(continued on following page)

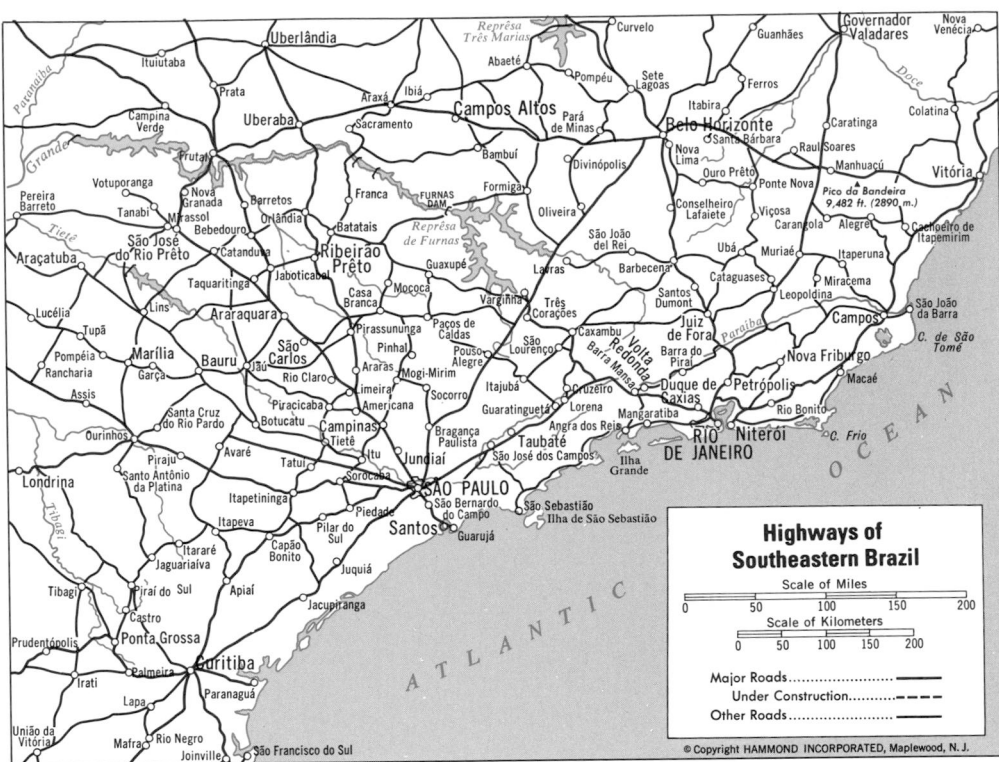

Highways of Southeastern Brazil

Scale of Miles
0   50   100   150   200

Scale of Kilometers
0   50   100   150   200

Major Roads ....
Under Construction ....
Other Roads ....

© Copyright HAMMOND INCORPORATED, Maplewood, N.J.

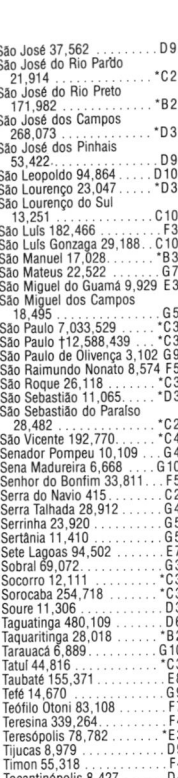

Agriculture, Industry and Resources

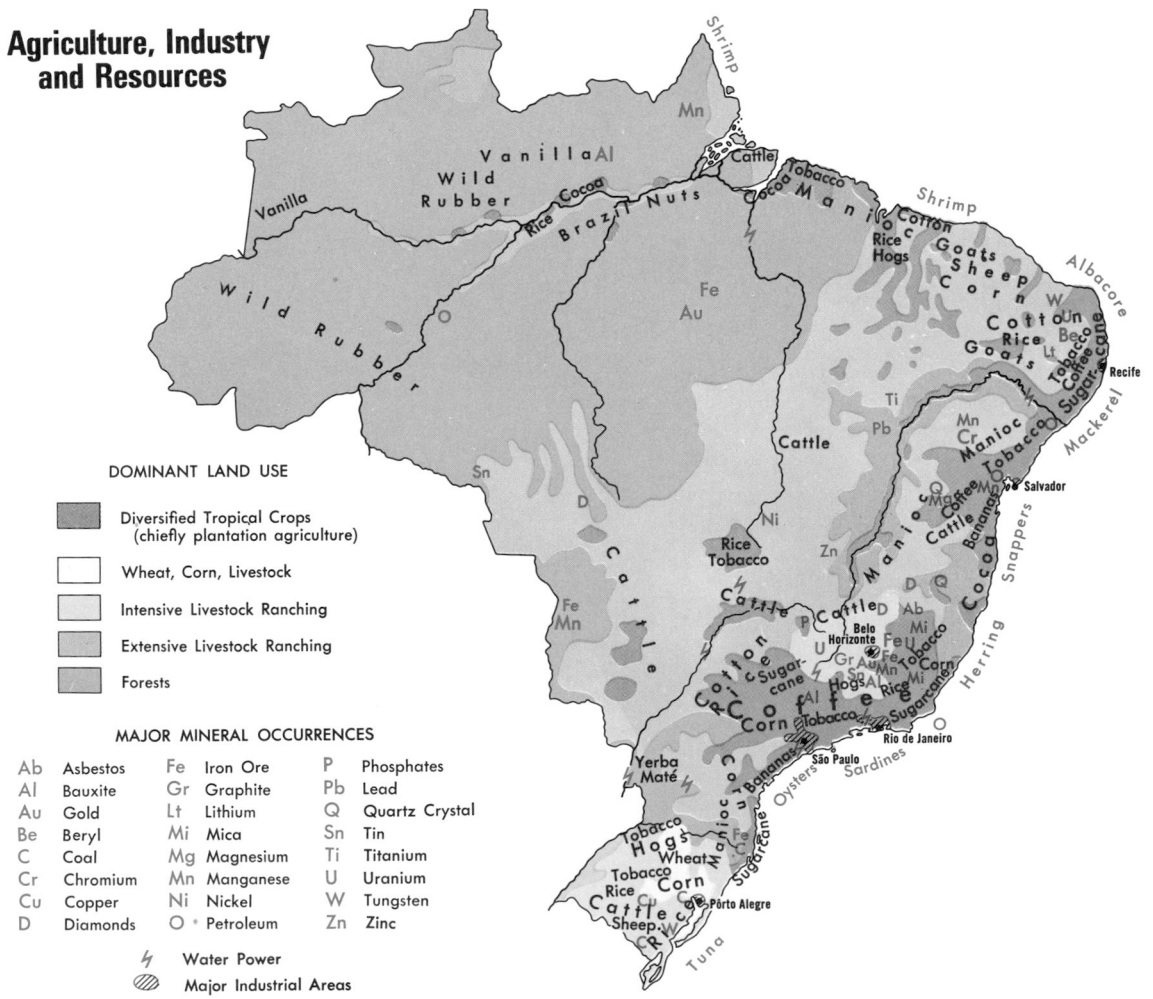

DOMINANT LAND USE

Diversified Tropical Crops
(chiefly plantation agriculture)

Wheat, Corn, Livestock

Intensive Livestock Ranching

Extensive Livestock Ranching

Forests

MAJOR MINERAL OCCURRENCES

Ab	Asbestos	Fe	Iron Ore	P	Phosphates
Al	Bauxite	Gr	Graphite	Pb	Lead
Au	Gold	Lt	Lithium	Q	Quartz Crystal
Be	Beryl	Mi	Mica	Sn	Tin
C	Coal	Mg	Magnesium	Ti	Titanium
Cr	Chromium	Mn	Manganese	U	Uranium
Cu	Copper	Ni	Nickel	W	Tungsten
D	Diamonds	O	Petroleum	Zn	Zinc

⚡ Water Power

▨ Major Industrial Areas

Três Corações 36,179 . . . . . *D2
Três Lagoas 45,171 . . . . . . C8
Três Pontas 24,225 . . . . . *D2
Três Rios 47,497 . . . . *E3
Trindade 22,321 . . . . D7
Tubarão 64,585 . . . . D10
Tucuruí 27,209 . . . . D3
Tupã 44,450 . . . . *A2
Tupancíretã 13,103 . . . . . C10
Tutóia 4,766 . . . . F3
Ubá 43,080 . . . . *E2
Ubaitaba 9,413 . . . . G6
Ubatuba 23,078 . . . . *D3
Uberaba 180,296 . . . . *C1
Uberlândia 230,400 . . . . . E7
Unaí 28,148 . . . . E7
União 9,396 . . . . F4
União da Vitória 22,682 . . . D9
União dos Palmares 20,876 . H5
Uruaçu 19,607 . . . . D6
Uruçuí 6,047 . . . . E4
Uruguaiana 79,059 . . . . . . B10
Vacaria 37,370 . . . . D10
Valença 34,231 . . . . *E3
Varginha 57,448 . . . . *D2
Viana 9,753 . . . . E3
Viçosa 9,843 . . . . G5
Viçosa 29,198 . . . . *E2
Vigia 14,749 . . . . E3
Vila Velha Argolas 74,166 . . F8
Vilhena 12,565 . . . . H10
Visconde dos Rio Branco
  17,295 . . . . *E2
Vitória 144,143 . . . . G8
Vitória da Conquista 125,717 F6
Vitória de Santo Antão
  62,890 . . . . G4
Volta Redonda 177,772 . . . *D3
Votuporanga 44,169 . . . . . *B2
Xapuri 3,122 . . . . G10
Xique-Xique 17,625 . . . . . . F5

OTHER FEATURES

Abacaxis (riv.) B4
Abunã (riv.) G10
Acaraí, Serra do (range) . . B2
Acre (riv.) G10
Aiama (lake) H9
Amambaí, Serra de (range) . C7
Amapari (riv.) C2
Amazon (riv.) C3

Anauá (riv.) B2
Aporé (riv.) D7
Araguaia (riv.) D4
Araguari (riv.) D2
Araruama (lake) *E3
Arinos (riv.) D3
Aripuanã (riv.) A4
Armando Laydner (res.) . . *B3
Bailique (isl.) C2
Balsas (riv.) E5
Bananal (isl.) D5
Bandeira, Pico da (mt.) . *E2, F8
Braço Maior do Araguaia
  (riv.) D5
Braço Menor do Araguaia
  (riv.) D6
Branco (riv.) H3
Buzios (cape) *F3
Canumã (riv.) B4
Capim (riv.) D3
Carajás, Serra dos (range) . C4
Cardoso (isl.) *C4
Cassiporé (cape) C2
Caviana (isl.) D2
Chavantes, Serra dos
  (range) D7
Claro (riv.) D7
Comprida (isl.) *C4
Cuiabá (riv.) B7
Culuene (riv.) C6
Curuá (riv.) C4
Doce (riv.) *E2, F7
Dois Irmãos, Serra (range) . F5
Espigão Mestre (Geral
  de Goiás) (range) E6
Espinhaço, Serra do (range) . F7
Estrondo, Serra do (range) . D4
Feia (lake) *F3
Feio (riv.) *B2
Formosa, Serra (range) . . . C5
Frio (cape) *F3
Furnas (lake) *C2
Geral de Goiás, Serra
  (range) E6
Gi-Paraná (riv.) H10
Gradaús, Serra do (range) . D4
Grajaú (riv.) E4
Grande (isl.) *D3
Grande (riv.) *B2, E8
Guanabara (bay) *E3
Guaporé (riv.) H10

Gurguéia (riv.) E5
Gurupi, Serra do (range) . . E4
Gurupi (riv.) E3
Ibicuí (riv.) C10
Içá (riv.) G9
Iguaçu (riv.) C9
Iguazú (falls) C9
Pará (riv.) D3
Paracatu (riv.) E7
Ilha Grande (bay) *D3
Iriri (riv.) C4
Itaipu (dam) C9
Itaipu (res.) C9
Itapecuru (riv.) F4
Itapi (riv.) B3
Itapicuru (riv.) G5
Itararé (riv.) *B3
Ivaí (riv.) C8
Jaculpe (riv.) F5
Jaguaribe (riv.) G4
Jamanxim (riv.) C4
Japurá (riv.) G9
Jari (riv.) C3
Jauari, Serra (mts.) C3
Javari (riv.) F9
Jequitinhonha (riv.) F7
Juruá (riv.) G10
Juruena (riv.) B5
Jutaí (riv.) G9
Lombarda, Serra (mts.) . . . D2
Madeira (riv.) A4
Mangueira (lag.) D11
Manso (riv.) C6
Mantiqueira (range) *D3
Mapuera (riv.) B3
Mar, Serra do (range) . *C4, E9
Maracá (isl.) C2
Marajó (bay) E2
Marajó (isl.) 147,895 . . . . D3
Mato Grosso, Planalto de
  (plat.) B6
Maués-Açu (riv.) B4
Mearim (riv.) E4
Mexiana (isl.) D2
Miranda (riv.) B8
Mirim (lag.) C11
Mogi Guaçu (riv.) *C2
Mortes (Manso) (riv.) D6
Neblina, Pico da (peak) . . . G8
Negro (riv.) H9
Nhamundá (riv.) B3
Norte, Serra do (range) . . . B5
Oiapoque (Oyapock) (riv.) . C2

Orange (cape) D1
Órgãos (range) *E3
Oyapock (riv.) C2
Pacajá Grande (riv.) D4
Pacaraimã, Serra da (mts.) . H8
Papagaio (riv.) B6
Pará (riv.) D3
Paracatu (riv.) E7
Paraguaçu (riv.) F6
Paraguaí (riv.) B8
Paraíba (riv.) *D3
Paraná (riv.) C8
Paraná (riv.) C9
Paranapanema (riv.) . . *B3, C8
Paranapiacaba (range) . . . *B4
Paranatinga (riv.) C6
Pardo (riv.) *B2, D8
Pardo (riv.) C8
Pardo (riv.) F6
Parecís, Serra dos (range) . B6
Parnaíba (riv.) F3
Paru (riv.) C3
Patos (lag.) D10
Penitente, Serra do (range) . E5
Piauí, Serra do (range) . . . F5
Piauí (riv.) F5
Purus (riv.) H9
Ribeira (riv.) *B4
Roncador, Serra do (range) . D5
Roosevelt (riv.) A5
Santa Catarina (isl.) 138,556 E9
São Lourenço (riv.) C7
São Marcos (bay) F3
São Roque (cape) H4
São Francisco (riv.) . . *D2, G5
São Sebastião (isl.) 5,724 . *D3, E8
São Tomé (cape) F8
Sapucaí (riv.) *D2
Sepetiba (bay) *D3
Sete Quedas (falls) C9
Sete Quedas (Grande) (isl.) . C8
Sobradino (res.) F5
Sono (riv.) E5
Sul (chan.) D2
Tacutu (riv.) B2
Tapajós (riv.) B4
Tapuari (riv.) C7
Tefé (riv.) G9
Teles Pires (riv.) B5

Tibagi (riv.) *A4
Tietê (riv.) *B2, D8
Tiracambu, Serra (range) . . E3
Tocantins (riv.) D3
Tombador, Serra do (range) . B6
Trombetas (riv.) B3
Tucuruí (res.) D4
Tumucumaque, Serra de
  (range) C2

Turvo (riv.) *B2
Uaupés (riv.) G9
Uraricoera (riv.) H8
Urubu (riv.) A3
Urubupungá (dam) B6
Urucún, Morro do (mt.) . . . B7
Uruguai (riv.) D4
Vasa Barris (riv.) G5
Velhas (riv.) E7

Verde (riv.) C7
Verdinho (riv.) D7
Xavantes (res.) *B3
Xingu (riv.) C3

†Population of met. area.
*preceding reference indicates
that the name will be found on
S.E. Brazil map, page 135.

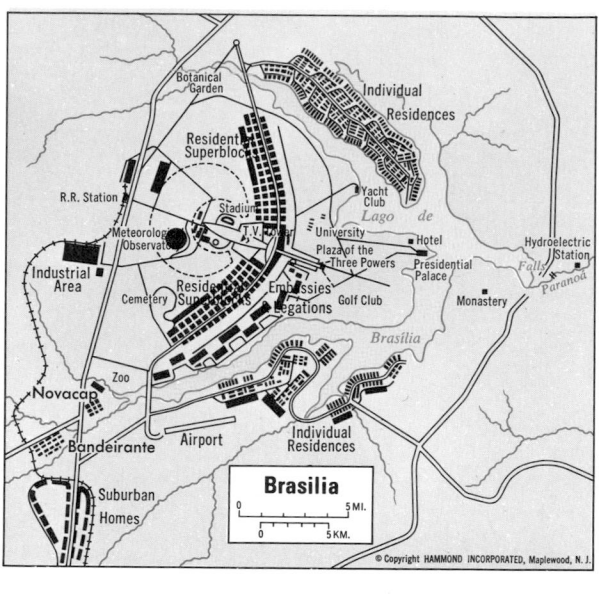

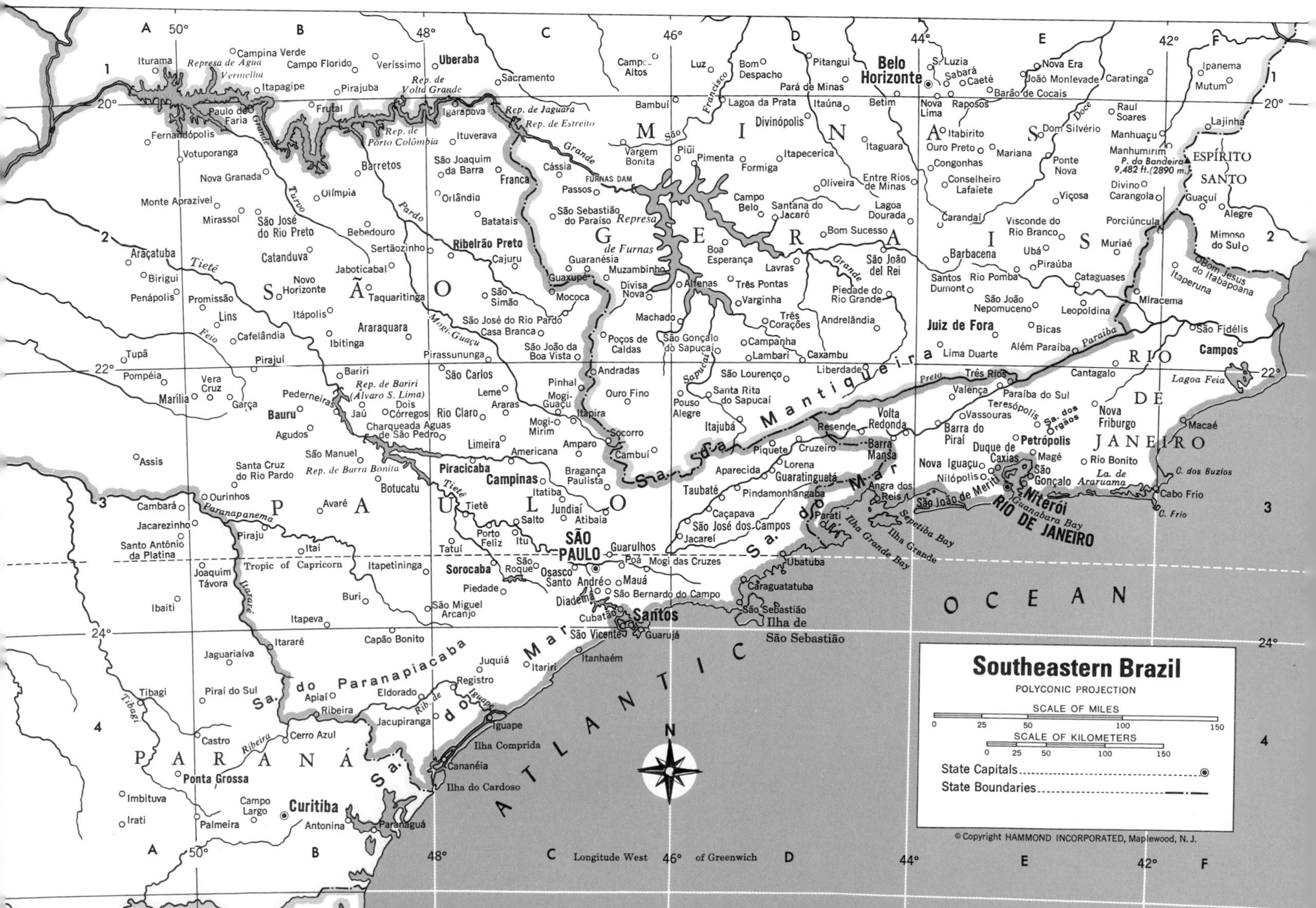

Brasilia

© Copyright HAMMOND INCORPORATED, Maplewood, N.J.

Southeastern Brazil

POLYCONIC PROJECTION

SCALE OF MILES

SCALE OF KILOMETERS

State Capitals . . . . ⊙
State Boundaries . . . . — —

© Copyright HAMMOND INCORPORATED, Maplewood, N.J.

DEPARTMENTS

Beni, El 168,367 ....C3
Chuquisaca 358,516 ....C6
Cochabamba 720,952 ......C5
La Paz 1,465,078 ....A4
Oruro 310,409 ....A6
Pando 34,493 ....B2
Potosí 657,743 ....B7
Santa Cruz 710,724 ....E5
Tarija 187,204 ....D7

CITIES and TOWNS

Achacachi 3,621 ....A5
Aiquile 3,465 ....C5
Alto Seco 3,414 ....D6
Amarete 992 ....A5
Ancoraimes 769 ....A4
Añez (Ascención) D4
Anzaldo 1,056 ....C6
Apolo 1,043 ....A4
Araca‡ 3,537 ....B5

Arampampa 829 ....B5
Arani 2,200 ....C5
Arcopongo‡ 2,223 ....B5
Aromat 873 ....B6
Arque 1,254 ....B5
Ascención (Añez) 2,097 ....D4
Atocha‡ 3,964 ....B7
Ayacucho 729 ....D5
Azurduy 1,234 ....C6
Baures 592 ....D3
Berenguela‡ 2,412 ....A5
Betanzos 1,097 ....C6

Boyuibe 537 ....D7
Cachuela Esperanza 1,073 .....C2
Caiza 838 ....C7
Calamarca 802 ....A5
Callapa 636 ....A5
Camacho‡ 875 ....C7
Camargo 1,609 ....C7
Camatindi‡ 297 ....D7
Camiri 4,969 ....C6
Capinota 1,734 ....B5
Caquiaviri 760 ....A5
Carabuco 626 ....A4

Caracollo 909 ....B5
Caranavi‡ 525 ....B4
Carandaiti 1,403 ....D7
Carmen‡ 845 ....B2
Cataricahua 3,240 ....A5
Cavinas‡ 1,011 ....B3
Chaguaya 643 ....C7
Challana‡ 1,206 ....A4
Challapata 2,529 ....B6
Charagua 1,185 ....D6
Charaña 794 ....A5
Chayanta 1,272 ....B6

Choquecut‡ 1,976 ....A6
Chulumani 2,362 ....B5
Chuma 931 ....B4
Chuquichambi‡ 1,094 ....B5
Chuquichuqui‡ 1,892 ....C6
Cliza 3,121 ....B5
Cobija 3,650 ....A2
Cocani‡ 658 ....C5
Cocapata‡ 2,855 ....B5
Cochabamba 204,684 ....C5
Cohoni 890 ....B5
Colquechaca 1,070 ....B6

Colquiri 806 ....B5
Comarapa 1,096 ....C5
Concepción 1,056 ....D5
Condo‡ 5,525 ....B6
Conquista‡ 1,162 ....B2
Copacabana 1,981 ....A5
Coripata 1,647 ....B5
Corocoro 4,431 ....A5
Coroico 2,235 ....B5
Cotagaita 1,353 ....C7
Cotoca 915 ....D5
Cuevo 902 ....D7

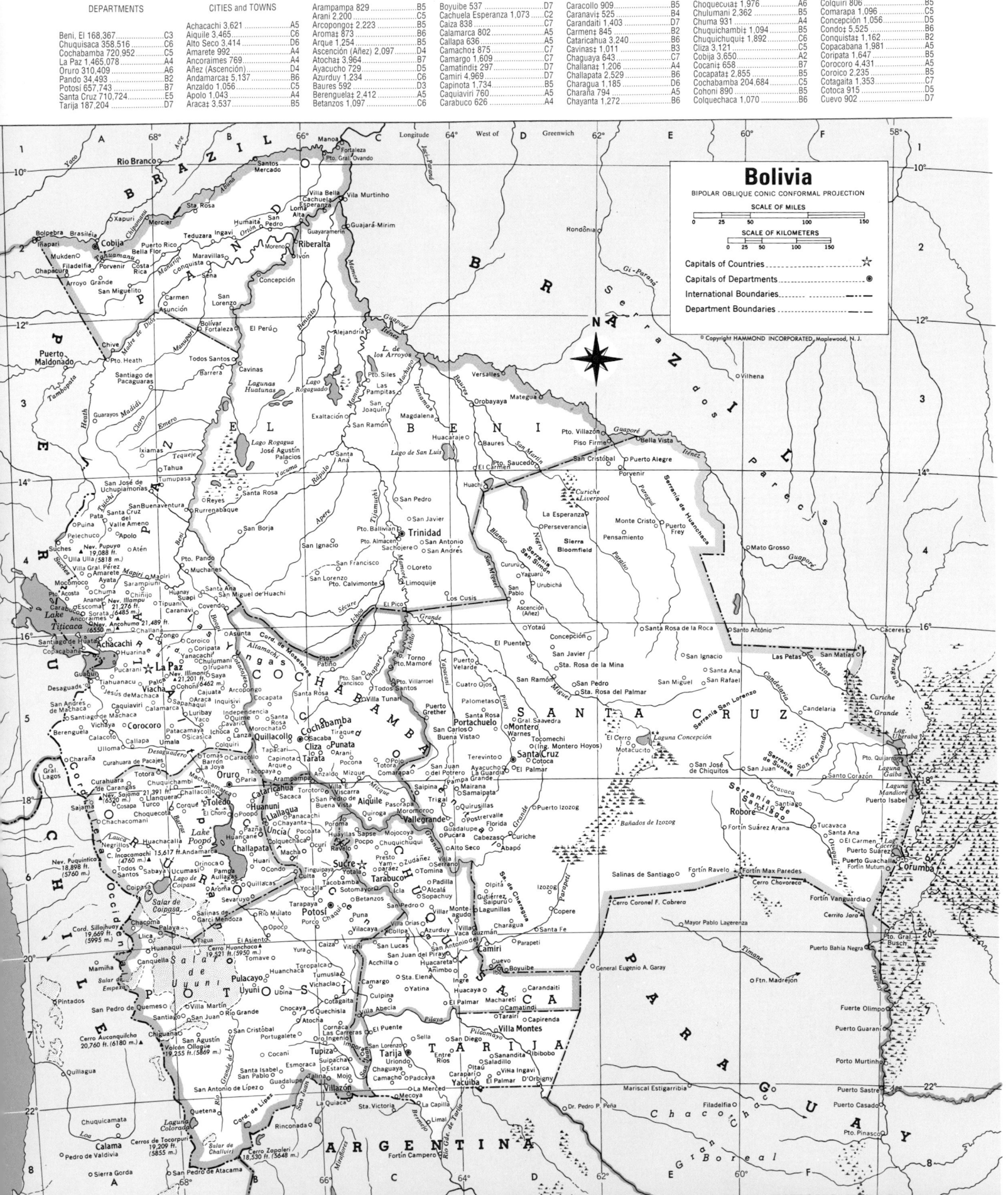

Culpina 981 .... C7
Culta‡ 4,412 .... B6
Curahuara de Pacajes 510 .... A5
El Palmar, Chuquisaca‡ 772 .... D7
El Palmar, Tarija 832 .... D7
El Puente, Santa Cruz‡ 1,185 .... D5
El Puente, Tarija‡ 1,310 .... C7
Entre Ríos 1,011 .... C7
Esmoraca‡ 1,137 .... B7
Estarca‡ 2,331 .... C7
Filadelfia‡ 942 .... A2
Fortaleza‡ 765 .... B3
Fortín Mutum F6
General Saavedra 1,006 .... D5
Guadalupe 2,355 .... C6
Guaqui 2,266 .... A5
Guayaramerín 1,470 .... C2
Huacaraje 673 .... D3
Huachacalla 801 .... A6
Huanay 574 .... B4
Huanchaca B7
Huanuni 5,696 .... B6
Huari 1,070 .... B6
Huarina 1,151 .... A5
Ichoca 591 .... B5
Independencia 1,742 .... B5
Ingeniero Montero Hoyos (Tocomechi) 575 .... D5
Inquisivi 530 .... B5
Irupana 1,937 .... B5
Ivón‡ 772 .... C2
Izozog‡ 2,759 .... D6
Jesús de Machaca 529 .... A5
José Agustín Palacios‡ 2,273 .... B3
La Capilla‡ 1,870 .... C8
Lagunillas 840 .... D6
La Merced‡ 688 .... C8
Lanza 526 .... B5
La Paz (cap.) 635,283 .... B5
Limal‡ 524 .... C8
Llallagua 6,719 .... B6
Llanquera 613 .... A6
Llica 560 .... A6
Loreto 589 .... C4
Macha 1,050 .... B6
Machacamarca 1,746 .... B5
Macharetí‡ 1,164 .... D7
Magdalena 1,724 .... C3
Mairana 508 .... D6
Mecoya‡ 585 .... C8
Mizque 870 .... C5
Mocomoco 977 .... A4
Mojo 469 .... C7
Mojocoya 498 .... C6
Monteagudo 971 .... D6
Montero 2,713 .... D5
Morochata 461 .... B5
Moromoro 556 .... C6
Motacucito‡ 585 .... E5
Ocurí 1,531 .... C6
Orinoca‡ 2,380 .... B6
Orobayaya‡ 1,132 .... D3
Oro Ingenio‡ 945 .... C7
Oruro 124,213 .... B5
Padcaya 324 .... C7
Padilla 2,462 .... C6
Palaya 300 .... A6
Palca 887 .... A5
Palometas‡ 3,453 .... D5
Pampa Aullagas‡ 1,834 .... B6
Pampa Grande 727 .... D5
Panacachi 952 .... B6
Paria 335 .... B5
Pasorapa 1,016 .... C6
Pata 122 .... A4
Patacamaya 1,278 .... B5
Pazña 671 .... B6
Pelechuco 873 .... A4
Pocoata 859 .... B6
Pocona 518 .... C5
Pocpo‡ 2,791 .... C6
Pojo 1,047 .... C5
Poopó 736 .... B6
Porco 817 .... B6
Poroma 171 .... C6
Portachuelo 2,456 .... D5
Portugalete‡ 1,590 .... B7
Porvenir‡ 846 .... A2
Postrervalle 750 .... D6
Potosí 77,397 .... C6
Presto 725 .... C6
Pucara 762 .... C6
Pucarani 1,041 .... A5
Puerto Acosta 1,302 .... A4
Puerto Almacen 358 .... C4
Puerto General Ovando 658 .... C1
Puerto Heath‡ 570 .... A3
Puerto Rico‡ 539 .... B2
Puerto Siles 357 .... C3
Puerto Suárez 1,159 .... F6
Pulacayo 7,984 .... B7
Puna 852 .... C6
Punata 5,014 .... C5
Quechisla 171 .... C7
Queteña 183 .... B8
Quillacas 1,170 .... B6
Quillacollo 9,123 .... B5
Quime 1,256 .... B5
Quiroga‡ 3,467 .... C6
Quirusillas 433 .... D6
Ravelo 907 .... C6
Reyes 1,404 .... B4
Riberalta 6,549 .... C2
Río Grande 281 .... B7
Río Mulato 381 .... B6
Roboré 3,715 .... F6
Rurrenabaque 1,225 .... B4
Sabaya 649 .... A6
Sacaba 2,752 .... C5
Sacaca 1,778 .... B6
Sachojere 401 .... C4
Saipina 573 .... C6
Sajama 231 .... A6
Saladillo‡ 1,315 .... D7
Salinas de Garci Mendoza 335 .... B6
Samaipata 1,656 .... D6
San Agustín‡ 810 .... B7
Sanandita 379 .... D7
San Andrés 399 .... C4
San Andrés de Machaca 101 .... A5
San Antonio, El Beni 436 .... C4
San Antonio de Lípez‡ 177 .... B7
San Antonio del Parapetí 497 .... D7
San Borja 708 .... B4
San Buenaventura 307 .... A4
San Carlos 570 .... D5
San Cristóbal‡ 1,200 .... B7
San Diego‡ 773 .... D7
San Francisco 185 .... C4
San Ignacio, El Beni 1,757 .... C4
San Ignacio, Santa Cruz 1,819 .... E5
San Javier, El Beni 233 .... C4
San Javier, Santa Cruz 564 .... D5
San Joaquín 1,959 .... C3
San José de Chiquitos 1,933 .... E5
San José de Uchupiamonas 277 .... A4
San Juan, Potosí 131 .... B7
San Juan, Santa Cruz‡ 1,482 .... F5
San Juan del Piray 541 .... C7
San Juan del Potrero 263 .... C5
San Lorenzo, El Beni 496 .... C4
San Lorenzo, Pando‡ 317 .... B2
San Lorenzo, Tarija 785 .... C7
San Lucas 025 .... C7
San Matías 887 .... F5
San Miguel 502 .... E5
San Miguel de Huachi 25 .... B4
San Pablo 11 .... B7
San Pedro, Chuquisaca 182 .... C6
San Pedro, El Beni 262 .... C4
San Pedro, Pando‡ 312 .... B2
San Pedro, Santa Cruz 80 .... D5
San Pedro de Buena Vista 1,094 .... C6
San Pedro de Quemes‡ 290 .... A7
San Rafael‡ 1,282 .... E5
San Ramón, El Beni 1,161 .... C3
San Ramón, Santa Cruz 379 .... D5
Santa Ana, El Beni 2,225 .... C3
Santa Ana, La Paz 171 .... B4
Santa Ana, Santa Cruz 275 .... E5
Santa Ana, Santa Cruz 2,225 .... F6
Santa Cruz 254,682 .... D5
Santa Cruz del Valle Ameno 442 .... A4
Santa Elena‡ 4,474 .... C7
Santa Isabel‡ 323 .... B7
Santa Rosa, Cochabamba‡ 942 .... B5
Santa Rosa, Cochabamba‡ 276 .... C5
Santa Rosa, El Beni 765 .... B4
Santa Rosa, Pando‡ 105 .... B2
Santa Rosa, Santa Cruz 995 .... D5
Santa Rosa de la Mina 99 .... D5
Santa Rosa de la Roca 101 .... E5
Santa Rosa del Palmar 441 .... E5
Santiago, Potosí 172 .... A7
Santiago, Santa Cruz 765 .... F6
Santiago de Huata 948 .... A5
Santiago de Machaca 218 .... A5
Santo Corazón‡ 963 .... F5
Sapahaqui 55 .... B5
Sapse‡ 89 .... C6
Sarampiuni 138 .... A4
Saya 339 .... B5
Sena‡ 660 .... B2
Sevaruyo 475 .... B6
Sicasica 1,486 .... B5
Sopachuy 713 .... C6
Sorata 2,087 .... A4
Sotomayor 510 .... C6
Suapi‡ 1,750 .... B4
Suches‡ 231 .... A4
Sucre (cap.) 63,625 .... C6
Suipacha‡ 2,701 .... C7
Tacobamba‡ 6,933 .... C6
Tacopaya 795 .... B5
Talina 122 .... B7
Tapacarí 980 .... B5
Tarabuco 2,833 .... C6
Tarairí‡ 394 .... D7
Tarapaya 357 .... B6
Tarata 3,016 .... C5
Tarija 38,916 .... C7
Teduzara‡ 271 .... B2
Terevinto‡ 3,790 .... D5
Tiahuanacu 1,227 .... A5
Tinguipaya 766 .... C6
Tipuani‡ 1,216 .... B4
Tiraque 1,390 .... C5
Tocomechi 575 .... D5
Todos Santos, Cochabamba 408 .... C5
Todos Santos, Oruro 68 .... A6
Toledo 3,273 .... B6
Tomás Barrón 1,852 .... B5
Tomave 201 .... B7
Tomina 708 .... C6
Toropalca‡ 199 .... B7
Torotoro 1,233 .... C6
Totora C5
Trigal 749 .... C6
Trinidad 14,505 .... C4
Tumupasa 349 .... B4
Tumusla‡ 526 .... C7
Tupiza 8,248 .... C7
Turco 131 .... A6
Ubina‡ 462 .... B7
Ucumasi‡ 1,040 .... B6
Ulla Ulla 52 .... A4
Ulloma 116 .... A5
Umala 481 .... B5
Uncía 4,507 .... B6
Uriondo 860 .... C7
Urubichá 1,369 .... D4
Uyuni 6,968 .... B7
Vallegrande 5,094 .... C6
Versalles 83 .... D3
Viacha 6,607 .... A5
Vichacla 317 .... C7
Vichaya 422 .... A5
Vilacaya 200 .... C6
Villa Abecia 539 .... C7
Villa Bella 88 .... C2
Villa E. Viscarra 658 .... C6
Villa General Pérez 802 .... A4
Villa Ingavi 122 .... D7
Villa Martín 543 .... B7
Villa Montes 3,105 .... D7
Villa Orías 404 .... C6
Villar 322 .... C6
Villa Serrano 1,570 .... C6
Villa Tunari 510 .... C5
Villa Vaca Guzmán 609 .... D6
Villazón 6,261 .... C7
Vitichi 1,515 .... C7
Warnes 1,571 .... D5
Yaco 835 .... B5
Yacuiba 5,027 .... D7
Yamparaéz 725 .... C6
Yanacachi‡ 1,964 .... B5
Yatina‡ 1,850 .... C7
Yocalla‡ 1,014 .... D6
Yotala 1,554 .... C6
Yura 136 .... B7
Zongo 141 .... B5
Zudáñez 1,868 .... C6

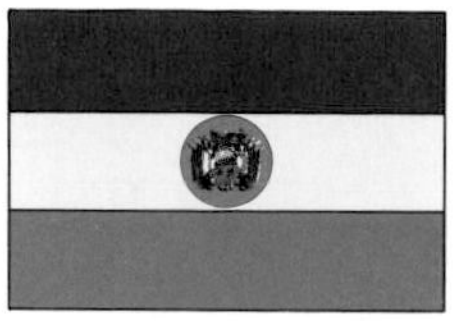

AREA 424,163 sq. mi. (1,098,582 sq. km.)
POPULATION 7,193,000
CAPITALS La Paz, Sucre
LARGEST CITY La Paz
HIGHEST POINT Nevada Ancohuma 21,489 ft. (6,550 m.)
MONETARY UNIT Bolivian peso
MAJOR LANGUAGES Spanish, Quechua, Aymara
MAJOR RELIGION Roman Catholicism

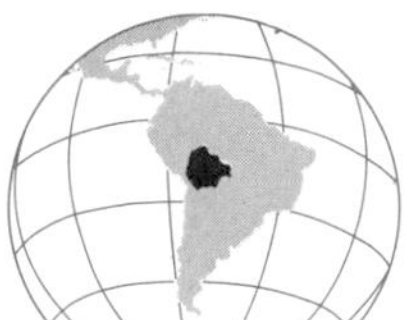

Topography

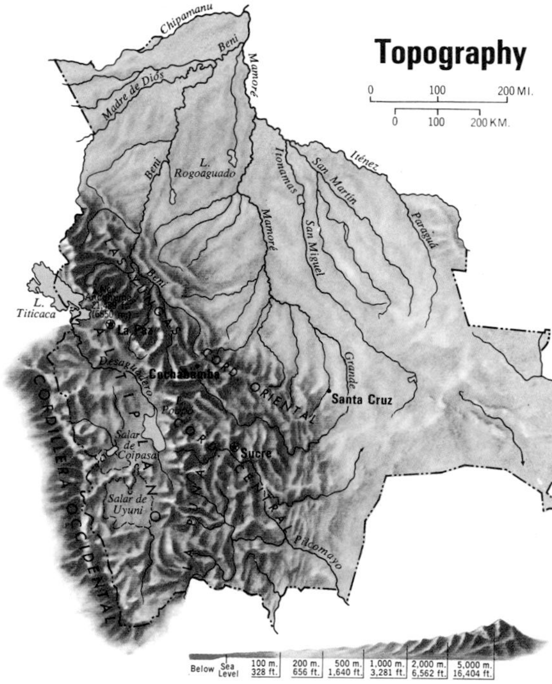

0 100 200 MI.
0 100 200 KM.
Chipamanu
Beni
Madre de Dios
Mamoré
Iténez
San Martín
Paraguá
L. Rogoaguado
Itonamas
San Miguel
L. Titicaca
La Paz
Cochabamba
Santa Cruz
Grande
Sucre
Salar de Coipasa
Salar de Uyuni
Pilcomayo
CORDILLERA OCCIDENTAL
CORDILLERA ORIENTAL
Below Sea Level
100 m. 328 ft.
200 m. 656 ft.
500 m. 1,640 ft.
1,000 m. 3,281 ft.
2,000 m. 6,562 ft.
5,000 m. 16,404 ft.

OTHER FEATURES

Abuná (riv.) B2
Altamachi (riv.) B5
Ancohuma, Nevada (mt.) A4
Apere (riv.) C4
Arroyas, Los (lake) C3
Barrás (riv.) B6
Baures (riv.) D3
Beni (riv.) B4
Benicito (riv.) C3
Bermejo (riv.) C8
Blanco (riv.) D4
Bloomfield, Sierra (mts.) D4
Boopi (riv.) B4
Cáceres (lag.) G6
Candelaria (riv.) F5
Capitán Ustarés, Cerro (mt.) E6
Central, Cordillera (range) C6
Challviri (salt dep.) B8
Chaparé (riv.) C5
Charagua, Sierra de (mts.) D6
Chipamanu (riv.) A2
Chovoreca, Cerro (mt.) F6
Claro (riv.) A3
Coipasa (lake) B6
Coipasa (salt dep.) A6
Colorada (lag.) A8
Concepción (lag.) E5
Coronel F. Gabrera E6
Cotacajes (riv.) B5
Desaguadero (riv.) B5
Emero (riv.) B3
Empexa (salt dep.) A7
Gaiba (lag.) F5
Grande (marsh) F5
Grande (riv.) C4
Grande (riv.) C6
Grande de Lípez (riv.) B7
Guaporé (riv.) C3
Heath (riv.) A3
Huanchaca, Cerro (mt.) B7
Huanchaca, Serranía de (mts.) E4
Huatunas (lag.) B3
Ichilo (riv.) C5
Ichoa (riv.) C4
Illampu, Nevada (mt.) A4
Illimani, Nevada (mt.) B5
Incacamachi, Cerro (mt.) A6
Isiboro (riv.) C5
Iténez (Guaporé) (riv.) C3
Itonamas (riv.) C3
Izozog (swamp) E6
Jara, Cerrito (mt.) F6
Lauca (riv.) A6
Lípez, Cordillera de (range) B8
Liverpool (swamp) D4
Machupo (riv.) C3
Madidi (riv.) A3
Madre de Diós (riv.) A3
Mamoré (riv.) C2
Mandioré (lag.) F6
Manupari (riv.) B3
Manuripi (riv.) B2
Mapiri (riv.) A4
Mizque (riv.) C6
Mosetenes, Cordillera de (range) B5
Negro (riv.) D4
Occidental, Cordillera (range) A6
Ollagüe (vol.) B7
Oriental, Cordillera (range) C5
Ortón (riv.) B2
Otuquis (riv.) F6
Paraguá (riv.) E4
Paraguay (riv.) F7
Paraíso (riv.) E4
Parapetí (riv.) D6
Petas, Las (riv.) F5
Pilaya (riv.) C7
Pilcomayo (riv.) D7
Piray (riv.) D5
Poopó (lake) B6
Pupuya, Nevada (mt.) A4
Puquintica, Nevado (mt.) A6
Rápulo (riv.) C4
Real, Cordillera (range) A5
Rogagua (lake) B3
Rogaguado (lake) C3
Sajama, Nevada (mt.) A6
San Fernando (riv.) F5
San Juan (riv.) C7
San Lorenzo, Serranía (mts.) E5
San Luis (lake) C3
San Martín (riv.) D3
San Miguel (riv.) D4
San Simón, Serranía (mts.) D4
Santiago, Serranía de (mts.) F6
Sécure (riv.) C4
Sillajhuay, Cordillera (mt.) A6
Suches (riv.) A4
Sunsas, Serranía de (mts.) F5
Tahuamanu (riv.) A2
Tarija, Rio Grande de (riv.) C8
Tequeje (riv.) B3
Tijamuchi (riv.) C4
Titicaca (lake) A4
Tocorpuri, Cerros de (mt.) A8
Tucavaca (riv.) F6
Tuichi (riv.) A4
Uberaba (lag.) G5
Uyuni (salt dep.) B7
Yacuma (riv.) B3
Yapacani (riv.) C5
Yata (riv.) C3
Yungas, Las (reg.) B5
Zapaleri, Cerro (mt.) B8

‡Population of canton.

Agriculture, Industry and Resources

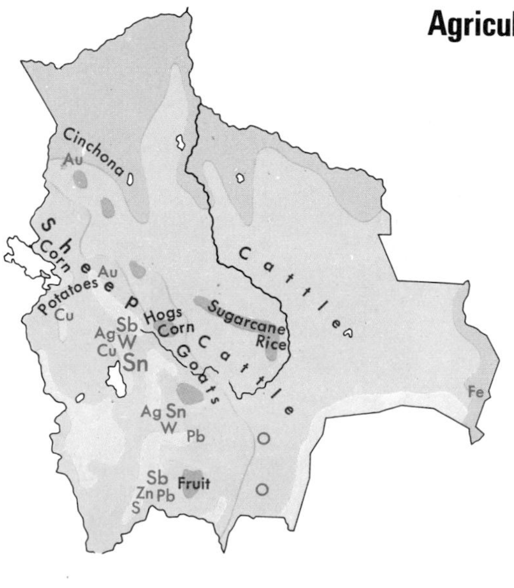

Cinchona
Au
Sheep
Corn
Potatoes
Cu
Ag
Sb
W
Sn
Hogs
Corn
Cattle
Sugarcane
Rice
Cattle
Goats
Pb
Fruit
Zn
S
Fe

DOMINANT LAND USE

- Diversified Tropical Crops (chiefly plantation agriculture)
- Upland Cultivated Areas
- Upland Livestock Grazing, Limited Agriculture
- Extensive Livestock Ranching
- Forests
- Nonagricultural Land

MAJOR MINERAL OCCURRENCES

Ag	Silver	G	Natural Gas	Sb	Antimony
Au	Gold	O	Petroleum	Sn	Tin
Cu	Copper	Pb	Lead	W	Tungsten
Fe	Iron Ore	S	Sulfur	Zn	Zinc

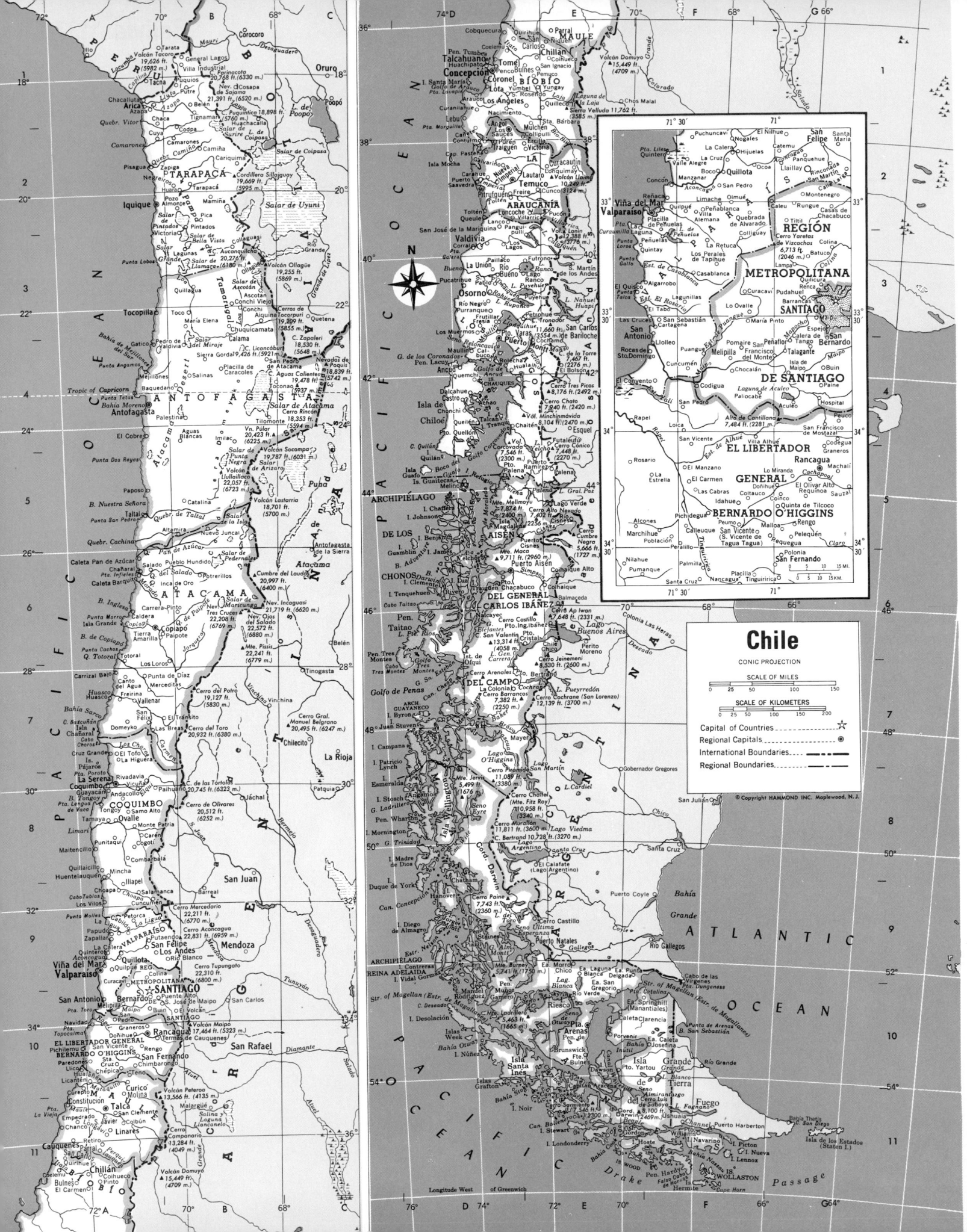

Chile

CONIC PROJECTION

SCALE OF MILES

| 0 | 25 | 50 | 100 | 150 |

SCALE OF KILOMETERS

| 0 | 25 | 50 | 100 | 150 | 200 |

Capital of Countries .... ★
Regional Capitals .... ◉
International Boundaries ....
Regional Boundaries ....

© Copyright HAMMOND INC. Maplewood, N.J.

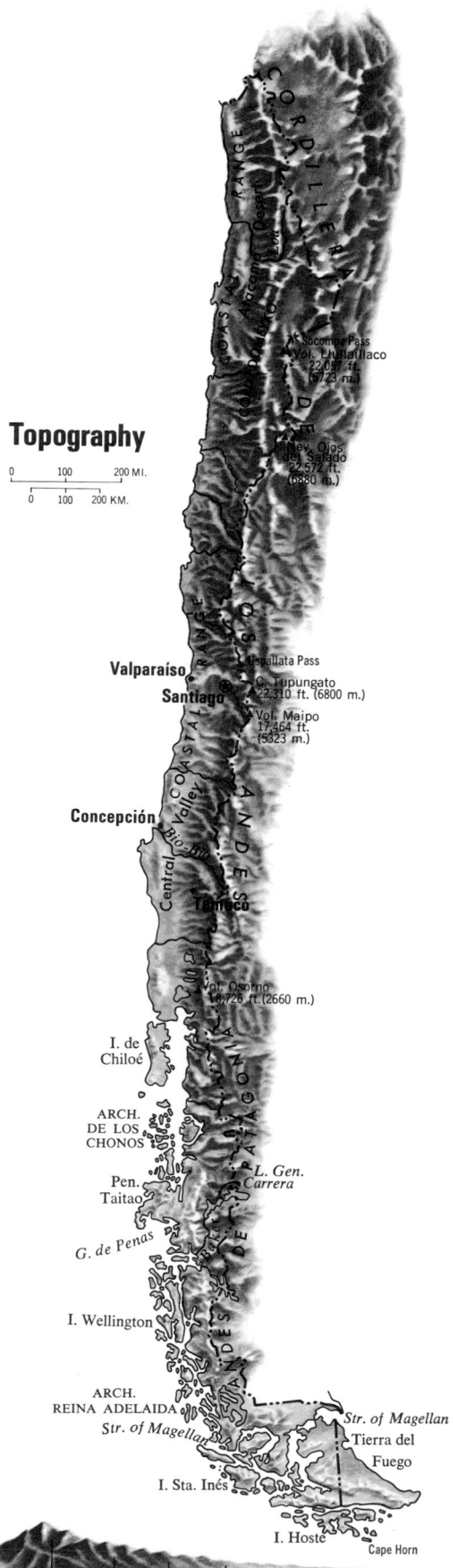

Topography

AREA 292,257 sq. mi. (756,946 sq. km.)
POPULATION 12,961,000
CAPITAL Santiago
LARGEST CITY Santiago
HIGHEST POINT Ojos del Salado 22,572 ft.
(6,880 m.)
MONETARY UNIT Chilean peso
MAJOR LANGUAGE Spanish
MAJOR RELIGION Roman Catholicism

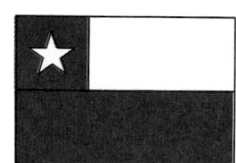

Cordillera (Range)
Vol. Llullaillaco 22,057 ft. (6723 m.)
Sacompe Pass
Vol. Ojos del Salado 22,572 ft. (6880 m.)

Valparaíso
Santiago
C. Tupungato 22,310 ft. (6800 m.)
Uspallata Pass
Vol. Maipo 17,464 ft. (5323 m.)

Concepción
Central Valley
Coastal Range
Bío Bío R.

Talca

Vol. Osorno 8,726 ft.(2660 m.)

I. de Chiloé

ARCH. DE LOS CHONOS

Pen. Taitao
L. Gen. Carrera

G. de Penas

I. Wellington

ARCH. REINA ADELAIDA
Str. of Magellan
Str. of Magellan
Tierra del Fuego
I. Sta. Inés
I. Hoste
Cape Horn

0	100	200 MI.
0	100	200 KM.

| 5,000 m. 16,404 ft. | 2,000 m. 6,562 ft. | 1,000 m. 3,281 ft. | 500 m. 1,640 ft. | 200 m. 656 ft. | 100 m. 328 ft. | Sea Level | Below |

REGIONS

Aisén del General Carlos
  Ibáñez del Campo
  65,478 .... E6
Antofagasta 341,203 ...... B4
Atacama 183,071 .... B6
Bíobío 1,516,552 .... E1
Coquimbo 419,178 .... A8
El Libertador General
  Bernardo O'Higgins
  584,989 .... A10
La Araucanía 692,924 ... E2
Los Lagos 843,430 ...... D3
Magallanes 132,333 ..... E10
Maule 723,224 .... A11
Santiago, Región
  Metropolitana de (Santiago
  Metropolitan Region)
  4,294,938 .... A9
Tarapacá 273,427 .... B2
Valparaíso 1,204,693 ..... A9

CITIES and TOWNS

Achao ○11,501 .... D4
Aguas Blancas ○203 ...... B4
Algarrobo ○3,941 .... F3
Ancud 11,900 .... D4
Andacollo 6,000 .... A8
Angol 42,670 .... D1
Antofagasta 125,100 ..... A4
Arauco 5,400 .... D1
Arica 87,700 .... A1
Ascotán B3
Barrancas ○184,241 ..... G3
Belén ○925 .... B1
Buin 11,800 .... G4
Bulnes 6,900 .... E1
Cabildo 5,800 .... A9
Calama 45,900 .... B3
Calbuco ○21,673 .... D4
Caldera ○3,268 .... A6
Calera de Tango ○6,198 . G4
Calle Larga ○7,172 .... G2
Cañete 7,900 .... D2
Carahue ○12,733 ...... D2
Cartagena ○7,124 ..... F3
Casablanca 5,500 ..... F3
Casas de Chacabuco ... G2
Castro 11,200 .... D4
Catalina ○1,637 ...... B5
Catemu ○8,728 .... G2
Cauquenes 20,200 ... A11
Cerro Castillo ○537 .. E9
Cerro Manantiales F10
Chaitén ○4,067 ...... E4
Chañaral ○36,949 .... A6
Chanco ○12,433 ..... A11
Chépica ○11,199 .... A10
Chillán 128,515 .... A11
Chimbarongo 5,300 .. A10
Chonchi ○8,911 ..... D4
Chuquicamata 22,100 . B3
Cobquecura ○6,298 .. D1
Cochamó ○5,042 .... E3
Codegua ○6,757 .... G4
Codpa ○950 .... B1
Coelemu 5,400 ..... D1
Coihaique 32,129 ... E6
Coihueco ○17,276 .. A11
Coinco ○4,942 ..... G5
Colbún ○12,924 .... A11
Colina 7,400 ...... G3
Collipulli 7,200 .... E2
Coltauco ○11,857 .. F5
Combarbalá ○17,332 . A8
Concepción 206,226 . D1
Constitución 11,500 . A11
Contulmo ○13,987 .. D2
Copiapó 45,200 .... B6
Coquimbo 73,953 ... A8
Coronel 37,300 .... D1
Corral ○5,533 ..... D3
Cunco ○18,836 .... E2
Curacautín 9,800 .. E2
Curacaví 5,800 .... G3
Curanilahue 13,200 . D1
Curepto ○13,020 .. A10
Curicó 41,300 .... A10
Dalcahue ○7,084 .. D4
Domeiko A7
Doñihue ○8,837 ... G5
El Carmen ○13,226 . A11
El Monte 7,000 ... G4
El Quisco ○2,152 . E3
El Salto ○2,180 .. F3
El Tofo A7
Empedrado ○7,887 . A11
Ercilla ○8,061 ... E2
Estancia Caleta
  Josefina ○1,042 . F10
Estancia Morro Chico ○785 . E9
Estancia San Gregorio
  ○1,156 .... E9
Estancia Springhill
  (Cerro Manantiales) F10

Freire ○23,313 .... E2
Freirina ○5,523 .... A7
Fresia ○15,359 .... D3
Frutillar ○12,721 .... D3
Futaleufú ○2,366 .... E4
Futrono ○7,109 .... E3
Galvarino ○9,495 .... D2
General Lagos ○810 ...... B1
Graneros 8,900 .... G5
Guayacán A8
Hijuelas ○7,128 .... F2
Hualañé ○6,912 .... A10
Huara ○1,934 .... B2
Huasco ○4,971 .... A7
Illapel 12,200 .... A8
Inca de Oro 1,406 ..... B6
Iquique 64,500 .... A2
Isla de Maipo ○12,903 . G4
La Calera 24,600 ...... F2
La Cruz ○8,907 .... F2
La Estrella ○3,707 .... G5
Lago Ranco ○12,767 ... E3
Lagunas ○5,653 .... B3
La Higuera ○6,991 ..... A7
La Ligua 7,500 .... A9
Lampa ○10,220 ...... G3
Lanco 5,200 .... D2
Las Cabras ○12,119 ... F5
La Serena 99,908 .... A8
La Unión 15,200 .... D3
Lautaro 11,900 ..... E2
Lebu 12,500 .... D1
Licantén ○6,354 ... A10
Limache 15,200 ... F2
Linares 37,900 .... A11
Llay-Llay 9,700 ... G2
Loica G4
Loncoche ○17,539 . D2
Longaví ○15,909 .. A11
Lonquimay ○9,524 . E2
Los Andes 23,500 . G2
Los Ángeles 49,500 . D1
Los Lagos ○14,934 . D3
Los Muermos ○9,296 . D3
Los Sauces ○7,613 . D2
Los Vilos ○10,453 . A9
Lota 48,100 ...... D1
Machalí 5,800 .... G4
Maipú ○117,872 .. G3
Malloa ○9,742 ... G5
Marchigüe ○4,451 . F5
Marla Elena 5,900 . B3
Marla Pinto ○5,980 . G3
Maullín ○14,544 .. D4
Mejillones ○3,333 . A4
Melipilla 23,900 .. F4
Mincha ○11,329 .. A8
Molina 9,400 ... A10
Monte Patria ○18,927 . A8
Mulchén 13,700 ... E1
Nacimiento ○17,651 . D1
Nancagua ○11,076 .. F6
Navidad ○6,618 ... A10
Negreiros ○1,144 .. B2
Ñiquén ○13,640 ... E1
Nogales ○18,529 .. F2
Nueva Imperial 8,000 . D2
Olivar Alto ○5,414 . G5
Ollagüe B3
Olmué ○8,804 .... F2
Osorno 68,800 ... D3
Ovalle 31,700 ... A8
Paihuano ○6,048 . B8
Paillaco 5,200 ... D3
Paine ○21,876 ... G4
Palena ○2,508 ... E5
Palmilla ○7,965 . F4
Panguipulli 5,700 . E2
Panquehue ○4,230 . G2
Papudo ○2,594 ... A9
Paredones ○7,404 . A10
Parral 17,000 ... A11
Pedro de Valdivia 6,200 . B4
Pemuco ○7,577 ... E1
Peñaflor 15,500 . G4
Penco ○33,962 .. D1
Peñuelas F3
Petorca ○8,343 . A9
Petrohué E3
Peumo ○11,308 .. F5
Pica ○1,487 .... B2
Pichidegua ○13,550 . F5
Pichilemu ○8,042 .. A10
Pinto ○8,687 ... A11
Pisagua ○1,880 . A2
Pitrufquén 7,800 . D2
Placilla ○6,441 . F6
Porvenir ○4,000 . E10
Potrerillos 5,800 . B6
Pozo Almonte ○1,798 . B2
Puchuncaví ○7,542 . F2
Pucón 18,000 ... E2
Pudahuel G3
Pueblo Hundido 6,200 . B6
Puente Alto 65,100 .. B10
Puerto Aisén 17,848 .. E6
Puerto Cisnes ○2,800 . E5

Puerto Ingeniero
  Ibáñez ○1,900 .... E6
Puerto Montt 119,059 .... E4
Puerto Natales 17,280 ... E9
Puerto Quellón ○7,734 .. D4
Puerto Varas 10,900 .... E3
Puerto Williams ○949 .. F11
Pumanque ○3,137 ...... F6
Punitaqui ○16,167 ..... A8
Punta Arenas 2,140 ... E10
Purén ○11,604 .... D2
Purranque 5,900 ...... D3
Putaendo ○12,806 ..... A9
Putre ○855 .... B1
Puyehue E3
Queilén ○6,055 ...... D4
Quemchi ○6,707 ..... D4
Quilicura 8,100 ..... G3
Quillagua B3
Quilleco ○16,043 ... E1
Quillota 36,500 ... F2
Quilpué 40,600 .... F2
Quinta de Tilcoco ○6,513 . G5
Quintero 9,900 ... F2
Quirihue ○11,178 . E1
Rancagua 140,589 . G5
Renca ○67,168 .... G3
Rengo 12,400 .... G5
Requinoa ○10,730 . G5
Retiro ○15,146 .. A11
Rinconada San Martín
  ○4,118 .... G2
Río Blanco B9
Río Bueno 9,600 . D3
Río Negro 5,100 . D3
Río Verde ○554 . E10
Rocas de Santo
  Domingo ○4,114 . F4
Rosario ○3,383 . F5
Salamanca 18,741 . A9
Samo Alto ○5,689 . A8
San Antonio 46,700 . F3
San Bernardo ○117,766 . G4
San Carlos 17,000 ... E1
San Clemente ○23,273 . A11
San Felipe 26,100 ... G2
San Fernando 23,600 . G6
San Francisco de
  Mostazal ○11,439 ... G4
San Ignacio ○13,523 .. E1
San Javier 10,800 ... A11
San José de
  Maipo ○9,601 .... B10
San Pablo ○7,978 ... D3
San Pedro ○8,255 ... F4
San Pedro de Atacama . C4
San Rosendo ○14,337 . E1
Santa Bárbara ○14,345 . E1
Santa Cruz 8,600 ... F6
Santa Marla ○8,162 .. G2
Santiago (cap.) 3,614,947 . G3
Santiago *3,672,374 ... G3
San Vicente F4
San Vicente (San Vicente
  de Tagua Tagua) ○28,333 . F5
Sierra Gorda ○8,805 .. B4
Talagante 16,500 ... G4
Talca 133,160 ..... A11
Talcahuano 148,300 . D1
Taltal 6,400 ..... A5
Tamaya A8
Tarapacá B2
Temuco 197,232 ... E2
Teno ○17,675 .... A10
Termàs de Cauquenes . B10
Tierra Amarilla ○7,899 . A6
Titil ○9,198 ...... G2
Toco ○8,734 ..... B3
Toconao C4
Tocopilla 22,000 ... A3
Toltén ○16,265 .. D1
Tomé 29,600 .... D1
Traiguén 11,400 .. D2
Valdivia 115,536 .. D3
Vallenar 26,800 .. A7
Valparaíso 271,580 . A7

Victoria 16,500 ...... D2
Vicuña 5,100 .... A8
Villa Alemana 29,600 .. F2
Villa Alhué ○5,078 ... G4
Villarrica 25,091 .... E2
Viña del Mar 281,361 . F2
Yumbel ○21,858 .... E1
Yungay ○10,725 .... E1
Zapallar ○2,894 .... A9
Zapiga B2

OTHER FEATURES

Aconcagua (riv.) F2
Aculeo (lag.) G4
Adventure (bay) D5
Aguas Calientes, Cerro (mt.) . C4
Almirantazgo (bay) .. F11
Almirante Montt (gulf) . D9
Ancud (gulf) D4
Angamos (isl.) D8
Angamos (pt.) A4
Ap Iwan, Cerro (mt.) . E6
Arauco (gulf) D1
Arenales, Cerro (mt.) . D7
Atacama (des.) B4
Atacama, Salar de
  (salt dep.) C4
Aucanquilcha, Cerro (mt.) . B3
Azapa, Quebrada (riv.) . B1
Baker (riv.) D7
Ballenero (chan.) .. E11
Bascuñán (cape) ... A7
Beagle (chan.) ... E11
Bella Vista, Salar de
  (salt dep.) B3
Benjamín (isl.) ... D5
Bío-Bío (riv.) E2
Blanca (lag.) E10
Blanco (lake) ... F10
Bravo (riv.) D7
Brunswick (pen.) . E10
Bueno (riv.) D3
Buenos Aires (lake) . E6
Byron (isl.) D7
Cachapoal (riv.) . G5
Cachina, Quebrada (riv.) . A6
Cachos (pt.) A6
Calafquén (lake) . E3
Camarones (riv.) . A2
Camiña, Quebrada (riv.) . B2
Campana (isl.) .. D7
Campanario, Cerro (mt.) . A10
Capitán Aracena (isl.) . E10
Carmen (riv.) .. B7
Castillo, Cerro (mt.) . E6
Catalina (pt.) .. F10
Chaffers (isl.) .. D5
Chaltel, Cerro (mt.) . E8
Chañaral (isl.) .. A7
Chatham (isl.) .. D9
Chauques (isls.) . D4
Cheap (chan.) .. D7
Chiloé (isl.) 119,286 . D4
Choapa (riv.) .. A9
Chonos (arch.) . D6
Choros (cape) .. A7
Cisnes (riv.) .. E5
Clarence (isl.) . E10
Clemente (isl.) . D6
Cochrane (lake) . E7
Cochrane, Cerro (mt.) . E7
Cockburn (chan.) . E11
Concepción (chan.) . D9
Cónico, Cerro (mt.) . E4
Contreras (isl.) . D9
Cook (bay) E11
Copiapó (bay) .. A6
Copiapó (riv.) . A6
Corcovado (gulf) . D4
Corcovado (vol.) . D5
Coronados (gulf) . D4
Curaumilla (pt.) . F2
Darwin (bay) ... D6
Darwin, Cordillera (mts.) . D8
Darwin, Cordillera (mts.) . E11

(continued on following page)

Agriculture, Industry and Resources

DOMINANT LAND USE

- Cereals, Livestock
- Mediterranean Agriculture (cereals, fruit, livestock)
- Pasture Livestock
- Extensive Livestock Ranching
- Limited Seasonal Grazing
- Forests
- Nonagricultural Land

MAJOR MINERAL OCCURRENCES

Ag	Silver	Hg	Mercury
Au	Gold	Id	Iodine
C	Coal	Mn	Manganese
Cu	Copper	Mo	Molybdenum
Fe	Iron Ore	N	Nitrates
G	Natural Gas	Na	Salt
Gp	Gypsum	O	Petroleum
		S	Sulfur

⚡ Water Power   ▨ Major Industrial Areas

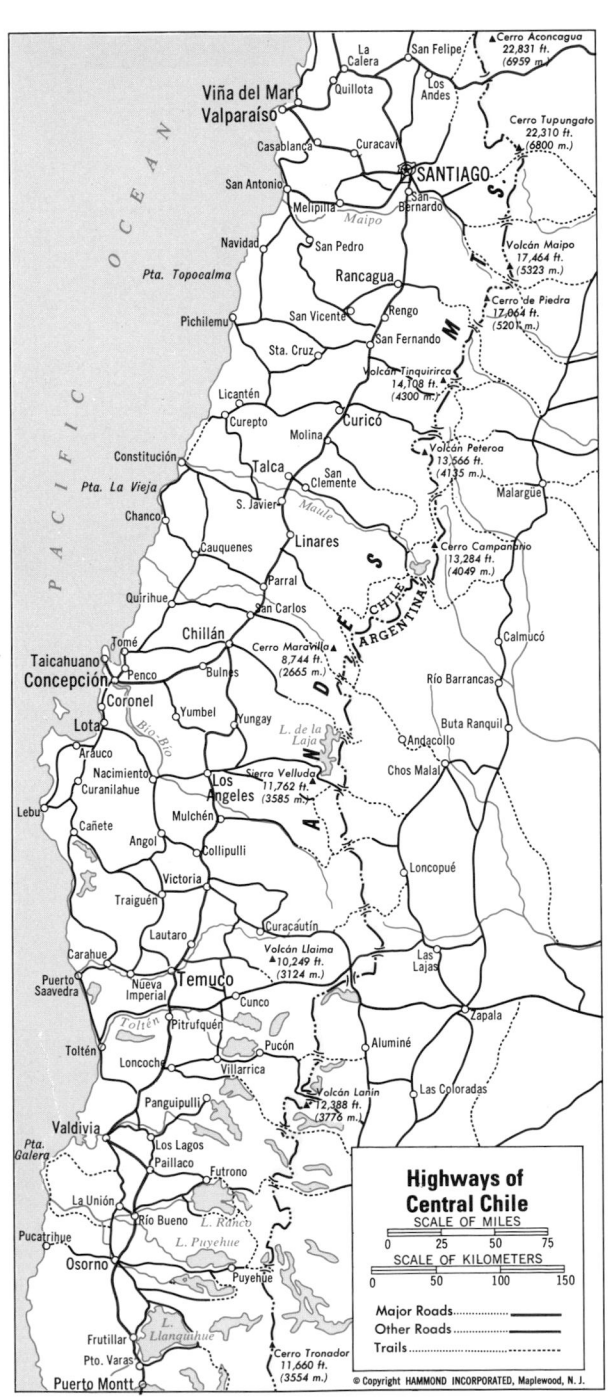

Highways of Central Chile

SCALE OF MILES
0   25   50   75

SCALE OF KILOMETERS
0   50   100   150

Major Roads ————
Other Roads ————
Trails -------

© Copyright HAMMOND INCORPORATED, Maplewood, N.J.

PROVINCES

Buenos Aires 10,796,036...D 4
Catamarca 206,204......C2
Chaco 692,410.......D2
Chubut 262,196......C5
Córdoba 2,407,135....D3
Corrientes 657,716.....E2
Distrito Federal 2,908,001..H7
Entre Ríos 902,241......E3
Formosa 292,479.....D1
Jujuy 408,514........C1
La Pampa 207,132......C4
La Rioja 163,342......C2
Mendoza 1,187,305.....C4
Misiones 579,579......F2
Neuquén 241,904......C4
Río Negro 383,896.....C5
Salta 662,369........D1
San Juan 469,973......C3
San Luis 212,837.....C3
Santa Cruz 114,479.....C6
Santa Fe 2,457,188.....D2
Santiago del Estero 652,318 D2
Tierra del Fuego, Antártida,
  e Islas del Atlántico
  Sur 29,451..........C7
Tucumán 968,066.......C2

CITIES and TOWNS

Abra Pampa 2,929........C1
Adolfo Alsina 7,707.......D4
Aguaray 4,802............D1
Aguilares 20,286.........C2
Aimogasta 4,640.........C2
Alberti 6,440............G7
Alcorta 5,818............F6
Algarrobo del Águila.....C4
Allen 14,041.............C4
Alpachiri 1,657..........D4
Alta Gracia 30,628.......D3
Aluminé 1,560...........B4
Alvear 5,419............E2
Ameghino 2,775..........D3
Añatuya 15,025..........D2
Andalgalá 6,853.........C2
Antofagasta de la Sierra..C2
Apóstoles 11,252........E2
Arrecifes 17,719.........F7
Arroyo Seco 12,886......F6
Ascensión 3,031.........F7
Avellaneda 330,654......G7
Ayacucho 12,363.........E4
Azul 43,582.............E4
Bahía Blanca 220,765.....D4
Bahía Bustamante........C6
Bahía Thetis............C7
Balcarce 28,985.........E4
Balnearia 4,531.........D3
Baradero 20,103.........G6
Barrancas 3,602.........F6
Barranqueras............E2
Barreal 2,739...........C3
Basavilbaso 7,657.......G6
Belén 7,411............C2
Bella Vista, Corrientes
  14,229...............E2
Bella Vista, Tucumán 9,177 .D2
Bell Ville 26,559.........D3
Bolívar 16,382..........D4
Bovril 4,735...........G5
Bragado 27,101.........F7
Buenos Aires (cap.)
  2,908,001............H7
Buenos Aires *9,927,404...H7
Cafayate 5,048..........C2
Calafate...............B7
Calchaquí 5,958.........F5
Caleta Olivia 20,141.....C6
Camarones.............C5
Campana 51,498.........G7
Cañada de Gómez 24,706...F6
Canals 6,627...........D3
Cañuelas 14,831.........G7
Carcarañá 11,121........F6
Carlos Casares 13,286....F7
Carlos Tejedor 4,421.....D4
Carmen de Areco 7,882....F7
Carmen de Patagones
  13,981...............D5
Casilda 23,492..........F6
Castelli 4,507..........H7
Catamarca 88,432........C2
Caucete 14,512.........C3
Ceres 10,743...........D2
Chabás 5,156...........F6
Chacabuco 26,492........F7
Chajarí 15,242..........G5
Chamical 6,333..........C3
Charadai 1,078.........D2
Charata 13,070.........D2
Chascomús 21,864........H7
Chepes 4,775...........C3
Chicoana 1,844.........C2
Chilecito 14,010........C2
Chilvicoy 43,779........F7
Choele-Choel 6,191......C4
Chos-Malal 4,823........C4
Cinco Saltos 15,094......C4
Cipolletti 40,123........C4
Clorinda 21,008.........E2
Colón, Buenos Aires 16,070. F6
Colón, Entre Ríos 11,648...G6
Colonia Las Heras 3,176...C6
Comandante Fontana 4,468 .D2
Comandante Luis Piedrabuena
  2,492...............C6
Comodoro Rivadavia 96,865. C6
Concepción 29,359.......C2
Concepción de
  la Sierra 2,778.......E2
Concepción del
  Uruguay 46,065.......G6
Concordia 93,618........G5
Constanza 1,313........G6
Córdoba 982,018........D3
Coronda 11,554.........F6
Coronel Brandsen 10,484...H7
Coronel Dorrego 10,661...D4
Coronel Pringles 16,592...D4
Coronel Suárez 16,359....D4

AREA 1,072,070 sq. mi. (2,776,661 sq. km.)
POPULATION 31,929,000
CAPITAL Buenos Aires
LARGEST CITY Buenos Aires
HIGHEST POINT Cerro Aconcagua 22,831 ft.
  (6,959 m.)
MONETARY UNIT austral
MAJOR LANGUAGE Spanish
MAJOR RELIGION Roman Catholicism

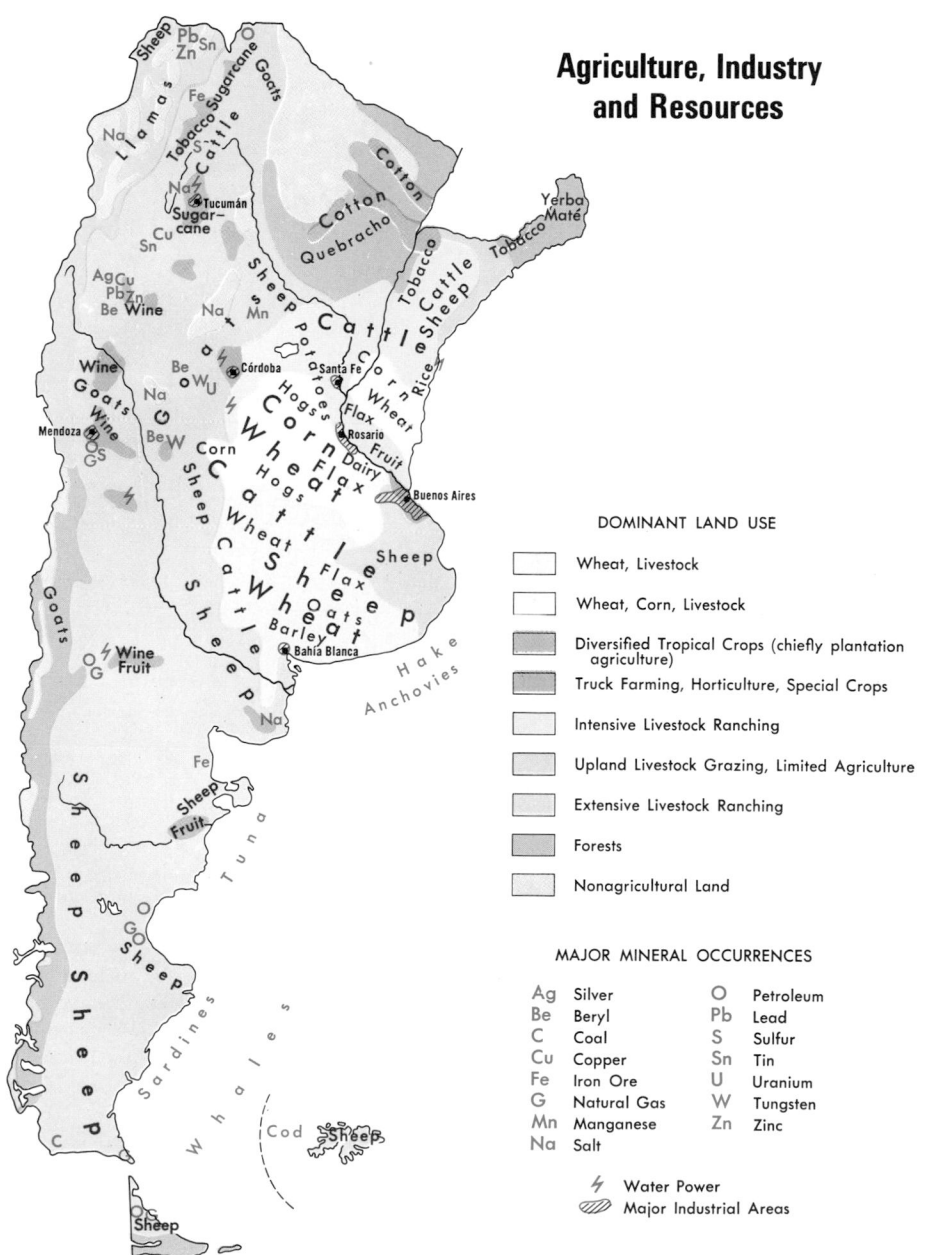

Agriculture, Industry and Resources

DOMINANT LAND USE

Wheat, Livestock
Wheat, Corn, Livestock
Diversified Tropical Crops (chiefly plantation agriculture)
Truck Farming, Horticulture, Special Crops
Intensive Livestock Ranching
Upland Livestock Grazing, Limited Agriculture
Extensive Livestock Ranching
Forests
Nonagricultural Land

MAJOR MINERAL OCCURRENCES

Ag Silver
Be Beryl
C   Coal
Cu Copper
Fe Iron Ore
G   Natural Gas
Mn Manganese
Na Salt
O   Petroleum
Pb Lead
S   Sulfur
Sn Tin
U   Uranium
W   Tungsten
Zn Zinc

⚡ Water Power
▨ Major Industrial Areas

Coronel Vidal 4,774.......E4
Corral de Bustos 8,613...D3
Corrientes 179,590.......E2
Cosquín 13,929..........D3
Crespo 10,668..........F6
Cruz del Eje 23,473......C3
Curuzú Cuatiá 24,955....G5
Cutral-Có 25,870........C4
Daireaux 8,150..........D4
Deán Funes 16,306......D3
Diamante 13,464........F6
Dolavon 1,778..........C5
Dolores 19,307.........E4
Eduardo Castex 5,397....D4
El Bolsón 5,001.........B5
Eldorado 22,821........F2
El Maitén 2,350.........B5
Elortondo 4,939........F6
El Quebrachal 2,202.....D2
Embarcación 9,016......D1
Empedrado 4,732........E2
Escobar 70,829.........G7
Esperanza 22,838.......F5
Esquel 17,228..........R5
Esquina 10,380.........G5
Famatina 1,237.........C2
Federación 7,259.......G5
Felipe Yofré 1,140......G4
Fernández 6,062........D2
Fiambalá 1,201.........C2
Firmat 13,588..........F6
Formosa 95,067........E2
Fortín Olmos 1,101......F4
Frías 20,901...........D2
Gaiman 2,651..........C5
Gálvez 14,711..........F6
General Acha 7,647......C4
General Alvear, Buenos Aires
  5,481...............F7
General Alvear,
  Mendoza 21,250.......C3
General Arenales 3,332...F7
General Belgrano 10,909..G7
General Conesa 3,566....C5
General Galarza 3,057....G6
General Güemes 15,534...D1
General José de
  San Martín 16,296.....E2
General Juan Madariaga
  13,409...............E4
General La Madrid 5,154..D4
General Las Heras 6,005..G7
General Paz 5,127.......H7
General Pico 30,180......D4
General Ramírez 5,393...F6
General Roca 38,296.....C4
General San Martín, Buenos
  Aires 384,306........G7
General San Martín,
  La Pampa 2,168.......C4
General Viamonte 10,112..F7
General Villegas 11,307...D4
Gobernador Crespo 2,972..F5
Godoy Cruz 141,553......C3
Goya 47,357...........G4
Gualeguay 24,883.......G6
Gualeguaychú 51,057.....G6
Guandacol 1,351........C2
Hasenkamp 2,804.......F5
Helvecia 3,927.........F5
Hernandarias 3,002......F5
Hernando 8,619.........D3
Huinca Renancó 7,187....D3
Humahuaca 3,963.......C1
Humberto (Humberto
  Primo) 4,163.........F5
Ibarreta 5,262.........D2
Ibicuy 3,082...........G6
Ingeniero Huergo 3,385...C4
Ingeniero Jacobacci 4,045. C5
Ingeniero Luiggi 3,002....D4
Intendente Alvear 3,640...D4
Itatí 3,269............E2
Ituzaingó 8,687........E2
Jáchal 8,832...........C3
Jesús María 17,594......D3
Joaquín V. González 6,054. D2
Juárez 11,798..........E4
Jujuy 124,487..........C1
Junín 62,080...........F7
Junín de los Andes 5,638..B4
La Banda 46,994........D2
Laboulaye 16,883.......D3
La Carlota 8,614........D3
La Cruz 4,132..........G4
La Cumbre 6,110........C3
La Falda 12,502........C3
Laguna Paiva 11,129.....F5
Lanús 465,891.........H7
La Paz, Entre Ríos 14,920. G5
La Paz, Mendoza 4,604...C3
La Plata 560,341........H7
Laprida 6,495..........D4
La Quiaca 8,289........C1
La Rioja 66,826........C2
Larroque 3,147.........F5
Las Flores 18,287.......E4
Las Lomitas 4,047......D1
Las Palmas 5,061.......E2
Las Parejas 7,430.......F6
Las Rosas 9,725.......F6
Las Varillas 10,605......D3
La Toma 4,325.........C3
Lincoln 19,009.........F7
Lobería 8,898..........E4
Lobos 20,798..........G7
Lomas de Zamora 508,620. G7
Lucas González 3,015....G6
Luján 38,919...........G7
Lules 11,391...........C2
Maciel 4,066...........F6
Magdalena 7,135........H7
Malabrigo 3,294........F4
Malargüe 9,496.........C4
Maquinchao 1,299.......C5
Marcos Juárez 19,827....D3
Mar del Plata 407,024....E4
Máximo Paz 3,216.......F6
Mburucuyá 3,044.......E2
Médanos 4,511.........D4
Mendoza 596,796.......C3
Mercedes, Buenos Aires
  46,581...............G7
Mercedes, Corrientes
  20,603...............G4
Mercedes, San Luis 50,856. C3
Merlo 293,059.........G7
Metán 18,928..........D2
Miramar 15,473........E4
Monte Caseros 18,247....G5
Monteros 15,832........C2
Monte Quemado 4,707....D2
Morón 596,769.........G7
Morteros 11,456........D3
Navarro 7,176.........G7
Necochea 50,939.......E4
Neuquén 90,037........C4
Nogoyá 15,862.........F6
Norquincó............B5
Nueve de Julio 26,608....F7
Oberá 27,311..........F2
Olavarría 63,686.......D4
Oliva 9,231...........D3
Palo Santo 3,088.......E2
Paraná 159,581........F5
Paso de Los Libres 24,112 . E4
Pedro Luro 3,142.......D4
Pehuajó 25,613........D4
Pellegrini 3,940.......D4
Pergamino 68,989......F6
Pico Truncado 9,626.....C6
Pigüé 10,793..........D4
Pilar 3,805............F5
Pirané 9,039...........E2
Plaza Huincul 7,988.....B4

(continued on following page)

Topography

0 ... 150 ... 300 MI.
0 ... 150 ... 300 KM.

5,000 m. 16,404 ft.	2,000 m. 6,562 ft.	1,000 m. 3,281 ft.	500 m. 1,640 ft.	200 m. 656 ft.	100 m. 328 ft.	Sea Level	Below

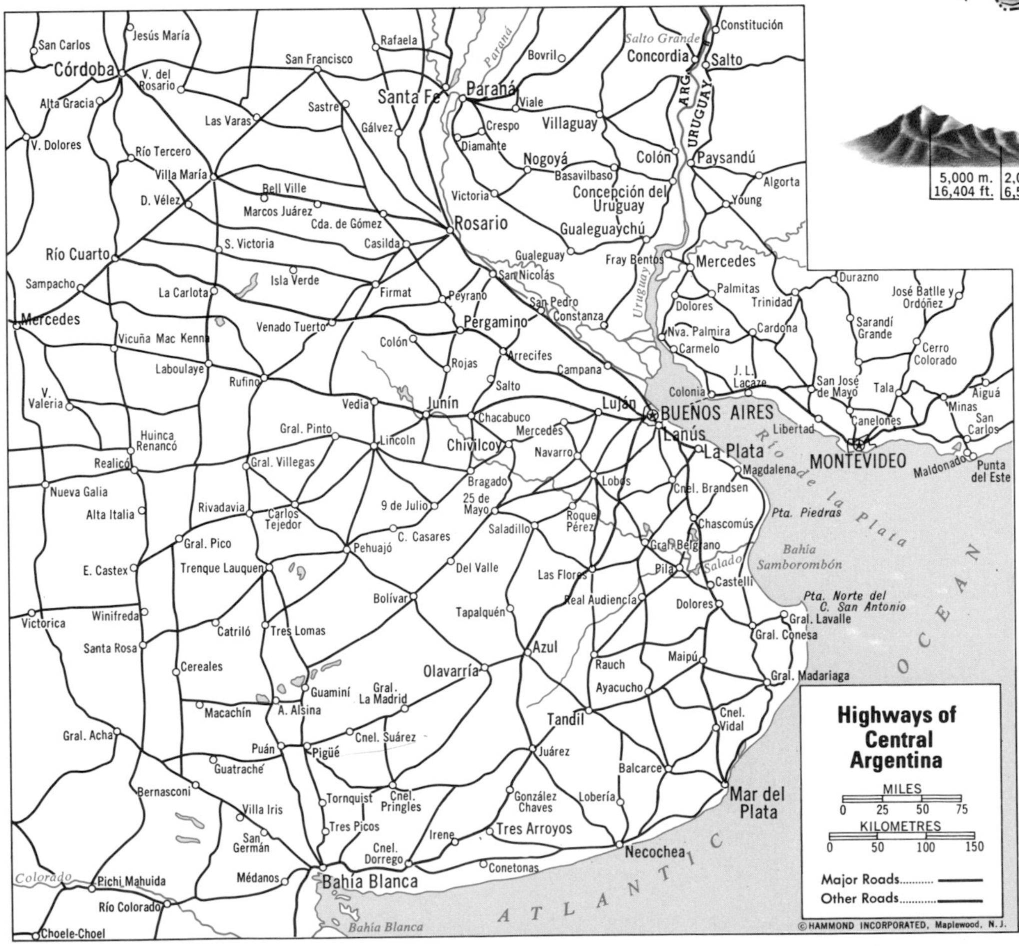

Highways of Central Argentina

MILES
0 ... 25 ... 50 ... 75
KILOMETRES
0 ... 50 ... 100 ... 150

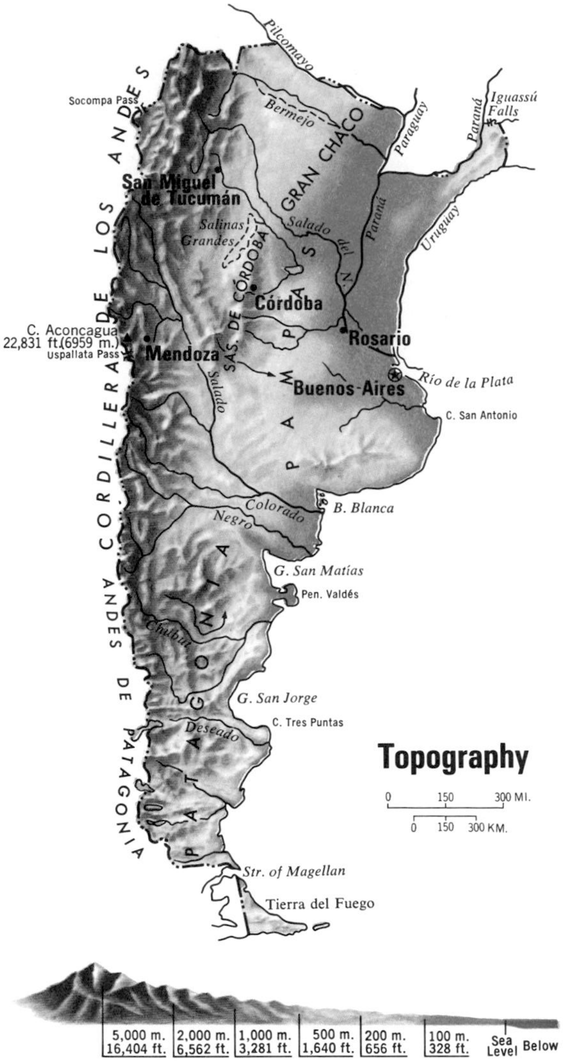

Major Roads ....
Other Roads ....

© HAMMOND INCORPORATED, Maplewood, N.J.

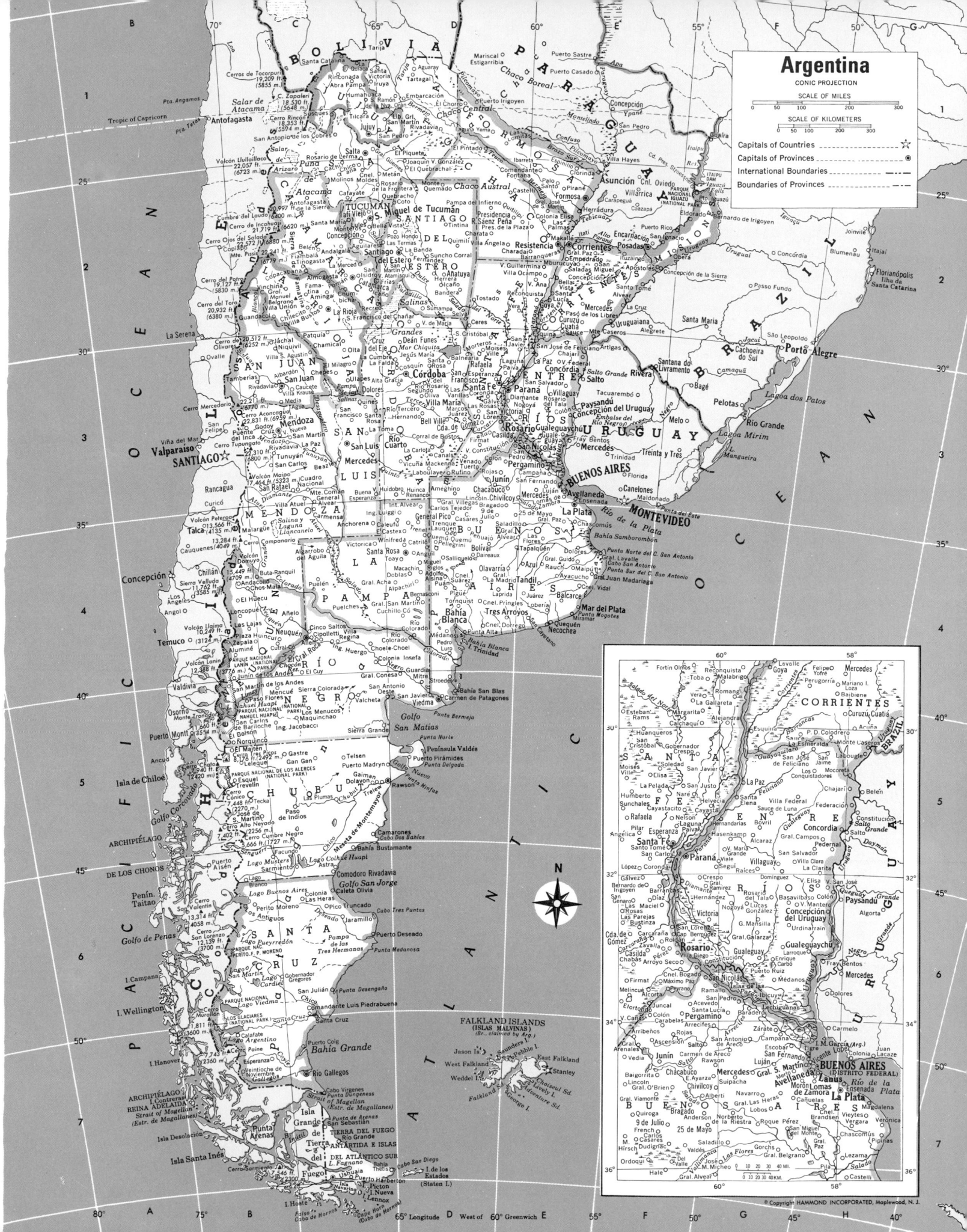

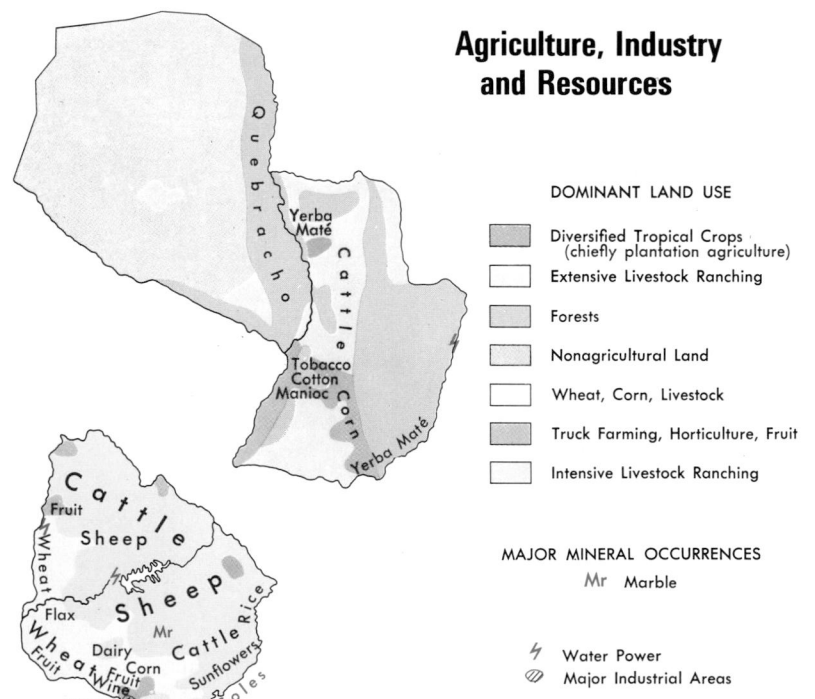

Paraguay
CONIC PROJECTION

SCALE OF MILES
0 20 40 60 80 100 120 140

SCALE OF KILOMETERS
0 20 40 60 80 100 140

★ Capitals of Countries
◉ Capitals of Departments
— · — · — International Boundaries
— — — Department Boundaries

© Copyright HAMMOND INCORPORATED, Maplewood, N.J.

PARAGUAY

DEPARTMENTS

Alto Paraguay	C2
Alto Paraná	E4
Amambay	D3
Asunción	A4
Boquerón	B3
Caaguazú	D-E4
Caazapá	D-E5
Canendiyu	E4
Central	D4
Chaco	B-C2
Concepción	D3
Cordillera	D4
Guaira	D4
Itapúa	E5
Misiones	D5
Ñeembucú	C-D5
Nueva Asunción	B2
Paraguarí	D 4-5
Presidente Hayes	C3
San Pedro	D 4-5

CITIES and TOWNS

Abaí 1,507	E4
Acahay 1,937	B5
Alberdi 2,346	D5
Altos 1,441	B4
Antequera 1,281	D4
Aregua 3,941	B4
Arroyos y Esteros 1,253	B4
Asunción (cap.) 387,676	A4
Atyrá 1,427	B4
Belén 1,219	D3
Bella Vista 3,101	D3
Bella Vista 1,421	E5
Benjamín Aceval 2,877	C4
Buena Vista 1,353	D5
Caacupé 7,278	B5
Caaguazú 7,950	D4
Caapucú 1,400	D5
Caazapá 3,132	D5
Capiatá 2,827	B4
Carapeguá 3,416	B5
Carmen del Paraná 1,980	D5
Ciudad Presidente Stroessner 7,085	E4
Concepción 19,392	D3
Coronel Bogado 3,973	D5
Coronel Martínez 1,598	B5
Coronel Oviedo 13,786	C5
Doctor Cecilio Báez 1,300	D4
Doctor Juan L. Mallorquín 1,913	E4
Doctor Juan Manuel Frutos 1,494	E4
Encarnación 23,343	E5
Eusebio Ayala 4,328	B4
Fernando de la Mora 36,834	B4
Filadelfia 1,438	B3
Fuerte Olimpo 3,063	C2
General Artigas 3,542	D5
General Elizardo Aquino 1,304	D4
Guarambaré 3,640	B5
Hernandarias 3,898	E4
Horqueta 4,328	D3
Isla Pucú 1,766	B4
Itá 7,041	B5
Itacurubí 1,997	B5
Itacurubí del Rosario 2,467	D4
Itapé 1,376	C5
Itauguá 3,767	B5
Iturbe 3,413	C5
Jesús 1,495	E5
La Colmena 1,804	B5
Lambaré 31,656	A4
Limpio 2,219	B4
Loreto 1,258	D3
Luque 13,921	B4
Mariano Roque Alonso 1,492	A4
Mariscal Estigarribia 3,150	B3
Mbuyapey 1,560	D5

Natalicio Talavera 1,228	D4
Nueva Italia 1,517	B5
Paraguarí 5,036	B5
Pirayú 2,698	B5
Piribebuy 4,497	B5
Primero de Marzo 696	B4
Puerto Casado 4,078	C3
Puerto Guaraní 302	C2
Puerto Pinasco 5,477	C3
Puerto Presidente Franco 4,152	E4
Quiindy 2,664	B5
Quindy 3,186	D4
Roque González de Santa Cruz 1,375	D4
Rosario 4,165	D4
San Antonio 4,906	A5
San Estanislao 4,753	D4
San Ignacio 6,116	D5
San José 3,102	B5
San Juan Bautista 6,457	D5
San Juan Nepomuceno 2,974	E5
San Lázaro 1,767	D3
San Lorenzo 11,616	B4
San Pedro 3,186	D3
San Pedro del Paraná 2,723	D5
San Salvador 1,393	C5
Santa Elena 1,439	B4
Santa Rosa 3,736	D5
Santiago 1,265	D5
Sapucai 1,864	B5
Tobatí 4,983	B4
Unión 1,286	D4
Valenzuela 1,108	B4
Valle Mi 1,318	D3
Villa Florida 1,261	D5
Villa Hayes 4,749	A4
Villarrica 17,687	C5
Villeta 3,156	A5
Yaguarón 3,368	B5
Ybycuí 1,736	B5
Ypacaraí 5,195	B5
Ypané 1,474	B5
Yuty 2,392	D5

OTHER FEATURES

Acaray (riv.)	E4
Alto Paraná (riv.)	D5
Amambay, Cordillera de (mts.)	D3
Ao Paray (riv.)	A5
Apa (riv.)	D3
Aquidabán (riv.)	D3
Cabral (lake)	A5
Carapa (riv.)	E4
Chaco Boreal (reg.)	B2
Chovoreca (mt.)	C1
Confuso (riv.)	C4
Coronel F. Cabrera (mt.)	B1
Galván (mt.)	C3
González, Riacho (riv.)	C3
Gran Chaco (reg.)	B2
Itaipu (dam)	E4
Itaipu (res.)	E4
Jara (hill)	C1
Jejui-Guazú (riv.)	C4
La Bella (lag.)	B4
León (mt.)	B2
Mbaracayú, Cordillera de (mts.)	E3
Monday (riv.)	E4
Montelindo (riv.)	C3
Mosquito, Riacho (riv.)	C3
Negro (riv.)	C4
Paraguay (riv.)	C4
Pilcomayo (riv.)	C4
Piribebuy (riv.)	B4
Tebicuary (riv.)	C5
Tebicuary Mi (riv.)	C5
Tímane (riv.)	B2
Vera (lag.)	D3
Verde (riv.)	C3
Ypané (riv.)	D3
Ypoá (lake)	B5

Agriculture, Industry and Resources

DOMINANT LAND USE

- Diversified Tropical Crops (chiefly plantation agriculture)
- Extensive Livestock Ranching
- Forests
- Nonagricultural Land
- Wheat, Corn, Livestock
- Truck Farming, Horticulture, Fruit
- Intensive Livestock Ranching

MAJOR MINERAL OCCURRENCES

Mr Marble

⚡ Water Power
⚙ Major Industrial Areas

Topography

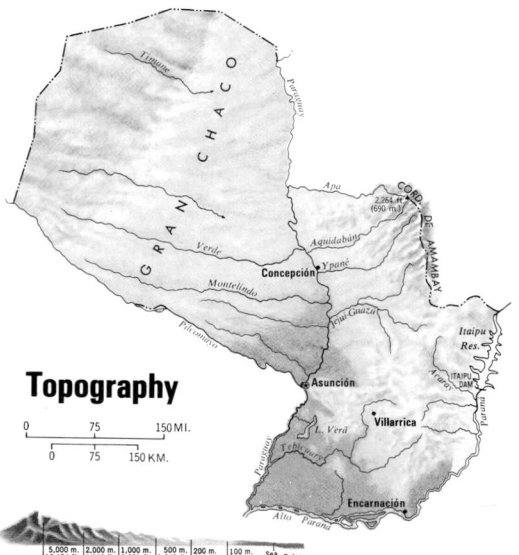

5,000 m. 2,000 m. 1,000 m. 500 m. 200 m. 100 m. Sea Level Below
16,404 ft. 6,562 ft. 3,281 ft. 1,640 ft. 656 ft. 328 ft.

URUGUAY

DEPARTMENTS

PARAGUAY

AREA 157.047 sq. mi. (406,752 sq. km.)
POPULATION 4,157,000
CAPITAL Asunción
LARGEST CITY Asunción
HIGHEST POINT Amambay Range
  2.264 ft. (690 m.)
MONETARY UNIT guaraní
MAJOR LANGUAGES Spanish, Guaraní
MAJOR RELIGION Roman Catholicism

URUGUAY

AREA 72,172 sq. mi. (186,925 sq. km.)
POPULATION 3,077,000
CAPITAL Montevideo
LARGEST CITY Montevideo
HIGHEST POINT Mirador Nacional 1,644 ft.
  (501 m.)
MONETARY UNIT Uruguayan peso
MAJOR LANGUAGE Spanish
MAJOR RELIGION Roman Catholicism

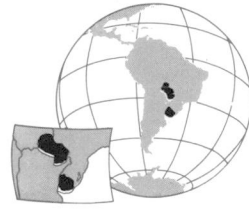

PARAGUAY

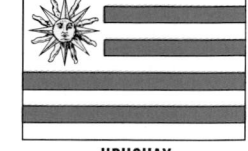

URUGUAY

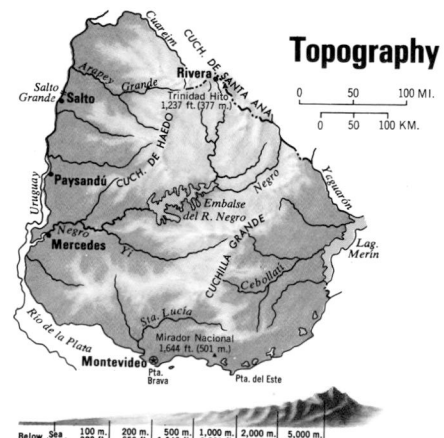

Topography

0	50	100 MI.
0	50	100 KM.

Below sea Level — 100 m. 328 ft. — 200 m. 656 ft. — 500 m. 1,640 ft. — 1,000 m. 3,281 ft. — 2,000 m. 6,562 ft. — 5,000 m. 16,404 ft.

Uruguay

CONIC PROJECTION

SCALE OF MILES
0   20   40   60

SCALE OF KILOMETERS
0   20   40   60

Capitals of Countries ....☆
Department Capitals ....◉
International Boundaries ....
Department Boundaries ....

© Copyright HAMMOND INCORPORATED, Maplewood, N.J.

North America

LAMBERT AZIMUTHAL EQUAL-AREA PROJECTION

MILES
0 100 200   400   600   800

KILOMETERS
0 100 200 400   600   800

Capitals of Countries ....⦿
Other Capitals ....◉
International Boundaries .... —·—·—
Other Boundaries .... ——————

© Copyright HAMMOND INCORPORATED, Maplewood, N.J.

Population Distribution

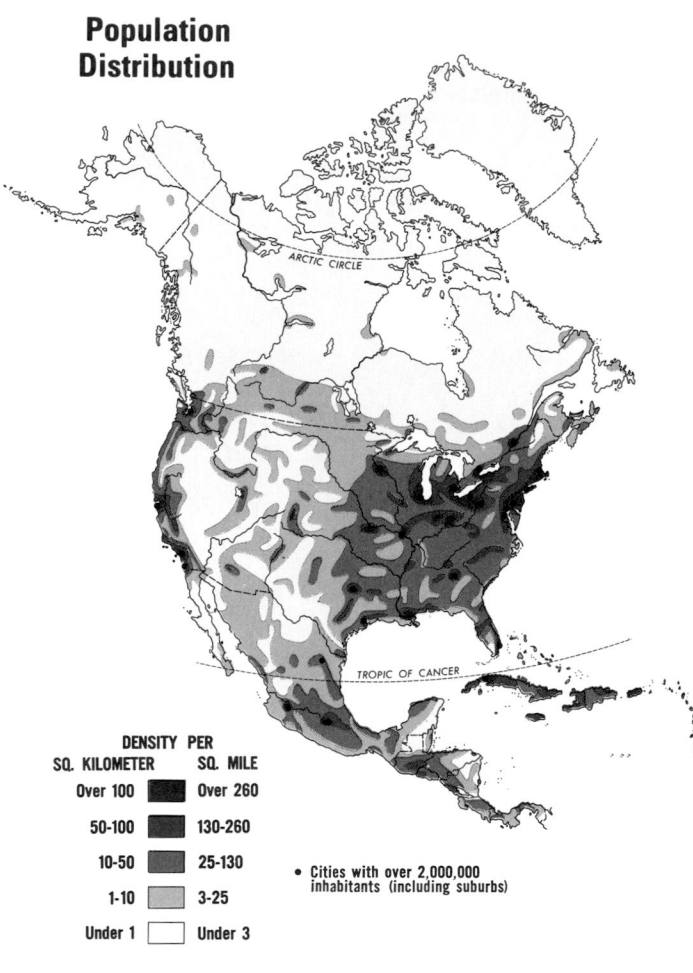

AREA   9,363,000 sq. mi. (24,250,170 sq. km.)
POPULATION   443,438.000
LARGEST CITY   New York
HIGHEST POINT   Mt. McKinley 20,320 ft. (6,194 m.)
LOWEST POINT   Death Valley -282 ft. (-86 m.)

Vegetation

DENSITY PER

SQ. KILOMETER	SQ. MILE
Over 100	Over 260
50-100	130-260
10-50	25-130
1-10	3-25
Under 1	Under 3

• Cities with over 2,000,000 inhabitants (including suburbs)

MID-LATITUDE FOREST
Coniferous Forest
Broadleaf Forest
Mixed Coniferous and Broadleaf Forest
Woodland and Shrub (Mediterranean)

MID-LATITUDE GRASSLAND
Short Grass (Steppe)
Tall Grass (Prairie)

TROPICAL FOREST
Tropical Rainforest
Light Tropical Forest

TROPICAL GRASSLAND
Wooded Savanna

DESERT AND DESERT SHRUB

TUNDRA AND ALPINE

PERMANENT ICE

Average January Temperature

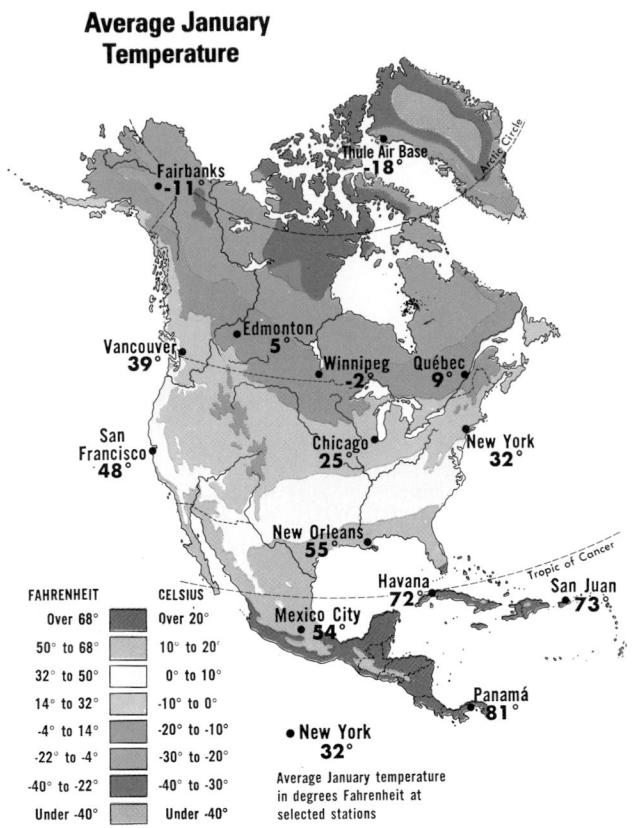

Thule Air Base -18°
Fairbanks -11°
Edmonton 5°
Vancouver 39°
Winnipeg -2°
Québec 9°
San Francisco 48°
Chicago 25°
New York 32°
New Orleans 55°
Havana 72°
San Juan 73°
Mexico City 54°
Panamá 81°

FAHRENHEIT	CELSIUS
Over 68°	Over 20°
50° to 68°	10° to 20°
32° to 50°	0° to 10°
14° to 32°	-10° to 0°
-4° to 14°	-20° to -10°
-22° to -4°	-30° to -20°
-40° to -22°	-40° to -30°
Under -40°	Under -40°

• New York
32°

Average January temperature in degrees Fahrenheit at selected stations

Average July Temperature

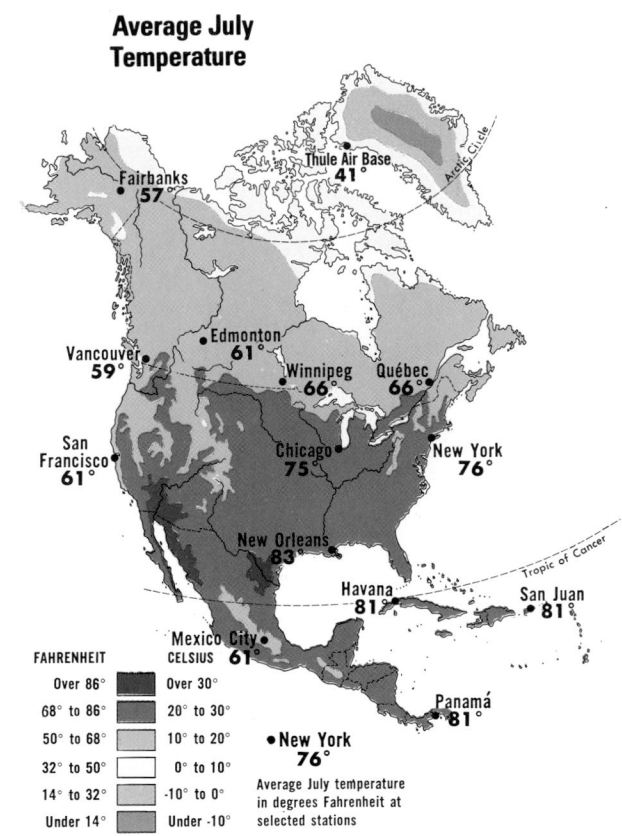

Thule Air Base 41°
Fairbanks 57°
Edmonton 61°
Vancouver 59°
Winnipeg 66°
Québec 66°
San Francisco 61°
Chicago 75°
New York 76°
New Orleans 83°
Havana 81°
San Juan 81°
Mexico City 61°
Panamá 81°

FAHRENHEIT	CELSIUS
Over 86°	Over 30°
68° to 86°	20° to 30°
50° to 68°	10° to 20°
32° to 50°	0° to 10°
14° to 32°	-10° to 0°
Under 14°	Under -10°

• New York
76°

Average July temperature in degrees Fahrenheit at selected stations

Rainfall

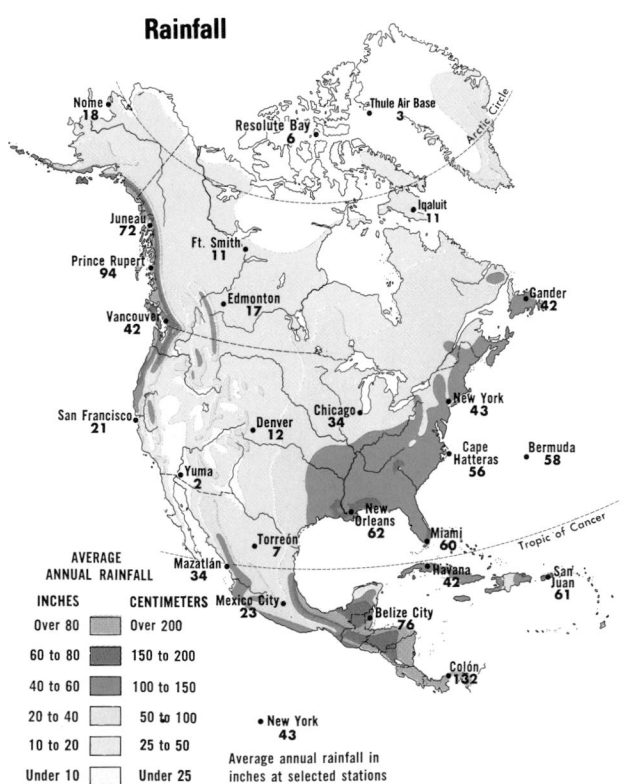

Nome 18
Resolute Bay 6
Thule Air Base 3
Iqaluit 11
Juneau 72
Ft. Smith 11
Prince Rupert 94
Edmonton 17
Gander 42
Vancouver 42
San Francisco 21
Denver 12
Chicago 34
New York 43
Cape Hatteras 56
Bermuda 58
Yuma 2
New Orleans 62
Miami 60
Torreón 7
Havana 42
San Juan 61
Mazatlán 34
Mexico City 23
Belize City 76
Colón 132

AVERAGE ANNUAL RAINFALL		
INCHES	CENTIMETERS
Over 80	Over 200
60 to 80	150 to 200
40 to 60	100 to 150
20 to 40	50 to 100
10 to 20	25 to 50
Under 10	Under 25

• New York
43

Average annual rainfall in inches at selected stations

Vegetation/Relief

SCALE OF MILES
0 200 400 600 800 1000

SCALE OF KILOMETERS
0 200 400 600 800 1000

Capitals of Countries.................⊛
Other Capitals..........................◉
International Boundaries.............—·—·—
Canals.......................................

Depths in Fathoms

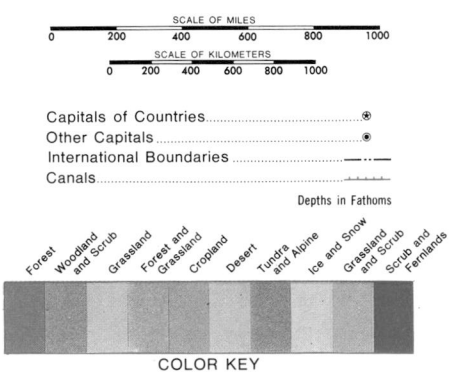

Forest | Woodland and Scrub | Grassland | Forest and Grassland | Cropland | Desert | Tundra and Alpine | Ice and Snow | Grassland Scrub and | Scrub and Fernlands

COLOR KEY

Longitude 90° West of Greenwich

Topography

0   150   300 MI.

0   150   300 KM.

5,000 m. | 2,000 m. | 1,000 m. | 500 m. | 200 m. | 100 m. | Sea Level | Below
16,404 ft. | 6,562 ft. | 3,281 ft. | 1,640 ft. | 656 ft. | 328 ft. |

Monterrey 1,006,221	J4	
Morelia 199,099	J7	
Moroleón 25,620	J6	
Motozintla de Mendoza 4,682	N9	
Motul de Felipe Carrillo		
Puerto 12,949	P6	
Muna 5,491	P6	
Naica 7,190	G2	
Namiquipa 4,875	F2	
Nanacamilpa 6,356	M1	
Naranjos 14,732	L6	
Naucalpan de Juárez 9,425	L1	
Navojoa 43,817	E3	
Navolato 12,799	E4	
Netzahualcóyotl 580,436	L1	
Nochistlán 8,780	H6	
Nogales 14,254	D1	
Nueva Casas Grandes 20,023	F1	
Nueva Italia de Ruiz 14,718	J7	
Nueva Rosita 34,706	J2	
Nuevo Ideal 5,252	G4	
Nuevo Laredo 184,622	J3	
Oaxaca de Juárez 114,948	L8	
Ocampo 4,801	K5	
Ocotlán 35,361	H6	
Ocotlán de Morelos 5,882	L8	
Ojinaga 12,757	G2	
Ojocaliente 7,582	H5	
Ometepec 7,342	K8	
Oriental 6,009	O1	
Orizaba 105,150	P2	
Oxkutzcab 8,182	P6	
Ozumba de Alzate 6,876	M1	
Pachuca de Soto 83,892	K6	
Padilla 4,581	K5	
Palenque 2,595	O8	
Pánuco 14,277	L6	
Papantla de Olarte 26,773	L6	
Paraíso 7,561	N7	
Parras de la Fuente 18,207	H4	
Paso de Ovejas 4,371	Q2	
Pátzcuaro 17,299	J7	
Pedro Montoya 4,563	K6	
Pénjamo 9,245	J6	
Pericos 4,445	E4	
Perote 12,742	O1	
Petatlán 9,419	J8	
Peto 8,362	P6	
Pichucalco 4,615	N8	
Piedras Negras, Coahuila		
41,033	J2	
Piedras Negras, Veracruz		
4,099	Q2	
Pijijiapan 5,053	N9	
Poza Rica de Hidalgo		
152,276	L6	
Profesor Rafael Ramírez		
5,338	O1	
Progreso 17,518	P6	

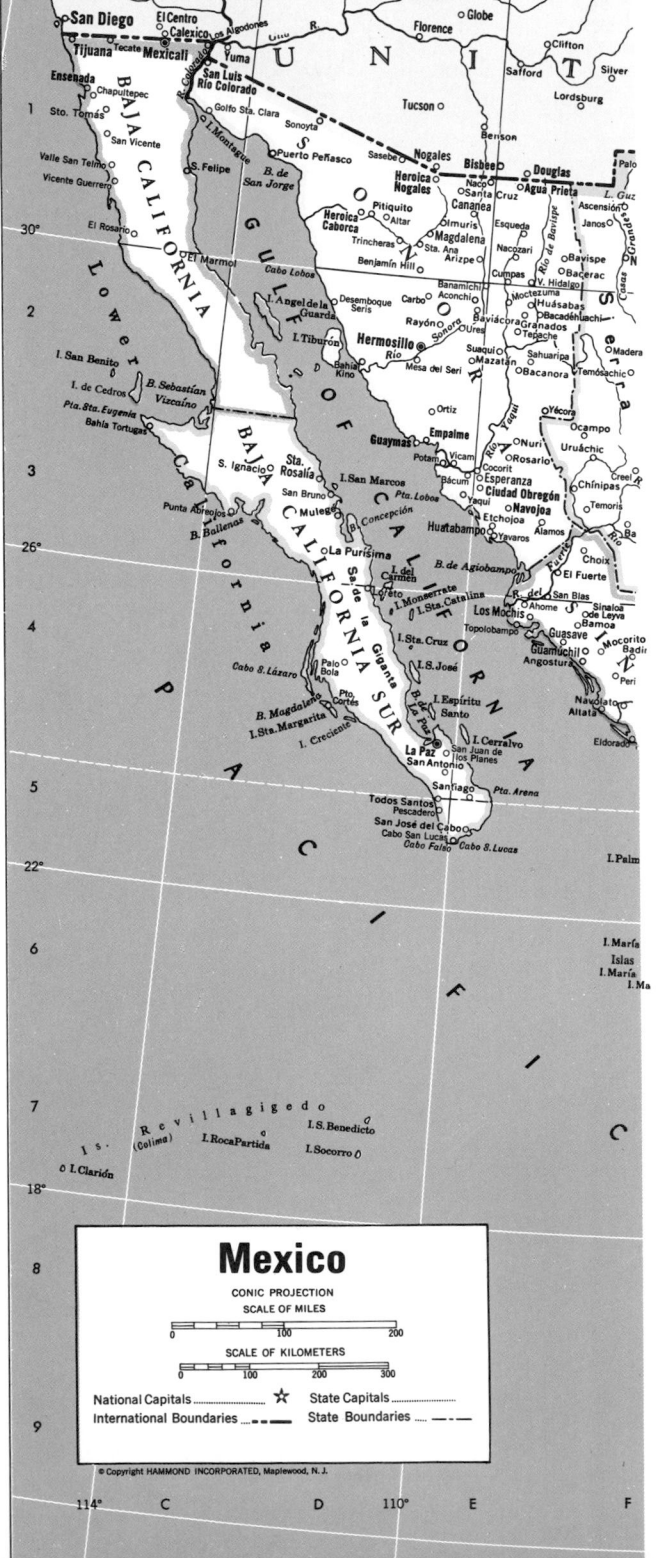

Mexico

CONIC PROJECTION

SCALE OF MILES

0   100   200

SCALE OF KILOMETERS

0   100   200   300

National Capitals .... ☆   State Capitals .... ●

International Boundaries ___ ___   State Boundaries _ _ _ _

© Copyright HAMMOND INCORPORATED, Maplewood, N.J.

STATES

Aguascalientes 504,300	H6
Baja California 1,227,400	B1
Baja California Sur 221,000	C3
Campeche 371,800	O7
Chiapas 2,097,500	N8
Chihuahua 1,935,100	F2
Coahuila 1,561,000	H3
Colima 339,400	G7
Distrito Federal 9,377,300	L1
Durango 1,160,300	G4
Guanajuato 3,045,600	J6
Guerrero 2,174,200	J8
Hidalgo 1,518,200	K6
Jalisco 4,296,500	H6
México 7,542,300	K7
Michoacán 3,049,400	H7
Morelos 931,400	K7
Nayarit 729,500	G6
Nuevo León 2,463,500	K4
Oaxaca 2,517,500	L8
Puebla 3,285,300	L7
Querétaro 730,900	J6
Quintana Roo 209,900	P7
San Luis Potosí 1,669,900	J5
Sinaloa 1,882,200	F4
Sonora 1,498,100	D2
Tabasco 1,150,000	N7
Tamaulipas 1,924,900	K4
Tlaxcala 548,500	N1
Veracruz 5,263,800	L7
Yucatán 1,034,300	P6
Zacatecas 1,144,700	H5

CITIES and TOWNS

Acala 11,483	N8
Acámbaro 32,257	J7
Acaponeta 11,844	G5
Acapulco de Juárez 309,254	K8
Acatlán de Osorio 7,624	K7
Acatzingo de Hidalgo 6,905	N2
Acayucan 21,173	M8
Actopan 11,037	K6
Agua Dulce 21,060	M7
Agua Prieta 20,754	E1
Aguascalientes 181,277	H6
Aguililla 5,715	H7
Ahuacatitlán 6,436	L1
Ahuacatlán 5,350	G6
Ahumada 6,466	F1
Ajalpan 8,238	L7
Álamo 9,954	L6
Aldama 6,047	G2
Allende, Coahuila 11,076	J2
Allende, Nuevo León 9,914	J4
Altamira 6,053	L5
Altepexi 6,661	L7
Altotonga 6,754	P1
Alvarado 15,792	M7
Ameca 21,018	H6
Amecameca de Juárez	
16,276	L1
Amozoc de Mota 9,203	N2
Anáhuac, Chihuahua 10,886	F2
Anáhuac, Nuevo León 8,168	J3
Apan 13,705	M1
Apatzingán de la Constitución	
44,849	H7
Apizaco 21,189	N1
Arandas 18,934	H6
Arcelia 10,024	J7
Ario de Rosales 8,774	J7
Armería 10,616	G7
Arriaga 13,193	N8
Arteaga 5,324	H7
Atlixco 41,967	L7
Atotonilco el Alto 16,271	H6
Atoyac de Álvarez 8,874	J8
Autlán de Navarro 20,308	G7
Axochiapan 8,283	M2

Azcapotzalco 534,554	L1
Bamoa 5,866	E4
Benjamín Hill 5,366	D1
Bernardino de Sahagún	
12,327	M1
Cabo San Lucas 1,534	E5
Cacahoatán 5,079	N9
Cadereyta Jiménez 13,586	K4
Calkiní 6,870	O6
Calpulálpan 8,659	M1
Calvillo 6,453	H6
Campeche 69,506	O7
Cananea 17,518	D1
Canatlán 5,983	G4
Cancún 326	Q6
Cañitas de Felipe Pescador	
4,885	H5
Capulhuac de Mirafuentes	
8,289	K1
Cárdenas, San Luis Potosí	
12,020	K6
Cárdenas, Tabasco 15,643	N8
Castaños 8,996	J3
Catemaco 11,786	M7
Celaya 79,977	J6
Cerritos 10,421	J5
Cerro Azul 20,259	L6
Chahuites 5,218	M8
Chalco de Díaz Covarrubias	
12,172	M1
Champotón 6,606	O7
Charcas 10,491	J5
Chetumal 23,685	Q7
Chiapa de Corzo 8,571	N8
Chiautempan 12,327	N1
Chietla 4,602	M2
Chihuahua 327,313	F2
Chilapa de Álvarez 9,204	K8
Chilpancingo de los Bravos	
36,193	K8
China, Nuevo León 4,958	K4
Chocomán 5,114	P2
Cholula de Rivadavia 15,399	M1
Cihuatlán 9,451	G7
Cintalapa de Figueroa 12,036	N8
Ciudad Acuña (Villa Acuña)	
30,276	J2
Ciudad Altamirano 8,694	J7
Ciudad Camargo, Chihuahua	
24,030	G3
Ciudad Camargo, Tamaulipas	
5,953	K3
Ciudad de Río Grande 11,651	H5
Ciudad del Carmen 34,656	N7
Ciudad del Maíz 5,241	K5
Ciudad Delicias 52,446	G2
Ciudad Guzmán 48,166	H7
Ciudad Hidalgo, Chiapas	
4,105	N9
Ciudad Hidalgo, Michoacán	
24,692	J7
Ciudad Juárez 424,135	F1
Ciudad Lerdo 19,803	H4
Ciudad Madero 115,302	L5
Ciudad Mante 51,247	K5
Ciudad Mendoza 18,696	O2
Ciudad Miguel Alemán	
11,299	K3
Ciudad Obregón 144,795	E3
Ciudad Río Bravo 39,018	K4
Ciudad Satélite 35,083	L1
Ciudad Serdán 9,581	O2
Ciudad Valles 47,587	K5
Ciudad Victoria 83,897	K5
Coalcomán de Matamoros	
4,875	H7
Coatepec 21,542	P1
Coatetelco 5,268	K7
Coatzacoalcos 69,753	M7
Cocorit 4,478	E3
Colima 58,450	H7
Colotlán 6,135	H5

Comala 5,592	H7
Comalcalco 14,963	N7
Comitán de Domínguez	
21,249	O8
Compostela 9,801	G6
Concepción del Oro 8,144	J4
Contla 7,517	N1
Coquimatlán 6,212	G7
Córdoba 78,495	P2
Cosamaloapan de Carpio	
19,766	M7
Coscomatepec de Bravo	
6,023	P2
Costa Rica 11,795	F4
Cotija de la Paz 9,178	H7
Coyoacán 339,446	L1
Coyotepec 8,888	L1
Coyuca de Benítez 6,328	J8
Cozumel 5,858	Q6
Cuatrociénegas de Carranza	
5,523	H3
Cuauhtémoc 26,598	F2
Cuautepec de Hinojosa 5,501	K6
Cuautitlán de Romero Rubio	
11,439	L1
Cuautla Morelos 13,946	L2
Cuernavaca 239,813	L2
Cuitláhuac 4,813	P2
Culiacán 228,001	F4
Dolores Hidalgo de la	
Independencia Naci 16,849	J6
Durango 182,633	G4
Dzidzantún 7,064	P6
Dzitbalché 4,393	P6
Ebano 17,489	L5
Ecatepec de Morelos 11,899	L1
Ejutla de Crespo 5,263	L8
Eldorado 8,115	E4
El Fuerte 7,179	E3
El Salto 7,818	G5
Empalme 24,927	D2
Encarnación de Díaz 10,474	H6
Ensenada 77,687	A1
Escárcega 7,248	O7
Escuinapa de Hidalgo 16,442	G5
Escuintla 4,111	N9
Espita 5,894	P6
Fortín de las Flores 9,358	P2
Francisco I. Madero 12,613	H4
Fresnillo de González	
Echeverría 44,475	H5
Frontera 10,066	N7
General Terán 5,354	K4
Gómez Palacio 79,650	G4
González 6,440	K5
Guadalajara 1,478,383	H6
Guadalupe, Nuevo León	
51,899	K4
Guadalupe, Zacatecas 13,246	H5
Guadalupe Victoria, Durango	
7,931	G4
Guamúchil 17,151	E4
Guanajuato 36,809	J6
Guasave 26,080	E4
Guaymas 57,492	D3
Gustavo Díaz Ordaz 10,154	K3
Gutiérrez Zamora 9,099	L6
Halachó 4,804	O6
Hermosillo 232,691	D2
Heroica Caborca 20,771	C1
Heroica Nogales 14,254	D1
Hidalgo del Parral (Parral)	
57,619	G3
Huachinango 16,826	K7
Huajuapan de León 13,822	L8
Huamantla 15,565	N1
Huatabampo 18,506	D3
Huatusco de Chicuellar 9,501	P2
Huauchinango 16,826	L6
Huautla de Jiménez 6,132	L7
Huejotzingo 8,552	M1

Huejutla 6,854	K6
Huetamo 9,333	J7
Huimanguillo 7,075	N8
Huitzuco de los Figueroa	
9,406	K7
Huixtepec 5,927	L8
Huixtla 15,737	N9
Hunucmá 8,020	O6
Iguala de la Independencia	
45,355	K7
Irapuato 135,596	J6
Isla, Veracruz 8,075	M7
Isla Mujeres 2,663	Q6
Ixmiquilpan 6,048	K6
Ixtapa	J8
Ixtapalapa 522,095	L1
Ixtenco 5,035	N1
Ixtepec 14,025	M8
Ixtlán del Río 10,986	G6
Izamal 9,749	P6
Izúcar de Matamoros 21,164	M2
Jala 4,535	G6
Jalapa Enríquez 161,352	P1
Jalpa 9,904	H6
Jalpa de Méndez 4,785	N7
Jáltipan de Morelos 15,170	M8
Jerez de García Salinas	
20,325	H5
Jico 7,269	P1
Jiménez, Chihuahua 18,095	G3
Jojutla de Juárez 14,438	L2
José Cardel 5,396	Q1
Juan Aldama 9,667	H4
Juchipila 6,328	H6
Juchitán de Zaragoza 30,218	M8
La Barca 18,055	H6
Lagos de Moreno 33,782	J6
La Paz 46,011	D5
La Piedad Cavadas 34,963	H6
Las Choapas 20,166	M7
Las Rosas 7,658	N8
León 468,887	J6
Lerdo de Tejada 11,628	M8
Libres 4,830	O1
Linares 24,456	K4
Loma Bonita 15,804	M7
Loreto 7,132	J5
Los Mochis 67,953	E4
Los Reyes de Salgado	
19,452	H7
Macuspana 12,293	N8
Madera 9,759	F2
Magdalena de Kino 10,281	D1
Maltrata 5,457	O2
Manzanillo 20,777	G7
Mapastepec 5,907	N9
Martínez de la Torre 17,203	L6
Mascota 5,674	G6
Matamoros, Coahuila 15,125	H4
Matamoros, Tamaulipas	
165,124	L4
Matehuala 28,799	J5
Matías Romero 13,200	M8
Maxcanú 6,505	O6
Mazatlán 147,010	F5
Melchor Múzquiz 18,868	H3
Melchor Ocampo del Balsas	
4,766	H8
Meoquí 12,308	G2
Mérida 233,912	P6
Metepec 4,625	M2
Mexicali 317,228	B1
Mexico City (cap.) 9,377,300	L1
Miahuatlán de Porfirio Díaz	
5,714	L8
Mier 5,636	K3
Miguel Auza 9,303	H4
Minatitlán 68,397	M8
Mineral del Monte 8,887	K6
Misantla 8,799	P1
Monclova 78,134	H3
Montemorelos 18,642	K4

(continued on following page)

AREA 761,601 sq. mi. (1,972,546 sq. km.)
POPULATION 86,154,000
CAPITAL Mexico City
LARGEST CITY Mexico City
HIGHEST POINT Citlaltépetl 18,700 ft. (5,700 m.)
MONETARY UNIT Mexican peso
MAJOR LANGUAGE Spanish
MAJOR RELIGION Roman Catholicism

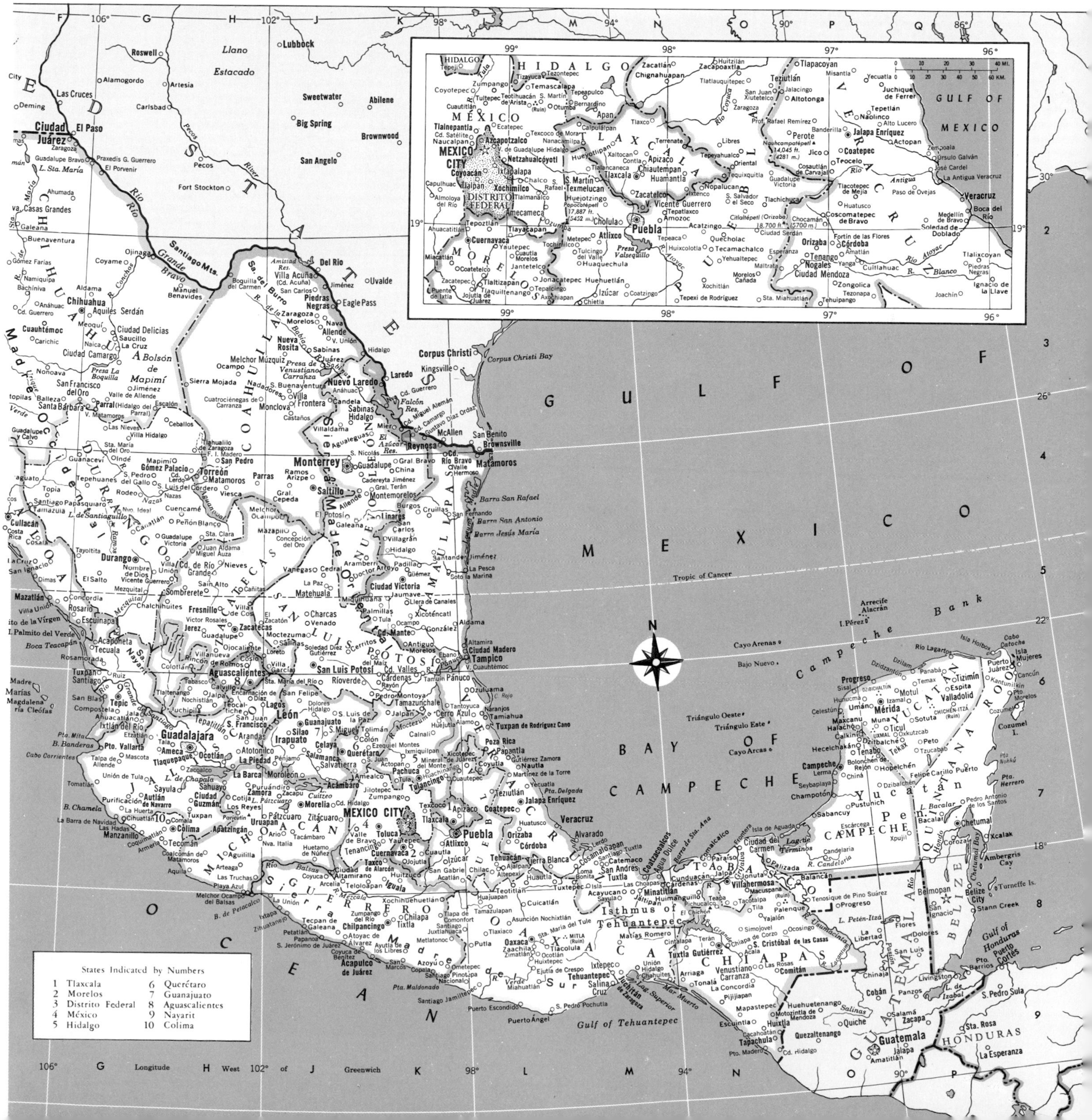

States Indicated by Numbers

1	Tlaxcala	6	Querétaro
2	Morelos	7	Guanajuato
3	Distrito Federal	8	Aguascalientes
4	México	9	Nayarit
5	Hidalgo	10	Colima

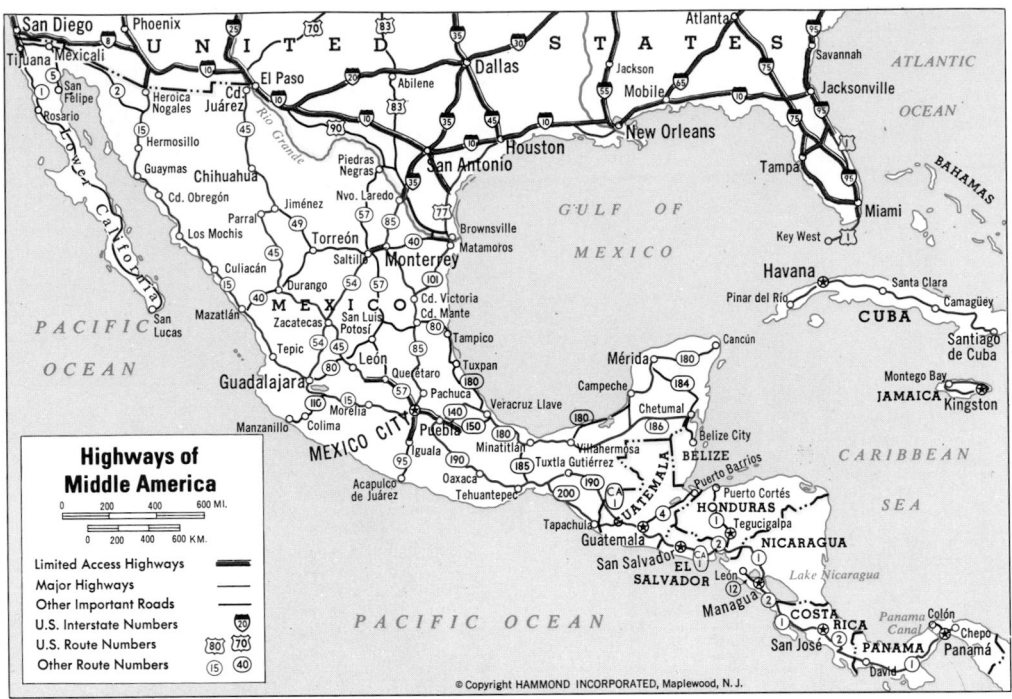

Highways of Middle America

0 200 400 600 MI.
0 200 400 600 KM.

Limited Access Highways
Major Highways
Other Important Roads
U.S. Interstate Numbers
U.S. Route Numbers
Other Route Numbers

© Copyright HAMMOND INCORPORATED, Maplewood, N.J.

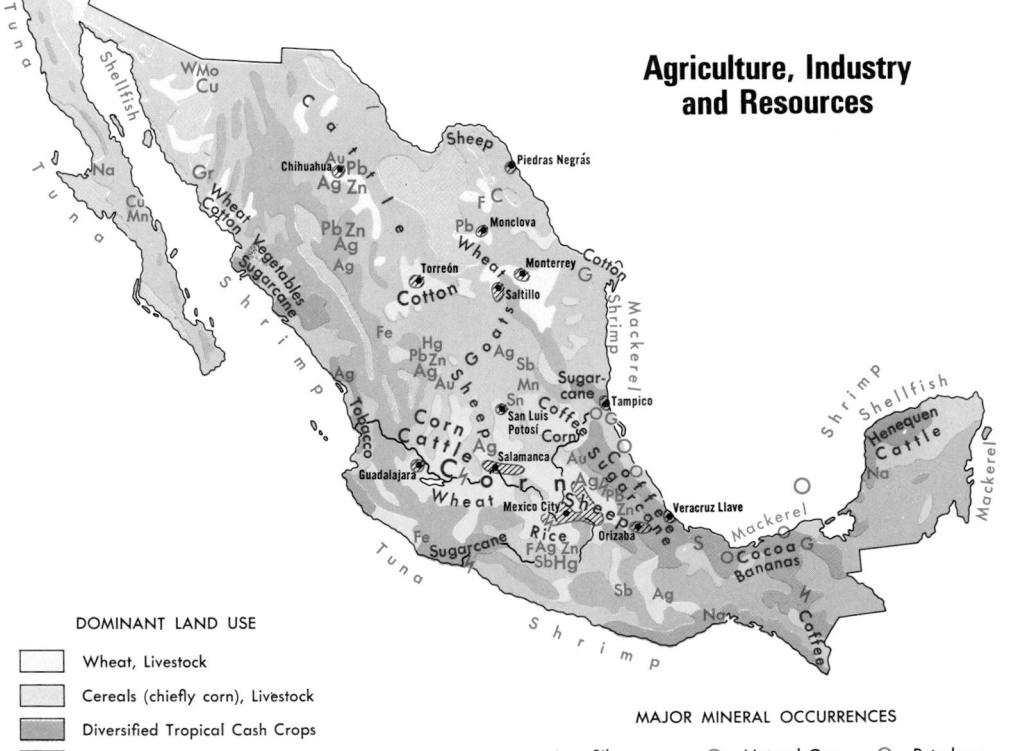

Agriculture, Industry and Resources

DOMINANT LAND USE

- Wheat, Livestock
- Cereals (chiefly corn), Livestock
- Diversified Tropical Cash Crops
- Cotton, Mixed Cereals
- Livestock, Limited Agriculture
- Range Livestock
- Forests
- Nonagricultural Land

MAJOR MINERAL OCCURRENCES

Ag Silver
Au Gold
C Coal
Cu Copper
F Fluorspar
Fe Iron Ore
G Natural Gas
Gr Graphite
Hg Mercury
Mn Manganese
Mo Molybdenum
Na Salt
O Petroleum
Pb Lead
S Sulfur
Sb Antimony
Sn Tin
W Tungsten
Zn Zinc

Water Power
Major Industrial Areas

GUATEMALA

AREA 42,042 sq. mi. (108,889 sq. km.)
POPULATION 9,197,000
CAPITAL Guatemala
LARGEST CITY Guatemala
HIGHEST POINT Tajumulco 13,845 ft.
(4,220 m.)
MONETARY UNIT quetzal
MAJOR LANGUAGES Spanish, Quiché
MAJOR RELIGION Roman Catholicism

BELIZE

AREA 8,867 sq. mi. (22,966 sq. km.)
POPULATION 180,000
CAPITAL Belmopan
LARGEST CITY Belize City
HIGHEST POINT Victoria Peak 3,681 ft. (1,122 m.)
MONETARY UNIT Belize dollar
MAJOR LANGUAGES English, Spanish, Mayan
MAJOR RELIGIONS Roman Catholicism, Protestantism

EL SALVADOR

AREA 8,260 sq. mi. (21,393 sq. km.)
POPULATION 5,207,000
CAPITAL San Salvador
LARGEST CITY San Salvador
HIGHEST POINT Santa Ana 7,825 ft.
(2,385 m.)
MONETARY UNIT colón
MAJOR LANGUAGE Spanish
MAJOR RELIGION Roman Catholicism

HONDURAS

AREA 43,277 sq. mi. (112,087 sq. km.)
POPULATION 4,951,000
CAPITAL Tegucigalpa
LARGEST CITY Tegucigalpa
HIGHEST POINT Las Minas 9,347 ft.
(2,849 m.)
MONETARY UNIT lempira
MAJOR LANGUAGE Spanish
MAJOR RELIGION Roman Catholicism

NICARAGUA

AREA 45,698 sq. mi. (118,358 sq. km.)
POPULATION 3,384,000
CAPITAL Managua
LARGEST CITY Managua
HIGHEST POINT Cerro Mocotón 6,913 ft.
(2,107 m.)
MONETARY UNIT córdoba
MAJOR LANGUAGE Spanish
MAJOR RELIGION Roman Catholicism

COSTA RICA

AREA 19,575 sq. mi. (50,700 sq. km.)
POPULATION 2,959,000
CAPITAL San José
LARGEST CITY San José
HIGHEST POINT Chirripó Grande
12,530 ft. (3,819 m.)
MONETARY UNIT colón
MAJOR LANGUAGE Spanish
MAJOR RELIGION Roman Catholicism

PANAMA

AREA 29,761 sq. mi. (77,082 sq. km.)
POPULATION 2,418,000
CAPITAL Panamá
LARGEST CITY Panamá
HIGHEST POINT Vol. Baru 11,401 ft.
(3,475 m.)
MONETARY UNIT balboa
MAJOR LANGUAGE Spanish
MAJOR RELIGION Roman Catholicism

Agriculture, Industry and Resources

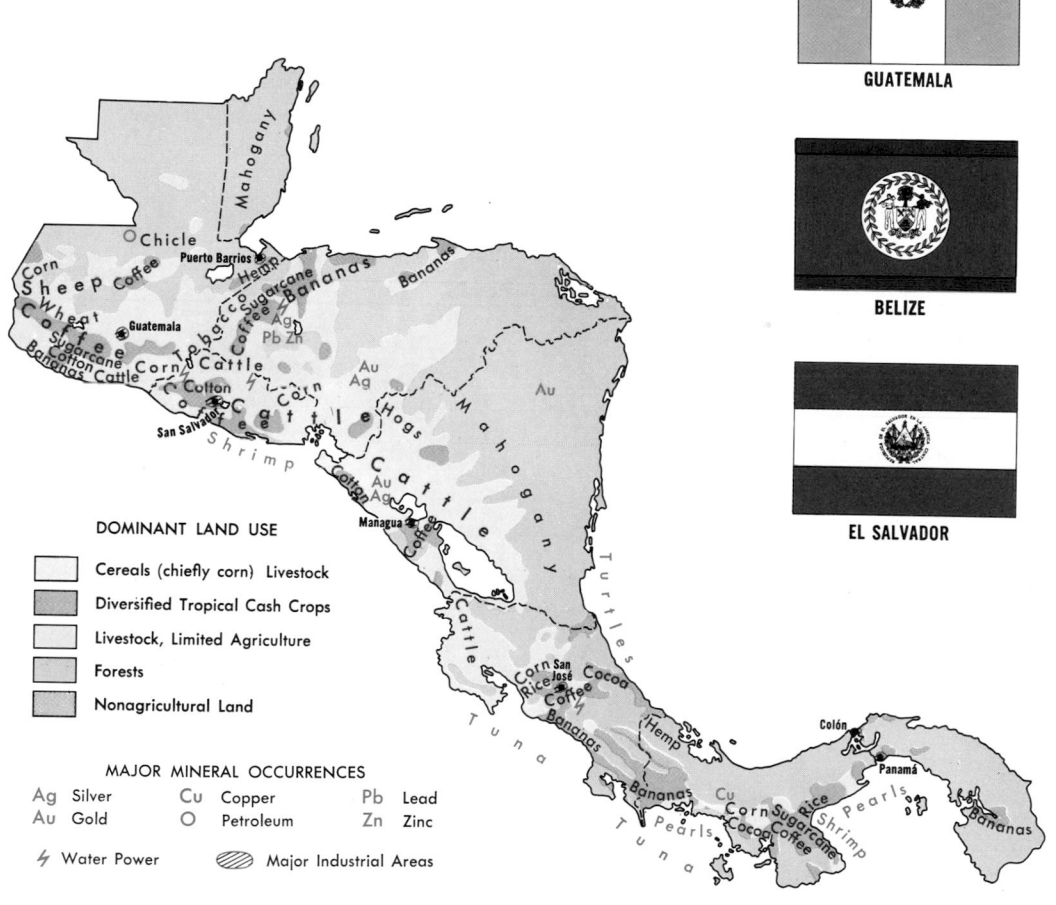

DOMINANT LAND USE

- Cereals (chiefly corn) Livestock
- Diversified Tropical Cash Crops
- Livestock, Limited Agriculture
- Forests
- Nonagricultural Land

MAJOR MINERAL OCCURRENCES

Ag Silver
Au Gold
Cu Copper
O Petroleum
Pb Lead
Zn Zinc

⚡ Water Power   ▨ Major Industrial Areas

GUATEMALA

BELIZE

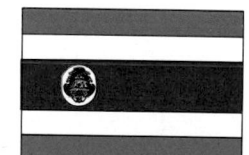
EL SALVADOR

HONDURAS

NICARAGUA

COSTA RICA

PANAMA

(continued on following page)

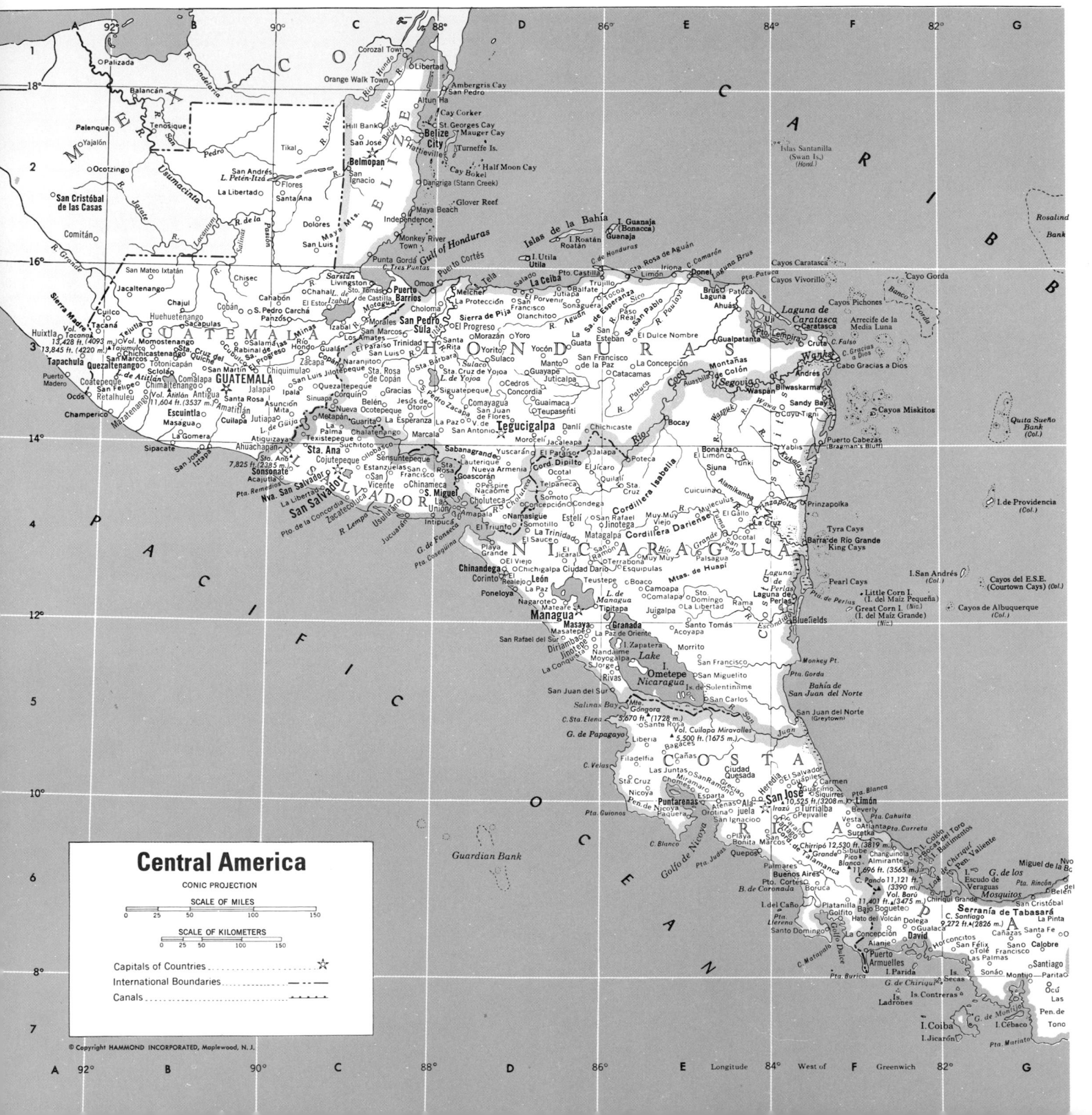

Central America

CONIC PROJECTION

SCALE OF MILES

0   25   50   100   150

SCALE OF KILOMETERS

0 25 50   100   150

Capitals of Countries .... ★

International Boundaries ...... -----

Canals ...... ••••••

© Copyright HAMMOND INCORPORATED, Maplewood, N. J.

San Pedro (riv.) B2
Sarstún (riv.) C3
Tacaná (vol.) A3
Tajumulco (vol.) B3
Tres Puntas (cape) C3
Usumacinta (riv.) B2

Corquín 2,629 ....C3
Danlí 10,825 ....D3
El Dulce Nombre 1,297 ....E3
El Paraíso 6,709 ....D4
El Paraíso 2,164 ....D4
El Porvenir 1,076 ....D3
El Progreso 28,105 ....D3
El Triunfo 2,925 ....D4
Goascorán 996 ....D4
Gracias 2,299 ....C3
Guaimaca 3,953 ....D3
Guanaja 1,947 ....E2
Guarita 419 ....C3
Guayape 804 ....D3
Jacaleapa 1,609 ....D3
Jesús de Otoro 2,976 ......C3
Jutiapa 1,126 ....D3
Juticalpa 10,075 ....D3
La Ceiba 38,788 ....D3
La Esperanza 2,146 ....C3

HONDURAS

CITIES and TOWNS

Amapala 2,274 ....D4
Brus Laguna 933 ....E3
Catacamas 9,134 ....E3
Cedros 917 ....D3
Choloma 961 ....C3
Choluteca 26,152 ....D3
Comayagua 15,941 ....D3
Concepción de María 579 .D4
Concordia 646 ....D3

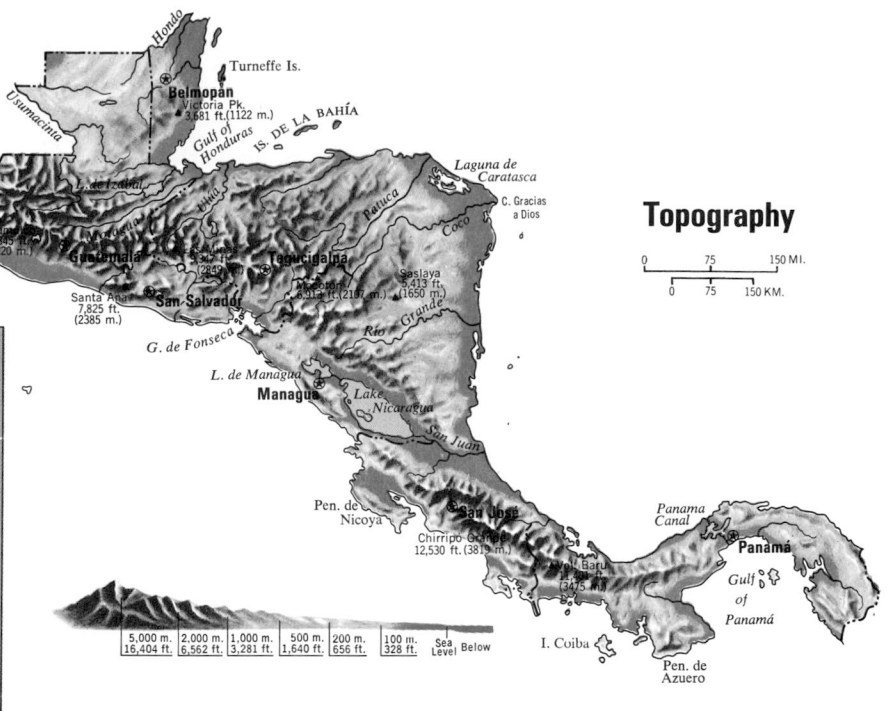

Topography

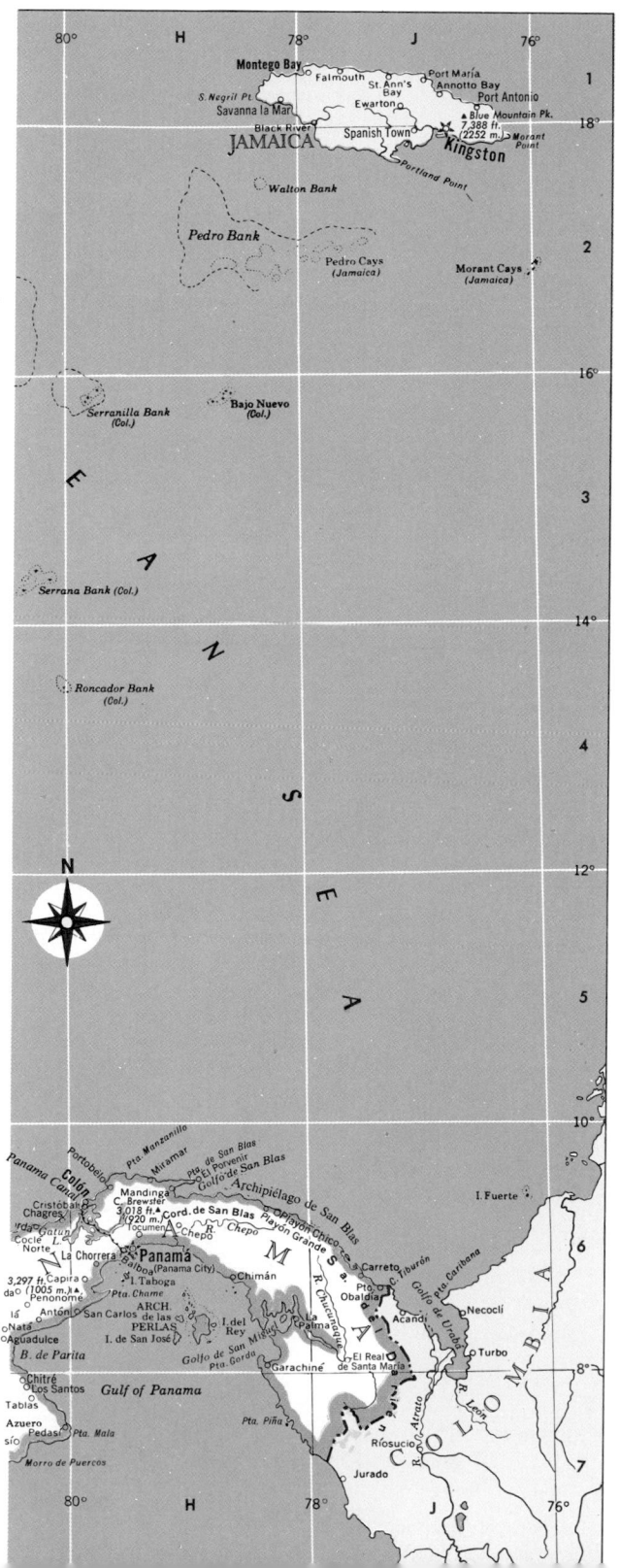

La Paz 6,811 ....D3
Limón 1,704 ....E3
Marcala 3,183 ....C3
Morazán 4,367 ....D3
Morocelí 1,442 ....D3
Nacaome 6,159 ....D4
Namasigüe 816 ....D4
Naranjito 2,770 ....C3
Nueva Armenia 670 ....D4
Nueva Ocotepeque 4,724 ..C3
Olanchito 7,411 ....D3
Omoa 9,161 ....C3
Pespire 1,895 ....D4
Puerto Cortés 25,817 ....D2
Puerto Lempira 727 ....F3
Roatán 1,943 ....D3
Sabanagrande 1,446 ....D3
San Esteban 610 ....D3
San Francisco 1,557 ....D3
San Francisco de la Paz 2,291 D3
San Juan de Flores 1,184 ..D3
San Luis 2,237 ....C3
San Marcos 2,499 ....C3
San Pedro Sula 150,991 ....C3
San Pedro Zacapa 648 ......D3
Santa Bárbara 5,883 ....C3
Santa Cruz de Yojoa 1,848 .D3
Santa Rita 5,298 ....D3
Santa Rosa de Aguán 1,622 E2
Santa Rosa de Copán 12,413 C3
Siguatepeque 12,456 ....C3
Sinuapa 831 ....C3
Sonaguera 2,264 ....D3
Sulaco 1,121 ....D3
Tegucigalpa (cap.) 273,894 D3
Tela 19,055 ....D3
Teupasenti 2,003 ....D3
Tocoa 2,803 ....E3
Trinidad 1,598 ....C3
Trujillo 3,961 ....E3
Utila 1,177 ....D2
Villa de San Antonio 2,359 .D3
Yoro 4,449 ....D3
Yuscarán 1,835 ....D4

OTHER FEATURES

Aguán (riv.) D3
Bahía (isls.) D2
Brus (lag.) E2
Camarón (pt.) E2
Caratasca (lag.) F3
Choluteca (riv.) D4
Coco (riv.) E3
Colón (mts.) E3
Esperanza (mts.) E3
Fonseca (gulf) D4
Gorda (bank) F3
Guanaja (isl.) E2
Honduras (cape) E2
Honduras (gulf) D2
Patuca (pt.) E3
Patuca (riv.) E3
Paulaya (riv.) E3
Pija, Sierra de (mts.) D3
Roatán (isl.) D2
San Pablo, Sierra (mts.) D3
Santanilla (Swan) (isls.) F2
Sico (riv.) E3
Sulaco (riv.) D3
Ulúa (riv.) D3
Utila (isl.) D2
Vivorillo (cays) F3
Yojoa (lake) D3

NICARAGUA

CITIES and TOWNS

Acoyapa 2,588 ....E5
Barra de Río Grande F4
Bilwaskarma F3
Bluefields 14,252 ....F4
Boaco 6,372 ....E4
Bonanza E4
Bragmans Bluff
  (Puerto Cabezas) 5,457 ..F3
Cabo Gracias a Dios 3,846 F3
Camoapa 4,385 ....E4
Chichigalpa 14,498 ....D4
Chinandega 30,441 ....D4
Ciudad Darío 5,304 ....D4
Comalapa 508 ....E4
Condega 3,414 ....D4
Corinto 13,404 ....D4
Diriamba 10,085 ....D5
El Jícaro 1,660 ....D4
El Jicaral 428 ....D4
El Limón E4
El Realejo 2,229 ....D4
El Sauce 3,202 ....D4
El Viejo 8,507 ....D4
Esquipulas 2,232 ....E4
Estelí 20,222 ....D4
Granada 34,976 ....E5
Greytown
  (San Juan del Norte) 294 .F5
Jalapa 3,633 ....E4
Jinotega 9,506 ....E4
Jinotepe 12,473 ....D4
Juigalpa 8,497 ....E4
La Conquista 458 ....D5
La Cruz 150 ....D4
La Libertad 1,286 ....E4
La Paz de Oriente 957 ....E5
La Trinidad 3,548 ....D4
León 55,625 ....D4
Managua (cap.) 398,514 ...D4
Masatepe 6,307 ....D5
Masaya 30,753 ....D5
Matagalpa 21,385 ....E4
Mateare 1,405 ....D4
Morrito 368 ....E5
Moyogalpa 1,551 ....E5
Muy Muy 1,373 ....E4
Nagarote 7,185 ....D4
Nandaime 5,631 ....E5
Ocotal 8,215 ....D4
Palsaguna E4
Poneloya D4
Prinzapolka 8,979 ....F4
Puerto Cabezas 5,457 ....F3
Quilalí 1,245 ....E4
Rama 1,341 ....E4
Rivas 10,125 ....E5
San Carlos 2,022 ....E5
San Jorge 2,874 ....E5
San Juan del Norte 294 .....F5
San Juan del Sur 2,393 .....D5
San Miguelito 1,312 ....E5
San Rafael del Norte 1,938 E4
San Rafael del Sur 2,914 ...D5
San Ramón 477 ....E4
Santo Domingo 1,949 ....E4
Santo Tomás 2,309 ....E4
Siuna E4
Somotillo 1,864 ....D4
Somoto 5,847 ....D4
Telpaneca 991 ....D4
Terrabona 904 ....E4
Teustepe 1,060 ....E4
Tipitapa 5,758 ....E4
Waspán 1,246 ....E3
Yablis F4

OTHER FEATURES

Coco (riv.) E3
Coseguína (pt.) D4
Dariense, Cordillera (range) E4
Dipilto, Cordillera (range) ..E4
Escondido (riv.) F4
Fonseca (gulf) D4
Gracias a Dios (cape) F3
Grande (riv.) E4
Great Corn (isl.) F4
Isabelia, Cordillera (range) E4
Kukalaya (riv.) F4
Little Corn (isl.) F4
Managua (lake) D4
Miskitos (cays) F3
Monkey (pt.) F5
Mosquitos, Costa de (reg.) E4
Nicaragua (lake) E5
Ometepe (isl.) E5
Perlas (lag.) F4
Perlas (pt.) F4
Prinzapolca (riv.) F4
Salinas (bay) D5
San Juan (riv.) E5
San Juan del Norte (bay) ...F5
Segovia (riv.) F4
Tuma (riv.) E4
Tyra (cays) F4
Waspuk (riv.) E3
Wawa (riv.) F4
Zapatera (isl.) E5

PANAMA

CITIES and TOWNS

Aguadulce 10,659 ....G6
Alanje 866 ....F6
Almirante 4,664 ....F6
Antón 4,259 ....G6
Bajo Boquete 2,831 ....F6
Balboa 1,952 ....H6
Bocas del Toro 2,515 ....F6
Calobre 609 ....G6
Cañazas 1,526 ....G6
Capira 1,749 ....G6
Changuinola 9,528 ....F6
Chepo 4,529 ....H6
Chiriquí Grande F6
Chitré 17,156 ....G7
Coclé del Norte G6
Colón 59,832 ....H6
Cristóbal* 7,959 ....G6
David 50,621 ....F6
Dolega 1,019 ....F6
El Porvenir H6
El Real de Santa María 912 J6
Garachiné 1,116 ....H7
Gualaca 1,510 ....F6
Hato del Volcán F6
Horconcitos 1,090 ....F6
La Chorrera 36,971 ....H6
La Concepción 10,460 ....F6
La Palma 164 ....H6
La Pintada 1,100 ....G6
Las Palmas 738 ....G6
Las Tablas 5,230 ....G7
Los Santos 4,644 ....G7
Mandinga 81 ....H6
Montijo 1,152 ....G6
Natá 5,603 ....G6
Ocú 2,353 ....G7
Panamá (cap.) 388,638 .....H6
Panamá* 498,624 ....H6
Parita 1,616 ....G7
Pedasí 934 ....G7
Penonomé 7,389 ....G6
Playón Chico 1,395 ....H6
Portobelo 551 ....H6
Puerto Armuelles 12,488 ...F6
San Carlos 562 ....G6
San Félix 617 ....G6
San Francisco 990 ....G6
Santa Fe 490 ....G6
Santiago 21,809 ....G6
Soná 4,471 ....G6
Tocumen⊙ 21,745 ....H6
Tolé 1,052 ....G6
Tonosí 891 ....G7

OTHER FEATURES

Azuero (pen.) G7
Barú (vol.) F6
Bastimentos (isl.) G6
Brewster, Cerro (mt.) H6
Burica, Punta (cape) F6
Cébaco (isl.) G7
Chame (pt.) H6
Chepo (riv.) H6
Chiriquí (lag.) F6
Chiriquí (gulf) F7
Chucunaque (riv.) J6
Coiba, Isla de (isl.) F7
Colón, Isla de (isl.) F6
Contreras (isls.) F7
Darién (mts.) J6
Escudo de Veraguas (isl.) .G6
Gatun (lake) H6
Gorda (pt.) H6
Jicarón (isl.) F7
Mala, Punta (cape) H7
Mariato, Punta (cape) G7
Montijo (gulf) G7
Mosquitos, Golfo de los
  (gulf) G6
Panama (canal) H6
Panama (gulf) H7
Pando, Cerro (mt.) F6
Parida (isl.) F6
Parita (bay) G7
Perlas (arch.) H6
Rey (isl.) H6
San Blas, Archipiélago de
  (arch.) J7
San Blas, Cordillera de
  (mts.) H6
San Blas, Golfo de (bay) H6
San Blas, Pta. de (pt.) H6
San José (isl.) H6
San Miguel, Golfo de (bay) H6
Santiago, Cerro (mt.) G6
Secas (isls.) F6
Tabasará (mts.) G6
Taboga (isl.) H6
Tiburón (pt.) J6
Valiente (pen.) G6

* City and suburbs
⊙ Population of district

CUBA

HAITI

DOMINICAN REPUBLIC

JAMAICA

TRINIDAD AND TOBAGO

BARBADOS

GRENADA

BAHAMAS

DOMINICA

ST. LUCIA

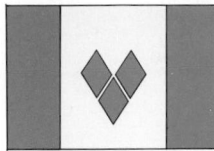
ST. VINC. & GRENS.

ANTIGUA AND BARBUDA

CUBA
AREA 44,206 sq. mi. (114,494 sq. km.)
POPULATION 10,617,000
CAPITAL Havana
LARGEST CITY Havana
HIGHEST POINT Pico Turquino
  6,561 ft. (2,000 m.)
MONETARY UNIT Cuban peso
MAJOR LANGUAGE Spanish
MAJOR RELIGION Roman Catholicism

HAITI
AREA 10,694 sq. mi. (27,697 sq. km.)
POPULATION 5,609,000
CAPITAL Port-au-Prince
LARGEST CITY Port-au-Prince
HIGHEST POINT Pic La Selle 8,793 ft. (2,680 m.)
MONETARY UNIT gourde
MAJOR LANGUAGES Creole French, French
MAJOR RELIGION Roman Catholicism

DOMINICAN REPUBLIC
AREA 18,704 sq. mi. (48,443 sq. km.)
POPULATION 6,867,000
CAPITAL Santo Domingo
LARGEST CITY Santo Domingo
HIGHEST POINT Pico Duarte
  10,417 ft. (3,175 m.)
MONETARY UNIT Dominican peso
MAJOR LANGUAGE Spanish
MAJOR RELIGION Roman Catholicism

JAMAICA
AREA 4,411 sq. mi. (11,424 sq. km.)
POPULATION 2,392,000
CAPITAL Kingston
LARGEST CITY Kingston
HIGHEST POINT Blue Mountain Peak
  7,402 ft. (2,256 m.)
MONETARY UNIT Jamaican dollar
MAJOR LANGUAGE English
MAJOR RELIGIONS Protestantism,
  Roman Catholicism

PUERTO RICO
AREA 3,515 sq. mi. (9,104 sq. km.)
POPULATION 3,522,037
CAPITAL San Juan
MONETARY UNIT U.S. dollar
MAJOR LANGUAGES Spanish, English
MAJOR RELIGION Roman Catholicism

NETHERLANDS ANTILLES
AREA 390 sq. mi. (1,010 sq. km.)
POPULATION 246,000
CAPITAL Willemstad
MONETARY UNIT Antilles guilder
MAJOR LANGUAGES Dutch, Papiamento, English
MAJOR RELIGIONS Roman Catholicism,
  Protestantism

BERMUDA
AREA 21 sq. mi. (54 sq. km.)
POPULATION 67,761
CAPITAL Hamilton
MONETARY UNIT Bermuda dollar
MAJOR LANGUAGE English
MAJOR RELIGION Protestantism

ARUBA
AREA 75 sq. mi (193 sq. km.)
POPULATION 66,790
CAPITAL Oranjestad
MONETARY UNIT Aruba guilder
MAJOR LANGUAGES Dutch, Papiamento
MAJOR RELIGION Roman Catholic

Topography

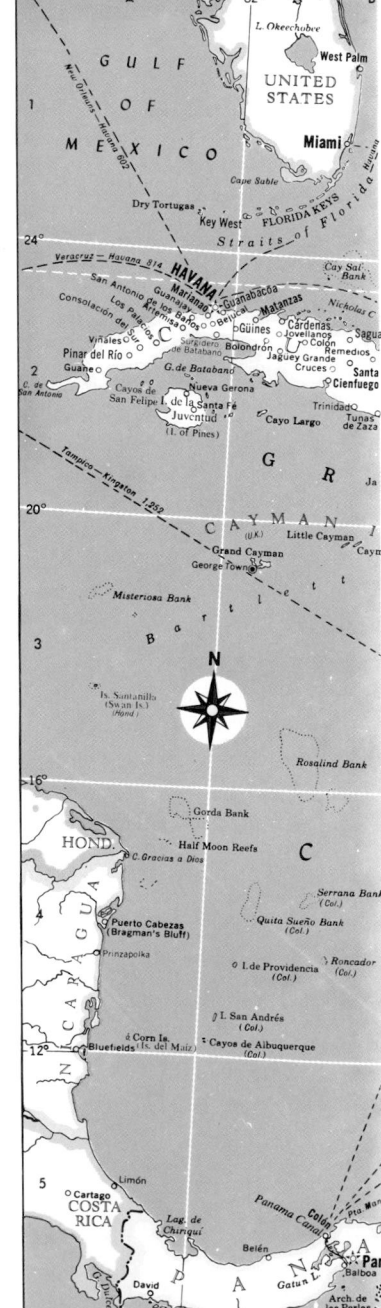

West Indies 157

TRINIDAD AND TOBAGO
AREA 1,980 sq. mi. (5,128 sq. km.)
POPULATION 1,212,000
CAPITAL Port of Spain
LARGEST CITY Port of Spain
HIGHEST POINT Mt. Aripo 3,084 ft. (940 m.)
MONETARY UNIT Trinidad and Tobago dollar
MAJOR LANGUAGES English, Hindi
MAJOR RELIGIONS Roman Catholicism,
Protestantism, Hinduism, Islam

SAINT KITTS AND NEVIS

BARBADOS
AREA 166 sq. mi. (430 sq. km.)
POPULATION 256,000
CAPITAL Bridgetown
LARGEST CITY Bridgetown
HIGHEST POINT Mt. Hillaby 1,104 ft. (336 m.)
MONETARY UNIT Barbadian dollar
MAJOR LANGUAGE English
MAJOR RELIGION Protestantism

BAHAMAS
AREA 5,382 sq. mi. (13,939 sq. km.)
POPULATION 253,000
CAPITAL Nassau
LARGEST CITY Nassau
HIGHEST POINT Mt. Alvernia 206 ft. (63 m.)
MONETARY UNIT Bahamian dollar
MAJOR LANGUAGE English
MAJOR RELIGIONS Roman Catholicism, Protestantism

GRENADA
AREA 133 sq. mi. (344 sq. km.)
POPULATION 103,103
CAPITAL St. George's
LARGEST CITY St. George's
HIGHEST POINT Mt. St. Catherine 2,757 ft. (840 m.)
MONETARY UNIT East Caribbean dollar
MAJOR LANGUAGES English, French patois
MAJOR RELIGIONS Roman Catholicism, Protestantism

DOMINICA
AREA 290 sq. mi. (751 sq. km.)
POPULATION 81,000
CAPITAL Roseau
HIGHEST POINT Morne Diablotin 4,747 ft. (1,447 m.)
MONETARY UNIT Dominican dollar
MAJOR LANGUAGES English, French patois
MAJOR RELIGIONS Roman Catholicism, Protestantism

SAINT LUCIA
AREA 238 sq. mi. (616 sq. km.)
POPULATION 148,000
CAPITAL Castries
HIGHEST POINT Mt. Gimie 3,117 ft. (950 m.)
MONETARY UNIT East Caribbean dollar
MAJOR LANGUAGES English, French patois
MAJOR RELIGIONS Roman Catholicism, Protestantism

SAINT VINCENT AND THE GRENADINES
AREA 150 sq. mi. (388 sq. km.)
POPULATION 124,000
CAPITAL Kingstown
HIGHEST POINT Soufrière 4,000 ft. (1,219 m.)
MONETARY UNIT East Caribbean dollar
MAJOR LANGUAGE English
MAJOR RELIGIONS Protestantism, Roman Catholicism

ANTIGUA AND BARBUDA
AREA 171 sq. mi. (443 sq. km.)
POPULATION 76,000
CAPITAL St. John's
HIGHEST POINT Boggy Peak 1,319 ft. (402 m.)
MONETARY UNIT East Caribbean dollar
MAJOR LANGUAGE English
MAJOR RELIGION Protestantism

SAINT KITTS & NEVIS
AREA 104 sq. mi. (269 sq. km.)
POPULATION 44,404
CAPITAL Basseterre
HIGHEST POINT Mt. Misery 4,314 ft. (1,315 m.)
MONETARY UNIT East Caribbean dollar
MAJOR LANGUAGE English
MAJOR RELIGIONS Protestantism, Roman Catholicism

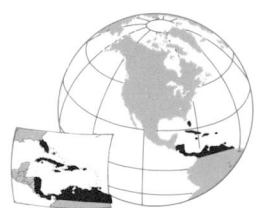

The West Indies
CONIC PROJECTION

SCALE OF MILES
0   50   100   150   200

SCALE OF KILOMETERS
0   50   100   200   300

Capitals of Countries _____ ★
Other Capitals _____ ◉

Puerto Rico

Bermuda Islands

© Copyright HAMMOND INCORPORATED, Maplewood, N.J.

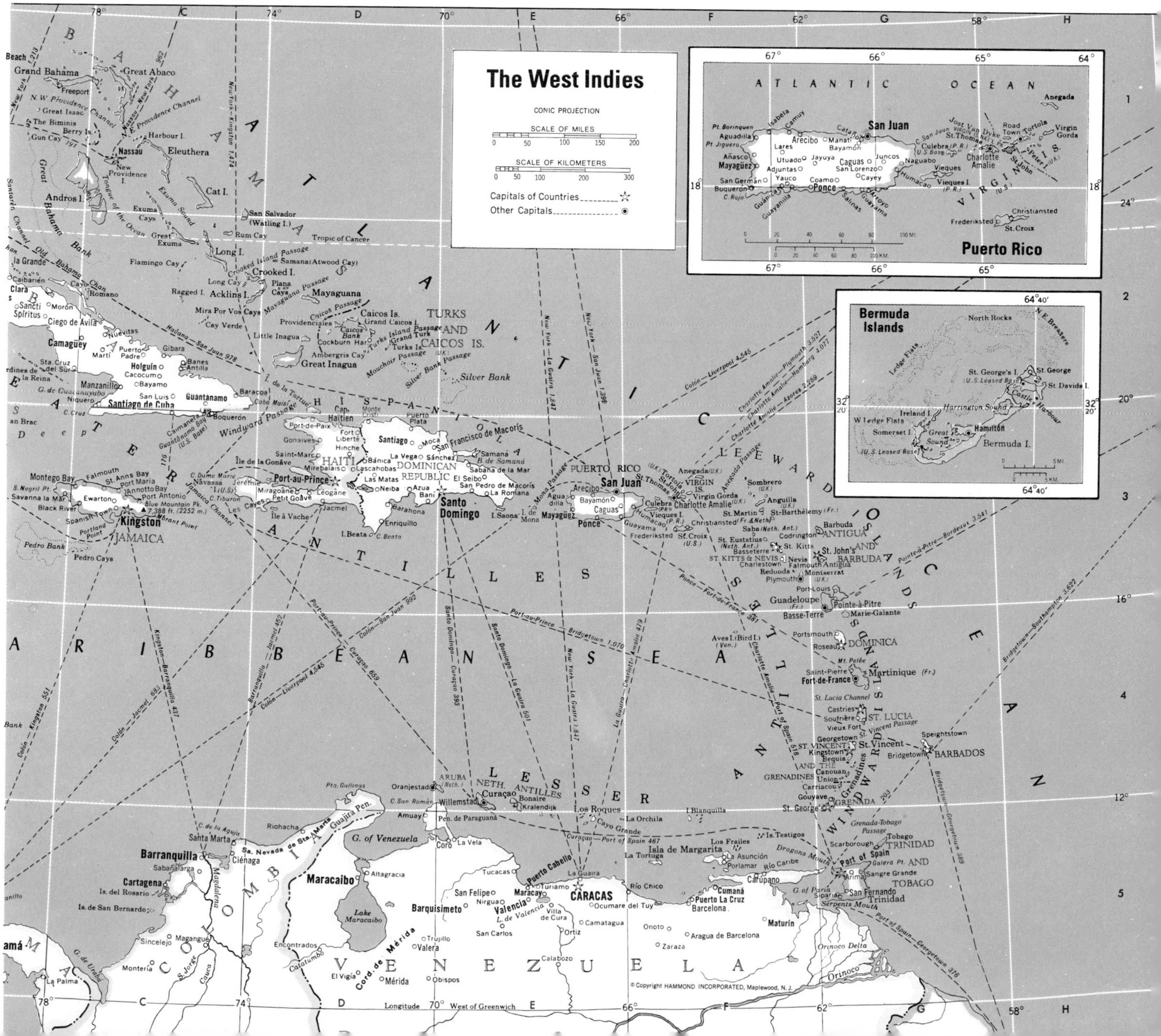

CUBA

PROVINCES

Camagüey, 664,566 . . . . .G2
Ciego de Avila 320,961 . . . . . . .F2
Cienfuegos 326,412 . . . . .E2
Granma 739,335 . . . . .H4
Guantánamo 466,609 . . . . .K4
Holguín 911,034 . . . . .J3
Juventud (municipio
  especial) 57,879 . . . . .C2
La Habana, Ciudad de
  Habana 1,924,886 . . . . .C1
La Habana (Havana) 586,029 . . .C1
Las Tunas 436,341 . . . . .H3
Matanzas 557,628 . . . . .D1
Pinar del Río 640,740 . . . . .A2
Sancti Spíritus 399,700 . . . . . . .F2
Santiago de Cuba 909,506 . . . . .J4
Villa Clara 764,743 . . . . .E1

CITIES and TOWNS

Abreus 14,267 . . . . .D2
Agramonte 4,603 . . . . .D2
Aguada de Pasajeros 20,219 D2
Alacranes 4,959 . . . . .C1
Alonso Rojas 1,427 . . . . .B2
Alquízar 12,691 . . . . .C1
Altagracia 1,722 . . . . .G3
Alto Songo-La Maya 25,188 . .J4

Amarillas 2,767 . . . . .D2
Amazonas 1,066 . . . . .F2
Antilla 10,052 . . . . .J3
Arroyo Blanco 1,431 . . . . .F2
Artemisa 45,689 . . . . .B1
Báez 4,178 . . . . .E2
Báguanos 12,678 . . . . .J3
Bahía Honda 16,901 . . . . .B1
Baire 4,879 . . . . .H4
Banao 803 . . . . .F2
Banes 38,905 . . . . .J3
Baracoa 36,702 . . . . .K4
Baraguá 12,633 . . . . .F2
Bauta 26,826 . . . . .C1
Bayamo 109,201 . . . . .H4
Bejucal 15,649 . . . . .C1
Bolondrón 5,840 . . . . .D1
Buenaventura 4,711 . . . . .H3
Buenavista 1,303 . . . . .F2
Buey Arriba 8,017 . . . . .H4
Cabaiguán 36,544 . . . . .F2
Cabañas 4,897 . . . . .B1
Cabezas 5,262 . . . . .C1
Caocum 14,145 . . . . .H3
Caibarién 32,094 . . . . .E1
Caimanera 6,664 . . . . .J4
Calabazar de Sagua 9,023 . . . . .E1
Calimete 19,925 . . . . .D1
Camagüey 245,235 . . . . .G2
Camajuaní 26,653 . . . . .E2
Campechuela 20,743 . . . . .G4
Canasí 1,637 . . . . .C1

Candelaria 10,810 . . . . .B1
Cárdenas 65,585 . . . . .D1
Cartagena 2,166 . . . . .D2
Cascajal 3,530 . . . . .E1
Cauto del Embarcadero 949 . .H4
Cauto el Cristo 1,626 . . . . .J3
Central Amancio Rodríguez
  22,506 . . . . .G3
Central Bolivia 6,301 . . . . .G2
Central Brasil 4,904 . . . . .G2
Central Cándido González
  3,414 . . . . .G3
Central Colombia 16,799 . . . . . .G3
Central Frank Pals 9,066 . . . . . .K3
Central Guatemala 5,584 . . . . . .J3
Central Haití 3,609 . . . . .G3
Central Los Reynaldos 3,997 J4
Central Loynaz Echevarría
  3,245 . . . . .J4
Central Manuel Tames 7,864 K4
Céspedes 6,634 . . . . .F2
Chambas 19,877 . . . . .F2
Chaparra 8,428 . . . . .H3
Cidra 3,567 . . . . .D1
Ciego de Avila 80,010 . . . . .F2
Cienfuegos 107,396 . . . . .D2
Colón 47,010 . . . . .D1
Condado 3,571 . . . . .D1
Consolación del Norte 4,681 . . .B1
Consolación del Sur 34,334 . . . .B2
Contramaestre 44,991 . . . . .J4
Corralillo 15,822 . . . . .D1

Cruces 20,324 . . . . .E2
Cueto 23,183 . . . . .J3
Cumanayagua 25,338 . . . . .E2
Daiquirí J4
Delicias 10,562 . . . . .H3
Dos Caminos 3,772 . . . . .J4
Dos Ríos 1,786 . . . . .J4
El Caney 3,921 . . . . .J4
El Cobre 3,952 . . . . .J4
El Santo 2,473 . . . . .E1
Encrucijada 23,029 . . . . .E1
Esmeralda 17,205 . . . . .G1
Esperanza 9,241 . . . . .E2
Florencia 6,979 . . . . .F2
Florida 43,881 . . . . .G3
Fomento 17,310 . . . . .F2
Gaspar 2,682 . . . . .F2
Gibara 23,137 . . . . .J3
Guáimaro 29,712 . . . . .G3
Guanabacoa 89,741 . . . . .C1
Guanajay 21,042 . . . . .B1
Guane 14,126 . . . . .A2
Guantánamo 178,129 . . . . .K4
Guaro 3,086 . . . . .J3
Guasimal 3,057 . . . . .E2
Guayabal 3,703 . . . . .G3
Guayos 6,753 . . . . .F2
Güines 51,691 . . . . .C1
Güira de Melena 19,851 . . . . . .C1
Guisa 15,182 . . . . .H4
Havana (cap.) 1,924,886 . . . . . .C1
Herradura 3,762 . . . . .B1

Holguín 190,155 . . . . .J3
Ignacio Agramonte 1,487 . . . . .G3
Isabela de Sagua 3,721 . . . . . . .E1
Jagüey Grande 30,205 . . . . .D2
Jamaica 5,128 . . . . .C1
Jaruco 16,844 . . . . .C1
Jatibonico 17,047 . . . . .F2
Jíbaro 1,263 . . . . .F2
Jiguaní 25,069 . . . . .H4
Jobabo 14,899 . . . . .H3
Jovellanos 35,043 . . . . .D1
La Coloma 3,462 . . . . .B2
La Maya-Alto Songo 25,188 . .J4
Las Martinas 4,511 . . . . .A2
Limonar 4,491 . . . . .D1
Los Arabos 10,664 . . . . .E1
Los Palacios 21,884 . . . . .B1
Lugareño 4,396 . . . . .G3
Mabay 6,176 . . . . .H4
Maceo 2,652 . . . . .H3
Majagua 9,110 . . . . .F2
Manacas 5,914 . . . . .E1
Manatí 11,054 . . . . .H3
Manguito 2,739 . . . . .D1
Manicaragua 33,900 . . . . .E2
Mantua 9,165 . . . . .A2
Mapos (Amazonas) 1,066 . . . . .F2
Manzanillo 95,420 . . . . .H4
Mariano ○127,563 . . . . .C1
Mariel 24,115 . . . . .B1
Martí 11,474 . . . . .D1

Matanzas 103,302 . . . . .C1
Máximo Gómez, Ciego
  de Avila 5,116 . . . . .F2
Máximo Gómez, Matanzas
  4,970 . . . . .D1
Mayajigua 4,425 . . . . .F2
Mayarí 54,699 . . . . .J3
Mayarí Arriba 2,302 . . . . .J4
Media Luna 13,794 . . . . .H4
Mendoza 2,914 . . . . .A2
Meneses 4,768 . . . . .F2
Minas 17,675 . . . . .G2
Minas de Matahambre
  14,976 . . . . .A1
Moa 28,696 . . . . .K3
Morón 40,396 . . . . .F2
Nicaro 9,506 . . . . .J3
Niquero 15,544 . . . . .G4
Nueva Gerona 17,175 . . . . .C2
Nuevitas 35,103 . . . . .G2
Orozco 4,256 . . . . .B1
Palma Soriano 66,222 . . . . .J4
Palmira 19,680 . . . . .D2
Pedro Betancourt 22,915 . . . . . .D1
Perico 20,633 . . . . .D1
Pilón 10,194 . . . . .H4
Pinar del Río 104,598 . . . . .B2
Placetas 46,038 . . . . .E2
Primero Enero 14,807 . . . . .F2
Puerto Esperanza 3,499 . . . . . . .A1
Puerto Padre 46,806 . . . . .H3
Quemado de Güines 11,208 E1

Rancho Veloz 3,966 . . . . .D1
Ranchuelo 24,255 . . . . .E2
Regla 38,491 . . . . .C1
Remedios 27,722 . . . . .E2
Repúbliica Dominicana
  2,540 . . . . .E2
Río Cauto 19,550 . . . . .H4
Rodas 16,350 . . . . .D2
Sagua de Tánamo 15,327 . . . . . .K3
Sagua la Grande 52,315 . . . . . .E1
San Andrés 2,127 . . . . .H3
San Antonio de los Baños
  28,137 . . . . .C1
San Cristóbal 30,769 . . . . .B1
Sancti Spíritus 79,542 . . . . .E2
San Diego de los Baños
  1,430 . . . . .B1
San Germán 12,362 . . . . .J3
San José de las Lajas
  37,148 . . . . .C1
San José de los Ramos
  1,726 . . . . .D1
San Juan y Martínez 13,227 . . . .B2
San Luis, Pinar del Río
  5,677 . . . . .B2
San Luis, Santiago de Cuba
  32,826 . . . . .J4
San Nicolás 12,368 . . . . .C1
San Ramón 2,676 . . . . .H4
Santa Clara 175,113 . . . . .E2
Santa Cruz del Norte
  15,239 . . . . .C1

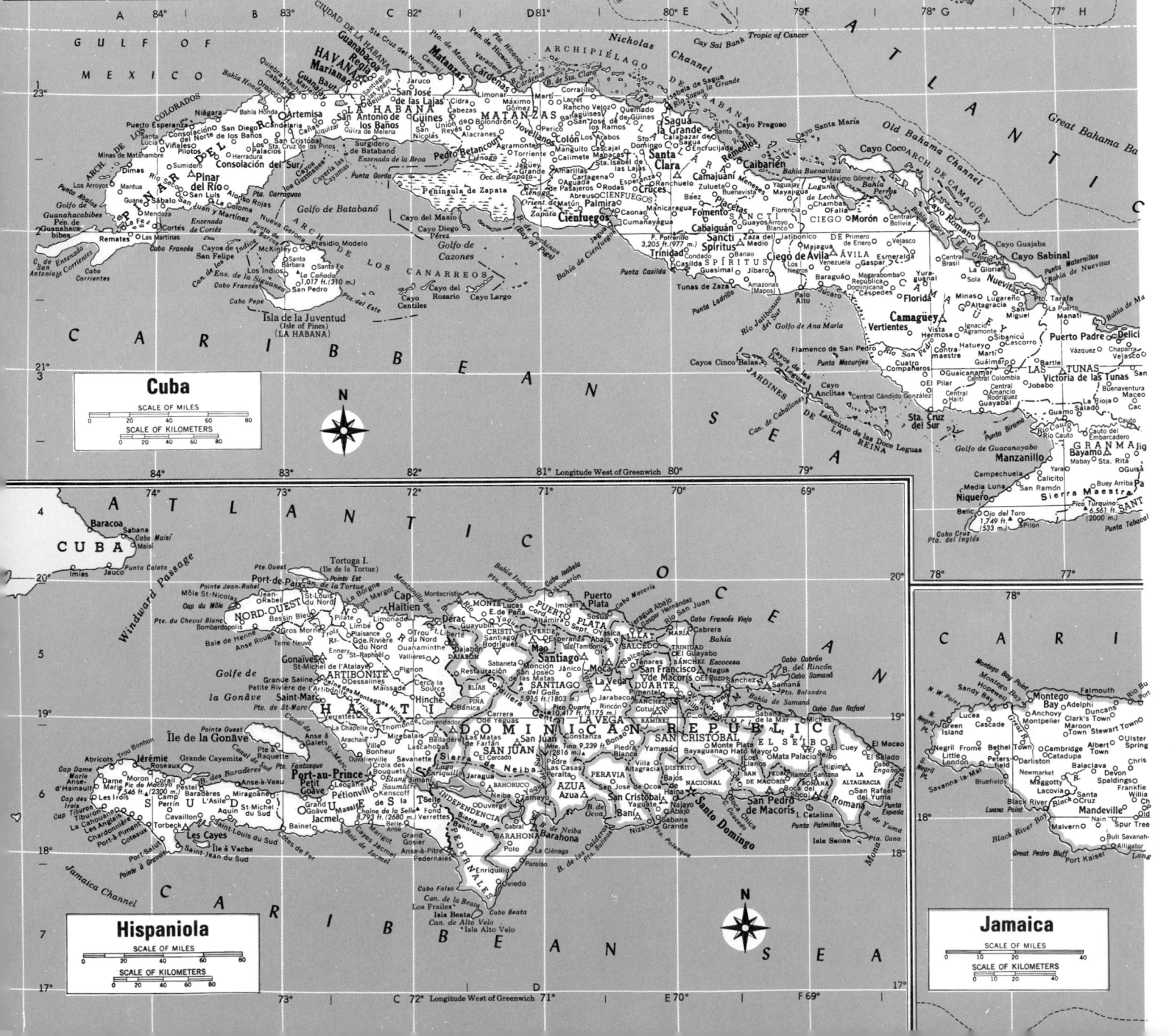

Cuba

SCALE OF MILES

SCALE OF KILOMETERS

Hispaniola

SCALE OF MILES

SCALE OF KILOMETERS

Jamaica

SCALE OF MILES

SCALE OF KILOMETERS

Santa Cruz de los Pinos 3,545 .... B1
Santa Cruz del Sur 27,142 .. G3
Santa Fe 3,925 .... B2
Santa Isabel de las Lajas 7,279 .... E2
Santa Lucía 3,734 .. J3
Santa Rita 6,358 .. H4
Santiago de Cuba 362,432 .. J4
Santiago de las Vegas 29,325 .... C1
Santo Domingo 32,950 .. E1
Sibanicú 14,252 .. G3
Sola 2,436 .... G2
Sumidero 980 .. A2
Surgidero de Batabanó 11,533 .... C1
Tacajó 4,469 .... J3
Torriente 1,759 .. D11
Trinidad 42,080 .. E2
Unión de Reyes 28,422 .. C1
Varadero 14,737 .. D1
Vázquez 3,851 .. H3
Velasco 5,618 .. H3
Venezuela 13,744 .. G3
Vertientes 25,178 .. G3
Victoria de las Tunas 87,522 H3
Viñales 2,049 .. A1
Yaguajay 30,720 .. F2
Yara 238,879 .. H4
Zaza del Medio 7,495 .. F2
Zulueta 5,425 .. E2

OTHER FEATURES

Abalos (pt.) A2
Ana María (gulf) .. F3
Anclitas (cay) .. F3
Batabanó (gulf) .. C1
Birama (pt.) G4
Broa (inlet) .. C1
Buenavista (bay) .. F2
Caballones (chan.) .. G3
Camagüey (arch.) .. G3
Cantiles (cay) .. C3
Cárdenas (bay) .. D1
Carraguao (pt.) .. G4
Casilda (pt.) .. E2
Cauto (riv.) .. H3
Cayamas (cays) .. C2
Cazones (gulf) .. E3
Cienfuegos (bay) .. D2
Cinco Balas (cays) .. E3
Cochinos (bay) .. D2
Coco (cay) .. G4
Corrientes (cape) .. A2
Corrientes (inlet) .. A2
Cortés (inlet) .. B2
Cristal, Sierra del (mts.) .. J3
Cruz (cape) .. G4
Diego Pérez (cay) .. C3
Doce Leguas (cays) .. F3
Este (pt.) .. C3
Fragoso (cay) .. F1
Francés (cape) .. E2

Gorda (pt.) C2
Gran Piedra (mt.) .. J4
Guacanayabo (gulf) .. G4
Guajaba (cay) .. G2
Guanahacabibes (gulf) .. A2
Guanahacabibes (pen.) .. A2
Guantánamo (bay) .. J4
Guantánamo Bay U.S. Nav. Reserve .. K4
Guarico (pt.) .. K3
Guzmanes (cays) .. B2
Hicacos (pen.) .. D1
Hicacos (pt.) .. D1
Honda (bay) .. B1
Indios (chan.) .. B2
Inglés (pt.) .. G4
Jardines de la Reina (arch.) .. F3
Jatibonico del Sur (riv.) .. F3
Jiguey (bay) .. G2
Juventud, Isla de la (Pines) (isl.) 57,879 .. B3
Laberinto de las Doce Leguas (cays) .. F3
Ladrillo (pt.) .. E3
Largo (cay) .. D2
Leche (lag.) .. F2
Los Barcos (pt.) .. B2
Los Canarreos (arch.) .. C2
Los Colorados (arch.) .. A1
Lucrecia (cape) .. J3
Macurijes (pt.) .. F3
Maestra, Sierra (mts.) .. H4
Maisí (cape) .. K4
Mangle (pt.) .. J3
Maslo (bay) .. C2
Matanzas (bay) .. D1
Nicholas (chan.) .. E1
Nipe (bay) .. J3
Nuevitas (bay) .. H2
Ojo del Toro (mt.) .. G4
Old Bahama (chan.) .. G1
Pepe (cape) .. B3
Perros (bay) .. G2
Pigs (Cochinos) (bay) .. D2
Pines (Isla de la Juventud) (isl.) 7,879 .. B3
Potrerillo (peak) .. E2
Quemado (pt.) .. K4
Romano (cay) .. G2
Rosario (cay) .. C2
Sabana (arch.) .. E1
Sabinal (cay) .. H2
Sagua la Grande (riv.) .. E1
San Antonio (cape) .. A2
San Felipe (cays) .. B2
San Pedro (riv.) .. G3
Santa Clara (bay) .. D1
Santa María (cay) .. F1
Siguanea (bay) .. B3
Tabacal (pt.) .. H4
Toa, Cuchillas de (mts.) .. K4
Tortuguilla (pt.) .. K4
Turquino (peak) .. H4
Zapata (pen.) .. C2
Zapata Occidental (swamp) .. D2
Zapata Oriental (swamp) .. D2

DOMINICAN REPUBLIC
PROVINCES

Azua 142,770 .... D6

Bahoruco 78,636 .... D6
Barahona 137,160 .. D6
Dajabón 57,709 .. D5
Distrito Nacional 1,550,739 .. E6
Duarte 235,544 .. E5
Elías Piña 65,384 .. D6
El Seibo 157,866 .. F6
Espaillat 164,017 .. E5
Independencia 38,768 .. D6
La Altagracia 100,112 .. F6
La Romana 109,769 .. F6
La Vega 385,043 .. D6
María Trinidad Sánchez 112,629 .. E5
Monte Cristi 83,407 .. D5
Pedernales 17,006 .. D7
Peravia 168,123 .. E6
Puerto Plata 206,757 .. D5
Salcedo 99,191 .. E5
Samaná 65,699 .. E5
Sánchez Ramírez 126,567 .. E5
San Cristóbal 446,132 .. E6
San Juan 239,957 .. D6
San Pedro de Macorís 152,890 .. F6
Santiago 550,372 .. D5
Santiago Rodríguez 55,411 .. D5
Valverde 100,319 .. D5

CITIES and TOWNS

Altamira 2,759 .... D5
Azua 31,481 .. D6
Bajos de Haina 33,135 .. E6
Baní 36,705 .. E6
Barahona 49,334 .. D6
Bonao 44,486 .. E5
Cabrera 2,542 .. E5
Comendador 5,962 .. D6
Constanza 15,141 .. D6
Cotuí 16,688 .. E5
Dajabón 8,808 .. D5
El Seibo 13,511 .. F6
Hato Mayor 17,859 .. F6
Higüey 33,501 .. F6
Imbert 5,315 .. D5
Jarabacoa 13,416 .. E5
Jimaní 3,327 .. C6
La Romana 91,571 .. F6
La Vega 52,432 .. E5
Luperón 2,500 .. D5
Mao 33,527 .. D5
Moca 31,176 .. E5
Monción 3,344 .. D5
Nagua 20,912 .. E5
Puerto Plata 45,348 .. D5
Sabana de la Mar 9,983 .. F5
Sabaneta 9,170 .. D5
Samaná 5,023 .. E5
Sánchez 7,919 .. E5
San Cristóbal 58,520 .. E6
San Francisco de Macorís 64,906 .. E5
San Juan 49,764 .. D6
San Pedro de Macorís 78,562 .. F6
Santiago 278,638 .. D5
Santo Domingo (cap.) 1,313,172 .. E6
Tenares 4,065 .. E5
Villa Altagracia 20,890 .. E6

OTHER FEATURES

Alto Velo (chan.) C7
Alto Velo (isl.) .. D7
Balandra (pt.) .. D7
Beata (cape) .. D7
Beata (chan.) .. D7
Beata (isl.) .. D7
Cabrón (cape) .. F5
Calderas (bay) .. E6
Cana (pt.) .. F6
Catalina (isl.) .. F6
Caucedo (cape) .. E6
Central, Cordillera (range) .. D5
Duarte (peak) .. D5
Engaño (cape) .. F6
Enriquillo (lake) .. D6
Escocesa (bay) .. E5
Espada (pt.) .. F6
Falso (cape) .. C7
Francés Viejo (cape) .. E5
Gallo (mt.) .. D5
Isabela (bay) .. D5
Isabela (cape) .. D5
Los Frailes (isl.) .. C7
Macorís (cape) .. C5
Manzanillo (bay) .. C5
Mona (passg.) .. G6
Neiba (bay) .. D6
Neiba, Sierra de (mts.) .. D6
Ocoa (bay) .. E6
Oriental, Cordillera (range) .. F6
Palenque (pt.) .. E6
Palmillas (pt.) .. F5
Rincón (bay) .. F5
Rucia (pt.) .. D6
Salinas (pt.) .. D6
Samaná (bay) .. F5
Samaná (cape) .. F5
San Rafael (cape) .. F5
Saona (isl.) .. F6
Septentrional, Cordillera (range) .. D5
Tina (mt.) .. D6
Yaque del Norte (riv.) .. D5
Yaque del Sur (riv.) .. D6
Yuma (bay) .. F6
Yuna (riv.) .. E5

HAITI
DEPARTMENTS

Artibonite C5
Nord .. C5
Nord-Ouest .. B5
Ouest .. C6
Sud .. A6

CITIES and TOWNS

Anse-à-Galets 3,623 .. B6
Anse-d'Hainault 5,220 .. A6
Aquin 3,820 .. B6
Cap-Haïtien 64,406 .. C5
Croix des Bouquets 4,365 .. C6
Dame Marie 4,320 .. A6
Dérac 1,300 .. C5

Dessalines 7,984 .... C5
Fort Liberté 5,012 .. C5
Gonaïves 34,209 .. B5
Grande Rivière du Nord 6,007 .. C5
Gros Morne 4,739 .. B5
Hinche 10,070 .. C5
Jacmel 13,730 .. C6
Jérémie 18,493 .. A6
Kenscoff 2,605 .. C6
Lascahobas 3,805 .. C6
Léogâne 5,782 .. C6
Les Cayes 34,090 .. B6
Limbé 10,476 .. C5
Miragoâne 4,327 .. B6
Mirebalais 6,069 .. C6
Ouanaminthe 7,276 .. C5
Pétionville 35,333 .. C6
Petite Rivière de l'Artibonite 10,099 .. B5
Petit Goâve 7,310 .. B6
Pignon 4,576 .. C5
Port-au-Prince (cap.) 449,831 .. C6
Port-de-Paix 15,540 .. B5
Saint-Louis du Nord 7,203 .. B5
Saint-Marc 24,165 .. B5
Saint-Michel de l'Atalaye 7,559 .. C5
Saint-Raphaël 3,889 .. C5
Trou du Nord 7,637 .. C5
Verrettes 3,670 .. C5

OTHER FEATURES

Artibonite (riv.) C5
Baradères (bay) .. B6
Cheval Blanc (pt.) .. B5
Dame Marie (cape) .. A6
Est (pt.) .. C4
Fantasque (pt.) .. B6
Gonâve (gulf) .. B6
Gonâve (isl.) .. B6
Grande Cayemite (isl.) .. B6
Gravois (pt.) .. A7
Irois (cape) .. A6
Jean-Rabel (pt.) .. B5
Macaya (mt.) .. A6
Manzanillo (bay) .. C5
Môle (cape) .. B5
Noires (mts.) .. C5
Ouest (pt.) .. B4
Ouest (pt.) .. B6
Saint-Marc (chan.) .. B6
Saint-Marc (pt.) .. C5
Saumâtre (lake) .. C6
Selle (peak) .. C6
Sud (pt.) .. B6
Tortue (chan.) .. C5
Tortue (Tortuga) (isl.) .. C4
Tortuga (isl.) .. C4
Trois-Rivières (riv.) .. B5
Vache (isl.) .. B6
Windward (passg.) .. A5

JAMAICA
CITIES and TOWNS

Alley J7

Alligator Pond H6
Anchovy 2,558 .. H5
Annotto Bay .. K6
Bamboo 2,971 .. J6
Bath .. K6
Black River 2,701 .. H6
Bog Walk .. K6
Bowden .. K6
Browns Town 5,479 .. J6
Bull Savanna-Junction 5,110 .. H6
Cambridge 2,449 .. H6
Catadupa .. H6
Christiana .. H6
Discovery Bay 1,814 .. J5
Falmouth 3,937 .. H5
Green Island .. G5
Hope Bay .. K6
Kingston (cap.) 106,791 .. K6
Kingston *516,865 .. J7
Linstead .. K6
Lucea 3,635 .. G5
Mandeville 14,421 .. H6
Maroon Town 2,717 .. H6
May Pen 26,074 .. J6
Montego Bay 43,521 .. H5
Montpelier .. H5
Morant Bay 7,465 .. K7
Negril .. G6
Ocho Rios 5,851 .. J6
Oracabessa .. K6
Port Antonio 10,538 .. K6
Port Kaiser .. H7
Port Maria 5,259 .. K6
Port Morant .. K7
Saint Ann's Bay 7,101 .. J5
Saint Margaret's Bay .. K6
Savanna-la-Mar 11,759 .. G6
Spanish Town 40,731 .. J6
Williamsfield .. H6

OTHER FEATURES

Black (riv.) H6
Black River (bay) .. H6
Blue (mts.) .. J6
Blue Mountain (peak) .. J6
Galina (pt.) .. J6
Grande (riv.) .. H6
Great (riv.) .. H6
Great Pedro Bluff (prom.) .. H7
Long (bay) .. H7
Luana (pt.) .. J6
Minho (riv.) .. J6
Montego (bay) .. G5
Montego Bay (pt.) .. G5
North East (pt.) .. K6
North Negril (pt.) .. G6
North West (pt.) .. G6
Old Harbour (bay) .. J6
Portland (pt.) .. J7
Sir John's (peak) .. K6
South East (pt.) .. K6
South Negril (pt.) .. G6

*City and Suburbs.
○ Population of municipality.

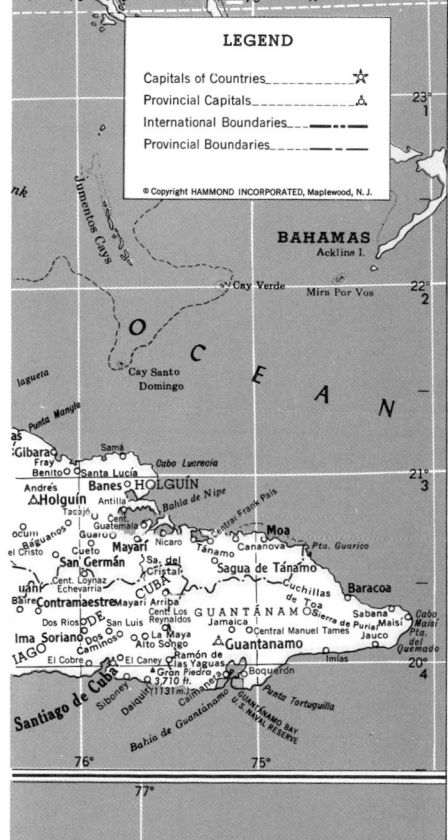

LEGEND

Capitals of Countries .... ☆
Provincial Capitals .... △
International Boundaries .... ▬▬▬
Provincial Boundaries ....

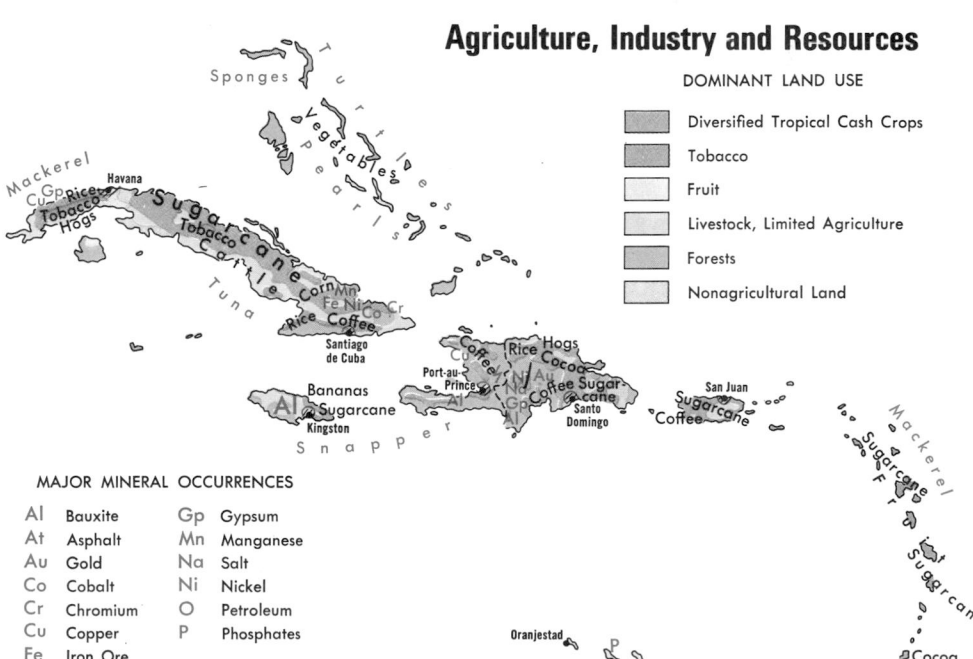

Agriculture, Industry and Resources

DOMINANT LAND USE

Diversified Tropical Cash Crops
Tobacco
Fruit
Livestock, Limited Agriculture
Forests
Nonagricultural Land

MAJOR MINERAL OCCURRENCES

Al	Bauxite	Gp	Gypsum
At	Asphalt	Mn	Manganese
Au	Gold	Na	Salt
Co	Cobalt	Ni	Nickel
Cr	Chromium	O	Petroleum
Cu	Copper	P	Phosphates
Fe	Iron Ore		

⚡ Water Power
Major Industrial Areas

(continued)

PUERTO RICO

DISTRICTS

Aguadilla A1
Arecibo C1
Bayamón D1
Guayama D2
Humacao E2
Mayagüez B2
Ponce C2
San Juan D1

CITIES and TOWNS

Adjuntas 5,239 B2
Aguada 5,025 A1
Aguadilla 22,039 A1
Aguas Buenas 3,766 E2
Aibonito 9,331 D2
Añasco 5,646 A1
Angeles ○2,817 B2
Arecibo 48,779 B1
Arroyo 8,435 E3
Bahomamey A1
Bajadero 3,678 C1
Barceloneta 4,502 C1
Barranquitas 3,618 D2
Bayamón 185,087 D1
Boquerón ○3,675 A3
Cabo Rojo 10,292 A2
Caguas 87,214 E2
Caguas †156,819 E2
Camuy 3,834 B1
Carolina 147,835 E1
Cataño 26,243 D1
Cayey 23,305 D2
Ceiba 4,973 F2
Central Aguirre 1,049 D3
Ciales 3,582 C1
Cidra 6,069 D2
Coamo 12,851 D2
Comerío 5,736 D2
Coquí 3,018 D3
Corozal 5,889 D1
Coto Laurel ○5,192 C2
Culebra (Dewey) 938 G1
Dorado 10,203 D1
Ensenada B3
Esperanza 1,130 G2
Fajardo 26,928 F1
Florida 3,641 C1
Guánica 9,628 B3
Guayama 21,097 E3
Guayanilla 6,163 B3
Guaynabo 65,075 D1
Gurabo 7,645 E2
Hatillo 5,019 B1
Hato Rey E1
Hormigueros 12,031 A2
Humacao 19,147 E2
Isabela 12,087 A1
Isabel Segunda 2,330 G2
Jayuya 3,588 C2
Jobos 4,194 D3
Juana Díaz 10,469 C2
Juncos 7,851 E2
Lajas 4,275 A2
Lares 5,224 B2
Las Piedras 4,857 E2
Levittown 31,613 D1
Loíza 3,932 E1
Loíza Aldea E1
Luquillo 4,531 F1
Manatí 17,347 C1
Maricao 1,390 B2
Mayagüez 82,968 A2
Mayagüez †98,155 A2
Moca 3,960 A1
Naguabo 4,135 F2
Naranjito 2,849 D1
Palmer 1,566 F1
Palo Seco 1,172 D1
Parguera A3
Patillas 3,172 E2
Peñuelas 4,235 B2
Playa de Fajardo F1
Playa de Humacao ○5,573 F2
Ponce 161,739 C3
Ponce †168,272 C3
Puerto Nuevo D1
Puerto Real 2,390 A2
Puerto Real (Playa de Fajardo) F1
Punta Santiago (Playa de Humacao) ○5,573 F2
Quebradillas 3,770 B1
Río Blanco 1,433 F2
Río Grande 12,047 E1
Río Piedras E1
Rosario A2
Sabana Grande 7,435 B2
Sabana Seca 11,431 D1
Salinas 6,220 D3
San Antonio 2,681 A1
San Germán 13,054 A2
San Juan (cap.) 424,600 E1
San Juan †1,081,193 E1
San Lorenzo 8,880 E2
San Sebastián 10,619 B1
Santa Isabel 6,948 C3
Santurce E1
Tallaboa 1,059 B3
Toa Alta 4,427 D1
Toa Baja 1,992 D1
Trujillo Alto 41,141 E1
Utuado 11,113 B2
Vega Alta 10,582 D1
Vega Baja 18,233 D1
Vieques (Isabel Segunda) 2,330 G2
Villalba 3,469 C2
Yabucoa 6,797 E2
Yauco 14,594 B2

OTHER FEATURES

Aguadilla (bay) A1
Algarrobo (pt.) A2
Añasco (bay) A1
Arenas (pt.) F2
Bauta (riv.) C2
Bayamón (riv.) D1
Boquerón (bay) A3
Borinquen (pt.) A1
Cabullones (pt.) C3
Caja de Muertos (isl.) C3
Camuy (riv.) B1
Canovanas (riv.) E1
Caonillas (lake) C2
Carite (lake) E2
Carraízo (lake) E1
Cayey, Sierra de (mts.) D2
Central, Cordillera (range) C2
Cerro Gordo (pt.) D1
Coamo (res.) D3
Coamo (riv.) D3
Culebra (isl.) 1,265 G1
Culebrinas (riv.) A1
Culebrita (isl.) G2
El Toro (mt.) F2
El Yunque (mt.) F1
Este (pt.) G2
Fajardo (riv.) F1
Figuras (pt.) E3
Fosforescente (bay) A3
Grande de Añasco (riv.) B2
Grande de Arecibo (riv.) C1
Grande de Loíza (riv.) E1
Grande de Manatí (riv.) C1
Guajataca (lake) B1
Guanajibo (pt.) A2
Guanajibo (riv.) A2
Guánica (lake) B3
Guaniquilla (pt.) A2
Guayabal (lake) C2
Guayanés (pt.) F2
Guayanés (riv.) E2
Guayanilla (bay) B3
Guayo (lake) B2
Guilarte (mt.) B2
Honda (bay) F2
Jacaguas (riv.) C2
Jaicoa, Cordillera (mts.) B1
Jiguero (pt.) A1
Jobos (bay) D3
Lima (pt.) F2
Luquillo, Sierra de (mts.) E2
Manglillo (pt.) B3
Mayagüez (bay) A2
Miquillo (pt.) F1
Molinos (pt.) G1
Mona (passg.) A2
Negra (pt.) G2
Nigua (riv.) D2
Ola Grande (pt.) D3
Palmas Altas (pt.) C1
Patillas (lake) E2
Petrona (pt.) D3
Pirata (mt.) F2
Plata (riv.) D2
Puerca (pt.) F2
Puerto Medio Mundo (bay) F2
Punta, Cerro de (mt.) C2
Ramey A.F.B. A1
Rincón (bay) D3
Rojo (cape) A3
Roosevelt Road Naval Res. F2
Salinas (pt.) D1
San José (lag.) E1
San Juan, Cabezas de (prom.) F1
San Juan Nat'l Hist. Site D1
Soldado (pt.) G2
Sucia (bay) A3
Tanamá (riv.) B1
Toro, El (mt.) F2
Torrecilla (lag.) E1
Tortuguero (lag.) D1
Tuna (pt.) E3
Vacía Talega (pt.) E1
Vieques (isl.) 7,662 G2
Vieques (passg.) F2
Vieques (sound) G2
Yagüez (riv.) A2
Yauco (lake) B2
Yeguas ((pt.) F3

ANTIGUA

CITIES and TOWNS

All Saints 1,796 E11
Cedar Grove 1,460 E11
Falmouth 1,134 E11
Freetown 1,250 E11
Jennings 1,370 D11
Liberta 2,394 E11
Old Road 1,244 D11
Parham 1,570 E11
Saint John's (cap.) 21,814 E11
Willikies 1,843 E11

OTHER FEATURES

Antigua (isl.) 76,213 E11
Boggy (peak) D11
Boon (pt.) E11
Green (isl.) E11
Guiana (isl.) E11
Long (isl.) E11
Saint John's (harb.) C11
Standfast (pt.) E11
Willoughby (bay) E11

ARUBA

CITIES and TOWNS

Aresji D9
Balashi E10
Bubali D10
Bushiribana E10
Druif D1
Oranjestad (cap.) Aruba 10,100 D10
Sint Nicolaas E10
Westpunt D10

OTHER FEATURES

Aruba (isl.) 66,790 E9
Basora (pt.) E10
Jamanota (mt.) E10
Paarden (bay) D10
Palm (beach) D10

BARBADOS

CITIES and TOWNS

Bathsheba B8
Belleplaine B8
Bridgetown (cap.) 7,552 B9
Carlton B8
Cave Hill B9
Checker Hall B8
Codrington B8
Crab Hill B8
Crane C9
Drax Hall B8
Ellerton B9
Greenland B8
Holetown B8
Kendal B8
Lodge Hill B8
Marchfield B9
Mount Standfast B8
Oistins B9
Rose Hill B8
Rouen B9
Saint Lawrence B9
Saint Martins C9
Scarboro B9
Seawell B9
Six Mens B8
Speightstown B8
Spring Hall B8
Welchman Hall B8

OTHER FEATURES

Carlisle (bay) B9
Hillaby (mt.) B8
Long (bay) B9
North (pt.) B8
Oistins (bay) B9
Pelican (isl.) B9
Ragged (pt.) C8
Sam Lord's Castle C9
South (pt.) B9

DOMINICA

CITIES and TOWNS

Barroui 1,480 E6
Castle Bruce 1,975 F6
Coulihaut 1,735 E6
Delice F7
Grand Bay 3,152 F7
Hampstead E5
La Plaine F6
Mahout 2,095 E6
Marigot 3,183 F6
Petit Soufrière F6
Portsmouth 2,329 E5
Rosalie F6
Roseau (cap.) 9,968 E7
Roseau *16,035 E7
Saint Joseph 2,643 E6
Salybia F6
Soufrière E7
Vieille Case E5
Wesley 2,002 F5

OTHER FEATURES

Capuchin (cape) E5
Carib Reserve F6
Clyde (riv.) F6
Crumpton (pt.) F5
Diablotin, Morne (mt.) E6
Dominica (passg.) E5
Douglas (bay) E5
Grand (bay) F7
Jaquet (pt.) E5
Layou (riv.) E6
Martinique (passg.) E7
Micotrin (mt.) F6
Pagoua (bay) F6
Prince Rupert (bay) E5
Scotts (head) E7
Soufrière (bay) E7
Trois Pitons, Morne (mt.) E6

GRENADA

CITIES and TOWNS

Gouyave 2,498 C8
Grand Roy C8
Grenville 1,723 D8
Hermitage D8
La Taste D8
Marquis D8
Mount Tivoli D8
Saint George's (cap.) 6,463 C9
Saint George's *34,624 C9
Sauteurs 605 D8
Victoria 1,673 D8
Woodford C8

OTHER FEATURES

Bedford (pt.) D8
David (pt.) D8
Great Bacolet (pt.) D8
Green (isl.) D8
Grenville (bay) D8
Gros (pt.) D8
Halifax (harb.) C8
Irvin's (bay) D8
Les Tantes (isls.) D7
Molinière (pt.) C8
Prickly (pt.) C9
Ronde (isl.) D7
Saint Catherine (mt.) D8
Saline (pt.) C9
Sinai (mt.) D8
Telescope (pt.) D8

GUADELOUPE
Total Population 329,017

CITIES and TOWNS

Anse-Bertrand 1,921 A5
Baie-Mahault 5,874 A6
Baillif 3,844 A7
Bananier A7
Basse-Terre (cap.) 13,397 A7
Bouillante 1,821 A6
Bourg-des-Saintes 907 A7
Capesterre 7,541 A7
Ferry A6
Gosier 13,741 B6
Gourbeyre 5,637 A7
Goyave 1,709 A6
Grand-Bourg 3,249 B7
Lamentin 2,319 A6
Les Abymes 51,837 B6
Morne-à-l'Eau 9,457 A6
Moule 9,800 B6
Petit-Bourg 5,097 A6
Petit-Canal 1,581 A6
Pigeon A6
Pointe-à-Pitre 25,151 B6
Pointe-Noire 2,180 A6
Port-Louis 4,517 B5
Saint-Claude 6,755 A7
Sainte-Anne 11,527 B6
Sainte-Marguerite B6
Sainte-Marie A6
Sainte-Rose 4,805 A6
Saint-François 3,141 B6
Trois-Rivières 7,881 A7
Vieux-Fort 1,073 B7
Vieux-Habitants 4,065 A7

OTHER FEATURES

Allègre (pt.) A6
Antigues (pt.) A5
Basse-Terre (isl.) 138,777 A6
Châteaux (pt.) B6
Constant, Morne (hill) B7
Désirade, La (isl.) 1,602 B6
Fajou (isl.) A6
Grand Cul-de-Sac Marin (bay) A6
Grande-Terre (isl.) B6
Grande Vigie (pt.) B5
Grand-Îlet (isl.) A7
Guadeloupe (isl.) 167,896 B6
Guadeloupe (passg.) A5
Guadeloupe Nat'l Park A6
Kahouanne (isl.) A6
Marie-Galante (isl.) 13,757 B7
Nord (pt.) B7
Nord-Est (bay) B6
Petit Cul-de-Sac Marin (bay) A6
Petite-Terre (isls.) B6
Saintes (chan.) A7
Saintes (isls.) 2,901 A7
Salée (riv.) A6
Sans Toucher (mt.) A6
Soufrière (mt.) A7
Terre-de-Bas (isl.) 1,427 A7
Terre-de-Haut (isl.) 1,453 A7
Vieux-Fort (pt.) A7

MARTINIQUE
Total Population 330,220

CITIES and TOWNS

Ajoupa-Bouillon 1,569 C5
Basse-Pointe 2,163 C5
Bellefontaine 818 C6
Case-Pilote 1,776 C6
Ducos 4,429 D6
Fond-Saint-Denis 962 C6
Fort-de-France (cap.) 96,649 C6
Grand' Rivière 1,053 C5
Gros-Morne 1,976 D6
La Trinité 3,380 D6
Le Carbet 2,321 C6
Le François 2,940 D6
Le Lamentin 6,872 D6
Le Lorrain 2,024 D6
Le Marin 2,651 D7
Le Morne-Rouge 2,650 C5
Le Prêcheur 1,350 C6
Le Robert 3,610 D6
Le Saint-Esprit 3,947 D6
Les Trois-Îlets 1,484 D6
Le Vauclin 3,054 D6
Macouba 1,142 C5
Marigot 1,765 D5
Rivière-Pilote 1,587 D7
Rivière-Salée 1,859 D7
Sainte-Luce 1,502 D7
Sainte-Marie 3,966 D5
Saint-Joseph 2,052 D6
Saint-Pierre 4,923 C6
Schoelcher 16,412 C6

OTHER FEATURES

Cabet, Pitons du (mt.) C6
Cabrits (isl.) D7
Caravelle (pen.) D6
Cul-de-Sac du Marin (bay) D7
Diable (pt.) D5
Ferré (cape) E7
Fort-de-France (bay) C6
Galion (bay) D6
Lézarde (riv.) D6
Long (isl.) D6
Lorrain (riv.) D5
Martinique (passg.) C5
Pelée (vol.) C5
Pilote (riv.) D7
Ramiers (isl.) C6
Ramville (isl.) D6
Robert (harb.) D6
Rose (pt.) D6
Saint-Martin (cape) C5
Saint-Pierre (bay) C6
Salines (pt.) D7
Salomon (pt.) C7
Vauclin (mt.) D6

NETHERLANDS ANTILLES

CITIES and TOWNS

Ascension F8
Bacuna E8
Boven Bolivia E8
Dokterstuin F8
Emmastad F9
Entrejo E8
Fontein E8
Groot Sint Joris G9
Hato G8
Kralendijk (cap.), Bonaire 2,500 E8
Lagoen F8
Montanja di Reij G9
New Port G9
Noord di Salinja E8
Onima E8
Otrabanda F9
Patrick F8
Rincon E8
Rooi E8
Santa Barbara G9
Santa Catharina G9
Savonet F8
Sint Kruis F8
Sint Martha F8
Sint Michiel F9
Sint Willebrordus F8
Terra Corra E8
Westpunt F8
Willemstad (cap.) 95,000 F9
Willemstad *130,000 F9

OTHER FEATURES

Bonaire (isl.) 8,087 E9
Bullen (bay) F8
Caracas (bay) G9
Curaçao (isl.) 145,430 G7
Goto (lake) E8
Kanon (pt.) G9
Klein Bonaire (isl.) E8
Kudarebe (pt.) D9
Lac (bay) D9
Lacre (pt.) E9
Malmok (mt.) E8
Noord (pt.) D8
Noord (pt.) E8
Pekelmeer (lake) E9
Piscadera (bay) F9
Schottegat (bay) G9
Sint Anna (bay) F9
Sint Christoffel (mt.) F8
Sint Joris (bay) G9
Slag (bay) D8
Vierkant (pt.) E8

SAINT KITTS and NEVIS

CITIES and TOWNS

Basseterre (cap.) 14,725 C10
Cayon C10
Charlestown 1,326 C11
Cotton Ground 471 C11
Dieppe Bay C10
Frigate Bay C10
Gingerland D11
Golden Rock C10
Newcastle D11
Old Road Town C10
Sadlers Village C10
Sandy Point 862 C10
Tabernacle C10
Zion Hill D11

OTHER FEATURES

Brimstone (hill) C10
Dogwood (pt.) D11
Fort (pt.) C11
Great Salt (pond) D10
Heldens (pt.) C10
Horse Shoe (pt.) C11
Misery (mt.) C10
Monkey (hill) C10
Narrows, The (str.) D11
Nevis (isl.) 9,300 D11
Nevis (peak) D11
North Friars (bay) D10
Pinney's (beach) D11
Saint Christopher (Saint Kitts) (isl.) 35,104 D10
South Friars (bay) C10

SAINT LUCIA

CITIES and TOWNS

Anse la Raye •5,007 F6
Canaries •2,075 G6
Castries (cap.) •42,770 G6
Choc G5
Choiseul •6,382 F7
Dauphin G5
Dennery •9,654 G6
Gros Islet •10,329 G5
Laborie •6,944 G7
Marigot G6
Marquis G6
Micoud •12,264 G6
Preslin G6
Soufrière •7,456 F6
Vieux Fort •10,675 G7

OTHER FEATURES

Beaumont (pt.) F6
Canaries, Piton (mt.) G6
Cannelles (pt.) G7
Cannelles (riv.) G6
Cap (pt.) G5
Choc (bay) G5
Fond d'Or (bay) G6
Gimie (mt.) G6
Grand Caille (pt.) F6
Grand Cul de Sac (riv.) G6
Gros Islet (bay) G5
Gros Piton (mt.) G6
La Sorcière (mt.) G6
Maria (isls.) G7
Ministre (pt.) G7
Moule-à-Chique (cape) G7
Petit Piton (mt.) G6
Pigeon (isl.) G5
Port Castries (harb.) G6
Port Praslin (bay) G6
Roseau (riv.) G6
Saint Lucia (chan.) G5
Saint Vincent (chan.) G7
Savannes (bay) G7
Sorcière, La (mt.) G6
Soufrière (bay) F6
Vierge (pt.) G6

SAINT VINCENT and THE GRENADINES

CITIES and TOWNS

Barrouallie 1,298 A9
Calliaqua 627 A9
Camden Park A9
Colonarie A9
Georgetown 1,100 A8
Kingstown (cap.) 17,117 A9
Kingstown *23,330 A9
Layou 1,147 A9
Wallibu A8

OTHER FEATURES

Colonarie (pt.) A9
Cumberland (bay) A8
Dark (head) A8
De Volet (pt.) A8
Espagnol (pt.) A8
Greathead (bay) A9
Kingstown (bay) A9
Owia (bay) A8
Porter (pt.) A8
Richmond (peak) A8
Saint Andrew (mt.) A9
Saint Vincent (passg.) A8
Soufrière (mt.) A8
Yambou (head) A9

TRINIDAD and TOBAGO

CITIES and TOWNS

Arima 11,390 B10
Arouca B10
Basse Terre B11
Biche B10
Blanchisseuse B10
California A11
Carapichaima B10
Caroni B10
Cedros A11
Chaguanas 6,122 B10
Chaguaramas A10
Couva 3,635 B10
Cunapo B10
Flanagin Town B10
Fullarton A11
Fyzabad 1,564 A11
Grande Rivière B10
Guaico B10
Guayaguayare B11
La Brea 1,487 A11
Marabella 18,158 A11
Matelot B10
Matura B10
Mayaro 2,638 B11
Moruga B11
Mucurapo A10
Palo Seco A11
Peñal 3,606 B11
Point Fortin 6,538 A11
Port-of-Spain (cap.) 67,978 A10
Princes Town 8,288 B11
Redhead B10
Rio Claro 2,423 B11
Saint Joseph 4,132 B10
Saint Joseph B11
San Fernando 33,490 A11
San Francique A11
Sangre Grande 8,948 B1
San Juan A10
Sans Souci B10
Siparia 5,773 B11
Tabaquite 2,309 B11
Talparo B10
Toco 1,287 B10
Tunapuna 10,251 B10
Upper Manzanilla B1
Valencia B10
Waterloo A10

OTHER FEATURES

Aripo, El Cerro del (mt.) B10
Boca Grande (passg.) A10
Chacachacare (isl.) A10
Chupara (pt.) B10
Cocos (bay) B10
Dragons Mouth (str.) A10
El Tucuche (mt.) B10
Erin (bay) A11
Galeota (pt.) B11
Galera (pt.) C10
Guapo (bay) A11
Guatuaro (pt.) B11
Icacos (pt.) A11
Maracas (bay) C10
Pitch (lake) A11

VIRGIN ISLANDS (Br.)

CITIES and TOWNS

Road Town (cap.) 2,200 D3
West End C4

OTHER FEATURES

Flanagan (passg.) D4
Frenchman (cay) C4
Great Thatch (isl.) C4
Great Tobago (isl.) B3
Jost Van Dyke (isl.) 135 C3
Little Tobago (isl.) B3
Narrows, The (str.) C4
Norman (isl.) D4
Peter (isl.) D4
Road (bay) D3
Sage (mt.) D4
Sir Francis Drake (chan.) D4
Tortola (isl.) 9,257 D3

VIRGIN ISLANDS (U.S.)

CITIES and TOWNS

Bethlehem E4
Canebay E3
Charlotte Amalie (cap.) 11,842 B4
Christiansted 2,914 F4
Cruz Bay 1,928 C4
Diamond F4
Eastend D4
Emmaus C4
Fredensdal F4
Frederiksted 1,046 E4
Grove Place 3,599 E4
Kingshill F4
Longford F4
Negro Bay E4

OTHER FEATURES

Altona (lag.) F4
Annaly (bay) E3
Baron Bluff (prom.) E3
Bordeaux (mt.) C4
Brass (isls.) A4
Buck (isl.) G3
Buck Island (chan.) F3
Buck Island Reef Nat'l Mon. G3
Butler (bay) E4
Caneel (bay) B4
Capella (isls.) B5
Christiansted Nat'l Hist. Site F4
Coral (bay) C4
Crown (mt.) A4
Dutch Cap (cay) A4
Eagle (mt.) E4
East (pt.) G4
Flanagan (passg.) D4
Flat (cays) A4
Grass (pt.) G4
Great (pond) F4
Great Pond (bay) F4
Green (cay) F4
Hams Bluff (prom.) E3
Hans Lollik (isls.) B4
Hassel (isl.) B4
Jersey (bay) B4
Krause Lagoon (chan.) F4
Leeward (passg.) B4
Long (pt.) B4
Long (pt.) E4
Lovango (cay) C4
Magens (bay) B4
Maho (bay) C4
Narrows, The (str.) C4
Nulliberg (mt.) B4
Perseverance (bay) A4
Picara (pt.) B4
Pillsbury (sound) B4
Privateer (pt.) D4
Pull (pt.) F3
Ram (head) C5
Red (pt.) D4
Reef (bay) C4
Saba (isl.) A4
Saint Croix (isl.) 49,725 G4
Saint James (isls.) B4
Saint John (isl.) 2,472 C4
Saint Thomas (harb.) B4
Saint Thomas (isl.) 44,372 A4
Salt (cay) A4
Salt (riv.) F4
Salt River (bay) F3
Sandy (pt.) D4
Savana (isl.) A4
Southwest (cape) E4
Tague (bay) G4
Thatch (cay) B4
Turner Hole (bay) G4
U.S. Nav. Air Sta. A4
Virgin (str.) A4
Virgin Isls. Nat'l Park C4
Water (isl.) A4
Westend Saltpond (lag.) E4

*City and suburbs.
• Population of district.
†Population of met. area.
○ Population of municipality.

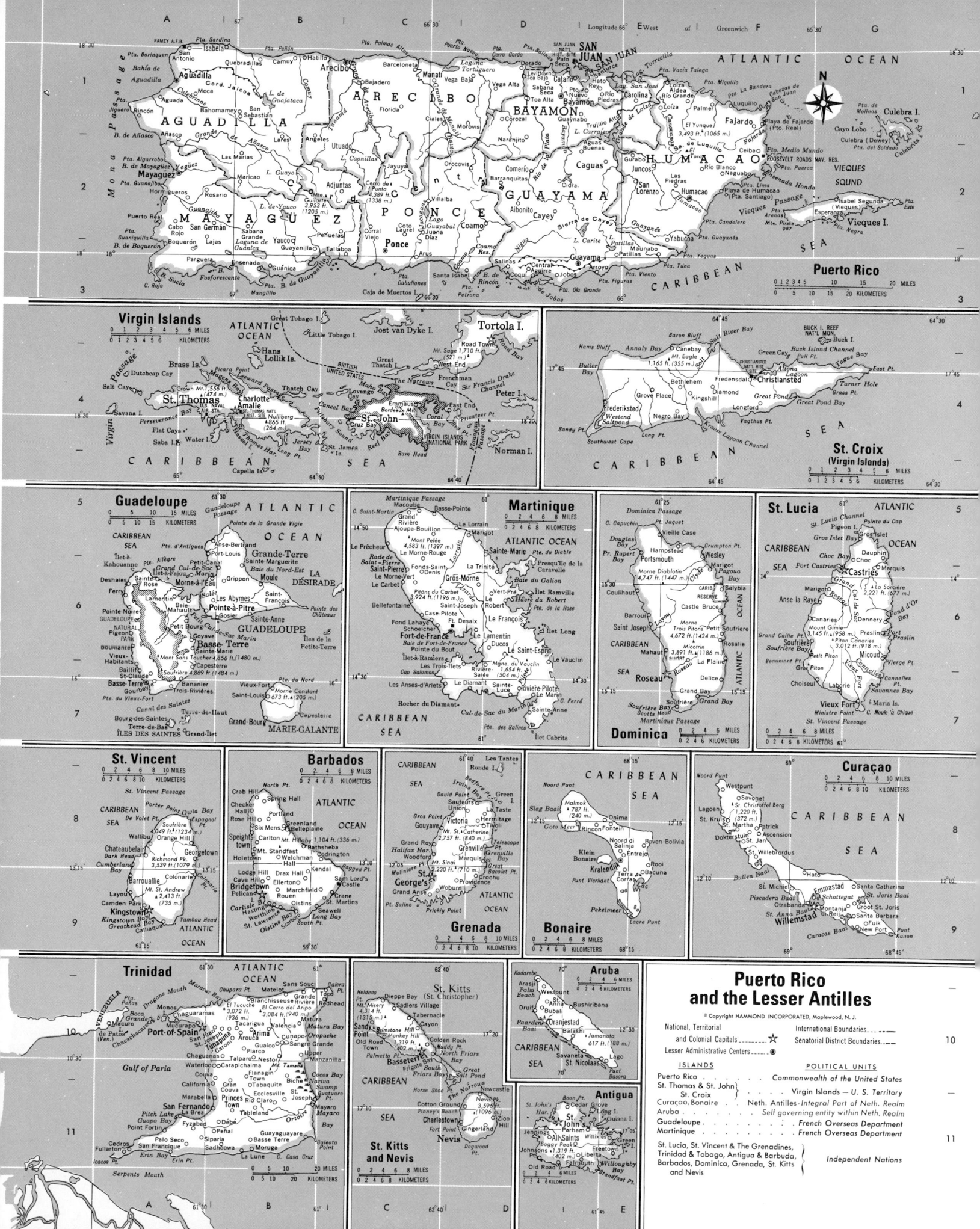

Puerto Rico and the Lesser Antilles

© Copyright HAMMOND INCORPORATED, Maplewood, N.J.

National, Territorial and Colonial Capitals .... ☆

Lesser Administrative Centers .... ◉

International Boundaries ....

Senatorial District Boundaries ....

ISLANDS	POLITICAL UNITS
Puerto Rico	Commonwealth of the United States
St. Thomas & St. John	Virgin Islands — U. S. Territory
St. Croix	
Curaçao, Bonaire	Neth. Antilles—Integral Part of Neth. Realm
Aruba	Self governing entity within Neth. Realm
Guadeloupe	French Overseas Department
Martinique	French Overseas Department

St. Lucia, St. Vincent & The Grenadines, Trinidad & Tobago, Antigua & Barbuda, Barbados, Dominica, Grenada, St. Kitts and Nevis — Independent Nations

Canada

CONIC PROJECTION

SCALE OF MILES
0 50 100   200   300

SCALE OF KILOMETERS
0 50 100 200   300   400   500

Capitals of Countries ....☆
Provincial & Territorial Capitals ....●
Administrative Centers ....◉
International Boundaries ....
Provincial Boundaries ....
Regional Boundaries............

© Copyright HAMMOND INCORPORATED, Maplewood, N. J.

AREA 3,851,787 sq. mi. (9,976,139 sq. km.)
POPULATION 29,123,194
CAPITAL Ottawa
LARGEST CITY Montréal
HIGHEST POINT Mt. Logan 19,524 ft. (5,951 m.)
MONETARY UNIT Canadian dollar
MAJOR LANGUAGES English, French
MAJOR RELIGIONS Protestantism, Roman Catholicism

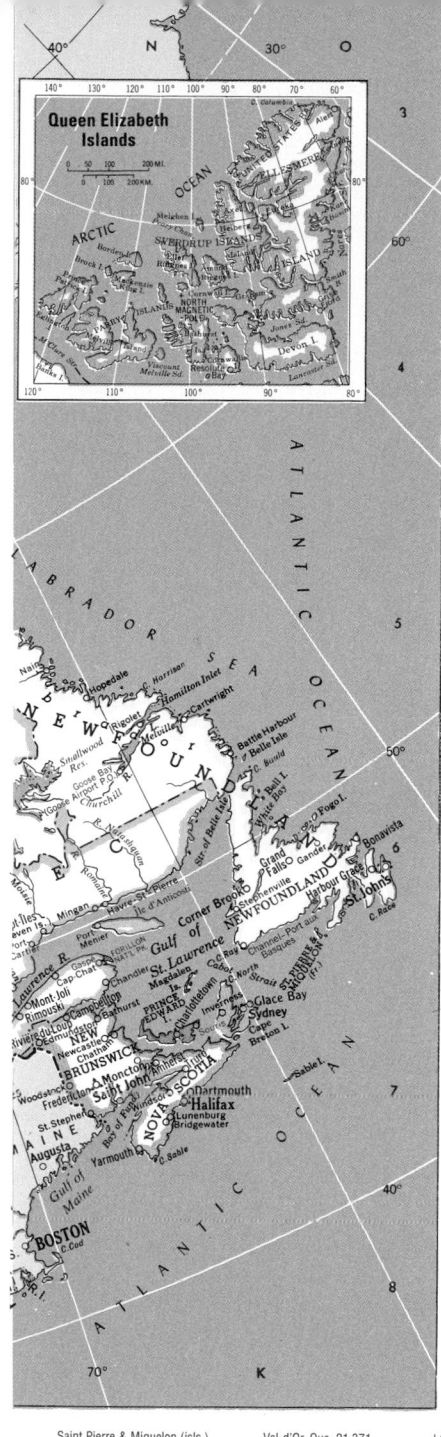

Population Distribution

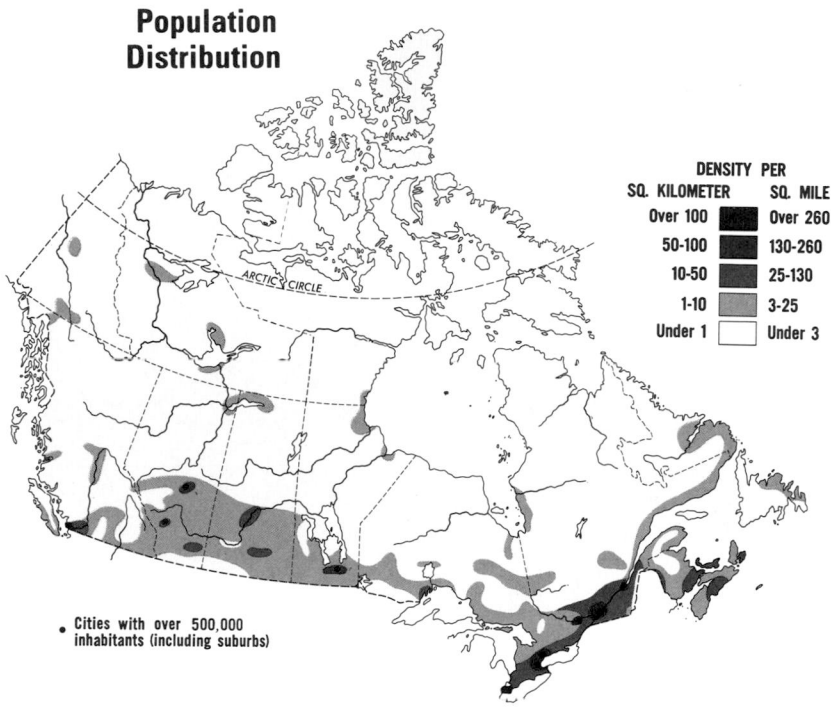

DENSITY PER	
SQ. KILOMETER	SQ. MILE
Over 100	Over 260
50-100	130-260
10-50	25-130
1-10	3-25
Under 1	Under 3

• Cities with over 500,000 inhabitants (including suburbs)

Vegetation

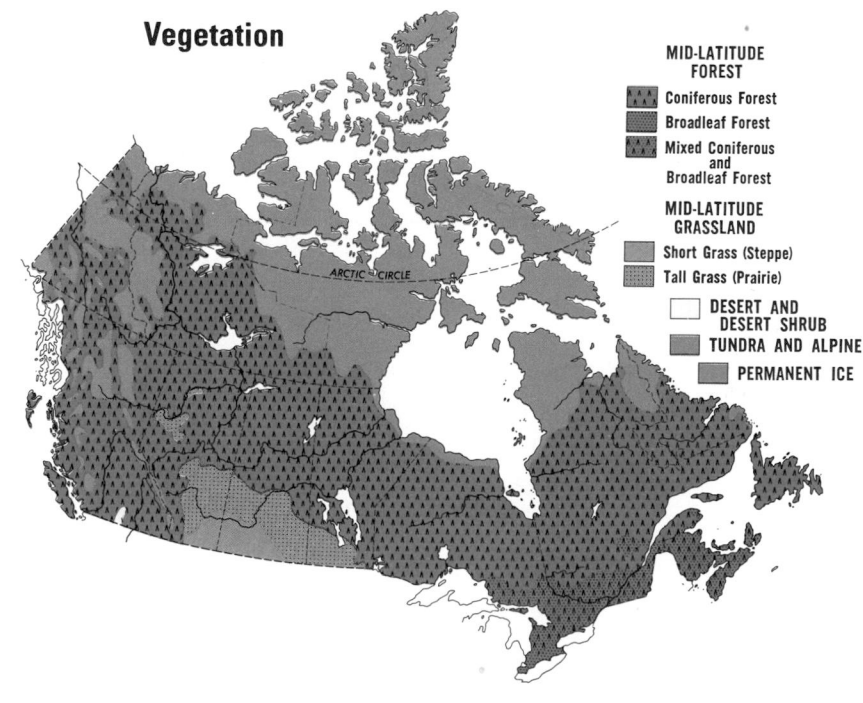

MID-LATITUDE FOREST
Coniferous Forest
Broadleaf Forest
Mixed Coniferous and Broadleaf Forest

MID-LATITUDE GRASSLAND
Short Grass (Steppe)
Tall Grass (Prairie)

DESERT AND DESERT SHRUB
TUNDRA AND ALPINE
PERMANENT ICE

Average January Temperature

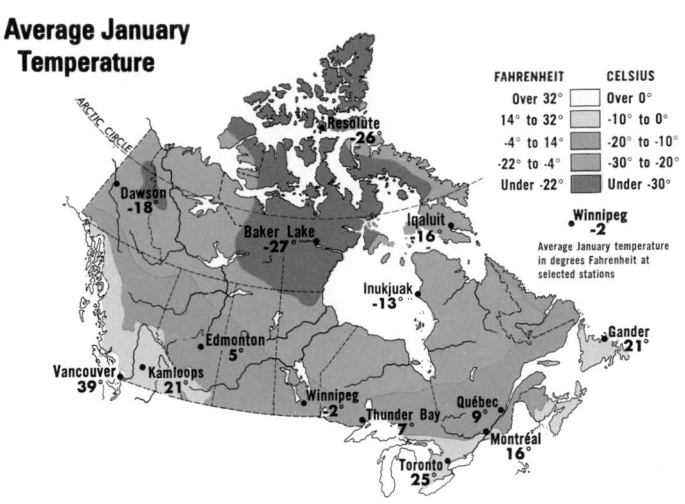

FAHRENHEIT CELSIUS
Over 32° Over 0°
14° to 32° -10° to 0°
-4° to 14° -20° to -10°
-22° to -4° -30° to -20°
Under -22° Under -30°
Winnipeg -2
Average January temperature in degrees Fahrenheit at selected stations
ARCTIC CIRCLE
Resolute -26°
Dawson -18°
Baker Lake -27°
Iqaluit -16°
Inukjuak -13°
Edmonton 5°
Vancouver 39°
Kamloops 21°
Winnipeg -2°
Thunder Bay 7°
Québec 9°
Montréal 16°
Toronto 25°
Gander 21°

Average July Temperature

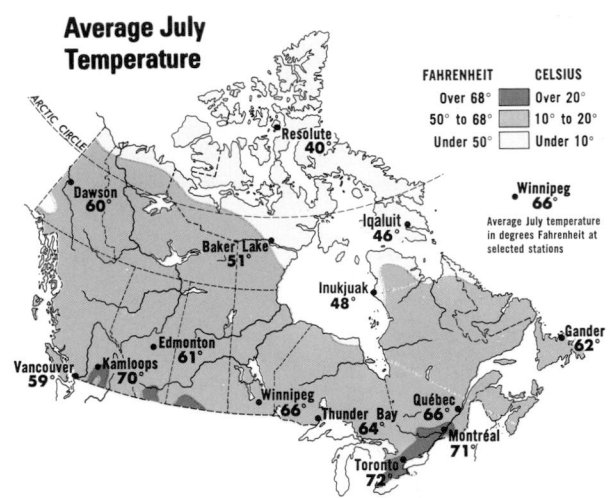

FAHRENHEIT CELSIUS
Over 68° Over 20°
50° to 68° 10° to 20°
Under 50° Under 10°
Winnipeg 66°
Average July temperature in degrees Fahrenheit at selected stations
ARCTIC CIRCLE
Resolute 40°
Dawson 60°
Iqaluit 46°
Baker Lake 51°
Inukjuak 48°
Edmonton 61°
Vancouver 59°
Kamloops 70°
Winnipeg 66°
Thunder Bay 64°
Québec 66°
Montréal 71°
Toronto 72°
Gander 62°

Agriculture, Industry and Resources

Furs
Timber
Salmon
Herring
Whales
Seals
Cod
Herring
Sheep
Oats
Barley
Wheat
Rye
Flax
Dairy
Cattle
Edmonton
Vancouver
Calgary
Winnipeg
Québec
Montréal
Toronto
Windsor

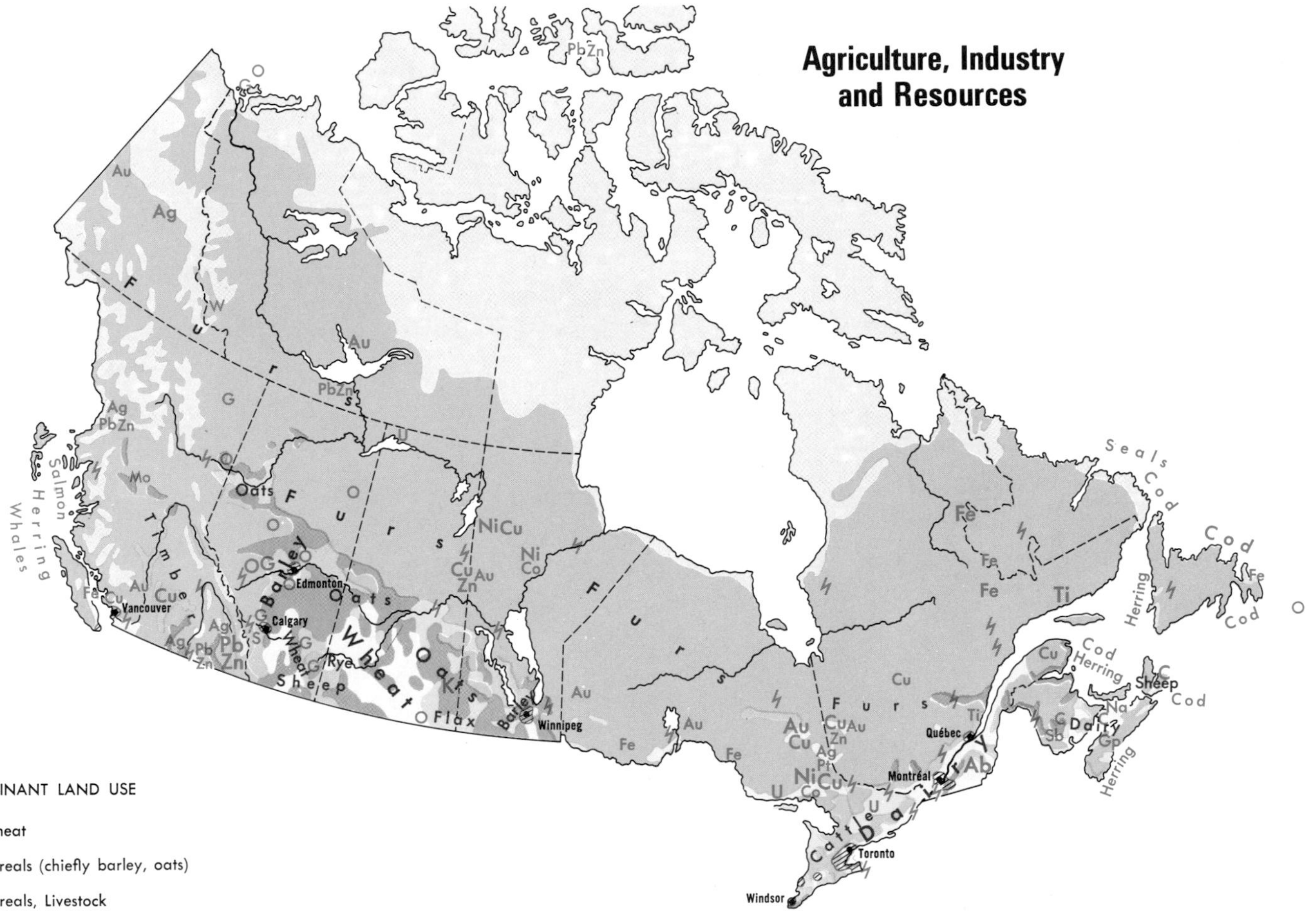

DOMINANT LAND USE

- Wheat
- Cereals (chiefly barley, oats)
- Cereals, Livestock
- General Farming, Livestock
- Dairy
- Fruit, Vegetables
- Pasture Livestock
- Range Livestock
- Forests
- Nonagricultural Land

MAJOR MINERAL OCCURRENCES

Ab	Asbestos	Fe	Iron Ore	Ni	Nickel	Sb	Antimony
Ag	Silver	G	Natural Gas	O	Petroleum	Ti	Titanium
Au	Gold	Gp	Gypsum	Pb	Lead	U	Uranium
C	Coal	K	Potash	Pt	Platinum	W	Tungsten
Co	Cobalt	Mo	Molybdenum	S	Sulfur	Zn	Zinc
Cu	Copper	Na	Salt				

Water Power

Major Industrial Areas

Rainfall

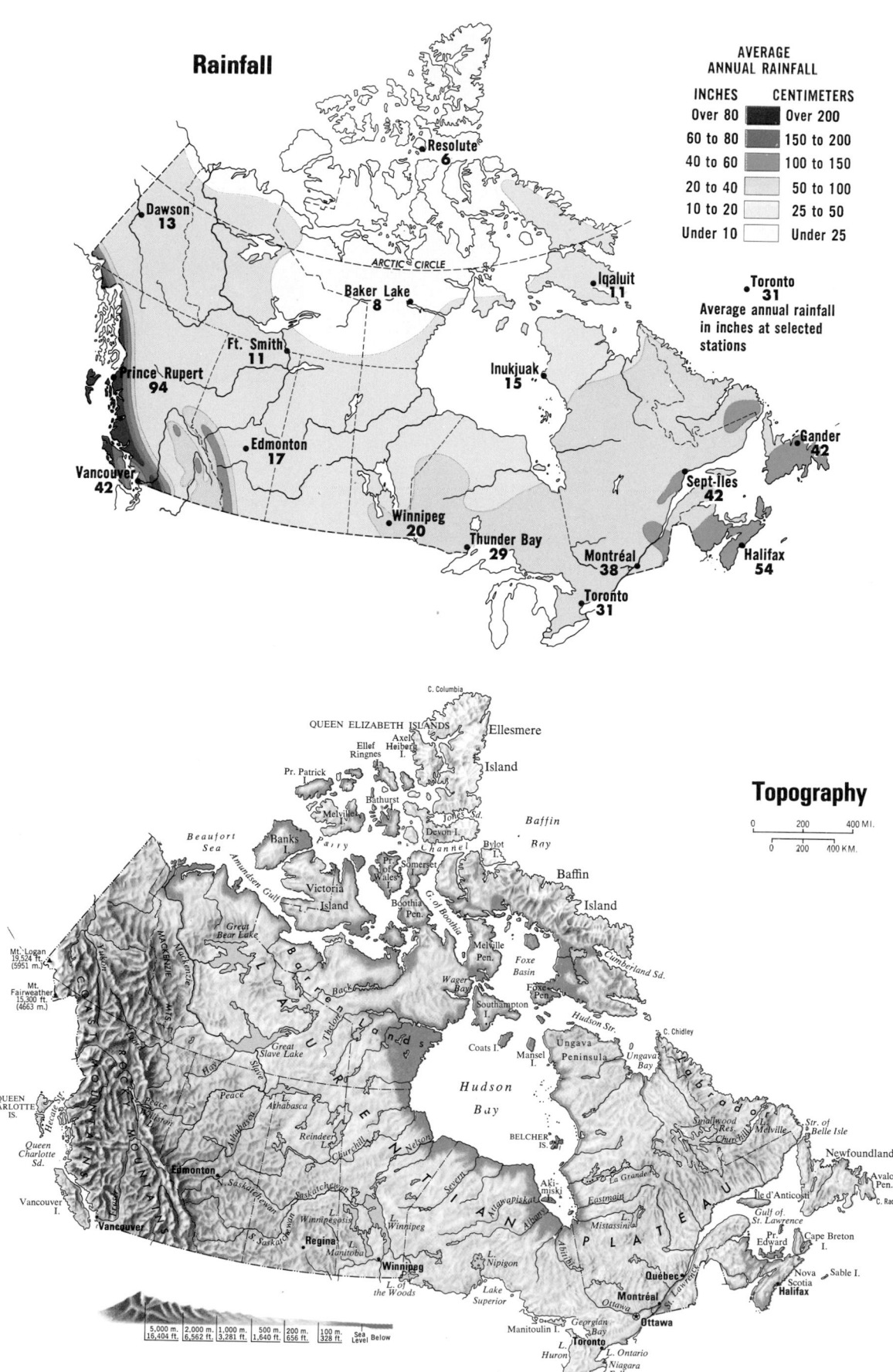

AVERAGE ANNUAL RAINFALL

INCHES	CENTIMETERS
Over 80	Over 200
60 to 80	150 to 200
40 to 60	100 to 150
20 to 40	50 to 100
10 to 20	25 to 50
Under 10	Under 25

Toronto
31
Average annual rainfall
in inches at selected
stations

Resolute
6

Dawson
13

ARCTIC CIRCLE

Baker Lake
8

Iqaluit
11

Ft. Smith
11

Prince Rupert
94

Inukjuak
15

Edmonton
17

Gander
42

Vancouver
42

Sept-Iles
42

Winnipeg
20

Thunder Bay
29

Montréal
38

Halifax
54

Toronto
31

Topography

0   200   400 MI.

0   200   400 KM.

C. Columbia

QUEEN ELIZABETH ISLANDS

Ellesmere

Axel
Heiberg
I.

Ellef
Ringnes I.

Island

Pr. Patrick

Bathurst

Baffin

Melville I.

Bay

Beaufort
Sea

Banks
I.

Parry

Devon I.

Jones Sd.

Channel

Pr. of
Wales I.

Somerset
I.

Bylot

Baffin

Victoria
Island

Boothia
Pen.

G. of Boothia

Island

Great
Bear Lake

Melville
Pen.

Cumberland Sd.

Amundsen Gulf

Mt. Logan
19,524 ft.
(5951 m.)

Back

Wager
Bay

Foxe
Basin

Mt.
Fairweather
15,300 ft.
(4663 m.)

Thelon

Foxe
Pen.

Hudson Str.

C. Chidley

Great
Slave Lake

Southampton
I.

QUEEN
CHARLOTTE
IS.

Hay

Liard

Coats I.

Mansel
I.

Ungava
Peninsula

Ungava
Bay

Queen
Charlotte Sd.

Peace

Slave

Athabasca

Reindeer L.

Churchill

Nelson

Hudson

Bay

BELCHER
IS.

Aki-
miski
I.

La Grande

Smallwood
Res.

Melville

Str. of
Belle Isle

Newfoundland

Vancouver I.

Edmonton

Saskatchewan

S. Saskat.

L.
Winnipegosis

L.
Manitoba

L.
Winnipeg

Regina

Winnipeg

L. of
the Woods

Attawapiskat

Albany

Eastmain

Mistassini

Avalon
Pen.

C. Race

Île d'Anticosti

Gulf of
St. Lawrence

Cape Breton
I.

Pr.
Edward
I.

Nova
Scotia

Sable I.

Vancouver

L. Nipigon

L.
Superior

Québec

St. Lawrence

Montréal

Ottawa

Nova
Scotia

Halifax

Georgian
Bay

Manitoulin I.

Toronto

L. Huron

L. Ontario

Niagara
Falls

5,000 m. | 2,000 m. | 1,000 m. | 500 m. | 200 m. | 100 m. | Sea
16,404 ft. | 6,562 ft. | 3,281 ft. | 1,640 ft. | 656 ft. | 328 ft. | Level
Below

Newfoundland
including Labrador

NEWFOUNDLAND

CITIES and TOWNS

Admiral's Beach 362 . . . D2
Admiral's Cove 99 . . . D2
Anchor Point 368 . . . C3
Aquaforte 200 . . . D2
Argentia 93 . . . C2
Arnold's Cove 1,124 . . . C2
Avondale 890 . . . D2
Badger 1,090 . . . C4
Badger's Quay-Valleyfield-Pool's Island 1,566 . . . D4
Baie Verte 2,491 . . . C4
Battle Harbour . . . C3
Bauline 423 . . . D2
Bay Bulls 1,081 . . . D2
Bay de Verde 786 . . . D2
Bay L'Argent 483 . . . D4
Bay Roberts 4,512 . . . D2
Bellburns 147 . . . C3
Belleoram 565 . . . C4
Bellevue 286 . . . D2
Bide Arm 339 . . . C3
Big Pond 167 . . . D2
Birchy Bay 707 . . . D4
Bird Cove 400 . . . C3
Bishop's Falls 4,395 . . . C4
Black Tickle 194 . . . C3
Blackhead Road 1,855 . . . D2
Blaketown 617 . . . D2
Bloomfield 715 . . . D2
Bonavista 4,460 . . . D2
Botwood 4,074 . . . C4
Branch 462 . . . D2
Brigus 898 . . . D2
Broad Cove 198 . . . D2
Brooklyn 197 . . . D2
Brownsdale 199 . . . D2
Buchans 1,655 . . . C4
Bunyan's Cove 590 . . . C2
Burgeo 2,504 . . . C4
Burin 2,904 . . . C4
Burnt Islands 991 . . . C4
Burnt Point 260 . . . D2
Calvert 482 . . . D2
Campbellton 703 . . . D4
Cape Broyle 698 . . . D2
Cape Ray 484 . . . C4
Caplin Cove 150 . . . D2
Carbonear 5,335 . . . D2
Carmanville 966 . . . D4
Cartwright 658 . . . C3
Catalina 1,162 . . . D2
Cavendish 343 . . . D2
Champney's West 141 . . . D2
Chance Cove 498 . . . D2
Change Islands 580 . . . D4
Channel-Port aux Basques 5,988 . . . C4
Chapel Arm 689 . . . D2
Charlottetown 330 . . . D2
Charlottetown 250 . . . C3
Churchill Falls 936 . . . B3
Clarenville 2,878 . . . C2
Clarke's Beach 1,009 . . . D2
Codroy 346 . . . C4
Colinet 310 . . . D2
Colliers 819 . . . D2
Come By Chance 337 . . . C2
Conception Harbour 917 . . . D2
Conche 464 . . . C3
Cook's Harbour 388 . . . C3
Corner Brook 24,339 . . . C4
Cow Head 695 . . . C4
Cox's Cove 980 . . . C4
Cupids 706 . . . D2
Daniell's Harbour 614 . . . C3
Dark Cove 1,344 . . . D4
Davis Inlet 240 . . . B2
Deep Bight 243 . . . C2
Deer Lake 4,348 . . . C4
Dildo 877 . . . D2
Dunville 1,817 . . . D2
Durrell 1,145 . . . D4
Eastport 597 . . . D1
Elliston 527 . . . D2
Embree 846 . . . C4
Englee 998 . . . C3
English Harbour 118 . . . D2
English Harbour West 327 . . . C4
Fermeuse 584 . . . D2
Ferryland 795 . . . D2
Flat Bay 322 . . . C4
Flat Rock 808 . . . D2
Fleur de Lys 616 . . . C3
Flowers Cove 459 . . . C3
Fogo 1,105 . . . D4
Forteau 520 . . . C3
Fortune 2,473 . . . C4
Fox Harbour 280 . . . C3
Fox Harbour 538 . . . D2
François 219 . . . C4
Freshwater 1,276 . . . C2
Freshwater 209 . . . D2
Gambo 2,932 . . . D4
Gander 10,404 . . . D4
Garnish 761 . . . C4
Gaskiers-Point la Haye 505 . . . D2
Gaultois 558 . . . C4
Georges Brook 356 . . . D2
Glenwood 1,129 . . . D4
Glovertown 2,165 . . . C1
Goobies 185 . . . D2
Goose Bay-Happy Valley 7,103 . . . B3
Gooseberry Cove 195 . . . C2
Goose Cove 134 . . . C2
Goose Cove 368 . . . C3
Goulds 4,242 . . . D2
Grand Bank 3,901 . . . C4
Grand Falls 8,765 . . . C4
Grates Cove 275 . . . D2
Green Island Cove 222 . . . C3
Green's Harbour 785 . . . D2
Greenspond 423 . . . D4
Grey River 234 . . . C4
Gull Island 362 . . . D2
Hampden 838 . . . C4
Hant's Harbour 542 . . . D2
Happy Adventure 352 . . . D2
Happy Valley-Goose Bay 7,103 . . . B3
Harbour Breton 2,464 . . . C4
Harbour Deep 278 . . . C3
Harbour Grace 2,988 . . . D2
Harbour Main-Chapel Cove-Lakeview 1,303 . . . D2
Hare Bay 1,520 . . . D4
Hawke's Bay 553 . . . C3
Head of Bay d'Espoir 586 . . . C4
Heart's Content 625 . . . D2
Heart's Delight Islington 899 . . . D2
Heart's Desire 416 . . . D2
Heatherton 328 . . . C4
Hermitage 863 . . . C4
Hickman's Harbour 479 . . . D2
Hillview 295 . . . D2
Hodge's Cove 438 . . . D2
Holyrood 1,789 . . . D2
Hopedale 425 . . . B2
Howley 456 . . . C4
Isle aux Morts 1,238 . . . C4
Jackson's Arm 623 . . . C4
Jeffrey's 270 . . . C4
Jerseyside 641 . . . B3
Job's Cove 201 . . . D2
Joe Batt's Arm-Barr'd Islands 1,155 . . . D4
Keels 129 . . . D1
Kelligrews (Foxtrap-Greeleytown-Peachtown-Kelligrews) 2,292 . . . D2
Kilbride 5,014 . . . D2
King's Cove 253 . . . D1
King's Point 825 . . . C4
Kippens 1,219 . . . C4
Labrador City 11,538 . . . A3
Lamaline 548 . . . C4
L'Anse-au-Clair 267 . . . C3
L'Anse-au-Loup 589 . . . C3
L'Anse au Meadow 66 . . . C3
La Poile 186 . . . C4
Lark Harbour 783 . . . C4
La Scie 1,422 . . . C4
Lawn 999 . . . C4
Lethbridge 686 . . . D2
Lewisporte 3,963 . . . C4
Little Bay Islands 407 . . . C4
Little Catalina 750 . . . D2
Little Heart's Ease 467 . . . D2
Lodge Bay 124 . . . C3
Long Harbour-Mount Arlington Heights 660 . . . D2
Lourdes 932 . . . C4
Lower Island Cove 415 . . . D2
Lumsden 645 . . . D4
Main Brook 514 . . . C3
Makkovik 347 . . . C2
Markland 344 . . . D2
Mary's Harbour 408 . . . C3
Marystown 6,299 . . . D4
McCallum 243 . . . C4
Melrose 416 . . . D2
Middle Arm, Green Bay 575 . . . C4
Millertown 228 . . . C4
Milltown-Head of Bay d'Espoir 1,376 . . . C4
Milton 258 . . . C2
Mobile 171 . . . D2
Mount Carmel-Mitchell's Brook-St. Catherine's 699 . . . D2
Mount Pearl 11,543 . . . D2
Musgrave Harbour 1,554 . . . D4
Musgravetown 635 . . . C2
Nain 938 . . . B2
New Bonaventure 106 . . . D2
New Chelsea 144 . . . D2
New Harbour 777 . . . D2
Newmans Cove 231 . . . D2
New Perlican 350 . . . D2
Newtown 511 . . . D4
Nippers Harbour 259 . . . C4
Norman's Cove-Long Cove 1,152 . . . D2
Norris Arm 1,216 . . . C4
Norris Point 1,033 . . . C4
North Harbour 161 . . . D2
North River 245 . . . D2
North West Brook 279 . . . C2
North West River 515 . . . B3
O'Donnells 280 . . . D2
Old Bonaventure 111 . . . D2
Old Perlican 709 . . . D2
Paradise 2,861 . . . D2
Parkers Cove 424 . . . D4
Parson's Pond 605 . . . C3
Pasadena 2,685 . . . C4
Patrick's Cove 155 . . . C2
Perry's Cove 141 . . . D2
Peterview 1,119 . . . C4
Petites 108 . . . C4
Petley 147 . . . D2
Petty Harbour-Maddox Cove 853 . . . D2
Picadilly 524 . . . C4
Pinware River 201 . . . C3
Placentia 2,204 . . . C2
Plate Cove 474 . . . D2
Point La Haye 195 . . . D2
Point Lance 141 . . . C2
Point Leamington 848 . . . C4
Point Verde 296 . . . C2
Pollards Point 502 . . . C4
Port au Bras 366 . . . D4
Port au Choix 1,311 . . . C3
Port au Port 603 . . . C4
Port Blandford 702 . . . C2
Port Hope Simpson 581 . . . C3
Port Kirwan 164 . . . D2
Port Rexton 489 . . . D2
Port Saunders 769 . . . C3
Portugal Cove 2,361 . . . D2
Portugal Cove South 371 . . . D2
Port Union 671 . . . D2
Postville 223 . . . B3
Pouch Cove 1,522 . . . D2
Princeton 204 . . . D2
Raleigh 373 . . . C3
Ramea 1,386 . . . C4
Red Bay 316 . . . C3
Red Head Cove 225 . . . D2
Rencontre East 230 . . . C4
Renews-Cappahayden 578 . . . D2
Rigolet 271 . . . C3
Riverhead 431 . . . D2
River of Ponds 304 . . . C3
Robert's Arm 1,005 . . . C4
Rocky Harbour 1,273 . . . C4
Roddickton 1,142 . . . C3
Rose Blanche-Harbour le Cou 975 . . . C4
Rushoon 520 . . . D4
Saint Alban's 1,968 . . . C4
Saint Andrew's 262 . . . C4
Saint Anthony 3,107 . . . C3
Saint Brendan's 468 . . . D4
Saint Bride's 599 . . . C2
Saint George's 1,756 . . . C4
St. John's (cap.) 83,770 . . . D2
Saint Joseph's 262 . . . D2
Saint Lawrence 2,012 . . . C4
Saint Lunaire-Griquet 1,010 . . . C3
Saint Mary's 701 . . . D2
Saint Paul's 454 . . . C4
Saint Phillips 1,365 . . . D2
Saint Shotts 239 . . . D2
Saint Vincent's-Saint Stephens-Peter's River 796 . . . D2
Sally's Cove 100 . . . C4
Salmon Cove 786 . . . D2
Seal Cove 751 . . . C3
Seal Cove-White Bay 498 . . . C4
Seldom-Little Seldom 560 . . . D4
Ship Harbour 265 . . . D2
Shoal Cove 223 . . . C3
Shoal Harbour 1,000 . . . C2
South Branch 264 . . . C4
South Brook, Hall's Bay Dist. 786 . . . C4
South Brook, Humber Dist. 477 . . . C4
Southern Harbour 772 . . . C2
South River 645 . . . D2
Spaniard's Bay 2,125 . . . D2
Springdale 3,501 . . . C4
Stephenville 8,876 . . . C4
Stephenville Crossing 2,172 . . . C4
Summerford 1,198 . . . C4
Summerville 346 . . . D2
Sunnyside 703 . . . D2
Sweet Bay 204 . . . D2
Swift Current 329 . . . C2
Terrenceville 796 . . . D4
Tilting 427 . . . D4
Torbay 3,394 . . . D2
Tors Cove 355 . . . D2
Traytown 383 . . . D1
Trepassey 1,473 . . . D2
Trinity 522 . . . D2
Trinity 375 . . . D4
Trout River 759 . . . C4
Twillingate 1,506 . . . C4
Upper Island Cove 2,025 . . . D2
Victoria 1,870 . . . D2
Wabana 4,254 . . . D2
Wabush 3,155 . . . A3
Wesleyville 1,125 . . . D4
Western Bay 463 . . . D2
West Saint Modeste 273 . . . C3
Whitbourne 1,233 . . . D2
Wild Cove 152 . . . C3
Windsor 5,747 . . . C4
Winterton 753 . . . D2
Witless Bay 907 . . . D2

OTHER FEATURES

Alexis (riv.) . . . C3
Anguille (cape) . . . C4
Annieopscotch (mts.) . . . C4
Ashuanipi (lake) . . . A3
Ashuanipi (riv.) . . . A3
Atikonak (lake) . . . B3
Attikamagen (lake) . . . A3
Avalon (pen.) . . . D2
Barachois Pond Prov. Park . . . C4
Bauld (cape) . . . C3
Bell (isl.) . . . C3
Bell (isl.) . . . D2
Belle Isle (isl.) . . . C3
Belle Isle (str.) . . . C3
Blackhead (bay) . . . D2
Bonavista (bay) . . . D1
Bonavista (cape) . . . D1
Bonne (bay) . . . C4
Branch (riv.) . . . C2
Broyle (cape) . . . D2
Bull Arm (inlet) . . . D2
Burin (pen.) . . . C4
Butter Pot Prov. Park . . . D2
Cabot (str.) . . . B4
Canada (bay) . . . C3
Chidley (cape) . . . B1
Churchill (falls) . . . B3
Churchill (riv.) . . . B3
Cirque (mt.) . . . B2
Clode (sound) . . . D2
Conception (bay) . . . D2
Deep (inlet) . . . B2
Double Mer (lake) . . . C3
Dyke (lake) . . . A3
Eagle (riv.) . . . C3
Espoir (bay) . . . C4
Exploits (riv.) . . . C4
Fogo (isl.) . . . D4
Fortune (bay) . . . C4
Freels (cape) . . . D3
Gander (lake) . . . D4
Gander (riv.) . . . D4
Glover (isl.) . . . C4
Goose (riv.) . . . B3
Grand (lake) . . . B3
Grand (lake) . . . C4
Grates (pt.) . . . D2
Great Colinet (isl.) . . . D2
Grey (isls.) . . . C3
Groais (isl.) . . . C3
Gros Morne (mt.) . . . C3
Gros Morne Nat'l Park . . . C4
Groswater (bay) . . . C3
Hamilton (inlet) . . . C3
Hamilton (sound) . . . D4
Hare (bay) . . . C3
Hawke (hills) . . . D2
Hebron (fjord) . . . B2
Hermitage (bay) . . . C4
Holyrood (bay) . . . D2
Horse (isls.) . . . C3
Horse Chops (head) . . . D2
Humber (riv.) . . . C4
Ingornachoix (bay) . . . C3
Ireland's Eye (isl.) . . . D2
Islands (bay) . . . C4
Kaipokok (bay) . . . B2
Kanairiktok (riv.) . . . B3
Kaumajet (mts.) . . . B2
Kingurutik (mesa) . . . B2
Labrador (reg.) . . . B2
Labrador (sea) . . . C2
La Manche Valley Prov. Park . . . D2
La Poile (bay) . . . C4
Little Mecatina (riv.) . . . B3
Long (isl.) . . . C2
Long (lake) . . . A3
Long (pt.) . . . C4
Long Range (mts.) . . . C4
Main Topsail (mt.) . . . C4
Makkovik (cape) . . . C2
McLelan (str.) . . . B1
Mealy (lake) . . . C3
Meelpaeg (lake) . . . C4
Melville (lake) . . . C3
Menihek (lakes) . . . A3
Merasheen (isl.) . . . C2
Mistaken (pt.) . . . D2
Mistastin (lake) . . . B2
Nachvak (fjord) . . . B2
Naskaupi (riv.) . . . B3
Newfoundland (isl.) . . . C4
Newman (sound) . . . D2
New World (isl.) . . . C4
Norman (cape) . . . C3
North Aulatsivik (isl.) . . . B2
Notre Dame (bay) . . . C4
Okak (bay) . . . B2
Ossokmanuan (res.) . . . B3
Petitsikapau (lake) . . . A3
Pine (cape) . . . D2
Pinware (riv.) . . . C3
Pistolet (bay) . . . C3
Placentia (bay) . . . C2
Ponds (isl.) . . . C3
Port au Port (bay) . . . C4
Port au Port (pen.) . . . C4
Port Manvers (harb.) . . . B2
Race (cape) . . . D2
Ramah (bay) . . . B2
Ramea (isls.) . . . C4
Random (isl.) . . . D2
Random (sound) . . . D2
Ray (cape) . . . C4
Red (isl.) . . . C2
Red Indian (lake) . . . C4
Red Wine (riv.) . . . B3
Rocky (riv.) . . . D2
Round (pond) . . . C4
Saglek (bay) . . . B2
Saint Francis (cape) . . . D2
Saint George (cape) . . . C4
Saint George's (bay) . . . C4
Saint John (bay) . . . C3
Saint John (cape) . . . C3
Saint Lawrence (gulf) . . . B4
Saint Lewis (cape) . . . C3
Saint Mary's (bay) . . . C2
Saint Mary's (cape) . . . C2
Saint Michaels (bay) . . . C3
Salmonier (riv.) . . . D2
Sandwich (bay) . . . C3
Shabogamo (lake) . . . A3
Shoal (bay) . . . D2
Smallwood (res.) . . . B3
Smith (sound) . . . D2
South Aulatsivik (isl.) . . . B2
Spear (cape) . . . D2
Squires Mem. Park . . . C4
Swale (isl.) . . . D1
Terra Nova (riv.) . . . C2
Terra Nova Nat'l Park . . . D2
Territok (cape) . . . B2
Thoresby (mt.) . . . B2
Torbay (pt.) . . . D2
Torngat (mts.) . . . B2
Trespassey (bay) . . . D2
Trinity (bay) . . . D2
Tunungayualok (isl.) . . . B2
Ukasiksalik (isl.) . . . B2
Victoria (lake) . . . C4
White (bay) . . . C3
White Bear (lake) . . . C4
White Handkerchief (cape) . . . B2

SAINT PIERRE and MIQUELON

CITIES and TOWNS

Saint-Pierre (cap.) 5,415 . . . C4

OTHER FEATURES

Miquelon (isl.) 626 . . . C4
Saint Pierre (isl.) 5,415 . . . C4

AREA 156,184 sq. mi. (404,517 sq. km.)
POPULATION 568,349
CAPITAL St. John's
LARGEST CITY St. John's
HIGHEST POINT in Torngat Mountains 5,420 ft. (1,652 m.)
SETTLED IN 1610
ADMITTED TO CONFEDERATION 1949
PROVINCIAL FLOWER Pitcher Plant

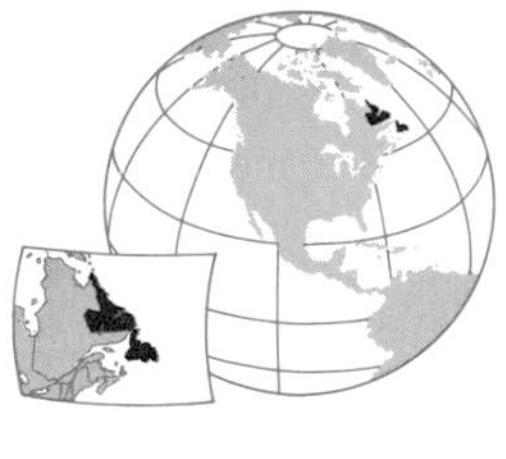

Agriculture, Industry and Resources

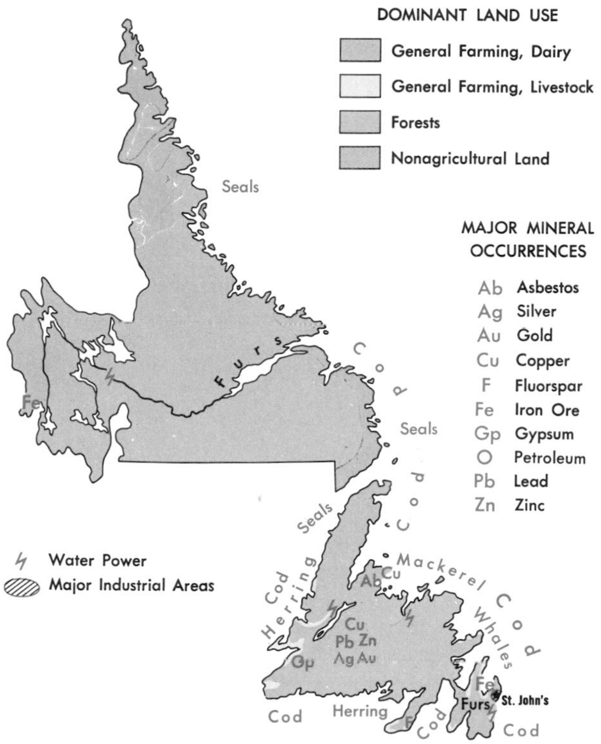
DOMINANT LAND USE
General Farming, Dairy
General Farming, Livestock
Forests
Nonagricultural Land
MAJOR MINERAL OCCURRENCES
Ab Asbestos
Ag Silver
Au Gold
Cu Copper
F Fluorspar
Fe Iron Ore
Gp Gypsum
O Petroleum
Pb Lead
Zn Zinc
Water Power
Major Industrial Areas
Seals
Furs
Cod
Mackerel
Herring
Whales
St. John's

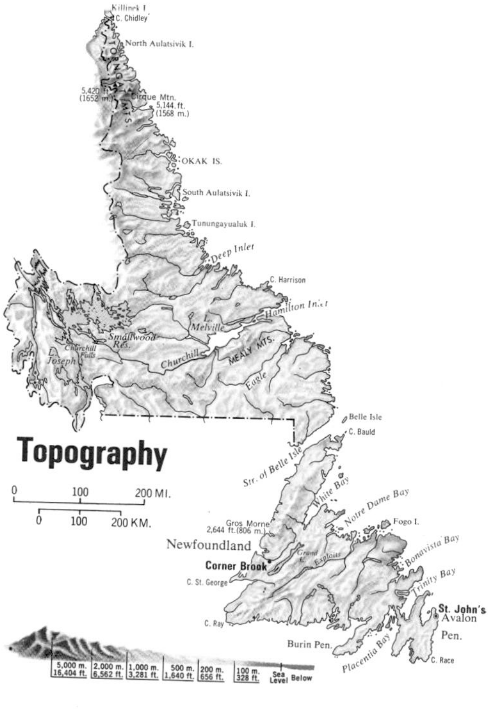
Topography
0 100 200 MI.
0 100 200 KM.
C. Chidley
North Aulatsivik I.
OKAK IS.
South Aulatsivik I.
Tunungayualuk I.
Deep Inlet
C. Harrison
Hamilton Inlet
Melville
Smallwood Res.
Churchill
MEALY MTS.
Eagle
Belle Isle
C. Bauld
Str. of Belle Isle
White Bay
Notre Dame Bay
Fogo I.
Gros Morne 2,644 ft. (806 m.)
Newfoundland
Corner Brook
C. St. George
C. Ray
Bonavista Bay
Trinity Bay
St. John's
Avalon Pen.
Burin Pen.
Placentia Bay
C. Race
5,000 m. 16,404 ft.
2,000 m. 6,562 ft.
1,000 m. 3,281 ft.
500 m. 1,640 ft.
200 m. 656 ft.
100 m. 328 ft.
Sea Level
Below

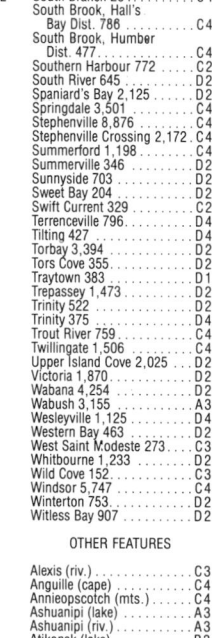

NOVA SCOTIA

COUNTIES

Annapolis 22,522 .... C 4
Antigonish 18,110 .... F 3
Cape Breton 127,035 .... H 3
Colchester 43,224 .... D 3
Cumberland 35,231 .... E 3
Digby 21,689 .... F 3
Guysborough 12,752 .... F 3
Halifax 288,126 .... D 4
Hants 33,121 .... D 4
Inverness 22,337 .... G 2
Kings 49,739 .... C 4
Lunenburg 45,746 .... D 4
Pictou 50,350 .... F 3
Queens 13,126 .... D 4
Richmond 12,284 .... H 3
Shelburne 17,328 .... C 5
Victoria 8,432 .... H 2
Yarmouth 26,290 .... C 5

CITIES and TOWNS

Alder Point 651 .... H 2
Aldershot .... H 2
Amherst◉ 9,684 .... D 3
Annapolis Royal◉ 631 .... C 4
Antigonish◉ 5,205 .... F 3
Arichat 824 .... H 3
Aylesford 744 .... D 3
Baddeck◉ 972 .... H 2
Barrington Passage 722 ...... C 5
Bear River-Sissiboo 854 ...... C 4
Beaverbank 1,322 .... E 4
Berwick 1,699 .... C 4
Bridgetown 1,047 .... C 4
Bridgewater 6,669 .... D 4
Brookfield 619 .... E 3
Brooklyn 1,269 .... D 4
Cambridge Station 799 .... D 3
Canning 763 .... D 3
Canso 1,255 .... H 3
Centreville 765 .... D 3
Chéticamp 1,022 .... G 2
Chester 1,131 .... D 4
Chester Basin 639 .... D 4
Church Point 318 .... B 4
Clark's Harbour 1,059 .... C 5
Coldbrook Station 617 .... D 3
Cow Bay 670 .... E 4
Dartmouth 62,277 .... E 4
Debert 618 .... E 3
Digby◉ 2,558 .... C 4
Dominion 2,856 .... J 2
Donkin 873 .... J 2
Ellershouse-Hartville 662 .... D 4
Elmsdale 1,172 .... E 4
Enfield 1,510 .... E 4
Fall River 1,897 .... E 4
Falmouth 1,110 .... D 3
Glace Bay 21,466 .... J 2
Guysborough◉ 496 .... G 3
Halifax (cap.)◉ 114,594 ...... E 4
Halifax *277,727 .... E 4
Hantsport 1,395 .... D 3
Herring Cove 1,323 .... E 4
Hilden 1,262 .... E 3
Ingonish 471 .... H 2
Inverness 2,013 .... G 2
Judique 925 .... G 3
Kentville◉ 4,974 .... D 3
Kingston 1,612 .... C 4
Lakeside 936 .... E 4
Lantz 1,172 .... E 4
Liverpool◉ 3,304 .... D 4
Lockeport 929 .... C 5
Louisbourg 1,410 .... J 3
Louisdale 979 .... G 3
Lower West Pubnico 790 .... C 5
Lunenburg◉ 3,014 .... D 4
Mahone Bay 1,228 .... D 4
Meteghan 890 .... C 4
Middleton 1,834 .... E 3
Milford Station 748 .... D 3
Milton 1,678 .... D 4
Mount Uniacke 1,145 .... D 4
Mulgrave 1,099 .... G 3
Musquodoboit Harbour 936 . E 4
New Glasgow 10,464 .... F 3
New Victoria 1,374 .... H 2
New Waterford 8,808 .... J 2
North Sydney 7,820 .... H 2
Oxford 1,470 .... E 3
Parrsboro 1,799 .... D 3
Pictou◉ 4,628 .... F 3
Porters Lake 893 .... E 4
Port Hastings 312 .... G 3
Port Hawkesbury 3,850 .... G 3
Port Hood◉ 701 .... G 3
Port Morien 717 .... J 2
Port Williams 1,227 .... D 3
Prospect 693 .... E 4
Pugwash 648 .... E 3
Reserve Mines 2,472 ...... H 2
River Hébert 835 .... D 3
Saint Peters 669 .... H 3
Sandy Point 691 .... C 5
Scotchtown 2,037 .... H 2
Sheet Harbour 819 .... F 4
Shelburne◉ 2,303 .... C 5
Shubenacadie 984 .... E 3
Springhill 4,896 .... E 3
Stellarton 5,435 .... F 3
Stewiacke 1,174 .... E 3
Sydney◉ 29,444 .... H 2
Sydney Mines 8,501 .... H 2
Terence Bay 960 .... E 4
Thorburn 1,014 .... F 3
Three Mile Plains 1,355 ... D 3
Timberlea 1,159 .... E 4
Trenton 3,154 .... F 3
Truro◉ 12,552 .... E 3
Waterville 687 .... D 3
Waverley 1,699 .... E 4
Wedgeport 827 .... C 5
Western Shore 1,712 ...... D 4
Westmount 3,097 .... H 2
Westville 4,522 .... F 3
Wileville 746 .... D 4
Windsor◉ 3,646 .... D 3
Wolfville 3,235 .... D 3
Yarmouth◉ 7,475 .... B 5

OTHER FEATURES

Advocate (bay) .... D 3
Ainslie (lake) .... G 2
Amet (sound) .... E 3
Andrew (isl.) .... H 3
Annapolis (basin) .... C 4
Annapolis (riv.) .... C 4
Antigonish (harb.) .... G 3
Argos (cape) .... G 3
Aspy (bay) .... H 2
Avon (riv.) .... D 4
Baccaro (pt.) .... C 5
Baddeck (riv.) .... H 2
Barachois (pt.) .... G 4
Barren (isl.) .... G 4
Barrington (bay) .... C 5
Berry (head) .... G 3
Bedford (basin) .... E 4
Boularderie (isl.) .... H 2
Bras d'Or (lake) .... H 3
Breton (cape) .... J 3
Brier (isl.) .... B 4
Canso (cape) .... H 3
Canso (str.) .... G 3
Cap d'Or (cape) .... D 3

© Copyright HAMMOND INCORPORATED, Maplewood, N.J.

Nova Scotia and Prince Edward Island

SCALE

0 10 20 30 40 50 MI.

0 10 20 30 40 50 KM.

Provincial Capitals .... ✪   Provincial Boundaries ___.___
County Seats .... ◉   County Boundaries _____

Cape Breton (isl.)	J 2	Craignish (hills)	G 3
Cape Breton Highlands Nat'l Park	H 2	Cross (isl.)	D 4
Cape Negro (isl.)	C 5	Cumberland (basin)	D 3
Cape Sable (isl.)	C 5	Dalhousie (mt.)	E 3
Capstan (cape)	D 3	Dauphin (cape)	H 2
Caribou (isl.)	F 3	Digby Gut (chan.)	C 4
Carleton (riv.)	C 4	Digby Neck (pen.)	B 4
Charlotte (lake)	F 4	East (bay)	H 3
Chebogue (harb.)	B 5	East (riv.)	F 3
Chedabucto (isl.)	G 3	East Bay (hills)	H 3
Chéticamp (isl.)	G 2	Egmont (cape)	H 2
Chignecto (bay)	D 3	Eigg (mt.)	F 3
Chignecto (cape)	C 3	Fisher (lake)	C 4
Chignecto (isth.)	D 3	Five (isls.)	D 3
Clam (bay)	F 4	Forchu (harb.)	H 3
Cliff (cape)	E 3	Forchu (cape)	B 5
Clyde (riv.)	C 5	Framboise Cove (bay)	H 3
Cobequid (bay)	E 3	Fundy (bay)	C 3
Coddle (harb.)	G 3	Gabarus (bay)	H 3
Coldspring (head)	E 3	Gabarus (cape)	J 3
Cole (harb.)	E 4	Gaspereau (lake)	D 4
Country (harb.)	G 3	George (cape)	G 3
		George (lake)	B 5

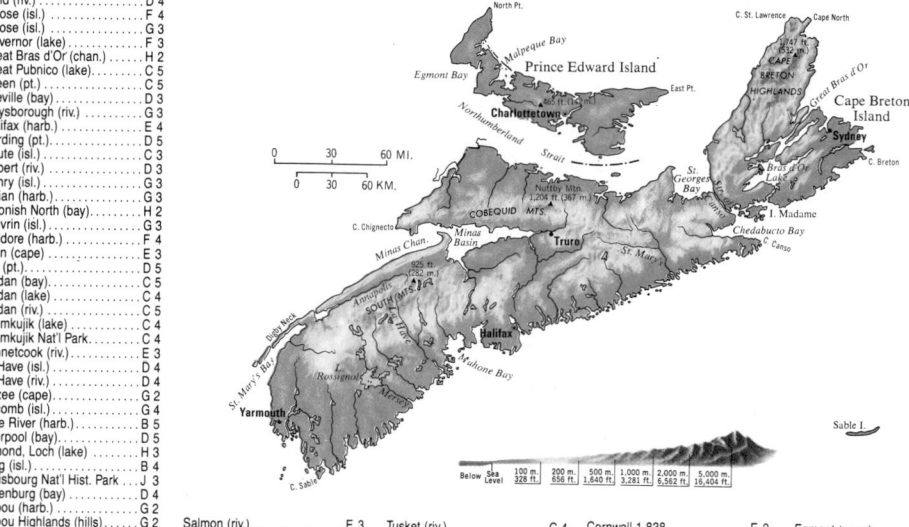

Gold (riv.)	D 4	Salmon (riv.)	E 3
Goose (isl.)	F 4	Salmon (riv.)	G 3
Goose (isl.)	G 3	Scatarie (isl.)	J 2
Governor (lake)	F 3	Wallace (harb.)	E 3
Great Bras d'Or (chan.)	H 2	Scots (bay)	D 3
Great Pubnico (lake)	C 5	Seal (isl.)	B 5
Green (pt.)	C 5	Sheet (harb.)	F 4
Greville (bay)	D 3	Sherbrooke (lake)	D 4
Guysborough (riv.)	G 3	Sherbrooke (riv.)	D 4
Halifax (harb.)	E 4	Shoal (bay)	F 4
Harding (pt.)	D 5	Shubenacadie (lake)	E 4
Haute (isl.)	C 3	Shubenacadie (riv.)	E 3
Hébert (riv.)	D 3	Sissiboo (riv.)	C 4
Henry (pt.)	G 3	Smoky (cape)	H 2
Indian (harb.)	G 3	Sober (isl.)	F 4
Ingonish North (bay)	H 2	South West Margaree (riv.)	G 2
Janvrin (isl.)	G 3	Split (cape)	D 3
Jeddore (harb.)	F 4	Spry (harb.)	F 4
John (cape)	E 3	Stewiacke (riv.)	E 3
Joli (pt.)	D 5	Sydney (harb.)	H 2
Jordan (bay)	C 5	Tangier (riv.)	F 4
Jordan (lake)	C 4	Taylor (head)	F 4
Jordan (riv.)	C 5	Tracadie (lake)	C 4
Kejimkujik (lake)	C 4	Tor (bay)	G 3
Kejimkujik Nat'l Park	C 4	Tupper (lake)	D 4
Kennetcook (riv.)	E 3	Tusket (isl.)	B 5
La Have (isl.)	D 4	Tusket (riv.)	C 4
La Have (riv.)	D 4	Verte (bay)	D 2
Linzee (cape)	G 2	West (bay)	G 3
Liscomb (isl.)	G 4	West (pt.)	H 5
Little River (harb.)	B 5	West (riv.)	F 3
Liverpool (bay)	D 5	Western (head)	D 5
Lomond, Loch (lake)	H 3	West Liscomb (riv.)	F 3
Long (isl.)	B 4	West Saint Mary's (riv.)	F 3
Louisbourg Nat'l Hist. Park	J 3	Whitehaven (harb.)	G 3
Lunenburg (bay)	D 4	Yarmouth (sound)	B 5
Mabou (harb.)	G 2		
Mabou Highlands (hills)	G 2		
Madame (isl.)	H 3		
Mahone (bay)	D 4		
Malagash (pt.)	E 3		
Margaree (isl.)	F 4		
McNutt (isl.)	C 5		
Medway (harb.)	D 4		
Medway (riv.)	D 4		
Merigomish (harb.)	F 3		
Mersey (riv.)	D 4		
Michaud (pt.)	H 3		
Minas (basin)	D 3		
Minas (chan.)	D 3		
Mira (bay)	J 2		
Mira (riv.)	H 3		
Mocodome (cape)	G 3		
Molega (lake)	D 4		
Morien (cape)	J 2		
Mouton (isl.)	D 5		
Mud (isl.)	B 5		
Mulgrave (lake)	F 3		
Musquodoboit (riv.)	F 4		
Necum Teuch (harb.)	F 4		
Nichol (isl.)	F 4		
North (cape)	H 1		
North (mt.)	D 3		
North Aspy (riv.)	H 2		
North Bay Ingonish (bay)	H 2		
North East Margaree (riv.)	H 2		
Northumberland (str.)	E 3		
Nuttby (mt.)	E 3		
Oak (isl.)	E 3		
Ocean (lake)	G 3		
Ohio (riv.)	E 3		
Panuke (lake)	D 4		
Paradise (lake)	E 3		
Pennant (pt.)	E 4		
Percé (cape)	J 2		
Peskowesk (lake)	C 4		
Petit-de-Grat (isl.)	H 3		
Petpeswick (head)	E 4		
Philip (riv.)	E 3		
Pictou (harb.)	F 3		
Pictou (isl.)	F 3		
Pleasant (bay)	H 2		
Ponhook (lake)	D 4		
Porters (lake)	E 4		
Port Hebert (harb.)	D 5		
Port Hood (isl.)	G 2		
Port Joli (harb.)	D 5		
Port Mouton (harb.)	D 5		
Poulet Cove (bay)	H 2		
Prim (pt.)	C 3		
Pubnico (lake)	C 5		
Pugwash (harb.)	E 3		
Roseway (riv.)	C 4		
Rossignol (lake)	C 4		
Sable (cape)	C 5		
Sable (isl.)	J 5		
Saint Andrews (chan.)	H 2		
Saint Anns (bay)	H 2		
Saint Georges (bay)	G 3		
Saint Lawrence (bay)	H 1		
Saint Lawrence (gulf)	H 1		
Saint Margarets (bay)	E 4		
Saint Mary (cape)	B 4		
Saint Marys (bay)	B 4		
Saint Mary's (riv.)	F 3		
Saint Patrick (chan.)	G 3		
Saint Paul (isl.)	H 1		
Saint Peters (bay)	H 3		

PRINCE EDWARD ISLAND

Cornwall 1,838	E 2	Egmont (cape)	D 2
Georgetown⊛ 737	F 2	Hillsborough (bay)	E 2
Kensington 1,143	E 2	Hog (isl.)	E 2
Miscouche 752	E 2	Kildare (cape)	E 2
Montague 1,957	F 2	Lennox (isl.)	E 2
Murray Harbour 443	F 2	Malpeque (bay)	E 2
North Rustico 688	E 2	New London (bay)	E 2
O'Leary 736	D 2	North (cape)	E 1
Parkdale 2,018	E 2	Northumberland (str.)	D 2
Saint Edward 650	E 2	Panmure (isl.)	F 2
Saint Eleanors 2,716	E 2	Prim (pt.)	E 2
Sherwood 5,681	E 2	Prince Edward Island Nat'l Park	F 2
Gouris 1,413	F 2	Rollo (bay)	F 2
Summerside⊛ 7,828	E 2	Saint Lawrence (gulf)	F 2
Tignish 982	D 2	Saint Peters (bay)	F 2
Wilmot 1,563	E 2	Saint Peters (isl.)	E 2
		Savage (harb.)	F 2
COUNTIES		Tracadie (bay)	F 2
Kings 19,215	F 2	West (pt.)	D 2
Prince 42,821	D 2	Wood (isls.)	F 3
Queens 60,470	E 2		
		OTHER FEATURES	
CITIES and TOWNS		Bedeque (bay)	E 2
Alberton 1,020	E 2	Boughton (isl.)	F 2
Bunbury 1,024	E 2	Cardigan (bay)	F 2
Charlottetown (cap.)⊛ 15,282	E 2	Cascumpeque (bay)	E 2
		East (pt.)	G 2
		Egmont (bay)	D 2

⊛County seat.
*Population of metropolitan area.

Agriculture, Industry and Resources

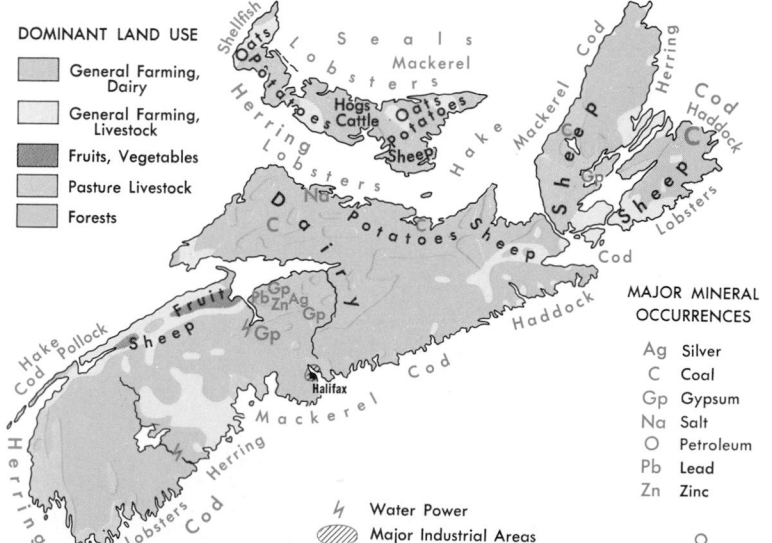

DOMINANT LAND USE

- General Farming, Dairy
- General Farming, Livestock
- Fruits, Vegetables
- Pasture Livestock
- Forests

MAJOR MINERAL OCCURRENCES

- Ag Silver
- C   Coal
- Gp Gypsum
- Na Salt
- O   Petroleum
- Pb Lead
- Zn Zinc

⚡ Water Power
▨ Major Industrial Areas

Havelock 439 E 3
Hayesville 107 D 2
Hazeldean 108 C 2
Head of Millstream 61 E 3
Hillman 69 C 2
Hillsborough 1,239 F 3
Holmesville 146 C 2
Holtville 222 D 2
Honeydale 77 C 3
Hopewell Cape⊛ 144 F 3
Hopewell Hill 172 F 3
Howard 77 E 2
Howland Ridge 55 C 2
Hoyt 114 D 3
Inkerman 396 F 1
Irishtown 605 F 2
Island View 240 D 3
Jacksonville 363 C 2
Jacquet River 778 E 1
Janeville 204 E 1
Jeanne Mance 89 E 1
Jemseg 228 D 3
Jolicure 96 F 3
Juniper 525 C 2
Kedgwick 1,222 C 1
Keenan Siding 86 E 2
Kent Junction 112 E 2
Kent Lake 57 E 2
Keswick 260 D 3
Kilburn 134 C 2
Killam 60 E 2
Kingsclear 250 D 3
Kingsley 145 D 2
Kirkland 69 C 3
Knowlesville 82 C 2
Kouchibouguac 213 F 2
Lac Baker 292 B 1
Lagacéville 227 E 1
Lake George 170 C 3
Laketon 81 E 2
Lakeville 201 C 2
Lambertville 109 C 3
Lamèque 1,571 F 1
Landry 281 E 1
Laplante 197 E 1
Lavillette 576 E 1
Lawrence Station 229 C 3
Leech 584 E 1
Léger Brook F 2
Légerville 184 F 2
Le Goulet 1,173 F 1
Leonardville 158 C 4
Lepreau 208 D 3
Levesque 77 C 1
Little Cape 513 F 2
Little Shippegan 131 F 1
Loggieville 781 E 1
Lorne 937 D 1
Lower Coverdale 616 F 2
Lower Derby 206 E 2
Lower Durham 52 D 2
Lower Hainesville 66 C 2
Lower Kars 30 E 3
Lower Millstream 184 E 3
Lower Sapin F 2
Lower Southampton C 3
Ludlow 100 D 2
Maces Bay 182 D 3
Madran 247 E 1
Magaguadavic 126 C 3
Maisonnette 757 E 1
Malden 93 G 2
Manners Sutton 159 D 3
Manuels 332 F 1
Mapleview 65 C 2
Marcelville 61 E 2
Martin 104 C 1
Maugerville 249 D 3
Maxwell 64 C 3
McAdam 1,837 C 3
McGivney 156 D 2
McKendrick 608 D 1
McNamee 147 D 2
Meductic 234 C 3
Melrose 121 F 2
Memramcook 276 F 2
Menneval 110 C 1
Midgic Station 208 F 3
Mill Cove 253 D 3
Millerton 130 E 2
Millville 309 C 2
Minto 3,399 D 2
Miscou Centre 554 F 1
Miscou Harbour 106 F 1
Mispec 180 E 3
Moncton 54,743 F 2
Moores Mills 117 C 3
Morrisdale 202 D 3
Moulin-Morneault 459 B 1
Murray Corner 233 G 2
Nackawic 1,357 C 2
Napadogan 103 D 2
Nash Creek 235 D 1
Nashwaak Bridge 142 D 2
Nashwaak Village 258 D 2
Nauwigewauk 139 E 3
Neguac 1,755 E 1
Nelson-Miramichi 1,452 E 2
Newcastle⊛ 6,284 E 2
Newcastle Creek 210 D 2
New Denmark 112 C 1
New Jersey 65 E 1
New Market 143 D 3
New Maryland 485 D 3
New River Beach 33 D 3
Newtown 154 E 3
New Zion 171 D 2
Nicholas Denys 170 D 1
Nictau 30 C 1
Nigadoo 1,075 E 1
Noinville 50 E 2
Nordin 393 E 1
North Head 661 D 4
Norton 1,372 E 3
Notre-Dame 344 F 2
Oak Bay 183 C 3
Oak Point 83 D 3
Oromocto 9,064 D 3
Paquetville 626 E 1
Peel 117 C 2
Pelletier Mills 88 B 1
Pennfield D 3
Penniac 179 D 2
Penobsquis 259 E 3
Perth-Andover⊛ 1,872 C 2
Petitcodiac 1,401 E 3
Petite-Rivière-de-l'Île 549 F 1
Petit Rocher 1,860 E 1
Petit Rocher Sud E 1
Pigeon Hill 595 F 1
Plaster Rock 1,222 C 2
Pocologan 150 D 3
Point de Bute 155 F 3
Pointe-du-Chêne 482 F 2
Pointe-Sapin 331 F 2
Pointe-Verte 1,335 E 1
Pollett River 73 E 3
Pontgrave 229 F 1
Pont-Lafrance 875 E 1
Pont-Landry 444 F 1
Port Elgin 504 F 2
Prime 89 B 1
Prince of Wales 138 D 3
Prince William 225 C 3
Quarryville 205 E 2
Queenstown 112 D 3
Quispamsis 6,022 E 3
Red Bank 141 E 2
Renforth 1,490 E 3
Renous 192 E 2
Rexton 928 F 2
Richardsville D 1
Richibucto⊛ 1,722 F 2
Richibucto Village 442 F 2
Richmond Corner 84 C 2
Riley Brook 126 C 1
Ripples 233 D 3
River de Chute 22 C 2
River Glade 268 E 3
Riverside-Albert 478 F 3
Riverview 14,907 F 2
Rivière-du-Portage 661 F 1
Rivière Verte 1,054 B 1
Robertville 733 E 1
Robichaud 485 F 2
Robinsonville 206 C 1
Rogersville 1,237 E 2
Rollingdam 65 C 3
Rosaireville 86 E 2
Rothesay 1,764 E 3
Rowena 73 C 2
Roy 173 F 2
Royal Road 41 D 2
Rusagonis 231 D 3
Sackville 5,654 F 3
Saint Almo 17 C 2
Saint-André 385 C 1
Saint Andrews⊛ 1,760 C 3
Saint-Antoine 1,217 F 2
Saint Arthur 369 D 1
Saint-Basile 3,214 B 1
Saint-Charles 355 F 2
Saint Croix 86 C 3
Sainte-Anne 329 E 1
Sainte-Anne-de-Kent 337 F 2
Sainte-Anne-de-Madawaska 1,332 B 1
Saint-Édouard-de-Kent 157 F 2
Sainte-Marie-de-Kent 283 F 2
Sainte-Marie-sur-Mer 539 F 1
Sainte-Rose-Gloucester 410 F 1
Saint-François-de-Madawaska 753 B 1
Saint George 1,163 D 3
Saint Hilaire 244 B 1
Saint-Ignace 96 F 2
Saint-Isidore 794 E 1
Saint-Jacques 2,297 B 1
Saint-Jean-Baptiste-de-Restigouche 228 C 1
Saint John⊛ 80,521 E 3
Saint-Joseph 630 F 3
Saint-Joseph-de-Madawaska 173 B 1
Saint-Léolin 799 E 1
Saint Leonard 1,566 C 1
Saint-Louis-de-Kent 1,166 F 2
Saint Margarets 63 E 2
Saint Martin de Restigouche 124 C 1
Saint Martins 530 E 3
Saint-Paul 365 E 2
Saint Quentin 2,334 C 1
Saint-Raphaël-sur-Mer 562 F 1
Saint Sauveur 252 E 1
Saint Stephen 5,120 C 3
Saint Wilfred E 1
Salisbury 1,672 E 2
Salmon Beach 277 E 1
Salmon Creek 38 E 2
Saumarez 690 E 1
Scoudouc 207 F 2
Seal Cove 548 D 4
Shannon 39 E 3
Shediac 4,285 F 2
Shediac Bridge 441 F 2
Sheffield 112 D 3
Sheila 1,172 F 1
Shemogue 199 F 2
Shepody 86 F 3
Shippegan 2,471 F 1
Siegas 227 C 1
Sillikers 292 E 2
Simonds 221 C 2
Sisson Ridge 170 C 2
Six Roads 239 F 1
Smiths Creek 163 E 3
Somerville 326 C 2
South Branch 86 F 2
Springfield, King's 116 E 3
Springfield, York 130 C 2
Stanley 432 D 2
Stickney 232 C 2
Storeytown 140 D 2
Sunny Corner 405 E 2
Sunnyside 87 D 1
Sussex 3,972 E 3
Sussex Corner 1,023 E 3
Tabusintac 231 E 1

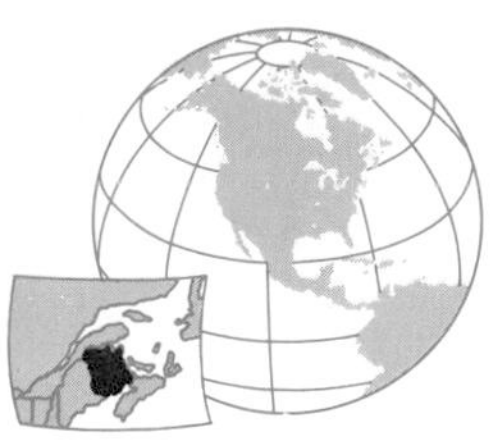

AREA 28,354 sq. mi. (73,437 sq. km.)
POPULATION 709,442
CAPITAL Fredericton
LARGEST CITY Saint John
HIGHEST POINT Mt. Carleton 2,690 ft. (820 m.)
SETTLED IN 1611
ADMITTED TO CONFEDERATION 1867
PROVINCIAL FLOWER Purple Violet

Topography

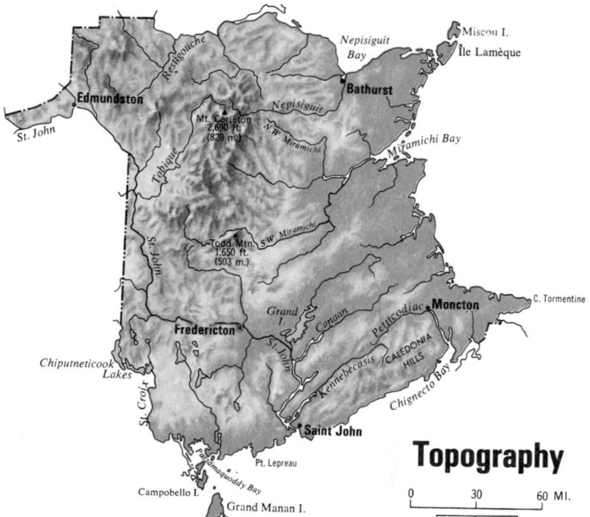

Miscou I.
Île Lamèque
Nepisiguit Bay
Bathurst
Restigouche
Edmundston
St. John
Nepisiguit
Mt. Carleton 2,690 ft. (820 m.)
N.W. Miramichi
Miramichi Bay
Tobique
Todd Mtn. 1,650 ft. (503 m.)
S.W. Miramichi
St. John
Grand L.
Fredericton
Canaan
Petitcodiac
Moncton
C. Tormentine
Chiputneticook Lakes
St. Croix
Kennebecasis
CALEDONIA HILLS
Chignecto Bay
Saint John
Pt. Lepreau
Passamaquoddy Bay
Campobello I.
Grand Manan I.
Southwest Hd.
0 30 60 MI.
0 30 60 KM.

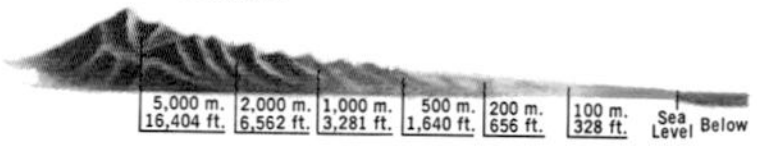

5,000 m. 16,404 ft.
2,000 m. 6,562 ft.
1,000 m. 3,281 ft.
500 m. 1,640 ft.
200 m. 656 ft.
100 m. 328 ft.
Sea Level
Below

Agriculture, Industry and Resources

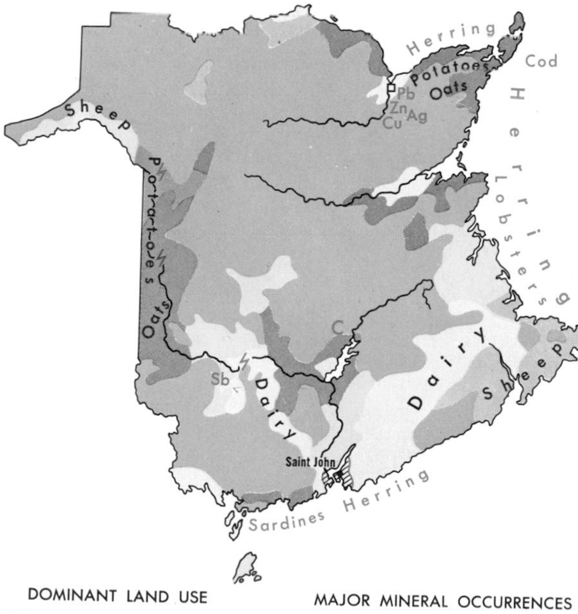

Herring
Potatoes
Oats
Cod
Pb
Zn
Ag
Cu
Sheep
Herring
Lobsters
Potatoes
Oats
C
Sb
Dairy
Dairy
Sheep
Saint John
Herring
Sardines

DOMINANT LAND USE

- Cereals, Livestock
- Dairy
- Potatoes
- General Farming, Livestock
- Pasture Livestock
- Forests

MAJOR MINERAL OCCURRENCES

- Ag Silver
- C Coal
- Cu Copper
- Pb Lead
- Sb Antimony
- Zn Zinc
- Water Power
- Major Industrial Areas

Taxis River 118 D 2
Tay Creek 161 D 2
Taymouth 301 D 2
Temperance Vale 357 C 2
The Range 58 E 2
Thibault 300 C 1
Tide Head 952 D 1
Tilley 95 C 2
Tobique Narrows 140 C 2
Tracadie 2,452 F 1
Tracy 636 D 3
Turtle Creek 81 F 3
Tweedside 87 C 3
Upham 107 E 3
Upper Blackville 60 E 2
Upper Buctouche 158 F 2
Upper Gagetown 236 D 3
Upper Hainesville 189 C 2
Upper Kent 203 C 2
Upper Maugerville 543 D 3
Upper Mills 153 C 3
Upper Rockport 18 F 3
Upper Sheila 706 E 1
Upper Woodstock 257 C 2
Upsalquitch 112 D 1
Val-Comeau 534 F 1
Val d'Amour 462 D 1
Val Doucet 505 E 1
Verret 637 B 1
Village-Saint-Laurent 187 E 1
Waasis 264 D 3
Wapske 195 C 2
Waterford 120 E 3
Waterville 181 C 2
Waweig C 3
Wayerton 188 E 1
Weaver 86 E 2
Weldon 227 F 3
Welsford 230 D 3
Welshpool 260 D 4
Westfield 1,100 D 3
West Quaco 48 E 3
White Head 185 D 4
White Rapids 238 E 2
Whitney 216 E 2
Wickham 72 D 3
Wicklow 143 C 2
Williamsburg 258 D 2
Williamstown 156 C 2
Willow Grove 509 E 3
Wilmot 57 C 3
Wilson Point 45 F 1
Wilsons Beach 844 D 4
Windsor 43 C 2
Wirral 110 D 3
Woodstock⊛ 4,649 C 2
Woodwards Cove 146 D 4
Youngs Cove 65 E 3
Zealand 458 D 2

OTHER FEATURES

Bald (mt.) C 1
Bartibog (riv.) E 1
Bay du Vin (riv.) E 2
Big Tracadie (riv.) E 1
Buctouche (harb.) F 2
Buctouche (riv.) F 2
Campobello (isl.) D 4
Canaan (riv.) E 2
Carleton (mt.) D 1
Chaleur (bay) E 1
Chignecto (bay) F 3
Chiputneticook (lakes) C 3
Cocagne (isl.) F 2
Cumberland (basin) F 3
Deer (isl.) D 4
Digdeguash (riv.) C 3
Escuminac (bay) D 1
Escuminac (pt.) F 1
Fundy (bay) E 3
Fundy Nat'l Park E 3
Gaspereau (riv.) D 2
Grand (bay) D 3
Grand (lake) C 3
Grand (lake) D 3
Grand Manan (chan.) C 4
Grand Manan (isl.) D 4
Grande (riv.) C 1
Green (riv.) B 1
Hammond (riv.) E 3
Harvey (lake) C 3
Heron (isl.) D 1
Kedgwick (riv.) C 1
Kennebecasis (riv.) E 3
Keswick (riv.) C 2
Kouchibouguac (bay) F 2
Kouchibouguacis (riv.) E 2
Kouchibouguac Nat'l Park F 2
Lamèque (isl.) F 1
Lepreau (riv.) D 3
Little (riv.) D 2
Long (isl.) D 3
Long Reach (inlet) D 3
Maces (bay) D 3
Mactaquac (lake) C 3
Madawaska (riv.) B 1
Magaguadavic (lake) C 3
Magaguadavic (riv.) C 3
Miramichi (bay) E 1
Miscou (isl.) F 1
Miscou (pt.) F 1
Mount Carleton Prov. Park D 1
Musquash (harb.) D 3
Nashwaak (riv.) D 2
Nepisiguit (bay) E 1
Nepisiguit (riv.) D 1
Nerepis (riv.) D 3
Northern (head) D 4
North Sevogle (riv.) D 1
Northumberland (str.) F 2
Northwest Miramichi (riv.) D 1
Oromocto (lake) C 3
Oromocto (riv.) D 3
Passamaquoddy (bay) C 3
Patapédia (riv.) C 1
Petitcodiac (riv.) F 3
Pokemouche (riv.) E 1
Pokesudie (isl.) F 1
Pollett (riv.) E 3
Quaco (head) E 3
Renous (riv.) D 2
Restigouche (riv.) C 1
Richibucto (harb.) F 2
Richibucto (riv.) E 2
Roosevelt Campobello Int'l Park D 4
Saint Croix (riv.) C 3
Saint Francis (riv.) A 1
Saint John (harb.) E 3
Saint John (riv.) C 2
Saint Lawrence (gulf) F 1
Salisbury (bay) F 3
Salmon (riv.) C 1
Salmon (riv.) E 2
Shediac (isl.) F 2
Shepody (bay) F 3
Shippegan (bay) E 1
Shippegan Gully (str.) F 1
South Sevogle (riv.) D 1
Southwest (head) D 4
Southwest Miramichi (riv.) D 2
Spear (cape) G 2
Spednik (lake) C 3
Spencer (cape) E 3
Tabusintac (riv.) E 1
Tabusintac Gully (str.) F 1
Tetagouche (riv.) D 1
Tobique (riv.) C 2
Upsalquitch (riv.) D 1
Utopia (lake) D 3
Verte (bay) G 2
Washademoak (lake) E 3
West (isls.) D 4
White Head (isl.) D 4

⊛County seat.

Topography

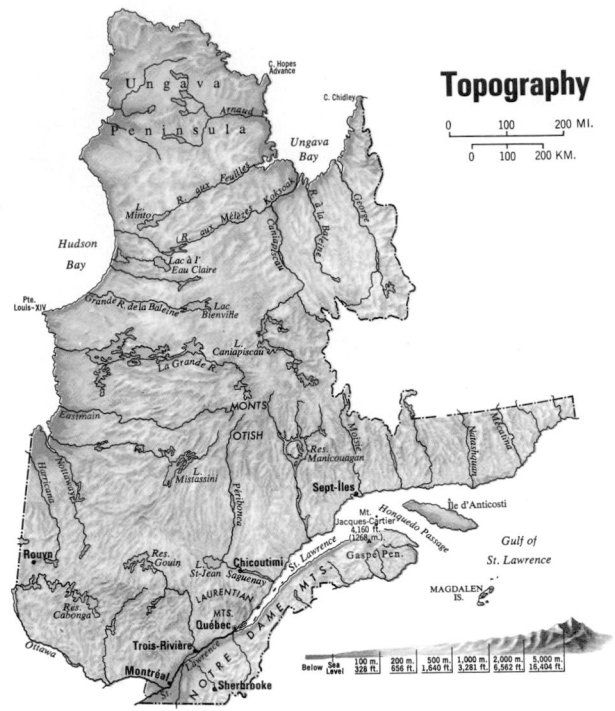

0   100   200 MI.

0   100   200 KM.

Sea Level Below | 100 m. 328 ft. | 200 m. 656 ft. | 500 m. 1,640 ft. | 1,000 m. 3,281 ft. | 2,000 m. 6,562 ft. | 5,000 m. 16,404 ft.

Agriculture, Industry and Resources

MAJOR MINERAL OCCURRENCES

Ab	Asbestos	Ni	Nickel
Au	Gold	Pb	Lead
Cu	Copper	Py	Pyrites
Fe	Iron Ore	Ti	Titanium
Mi	Mica	Zn	Zinc
Mo	Molybdenum		

⚡ Water Power

▨ Major Industrial Areas

DOMINANT LAND USE

- ▨ Cereals, Livestock
- ▨ Dairy
- ▨ Nonagricultural Land
- ▨ Pasture Livestock, Dairy
- ▨ Forests

COUNTIES

Argenteuil 32,454 .... C 4
Arthabaska 59,277 .... E 4
Bagot 26,840 .... D 4
Beauce 73,427 .... G 3
Beauharnois 54,034 .... C 4
Bellechasse 23,559 .... G 3
Berthier 31,096 .... C 3
Bonaventure 40,487 .... C 2
Brome 17,436 .... E 4
Chambly 307,090 .... J 4
Champlain 119,595 .... E 2
Charlevoix-Est 17,448 ...... G 2
Charlevoix-Ouest 14,172 ... G 2
Châteauguay 59,968 .... D 4
Chicoutimi 174,441 .... G 1
Compton 20,536 .... E 4
Deux-Montagnes 71,252 ... C 4
Dorchester 33,949 .... G 3
Drummond 69,770 .... E 4
Frontenac 26,814 .... G 4

Gaspé-Est 41,173 .... D 1
Gaspé-Ouest 18,943 .... C 1
Gatineau 54,229 .... B 3
Hull 131,213 .... B 4
Huntingdon 16,953 .... C 4
Iberville 23,180 .... D 4
Île-de-Montréal 1,760,122 . H 4
Île-Jésus 268,335 .... H 4
Joliette 60,384 .... C 3
Kamouraska 28,642 .... H 2
Labelle 34,395 .... B 3
Lac-Saint-Jean-Est 47,891 . F 1
Lac-Saint-Jean-Ouest 62,952 . E 1
Laprairie 105,962 .... H 4
L'Assomption 109,705 ...... D 4
Lévis 94,104 .... J 3
L'Islet 22,062 .... G 2
Lotbinière 29,653 .... F 3
Maskinongé 20,763 .... D 3
Matane 29,955 .... B 1
Matapédia 23,715 .... B 2
Mégantic 57,892 .... F 3

Missisquoi 36,161 .... D 4
Montcalm 27,557 .... C 3
Montmagny 25,622 .... G 3
Montmorency No 1 23,048 . F 2
Montmorency No 2 6,436 .. G 3
Napierville 13,562 .... D 4
Nicolet 33,513 .... E 3
Papineau 37,975 .... B 4
Pontiac 20,283 .... A 3
Portneuf 58,843 .... E 3
Québec 458,980 .... F 3
Richelieu 53,058 .... D 4
Richmond 40,871 .... E 4
Rimouski 69,099 .... J 1
Rivière-du-Loup 41,250 .... H 2
Rouville 42,391 .... D 4
Saguenay 115,881 .... H 1
Saint-Hyacinthe 55,888 .... D 4
Saint-Jean 55,576 .... D 4
Saint-Maurice 107,703 ..... D 3
Shefford 70,733 .... E 4
Sherbrooke 115,983 .... E 4

Soulanges 15,429 .... C 4
Stanstead 38,186 .... F 4
Témiscouata 52,570 .... J 2
Terrebonne 193,865 .... H 4
Vaudreuil 50,043 .... C 4
Verchères 63,353 .... J 4
Wolfe 15,635 .... F 4
Yamaska 14,797 .... E 3

CITIES and TOWNS

Acton Vale 4,371 .... E 4
Albanel 992 .... E 1
Alma⊙ 26,322 .... F 1
Amqui⊙ 4,048 .... B 2
Ancienne-Lorette 12,935 .. H 3
Angers .... B 4
Anjou 37,346 .... H 4
Annaville 712 .... E 3
Armagh 878 .... G 3
Arthabaska⊙ 6,827 .... F 3
Arvida .... F 1
Asbestos 7,967 .... F 4
Ascot Corner 847 .... E 4
Audet 760 .... G 4
Ayer's Cliff 810 .... E 4
Aylmer 26,695 .... B 4
Baie-Comeau 12,866 ...... A 1
Baie-d'Urfé 3,674 .... G 4
Baie-Saint-Paul⊙ 3,961 ... B 1
Baie-Trinité 749 .... H 4
Beaconsfield 19,613 ...... H 4
Beauceville⊙ 4,302 .... G 3
Beauharnois⊙ 7,025 ...... F 3
Beaumont 791 .... J 3
Beauport 60,447 .... H 4
Beaupré 2,740 .... G 2
Bécancour⊙ 10,247 ...... E 3
Bedford⊙ 2,832 .... E 4
Beebe Plain 1,072 .... E 4
Bélair (Val-Bélair) 12,695 . H 3
Beloeil 17,540 .... H 4
Bernierville 2,120 .... F 3
Berthier-en-Bas 562 ...... G 3
Berthierville⊙ 4,049 ...... C 3
Bic 2,994 .... J 1
Biencourt 824 .... J 2
Black Lake 5,148 .... F 3
Blainville 14,682 .... H 4
Boischatel 3,345 .... J 3
Bois-des-Filion 4,943 ..... H 4
Bolduc 1,565 .... G 4
Bonaventure 1,371 .... C 2
Boucherville 29,704 ...... J 4
Bromont 2,731 .... E 4
Bromptonville 3,035 ...... E 4
Brossard 52,232 .... H 4
Brownsburg 2,875 .... C 4
Buckingham 7,992 .... B 4
Cabano 3,291 .... J 2
Cacouna 1,160 .... H 2
Calumet 729 .... C 4
Candiac 8,502 .... J 4
Cap-à-l'Aigle 819 .... G 2
Cap-Chat 3,464 .... C 1
Cap-de-la-Madeleine 32,626 . E 3
Caplan-Rivière Caplan 1,139 . C 2
Cap-Saint-Ignace 1,485 .. G 2
Cap-Santé⊙ 671 .... F 3
Carignan 4,544 .... J 4
Carleton 2,710 .... C 2
Causapscal 2,501 .... B 2
Chambly 12,190 .... J 4
Chambord 961 .... F 1

Chandler 3,946 .... D 2
Charlemagne 4,827 .... H 4
Charlesbourg 68,326 ..... J 3
Charny 8,240 .... J 3
Châteauguay 36,928 ..... H 4
Château-Richer⊙ 3,628 .. J 3
Chénéville 633 .... B 4
Chicoutimi⊙ 60,064 ..... G 1
Chicoutimi-Jonquière
  *135,172 .... G 1
Chute-aux-Outardes 2,280 . A 1
Clermont 3,621 .... G 2
Coaticook 6,271 .... F 4
Coleraine 1,660 .... F 4
Compton 728 .... D 4
Contrecoeur 5,449 .... D 4
Cookshire⊙ 1,480 .... F 4
Coteau-du-Lac 1,247 .... C 4
Coteau-Landing⊙ 1,386 . C 4
Côte-Saint-Luc 27,531 ... H 4
Courcelles 608 .... G 4
Courville .... J 3
Cowansville 12,240 ...... E 4
Crabtree 1,950 .... D 4
Danville 2,200 .... E 4
Daveluyville 1,257 .... E 3
Deauville 942 .... E 4
Dégelis 3,477 .... J 2
Delisle 4,011 .... F 1
Delson 4,935 .... H 4
Desbiens 1,541 .... F 1
Deschaillons-sur-Saint-
  Laurent 950 .... E 3
Deschambault 977 .... E 3
Deschênes .... B 4
Deux-Montagnes 9,944 .. H 4
Didyme 667 .... F 1
Disraëli 3,181 .... F 4
Dolbeau 8,766 .... E 1
Dollard-des-Ormeaux 39,940 . H 4
Donnacona 5,731 .... F 3
Dorion 5,749 .... C 4
Dorval 17,727 .... H 4
Dosquet 703 .... F 3
Douville .... D 4
Drummondville 27,347 ... E 4
Drummondville-Sud 9,220 . E 4
Dunham 2,887 .... E 4
Durham-Sud 1,045 .... E 4
East Angus 4,016 .... F 4
East Broughton 2,587 .... F 3
East Broughton Station 1,302 . F 3
Eastman 612 .... E 4
Entrelacs 1,735 .... C 3
Farnham 6,498 .... E 4
Ferme-Neuve 2,266 ...... B 3
Forestville 4,271 .... H 1
Frampton 684 .... G 3
Francoeur 1,422 .... F 3
Gaspé 17,261 .... D 1
Gatineau 74,988 .... B 4
Giffard .... J 3
Girardville 1,128 .... E 1
Gracefield 869 .... A 3
Granby 38,069 .... E 4
Grand'Mère 15,442 ...... E 3
Grande-Rivière 4,420 .... D 2
Grandes-Bergeronnes 748 . H 1
Grande-Vallée 700 .... D 1
Greenfield Park 18,527 ... J 4
Grenville 1,417 .... C 4
Gros-Morne 672 .... C 1
Hampstead 7,598 .... H 4
Ham-Sud 62 .... F 4
Hauterive 13,995 .... A 1
Hébertville 2,515 .... F 1
Hébertville-Station 1,442 . F 1
Hemmingford 737 .... D 4
Henryville 595 .... D 4
Howick 639 .... D 4
Hudson 4,414 .... C 4
Hull⊙ 56,225 .... B 4
Huntingdon⊙ 3,018 .... C 4
Île-Perrot 5,945 .... C 4
Iberville⊙ 8,587 .... D 4
Inverness 329 .... F 3
Joliette⊙ 16,987 .... D 3
Jonquière 60,354 ...... F 1
Jonquière-Chicoutimi
  *135,172 .... F 1
Kingsey Falls 818 ...... E 4
Kirkland 10,476 .... H 4
Knowlton (Lac-Brome)⊙
  4,316 .... E 4
La Baie 20,935 .... G 1
Labelle 1,534 .... C 3
Lac-à-la-Croix 1,017 ... F 1
Lac-Alouette-Lac-Brière 1,356 . D 4
Lac-au-Saumon 1,332 .. B 2
Lac-aux-Sables 838 .... E 3
Lac-Beaufort .... F 3
Lac-Bouchette 1,703 .. E 1
Lac-Carré 717 .... C 3
Lac-des-Écorces 766 .. B 3
Lac-Drolet 1,120 ...... G 4
Lac-Etchemin 2,729 ... G 3
Lachenaie 8,631 .... D 4
Lachine 37,521 .... H 4
Lachute⊙ 11,729 ...... C 4
Lacolle 1,319 .... C 4
Lac-Mégantic⊙ 6,119 . G 4
Lac-Saint-Charles 5,837 . H 3
Lafontaine 4,799 ...... C 4
La Guadeloupe 1,692 . F 4
La Malbaie⊙ 4,030 ... G 2
Lambton 1,559 .... F 4
L'Annonciation 2,384 . C 3
Lanoraie (Lanoraie-d'Autry)
  1,613 .... D 4
La Pêche 4,977 .... B 4
La Pérade 1,039 ...... E 3
La Pocatière 4,560 ... H 2

La Prairie⊙ 10,627 ...... J 4
La Providence .... E 4
Larouche 662 .... F 1
La Salle 76,299 .... H 4
L'Ascension 1,287 ...... F 1
L'Assomption 4,844 .... D 4
La Station-du-Coteau 892 . C 4
Laterrière 788 .... F 1
La Tuque 11,556 .... E 2
Laurentides 1,947 ...... D 4
Laurier-Station 1,123 ... F 3
Laurierville 939 .... F 3
Lauzon 13,362 .... J 3
Laval 268,335 .... H 4
Lavaltrie 2,053 .... D 4
L'Avenir 1,116 .... E 4
Lawrenceville 562 .... E 4
Le Moyne 6,137 ...... J 4
L'Épiphanie 2,971 .... D 4
Léry 2,239 .... H 4
Lévis 17,895 .... J 3
Lennoxville 3,922 .... F 4
Les Méchins 803 .... B 1
Linière 1,168 .... G 3
L'Islet 1,070 .... G 2
L'Islet-sur-Mer 774 .. G 2
L'Isle-Verte 1,142 ... G 1
Longueuil 124,320 .. J 4
Loretteville 15,060 .. H 3
Lorraine 6,881 ...... H 4
Louiseville⊙ 3,735 .. E 3
Luceville 1,524 ..... J 1
Lyster 830 .... F 3
Magog 13,604 ..... E 4

Maniwaki⊙ 5,424 ..... B 3
Manseau 626 .... E 3
Maple Grove 2,009 ... H 4
Maria 1,178 .... C 2
Marieville⊙ 4,877 .... D 4
Mascouche 20,345 ... H 4
Maskinongé⊙ 1,005 . E 3
Masson 4,264 .... B 4
Massueville 671 ..... E 4
Matagami 13,612 .... B 3
Matapédia 586 ...... B 2
Melocheville 1,892 .. C 4
Mercier 6,352 .... H 4
Metabetchouan 3,406 . F 1
Mirabel 14,080 ..... H 4
Mistassini 6,682 .... E 1
Montauban 557 ..... E 3
Mont-Carmel 807 ... H 2
Montcerf 570 .... A 3
Mont-Joli 6,359 .... J 1
Mont-Laurier⊙ 8,405 . B 3
Montmagny⊙ 12,405 . G 2
Montréal⊙ 980,354 . H 4
Montréal *2,828,349 . H 4
Montréal-Est 3,778 . J 4
Montréal-Nord 94,914 . H 4
Mont-Rolland 1,517 . C 4
Mont-Royal 19,247 . H 4
Mont-Saint-Hilaire 10,066 . D 4
Morin Heights 592 . C 4
Murdochville 3,396 . C 1
Nantes 1,167 ...... F 4

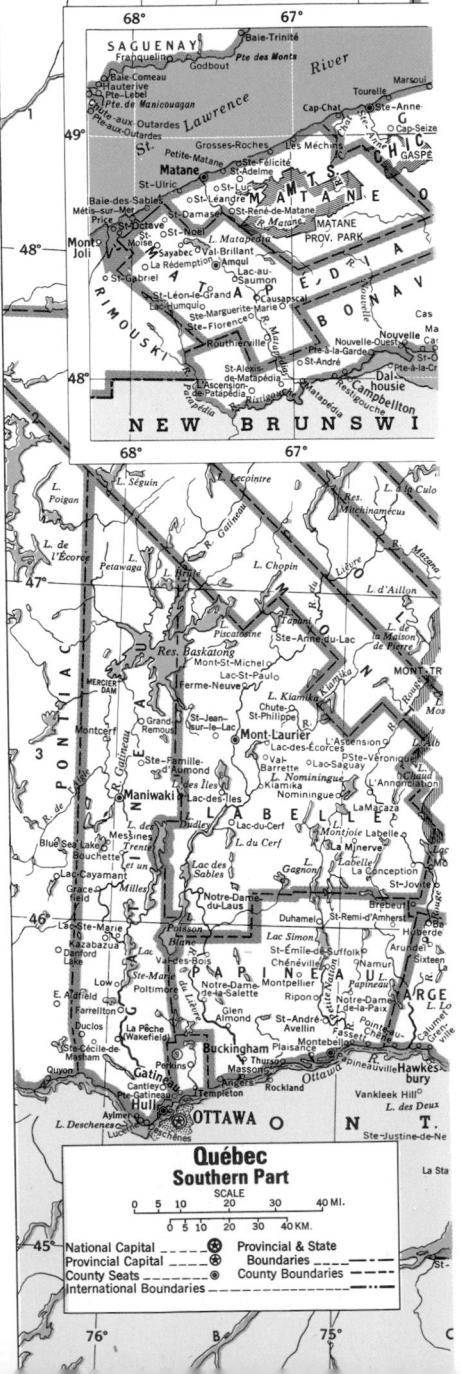

Québec
Southern Part

SCALE
0 5 10   20   30   40 MI.

⊛ National Capital ___ ___
⊛ Provincial Capital
● County Seats
   International Boundaries ___ ___
   Provincial & State Boundaries ___ ___ ___
   County Boundaries ___ ___ ___

Napierville⊙ 2,343 . . . . D 4
Neuville 996 . . . . F 3
New Carlisle⊙ 1,292 . . . . . . D 2
New Richmond 4,257 . . . . . . C 2
Nicolet 4,880 . . . . E 3
Nominingue 881 . . . . B 3
Normandin 4,041 . . . . E 1
North Hatley 689 . . . . E 4
Notre-Dame-de-la-Doré 1,064 E 1
Notre-Dame-des-Laurentides H 3
Notre-Dame-des-Prairies
 6,150 . . . . D 3
Notre-Dame-du-Bon-Conseil
 1,089 . . . . E 4
Notre-Dame-du-Lac⊙ 2,258 . J 2
Nouvelle 669 . . . . C 2
Oka 1,538 . . . . C 4
Omerville 1,398 . . . . E 4
Ormstown 1,659 . . . . D 4
Orsainville . . . . H 3
Otis 673 . . . . G 1
Otterburn Park 4,268 . . . . . . D 4
Outremont 24,338 . . . . H 4
Pabos 1,295 . . . . D 2
Pabos-Mills 1,565 . . . . D 2
Papineauville 1,481 . . . . C 4
Paspébiac 1,914 . . . . D 2
Percé 4,839 . . . . D 1
Petit-Cap 1,023 . . . . D 1
Petite-Matane 1,065 . . . . B 1
Petit-Saguenay (Saint-
 François-d'Assise) 804 . . G 1
Pierrefonds 38,390 . . . . H 4
Pierreville 1,212 . . . . E 3

Pincourt 8,750 . . . . D 4
Pintendre 1,849 . . . . J 3
Plaisance 748 . . . . B 4
Plessisville 7,249 . . . . F 3
Pohénégamooke 3,702 . . . . . H 2
Pointe-à-la-Croix 1,481 . . . . C 2
Pointe-au-Père 796 . . . . J 1
Pointe-au-Pic 1,054 . . . . G 2
Pointe-aux-Outardes 1,056 . . A 1
Pointe-aux-Trembles 36,270 . H 4
Pointe-Calumet 2,935 . . . . . G 4
Pointe-Claire 24,571 . . . . . . H 4
Pointe-du-Lac 5,359 . . . . . . E 3
Pointe-Gatineau . . . . B 4
Pointe-Lebel 1,573 . . . . A 1
Pont-Rouge 3,580 . . . . F 3
Port-Alfred 8,621 . . . . G 1
Portneuf 1,333 . . . . F 3
Portneuf-sur-Mer (Rivière-
 Portneuf-sur-Mer) 1,255 . H 1
Price 2,273 . . . . A 1
Princeville 4,023 . . . . F 3
Proulxville 588 . . . . E 3
Québec (cap.) 166,474 . . . . . H 3
Québec ⊙576,075 . . . . H 3
Quyon 744 . . . . A 4
Rawdon 2,958 . . . . D 3
Repentigny 34,419 . . . . J 4
Richelieu 1,531 . . . . D 4
Richmond⊙ 3,568 . . . . E 4
Rigaud 2,268 . . . . C 4
Rimouski⊙ 29,120 . . . . J 1
Rimouski-Est 2,506 . . . . J 1
Ripon 620 . . . . B 4

Rivière-à-Pierre 615 . . . . . . E 3
Rivière-au-Renard 2,211 . . . . D 1
Rivière-Bleue 1,690 . . . . J 2
Rivière-Bois-Clair 604 . . . . . F 3
Rivière-du-Loup⊙ 13,459 . . . H 2
Rivière-du-Moulin . . . . G 1
Rivière-Éternité 659 . . . . . . G 1
Rivière-Portneuf-Portneuf-sur-
 Mer 1,255 . . . . H 1
Robertsonville 1,987 . . . . . . F 3
Roberval⊙ 11,429 . . . . E 1
Rock Island 1,179 . . . . E 4
Rosemère 7,778 . . . . H 4
Rougemont 972 . . . . D 4
Roxboro 6,292 . . . . H 4
Roxton Falls 1,245 . . . . E 4
Sacré-Coeur-de-Saguenay
 1,678 . . . . H 1
Saint-Adelme 618 . . . . B 1
Saint-Adelphe 1,159 . . . . . . E 3
Saint-Adolphe-d'Howard
 1,686 . . . . C 4
Saint-Adrien 597 . . . . E 4
Saint-Agapithe 2,954 . . . . . . F 3
Saint-Aimé-des-Lacs 861 . . . G 2
Saint-Alban 673 . . . . E 3
Saint-Alexandre-de-
 Kamouraska 1,048 . . . . . H 2
Saint-Alexis-des-Monts 1,984 . D 3
Saint-Amable 2,424 . . . . J 4
Saint-Ambroise 3,606 . . . . . F 1
Saint-Anaclet 1,377 . . . . J 1
Saint-André-Avellin 1,312 . . . B 4
Saint-André-Est 1,293 . . . . . C 4

Saint-Anselme 1,808 . . . . . . F 3
Saint-Antoine 7,012 . . . . H 4
Saint-Antonin 941 . . . . H 2
Saint-Aubert 884 . . . . G 2
Saint-Augustin-de-Québec
 2,475 . . . . E 3
Saint-Basile-Sud 1,719 . . . . . E 3
Saint-Basile-le-Grand 7,658 . J 4
Saint-Benjamin 1,027 . . . . . . G 3
Saint-Bernard 585 . . . . G 3
Saint-Bernard-sur-Mer 711 . . G 2
Saint-Boniface-de-Shawinigan
 3,164 . . . . D 3
Saint-Bruno 2,580 . . . . H 4
Saint-Bruno-de-Montarville
 22,880 . . . . J 4
Saint-Camille-de-Bellechasse
 1,521 . . . . C 3
Saint-Casimir 1,133 . . . . C 3
Saint-Césaire 2,935 . . . . D 4
Saint-Charles 1,019 . . . . G 3
Saint-Charles-de-Mandeville
 1,392 . . . . D 3
Saint-Chrysostome 1,018 . . . D 4
Saint-Côme 660 . . . . D 3
Saint-Constant 9,938 . . . . . . H 4
Saint-Cyprien 860 . . . . J 2
Saint-Cyrille 1,041 . . . . E 4
Saint-Damien-de-Buckland
 1,522 . . . . G 3
Saint-David 5,380 . . . . J 3
Saint-David-de-Falardeau
 1,876 . . . . F 1
Saint-Denis 861 . . . . D 4

Saint-Dominique 2,068 . . . . . E 4
Saint-Donat-de-Montcalm
 1,521 . . . . C 3
Sainte-Adèle 4,675 . . . . C 4
Sainte-Agathe 709 . . . . F 3
Sainte-Agathe-des-Monts
 5,641 . . . . C 4
Sainte-Anne-de-Beaupré
 3,292 . . . . G 2
Sainte-Anne-de-Bellevue
 3,981 . . . . H 4
Sainte-Anne-des-Monts⊙
 6,062 . . . . C 1
Sainte-Anne-des-Plaines
 4,258 . . . . H 4
Sainte-Anne-du-Lac 686 . . . . B 3
Sainte-Aurélie 1,045 . . . . . . G 3
Sainte-Blandine 849 . . . . . . J 1

Sainte-Catherine 1,474 . . . . . F 3
Sainte-Claire 1,566 . . . . G 3
Sainte-Croix⊙ 1,814 . . . . . . F 3
Sainte-Félicité 711 . . . . B 1
Sainte-Foy 68,883 . . . . H 3
Sainte-Geneviève 2,573 . . . . H 4
Sainte-Geneviève-de-
 Batiscan⊙ 356 . . . . E 3
Sainte-Hélène-de-Bagot
 1,328 . . . . E 4
Sainte-Hénédine⊙ 639 . . . . . G 3
Sainte-Julie-de-Verchères
 14,243 . . . . J 4
Sainte-Julienne⊙ 750 . . . . . . D 4
Saint-Élie 639 . . . . E 3
Sainte-Justine 1,080 . . . . . . G 3
Saint-Élzéar 743 . . . . F 3
Sainte-Marie 8,937 . . . . G 3

Sainte-Martine⊙ 2,196 . . . . . D 4
Sainte-Émile 5,216 . . . . H 3
Sainte-Monique 705 . . . . F 1
Sainte-Pétronille 982 . . . . . . J 3
Saint-Épréme-de-Tring 973 . G 3
Saint-Épiphane 647 . . . . H 2
Saint-Esprit 1,068 . . . . E 4
Saint-Étienne-de-L'Islet
 1,232 . . . . H 2
Saint-Éphrem-de-Tring 973 . G 3
Saint-Épiphane 647 . . . . H 2
Sainte-Pudentienne 866 . . . . E 4
Sainte-Rosalie 2,862 . . . . . . E 4
Saint-Esprit 1,068 . . . . E 4
Sainte-Thérèse 18,750 . . . . . H 4
Sainte-Thérèse-Ouest
 (Boisbriand) 13,471 . . . . H 4
Sainte-Thècle 1,703 . . . . . . E 3
Saint-Étienne-de-Grès 845 . . E 3
Saint-Étienne-de-Lauzon
 1,218 . . . . J 3

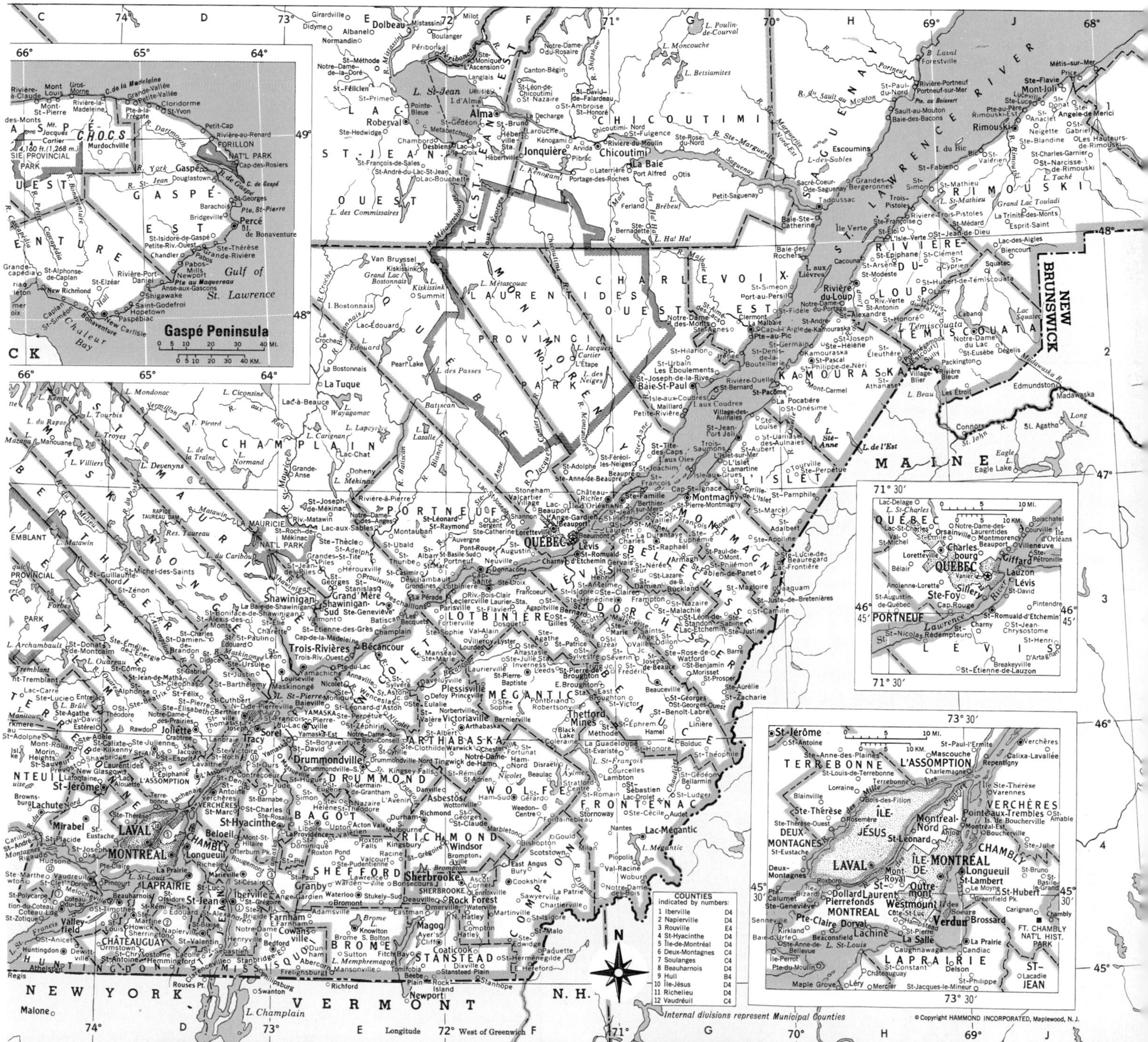

AREA 594,857 sq. mi. (1,540,680 sq. km.)
POPULATION 6,532,461
CAPITAL Québec
LARGEST CITY Montréal
HIGHEST POINT Mont D'Iberville 5,420 ft.
 (1,652 m.)
SETTLED IN 1608
ADMITTED TO CONFEDERATION 1867
PROVINCIAL FLOWER White Garden Lily

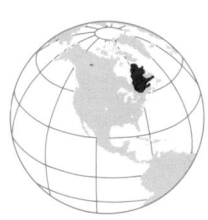

COUNTIES
(indicated by numbers)
1 Iberville . . . . D 4
2 Napierville . . . . D 4
3 Rouville . . . . E 4
4 St-Hyacinthe . . . . . D 4
5 Île-de-Montréal . . . . H 4
6 Deux-Montagnes . . H 4
7 Soulanges . . . . G 4
8 Beauharnois . . . . . . D 4
9 Hull . . . . B 4
10 Île-Jésus . . . . H 4
11 Richelieu . . . . D 4
12 Vaudreuil . . . . G 4

Internal divisions represent Municipal Counties

© Copyright HAMMOND INCORPORATED, Maplewood, N.J.

Gaspé Peninsula

PORTNEUF

MONTREAL

(continued)

Saint-Eustache 29,716 H 4
Saint-Fabien 1,361 J 1
Saint-Félicien 9,058 E 1
Saint-Félix-de-Valois 1,462 D 3
Saint-Ferréol-les-Neiges 1,758 G 2
Saint-Flavien 734 F 3
Saint-François-de-Sales 831 E 1
Saint-François-du-Lac⊙ 942 E 3
Saint-Fulgence 950 G 1
Saint-Gabriel 3,161 D 3
Saint-Gabriel-de-Rimouski 779 J 1
Saint-Gédéon, Frontenac 1,569 G 4
Saint-Gédéon, Lac-St-Jean-E. 1,000 F 1
Saint-Georges, Beauce 10,342 G 3
Saint-Georges, Champlain 3,344 E 3
Saint-Georges-Ouest 6,378 G 3
Saint-Germain-de-Grantham 1,373 E 4
Saint-Gervais 973 G 3
Saint-Gilles 912 F 3
Saint-Grégoire (Mont-St-Grégoire) 740 D 4
Saint-Henri 1,970 J 3
Saint-Honoré, Beauce 1,116 G 4
Saint-Honoré, Chicoutimi 1,790 F 1
Saint-Hubert 60,573 J 4
Saint-Hubert-de-Témiscouata 871 J 2
Saint-Hyacinthe⊙ 38,246 D 4
Saint-Isidore 811 F 3
Saint-Isidore-de-Laprairie 769 D 4
Saint-Jacques 2,152 D 4
Saint-Jacques-le-Mineur 1,203 H 4
Saint-Jean-Chrysostome 6,930 J 3
Saint-Jean-de-Dieu 1,377 J 1
Saint-Jean-de-Matha 931 D 3
Saint-Jean-Port-Joli⊙ 1,813 G 2
Saint-Jean-sur-Richelieu⊙ 35,640 D 4
Saint-Jérôme 25,123 H 4
Saint-Joachim 1,139 G 2
Saint-Joseph-de-Beauce 3,216 G 3
Saint-Joseph-de-Sorel 2,545 D 3
Saint-Jovite 3,841 C 3
Saint-Lambert 20,557 J 4
Saint-Laurent 65,900 H 4
Saint-Lazare 731 G 3
Saint-Léonard 79,429 H 4
Saint-Léonard-d'Aston 992 E 3
Saint-Léon-de-Chicoutimi 749 F 1
Saint-Léon-de-Standon 816 G 3
Saint-Léon-le-Grand 722 B 2
Saint-Liboire⊙ 746 E 4
Saint-Louis-de-Gonzague 615 D 4
Saint-Louis-de-Terrebonne 14,172 H 4
Saint-Louis-du-Ha! Ha! 809 H 2
Saint-Luc 8,815 D 4
Saint-Luc-de-Matane 598 B 1
Saint-Marc-des-Carrières 2,822 E 3
Saint-Méthode-de-Frontenac 925 F 3
Saint-Michel-de-Bellechasse 963 G 3
Saint-Michel-des-Saints 1,584 D 3
Saint-Nazaire-de-Chicoutimi 962 F 1
Saint-Nérée 970 G 3
Saint-Nicolas 5,074 H 3
Saint-Noël 666 B 1
Saint-Odilon 580 G 3
Saint-Omer 718 C 2
Saint-Ours 625 D 4
Saint-Pacôme 1,996 G 2
Saint-Pamphile 3,428 H 3
Saint-Pascal⊙ 2,763 H 2
Saint-Paul-de-Montminy 602 G 3
Saint-Paulin 663 D 3
Saint-Paul-l'Ermite (Le Gardeur) 8,312 J 4
Saint-Philippe-de-Néri 715 H 2
Saint-Pie 1,725 E 4
Saint-Pierre 5,305 H 4
Saint-Pierre-d'Orléans 880 G 3
Saint-Polycarpe 602 C 4
Saint-Prime 2,522 E 1
Saint-Prosper-de-Dorchester 2,150 G 3
Saint-Raphaël⊙ 1,346 G 3
Saint-Raymond 3,605 F 3
Saint-Rédempteur 4,463 J 3
Saint-Régis 1,370 C 4
Saint-Rémi 5,146 D 4
Saint-Roch-de-l'Achigan 1,160 D 4
Saint-Roch-de-Richelieu 1,650 D 4
Saint-Romuald-d'Etchemin⊙ 9,849 J 3
Saint-Sauveur-des-Monts 2,348 C 4
Saint-Siméon 1,152 G 2
Saint-Simon 602 H 1
Saint-Stanislas 1,443 E 3
Saint-Sylvère 1,006 E 3
Saint-Timothée 2,113 D 4
Saint-Tite 3,031 E 3
Saint-Tite-des-Caps 626 G 2
Saint-Ubald 1,605 E 3
Saint-Ulric 792 B 1
Saint-Urbain-de-Charlevoix 1,079 G 2
Saint-Victor 1,104 G 3
Saint-Zacharie 1,284 G 3
Saint-Zotique 1,774 C 4
Sault-au-Mouton 828 H 1
Sawyerville 939 F 4
Sayabec 1,721 B 2
Scotstown 762 F 4
Senneville 1,221 G 4
Shannon 3,488 F 3
Shawbridge 942 C 4
Shawinigan 23,011 E 3
Shawinigan-Sud 11,325 E 3
Shawville 1,608 A 4
Sherbrooke⊙ 74,075 E 4
Sherrington 614 D 4
Sillery 12,825 J 3
Sorel⊙ 20,347 D 4
Squatec 1,000 J 2
Stanstead Plain 1,093 F 4
Sutton 1,599 E 4
Tadoussac⊙ 900 H 1
Templeton B 4
Terrebonne 11,769 H 4
Thetford Mines 19,965 F 3
Thurso 2,780 B 4
Tourelle (Tourelle-Grand-Tourelle) 942 C 1
Tourville 659 H 2
Tracy 12,843 D 3
Tring-Jonction 1,315 F 3
Trois-Pistoles 4,445 H 1
Trois-Rivières 50,466 E 3
Trois-Rivières *111,453 E 3
Trois-Rivières-Ouest 13,107 E 3
Upton 926 E 4
Val-Barrette 609 B 3
Val-Brillant 687 B 1
Valcourt 2,601 E 4
Val-David 2,336 C 3
Vallée-Jonction 1,200 G 3
Valleyfield (Salaberry-de-Valleyfield) 29,574 C 4
Vanier 10,725 J 3
Varennes 8,764 J 4
Vaudreuil⊙ 7,608 C 4
Verchères⊙ 4,473 J 4
Verdun 61,287 H 4
Victoriaville 21,838 F 3
Villeneuve J 3
Warwick 2,847 F 4
Waterloo⊙ 4,664 E 4
Waterville 1,397 F 4
Weedon-Centre 1,263 F 4
Westmount 20,480 H 4
Wickham 2,043 E 4
Windsor 5,233 F 4
Wottonville 673 F 4
Yamachiche⊙ 1,258 E 3

OTHER FEATURES

Alma (isl.) F 1
Aylmer (lake) F 4
Baskatong (res.) B 3
Batiscan (riv.) E 2
Bécancour (riv.) F 3
Bonaventure (isl.) D 1
Bonaventure (riv.) C 1
Brome (lake) E 4
Brompton (lake) E 4
Cascapédia (riv.) C 1
Chaleur (bay) C 2
Champlain (lake) D 4
Chaudière (riv.) G 4
Chic-Chocs (mts.) C 1
Chicoutimi (riv.) F 2
Coudres (isl.) G 2
Deschênes (lake) A 4
Deux Montagnes (lake) C 4
Ditton (riv.) F 4
Forillon Nat'l Park D 1
Fort Chambly Nat'l Hist. Park J 4
Gaspé (bay) D 1
Gaspé (cape) D 1
Gaspé (pen.) D 2
Gaspésie Prov. Park C 1
Gatineau (riv.) B 3
Îles (lake) B 3
Jacques-Cartier (mt.) C 1
Jacques-Cartier (riv.) F 2
Kénogami (lake) F 1
Kiamika (lake) B 3
La Maurice Nat'l Park D 3
Laurentides Prov. Park F 2
Lièvre (riv.) B 4
Lièvres (isl.) H 2
Maskinongé (riv.) D 3
Matane (riv.) B 1
Matane Prov. Park B 1
Matapédia (riv.) B 2
Mégantic (lake) G 4
Memphremagog (lake) E 4
Mercier (dam) A 3
Métabetchouane (riv.) F 1
Mille Îles (riv.) H 4
Montmorency (riv.) F 2
Mont-Tremblant Prov. Park C 3
Nicolet (riv.) E 3
Nominingue (lake) B 3
Nord (riv.) C 4
Orléans (isl.) F 3
Ottawa (riv.) B 4
Ouareau (riv.) D 3
Ouelle (riv.) H 2
Patapédia (riv.) B 2
Péribonca (riv.) F 1
Petite Nation (riv.) B 4
Prairies (riv.) H 4
Rimouski (riv.) J 1
Ristigouche (riv.) B 2
Saguenay (riv.) G 1
Sainte-Anne (riv.) F 3
Sainte-Anne (riv.) G 2
Saint-François (lake) F 4
Saint-François (riv.) E 4
Saint-Jean (lake) E 1
Saint Lawrence (gulf) D 2
Saint Lawrence (riv.) H 1
Saint-Louis (lake) H 4
Saint-Maurice (riv.) E 2
Saint-Pierre (lake) E 3
Shawinigan (riv.) E 3
Shipshaw (riv.) F 1
Soeurs (isl.) H 4
Témiscouata (lake) H 2
Tremblant (lake) C 3
Trente et un Milles (lake) B 3
Verte (isl.) H 1
Yamaska (riv.) E 4
York (riv.) D 1

⊙County seat.
*Population of metropolitan area.

QUÉBEC, NORTHERN

INTERNAL DIVISIONS

Abitibi (county) 93,529 B 2
Abitibi (terr.) B 3
Berthier (county) 31,096 B 3
Bonaventure (county) 40,487 D 3
Champlain (county) 119,595 C 3
Charlevoix-Est (co.) 17,448 C 3
Charlevoix-Ouest (county) 14,172 C 3
Chicoutimi (county) 174,441 C 2
Gaspé-Est (county) 41,173 E 3
Gaspé-Ouest (county) 18,943 D 3
Gatineau (county) 54,229 B 3
Joliette (county) 60,384 B 3
Lac-Saint-Jean-Est (county) 47,891 C 3
Lac-Saint-Jean-Ouest (county) 62,952 C 2
Maskinongé (county) 20,763 C 3
Matane (county) 29,955 D 3
Matapédia (county) 23,715 D 3
Mistassini (terr.) B 2
Montcalm (county) 27,557 B 3
Montmorency No. I (county) 23,048 C 3
Nouveau-Québec (terr.) E 1
Pontiac (county) 20,283 B 3
Portneuf (county) 58,843 C 3
Québec (county) 458,980 C 3
Rimouski (county) 69,099 D 3
Saguenay (county) 115,881 D 2
Saint-Maurice (co.) 107,703 C 3
Témiscamingue (co.) 52,570 B 3

CITIES and TOWNS

Alma⊙ 26,322 C 3
Amos⊙ 9,421 B 3
Baie-Comeau 12,866 D 3
Baie-du-Poste 1,690 C 2
Chicoutimi⊙ 60,064 C 3
Gaspé 17,261 E 3
Hauterive 13,995 D 3
Jonquière 60,354 C 3
Lévis 17,895 C 3
La Tuque 11,556 C 3
Manicouagan D 2
Maniwaki⊙ 5,424 B 3
Matane⊙ 13,612 D 3
Mistassini (Baie-du-Poste) 1,690 C 2
Mont-Laurier⊙ 8,405 B 3
Montmagny⊙ 12,405 C 3
New Carlisle⊙ 781 E 3
Perce⊙ 4,839 E 3
Port-Cartier-Ouest D 3
Port-Menier⊙ 275 E 3
Povungnituk 745 E 1
Québec (cap.)⊙ 166,474 C 3
Rimouski⊙ 29,120 D 3
Rivière-au-Tonnerre 480 D 2
Rivière-du-Loup 13,459 D 3
Rouyn 17,224 B 3
Sept-Îles 29,262 D 2
Shawinigan 23,011 C 3
Tadoussac 900 C 3
Val d'Or 21,371 B 3
Ville-Marie 2,651 B 3
Wemindji B 2

OTHER FEATURES

Allard (lake) E 2
Anticosti (isl.) E 3
Baleine, Grand Rivière de la (riv.) B 1
Bell (riv.) B 3
Betsiamites (riv.) C 2
Bienville (lake) C 2
Broadback (riv.) B 2
Cabonga (res.) B 3
Caniapiscau (riv.) D 1
Eastmain (riv.) B 2
Eau Claire (lake) C 1
Feuilles (riv.) C 1
Gaspésie Prov. Park D 3
George (riv.) F 2
Gouin (res.) C 3
Grande Rivière, La (riv.) B 2
Honguedo (passage) E 3
Hudson (bay) A 1
Hudson (str.) F 1
Jacques-Cartier (passage) E 3
James (bay) A 2
Koksoak (riv.) D 1
Laurentides Prov. Park C 3
Louis-XIV (pt.) B 2
Manicouagan (res.) D 2
Minto (lake) E 2
Mistassibi (riv.) C 3
Mistassini (lake) C 2
Moisie (riv.) D 2
Natashquan (riv.) E 2
Nottaway (riv.) B 2
Nouveau-Québec (crater) F 1
Otish (mts.) C 2
Ottawa (riv.) B 3
Péribonca (riv.) C 3
Plétipi (lake) C 2
Saguenay (riv.) C 3
Saint-Jean (lake) C 3
Saint Lawrence (gulf) E 3
Saint Lawrence (riv.) D 3
Ungava (pen.) E 1

⊙County seat.
*Population of metropolitan area.

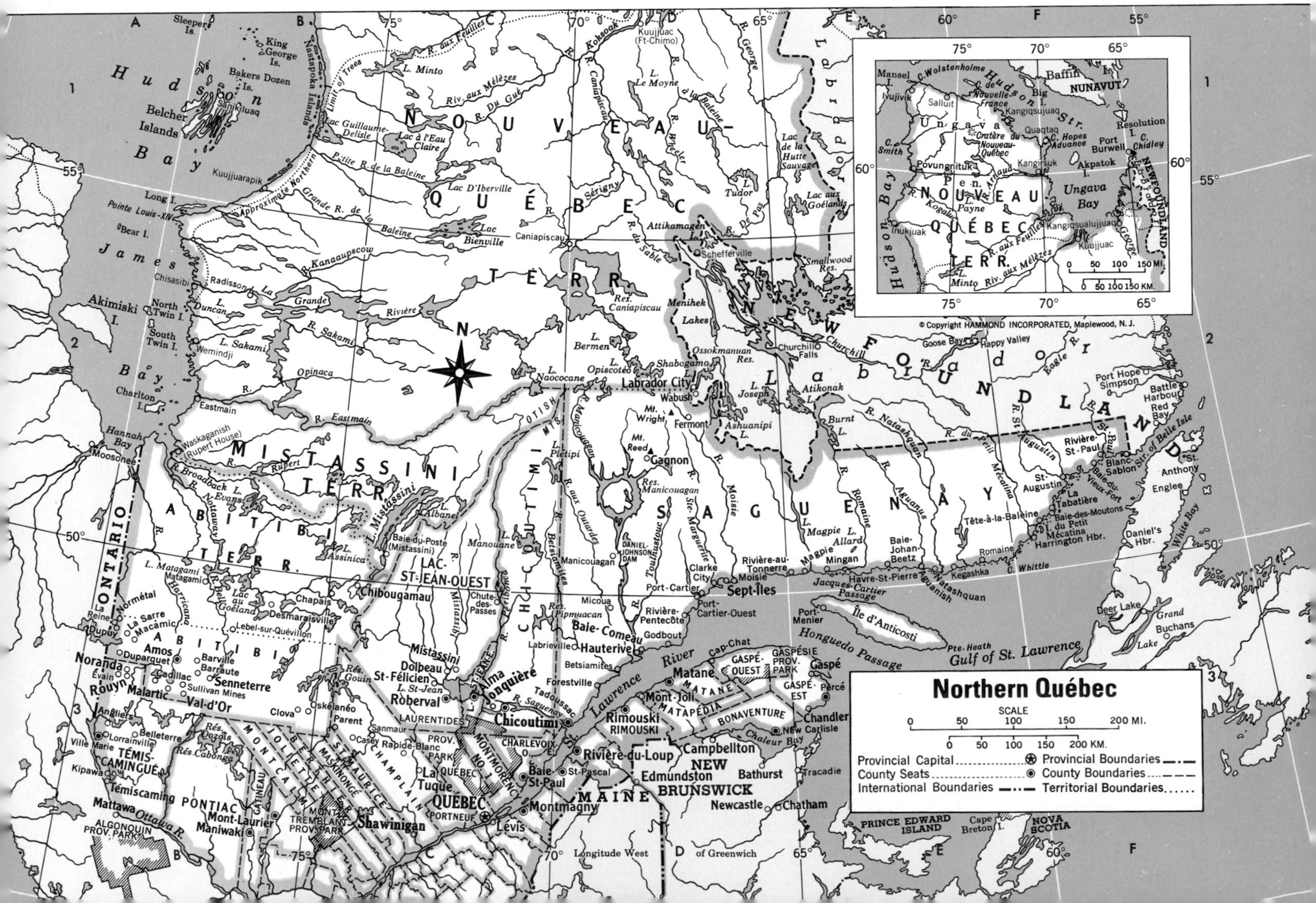
Northern Québec
SCALE
0 50 100 150 200 MI.
0 50 100 150 200 KM.
Provincial Capital
Province Boundaries
County Seats
County Boundaries
International Boundaries
Territorial Boundaries
Longitude West of Greenwich
© Copyright HAMMOND INCORPORATED, Maplewood, N. J.
Hudson Bay
James Bay
NOUVEAU-QUÉBEC TERR.
MISTASSINI TERR.
ABITIBI TERR.
SAGUENAY
CHICOUTIMI
LAC-ST-JEAN-OUEST
NEWFOUNDLAND
Labrador
ONTARIO
MAINE
NEW BRUNSWICK
NOVA SCOTIA
PRINCE EDWARD ISLAND
Gulf of St. Lawrence
Honguedo Passage
Île d'Anticosti
Kuujjuac (Ft-Chimo)
Schefferville
Labrador City
Gagnon
Sept-Îles
Baie-Comeau
Chibougamau
Chicoutimi
Jonquière
Roberval
St-Félicien
Rivière-du-Loup
Rimouski
Matane
Gaspé
Val-d'Or
Rouyn
Noranda
Amos
Senneterre
Shawinigan
QUÉBEC
Lévis
La Tuque
Mont-Laurier
Maniwaki
Campbellton
Edmundston
Bathurst
Chatham
Newcastle
Churchill Falls
Happy Valley
Goose Bay

AREA 412,580 sq. mi. (1,068,582 sq. km.)
POPULATION 9,101,694
CAPITAL Toronto
LARGEST CITY Toronto
HIGHEST POINT in Timiskaming Dist. 2,275 ft. (693 m.)
SETTLED IN 1749
ADMITTED TO CONFEDERATION 1867
PROVINCIAL FLOWER White Trillium

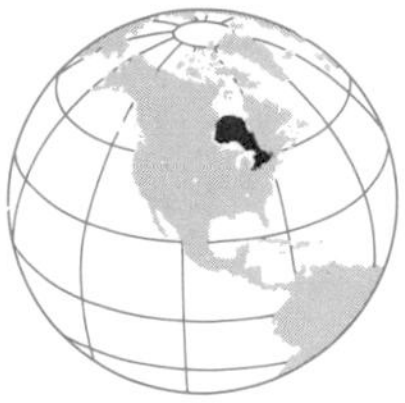

ONTARIO, NORTHERN

INTERNAL DIVISIONS

Algoma (terr. dist.) 133,553 . . . D 3
Cochrane (terr. dist.) 96,875 . . D 2
Kenora (terr. dist.) 59,421 . . . . C 2
Manitoulin (terr. dist.) 11,001 . D 3
Nipissing (terr. dist.) 80,268 . . E 3
Parry Sound (terr. dist.) 33,528 . . . . E 3
Rainy River (terr. dist.) 22,798 B 3
Renfrew (county) 87,484 . . . . . E 3
Sudbury (reg. munic.) 159,779 . . . . D 3
Sudbury (terr. dist.) 27,068 . . . D 3
Thunder Bay (terr. dist.) 153,997 . . . . C 3
Timiskaming (terr. dist.) 41,288 . . . . D 3

CITIES and TOWNS

Chalk River 1,010 . . . . E 3
Elliot Lake 16,723 . . . . D 3
Fort Albany 482 . . . . D 2
Fort Frances◎ 8,906 . . . . B 3
Kapuskasing 12,014 . . . . D 3
Kenora◎ 9,817 . . . . B 3
Kirkland Lake 12,219 . . . . D 3
Moose Factory 1,452 . . . . D 2
Moosonee 1,433 . . . . D 2
Nickel Centre 12,318 . . . . D 3
North Bay◎ 51,268 . . . . E 3
Pembroke◎ 14,026 . . . . E 3
Sault Sainte Marie◎ 82,697 . . D 3
Sudbury 91,829 . . . . D 3
Thunder Bay◎ 112,486 . . . . . . C 3
Timmins 46,114 . . . . D 3
Valley East 20,433 . . . . D 3

OTHER FEATURES

Abitibi (lake) . . . . E 3
Abitibi (riv.) . . . . D 2
Albany (riv.) . . . . C 2
Algonquin Prov. Park . . . . E 3
Asheweig (riv.) . . . . C 2
Attawapiskat (lake) . . . . C 2
Attawapiskat (riv.) . . . . C 2
Basswood (lake) . . . . B 3
Berens (riv.) . . . . A 2
Big Trout (lake) . . . . B 2
Black Duck (riv.) . . . . C 1
Bloodvein (riv.) . . . . A 2
Caribou (isl.) . . . . C 3
Cobham (riv.) . . . . A 2
Eabamet (lake) . . . . C 2
Ekwan (riv.) . . . . C 2
English (riv.) . . . . B 2
Fawn (riv.) . . . . C 2
Finger (lake) . . . . B 2
Georgian (bay) . . . . D 3
Hannah (bay) . . . . D 2
Henrietta Maria (cape) . . . . D 1
Hudson (bay) . . . . D 1
Huron (lake) . . . . D 3
James (bay) . . . . D 2
Kapiskau (riv.) . . . . D 2
Kapuskasing (riv.) . . . . D 3
Kenogami (riv.) . . . . C 2
Kesagami (riv.) . . . . E 2
Lake of the Woods (lake) . . . . . B 3
Lake Superior Prov. Park . . . . . D 3
Little Current (riv.) . . . . C 2
Long (lake) . . . . C 3
Manitoulin (isl.) . . . . D 3
Mattagami (riv.) . . . . D 3
Michipicoten (isl.) . . . . C 3
Mille Lacs (lake) . . . . B 3
Missinaibi (lake) . . . . D 3
Missinaibi (riv.) . . . . D 2
Missisa (lake) . . . . D 2
Nipigon (lake) . . . . C 3
Nipissing (lake) . . . . E 3
North (chan.) . . . . D 3
North Caribou (lake) . . . . B 2
Nungesser (lake) . . . . B 2
Ogidaki (mt.) . . . . D 3
Ogoki (riv.) . . . . C 2
Opazatika (riv.) . . . . D 3
Opinnagau (riv.) . . . . D 2
Otoskwin (riv.) . . . . B 2
Ottawa (riv.) . . . . E 3
Pipestone (riv.) . . . . B 2
Polar Bear Prov. Park . . . . D 2
Pukaskwa Prov. Park . . . . C 3
Quetico Prov. Park . . . . B 3
Rainy (lake) . . . . B 3
Red (lake) . . . . B 2
Sachigo (riv.) . . . . B 2
Saganaga (lake) . . . . B 3
Saint Ignace (isl.) . . . . C 3
Saint Joseph (lake) . . . . B 2
Sandy (lake) . . . . B 2
Savant (lake) . . . . B 2
Seine (riv.) . . . . B 3
Seul (lake) . . . . B 2
Severn (lake) . . . . B 2
Severn (riv.) . . . . B 2
Shamattawa (riv.) . . . . C 2
Shibogama (lake) . . . . C 2
Sibley Prov. Park . . . . C 3
Slate (isls.) . . . . C 3
Stout (lake) . . . . B 2
Superior (lake) . . . . C 3
Sutton (lake) . . . . D 2
Sutton (riv.) . . . . D 2
Temigami (lake) . . . . D 3
Timiskaming (lake) . . . . E 3
Trout (lake) . . . . B 2
Wabuk (pt.) . . . . D 1
Winisk (lake) . . . . C 2
Winisk (riv.) . . . . C 2
Winnipeg (riv.) . . . . A 2
Woods (lake) . . . . B 3

ONTARIO

INTERNAL DIVISIONS

Algoma (terr. dist.) 133,553 . . . J 5
Brant (county) 104,427 . . . . . . D 4
Bruce (county) 60,020 . . . . C 3
Cochrane (terr. dist.) 96,875 . . J 4
Dufferin (county) 31,145 . . . . . D 3
Dundas (county) 18,946 . . . . . J 2
Durham (reg. munic.) 283,639 F 3
Elgin (county) 69,707 . . . . C 5
Essex (county) 312,467 . . . . . . B 5
Frontenac (county) 108,133 . . H 3
Glengarry (county) 20,254 . . . K 2
Grenville (county) 27,176 . . . . J 3
Grey (county) 73,824 . . . . D 3
Haldimand-Norfolk (reg. munic.) 89,456 . . . . E 5
Haliburton (county) 11,361 . . . F 2
Halton (reg. munic.) 253,883 . E 4
Hamilton-Wentworth (reg. munic.) 411,445 . . . . D 4
Hastings (county) 106,883 . . . G 3
Huron (county) 56,127 . . . . C 4
Kenora (terr. dist.) 59,421 . . . . G 5
Kent (county) 107,022 . . . . B 5
Lambton (county) 123,445 . . . B 5
Lanark (county) 45,676 . . . . . . H 3
Leeds (county) 53,765 . . . . H 3
Lennox and Addington (county) 33,040 . . . . G 3
Manitoulin (terr. dist.) 11,001 . B 2
Middlesex (county) 318,184 . . C 4
Muskoka (dist. munic.) 38,370 . . . . E 3
Niagara (reg. munic.) 368,288 E 4
Nipissing (terr. dist.) 80,268 . . F 2
Northumberland (county) 64,966 . . . . G 3
Ottawa-Carleton (reg. munic.) 546,849 . . . . J 2
Oxford (county) 85,920 . . . . . . D 4
Parry Sound (terr. dist.) 33,528 . . . . D 2
Peel (reg. munic.) 490,731 . . . E 4
Perth (county) 66,096 . . . . C 4
Peterborough (county) 102,452 . . . . F 3
Prescott (county) 30,365 . . . . . K 2
Prince Edward (county) 22,336 . . . . G 3
Rainy River (terr. dist.) 22,798 G 5
Renfrew (county) 87,484 . . . . . G 2
Russell (county) 22,412 . . . . . . J 2
Simcoe (county) 225,071 . . . . E 3
Stormont (county) 61,927 . . . . K 2
Sudbury (reg. munic.) 159,779 . . . . K 6
Sudbury (terr. dist.) 27,068 . . . J 5
Thunder Bay (terr. dist.) 153,997 . . . . H 5
Timiskaming (terr. dist.) 41,288 . . . . K 5
Toronto (metro. munic.) 2,137,395 . . . . K 4
Victoria (county) 47,854 . . . . . . F 3
Waterloo (reg. munic.) 305,496 . . . . D 4
Wellington (county) 129,432 . . D 4
York (reg. munic.) 252,053 . . . E 4

CITIES and TOWNS

Ailsa Craig 765 . . . . C 4
Ajax 25,475 . . . . E 4
Alban 342 . . . . D 1
Alexandria 3,271 . . . . K 2
Alfred 1,057 . . . . K 2
Alliston 4,712 . . . . E 3
Almonte 3,855 . . . . H 2
Alvinston 736 . . . . B 5
Amherstburg 5,685 . . . . A 5
Amherst View 6,110 . . . . H 3
Ancaster 14,428 . . . . D 4
Angus 3,085 . . . . E 3
Apsley 264 . . . . F 3
Arkona 473 . . . . C 4
Armstrong 378 . . . . H 4
Arnprior 5,828 . . . . H 2
Aroland 291 . . . . H 4
Arthur 1,700 . . . . D 4
Astorville 340 . . . . E 1
Athens 948 . . . . J 3
Atherley 366 . . . . E 3
Atikokan 4,452 . . . . G 5
Atwood 723 . . . . D 4
Aurora 16,267 . . . . J 3
Avonmore 273 . . . . K 2
Aylmer 5,254 . . . . C 5
Ayr 1,295 . . . . D 4
Ayton 424 . . . . D 3
Baden 945 . . . . D 4
Bala 577 . . . . E 2
Bancroft 2,329 . . . . G 2
Barrie◎ 38,423 . . . . E 3
Barry's Bay 1,216 . . . . G 2
Batawa 430 . . . . G 3
Bath 1,071 . . . . H 3
Bayfield 649 . . . . C 4
Beachburg 682 . . . . H 2
Beachville 917 . . . . D 4
Beardmore 583 . . . . H 5
Beaverton 1,952 . . . . E 3
Beeton 1,989 . . . . E 3
Belle River 3,568 . . . . B 5
Belleville◎ 34,881 . . . . G 3
Belmont 831 . . . . C 5
Bethany 365 . . . . F 3
Bewdley 508 . . . . F 3
Binbrook 306 . . . . E 4
Blackstock 720 . . . . F 3
Blenheim 4,044 . . . . C 5
Blind River 3,444 . . . . J 5
Bloomfield 718 . . . . G 4
Blyth 926 . . . . C 4
Bobcaygeon 1,625 . . . . F 3
Bonfield 540 . . . . E 1
Bothwell 915 . . . . C 5
Bourget 1,057 . . . . J 2
Bracebridge◎ 9,063 . . . . E 2
Bradford 7,370 . . . . E 3
Braeside 492 . . . . H 2
Brampton◎ 149,030 . . . . J 4
Brantford◎ 74,315 . . . . D 4
Bridgenorth 1,633 . . . . F 3
Brigden 635 . . . . B 5
Brighton 3,147 . . . . G 3
Britt 419 . . . . D 2
Brockville◎ 19,896 . . . . J 3
Bruce Mines 635 . . . . J 5
Brussels 962 . . . . C 4
Burford 1,461 . . . . D 4
Burgessville 302 . . . . D 4
Burk's Falls 922 . . . . E 2
Burlington 114,853 . . . . E 4
Cache Bay 665 . . . . D 1
Caesarea 551 . . . . F 3
Calabogie 256 . . . . H 2
Caledon 26,645 . . . . E 4
Callander 1,158 . . . . E 1
Cambridge 77,183 . . . . D 4
Campbellford 3,409 . . . . G 3
Cannington 1,623 . . . . E 3
Capreol 3,845 . . . . K 5
Caramat 265 . . . . H 5
Cardinal 1,753 . . . . J 3
Carleton Place 5,626 . . . . H 2
Carlisle 781 . . . . D 4
Carlsbad Springs 616 . . . . J 2
Carp 707 . . . . H 2
Cartier 590 . . . . J 5
Casselman 1,675 . . . . J 2
Castleton 346 . . . . F 3
Chalk River 1,010 . . . . G 1
Chapleau 3,243 . . . . J 5
Charing Cross 443 . . . . B 5
Chatham◎ 40,952 . . . . B 5
Chatsworth 383 . . . . D 3
Cherry Valley 289 . . . . G 4
Chesley 1,840 . . . . C 3
Chesterville 1,430 . . . . J 2
Chute-à-Blondeau 365 . . . . K 2
City View . . . . J 2
Clarence Creek 796 . . . . J 2
Clarksburg 508 . . . . D 3
Clifford 645 . . . . D 4
Clinton 3,081 . . . . C 4
Cobalt 1,759 . . . . K 5
Cobden 997 . . . . H 2
Coboconk 426 . . . . F 3
Cobourg◎ 11,385 . . . . F 4
Cochrane◎ 4,848 . . . . K 5
Colborne 1,796 . . . . G 4
Colchester 711 . . . . B 6
Coldwater 964 . . . . E 3
Collingwood 12,064 . . . . D 3
Comber 667 . . . . B 5
Consecon 295 . . . . G 3
Cookstown 918 . . . . E 3
Cornwall◎ 46,144 . . . . K 2
Cottam 404 . . . . B 5
Courtland 647 . . . . D 5
Courtright 1,024 . . . . B 5
Crediton 370 . . . . C 4
Creemore 1,182 . . . . D 3
Crysler 540 . . . . J 2
Cumberland 518 . . . . J 2
Cumberland Beach-Bramshot-Buena Vista 679 . . . . E 3
Dashwood 426 . . . . C 4
Deep River 5,095 . . . . G 1
Delaware 481 . . . . C 5
Delhi 4,043 . . . . D 5
Delta 360 . . . . H 3
Deseronto 1,740 . . . . G 3
Douglas 303 . . . . H 2
Drayton 809 . . . . D 4
Dresden 2,550 . . . . B 5
Drumbo 476 . . . . D 4
Dryden 6,640 . . . . G 4
Dublin 295 . . . . C 4
Dubreuilville △988 . . . . J 5
Dundalk 1,250 . . . . D 3
Dundas 19,586 . . . . D 4
Dungannon 284 . . . . C 4
Dunnville 11,353 . . . . E 5
Durham 2,458 . . . . D 3
Dutton 1,115 . . . . C 5
Earlton 1,028 . . . . K 5
East York 101,974 . . . . J 4
Echo Bay 786 . . . . J 5
Eden Mills 318 . . . . D 4
Eganville 1,245 . . . . G 2
Egmondville 465 . . . . C 4
Elgin 327 . . . . H 3
Elk Lake 526 . . . . K 5
Elliot Lake 16,723 . . . . B 1
Elmira 7,063 . . . . D 4
Elmvale 1,183 . . . . E 3
Elmwood 364 . . . . C 3
Elora 2,666 . . . . D 4
Embro 727 . . . . C 4
Embrun 1,883 . . . . J 2
Emeryville-Puce 1,611 . . . . B 5
Emo 762 . . . . F 5
Englehart 1,689 . . . . K 5
Enterprise 357 . . . . H 3
Erieau 430 . . . . C 5
Erin 2,313 . . . . D 4
Espanola 5,836 . . . . J 5
Essex 6,295 . . . . B 5
Etobicoke 298,713 . . . . J 4
Everett 570 . . . . E 3
Exeter 3,732 . . . . C 4
Fauquier 561 . . . . J 5
Fenelon Falls 1,701 . . . . F 3
Fergus 6,064 . . . . D 4
Field 462 . . . . E 1
Finch 353 . . . . J 2
Fingal 380 . . . . C 5
Fitzroy Harbour 446 . . . . H 2
Flesherton 565 . . . . D 3
Foleyet 484 . . . . J 5
Fordwich 365 . . . . C 4
Forest 2,671 . . . . C 4
Formosa 393 . . . . C 3
Fort Erie 24,096 . . . . E 5
Fort Frances◎ 8,906 . . . . F 5
Foxboro 597 . . . . G 3
Frankford 1,919 . . . . G 3
Fraserdale 303 . . . . J 5
Freelton 307 . . . . D 4
Gananoque 4,863 . . . . H 3
Garden Village 270 . . . . E 1
Geraldton 2,956 . . . . H 5
Glencoe 1,694 . . . . C 5
Glen Miller 639 . . . . G 3
Glen Robertson 378 . . . . K 2
Glen Walter 710 . . . . K 2
Goderich◎ 7,322 . . . . C 4
Gogama 652 . . . . J 5
Goodwood 335 . . . . E 3
Gore Bay◎ 777 . . . . B 2
Gorrie 468 . . . . C 4
Grafton 409 . . . . G 4
Grand Bend 680 . . . . C 4
Grand Valley 1,226 . . . . D 4
Granton 315 . . . . C 4
Gravenhurst 8,532 . . . . E 3
Greely 567 . . . . J 2
Green Valley 459 . . . . K 2
Grimsby 15,797 . . . . E 4
Guelph◎ 71,207 . . . . D 4

(continued on following page)

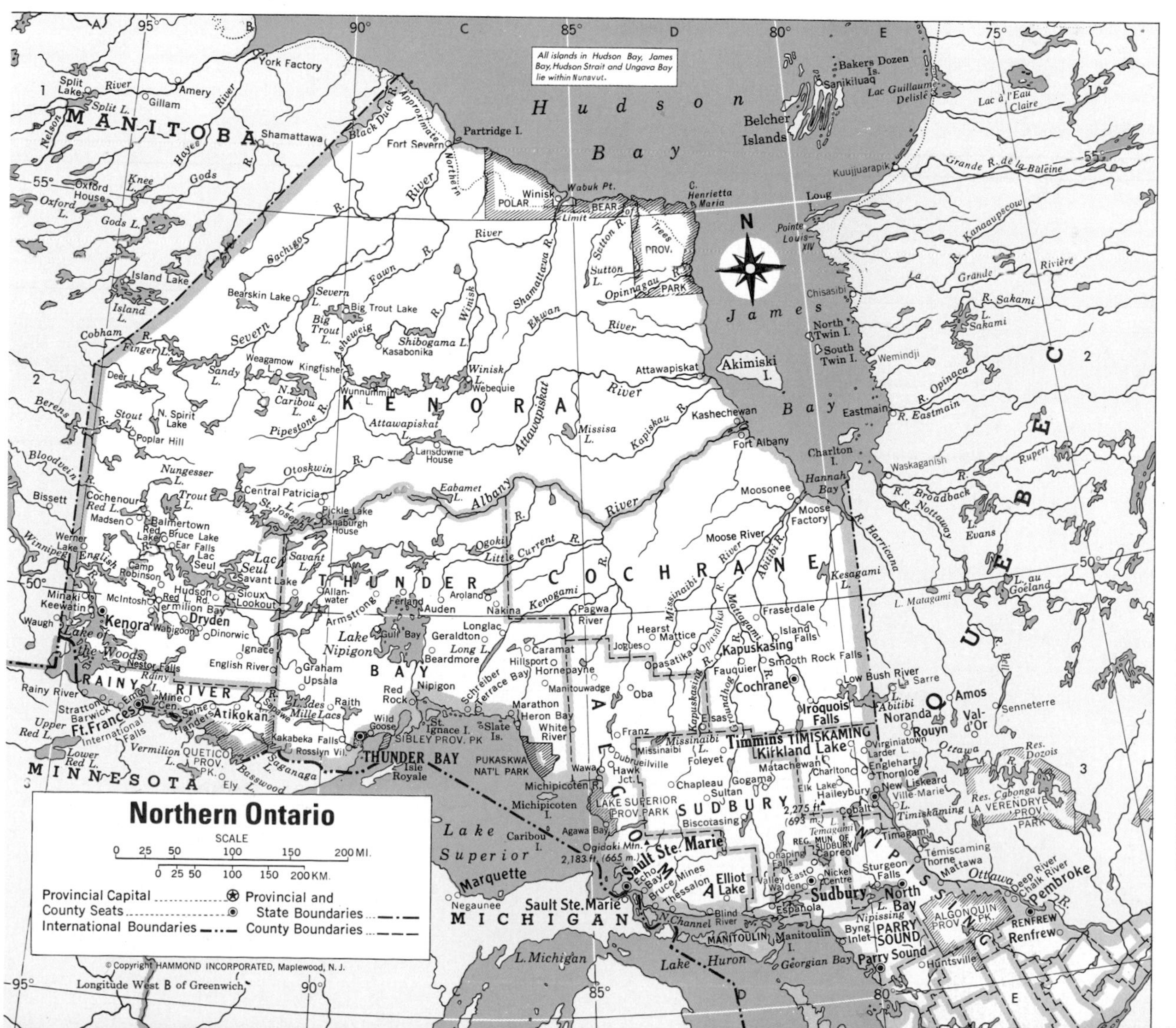

Northern Ontario
SCALE
0 25 50 100 150 200 MI.
0 25 50 100 150 200 KM.
Provincial Capital
County Seats
International Boundaries
Provincial and State Boundaries
County Boundaries
© Copyright HAMMOND INCORPORATED, Maplewood, N. J.
Longitude West B of Greenwich
All islands in Hudson Bay, James Bay, Hudson Strait and Ungava Bay lie within Nunavut.
Hudson Bay
James Bay
MANITOBA
KENORA
THUNDER BAY
COCHRANE
SUDBURY
ALGOMA
NIPISSING
TIMISKAMING
RAINY RIVER
QUEBEC
MINNESOTA
MICHIGAN
Lake Superior
Lake Nipigon
Lake Huron
Georgian Bay
L. Michigan
Lake of the Woods
York Factory
Fort Severn
Winisk
Attawapiskat
Fort Albany
Moosonee
Moose Factory
Kenora
Dryden
Ft. Frances
Atikokan
THUNDER BAY
Geraldton
Marathon
Wawa
Hearst
Kapuskasing
Cochrane
Timmins
Kirkland Lake
Iroquois Falls
Chapleau
Sault Ste. Marie
Elliot Lake
Sudbury
North Bay
Parry Sound
Pembroke
Renfrew
Huntsville
Rouyn
Noranda
Val-d'Or
Amos
Akimiski I.
Belcher Islands
Bakers Dozen Is.
Sanikiluaq
POLAR BEAR PROV. PARK
QUETICO PROV. PK.
SIBLEY PROV. PK.
PUKASKWA NAT'L PARK
LAKE SUPERIOR PROV. PARK
ALGONQUIN PROV. PK.
Isle Royale
Manitoulin

Haileybury® 4,925 . . . . K 5
Haldimand 16,866 . . . . E 5
Haliburton 1,443 . . . . F 2
Halton Hills 35,190 . . . . . . E 4
Hamilton® 306,434 . . . . . . E 4
Hamilton *542,095 . . . . . . E 4
Hanover 6,316 . . . . C 3
Harriston 1,954 . . . . D 4
Harrow 2,274 . . . . B 6
Harrowsmith 599 . . . . H 3
Harwood 332 . . . . F 3
Hastings 975 . . . . G 3
Havelock 1,385 . . . . G 3
Hawkesbury 9,877 . . . . . . K 2
Hawkestone 275 . . . . E 3
Hawk Junction 349 . . . . . . J 5
Hearst 5,533 . . . . H 5
Hensall 973 . . . . C 4
Hepworth 393 . . . . C 3
Hickson 263 . . . . D 4
Highgate 435 . . . . C 5
Hillsburgh 1,065 . . . . D 4
Hillsdale 370 . . . . E 3
Holland Landing 2,771 . . . . E 3
Honey Harbour 549 . . . . . . E 3
Hornepayne 1,848 . . . . . . J 5
Hudson 515 . . . . G 5
Huntsville 11,467 . . . . E 2
Huron Park 1,104 . . . . C 4
Ignace 2,499 . . . . G 5
Ilderton 301 . . . . C 4
Ingersoll 8,494 . . . . D 4
Ingleside 1,400 . . . . K 2
Innerkip 715 . . . . D 4
Inverhuron 438 . . . . A 1
Iron Bridge 821 . . . . A 1

Iroquois 1,211 . . . . J 3
Iroquois Falls 6,339 . . . . . J 5
Johnstown 789 . . . . J 3
Kakabeka Falls 300 . . . . . G 5
Kanata 19,728 . . . . J 2
Kapuskasing 12,014 . . . . . J 5
Kars 449 . . . . J 2
Kearney 538 . . . . E 2
Keene 353 . . . . F 3
Keewatin 1,863 . . . . F 5
Kemptville 2,362 . . . . J 2
Kenora® 9,817 . . . . F 4
Killaloe Station 634 . . . . . G 2
Killarney 433 . . . . C 2
Kincardine 5,775 . . . . C 3
Kingsville 5,134 . . . . B 6
Kingston® 52,616 . . . . . . H 3
Kinmount 262 . . . . F 2
Kirkland Lake 12,219 . . . . K 5
Kitchener® 139,734 . . . . . D 4
Kitchener *287,801 . . . . . D 4
Komoka 1,152 . . . . C 5
Lakefield 2,374 . . . . F 3
Lanark 753 . . . . H 2
Lancaster 637 . . . . K 2
Langton 348 . . . . D 5
Lansdowne 540 . . . . H 3
Larder Lake 1,084 . . . . . . K 5
Latchford 397 . . . . K 5
Leamington 12,528 . . . . . . B 5
Limoges 930 . . . . J 2
Lincoln 14,196 . . . . E 4
Linden Beach 579 . . . . . . B 6
Lindsay® 13,596 . . . . F 3
Linwood 450 . . . . D 4
Lion's Head 467 . . . . C 2

Lisle 265 . . . . E 3
Listowel 5,026 . . . . D 4
Little Britain 265 . . . . F 3
Little Current 1,507 . . . . . B 2
London 254,280 . . . . C 5
London *283,668 . . . . C 5
Longlac 2,431 . . . . H 5
Long Sault 1,227 . . . . K 2
L'Orignal® 1,819 . . . . K 2
Lucan 1,616 . . . . C 4
Lucknow 1,088 . . . . C 4
Lyn 518 . . . . J 3
Lynden 541 . . . . D 4
Lynhurst 685 . . . . C 5
MacGregor's Bay 861 . . . . G 2
MacTier 647 . . . . E 2
Madawaska 264 . . . . F 2
Madoc 1,249 . . . . G 3
Maitland 667 . . . . J 3
Mallorytown 368 . . . . J 3
Manitouwadge 3,155 . . . . . H 5
Manitowaning 518 . . . . . . C 2
Manotick-Hillside Gardens
  2,694 . . . . J 2
Marathon 2,271 . . . . H 5
Markdale 1,289 . . . . D 3
Markham 77,037 . . . . K 4
Markstay 444 . . . . D 1
Marmora 1,304 . . . . G 3
Martintown 388 . . . . K 2
Massey 1,274 . . . . C 1
Matachewan 444 . . . . J 5
Matheson 966 . . . . K 5
Mattawa 2,652 . . . . F 1
Mattice 803 . . . . J 5
Maxville 615 . . . . K 2

Maynooth 277 . . . . G 2
McGregor 1,145 . . . . B 5
McKerrow 260 . . . . C 1
Meaford 4,367 . . . . D 3
Melbourne 346 . . . . C 5
Merlin 745 . . . . B 5
Merrickville 984 . . . . J 2
Metcalfe 687 . . . . J 2
Midhurst 1,457 . . . . E 3
Midland 12,132 . . . . D 3
Mildmay 928 . . . . C 3
Milford Bay 401 . . . . E 2
Millbank 337 . . . . D 4
Millbrook 927 . . . . F 3
Milton® 28,067 . . . . D 4
Milverton 1,463 . . . . D 4
Minaki 319 . . . . F 4
Mindemoya 376 . . . . B 2
Minden® 838 . . . . F 2
Mississauga 315,056 . . . . J 4
Mitchell 2,777 . . . . C 4
Monkton 520 . . . . C 4
Moonbeam 838 . . . . J 5
Moorefield 308 . . . . D 4
Mooretown 344 . . . . B 5
Moose Creek 393 . . . . K 2
Morewood 264 . . . . J 2
Morpeth 284 . . . . C 5
Morrisburg 2,308 . . . . J 3
Mount Albert 1,165 . . . . . . E 3
Mount Brydges 1,557 . . . . C 5
Mount Forest 3,474 . . . . . D 4
Mount Hope 557 . . . . D 4
Munster 1,531 . . . . J 2
Nakina 936 . . . . H 4
Nanticoke® 19,816 . . . . . . E 5

Napanee 4,803 . . . . G 3
Navan 419 . . . . J 2
Neustadt 511 . . . . C 3
Newboro 260 . . . . H 3
Newburgh 617 . . . . H 3
Newbury 441 . . . . C 5
Newcastle 32,229 . . . . . . F 4
New Hamburg 3,923 . . . . . D 4
New Liskeard 5,551 . . . . . K 5
Newmarket® 29,753 . . . . . E 3
Niagara Falls 70,960 . . . . E 4
Niagara-on-the-Lake 12,186 . E 4
Nickel Centre 12,318 . . . . D 1
Nipigon 2,377 . . . . H 5
Nobel 386 . . . . E 2
Nobleton 1,861 . . . . J 3
Noelville 702 . . . . D 1
North Bay® 51,268 . . . . . E 1
North York 559,521 . . . . . J 4
Norwich 2,117 . . . . D 5
Norwood 1,278 . . . . F 3
Nottawa 360 . . . . D 3
Oakville 75,773 . . . . E 4
Oakwood 404 . . . . F 3
Odessa 849 . . . . H 3
Oil City 266 . . . . B 5
Oil Springs 627 . . . . B 5
Omemee 819 . . . . F 3
Onaping Falls 6,198 . . . . . J 5
Opasatika 413 . . . . J 5
Orangeville® 13,740 . . . . . D 4
Orillia 23,955 . . . . E 3
Oshawa 117,519 . . . . F 4
Oshawa *154,217 . . . . . . F 4

Ottawa® (cap.), Canada
  295,163 . . . . J 2
Ottawa-Hull *717,978 . . . . J 2
Otterville 776 . . . . D 5
Owen Sound® 19,883 . . . . D 3
Paincourt 414 . . . . B 5
Paisley 1,039 . . . . C 3
Pakenham 367 . . . . J 2
Palmerston 1,989 . . . . . . D 4
Paris 7,485 . . . . D 4
Parkhill 1,358 . . . . C 4
Parry Sound® 6,124 . . . . . E 2
Pefferlaw 857 . . . . E 3
Pelham 11,104 . . . . E 4
Pembroke® 14,026 . . . . . . G 2
Penetanguishene 5,315 . . . D 3
Perth® 5,655 . . . . H 3
Petawawa 5,520 . . . . G 2
Peterborough® 60,620 . . . . F 3
Petrolia 4,234 . . . . B 5
Pickering 37,754 . . . . K 4
Picton® 4,361 . . . . G 3
Plantagenet 870 . . . . K 2
Plattsville 495 . . . . D 4
Point Edward 2,383 . . . . . B 4
Pontypool 759 . . . . F 3
Port Burwell 655 . . . . D 5
Port Carling 629 . . . . E 2
Port Colborne 19,225 . . . . E 5
Port Elgin 6,131 . . . . C 3
Port Franks 547 . . . . C 4
Port Hope 9,992 . . . . F 4
Port Lambton 921 . . . . . . B 5
Port McNicoll 1,883 . . . . . E 3
Port Perry 4,712 . . . . E 3

Port Rowan 811 . . . . D 5
Port Stanley 1,891 . . . . . . C 5
Pottageville 286 . . . . J 3
Powassan 1,169 . . . . E 1
Prescott® 4,670 . . . . J 3
Princeton 462 . . . . D 4
Puce-Emeryville 1,611 . . . . B 5
Rainy River 1,061 . . . . . . F 5
Ramore 382 . . . . K 5
Rayside-Balfour 15,017 . . . J 5
Red Rock 1,260 . . . . H 5
Renfrew 8,283 . . . . H 2
Richards Landing 405 . . . . J 5
Richmond 2,880 . . . . J 2
Richmond Hill 37,778 . . . . J 4
Ridgetown 3,062 . . . . C 5
Ripley 591 . . . . C 3
River Valley 275 . . . . D 1
Rockcliffe Park 1,869 . . . . J 2
Rockland 3,961 . . . . J 2
Rockwood 1,068 . . . . D 4
Rodney 1,007 . . . . C 5
Rosslyn Village 362 . . . . . G 5
Round Lake Centre 255 . . . G 2
Russell 1,099 . . . . J 2
Ruthven 649 . . . . B 6
Saint Albert 254 . . . . J 2
Saint Catharines® 124,018 . E 4
Saint Catharines-Niagara
  *304,353 . . . . E 4
Saint Charles 382 . . . . . . D 1
Saint Clair Beach 2,845 . . . B 5
Saint Clements 520 . . . . . D 4
Saint-Eugène 470 . . . . . . K 2
Saint George 865 . . . . . . D 4
Saint Isidore de Prescott 746 . K 2

Saint Jacobs 1,189 . . . . D 4
Saint Mary's 4,883 . . . . C 4
Saint Thomas◎ 28,165 . . . . . . C 5
Saint Williams 442 . . . . D 5
Salem 825 . . . . D 4
Sarnia◎ 50,892 . . . . B 5
Sauble Beach 729 . . . . C 3
Sault Sainte Marie◎ 82,697 . . . J 5
Scarborough 443,353 . . . . K 4
Schomberg 923 . . . . J 3
Schreiber 1,968 . . . . H 5
Scotland 600 . . . . D 4
Seaforth 2,114 . . . . C 4
Searchmont 384 . . . . J 5
Sebringville 579 . . . . C 4
Seeleys Bay 503 . . . . H 3
Shakespeare 602 . . . . D 4
Shallow Lake 418 . . . . C 3
Shannonville 314 . . . . G 3
Shanty Bay 358 . . . . E 3
Sharbot Lake 495 . . . . H 3
Shedden 292 . . . . C 5
Shelburne 2,862 . . . . D 3
Simcoe◎ 14,326 . . . . D 5
Sioux Lookout 3,074 . . . . G 4
Sioux Narrows 394 . . . . F 5
Smithfield 349 . . . . G 3
Smiths Falls 8,831 . . . . H 3
Smithville 1,936 . . . . E 4
Smooth Rock Falls 2,352 . . . . . J 5
Sombra 420 . . . . B 5
Southampton 2,830 . . . . C 3
South Mountain 285 . . . . J 3
South River 1,109 . . . . E 2
Spanish 1,063 . . . . J 5
Sparta 283 . . . . C 5

Spencerville 438 . . . . J 3
Springfield 555 . . . . C 5
Springford 309 . . . . D 5
Stayner 2,530 . . . . E 3
Stirling 1,638 . . . . G 3
Stittsville 2,652 . . . . J 2
Stoney Creek 36,762 . . . . E 4
Stoney Point 1,090 . . . . B 5
Straffordville 752 . . . . D 5
Stratford◎ 26,262 . . . . C 4
Strathroy 8,748 . . . . C 5
Sturgeon Falls 6,045 . . . . E 1
Sudbury◎ 91,829 . . . . K 5
Sudbury *149,923 . . . . K 5
Sunderland 703 . . . . E 3
Sundridge 734 . . . . E 2
Sydenham 595 . . . . H 3
Tamworth 402 . . . . H 3
Tara 687 . . . . C 3
Tavistock 1,885 . . . . D 4
Tecumseh 6,364 . . . . B 5
Teeswater 1,026 . . . . C 3
Terrace Bay 2,639 . . . . H 5
Thamesford 1,920 . . . . C 4
Thamesville 961 . . . . C 5
Thedford 694 . . . . C 4
Thessalon 1,620 . . . . J 5
Thornbury 1,435 . . . . D 3
Thorndale 581 . . . . C 4
Thornton 414 . . . . E 3
Thorold 15,412 . . . . E 4
Thunder Bay◎ 112,486 . . . . H 5
Thunder Bay *121,379 . . . . H 5
Tilbury 4,298 . . . . B 5
Tillsonburg 10,487 . . . . D 5
Timmins 46,114 . . . . J 5

Tiverton 806 . . . . C 3
Tobermory 282 . . . . C 2
Toronto (cap.)◎ 599,217 . . . . . . K 4
Toronto *2,998,947 . . . . K 4
Tottenham 3,022 . . . . E 3
Trenton 15,085 . . . . G 3
Trout Creek 652 . . . . E 2
Turkey Point 407 . . . . D 5
Tweed 1,574 . . . . G 3
Udora 375 . . . . E 3
Union 485 . . . . C 5
Uxbridge 4,209 . . . . E 3
Valley East 20,433 . . . . J 5
Vanier 18,792 . . . . J 2
Vankleek Hill 1,774 . . . . K 2
Vars 527 . . . . J 2
Vaughan 29,674 . . . . J 4
Verner 1,076 . . . . D 1
Vernon 303 . . . . J 2
Verona 754 . . . . H 3
Victoria Harbour 1,125 . . . . E 3
Vienna 369 . . . . D 5
Virginiatown 1,010 . . . . K 5
Vittoria 420 . . . . D 5
Wabigoon 268 . . . . G 5
Walden 10,139 . . . . J 5
Walkerton◎ 4,682 . . . . C 3
Wallaceburg 11,506 . . . . B 5
Wardsville 450 . . . . C 5
Warkworth 618 . . . . G 3
Warren 579 . . . . D 1
Warsaw 314 . . . . F 3
Wasaga Beach 4,705 . . . . D 3
Washago 569 . . . . E 3
Waterloo 49,428 . . . . D 4
Watford 1,402 . . . . C 5
Waubaushene 878 . . . . E 3
Wawa 4,206 . . . . J 5
Webbwood 519 . . . . C 1
Welcome 293 . . . . F 4
Welland 454,448 . . . . E 5
Wellesley 997 . . . . D 4
Wellington 1,082 . . . . G 4
Wendover 369 . . . . J 2
West Lorne 1,258 . . . . C 5
Westmeath 262 . . . . H 2
Westport 621 . . . . H 3
Wheatley 1,638 . . . . B 5
Whitby◎ 36,698 . . . . F 4
Whitchurch-Stouffville 13,557 . . J 3
White River △1,006 . . . . J 5
Whitney 766 . . . . F 2
Wiarton 2,074 . . . . C 3
Wikwemikong 1,030 . . . . C 2
Williamsburg 407 . . . . J 3
Williamsford 256 . . . . D 3
Williamstown 328 . . . . K 2
Winchester 2,001 . . . . J 2
Windsor◎ 192,083 . . . . B 5
Windsor *246,110 . . . . B 5
Wingham 2,897 . . . . C 4
Wolfe Island 271 . . . . H 3
Woodstock◎ 26,603 . . . . D 4
Woodville 575 . . . . F 3
Wroxeter 350 . . . . C 4
Wyoming 1,682 . . . . B 5
Yarker 319 . . . . H 3
York 134,617 . . . . J 4
Zephyr 330 . . . . E 3
Zurich 795 . . . . C 4

OTHER FEATURES

Abitibi (riv.) . . . . J 5
Algonquin Prov. Park . . . . F 2
Amherst (isl.) . . . . H 3
Balsam (lake) . . . . F 3
Barrie (isl.) . . . . B 1
Bays (lake) . . . . F 2
Big Rideau (lake) . . . . H 3
Black (riv.) . . . . E 3
Bruce (pen.) . . . . C 2
Buckhorn (lake) . . . . F 3
Cabot (head) . . . . C 2
Charleston (lake) . . . . J 3
Christian (isl.) . . . . D 3
Clear (lake) . . . . F 3
Cockburn (isl.) . . . . A 2
Couchiching (lake) . . . . E 3
Croker (cape) . . . . D 3

Don (riv.) . . . . J 4
Doré (lake) . . . . G 2
Douglas (pt.) . . . . C 3
Erie (lake) . . . . E 5
Flowerpot (isl.) . . . . C 2
French (riv.) . . . . D 1
Georgian (bay) . . . . D 2
Georgian Bay Is.
  Nat'l Park . . . . C 2, D 3
Georgina (isl.) . . . . E 3
Grand (riv.) . . . . D 4
Humber (riv.) . . . . J 4
Hurd (cape) . . . . C 2
Huron (lake) . . . . B 3
Ipperwash Prov. Park . . . . C 4
Joseph (lake) . . . . E 2
Killarney Prov. Park . . . . C 1
Killbear Point Prov. Park . . . . . D 2
Lake of the Woods (lake) . . . . . F 5

Lake Superior Prov. Park . . . . . J 5
Lonely (isl.) . . . . C 2
Long (pt.) . . . . D 5
Long Point (bay) . . . . D 5
Madawaska (riv.) . . . . G 2
Magnetawan (riv.) . . . . D 2
Main (chan.) . . . . C 2
Manitou (lake) . . . . C 2
Manitoulin (isl.) . . . . B 2
Mattagami (riv.) . . . . J 5
Michipicoten (isl.) . . . . J 5
Missinaibi (riv.) . . . . J 5
Mississagi (riv.) . . . . A 1
Mississippi (riv.) . . . . H 2
Muskoka (lake) . . . . E 2
Niagara (riv.) . . . . E 4
Nipigon (lake) . . . . H 5
Nipissing (lake) . . . . E 1
North (chan.) . . . . A 1
Nottawasaga (bay) . . . . D 3
Ogidaki (mt.) . . . . J 5
Ontario (lake) . . . . G 4
Opeongo (lake) . . . . F 2
Ottawa (riv.) . . . . H 2
Owen (sound) . . . . D 3
Panache (lake) . . . . C 1
Parry (isl.) . . . . D 2
Parry (sound) . . . . D 2
Pelee (pt.) . . . . B 6
Petre (pt.) . . . . G 4
Point Pelee Nat'l Park . . . . B 5
Presqu'ile Prov. Park . . . . G 4
Pukaskwa Prov. Park . . . . H 5
Quetico Prov. Park . . . . G 5

Rainy (lake) . . . . G 5
Rice (lake) . . . . F 3
Rideau (lake) . . . . H 3
Rondeau Prov. Park . . . . C 5
Rosseau (lake) . . . . E 2
Saint Clair (lake) . . . . B 5
Saint Clair (riv.) . . . . B 5
Saint Lawrence (lake) . . . . K 3
Saint Lawrence (riv.) . . . . J 3
Saint Lawrence Is. Nat'l Park . . J 3
Saugeen (riv.) . . . . C 3
Scugog (lake) . . . . F 3
Seul (lake) . . . . G 4
Severn (riv.) . . . . E 3
Sibley Prov. Park . . . . H 5
Simcoe (lake) . . . . E 3
South (bay) . . . . C 2
Spanish (riv.) . . . . C 1
Stony (lake) . . . . G 3
Superior (lake) . . . . H 5
Sydenham (riv.) . . . . B 5
Thames (riv.) . . . . B 5
Theano (pt.) . . . . J 5
Thousand (isls.) . . . . H 3
Timagami (lake) . . . . K 5
Trout (lake) . . . . E 1
Vernon (lake) . . . . E 2
Walpole (isl.) . . . . B 5
Welland (canal) . . . . E 5
Woods (lake) . . . . F 5

◎County seat.
*Population of metropolitan area.
△Population of town or township.

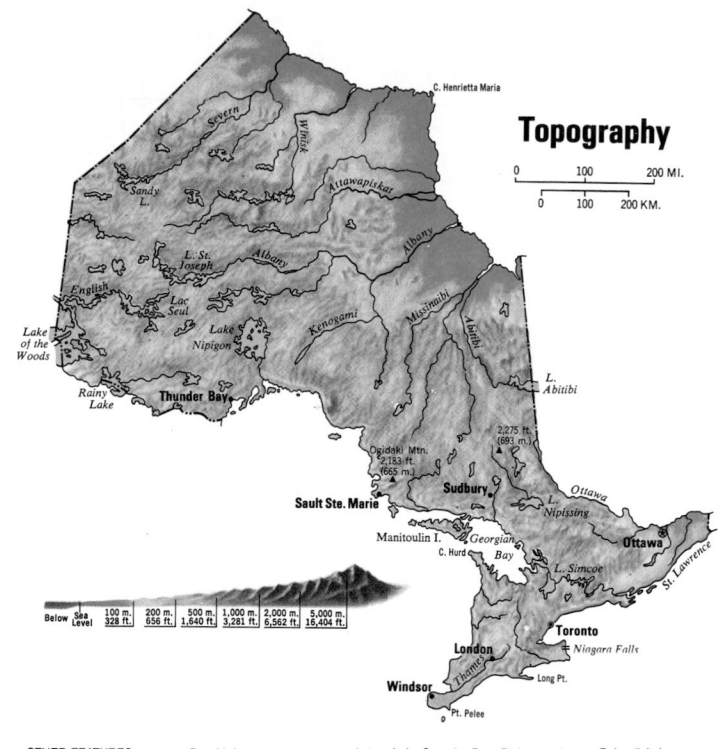

Topography

0   100   200 MI.
0   100   200 KM.

Below Sea Level | 100 m. 328 ft. | 200 m. 656 ft. | 500 m. 1,640 ft. | 1,000 m. 3,281 ft. | 2,000 m. 6,562 ft. | 5,000 m. 16,404 ft.

Ontario
Southern Part

SCALE
0 10 20 30 40 50 MI.
0 10 20 30 40 50 KM.

National Capital . . . . ⊛
Provincial Capital . . . . . . ⊛
County Seats . . . . ⊛
International Boundaries . . . — · · —
Provincial & State Boundaries . . . ———
County Boundaries . . . — — —
Canals . . . .

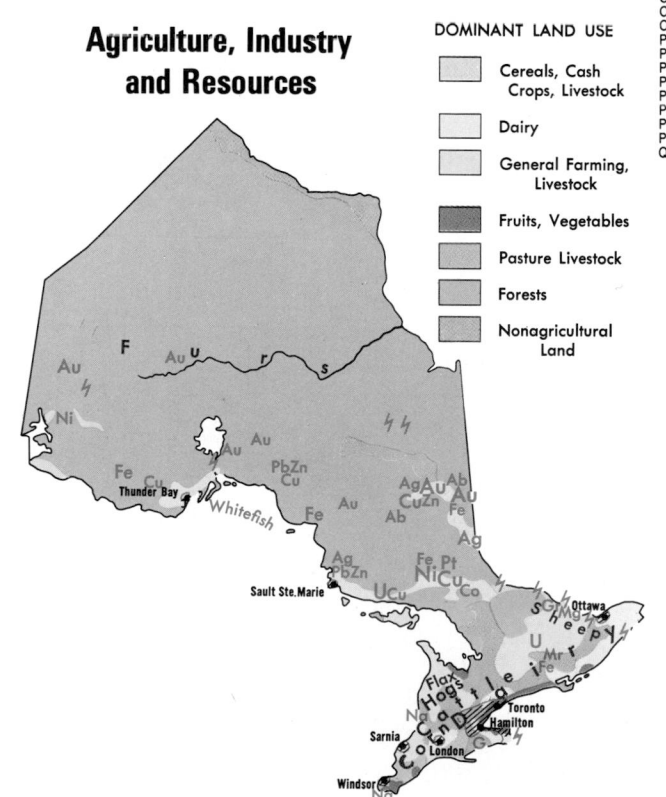

Agriculture, Industry and Resources

DOMINANT LAND USE

- Cereals, Cash Crops, Livestock
- Dairy
- General Farming, Livestock
- Fruits, Vegetables
- Pasture Livestock
- Forests
- Nonagricultural Land

MAJOR MINERAL OCCURRENCES

Ab Asbestos
Ag Silver
Au Gold
Co Cobalt
Cu Copper
Fe Iron Ore
G   Natural Gas
Gr Graphite

Mg Magnesium
Mr Marble
Na Salt
Ni Nickel
Pb Lead
Pt Platinum
U   Uranium
Zn Zinc

⚡ Water Power
 Major Industrial Areas

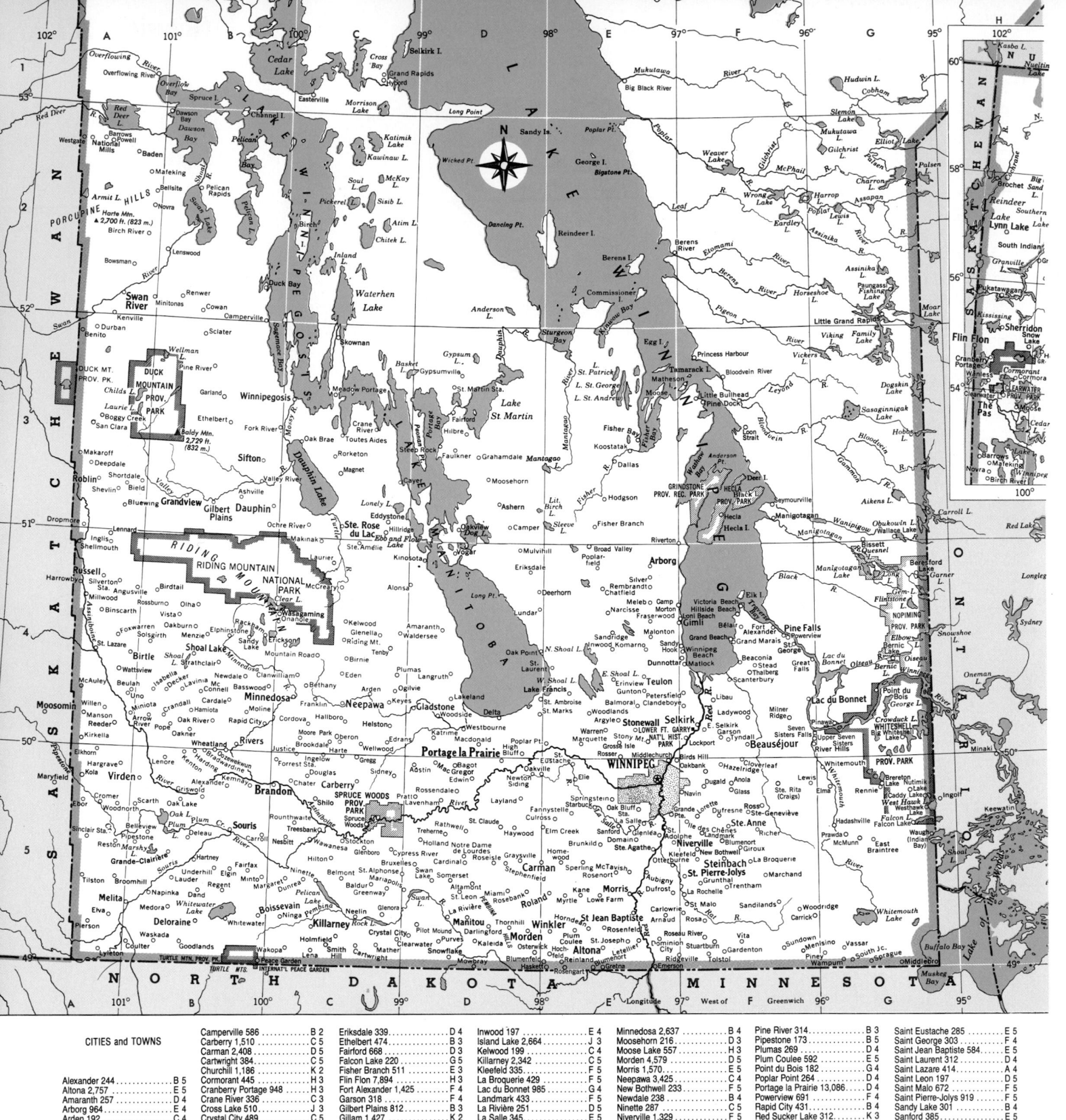

CITIES and TOWNS

Manitoba
Northern Part

0 40 80 120 MI.

0 40 80 120 KM.

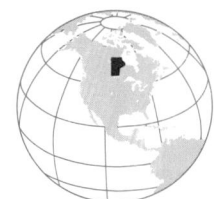

Manitoba
Southern Part

SCALE

0 5 10 20   40   60 MI.

0 5 10 20   40   60 KM.

Provincial Capital _____ ⊛
International Boundaries ___ · ___
Provincial Boundaries ___ · ___

© Copyright HAMMOND INCORPORATED, Maplewood, N.J.

The Pas 6,390 .... H 3
Thicket Portage 195 .... J 3
Thompson 14,288 .... J 2
Treherne 743 .... D 5
Tyndall 421 .... F 4
Virden 2,940 .... A 5
Vita 364 .... F 5
Wabowden 655 .... J 3
Wallace Lake ●2,044 ...... G 3
Wanless 193 .... H 3
Warren 459 .... E 4
Waskada 239 .... B 5
Wawanesa 492 .... C 5
Whitemouth 320 .... G 5
Whitewater ●856 .... B 5
Winkler 5,046 .... E 5
Winnipeg (cap.) 564,473 .. E 5
Winnipeg ●584,842 .... E 5
Winnipeg Beach 565 ...... F 4
Winnipegosis 855 .... B 3
Woodlands 185 .... E 4
Wooodridge 170 .... G 4
York Landing 229 .... J 2

OTHER FEATURES

Aikens (lake) .... G 3
Anderson (lake) .... D 2
Anderson (pt.) .... F 3
Armit (lake) .... A 2
Assapan (riv.) .... G 2
Assiniboine (riv.) .... C 5
Assinika (lake) .... G 2
Assinika (riv.) .... G 2
Atim (lake) .... C 2
Baldy (mt.) .... B 3
Basket (lake) .... C 3
Beaverhill (lake) .... J 3
Berens (isl.) .... E 2
Berens (riv.) .... E 2
Bernic (lake) .... G 4
Big Sand (lake) .... H 2
Bigstone (lake) .... J 3
Bigstone (pt.) .... E 2
Bigstone (riv.) .... J 3
Birch (isl.) .... C 2
Black (isl.) .... F 3
Black (riv.) .... F 4
Bloodvein (riv.) .... F 3
Bonnet (lake) .... G 4
Buffalo (bay) .... G 5
Burntwood (riv.) .... J 2
Caribou (riv.) .... J 1
Carroll (lake) .... G 3
Cedar (lake) .... B 1
Channel (isl.) .... B 2
Charron (lake) .... G 2
Childs (lake) .... A 3
Chitek (lake) .... C 2
Churchill (cape) .... K 2
Churchill (riv.) .... J 2
Clear (lake) .... C 4
Clearwater Lake Prov. Park .. H 3
Cobham (riv.) .... G 1
Cochrane (riv.) .... H 2
Commissioner (isl.) ...... E 2
Cormorant (lake) .... H 3
Cross (bay) .... C 1
Cross (lake) .... J 3
Crowduck (lake) .... G 4
Dancing (pt.) .... D 2
Dauphin (lake) .... C 3
Dauphin (riv.) .... D 3
Dawson (bay) .... B 2
Dog (lake) .... D 3
Dogskin (lake) .... G 3
Duck Mountain Prov. Park .. B 3
Eardley (lake) .... F 2

East Shoal (lake) .... E 4
Ebb and Flow (lake) ...... C 3
Egg (isl.) .... E 3
Elbow (lake) .... G 4
Elk (isl.) .... F 4
Elliot (lake) .... G 2
Etawney (lake) .... J 2
Etomami (riv.) .... F 2
Falcon (lake) .... G 5
Family (lake) .... G 3
Fisher (bay) .... E 3
Fisher (riv.) .... E 3
Fishing (lake) .... G 2
Flintstone (lake) .... G 2
Fox (riv.) .... K 2
Gammon (riv.) .... G 3
Garner (lake) .... G 4
Gem (lake) .... G 4
George (isl.) .... E 2
George (lake) .... G 4
Gilchrist (creek) ...... F 2
Gilchrist (lake) .... G 2
Gods (lake) .... K 3
Gods (riv.) .... K 3
Granville (lake) .... H 2
Grass (riv.) .... J 3
Grass River Prov. Park .. H 3
Grindstone Prov. Rec. Park .. F 3
Gunisao (lake) .... J 3
Gypsum (lake) .... D 3
Harrop (lake) .... J 3
Harte (mt.) .... A 2
Hayes (riv.) .... K 2
Hecla (isl.) .... E 3
Hecla Prov. Park ..... F 3
Hobbs (lake) .... G 2
Horseshoe (lake) .... J 3
Hubbart (pt.) .... K 2
Hudson (bay) .... H 1
Hudwin (lake) ...... G 1
Inland (lake) .... F 2
International Peace Garden .. B 5
Island (lake) .... K 3
Katimik (lake) ..... C 2
Kawinaw (lake) .... C 2
Kinwow (bay) ..... E 2
Kississing (lake) .. H 2
Knee (lake) .... J 3
Lake of the Woods (lake) .. H 5
La Salle (riv.) ..... E 5
Laurie (lake) ...... A 3
Leaf (riv.) .... F 2
Lewis (lake) ...... F 3
Leyond (riv.) ..... F 3
Little Birch (lake) . E 3
Lonely (lake) ..... C 3
Long (lake) ...... G 4
Long (pt.) .... D 1
Long (pt.) .... D 4
Manigotagan (lake) .. G 4

Manigotagan (riv.) ...... G 3
Manitoba (lake) .... D 4
Mantagao (riv.) .... D 3
Marshy (riv.) .... B 5
McKay (lake) .... F 2
McPhail (riv.) .... F 2
Minnedosa (riv.) ...... B 4
Moar (lake) .... G 2
Molson (lake) .... J 3
Moose (isl.) .... E 3
Morrison (lake) ...... C 1
Mossy (riv.) .... C 3
Mukutawa (lake) .... G 2
Mukutawa (riv.) ..... E 1
Muskeg (bay) .... G 6
Nejanilini (lake) .... J 1
Nelson (riv.) .... J 2
Nopiming Prov. Park .. G 4
Northern Indian (lake) .. J 2
North Knife (lake) ... J 2
North Seal (riv.) .... H 2
North Shoal (lake) .. E 4
Nueltin (lake) ...... H 1
Oak (lake) .... B 5
Obukowin (lake) ... G 3
Oiseau (lake) ...... G 4
Oiseau (riv.) ...... G 4
Overflow (bay) .... A 1
Overflowing (riv.) .. A 1
Owl (riv.) .... K 2
Oxford (lake) ..... J 3
Paint (lake) .... J 3
Palsen (riv.) ...... B 2
Pelican (bay) ..... B 2
Pelican (lake) .... B 2
Pelican (lake) .... C 5
Pembina (hills) ... D 5
Pembina (riv.) ... C 5
Peonan (pt.) .... D 3
Pickerel (lake) .. C 2
Pigeon (riv.) ... F 2
Pipestone (creek) .. A 5
Plum (creek) ... B 5
Plum (lake) .... B 5
Poplar (riv.) ... E 2
Porcupine (hills) .. A 2
Portage (bay) .. D 3
Punk (isl.) .... F 3
Quesnel (lake) .. G 4
Rat (riv.) ..... F 5
Red (riv.) ..... F 4
Red Deer (lake) .. A 2
Red Deer (riv.) .. A 2
Reindeer (isl.) .. E 2
Reindeer (lake) .. H 2
Riding (mt.) ... B 4
Riding Mountain Nat'l Park .. B 4
Rock (lake) ... C 5
Ross (isl.) ... J 3
Sagemace (bay) .. B 3

Saint Andrew (lake) ..... E 3
Saint George (lake) ..... E 3
Saint Martin (lake) ..... D 3
Saint Patrick (lake) .... E 3
Saie (riv.) .... E 5
Sandy (isls.) .... D 2
Sasaginnigak (lake) .. G 3
Seal (riv.) .... J 2
Selkirk (isl.) .... J 2
Setting (lake) ...... H 3
Shoal (lake) .... G 5
Shoal (riv.) .... B 2
Sipiwesk (lake) ... J 3
Sisib (lake) ...... C 2
Sleeve (lake) .... E 3
Slemon (lake) ... G 1
Snowshoe (lake) .. G 4
Soul (lake) ..... C 2
Souris (riv.) .... B 5
Southern Indian (lake) .. H 2
South Knife (riv.) .. J 2
South Seal (riv.) .. J 2
Split (lake) ..... J 2
Spruce (isl.) .... B 1
Spruce Woods Prov. Park .. C 5
Stevenson (lake) .. J 3
Sturgeon (bay) ... E 3
Swan (lake) .... B 2
Swan (lake) .... D 5
Swan (riv.) .... A 3
Tadoule (lake) .. J 2
Tamarack (isl.) .. F 3
Tatnam (cape) .. K 2
Traverse (bay) .. F 4
Turtle (mts.) ... B 5
Turtle (riv.) ... C 3
Turtle Mountain Prov. Park .. B 5
Valley (riv.) ... B 3
Vickers (lake) .. F 3
Viking (lake) .. G 3
Wanipigow (riv.) .. G 3
Washow (bay) .. F 3
Waterhen (lake) .. C 2
Weaver (lake) .. F 2
Wellman (lake) .. B 3
West Hawk (lake) .. G 5
West Shoal (lake) .. E 4
Whitemouth (lake) .. G 5
Whitemouth (riv.) .. G 5
Whiteshell Prov. Park .. G 4
Whitewater (lake) .. B 5
Wicked (pt.) ... D 2
Winnipeg (lake) .. E 2
Winnipeg (riv.) .. G 4
Winnipegosis (lake) .. C 2
Woods (lake) ... H 5
Wrong (lake) ... F 3

*Population of metropolitan area.
●Population of rural municipality.

AREA 250.999 sq. mi. (650,087 sq. km.)
POPULATION 1,063,016
CAPITAL Winnipeg
LARGEST CITY Winnipeg
HIGHEST POINT Baldy Mtn. 2,729 ft. (832 m.)
SETTLED IN 1812
ADMITTED TO CONFEDERATION 1870
PROVINCIAL FLOWER Prairie Crocus

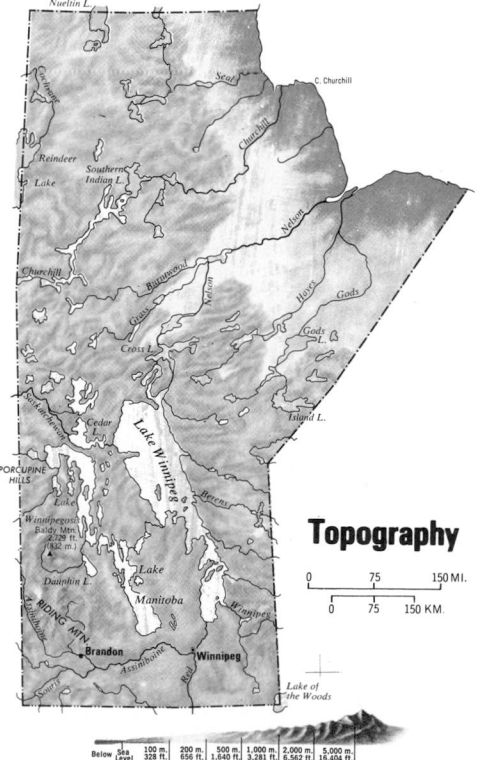

Topography

0   75   150 MI.

0   75   150 KM.

Below Sea Level | 100 m. 328 ft. | 200 m. 656 ft. | 500 m. 1,640 ft. | 1,000 m. 3,281 ft. | 2,000 m. 6,562 ft. | 5,000 m. 16,404 ft.

Agriculture, Industry and Resources

DOMINANT LAND USE

- Cereals (chiefly barley, oats)
- Cereals, Livestock
- Dairy
- Livestock
- Forests
- Nonagricultural Land

MAJOR MINERAL OCCURRENCES

Au Gold
Co Cobalt
Cu Copper
Na Salt

Ni Nickel
O Petroleum
Pb Lead
Pt Platinum
Zn Zinc

⚡ Water Power
▨ Major Industrial Areas

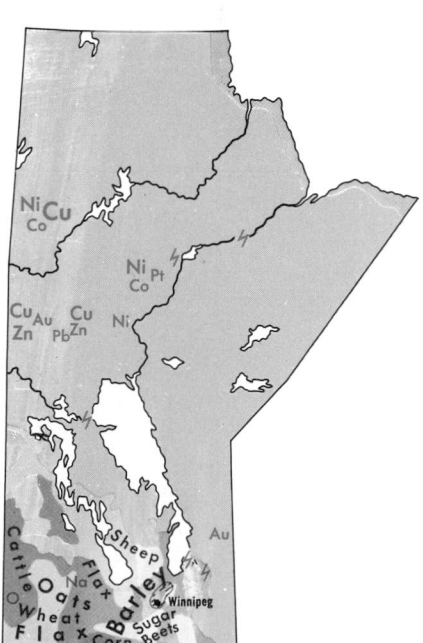

Topography

0   60   120 MI.

0   60   120 KM.

Tazin L.
Selwyn L.
L. Athabasca
Black L.
Fond du Lac
Wollaston L.
Cree L.
Reindeer L.
Frobisher L.
Peter Pond L.
Lac Ile-à-la-Crosse
Churchill
Lac La Ronge
Primrose L.
Doré L.
Beaver
Montreal L.
WAPAWEKKA HILLS
Amisk L.
Cumberland L.
Red Deer
PASQUIA HILLS
Prince Albert
North Battleford
Saskatoon
Quill Lakes
Assiniboine
Last Mountain L.
GREAT SAND HILLS
COTEAU HILLS
Moose Jaw
Old Wives L.
Regina
Qu'Appelle
Swift Current
CYPRESS HILLS
(1392 m.)
(4,567 ft.)
Souris

5,000 m. 2,000 m. 1,000 m. 500 m. 200 m. 100 m. Sea Level Below
16,404 ft. 6,562 ft. 3,281 ft. 1,640 ft. 656 ft. 328 ft.

CITIES and TOWNS

Abbey 218	C 5
Aberdeen 496	E 3
Abernethy 300	H 5
Air Ronge 557	M 3
Alameda 318	J 6
Alida 169	K 6
Allan 871	E 4
Alsask 652	B 4
Annaheim 209	G 3
Antelope ●231	C 5
Arborfield 439	H 2
Archerwill 286	H 3
Arcola 493	J 6
Arlington Beach ●432	F 4
Asquith 507	D 3
Assiniboia 2,924	E 6
Avonlea 442	G 5
Baildon ●799	F 5
Balcarres 739	H 5
Balgonie 777	G 5
Batoche	E 3
Battleford 3,565	C 3
Beauval 606	L 3
Beechy 279	D 5
Bengough 536	F 6
Bethune 369	F 5
Bienfait 835	J 6
Biggar 2,561	C 3
Big River 819	D 2
Birch Hills 957	F 3
Bjorkdale 269	H 3
Blaine Lake 653	D 3
Borden 197	D 3
Brabant Lake 245	M 3
Bradwell 168	E 4
Bredenbury 467	K 5
Briercrest 151	F 5
Broadview 840	J 5
Brock 184	C 4
Browning ●687	J 6
Bruno 772	F 3
Buchanan 392	J 4
Buffalo Gap ●598	F 6
Buffalo Narrows 1,088	L 3
Burstall 550	B 5
Cabri 632	C 5
Cadillac 173	D 6
Calder 164	K 4
Cana ●1,238	J 5
Candle Lake 219	F 2
Cando 163	C 3
Canoe Lake 182	L 3
Canora 2,667	J 4
Canwood 340	E 2
Carievale 246	K 6
Carlyle 1,074	J 6
Carnduff 1,043	K 6
Carrot River 1,169	H 2
Central Butte 548	E 5
Ceylon 184	G 6
Chaplin 389	E 5
Chitek Lake 170	D 2
Choiceland 543	G 2
Christopher Lake 227	F 2
Churchbridge 972	J 5
Clavet 234	E 4
Climax 293	C 6
Cochin 221	C 2
Codette 236	H 2
Coleville 383	B 4
Colonsay 594	F 4
Connaught Heights ●982	G 3
Conquest 256	D 4
Consul 153	B 6
Coronach 1,032	F 6
Craik 565	F 4
Craven 206	G 5
Creelman 184	H 6
Creighton 1,636	N 4
Cudworth 947	F 3
Cumberland House 831	J 2
Cupar 669	G 5
Cut Knife 624	B 3
Dalmeny 1,064	E 3
Davidson 1,166	E 4
Debden 403	E 2
Delisle 980	D 4
Denare Beach 592	M 4
Denzil 199	B 3
Deschambault Lake 386	M 3
Dinsmore 398	D 4
Dodsland 272	C 4
Domremy 209	F 3
Drake 211	G 4
Duck Lake 699	E 3
Dundurn 531	E 4
Dysart 275	H 5
Earl Grey 303	G 5
Eastend 723	C 6
Eatonia 528	B 4
Ebenezer 164	J 4
Edam 384	C 2
Edenwold 143	G 5
Elbow 313	E 4
Eldorado 229	L 2
Elfros 199	H 4
Elrose 624	D 4
Elstow 143	E 4
Endeavour 199	J 3
Englefeld 271	G 3
Erwood 149	J 3
Esterhazy 3,065	J 5
Eston 1,413	C 4
Estevan 9,174	J 6
Eyebrow 168	E 5
Fillmore 396	H 5
Fleming 141	K 5
Flin Flon 367	N 4

Foam Lake 1,452	H 4
Fond du Lac 494	L 2
Fort Qu'Appelle 1,827	H 5
Fox Valley 380	B 5
Francis 182	H 5
Frobisher 166	J 6
Frontier 619	C 6
Gainsborough 308	K 6
Gerald 197	K 5
Glaslyn 430	C 2
Glenavon 284	J 5
Glen Ewen 168	J 6
Goodsoil 263	L 3
Govan 394	G 5
Grand Coulee 208	G 6
Gravelbourg 1,338	E 6
Grayson 264	J 5
Green Acres 139	L 4
Green Lake 634	L 3
Grenfell 1,307	J 5
Guernsey 198	F 4
Gull Lake 1,095	C 5
Hafford 557	D 3
Hague 625	E 3
Hanley 484	E 4
Harris 259	D 4
Hawarden 137	E 4
Hearts Hill ●552	B 3
Hepburn 411	E 3
Herbert 1,019	D 5
Hodgeville 329	E 5
Holdfast 297	F 5
Hudson Bay 2,361	J 3
Humboldt 4,705	F 3
Hyas 165	J 3
Ile-à-la-Crosse 1,035	L 3
Imperial 501	F 4
Indian Head 1,889	H 5
Invermay 353	H 4
Ituna 870	H 4
Jansen 223	G 4
Jasmin ●14	H 4
Kamsack 2,688	K 4
Kelliher 397	H 4
Kelvington 1,054	H 3
Kenaston 345	E 4
Kennedy 275	J 5
Kerrobert 1,141	C 4
Kincaid 256	D 6
Kindersley 3,969	B 4
Kinistino 783	F 3
Kipling 1,016	J 5
Kisbey 228	J 6
Kronau 154	G 5
Kyle 516	C 5
Lac Pelletier ●586	C 6
Lafleche 583	E 6
Laird 233	E 3
Lake Lenore 361	G 3
La Loche 1,632	L 3
Lampman 651	J 6
Lancer 156	C 5
Landis 277	C 3
Lang 219	G 6
Langenburg 1,324	K 5
Lanigan 1,732	F 4
La Ronge 2,579	L 3
Lashburn 813	B 2
Leader 1,108	B 5
Leask 478	E 2
Lebret 274	H 5
Lemberg 414	H 5
Leoville 393	D 2
Leroy 504	G 4
Lestock 402	G 4
Limerick 164	E 6
Lintlaw 234	H 3

Lipton 364	H 5
Lloydminster 6,034	A 2
Loon Lake 369	B 1
Loreburn 201	E 4
Lucky Lake 333	D 5
Lumsden 1,303	G 5
Luseland 704	B 3
Macdowall 171	E 2
Macklin 976	A 3
Macoun 190	H 6
Maidstone 1,001	B 2
Mankota 375	D 6
Manor 368	J 6
Maple Creek 2,470	B 6
Marcelin 238	E 3
Margo 153	H 4
Marriott ●627	J 4
Marsden 229	B 3
Marshall 453	E 5
Martensville 1,966	E 3
Maryfield 431	K 6
Maymont 212	D 3
McLean 189	G 5
Meacham 178	F 3
Meadow Lake 3,857	C 1
Meath Park 262	F 2
Medstead 163	C 2
Melfort 6,010	G 3
Melville 5,092	J 5
Meota 235	C 2
Mervin 155	C 2
Midale 564	H 6
Middle Lake 275	G 3
Milden 251	D 4
Milestone 602	G 5
Montmartre 544	H 5
Montreal Lake 448	L 4
Moose Jaw 33,941	F 5
Moose Range ●679	J 2
Moosomin 2,579	K 5
Morse 416	D 5
Mortlach 293	E 5
Mossbank 464	F 6
Muenster 385	F 3
Naicam 886	G 3
Neilburg 354	B 3
Neuanlage 144	E 3
Neudorf 425	J 5
Neuhorst 146	E 3
Nipawin 4,376	H 2
Nokomis 524	F 4
Norquay 552	J 4
North Battleford 14,030	C 3
North Portal 164	J 6
Odessa 232	H 5
Ogema 441	G 6
Osler 527	E 3
Outlook 1,976	E 4
Oxbow 1,191	J 6
Paddockwood 211	F 2
Pangman 227	G 6
Paradise Hill 421	B 2
Patuanak 173	L 3
Paynton 210	B 2
Pelican Narrows 331	N 3
Pelly 391	K 4
Pennant 202	C 5
Pense 472	G 5
Perdue 407	D 3
Pierceland 425	K 4
Pilger 150	F 3
Pilot Butte 1,255	G 5
Pine House 612	M 3
Plenty 175	C 4
Plunkett 150	F 4
Ponteix 769	D 6
Porcupine Plain 937	H 3
Preeceville 1,243	J 4

Prelate 317	B 5
Prince Albert 31,380	F 2
Prud'homme 222	F 3
Punnichy 394	G 4
Qu'Appelle 653	H 5
Quill Lake 514	G 4
Quinton 169	G 4
Rabbit Lake 159	D 2
Radisson 439	D 3
Radville 1,012	G 6
Rama 133	H 4
Raymore 635	G 4
Redvers 895	K 6
Regina (cap.) 162,613	G 5
Regina *164,313	G 5
Regina Beach 603	F 5
Rhein 271	J 4
Richmound 188	B 5
Riverhurst 193	E 5
Rocanville 934	K 5
Roche Percé 142	J 6
Rockglen 511	F 6
Rosetown 2,664	D 4
Rose Valley 538	H 3
Rosthern 1,609	E 3
Rouleau 443	G 5
Saint Benedict 157	F 3
Saint Brieux 401	G 3
Saint Louis 448	F 3
Saint Philips ●538	K 4
Saint Walburg 802	J 2
Saltcoats 549	J 4
Sandy Bay 756	N 3
Saskatoon 154,210	E 3
Saskatoon *154,210	E 3
Sceptre 169	B 5
Scott 203	C 3
Sedley 373	H 5
Semans 344	G 4
Shaunavon 2,112	C 6
Sheho 285	H 4
Shell Lake 220	D 2
Shellbrook 1,228	E 2
Simpson 231	F 4
Sintaluta 215	H 5
Smeaton 246	G 2
Southey 697	G 5
Spalding 337	G 3
Spiritwood 926	D 2
Springside 533	J 4
Spy Hill 354	K 5
Star City 527	G 3
Stenen 143	J 4
Stockholm 391	J 5
Stonehenge ●701	F 6
Storthoaks 142	K 6
Stoughton 716	J 6
Strasbourg 842	G 4
Sturgis 789	J 4
Swift Current 14,747	D 5
Tantallon 196	K 5
Theodore 473	J 4
Timber Bay 152	F 1
Tisdale 3,107	H 3
Togo 181	K 4
Tompkins 275	C 5
Torch River ●2,440	G 2
Torquay 311	H 6
Tramping Lake 178	B 3
Tugaske 175	E 5
Turnor Lake 166	L 3
Turtleford 505	B 2
Unity 2,408	B 3
Uranium City 2,507	L 2
Val Marie 236	D 6
Vanguard 292	D 6
Vanscoy 298	D 4
Vibank 369	H 5

Viscount 386	F 4
Vonda 313	F 3
Wadena 1,495	H 4
Wakaw 1,030	F 3
Waldeck 292	D 5
Waldheim 758	E 3
Walpole ●711	K 6
Wapella 487	K 5
Warman 2,076	E 3
Waseca 169	B 2
Waskesiu Lake 176	E 2
Watrous 1,830	F 4
Watson 901	G 3
Wawota 622	J 6
Weldon 279	F 2
Welwyn 170	K 5
Weyburn 9,523	H 6
White City 602	G 5
White Fox 394	H 2
Whitewood 1,003	J 5
Wilcox 202	G 5
Wilkie 1,501	C 3
Willow Bunch 494	F 6
Willow Creek ●1,218	B 6
Windthorst 254	J 5
Wiseton 195	D 4
Wishart 212	H 4
Wollaston Lake 248	N 2
Wolseley 904	H 5
Wymark 162	D 5
Wynyard 2,147	G 4
Yarbo 158	K 5

Yellow Grass 477	H 6
Yorkton 15,339	J 4
Young 456	F 4
Zenon Park 273	H 2

OTHER FEATURES

Allan (hills)	E 4
Amisk (lake)	M 4
Antelope (lake)	C 5
Antler (riv.)	K 6
Arm (riv.)	F 5
Assiniboine (riv.)	J 3
Athabasca (lake)	L 2
Bad (lake)	C 4
Bad (riv.)	C 4
Bad (hills)	C 4
Batoche Nat'l Hist. Site	E 3
Battle (creek)	B 6
Battle (riv.)	B 3
Bear (hills)	C 4
Bear (lake)	H 4
Beaver (hills)	B 1
Beaver (riv.)	L 4
Beaverlodge (lake)	L 2
Big Muddy (lake)	G 6
Bigstick (lake)	B 5
Birch (lake)	C 2
Bitter (lake)	B 6
Black (lake)	M 2
Boundary (plat.)	C 6
Brightsand (lake)	C 2
Bronson (lake)	B 2

Agriculture, Industry and Resources

Furs
Cu
Au
Zn
Oats
Na
Rye
OG
W
He
Hogs
Barley
Wheat
Regina
K
O
Cattle
Sheep
Wheat
Lg Flax

DOMINANT LAND USE

Wheat	Cereals, Livestock	
Cereals (chiefly barley, oats)	Livestock	
Forests		

MAJOR MINERAL OCCURRENCES

Au	Gold		Na	Salt
Cu	Copper		O	Petroleum
G	Natural Gas		S	Sulfur
He	Helium		U	Uranium
K	Potash		Zn	Zinc
Lg	Lignite			

⚡ Water Power

Major Industrial Areas

Buffalo Pound Prov. Park . . . . F 5
Cabri (lake) . . . . B 4
Cactus (hills) . . . . F 5
Candle (lake) . . . . F 2
Cannington Manon Hist. Park . J 6
Canoe (lake) . . . . L 3
Carrot (riv.) . . . . J 2
Chaplin (lake) . . . . E 5
Chipman (riv.) . . . . M 2
Chitek (lake) . . . . D 2
Churchill (riv.) . . . . M 3
Clearwater (riv.) . . . . L 3
Cochrane (riv.) . . . . N 2
Coteau (hills) . . . . D 4
Cowan (lake) . . . . D 2
Crane (lake) . . . . B 5
Crean (lake) . . . . E 1
Cree (lake) . . . . L 3
Cree (riv.) . . . . M 2
Cumberland (lake) . . . . J 1
Cypress (hills) . . . . B 6
Cypress (hills) . . . . B 6
Cypress Hills Prov. Park . . . . . B 6
Danielson Prov. Park . . . . E 4
Delaronde (lake) . . . . E 1
Diefenbaker (lake) . . . . E 4
Doré (lake) . . . . L 3
Douglas Prov. Park . . . . E 4
Duck Lake Hist. Park . . . . E 3
Duck Mountain Prov. Park . . . K 4
Eagle (hills) . . . . C 3
Eaglehill (creek) . . . . D 4

Ear (lake) . . . . B 3
Echo Valley Prov. Park . . . . . . G 5
Etomami (riv.) . . . . J 3
Eyebrow (lake) . . . . E 5
Eyehill (creek) . . . . B 3
Fife (lake) . . . . E 6
File (hills) . . . . H 5
Fir (riv.) . . . . J 3
Fond du Lac (riv.) . . . . M 2
Forrest (lake) . . . . L 3
Fort Battleford Nat'l Hist. Park C 3
Fort Carlton Hist. Park . . . . . . E 3
Fort Pitt Hist. Park . . . . B 3
Fort Walsh Nat'l Hist. Park . . . A 6
Foster (lake) . . . . L 3
Frenchman (riv.) . . . . C 6
Frobisher (lake) . . . . L 3
Gap (creek) . . . . B 3
Gardiner (dam) . . . . D 4
Geikie (riv.) . . . . M 3
Good Spirit (lake) . . . . J 4
Goodspirit Lake Prov. Park . . . J 4
Great Sand (hills) . . . . B 5
Green (lake) . . . . D 1
Greenwater Lake Prov. Park . . J 3
Haultain (riv.) . . . . L 3
Ile-à-la-Crosse (lake) . . . . L 3
Ironspring (creek) . . . . G 3
Jackfish (lake) . . . . C 3
Katepwa (riv.) . . . . H 5
Kingsmere (lake) . . . . E 1
Kiyiu (lake) . . . . C 4

Lac La Ronge Prov. Park . . . . M 3
Lanigan (creek) . . . . F 4
Last Mountain (lake) . . . . F 4
Leaf (lake) . . . . J 2
Leech (lake) . . . . J 4
Lenore (lake) . . . . J 3
Little Manitou (lake) . . . . F 4
Lodge (creek) . . . . B 6
Long (creek) . . . . H 6
Loon (riv.) . . . . G 4
Makwa (lake) . . . . B 1
Makwa (riv.) . . . . B 1
Manito (lake) . . . . B 3
Maple (creek) . . . . B 5
McFarlane (riv.) . . . . L 2
Meadow (lake) . . . . C 1
Meadow Lake Prov. Park . . . . K 4
Meeting (lake) . . . . D 2
Midnight (lake) . . . . B 3
Ministikwan (lake) . . . . B 1
Missouri Coteau (hills) . . . . . . D 5
Montreal (lake) . . . . F 1
Moose (mt.) . . . . J 6
Moose Jaw (riv.) . . . . G 5
Moose Mountain (creek) . . . . J 6
Moose Mountain Prov. Park . . J 6
Mossy (riv.) . . . . H 1
Muddy (lake) . . . . B 3
Mudjatik (riv.) . . . . L 3
Nipawin Prov. Park . . . . G 1
North Saskatchewan (riv.) . . . D 3
Notukeu (creek) . . . . D 5

Oldman (riv.) . . . . L 2
Old Wives (lake) . . . . E 5
Opuntia (lake) . . . . C 4
Overflowing (riv.) . . . . K 2
Pasquia (hills) . . . . J 2
Pasquia (riv.) . . . . K 2
Pelican (lake) . . . . E 5
Peter Pond (lake) . . . . L 3
Pheasant (hills) . . . . J 5
Pine Lake Prov. Park . . . . E 4
Pinto (creek) . . . . D 6
Pipestone (creek) . . . . K 5
Pipestone (riv.) . . . . K 2
Ponass (lakes) . . . . H 3
Poplar (riv.) . . . . E 6
Porcupine (hills) . . . . K 3
Primrose (lake) . . . . L 3
Primrose Lake Air Weapons
   Range . . . . L 3
Prince Albert Nat'l Park . . . . . E 1
Qu'Appelle (riv.) . . . . J 5
Red Deer (riv.) . . . . A 5
Red Deer (riv.) . . . . K 3
Reindeer (lake) . . . . N 3
Reindeer (riv.) . . . . M 3
Riou (lake) . . . . M 2
Rivers (lake) . . . . F 6
Ronge, La (lake) . . . . M 3
Rowans Ravine Prov. Park . . . F 4
St. Victor Petroglyphs Hist.
   Park . . . . E 6

Saskatchewan (riv.) . . . . H 2
Saskatchewan Landing Prov.
   Park . . . . C 5
Saskeram (lake) . . . . K 2
Scott (lake) . . . . L 2
Selwyn (lake) . . . . M 2
Souris (riv.) . . . . K 3
South Saskatchewan (riv.) . . . C 5
Steele Narrows Hist. Park . . . . B 2
Stripe (lake) . . . . C 4
Sturgeon (riv.) . . . . E 2
Swan (riv.) . . . . J 3
Swift Current (creek) . . . . D 5
Tazin (riv.) . . . . L 2
The Battlefords Prov. Park . . . C 2

Thickwood (hills) . . . . D 2
Thunder (hills) . . . . L 4
Tobin (lake) . . . . H 2
Torch (riv.) . . . . H 2
Touchwood (hills) . . . . G 4
Tramping (lake) . . . . C 3
Trout (riv.) . . . . L 2
Turtle (lake) . . . . C 2
Twelvemile (lake) . . . . E 6
Vermilion (hills) . . . . E 4
Wapawekka (hills) . . . . M 4
Waskana (creek) . . . . G 5
Waskesiu (lake) . . . . E 2
Wathaman (riv.) . . . . M 3
Weed (hills) . . . . J 5

White Fox (riv.) . . . . G 2
White Gull (creek) . . . . G 2
Whiteshore (lake) . . . . C 3
Whiteswan (lakes) . . . . F 1
William (riv.) . . . . L 2
Willow Bunch (lake) . . . . F 6
Witchekan (lake) . . . . D 2
Wollaston (lake) . . . . N 2
Wood (mt.) . . . . E 6
Wood (riv.) . . . . E 6
Wood Mountain Hist. Park . . . E 6

AREA 251,699 sq. mi. (651,900 sq. km.)
POPULATION 1,009,613
CAPITAL Regina
LARGEST CITY Regina
HIGHEST POINT Cypress Hills 4,567 ft.
   (1,392 m.)
SETTLED IN 1774
ADMITTED TO CONFEDERATION 1905
PROVINCIAL FLOWER Prairie Lily

*Population of metropolitan area.
•Population of rural municipality.

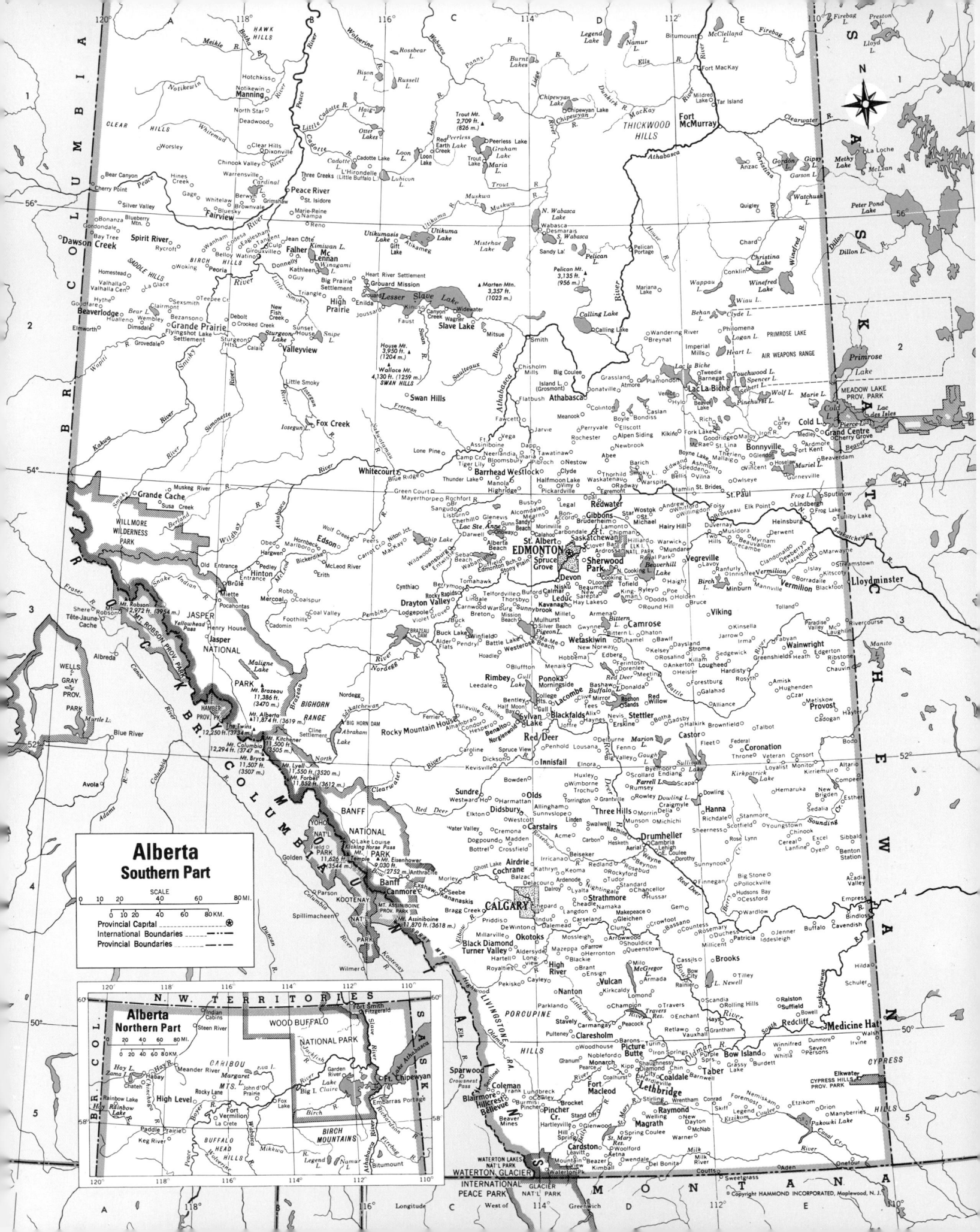

Alberta 183

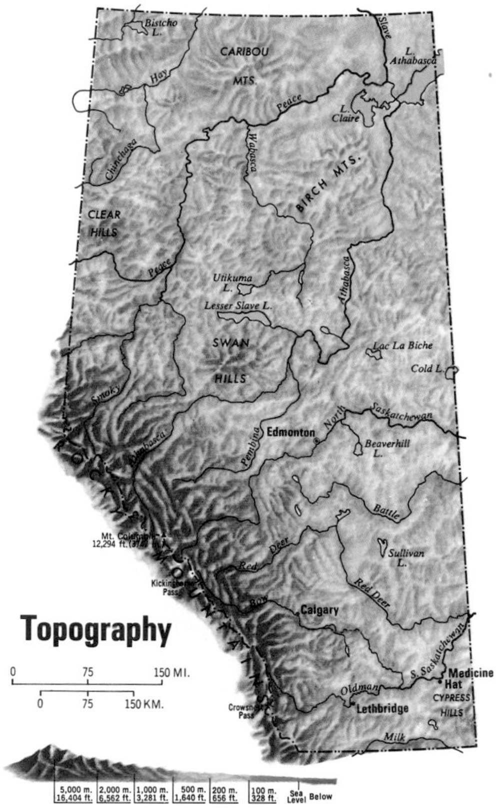
Bistcho L.
CARIBOU MTS
Hay
Slave
L. Athabasca
Peace
L. Claire
Wabasca
BIRCH MTS.
Chinchaga
CLEAR HILLS
Utikuma L.
Lesser Slave L.
Athabasca
SWAN HILLS
Lac La Biche
Cold L.
Smoky
North Saskatchewan
Edmonton
Beaverhill L.
Pembina
Battle
Sullivan L.
Red Deer
Mt. Columbia 12,294 ft.
Calgary
Bow
S. Saskatchewan
Medicine Hat
CYPRESS HILLS
Oldman
Lethbridge
Crowsnest Pass
Milk
0 75 150 MI.
0 75 150 KM.
5,000 m. 16,404 ft.
2,000 m. 6,562 ft.
1,000 m. 3,281 ft.
500 m. 1,640 ft.
200 m. 656 ft.
100 m. 328 ft.
Sea Level
Below

Topography

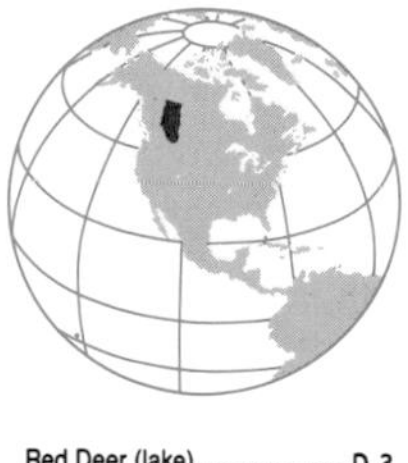

AREA 255,285 sq. mi. (661,185 sq. km.)
POPULATION 2,365,825
CAPITAL Edmonton
LARGEST CITY Edmonton
HIGHEST POINT Mt. Columbia 12,294 ft. (3,747 m.)
SETTLED IN 1861
ADMITTED TO CONFEDERATION 1905
PROVINCIAL FLOWER Wild Rose

CITIES and TOWNS

Acme 457 .... D 4
Airdrie 8,414 .... C 4
Alberta Beach 485 .... C 3
Alix 837 .... D 3
Andrew 548 .... D 3
Antler Lake 334 .... D 3
Ardmore 224 .... E 2
Arrowwood 156 .... D 4
Athabasca 1,731 .... D 2
Banff 4,208 .... C 4
Barnwell 359 .... D 5
Barons 315 .... D 4
Barrhead 3,736 .... C 2
Bashaw 875 .... D 3
Bassano 1,200 .... D 4
Bawlf 350 .... D 3
Beaumont 2,638 .... D 3
Beaverlodge 1,937 .... A 2
Beiseker 580 .... D 4
Bentley 823 .... C 3
Berwyn 557 .... B 1
Big Valley 360 .... D 3
Black Diamond 1,444 .... C 4
Blackfalds 1,488 .... D 3
Blackfoot 220 .... E 3
Blackie 298 .... D 4
Bon Accord 1,376 .... D 3
Bonnyville 4,454 .... E 2
Bowden 989 .... C 4
Bow Island 1,491 .... E 5
Boyle 638 .... D 2
Bragg Creek 505 .... C 4
Breton 552 .... C 3
Brooks 9,421 .... E 4
Bruce 88 .... E 3
Bruderheim 1,136 .... D 3
Burdett 220 .... E 5
Calgary 592,743 .... C 4
Calgary *592,743 .... C 4
Calmar 1,003 .... D 3
Camrose 12,570 .... D 3
Canmore 3,484 .... C 4
Carbon 434 .... D 4
Cardston 3,267 .... D 5
Carmangay 266 .... D 4
Caroline 436 .... C 3
Carseland 484 .... D 4
Carstairs 1,587 .... D 4
Castor 1,123 .... D 3
Cereal 249 .... E 4
Champion 339 .... D 4
Chauvin 298 .... E 3
Chipman 266 .... D 3
Clairmont 469 .... A 2
Claresholm 3,493 .... D 4
Clive 364 .... D 3
Clyde 364 .... D 2
Coaldale 4,579 .... D 5
Coalhurst 882 .... D 5
Cochrane 3,544 .... C 4
Cold Lake 2,110 .... E 2
College Heights 267 .... D 3
Consort 632 .... E 3
Cooking Lake 218 .... D 3
Coronation 1,309 .... E 3
Coutts 400 .... D 5
Cowley 304 .... D 5
Cremona 382 .... C 4
Crossfield 1,217 .... C 4
Daysland 679 .... D 3
Delburne 574 .... D 3
Desmarais 260 .... D 2
Devon 3,885 .... D 3
Didsbury 3,095 .... C 4
Donalda 280 .... D 3
Donnelly 336 .... B 2
Drayton Valley 5,042 .... C 3
Drumheller 6,508 .... D 4
Duchess 429 .... E 4
East Coulee 218 .... D 4
Eckville 870 .... C 3
Edgerton 387 .... E 3
Edmonton (cap.) 532,246 .... D 3
Edmonton *657,057 .... D 3
Edmonton Beach 280 .... C 3
Edson 5,835 .... B 3
Elk Point 1,022 .... E 3
Elnora 249 .... D 3
Entwistle 462 .... C 3
Erskine 259 .... D 3
Evansburg 779 .... C 3
Exshaw 353 .... C 4
Fairview 2,869 .... A 1
Falher 1,102 .... B 2
Faust 399 .... C 2
Foremost 568 .... E 5
Forestburg 924 .... E 3
Fort Assiniboine 207 .... C 2
Fort Chipewyan 944 .... C 5
Fort Macleod 3,139 .... D 5
Fort McKay 267 .... E 1
Fort McMurray 31,000 .... E 1
Fort Saskatchewan 12,169 .... D 3
Fort Vermilion 752 .... B 5
Fox Creek 1,978 .... B 2
Fox Lake 634 .... B 5
Gibbons 2,276 .... D 3
Gift Lake 428 .... C 2
Girouxville 325 .... B 2
Gleichen 381 .... D 4
Glendon 430 .... E 2
Glenwood 259 .... D 5
Grand Centre 3,146 .... E 2
Grande Cache 4,523 .... A 3
Grande Prairie 24,263 .... A 2
Granum 399 .... D 5
Grimshaw 2,316 .... B 1
Grouard Mission 221 .... C 2
Hanna 2,806 .... E 4
Hardisty 641 .... E 3
Hay Lakes 302 .... D 3
Heisler 212 .... D 3
High Level 2,194 .... A 5
High Prairie 2,506 .... B 2
High River 4,792 .... D 4
Hines Creek 575 .... A 1
Hinton 8,342 .... B 3
Holden 430 .... D 3
Hughenden 267 .... E 3
Hythe 639 .... A 2
Innisfail 5,247 .... D 3
Innisfree 255 .... E 3
Irma 474 .... E 3
Irricana 558 .... D 4
Irvine 360 .... E 5
Jasper 3,269 .... B 3
John d'Or Prairie 437 .... B 5
Joussard 330 .... B 2
Killam 1,005 .... E 3
Kinuso 285 .... C 2
Kitscoty 497 .... E 3
Lac La Biche 2,007 .... E 2
Lacombe 5,591 .... D 3
La Crete 479 .... B 5
Lake Louise 355 .... B 4
Lamont 1,563 .... D 3
Leduc 12,471 .... D 3
Legal 1,022 .... D 3
Lethbridge 54,072 .... D 5
Linden 407 .... D 4
Little Buffalo Lake 253 .... B 1
Lloydminster 8,997 .... E 3
Longview 301 .... C 4
Lougheed 226 .... E 3
Lundbreck 244 .... C 5
Magrath 1,576 .... D 5
Manning 1,173 .... B 1
Mannville 788 .... E 3
Marlboro 211 .... B 3
Marwayne 500 .... E 3
Mayerthorpe 1,475 .... C 3
McLennan 1,125 .... B 2
Medicine Hat 40,380 .... E 4
Milk River 894 .... D 5
Millet 1,120 .... D 3
Mirror 507 .... D 3
Monarch 212 .... D 5
Morinville 4,657 .... D 3
Morrin 244 .... D 4
Mundare 604 .... D 3
Myrnam 397 .... E 3
Nacmine 369 .... D 4
Nampa 334 .... B 1
Nanton 1,641 .... D 4
New Norway 291 .... D 3
New Sarepta 417 .... D 3
Nobleford 534 .... D 5
North Calling Lake 234 .... D 2
Okotoks 3,847 .... C 4
Olds 4,813 .... D 4
Onoway 621 .... C 3
Oyen 975 .... E 4
Peace River 5,907 .... B 1
Penhold 1,531 .... D 3
Picture Butte 1,404 .... D 5
Pincher Creek 3,757 .... D 5
Plamondon 259 .... D 2
Pollockville 19 .... E 4
Ponoka 5,221 .... D 3
Provost 1,645 .... E 3
Rainbow Lake 504 .... A 5
Ralston 357 .... E 4
Raymond 2,837 .... D 5
Redcliff 3,876 .... E 4
Red Deer 46,393 .... D 3
Redwater 1,932 .... D 3
Rimbey 1,685 .... C 3
Robb 230 .... B 3
Rockyford 329 .... D 4
Rocky Mountain House 4,698 .... C 3
Rosemary 328 .... E 4
Rycroft 649 .... A 2
Ryley 483 .... D 3
Saint Albert 31,996 .... D 3
Saint Paul 4,884 .... E 3
Sangudo 398 .... C 3
Sedgewick 879 .... E 3
Sexsmith 1,180 .... A 2
Shaughnessy 270 .... D 5
Sherwood Park 29,285 .... D 3
Slave Lake 4,506 .... C 2
Smith 216 .... D 2
Smoky Lake 1,074 .... D 2
Spirit River 1,104 .... A 2
Spruce Grove 10,326 .... D 3
Standard 379 .... D 4
Stavely 504 .... D 4
Stettler 5,136 .... D 3
Stirling 688 .... D 5
Stony Plain 4,839 .... C 3
Strathmore 2,986 .... D 4
Strome 281 .... E 3
Sundre 1,742 .... C 4
Swan Hills 2,497 .... C 2
Sylvan Lake 3,779 .... C 3
Taber 5,988 .... E 5
Thorhild 576 .... D 2
Thorsby 737 .... C 3
Three Hills 1,787 .... D 4
Tilley 345 .... E 4
Tofield 1,504 .... D 3
Trochu 880 .... D 4
Turner Valley 1,311 .... C 4
Two Hills 1,193 .... E 3
Valleyview 2,061 .... B 2
Vauxhall 1,049 .... D 4
Vegreville 5,251 .... E 3
Vermilion 3,766 .... E 3
Veteran 314 .... E 3
Viking 1,232 .... E 3
Vilna 345 .... E 2
Vulcan 1,489 .... D 4
Wabamun 662 .... C 3
Wabasca 701 .... D 2
Wainwright 4,266 .... E 3
Warburg 501 .... C 3
Warner 477 .... D 5
Waskatenau 290 .... D 2
Wembley 1,169 .... A 2
Westlock 4,424 .... C 2
Wetaskiwin 9,597 .... D 3
Whitecourt 5,585 .... C 2
Wildwood 441 .... C 3
Willingdon 366 .... E 3
Youngstown 297 .... E 4

OTHER FEATURES

Abraham (lake) .... B 3
Alberta (mt.) .... B 3
Assiniboine (mt.) .... C 4
Athabasca (lake) .... C 5
Athabasca (riv.) .... D 1
Banff Nat'l Park .... B 4
Battle (riv.) .... D 3
Bear (lake) .... A 2
Beaver (riv.) .... E 2
Beaverhill (lake) .... D 3
Behan (lake) .... E 2
Belly (riv.) .... D 5
Berland (riv.) .... A 3
Berry (creek) .... E 4
Biche (lake) .... E 2
Big (isl.) .... B 5
Big Horn (dam) .... B 3
Bighorn (range) .... B 3
Birch (hills) .... A 2
Birch (lake) .... E 3
Birch (mts.) .... B 5
Birch (riv.) .... B 5
Bison (lake) .... B 1
Bittern (lake) .... D 3
Botha (riv.) .... B 1
Bow (riv.) .... D 4
Boyer (riv.) .... A 5
Brazeau (mt.) .... B 3
Brazeau (riv.) .... B 3
Buffalo (lake) .... D 3
Buffalo Head (hills) .... B 5
Burnt (lakes) .... C 1
Cadotte (lake) .... B 1
Cadotte (riv.) .... B 1
Calling (lake) .... D 2
Canal (creek) .... E 5
Cardinal (lake) .... B 1
Caribou (mts.) .... B 5
Chinchaga (riv.) .... A 5
Chip (lake) .... C 3
Chipewyan (lake) .... D 1
Chipewyan (riv.) .... D 1
Christina (lake) .... E 2
Christina (riv.) .... E 1
Claire (lake) .... B 5
Clear (hills) .... A 1
Clearwater (riv.) .... C 4
Clearwater (riv.) .... E 1
Clyde (lake) .... E 2
Cold (lake) .... E 2
Columbia (mt.) .... B 3
Crowsnest (pass) .... C 5
Cypress (hills) .... E 5
Cypress Hills Prov. Park .... E 5
Dillon (riv.) .... E 2
Dowling (lake) .... D 4
Dunkirk (riv.) .... D 1
Eisenhower (mt.) .... C 4
Elbow (riv.) .... C 4
Elk Island Nat'l Park .... D 3
Ells (riv.) .... D 1
Etzikom Coulee (riv.) .... E 5
Eva (lake) .... B 5
Farrell (lake) .... D 4
Firebag (riv.) .... E 1
Forbes (mt.) .... B 4
Freeman (riv.) .... C 2
Frog (lake) .... E 3
Garson (lake) .... E 1
Gipsy (lake) .... E 1
Gordon (lake) .... E 1
Gough (lake) .... D 3
Graham (lake) .... C 1
Gull (lake) .... C 3
Haig (lake) .... B 1
Hawk (hills) .... B 1
Hay (lake) .... A 5
Hay (riv.) .... A 5
Heart (lake) .... E 2
Highwood (riv.) .... C 4
House (mt.) .... C 2
House (riv.) .... D 2
Iosegun (lake) .... B 2
Iosegun (riv.) .... B 2
Jackfish (riv.) .... B 5
Jasper Nat'l Park .... A 3
Kakwa (riv.) .... A 2
Kickinghorse (pass) .... B 4
Kimiwan (lake) .... B 2
Kirkpatrick (lake) .... E 4
Kitchener (mt.) .... B 3
Legend (lake) .... D 1
Lesser Slave (lake) .... C 2
Liége (riv.) .... D 1
Little Bow (riv.) .... D 4
Little Cadotte (riv.) .... B 1
Little Smoky (riv.) .... B 2
Livingstone (range) .... C 4
Logan (lake) .... E 2
Loon (lake) .... C 1
Loon (riv.) .... C 1
Lubicon (lake) .... C 1
Lyell (mt.) .... B 4
MacKay (riv.) .... D 1
Maligne (lake) .... B 3
Margaret (lake) .... B 5
Marie (lake) .... E 2
Marlon (lake) .... D 3
Marten (mt.) .... C 2
McClelland (lake) .... E 1
McGregor (lake) .... D 4
McLeod (riv.) .... B 3
Meikle (riv.) .... A 1
Mikkwa (riv.) .... B 5
Milk (riv.) .... D 5
Mistehae (lake) .... C 2
Muriel (lake) .... E 2
Muskwa (lake) .... C 1
Muskwa (riv.) .... C 1
Namur (lake) .... D 1
Newell (lake) .... E 4
Nordegg (riv.) .... C 3
North Saskatchewan (riv.) .... E 3
North Wabasca (lake) .... D 1
Notikewin (riv.) .... A 1
Oldman (riv.) .... D 5
Otter (lakes) .... B 1
Pakowki (lake) .... E 5
Panny (riv.) .... C 1
Peace (riv.) .... B 1
Peerless (lake) .... C 1
Pelican (lake) .... D 2
Pelican (mts.) .... D 2
Pembina (riv.) .... C 3
Pigeon (lake) .... D 3
Pinehurst (lake) .... E 2
Porcupine (hills) .... C 4
Primrose (lake) .... E 2
Rainbow (lake) .... A 5
Red Deer (lake) .... D 3
Red Deer (riv.) .... D 4
Richardson (riv.) .... C 5
Rocky (mts.) .... B-C 4
Rosebud (riv.) .... D 4
Russell (lake) .... C 1
Saddle (hills) .... A 2
Sainte Anne (lake) .... C 3
Saint Mary (res.) .... D 5
Saint Mary (riv.) .... D 5
Saulteaux (riv.) .... C 2
Seibert (lake) .... E 2
Simonette (riv.) .... A 2
Slave (riv.) .... C 5
Smoky (riv.) .... A 2
Snake Indian (riv.) .... A 3
Snipe (lake) .... B 2
Sounding (creek) .... E 4
South Saskatchewan (riv.) .... E 4
South Wabasca (lake) .... D 2
Spencer (lake) .... E 2
Spray (mts.) .... C 4
Sturgeon (lake) .... B 2
Sullivan (lake) .... D 3
Swan (hills) .... C 2
Swan (riv.) .... C 2
Temple (mt.) .... B 4
The Twins (mt.) .... B 3
Thickwood (hills) .... D 1
Touchwood (lake) .... E 2
Travers (res.) .... D 4
Trout (mt.) .... C 1
Trout (riv.) .... C 1
Utikuma (lake) .... C 2
Utikuma (riv.) .... C 1
Utikumasis (lake) .... C 2
Vermilion (riv.) .... E 3
Wabasca (riv.) .... C 1
Wallace (mt.) .... C 2
Wapiti (riv.) .... A 2
Wappau (lake) .... E 2
Watchusk (lake) .... E 1
Waterton-Glacier Int'l Peace Park .... C 5
Waterton Lakes Nat'l Park .... C 5
Whitemud (riv.) .... A 1
Wildhay (riv.) .... B 3
Willmore Wilderness Prov. Park .... A 3
Winagami (lake) .... B 2
Winefred (lake) .... E 2
Winefred (riv.) .... E 2
Wolf (lake) .... E 2
Wolverine (riv.) .... D 1
Wood Buffalo Nat'l Park .... B 5
Yellowhead (pass) .... A 3
Zama (lake) .... A 5

*Population of metropolitan area.

Agriculture, Industry and Resources

DOMINANT LAND USE

- Wheat
- Cereals (chiefly barley, oats)
- Cereals, Livestock
- Dairy
- Pasture Livestock
- Range Livestock
- Forests
- Nonagricultural Land

MAJOR MINERAL OCCURRENCES

- C Coal
- G Natural Gas
- Na Salt
- O Petroleum
- S Sulfur
- Water Power
- Major Industrial Areas

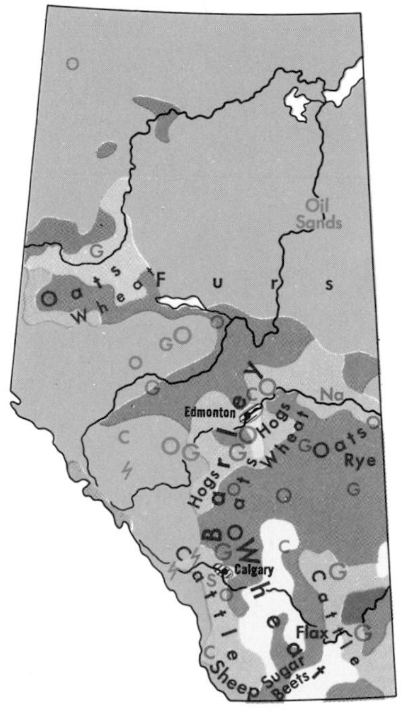
Oil Sands
Furs
Oats
Wheat
Edmonton
Hogs
Oats
Rye
Calgary
Cattle
Flax
Sheep
Sugar Beets

Topography

Mt. Fairweather 15,300 ft. (4663 m.)

Prince Rupert

QUEEN CHARLOTTE ISLANDS

Graham I.

Moresby I.

Prince George

Robson 12,972 ft. (3954 m.)

Vancouver Island

QUEEN CHARLOTTE SOUND

Kelowna

Vancouver

Victoria

Kicking Horse Pass

Crowsnest Pass

0   100   200 MI.

0   100   200 KM.

| Below Sea Level | 100 m. 328 ft. | 200 m. 656 ft. | 500 m. 1,640 ft. | 1,000 m. 3,281 ft. | 2,000 r. 6,562 ft. | 5,000 m. 16,404 ft. |

CITIES and TOWNS

Abbotsford 12,745	L 3	Cawston 785	H 5
Alert Bay 626	D 5	Central Saanich ○9,890	K 3
Armstrong 2,683	H 5	Chase 1,777	H 5
Ashcroft 2,156	G 5	Chemainus 2,069	J 3
Ashton Creek 452	H 5	Cherry Creek 450	G 5
Balfour 472	J 5	Chetwynd 2,553	G 2
Barlow 441	F 3	Chilliwack ○40,642	M 3
Barrière 1,370	H 4	Clearwater 1,461	G 4
Blueberry Creek 635	J 5	Clinton 804	G 4
Blue River 384	H 4	Comox 6,607	H 2
Boston Bar 498	G 5	Coquitlam ○61,077	K 3
Bowen Island 1,125	J 3	Courtenay 8,992	E 5
Brackendale 1,719	F 5	Cranbrook 15,915	K 5
Burnaby ○136,494	K 3	Creston 4,190	J 5
Burns Lake 1,777	D 3	Crofton 1,303	J 3
Cache Creek 1,308	G 5	Cultus Lake 481	M 3
Campbell River 15,370	E 5	Cumberland 1,947	E 5
Canal Flats 919	J 5	Dawson Creek 11,373	G 2
Canyon 698	J 5	Delta ○74,692	K 3
Cassiar 1,045	K 2	Duncan 4,228	J 3
Castlegar 6,902	J 5	Elkford 3,126	K 5
		Enderby 1,816	H 5
		Erickson 972	J 5

Errington 609	J 3	Hazelton 393	D 2
Falkland 478	H 5	Hedley 426	G 5
Fernie 5,444	K 5	Holberg 444	C 5
Forest Grove 444	G 4	Honeymoon Bay 474	J 3
Fort Fraser 574	E 3	Hope 3,205	M 3
Fort Langley 2,326	L 3	Hornby Island 474	H 2
Fort Nelson 3,724	M 2	Horsefly 430	G 4
Fort Saint James 2,284	E 3	Houston 1,714	D 3
Fort Saint John 13,891	G 2	Hudson Hope 984	F 2
Fraser Lake 1,543	E 3	Invermere 1,969	J 5
Fruitvale 1,904	J 5	Kaleden 998	H 5
Gabriola 1,627	J 3	Kamloops 64,048	G 5
Galiano 669	K 3	Kaslo 854	J 5
Ganges 1,118	K 3	Kelowna 59,196	H 5
Gibsons 2,594	K 3	Kent ○3,394	M 3
Gold River 2,225	D 5	Keremeos 830	J 5
Golden 3,476	J 4	Kimberley 7,375	K 5
Grand Forks 3,486	H 6	Kitimat 12,462	C 3
Granisle 1,430	D 3	Kitsault 554	C 2
Greenwood 856	H 5	Kitwanga 369	D 2
Hagensborg 350	J 5	Lac La Hache 647	G 4
Harrison Hot Springs 569	M 3	Ladysmith 4,558	J 3
Hatzic 1,055	L 3	Lake Cowichan 2,391	J 3
		Langley 15,124	L 3
		Lantzville 969	J 3
		Likely 425	G 4
		Lillooet 1,725	G 5
		Lion's Bay 1,078	K 3
		Logan Lake 2,637	G 5
		Lumby 1,266	H 5
		Lytton 428	G 5
		Mackenzie 5,797	F 2
		Mackenzie ○5,890	F 2
		Malakwa 392	H 5
		Maple Bay 393	K 3
		Maple Ridge ○32,232	L 3
		Masset 1,569	B 3
		Matsqui ○42,001	L 3
		Mayne 546	K 3
		McBride 641	G 3
		Merritt 6,110	G 5
		Midway 633	H 6
		Mill Bay 583	J 3
		Mission ○20,056	L 3
		Mission City 9,948	L 3
		Montrose 1,229	J 5
		Nakusp 1,495	J 5
		Nanaimo 47,069	H 5
		Naramata 876	H 5
		Nelson 9,143	J 5

Penticton 23,181	H 5	Chehalis (lake)	L 3
Pitt Meadows ○6,209	L 3	Chilcotin (riv.)	E 4
Port Alberni 19,892	H 3	Chilko (lake)	F 4
Port Alice 1,668	D 5	Chilko (riv.)	E 4
Port Clements 380	B 3	Chilkoot (pass)	J 1
Port Coquitlam 27,535	L 3	Chuchi (lake)	E 2
Port Edward 989	B 3	Churchill (peak)	M 2
Port Hardy ○3,778	D 5	Clayoquot (sound)	D 5
Port McNeill 2,474	D 5	Clearwater (lake)	G 4
Port Moody 14,917	L 3	Clearwater (riv.)	G 4
Pouce-Coupé 821	G 2	Coast (mts.)	D 3
Powell River ○13,423	E 5	Columbia (lake)	K 5
Prince George 67,559	F 3	Columbia (mt.)	J 4
Prince Rupert 16,197	B 3	Columbia (riv.)	H 4
Princeton 3,051	G 5	Columbia Reach (riv.)	H 4
Qualicum Beach 2,844	J 3	Cook (cape)	C 5
Queen Charlotte 1,070	A 3	Cowichan (lake)	J 3
Quesnel 8,240	F 4	Crowsnest (pass)	K 5
Radium Hot Springs 419	J 5	Cypress Prov. Park	K 3
Revelstoke 5,544	J 5	Dean (chan.)	D 4
Richmond ○96,154	K 3	Dean (riv.)	D 4
Roberts Creek 926	J 3	Dease (lake)	K 2
Robson 1,008	J 5	Dease (riv.)	K 2
Rossland 3,967	H 6	Devils Thumb (mt.)	A 1
Royston 754	H 2	Dixon Entrance (chan.)	A 3
Saanich ○78,710	K 3	Douglas (chan.)	C 3
Salmo 1,169	J 5	Duncan (riv.)	J 5
Salmon Arm 1,946	H 5	Dundas (isl.)	B 3
Salmon Arm ○10,780	H 5	Elk (riv.)	K 5
Saltair 1,356	J 3	Elk Lakes Prov. Park	K 5
Sandspit 794	B 3	Eutsuk (lake)	D 3
Sayward 482	D 5	Fairweather (mt.)	H 1
Sechelt 1,096	J 2	Finlay (riv.)	E 1
Shawnigan Lake 419	J 3	
Shoreacres 555	J 5	Fitzhugh (sound)	D 4
Sicamous 1,057	H 5	Flathead (riv.)	K 6
Sidney 7,946	K 3	Flores (isl.)	D 5
Slocan 351	J 5	Fontas (riv.)	M 2
Slocan Park 414	J 5	Forbes (mt.)	J 4
Smithers 4,570	D 3	Fort Nelson (riv.)	M 2
Sointula 567	D 5	François (lake)	D 3
Sooke 852	J 4	Fraser (lake)	E 3
Sorrento 659	H 5	Fraser (riv.)	F 4
South Hazelton 500	D 2	Fraser Reach (chan.)	C 3
South Wellington 620	J 3	Galiano (isl.)	K 3
Spallumcheen 4,213	H 5	Gardner (canal)	C 3
Sparwood 3,267	K 5	Garibaldi Prov. Park	F 5
Sproat Lake 440	H 3	Georgia (str.)	E 5
Squamish 1,590	F 5	Germansen (lake)	E 2
Stewart ○1,456	C 2	Gil (isl.)	C 4
Summerland ○7,473	G 5	Glacier Nat'l Park	J 4
Surrey ○147,138	K 3	Golden Ears Prov. Park	L 3
Tahsis 1,739	D 5	Gordon (riv.)	H 3
Taylor 966	G 2	Graham (isl.)	A 3
Telkwa 840	D 3	Graham Reach (chan.)	C 3
Terrace 8,893	C 3	Grenville (chan.)	C 3
Terrace ○10,914	C 3	Halfway (riv.)	F 2
Thornhill 4,999	C 3	Hamber Prov. Park	H 4
Thrums 360	J 5	Harrison (lake)	M 2
Tofino 705	E 5	Hawkesbury (isl.)	C 3
Trail 9,599	J 6	Hazelton (mts.)	C 2
Ucluelet 1,593	E 6	Hecate (str.)	B 3
Union Bay 601	H 2	Hobson (lake)	H 4
Valemount 1,130	H 4	Homathko (riv.)	E 4
Vancouver 414,281	K 3	Horsefly (lake)	G 4
Vancouver (Greater)		Howe (sound)	K 2
*1,169,831	K 3	Hunter (isl.)	C 4
Vanderhoof 2,323	E 3	
Vavenby 479	H 4	
Vernon 19,987	H 5	
Victoria (cap.) 64,379	K 4	
Victoria *233,481	K 4	
Warfield 1,969	J 5	
Wasa 345	K 5	
Wells 417	G 3	
Westbank 1,271	H 5	
West Vancouver ○35,728	K 3	
Westwold 409	G 5	
Whistler ○1,365	F 5	
White Rock 13,550	K 3	
Williams Lake 8,362	F 4	
Wilson Creek 611	J 2	
Windermere 611	J 5	
Winlaw 435	J 5	
Woss Lake 395	D 5	
Wynndel 566	J 5	
Yarrow 1,201	M 3	
Youbou 965	J 3	

OTHER FEATURES

Adams (lake)	H 4
Adams (riv.)	H 4
Alberni (inlet)	H 3
Alsek (riv.)	H 1
Aristazabal (isl.)	C 4
Assiniboine (mt.)	K 5
Atlin (lake)	J 1
Azure (lake)	G 4
Babine (lake)	E 3
Babine (riv.)	D 2
Banks (isl.)	B 3
Barkley (sound)	E 6
Beale (cape)	E 6
Beatton (riv.)	G 1
Bella Coola (riv.)	D 4
Bennett, W.A.C. (dam)	F 2
Birkenhead Lake Prov. Park	F 5
Bowron Lake Prov. Park	G 3
Bowser (lake)	C 2
Brooks (pen.)	C 5
Browning Entrance (str.)	B 3
Bryce (mt.)	H 4
Bugaboo Glacier Prov. Park	J 5
Bulkley (riv.)	D 2
Burke (chan.)	D 4
Burnaby (isl.)	B 4
Bute (inlet)	E 5
Caamaño (sound)	C 4
Calvert (isl.)	C 4
Canim (lake)	G 4
Canoe Reach (riv.)	H 4
Cariboo (mts.)	G 3
Carp Lake Prov. Park	F 3
Carpenter (lake)	F 5
Cassiar (mts.)	K 2
Castle (mt.)	A 2
Cathedral Prov. Park	H 5
Charlotte (lake)	E 4
Chatham (sound)	B 3

Agriculture, Industry and Resources

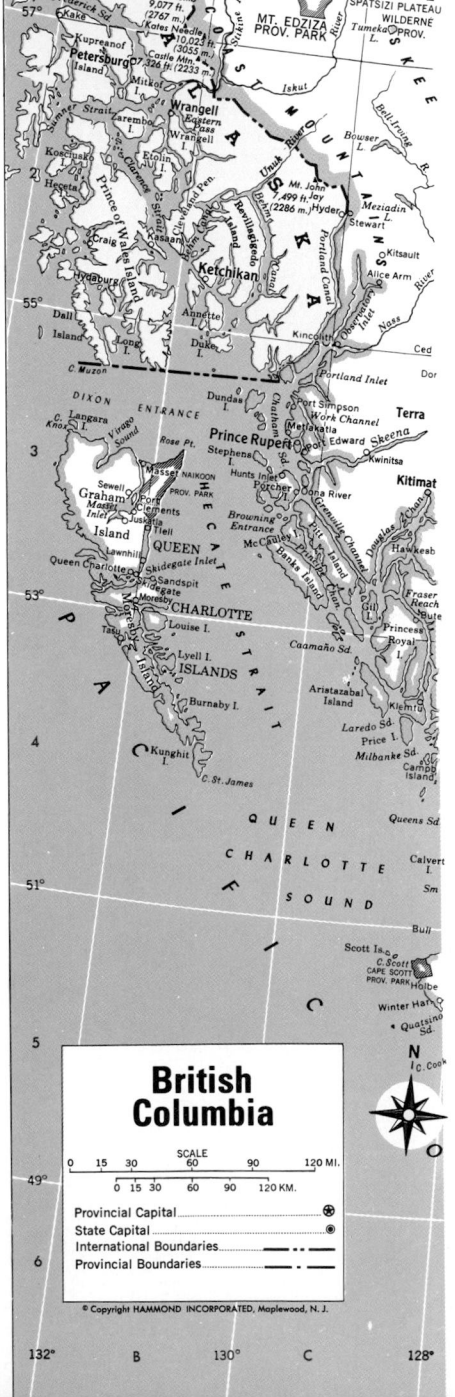

DOMINANT LAND USE

- Cereals, Livestock
- Dairy
- Fruits, Vegetables
- Pasture Livestock
- Forests
- Nonagricultural Land

MAJOR MINERAL OCCURRENCES

Ab	Asbestos	Gp	Gypsum
Ag	Silver	Mo	Molybdenum
Au	Gold	Ni	Nickel
C	Coal	O	Petroleum
Cu	Copper	Pb	Lead
Fe	Iron Ore	S	Sulfur
G	Natural Gas	Sn	Tin
		Zn	Zinc

⚡ Water Power

▨ Major Industrial Areas

British Columbia

SCALE

0 15 30 60 90 120 MI.

0 15 30 60 90 120 KM.

Provincial Capital ⊛

State Capital ⊚

International Boundaries

Provincial Boundaries

© Copyright HAMMOND INCORPORATED, Maplewood, N.J.

AREA 366,253 sq. mi. (948,596 sq. km.)
POPULATION 2,883,367
CAPITAL Victoria
LARGEST CITY Vancouver
HIGHEST POINT Mt. Fairweather 15,300 ft.
  (4,663 m.)
SETTLED IN 1806
ADMITTED TO CONFEDERATION 1871
PROVINCIAL FLOWER Dogwood

*Population of metropolitan area.
○Population of municipality.

NORTHWEST TERRITORIES

CITIES and TOWNS

Topography

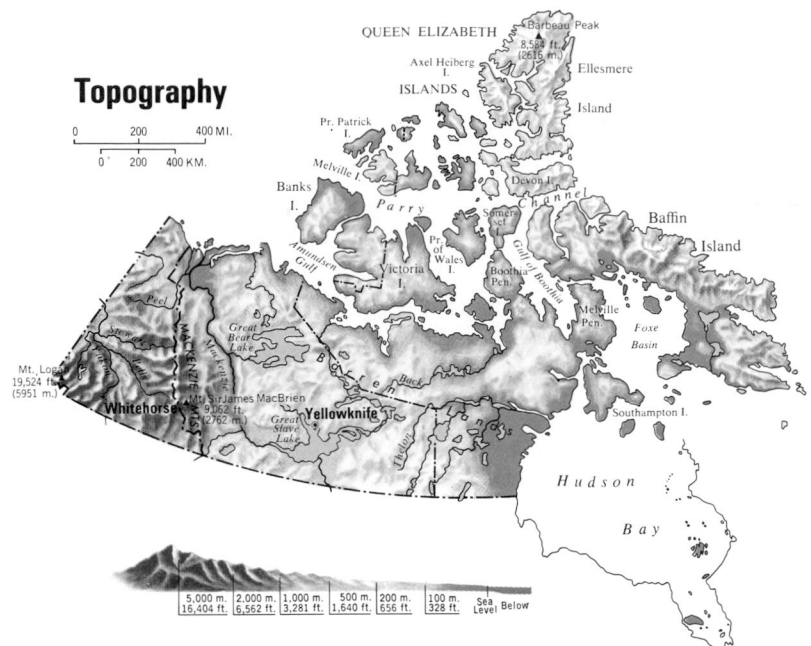

Agriculture, Industry and Resources

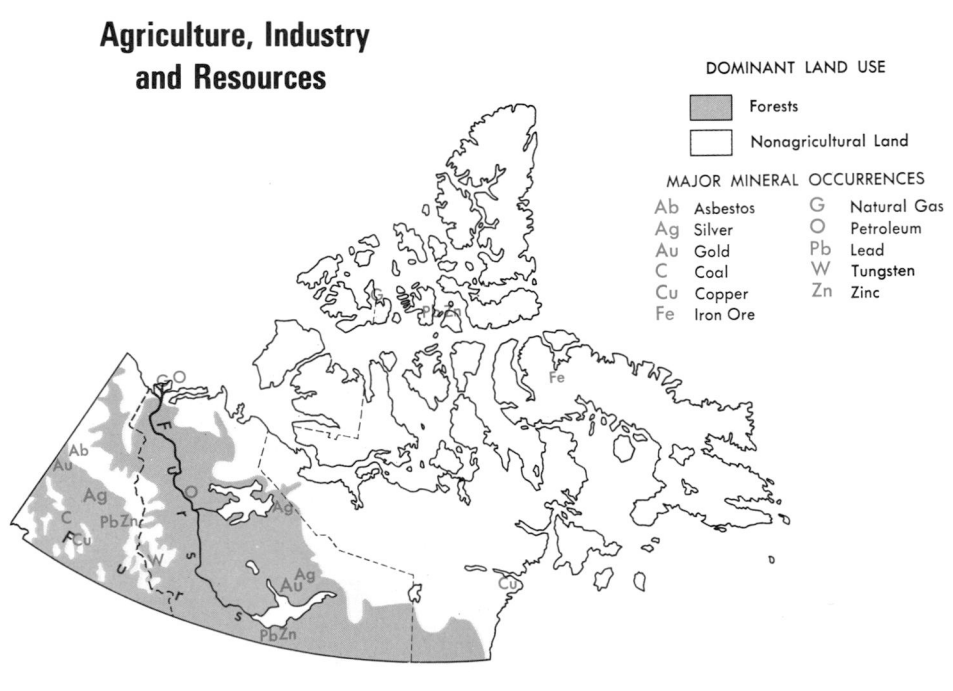

DOMINANT LAND USE

- Forests
- Nonagricultural Land

MAJOR MINERAL OCCURRENCES

Ab	Asbestos	G	Natural Gas
Ag	Silver	O	Petroleum
Au	Gold	Pb	Lead
C	Coal	W	Tungsten
Cu	Copper	Zn	Zinc
Fe	Iron Ore		

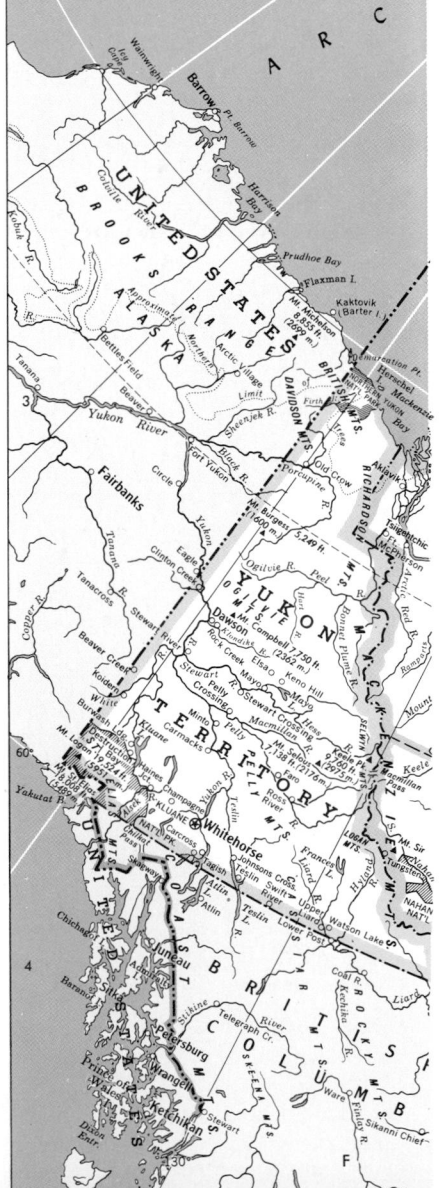

Mistake (bay) J3	Royal Geographic Society
Nansen (sound) J1	(isls.) J3
Nares (str.) L2	Russell (isl.) J2
Navy Board (inlet) K2	Sabine (pen.) H2
Nettilling (lake) L3	Salisbury (isl.) L3
North Magnetic Pole H2	Seahorse (pt.) L3
Norwegian (bay) J2	Simpson (pen.) K3
Nottingham (isl.) L3	Smith (bay) L2
Nueltin (lake) J3	Smith (cape) L3
Ommanney (bay) H2	Smith (sound) L2
Padloping (isl.) M3	Somerset (isl.) J2
Parry (bay) K3	South (bay) K3
Parry (chan.) G2	Southampton (isl.) K3
Parry (isls.) G2	Stallworthy (cape) J1
Peary (chan.) H2	Steensby (inlet) L2
Peel (sound) J2	Stefansson (isl.) H2
Pelly (bay) J3	Sverdrup (chan.) J1
Penny (str.) J2	Takijug (lake) G3
Pond (inlet) L2	Talbot (inlet) L2
Prince Charles (isl.) L3	Tha'ane (riv.) J3
Prince Gustav Adolf (sea) H2	Thelon (riv.) H3
Prince of Wales (isl.) J2	Thlewiasa (riv.) J3
Prince Regent (inlet) J2	Ungava (bay) M4
Queen Elizabeth (isls.) H1	Vansittart (isl.) K3
Queen Maud (gulf) H3	Victoria (isl.) G2
Queens (chan.) J2	Victoria (str.) H3
Raanes (pen.) K2	Viscount Melville (sound) ...G2
Rae (isth.) K3	Wager (bay) K3
Rae (riv.) G3	Wales (isl.) K3
Rae (str.) J3	Walsingham (cape) M3
Resolution (isl.) M3	Wellington (chan.) J3
Robeson (chan.) M1	Winter (harb.) H3
Ross Welcome (sound) K3	Wollaston (pen.) G3
Rowley (isl.) K3	Yathkyed (lake) J3

YUKON TERRITORY

AREA 186,660 sq. mi.
  (483,450 sq. km.)
POPULATION 27,797
CAPITAL Whitehorse
LARGEST CITY Whitehorse
HIGHEST POINT Mt. Logan 19,524 ft.
  (5,951 m.)
SETTLED IN 1897
ADMITTED TO CONFEDERATION 1898
PROVINCIAL FLOWER Fireweed

NORTHWEST TERRITORIES

AREA 589,315 sq. mi.
  (1,526,328 sq. km.)
POPULATION 39,672
CAPITAL Yellowknife
LARGEST CITY Yellowknife
HIGHEST POINT Mt. Sir James McBrien
  9,062 ft. (2,762 m.)
SETTLED IN 1800
ADMITTED TO CONFEDERATION 1870
PROVINCIAL FLOWER Mountain Avens

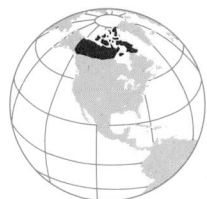

YUKON TERRITORY
CITIES and TOWNS

Beaver Creek 113 ....D3	Haines Junction 340 ....E3
Burwash Landing 64 ....D3	Johnson's Crossing 18 ......E3
Carcross 209 ....E3	Keno Hill 47 ....E3
Carmacks 280 ....E3	Koidern D3
Champagne 57 ....E3	Mayo 324 ....E3
Clinton Creek D3	Minto E3
Cowley E3	Old Crow 232 ....E3
Dawson 1,287 ....E3	Pelly Crossing 177 ....E3
Destruction Bay 48 ....E3	Rock Creek 75 ....E3
Elsa 294 ....E3	Ross River 352 ....E3
Faro 1251 ....E3	Stewart Crossing 40 ....E3
	Stewart River D3
	Swift River 5 ....E3
	Tagish 103 ....E3
	Teslin 181 ....E3
	Upper Liard 130 ....E3
	Watson Lake 993 ....F3
	Whitehorse (cap.) 19,157 ...E3

OTHER FEATURES

Alsek (riv.) E3	Keele (peak) E3
Bonnet Plume (riv.) E3	Klondike (riv.) E3
British (mts.) D3	Kluane (lake) E3
Campbell (mt.) E3	Kluane Nat'l Park E3
Cassiar (mts.) E3	Liard (riv.) E3
Frances (lake) E3	Logan (mt.) D3
Herschel (isl.) E3	Logan (mts.) F3
Hess (riv.) E3	Mackenzie (mts.) E3
Hyland (riv.) F3	Macmillan (riv.) E3
	Mayo (lake) E3
	Northern Yukon Nat'l Pk. ...E3
	Ogilvie (mts.) E3
	Ogilvie (riv.) E3
	Peel (riv.) E3
	Pelly (mts.) E3

Pelly (riv.) E3	
Porcupine (riv.) E3	
Richardson (mts.) E3	
Rocky (mts.) F4	
Saint Elias (mt.) E3	
Saint Elias (mts.) E3	
Selous (mt.) E3	
Selwyn (mts.) E3	
Stewart (riv.) E3	
Teslin (lake) E4	
Teslin (riv.) E3	
White (riv.) D3	
Yukon (riv.) E3	

• Population of district.

Map

Yukon and Northwest Territories

SCALE

0 50 100 200 300 MI.

0 50 100 200 300 KM.

Territorial Capitals .... ⊗
International Boundaries ....
Provincial & Territorial Boundaries ....
Regional Boundaries ....

United States

POLYCONIC PROJECTION

SCALE OF MILES

SCALE OF KILOMETERS

Capitals of Countries .... ☆
State Capitals .... △
International Boundaries .... — — —

Scale 1:17,400,000

© Copyright HAMMOND INCORPORATED, Maplewood, N.J.

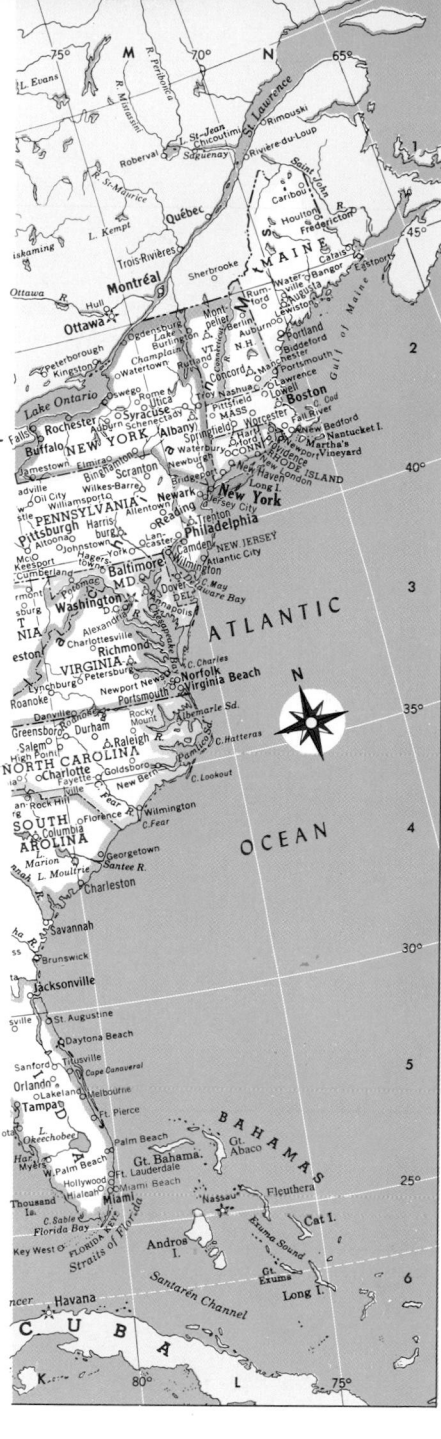

AREA 3,623,420 sq. mi.
(9,384,658 sq. km.)
POPULATION 249,632,692
CAPITAL Washington
LARGEST CITY New York
HIGHEST POINT Mt. McKinley 20,320 ft.
(6,194 m.)
MONETARY UNIT U.S. dollar
MAJOR LANGUAGE English
MAJOR RELIGIONS Protestantism,
Roman Catholicism, Judaism

Population Distribution

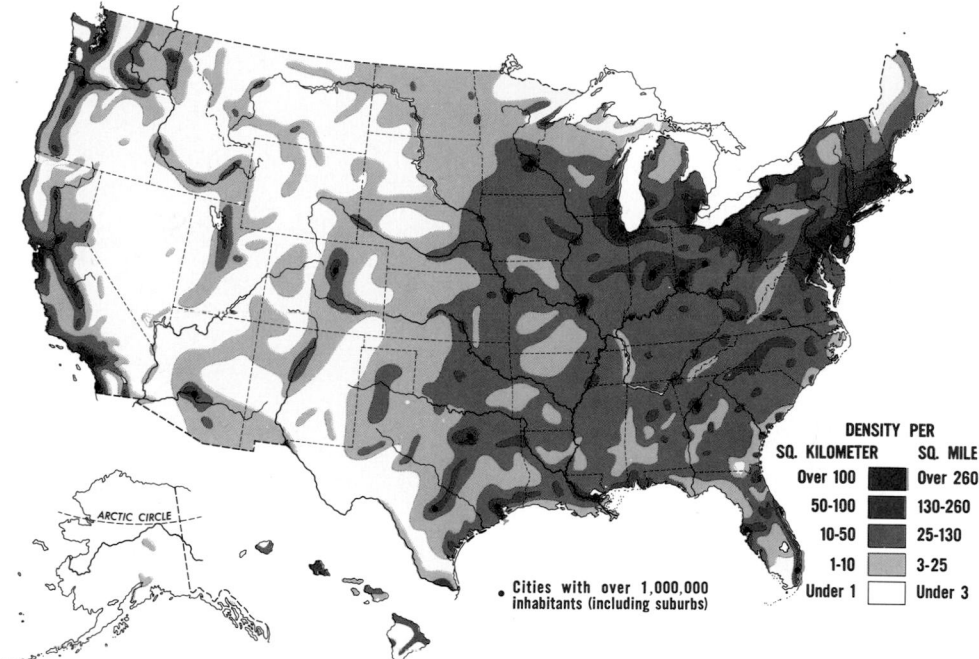

DENSITY PER	
SQ. KILOMETER	**SQ. MILE**
Over 100	Over 260
50-100	130-260
10-50	25-130
1-10	3-25
Under 1	Under 3

● Cities with over 1,000,000 inhabitants (including suburbs)

Vegetation

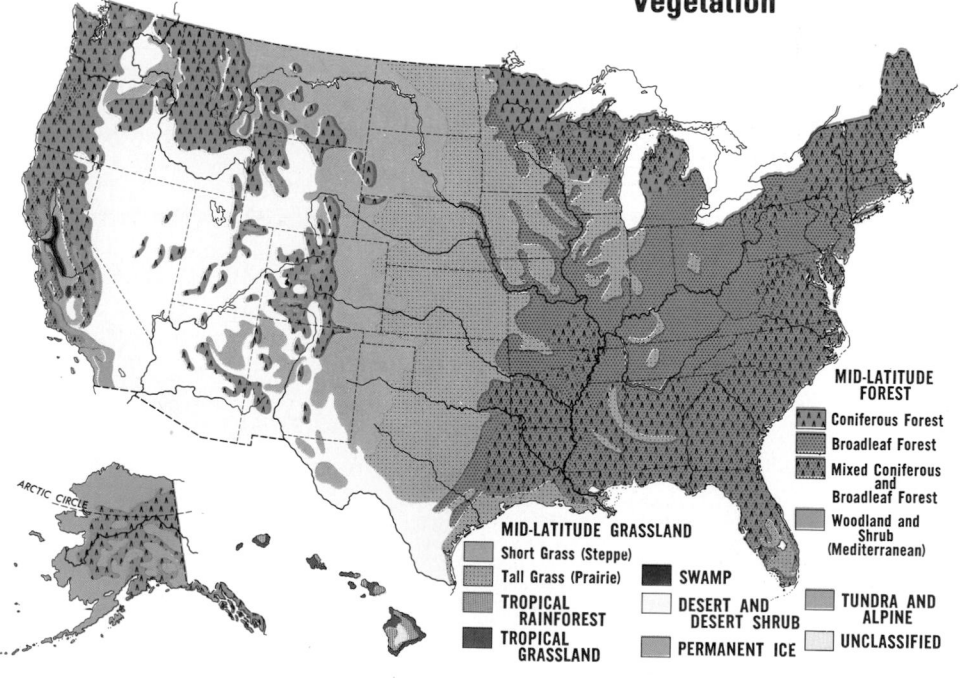

MID-LATITUDE FOREST
Coniferous Forest
Broadleaf Forest
Mixed Coniferous and Broadleaf Forest
Woodland and Shrub (Mediterranean)

MID-LATITUDE GRASSLAND
Short Grass (Steppe)
Tall Grass (Prairie)

TROPICAL RAINFOREST
TROPICAL GRASSLAND

SWAMP
DESERT AND DESERT SHRUB
PERMANENT ICE

TUNDRA AND ALPINE
UNCLASSIFIED

Rainfall

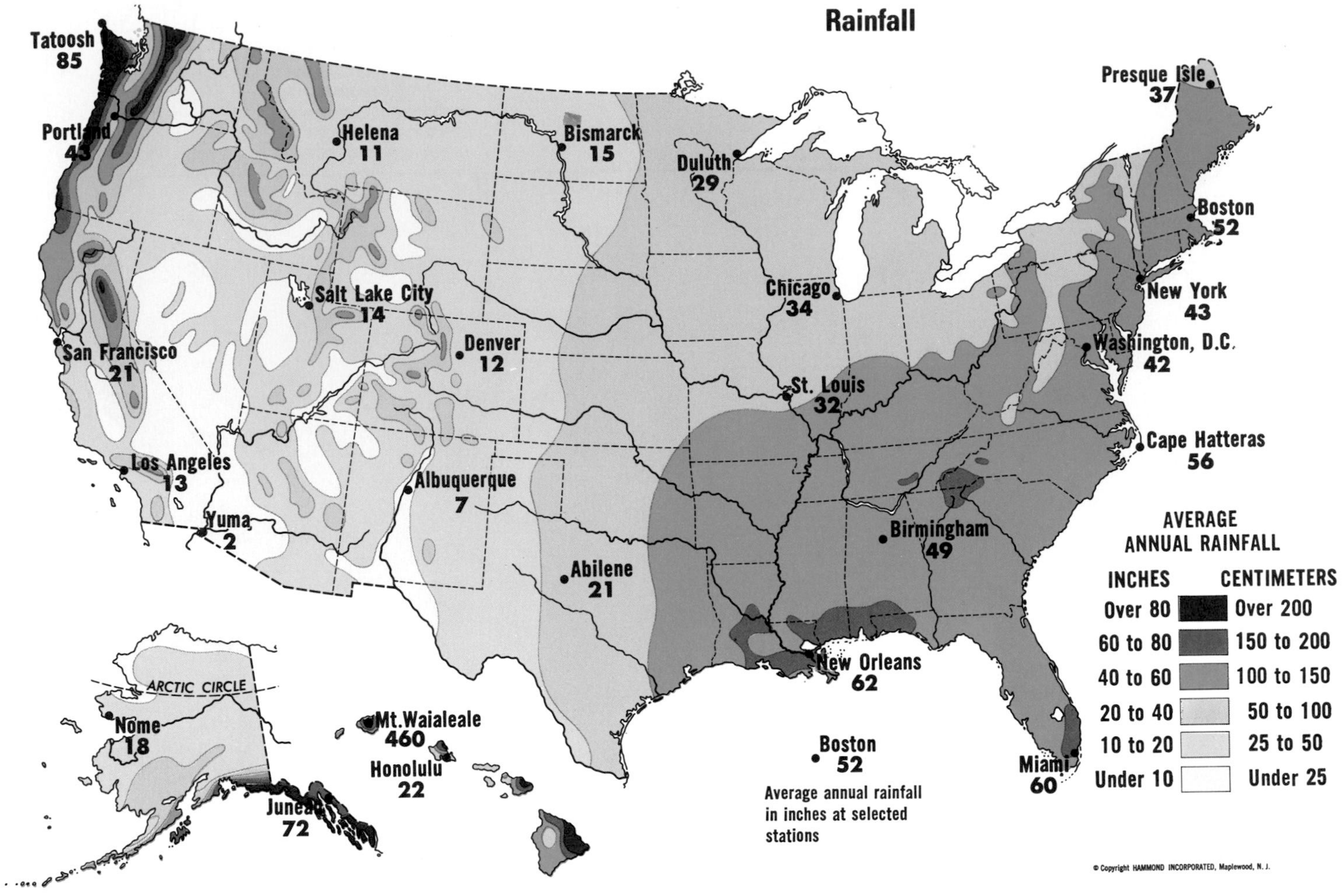

Tatoosh
85

Portland
43

Helena
11

Bismarck
15

Duluth
29

Presque Isle
37

Boston
52

Salt Lake City
14

Denver
12

Chicago
34

New York
43

Washington, D.C.
42

San Francisco
21

St. Louis
32

Cape Hatteras
56

Los Angeles
13

Albuquerque
7

Yuma
2

Abilene
21

Birmingham
49

New Orleans
62

Boston
52

Miami
60

AVERAGE ANNUAL RAINFALL

INCHES		CENTIMETERS
Over 80		Over 200
60 to 80		150 to 200
40 to 60		100 to 150
20 to 40		50 to 100
10 to 20		25 to 50
Under 10		Under 25

Average annual rainfall in inches at selected stations

ARCTIC CIRCLE

Nome
18

Mt. Waialeale
460

Honolulu
22

Juneau
72

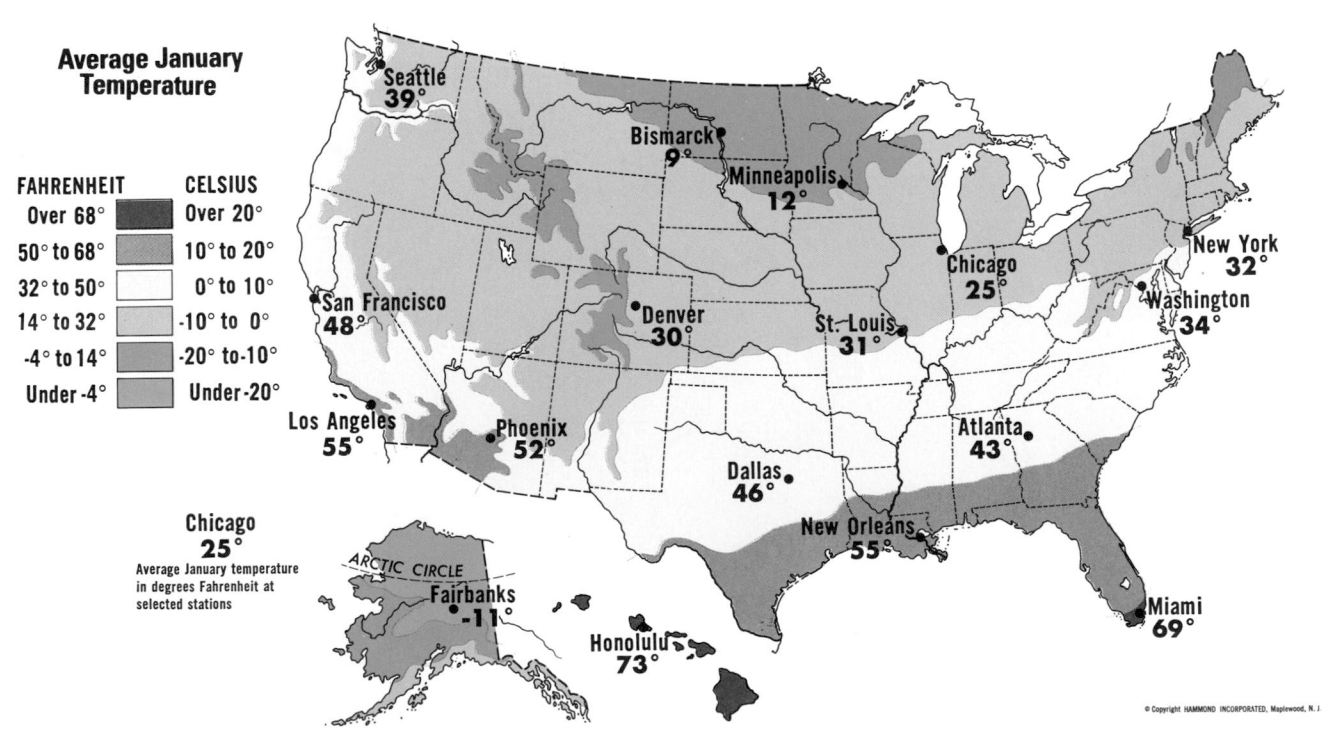

Average January Temperature

FAHRENHEIT	CELSIUS
Over 68°	Over 20°
50° to 68°	10° to 20°
32° to 50°	0° to 10°
14° to 32°	-10° to 0°
-4° to 14°	-20° to -10°
Under -4°	Under -20°

Seattle
39°

Bismarck
9°

Minneapolis
12°

New York
32°

San Francisco
48°

Denver
30°

Chicago
25°

St. Louis
31°

Washington
34°

Los Angeles
55°

Phoenix
52°

Atlanta
43°

Dallas
46°

New Orleans
55°

Chicago
25°

Average January temperature in degrees Fahrenheit at selected stations

ARCTIC CIRCLE

Fairbanks
-11°

Honolulu
73°

Miami
69°

Topography

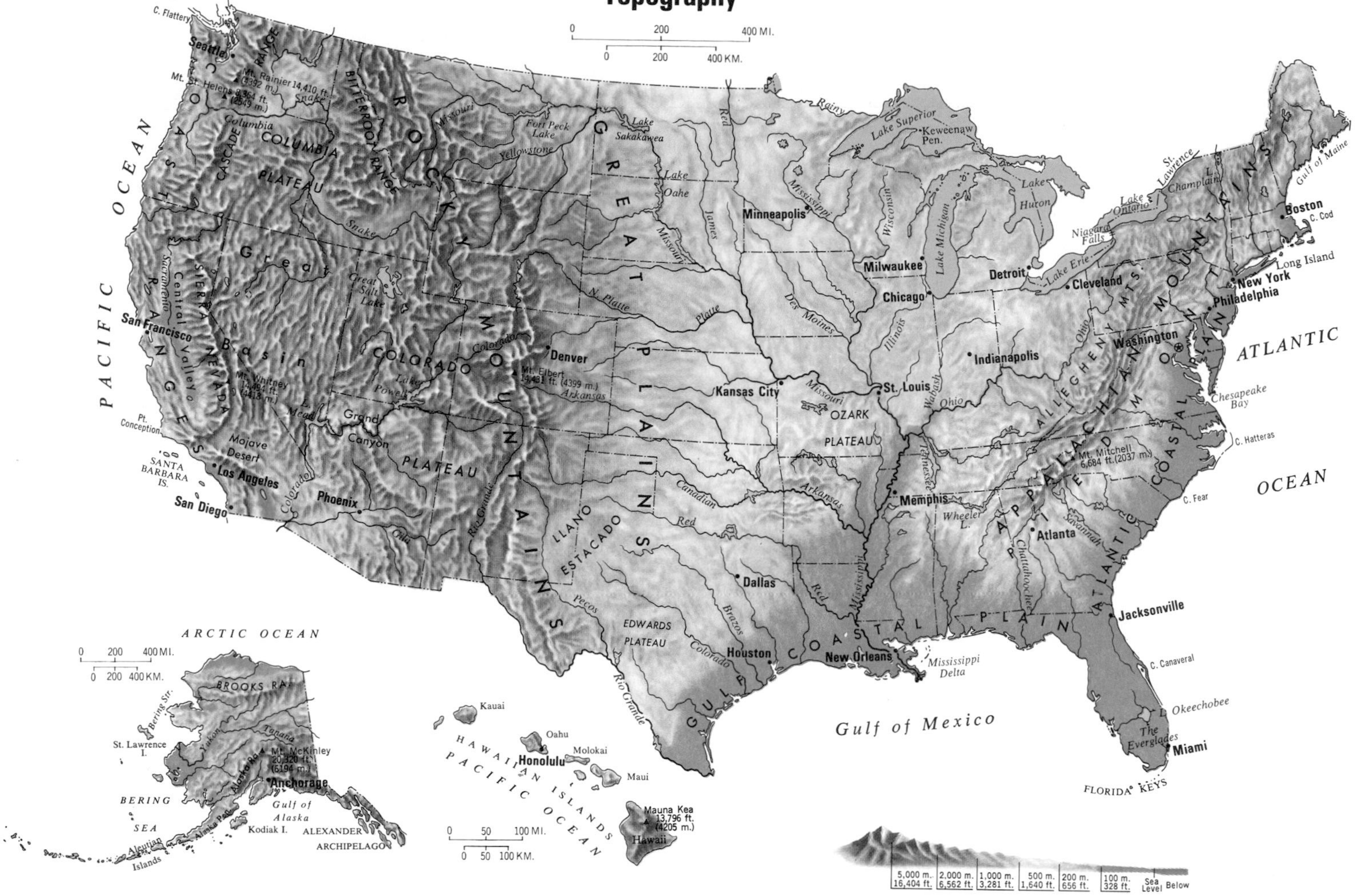

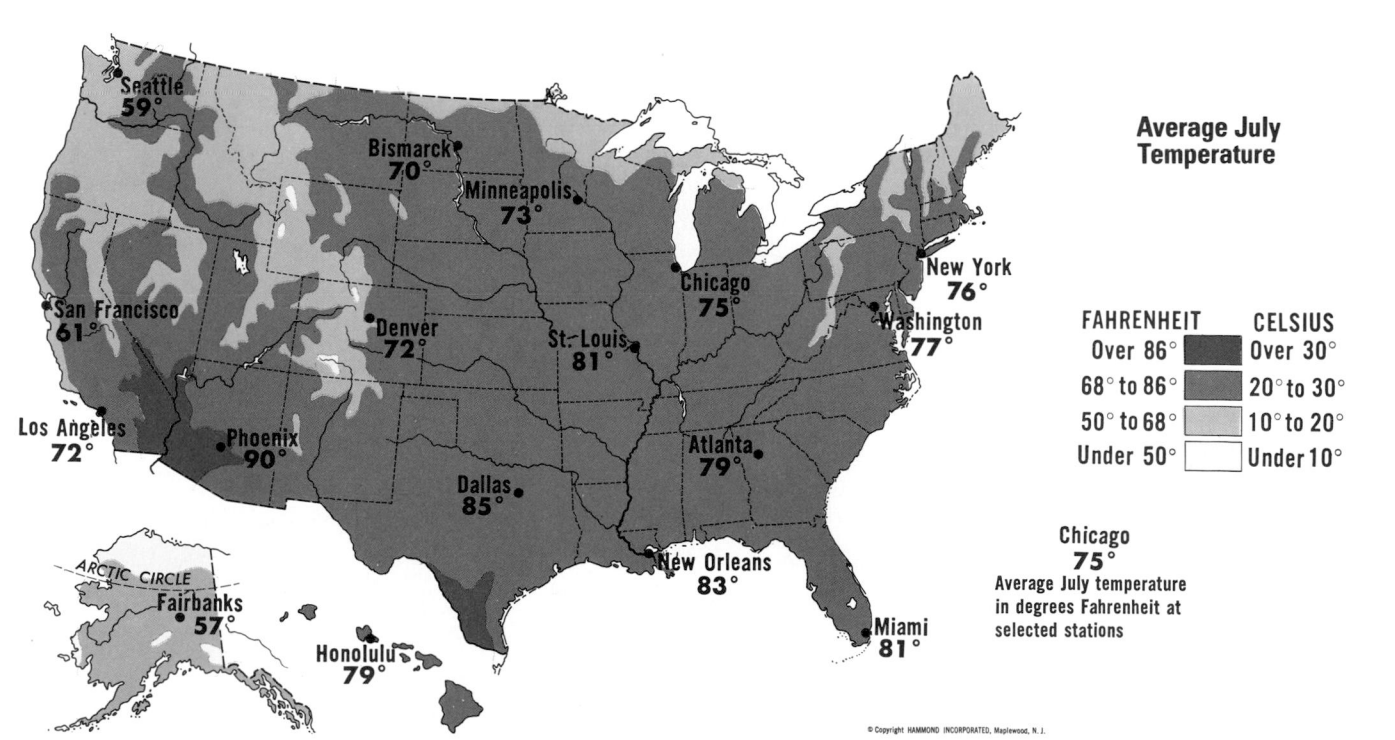

0   200   400 MI.

0   200   400 KM.

PACIFIC OCEAN

C. Flattery

Seattle

Mt. Rainier 14,410 ft.
(4392 m.)

Mt. St. Helens
8,364 ft.
(2549 m.)

Columbia

COASCADE RANGE

Snake

BITTERROOT RANGE

COLUMBIA PLATEAU

Yellowstone

Fort Peck Lake

Missouri

Rainy

Lake Superior

Keweenaw Pen.

Red

GREAT PLAINS

Lake Sakakawea

Minneapolis

Wisconsin

Milwaukee

Lake Michigan

Chicago

Lake Huron

Detroit

Lake Erie

Cleveland

Niagara Falls

Lake Ontario

Lake Champlain

St. Lawrence

Boston

C. Cod

Long Island

New York
Philadelphia

ATLANTIC

ALLEGHENY MTS.

APPALACHIAN MOUNTAINS

Washington

Indianapolis

St. Louis

Ohio

OZARK PLATEAU

Chesapeake Bay

C. Hatteras

OCEAN

Mt. Mitchell
6,684 ft. (2037 m.)

C. Fear

Atlanta

ATLANTIC COASTAL PLAIN

Savannah

Jacksonville

Great Salt Lake

ROCKY MOUNTAINS

Denver

Mt. Elbert
14,431 ft. (4399 m.)

Arkansas

Kansas City

Missouri

Memphis

Wheeler

N. Platte

Platte

Des Moines

Illinois

Wabash

Tennessee

Chattahoochee

SIERRA NEVADA

Sacramento

San Francisco

Central Valley

Mojave Desert

Los Angeles

SANTA BARBARA IS.

Pt. Conception

San Diego

Great Basin

Mt. Whitney
14,494 ft.
(4418 m.)

COLORADO PLATEAU

Grand Canyon

Phoenix

Colorado

Colorado

Gila

Pecos

Rio Grande

LLANO ESTACADO

EDWARDS PLATEAU

Red

Canadian

Arkansas

Dallas

Brazos

Colorado

Houston

GULF COASTAL PLAIN

New Orleans

Mississippi Delta

Red

Mississippi

Gulf of Mexico

Okeechobee

The Everglades

Miami

FLORIDA KEYS

ARCTIC OCEAN

0   200   400 MI.

0   200   400 KM.

BROOKS RANGE

St. Lawrence I.

Tanana

Yukon

Mt. McKinley
20,320 ft.
(6194 m.)

Anchorage

Gulf of Alaska

Kodiak I.

BERING SEA

Aleutian Islands

ALEXANDER ARCHIPELAGO

Kauai

Oahu

Honolulu

Molokai

Maui

HAWAIIAN ISLANDS

PACIFIC OCEAN

0   50   100 MI.

0   50   100 KM.

Mauna Kea
13,796 ft.
(4205 m.)

Hawaii

| 5,000 m. 16,404 ft. | 2,000 m. 6,562 ft. | 1,000 m. 3,281 ft. | 500 m. 1,640 ft. | 200 m. 656 ft. | 100 m. 328 ft. | Sea Level | Below |

Average July Temperature

Seattle 59°

Bismarck 70°

Minneapolis 73°

San Francisco 61°

Denver 72°

St. Louis 81°

Chicago 75°

New York 76°

Washington 77°

Los Angeles 72°

Phoenix 90°

Dallas 85°

Atlanta 79°

New Orleans 83°

Miami 81°

ARCTIC CIRCLE

Fairbanks 57°

Honolulu 79°

FAHRENHEIT	CELSIUS
Over 86°	Over 30°
68° to 86°	20° to 30°
50° to 68°	10° to 20°
Under 50°	Under 10°

Chicago
75°
Average July temperature
in degrees Fahrenheit at
selected stations

United States Standard Time Zones

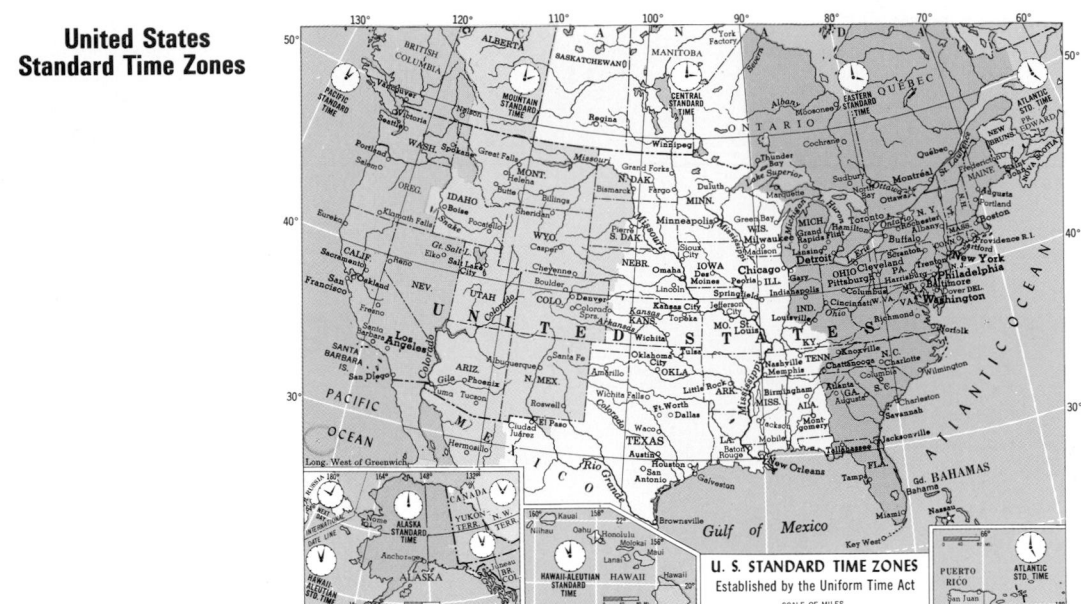

U. S. STANDARD TIME ZONES
Established by the Uniform Time Act

SCALE OF MILES
0 100 200 400 600 800

Agriculture, Industry and Resources

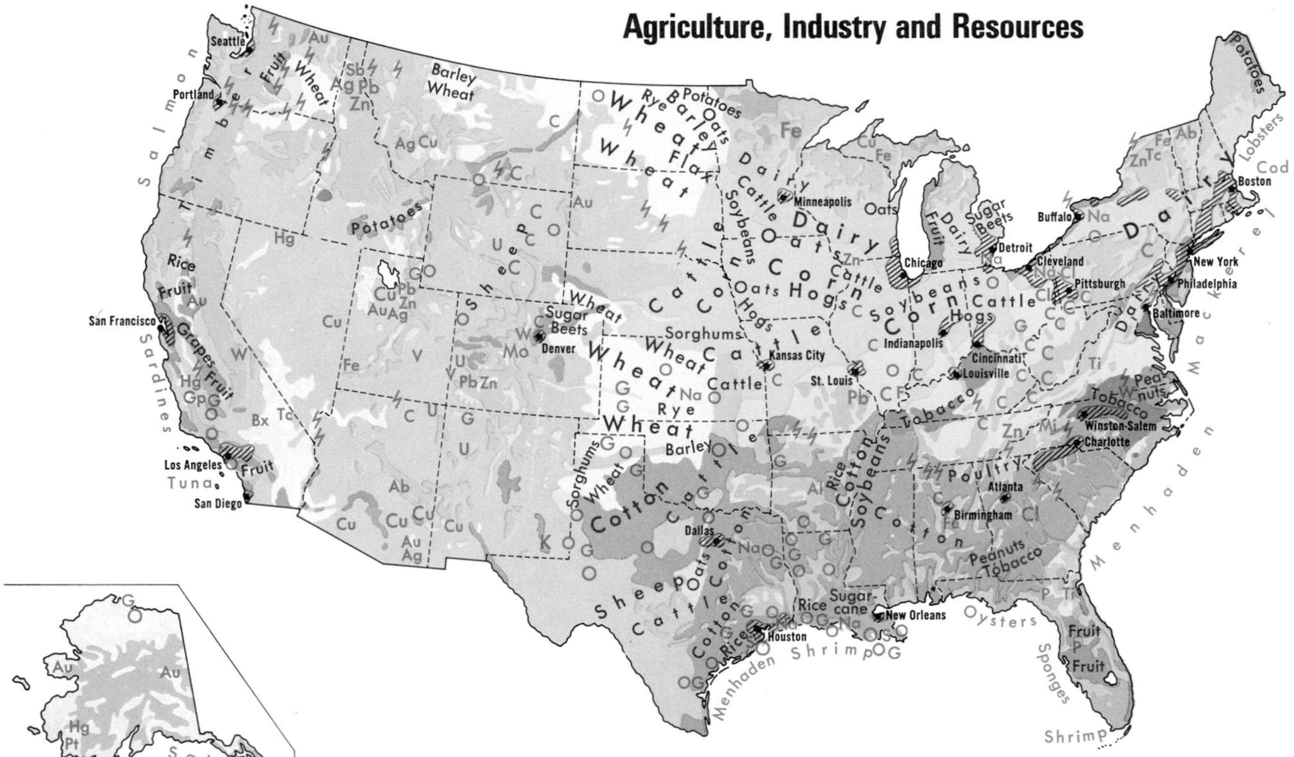

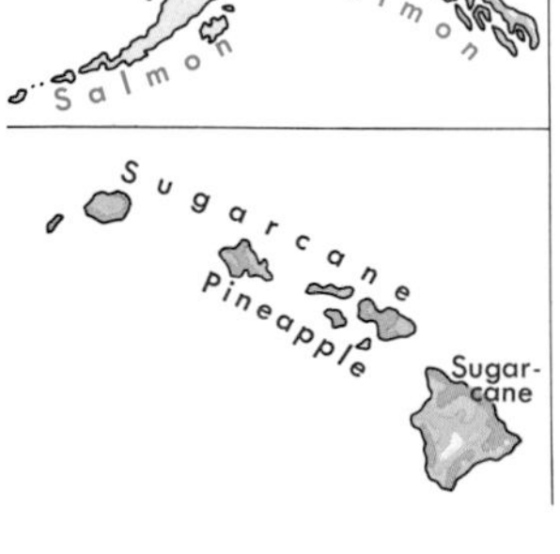

DOMINANT LAND USE

- Wheat and Small Grains
- Feed Grains and Livestock
- Dairy
- General Farming
- Cotton
- Fruit, Truck and Mixed Farming
- Tobacco and General Farming
- Special Crops and General Farming
- Range Livestock
- Forests
- Swampland
- Nonagricultural Land

MAJOR MINERAL OCCURRENCES

Ab	Asbestos	Gp	Gypsum	Sb	Antimony
Ag	Silver	Hg	Mercury	Tc	Talc
Al	Bauxite	K	Potash	Ti	Titanium
Au	Gold	Mi	Mica	U	Uranium
Bx	Borax	Mo	Molybdenum	V	Vanadium
C	Coal	Na	Salt	W	Tungsten
Cl	Clay	O	Petroleum	Zn	Zinc
Cu	Copper	P	Phosphates		
F	Fluorspar	Pb	Lead	⚡	Water Power
Fe	Iron Ore	Pt	Platinum	▨	Major Industrial Areas
G	Natural Gas	S	Sulfur		

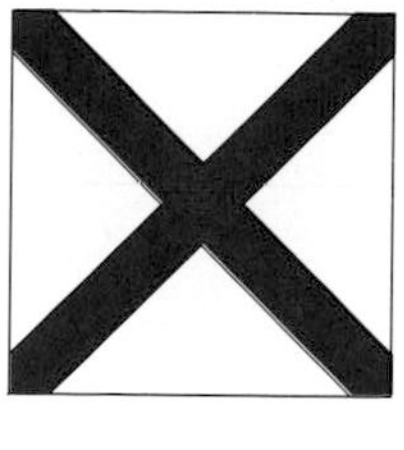

AREA 51,705 sq. mi. (133,916 sq. km.)
POPULATION 4,062,608
CAPITAL Montgomery
LARGEST CITY Birmingham
HIGHEST POINT Cheaha Mtn. 2,407 ft. (734 m.)
SETTLED IN 1702
ADMITTED TO UNION December 14, 1819
POPULAR NAME Heart of Dixie; Cotton State; Yellowhammer State
STATE FLOWER Camellia
STATE BIRD Yellowhammer

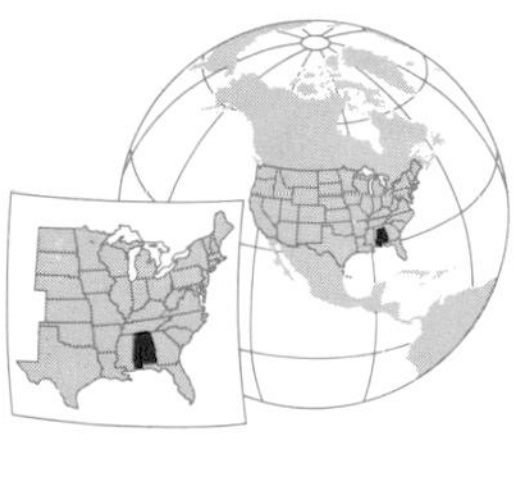

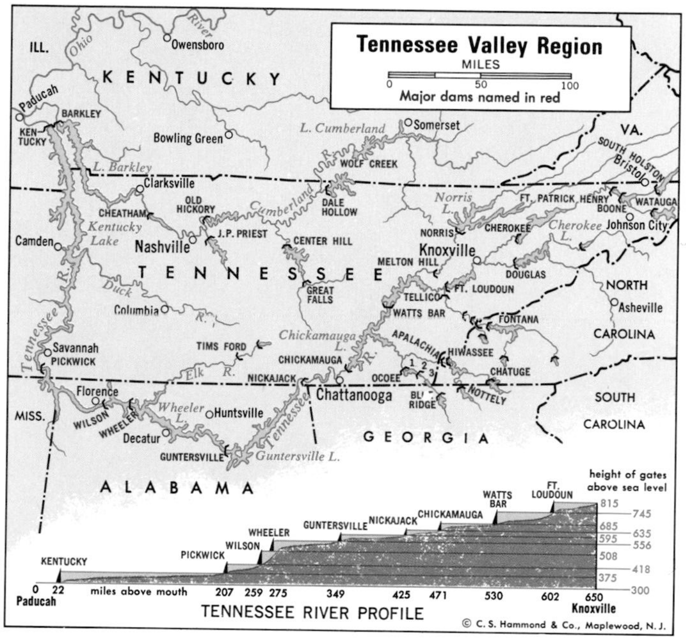

COUNTIES

Autauga 34,222 E5
Baldwin 98,280 C9
Barbour 25,417 H7
Bibb 16,576 D5
Blount 39,248 E2
Bullock 11,042 G6
Butler 21,892 E7
Calhoun 116,034 G3
Chambers 36,876 H5
Cherokee 19,543 G2
Chilton 32,458 E5
Choctaw 16,018 B6
Clarke 27,240 C7
Clay 13,252 G4
Cleburne 12,730 G3
Coffee 40,240 G8
Colbert 51,666 C1
Conecuh 14,054 E8
Coosa 11,063 F5
Covington 36,478 F8
Crenshaw 13,635 F7
Cullman 67,613 E2
Dale 49,633 G8
Dallas 48,130 D6
De Kalb 53,658 G2
Elmore 49,210 F5
Escambia 35,518 D8
Etowah 99,840 F2
Fayette 17,962 C3
Franklin 27,814 C2
Geneva 23,647 G8
Greene 10,153 C5
Hale 15,498 C5
Henry 15,374 H7
Houston 81,331 H8
Jackson 47,796 F1
Jefferson 651,525 E3
Lamar 15,715 B3
Lauderdale 79,661 C1
Lawrence 31,513 D1
Lee 87,146 H5
Limestone 54,135 E1
Lowndes 12,658 E6
Macon 24,928 G6
Madison 238,912 E1
Marengo 23,084 C6
Marion 29,830 C2
Marshall 70,832 F2
Mobile 378,643 B9
Monroe 23,968 D7
Montgomery 209,085 F6
Morgan 100,043 E2
Perry 12,759 D5
Pickens 20,699 B4
Pike 27,595 G7
Randolph 19,881 H4
Russell 46,860 H6
Saint Clair 41,205 F3
Shelby 99,358 E4
Sumter 16,174 B5
Talladega 74,107 F4
Tallapoosa 38,826 G5
Tuscaloosa 150,522 C4
Walker 67,670 D3
Washington 16,694 B8
Wilcox 13,568 D7
Winston 22,053 D2

CITIES and TOWNS

Abbeville▲ 3,173 H7
Abernant 405 D4
Adamsville 4,161 D3
Addison 626 D2
Adger 400 D4
Akron 468 C5
Alabaster 14,732 E4
Albertville 14,507 F2
Aldrich 500 E4
Alexander City 14,917 G5
Alexandria 600 G3
Aliceville 3,009 B4
Allgood 464 F3
Allsboro 300 B1
Alma 500 C8
Altoona 960 F2
Andalusia▲ 9,269 E8
Anderson 339 D1
Anniston▲ 26,623 G3
Arab 6,321 E2
Ardmore 1,090 E1
Argo 930 E3
Ariton 743 G7
Arley 338 D2
Ashby 500 E4
Ashford 1,926 H8
Ashland▲ 2,034 G4
Ashville▲ 1,494 F3
Athens▲ 16,901 E1
Atmore 8,046 C8
Attalla 6,859 F2
Auburn 33,830 H5
Autaugaville 681 E6
Avon 462 H8
Axis 500 B9
Babbie 576 F8
Baileyton 352 E2
Baker Hill 300 H7
Banks 195 G7
Barnwell 700 C10
Bay Minette▲ 7,168 C9
Bayou La Batre 2,456 B10
Bear Creek 913 C2
Beatrice 454 D7
Beaverton 319 B3
Belgreen 500 C2
Belk 255 C3
Bellamy 700 B6
Belle Mina 675 E1
Bellwood 400 G8
Benton 48 E6
Berry 1,218 C3
Bessemer 33,497 D4
Beulah 500 H5
Billingsley 150 E5
Birmingham▲ 265,968 D3
Black 174 G8
Blountsville 1,527 E2
Blue Mountain 221 G3
Blue Springs 108 G7
Boaz 6,928 F2
Boligee 268 C5
Bon Air 91 F4
Bon Secour 850 C10
Branchville 370 F3
Brantley 1,015 F7
Brent 2,776 D5
Brewton▲ 5,885 D8
Bridgeport 2,936 G1
Brighton 4,518 D4
Brilliant 751 C2
Brookside 1,365 E3
Brookwood 658 D4
Browns 375 D6
Brownville 2,386 C4
Brundidge 2,472 G7
Butler▲ 1,872 B6
Cahaba 4,778 D6
Calera 2,136 E4
Calhoun 950 F6
Calvert 600 B8
Camden▲ 2,414 D7
Camp Hill 1,415 G5
Canoe 560 D8
Carbon Hill 2,115 D3
Cardiff 72 E3
Carolina 201 E8
Carrollton▲ 1,170 B4
Carrville 820 G5
Carson 400 C8
Castleberry 669 D8
Cedar Bluff 1,174 G2
Centre▲ 2,893 G2
Centreville▲ 2,508 D5
Chatom▲ 1,094 B8
Chelsea 1,329 E4
Cherokee 1,479 C1
Chickasaw 6,649 B9
Childersburg 4,579 F4
Choccolocco 500 G3
Choctaw 600 B6
Chrysler 400 C8
Chunchula 700 B9
Citronelle 3,671 B8
Clanton▲ 7,669 E5
Clayhatchee 411 G8
Clayton▲ 1,564 G7
Cleveland 739 E3
Clio 1,365 G7
Coaling 400 D4
Coden 600 B10
Coffee Springs 294 G8
Coffeeville 431 B7
Coker 800 C4
Collinsville 1,429 G2
Columbia 922 H8
Columbiana▲ 2,968 E4
Coosada 912 F5
Cordova 2,623 D3
Cottondale 500 D4
Cottonton 324 H6
Cottonwood 1,385 H8
County Line 124 F8
County Line 199 E3
Courtland 803 D1
Cowarts 1,400 H8
Coy 950 D7
Crane Hill 355 D2
Creola 1,896 B9
Cromwell 650 B6
Crossville 1,350 G2
Cuba 390 B6
Cullman▲ 13,367 E2
Cullomburg 325 B7
Cusseta 650 H5
Dadeville▲ 3,276 G5
Daleville 5,117 G8
Daphne 11,290 C9
Dauphin Island 824 B10
Daviston 261 G4
Dayton 77 C6
De Armanville 350 G3
Decatur▲ 48,761 D1
Demopolis 7,512 C6
Detroit 291 B2
Dolomite D4
Dora 2,214 D3
Dothan▲ 53,589 H8
Double Springs▲ 1,138 D2
Douglas 474 F2
Dozier 483 F7
Dutton 243 G1
East Brewton 2,579 E8
Eclectic 1,087 F5
Edwardsville 118 H3
Elba▲ 4,011 F8
Elberta 458 C10
Eldridge 225 C3
Elkmont 389 E1
Elmore 600 F5
Elrod 746 C4
Emelle 44 B5
Empire 600 D3
Enterprise 20,123 G8
Epes 267 B5
Ethelsville 52 B4
Eufaula 13,220 H7
Eunola 199 G8
Eutaw▲ 2,281 C5
Eva 438 E2
Evergreen▲ 3,911 E8
Excel 571 D8
Fairfield 12,200 E4
Fairhope 8,485 C10
Fairview 383 E2
Falkville 1,337 E2
Faunsdale 96 C6
Fayette▲ 4,909 C3
Five Points 200 H4
Flat Rock 750 G1
Flint City 1,033 D1
Flomaton 1,811 D8
Florala 2,075 F8
Florence▲ 36,426 C1
Foley 4,937 C10
Forestdale 10,395 E3
Forkland 667 C5
Fort Davis 500 G6
Fort Deposit 1,240 E7
Fort Mitchell 900 H6
Fort Payne▲ 11,838 G2
Fosters 400 C4
Franklin 133 G6
Franklin 152 D7
Frisco City 1,581 D8
Fruitdale 500 B8
Fruithurst 177 G3
Fulton 384 C7
Fultondale 6,400 E3
Fyffe 1,094 G2
Gadsden▲ 42,523 G2
Gainesville 449 B5
Gallant 475 F2
Gantt 265 E8
Gantt's Quarry F4
Garden City 578 E2
Gardendale 9,251 E3
Gaylesville 149 G2
Geiger 270 B5
Geneva▲ 4,681 G8
Georgiana 1,933 E7
Geraldine 801 G2
Gilbertown 235 B7
Glen Allen 350 C3
Glencoe 4,670 G3
Glenwood 208 F7
Goldville 61 G4
Good Hope 1,700 E2
Goodsprings 360 D3
Goodwater 1,840 F4
Gordo 1,918 C4
Gordon 493 H8
Gorgas 500 D3
Goshen 302 F7
Gosport 500 C7
Grand Bay 3,383 B10
Grant 638 F1
Graysville 2,241 D3
Green Pond 750 D4
Greensboro▲ 3,047 C5
Greenville▲ 7,492 E7
Grimes 443 H8
Grove Hill▲ 1,551 C7
Gu-Win 243 C3
Guin 2,464 C3
Gulf Shores 3,261 C10
Guntersville▲ 7,038 F2
Gurley 1,007 F1
Hackleburg 1,161 C2
Haleburg 97 H8
Haleyville 4,452 C2
Hamilton▲ 5,787 C2
Hammondville 420 G1
Hanceville 2,246 E2
Hardaway 600 G6
Harpersville 772 F4
Hartford 2,448 G8
Hartselle 10,795 E2
Harvest 1,922 E1
Hatchechubbee 840 H6
Hatton 950 D1
Hayden 385 E3
Hayneville▲ 969 E6
Hazel Green 2,208 E1
Headland 3,266 H8
Heath 182 F8
Heflin▲ 2,906 G3
Heiberger 310 D5
Helena 3,918 E4
Henagar 1,934 G1
Higdon 925 G1
Highland Lake 304 F3
Hillsboro 587 D1
Hobson City 794 G3
Hodges 272 C2
Hokes Bluff 3,739 G3
Hollins 500 F4
Holly Pond 602 E2
Hollywood 916 G1
Holt 4,125 D4
Holy Trinity 400 H6
Homewood 22,922 E4
Hoover 39,788 E4
Hope Hull 975 F6
Horn Hill 186 F8
Hueytown 15,280 D4
Huntsville▲ 159,789 E1
Hurtsboro 707 H6
Hytop 350 F1
Ider 671 G1
Inverness 2,528 G6
Irondale 9,454 E3
Jack 5,819 F7
Jackson 789 C8
Jacksons Gap 800 G5
Jacksonville 10,283 G3
Jasper▲ 13,553 D3
Jemison 1,898 E5
Kansas 230 C3
Kellyton 375 F5
Kennedy 523 B3
Key 400 G2
Killen 1,047 D1
Kimberly 1,096 E3
Kinsey 1,670 H8
Kinston 595 F8
Laceys Spring 400 E1
Lafayette▲ 3,151 H5
Lakeview 166 G2
Lanett 8,985 H5
Langdale 2,034 H5
Langston 207 G1
Larkinsville 425 F1
Lavaca 500 B6
Leeds 9,946 E3
Leesburg 218 G2
Leighton 988 D1
Leroy 699 B8
Lester 89 D1
Level Plains 1,473 G8
Lexington 821 D1
Libertyville 133 F8
Lillian 350 D10
Lincoln 2,941 F3
Linden▲ 2,548 C6
Lineville 2,394 G4
Lipscomb 2,892 E4
Lisman 481 B6
Little River 400 C8
Little Shawmut 2,793 H5
Littleville 925 C1
Livingston▲ 3,530 B5
Loachapoka 259 G5
Lockhart 484 F8
Locust Fork 342 E3
Longview 475 E4
Louisville 728 G7
Lower Peach Tree 926 C7
Lowndesboro 139 E6
Loxley 1,161 C9
Luverne▲ 2,555 F7
Lynn 611 C2
Madison 14,904 E1
Madrid 211 H8
Magnolia Springs 800 C10
Malvern 570 G8
Manchester 400 D3
Maplesville 725 E5
Margaret 616 F3
Marion Junction 400 D6
Marion▲ 4,211 D5
Maylene 500 E4
McCalla 657 E4
McCullough 500 D8
McIntosh 250 B8
McKenzie 464 E7
McWilliams 306 D7
Memphis 54 B4
Mentone 474 G1
Meridianville 2,852 F1
Midfield 5,559 E4
Midland City 1,819 H8
Midway 455 H6
Mignon 1,548 F4
Millbrook 6,050 F6
Millerville 345 G4
Millport 1,203 B3
Millry 781 B7
Minter 450 D6
Mobile▲ 196,278 B9
Monroeville▲ 6,993 D7
Monrovia 500 E1
Montevallo 4,239 E4
Montgomery (cap.)▲ 187,106 F6
Montrose 750 C9
Moody 4,921 F3
Mooresville 54 E1
Morris 1,136 E3
Morvin 355 C7
Moulton▲ 3,248 D2
Moundville 1,348 C5
Mount Vernon 902 B8
Mountain Brook 19,810 E4
Mountainboro 261 F2
Munford 700 F3
Muscle Shoals 9,611 C1
Myrtlewood 197 C6
Nanafalia 500 B6
Napier Field 462 H8
Nauvoo 240 D3
Nectar 238 E3
Needham 99 B7
New Brockton 1,184 G8
New Hope 2,248 F1
New Market 1,094 F1
New Site 669 G4
Newbern 222 C5
Newton 1,580 G8
Newville 531 H8
North Johns 177 D4
Northport 17,366 C4
Notasulga 979 G5
Oak Grove 436 B9
Oak Grove 638 F4
Oak Hill 28 D7
Oakman 846 D3
Odenville 796 F3
Ohatchee 1,042 G3
Onoonta▲ 1,844 E3
Onycha 150 F8
Opelika▲ 22,122 H5
Opp 6,985 F8
Orange Beach 2,253 C10
Orrville 234 D6
Owens Cross Roads 695 E1
Oxford 9,362 G3
Ozark▲ 12,922 G8
Paint Rock 214 F1
Parrish 1,433 D3
Pelham 9,765 E4
Pell City▲ 8,118 F3
Pennington 302 B6
Perdido 500 C8
Peterman 600 D7
Peterson D4
Petrey 80 F7
Phenix City▲ 25,312 H6
Phil Campbell 1,317 C2
Pickensville 169 B4
Piedmont 5,288 G3
Pinckard 618 G8
Pine Apple 365 E7
Pine Hill 481 C7
Pinson 10,987 E3
Pisgah 652 G1
Plantersville 650 E5
Pleasant Grove 8,458 D4
Point Clear 2,125 C10
Pollard 100 D8
Powell's Crossroads 636 G1
Prattville▲ 19,587 E6
Priceville 1,323 E1
Prichard 34,311 B9
Providence 307 C6
Ragland 1,807 F3
Rainbow City 7,673 F3
Rainsville 3,875 G2
Ramer 680 F6
Ranburne 447 H3
Red Bay 3,451 B2
Red Level 588 E8
Reece City 657 G2
Reform 2,105 C4
Remlap 800 E3
Renfroe 400 F4
Repton 293 D8
Republic 500 E3
River Falls 710 E8

(continued on following page)

Agriculture, Industry and Resources

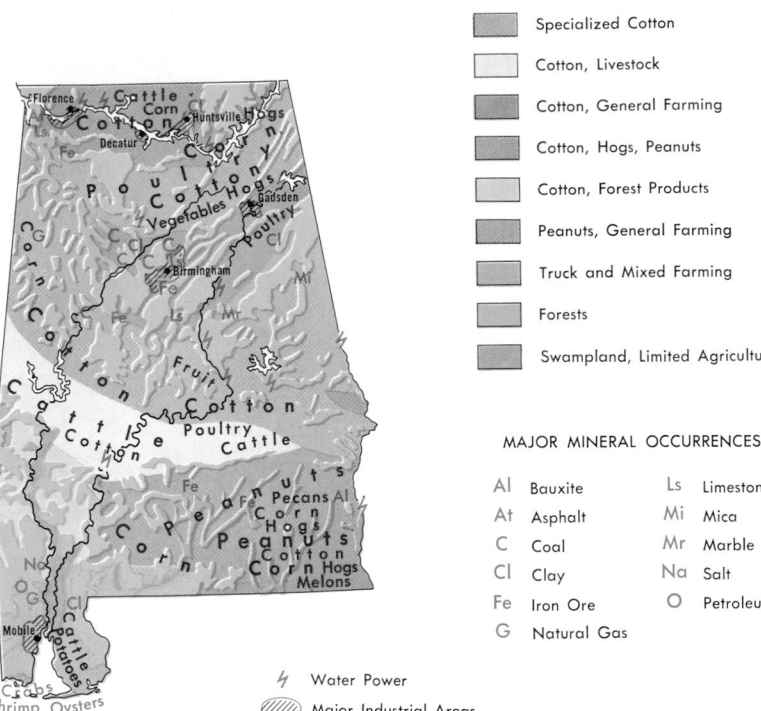

DOMINANT LAND USE

- Specialized Cotton
- Cotton, Livestock
- Cotton, General Farming
- Cotton, Hogs, Peanuts
- Cotton, Forest Products
- Peanuts, General Farming
- Truck and Mixed Farming
- Forests
- Swampland, Limited Agriculture

MAJOR MINERAL OCCURRENCES

Al	Bauxite	Ls	Limestone
At	Asphalt	Mi	Mica
C	Coal	Mr	Marble
Cl	Clay	Na	Salt
Fe	Iron Ore	O	Petroleum
G	Natural Gas		

⚡ Water Power

▨ Major Industrial Areas

Topography

0   30   60 MI.
0   30   60 KM.

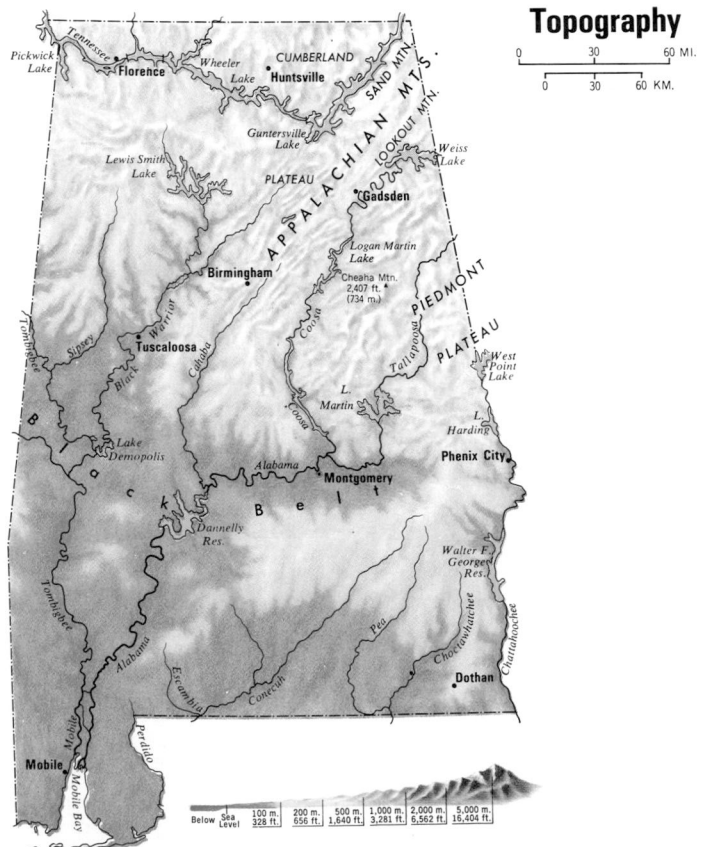

Below Sea Level | 100 m. 328 ft. | 200 m. 656 ft. | 500 m. 1,640 ft. | 1,000 m. 3,281 ft. | 2,000 m. 6,562 ft. | 5,000 m. 16,404 ft.

Agriculture, Industry and Resources

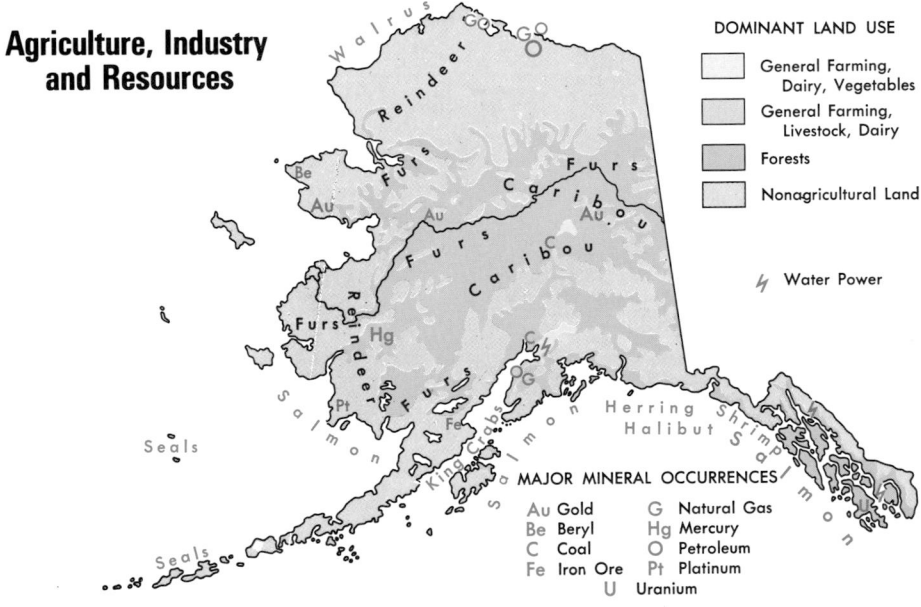

DOMINANT LAND USE

General Farming, Dairy, Vegetables

General Farming, Livestock, Dairy

Forests

Nonagricultural Land

⚡ Water Power

MAJOR MINERAL OCCURRENCES

Au Gold
Be Beryl
C Coal
Fe Iron Ore
G Natural Gas
Hg Mercury
O Petroleum
Pt Platinum
U Uranium

Topography

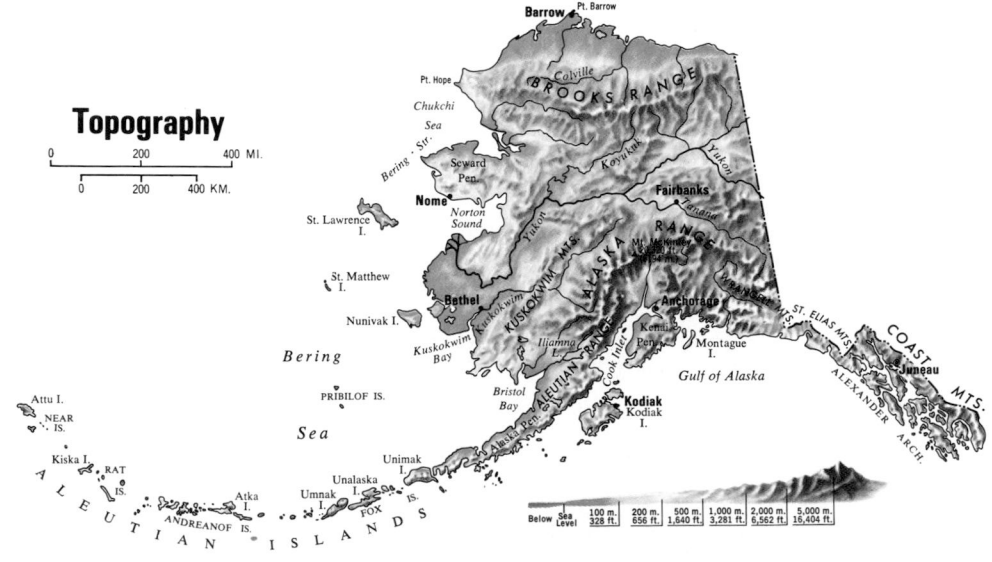

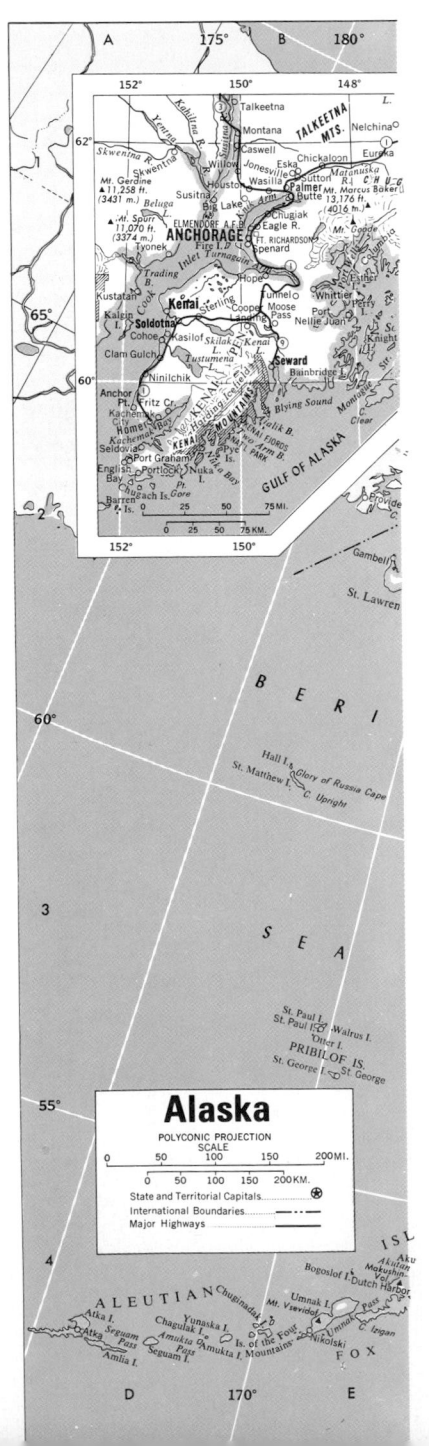

Alaska

POLYCONIC PROJECTION

SCALE

State and Territorial Capitals ....⊛
International Boundaries ....--·--·--
Major Highways

Marmot (isl.) H3	Port Clarence (inlet) E1	Shemya (isl.) J3	Tugidak (isl.) G3
Matanuska (riv.) C1	Port Heiden (inlet) G3	Shishaldin (vol.) E4	Turnagain Arm (inlet) B1
McKinley (mt.) H2	Portland Canal (inlet) N2	Shumagin (isl.) G4	Tustumena (lake) C1
Meade (riv.) G1	Port Moller (inlet) F3	Shuyak (isl.) H3	Two Arm (bay) C2
Mendenhall (cape) E3	Port Wells (inlet) C1	Sitka (sound) M1	Ugashik (lakes) G3
Mentasta (pass) K2	Pribilof (isls.) D3	Sitka Nat'l Hist. Park M1	Umnak (isl.) C4
Merrill (pass) H2	Prince of Wales (cape) E1	Sitkinak (str.) H3	Umnak (passage) E4
Michelson (mt.) K1	Prince of Wales (isl.) N2	Skilak (lake) C1	Unalaska (isl.) E4
Middleton (isl.) J3	Prince William (sound) D1	Skwentna (riv.) A1	Unga (isl.) E4
Misty Fjords Nat'l Mon. N2	Prudhoe (bay) J1	Smith (bay) H1	Unimak (isl.) E4
Mitkof (isl.) N2	Rat (isls.) K4	Spencer (cape) L1	Unimak (passage) E4
Montague (isl.) D1	Redoubt (vol.) H2	Stephens (passage) N1	Utukok (riv.) F1
Muir (glac.) M1	Revillagigedo (chan.) N2	Stevenson Entrance (str.) H3	Valley of Ten
Mulchatna (riv.) G2	Revillagigedo (isl.) N2	Stikine (riv.) N2	Thousand Smokes G3
Muzon (cape) M2	Romanzof (cape) E2	Stikine (str.) N2	Vancouver (mt.) L2
Naknek (lake) G3	Sagavanirktok (riv.) J1	Stony (riv.) G2	Veniaminof (crater) F3
Near (isls.) J4	Saint Elias (cape) K3	Stuart (isl.) F2	Vsevidof (mt.) E4
Nelson (isl.) E2	Saint Elias (mt.) K2	Suemez (isl.) M2	Walrus (mt.) E3
Newenham (cape) F1	Saint George (isl.) D3	Sumner (str.) M2	Walrus (isls.) F3
Noatak (riv.) F1	Saint Lawrence (isl.) C2	Susitna (riv.) B1	Waring (mts.) G1
Norton (bay) E2	Saint Matthew (isl.) D2	Sutwik (isl.) G3	West Point (mt.) K2
Norton (sound) E2	Saint Paul (isl.) D3	Taku (glac.) N1	White (mt.) K2
Nowitna (riv.) H2	Salisbury (sound) M1	Taku (riv.) N1	White (pass) N1
Nuka (bay) C2	Sanak (isl.) F4	Talkeetna (mts.) J2	White Mountains Nat'l
Nunivak (isl.) E3	Sanford (mt.) K2	Tanaga (isl.) K4	Rec .Area J1
Nushagak (riv.) G2	Schwatka (mts.) G1	Tanaga (vol.) K4	Witherspoon (mt.) C1
Nuyakuk (lake) F3	Seguam (isl.) D4	Tanana (riv.) J2	Wrangell (cape) H3
Ommaney (cape) M2	Selawik (lake) F1	Taylor (mts.) G2	Wrangell (isl.) N2
Otter (isl.) D3	Semichi (isls.) J3	Tazlina (lake) D1	Wrangell (mt.) K2
Pastol (bay) F2	Semidi (isls.) G3	Tazlina (riv.) D1	Wrangell-St. Elias Nat'l Park ..K2
Pavlof (bay) F3	Semisopochnoi (isl.) K4	Teshekpuk (lake) H1	Yakobi (isl.) M1
Pavlof (vol.) F3	Seward (pen.) E1	Tigalda (isl.) F4	Yakutat (bay) K3
Philip Smith (mts.) J1	Sheenjek (riv.) K1	Tikchik (lakes) G2	Yentna (riv.) A1
Porcupine (riv.) K1	Shelikof (str.) H3	Togiak (bay) F3	Yukon (riv.) F2

AREA 591,004 sq. mi. (1,530,700 sq. km.)
POPULATION 551,947
CAPITAL Juneau
LARGEST CITY Anchorage
HIGHEST POINT Mt. McKinley 20,320 ft. (6194 m.)
SETTLED IN 1801
ADMITTED TO UNION January 3, 1959
POPULAR NAME Great Land; Last Frontier
STATE FLOWER Forget-me-not
STATE BIRD Willow Ptarmigan

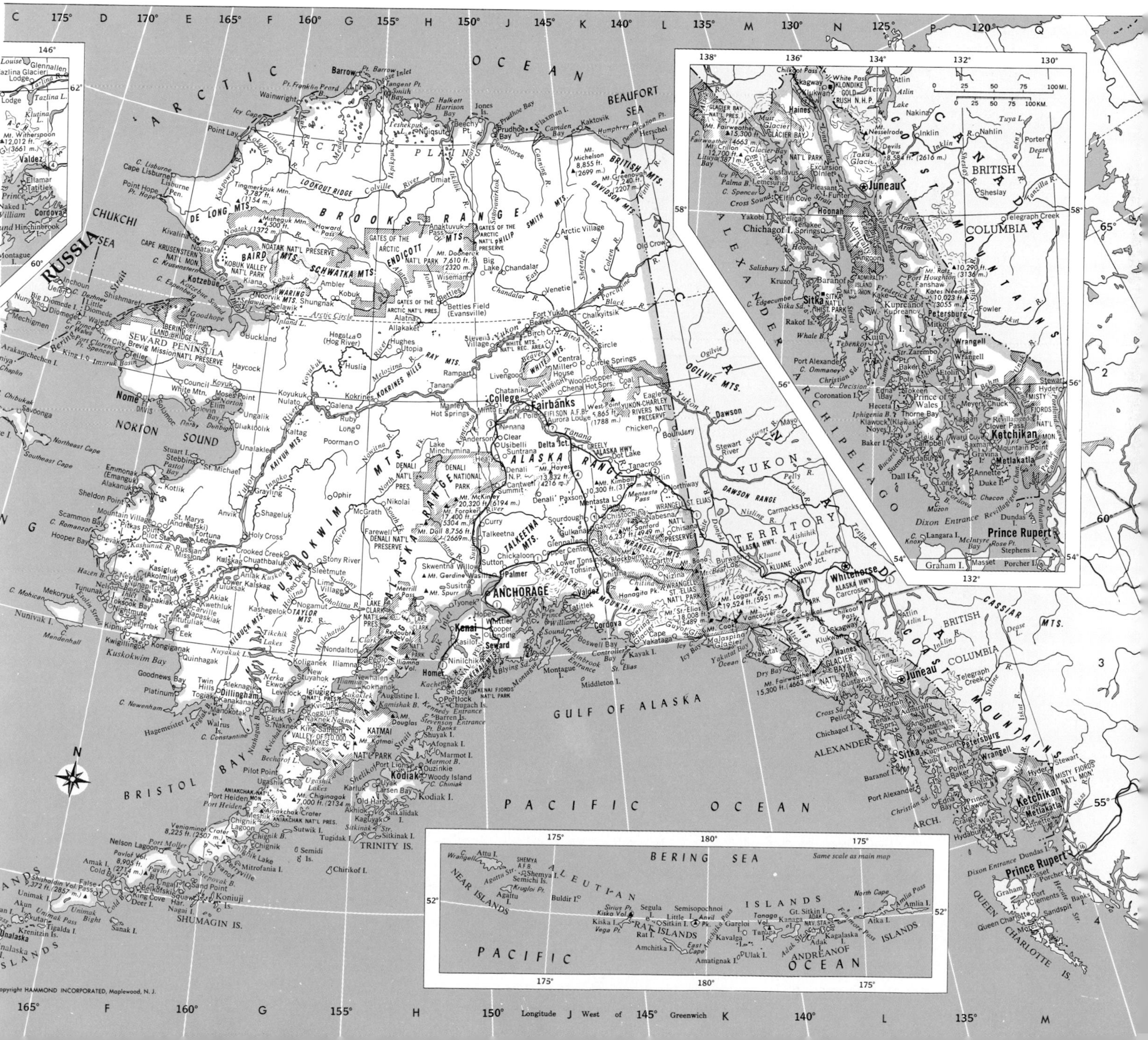

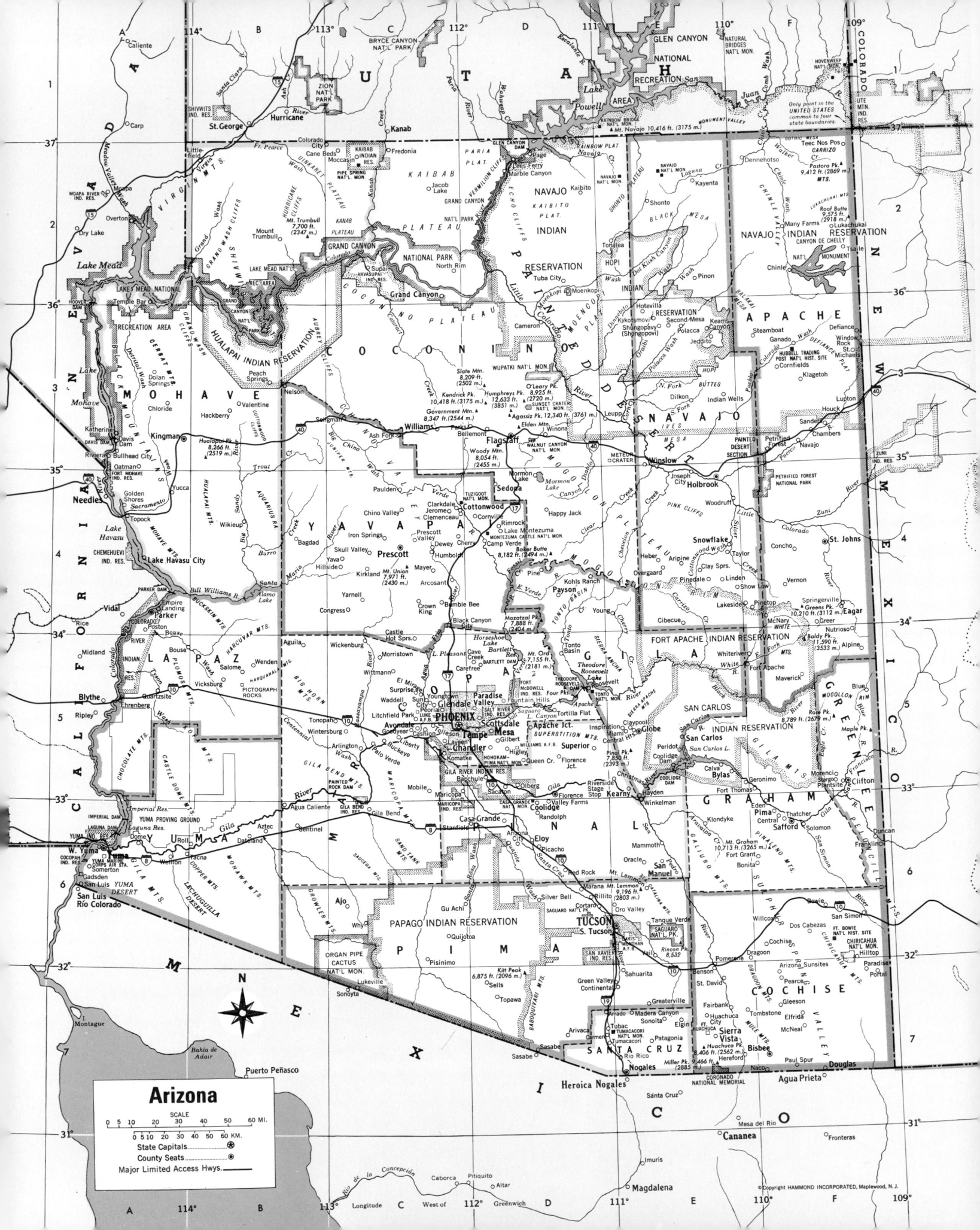

Arizona

SCALE

0 5 10   20   30   40   50   60 MI.

0 5 10 20 30 40 50 60 KM.

State Capitals ⊛
County Seats ⊙
Major Limited Access Hwys. ▬▬▬

© Copyright HAMMOND INCORPORATED, Maplewood, N.J.

Arizona 199

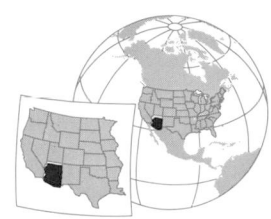

AREA 114,000 sq. mi. (295,260 sq. km.)
POPULATION 3,677,985
CAPITAL Phoenix
LARGEST CITY Phoenix
HIGHEST POINT Humphreys Pk. 12,633 ft. (3851 m.)
SETTLED IN 1752
ADMITTED TO UNION February 14, 1912
POPULAR NAME Grand Canyon State
STATE FLOWER Saguaro Cactus Blossom
STATE BIRD Cactus Wren

Agriculture, Industry and Resources

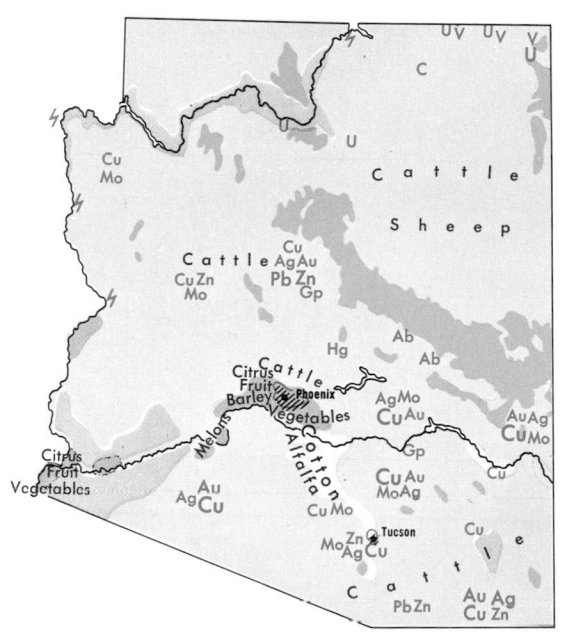

MAJOR MINERAL OCCURRENCES

Ab	Asbestos	Cu	Copper	Pb	Lead
Ag	Silver	Gp	Gypsum	U	Uranium
Au	Gold	Hg	Mercury	V	Vanadium
C	Coal	Mo	Molybdenum	Zn	Zinc

DOMINANT LAND USE

- Fruit, Truck and Mixed Farming
- Cotton and Alfalfa
- General Farming, Livestock, Special Crops
- Range Livestock
- Forests
- Nonagricultural Land

⚡ Water Power
〰 Major Industrial Areas

COUNTIES

Apache 61,591	F3
Cochise 97,624	F7
Coconino 96,591	C3
Gila 40,216	E5
Graham 26,554	E6
Greenlee 8,008	F5
La Paz 13,844	A5
Maricopa 2,122,101	C5
Mohave 93,497	A3
Navajo 77,658	E3
Pima 666,880	D6
Pinal 116,379	D6
Santa Cruz 29,676	E7
Yavapai 107,714	C4
Yuma 106,895	A5

CITIES and TOWNS

Agua Caliente 60	B6
Aguila 900	B5
Ajo 2,919	C6
Alpine 450	F5
Amado 75	D7
Apache Junction 18,100	D5
Arcosanti	C4
Aripine 25	E4
Arivaca 400	D7
Arizona City 1,940	D6
Arizona Sunsites 825	F7
Arlington 950	C5
Ash Fork 800	C3
Avondale 16,169	C5
Aztec 20	B6
Bagdad 1,858	B4
Bapchule 400	D5

Bellemont 210	D3
Benson 3,824	E7
Bisbee▲ 6,288	F7
Black Canyon City 1,811	C4
Blue 50	F5
Bonita 20	E6
Bouse 500	A5
Bowie 600	F6
Buckeye 5,038	C5
Bullhead City (Bullhead City-Riviera) 21,951	A3
Bumble Bee 15	C4
Bylas 1,219	E5
Calva 10	E5
Cameron 493	D3
Camp Verde 6,243	D4
Cane Beds 30	B2
Carefree 1,666	C5
Carmen 200	D7
Casa Grande 19,082	D6
Cashion 3,014	C5
Castle Hot Springs 50	C5
Cave Creek 2,925	D5
Central 300	F6
Central Heights (Central Heights-Midland City) 2,791	E5
Chambers 500	F3
Chandler 90,533	D5
Cherry 20	C4
Chinle 5,059	F2
Chino Valley 4,837	C4
Chloride 225	A3
Christmas 201	E5
Cibecue 1,254	E4
Clarkdale 2,144	C4

Clay Springs 500	E4
Claypool 1,942	E5
Clemenceau 300	C4
Clifton▲ 2,840	F5
Cochise 150	F6
Colorado City 2,426	B2
Concho 100	F4
Congress 800	C4
Continental 250	D7
Coolidge 6,927	D6
Coolidge Dam 42	E5
Cornfields 200	F3
Cornville 2,089	D4
Cortaro 375	D6
Cottonwood 5,918	D4
Crown King 100	C4
Dateland 100	B6
Davis Dam 125	A3
Dennehotso 616	F2
Dewey 100	C4
Dilkon 90	E3
Dolan Springs 1,090	A3
Dome 48	A6
Dos Cabezas 30	F6
Douglas 12,822	F7
Dragoon 150	F6
Duncan 662	F6
Eagar 4,025	F4
Eden 89	F6
Ehrenberg 1,226	A5
El Mirage 5,001	C5
Elfrida 700	F7
Elgin 525	E7
Eloy 7,211	D6
Empire Landing	A4
Fairbank 100	E7
Flagstaff 45,857	D3

(continued on following page)

Topography

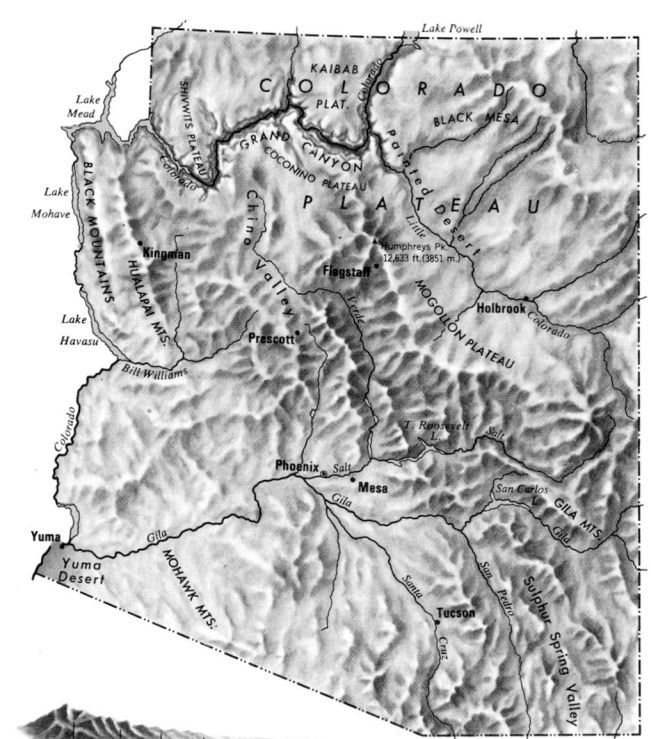

| 5,000 m. 16,404 ft. | 2,000 m. 6,562 ft. | 1,000 m. 3,281 ft. | 500 m. 1,640 ft. | 200 m. 656 ft. | 100 m. 328 ft. | Sea Level | Below |

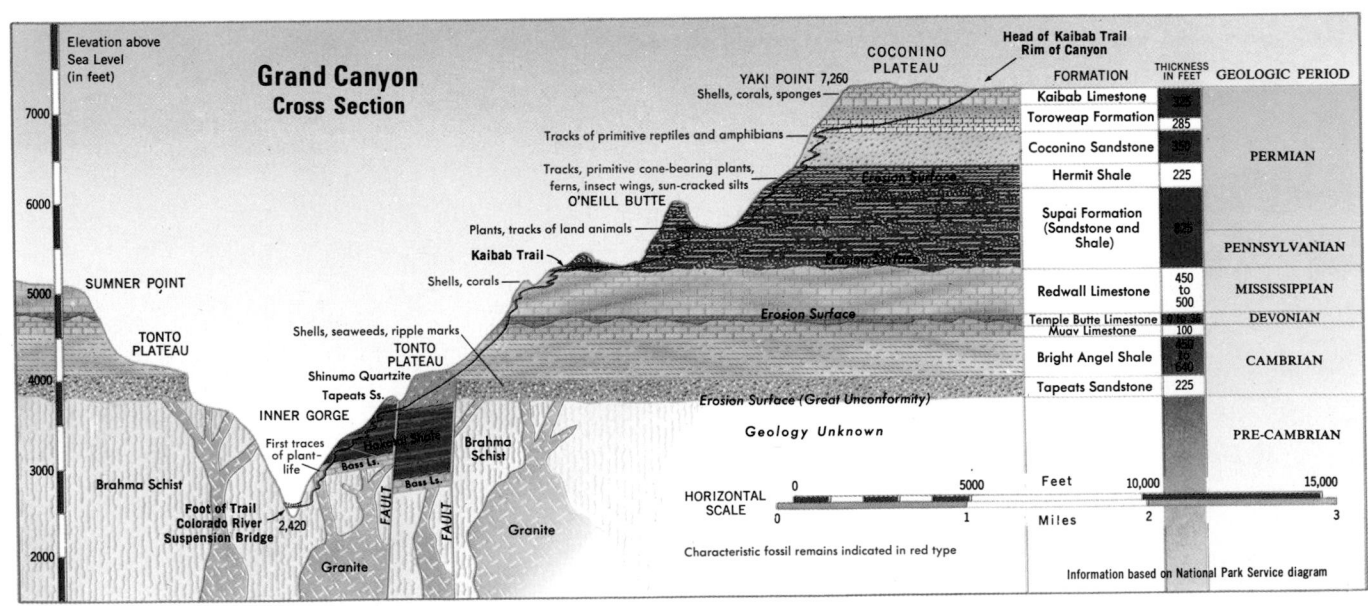

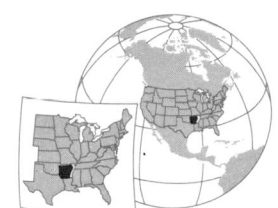

AREA 53,187 sq. mi. (137,754 sq. km.)
POPULATION 2,362,239
CAPITAL Little Rock
LARGEST CITY Little Rock
HIGHEST POINT Magazine Mtn. 2,753 ft. (839 m.)
SETTLED IN 1685
ADMITTED TO UNION June 15, 1836
POPULAR NAME Land of Opportunity
STATE FLOWER Apple Blossom
STATE BIRD Mockingbird

Agriculture, Industry and Resources

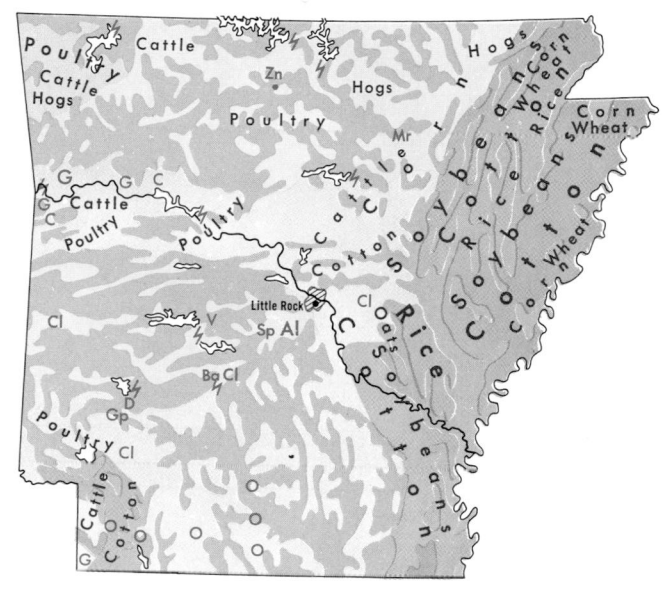

COUNTIES

Arkansas 21,653	H5
Ashley 24,319	G7
Baxter 31,186	F1
Benton 97,499	B1
Boone 28,297	D1
Bradley 11,793	F7
Calhoun 5,826	E6
Carroll 18,654	C1
Chicot 15,713	H7
Clark 21,437	D5
Clay 18,107	K1
Cleburne 19,411	F2
Cleveland 7,781	F6
Columbia 25,691	D7
Conway 19,151	E3
Craighead 68,956	J2
Crawford 42,493	B2
Crittenden 49,939	K3
Cross 19,225	J3
Dallas 9,614	E6
Desha 16,798	H6
Drew 17,369	G6
Faulkner 60,006	F3
Franklin 14,897	C2
Fulton 10,037	G1
Garland 73,397	D4
Grant 13,948	F5
Greene 31,804	J1
Hempstead 21,621	C6
Hot Spring 26,115	E5
Howard 13,569	C5
Independence 31,192	G2
Izard 11,364	G1
Jackson 18,944	H2
Jefferson 85,487	G5
Johnson 18,221	C2
Lafayette 9,643	C7
Lawrence 17,457	H1
Lee 13,053	J4
Lincoln 13,690	G6
Little River 13,966	B6
Logan 20,557	C3
Lonoke 39,268	G4
Madison 11,618	C1
Marion 12,001	E1
Miller 38,467	C7
Mississippi 57,525	K2
Monroe 11,333	H4
Montgomery 7,841	C4
Nevada 10,101	C6
Newton 7,666	D2
Ouachita 30,574	E6
Perry 7,969	E4
Phillips 28,838	J5
Pike 10,086	C5
Poinsett 24,664	J2
Polk 17,347	B5
Pope 45,883	D3
Prairie 9,518	G4
Pulaski 349,660	F4
Randolph 16,558	H1
Saint Francis 30,858	J3
Saline 64,183	E4
Scott 10,205	B4
Searcy 7,841	E2
Sebastian 99,590	B3
Sevier 13,637	B6
Sharp 14,109	G1
Stone 9,775	F2
Union 46,719	E7
Van Buren 14,008	E2
Washington 113,409	B2
White 54,676	G3
Woodruff 9,520	H3
Yell 17,759	D3

CITIES and TOWNS

Adona 146	E3
Alco 200	F2
Alexander 201	F4
Alicia 157	H2
Alix 225	C3
Alleene 200	B6
Allport 188	G4
Alma 2,959	B3
Almyra 311	H5
Alpena 319	D1
Altheimer 972	G5
Altus 433	C3
Amagon 108	H2
Amity 526	D5
Antoine 160	D5
Arkadelphia▲ 10,014	D5
Arkansas City▲ 523	H6
Armorel 500	L2
Ash Flat▲ 667	G1
Ashdown▲ 5,150	B6
Athens	C5
Atkins 2,834	E3
Aubrey 204	J4
Augusta▲ 2,759	H3
Austin 235	G4
Avoca 269	B1
Bald Knob 2,653	G3
Banks 88	F6

Barling 4,078	B3
Bassett 199	K2
Bates 9,187	B4
Batesville▲ 8,263	G2
Bauxite 412	F4
Bay 1,660	J2
Bearden 1,021	E6
Beaver 57	C1
Beebe 4,455	G3
Beedville 183	H3
Bella Vista 9,083	B1
Bellefonte 361	D1
Belleville 390	D3
Ben Lomond 157	B6
Benton▲ 18,177	E4
Bentonville▲ 11,257	B1
Bergman 324	E1
Berryville▲ 3,212	C1
Bethel Heights 281	B1
Bethesda 285	G2
Big Flat 93	F1
Bigelow 340	E3
Biggers 337	J1
Birdsong 104	K3
Birta	D3
Biscoe 486	H4
Black Oak 277	K2
Black Rock 736	H1
Black Springs 97	C5
Blevins 253	C6
Blue Eye 38	D1
Blue Mountain 146	C3
Bluff City 227	D6
Blytheville▲ 22,906	L2
Bodcaw 161	D6
Bonanza 520	B3
Bono 1,220	J2
Booneville▲ 3,804	C3
Bradford 874	G3
Bradley 585	C7
Branch 299	C3
Brickeys	J4
Brinkley 4,234	H4
Brookland 919	J2
Bryant 5,269	F4
Buckner 325	D7
Bull Shoals 1,534	E1
Burdette 148	L2
Cabot 8,319	F4
Caddo Valley 389	D5
Caldwell 334	J3
Cale 70	D6
Calico Rock 938	F1
Calion 558	E7
Camden▲ 14,380	E6
Cammack Village 828	E4
Campbell Station 247	H2
Canfield 365	C7
Caraway 1,178	K2
Carlisle 2,253	G4
Carthage 452	E5
Casa 200	D3
Cash 214	J2
Cass 225	C2
Casscoe 297	H4
Caulksville 224	C3
Cave City 1,503	G2
Cave Springs 465	B1
Cedarville 375	B2
Center Point	C5
Centerton 491	B1
Centerville 300	D3
Central City 419	B3
Charleston▲ 2,128	B3
Cherokee Village (Cherokee Village-Hidden Valley) 4,416	G1
Cherry Hill 250	B4
Cherry Valley 659	J3
Chester 125	B2
Chidester 489	D6
Clarendon▲ 2,072	H4
Clarkedale 300	K3
Clarksville▲ 5,833	D3
Cleveland	E3
Clinton▲ 2,213	F2
Coal Hill 912	C3
College City 339	J1
Collins	J3
Colt 334	J3
Columbus 265	C6
Concord 262	G2
Conway▲ 26,481	F3
Cord 250	H2
Corinth 63	C3
Corning▲ 3,323	J1
Cotter 867	E1
Cotton Plant 1,150	H3
Cove 346	B5
Coy 142	G4
Crawfordsville 617	K3
Crossett 6,282	G7
Crystal Springs 215	D5
Curtis 300	D6
Cushman 428	G2
Daisy 122	C5
Dalark	E5
Damascus 246	F3

Danville▲ 1,585	D3
Dardanelle▲ 3,722	D3
Datto 120	J1
De Queen▲ 4,633	B5
De Valls Bluff▲ 702	H4
De Witt▲ 3,553	H5
Decatur 918	A1
Delaplaine 146	J1
Delight 311	C5
Dell 258	K2
Denning 206	C3
Dermott 4,715	H7
Des Arc▲ 2,001	G4
Diamond City 601	E1
Diaz 1,363	H2
Dierks 1,263	B5
Donaldson 300	E5
Dover 1,055	D3
Dryden	J2
Dumas 5,520	H6
Dyer 502	B3
Dyess 466	K2
Earle 3,393	K3
East Camden 783	E6
Edmondson 286	K3
El Dorado▲ 23,146	E7
Elaine 846	J5
Elkins 692	C1
Elm Springs 893	B1
Emerson 317	D7
Emmet 446	D6
England 3,351	G4
Enola 179	F3
Eudora 3,155	H7
Eureka Springs▲ 1,900	C1
Evening Shade 328	G1
Everton 150	E1
Fargo 140	H4
Farmington 1,322	B1
Fayetteville▲ 42,099	B1
Felsenthal 95	F7
Fifty-Six 156	F2
Fisher 245	J2
Flippin 1,006	E1
Fordyce▲ 4,729	F6
Foreman 1,267	B6
Formosa 224	E3
Forrest City▲ 13,364	J3
Fort Smith▲ 72,708	B3
Fouke 634	C7
Fountain Hill 195	G7
Franklin 205	G1
Fredonia (Biscoe) 484	H4
Friendship 160	E5
Fulton 269	C6
Garfield 308	C1
Garland City 415	C7
Garner 191	G3
Gassville 1,167	F1
Gateway 65	C1
Genoa 350	C7
Gentry 1,726	A1
Georgetown 126	G3
Gillett 883	H5
Gillham 210	B5
Gilmore 331	K3
Glenwood 1,354	C5
Goodwin 225	J4
Goshen 589	C1
Gosnell 3,783	K2
Gould 1,470	G6
Grady 586	G5
Grannis 507	B5
Gravelly 300	C4
Gravette 1,412	B1
Green Forest 2,050	D1
Greenbrier 2,130	F3
Greenland 757	B1
Greenway 212	K1
Greenwood▲ 3,984	B3
Greers Ferry 724	F2
Griffithville 237	G3
Grubbs 528	H2
Guion 93	G2
Gum Springs 157	D5
Gurdon 2,199	D6
Guy 241	F3
Hackett 490	B3
Halley	H6
Hamburg▲ 3,098	G7
Hampton▲ 1,562	F6
Hardy 538	H1
Harrell 258	F6
Harrisburg▲ 1,943	J2
Harrison▲ 9,922	D1
Hartford 721	B3
Hartman 498	C3
Haskell 1,342	E4
Hatfield 414	B5
Havana 358	D3
Haynes 258	J4
Hazen 1,668	G4
Heber Springs▲ 5,628	G2
Hector 478	E3
Helena▲ 7,491	J4
Hensley 500	F4
Hermitage 639	F7
Hickory Ridge 436	J3

DOMINANT LAND USE

- Fruit and Mixed Farming
- Specialized Cotton
- Cotton, General Farming
- Rice, General Farming
- General Farming, Livestock, Truck Farming, Cotton
- Forests
- Swampland, Limited Agriculture

MAJOR MINERAL OCCURRENCES

Al	Bauxite		Gp	Gypsum
Ba	Barite		Mr	Marble
C	Coal		O	Petroleum
Cl	Clay		Sp	Soapstone
D	Diamonds		V	Vanadium
G	Natural Gas		Zn	Zinc
⚡	Water Power			Major Industrial Areas

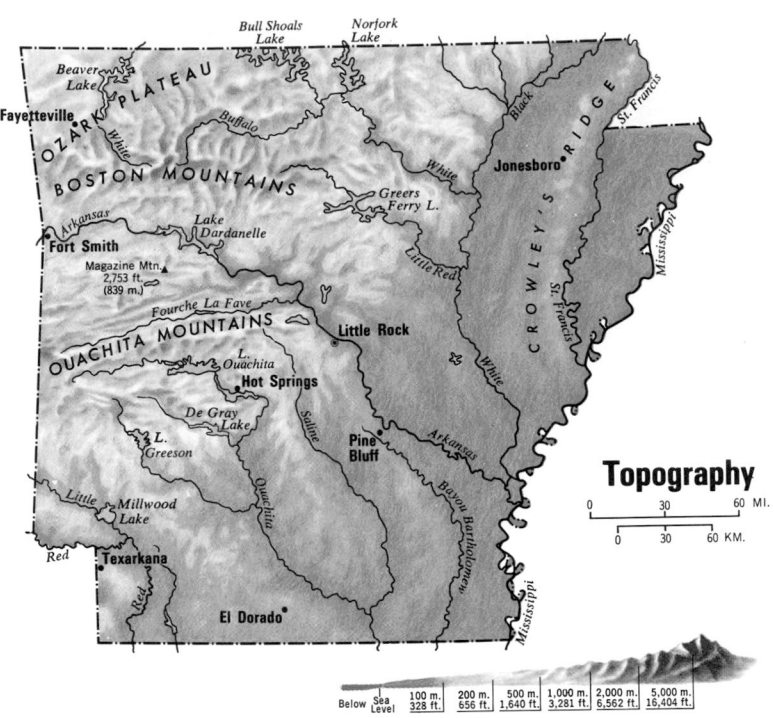

Topography

0 30 60 MI.

0 30 60 KM.

Below Sea Level	100 m. 328 ft.	200 m. 656 ft.	500 m. 1,640 ft.	1,000 m. 3,281 ft.	2,000 m. 6,562 ft.	5,000 m. 16,404 ft.

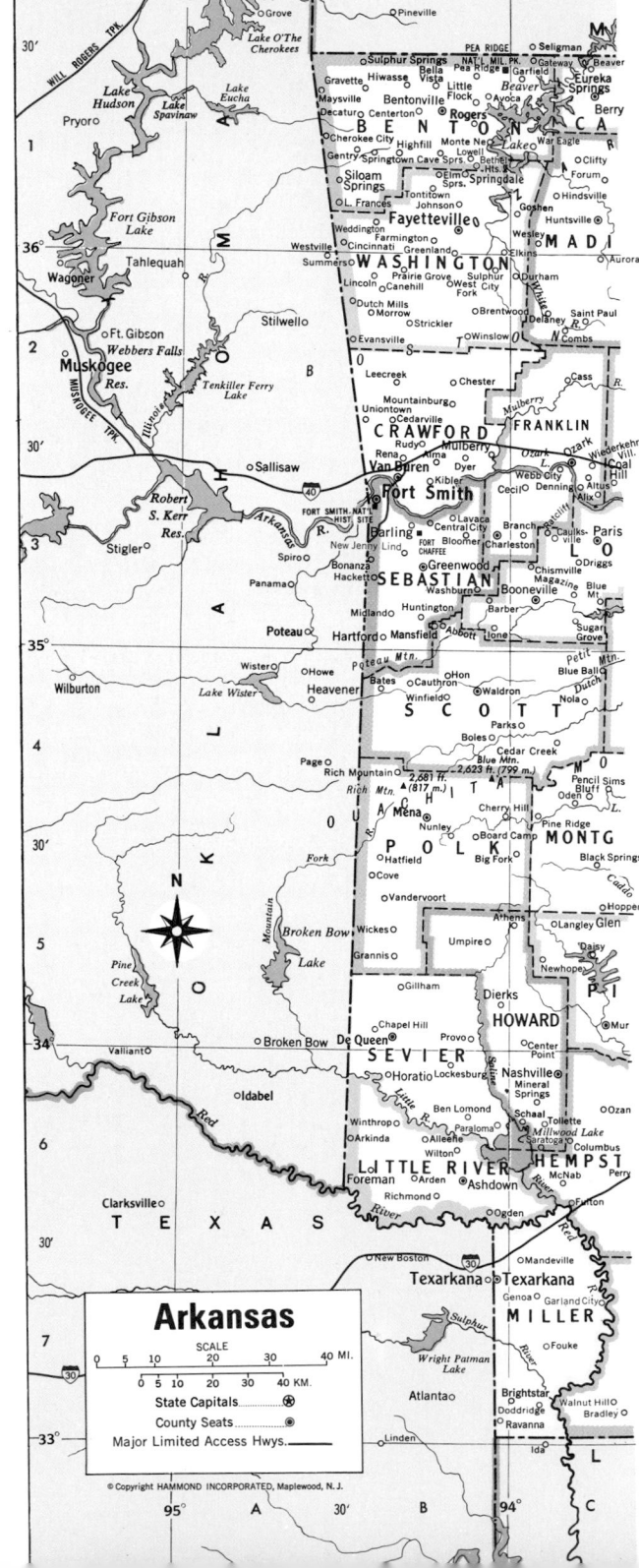

Arkansas

SCALE

0 5 10 20 30 40 MI.

0 5 10 20 30 40 KM.

State Capitals .... ⊛
County Seats .... ⊙
Major Limited Access Hwys. _____

© Copyright HAMMOND INCORPORATED, Maplewood, N.J.

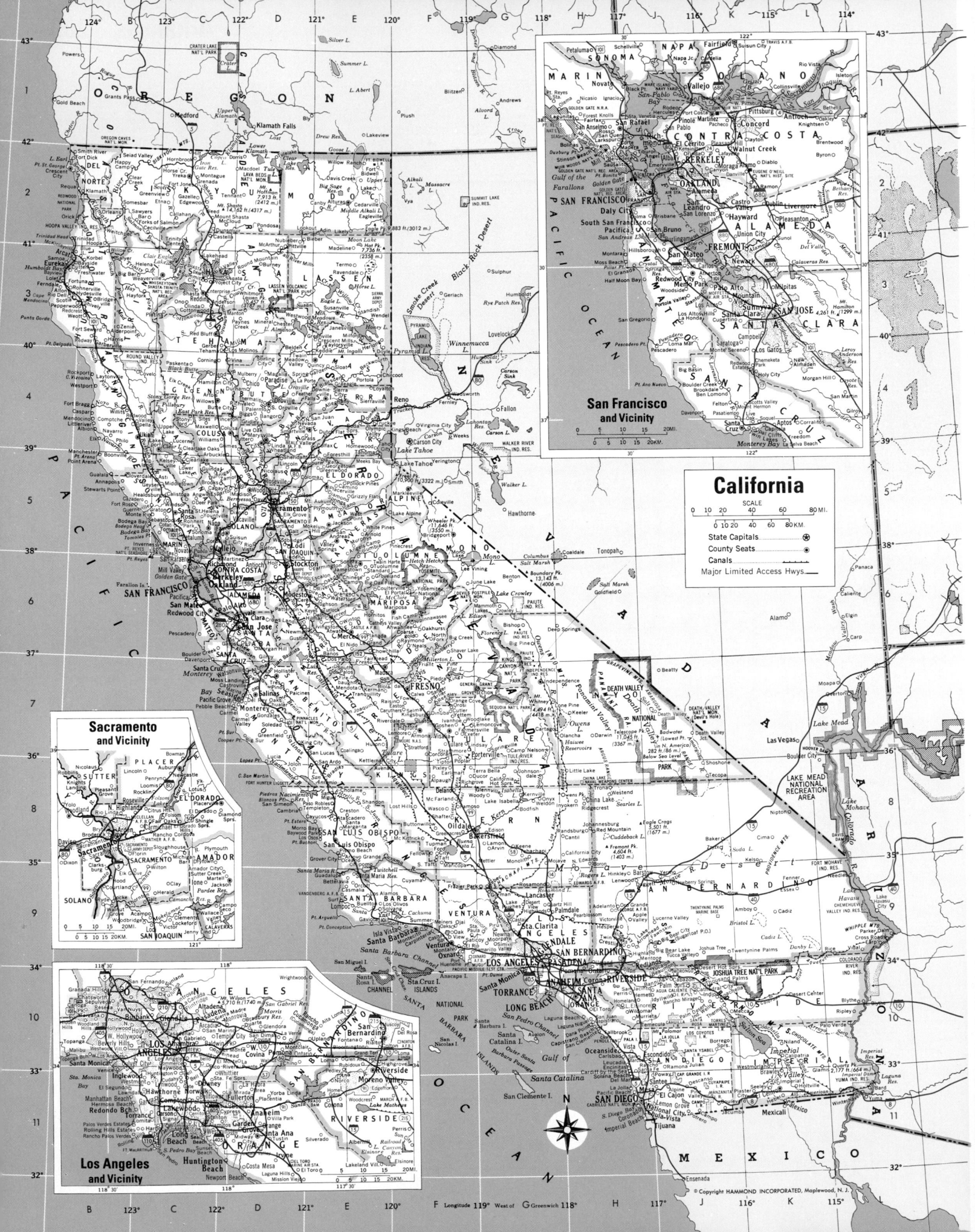

California

SCALE

0 10 20   40   60   80 MI.

0 10 20 40   60   80 KM.

State Capitals .... ⊛

County Seats .... ⊛

Canals ....

Major Limited Access Hwys. _____

San Francisco and Vicinity

0   5 10 15 20 MI.

0 5 10 15 20 KM.

Sacramento and Vicinity

0 5 10 15 20KM.

Los Angeles and Vicinity

0   5   10   15   20MI.

0 5 10 15 20 KM.

© Copyright HAMMOND INCORPORATED, Maplewood, N.J.

Longitude 119° West of Greenwich 118°

CALIFORNIA REPUBLIC

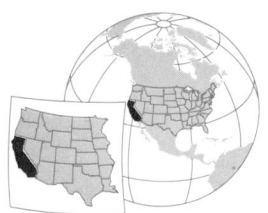

AREA 158,706 sq. mi. (411,049 sq. km.)
POPULATION 29,839,250
CAPITAL Sacramento
LARGEST CITY Los Angeles
HIGHEST POINT Mt. Whitney 14,494 ft.
(4418 m.)
SETTLED IN 1769
ADMITTED TO UNION September 9, 1850
POPULAR NAME Golden State
STATE FLOWER Golden Poppy
STATE BIRD California Valley Quail

COUNTIES

Alameda 1,279,182 ....D6
Alpine 1,113 ....F5
Amador 30,039 ....E5
Butte 182,120 ....D4
Calaveras 31,998 ....E5
Colusa 16,275 ....C4
Contra Costa 803,732 ....D6
Del Norte 23,460 ....B2
El Dorado 125,995 ....E5
Fresno 667,490 ....E7
Glenn 24,798 ....C4
Humboldt 119,118 ....B3
Imperial 109,303 ....K1
Inyo 18,281 ....H7
Kern 543,477 ....G8
Kings 101,469 ....E8
Lake 50,631 ....E3
Lassen 27,598 ....E3
Los Angeles
8,863,164 ....G9
Madera 88,090 ....F6
Marin 230,096 ....C5
Mariposa 14,302 ....F6
Mendocino 80,345 ....B4
Merced 178,403 ....E6
Modoc 9,678 ....E2
Mono 9,956 ....F6
Monterey 355,660 ....D7
Napa 110,765 ....C5
Nevada 78,510 ....E4
Orange 2,410,556 ....H9
Placer 172,796 ....E4
Plumas 19,739 ....E4
Riverside 1,170,413 ....J1
Sacramento 1,041,219 ....D5
San Benito 36,697 ....D7
San Bernardino 1,418,380 .....J9
San Diego 2,498,016 ....J1
San Francisco 723,959 ....J2
San Joaquin 480,628 ....D5
San Luis Obispo 217,162 ......E8
San Mateo 649,623 ....J3
Santa Barbara 369,608 ....F9
Santa Clara 1,497,577 ....D6
Santa Cruz 229,734 ....C6
Shasta 147,036 ....C3
Sierra 3,318 ....E4
Siskiyou 43,531 ....C2
Solano 340,421 ....D5
Sonoma 388,222 ....C5
Stanislaus 370,522 ....D6
Sutter 64,415 ....D4
Tehama 49,625 ....C3
Trinity 13,063 ....B3
Tulare 311,921 ....F7
Tuolumne 48,456 ....F5
Ventura 669,016 ....F9
Yolo 141,092 ....D5
Yuba 58,228 ....D4

CITIES and TOWNS

Adelanto 8,517 ....H9
Alameda 76,459 ....J2
Alamo 12,277 ....K2
Albany 16,327 ....J2
Alhambra 82,106 ....C10
Alpine 9,695 ....J11
Alta Loma E10
Altadena 42,658 ....C10
Alturas▲ 3,231 ....E2
Amador City 196 ....C9
Anaheim 266,406 ....D11
Anderson 8,299 ....C3
Angels Camp 2,302 ....E5
Angwin 3,503 ....C5
Antioch 62,195 ....L1
Apple Valley 46,079 ....H9
Aptos 9,061 ....K4
Arbuckle 1,912 ....C4
Arcadia 48,290 ....C10
Arcata 15,197 ....A3
Arden-Arcade 92,040 ....B8
Armona 3,122 ....E7
Arnold 3,788 ....E5
Aromas 2,275 ....D7
Arroyo Grande 14,378 ....E8
Artesia 15,464 ....C11
Arvin 9,286 ....G8
Ashland 16,590 ....K2
Asti 75 ....C5
Atascadero 23,138 ....E8
Atherton 7,163 ....K3
Atwater 22,282 ....E6
Auberry 1,866 ....F6
Auburn▲ 10,592 ....E4
Avalon 2,918 ....G10
Avenal 9,770 ....E8
Azusa 41,333 ....D10
Baker 174,820 ....J8
Bakersfield▲ 105,611 ....G0
Baldwin Park 69,330 ....D10
Banning 20,570 ....J10
Barstow 21,472 ....I9
Bayview 1,318 ....A3
Baywood Park (Baywood Park–
Los Osos) 10,933 ....E8
Beaumont 9,685 ....J10
Bell 34,365 ....C11
Bell Gardens 42,355 ....C11
Bellflower 61,815 ....C11
Belmont 24,127 ....J3
Belvedere 2,147 ....H2
Ben Lomond 7,884 ....K4
Benicia 24,437 ....K1
Berkeley 102,724 ....J2
Bethel Island 2,115 ....L1
Beverly Hills 31,971 ....B10
Big Bear City (Sugarloaf
Post Office) 4,920 ....J10
Big Bear Lake 5,351 ....J9

Big Pine 1,158 ....G6
Biggs 1,581 ....D4
Bishop 3,475 ....G6
Bloomington 15,116 ....E10
Blue Lake 1,235 ....B3
Blythe 8,428 ....L10
Bodfish 1,283 ....G8
Bolinas 1,098 ....H1
Boron 2,101 ....H8
Borrego Springs 2,244 ....J10
Boulder Creek 6,725 ....J4
Bowman C7
Brawley 18,923 ....K11
Brea 32,873 ....D11
Brentwood 7,563 ....C6
Bridgeport▲ 525 ....F5
Brisbane 2,952 ....J2
Broderick (Broderick-Bryte)
10,194 ....B8
Bryte (Bryte-Broderick)
10,194 ....B8
Buellton 3,506 ....E9
Buena Park 68,784 ....D11
Burbank 93,643 ....C10
Burlingame 26,801 ....J2
Burney 3,423 ....D3
Buttonwillow 1,301 ....F8
Cabazon 1,588 ....J10
Calabasas B10
Calexico 18,633 ....K11
California City 5,955 ....H8
Calipatria 2,690 ....K10
Calistoga 4,468 ....C5
Calwa 6,640 ....F7
Camarillo 52,303 ....G9
Cambria 5,382 ....D8
Campbell 36,048 ....K3
Canoga Park B10
Canyon 7,938 ....K2
Capistrano Beach 6,168 .....H10
Capitola 10,171 ....K4
Cardiff-by-the-Sea 10,054 ...H10
Carlsbad 63,126 ....H10
Carmel 4,407 ....D7
Carmel Valley 4,013 ....D7
Carmichael 48,702 ....C8
Carpinteria 13,747 ....F9
Carson 83,995 ....C11
Caruthers 1,603 ....E7
Casitas Springs 1,038 ....F9
Castro Valley 48,619 ....K2
Castroville 5,272 ....D7
Cathedral City 30,085 ....J10
Cayucos 2,960 ....E8
Central Valley 4,340 ....C3
Ceres 26,314 ....D6
Cerritos 53,240 ....C11
Chatsworth B10
Chemeketa Park (Chemeketa
Park–Redwood Estates)
1,847 ....K4
Cherryland 11,088 ....K2
Chester 2,082 ....D3
Chico 40,079 ....D4

China Lake 4,275 ....H8
Chinese Camp 150 ....E6
Chino 59,682 ....D10
Chowchilla 5,930 ....E6
Chula Vista 135,163 ....J11
Citrus Heights 107,439 ....C8
Claremont 32,503 ....D10
Clay 7,317 ....C9
Clayton 4,325 ....K2
Clearlake 11,804 ....C5
Clearlake Oaks 2,419 ....C4
Cloverdale 4,924 ....B5
Clovis 50,323 ....F7
Coachella 16,896 ....J10
Coalinga 8,212 ....E7
Colfax 1,306 ....E4
Colton 40,213 ....E10
Columbia 1,799 ....E5
Colusa▲ 4,934 ....C4
Commerce 12,135 ....C10
Compton 90,454 ....C11
Concord 111,348 ....K1
Corcoran 13,364 ....F7
Corning 5,870 ....C4
Corona 76,095 ....E11
Coronado 26,540 ....H11
Corte Madera 8,272 ....J2
Costa Mesa 96,357 ....D11
Cotati 5,714 ....C5
Cottonwood 1,747 ....C3
Covina 43,207 ....D10
Crescent City▲ 4,380 ....A2
Crestline 8,594 ....H9
Crockett 3,228 ....J1
Crowley Lake G6
Cudahy 22,817 ....C11
Culver City 38,793 ....B10
Cutler 4,450 ....F7
Cutten 1,516 ....A3
Cypress 42,655 ....D11
Daly City 92,311 ....H2
Dana Point 31,896 ....H10
Danville 31,306 ....K2
Davis 46,209 ....B9
Death Valley Junction J7
Deer Park 1,825 ....C5
Del Mar 4,860 ....H11
Del Rey Oaks 1,661 ....D7
Del Rosa E10
Delano 22,762 ....F8
Delhi 3,280 ....E6
Desert Hot Springs 11,668 ...J10
Desert View Highlands 2,154 ..G9
Diamond Springs 2,872 ......D8
Dinuba 12,743 ....F7
Dixon 10,401 ....B9
Dorris 892 ....D2
Dos Palos 4,196 ....E6
Downey 91,444 ....C11
Downieville▲ 500 ....E4
Duarte 20,688 ....D10

Dublin 23,229 ....K2
Dunsmuir 2,129 ....C2
Durham 4,784 ....D4
Earlimart 5,881 ....F8
East Blythe 1,511 ....L10
East Los Angeles 126,379 ...C10
Easton 1,877 ....F7
Edgemont E11
Edison G8
El Cajon 88,693 ....J11
El Centro▲ 31,384 ....K11
El Cerrito 4,490 ....J2
El Dorado 6,395 ....C8
El Dorado Hills 3,453 ....C8
El Granada 4,426 ....H3
El Monte 106,209 ....D10
El Rio 6,419 ....F9
El Segundo 15,223 ....B11
El Toro 62,685 ....E11
Elk 17,483 ....B4
Elk Grove 10,959 ....B9
Emeryville 5,740 ....J2
Empire D6
Encinitas 55,386 ....H10
Encino B10
Enterprise C3
Escalon 4,437 ....E6
Escondido 108,635 ....J10
Esparto 1,487 ....C5
Eureka▲ 27,025 ....A3
Exeter 7,276 ....F7
Fair Oaks 26,867 ....C8
Fairfax 6,931 ....H1
Fairfield▲ 77,211 ....K1
Fallbrook 22,095 ....H10
Farmersville 6,235 ....F7
Felton 5,350 ....K4
Ferndale 1,331 ....A3
Fillmore 11,992 ....G9
Firebaugh 4,429 ....E7
Florin 24,330 ....B8
Folsom 29,802 ....C8
Fontana 87,535 ....E10
Ford City 3,781 ....F8
Forest Knolls (Forest Knolls–
Lagunitas) H1
Foresthill 1,409 ....E4
Fort Bragg 6,078 ....B4
Fortuna 8,788 ....A3
Foster City 28,176 ....J2
Fountain Valley 53,691 .....D11
Fowler 3,208 ....F7
Frazier Park 2,201 ....F9
Freedom 8,361 ....I 4
Fremont 173,339 ....K3
Fresno▲ 354,202 ....F7
Galt 8,889 ....C9
Garden Grove 143,050 ......D11
Gardena 49,847 ....C11
Glen Avon Heights 8,444 ...E10
Glendale 180,038 ....C10
Glendora 47,828 ....D10
Goleta F9
Gonzales 4,660 ....D7
Goshen 1,809 ....F7
Granada Hills B10
Grand Terrace 10,946 ....E10
Grass Valley 9,048 ....D4
Graton 1,409 ....C5
Greenacres 7,379 ....F8
Greenfield 7,464 ....D7
Greenville 1,396 ....E3
Gridley 4,631 ....D4
Groveland 2,753 ....E6
Grover City 11,656 ....E8
Guadalupe 5,479 ....E9
Guerneville 1,966 ....B5
Gustine 3,931 ....D6
Half Moon Bay 8,886 ....H3
Hamilton City 1,811 ....C4
Hanford▲ 30,897 ....F7
Harbor City C11
Hawthorne 71,349 ....C11
Hayfork 2,605 ....B3
Hayward 111,498 ....K2
Healdsburg 9,469 ....B5
Heber 2,566 ....K11
Hemet 36,094 ....H10
Hercules 16,829 ....J1
Herlong 1,188 ....E3
Hermosa Beach 18,219 .....B11
Hesperia 50,418 ....H9
Hidden Hills 1,729 ....B10
Highgrove 3,175 ....E10
Highland 34,439 ....H9
Hillsborough 10,667 ....J2
Hilmar (Hilmar-Irwin) 3,392 ..E6
Hollister▲ 19,212 ....D7
Hollywood C10
Holt 4,820 ....D6
Holtville 4,399 ....K11
Home Gardens 7,780 ....E11
Homeland 3,312 ....H10
Hughson 3,259 ....D6
Huntington Beach 181,519 ...C11

Huntington Park 56,065 ......C11
Huron 4,766 ....E7
Idyllwild (Idyllwild–
Pine Cove) 2,853 ....J10
Imperial 4,113 ....K11
Imperial Beach 26,512 ....H11
Independence▲ 748 ....J10
Indian Wells 2,647 ....J10
Indio 36,793 ....J10
Inglewood 109,602 ....B11
Inverness 1,422 ....B5
Ione 6,516 ....C9
Irvine 110,330 ....D11
Isla Vista 20,395 ....E9
Ivanhoe 3,293 ....F7
Jackson▲ 3,545 ....C9
Jamestown 2,178 ....E6
Joshua Tree 3,898 ....J9
Julian 1,284 ....J10
Kelseyville 2,861 ....C5
Kensington 4,974 ....J2
Kerman 5,448 ....E7
Kernville 1,656 ....G8
Kettleman City 1,411 ....E7
Keyes 2,878 ....E6
King City 7,634 ....D7
Kings Beach 2,796 ....F4
Kingsburg 7,205 ....F7
La Cañada Flintridge 19,378 ..C10
La Crescenta (La Crescenta–
Montrose) 16,968 ....C10
La Habra 51,266 ....D11
La Mesa 52,931 ....H11
La Mirada 40,452 ....D11
La Puente 36,955 ....D10
La Selva Beach 1,603 ....K4
La Verne 30,897 ....D10
Lafayette 23,501 ....K2
Laguna Beach 23,170 ....D10
Laguna Hills 46,731 ....D11
Laguna Niguel 44,400 ....H10
Lagunitas (Lagunitas–
Forest Knolls) 1,821 ......H1
Lake Arrowhead 6,539 ....H9
Lake Elsinore 18,285 ....H10
Lake Isabella 3,323 ....G8
Lakeland Village 5,159 ....E11
Lakeport▲ 4,390 ....C4
Lakewood 73,557 ....C11
Lamont 11,517 ....G8
Lancaster 97,291 ....G9
Larkspur 11,070 ....H1
Lathrop 6,841 ....D6
Laton 1,415 ....F7
Lawndale 27,331 ....B11
Le Grand 1,205 ....E6
Lemon Grove 23,984 ....J11
Lemoore 13,622 ....F7
Lenwood 3,190 ....H9
Leucadia 9,478 ....H10
Lewiston 1,187 ....C3
Lincoln 7,248 ....B8
Linda 13,033 ....D4
Linden 1,339 ....D5
Lindsay 8,338 ....F7
Live Oak 11,482 ....K4
Live Oak 3,103 ....D4
Live Oak 4,320 ....K4
Livermore 56,741 ....L2
Livingston 7,317 ....E6
Locke 2,722 ....K1
Lockeford 1,852 ....C9
Lodi 51,874 ....C9
Loma Linda 17,400 ....F10
Lomita 19,382 ....C11
Lompoc 37,649 ....E9
Lone Pine 1,818 ....H7
Long Beach 429,433 ....C11
Loomis 5,705 ....C8
Los Alamitos 11,676 ....D11
Los Altos 26,303 ....K3
Los Altos Hills 7,514 ....J3
Los Angeles▲ 3,485,398 ...C10
Los Banos 14,519 ....E6
Los Gatos 27,357 ....K4
Los Molinos 1,709 ....D3
Los Osos (Los Osos–
Baywood Park) 10,933 ...E8
Lost Hills 1,212 ....F8
Lower Lake 1,217 ....C5
Lucerne 2,011 ....C4
Lynwood 61,945 ....C11
Madera▲ 29,281 ....E7
Magalia 8,987 ....D4
Mammoth Lakes 4,785 ......G6
Manhattan Beach 32,063 ...B11
Manteca 40,773 ....D6
Maricopa 1,193 ....F8
Marina 26,436 ....D7
Mariposa▲ 1,152 ....F6
Markleeville▲ 500 ....F5
Martinez▲ 31,808 ....K1
Marysville▲ 12,324 ....D4
Maywood 27,850 ....C10
McCloud 1,555 ....C2
McFarland 7,005 ....F8
McKinleyville 10,749 ....A3

Mecca 1,966 ....K10
Meiners Oaks (Meiners Oaks–
Mira Monte) 3,329 ....F9
Mendota 6,821 ....E7
Menlo Park 28,040 ....J3
Mentone 5,675 ....H9
Merced▲ 56,216 ....E6
Mill Valley 13,038 ....H2
Millbrae 20,412 ....J2
Milpitas 50,686 ....L3
Mira Loma 15,786 ....E10
Mission Viejo 72,820 ....D11
Modesto▲ 164,730 ....D6
Mojave 3,763 ....G8
Monrovia 35,761 ....D10
Montague 1,415 ....C2
Montara 2,552 ....H3
Montclair 28,434 ....D10
Monte Sereno 3,287 ....K4
Montebello 59,564 ....C10
Monterey 31,954 ....D7
Monterey Park 60,738 ....C10
Montrose (Montrose–La
Crescenta) C10
Moorpark 25,494 ....G9
Moraga 15,852 ....K2
Moreno Valley 118,779 ......H10
Morgan Hill 23,928 ....L4
Morro Bay 9,664 ....D8
Moss Beach 3,002 ....H3
Mount Shasta 3,460 ....C2
Mountain View 67,460 ....K3
Mulberry 1,946 ....D4
Murphys 1,517 ....E5
Murrieta 1,608 ....H10
Muscoy 7,541 ....E10
Napa▲ 61,842 ....C5
National City 54,249 ....J11
Needles 5,191 ....L9
Nevada City▲ 2,855 ....D4
Newark 37,861 ....K3
Newhall 12,029 ....G9
Newman 4,151 ....D6
Newport Beach 66,643 ......D11
Nipomo 7,109 ....E8
Norco 23,302 ....E11
North Edwards 1,259 ....H8
North Highlands 42,105 ....B8
Norwalk 94,279 ....C11
Novato 47,585 ....H1
Oak View 4,066 ....F9
Oakdale 11,961 ....E6
Oakhurst 2,602 ....F6
Oakland▲ 372,242 ....J2
Oakley 18,374 ....L1
Oceano 6,169 ....E8
Oceanside 128,398 ....H10
Oildale 26,553 ....F8
Ojai 7,613 ....F9
Ontario 133,179 ....D10
Opal Cliffs 5,940 ....K4
Orange 110,658 ....D11
Orange Cove 5,604 ....F7
Orinda 16,642 ....J2
Orland 5,052 ....C4
Orosi 5,486 ....F7
Oroville▲ 11,960 ....D4
Oxnard 142,216 ....F9
Pacheco (Pacheco–Vine Hill)
3,325 ....K1
Pacific Grove 16,117 ....D7
Pacifica 37,670 ....H2
Pajaro 3,332 ....D7
Palermo 5,260 ....D4
Palm Desert 23,252 ....J10
Palm Springs 40,181 ....J10
Palmdale 68,842 ....G9
Palo Alto 55,900 ....K3
Palos Verdes Estates
13,512 ....B11
Paradise 25,408 ....D4
Paramount 47,669 ....C11
Parlier 7,938 ....F7
Pasadena 131,591 ....C10
Paso Robles 18,583 ....E8
Patterson 8,626 ....D6
Pebble Beach D7
Pedley 8,869 ....E10
Perris 21,460 ....H10
Petaluma 43,184 ....H1
Pico Rivera 59,177 ....C10
Piedmont 10,602 ....J2
Pine Valley 1,297 ....J11
Pinole 17,460 ....J1
Piru 1,157 ....G9
Pismo Beach 7,669 ....E8
Pittsburg 47,564 ....L1
Pixley 2,457 ....F8
Placentia 41,259 ....D11
Placerville▲ 8,355 ....D8
Planada 3,531 ....E6
Pleasant Hill 31,585 ....K2
Pleasanton 50,553 ....L2
Pollock Pines 4,291 ....E5
Pomona 131,723 ....D10
Poplar (Poplar–Cotton Center)
1,901 ....F7

(continued on following page)

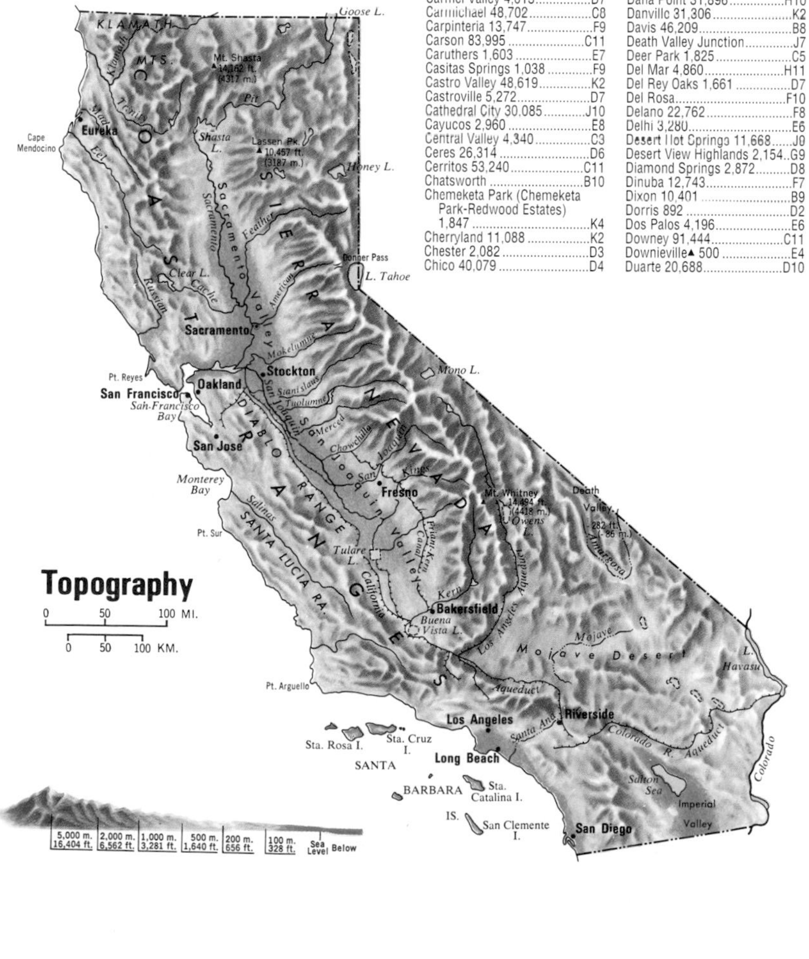

Topography

0   50   100 MI.
0   50   100 KM.

KLAMATH MTS.
Mt. Shasta
Shasta L.
Honey L.
Goose L.
Cape Mendocino
Eureka
SIERRA NEVADA
Lassen Pk. 10,457 ft. (3187 m.)
Pit
Sacramento
Feather
Clear Lake
Yuba
Pyramid
Donner Pass
L. Tahoe
American
Sacramento Valley
Stockton
Oakland
San Francisco
San Francisco Bay
San Jose
Pt. Reyes
Mono L.
DIABLO RANGE
San Joaquin Valley
Fresno
Mt. Whitney 14,494 ft. (4418 m.)
Owens
Death Valley 282 ft. (86 m.)
Monterey Bay
Pt. Sur
SANTA LUCIA RA.
Salinas
Tulare L.
Bakersfield
Buena Vista L.
Kern
Mojave Desert
Pt. Arguello
Sta. Rosa I.
Sta. Cruz I.
SANTA BARBARA IS.
San Clemente I.
Sta. Catalina I.
Los Angeles
Long Beach
Riverside
Santa Ana
San Bernardino
San Gabriel
Salton Sea
Colorado
Aqueduct
Havasu L.
Imperial Valley
San Diego

5,000 m. 16,404 ft. | 2,000 m. 6,562 ft. | 1,000 m. 3,281 ft. | 500 m. 1,640 ft. | 200 m. 656 ft. | 100 m. 328 ft. | Sea Level | Below

Porterville 29,563 ... G7
Port Hueneme 20,319 ... F9
Portola 2,193 ... E4
Portola Valley 4,194 ... J3
Poway 43,516 ... J11
Project City 1,657 ... C3
Quartz Hill 9,626 ... G9
Quincy▲ (Quincy-East Quincy) 4,271 ... E4
Ramona 13,040 ... J10
Rancho Cordova 48,731 ... C8
Rancho Cucamonga (Cucamonga) 101,409 ... E10
Rancho Mirage 9,778 ... J10
Rancho Palos Verdes 41,659 ... B11
Rancho Santa Fe 4,014 ... H10
Red Bluff▲ 12,363 ... C3
Redding▲ 66,462 ... C3
Redlands 60,394 ... H9
Redondo Beach 60,167 ... B11
Redway 1,212 ... B3
Redwood City▲ 66,072 ... J3
Redwood Estates (Redwood Estates-Chemeketa Park) 1,847 ... K4
Reedley 15,791 ... F7
Rialto 72,388 ... E10
Richgrove 1,899 ... F8
Richmond 87,425 ... J1
Ridgecrest 27,725 ... H8
Rio Dell 3,012 ... A3
Rio Linda 9,481 ... B8
Rio Vista 3,316 ... L1
Ripon 7,455 ... D6
Riverbank 8,547 ... E6
Riverdale 1,980 ... E7
Riverside▲ 226,505 ... E11
Rocklin 19,033 ... B8
Rodeo 7,589 ... J1
Rohnert Park 36,326 ... C5
Rolling Hills 1,871 ... B11
Rolling Hills Estates 7,789 ... B11
Rosamond 7,430 ... G9
Rosemead 51,638 ... C10
Roseville 44,685 ... B8
Ross 2,123 ... H1
Rubidoux 24,367 ... E10
Sacramento (cap.)▲ 369,365 ... B8
Saint Helena 4,990 ... C5
Salinas▲ 108,777 ... D7
San Andreas▲ 2,115 ... E5
San Anselmo 11,743 ... H1
San Bernardino▲ 164,164 ... E10
San Bruno 38,961 ... J2
San Carlos 26,167 ... J3
San Clemente 41,100 ... H10
San Diego▲ 1,110,549 ... H11
San Dimas 32,397 ... D10
San Fernando 22,580 ... C10
San Francisco▲ 723,959 ... H2
San Gabriel 37,120 ... C10
Sanger 16,839 ... F7
San Jacinto 16,210 ... H10
San Joaquin 2,311 ... E7
San Jose▲ 782,248 ... L3
San Juan Bautista 1,570 ... D7
San Juan Capistrano 26,183 ... H10
San Leandro 68,223 ... J2
San Lorenzo 19,987 ... K2
San Luis Obispo▲ 41,958 ... E8
San Marcos 38,974 ... H10
San Marino 12,959 ... C10
San Martin 1,713 ... L4
San Mateo 85,486 ... J3
San Pablo 25,158 ... J1
San Rafael▲ 48,404 ... J1
San Ramon 35,303 ... K2
Santa Ana▲ 293,742 ... D11
Santa Barbara▲ 85,571 ... F9
Santa Clara 93,613 ... K3
Santa Clarita 110,642 ... G9
Santa Cruz▲ 49,040 ... K4
Santa Fe Springs 15,520 ... C11
Santa Maria 61,284 ... E9
Santa Monica 86,905 ... B10
Santa Paula 25,062 ... F9
Santa Rosa▲ 113,313 ... C5
Santa Venetia 3,362 ... J1
Santee 52,902 ... J11
Saratoga 28,061 ... K4
Sausalito 7,152 ... H2
Scotts Valley 8,615 ... K4
Seal Beach 25,098 ... C11
Seaside 38,901 ... D7
Sebastopol 7,004 ... C5
Seeley 1,228 ... K11
Selma 14,757 ... F7
Shafter 8,409 ... F8
Shingle Springs 2,049 ... C8
Sierra Madre 10,762 ... D10
Signal Hill 8,371 ... C11
Simi Valley 100,217 ... G9
Solana Beach 12,962 ... H11
Soledad 7,146 ... D7
Solvang 4,741 ... E9
Sonoma 8,121 ... C5
Sonora▲ 4,153 ... E6
Soquel 9,188 ... K4
South Dos Palos 1,214 ... E7
South El Monte 20,850 ... C10
South Gate 86,284 ... C11
South Lake Tahoe 21,586 ... F5
South Oroville 7,463 ... D4
South Pasadena 23,936 ... C10
South San Francisco 54,312 ... J2
South Taft 2,170 ... F8
Stanford 18,097 ... J3
Stanton 30,491 ... D11
Stockton▲ 210,943 ... D6
Strathmore 2,353 ... F7
Suisun City 22,686 ... K1
Summit City 1,136 ... C3
Sun City 14,930 ... F11
Sunnyvale 117,229 ... K3
Susanville▲ 7,279 ... E3
Sutter 2,606 ... D4
Sutter Creek 1,835 ... C9
Taft 5,902 ... F8
Tehachapi 5,791 ... G8
Temecula 27,099 ... H10
Temple City 31,100 ... D10
Templeton 2,887 ... E8
Terra Bella 2,740 ... G8
Thermal 5,646 ... J10
Thermalito 4,961 ... D4
Thousand Oaks 104,352 ... G9
Thousand Palms 4,122 ... J10
Tiburon 7,532 ... J2
Tipton 1,383 ... F7
Torrance 133,107 ... C11
Tracy 33,558 ... D6
Truckee 3,484 ... E4
Tulare 33,249 ... F7
Tulelake 1,010 ... D2
Tuolumne 1,686 ... E6
Turlock 42,198 ... E6
Tustin 50,689 ... D11
Twain 2,170 ... D4
Twain Harte 1,369 ... E6
Twentynine Palms 11,821 ... K9
Twin Lakes 5,379 ... K4
Ukiah▲ 14,599 ... B4
Union City 53,762 ... K2
Upland 63,374 ... E10
Vacaville 71,479 ... D5
Valencia 12,163 ... G9
Vallejo 109,199 ... J1
Ventura▲ 92,575 ... F9
Victor 40,674 ... C9
Victorville 14,220 ... H9
Villa Park 6,299 ... D11
Visalia▲ 75,636 ... F7
Vista 71,872 ... H10
Walnut 29,105 ... D10
Walnut Creek 60,569 ... K2
Wasco 12,412 ... F8
Waterford 4,771 ... E6
Watsonville 31,099 ... D7
Weaverville▲ 3,370 ... B3
Weed 3,062 ... C2
West Covina 96,086 ... D10
West Hollywood 36,118 ... B10
Westminster 78,118 ... D11
Westmont 31,044 ... C11
Westmorland 1,380 ... K10
West Pittsburg 17,453 ... K1
West Sacramento 28,898 ... B8
Westwood 2,017 ... D3
Wheatland 1,631 ... D4
Whittier 77,671 ... D11
Wildomar 10,411 ... H10
Williams 2,297 ... C4
Willits 5,027 ... B4
Willow Creek 1,576 ... B3
Willows▲ 5,988 ... C4
Wilton 3,858 ... C9
Windsor 13,371 ... C5
Winters 4,639 ... D5
Winton 7,559 ... E6
Woodbridge 3,456 ... B9
Woodcrest 7,796 ... E11
Woodlake 5,678 ... G7
Woodland▲ 39,802 ... B8
Woodside 5,035 ... J3
Wrightwood 3,308 ... D10
Yorba Linda 52,422 ... D11
Yountville 3,259 ... C5
Yreka▲ 6,948 ... C2
Yuba City▲ 27,437 ... D4
Yucaipa 32,824 ... J9
Yucca Valley 13,701 ... J9

OTHER FEATURES

Agua Caliente Ind. Res. ... J10
Alameda (creek) ... K3
Alamo (riv.) ... K10
Alcatraz (isl.) ... J2
Alkali (lakes) ... E2
All American (canal) ... K11
Almanor (lake) ... D3
Amargosa (range) ... J7
Amargosa (riv.) ... J7
American (riv.) ... C8
Anacapa (isl.) ... F10
Angel (isl.) ... J2
Ano Nuevo (pt.) ... J4
Arena (pt.) ... B5
Arguello (pt.) ... E9
Argus (range) ... H7
Arroyo del Valle (dry riv.) ... L3
Arroyo Hondo (dry riv.) ... L3
Arroyo Mocho (dry riv.) ... L2
Arroyo Seco (dry riv.) ... K10
Beale A.F.B. ... D4
Berryessa (lake) ... D5
Bethany (res.) ... L2
Big Sage (res.) ... E2
Black Butte (lake) ... C4
Bodega (bay) ... B5
Bonita (pt.) ... H2
Bristol (lake) ... K9
Buchon (pt.) ... D8
Buena Vista (lake) ... F8
Cabrillo Nat'l Mon. ... H11
Cachuma (lake) ... F9
Cadiz (lake) ... K9
Cahuilla Ind. Res. ... J10
Calaveras (res.) ... L3
California Aqueduct ... E7
Camanche (res.) ... C9
Campo Ind. Res. ... J11
Camp Pendleton 21,672 ... H10
Capitan Grande Ind. Res. ... J11
Cascade (range) ... D1
Castle A.F.B. ... E6
Channel Islands Nat'l Park ... E10
Chemehuevi Valley Ind. Res. ... L9
China Lake Naval Weapons Center ... H8
Chocolate (mts.) ... K10
Clair Engle (lake) ... C3
Clear (lake) ... C4
Clear Lake (res.) ... D2
Coachella (canal) ... K10
Coast (ranges) ... D7
Colorado (riv.) ... L8
Colorado River Aqueduct ... K10
Colorado River Ind. Res. ... L10
Conception (pt.) ... E9
Cooper (pt.) ... D7
Copco (lake) ... C2
Cosumnes (riv.) ... C9
Cottonwood (creek) ... C3
Coyote (res.) ... L4
Crowley (lake) ... G6
Crystal Springs (res.) ... J3
Cuyama (riv.) ... E8
Cuyapaipe Ind. Res. ... J11
Danby (lake) ... K9
Death (valley) ... H7
Death Valley Nat'l Park ... H7
Delgada (pt.) ... A3
Del Valle (lake) ... L3
Devils Postpile Nat'l Mon. ... F6
Donner (pass) ... E4
Dume (pt.) ... G10
Duxbury (pt.) ... H2
Eagle (lake) ... E3
Eagle (peak) ... E2
Eagle Crags (mt.) ... J8
Edison (lake) ... F6
Edwards A.F.B. ... H9
Eel (riv.) ... B4
Elsinore (lake) ... E11
El Toro Marine Air Station ... D11
Estero (pt.) ... D8
Estrella (riv.) ... E8
Eugene O'Neill Nat'l Hist. Site ... K2
Farallon (isls.) ... B6
Farallons, The (gulf) ... H2
Feather (riv.) ... D4
Florence (lake) ... G6
Folsom (lake) ... C8
Fort Bidwell Ind. Res. ... E2
Fort Hunter Liggett ... D8
Fort Independence Ind. Res. ... G7
Fort MacArthur ... C11
Fort Mohave Ind. Res. ... L9
Fort Ord ... D7
Fort Point Nat'l Hist. Site ... J2
Freel (peak) ... F5
Fremont (peak) ... H8
Fresno (riv.) ... E7
Friant-Kern (canal) ... F8
General Grant Grove Section (King's Canyon) ... G7
George A.F.B. ... H9
Golden Gate (chan.) ... H2
Golden Gate Nat'l Rec. Area ... H2
Goose (lake) ... E1
Grapevine (mts.) ... H7
Grizzly (bay) ... K1
Guadalupe (riv.) ... K3
Haiwee (res.) ... H7
Hamilton (mt.) ... L3
Hat (peak) ... E2
Havasu (lake) ... L9
Hay Fork, Trinity (riv.) ... B3
Hetch Hetchy (res.) ... F6
Hoffman (mt.) ... D2
Honey (lake) ... E3
Hoopa Valley Ind. Res. ... A2
Humboldt (bay) ... A3
Imperial (res.) ... L10
Imperial (valley) ... K10
Ingalls (mt.) ... E3
Inyo (mts.) ... G6
Iron Gate (res.) ... C2
Isabella (lake) ... G8
John Muir Nat'l Hist. Site ... K1
Joshua Tree Nat'l Park ... J10
Kern (riv.) ... G8
Kings (riv.) ... F7
Kings Canyon Nat'l Park ... G7
Klamath (riv.) ... B2
Laguna (res.) ... L11
La Jolla Ind. Res. ... J10
Lassen (peak) ... D3
Lassen Volcanic Nat'l Park ... D3
Lava Beds Nat'l Mon. ... D2
Lemoore N.A.S. ... F7
Leroy Anderson (res.) ... L4
Lopez (pt.) ... D7
Los Angeles Aqueduct ... G8
Los Coyotes Ind. Res. ... J10
Lost (riv.) ... D1
Lower Alkali (lake) ... E2
Lower Klamath (lake) ... D2
Mad (riv.) ... B3
Manzanita Ind. Res. ... J11
March A.F.B. ... E11
Mare Island Navy Yard ... J1
Mather A.F.B. ... C8
Mathews (lake) ... E11
McClellan A.F.B. ... B8
McClure (lake) ... E6
Mendocino (cape) ... A3
Merced (riv.) ... E6
Middle Alkali (lake) ... E2
Mill (creek) ... D3
Millerton (lake) ... F6
Moffett N.A.S. ... K3
Mojave (des.) ... H9
Mojave (riv.) ... J9
Mokelumne (riv.) ... C9
Mono (lsake) ... G5
Monterey (bay) ... K4
Moon (lake) ... E2
Morongo Ind. Res. ... J10
Mountain Meadows (res.) ... E3
Muir Woods Nat'l Mon. ... H2
Nacimiento (riv.) ... D8
Navarro (riv.) ... B4
Nevada, Sierra (mts.) ... E4
New (riv.) ... K11
Norton A.F.B. ... F10
Noyo (riv.) ... B4
Oakland Army Base ... J2
Old (riv.) ... L1
Oroville (lake) ... D4
Owens (lake) ... H7
Owens (peak) ... H8
Owens (riv.) ... G6
Oxnard A.F.B. ... F9
Pala Ind. Res. ... H10
Palomar (mt.) ... J10
Panamint (range) ... H7
Panamint (valley) ... H7
Pescadero (pt.) ... J3
Piedras Blancas (pt.) ... D8
Pillar (pt.) ... H3
Pillsbury (lake) ... C4
Pine (creek) ... D3
Pine Flat (lake) ... F7
Pinnacles Nat'l Mon. ... D7
Pit (riv.) ... D2
Point Mugu Pacific Missile Test Center ... F9
Point Reyes Nat'l Seashore ... H1
Presidio ... J2
Providence (mts.) ... K8
Punta Gorda (pt.) ... A3
Quartz (peak) ... L11
Railroad Canyon (res.) ... E11
Redwood Nat'l Park ... A2
Reyes (pt.) ... B6
Rogers (lake) ... H9
Rosamond (lake) ... G9
Round Valley Ind. Res. ... B4
Russian (riv.) ... B4
Sacramento (riv.) ... D5
Sacramento Army Depot ... B8
Saint George (pt.) ... A2
Salinas (riv.) ... D7
Salmon (riv.) ... B2
Salton Sea (lake) ... K10
San Andreas (lake) ... H2
San Antonio (lake) ... E8
San Benito (riv.) ... D7
San Bernardino (mts.) ... J10
San Clemente (isl.) ... G11
San Diego (bay) ... H11
San Francisco (bay) ... J2
San Gabriel (res.) ... D10
San Joaquin (riv.) ... E6
San Joaquin (valley) ... D6
San Lorenzo (riv.) ... K4
San Luis (res.) ... E7
San Martin (cape) ... D8
San Miguel (isl.) ... E9
San Nicolas (isl.) ... F10
San Pablo (bay) ... J1
San Pedro (bay) ... C11
Santa Ana (riv.) ... E11
Santa Barbara (chan.) ... E9
Santa Barbara (isl.) ... G10
Santa Barbara (isls.) ... F10
Santa Catalina (gulf) ... G11
Santa Catalina (isl.) ... G10
Santa Cruz (chan.) ... F10
Santa Cruz (isl.) ... F10
Santa Maria (riv.) ... E9
Santa Monica (bay) ... B11
Santa Rosa (isl.) ... E10
Santa Rosa Ind. Res. ... J10
Santa Ynez (riv.) ... E9
Santa Ysabel Ind. Res. ... J10
Searles (lake) ... H8
Sequoia Nat'l Park ... G7
Sharpe Army Depot ... D6
Shasta (lake) ... C3
Shasta (mt.) ... C2
Shasta (riv.) ... C2
Sierra Army Depot ... E3
Sierra Nevada (mts.) ... E4
Siskiyou (mts.) ... C2
Smith (riv.) ... A2
Soda (lake) ... K8
South Bay Aqueduct ... L2
South Cow (creek) ... C3
Stony Gorge (res.) ... C4
Suisun (bay) ... K1
Sur (pt.) ... D7
Susan (riv.) ... D3
Tahoe (lake) ... F4
Tamalpais (mt.) ... H1
Tehachapi (mts.) ... G9
Telescope (peak) ... H7
Tomales (pt.) ... B5
Torres Martinez Ind. Res. ... J10
Travis A.F.B. ... L1
Trinidad (head) ... A2
Trinity (riv.) ... B3
Truckee (riv.) ... F4
Tulare (lake) ... F7
Tule (lake) ... D2
Tule River Ind. Res. ... G7
Twentynine Palms Marine Base ... J9
Twitchell (res.) ... E9
Upper Alkali (lake) ... E2
Vandenberg A.F.B. ... E9
Vizcaino (cape) ... B4
Walnut (creek) ... K1
Wheeler (peak) ... F5
Whipple (mts.) ... L9
Whiskeytown-Shasta-Trinity Nat'l Rec. Area ... C3
Whitney (mt.) ... G7
Willow (creek) ... E3
Wilson (mt.) ... D10
Yosemite Nat'l Park ... F6
Yuba (riv.) ... D4
Yuma Ind. Res. ... L11

▲County seat

Agriculture, Industry and Resources

DOMINANT LAND USE

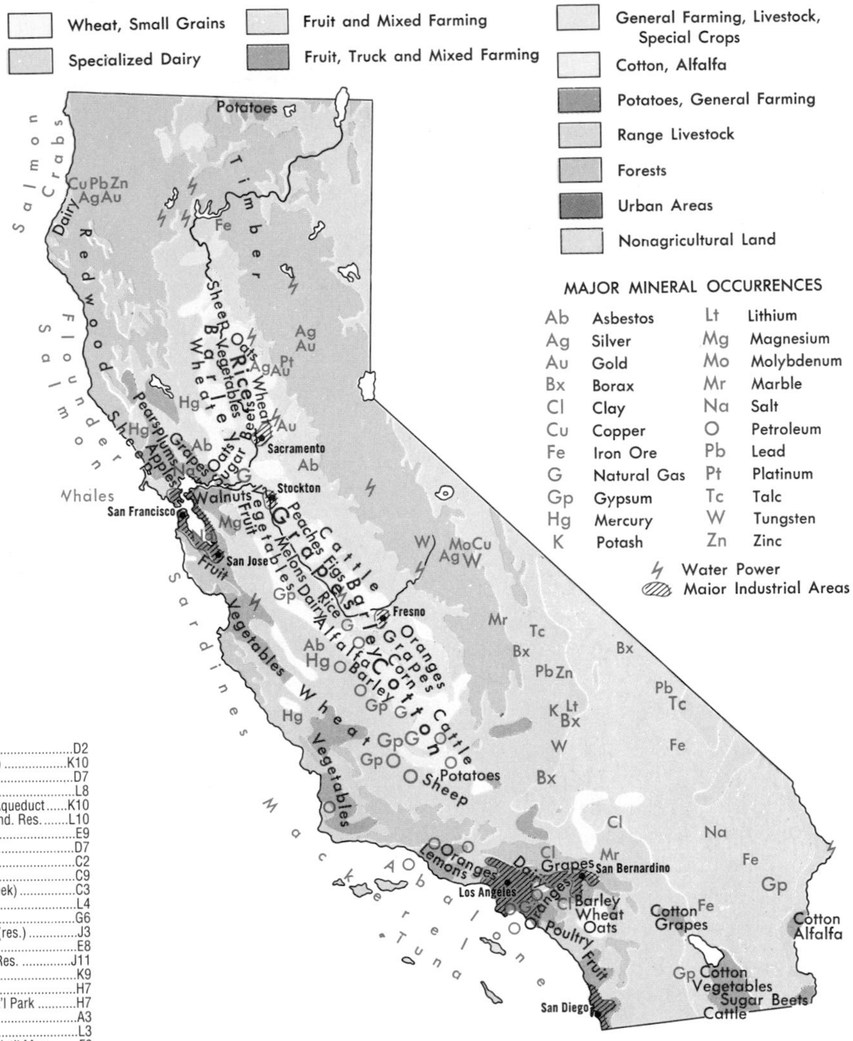

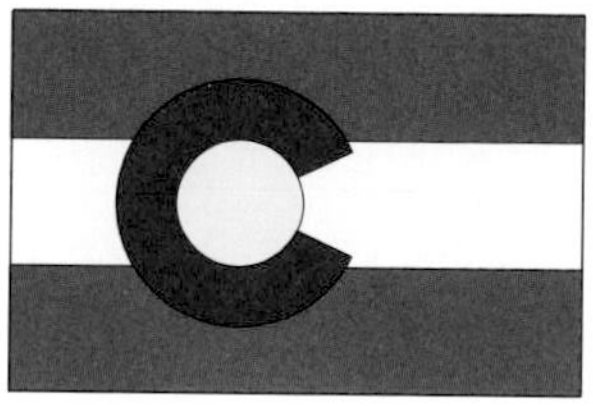

AREA 104,091 sq. mi. (269,596 sq. km.)
POPULATION 3,307,912
CAPITAL Denver
LARGEST CITY Denver
HIGHEST POINT Mt. Elbert 14,433 ft. (4399 m.)
SETTLED IN 1858
ADMITTED TO UNION August 1, 1876
POPULAR NAME Centennial State
STATE FLOWER Rocky Mountain Columbine
STATE BIRD Lark Bunting

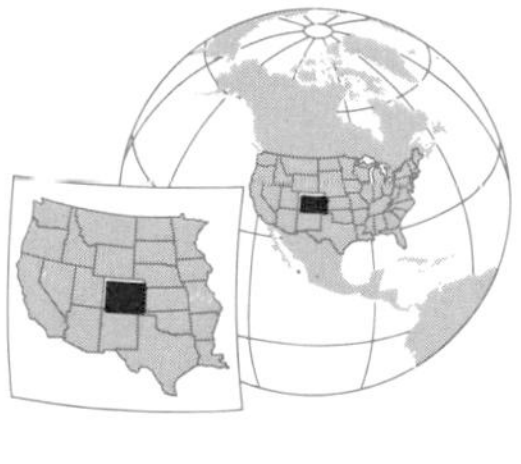

COUNTIES

Adams 265,038 L3
Alamosa 13,617 H7
Arapahoe 391,511 L3
Archuleta 5,345 E8
Baca 4,556 O8
Bent 5,048 N7
Boulder 225,339 J2
Chaffee 12,684 G5
Cheyenne 2,397 O5
Clear Creek 7,619 H3
Conejos 7,453 G8
Costilla 3,190 J8
Crowley 3,946 M6
Custer 1,926 J6
Delta 20,980 D5
Denver 467,610 K3
Dolores 1,504 C7
Douglas 60,391 K4
Eagle 21,928 F3
El Paso 397,014 K5
Elbert 9,646 L4
Fremont 32,273 J5
Garfield 29,974 C3
Gilpin 3,070 H3
Grand 7,966 G2
Gunnison 10,273 E5
Hinsdale 467 E7
Huerfano 6,009 K7
Jackson 1,605 G1
Jefferson 438,430 J3
Kiowa 1,688 O6
Kit Carson 7,140 O4
La Plata 32,284 D8
Lake 6,007 G4
Larimer 186,136 H1
Las Animas 13,765 L8
Lincoln 4,529 M5
Logan 17,567 N1
Mesa 93,145 B5
Mineral 558 F7
Moffat 11,357 C1
Montezuma 18,672 B8
Montrose 24,423 C6
Morgan 21,939 M2
Otero 20,185 M7
Ouray 2,295 D6
Park 7,174 H4
Phillips 4,189 P1
Pitkin 12,661 F4
Prowers 13,347 P7
Pueblo 123,051 K6
Rio Blanco 5,972 C3
Rio Grande 10,770 G7
Routt 14,088 E1
Saguache 4,619 G6
San Juan 745 D7
San Miguel 3,653 C6
Sedgwick 2,690 P1
Summit 12,881 G3
Teller 12,468 J5
Washington 4,812 N3
Weld 131,821 L1
Yuma 8,954 P2

CITIES and TOWNS

Agate 90 M4
Aguilar 520 K8
Akron▲ 1,599 N2
Alamosa▲ 7,579 H8
Allenspark 200 J2
Alma 148 G4
Almont 135 F5
Amherst 85 P1
Anton 875 N3
Antonito 1,103 H8
Arapahoe 300 P5
Arlington 37 N6
Arriba 220 N4
Arriola 5,672 B8
Arvada 89,235 J3
Aspen▲ 5,049 F4
Atwood 100 N1
Ault 1,107 K1
Aurora 222,103 K3
Austin D5
Avon 1,798 F3
Avondale 750 L6
Bailey 150 H4
Barnesville 20 L2
Basalt 1,128 E4
Bayfield 1,090 D8
Bedrock 45 B6
Beecher Island 5 P3
Bellvue 250 J1
Bennett 1,757 L3
Berthoud 2,990 J2
Berthoud Pass 40 H3
Bethune 173 P4
Beulah 650 K6
Black Forest 8,143 K4
Black Hawk 227 J3
Blanca 272 H8
Blue River 440 G4
Bonanza 16 G6
Boncarbo 200 K8
Bond 65 F3
Boone 341 L6
Boulder▲ 83,312 J2
Bowie 18 D5
Boyero 12 N5
Brandon 30 P6
Branson 50 M8
Breckenridge▲ 1,285 G4
Briggsdale 85 L1
Brighton▲ 14,203 K3
Bristol 200 P6
Brookside 183 J6
Broomfield 24,638 J3
Brush 4,165 M2
Buckingham 5 L1
Buena Vista 1,752 G5
Buffalo Creek 150 J4
Burlington▲ 2,941 P4
Burns 100 F3
Byers 1,065 L3
Cahone 200 B7
Calhan 562 L4
Campo 121 O8
Canon City▲ 12,687 J6
Capulin 600 G8
Carbondale 3,004 E4
Carr 49 K1
Cascade 1,479 K5
Castle Rock▲ 8,708 K4
Cedaredge 1,380 D5
Center 1,963 G7
Central City▲ 335 J3
Chama 239 J8
Cheraw 265 N6
Cheyenne Wells▲ 1,128 P5
Chimney Rock 76 E8
Chivington 20 O6
Chromo 115 F8
Cimarron 50 D6
Clark 20 F1
Clifton 12,671 C4
Climax 975 G4
Coal Creek 157 J6
Coaldale 153 H6
Coalmont 50 F1
Cokedale 116 K8
Collbran 228 C4
Colona 54 D6
Colorado City 1,149 K6
Colorado Springs▲ 281,140 K5
Columbine 23,969 E1
Commerce City 16,466 K3
Como 30 H4
Conejos▲ 200 G8
Cope 110 O3
Cornish 15 L2
Cortez▲ 7,284 B8
Cotopaxi 250 H6
Cowdrey 80 G1
Craig▲ 8,091 D2
Crawford 221 D5
Creede▲ 362 E7
Crested Butte 878 E5
Crestone 39 H7
Cripple Creek▲ 584 J5
Crook 148 O1
Crowley 225 M6
Cuchara 43 J8
Dacono 2,228 K2
Dailey 20 O1
De Beque 257 C4
Deckers 4 J4
Deer Trail 476 M3
Del Norte▲ 1,674 G7
Delhi 10 M7
Delta▲ 3,789 D5
Denver (cap.)▲ 467,610 K3
Deora 2 O7
Dillon 553 H3
Dinosaur 324 B2
Divide 700 J5
Dolores 866 C8
Dove Creek▲ 643 A7
Doyleville 75 F6
Drake 300 J2
Durango▲ 12,430 D8
Eads▲ 780 O6
Eagle▲ 1,580 F3
Eaton 1,959 K1
Eckley 211 P2
Edgewater 4,613 J3
Edwards 250 F3
Egnar 50 B7
Elbert 200 L4
Eldora 100 H3
Elizabeth 818 K4
Elk Springs 18 C2
Empire 401 H3
Englewood 29,387 K3
Erie 1,258 K2
Estes Park 3,184 J2
Eureka 25 D7
Evans 5,877 K2
Evergreen 7,582 J3
Fairplay▲ 387 H4
Farisita 116 J7
Federal Heights 9,342 J3
Firestone 1,358 K2
Firstview 6 O5
Flagler 564 N4
Fleming 344 O1
Florence 2,987 J6
Florissant 130 J5
Fort Collins▲ 87,758 J1
Fort Garland 700 J8
Fort Lupton 5,159 K2
Fort Lyon 500 N6
Fort Morgan▲ 9,068 M2
Fountain 9,984 K5
Fowler 1,154 L6
Foxton 12 J4
Franktown 200 K4
Fraser 575 H3
Frederick 988 K2
Freshwater (Guffey) 24 H5
Frisco 1,601 G3
Fruita 4,046 B4
Galeton 200 K1
Garcia 75 J8
Gardner 100 J7
Garfield 30 G5
Gateway 7,510 B5
Genoa 167 N4
Georgetown▲ 891 H3
Gilcrest 1,084 K2
Gill 250 L2
Gilman 160 G3
Glade Park 100 B5
Glen Haven 110 H2
Glendevey 50 H1
Glenwood Springs▲ 6,561 E4
Golden▲ 13,116 J3
Goodrich 85 M2
Gould 12 G2
Granada 513 P6
Granby 966 H2
Grand Junction▲ 29,034 B4
Grand Lake 259 H2
Granite 47 G4
Grant 50 H4
Greeley▲ 60,536 K2
Green Mountain Falls 663 K5
Greenland 21 K4
Greystone 2 B1
Grover 135 L1
Guffey 24 H5
Gulnare 6 K8
Gunnison▲ 4,636 E5
Gypsum 1,750 F3
Hale 4 P3
Hamilton 100 D2
Hartman 108 P6
Hartsel 69 H4
Hasty 150 O6
Haswell 62 N6
Haxtun 952 O1
Hayden 1,444 E2
Hereford 50 L1
Hesperus 250 C8
Hillrose 169 N2
Hillside 79 H6
Hoehne 400 L8
Holly 877 P6
Holyoke▲ 1,931 P1
Hooper 112 H7
Hot Sulphur Springs▲ 347 H2
Hotchkiss 744 D5
Howard 200 H6
Hoyt 60 L2
Hudson 918 K2
Hugo▲ 660 N4
Hygiene 450 J2
Idaho Springs 1,834 H3
Idalia 125 P3
Ignacio 720 D8
Iliff 174 N1
Jamestown 251 J2
Jansen 267 K8
Jaroso 50 H8
Jefferson 50 H4
Joes 100 O3
Johnstown 1,579 K2
Julesburg▲ 1,295 P1
Karval 51 N5
Keenesburg 570 L2
Keota 5 L1
Kersey 980 L2
Kim 76 N8
Kiowa▲ 275 L4
Kirk 30 P3
Kit Carson 305 O5
Kremmling 1,166 G2
Kutch 2 M5
La Garita 10 G7
La Jara 725 H8
La Junta▲ 7,637 M7
La Salle 1,783 K2
La Veta 726 J8
Lafayette 14,548 K3
Laird 105 P2
Lake City▲ 223 E6
Lake George 500 J5
Lakewood 126,481 J3
Lamar▲ 8,343 O6
Laporte 950 J1
Larkspur 232 K4
Las Animas▲ 2,481 N6
Lasauces 150 H8
Lavalley 237 J8
Lawson 108 H3
Lay 40 D2
Lazear 60 D5
Leadville▲ 2,629 G4
Lebanon 50 B8
Lewis 150 B8
Limon 1,831 M4
Lincoln Park 3,728 J6
Lindon 60 N3
Littleton▲ 33,685 K3
Livermore 150 J1
Lochbuie 1,168 K2
Log Lane Village 667 M2
Loma 265 B4
Longmont 42,942 J2
Longview 10 J4
Louisville 12,361 J3
Louviers 300 K4
Loveland 37,352 J2
Lucerne 135 K2
Lycan 4 P7
Lyons 1,227 J2
Mack 380 B4
Maher 75 D5
Malta 200 G4
Manassa 988 H8
Mancos 842 C8
Manitou Springs 4,535 J5
Manzanola 437 M6
Marble 64 E4
Marvel 176 C8
Masonville 200 J2
Masters 50 L2

(continued on following page)

Agriculture, Industry and Resources

DOMINANT LAND USE

- Specialized Wheat
- Wheat, Range Livestock
- Wheat, Grain Sorghums, Range Livestock
- Dry Beans, General Farming
- Sugar Beets, Dry Beans, Livestock, General Farming
- Fruit, Mixed Farming
- General Farming, Livestock, Special Crops
- Range Livestock
- Forests
- Urban Areas
- Nonagricultural Land

MAJOR MINERAL OCCURRENCES

Ag	Silver	Mi	Mica
Au	Gold	Mo	Molybdenum
Be	Beryl	Mr	Marble
C	Coal	O	Petroleum
Cl	Clay	Pb	Lead
Cu	Copper	U	Uranium
F	Fluorspar	V	Vanadium
Fe	Iron Ore	W	Tungsten
G	Natural Gas	Zn	Zinc

Water Power
Major Industrial Areas

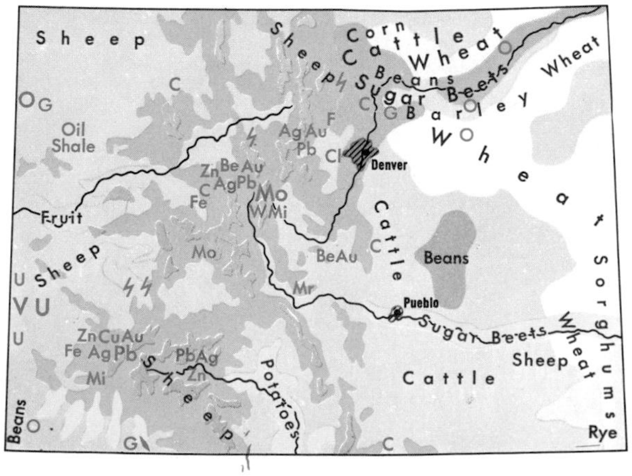

Topography

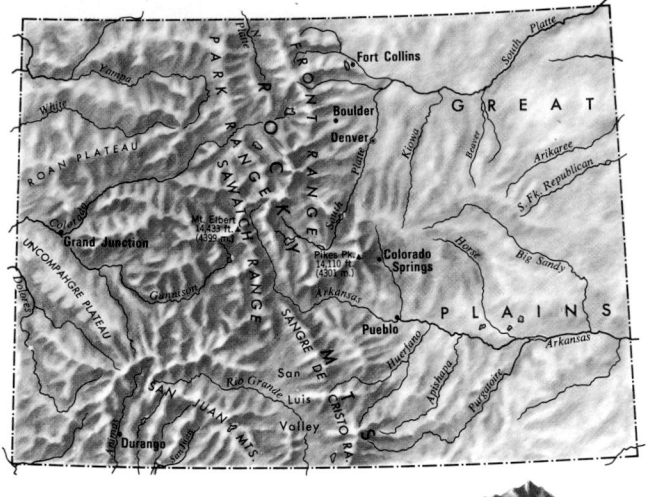

Below Sea Level | 100 m. 328 ft. | 200 m. 656 ft. | 500 m. 1,640 ft. | 1,000 m. 3,281 ft. | 2,000 m. 6,562 ft. | 5,000 m. 16,404 ft.

Colorado

SCALE
0 5 10 20 30 40MI.
0 5 10 20 30 40KM.

State Capitals .... ⊛
County Seats .... ⊛
Major Limited Access Hwys. ———

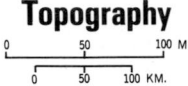

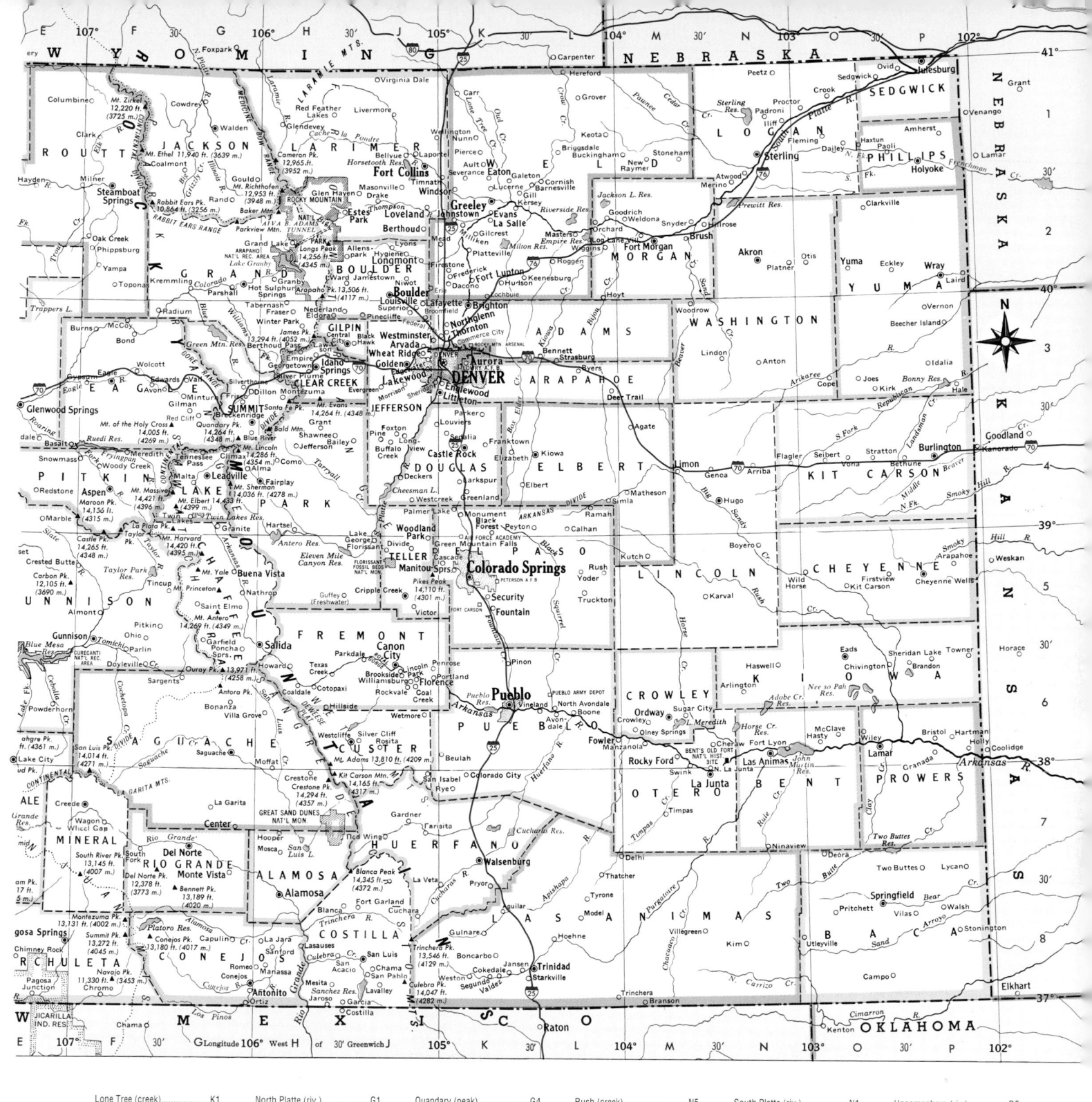

Lone Tree (creek)................K1
Longs (peak)........................H2
Los Pinos (riv.)...................G8
Lowry A.F.B.........................K3
Mancos (riv.).......................B8
Maroon (peak)......................F4
Massive (mt.).......................F4
McElmo (creek).....................B8
Medicine Bow (range)............G1
Meredith (lake)....................M6
Mesa Verde Nat'l Park...........C8
Middle Beaver (creek)............P4
Milton (res.).........................K2
Montezuma (peak).................F8
Morrow Point (res.)...............E6
Muddy (creek)......................E4
Navajo (peak).......................F8
Navajo (res.)........................D8
Nee so Pah (res.)..................D6
North Carrizo (creek)............N8

North Platte (riv.)................G1
Ouray (peak)........................G6
Owl (creek)..........................K1
Pagoda (peak)......................E2
Park (range)........................F1
Parkview (mt.).....................G2
Pawnee (creek)....................M1
Peterson A.F.B......................K5
Piceance (creek)...................C3
Piedra (riv.)........................E8
Pikes (peak)........................J5
Pinos (riv.)..........................D8
Plateau (creek).....................C4
Platoro (res.)........................F8
Pot (creek)...........................A1
Prewitt (res.).......................N2
Princeton (mt.).....................G5
Pueblo (res.)........................K6
Pueblo Army Depot...............L6
Purgatoire (riv.)...................M8

Quandary (peak)..................G4
Rabbit Ears (peak)................G2
Rabbit Ears (range)...............F2
Redcloud (peak)...................E6
Republican (riv.)...................P3
Richthofen (mt.)...................D3
Rifle (creek)........................D3
Rio Grande (res.)..................E7
Rio Grande (riv.)..................H7
Rio Grande Pyramid (mt.).....E7
Riverside (res.).....................L2
Roan (creek)........................C4
Roan (plat.).........................B3
Roaring Fork, Colorado (riv.)..E4
Rocky (mts.).........................F1
Rocky Mountain Arsenal.......K3
Rocky Mountain Nat'l Park....H2
Royal Gorge (canyon)...........J6
Ruedi (res.).........................F4
Rule (creek).........................N7

Rush (creek)........................N5
Saguache (creek)..................F6
Sanchez (res.).......................H8
Sand Arroyo (dry riv.)...........O8
Sangre de Cristo (mts.)..........H6
San Juan (mts.)....................F7
San Juan (riv.)......................E8
San Luis (creek)....................H6
San Luis (lake).....................H7
San Luis (res.)......................F6
San Miguel (mts.).................C7
San Miguel (riv.)..................B6
Santa Fe (peak)....................H4
Sawatch (range)...................G4
Sheep (mt.)..........................E6
Sherman (mt.)......................G4
Slate (riv.)...........................E5
Smoky Hill (riv.)..................P5
Smoky Hill, North Fork (riv.)..P4
Sneffels (mt.).......................D7

South Platte (riv.).................N1
South River (peak)................F7
Southern Ute Ind. Res...........D8
Sterling (res.).......................N1
Summit (res.).......................F8
Tarryall (creek)....................H4
Taylor (peak).......................F5
Taylor (riv.)........................F5
Taylor Park (res.).................F5
Timpas (creek).....................M7
Tomichi (creek)....................F5
Trappers (lake).....................E3
Trinchera (creek)..................J8
Trinchera (riv.).....................J7
Trout (creek)........................E2
Twin Lakes (res.)..................G4
Two Butte (creek).................N7
Two Buttes (res.)..................O7
Uncompahgre (peak).............E6
Uncompahgre (plat.).............B5

Uncompahgre (riv.)...............D5
Ute Mountain Ind. Res..........B8
Vallecito (res.)......................D8
Wet (mts.)...........................J6
Wetterhorn (peak)................D6
White (riv.)..........................B2
Williams Fork, Colorado (riv.)..G3
Williams Fork, Yampa (riv.)....E2
Wilson (mt.).........................C7
Windom (peak).....................D7
Yale (mt.)............................G5
Yampa (riv.).........................B2
Yellow (creek)......................C3
Yucca House Nat'l Mon..........B8
Zenobia (peak).....................B1
Zirkel (mt.)..........................F1

▲County seat

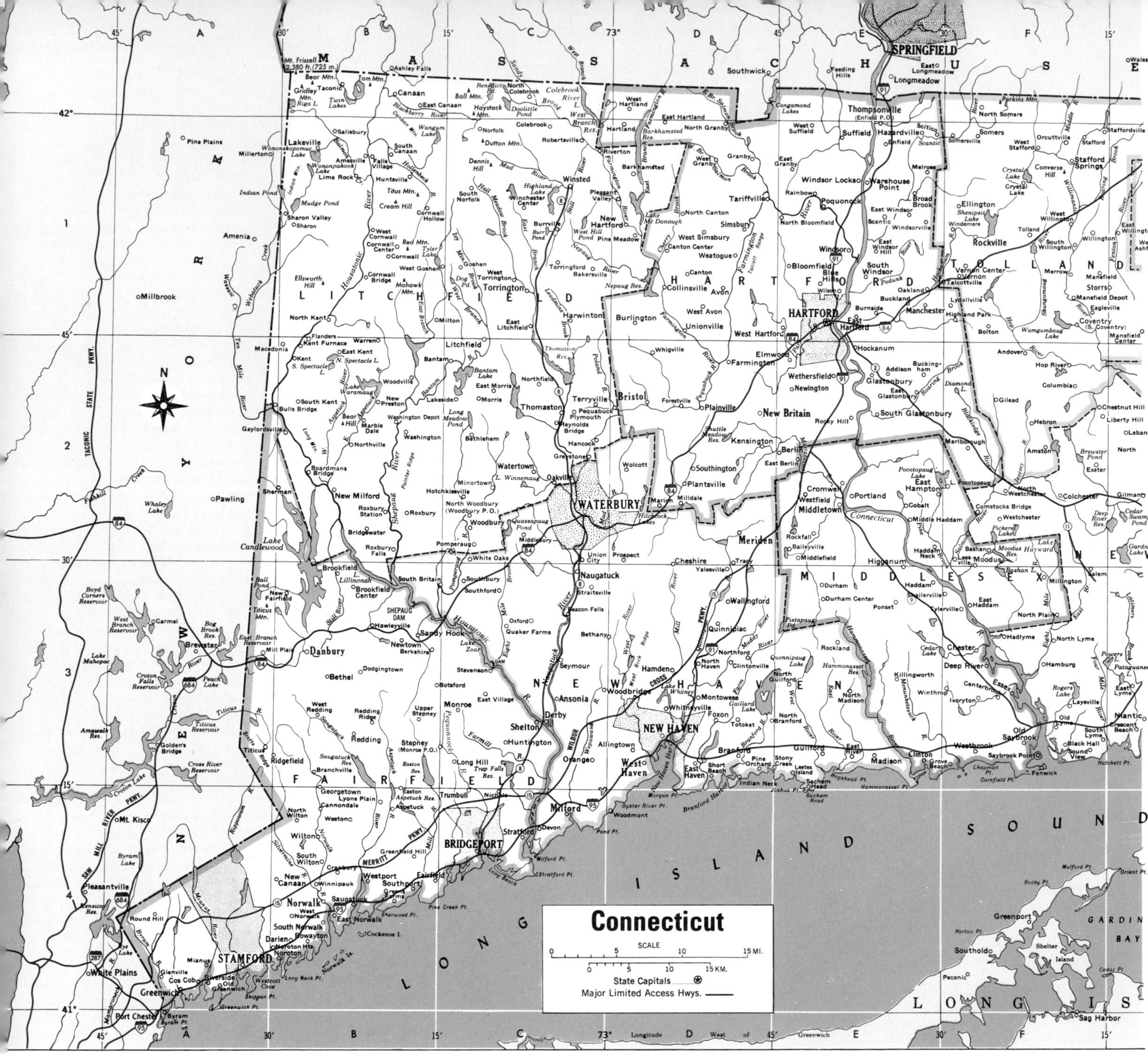

Connecticut

SCALE
0 — 5 — 10 — 15 MI.
0 — 5 — 10 — 15 KM.
State Capitals ⊛
Major Limited Access Hwys. ——

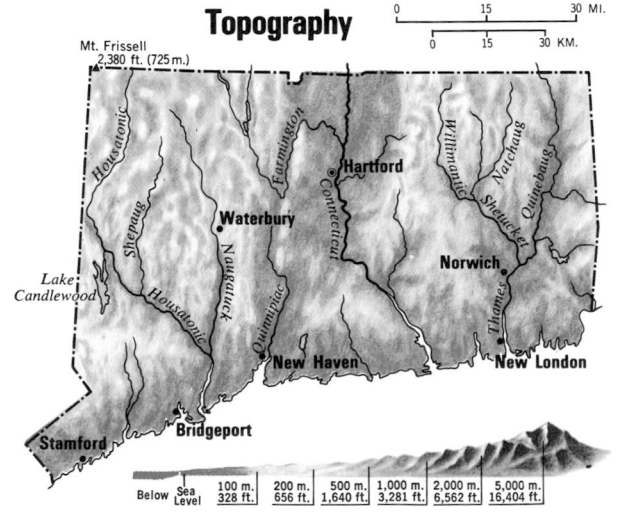

Topography

Mt. Frissell
2,380 ft. (725 m.)

0 — 15 — 30 MI.
0 — 15 — 30 KM.

Below Sea Level	100 m. 328 ft.	200 m. 656 ft.	500 m. 1,640 ft.	1,000 m. 3,281 ft.	2,000 m. 6,562 ft.	5,000 m. 16,404 ft.

COUNTIES

Fairfield 827,645 ....B3
Hartford 851,783 ....D1
Litchfield 174,092 ....B1
Middlesex 143,196 ....E3
New Haven 804,219 ....C3
New London 254,957 ....G2
Tolland 128,699 ....F1
Windham 102,525 ....H1

CITIES and TOWNS

Abington 600 ....G1
Addison 700 ....E2
Allingtown D3
Amston 900 ....F2
Andover • 2,540 ....F2
Ansonia 18,403 ....C3
Ashford P.O. (Warrenville)
  500 ....G1
Ashford • 3,765 ....G1
Avon 1,434 ....C1
Avon • 13,937 ....C1
Bakersville 750 ....D1
Ballouville 800 ....H1
Baltic G2
Bantam 757 ....B2
Barkhamsted • 3,369 ....D1
Beacon Falls • 5,083 ....C3
Berkshire 500 ....B3
Berlin • 16,787 ....E2

Bethany • 4,608 ....C3
Bethel 8,835 ....B3
Bethel • 17,541 ....B3
Bethlehem 1,762 ....C2
Bethlehem • 3,071 ....C2
Bloomfield • 19,483 ....E1
Blue Hills 3,206 ....E1
Bolton • 4,575 ....F1
Branchville 600 ....B3
Branford 5,688 ....D3
Branford • 27,603 ....D3
Bridgeport 141,686 ....C4
Bridgewater • 1,654 ....B2
Bristol 60,640 ....D2
Broad Brook 3,585 ....E1
Brookfield • 14,113 ....B3
Brookfield Center B3
Brooklyn • 6,681 ....H1
Buckingham 800 ....E2
Burlington • 7,026 ....D1
Burnside E1
Byram A4
Canaan 1,057 ....B1
Canaan • 1,194 ....B1
Canterbury • 4,467 ....H2
Canton 1,680 ....D1
Canton • 8,268 ....D1
Center Groton 600 ....G3
Centerbrook 800 ....F3
Central Village 950 ....H2
Chaplin • 2,048 ....G1
Cheshire 5,759 ....D2

Cheshire 25,684 ....D2
Chester 1,563 ....F3
Chester • 3,417 ....F3
Clinton 3,439 ....E3
Clinton • 12,767 ....E3
Clintonville D3
Cobalt 700 ....E2
Colchester 3,212 ....F2
Colchester • 10,980 ....F2
Colebrook 1,365 ....C1
Collinsville 2,591 ....D1
Columbia • 4,510 ....F1
Cornwall • 1,414 ....B1
Cos Cob A4
Coventry 3,769 ....F1
Coventry • 10,063 ....F1
Cranbury 700 ....B4
Cromwell • 12,286 ....E2
Crystal Lake 1,175 ....F1
Danbury 65,585 ....A3
Danielson 4,441 ....H1
Darien • 18,196 ....A4
Dayville H1
Deep River 2,520 ....F3
Deep River • 4,332 ....F3
Derby 12,199 ....C3
Devon C4
Durham 2,650 ....E3
Durham • 5,732 ....E3
East Berlin 950 ....E2
East Brooklyn 1,481 ....H1
Cheshire 5,759 ....D2

East Canaan 800 ....B1
East Granby • 4,302 ....E1
East Haddam • 6,676 ....F3
East Hampton 2,167 ....E2
East Hampton • 10,428 ....E2
East Hartford 50,452 ....E1
East Hartland 900 ....D1
East Haven • 26,144 ....D3
East Killingly 900 ....H1
East Lyme • 15,340 ....G3
East Morris 800 ....C2
East Norwalk B4
East Putnam 500 ....H1
East River 500 ....E3
East Windsor • 10,081 ....E1
East Windsor Hill 500 .....E1
Eastford • 1,314 ....G1
Easton • 6,303 ....B4
Ellington • 11,197 ....F1
Elmwood D2
Enfield 8,151 ....E1
Enfield • 45,532 ....E1
Essex 2,500 ....F3
Essex • 5,904 ....F3
Fabyan 600 ....H1
Fairfield • 53,418 ....B4
Falls Village 600 ....B1
Farmington 20,608 ....D2
Fenwick 89 ....F3
Forestville D2
Foxon D2
Franklin • 1,810 ....G2

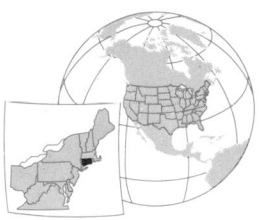

AREA 5,018 sq. mi. (12,997 sq. km.)
POPULATION 3,295,669
CAPITAL Hartford
LARGEST CITY Bridgeport
HIGHEST POINT Mt. Frissell (S. Slope) 2,380 ft. (725 m.)
SETTLED IN 1635
ADMITTED TO UNION January 9, 1788
POPULAR NAME Constitution State; Nutmeg State
STATE FLOWER Mountain Laurel
STATE BIRD Robin

Milldale 975	D2
Milton 600	C1
Mohegan 700	G3
Monroe • 16,896	C3
Monroe P.O. (Stepney)	B3
Montowese	D3
Montville 1,711	G3
Montville • 16,673	G3
Moodus 1,170	F2
Moosup 3,289	H2
Morningside Park	G3
Morris • 2,039	C2
Mystic 2,618	H3
Naugatuck 30,625	C3
New Britain 75,491	C1
New Canaan • 17,864	B4
New Fairfield • 12,911	B3
New Hartford 1,269	C1
New Hartford • 5,769	C1
New Haven 130,474	D3
New London 28,540	G3
New Milford 5,775	B2
New Milford • 23,629	B2
New Preston 1,217	B2
Newington • 29,208	D1
Newtown 1,800	B3
Newtown • 20,779	B3
Niantic 3,048	G3
Nichols	C4
Noank 1,406	G3
Norfolk • 2,060	B1
Noroton	B4
Noroton Heights	B4
North Bloomfield 500	E1
North Branford • 12,996	D3
North Franklin 500	G2
North Granby 1,455	D1
North Grosvenor Dale 1,705	H1
North Guilford	D3
North Haven • 22,249	D3
North Lyme	F3
North Stonington • 4,884	H3
North Wilton 900	B4
North Woodbury 900	C2
Northfield 600	C2
Northford	D3
Northville 700	B2
Norwalk 78,331	B4
Norwich 37,391	G2
Norwichtown	G2
Oakdale 608	G3
Oakville 8,741	C2
Occum	G2
Old Greenwich	A4
Old Lyme • 6,535	F3
Old Mystic 600	H3
Old Saybrook 1,820	F3
Old Saybrook • 9,552	F3
Oneco 550	H2
Orange • 12,830	C3
Oxford • 8,685	C3
Pawcatuck 5,289	H3
Pequabuck 642	C2
Plainfield 2,856	H2
Plainfield • 14,363	H2
Plainville • 17,392	D2
Plantsville	D2
Pleasure Beach 1,356	G3
Plymouth • 11,822	C2
Pomfret • 3,102	H1
Poquonock	E1

Poquonock Bridge 2,770	G3
Portland 5,645	E2
Portland • 8,418	E2
Preston 5,006	H2
Prospect • 7,775	D2
Putnam 6,835	H1
Putnam • 9,031	H1
Putnam Heights 500	H1
Quaker Hill 2,052	G3
Quinebaug 1,031	H1
Quinnipiac	D3
Redding • 7,927	B3
Redding Ridge 550	B3
Ridgefield 6,363	B3
Ridgefield • 20,919	B3
Riverside	A4
Rockfall 900	E2
Rocky Hill • 16,554	E2
Rogers 650	H1
Round Hill 900	A4
Rowayton	B4
Roxbury • 1,825	B2
Salem • 3,310	F3
Salisbury • 4,000	B1
Sandy Hook	B3
Saugatuck	B4
Saybrook Point 700	F3
Scantic 500	E1
Scotland • 1,215	G2
Seymour • 14,288	C3
Sharon • 2,928	B1
Shelton 35,418	C3
Sherman • 2,809	B2
Short Beach	D3
Simsbury 5,577	D1
Simsbury • 22,023	D1
Somers 1,643	F1
Somers • 9,108	F1
Somersville 750	F1
South Coventry (Coventry) 1,257	F1
South Glastonbury	E2
South Killingly 500	H1
South Norwalk	B4
South Wilton	B4
South Windham 1,644	G2
South Windsor • 22,090	E1
South Woodstock 1,112	G1
Southbury • 15,818	C3
Southington • 38,518	D2
Southport	B4
Stafford • 11,091	F1
Stafford Springs 4,100	F1
Staffordville 500	F1
Stamford 108,056	A4
Stepney	B3
Sterling • 2,357	H2
Stonington 1,100	H3
Stonington • 16,919	H3
Stony Creek	E3
Storrs 12,198	F1
Stratford • 49,389	C4
Suffield 1,353	E1
Suffield • 11,427	E1
Taftville	G2
Talcottville 875	E1
Tariffville 1,477	D1
Terryville 5,426	C2
Thamesville	G2
Thomaston • 6,947	C2

Thompson • 8,668	H1
Thompsonville 8,458	E1
Tolland 11,001	F1
Torringford	C1
Torrington 33,687	C1
Totoket 950	D3
Trumbull • 32,016	C4
Uncasville 1,597	G3
Union • 612	G1
Union City	C2
Unionville	D1
Vernon Center	F1
Vernon • 29,841	F1
Versailles 540	G2
Voluntown • 2,113	H2
Wallingford 17,827	D3
Wallingford • 40,822	D3
Warehouse Point	E1
Warren • 1,226	B2
Washington • 3,905	B2
Washington Depot 900	B2
Waterbury 108,961	C2
Waterford 2,736	G3
Waterford • 17,930	G3
Watertown 20,456	C2
Wauregan 1,079	H2
Weatogue 2,521	D1
West Avon	D1
West Granby 567	D1
West Hartford • 60,110	D1
West Haven 54,021	D3
West Mystic 3,595	H3
West Norwalk 950	B4
West Simsbury 2,149	D1
West Suffield	E1
Westbrook 2,000	F3
Westbrook • 5,414	F3
Westfield	E2
Weston • 8,648	B4
Westport • 24,410	B4
Wethersfield • 25,651	E2
Whitneyville	D3
Willimantic 14,746	G2
Willington • 5,979	F1
Wilton 15,989	B4
Winchester • 11,524	C1
Windham • 22,039	G2
Windsor 17,517	E1
Windsor • 27,817	E1
Windsor Locks • 12,358	E1
Winnipauk 650	B4
Winsted 8,254	C1
Winthrop 750	E3
Wolcott • 13,700	D2
Woodbridge • 7,924	D3
Woodbury 1,212	C2
Woodbury • 8,131	C2
Woodmont 1,770	D4
Woodstock • 6,008	H1
Yalesville	D3
Yantic 500	G2

OTHER FEATURES	
Aspetuck (res.)	B4
Bantam (lake)	C2
Barkhamsted (res.)	D1
Bear (mt.)	B1
Byram (riv.)	A4
Candlewood (lake)	A2
Coast Guard Academy	G3

Colebrook River (lake)	C1
Congamond (lakes)	E1
Connecticut (riv.)	D1
Dennis (hill)	C1
Easton (res.)	B3
Eight Mile (riv.)	F3
Farmington (riv.)	D1
French (riv.)	H1
Frissell (mt.)	B1
Gaillard (lake)	D3
Gardner (lake)	G3
Hammonasset (pt.)	E3
Hammonasset (res.)	E3
Haystack (mt.)	C1
Highland (lake)	C1
Hockanum (riv.)	E1
Hop (riv.)	F1
Housatonic (riv.)	C1
Lillinonah (lake)	B3
Little (riv.)	H1
Long Island (sound)	C4
Mad (riv.)	C2
Mashapaug (lake)	G1
Mason (isl.)	H3
Mattabesset (riv.)	E2
Mianus (riv.)	A4
Mohawk (mt.)	B1
Moosup (riv.)	H2
Mount Hope (riv.)	G1
Mudge (riv.)	B1
Mystic (riv.)	H3
Natchaug (riv.)	G2
Naugatuck (riv.)	C3
Nepaug (riv.)	C1
Niantic (riv.)	G3
Norwalk (riv.)	B4
Pachaug (pond)	H2
Pawcatuck (riv.)	H3
Pequabuck (riv.)	D2
Pequonnock (riv.)	C4
Pocotopaug (lake)	E2
Quaddick (res.)	H1
Quinebaug (riv.)	H2
Quinnipiac (riv.)	D3
Rippowam (riv.)	A4
Sachem (head)	E4
Salmon (brook)	D1
Salmon (riv.)	F2
Saugatuck (res.)	B3
Scantic (riv.)	E1
Shenipsit (lake)	F1
Shepaug (riv.)	B2
Shetucket (riv.)	G2
Silvermine (riv.)	B4
Spectacle (lakes)	B2
Still (riv.)	B3
Still (riv.)	C1
Tolcott (range)	D2
Thames (riv.)	G3
Thomaston (res.)	C2
Titicus (riv.)	A3
Trap Falls (res.)	C3
Twin (lakes)	B1
Wamgumbaug (lake)	F1
Waramaug (lake)	B2
West Rock Ridge (hills)	D3
Willimantic (riv.)	F1
Wononskopomuc (lake)	B1
Yantic (riv.)	G2

• Population of town or township

Gales Ferry 1,191	G3
Gaylordsville 960	A2
Georgetown 1,694	B4
Glastonbury 7,082	E2
Glastonbury • 27,901	E2
Glenville	A4
Goshen • 2,329	C1
Granby 1,912	D1
Granby • 9,369	D1
Greenfield Hill	B4
Greenwich • 58,441	A4
Grosvenor Dale 700	H1
Groton 9,837	G3
Groton • 45,144	G3
Guilford 2,588	E3
Guilford • 19,848	E3
Haddam • 6,769	E3
Hamden • 52,434	D3
Hampton • 1,578	G1
Hanover 500	G2
Hartford (cap.) 139,739	E1
Hartland • 1,866	D1
Harwinton 3,293	C1
Harwinton • 5,228	C1
Hawleyville 600	B3
Hazardville 5,179	E1
Hebron • 7,079	F2
Higganum 1,692	E2
Highland Park 500	F1
Hockanum	E2
Huntington	C3
Indian Neck	D3

Ivoryton	F3
Jewett City 3,349	H2
Kensington 8,306	D2
Kent • 2,918	B2
Killingly • 15,889	H1
Killingworth • 4,814	E3
Lake Pocotopaug 3,029	F2
Lakeville	B1
Lebanon • 6,041	G2
Ledyard • 14,913	G3
Leetes Island 500	E3
Lisbon • 3,790	G2
Litchfield 1,378	C2
Litchfield • 8,365	C2
Long Hill	C3
Lords Point 500	H3
Lyons Plain 700	B4
Madison 2,139	E3
Madison • 15,485	E3
Manchester 31,058	E1
Manchester • 51,618	E1
Mansfield • 21,103	F1
Mansfield Center 1,043	G1
Marion 900	D2
Marlborough 1,039	F2
Marlborough • 5,535	F2
Meriden 59,479	D2
Middlebury • 6,145	C2
Middlefield • 3,925	E2
Middletown 42,762	E2
Milford 48,168	C4
Mill Plain 750	A3

Agriculture, Industry and Resources

DOMINANT LAND USE

- Specialized Dairy
- Dairy, Poultry, Mixed Farming
- Forests
- Urban Areas

MAJOR MINERAL OCCURRENCES

Cl Clay   Mi Mica

Major Industrial Areas

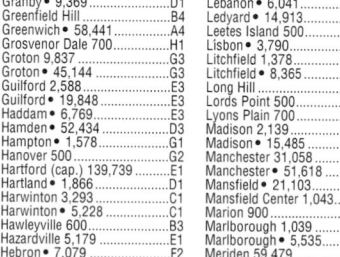

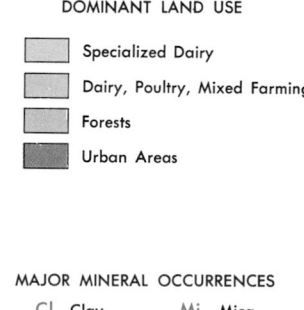

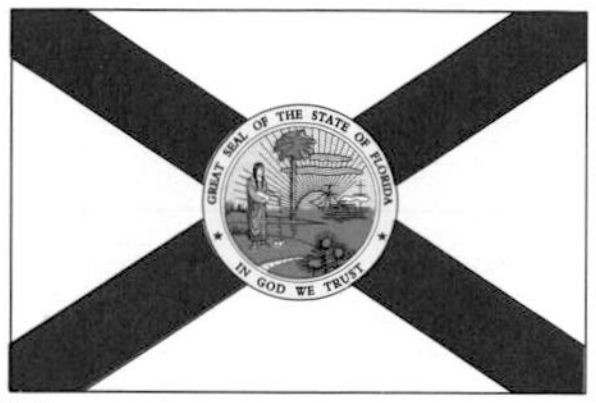

AREA 58,664 sq. mi. (151,940 sq. km.)
POPULATION 13,003,362
CAPITAL Tallahassee
LARGEST CITY Jacksonville
HIGHEST POINT (Walton County) 345 ft. (105 m.)
SETTLED IN 1565
ADMITTED TO UNION March 3, 1845
POPULAR NAME Sunshine State; Peninsula State
STATE FLOWER Orange Blossom
STATE BIRD Mockingbird

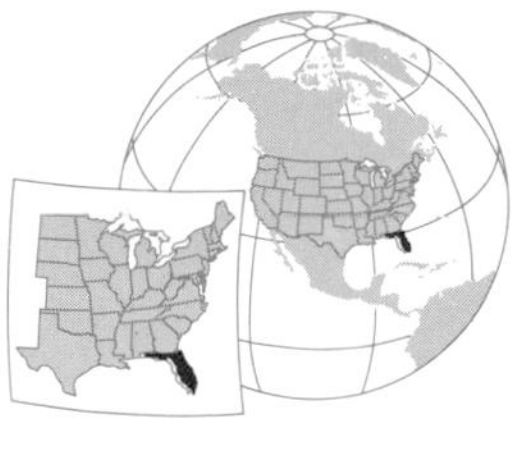

Topography

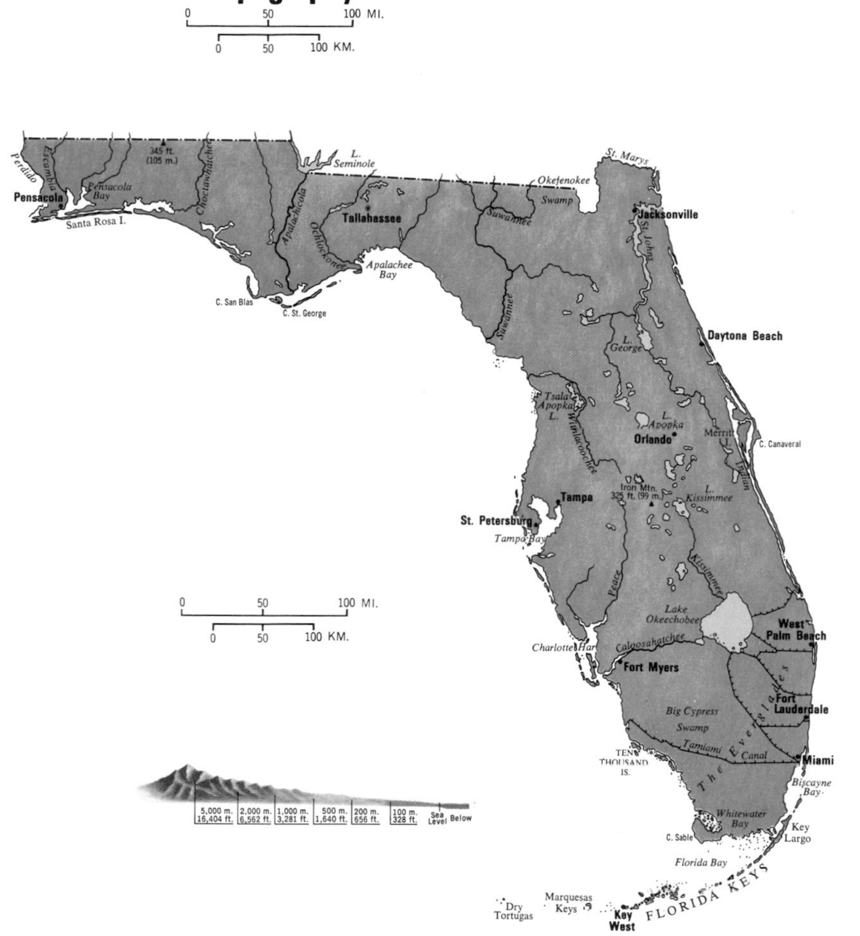

0 50 100 MI.
0 50 100 KM.
Perdido
Escambia
345 ft. (105 m.)
Pensacola
Pensacola Bay
Santa Rosa I.
Choctawhatchee
Apalachicola
L. Seminole
Tallahassee
Ochlockonee
Apalachee Bay
C. San Blas
C. St. George
Okefenokee Swamp
St. Marys
Suwannee
Jacksonville
St. Johns
L. George
Daytona Beach
Tsala Apopka L.
L. Apopka
Orlando
Merritt I.
C. Canaveral
Iron Mtn. 325 ft. (99 m.)
L. Kissimmee
Tampa
St. Petersburg
Tampa Bay
Peace
Kissimmee
Lake Okeechobee
West Palm Beach
Charlotte Har.
Caloosahatchee
Fort Myers
Fort Lauderdale
Big Cypress Swamp
Tamiami Canal
The Everglades
Miami
Ten Thousand Is.
Biscayne Bay
Whitewater Bay
C. Sable
Key Largo
Florida Bay
Dry Tortugas
Marquesas Keys
Key West
FLORIDA KEYS
5,000 m. 16,404 ft.
2,000 m. 6,562 ft.
1,000 m. 3,281 ft.
500 m. 1,640 ft.
200 m. 656 ft.
100 m. 328 ft.
Sea Level
Below

COUNTIES

Alachua 181,596 D2
Baker 18,486 D1
Bay 126,994 C6
Bradford 22,515 D2
Brevard 398,978 F3
Broward 1,255,488 F5
Calhoun 11,011 D6
Charlotte 110,975 E5
Citrus 93,515 D3
Clay 105,986 E2
Collier 152,099 E5
Columbia 42,613 D1
Dade 1,937,094 F6
De Soto 19,039 E4
Dixie 10,585 C2
Duval 672,971 E1
Escambia 262,798 B6
Flagler 28,701 E2
Franklin 8,967 B2
Gadsden 41,105 B1
Gilchrist 9,667 D2
Glades 7,591 E5
Gulf 11,504 D7
Hamilton 10,930 D1
Hardee 19,499 E4
Hendry 25,773 E5
Hernando 101,115 D3
Highlands 68,432 E4
Hillsborough 834,054 D4
Holmes 15,778 C5
Indian River 90,208 F4
Jackson 41,375 D5
Jefferson 11,296 C1
Lafayette 5,578 C2
Lake 152,104 E3
Lee 335,113 E5
Leon 192,493 B1
Levy 25,923 D2
Liberty 5,569 B1
Madison 16,569 C1
Manatee 211,707 D4
Marion 194,833 D2
Martin 100,900 F4
Monroe 78,024 E7
Nassau 43,941 E1
Okaloosa 143,776 C6
Okeechobee 29,627 F4
Orange 677,491 E3
Osceola 107,728 E3
Palm Beach 863,518 F5
Pasco 281,131 D3
Pinellas 851,659 D4
Polk 405,382 E4
Putnam 65,070 E2
Saint Johns 51,303 E2
Saint Lucie 87,182 F4
Santa Rosa 81,608 B6
Sarasota 277,776 D4
Seminole 287,529 E3
Sumter 31,577 D3
Suwannee 26,780 C1
Taylor 17,111 C1
Union 10,252 D1
Volusia 370,712 E2
Wakulla 14,202 B1
Walton 27,760 C6
Washington 16,919 C6

CITIES and TOWNS

Alachua 4,529 D2
Alford 472 D6
Altamonte Springs 34,879 E3
Altha 497 A1
Altoona 800 E3
Alturas 900 E4
Alva 1,036 E5
Anna Maria 1,744 D4
Anthony 500 D2
Apalachicola▲ 2,602 A2
Apollo Beach 6,025 C3
Apopka 13,512 E3
Arcadia▲ 6,488 E4
Archer 1,372 D2
Aripeka 450 D3
Astatula 981 E3
Astor 1,273 E2
Atlantic Beach 11,636 E1
Auburndale 8,858 E3
Avon Park 8,042 E4
Azalea Park 8,926 E3
Babson Park 1,125 E4
Bagdad 1,457 B6
Baker 500 C5
Bal Harbour 3,045 C4
Baldwin 1,450 E1
Barberville 500 E2
Bartow▲ 14,716 E4
Bascom 90 A1
Basinger 300 F4
Bay Harbor Islands 4,703 B4
Bay Lake E3
Bay Pines 4,171 B3
Bayshore 17,062 E5
Bayshore Gardens 14,945 D4
Bee Ridge 6,406 D4
Bell 267 D2
Belle Glade 16,177 F5
Belle Glade Camp 1,616 F5
Belle Isle 5,272 E3
Belleair 3,968 B2
Belleair Beach 2,070 B2
Belleair Bluffs 2,128 B3
Belleair Shore 80 B3
Belleview 2,666 D2
Beverly Beach 312 E2
Biscayne Park 3,068 B4
Bithlo 4,834 E3
Blountstown▲ 2,404 A1
Boca Grande 900 D5
Boca Raton 61,492 F5
Bokeelia 750 D5
Bonifay▲ 2,612 C5
Bonita Sings 5,435 E5
Bostwick 500 E2
Boulogne E1
Bowling Green 1,836 E4
Boynton Beach 46,194 F5
Bradenton Beach 1,657 D4
Bradenton▲ 43,779 D4
Bradley 1,108 D4
Brandon 57,985 D4
Branford 670 D2
Briny Breezes 400 G5
Bristol▲ 937 B1
Broadview Park-Rock Hill
6,022 B4
Bronson▲ 875 D2
Brooker 312 D2
Brooksville▲ 7,440 D3
Browardale 6,257 B4
Browns Village B5
Bruce 221 C6
Bunche Park 4,388 B4
Bunnell▲ 1,873 E2
Bushnell▲ 1,998 D3
Callahan 946 E1
Callaway 12,253 D6
Campbellton 202 D5
Canal Point 900 F5
Candler 275 E2
Cantonment B6
Cape Canaveral 8,014 F3
Cape Coral 74,991 E5
Carol City 53,331 B4
Carrabelle 1,200 B2
Caryville 631 C6
Cassadaga 325 E3
Casselberry 18,911 E3
Cedar Grove 1,479 D6
Cedar Key 668 C2
Center Hill 735 D3
Century 1,989 B5
Charlotte Harbor 3,327 E5
Chattahoochee 4,382 B1
Cherry Lake Farms 400 C1
Chiefland 1,917 D2
Chipley▲ 3,866 D6
Chokoloskee 600 E6
Christmas 800 E3
Cinco Bayou 322 B6
Citra 500 D2
Clarksville 350 D6
Clearwater▲ 98,784 B2
Clermont 6,910 E3
Cleveland 2,896 E5
Clewiston 6,085 E5
Cocoa 17,722 F3
Cocoa Beach 12,123 F3
Coconut Creek 27,485 F5
Coleman 857 D3
Compass Lake 296 D6
Concord 300 B1
Cooper City 20,791 B4
Copeland 350 E6
Coral Cove 2,042 D4
Coral Gables 40,091 B5
Coral Springs 79,443 F5
Cornwell 700 E4
Cortez 4,509 D4
Cottagehill 500 B6
Cottondale 900 D6
Crawfordville▲ 1,110 B1
Crescent City 1,859 E2
Crestview▲ 9,886 C6
Cross City▲ 2,041 C2
Crystal Lake 5,300 D6
Crystal River 4,044 D3
Crystal Springs 800 D3
Cutler Ridge 21,268 F6
Cypress 9,188 A1
Cypress Gardens 8,043 E3
Cypress Quarters 1,343 F4
Dade City▲ 5,633 D3
Dania 13,024 B4
Davenport 1,529 E3
Davie 47,217 B4
Day 61,921 C1
Daytona Beach 2,335 F2
Daytona Beach Shores 1,324 F2
De Bary 7,176 E3
De Funiak Springs▲ 5,120 C6
De Land▲ 16,491 E2
De Leon Springs 1,481 E2
Deer Park 250 F3
Deerfield Beach 46,325 F5
Delray Beach 47,181 F5
Deltona 50,828 E3
Destin 8,080 C6
Doctors Inlet 800 E1
Dover 2,606 D4
Dowling Park 250 C1
Dundee 2,335 E3
Dunedin 34,012 B2
Dunnellon 1,624 D2
Eagle Lake 1,758 E4
Earleton 350 D2
East Lake-Orient Park 6,171 C2
East Naples 22,951 E5
East Palatka 1,989 E2
Eastpoint 1,577 B2
Eatonville 2,170 E3
Ebro 255 C6
Edgewater 15,337 F3
Edgewood 1,062 E3
Egypt Lake 14,580 C2
El Portal 2,457 B4
Elfers 12,356 D3
Elkton 240 E2
Englewood 15,025 D5
Ensley 16,362 B6
Espanola 300 E2
Estero 3,177 E5
Esto 253 C5
Eustis 12,967 E3
Everglades City 524 E6
Fairbanks 300 D2
Fairfield 450 D2
Fanning Springs 493 C2
Felda 500 E5
Fellsmere 2,179 F4
Fernandina Beach▲ 8,765 E1
Five Points 1,136 D1
Flagler Beach 3,820 E2
Florahome 400 E2
Floral City 2,609 D3
Florida City 5,806 F6
Florida Ridge 12,218 F4
Foley 525 C1
Fort Denaud 600 E5
Fort Green 300 E4
Fort Lauderdale▲ 149,377 C4
Fort McCoy 600 E2
Fort Meade 4,976 E4
Fort Myers Beach 9,284 E5
Fort Myers▲ 45,206 E5
Fort Ogden 900 E4
Fort Pierce▲ 36,830 F4
Fort Walton Beach 21,471 C6
Fort White 268 D2
Fountain 900 D6
Freeport 843 C6
Frink 275 D6
Frostproof 2,808 E4
Fruitland Park 2,754 D3
Fruitville 9,808 D4
Gainesville▲ 84,770 D2
Geneva 1,120 E3
Georgetown 687 E2
Gibsonton 7,706 C3
Gifford 6,278 F4
Glen Saint Mary 462 D1
Glenwood 400 E2
Golden Beach 774 C4
Golden Gate 14,148 E5
Golf 234 F5
Gomez 400 F4
Gonzalez 7,669 B6
Goodland 600 E6
Goulding 4,159 B6
Goulds 7,284 F6
Graceville 2,675 D5
Graham 225 D2
Grand Ridge 536 A1
Grandin 250 E2
Grant 500 F4
Green Cove Springs▲ 4,497 E2
Greenacres City 18,683 F5
Greensboro 586 B1
Greenville 950 C1
Greenwood 474 A1
Gretna 1,981 B1
Grove City 2,374 D5
Groveland 2,300 E3
Gulf Breeze 5,530 B6
Gulf Hammock 325 D2
Gulf Harbors D3
Gulf Stream 690 F5
Gulfport 11,727 B3
Haines City 11,683 E3
Hallandale 30,996 B4
Hampton 296 D2
Harlem 2,826 F5
Harold 500 B6
Hastings 595 E2
Havana 1,654 B1
Hawthorne 1,305 D2
Hernando 2,103 D3
Hialeah 188,004 B4
Hialeah Gardens 7,713 B4
High Point 2,288 B3
High Springs 3,144 D2
Highland Beach 3,209 F5
Highland City 1,919 E4
Highland Park 155 E4
Hiland Park 3,865 C6
Hillcrest Heights 221 E4
Hilliard 1,751 E1
Hillsboro Beach 1,748 F5
Hinson 250 B1
Hobe Sound 11,507 F4
Holder 350 D3
Hollister 980 E2
Holly Hill 11,141 E2
Hollywood 121,697 B4
Holmes Beach 4,810 D4
Holt 850 C6
Homestead 26,866 F6
Homosassa 2,113 D3
Homosassa Springs 6,271 D3
Horseshoe Beach 252 C2
Hosford 750 B1
Howey In The Hills 724 E3
Hudson 7,344 D3
Hurlburt B6
Hypoluxo 830 F5
Immokalee 14,120 E5
Indialantic 2,844 F3
Indian Creek 44 B4
Indian Harbour Beach 6,933 F3
Indian River Shores 2,278 F4
Indian Rocks Beach 3,963 B3
Indian Shores 1,405 B3
Indiantown 4,794 F4
Inglis 1,241 D2
Intercession City 600 E3
Interlachen 1,160 E2
Inverness▲ 5,797 D3
Islamorada 1,220 F7
Islandia 13 F6
Jacksonville Beach 17,839 E1
Jacksonville▲ 672,971 E1
Jasmine Estates 17,136 D3
Jasper▲ 2,099 D1
Jay 666 B5
Jennings 712 C1
Jensen Beach 9,884 F4
June Park 4,080 F3
Juno Beach 2,121 F5
Jupiter 24,986 F5
Jupiter Island 549 F4
Kathleen 2,743 D3
Kenansville 650 F4
Kendall 87,271 B5
Kenneth City 4,462 B3
Key Biscayne 8,854 B5
Key Colony Beach 977 F7
Key Largo 11,336 F6
Key West▲ 24,832 E7
Keystone Heights 1,315 E2
Kinard 295 D6
Kissimmee▲ 30,050 E3
La Belle▲ 2,703 E5
La Crosse 122 D2
Lacoochee 2,072 D3
Lady Lake 8,071 E3
Lake Alfred 3,622 E3
Lake Buena Vista 1,776 E3
Lake Butler▲ 2,116 D1
Lake Carroll 13,012 C2
Lake City▲ 10,005 D1
Lake Como 340 E2
Lake Forest B4
Lake Harbor 600 F5
Lake Helen 2,344 E3
Lake Jem 314 E3
Lake Magdalene 15,973 D3
Lake Mary 5,929 E3
Lake Monroe 500 E3
Lake Park 6,704 F5
Lake Placid 1,158 E4
Lake Wales 9,670 E4
Lake Worth 28,564 G5
Lakeland 70,576 D3
Lakeport 375 E5
Lakewood 7,211 C5
Land O'Lakes 7,892 D3
Lantana 8,392 F5
Largo 65,674 B3
Lauderdale Lakes 27,341 B3
Lauderdale-by-the-Sea 2,990 C3
Lauderhill 49,708 B3
Laurel 8,245 D4
Laurel Hill 543 C5
Lawtey 676 D1
Layton 183 F7
Lazy Lake 33 B3
Lecanto 1,243 D3
Lee 306 C1
Leesburg 14,903 E3

(continued on following page)

(continued)

Lehigh Acres 13,611 ... E5
Leisure City 19,379 ... F6
Leonia 350 ... C5
Leto ... C2
Lighthouse Point 10,378 ... F5
Live Oak▲ 6,332 ... D1
Lloyd 500 ... C1
Lochloosa 400 ... E2
Longboat Key 5,937 ... D4
Longwood 13,316 ... E3
Lorida 950 ... E4
Loughman 1,214 ... E3
Lowell 250 ... D2
Loxahatchee 950 ... F5
Lutz 10,552 ... D3
Lynn Haven 9,298 ... C6
Macclenny▲ 3,966 ... D1
Madeira Beach 4,225 ... B3
Madison▲ 3,345 ... C1
Maitland 9,110 ... E3
Malabar 1,977 ... F3
Malone 765 ... A1
Mango 8,700 ... D4
Marathon 8,857 ... E7
Marco (Marco Island) 9,493 ... E6
Margate 42,985 ... F5
Marianna▲ 6,292 ... A1
Marineland 21 ... E2
Mary Esther 4,139 ... B6
Masaryktown 389 ... D3
Mascotte 1,761 ... E3
Mayo▲ 917 ... C1
McDavid 500 ... B5
McIntosh 411 ... D2
Medley 663 ... B4
Melbourne 59,646 ... F3
Melbourne Beach 3,021 ... F3
Melrose 6,477 ... D2
Melrose Park 5,672 ... B4
Memphis 6,760 ... D4
Merritt Island 32,886 ... F3
Mexico Beach 992 ... D6
Miami▲ 358,548 ... B5
Miami Beach 92,639 ... C5
Miami Lakes 12,750 ... B4
Miami Shores 10,084 ... B4
Miami Springs 13,268 ... B5
Micanopy 612 ... D2
Micco 8,757 ... F4
Miccosukee 300 ... B1
Middleburg 6,223 ... E1
Midway 852 ... B1
Milligan 950 ... C6
Milton▲ 7,216 ... B6
Mims 9,412 ... F3
Minneola 1,515 ... E3
Miramar 40,663 ... B4
Molino 1,207 ... B6
Montbrook 250 ... D2
Monticello▲ 2,573 ... C1
Montverde 890 ... E3
Moore Haven▲ 1,432 ... E5
Mossy Head 280 ... C6
Mount Dora 7,196 ... E3
Mulberry 2,988 ... E4
Murdock 272 ... D4
Myakka City 672 ... D4
Myrtle Grove 17,402 ... B6
Naples▲ 19,505 ... E5
Naples Park 8,002 ... E5
Naranja 5,790 ... F6
Neptune Beach 6,816 ... E1
Newberry 1,644 ... D2
New Port Richey 14,044 ... D3
New Smyrna Beach 16,543 ... F2
Niceville 10,507 ... C6
Nichols 300 ... E4
Nocatee 950 ... E4
Nokomis 3,448 ... D4
Noma 207 ... C5
Norland 22,109 ... B4
North Bay Village 5,383 ... B4
North Fort Myers 30,027 ... E5
North Lauderdale 26,506 ... B3
North Miami 49,998 ... B4
North Miami Beach 35,359 ... C4
North Naples 13,422 ... E5
North Palm Beach 11,343 ... F5
North Port 11,973 ... D4
North Redington Beach 1,135 ... B3
Oak Hill 917 ... F3
Oakland 700 ... E3
Oakland Park 26,326 ... B3
Ocala▲ 42,045 ... D2
Ocean Breeze Park 519 ... F4
Ocean Ridge 1,570 ... F5
Ochopee 750 ... E6
Ocoee 12,778 ... E3
Odessa 500 ... D3
Ojus 15,519 ... B4
Okahumpka 900 ... D3
Okeechobee▲ 4,943 ... F4
Oklawaha 700 ... E2
Old Town 850 ... C2
Oldsmar 8,361 ... B2
Olustee 400 ... D1
Ona ... E4
Oneco ... D4
Opa Locka 15,283 ... B4
Orange ... B1
Orange City 5,347 ... E3
Orange Lake 900 ... D2
Orange Park 9,488 ... E1
Orange Springs 500 ... E2
Orchid 10 ... F4
Orlando▲ 164,693 ... E3
Ormond Beach 29,721 ... E2
Ormond-by-the-Sea 8,157 ... E2
Osprey 2,597 ... D4
Osteen 875 ... E3
Otter Creek 136 ... D2
Oviedo 11,114 ... E3
Oxford ... D3
Ozona 900 ... D3
Pace 6,277 ... B6
Pahokee 6,822 ... F5
Palatka▲ 10,201 ... E2
Palm Bay 62,632 ... F3
Palm Beach 9,814 ... G5
Palm Beach Gardens 22,965 ... F5
Palm Beach Shores 1,040 ... G5
Palm City 3,925 ... F4
Palm Coast 14,287 ... E2
Palmetto 9,268 ... D4
Palm Harbor 50,256 ... D3
Palm River-Clair Mel 13,691 ... C3
Palm Shores 210 ... F3
Palm Springs 9,763 ... F5
Panacea 950 ... B1
Panama City▲ 34,378 ... C6
Panama City Beach 4,051 ... C6
Parker 4,598 ... C6
Parkland 3,558 ... F5
Parrish 950 ... D4
Paxton 600 ... C5
Pembroke Park 4,933 ... B4
Pembroke Pines 65,452 ... B4
Penney Farms 609 ... E2
Pennsuco 15 ... B4
Pensacola▲ 58,165 ... B6
Perrine 15,576 ... F6
Perry▲ 7,151 ... C1
Pierce 500 ... E4
Pierson 2,988 ... E2
Pine Hills 35,322 ... E3
Pineland 700 ... D5
Pinellas Park 43,426 ... B3
Placida 250 ... D5
Plantation 1,885 ... B4
Plant City 22,754 ... D3
Plymouth 950 ... E3
Polk City 1,439 ... E3
Pomona Park 663 ... E2
Pompano Beach 72,411 ... F5
Ponce de Leon 406 ... C6
Ponce Inlet 1,704 ... F2
Ponte Vedra Beach ... E1
Port Charlotte 41,535 ... D5
Portland 300 ... C6
Port Mayaca 400 ... F5
Port Orange 35,317 ... F2
Port Richey 2,523 ... D3
Port Saint Joe 4,044 ... D6
Port Saint Lucie 55,866 ... F4
Port Salerno 7,786 ... F4
Princeton 7,073 ... F6
Progress Village ... C3
Punta Gorda▲ 10,747 ... E5
Quincy▲ 7,444 ... B1
Raiford 198 ... D1
Raleigh 275 ... D2
Red Bay 300 ... C6
Reddick 554 ... D2
Redington Beach 1,626 ... B3
Redington Shores 2,366 ... B3
Richland 250 ... D3
Richmond Heights 8,583 ... F6
Riverland 5,376 ... B4
Riverview 6,478 ... D4
Riviera Beach 27,639 ... G5
Rockledge 16,023 ... F3
Roseland 1,379 ... F4
Round Lake 275 ... D6
Ruskin 6,046 ... C3
Safety Harbor 15,124 ... B2
Saint Augustine▲ 11,692 ... E2
Saint Augustine Beach 3,657 ... E2
Saint Catherine 486 ... D3
Saint Cloud 12,453 ... E3
Saint James City 1,904 ... D5
Saint Leo 1,009 ... D3
Saint Lucie 584 ... F4
Saint Marks 307 ... B1
Saint Petersburg 238,629 ... B3
Saint Petersburg Beach 9,200 B3
Samoset 3,119 ... D4
Samsula (Samsula-Spruce Creek) 3,404 ... E2
San Antonio 776 ... D3
Sanderson 800 ... D1
Sanford▲ 32,387 ... E3
Sanibel 5,468 ... D5
San Mateo 975 ... E2
Sarasota▲ 50,961 ... D4
Sarasota Springs 16,088 ... D4
Satellite Beach 9,889 ... F3
Satsuma 610 ... E2
Scottsmoor 900 ... F3
Sea Ranch Lakes 619 ... C3
Sebastian 10,205 ... F4
Sebring▲ 8,900 ... E4
Seffner 5,371 ... D4
Seminole 9,251 ... B3
Seville 500 ... E2
Sewall's Point 1,588 ... F4
Shalimar 341 ... C6
Sharpes 3,348 ... F3
Siesta Key 7,772 ... D4
Silver Springs ... D2
Sneads 1,746 ... B1
Sopchoppy 367 ... B1
Sorrento 500 ... E3
South Bay 3,558 ... F5
South Daytona 12,482 ... F2
South Miami 10,404 ... B5
South Miami Heights 30,030 ... F6
South Pasadena 5,644 ... B3
South Patrick Shores 10,249 ... F3
Southport 1,992 ... C6
South Venice 11,951 ... D4
Sparr 902 ... D2
Springfield 8,715 ... D6
Starke▲ 5,226 ... D2
Steinhatchee 800 ... C2
Stuart▲ 11,936 ... F4
Summerfield 780 ... D2
Summerland Key 350 ... E7
Sun City ... D4
Sun City Center 8,326 ... C3
Sunny Isles 11,772 ... C4
Sunnyside 1,008 ... C6
Sunrise 64,407 ... B4
Surfside 4,108 ... B4
Suwannee 365 ... C2
Sweetwater 13,909 ... B5
Switzerland ... E1
Taft 900 ... E3
Tallahassee (cap.)▲ 124,773 ... B1
Tamarac 44,822 ... B3
Tampa▲ 280,015 ... C2
Tarpon Springs 17,906 ... D3
Tavares▲ 7,383 ... E3
Tavernier 2,433 ... F6
Telogia 400 ... B1
Temple Terrace 16,444 ... C2
Tequesta 4,499 ... F5
Terra Ceia 450 ... D4
Thonotosassa 900 ... D3
Tice 3,971 ... E5
Titusville▲ 39,394 ... F3
Town'n Country 60,946 ... B2
Treasure Island 7,266 ... B3
Trenton▲ 1,287 ... D2
Trilby 930 ... D3
Umatilla 2,350 ... E3
University 23,760 ... C2
Valparaiso 4,672 ... C6
Venice 16,922 ... D4
Venus 500 ... E4
Vernon 778 ... C6
Vero Beach▲ 17,350 ... F4
Villa Tasso 365 ... C6
Virginia Gardens 2,212 ... B5
Wabasso 1,145 ... F4
Wacissa 350 ... B1
Wakulla 225 ... B1
Waldo 1,017 ... D2
Walnut Hill 500 ... B5
Ward Ridge 104 ... D7
Warrington 16,040 ... B6
Watertown 3,340 ... D1
Wauchula▲ 3,253 ... E4
Wausau 313 ... D6
Waverly 2,071 ... E4
Webster 746 ... D3
Weeki Wachee 53 ... D3
Weirsdale 995 ... D3
Welaka 533 ... E2
Wellborn 500 ... D1
West Bay 500 ... C6
West Eau Gallie ... F3
West Melbourne 8,399 ... F3
West Miami 5,727 ... B5
West Palm Beach▲ 67,643 ... F5
West Pensacola 22,107 ... B6
Westville 257 ... C6
Westwood Lakes 11,522 ... B5
Wewahitchka▲ 1,779 ... D6
White City 4,645 ... F4
White Springs 704 ... D1
Wildwood 3,421 ... D3
Williston 2,179 ... D2
Wilton Manors 11,804 ... B3
Wimauma 2,932 ... D4
Windermere 1,371 ... E3
Winter Beach 350 ... F4
Winter Garden 9,745 ... E3
Winter Haven 24,725 ... E3
Winter Park 22,242 ... E3
Winter Springs 22,151 ... E3
Woodville 2,760 ... B1
Worthington Springs 178 ... D2
Yalaha 1,168 ... E3
Yankeetown 635 ... D2
Youngstown 900 ... D6
Yulee 6,915 ... E1
Zellwood 1,760 ... E3
Zephyrhills 8,220 ... D3
Zolfo Springs 1,219 ... E4

OTHER FEATURES

Alapaha (riv.) ... C1
Alligator (lake) ... E3
Amelia (isl.) ... E1
Anastasia (isl.) ... E2
Anclote (keys) ... D3
Apalachee (bay) ... B2
Apalachicola (bay) ... B2
Apalachicola (riv.) ... A1
Apopka (lake) ... E3
Arbuckle (lake) ... E4
Aucilla (riv.) ... C1
Banana (riv.) ... F3
Beresford (lake) ... E3
Big Cypress (swamp) ... E5
Big Cypress Nat'l Preserve ... E5
Biscayne (bay) ... F6
Biscayne (key) ... B5
Biscayne Nat'l Park ... F6
Blackwater (riv.) ... B6
Blue Cypress (lake) ... F4
Boca Chica (key) ... E7
Boca Ciega (key) ... B3
Boca Grande (key) ... D7
Bryant (lake) ... E2
Caloosahatchee (riv.) ... E5
Canaveral (cape) ... F3
Captiva (isl.) ... D5
Casey (key) ... D4
Castillo de San Marcos Nat'l Mon. ... E2
Cecil Field Naval Air Sta. ... E1
Charlotte (harb.) ... D5
Chattahoochee (riv.) ... B1
Chipola (riv.) ... D6
Choctawhatchee (riv.) ... C6
Crescent (lake) ... E2
Cumberland Island Nat'l Seashore ... E1
Cypress (lake) ... E3
De Soto Nat'l Mem. ... D4
Dead (lake) ... D6
Dexter (lake) ... E2
Dog (isl.) ... B2
Dorr (lake) ... E2
Dry Tortugas (keys) ... D7
Dry Tortugas Nat'l Park ... C7
Dumfoundling (bay) ... C4
East (pt.) ... E6
Eglin A.F.B 8,347. ... C6
Egmont (key) ... D4
Elliott (key) ... F6
Escambia (riv.) ... B6
Estero (isl.) ... E5
Eureka (res.) ... E2
Everglades, The (swamp) ... F6
Everglades Nat'l Park ... E6
Fenholloway (riv.) ... C1
Florida (bay) ... F6
Florida (cape) ... F6
Florida (keys) ... E7
Florida (strs.) ... F7
Fort Caroline Nat'l Mem. ... E1
Fort Matanzas Nat'l Mon. ... E2
Gasparilla (isl.) ... D5
George (lake) ... E2
Grassy (key) ... F7
Gulf Islands Nat'l Seashore ... B6
Harney (lake) ... F3
Hart (lake) ... E3
Hillsborough (bay) ... C3
Hillsborough (canal) ... F5
Hillsborough (riv.) ... C2
Homestead A.F.B 5,153. ... F6
Homosassa (isls.) ... D3
Iamonia (lake) ... B1
Indian (riv.) ... F3
Iron (mt.) ... E4
Istokpoga (lake) ... E4
Jackson (lake) ... B1
Jackson (lake) ... E4
Jacksonville Naval Air Sta. ... E1
John F. Kennedy Space Center ... F3
June in Winter (lake) ... E4
Kerr (lake) ... E2
Key Largo (key) ... F6
Key Vaca (key) ... E7
Key West Naval Air Sta. ... E7
Kissimmee (lake) ... E4
Kissimmee (riv.) ... E4
Largo (key) ... F6
Levy (lake) ... D2
Lochloosa (lake) ... D2
Long (key) ... B3
Long (key) ... F7
Longboat (key) ... D4
Lower Matecumbe (key) ... F7
Lowery (lake) ... E3
MacDill A.F.B. ... C3
Manatee (riv.) ... D4
Marco (isl.) ... E6
Marian (lake) ... E4
Marquesas (keys) ... D7
Matanzas (inlet) ... E2
Mayport Naval Air Sta. ... E1
McCoy A.F.B. ... E3
Merritt (isl.) ... F3
Mexico (gulf) ... C4
Miami (canal) ... F5
Miami (riv.) ... B5
Miccosukee (lake) ... B1
Monroe (lake) ... E3
Mosquito (lag.) ... F3
Mullet (key) ... D4
Myakka (riv.) ... D4
Nassau (riv.) ... E1
Nassau (sound) ... E1
New (riv.) ... B1
New (riv.) ... D1
Newnans (lake) ... D2
North Merritt (isl.) ... F3
North New River (canal) ... F5
Ochlockonee (riv.) ... B1
Okaloacoochee Slough (swamp) ... E5
Okeechobee (lake) ... F5
Okefenokee (swamp) ... D1
Oklawaha (riv.) ... E2
Old Rhodes (key) ... F6
Old Tampa (bay) ... B3
Olustee (riv.) ... D1
Orange (lake) ... D2
Patrick A.F.B. ... F3
Peace (riv.) ... E4
Pensacola (bay) ... B6
Pensacola Naval Air Sta. ... B6
Perdido (riv.) ... B6
Pine (isl.) ... D5
Pine Island (sound) ... D5
Pinellas (pt.) ... B3
Piney (isl.) ... B1
Piney (pt.) ... C2
Placid (lake) ... E4
Plantation (key) ... F7
Poinsett (lake) ... F3
Ponce de Leon (bay) ... E6
Port Everglades (harb.) ... C4
Poet Tampa (harb.) ... B3
Raccoon (pt.) ... D3
Reedy (lake) ... E4
Romano (cape) ... E6
Sable (cape) ... E6
Saint Andrew (pt.) ... D6
Saint George (cape) ... A2
Saint George (isl.) ... B2
Saint George (sound) ... B2
Saint Johns (riv.) ... E2
Saint Joseph (bay) ... D6
Saint Joseph (pt.) ... D6
Saint Lucie (canal) ... F4
Saint Lucie (inlet) ... F4
Saint Marys (riv.) ... D1
Saint Marys Entrance (inlet) ... E1
Saint Vincent (isl.) ... D7
San Blas (cape) ... D7
Sand (key) ... B3
Sands (key) ... F6
Sanibel (isl.) ... D5
Santa Fe (lake) ... D2
Santa Fe (riv.) ... D2
Santa Rosa (isl.) ... B6
Santa Rosa (sound) ... B6
Sarasota (pt.) ... D4
Seminole (lake) ... B1
Seminole Ind. Res. ... E4
Seminole Ind. Res. ... E5
Shark (pt.) ... E6
Shoal (riv.) ... C6
Snake Creek (canal) ... B4
South New River (canal) ... F5
Stafford (lake) ... D2
Sugarloaf (key) ... E7
Suwannee (riv.) ... C2
Suwannee (sound) ... C2
Talbot (isl.) ... E1
Talquin (lake) ... B1
Tamiami (canal) ... E5
Tampa (bay) ... D4
Ten Thousand (isls.) ... E6
Timucuan Ecological and Historical Preserve ... E1
Torch (key) ... E7
Treasure (isl.) ... B3
Tsala Apopka (lake) ... D3
Tyndall A.F.B. ... C6
Upper Matecumbe (key) ... F7
Vaca (key) ... E7
Virginia (key) ... B5
Waccasassa (bay) ... D2
Waccasassa (riv.) ... D2
Washington (lake) ... F3
Weir (lake) ... E2
Weohyakapka (lake) ... E4
West Palm Beach (canal) ... F5
Whitewater (bay) ... F6
Whiting Field Naval Air Sta. ... B6
Wimico (lake) ... A2
Winder (lake) ... F3
Withlacoochee (riv.) ... C1
Withlacoochee (riv.) ... D2
Yale (lake) ... E3
Yellow (riv.) ... B6

▲County seat

Agriculture, Industry and Resources

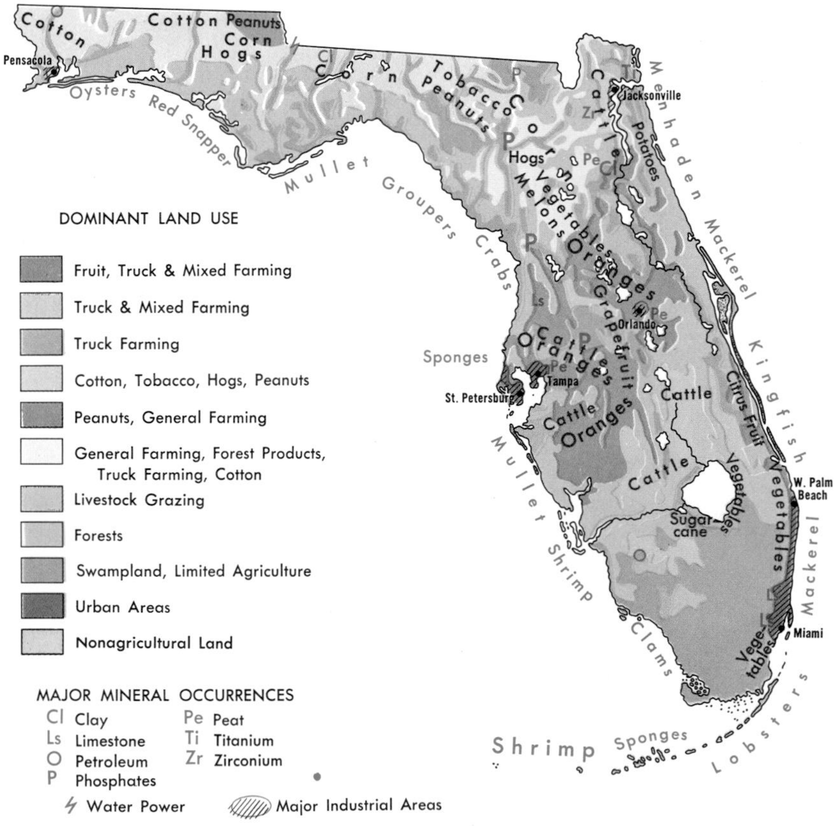

Cotton
Cotton Peanuts
Corn
Hogs
Pensacola
Oysters
Red Snapper
Mullet
Groupers
Crabs
Tobacco
Peanuts
Corn
Cotton
Cattle
Jacksonville
Potatoes
Menhaden
Hogs
Melons
Vegetables
Oranges
Grapefruit
Mackerel
Orlando
Cattle
Oranges
Sponges
Tampa
St. Petersburg
Cattle
Oranges
Cattle
Citrus Fruit
Kingfish
Cattle
Vegetables
W. Palm Beach
Sugar cane
Vegetables
Mackerel
Mullet
Shrimp
Clams
Vegetables
Miami
Shrimp
Sponges
Lobsters
DOMINANT LAND USE
Fruit, Truck & Mixed Farming
Truck & Mixed Farming
Truck Farming
Cotton, Tobacco, Hogs, Peanuts
Peanuts, General Farming
General Farming, Forest Products, Truck Farming, Cotton
Livestock Grazing
Forests
Swampland, Limited Agriculture
Urban Areas
Nonagricultural Land
MAJOR MINERAL OCCURRENCES
Cl Clay
Ls Limestone
O Petroleum
P Phosphates
Pe Peat
Ti Titanium
Zr Zirconium
Water Power
Major Industrial Areas

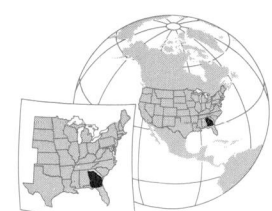

AREA 58,910 sq. mi. (152,577 sq. km.)
POPULATION 6,508,419
CAPITAL Atlanta
LARGEST CITY Atlanta
HIGHEST POINT Brasstown Bald 4,784 ft. (1458 m.)
SETTLED IN 1733
ADMITTED TO UNION January 2, 1788
POPULAR NAME Empire State of the South; Peach State
STATE FLOWER Cherokee Rose
STATE BIRD Brown Thrasher

COUNTIES

Appling 15,744	H7
Atkinson 6,213	G8
Bacon 9,566	G7
Baker 3,615	D8
Baldwin 39,530	F4
Banks 10,308	E2
Barrow 29,721	E2
Bartow 55,911	C2
Ben Hill 16,245	F7
Berrien 14,153	F7
Bibb 149,967	E5
Bleckley 10,430	F6
Brantley 11,077	J8
Brooks 15,398	E9
Bryan 15,438	K6
Bulloch 43,125	J6
Burke 20,579	J4
Butts 15,326	E4
Calhoun 5,013	C7
Camden 30,167	J9
Candler 7,744	H6
Carroll 71,422	B3
Catoosa 42,464	B1
Charlton 8,496	H9
Chatham 216,935	K6
Chattahoochee 16,934	C6
Chattooga 22,242	B1
Cherokee 90,204	D2
Clarke 87,594	F3
Clay 3,364	B7
Clayton 182,052	D3
Clinch 6,160	G9
Cobb 447,745	C3
Coffee 29,592	G8
Colquitt 36,645	E8
Columbia 66,031	H3
Cook 13,456	F8
Coweta 53,853	C4
Crawford 8,991	E5
Crisp 20,011	E7
Dade 13,147	A1
Dawson 9,429	D2
De Kalb 483,024	D3
Decatur 25,511	C9
Dodge 17,607	F6
Dooly 9,901	E6
Dougherty 96,311	D7
Douglas 71,120	C3
Early 11,854	C8
Echols 2,334	G9
Effingham 25,687	K6
Elbert 18,949	G2
Emanuel 20,546	H5
Evans 8,724	J6
Fannin 15,992	D1
Fayette 62,415	C4
Floyd 81,251	B2
Forsyth 44,083	D2
Franklin 16,650	F2
Fulton 648,951	D3
Gilmer 13,368	D1
Glascock 2,357	G4
Glynn 62,496	J8
Gordon 35,072	C2
Grady 20,279	D9
Greene 11,793	F3
Gwinnett 352,910	D2
Habersham 27,621	E1
Hall 95,428	E2
Hancock 8,908	G4
Haralson 21,966	B3
Harris 17,788	C5
Hart 19,712	G2
Heard 8,628	B4
Henry 58,741	D4
Houston 89,208	E6
Irwin 8,649	F7
Jackson 30,005	E2
Jasper 8,453	E4
Jeff Davis 12,032	G7
Jefferson 17,408	H4
Jenkins 8,247	J5
Johnson 8,329	G5
Jones 20,739	E5
Lamar 13,038	D4
Lanier 5,531	F8
Laurens 39,988	G6
Lee 16,250	D7
Liberty 52,745	J7
Lincoln 7,442	H3
Long 6,202	J7
Lowndes 75,981	F9
Lumpkin 14,573	D1
Macon 13,114	D6
Madison 21,050	F2
Marion 5,590	C6
McDuffie 20,119	H4
McIntosh 8,634	K7
Meriwether 22,411	C4
Miller 6,280	C8
Mitchell 20,275	D8
Monroe 17,113	E4
Montgomery 7,163	G6
Morgan 12,883	F3
Murray 26,147	C1
Muscogee 179,278	C6
Newton 41,808	E3
Oconee 17,618	F3
Oglethorpe 8,929	F3
Paulding 41,611	C3
Peach 21,189	E5
Pickens 14,432	D2
Pierce 13,328	H8
Pike 10,224	D4
Polk 33,815	B3
Pulaski 8,108	E6
Putnam 14,137	F4
Quitman 2,209	B7
Rabun 11,648	F1
Randolph 8,023	C7
Richmond 189,719	H4
Rockdale 54,091	D3
Schley 3,588	D6
Screven 13,842	J5
Seminole 9,010	C9
Spalding 54,457	D4
Stephens 23,257	F1
Stewart 5,654	C6
Sumter 30,228	D6
Talbot 6,524	C5
Taliaferro 1,915	G3
Tattnall 17,722	H6
Taylor 7,642	D5
Telfair 11,000	G7
Terrell 10,653	D7
Thomas 38,986	E9
Tift 34,998	E7
Toombs 24,072	H6
Towns 6,754	E1
Treutlen 5,994	G6
Troup 55,536	B4
Turner 8,703	E7
Twiggs 9,806	F5
Union 11,993	E1
Upson 26,300	D5
Walker 58,340	B1
Walton 38,586	E3
Ware 35,471	H8
Warren 6,078	G4
Washington 19,112	G4
Wayne 22,356	J7
Webster 2,263	C6
Wheeler 4,903	G6
White 13,006	E1
Whitfield 72,462	B1
Wilcox 7,008	F7
Wilkes 10,597	G3
Wilkinson 10,228	F5
Worth 19,745	E8

CITIES and TOWNS

Abbeville▲ 907	F7
Acworth 4,519	C2
Adairsville 2,131	C2
Adel▲ 5,093	F8
Adrian 615	G5
Ailey 579	G6
Alamo▲ 855	G6
Alapaha 812	F7
Albany▲ 78,122	D7
Aldora 127	D4
Allenhurst 594	J7
Allentown 273	F5
Alma▲ 3,663	G7
Alpharetta 13,002	D2
Alston 160	H6
Alto 651	E2
Alvaton 91	C4
Ambrose 288	G7
Americus▲ 16,512	D6
Andersonville 277	D6
Appling▲ 150	H3
Arabi 433	E7
Aragon 902	B2
Arcade 697	E2
Arco 6,189	J8
Argyle 206	G8
Arlington 1,513	C8
Armuchee 600	B2
Arnoldsville 275	F3
Ashburn▲ 4,827	E7
Athens▲ 45,734	F3
Atlanta (cap.)▲ 394,017	K1
Attapulgus 380	D9
Auburn 3,139	E2
Augusta▲ 44,639	J4
Austell 4,173	J1
Avalon 159	F1
Avera 215	G4
Avondale Estates 2,209	L1
Baconton 623	D8
Bainbridge▲ 10,712	C9
Baldwin 1,439	E2
Ball Ground 905	D2
Barnesville▲ 4,747	D4
Barney 146	E8
Bartow 292	G5
Barwick 385	E9
Baxley▲ 3,841	H7
Bellville 192	H6
Belvedere 18,089	L1
Benevolence 138	C7
Berkeley Lake 791	D3
Berlin 480	E8
Bethlehem 348	E3
Between 82	E3
Bibb City 597	B5
Bishop 158	F3
Blackshear▲ 3,263	H8
Blairsville▲ 564	E1
Blakely▲ 5,595	C8
Bloomingdale 2,271	K6
Blue Ridge▲ 1,336	D1
Bluffton 138	C7
Blythe 300	H4
Bogart 1,018	E3
Boston 1,395	E9
Bostwick 307	E3
Bowdon 1,981	B3
Bowersville 311	F2
Bowman 791	G2
Box Springs 518	C5
Braselton 418	E2
Braswell 247	C3
Bremen 4,356	B3
Brinson 238	C9
Bronwood 513	D7
Brookfield 600	F8
Brookhaven	K1
Brooklet 1,013	J6
Brooks 328	D4
Broxton 1,211	G7
Brunswick▲ 16,433	K8
Buchanan▲ 1,009	B3
Buckhead 176	F3
Buena Vista▲ 1,472	D6
Buford 8,771	D2
Butler▲ 1,673	D5
Byromville 452	E6
Byron 2,276	E5
Cadwell 458	G6
Cairo▲ 9,035	D9
Calhoun▲ 7,135	C1
Calvary 500	D9
Camak 220	G4
Camilla▲ 5,008	D8
Campton	E3
Canon 737	F2
Canton▲ 4,817	C2
Carl 263	E3
Carlton 282	F2
Carnesville▲ 514	F2
Carrollton▲ 16,029	C3
Carters 12,035	C1
Cartersville▲ 9,247	C2
Cataula 500	C5
Cave Spring 950	B2
Cecil 376	F8
Cedar Grove	A1
Cedartown▲ 7,978	B2
Center 3,251	F2
Centerville 2,622	E5
Centralhatchee 301	B4
Chalybeate Springs 265	C5
Chamblee 7,668	K1
Charles	H6
Chatsworth▲ 2,865	C1
Chauncey 312	F6
Chester 1,072	F6
Chickamauga 2,149	B1
Chula 500	E7
Clarkesville▲ 1,151	F1
Clarkston 5,385	L1
Claxton▲ 2,464	J6
Clayton▲ 1,613	F1
Clermont 402	E2
Cleveland▲ 1,653	E1
Climax 226	D9
Clyattville 500	F9
Cobb 338	E7
Cobbtown 494	H6
Cochran▲ 4,390	F6
Cohutta 529	C1
Colbert 443	F2
Coleman 137	C7
Colemans Lake	H5
College Park 20,457	K2
Collins 528	H6
Colquitt▲ 1,991	C8
Columbus▲ 179,278	C6
Comer 939	F2
Commerce 4,108	E2
Concord 211	D4
Conley 5,528	K2
Constitution	K2
Conyers▲ 7,380	D3
Coolidge 610	E8
Coosa 600	B2
Cordele▲ 10,321	E6
Corinth 136	B4
Cornelia 3,219	E1
Cotton 122	D8
Covington▲ 10,026	E3
Crandall	C1
Crawford 694	F3
Crawfordville▲ 577	G3
Crosland	E8
Crystal Springs 500	B2
Culloden 242	D5
Cumming▲ 2,828	D2
Cusseta▲ 1,107	C6
Cuthbert▲ 3,730	C7
Dacula 2,217	E3
Dahlonega▲ 3,086	D1
Daisy 138	J6
Dallas▲ 2,810	C3
Dalton▲ 21,761	C1
Damascus 290	C8
Danielsville▲ 318	F2
Danville 480	F5
Darien▲ 1,783	K8
Dasher 659	F9
Davisboro 407	G5
Dawson▲ 5,295	D7
Dawsonville▲ 467	D2
De Soto 258	D7
Dearing 547	H4
Decatur▲ 17,336	K1
Deenwood 2,055	H8
Deepstep 111	G4
Demorest 1,088	F1
Denton 335	G7
Dexter 475	G6
Dickey	C7
Dillard 199	F1
Dixie 259	E9
Dock Junction (Arco)	J8
Doerun 899	D8
Donalsonville▲ 2,761	C8
Dooling 28	E6
Doraville 7,626	K1
Douglas▲ 10,464	G7
Douglasville▲ 11,635	C3
Dry Branch 700	F5
Du Pont 177	G9
Dublin▲ 16,312	G5
Ducktown	D9
Dudley 430	F5
Duluth 9,029	D2
Dunwoody 26,302	K1
Durand 206	C4
East Dublin 2,524	G5
East Ellijay 303	C1
East Juliette	C4
East Newnan 1,173	C4
East Point 34,402	K2
Eastman▲ 5,153	F6
Eastville	
Eatonton▲ 4,737	F4
Eden 990	K6
Edge Hill 22	G4
Edison 1,182	C8
Elberta 1,559	E5
Elberton▲ 5,682	G2
Elizabeth 950	J1
Ellabell 500	K6
Ellaville▲ 1,724	D6
Ellenton 227	E8
Ellenwood	L2
Ellerslie 700	C5
Ellijay▲ 1,178	D1
Emerson 1,201	C2
Enigma 611	F8
Ephesus 324	B4

(continued on following page)

Agriculture, Industry and Resources

DOMINANT LAND USE

- Specialized Cotton
- Cotton, General Farming
- Cotton, Tobacco, Hogs, Peanuts
- Peanuts, General Farming
- General Farming, Livestock, Fruit, Tobacco
- General Farming, Forest Products, Cotton, Truck Farming
- Forests
- Swampland, Limited Agriculture
- Urban Areas

MAJOR MINERAL OCCURRENCES

Al	Bauxite
Ba	Barite
C	Coal
Cl	Clay
Fe	Iron Ore
Gn	Granite
Mi	Mica
Mn	Manganese
Mr	Marble
Sl	Slate
Tc	Talc
Ti	Titanium

Water Power   Major Industrial Areas

Eton 315 C1
Euharlee 850 C2
Evans 13,713 H3
Experiment 3,762 D4
Fair Oaks 6,996 J1
Fairburn 4,013 J2
Fairmount 657 C2
Fargo 800 G9
Farmington F3
Farrar E4
Fayetteville▲ 5,827 C4
Felton 500 B3
Finleyson 101 F6
Fitzgerald▲ 8,612 F7
Fleming 279 K7
Flemington 440 K7
Flippen 600 D3
Flovilla 602 E4
Flowery Branch 1,251 E2
Floyd J1
Folkston▲ 2,285 H9
Forest Park 16,925 K2
Forsyth▲ 4,268 E4
Fort Gaines▲ 1,248 C7
Fort Oglethorpe 5,880 B1
Fort Valley▲ 8,198 E5
Franklin Springs 475 F2
Franklin▲ 876 B4
Funston 248 E8
Gainesville▲ 17,885 E2
Garden City 7,410 K6
Garfield 255 H5
Gay 133 C4
Geneva 182 C5
Georgetown▲ 913 B7
Gibson▲ 679 G4
Gillsville 113 E2
Gilmore J1
Girard 195 J4
Glenn 3,676 B4
Glennville 4,144 J7
Glenwood 824 G6
Glenwood 881 L1
Glynco J8
Good Hope 181 E3
Gordon 2,468 F5
Grantville 1,180 C4
Gray▲ 2,189 F4
Grayson 529 E3
Graysville 193 B1
Greensboro▲ 2,860 F3
Greenville▲ 1,167 C4
Griffin▲ 21,347 D4
Grovetown 3,596 H4
Gumbranch 291 J7
Guyton 740 K6
Haddock 800 F4
Hagan 787 J6
Hahira 1,353 F9
Hamilton▲ 454 C5
Hampton 2,694 D4
Hapeville 5,483 K2
Haralson 139 C4
Hardwick (Midway-
Hardwick) 8,977 F4
Harlem 2,199 H4
Harrison 414 G5
Hartwell▲ 4,555 G2
Hawkinsville▲ 3,527 E6
Hazlehurst▲ 4,202 G7
Helen 300 E1
Helena 1,256 G6
Hephzibah 2,466 H4
Hiawassee▲ 547 E1
Higgston 274 G6
Hilltonia 402 J5
Hinesville▲ 21,603 J7
Hiram 1,389 C3
Hoboken 440 H8
Hogansville 2,976 C4
Holly Springs 2,406 D2
Homeland 981 H9
Homer▲ 742 F2
Homerville▲ 2,560 G8
Hoschton 642 E2
Howell F9
Hull 156 F2
Ideal 554 D6
Ila 297 F2
Indian Springs 1,273 E4
Industrial City 1,054 C1
Inman 500 D4
Iron City 503 C8
Irwinton▲ 641 F5
Isle of Hope 975 K7
Ivey 1,053 F5
Jackson▲ 4,076 E4
Jacksonville 128 G7
Jakin 137 C8
Jasper▲ 1,772 D2
Jefferson▲ 2,763 F2
Jeffersonville▲ 1,545 F5
Jenkinsburg 213 E4
Jersey 149 E3
Jesup▲ 8,958 J7
Jonesboro▲ 3,635 D4
Juliette 600 E4
Junction City 182 C5
Juno 522 D2
Kennesaw 8,936 C2
Keysville 284 H4
Kingsland 4,699 J9
Kingston 616 C2
Kite 297 G5
Knoxville▲ 75 E5
La Fayette▲ 6,313 B1
La Grange▲ 25,597 B4
Lake City 2,733 K2
Lake Park 500 F9
Lakeland▲ 2,467 F8
Lavonia 1,840 F2
Lawrenceville▲ 16,848 D3
Leary 701 C8
Lebanon 800 D2
Leesburg▲ 1,452 D7
Leland J1
Lenox 783 F8
Leslie 445 D7
Lexington▲ 230 F3
Lilburn 9,301 D3
Lilly 138 E6
Lincoln Park 1,755 D5
Lincolnton▲ 1,476 G3
Lindale 4,187 B2
Linwood 342 B1
Lithia Springs 11,403 C3
Lithonia 2,448 D3
Lizella 975 E5
Locust Grove 1,681 D4
Loganville 3,180 E3
Lollie G6
Lone Oak 161 C4
Lookout Mountain 1,636 B1
Louisville▲ 2,429 H4
Lovejoy 754 D4
Lovett G5
Ludowici▲ 1,291 J7
Lula 1,018 E2
Lumber City 1,429 G7
Lumpkin▲ 1,250 C6
Luthersville 741 C4
Lyerly 493 B2
Lyons▲ 4,502 H6
Mableton 25,725 J1
Macon▲ 106,612 E5
Madison▲ 3,483 F3
Manassas 123 H6
Manchester 4,104 C5
Mansfield 341 E4
Marietta▲ 44,129 J1
Marlow 500 K6
Marshallville 1,457 D6
Martin 243 F2
Martinez 33,731 H3
Matthews H4
Maxeys 180 F3
Maysville 728 E2
McCaysville 1,065 D1
McDonough▲ 2,929 D4
McIntosh 500 K7
McIntyre 552 F5
McRae▲ 3,007 G6
Meansville 250 D4
Mechanicsville L1
Meigs 1,120 D8
Meldrim 510 K6
Menlo 538 B2
Merrillville E9
Metcalf E9
Metter▲ 3,707 H6
Middleton G2
Midville 620 H5
Midway 863 K7
Milan 1,056 G6
Milledgeville▲ 17,727 F4
Millen▲ 3,808 J5
Milner 321 D4
Milstead D3
Mineral Bluff 153 D1
Mitchell 181 G4
Modoc H5
Molena 439 D4
Monroe▲ 9,759 E3
Montezuma 4,506 E6
Monticello▲ 2,289 E4
Montrose 117 F5
Moreland 366 C4
Morgan▲ 252 C7
Morganton 295 D1
Morrow 5,168 K2
Morven 536 E9
Moultrie▲ 14,865 E8
Mount Airy 543 F1
Mount Berry B2
Mount Bethel K1
Mount Vernon▲ 1,914 G6
Mount Zion 511 B3
Mountain City 784 F1
Mountain Park 554 D2
Mountain View K2
Mountville 168 C4
Murrayville 550 E2
Nahunta▲ 1,049 H8
Nashville▲ 4,782 F8
Naylor 111 F9
Nelson 486 D2
New Holland 950 E2
Newborn 404 E3
Newington 319 J5
Newnan▲ 12,497 C4
Newton▲ 703 D8
Nicholls 1,003 G7
Nicholson 535 F2
Norcross 5,947 D3
Norman Park 711 E8
Normantown H6
North Canton 950 C2
North High Shoals 268 F3
Norwood 238 G4
Nunez 135 H5
Oak Park 269 H6
Oakfield 113 E7
Oakman 150 C1
Oakwood 1,464 E2
Ochlocknee 588 E9
Ocilla▲ 3,182 F7
Oconee 234 G5
Odessadale 142 C5
Odum 388 H7
Oglethorpe▲ 1,302 D6
Ohoopee H6
Oliver 242 J5
Omaha 116 C6
Omega 912 E8
Orchard Hill 239 D4
Oxford 1,945 E3
Palmetto 2,612 C3
Panthersville 9,874 L1
Parrott 140 D7
Patterson 626 H8
Pavo 774 E9
Payne 192 E5
Peachtree City 19,027 C4
Pearson▲ 1,714 G8
Pelham 3,869 D8
Pembroke▲ 1,503 J6
Pendergrass 298 E2
Penfield F3
Perry▲ 9,452 E6
Phillipsburg 1,044 E8
Piedmont D4
Pine Lake 810 D3
Pine Mountain 875 C5
Pine Park D9
Pinehurst 388 E6
Pineora 387 K6
Pineview 594 F6
Pitts 214 E7
Pittsburg L1
Plainfield 128 F6
Plains 716 D6
Plainville 231 C2
Pocotalago F2
Pooler 4,453 K6
Port Wentworth 4,012 K6
Portal 522 J5
Porterdale 1,278 E3
Poulan 962 E8
Powder Springs 6,893 C3
Preston▲ 388 C6
Primrose 30 C4
Pulaski 264 J6
Putney 3,108 D8
Quitman▲ 5,292 E9
Raleigh C5
Ranger 153 C2
Ray City 603 F8
Rayle 107 G3
Rebecca 148 E7
Red Oak 950 J2
Register 195 J6
Reidsville▲ 2,469 H6
Remerton 463 F9
Reno D9
Rentz 364 G6
Resaca 410 C1
Rest Haven 176 E2
Reynolds 1,166 D5
Rhine 466 F7
Riceboro 745 K7
Richland 1,668 C6
Richmond Hill 2,934 K7
Riddleville 79 G5
Rincon 2,697 K6
Ringgold▲ 1,675 B1
Riverdale 9,359 K2
Riverside 74 B2
Riverside 99 E8
Roberta 939 D5
Rochelle 1,510 F7
Rockmart 3,356 B2
Rocky Face 500 C1
Rocky Ford 197 J5
Rocky Mount 56 C4
Rome▲ 30,326 B2
Roopville 248 B4
Rossville 3,601 B1
Roswell 47,923 D2
Royston 2,758 F2
Ruckersville G2
Russell 871 E3
Rutledge 659 E3
Saint George 600 H9
Saint Marks 36 C4
Saint Marys 8,187 J9
Saint Simons Island 12,026 K8
Sale City 324 D8
Sandersville▲ 6,290 G5
Sandy Springs 67,842 K1
Santa Claus 154 H6
Sardis 1,116 J5
Sargent 800 C4
Sasser 335 D7
Savannah▲ 137,560 L6
Scotland 244 G6
Scott 8,636 G5
Scottdale 8,770 L1
Screven 819 H7
Sea Island 600 K8
Senoia 956 C4
Seville 209 E7
Shady Dale 180 E4
Shannon 1,703 B2
Sharon 94 G3
Sharpsburg 224 C4
Shellman 1,162 C7
Shiloh 329 C5
Siloam 329 F3
Silver Creek 500 B2
Six Flags Over Georgia J1
Sky Valley 187 F1
Smithonia F2
Smithville 804 D7
Smyrna 30,981 K1
Snellville 12,084 D3
Social Circle 2,755 E3
Soperton▲ 2,797 G6
Sparks 1,205 F8
Sparta▲ 1,710 F4
Spring Place 246 C1
Springfield▲ 1,415 K6
Stapleton 330 H4
Statenville▲ 700 G9
Statesboro▲ 15,854 J6
Statham 1,360 E3
Stillmore 615 H6
Stockbridge 3,359 D3
Stockton 532 G9
Stone Mountain 6,494 D3
Stonewall 950 J2
Sugar Hill 4,557 E2
Sugar Valley C1
Summertown 153 H5
Summerville▲ 5,025 B2
Sumner 209 E7
Sunny Side 215 D4
Surrency 253 H7
Suwanee 2,412 D2
Swainsboro▲ 7,361 H5
Sycamore 417 E7
Sylvania▲ 2,871 J5
Sylvester▲ 5,702 E7
Talbotton▲ 1,046 C5
Talking Rock 62 D1
Tallapoosa 2,805 B3
Tallulah Falls 147 F1
Talmo 189 E2
Tarrytown 130 H6
Tate 950 D2
Taylorsville 269 C2
Tazewell D6
Tell J2
Temple 1,870 B3
Tennille 1,552 G5
The Rock 88 D5
Thomaston▲ 9,127 D5
Thomasville▲ 17,457 E9
Thomson▲ 6,862 H4
Thunderbolt 2,786 K6
Tifton▲ 14,215 F8
Tiger 301 F1
Tignall 711 G3
Toccoa▲ 8,266 F1
Toco Hills K1
Toomsboro 617 F5
Towns G7
Trenton▲ 1,994 A1
Trion 1,661 B1
Tunnel Hill 970 C1
Turin 189 C4
Twin City 1,466 H5
Ty Ty 579 E8
Tybee Island 2,842 L6
Tyrone 2,724 C4
Unadilla 1,620 E6
Union City 8,375 J2
Union Point 1,753 F3
Unionville 2,710 F8
Uvalda 561 H6
Valdosta▲ 39,806 F9
Van Wert 303 B3
Vanna F2
Varnell 358 C1
Vernonburg 74 K7
Vidalia 11,078 H6
Vidette H4
Vienna▲ 2,708 E6
Villa Rica 6,542 C3
Vinings 7,417 K1
Waco 461 B3
Wadley 2,473 H5
Waleska 700 D2
Walnut Grove 458 E3
Walthourville 2,024 J7
Waresboro 582 H8
Warm Springs 407 C5
Warner Robins 43,726 E5
Warrenton▲ 2,056 G4
Warwick 501 E7
Watkinsville▲ 1,600 E3
Waverly 769 J8
Waverly Hall 913 C5
Waycross▲ 16,410 H8
Waynesboro▲ 5,701 J4
Welcome All J2
Wesley H6
West Point 3,571 B5
Weston 42 C7
Whigham 605 D9
White 542 C2
White Plains 286 F4
White Sulphur Springs 118 C5
Whitesburg 643 B4
Willacoochee 1,205 G8
Williamson 295 D4
Wilmington Island 11,230 L7
Winder▲ 7,373 E3
Winterville 876 F3
Woodbine▲ 1,212 J9
Woodbury 1,429 C5
Woodland 552 D5
Woodstock 4,361 D2
Woodville 415 F3
Woolsey 120 D4
Wrens 2,414 H4
Wrightsville▲ 2,331 G5
Yatesville 409 D5
Young Harris 604 E1
Zebulon▲ 1,035 D4

OTHER FEATURES

Alapaha (riv.) F7
Allatoona (lake) C2
Altamaha (riv.) H7
Andersonville Nat'l Hist. Site D6
Atlanta Naval Air Sta. J1
Banks (lake) F9
Bartletts Ferry (dam) B5
Blackshear (lake) E7
Blue Ridge (mts.) D1
Brasstown Bald (mt.) E1
Burton (lake) E1
Carters (lake) C1
Chattahoochee (riv.) B8
Chattahoochee River
Nat'l Rec. Area K1
Chattooga (riv.) A2
Chattooga (riv.) F1
Chatuge (lake) E1
Chickamauga and Chattanooga
Nat'l Mil. Park B1
Coosa (riv.) A2
Coosawattee (riv.) C1
Cumberland (isl.) K9
Cumberland Island
Nat'l Seashore K9
Dobbins A.F.B. J1
Doboy (sound) K8
Etowah (riv.) C2
Flint (riv.) D8
Fort Benning B6
Fort Frederica Nat'l Mon. K8
Fort Gordon 9,140 H4
Fort McPherson K1
Fort Pulaski Nat'l Mon. L6
Fort Stewart 13,774 J7
Goat Rock (lake) B5
Harding (lake) B5
Hartwell (lake) G2
Jekyll (isl.) K8
Jimmy Carter Nat'l Hist. Site D6
Kennesaw Mtn. Nat'l
Battlefield Park J1
Martin Luther King, Jr.,
Nat'l Hist. Site K1
Moody A.F.B.1,288 F9
Morgan Falls (dam) K1
Nottely (lake) D1
Ochlockonee (riv.) 10
Ocmulgee (riv.) E5
Ocmulgee Nat'l Mon. F5
Oconee (riv.) F5
Ogeechee (riv.) J5
Okefenokee (swamp) H9
Oliver (lake) B5
Oostanaula (riv.) B2
Ossabaw (sound) K7
Rabun (lake) E1
Robins A.F.B. 3,092 F5
Saint Andrew (sound) K9
Saint Catherines (isl.) K7
Saint Mary's (riv.) J9
Saint Simons (isl.) K8
Sapelo (isl.) K8
Satilla (riv.) G8
Savannah (riv.) K5
Sea (isls.) K9
Seminole (lake) B9
Sidney Lanier (lake) D2
Sinclair (lake) F4
Skidaway (isl.) L7
Springer (mt.) D1
Strom Thurmond (lakes) H3
Suwannee (riv.) G 10
Walter F. George (res.) B7
Wassaw (sound) L7
Weiss (lake) A2
West Point (lake) B4

▲County seat

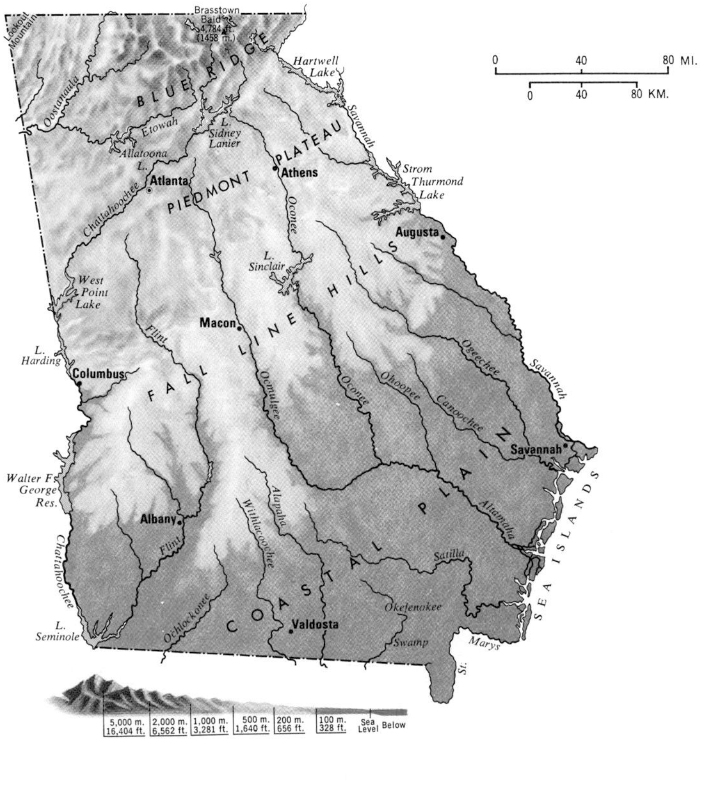

Brasstown Bald 4,784 ft. (1458 m.)
Lookout Mountain
BLUE RIDGE
Hartwell Lake
Oostanaula
Etowah
L. Sidney Lanier
Allatoona L.
Atlanta
Athens
PIEDMONT
PLATEAU
Savannah
Strom Thurmond Lake
Chattahoochee
Oconee
Augusta
L. Sinclair
West Point Lake
Macon
FALL LINE HILLS
L. Harding
Columbus
Flint
Ocmulgee
Ogeechee
Ohoopee
Canoochee
Savannah
COASTAL PLAIN
Walter F. George Res.
Albany
Alapaha
Withlacoochee
Altamaha
SEA ISLANDS
Satilla
Okefenokee
Swamp
Chattahoochee
Ochlockonee
Valdosta
L. Seminole
St. Marys
5,000 m. 16,404 ft.
2,000 m. 6,562 ft.
1,000 m. 3,281 ft.
500 m. 1,640 ft.
200 m. 656 ft.
100 m. 328 ft.
Sea Level
Below
0 40 80 MI.
0 40 80 KM.

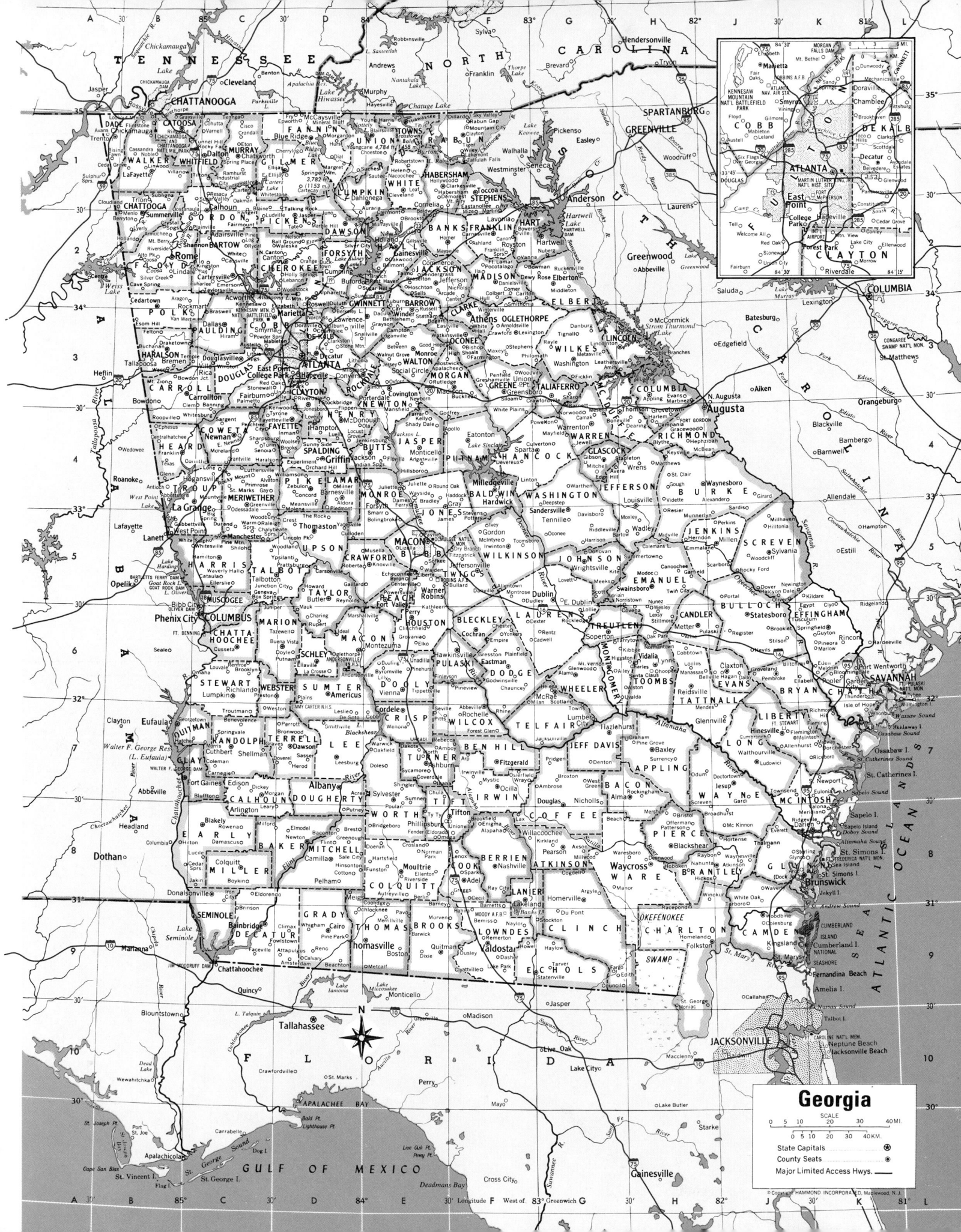

Georgia

SCALE

0 5 10   20   30   40 MI.

0 5 10   20   30   40 KM.

⊛ State Capitals

○ County Seats

Major Limited Access Hwys. ——

COUNTIES

Hawaii 120,317	K7
Honolulu 836,231	D3
Kalawao 130	G1
Kauai 51,177	A1
Maui 100,374	J1

CITIES and TOWNS

Aiea 8,906	B3
Aina Haina	F2
Ala Moana	C4
Anahola 1,181	C1
Barbers Point 2,218	E2
Captain Cook 2,595	G5
Eleele 1,489	C2
Ewa 14,315	A4
Ewa Beach 14,369	A4
Haena 200	C1
Haiku 4,509	J2
Haina 333	H3
Hakalau	J4
Halawa Heights	B3
Halawa, Hawaii 50	J2
Haleiwa 2,442	E1
Halfway House 150	H6
Haliimaile 841	J2
Hana 683	K2
Hanalei 461	C1
Hanamaulu 3,611	C1
Hanapepe 1,395	C2
Hauula 3,479	E1
Hawaii Kai	F2
Hawaii National Park 250	J6
Hawi 924	G3
Hickam Housing 6,553	B4
Hilo▲ 37,808	J5
Holualoa 3,834	G5
Honaunau 2,373	G6
Honohina 125	J4
Honokaa 2,186	H4
Honokahua 309	H1
Honokohau 200	G5
Honokohau 309	J1
Honolulu (cap.)▲ 365,272	C4
Honomu 532	J4
Honouliuli 600	A3
Hoolehua	G1
Huehue 100	G5
Hulopoe Bay	H2
Huumula 50	H5
Iroquois Point 4,188	A4
Iwilei	C4
Kaaawa 1,138	F1
Kaanapali 579	H2
Kahakuloa 75	J1
Kahala	D5
Kahaluu 3,068	E2
Kahuku 2,063	E1
Kahului 16,889	J2
Kailua (Kailua Kona), Hawaii 9,126	F5
Kailua Kona	F5
Kailua, Oahu 36,818	F2
Kaimuki	D4
Kainaliu 512	G5
Kalae 150	G1
Kalaheo 3,592	C2
Kalapa 4,490	G5
Kalapana 75	J6
Kalaupapa▲ 170	G1
Kalihi 435	C4
Kalihi 60	H1
Kamalo 500	H1
Kamuela 1,179	G4
Kapaa 8,149	D1
Kapaau 850	J6
Kapaau 1,083	G3
Kapalama	C4
Kapoho 300	K5
Kapulena 125	H4
Kaumakani 803	C2
Kaumalapau Harbor	G2
Kaunakakai 2,658	G1
Kaupakulua 600	K2
Kaupo 65	K2
Kawaihae 50	G4
Kawailoa 200	E1
Keaau 1,584	J5
Kealakekua 1,453	G5
Kealia 550	G6
Kealia, Kauai 300	D1
Keanae 280	K2
Keauhou	F5
Kekaha 3,506	C2
Keokea 500	G6
Keokea 750	J2
Kihei 11,107	J2
Kilauea 1,685	C1
Kipahulu 75	K2
Koali 60	G1
Kohala (Kapaau)	G3
Kokomo 500	K2
Koloa 1,791	C2
Koloa Landing	C2
Kualapuu 1,661	G1
Kukuihaele 316	H3
Kula 800	J2
Kunia 550	E2
Kurtistown 910	J5
Lahaina 9,073	H2
Laie 5,577	E1
Lanai City 2,400	H2
Laupahoehoe 508	J4
Lawai 1,787	C2
Lihue▲ 5,536	C2
Lower Paia 1,500	J1
Maalaea 443	J2
Maili 6,059	D2
Makaha 7,990	D2
Makaiwa	H2
Makakilo 9,828	E2
Makalapa	G3
Makapala	K2
Makawao 5,405	J2
Makaweli 500	C2
Makena 100	J2
Makiki	C4
Mana	B2
Manele Bay	H2
Maunaloa 405	G1
Maunawili 4,847	F2
Mililani Town 29,359	E2
Miloiii 120	G6
Moiliili	C4
Mokapu 11,615	F2
Mokuleia 1,776	D1
Mountain View 3,075	J5
Naalehu 1,027	H7
Nanakuli 9,575	D2
Napili-Honokowai 4,332	H1
Ninole 75	J4
Olowalu 750	H2
Ookala 401	H4
Opihikao 125	K6
Paauhau 350	H4
Paauilo 620	H4
Pacific Heights 5,305	C4
Pacific Palisades	E2
Pahala 1,520	H6
Pahoa 7,990	D2
Paia 2,091	J5
Papa 1,634	G6
Papaaloa	J4
Papaikou 1,567	J5
Paukaa 495	J5
Pauwela 468	K2
Peahi 308	K2
Pearl City 30,993	B3
Pepeekeo 1,813	J4
Poipu 975	C2
Princeville 1,244	C1
Puako 397	G4
Puhi 1,210	C2
Pukalani 5,879	J2
Punaluu 672	H7
Puuanahulu 56	G4
Puuiki 75	K2
Puunene 572	J2
Puunui	C4
Puuwai 200	A3
Schofield Barracks 19,597	E2
Spreckelsville 350	J1
Sunset Beach	E1
Ulumalu 201	K2
Ulupalakua 75	J2
Volcano 1,516	J6
Wahiawa 17,386	E2
Waiakoa	J2
Waialae	D4
Waialua, Oahu 3,943	E1
Waianae 8,758	D2
Waihee 4,004	J2
Waikane 717	E2
Waikapu 729	J2
Waikiki 50	H4
Waikiki	C4
Wailea, Hawaii 150	J4
Wailea-Makena, Maui 3,799	J2
Wailua 2,018	D2
Wailuku▲ 10,688	J2
Waimalu 29,967	B3
Waimanalo 3,508	F2
Waimanalo Beach 4,185	F2
Waimea (Kamuela), Hawaii 1,840	G3
Waimea 200	E1
Waimea, Kauai 5,972	B2
Wainaku 1,243	J5
Wainiha 175	C1
Waiohinu 200	G7
Waipahu 31,435	A3
Waipio 11,812	H3
Waipio Acres 5,304	E2
Whitmore Village 3,373	E1

OTHER FEATURES

Alalakeiki (chan.)	J3

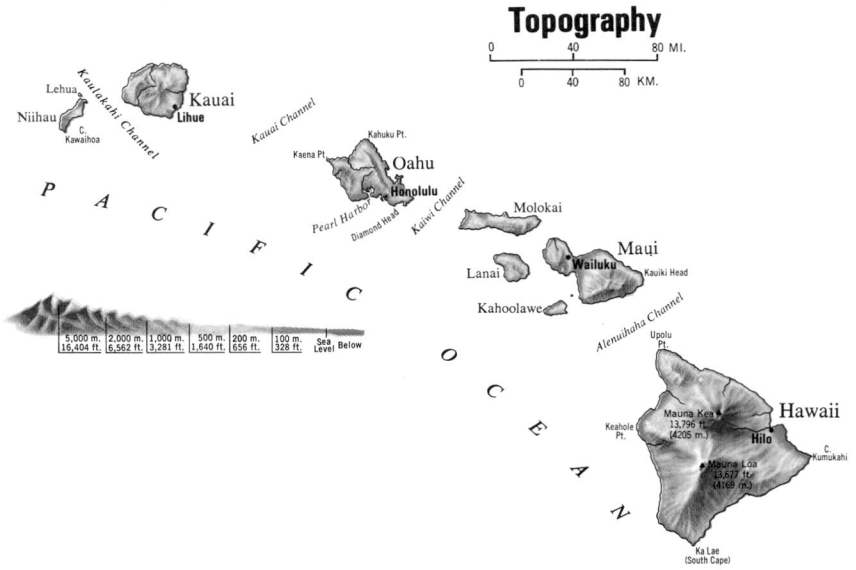

Topography

Agriculture, Industry and Resources

DOMINANT LAND USE

- Diversified Tropical Cash Crops
- Livestock Grazing
- Forests
- Urban Areas
- Nonagricultural Land

Major Industrial Areas

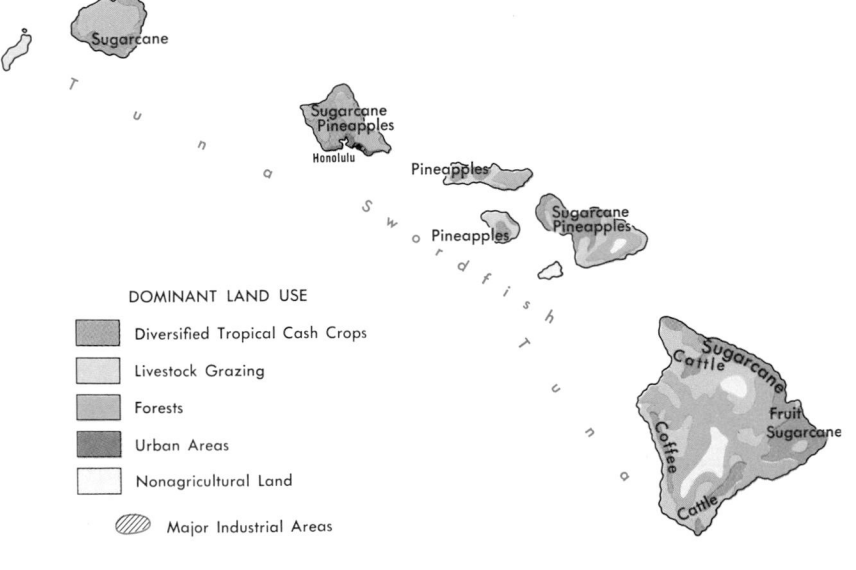

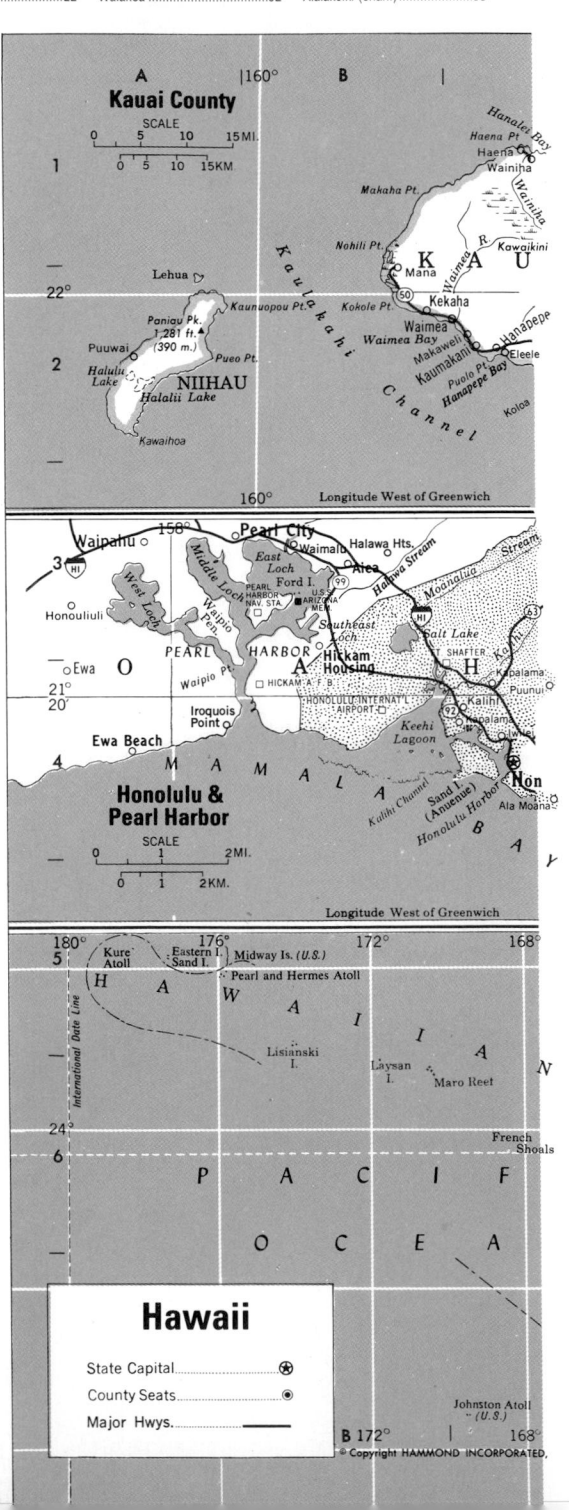

Kauai County

Honolulu & Pearl Harbor

Hawaii

- State Capital ⊛
- County Seats ⊙
- Major Hwys. ▬

© Copyright HAMMOND INCORPORATED,

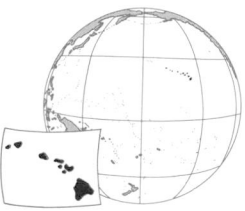

HAWAII

AREA 6,471 sq. mi. (16,760 sq. km.)
POPULATION 1,115,274
CAPITAL Honolulu
LARGEST CITY Honolulu
HIGHEST POINT Mauna Kea 13,796 ft. (4205 m.)
SETTLED IN —
ADMITTED TO UNION August 21, 1959
POPULAR NAME Aloha State
STATE FLOWER Hibiscus
STATE BIRD Nene (Hawaiian Goose)

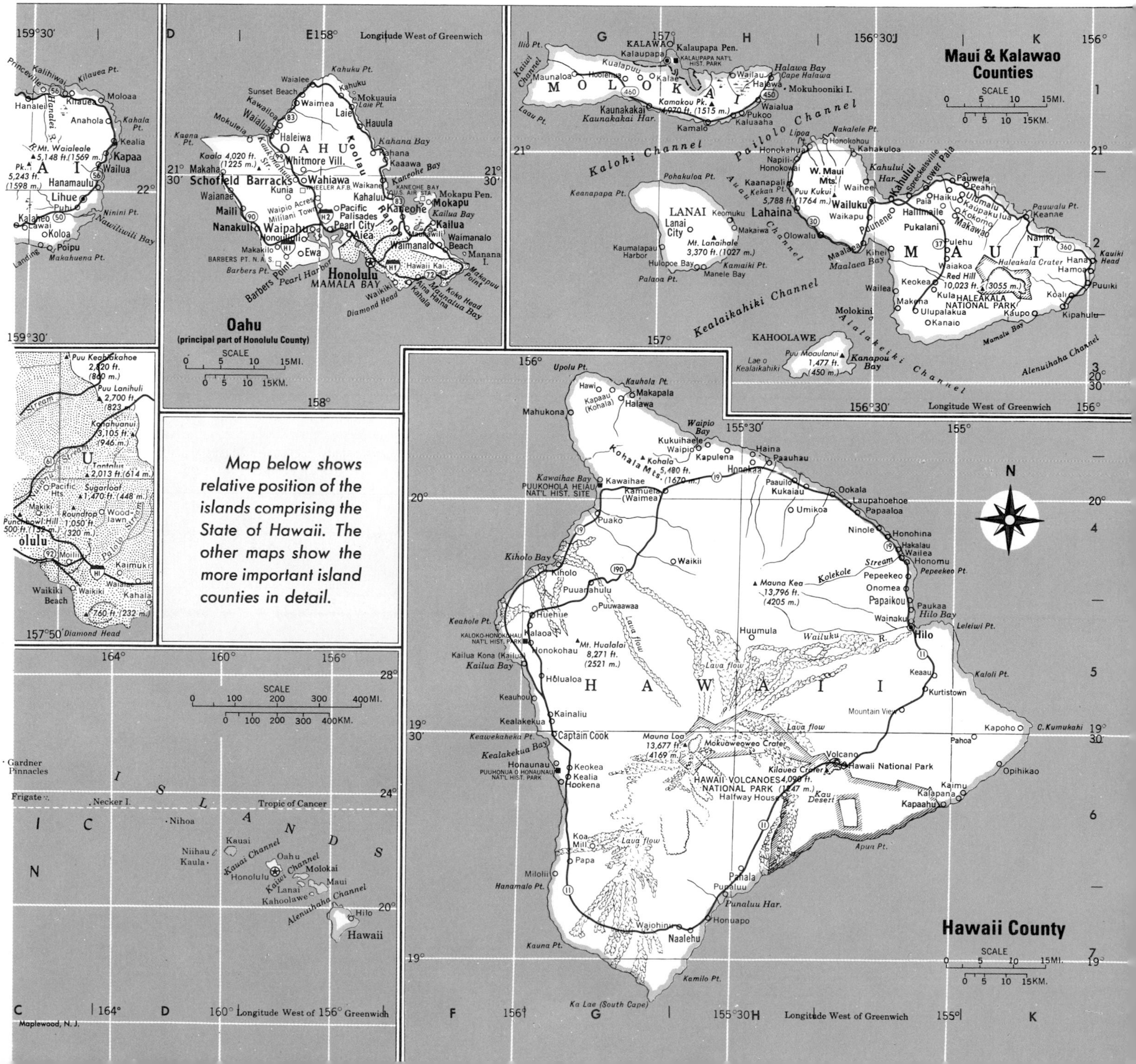

Oahu
(principal part of Honolulu County)

Maui & Kalawao Counties

Hawaii County

Map below shows relative position of the islands comprising the State of Hawaii. The other maps show the more important island counties in detail.

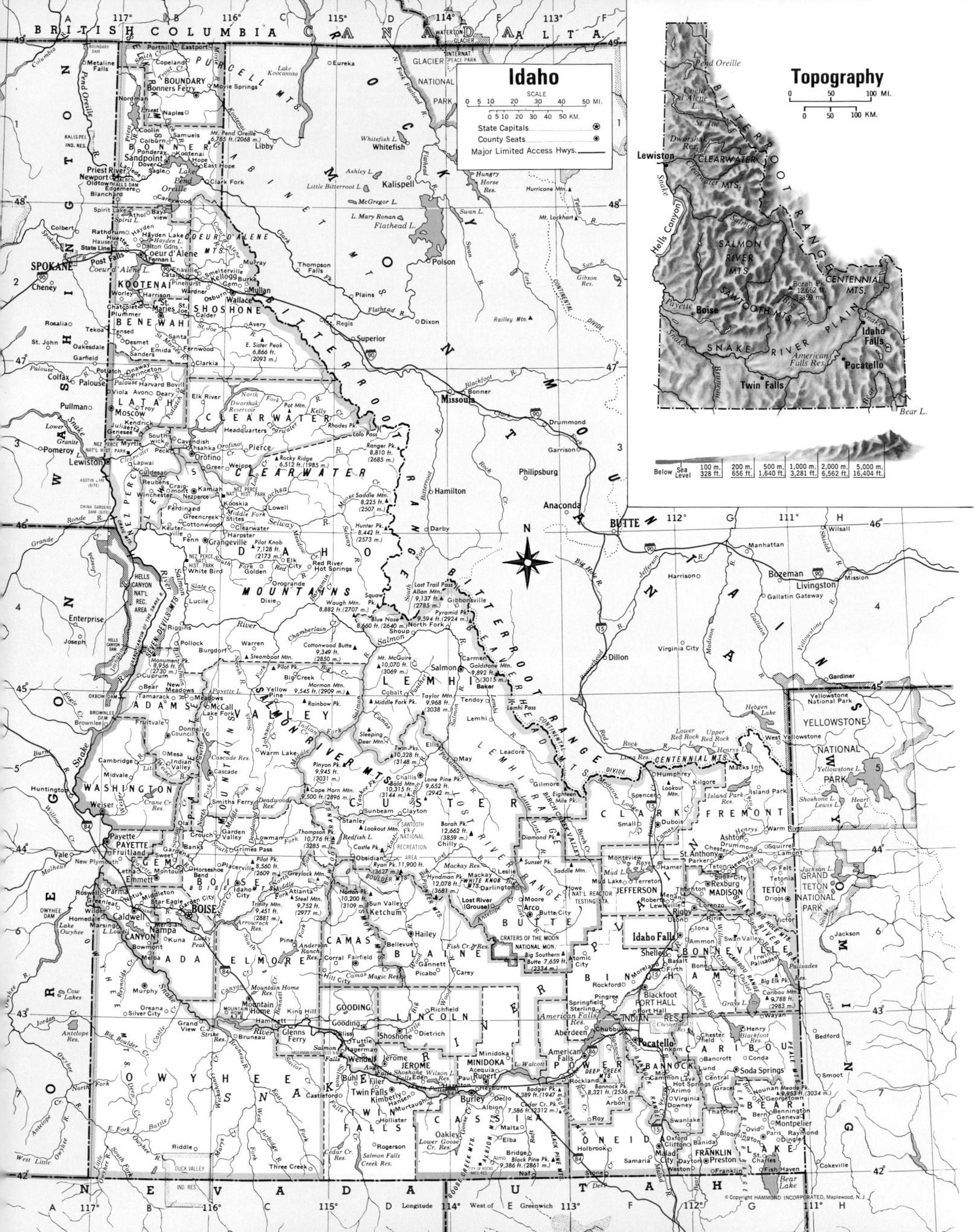

Idaho

SCALE

| 0 5 10 | 20 | 30 | 40 | 50 MI. |

| 0 5 10 | 20 | 30 | 40 | 50 KM. |

State Capitals .... ⊛
County Seats .... ◉
Major Limited Access Hwys. ———

Topography

0   50   100 MI.

0   50   100 KM.

| Below Sea Level | 100 m. 328 ft. | 200 m. 656 ft. | 500 m. 1,640 ft. | 1,000 m. 3,281 ft. | 2,000 m. 6,562 ft. | 5,000 m. 16,404 ft. |

© Copyright HAMMOND INCORPORATED, Maplewood, N.J.

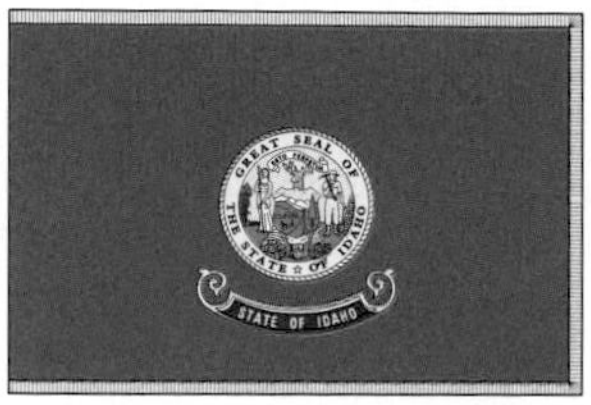
STATE OF IDAHO

AREA 83,564 sq. mi. (216,431 sq. km.)
POPULATION 1,011,986
CAPITAL Boise
LARGEST CITY Boise
HIGHEST POINT Borah Pk. 12,662 ft. (3859 m.)
SETTLED IN 1842
ADMITTED TO UNION July 3, 1890
POPULAR NAME Gem State
STATE FLOWER Syringa
STATE BIRD Mountain Bluebird

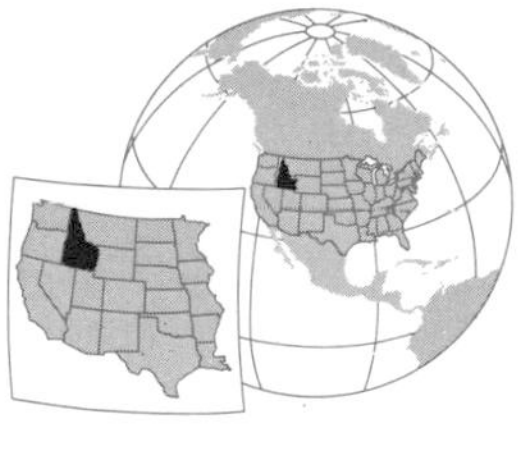

COUNTIES

Ada 205,775 B6
Adams 3,254 B5
Bannock 66,026 F7
Bear Lake 6,084 G7
Benewah 7,937 B2
Bingham 37,583 F6
Blaine 13,552 D6
Boise 3,509 C6
Bonner 26,622 B1
Bonneville 72,207 G6
Boundary 8,332 B1
Butte 2,918 E6
Camas 727 D6
Canyon 90,076 B6
Caribou 6,963 G7
Cassia 19,532 E7
Clark 762 F5
Clearwater 8,505 C3
Custer 4,133 D5
Elmore 21,205 C6
Franklin 9,232 G7
Fremont 10,937 G5
Gem 11,844 B6
Gooding 11,633 D6
Idaho 13,783 C4
Jefferson 16,543 F6
Jerome 15,138 D7
Kootenai 69,795 B2
Latah 30,617 B3
Lemhi 6,899 D4
Lewis 3,516 B3
Lincoln 3,308 D6
Madison 23,674 G6
Minidoka 19,361 E7
Nez Perce 33,754 B3
Oneida 3,492 F7
Owyhee 8,392 B7
Payette 16,434 B5
Power 7,086 F7
Shoshone 13,931 B2
Teton 3,439 G6
Twin Falls 53,580 D7
Valley 6,109 C5
Washington 8,550 B5

CITIES and TOWNS

Aberdeen 1,406 F7
Acequia 106 E7
Ahsahka 160 B3
Albion 305 E7
American Falls▲ 3,757 E7
Ammon 5,002 G6
Arco▲ 1,016 E6
Arimo 311 F7
Ashton 1,114 G5
Athol 346 B2
Atomic City 25 F6
Bancroft 393 G7
Basalt 407 F6
Bayview 350 B2
Bellevue 1,275 D6
Bern 154 G7
Blackfoot▲ 9,646 F6
Bliss 185 D7
Bloomington 197 G7
Boise (cap.)▲ 102,160 B6
Bonners Ferry▲ 2,193 B1
Bovill 256 B3
Bruneau 160 C7
Buhl 3,516 D7
Burgdorf B4
Burke 150 C2
Burley▲ 8,702 E7
Butte City 59 E6
Calder 200 B2
Caldwell▲ 18,400 B6
Cambridge 374 B5
Carey 800 E6
Cascade▲ 877 C5
Castleford 179 C7
Cataldo 150 B2
Challis▲ 1,073 D5
Chatcolet 72 B2
Chester 300 G5
Chilly E5
Chubbuck 7,791 F7
Clark Fork 448 B1
Clarkia 175 B2
Clayton 26 D5
Clifton 228 F7
Coeur d'Alene▲ 24,563 B2
Colburn 250 B1
Conda 200 G7
Coolin 150 B1
Cottonwood 822 B3
Council▲ 831 B5
Craigmont 542 B3
Crouch 75 B5
Culdesac 280 B3
Dalton Gardens 1,951 B2
Dayton 357 F7
Deary 529 B3
Declo 279 E7
Dietrich 127 D7
Dingle 300 G7
Donnelly 135 B5
Dover 294 B1
Downey 626 F7
Driggs▲ 846 G6
Drummond 37 G5
Dubois▲ 420 F5
Eagle 3,327 B6
East Hope 215 B1
Eden 314 D7
Elk City 500 C4
Elk River 149 B3
Emida 175 B2
Emmett▲ 4,601 B6
Fairfield▲ 371 D6
Ferdinand 135 B3
Fernan Lake 178 B2
Fernwood 608 B2
Filer 1,511 D7
Firth 429 F6
Fort Hall 2,681 F6
Franklin 478 G7
Fruitland 2,400 B6
Fruitvale 200 B5
Garden City 6,369 B6
Garden Valley 250 C5
Genesee 725 B3
Geneva 220 G7
Georgetown 558 G7
Gilmore E5
Glenns Ferry 1,304 C7
Gooding▲ 2,820 D7
Grace 973 G7
Grand View 330 B7
Grangeville▲ 3,226 B4
Greenleaf 648 B6
Grimes Pass C5
Hagerman 600 D7
Hailey▲ 3,687 D6
Hamer 79 F6
Hammett 180 C7
Hansen 848 D7
Harrison 226 B2
Hauser 380 A2
Hayden 3,744 B2
Hayden Lake 338 B2
Hazelton 394 E7
Headquarters 165 C3
Heise 84 G6
Heyburn 2,714 E7
Hollister 144 D7
Homedale 1,963 A6
Hope 99 B1
Horseshoe Bend 643 B6
Huetter 82 B2
Idaho City▲ 322 C6
Idaho Falls▲ 43,929 F6
Inkom 769 F7
Iona 1,049 G6
Irwin 108 G6
Island Park 159 G5
Jerome▲ 6,529 D7
Juliaetta 488 B3
Kamiah 1,157 B3
Kellogg 2,591 B2
Kendrick 325 B3
Ketchum 2,523 D6
Kimberly 2,367 D7
Kooskia 692 C3
Kootenai 327 B1
Kuna 1,955 B6
Laclede 400 B1
Lake Fork 250 B5
Lapwai 932 B3
Lava Hot Springs 420 F7
Leadore 74 E5
Lewiston▲ 28,082 A3
Lewisville 471 F6
Lost River (Grouse) 29 E6
Lowman 180 C5
Mackay 574 E6
Macks Inn 200 G5
Malad City▲ 1,946 F7
Malta 171 E7
Marsing 798 B6
McCall 2,005 C5
McCammon 722 F7
Meadows 250 B5
Melba 252 B6
Menan 601 F6
Meridian 9,596 B6
Middleton 1,851 B6
Midvale 110 B5
Minidoka 67 E7
Monteview 200 F6
Montpelier 2,656 G7
Moore 190 E6
Moreland 600 F6
Moscow▲ 18,519 B3
Mountain Home▲ 7,913 C6
Moyie Springs 415 B1
Mud Lake 179 F6
Mullan 821 C2
Murphy▲ 200 B6
Murtaugh 114 D7
Nampa 28,365 B6
Naples 250 B1
New Meadows 534 B4
New Plymouth 1,313 B6
Newdale 377 G6
Nezperce▲ 453 B3
Nordman 300 B1
North Fork 250 D4
Notus 380 B6
Oakley 635 D7
Ola 175 B5
Oldtown 151 A1
Onaway 203 B3
Orofino▲ 2,868 B3
Osburn 1,579 B2
Oxford 44 F7
Paris▲ 581 G7
Parker 288 G6
Parma 1,597 B6
Patterson 4 E5
Paul 901 E7
Payette▲ 5,592 B5
Pearl 8 B6
Peck 160 B3
Pierce 746 C3
Pinehurst 1,722 B2
Placerville 14 C6
Plummer 804 B2
Pocatello▲ 46,080 F7
Ponderay 449 B1
Post Falls 7,349 A2
Potlatch 790 A3
Preston▲ 3,710 G7
Priest River 1,560 A1
Rathdrum 2,000 A2
Reubens 46 B3
Rexburg▲ 14,302 G6
Richfield 383 D6
Rigby▲ 2,681 F6
Riggins 443 B4
Ririe 596 G6
Roberts 557 F6
Rockland 264 F7
Rupert▲ 5,455 E7
Sagle 600 B1
Saint Anthony▲ 3,010 G6
Saint Charles 211 G7
Saint Maries▲ 2,442 B2
Salmon▲ 2,941 D4
Samuels 467 B1
Sandpoint▲ 5,203 B1
Shelley 3,536 F6
Shoshone▲ 1,249 D7
Silver City 1 B6
Smelterville 464 B2
Soda Springs▲ 3,111 G7
Spencer 11 F5
Spirit Lake 790 A2
Stanley 71 D5
Star 500 B6
State Line 26 A2
Stites 204 C3
Sugar City 1,275 G6
Sun Valley 938 D6
Swan Valley 141 G6
Sweet 290 B6
Tendoy 155 E5
Tensed 90 B2
Terreton 400 F6
Teton 570 G6
Tetonia 132 G6
Thatcher 300 G7
Thornton 177 G6
Troy 699 B3
Twin Falls▲ 27,591 D7
Ucon 895 F6
Victor 292 G6
Wallace▲ 1,010 C2
Wardner 246 B2
Warm Lake 200 C5
Warm River 9 G5
Wayan 175 G7
Weippe 532 C3
Weiser▲ 4,571 B5
Wendell 1,963 D7
Weston 390 F7
White Bird 108 B4
Wilder 1,232 A6
Winchester 262 B3
Worley 182 B2

OTHER FEATURES

Albeni Falls (dam) B1
Albion (mts.) E7
Allan (mt.) D4
American Falls (res.) F6
Anderson Ranch (res.) C6
Antelope (creek) E6
Arrowrock (res.) C6
Auger (falls) D7
Badger (peak) E7
Bald (mt.) D5
Bannock (creek) F7
Bannock (peak) F7
Bannock (range) F7
Bargamin (creek) C4
Battle (creek) B7
Bear (lake) G7
Bear (riv.) G7
Bear River (range) G7
Beaver (creek) F5
Beaverhead (mts.) E4
Big (creek) C4
Big Boulder (creek) B7
Big Elk (peak) G6
Big Hole (mts.) G6
Big Lost (riv.) E6
Big Southern (butte) E6
Big Wood (riv.) D6
Birch (creek) F5
Birch Creek (valley) E5
Bitterroot (range) D3
Blackfoot (res.) G7
Black Pine (mts.) E7
Blue Nose (mt.) D4
Boise (mts.) B6
Boise (riv.) B6
Borah (peak) E5
Boulder (mts.) D6
Brownlee (dam) B5
Bruneau (riv.) C7
Camas (creek) D5
Camas (creek) D6
Camas (creek) F5
Canyon (creek) C6
Cape Horn (mt.) C5
Caribou (mt.) G6
Caribou (range) G6
Cascade (res.) C5
Castle (creek) B7
Castle (peak) D5
Cedar Creek (peak) E7
Cedar Creek (res.) D7
Centennial (mts.) F5
Chesterfield (res) F7
Clearwater (mts.) C3
Clearwater (riv.) B3
Coeur d'Alene (lake) B2
Coeur d'Alene (mts.) C2
Coeur d'Alene (riv.) B2
Cottonwood (butte) C4
Craig (mts.) B4
Crane Creek (res.) B5
Craters of the Moon Nat'l Mon. E6
Deadwood (res.) C5
Deep (creek) B7
Deep (creek) F7
Deep Creek (mts.) F7
Diamond (peak) E5
Duck Valley Ind. Res. B7
Dworshak (res.) C3
East Sister (peak) C2
Eighteen Mile (peak) E5
Fish Creek (res.) E6
Fort Hall Ind. Res. F6
Goldstone (mt.) E4
Goose (creek) E7
Goose Creek (mts.) E7
Grand Canyon of the Snake River (canyon) B4
Grays (lake) G6
Grays Lake Outlet (creek) G6
Greylock (mt.) C6
Hayden (lake) B2
Hells (canyon) B4
Hells Canyon Nat'l Rec. Area B4
Henrys (lake) G5
Henrys Fork, Snake (riv.) G5
Hunter (peak) D3
Hyndman (peak) D6
Indian (creek) C5
Island Park (res.) G5
Jarbidge (riv.) C7
Johnson (creek) C5
Jordan (creek) A7
Kootenai (riv.) C1
Lemhi (pass) E5
Lemhi (range) E5
Lemhi (riv.) E5
Little Lost (riv.) E5
Little Owyhee (riv.) B7
Little Salmon (riv.) B4
Little Weiser (riv.) B5
Little Wood (riv.) D6
Lochsa (riv.) C3
Lolo (creek) C3
Lolo (pass) D3
Lone Pine (peak) D5
Lookout (mt.) D5
Lookout (mt.) F5
Lost River (range) E5
Lost Trail (pass) D4
Lowell (lake) B6
Lower Goose Creek (res.) D7
Lower Granite (lake) A3
Lucky Peak (lake) B6
Mackay (res.) E6
Magic (res.) D6
Malad (riv.) F7
Marsh (creek) F7
McGuire (mt.) D4
Meade (peak) G7
Meadow (creek) C4
Medicine Lodge (creek) F5
Middle Fork (peak) D5
Monument (peak) B4
Moose (creek) D3
Mores (creek) C6
Mormon (mt.) C4
Mountain Home (res.) C6
Mountain Home A.F.B. 5,936 C6
Moyie (riv.) B1
Mud (lake) F6
National Reactor Testing Sta. F6
Nez Perce Nat'l Hist. Park C3
Norton (peak) D6
Orofino (creek) C3
Owyhee (mts.) B6
Owyhee, East Fork (riv.) B7
Oxbow (dam) B5
Pack (riv.) B1
Pahsimeroi (riv.) E5
Palisades (res.) G6
Palouse (riv.) B3
Panther (creek) D4
Payette (lake) C4
Payette (mts.) B5
Payette (riv.) B6
Peale (mts.) G7
Pend Oreille (lake) B1
Pend Oreille (mt.) B1
Pend Oreille (riv.) A1
Pilot (peak) C4
Pilot (peak) C6
Pilot Knob (mt.) C4
Pinyon (peak) C5
Pioneer (mts.) D6
Pot (mt.) C3
Potlatch (riv.) B3
Priest (lake) B1
Priest (riv.) B1
Purcell (mts.) B1
Pyramid (peak) E4
Raft (riv.) E7
Rainbow (mt.) C5
Ranger (peak) D3
Rays (lake) F6
Red (riv.) C4
Redfish (lake) D5
Reynolds (creek) B6
Rhodes (peak) D3
Rock (creek) F7
Rocky (mts.) D1
Rocky Ridge (mt.) C3
Ryan (peak) D6
Saddle (mt.) D3
Saddle (mt.) F6
Sailor (creek) C7
Saint Joe (riv.) B2
Saint Maries (riv.) B2
Salmon (falls) C7
Salmon (riv.) B4
Salmon Falls (creek) D7
Salmon Falls Creek (res.) D7
Salmon River (mts.) C5
Sawtooth (range) C6
Sawtooth Nat'l Rec. Area D5
Secesh (riv.) C4
Selkirk (mts.) B1
Selway (riv.) C3
Seven Devils (mts.) B4
Shoshone (falls) D7
Sleeping Deer (mt.) D5
Smith (creek) B1
Smoky (mts.) D6
Snake (riv.) A3
Snake River (plain) D7
Snake River (range) G6
Spirit (lake) B2
Squaw (creek) B5
Squaw (peak) D4
Steamboat (mt.) C4
Steel (mt.) C6
Strike, C.J. (res.) C7
Sublett (mts.) E7
Sunset (peak) E6
Taylor (mt.) D5
Teton (riv.) G6
Thompson (peak) C5
Trinity (mt.) C6
Trout (creek) B1
Twin (falls) D7
Twin Peaks (mt.) D5
Walcott (lake) E7
Waugh (mt.) D4
Weiser (riv.) B5
White Knob (mts.) E6
Wickahoney (creek) C7
Willow (creek) G6
Wilson Lake (res.) D7
Yankee Fork, Salmon (riv.) D5
Yellowstone Nat'l Park H5

▲County seat

Agriculture, Industry and Resources

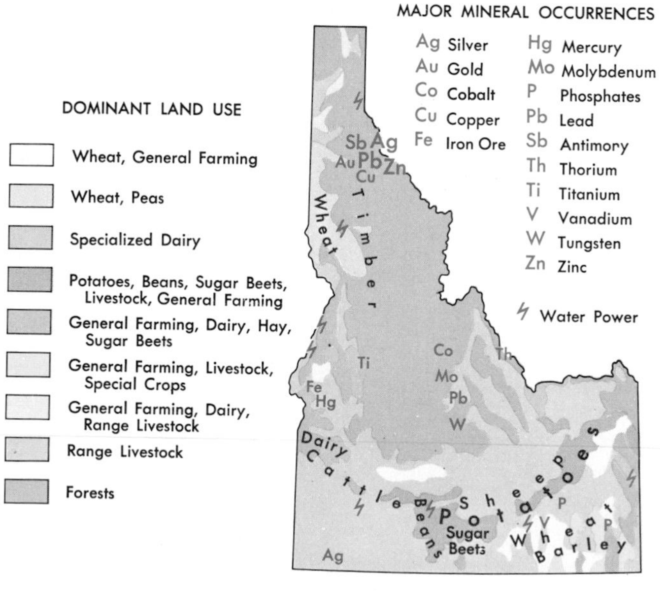
DOMINANT LAND USE
Wheat, General Farming
Wheat, Peas
Specialized Dairy
Potatoes, Beans, Sugar Beets, Livestock, General Farming
General Farming, Dairy, Hay, Sugar Beets
General Farming, Livestock, Special Crops
General Farming, Dairy, Range Livestock
Range Livestock
Forests
MAJOR MINERAL OCCURRENCES
Ag Silver
Au Gold
Co Cobalt
Cu Copper
Fe Iron Ore
Hg Mercury
Mo Molybdenum
P Phosphates
Pb Lead
Sb Antimony
Th Thorium
Ti Titanium
V Vanadium
W Tungsten
Zn Zinc
Water Power
Wheat
Timber
Dairy
Cattle
Sheep
Potatoes
Beans
Sugar Beets
Wheat
Barley

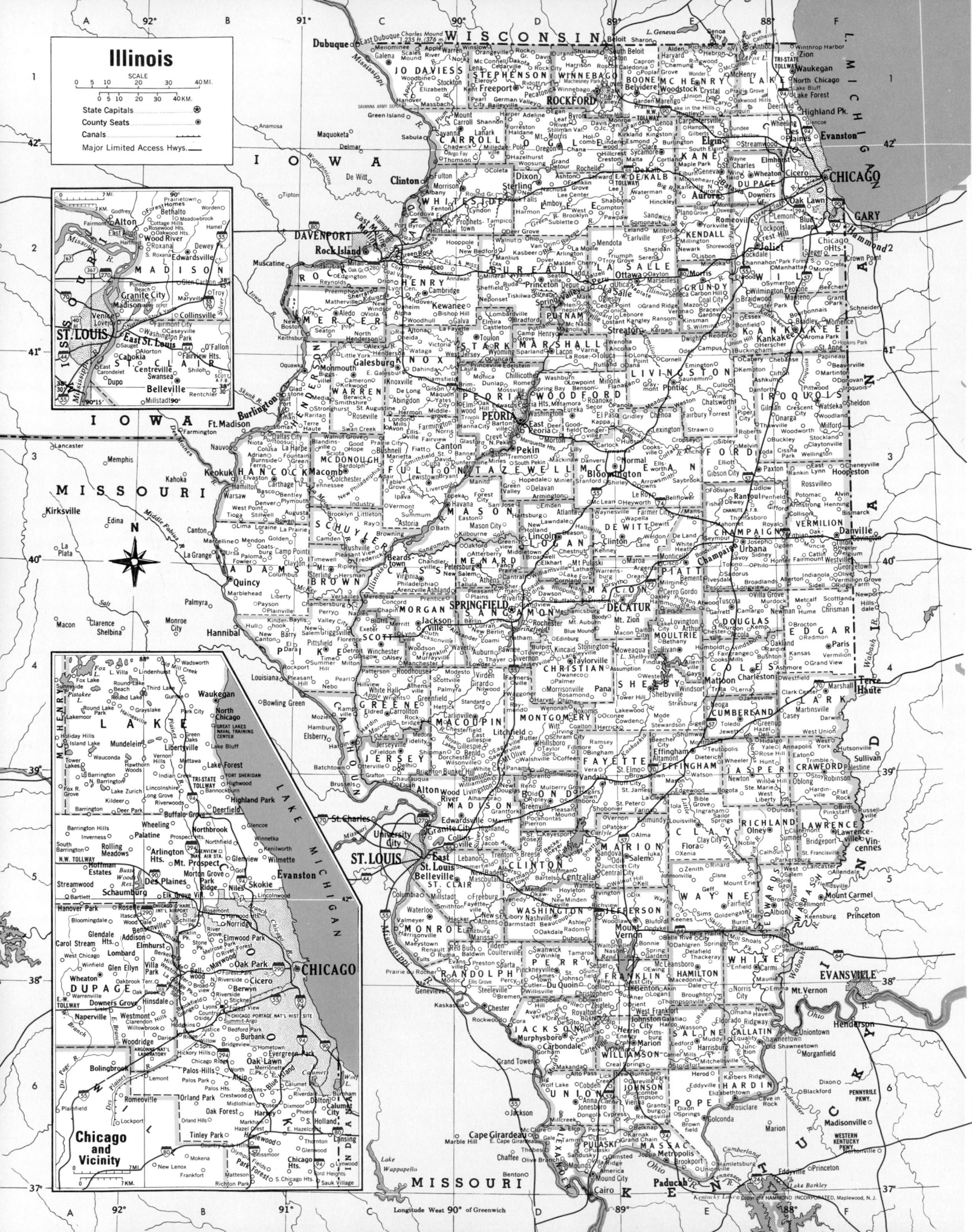

Illinois 223

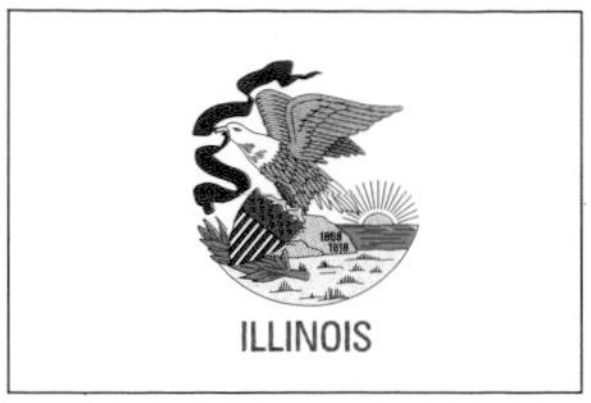

ILLINOIS

AREA 56,345 sq. mi. (145,934 sq. km.)
POPULATION 11,466,682
CAPITAL Springfield
LARGEST CITY Chicago
HIGHEST POINT Charles Mound 1,235 ft. (376 m.)
SETTLED IN 1720
ADMITTED TO UNION December 3, 1818
POPULAR NAME Prairie State; Land of Lincoln
STATE FLOWER Native Violet
STATE BIRD Cardinal

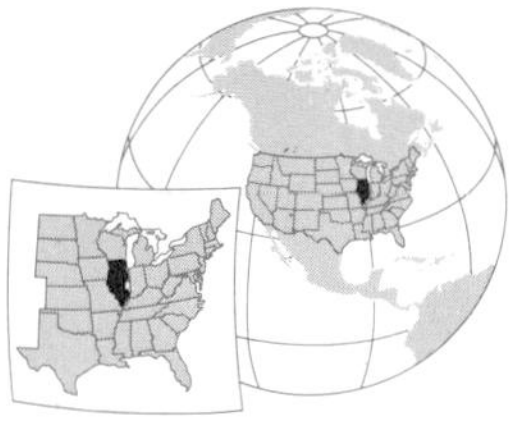

COUNTIES

Adams 66,090 B4
Alexander 10,626 D6
Bond 14,991 D5
Boone 30,806 E1
Brown 5,836 C4
Bureau 35,688 D2
Calhoun 5,322 C4
Carroll 16,805 D1
Cass 13,437 C4
Champaign 173,025 E3
Christian 34,418 D4
Clark 15,921 F4
Clay 14,460 E5
Clinton 33,944 D5
Coles 51,644 E4
Cook 5,105,067 F2
Crawford 19,464 F4
Cumberland 10,670 E4
De Kalb 74,624 E2
De Witt 16,516 E3
Douglas 19,464 E4
Du Page 658,858 E2
Edgar 19,595 F4
Edwards 7,440 E5
Effingham 31,704 E4
Fayette 20,893 D4
Ford 14,275 E3
Franklin 40,319 E5
Fulton 38,080 C3
Gallatin 6,909 E6
Greene 15,317 C4
Grundy 32,337 E2
Hamilton 8,499 E5
Hancock 21,373 B3
Hardin 5,189 E6
Henderson 8,096 C3
Henry 51,159 C2
Iroquois 30,787 F3
Jackson 61,067 D6
Jasper 10,609 E4
Jefferson 37,020 E5
Jersey 20,539 C4
Jo Daviess 21,821 C1
Johnson 11,347 E6
Kane 317,471 E2
Kankakee 96,255 F2
Kendall 39,413 E2
Knox 56,393 C3
La Salle 106,913 E2
Lake 516,418 E1
Lawrence 15,972 F5
Lee 34,392 D2
Livingston 39,301 E3
Logan 30,798 D3
Macon 117,206 E4
Macoupin 47,679 D4
Madison 249,238 D5
Marion 41,561 E5
Marshall 12,846 D2
Mason 16,269 D3
Massac 14,752 E6
McDonough 35,244 C3
McHenry 183,241 E1
McLean 129,180 E3
Menard 11,164 D3
Mercer 17,290 C2
Monroe 22,422 C5
Montgomery 30,728 D4
Morgan 36,397 C4
Moultrie 13,930 E4
Ogle 45,957 D1
Peoria 182,827 D3
Perry 21,412 D5
Piatt 15,548 E4
Pike 17,577 C4
Pope 4,373 E6
Pulaski 7,523 D6
Putnam 5,730 D2
Randolph 34,583 D5
Richland 16,545 E5
Rock Island 148,723 C2
Saint Clair 267,531 D5
Saline 26,551 E6
Sangamon 178,386 D4
Schuyler 7,498 C3
Scott 5,644 C4
Shelby 22,261 E4
Stark 6,534 D2
Stephenson 48,052 D1
Tazewell 123,692 D3
Union 17,619 D6
Vermilion 88,257 F3
Wabash 13,111 F5
Warren 19,181 C3
Washington 14,965 D5
Wayne 17,241 E5
White 16,522 E5
Whiteside 60,186 D2
Will 357,313 F2
Williamson 57,733 E6
Winnebago 252,913 D1
Woodford 32,653 D3

CITIES and TOWNS

Abingdon 3,597 C3
Addison 32,058 B5
Albany 835 C2
Albers 700 D5
Albion▲ 2,116 E5
Aledo▲ 3,681 C2
Alexis 908 C2
Algonquin 11,663 E1
Alhambra 709 D5
Allendale 476 F5
Alorton 2,960 B2
Alpha 753 C2
Alsip 18,227 B6
Altamont 2,296 E4
Alton 32,905 A2
Altona 559 C2
Amboy 2,377 D2
Andalusia 1,052 C2
Andover 579 C2
Anna 4,805 D6
Annawan 802 C2
Antioch 6,105 E1
Arcola 2,678 E4
Arenzville 432 C4
Argenta 940 E4
Arlington Heights 75,460 B5
Aroma Park 690 F2
Arthur 2,112 E4
Ashkum 650 E3
Ashland 1,257 C4
Ashley 583 D5
Ashmore 800 F4
Ashton 1,042 D2
Assumption 1,244 E4
Astoria 1,205 C3
Athens 1,404 D4
Atkinson 950 C2
Atlanta 1,616 D3
Atwood 1,253 E4
Auburn 3,724 D4
Augusta 614 C3
Aurora 99,581 E2
Ava 674 D6
Aviston 924 D5
Avon 957 C3
Baldwin 426 D5
Bannockburn 1,388 B5
Barrington 9,504 A5
Barrington Hills 4,202 A5
Barry 1,391 B4
Bartlett 19,373 A5
Bartonville 5,643 D3
Batavia 17,076 E2
Beardstown 5,270 C3
Beckemeyer 1,070 D5
Bedford Park 566 B6
Beecher 2,032 F2
Beecher City 437 E4
Belgium 511 F3
Belleville▲ 42,785 B3
Bellwood 20,241 B5
Belvidere▲ 15,958 E1
Bement 1,668 E4
Benld 1,604 D4
Bensenville 17,767 B5
Benton▲ 7,216 E6
Berkeley 5,137 B5
Berwyn 45,426 B6
Bethalto 9,507 B2
Bethany 1,369 E4
Blandinsville 762 C3
Bloomingdale 16,614 A5
Bloomington▲ 51,972 D3
Blue Island 21,203 B6
Blue Mound 1,161 D4
Bluffs 774 C4
Bluford 747 E5
Bolingbrook 40,843 A6
Bourbon 13,934 E4
Bourbonnais 13,280 F2
Bowen 462 B3
Braceville 587 E2
Bradford 678 D2
Bradley 10,792 F2
Braidwood 3,584 E2
Breese 3,567 D5
Bridgeport 2,118 F5
Bridgeview 14,402 B6
Brighton 2,270 C4
Brimfield 797 D3
Broadview 8,713 B6
Brookfield 18,876 B6
Brooklyn (Lovejoy) 1,144 A2
Brookport 1,070 E6
Brownstown 668 E5
Buckley 557 F3
Buckner 478 E6
Buda 563 D2
Buffalo 503 D4
Buffalo Grove 36,427 B5
Bunker Hill 1,722 D4
Burbank 27,600 B6
Burnham 3,916 C6
Burr Ridge 7,669 B6
Bushnell 3,288 C3
Byron 2,284 D1
Cahokia 17,550 A3
Cairo▲ 4,846 D6
Calumet City 37,840 C6
Calumet Park 8,418 C6
Cambria 1,230 D6
Cambridge▲ 2,124 C2
Camp Point 1,230 B3
Canton 13,922 D3
Capron 682 E1
Carbon Cliff 1,492 C2
Carbondale 27,033 D6
Carlinville▲ 5,416 D4
Carlyle▲ 3,474 D5
Carmi▲ 5,564 E5
Carol Stream 31,716 A5
Carpentersville 23,049 E1
Carrier Mills 2,268 E6
Carrollton▲ 2,507 C4
Carterville 3,630 D6
Carthage▲ 2,657 B3
Cary 10,043 E1
Casey 2,914 F4
Caseyville 4,419 B2
Catlin 2,173 F3
Cave in Rock 381 E6
Cedarville 751 D1
Central City 1,390 D5
Centralia 14,274 D5
Centreville 7,489 B3
Cerro Gordo 1,436 E4
Chadwick 557 D1
Champaign 63,502 E3
Chandlerville 689 C3
Channahon 4,266 E2
Chapin 632 C4
Charleston▲ 20,398 E4
Chatham 6,074 D4
Chatsworth 1,186 E3
Chebanse 1,082 F3
Chenoa 1,732 E3
Cherry 487 D2
Cherry Valley 1,615 D1
Chester▲ 8,194 D6
Chicago Heights 33,072 C6
Chicago Ridge 13,643 B6
Chicago▲ 2,783,726 C5
Chillicothe 5,959 D3
Chrisman 1,136 F4
Christopher 2,774 D6
Cicero 67,436 B5
Cisne 645 E5
Cissna Park 805 F3
Clarendon Hills 6,994 B6
Clay City 929 E5
Clayton 726 B3
Clifton 1,347 F3
Clinton▲ 7,437 E3
Coal City 3,907 E2
Coal Valley 2,683 C2
Cobden 1,090 D6
Coffeen 736 D4
Colchester 1,645 C3
Colfax 854 E3
Collinsville 22,446 B2
Colona 2,237 C2
Columbia 5,524 C5
Cordova 638 C2
Cornell 556 E3
Cortland 963 E2
Coulterville 984 D5
Country Club Hills 15,431 B6
Countryside 5,716 B6
Cowden 599 E4
Creal Springs 791 E6
Crescent City 541 F3
Crest Hill 10,643 E2
Creston 535 D2
Crestwood 10,823 B6
Crete 6,773 F2
Creve Coeur 5,938 D3
Crossville 805 F5
Crystal Lake 24,512 E1
Cuba 1,440 C3
Cullom 568 E3
Cutler 523 D5
Dahlgren 512 E5
Dakota 549 D1
Dallas City 1,037 B3
Dalton City 573 E4
Dalzell 587 D2
Danforth 457 E3
Danvers 981 D3
Danville▲ 33,828 F3
Darien 18,341 B6
Davis 541 D1
Dawson 536 D4
De Kalb 34,925 E2
De Land 458 E3
De Soto 1,500 D6
Decatur▲ 83,885 E4
Deer Creek 630 D3
Deer Park 2,887 A5
Deerfield 17,327 B5
Delavan 1,642 D3
Depue 1,729 D2
Des Plaines 53,223 B5
Dieterich 568 E4
Divernon 1,178 D4
Dix 456 E5
Dixmoor 3,647 C6
Dixon▲ 15,144 D2
Dolton 23,930 C6
Dongola 728 D6
Dow 465 C4
Dowell 480 D6
Downers Grove 46,858 A6
Downs 620 E3
Du Quoin 6,697 D5
Dundee (East and West Dundee) 6,169 E1
Dunlap 851 D3
Dupo 3,164 A3
Durand 1,100 D1
Dwight 4,230 E2
Earlville 1,435 E2
East Alton 7,063 A2
East Cape Girardeau 451 D6
East Carondelet 630 A3
East Dubuque 1,914 C1
East Dundee (Dundee) 2,721 E1
East Galesburg 813 C3
East Hazelcrest 1,570 C6
East Moline 20,147 C2
East Peoria 21,378 D3
East Saint Louis 40,944 A2
Edgewood 502 E5
Edinburg 982 D4
Edwards 14,579 D3
Edwardsville▲ 12,480 B2
Effingham▲ 11,851 E4
El Paso 2,499 D3
Elburn 1,275 E2
Eldorado 4,536 E6
Elgin 77,010 E1
Elizabeth 641 C1
Elizabethtown▲ 427 E6
Elk Grove Village 33,429 B5
Elkhart 475 D3
Elkville 958 D6
Elmhurst 42,029 B5
Elmwood 1,841 D3
Elmwood Park 23,206 B5
Elsah 851 C5
Elwood 951 E2
Emden 459 D3
Energy 1,106 E6
Enfield 683 E5
Equality 748 E6
Erie 1,572 C2
Essex 482 E2
Eureka▲ 4,435 D3
Evanston 73,233 B5
Evansville 844 D5
Evergreen Park 20,874 B6
Fairbury 3,643 E3
Fairfield▲ 5,439 E5
Fairmont 2,894 A2
Fairmont City 2,140 B2
Fairmount 678 F3
Fairview 510 C3
Fairview Heights 14,351 B3
Farina 575 E5
Farmer City 2,114 E3
Farmersville 698 D4
Farmington 2,535 C3
Findlay 787 E4
Fisher 1,526 E3
Fithian 512 F3
Flanagan 987 E3
Flat Rock 421 F5
Flora 5,054 E5
Flossmoor 8,651 B6
Ford Heights 4,259 C6
Forest Homes 1,701 B2
Forest Park 14,918 B5
Forest View 743 B6
Forrest 1,124 E3
Forreston 1,361 D1
Forsyth 1,275 D4
Fox Lake 7,478 A4
Fox River Grove 3,551 A5
Frankfort 7,180 B6
Franklin 634 C4
Franklin Grove 968 D2
Franklin Park 18,485 B5
Freeburg 3,115 D5
Freeport▲ 25,840 D1
Fulton 3,698 C2
Galatia 983 E6
Gale 3,647 D6
Galena▲ 3,876 C1
Galesburg▲ 33,530 C3
Galva 2,742 D2
Gardner 1,237 E2
Geneseo 5,990 C2
Geneva▲ 12,617 E2
Genoa 3,083 E1
Georgetown 3,678 F4
German Valley 480 D1
Germantown 1,167 D5
Gibson City 3,498 E3
Gifford 845 E3
Gilberts 987 E1
Gillespie 3,645 D4
Gilman 1,816 E3
Glasford 1,115 D3
Glen Carbon 7,731 B2
Glen Ellyn 24,944 A5
Glencoe 8,499 B5
Glendale Heights 27,973 A5
Glenview 37,093 B5
Glenwood 9,289 C6
Godfrey 5,436 A2
Golconda▲ 823 E6
Golden 565 B3
Golf 454 B5
Goodfield 454 D3
Goreville 872 E6
Grafton 918 C5
Grand Ridge 560 E2
Grand Tower 775 D6
Grandview 1,647 D4
Granite City 32,862 A2
Grant Park 1,024 F2
Granville 1,407 D2
Grayslake 7,388 B4
Grayville 2,043 E5
Green Oaks 2,101 B4
Green Rock 2,615 C2
Green Valley 745 D3
Greenfield 1,162 C4
Greenup 1,616 E4
Greenview 848 D3
Greenville▲ 4,806 D5
Gridley 1,304 E3
Griggsville 1,218 C4
Gurnee 13,701 B4
Hamel 530 B2
Hamilton 3,281 B3
Hammond 527 E4
Hampshire 1,843 E1
Hampton 1,601 C2
Hanna City 1,205 D3
Hanover 908 C1
Hanover Park 32,895 A5
Hardin▲ 1,071 C4
Harrisburg▲ 9,289 E6
Harristown 1,319 D4
Hartford 1,676 A2
Harvard 5,975 E1
Harvey 29,771 B6
Harwood Heights 7,680 B5
Havana▲ 3,610 D3
Hawthorn Woods 4,423 B5
Hazel Crest 13,334 B6
Hebron 809 E1
Hecker 534 D5
Hegeler 1,853 F3
Hennepin▲ 669 D2
Henry 2,591 D2
Herrick 466 D4
Herrin 10,857 E6
Herscher 1,278 E2
Heyworth 1,627 E3
Hickory Hills 13,021 B6
Highland 7,525 D5
Highland Park 30,575 B5
Highwood 5,331 B5
Hillcrest 828 D2
Hillsboro▲ 4,400 D4
Hillsdale 489 C2
Hillside 7,672 B5
Hinckley 1,682 E2
Hinsdale 16,029 B6
Hodgkins 1,963 B6
Hoffman 492 D5
Hoffman Estates 46,561 A5
Holiday Hills 807 A4
Homer 1,264 F3
Hometown 4,769 B6
Homewood 19,278 B6
Hoopeston 5,871 F3
Hopedale 805 D3
Hopkins Park 601 F2
Hoyleton 508 D5
Hudson 1,006 E3
Hull 514 B4
Humboldt 470 E4
Hunt 2,453 E4
Huntley 1,646 E1
Hurst 842 D6
Hutsonville 622 F4
Illiopolis 934 D4
Ina 489 E5
Industry 571 C3
Inverness 6,503 A5
Ipava 483 C3
Irving 516 D4
Irvington 827 D5
Island Lake 4,449 A4
Itasca 6,947 B5
Jacksonville▲ 19,324 C4
Jerome 1,206 D4
Jerseyville▲ 7,382 C4
Johnston City 3,706 E6
Joliet▲ 76,836 E2
Jonesboro▲ 1,728 D6
Joppa 492 E6
Joy 452 C2
Junction City 539 D5
Justice 11,137 B6

(continued on following page)

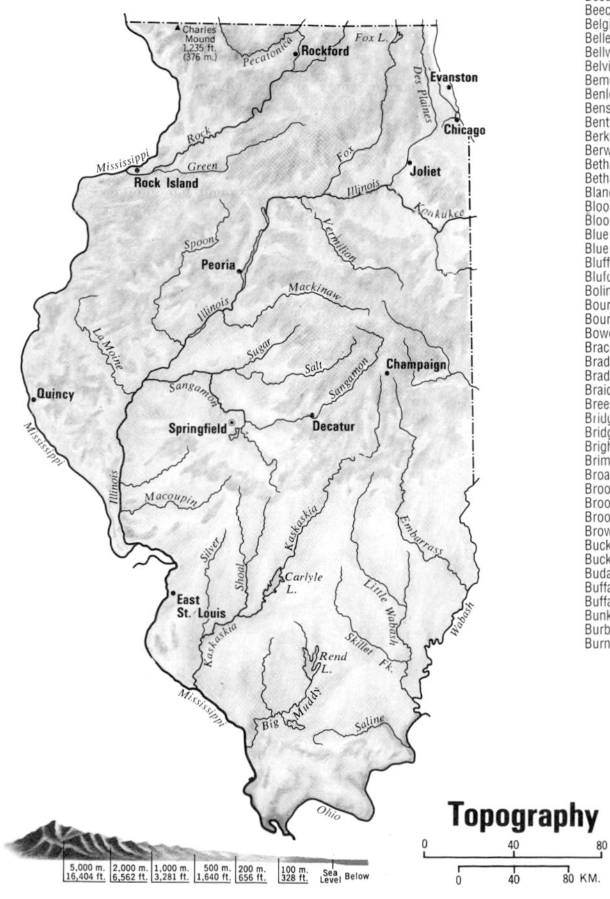

Charles Mound 1,235 ft. (376 m.)
Rockford
Pecatonica
Fox L.
Des Plaines
Evanston
Chicago
Rock
Fox
Joliet
Mississippi
Green
Rock Island
Illinois
Kankakee
Vermilion
Spoon
Peoria
Mackinaw
Illinois
La Moine
Sugar
Salt
Champaign
Sangamon
Quincy
Sangamon
Springfield
Decatur
Mississippi
Illinois
Macoupin
Embarrass
Silver
Shoal
Kaskaskia
Carlyle L.
Little Wabash
Wabash
East St. Louis
Kaskaskia
Skillet Fk.
Rend L.
Mississippi
Big Muddy
Saline
Ohio
5,000 m. 16,404 ft.
2,000 m. 6,562 ft.
1,000 m. 3,281 ft.
500 m. 1,640 ft.
200 m. 656 ft.
100 m. 328 ft.
Sea Level
Below
0 40 80 MI.
0 40 80 KM.

Topography

Agriculture, Industry and Resources

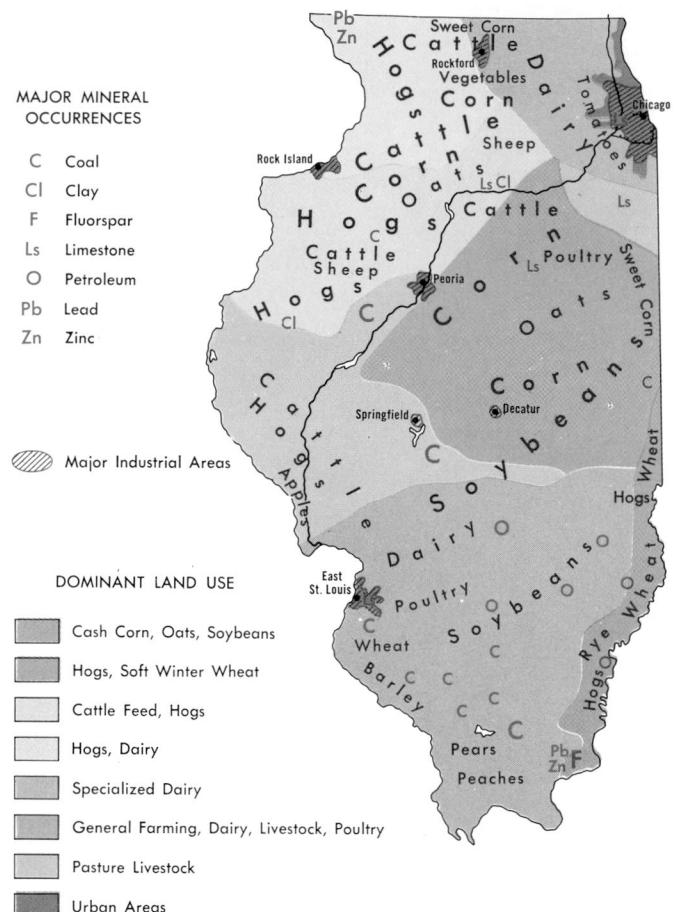

MAJOR MINERAL OCCURRENCES

C   Coal
Cl   Clay
F   Fluorspar
Ls   Limestone
O   Petroleum
Pb   Lead
Zn   Zinc

Major Industrial Areas

DOMINANT LAND USE

Cash Corn, Oats, Soybeans
Hogs, Soft Winter Wheat
Cattle Feed, Hogs
Hogs, Dairy
Specialized Dairy
General Farming, Dairy, Livestock, Poultry
Pasture Livestock
Urban Areas

▲County seat

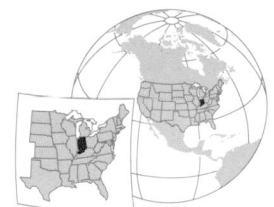

AREA   36,185 sq. mi. (93,719 sq. km.)
POPULATION   5,564,228
CAPITAL   Indianapolis
LARGEST CITY   Indianapolis
HIGHEST POINT   1,257 ft. (383 m.) (Wayne County)
SETTLED IN   1730
ADMITTED TO UNION   December 11, 1816
POPULAR NAME   Hoosier State
STATE FLOWER   Peony
STATE BIRD   Cardinal

COUNTIES

Adams 31,095	H3
Allen 300,836	G2
Bartholomew 63,657	F6
Benton 9,441	C3
Blackford 14,067	G4
Boone 38,147	E4
Brown 14,080	E6
Carroll 18,809	D3
Cass 38,413	E3
Clark 87,777	F8
Clay 24,705	C6
Clinton 30,974	E4
Crawford 9,914	E8
Daviess 27,533	C7
De Kalb 35,324	H2
Dearborn 38,835	H6
Decatur 23,645	G6
Delaware 119,659	G4
Dubois 36,616	D8
Elkhart 156,198	F1
Fayette 26,015	G5
Floyd 64,404	F8
Fountain 17,808	C4
Franklin 19,580	G6
Fulton 18,840	E2
Gibson 31,913	B8
Grant 74,169	F3
Greene 30,410	D6
Hamilton 108,936	E4
Hancock 45,527	F5
Harrison 29,890	E8
Hendricks 75,717	E5
Henry 48,139	G5
Howard 80,827	E4
Huntington 35,427	G3
Jackson 37,730	E7
Jasper 24,960	C2
Jay 21,512	H4
Jefferson 29,797	G7
Jennings 23,661	F7
Johnson 88,109	E6
Knox 39,884	C7
Kosciusko 65,294	F2
LaPorte 108,632	D1
Lagrange 29,477	G1
Lake 475,594	C2
Lawrence 42,836	E7
Madison 130,669	F4
Marion 797,159	E5
Marshall 42,182	E2
Martin 10,369	D7
Miami 36,897	E3
Monroe 108,978	D6
Montgomery 34,436	D4
Morgan 55,920	E6
Newton 13,551	C3
Noble 37,877	G2
Ohio 5,315	H7
Orange 18,409	E7
Owen 17,281	D6
Parke 15,410	C5
Perry 19,107	D8
Pike 12,509	C8
Porter 128,932	C2
Posey 25,968	B8
Pulaski 12,643	D2
Putnam 30,315	D5
Randolph 27,148	G4
Ripley 24,616	G6
Rush 18,129	G5
Saint Joseph 241,617	E1
Scott 20,991	F7
Shelby 40,307	F5
Spencer 19,490	C9
Starke 22,747	D2
Steuben 27,446	G1
Sullivan 18,993	C6
Switzerland 7,738	G7
Tippecanoe 130,598	D4
Tipton 16,119	E4
Union 6,976	H5
Vanderburgh 165,058	B8
Vermillion 16,773	C5
Vigo 106,107	C6
Wabash 35,069	F3
Warren 8,176	C4
Warrick 44,920	C8
Washington 23,717	E7
Wayne 71,951	G5
Wells 25,948	G3
White 23,265	D3
Whitley 27,651	F2

CITIES and TOWNS

Abington 200	H5
Adams 250	F6
Adamsboro 325	E3
Advance 520	D5
Akron 1,001	E2
Alamo 112	C5
Albany 2,357	G4
Albion▲ 1,823	G2
Alexandria 5,709	F4
Altona 156	G2

Ambia 249	C4
Amboy 370	F3
Americus 150	D3
Amity 200	E6
Amo 380	D5
Anderson▲ 59,459	F4
Andersonville 225	G5
Andrews 1,118	F3
Angola▲ 5,824	G1
Anthony 130	G4
Arcadia 1,468	E4
Arcola 300	G2
Ardmore 800	E1
Argos 1,642	E2
Arlington 500	F5
Ashley 767	G1
Athens 145	E2
Atlanta 703	E4
Attica 3,457	C4
Atwood 300	F2
Auburn▲ 9,379	G2
Aurora 3,825	H6
Austin 4,310	F7
Avilla 1,366	G2
Avoca 400	D7
Azalia 194	F6
Bainbridge 682	D5
Bargersville 1,681	E5
Batesville 4,720	G6
Battle Ground 806	D3
Bear Branch 150	G7
Bedford▲ 13,817	E7
Beech Grove 13,383	E5
Bellmore 160	C5
Bennetts Switch 138	E3
Benton 220	F2
Berne 3,559	H3
Bethany 90	E5
Beverly Shores 622	D1
Bicknell 3,357	C7
Bippus 300	F3
Birdseye 472	D8
Black Oak	C1
Blanford 500	B5
Blocher 400	F7
Bloomfield▲ 2,592	D6
Blooming Grove 300	G5
Bloomingdale 341	C5
Bloomington▲ 60,633	D6
Blountsville 155	G4
Blue Ridge 219	F5
Bluffton▲ 9,020	G3
Boggstown 200	F5
Boone Grove 220	C2
Boonville▲ 6,724	C8
Borden	F8
Boston 159	H5
Bourbon 1,672	E2
Bowling Green 200	D6
Bradford 350	E8
Brazil▲ 7,640	C5
Bremen 4,725	E2
Bridgeton 250	C5
Bright 3,945	H6
Brimfield 292	G2
Bringhurst 275	E3
Bristol 1,133	F1
Brook 899	C3
Brooklyn 1,162	E5
Brooksburg 79	G7
Brookston 1,804	D3
Brookville▲ 2,529	G6
Brownsburg 7,628	E5
Brownstown▲ 2,872	F7
Brownsville 250	H5
Bruceville 471	C7
Bryant 273	G3
Buck Creek 225	D4
Buckskin 200	C8
Buffalo 500	D3
Bunker Hill 1,010	E3
Burket 200	F2
Burlington 568	E4
Burnettsville 401	D3
Burney 300	F6
Burns City 140	D7
Burns Harbor 788	C1
Burrows 250	E3
Butler 2,601	H2
Butlerville 300	F6
Byron 200	C5
Cadiz 202	G5
Cambridge City 2,091	G5
Camden 607	D3
Cammack 250	G4
Campbellsburg 606	E7
Cannelburg 97	C7
Cannelton▲ 1,786	D9
Carbon 350	C5
Carefree 26	E8
Carlisle 613	C7
Carmel 25,380	E5
Cartersburg 300	E5
Carthage 887	F5
Cassville 159	E3
Cates 125	C4

Cayuga 1,083	C5
Cedar Grove 246	H6
Cedar Lake 8,885	C2
Celestine 150	D8
Centenary 150	B5
Center 278	E4
Centerpoint 242	C6
Centerton 250	E5
Centerville 2,398	H5
Chalmers 525	D3
Chandler 3,099	C8
Chapel Hill 175	E6
Charlestown 5,889	F8
Charlottesville 300	F5
Chelsea 200	F7
Chester 2,730	H5
Chesterfield 2,701	F4
Chesterton 9,124	D1
Chili 280	F3
Chrisney 511	C8
Churubusco 1,781	G2
Cicero 3,268	E4
Clarks Hill 716	D4
Clarksburg 300	G6
Clarksville 19,833	F8
Clay City 929	C6
Claypool 411	F2
Clayton 610	D5
Clear Creek 200	E6
Clear Lake 272	H1
Clifford 308	F6
Clifton 5,040	C5
Cloverdale 1,681	D5
Cloverland 175	C6
Clymers 150	E3
Coal City 225	D6
Coalmont 450	C6
Coatesville 469	D5

Coesse 150	G2
Colburn 300	D3
Colfax 727	D4
Collegeville 993	C3
Columbia City▲ 5,706	G2
Columbus▲ 31,802	F6
Commiskey 150	F7
Connersville▲ 15,550	G5
Converse 1,144	F3
Correct 131	G7
Cortland 175	F7
Corunna 241	G2
Cory 2,661	C6
Corydon▲ 2,724	E8
Covington▲ 2,747	C4
Cowan 428	G4
Craigville 130	G3
Crandall 147	E8
Crane 216	D7
Crawfordsville▲ 13,584	D4
Cromwell 520	F2
Cross Plains 254	G7
Crothersville 1,687	F7
Crown Point▲ 17,728	C2
Crumstown 175	F1
Culver 1,404	E2
Cumberland 1,624	F5
Cutler 140	D4
Cynthiana 669	B8
Dale 1,553	D8
Daleville 1,681	G4
Dana 612	C5
Danville▲ 4,345	D5
Darlington 740	D4
Darmstadt 1,346	B8
Dayton 996	D4
Decatur▲ 8,644	H3
Decker 281	B7

Deer Creek 250	E3
Deerfield 300	H4
Delaware 135	G6
Delong 156	E2
Delphi▲ 2,531	D3
Demotte 2,482	C2
Denham 140	D2
Denver 504	F3
Depauw 150	E8
Deputy 200	F7
Desoto 385	G4
Dillsboro 1,200	G6
Donaldson 320	E2
Doolittle Mills 200	D8
Dublin 805	G5
Dubois 550	D8
Dugger 936	C6
Dundee 160	F4
Dune Acres 263	C1
Dunkirk 2,739	G4
Dunlap 5,705	F1
Dunreith 205	F5
Dupont 391	G7
Dyer 10,923	C1
Fagletown 306	E4
Earl Park 443	C3
East Chicago 33,892	C1
East Enterprise 250	H7
East Germantown (Pershing) 372	G5
Eaton 1,614	G4
Economy 151	G5
Edgewood 2,057	F4
Edinburgh 4,536	E6
Edwardsport 380	C7
Edwardsville 700	F8
Elberfeld 635	C8
Elizabeth 153	F8

Elizabethtown 495	F6
Elkhart 43,627	F1
Ellettsville 3,275	D6
Elnora 679	C7
Elrod 200	G6
Elston 500	D4
Elwood 9,494	F4
Eminence 200	D5
English▲ 614	E8
Etna 578	F2
Etna Green 522	E2
Eugene 400	B5
Evansville▲ 126,272	C9
Everton 500	G5
Fair Oaks 175	C2
Fairbanks 165	B6
Fairland 1,348	F5
Fairmount 3,130	F4
Fairview 1,446	G7
Fairview Park 1,545	C5
Farmersburg 1,159	C6
Farmland 1,412	G4
Fayetteville 180	D7
Ferdinand 2,318	D8
Fillmore 497	D5
Finly 400	F5
Fishers 7,508	E5
Flat Rock 323	F6
Flora 2,179	E3
Florence 155	H7
Floyds Knobs 500	F8
Fontanet 325	C5
Forest 400	E4
Fort Branch 2,447	B8
Fort Wayne▲ 173,072	G2
Fortville 2,690	F5
Fountain 766	C4
Fountain City 839	H5

Fountaintown 225	F5
Fowler▲ 2,333	C3
Fowlerton 306	F4
Francesville 969	D3
Francisco 560	B8
Frankfort▲ 14,754	E4
Franklin▲ 12,907	E6
Frankton 1,736	F4
Fredericksburg 155	E8
Freelandville 600	C7
Freetown 600	E7
Fremont 1,407	H1
French Lick 2,087	D7
Fulton 371	E3
Galena 751	F8
Galveston 1,609	E3
Garrett 5,349	G2
Gary 116,646	C1
Gas City 6,296	F4
Gaston 979	G4
Geneva 1,280	H3
Gentryville 277	C8
Georgetown 2,092	F8
Gessie 144	C4
Glenwood 285	G5
Glezen 300	C8
Goldsmith 235	E4
Goodland 1,033	C3
Goshen▲ 23,797	F1
Gosport 764	D6
Grabill 751	H2
Grandview 761	C9
Granger 20,241	E1
Grantsburg 189	D8
Gravelton 150	F2
Greencastle▲ 8,984	D5
Greendale 3,881	H6
Greenfield▲ 11,657	F5

(continued on following page)

Agriculture, Industry and Resources

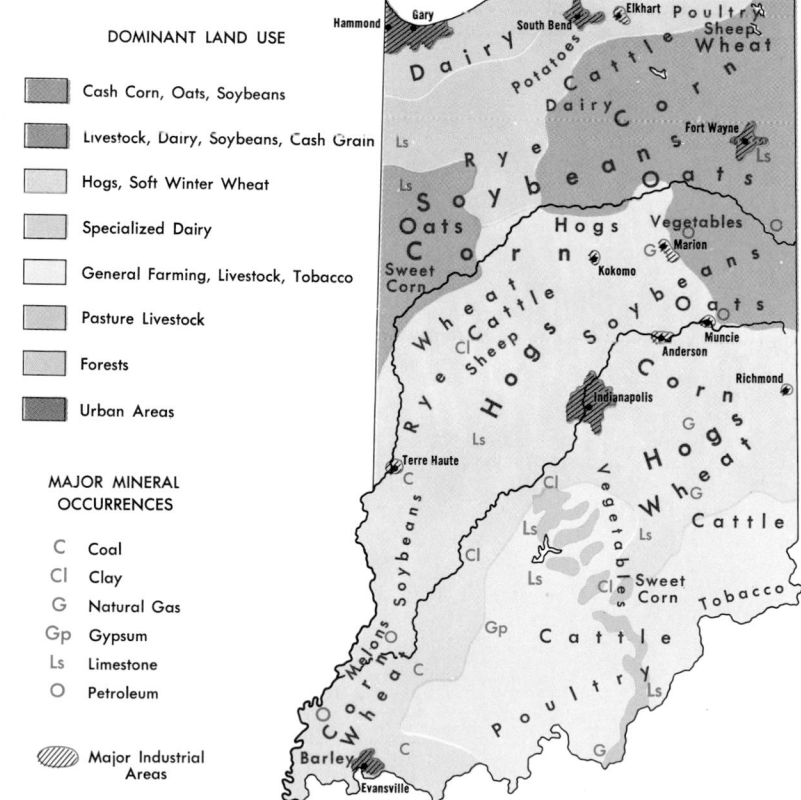

DOMINANT LAND USE

- Cash Corn, Oats, Soybeans
- Livestock, Dairy, Soybeans, Cash Grain
- Hogs, Soft Winter Wheat
- Specialized Dairy
- General Farming, Livestock, Tobacco
- Pasture Livestock
- Forests
- Urban Areas

MAJOR MINERAL OCCURRENCES

- C   Coal
- Cl   Clay
- G   Natural Gas
- Gp   Gypsum
- Ls   Limestone
- O   Petroleum

Major Industrial Areas

Topography

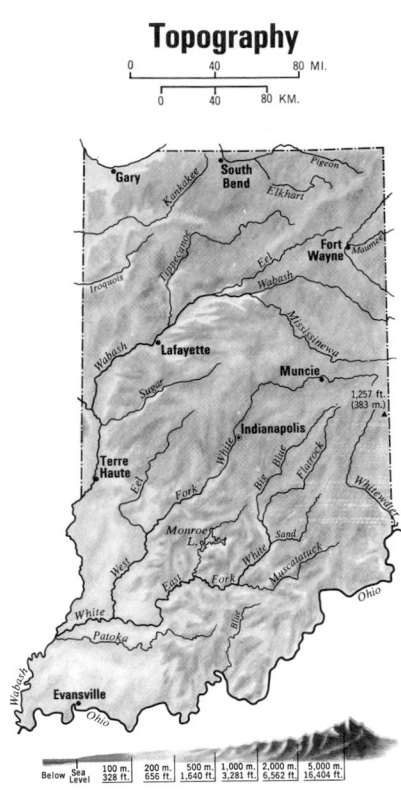

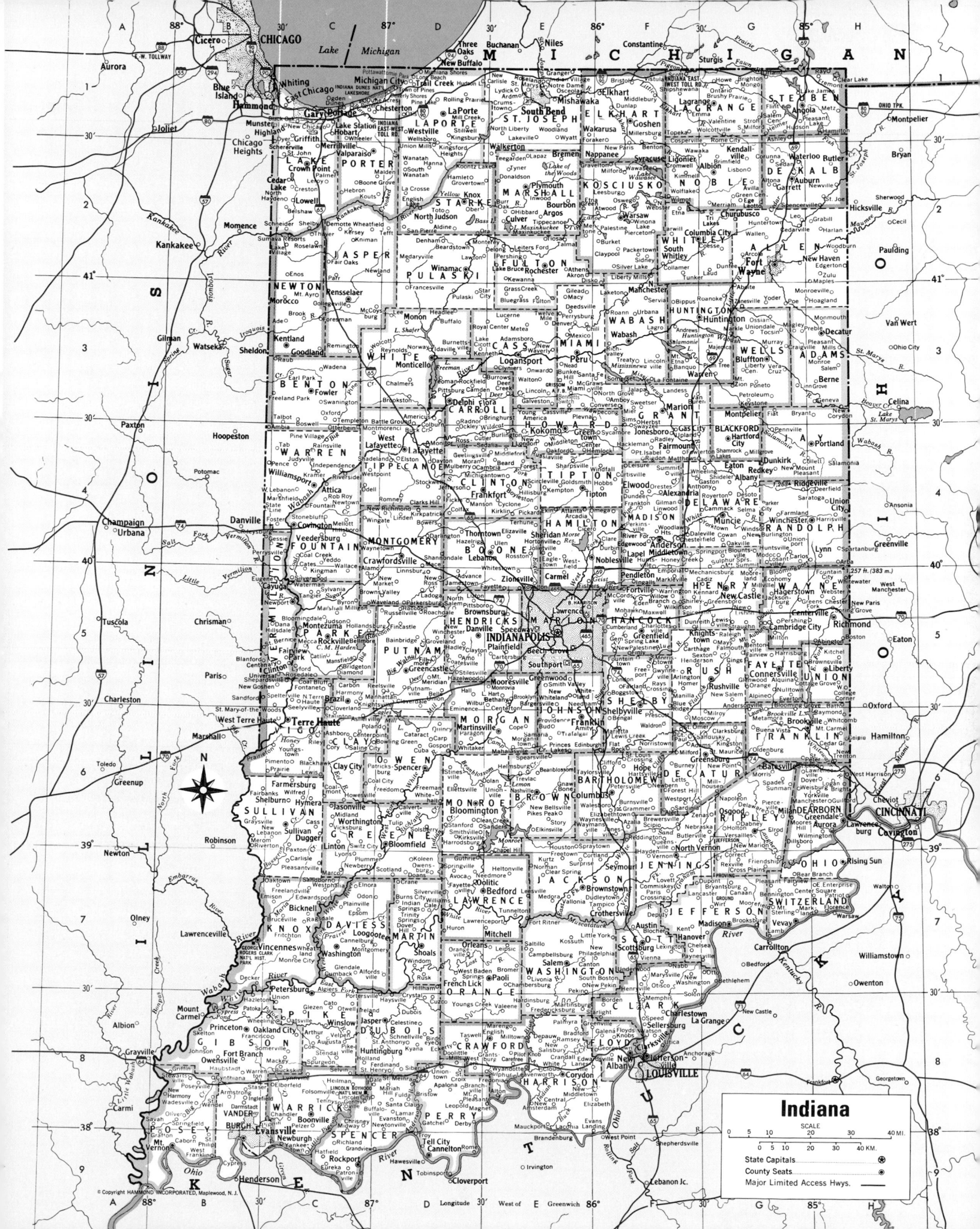

COUNTIES

County	Pop.	Ref.
Adair	8,409	E6
Adams	4,866	D6
Allamakee	13,855	L2
Appanoose	13,743	H7
Audubon	7,334	C5
Benton	22,429	J4
Black Hawk	123,798	F5
Boone	25,186	E4
Bremer	22,813	K4
Buchanan	20,844	K4
Buena Vista	19,965	H3
Butler	15,731	D4
Calhoun	11,508	D4
Carroll	21,423	D6
Cass	15,128	L5
Cedar	17,381	G2
Cerro Gordo	46,733	B3
Cherokee	14,098	J2
Chickasaw	13,295	F6
Clarke	8,287	C2
Clay	17,585	L3
Clayton	19,054	L3
Clinton	51,040	M5
Crawford	16,775	C4
Dallas	29,755	E5
Davis	8,312	J7
Decatur	8,338	F7
Delaware	18,035	L4
Des Moines	42,614	L7
Dickinson	14,909	M4
Dubuque	86,403	M4
Emmet	11,569	D2
Fayette	21,843	K3
Floyd	17,058	H2
Franklin	11,364	G3
Fremont	8,226	B7
Greene	10,045	E5
Grundy	12,029	H4
Guthrie	10,935	D5
Hamilton	16,071	F4
Hardin	19,094	G4
Harrison	14,730	B5
Henry	19,226	K6
Humboldt	10,756	E3
Ida	8,365	C4
Iowa	14,630	J5
Iowa	2,913,808	J5
Jackson	19,950	M4
Jasper	34,795	G5
Jefferson	16,310	K6
Johnson	96,119	K5
Jones	19,444	L4
Keokuk	11,624	J6
Kossuth	18,591	E2
Lee	38,687	L7
Linn	168,767	K4
Louisa	11,592	L6
Lucas	9,070	G6
Lyon	11,952	A2
Madison	12,483	E6
Marion	30,001	G5
Marshall	38,276	G4
Mills	13,202	B6
Mitchell	10,928	H2
Monona	10,381	B4
Monroe	8,114	H7
Montgomery	12,076	C6
Muscatine	39,907	L5
O'Brien	16,972	B2
Osceola	7,267	B2
Page	16,870	C7
Palo Alto	10,669	D2
Plymouth	23,388	A3
Pocahontas	9,525	D3
Polk	327,140	F5
Pottawattamie	82,628	B6
Poweshiek	19,033	H4
Ringgold	5,420	E7
Sac	12,324	C4
Scott	150,979	M5
Shelby	13,230	C5
Sioux	29,903	A2
Story	74,252	F4
Tama	17,419	H4
Taylor	7,114	D7
Union	12,750	E7
Van Buren	7,676	K7
Wapello	35,687	J6
Warren	36,033	F6
Washington	19,612	K6
Wayne	7,067	G7
Webster	40,342	E4
Winnebago	12,122	F2
Winneshiek	20,847	K2
Woodbury	98,276	B4
Worth	7,991	G2
Wright	14,269	F3

CITIES and TOWNS

Place	Pop.	Ref.
Ackley	1,696	G3
Adair	894	D6
Adel▲	3,304	E5
Afton	953	E6
Agency	616	J7
Ainsworth	506	K6
Akron	1,450	A3
Albert City	779	C3
Albia▲	3,870	H6
Albion	585	G4
Alden	855	G3
Alexander	170	G3
Algona▲	6,015	E2
Alleman	340	F5
Allerton	599	G7
Allison▲	1,000	H3
Alta	1,820	C3
Alta Vista	246	J2
Alton	1,063	A3
Altoona	7,191	G5
Alvord	204	A2
Amana	300	K5
Ames	47,198	F4
Anamosa▲	5,100	L4
Andrew	319	M4
Ankeny	18,482	F5
Anthon	638	B4
Aplington	1,034	H3
Arcadia	485	C4
Arion	148	B5
Arlington	465	K3
Armstrong	1,025	D2
Arnolds Park	953	C2
Arthur	272	M4
Asbury	2,013	M4
Ashton	462	B2
Atalissa	357	L5
Atkins	637	K4
Atlantic	7,432	D6
Auburn	283	D4
Audubon▲	2,524	D5
Aurelia	1,034	C3
Aurora	196	K3
Avoca	1,497	C6
Ayrshire	195	D2
Badger	569	E3
Bagley	303	E5
Baldwin	137	M4
Bancroft	857	E2
Barnes City	221	H6
Barnum	174	E3
Batavia	520	J7
Battle Creek	818	B4
Baxter	938	G5
Bayard	511	D5
Beacon	509	H6
Beaman	183	H4
Bedford▲	1,528	D7
Belle Plaine	2,834	J4
Bellevue	2,239	M4
Belmond	2,500	G3
Bennett	395	L5

AREA 56,275 sq. mi. (145,752 sq. km.)
POPULATION 2,787,424
CAPITAL Des Moines
LARGEST CITY Des Moines
HIGHEST POINT (Osceola Co.) 1670 ft. (509 m.)
SETTLED IN 1788
ADMITTED TO UNION December 28, 1846
POPULAR NAME Hawkeye State
STATE FLOWER Wild Rose
STATE BIRD Eastern Goldfinch

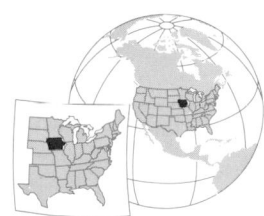

Iowa

SCALE
0 5 10 20 30 40 MI.
0 5 10 20 30 40 KM.

State Capitals .... ⊛
County Seats .... ○
Major Limited Access Hwys. ──

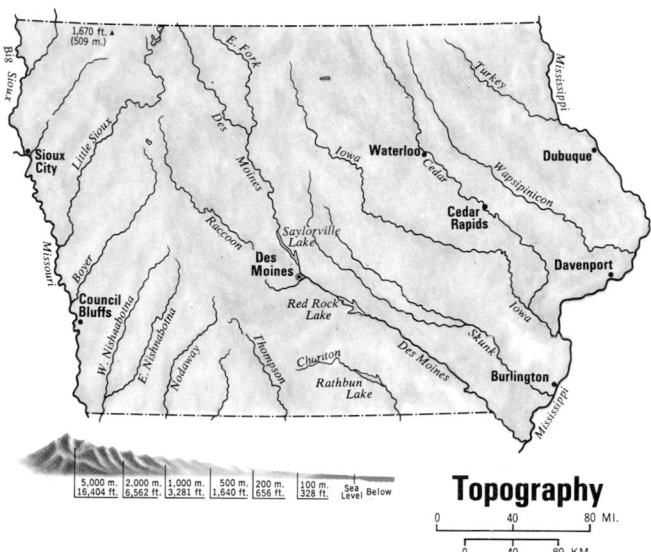

Topography

0 40 80 MI.
0 40 80 KM.

5,000 m. 16,404 ft. | 2,000 m. 6,562 ft. | 1,000 m. 3,281 ft. | 500 m. 1,640 ft. | 200 m. 656 ft. | 100 m. 328 ft. | Sea Level | Below

(continued on following page)

Agriculture, Industry and Resources

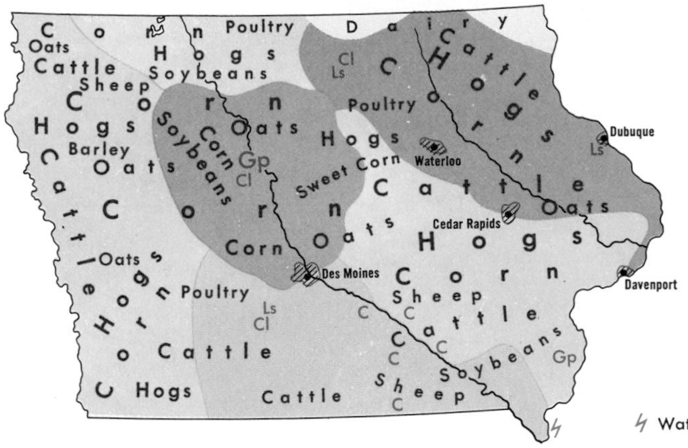

Corn
Oats
Cattle
Sheep
Hogs
Soybeans
Poultry
Dairy
Barley
Sweet Corn
Cl
Ls
Gp
C
Dubuque
Waterloo
Cedar Rapids
Des Moines
Davenport

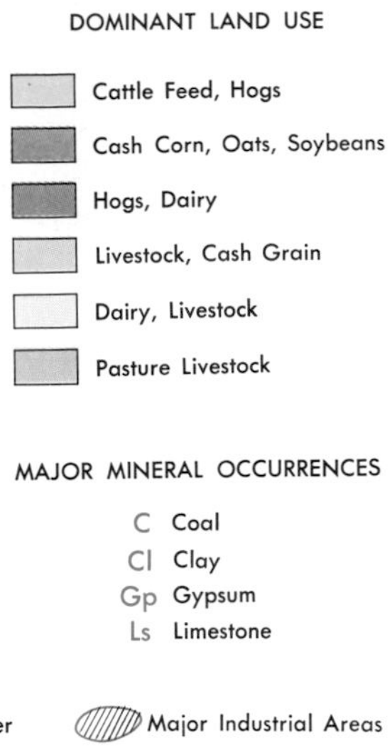

DOMINANT LAND USE
Cattle Feed, Hogs
Cash Corn, Oats, Soybeans
Hogs, Dairy
Livestock, Cash Grain
Dairy, Livestock
Pasture Livestock
MAJOR MINERAL OCCURRENCES
C Coal
Cl Clay
Gp Gypsum
Ls Limestone
Water Power
Major Industrial Areas

Guthrie Center▲ 1,614 ....D5
Guttenberg 2,257 ....L3
Halbur 215 ....D4
Hamburg 1,248 ....B7
Hampton▲ 4,133 ....G3
Hancock 201 ....C6
Hanlontown 193 ....G2
Harcourt 306 ....E4
Harlan▲ 5,148 ....C5
Harper 147 ....J6
Harpers Ferry 284 ....L2
Harris 170 ....C2
Hartford 768 ....G6
Hartley 1,632 ....C2
Harvey 235 ....H6
Hastings 187 ....C6
Havelock 217 ....D3
Haverhill 144 ....H5
Hawarden 2,439 ....A2
Hawkeye 460 ....J3
Hazleton 733 ....K3
Hedrick 810 ....J6
Henderson 206 ....B6
Hiawatha 4,986 ....K4
Hills 662 ....K5
Hillsboro 151 ....K7
Hinton 697 ....A3
Holland 215 ....H4
Holstein 1,449 ....B4
Holy Cross 304 ....L3
Hopkinton 695 ....L4
Hornick 222 ....A4
Hospers 643 ....B2
Hubbard 814 ....G4
Hudson 2,037 ....H4
Hull 1,724 ....A2
Humboldt 4,438 ....E3
Humeston 553 ....G7
Huxley 2,047 ....F5
Ida Grove▲ 2,357 ....B4
Independence▲ 5,972 ....K4
Indianola▲ 11,340 ....F6
Inwood 824 ....A2
Ionia 304 ....J2
Iowa City▲ 59,738 ....L5
Iowa Falls 5,424 ....G3
Ireton 597 ....A3
Irwin 394 ....C5
Jamaica 232 ....E5
Janesville 822 ....J3
Jefferson▲ 4,292 ....E4
Jesup 2,121 ....J4
Jewell 1,106 ....F4
Johnston 4,702 ....F5
Joice 245 ....G2
Kalo 1,942 ....E4
Kalona 1,862 ....K6
Kamrar 203 ....F4
Kanawha 763 ....F3
Kellerton 314 ....E7
Kelley 246 ....F5
Kellogg 626 ....H5
Kensett 298 ....G2
Keokuk▲ 12,451 ....L8
Keosauqua▲ 1,020 ....J7
Keota 1,000 ....K6
Keswick 284 ....J6
Keystone 568 ....J5
Kimballton 289 ....D5
Kingsley 1,129 ....A3
Kirkville 177 ....H6
Kiron 301 ....C4
Klemme 587 ....F3
Knoxville▲ 8,232 ....G6
La Motte 219 ....M4
La Porte City 2,128 ....J4
Lacona 357 ....G6
Ladora 308 ....J5
Lake City 1,841 ....D4
Lake Mills 2,143 ....F2
Lake Park 996 ....C2
Lake View 1,303 ....C4
Lakeside 522 ....C3
Lakota 281 ....E2
Lambs Grove 212 ....G5
Lamoni 2,319 ....E7
Lamont 471 ....K3
Lanesboro 182 ....D4
Lansing 1,007 ....L2
Larchwood 739 ....A2
Larrabee 175 ....B3
Latimer 430 ....G3
Laurel 271 ....H5
Laurens 1,550 ....D3
Lawler 517 ....J2
Lawton 482 ....A4
Le Claire 2,734 ....N5
Le Grand 854 ....H5
Le Mars▲ 8,454 ....A3
Ledyard 164 ....E2
Lehigh 536 ....E4
Leighton 142 ....H6
Leland 311 ....F2
Lenox 1,303 ....D7
Leon▲ 2,047 ....F7
Lester 257 ....A2
Letts 390 ....L6
Lewis 433 ....C6
Libertyville 264 ....K7
Lidderdale 202 ....D4
Lime Springs 438 ....J2
Lincoln 173 ....H4
Linden 201 ....E5
Lineville 289 ....G7
Linn Grove 194 ....C3
Lisbon 1,452 ....L5
Liscomb 258 ....H4
Little Rock 493 ....B2
Little Sioux 205 ....B5
Livermore 436 ....E3
Lockridge 270 ....K7
Logan▲ 1,401 ....B5
Lohrville 453 ....D4
Lone Rock 185 ....E2
Lone Tree 979 ....L6
Long Grove 605 ....M5
Lorimor 377 ....E6
Lost Nation 467 ....M5
Lovilia 551 ....H6
Low Moor 280 ....N5
Lowden 726 ....L5
Lu Verne 328 ....E3
Luana 190 ....K2
Lucas 224 ....G6
Luther 154 ....F5
Luxemburg 257 ....L3
Lynnville 393 ....H5
Lytton 320 ....D4
Macedonia 262 ....C6
Madrid 2,395 ....F5
Magnolia 204 ....B5
Malcom 447 ....H5
Mallard 360 ....D3
Malvern 1,210 ....B7
Manchester▲ 5,137 ....L3
Manilla 898 ....C5
Manly 1,349 ....G2
Manning 1,484 ....C5
Manson 1,844 ....D3
Mapleton 1,294 ....B4
Maquoketa▲ 6,111 ....M4
Marathon 320 ....C3
Marble Rock 361 ....H3
Marcus 1,171 ....B3
Marengo▲ 2,270 ....J5
Marion 20,403 ....K4
Marne 149 ....C6
Marquette 479 ....L2
Marshalltown▲ 25,178 ....G4
Martelle 290 ....L4
Martensdale 491 ....F6
Martinsburg 157 ....J6
Mason City▲ 29,040 ....G2
Masonville 129 ....K4
Massena 372 ....D6
Maurice 243 ....A3
Maxwell 788 ....G5
Maynard 513 ....K3
Maysville 170 ....M5
McCallsburg 292 ....G4
McCausland 308 ....M5
McClelland 139 ....B6
McGregor 797 ....L2
McIntire 147 ....H2
Mechanicsville 1,012 ....L5
Mediapolis 1,637 ....L6
Melbourne 669 ....G5
Melcher 1,302 ....G6
Melrose 150 ....G7
Melvin 250 ....B2
Menlo 356 ....E5
Meriden 193 ....B3
Merrill 729 ....A3
Meservey 292 ....G3
Middle 386 ....K5
Middletown 487 ....L7
Miles 409 ....N4
Milford 2,170 ....C2
Miller 188 ....F2
Millersburg 184 ....J5
Milo 864 ....G6
Milton 506 ....J7
Minburn 346 ....E5
Minden 498 ....C6
Mingo 252 ....G5
Missouri Valley 2,888 ....B5
Mitchell 170 ....H2
Mitchellville 1,670 ....G5
Modale 289 ....B5
Mondamin 403 ....B5
Monmouth 169 ....M4
Monona 1,520 ....L2
Monroe 1,739 ....G5
Montezuma▲ 1,651 ....H5
Monticello 3,522 ....L4
Montour 312 ....H5
Montrose 957 ....L7
Moorhead 259 ....B5
Moorland 209 ....E4
Moravia 679 ....H7
Morning Sun 841 ....L6
Moulton 613 ....H7
Mount Auburn 134 ....J4
Mount Ayr▲ 1,796 ....E7
Mount Pleasant▲ 8,027 ....L7
Mount Union 140 ....L6
Mount Vernon 3,657 ....K5
Moville 1,306 ....A4
Murray 731 ....F6
Muscatine▲ 22,881 ....L6
Mystic 545 ....H7
Nashua 1,476 ....J3
Neola 894 ....B6
Nevada▲ 6,009 ....G5
New Albin 534 ....L2
New Hampton▲ 3,660 ....J2
New Hartford 683 ....H3
New Liberty 139 ....M5
New London 1,922 ....L7
New Market 454 ....D7
New Providence 240 ....G4
New Sharon 1,136 ....H6
New Vienna 376 ....L3
New Virginia 433 ....F6
Newell 1,089 ....D3
Newhall 854 ....K5
Newton▲ 14,789 ....H5
Nichols 366 ....L6
Nodaway 153 ....D7
Nora Springs 1,505 ....H2
North Buena Vista 145 ....L3
North English 944 ....J5
North Liberty 2,926 ....K5
Northwood▲ 1,940 ....G2
Norwalk 5,726 ....F6
Norway 583 ....K5
Numa 151 ....G7
Oakland 1,496 ....C6
Oakland Acres 152 ....H5
Oakville 442 ....L6
Ocheyedan 539 ....B2
Odebolt 1,158 ....C4
Oelwein 6,493 ....K3
Ogden 1,909 ....E4
Okoboji 775 ....C2
Olds 205 ....K6
Olin 663 ....L5
Ollie 207 ....J6
Onawa▲ 2,936 ....A4
Onslow 216 ....M4
Oran 4,940 ....J3
Orange City▲ 4,588 ....A2
Orient 376 ....E6
Orleans 560 ....C2
Osage▲ 3,439 ....H2
Osceola▲ 4,164 ....F6
Oskaloosa▲ 10,632 ....H6
Ossian 810 ....K2
Otho 529 ....E4
Ottumwa▲ 24,488 ....J6
Oxford 663 ....K5
Oxford Junction 581 ....M4
Pacific Junction 548 ....B6
Packwood 208 ....J6
Palmer 230 ....D3
Palo 514 ....K4
Panama 201 ....B5
Panora 1,100 ....E5
Parkersburg 1,804 ....H3
Parnell 209 ....J5
Paton 255 ....E4
Patterson 128 ....F6
Paullina 1,134 ....B3
Pella 9,270 ....H6
Peosta 128 ....M4
Perry 6,652 ....E5
Persia 312 ....B5
Peterson 390 ....C3
Pierson 341 ....B3
Pilot Mound 199 ....F4
Pisgah 268 ....B5
Plainfield 455 ....J3
Pleasant Hill 3,671 ....G5
Pleasant Plain 128 ....K6
Pleasantville 1,536 ....G6
Plymouth 453 ....G2
Pocahontas▲ 2,085 ....D3
Polk City 1,908 ....F5
Pomeroy 762 ....D3
Portsmouth 209 ....C5
Postville 1,472 ....K2
Prairie City 1,360 ....G5
Prairieburg 213 ....L4
Prescott 287 ....D6
Preston 1,025 ....N4
Primghar▲ 950 ....B2
Princeton 806 ....N5
Protivin 305 ....J2
Pulaski 221 ....J7
Quasqueton 579 ....K4
Quimby 334 ....B3
Radcliffe 574 ....G4
Rake 238 ....F2
Randall 161 ....F4
Randolph 243 ....B7
Raymond 619 ....J4
Readlyn 773 ....J3
Reasnor 191 ....G5
Red Oak▲ 6,264 ....C6
Redfield 883 ....E5
Reinbeck 1,605 ....H4
Rembrandt 229 ....C3
Remsen 1,513 ....B3
Renwick 287 ....E3
Rhodes 272 ....G5
Riceville 827 ....H2
Richland 522 ....K6
Rickardsville 171 ....M3
Ridgeway 295 ....K2
Ringsted 481 ....D2
Rippey 275 ....E5
Riverdale 433 ....N5
Riverside 824 ....K6
Riverton 333 ....B7
Robins 875 ....K4
Rock Falls 130 ....G2
Rock Rapids▲ 2,601 ....A2
Rock Valley 2,540 ....A2
Rockford 863 ....H2
Rockwell 1,008 ....G3
Rockwell City▲ 1,981 ....D4
Roland 1,035 ....F4
Rolfe 721 ....D3
Rose Hill 171 ....J6
Rowan 189 ....F3
Rowley 272 ....K4
Royal 466 ....C2
Rudd 429 ....H2
Runnells 306 ....G5
Russell 531 ....G7
Ruthven 707 ....D2
Rutland 149 ....E3
Ryan 382 ....K4
Sabula 710 ....N4
Sac City▲ 2,492 ....C4
Sageville 288 ....M3
Saint Ansgar 1,063 ....H2
Saint Anthony 112 ....G4
Saint Charles 537 ....F6
Saint Donatus 145 ....M4
Saint Lucas 174 ....K2
Saint Olaf 111 ....L3
Saint Paul 120 ....L7
Salem 453 ....K7
Salix 367 ....A4
Sanborn 1,345 ....B2
Schaller 768 ....C4
Schleswig 851 ....B4
Scranton 583 ....D4
Searsboro 164 ....H5
Sergeant Bluff 2,772 ....A4
Seymour 869 ....G7
Shambaugh 190 ....D7
Sheffield 1,174 ....G3
Shelby 637 ....C5
Sheldahl 315 ....F5
Sheldon 4,937 ....B2
Shell Rock 1,385 ....H3
Shellsburg 765 ....K4
Shenandoah 5,572 ....C7
Sherrill 148 ....M3
Shueyville 223 ....K5
Sibley▲ 2,815 ....B2
Sidney▲ 1,253 ....B7
Sigourney▲ 2,111 ....J6
Silver City 252 ....B6
Sioux Center 5,074 ....A2
Sioux City▲ 80,505 ....A3
Sioux Rapids 761 ....C3
Slater 1,268 ....F5
Sloan 938 ....A4
Smithland 235 ....B4
Soldier 205 ....B5
Solon 1,050 ....L5
Somers 161 ....E4
South English 224 ....J6
Spencer▲ 11,066 ....C2
Spillville 387 ....J2
Spirit Lake▲ 3,871 ....C2
Springville 1,068 ....L4
Stacyville 481 ....H2
Stanhope 447 ....F4
Stanton 692 ....C7
Stanwood 646 ....L5
State Center 1,248 ....G5
Steamboat Rock 335 ....G4
Stockport 260 ....K7
Stockton 187 ....M5
Storm Lake▲ 8,769 ....C3
Story City 2,959 ....F4
Stout 192 ....H3
Stratford 715 ....F4
Strawberry Point 1,357 ....K3
Stuart 1,522 ....E6
Sully 841 ....H5
Sumner 2,078 ....J3
Superior 128 ....D2
Sutherland 714 ....B3
Swaledale 190 ....G3
Swea City 634 ....E2
Swisher 645 ....K5
Tabor 957 ....B7
Tama 2,697 ....H5
Templeton 321 ....D5
Terril 383 ....C2
Thompson 498 ....F2
Thor 205 ....E3
Thornton 431 ....G3
Thurman 239 ....B7
Tiffin 460 ....K5
Tingley 179 ....E7
Tipton▲ 2,998 ....L5
Titonka 612 ....E2
Toledo▲ 2,380 ....H4
Traer 1,552 ....J4
Treynor 897 ....B6
Tripoli 1,188 ....J3
Truesdale 132 ....C3
Truro 391 ....F6
Underwood 515 ....B6
Union 448 ....G4
Unionville 133 ....H7
University Heights 1,042 ....K5
University Park 604 ....H6
Urbana 595 ....K4
Urbandale 23,500 ....F5
Ute 395 ....B4
Vail 388 ....C4
Van Horne 695 ....J4
Van Meter 751 ....E5
Van Wert 249 ....F7
Ventura 590 ....F2
Victor 966 ....J5
Villisca 1,332 ....C7
Vincent 185 ....E3
Vinton▲ 5,103 ....J4
Volga 306 ....L3
Wadena 236 ....K3
Wahpeton 484 ....C2
Walcott 1,356 ....M5
Walford 303 ....K5
Walker 673 ....K4
Wall Lake 875 ....C4
Wallingford 196 ....D2
Walnut 857 ....C6
Wapello▲ 2,013 ....L6
Washington▲ 7,074 ....K6
Washta 284 ....B3
Waterloo▲ 66,467 ....J4
Waterville 140 ....L2
Waucoma 277 ....J2
Waukee 2,512 ....F5
Waukon▲ 4,019 ....L2
Waverly▲ 8,539 ....J3
Wayland 838 ....K6
Webb 167 ....D3
Webster City▲ 7,894 ....F4
Weldon 151 ....F7
Wellman 1,085 ....K6
Wellsburg 682 ....H4
Welton 177 ....M5
Wesley 444 ....E2
West 862 ....J5
West Bend 941 ....D3
West Branch 1,908 ....L5
West Burlington 3,083 ....L7
West Chester 178 ....K6
West Des Moines 31,702 ....F5
West Liberty 2,935 ....L5
West Okoboji 263 ....C2
West Point 1,079 ....K7
West Union▲ 2,490 ....K3
Westfield 160 ....A3
Westgate 207 ....K3
Westphalia 144 ....C5
Westside 348 ....C4
What Cheer 762 ....J6
Wheatland 723 ....M5
Whiting 683 ....A4
Whittemore 535 ....E2
Whitten 137 ....H4
Williams 368 ....F3
Williamsburg 2,174 ....J5
Williamson 166 ....G6
Wilton 2,577 ....M5
Windsor Heights 5,190 ....F5
Winfield 1,051 ....L6
Winterset▲ 4,196 ....E6
Winthrop 742 ....K4
Wiota 160 ....D6
Woden 259 ....F2
Woodbine 1,500 ....B5
Woodburn 240 ....F7
Woodward 1,197 ....E5
Woolstock 212 ....F3
Worthington 439 ....L4
Wyoming 659 ....L4
Yale 220 ....E5
Zearing 614 ....G4

OTHER FEATURES

Big Sioux (riv.) A3
Boyer (riv.) B5
Cedar (riv.) K4
Chariton (riv.) G7
Clear (lake) G2
Des Moines (riv.) J7
Eagle (lake) F2
East Nishnabotna (riv.) C6
Effigy Mounds Nat'l Mon. L2
Five Island (lake) D2
Floyd (riv.) A3
Herbert Hoover Nat'l Hist. Site L5
Iowa (riv.) H4
Little Sioux (riv.) B3
Lost Island (lake) D2
Mississippi (riv.) L7
Missouri (riv.) A5
Nodaway (riv.) D7
Palo Alto (lake) D2
Platte (riv.) D8
Raccoon (riv.) D4
Rathbun (lake) G7
Red Rock (lake) G6
Rock (riv.) A2
Sac and Fox Ind. Res. H5
Skunk (riv.) K6
Spirit (lake) C2
Storm (lake) C3
Summit (lake) E6
Thompson (riv.) E7
Trumbull (lake) C2
Turkey (riv.) K2
Upper Iowa (riv.) K2
Wapsipinicon (riv.) J3
West Nishnabotna (riv.) C6

▲County seat

KANSAS

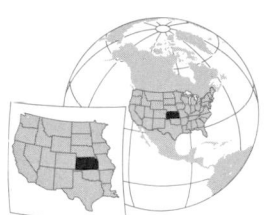

AREA 82,277 sq. mi. (213,097 sq. km.)
POPULATION 2,485,600
CAPITAL Topeka
LARGEST CITY Wichita
HIGHEST POINT Mt. Sunflower 4,039 ft. (1231 m.)
SETTLED IN 1831
ADMITTED TO UNION January 29, 1861
POPULAR NAME Sunflower State
STATE FLOWER Sunflower
STATE BIRD Western Meadowlark

Agriculture, Industry and Resources

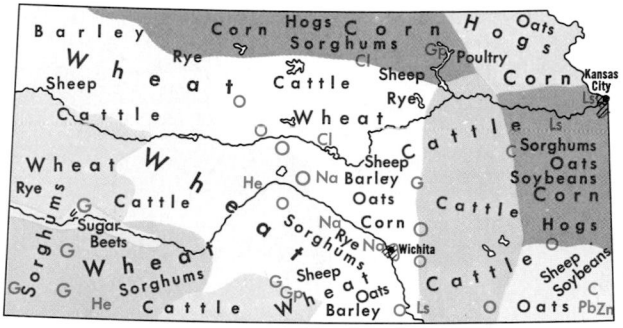

DOMINANT LAND USE

- Specialized Wheat
- Wheat, General Farming
- Wheat, Range Livestock
- Wheat, Grain Sorghums, Range Livestock
- Cattle Feed, Hogs
- Livestock, Cash Grain
- Livestock, Cash Grain, Dairy
- General Farming, Livestock, Cash Grain
- General Farming, Livestock, Special Crops
- Range Livestock

MAJOR MINERAL OCCURRENCES

C	Coal	Ls	Limestone
Cl	Clay	Na	Salt
G	Natural Gas	O	Petroleum
Gp	Gypsum	Pb	Lead
He	Helium	Zn	Zinc

▨ Major Industrial Areas

(continued on following page)

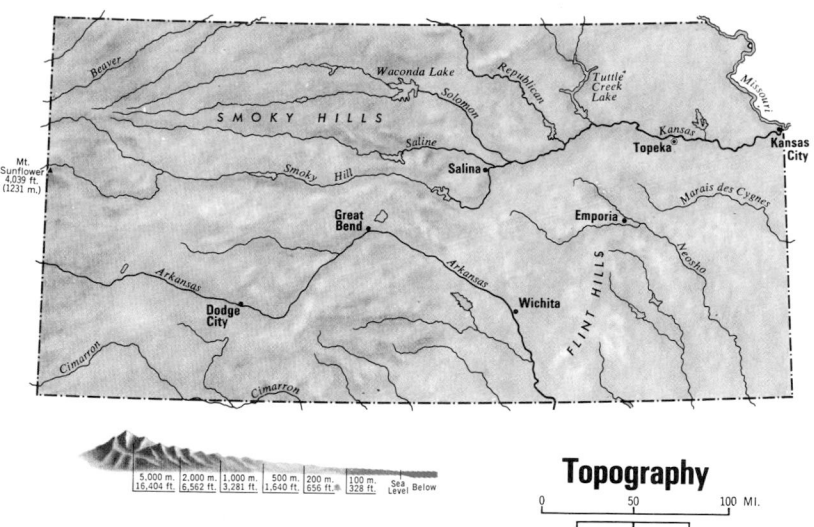

5,000 m. 2,000 m. 1,000 m. 500 m. 200 m. 100 m. Sea
16,404 ft. 6,562 ft. 3,281 ft. 1,640 ft. 656 ft. 328 ft. Level Below

Topography

0   50   100 MI.

0   50   100 KM.

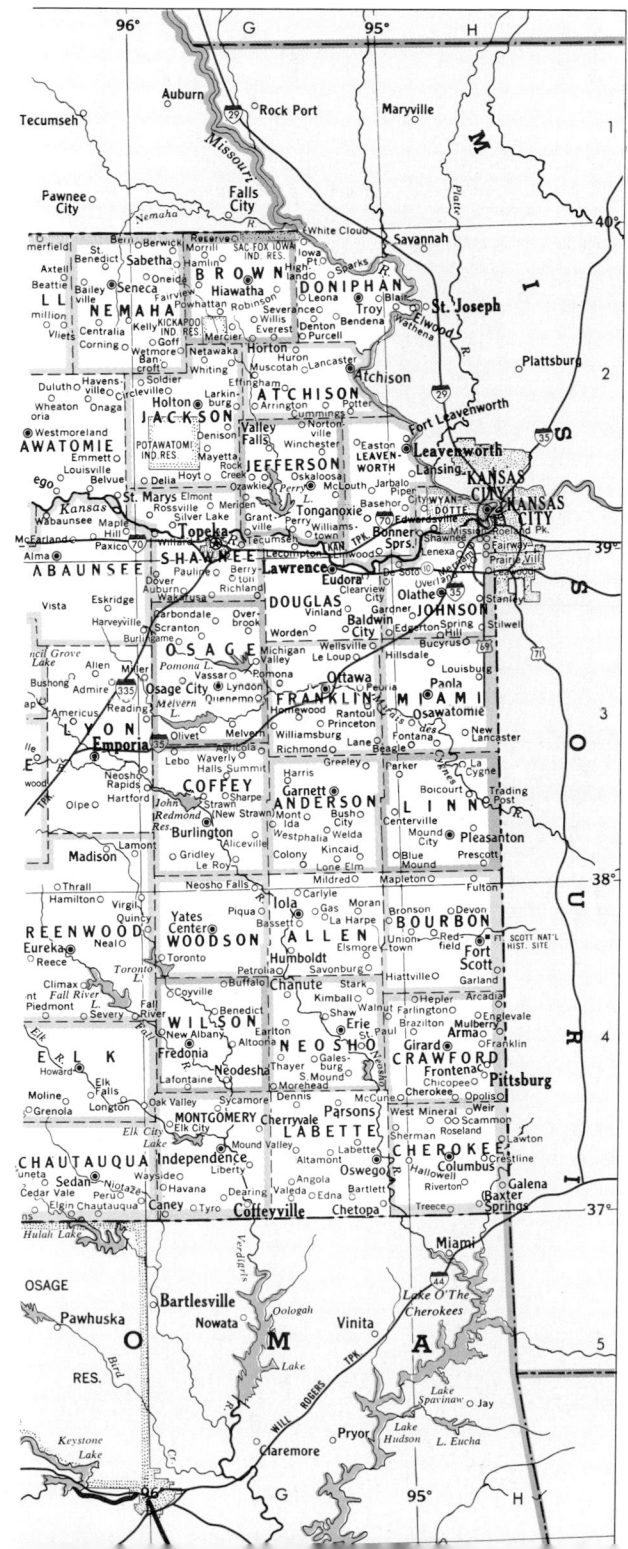

KENTUCKY

COUNTIES

Adair 15,360 ... L6
Allen 14,628 ... J7
Anderson 14,571 ... M5
Ballard 7,902 ... C6
Barren 34,001 ... K7
Bath 9,692 ... O4
Bell 31,506 ... O7
Boone 57,589 ... M3
Bourbon 19,236 ... N4
Boyd 51,150 ... R4
Boyle 25,641 ... M5
Bracken 7,766 ... N3
Breathitt 15,703 ... P5
Breckinridge 16,312 ... J5
Bullitt 47,567 ... K5
Butler 11,245 ... H6
Caldwell 13,232 ... F6
Calloway 30,735 ... E7
Campbell 83,866 ... N3
Carlisle 5,238 ... C7
Carroll 9,292 ... L3
Carter 24,340 ... P4
Casey 14,211 ... M6
Christian 68,941 ... F7
Clark 29,496 ... N4
Clay 21,746 ... O6
Clinton 9,135 ... L7
Crittenden 9,196 ... E6
Cumberland 6,784 ... L7
Daviess 87,189 ... G5
Edmonson 10,357 ... J6
Elliott 6,455 ... P4
Estill 14,614 ... O5
Fayette 225,366 ... M5
Fleming 12,292 ... O4
Floyd 43,586 ... R5
Franklin 43,781 ... M4
Fulton 8,271 ... C7
Gallatin 5,393 ... M3
Garrard 11,579 ... M5
Grant 15,737 ... M3
Graves 33,550 ... D7
Grayson 21,050 ... J5
Green 10,371 ... K6
Greenup 36,742 ... R3
Hancock 7,864 ... H5
Hardin 89,240 ... K5
Harlan 36,574 ... P7
Harrison 16,248 ... N4
Hart 14,890 ... K6
Henderson 43,044 ... F5
Henry 12,823 ... L4
Hickman 5,566 ... C7
Jackson 11,955 ... N6
Jefferson 664,937 ... K4
Jessamine 30,508 ... M5
Johnson 23,248 ... R5
Kenton 142,031 ... M3
Knott 17,906 ... R6
Knox 29,676 ... O7
Larue 11,679 ... K5
Laurel 43,438 ... N6
Lawrence 13,998 ... R4
Lee 7,422 ... O5
Leslie 13,642 ... P6
Letcher 27,000 ... R6
Lewis 13,029 ... P3
Lincoln 20,045 ... M6
Livingston 9,062 ... E6
Logan 24,416 ... H7
Lyon 6,624 ... E7
Madison 57,508 ... N5
Magoffin 13,077 ... P5
Marion 16,499 ... L5
Marshall 27,205 ... E7
Martin 12,526 ... R5
Mason 16,666 ... O3
McCracken 62,879 ... D6
McCreary 15,603 ... N7
McLean 9,628 ... G5
Meade 24,170 ... J5
Menifee 5,092 ... O5
Mercer 19,148 ... M5
Metcalfe 8,963 ... K7
Monroe 11,401 ... K7
Montgomery 19,561 ... O4
Morgan 11,648 ... P5
Muhlenberg 31,318 ... G6
Nelson 29,710 ... K5
Nicholas 6,725 ... N4
Ohio 21,105 ... H6
Oldham 33,263 ... L4
Owen 9,035 ... M3
Owsley 5,036 ... O6
Pendleton 12,036 ... N3
Perry 30,283 ... P6
Pike 72,583 ... S6
Powell 11,686 ... O5
Pulaski 49,489 ... M6
Robertson 2,124 ... N3
Rockcastle 14,803 ... N6
Rowan 20,353 ... P4
Russell 14,716 ... L6
Scott 23,867 ... M4
Shelby 24,824 ... L4
Simpson 15,145 ... H7
Spencer 6,801 ... L4
Taylor 21,146 ... L6
Todd 10,940 ... G7
Trigg 10,361 ... F7
Trimble 6,090 ... L3
Union 16,557 ... F5
Warren 76,673 ... H6
Washington 10,441 ... L5
Wayne 17,468 ... M7
Webster 13,955 ... F5
Whitley 33,326 ... N7
Wolfe 6,503 ... O5
Woodford 19,955 ... M4

CITIES and TOWNS

Adairville 906 ... H7
Ages 500 ... P7
Albany▲ 2,062 ... L7
Alexandria▲ 5,592 ... N3
Allen 229 ... R5
Allensville 218 ... G7
Amburgey 500 ... R6
Anchorage 2,082 ... L2
Annville 470 ... O6
Arjay 975 ... O7
Arlington 449 ... D7
Ashland 23,622 ... R4
Auburn 1,273 ... H7
Audubon Park 1,520 ... J2
Augusta 1,336 ... N3
Austin 500 ... K7
Auxier 900 ... R5
Bancroft 582 ... K1
Banner 950 ... R5
Barbourmeade 1,402 ... K1
Barbourville▲ 3,658 ... O7
Bardstown▲ 6,801 ... L5
Bardwell▲ 819 ... D7
Barlow 706 ... D6
Baskett 550 ... F5
Beattyville▲ 1,131 ... O5
Beauty 800 ... S5
Beaver Dam 2,904 ... H6
Bedford▲ 761 ... L3
Bee Spring 500 ... J6
Beechwood Village 1,263 ... K2
Belcher 500 ... S6
Belfry 800 ... S5
Bellemeade 927 ... L2
Bellevue 6,997 ... S1
Benham 717 ... R7
Benton▲ 3,899 ... E7
Berea 9,126 ... N5
Berry 240 ... N3
Betsy Layne 975 ... R5
Big Creek 700 ... O6
Blaine 271 ... R4
Blandville 95 ... D7
Bloomfield 845 ... L5
Blue Ridge Manor 565 ... L2
Boldman 510 ... R5
Bonnieville 300 ... K6
Bonnyman 800 ... P6
Boone 232 ... N5
Booneville▲ 191 ... O6
Bowling Green▲ 40,641 ... H7
Bradford 199 ... N3
Bradfordsville 331 ... L6
Brandenburg▲ 1,857 ... J4
Bremen 267 ... G6
Briensburg ... E7
Broadfields 273 ... K2
Brodhead 1,140 ... N6
Bromley 1,137 ... S2
Brooks 2,464 ... K4
Brooksville▲ 670 ... N3
Brownsboro Farm 670 ... L1
Brownsville 897 ... J6
Buechel 7,081 ... K2
Buffalo ... K6
Bulan 800 ... P6
Burgin 1,009 ... M5
Burkesville▲ 1,815 ... L7
Burlington▲ 6,070 ... R2
Burnside 695 ... M6
Butler 625 ... N3
Cadiz▲ 2,148 ... F7
Calhoun▲ 854 ... G5
California 130 ... N3
Calvert City 2,531 ... E6
Camargo 1,022 ... O4
Campbellsburg 604 ... L3
Campbellsville▲ 9,577 ... L6
Campton▲ 484 ... O5
Caney 549 ... P5
Caneyville 642 ... J6
Cannel City 600 ... P5
Carlisle▲ 1,639 ... N4
Carrollton▲ 3,715 ... L3
Carter ... P4
Catlettsburg▲ 2,231 ... R4
Cave City 1,953 ... K6
Cawood 800 ... P7
Center 383 ... K6
Centertown 462 ... G6
Centerville ... S6
Central City 4,979 ... G6
Cerulean ... F7
Clarkson 611 ... J6
Clay 1,173 ... F6
Clay City 1,258 ... O5
Clearfield 1,250 ... P4
Clinton▲ 1,547 ... D7
Clover Bottom 600 ... N5
Cloverport 1,207 ... H5
Coal Run 262 ... R5
Cold Spring 2,880 ... T2
Columbia▲ 3,845 ... L6
Columbus 252 ... C7
Combs 900 ... P6
Corbin 7,419 ... N7
Corinth 137 ... M3
Corydon 790 ... F5
Covington 43,264 ... S2
Crab Orchard 825 ... M6
Crescent Springs 2,179 ... R2
Crestview 356 ... S2
Crestview Hills 2,546 ... R2
Crestwood 1,435 ... L4
Crittenden 731 ... M3
Crofton 699 ... G6
Cumberland 3,112 ... R6
Cynthiana▲ 6,497 ... N4
Danville▲ 12,420 ... M5
Dawson Springs 3,129 ... F6
Dayton 6,576 ... T1
Devondale 1,164 ... K2
Dexter ... E7
Dixon▲ 552 ... F5
Dorton 750 ... R6
Douglass Hills 5,549 ... L2
Dover 297 ... O3
Drakesboro 565 ... H6
Dry Ridge 1,601 ... M3
Earlington 1,833 ... F6
East Bernstadt 550 ... N6
Echols 576 ... H6
Eddyville▲ 1,889 ... E6
Edgewood 8,143 ... S2
Edmonton▲ 1,477 ... K7
Elizabethtown▲ 18,167 ... K5
Elkhorn City 813 ... S6
Elkton▲ 1,789 ... G7
Elsmere 6,847 ... R2
Eminence 2,055 ... L4
Eolia 875 ... R6
Erlanger 15,979 ... R2
Essie 650 ... P6
Eubank 354 ... M6
Evarts 1,063 ... P7
Ewing 268 ... O4
Fairdale 6,563 ... K4
Fairfield 142 ... L5
Fairview 119 ... G7
Fairview 198 ... S2
Fallsburg ... R4
Falmouth▲ 2,378 ... N3
Fancy Farm 800 ... D7
Farmington 600 ... D7
Fedscreek 950 ... S6
Ferguson 934 ... M6
Fincastle 838 ... L1
Flat 7,799 ... O5
Flat Lick 600 ... O7
Flatwoods 8,354 ... R4
Fleming (Fleming-Neon) 759 ... R6
Flemingsburg▲ 3,071 ... O4
Florence 18,624 ... R2
Ford 522 ... N5
Fordsville 561 ... H5
Forest Hills 454 ... L2
Fort Knox 21,495 ... K5
Fort Mitchell 7,438 ... S2
Fort Thomas 16,032 ... S2
Fort Wright 6,570 ... S2
Fountain Run 259 ... K7
Frankfort (cap.)▲ 25,968 ... M4
Franklin▲ 7,607 ... J7
Fredonia 490 ... E6
Frenchburg▲ 625 ... O5
Fullerton 950 ... P3
Fulton 3,078 ... D7
Gamaliel 462 ... K7
Garrison 700 ... P3
Georgetown▲ 11,414 ... M4
Germantown 213 ... O3
Ghent 365 ... L3
Gilbertsville ... E7
Glasgow▲ 12,351 ... J7
Glencoe 257 ... M3
Glenview 653 ... K1
Goose Creek 321 ... L1
Goshen 2,447 ... K4
Gramoor 1,167 ... K1
Grand Rivers 351 ... E7
Gray 2,911 ... O7
Grayson▲ 3,510 ... R4
Greensburg▲ 1,990 ... K6
Greenup▲ 1,158 ... R3
Greenville▲ 4,689 ... G6
Guthrie 1,504 ... G7
Hammond 510 ... O7
Hanson 450 ... G6
Hardin 595 ... E7
Hardinsburg▲ 1,906 ... H5
Hardy 900 ... S5
Harlan▲ 2,686 ... P7
Harold 520 ... R5
Harrodsburg▲ 7,335 ... M5
Hartford▲ 2,532 ... H6
Hatfield 700 ... S5
Hawesville▲ 998 ... H5
Hazard▲ 5,416 ... P6
Hazel 460 ... E7
Hebron 930 ... R2
Helton 600 ... P7
Henderson▲ 25,945 ... F5
Hickman▲ 2,689 ... C7
Hickory 152 ... D7
Highland Heights 4,223 ... T2
Hima 600 ... O6
Himyar 545 ... O7
Hindman▲ 798 ... R6
Hiseville 220 ... K6
Hitchins 750 ... R4
Hodgenville▲ 2,721 ... K5
Hollow Creek 991 ... K4
Hopkinsville▲ 29,809 ... F7
Horse Cave 2,284 ... K6
Houston Acres 496 ... K2
Hustonville 313 ... M6
Hyden▲ 375 ... P6
Independence▲ 10,444 ... M3
Indian Hills 1,074 ... K1
Inez▲ 511 ... S5
Irvine▲ 2,836 ... O5
Irvington 1,180 ... J5
Island 446 ... G6
Ivel 850 ... R5
Jackson▲ 2,466 ... P5
Jamestown▲ 1,641 ... L7
Jeff 23,221 ... P6
Jeffersontown 15,795 ... L2
Jeffersonville 1,854 ... O5
Jenkins 2,751 ... R6
Junction City 1,983 ... M5
Keavy 900 ... N6
Keene 393 ... M5
Kenton 358 ... N3
Kenton Vale 145 ... S2
Kenvir 800 ... P7
Kevil 337 ... D6
King 399 ... O7
Kingsley 464 ... K2
Kitts 800 ... P7
Kuttawa 535 ... E6
La Center 1,040 ... C6
La Fayette 106 ... F7
La Grange▲ 3,853 ... L4
Lackey ... R6
Lake 3,131 ... O6
Lakeside Park 3,062 ... R2
Lancaster▲ 3,421 ... M5
Lawrenceburg▲ 5,911 ... M4
Leatherwood 800 ... P6
Lebanon Junction 1,741 ... K5
Lebanon▲ 5,695 ... L5
Leitchfield▲ 4,965 ... J6
Lejunior 597 ... P7
Lewisburg 772 ... G6
Lewisport 1,778 ... H5
Lexington▲ 204,165 ... N4
Liberty▲ 1,937 ... M6
Littcarr 645 ... R6
Livermore 1,534 ... G5
Livingston 241 ... N6
Lockport 84 ... M4
London▲ 5,757 ... N6
Lone Oak 465 ... D6
Lookout 600 ... S6
Lookout Heights ... S2
Loretto 820 ... L5
Lothair 600 ... P6
Louisa▲ 1,990 ... R4
Louisville▲ 269,063 ... J2
Loyall 1,100 ... P7
Ludlow 4,736 ... S2
Lynch 1,166 ... R7
Mackville 200 ... L5
Madisonville▲ 16,200 ... F6
Majestic 600 ... S5
Manchester▲ 1,634 ... O6
Marion▲ 3,320 ... E6
Marshes Siding 800 ... M7
Martha 650 ... R4
Martin 694 ... R5
Mary 177 ... O5
Mason 1,119 ... M3
Mayfield▲ 9,935 ... D7
Maysville▲ 7,169 ... O3
McAndrews 975 ... S5
McCarr 592 ... S5
McHenry 414 ... H6
McKee▲ 870 ... O6
McRoberts 1,101 ... R6
McVeigh 650 ... S5
Meadow Vale 798 ... L1
Meally 550 ... R5
Melbourne 660 ... T2
Mentor 169 ... N3
Meta 600 ... S5
Middlesboro 11,328 ... O7
Middletown 5,016 ... L2
Midway 1,290 ... M4
Millersburg 937 ... N4
Millstone 550 ... R6
Milton 563 ... L3
Minor Lane Heights 1,675 ... K4
Monterey 164 ... M4
Monticello▲ 5,357 ... M7
Moorland 467 ... L2
Morehead▲ 8,357 ... P4
Morgan 3,776 ... N3
Morganfield▲ 3,781 ... E5
Morgantown▲ 2,284 ... H6
Mortons Gap 987 ... F6
Mount Olivet▲ 384 ... N3
Mount Sterling▲ 5,362 ... N4
Mount Vernon▲ 2,654 ... N6
Mount Washington 5,226 ... K4
Mouthcard 900 ... S6
Muldraugh 1,376 ... J5
Munfordville▲ 1,556 ... J6
Murray▲ 14,439 ... E7
Nebo 227 ... F6
Neon (Neon-Fleming) ... R6
New Castle▲ 893 ... L4
New Concord 800 ... E7
New Haven 796 ... K5
New Hope ... L5
Newport 18,871 ... S2
Nicholasville▲ 13,603 ... N5
North Middletown 602 ... N4
Northfield 898 ... K1
Nortonville 1,209 ... G6
Oak Grove 2,863 ... G7
Oakland 202 ... J6
Oil Springs 900 ... P5
Okolona 18,902 ... K4
Oldtown 570 ... R4
Olive Hill 1,809 ... P4
Owensboro▲ 53,549 ... G5
Owenton▲ 1,306 ... M3
Owingsville▲ 1,491 ... O4
Paducah▲ 27,256 ... D6
Paintsville▲ 4,354 ... R5
Paris▲ 8,730 ... N4
Park City 549 ... J6
Park Hills 3,321 ... S2
Parksville 560 ... M5
Parkway Village 707 ... J2
Pembroke 640 ... G7
Perryville 815 ... M5
Petersburg ... M2
Pewee Valley 1,283 ... L4
Phelps 1,298 ... S6
Philpot 700 ... H5
Pikeville▲ 6,324 ... S6
Pine Knot 1,549 ... M7
Pineville▲ 2,198 ... O7
Pittsburg ... N6
Plantation 830 ... K1
Pleasure Ridge Park 25,131 ... J4
Pleasureville 761 ... L4
Plum Springs 361 ... J7
Powderly 748 ... G6
Premium 729 ... R6
Preston 3,558 ... O4
Prestonsburg▲ 4,011 ... R5
Prestonville 205 ... L3
Princeton▲ 6,940 ... F6
Prospect 2,788 ... K4
Providence 4,123 ... F6
Raceland 2,256 ... R3
Radcliff 19,772 ... K5
Ravenna 804 ... O5
Raywick 157 ... L5
Richmond▲ 21,155 ... N5
Riverwood 506 ... K1
Robards 701 ... F5
Rochester 191 ... H6
Rockholds 775 ... N7
Rockport 385 ... H6
Rolling Fields 593 ... K2
Rolling Hills 1,135 ... L1
Russell 4,014 ... R3
Russell Springs 2,363 ... L6
Russellville▲ 7,454 ... H7
Ryland Heights 279 ... M3
Sacramento 563 ... G6
Sadieville 255 ... M4
Saint Charles 316 ... F6
Saint Matthews 15,800 ... K2

Agriculture, Industry and Resources

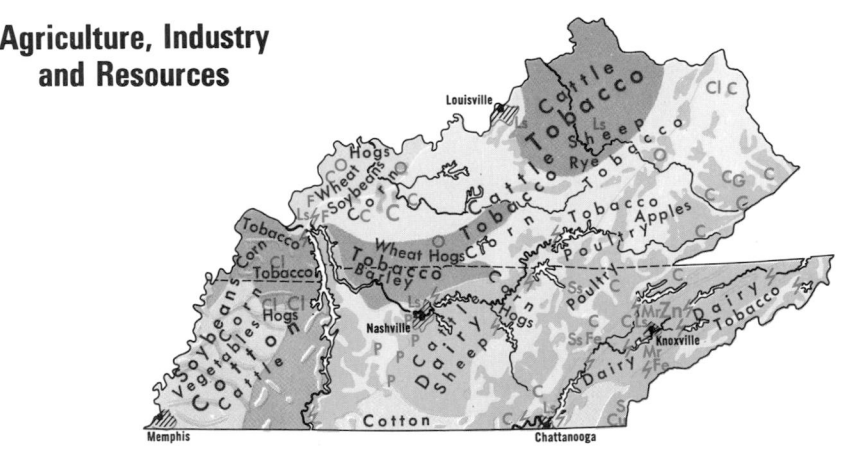

DOMINANT LAND USE

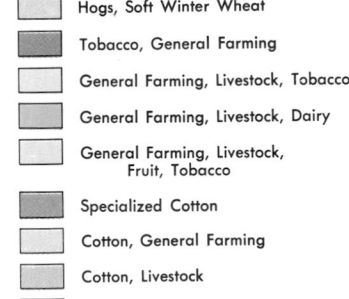

- Hogs, Soft Winter Wheat
- Tobacco, General Farming
- General Farming, Livestock, Tobacco
- General Farming, Livestock, Dairy
- General Farming, Livestock, Fruit, Tobacco
- Specialized Cotton
- Cotton, General Farming
- Cotton, Livestock
- Forests
- Swampland, Limited Agriculture

MAJOR MINERAL OCCURRENCES

C Coal
Cl Clay
Cu Copper
F Fluorspar
Fe Iron Ore
G Natural Gas
Ls Limestone
Mr Marble
O Petroleum
P Phosphates
S Pyrites
Ss Sandstone
Zn Zinc

Water Power
Major Industrial Areas

Saint Regis Park 1,756 .... K2
Salem 770 .... E6
Salt Lick 342 .... O4
Salyersville▲ 1,917 .... P5
Sanders 231 .... M3
Sandy Hook▲ 548 .... P4
Sardis 171 .... O3
Science Hill 628 .... M6
Scottsville▲ 4,278 .... J7
Sebree 1,510 .... F5
Seco R6
Sedalia D7
Seneca Gardens 684 .... K2
Sextons Creek 975 .... O6
Sharpsburg 315 .... O4
Shelbyville▲ 6,238 .... L4
Shepherdsville▲ 4,805 .... K4
Shively 15,535 .... K4
Silver Grove 1,102 .... T2
Simpson 907 .... P5
Simpsonville 642 .... L4
Slaughters 235 .... F6
Smilax 987 .... P6
Smithfield 115 .... L4
Smithland▲ 384 .... E6
Smiths Grove 703 .... J6
Somerset▲ 10,733 .... M6
Sonora 295 .... K5
South 202 .... J6
South Carrollton 262 .... G6
South Portsmouth 900 .... P3
South Shore 1,318 .... R3
South Williamson 1,016 .... S5
Southgate 3,266 .... T2
Sparta 133 .... M3
Spottsville 914 .... G5
Springfield▲ 2,875 .... L5
Springlee 451 .... K2
Staffordsville 700 .... R5
Stamping Ground 698 .... M4
Stanford▲ 2,686 .... M5
Stanton▲ 2,795 .... O5
Stearns 1,550 .... N7
Stone 900 .... S5
Strathmoor Village 361 .... K2
Sturgis 2,184 .... F5
Tateville 680 .... M7
Taylor Mill 5,530 .... S2
Taylorsville▲ 774 .... L4
Thealka 600 .... R5
Thornhill 146 .... K1
Tollesboro 808 .... O3
Tompkinsville▲ 2,861 .... K7
Trenton 378 .... G7
Tyner 590 .... O6
Union 1,001 .... M3
Uniontown 1,008 .... F5
Upton 719 .... K6
Valley Station 22,840 .... K4
Van 1,050 .... R6
Van Lear 2,035 .... R5
Vanceburg▲ 1,713 .... P3
Verda 1,133 .... P7
Versailles▲ 7,269 .... M4
Vicco 244 .... P6
Villa Hills 7,739 .... R2
Vine Grove 3,586 .... K5
Virgie 600 .... R6
Visalia 190 .... N3
Wallins Creek 261 .... O7
Walton 2,034 .... M3
Warfield 364 .... S5
Warsaw▲ 1,202 .... M3
Washington 795 .... O3
Water Valley 321 .... D7
Waverly 345 .... F5
Wayland 359 .... R6
Weeksbury 850 .... R6
Wellington 593 .... O5
Wellington 653 .... K2
West Buechel 1,587 .... K2
West Liberty▲ 1,887 .... P5
West Point 1,216 .... J4
West Somerset 850 .... M6
Westwood 734 .... R4
Westwood 826 .... L1
Wheatcroft 206 .... F5
Wheelwright 721 .... R6
White Plains 598 .... G6
Whitesburg▲ 1,636 .... R6
Whitesville 682 .... H5
Whitley City▲ 1,133 .... N7
Wickliffe▲ 851 .... C7
Wilders 633 .... S2
Willard R4
Williamsburg▲ 5,493 .... N7
Williamstown▲ 3,023 .... M3
Willisburg 223 .... L5
Wilmore 4,215 .... M5
Winchester▲ 15,799 .... N5
Windy Hills 2,452 .... K1
Wingo 568 .... D7
Winston Park S2
Wolf Creek 600 .... J4
Woodbine 900 .... N7
Woodburn 343 .... J7
Woodbury 117 .... H6
Woodland Hills 714 .... L2
Woodlawn (Oakdale) 308 .... D6
Woodlawn 331 .... T2
Woodlawn Park 1,099 .... K2
Wooton 750 .... P6
Worthington 1,751 .... R3
Worthville 191 .... L3
Wurtland 1,221 .... R3
Zebulon 750 .... S5

OTHER FEATURES

Abraham Lincoln Birthplace Nat'l Hist. Site K5
Barkley (dam) E6
Barkley (lake) F7
Barren (riv.) H6
Barren River (lake) J7
Beech Fork (riv.) L5
Big Sandy (riv.) R4
Black (mt.) R7
Buckhorn (lake) O6
Chaplin (riv.) L5
Clarks, East Fork (riv.) E7
Cove Run (lake) P4
Cumberland (lake) M7
Cumberland (mt.) P7
Cumberland (riv.) K8
Cumberland Gap Nat'l Hist. P7
Dale Hollow (lake) L7
Dewey (lake) R5
Dix (riv.) M5
Drakes (creek) J7
Dry (creek) R2
Eagle (creek) M3
Fishtrap (lake) S6
Fort Campbell G7
Grayson (lake) P4
Green (riv.) G6
Green River (lake) L6
Herrington (lake) M5
Hinkston (creek) N4
Kentucky (dam) E7
Kentucky (lake) E8
Kentucky (riv.) M3
Land Between The Lakes Rec. Area E7
Laurel River (lake) N6
Lexington Blue Grass Army Depot N4
Licking (riv.) N3
Mammoth Cave Nat'l Park J6
Mayfield (creek) C7
Mississippi (riv.) 10
Mud (riv.) H7
Nolin (lake) K6
Nolin (riv.) J6
Obion (creek) C7
Ohio (riv.) F5
Paint Lick (riv.) M5
Panther (creek) G5
Pine (mt.) O7
Pond (riv.) G6
Red (riv.) G7
Red (riv.) O5
Rockcastle (riv.) N6
Rolling Fork (riv.) K5
Rough (riv.) H5
Rough River (lake) J5
Salt (riv.) K5
Tennessee (riv.) D6
Tradewater (riv.) F6
Tug Fork (riv.) S5

KENTUCKY

KENTUCKY

AREA 40,409 sq. mi. (104,659 sq. km.)
POPULATION 3,698,969
CAPITAL Frankfort
LARGEST CITY Louisville
HIGHEST POINT Black Mtn. 4,145 ft. (1263 m.)
SETTLED IN 1774
ADMITTED TO UNION June 1, 1792
POPULAR NAME Bluegrass State
STATE FLOWER Goldenrod
STATE BIRD Cardinal

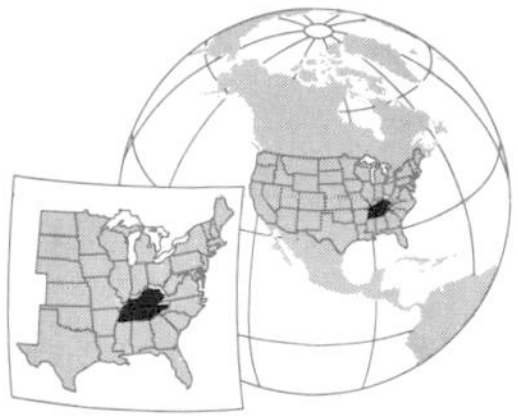

TENNESSEE

COUNTIES

Anderson 68,250 .... N8
Bedford 30,411 .... J9
Benton 14,524 .... E8
Bledsoe 9,669 .... L9
Blount 85,969 .... O9
Bradley 73,712 .... M1
Campbell 35,079 .... N8
Cannon 10,467 .... J9
Carroll 27,514 .... E9
Carter 51,505 .... S8
Cheatham 27,140 .... G8
Chester 12,819 .... D1
Claiborne 26,137 .... O8
Clay 7,238 .... K7
Cocke 29,141 .... P9
Coffee 40,339 .... J9
Crockett 13,378 .... C9
Cumberland 34,736 .... L9
Davidson 510,784 .... H8
De Kalb 13,589 .... K9
Decatur 10,472 .... E9
Dickson 35,061 .... G8
Dyer 34,854 .... C8
Fayette 25,559 .... C1
Fentress 14,669 .... M8
Franklin 34,725 .... J1
Gibson 46,315 .... D9
Giles 25,741 .... G1
Grainger 17,095 .... O8
Greene 55,853 .... R8
Grundy 13,362 .... K1
Hamblen 50,480 .... P8
Hamilton 285,536 .... L1
Hancock 6,739 .... P7
Hardeman 23,377 .... C1
Hardin 22,633 .... E1
Hawkins 44,565 .... P8
Haywood 19,437 .... C9
Henderson 21,844 .... E9
Henry 27,888 .... E8
Hickman 16,754 .... G9
Houston 7,018 .... F8
Humphreys 15,795 .... F8
Jackson 9,297 .... K8
Jefferson 33,016 .... P8
Johnson 13,766 .... T7
Knox 335,749 .... O9
Lake 7,129 .... B8
Lauderdale 23,491 .... B9
Lawrence 35,303 .... G1
Lewis 9,247 .... F9
Lincoln 28,157 .... H1
Loudon 31,255 .... N9
Macon 15,906 .... J7
Madison 77,982 .... D9
Marion 24,860 .... K1
Marshall 21,539 .... H1
Maury 54,812 .... G9
McMinn 42,383 .... M1
McNairy 22,422 .... D1
Meigs 8,033 .... M9
Monroe 30,541 .... N1
Montgomery 100,498 .... G8
Moore 4,721 .... J1
Morgan 17,300 .... M8
Obion 31,717 .... C8
Overton 17,636 .... L8
Perry 6,612 .... F9
Pickett 4,548 .... M7
Polk 13,643 .... N1
Putnam 51,373 .... K8
Rhea 24,344 .... M9
Roane 47,227 .... M9
Robertson 41,494 .... H7
Rutherford 118,570 .... J9
Scott 18,358 .... M8
Sequatchie 8,863 .... L1
Sevier 51,043 .... O9
Shelby 826,330 .... B1
Smith 14,143 .... J8
Stewart 9,479 .... F7
Sullivan 143,596 .... S7
Sumner 103,281 .... J8
Tipton 37,568 .... B9
Trousdale 5,920 .... J8
Unicoi 16,549 .... S8
Union 13,694 .... O8
Van Buren 4,846 .... L9
Warren 32,992 .... K9
Washington 92,315 .... R8
Wayne 13,935 .... F1
Weakley 31,972 .... D8
White 20,090 .... L9
Williamson 81,021 .... H9
Wilson 67,675 .... J8

TENNESSEE

TENNESSEE

AREA 42,144 sq. mi. (109,153 sq. km.)
POPULATION 4,896,641
CAPITAL Nashville
LARGEST CITY Memphis
HIGHEST POINT Clingmans Dome 6,643 ft. (2025 m.)
SETTLED IN 1757
ADMITTED TO UNION June 1, 1796
POPULAR NAME Volunteer State
STATE FLOWER Iris
STATE BIRD Mockingbird

CITIES and TOWNS

Adams 587 .... G7
Adamsville 1,745 .... E10
Afton 800 .... R8
Alamo▲ 2,426 .... C9
Alcoa 6,400 .... N9
Alexandria 730 .... J8
Algood 2,399 .... K8
Allardt 609 .... M8
Allons 600 .... L8
Altamont▲ 679 .... K10
Apison 750 .... L10
Ardmore 866 .... H10
Arlington 1,541 .... B10
Armathwaite 700 .... M8
Arthur 500 .... O7
Ashland City▲ 2,552 .... G8
Athens▲ 12,054 .... M10
Atoka 659 .... B10
Atwood 1,066 .... D9
Auburntown 240 .... J9
Baileyton 309 .... R8
Banner Hill 1,717 .... R8
Bartlett 26,989 .... B10
Bath Springs 800 .... E10
Baxter 1,289 .... K8
Bean Station 500 .... P8
Beechgrove 550 .... J9
Beersheba Springs 596 .... K10
Bell Buckle 326 .... J9
Belle Meade 2,839 .... H8
Bells 1,643 .... C9
Benton▲ 992 .... M10
Berry Hill 802 .... H8
Berry's Chapel 2,703 .... H9
Bethel Springs 755 .... D10
Big Sandy 505 .... E8
Birchwood 550 .... M10
Blaine 1,326 .... O8
Bloomingdale 10,953 .... R7
Bloomington Springs 800 .... K8
Blountville▲ 2,605 .... S7
Bluff City 1,390 .... S8
Bolivar▲ 5,969 .... C10
Braden 354 .... B10
Bradford 1,154 .... D8
Braemar S8
Brentwood 16,392 .... H8
Briceville 850 .... N8
Brighton 717 .... B10
Bristol 23,421 .... S7
Brownsville▲ 10,019 .... C9
Bruceton 1,586 .... E8
Buena Vista 500 .... E9
Bulls Gap 659 .... P8
Burlison 394 .... B9
Burns 1,127 .... G8
Butler 500 .... T8
Byrdstown▲ 998 .... L7
Calhoun 552 .... M10
Camden▲ 3,643 .... E8
Carthage▲ 2,386 .... K8
Caryville 1,751 .... N8
Castalian Springs 650 .... J8
Cedar Hill 347 .... H7
Celina▲ 1,493 .... K7
Centertown 332 .... K9
Centerville▲ 3,616 .... G9
Chapel Hill 833 .... H9
Charleston 653 .... M10
Charlotte▲ 854 .... G8
Chattanooga▲ 152,466 .... K10
Chuckey 500 .... R8
Church Hill 4,834 .... R7
Clairfield 650 .... O7
Clarksburg 321 .... E9
Clarksville▲ 75,494 .... G7
Cleveland▲ 30,354 .... M10
Clifton 620 .... F10
Clinton▲ 8,972 .... N8
Coalfield 712 .... N8
Coalmont 813 .... K10
Cokercreek 500 .... N10
College Grove 580 .... H9
Collegedale 5,048 .... M10
Collierville 14,427 .... B10
Collinwood 1,014 .... F10
Colonial Heights 6,716 .... R8
Columbia▲ 28,583 .... G9
Concord 8,569 .... N9
Cookeville▲ 21,744 .... L8
Copperhill 362 .... N10
Cordova 600 .... B10
Cornersville 683 .... H10
Corryton 500 .... O8
Counce 975 .... E10
Covington▲ 7,487 .... B9
Cowan 1,738 .... K10
Crab Orchard 876 .... M9
Crockett Mills 500 .... C9
Cross Plains 1,025 .... H7
Crossville▲ 6,930 .... L9
Crump 2,028 .... E10
Cumberland City 319 .... F8
Cumberland Gap 210 .... O8
Cypress Inn 500 .... F10
Dandridge▲ 1,540 .... O8
Dayton▲ 5,671 .... L9
Decatur▲ 1,361 .... M9
Decaturville▲ 879 .... E9
Dechero 2,196 .... J10
Dickson 8,791 .... G8
Dover▲ 1,341 .... F8
Dowelltown 308 .... K8
Doyle 345 .... K9
Dresden▲ 2,488 .... D8
Drummonds 800 .... A10
Duck River 750 .... G9
Ducktown 421 .... N10
Dunlap▲ 3,731 .... L10
Dyer 2,204 .... D8
Dyersburg▲ 16,317 .... C8
Eads 550 .... B10
Eagleton Village 5,169 .... O9
Eagleville 462 .... H9
East Ridge 21,101 .... L11
Eastview 563 .... D10
Elgin 700 .... M8
Elizabethton▲ 11,931 .... S8
Elk Valley 750 .... N7
Elkton 448 .... H10
Ellendale 850 .... B10
Embreeville Junction R8
Emory Gap 500 .... M9
Englewood 1,611 .... M10
Enville 211 .... E10
Erin▲ 1,586 .... F8
Erwin▲ 5,015 .... S8
Estill Springs 1,408 .... J10
Ethridge 565 .... G10
Etowah 3,815 .... M10
Eva 500 .... E8
Fairfield 2,209 .... J9
Fairview 4,210 .... G9
Fall Branch 1,203 .... R8
Farner 750 .... N10
Fayetteville▲ 6,921 .... H10
Finger 279 .... D10
Finley 1,014 .... B8
Flintville 500 .... H10
Forest Hills 4,231 .... H8
Fort Pillow 700 .... B9
Fowlkes 700 .... C9
Franklin▲ 20,098 .... H9
Friendship 467 .... C9
Friendsville 792 .... N9
Gadsden 561 .... D9
Gainesboro▲ 1,002 .... K8
Gallatin▲ 18,794 .... H8
Gallaway 762 .... B10
Garland 194 .... B9
Gates 608 .... C9
Gatlinburg 3,417 .... O9
Germantown 32,893 .... B10
Gibson 281 .... D9
Gilt Edge 447 .... B9
Gleason 1,402 .... D8
Goodlettsville 8,177 .... H8
Gordonsville 891 .... K8
Grand Junction 365 .... C10
Grandview M9
Graysville 1,301 .... L10
Greenback 611 .... N9
Greenbrier 2,873 .... H8
Greeneville▲ 13,532 .... R8
Greenfield 2,105 .... D8
Grimsley 650 .... L8
Gruetli 1,810 .... K10
Guys 497 .... D10
Habersham 750 .... N8
Halls 2,431 .... C9
Halls Crossroads O8
Hampshire 788 .... G9
Hampton 2,236 .... S8
Harriman 7,119 .... M9
Harris 7,191 .... C8
Harrison 6,206 .... L10
Harrogate (Shawanee) 2,657 .... O8
Hartsville▲ 2,188 .... J8
Helenwood 675 .... M8
Henderson▲ 4,760 .... D10
Hendersonville 32,188 .... H8
Henning 802 .... B9
Henry 317 .... E8
Hickory Valley 159 .... C10
Hixson L10
Hohenwald▲ 3,760 .... F9
Hollow Rock 902 .... E8
Hornbeak 445 .... C8
Hornsby 313 .... D10
Humboldt 9,651 .... D9
Huntingdon▲ 4,180 .... E8
Huntland 885 .... J10
Huntsville▲ 600 .... N8
Hurricane Mills 850 .... F9
Iron City 402 .... F10
Jacksboro▲ 1,568 .... N8
Jackson▲ 48,949 .... D9
Jamestown▲ 1,862 .... M8
Jasper▲ 2,780 .... K10
Jefferson City 5,494 .... P8
Jellico 2,447 .... N7
Johnson City 49,381 .... S8
Jones 3,091 .... C9
Jonesborough▲ 2,829 .... R8
Karns 1,458 .... N9
Kenton 1,366 .... C8
Kimball 1,243 .... K10
Kimberlin Heights 500 .... O9
Kingsport 36,365 .... R7
Kingston Springs 1,529 .... G8
Kingston▲ 4,552 .... N9
Knoxville▲ 165,121 .... O9
Kodak 700 .... O9
La Follette 7,192 .... N8
La Grange 167 .... C10
La Vergne 7,499 .... H9
Laager 675 .... K10
Lafayette▲ 3,641 .... J7
Lake City 2,166 .... N8
Lakeland 1,204 .... B10
Lakesite 732 .... L10
Lakewood 2,009 .... H8
Lawrenceburg▲ 10,412 .... G10
Lebanon▲ 15,208 .... J8
Lenoir City 6,147 .... N9
Leoma 600 .... G10
Lewisburg▲ 9,879 .... H10
Lexington▲ 5,810 .... E9
Liberty 391 .... K8
Linden▲ 1,099 .... F9
Livingston▲ 3,809 .... L8
Lobelville 830 .... F9
Long Island S7
Lookout Mountain 1,901 .... L11
Loretto 1,515 .... G10
Loudon▲ 4,026 .... N9
Louisville 500 .... N9
Luttrell 812 .... O8
Lutts 740 .... F10
Lyles 500 .... G9
Lynchburg▲ 668 .... J10
Lynnville 344 .... G10
Madisonville▲ 3,033 .... N9
Malesus 600 .... D9
Manchester▲ 7,709 .... J10
Martel 500 .... N9
Martin 8,600 .... D8
Maryville▲ 19,208 .... O9
Mascot 2,138 .... O8
Mason 337 .... B10
Maury City 782 .... C9
Maynardville▲ 1,298 .... O8
McDonald 500 .... M10
McEwen 1,442 .... F8
McKenzie 5,168 .... E8
McLemoresville 280 .... D9
McMinnville▲ 11,194 .... K9
Medina 658 .... D9
Medon 137 .... D10
Memphis▲ 610,337 .... B10
Michie 677 .... E10
Middleton 536 .... D10
Midway 2,953 .... P8
Milan 7,512 .... D9
Milledgeville 279 .... E10
Milligan College 600 .... S8
Millington 17,866 .... B10
Minor Hill 372 .... G10
Mitchellville 193 .... J7
Monteagle 1,138 .... K10
Monterey 2,559 .... L8
Morley 600 .... N7
Morrison 570 .... K9
Morrison City 2,032 .... R7
Morristown▲ 21,385 .... P8
Moscow 384 .... C10
Mosheim 1,451 .... R8
Mount Carmel 4,082 .... R8
Mount Juliet 5,389 .... H8
Mount Pleasant 4,278 .... G9
Mountain City▲ 2,169 .... T8
Munford 2,326 .... B10
Murfreesboro▲ 44,922 .... J9
Murray Lake Hills L10
Nashville (cap.)▲ 488,374 .... H8
Neubert 800 .... O9
New Hope 854 .... K11
New Johnsonville 1,643 .... E8
New Market 1,086 .... O8
New Tazewell 1,864 .... O8
Newbern 2,515 .... C8
Newport▲ 7,123 .... P9
Niota 745 .... M9
Norma 118 .... N8
Normandy 118 .... J10
Norris 1,303 .... N8
Oak Hill 4,301 .... H8
Oak Ridge 27,310 .... N8
Oakdale 268 .... M9
Oakland 392 .... B10
Obion 1,241 .... C8
Oliver Springs 3,433 .... N8
Oneida 3,502 .... N7
Ooltewah 4,903 .... M10
Orebank 1,284 .... R7
Orlinda 469 .... H7
Orme 150 .... K10
Pall Mall 750 .... M7
Palmer 769 .... K10
Paris▲ 9,332 .... E8
Parrotsville 121 .... P8
Parsons 2,033 .... E9
Pegram 1,371 .... H8
Petersburg 514 .... H10
Petros 1,286 .... M8
Philadelphia 463 .... M9
Pickwick Dam 650 .... E10
Pigeon Forge 3,027 .... O9
Pikeville▲ 1,771 .... L9
Piperton 612 .... B10
Pittman Center 478 .... P9
Pleasant Hill 494 .... L9
Pleasant View 625 .... G8
Portland 5,165 .... H7
Powder Springs 600 .... O8
Powell 7,534 .... N8
Powells Crossroads 1,098 .... L10
Primm Springs 750 .... G9
Pulaski▲ 7,895 .... G10
Puryear 592 .... E8
Ramer 337 .... D10
Red Bank 12,322 .... L10
Red Boiling Springs 905 .... K7
Rheatown R8
Ridgely 1,775 .... B8
Ridgeside 400 .... L10
Ripley▲ 6,188 .... B9
Rives 344 .... C8
Roan Mountain 1,220 .... S8
Rockford 646 .... O9
Rockwood 5,348 .... M9
Rogersville▲ 4,149 .... P8
Rosemark 950 .... B10
Rossville 291 .... B10
Russellville 1,069 .... P8
Rutherford 1,303 .... C8
Rutledge▲ 903 .... P8
Saint Joseph 789 .... G10
Sale Creek 900 .... L10
Saltillo 383 .... E10
Samburg 374 .... C8
Sardis 305 .... E10
Saulsbury 106 .... C10
Saundersville H8
Savannah▲ 6,547 .... E10
Scotts Hill 594 .... E10
Selmer▲ 3,838 .... D10
Sequatchie 800 .... K10
Sevierville▲ 7,178 .... P9
Sewanee 2,128 .... K10
Seymour 7,026 .... O9
Sharon 1,047 .... D8
Shelbyville▲ 14,049 .... H10
Sherwood 900 .... K10
Signal Mountain 7,034 .... L10
Smithville▲ 3,791 .... K9
Smyrna 13,647 .... H9
Sneedville▲ 1,446 .... P7
Soddy-Daisy (Daisy-Soddy) 8,240 .... L10
Somerville▲ 2,047 .... C10
South Carthage 851 .... K8
South Cleveland 5,372 .... M10
South Clinton 1,671 .... N8
South Fulton 2,688 .... D8
South Pittsburg 3,295 .... K10
Southside 800 .... G8
Sparta▲ 4,681 .... K9
Spencer▲ 1,125 .... L9
Spring City 2,199 .... M9
Spring Hill 1,464 .... H9
Springfield▲ 11,227 .... H8
Stanton 487 .... C10
Stantonville 264 .... E10
Strawberry Plains 800 .... O8
Sullivan Gardens 2,513 .... R8
Summertown 850 .... G10
Surgoinsville 1,499 .... R8
Sweetwater 5,066 .... N9
Talbott 975 .... P8
Tazewell▲ 2,150 .... O8
Tellico Plains 657 .... N10
Ten Mile 700 .... M9
Tennessee Ridge 1,271 .... F8
Tiftona L11
Tipton 2,149 .... B10
Tiptonville▲ 2,438 .... B8
Toone 279 .... D10
Townsend 329 .... O9
Tracy City 1,556 .... K10
Treadway 712 .... P8
Trenton▲ 4,836 .... D9
Trezevant 874 .... D8
Trimble 694 .... C8
Troy 1,047 .... C8
Tullahoma 16,761 .... J10
Tusculum 1,918 .... R8
Union City▲ 10,513 .... C8
Vanleer 369 .... G8
Victoria 800 .... K10
Viola 123 .... K9
Vonore 605 .... N9
Walden 1,523 .... L10
Walterhill 1,043 .... J9
Wartburg▲ 932 .... M8
Wartrace 494 .... J9

(continued on following page)

(continued)

Watauga 389............................S8
Watertown 1,250.....................J8
Waverly▲ 3,925.......................F8
Waynesboro▲ 1,824..............F10
Western Institute 850 ....C10
Westmoreland 1,726...............J7
White Bluff 1,988....................G8
White House 2,987 ....H8
White Pine 1,771 ....P8
Whiteville 1,050.....................C10
Whitwell 1,622.......................K10
Williston 427..........................C10
Winchester▲ 6,305................J10
Winfield 564...........................M7
Woodbury▲ 2,287 ....J9
Woodland Mills 398................C8
Yorkville 347...........................C8

OTHER FEATURES

Andrew Johnson
  Nat'l Hist. Site.....................R8
Appalachian (mts.)...............M10
Bald (mts.)...............................R9
Barkley (lake) F7
Big Sandy (riv.) E9
Boone (lake) S8
Buffalo (riv.)............................F9
Caney Fork (riv.) L9
Center Hill (lake) K9
Cheatham (dam).....................G8
Cheatham (lake) H8
Cherokee (dam) P8
Cherokee (lake)........................P8
Chickamauga (dam)..............L10
Chickamauga (lake)...............L10
Chilhowee (mt.) O9
Clinch (riv.)..............................N9
Clingmans Dome (mt.) P10
Collins (riv.)............................K9
Conasauga (riv.) M11
Cordell Hull (res.) K8
Cumberland (plat.) L9
Cumberland (riv.)....................K8
Cumberland Gap
  Nat\'l Hist. Park...................O7
Dale Hollow (lake)...................L7
Douglas (lake).........................P9
Duck (riv.) F9
Elk (riv.)................................H10
Emory (riv.)............................M8
Forked Deer (riv.)....................C9
Fort Campbell G7
Fort Donelson Nat'l Mil. Park...F8
Fort Loudoun (lake)................N9
French Broad (riv.) R9
Great Falls (dam) K9
Great Smoky (mts.) P9
Great Smoky Mountains
  Nat'l Park P9
Green (riv.)............................F10
Guyot (mt.) P9
Harpeth (riv.) G8
Hatchie (riv.)............................B9
Hiwassee (riv.)......................O10
Holston (riv.) O8
Iron (mts.) S8
Kentucky (lake) E8
Land Between The Lakes
  Rec. Area E7
Lick (creek)..............................R8
Little Tennessee (riv.)...........N10
Loosahatchie (riv.)................B10
Melton Hill (lake) N9
Memphis Naval Air Sta. B10
Meriwether Lewis Park,
  Natchez Trace Pkwy..........G10
Mississippi (riv.)....................A10
Nolichucky (riv.) R8
Norris (dam)............................N8
Norris (lake) O8
Obed (riv.)...............................M8
Obion (riv.) C8
Ocoee (riv.)...........................M10
Old Hickory (dam) H8
Old Hickory (lake)....................J8
Pickwick (lake)......................E11
Powell (riv.) P8
Priest, J. Percy (lake) J8
Red (riv.) G7
Reelfoot (lake) C8
Richland (creek) G10
Rutherford Fork, Obion (riv.) ..D8
Sequatchie (riv.)...................L10
Sewart A.F.B...........................J8
Shiloh Nat'l Mil. Park E10
Shoal (creek).........................F10
South Holston (lake)..............S7
Stone (mts.).............................T8
Stones (riv.) J9
Stones River Nat'l Battlefield ...J9
Sulphur Fork, Red (riv.)..........H8
Tellico (riv.) N10
Tennessee (riv.) E10
Tims Ford (lake)....................J10
Unaka (mts.)...........................S8
Unicoi (mts.) N10
Watauga (lake).........................T8
Watts Bar (dam) M9
Watts Bar (lake) M9
Whiteoak (creek).....................F8
Wolf (riv.) B10
Woods (res.) J10
Yellow (creek) F8

▲ County seat.

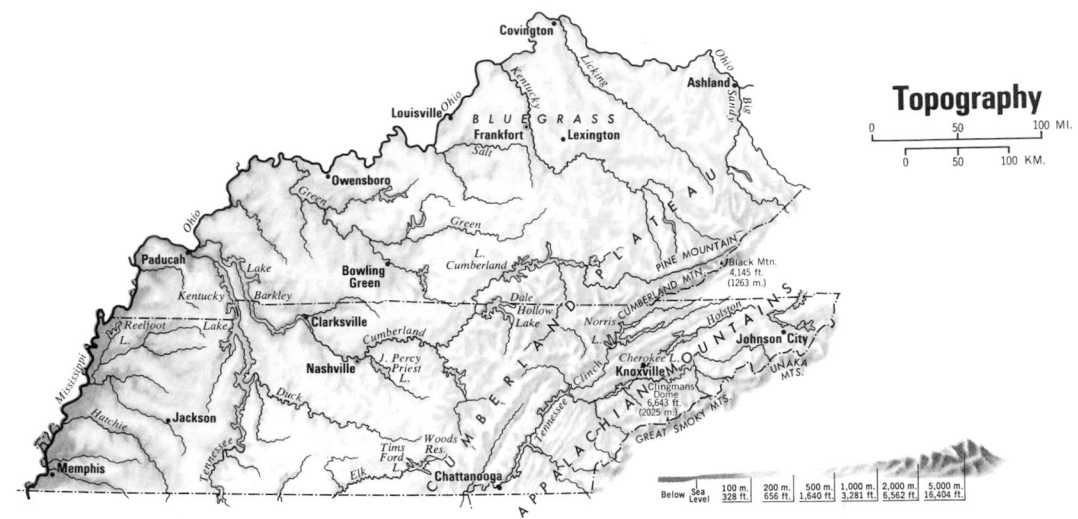

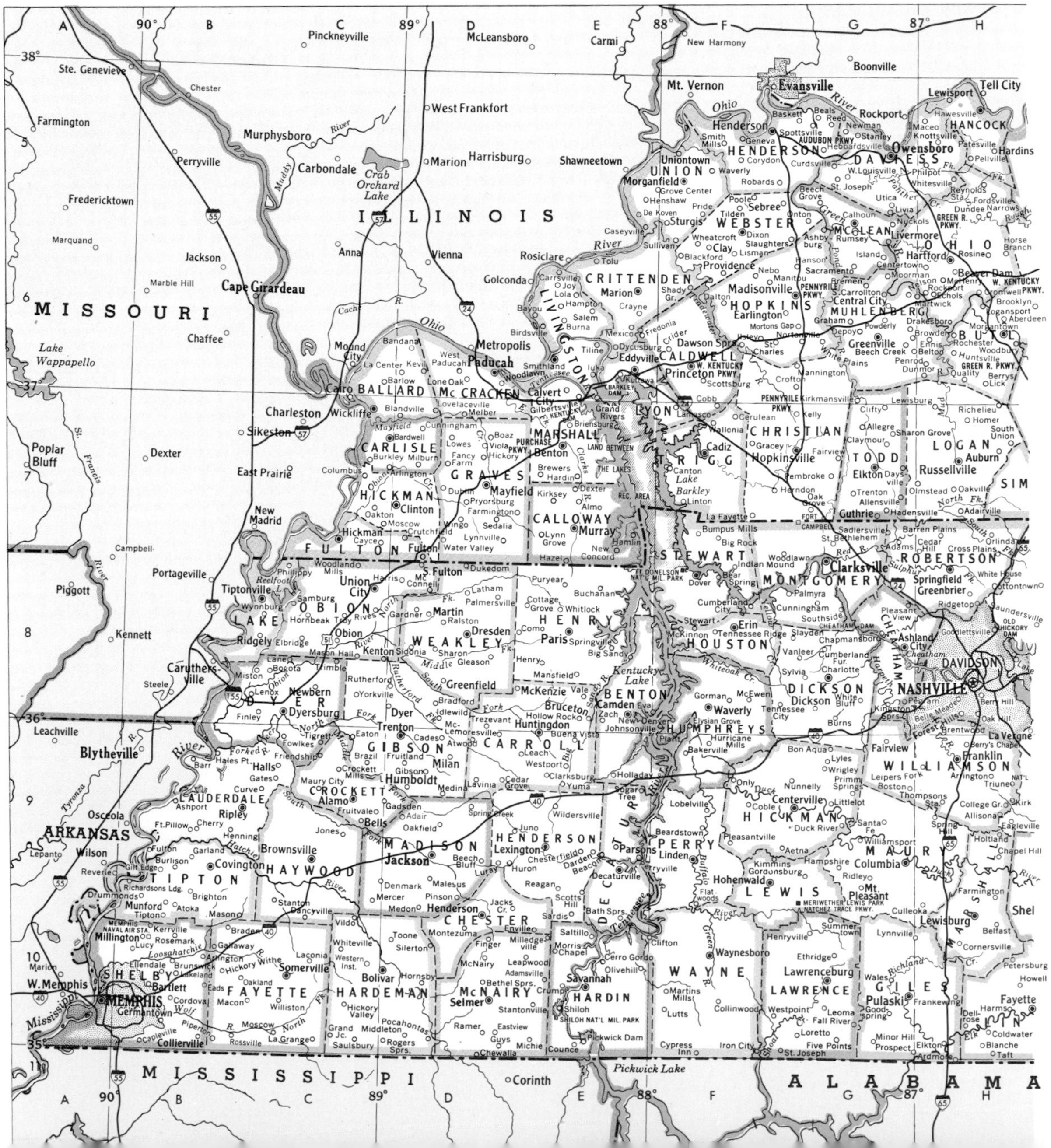

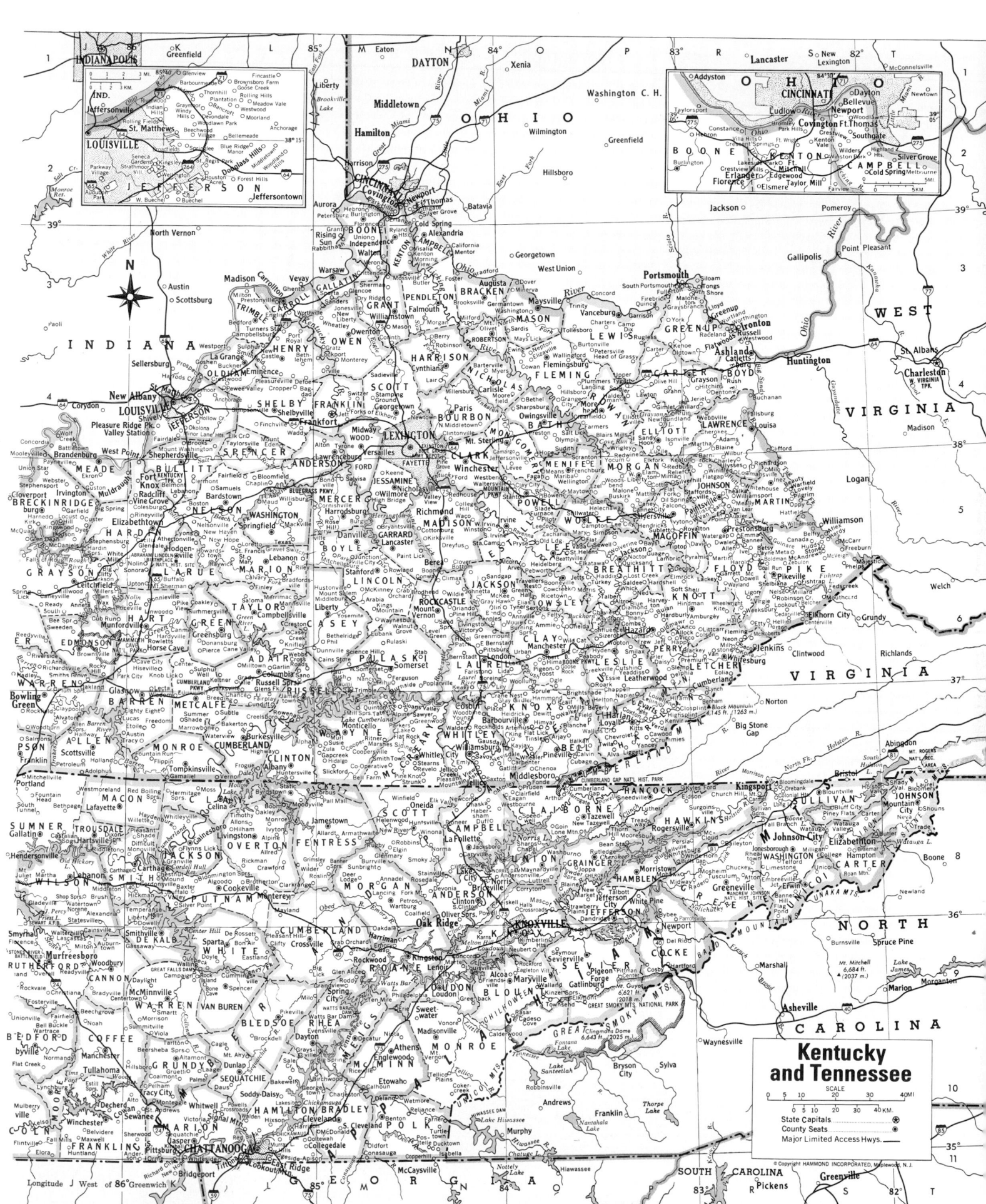

Kentucky
and Tennessee

SCALE
0 5 10   20   30   40 MI
0 5 10   20 30 40 KM.

State Capitals .... ✪
County Seats .... ◉
Major Limited Access Hwys. ——

© Copyright HAMMOND INCORPORATED, Maplewood, N.J.

Topography

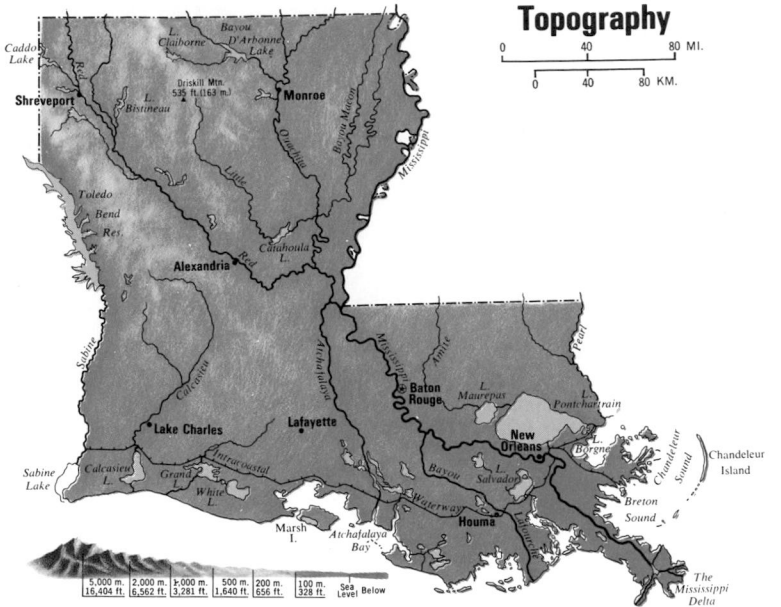

5,000 m. 2,000 m. 000 m. 500 m. 200 m. 100 m. Sea
16,404 ft. 6,562 ft. 3,281 ft. 1,640 ft. 656 ft. 328 ft. Level Below

PARISHES

Acadia 56,427 ....F6
Allen 21,390 ....E5
Ascension 50,068 ....L3
Assumption 22,084 ....H7
Avoyelles 41,393 ....G4
Beauregard 29,692 ....D5
Bienville 16,387 ....D2
Bossier 80,721 ....C1
Caddo 252,437 ....C1
Calcasieu 167,223 ....D6
Caldwell 10,761 ....F2
Cameron 9,336 ....D7
Catahoula 12,287 ....G3
Claiborne 17,095 ....D1
Concordia 22,981 ....G4
De Soto 25,727 ....C2
East Baton Rouge 366,191 ...K1
East Carroll 11,772 ....H1
East Feliciana 19,015 ....H5
Evangeline 33,343 ....F5
Franklin 24,141 ....G2
Grant 16,703 ....E4
Iberia 63,752 ....G7
Iberville 32,159 ....H6
Jackson 17,321 ....E2
Jefferson 454,592 ....K7
Jefferson Davis 32,168 .....F6
La Salle 17,004 ....F3
Lafayette 150,017 ....F6
Lafourche 82,483 ....K7
Lincoln 39,763 ....E1
Livingston 58,806 ....L2
Madison 15,682 ....H2
Morehouse 34,803 ....G1
Natchitoches 39,863 ....D3
Orleans 557,927 ....L6
Ouachita 139,241 ....G2
Plaquemines 26,049 ....L8
Pointe Coupee 24,045 ......G5
Rapides 135,282 ....E4
Red River 10,433 ....D2
Richland 22,187 ....G2
Sabine 25,280 ....C3
Saint Bernard 64,097 ....L7
Saint Charles 37,259 ....K7
Saint Helena 9,827 ....J5
Saint James 21,495 ....L3
Saint John the Baptist
  31,924 ....M3
Saint Landry 84,128 ....F5
Saint Martin 40,214 ....G6
Saint Mary 64,253 ....H7
Saint Tammany 110,869 ...L6
Tangipahoa 80,698 ....L5
Tensas 8,525 ....H2
Terrebonne 94,393 ....J8
Union 21,167 ....F1
Vermilion 48,458 ....F7
Vernon 53,475 ....D4
Washington 44,207 ....K5
Webster 43,631 ....D1
West Baton Rouge 19,086 ...H6
West Carroll 12,922 ....H1
West Feliciana 12,186 ....H5
Winn 17,253 ....E3

CITIES and TOWNS

Abbeville ▲ 11,187 ....F7
Abita Springs 1,296 ....L6
Acme 235 ....G4
Acy 570 ....L3
Addis 1,222 ....J2
Adeline 200 ....G7

Akers 150 ....N2
Albany 645 ....M1
Alberta 150 ....D2
Alexandria ▲ 49,188 ....E4
Allen 175 ....D3
Alto 132 ....G2
Alton 500 ....L6
Amelia 2,447 ....H7
Amite ▲ 4,301 ....K5
Anacoco 823 ....D4
Anandale F4
Andrew 100 ....F6
Angie 235 ....L5
Angola 600 ....G5
Ansley 100 ....E2
Arabi 8,787 ....P4
Arbroth 250 ....H5
Arcadia ▲ 3,079 ....E1
Archibald 425 ....G3
Arcola 280 ....K5
Arcola 200 ....K5
Arnaudville 1,444 ....G6
Ashland 289 ....D3
Athens 278 ....E1
Atlanta 118 ....E3
Avery Island 500 ....G7
Bains 400 ....H5
Baker 13,233 ....K1
Baldwin 2,379 ....H7
Ball 3,305 ....F4
Bancroft 114 ....C5
Baptist 150 ....M1
Baratia 1,160 ....K7
Basile 1,808 ....E5
Baskin 243 ....G2
Bastrop ▲ 13,916 ....G1
Batchelor 500 ....G5
Baton Rouge (cap.) ▲ 219,531 .K2
Bayou Barbary 200 ....M2
Bayou Cane 15,876 ....J7
Bayou Goula 850 ....J3
Bayou Vista 4,733 ....H7
Baywood 100 ....K1
Beaver 350 ....E5
Bekman 150 ....G1
Bel 150 ....D6
Belcher 249 ....C1
Bell City 400 ....D6
Belle Alliance H6
Belle Chasse 8,512 ....O4
Belle D'Eau 120 ....F4
Belle Rose 900 ....K3
Belmont 350 ....D3
Benson 200 ....C3
Bentley 120 ....E3
Benton ▲ 2,047 ....C1
Bernice 1,543 ....E1
Bertrandville 175 ....L7
Berwick 4,375 ....H7
Bethany 300 ....B2
Bienville 316 ....D2
Blanchard 1,175 ....C1
Bogalusa 14,280 ....L5
Bolinger 200 ....G1
Bonita 265 ....G1
Boothville 300 ....M8
Bordelonville 350 ....G4
Bosco 480 ....F2
Bossier City 52,721 ....C1
Boudreaux 275 ....J8
Bourg 2,073 ....J7
Boutte 2,702 ....N4
Boyce 1,361 ....E4
Braithwaite 350 ....P4
Branch 200 ....F6

Breaux Bridge 6,515 ....G6
Brittany 475 ....L3
Broussard 3,213 ....G6
Brusly 1,824 ....J2
Bryceland 103 ....E2
Buckeye 280 ....F4
Bunkie 5,044 ....F5
Buras (Buras-Triumph) 4,137 .L8
Burnside 500 ....L3
Bush 275 ....L5
Cade 175 ....G6
Calcasieu 400 ....E4
Calhoun 350 ....F2
Calumet 100 ....H7
Calvin 207 ....E3
Cameron ▲ 2,041 ....D7
Campti 929 ....D3
Cankton 323 ....F6
Carlisle 975 ....L7
Carencro 5,429 ....G6
Carville 1,108 ....K3
Castor 196 ....D2
Cecelia 550 ....G6
Center Point 850 ....F4
Centerville 600 ....H7
Central 100 ....L3
Chacahoula 150 ....J7
Chalmette ▲ 31,860 ....P4
Charenton 1,584 ....H7
Chase 200 ....G2
Chataignier 281 ....F5
Chatham 617 ....F2
Chauvin 3,375 ....J8
Cheneyville 1,005 ....F4
Chopin 175 ....E4
Choudrant 521 ....F1
Church Point 4,677 ....F6
Clarence 577 ....E3
Clarks 650 ....F2
Clay 400 ....E2
Clayton 917 ....H3
Clear Lake 100 ....E3
Clinton ▲ 1,904 ....J5
Clio 125 ....M2
Cloutierville 100 ....E3
Colfax ▲ 1,696 ....E3
Collinston 375 ....G1
Columbia ▲ 386 ....F2
Convent ▲ 400 ....L3
Converse 436 ....C3
Corey 110 ....F2
Cotton Valley 1,130 ....D1
Cottonport 2,600 ....F5
Couchwood 150 ....D1
Coushatta ▲ 1,845 ....D2
Covington ▲ 7,691 ....K5
Cow Island 200 ....F7
Cravens 200 ....E5
Crescent 300 ....J2
Creston 135 ....E3
Crowley ▲ 13,983 ....F6
Crowville 400 ....G2
Cullen 1,642 ....D1
Curtis 110 ....C2
Cut Off 5,325 ....K7
Dalcour 250 ....P4
Danville 100 ....E2
Davant 600 ....L7
De Quincy 3,474 ....D6
De Ridder ▲ 9,868 ....D5
Deerford 100 ....K1
Delcambre 1,978 ....G7
Delhi 3,169 ....H2
Delta 234 ....J2

Denham Springs 8,381 ....L2
Des Allemands 2,504 ......N4
Destrehan 8,031 ....N4
Deville 1,113 ....F4
Diamond 370 ....L7
Dixie 330 ....C1
Dixie Inn 347 ....D1
Dodson 350 ....E2
Donaldsonville ▲ 7,949 ...K3
Donner 500 ....J7
Downsville 101 ....F1
Doyline 884 ....D1
Dry Creek 300 ....D5
Dry Prong 380 ....E3
Dubach 843 ....E1
Dubberly 253 ....D1
Dulac 3,273 ....J8
Dunn 225 ....G2
Duplessis 350 ....K2
Duson 1,465 ....F6
East Hodge 421 ....E2
East Point 100 ....D3
Easton 365 ....F5
Echo 525 ....F4
Edgard ▲ 2,753 ....M3
Edgefield 207 ....D2
Edgerly 250 ....C6
Effie 300 ....F4
Elizabeth 414 ....E5
Elm Grove 100 ....C2
Elm Park 200 ....H5
Elmer 200 ....E4
Elton 1,277 ....E6
Empire 2,654 ....L8
Enterprise 375 ....G3
Epps 541 ....G1
Erath 2,428 ....F7
Eros 177 ....F2
Erwinville 790 ....H5
Esther 745 ....F7
Estherwood 745 ....F6
Ethel 250 ....H5
Eunice 11,162 ....E6
Eva 100 ....G4
Evangeline 400 ....F6
Evans 500 ....D5
Evergreen 283 ....F5
Extension 950 ....G3
Fairbanks 300 ....F1
Farmerville ▲ 3,334 ....F1
Fenton 265 ....E6
Ferriday 4,111 ....G3
Fields 125 ....D4
Fisher 277 ....D4
Flatwoods 360 ....E4
Flora 300 ....D3
Florien 626 ....D4
Fluker 400 ....K5
Folsom 469 ....L5
Forbing 100 ....C2
Fordoche 869 ....G5
Forest 263 ....H1
Forest Hill 408 ....E4
Fort Jesup 100 ....C3
Fort Necessity 150 ....G3
Franklin ▲ 9,004 ....G7
Franklinton ▲ 4,007 ....K5
French Settlement 829 ...L2
Frierson 700 ....C2
Frost 500 ....F2
Fryeburg 150 ....D2
Fullerton 300 ....D5
Galliano 4,294 ....K8
Galvez 200 ....L2
Garden City 225 ....H7
Garyville 3,181 ....M3

(continued)

Louisiana

SCALE
0 5 10 20 30 40 MI.
0 5 10 20 30 40 KM.

State Capitals .... ⊛
Parish Seats .... ◉
Canals
Major Limited Access Hwys. ──────

AREA 47,752 sq. mi. (123,678 sq. km.)
POPULATION 4,238,216
CAPITAL Baton Rouge
LARGEST CITY New Orleans
HIGHEST POINT Driskill Mtn. 535 ft. (163 m.)
SETTLED IN 1699
ADMITTED TO UNION April 30, 1812
POPULAR NAME Pelican State
STATE FLOWER Magnolia
STATE BIRD Eastern Brown Pelican

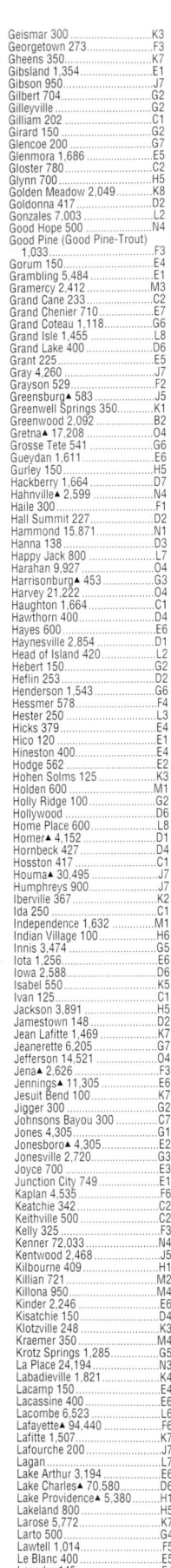

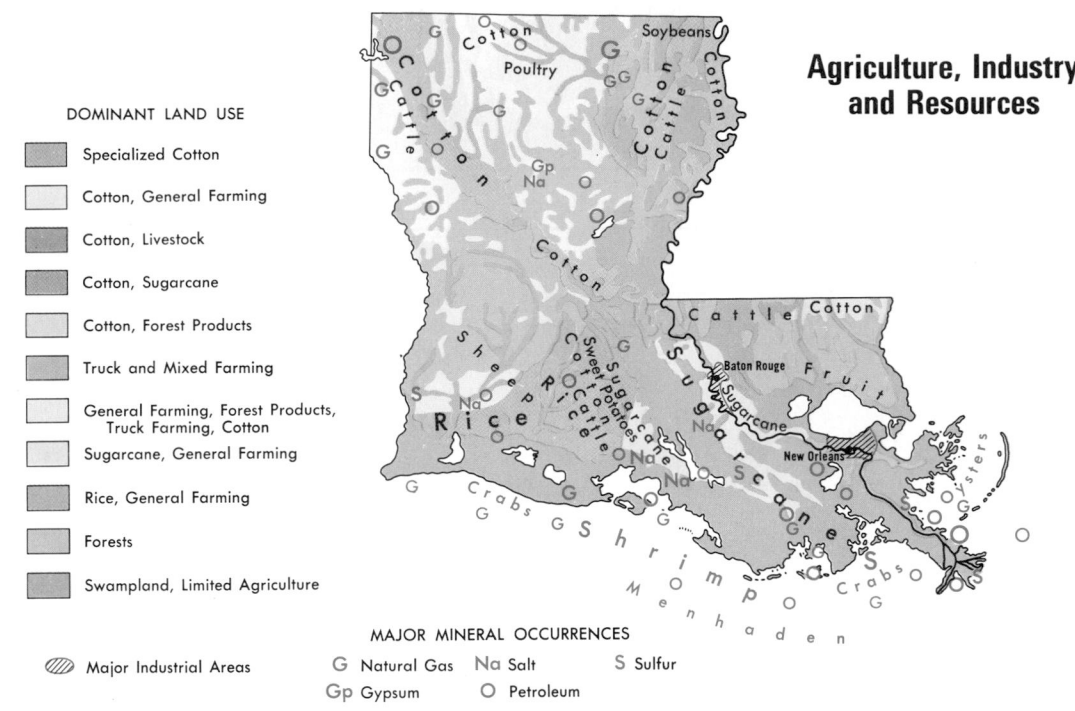

Agriculture, Industry and Resources

DOMINANT LAND USE

- Specialized Cotton
- Cotton, General Farming
- Cotton, Livestock
- Cotton, Sugarcane
- Cotton, Forest Products
- Truck and Mixed Farming
- General Farming, Forest Products, Truck Farming, Cotton
- Sugarcane, General Farming
- Rice, General Farming
- Forests
- Swampland, Limited Agriculture

Major Industrial Areas

MAJOR MINERAL OCCURRENCES

G Natural Gas   Na Salt   S Sulfur
Gp Gypsum   O Petroleum

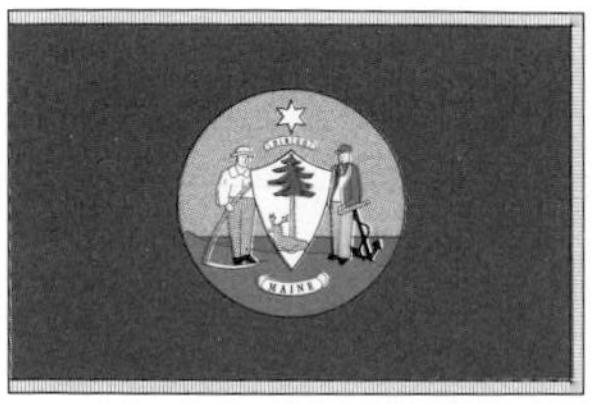

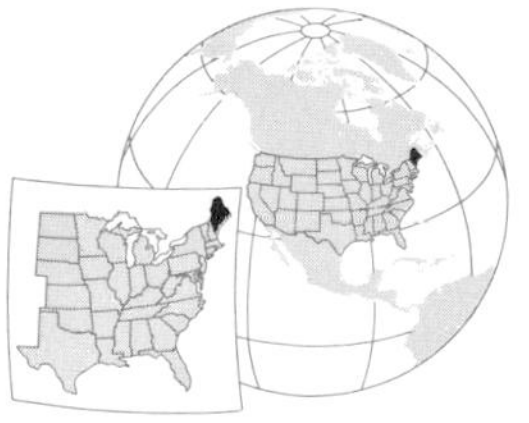

AREA 33,265 sq. mi. (86,156 sq. km.)
POPULATION 1,233,223
CAPITAL Augusta
LARGEST CITY Portland
HIGHEST POINT Katahdin 5,268 ft. (1606 m.)
SETTLED IN 1624
ADMITTED TO UNION March 15, 1820
POPULAR NAME Pine Tree State
STATE FLOWER White Pine Cone & Tassel
STATE BIRD Chickadee

COUNTIES

Androscoggin 105,259 C7
Aroostook 86,936 F2
Cumberland 243,135 C8
Franklin 29,008 B5
Hancock 46,948 G6
Kennebec 115,904 D7
Knox 36,310 E7
Lincoln 30,357 D7
Oxford 52,602 B7
Penobscot 146,601 F5
Piscataquis 18,653 E4
Sagadahoc 33,535 D7
Somerset 49,767 C4
Waldo 33,018 E6
Washington 35,308 H6
York 164,587 B9

CITIES and TOWNS

Abbot Village• 576 D5
Acton 850 B8
Acton• 1,727 B8
Addison 350 H6
Addison• 1,114 H6
Albion• 1,736 E6
Alexander• 478 H5
Alfred 1,890 B9
Alfred• 2,238 B9
Allagash• 359 F1
Alna• 571 D7
Alton• 771 F5
Amherst• 226 G6
Andover 350 B6
Andover• 953 B6
Anson 950 D6
Anson• 2,382 D6
Appleton• 1,069 E7
Argyle 202 F5
Ashland 750 G2
Ashland• 1,542 G2
Athens 300 D6
Athens• 897 D6
Atkinson• 332 E5
Auburn▲ 24,309 C7
Augusta (cap.)▲ 21,325 D7
Aurora• 82 G6
Bailey Island 500 D8
Bancroft H4
Bancroft• 66 H4
Bangor▲ 33,181 F6
Bar Harbor 2,685 G7
Bar Harbor• 2,768 G7
Bar Mills 800 C8
Baring 236 J5
Baring• 275 J5
Bass Harbor 450 G7
Bath▲ 9,799 D8
Bayside F7
Beals• 667 H7
Beddington• 43 H6
Belfast▲ 6,355 F7
Belgrade 950 D7
Belgrade• 2,375 D7
Belgrade Lakes 700 D6
Belmont• 652 E7
Benedicta• 225 G4
Benton• 2,312 D6
Berwick 2,378 B9
Berwick• 5,995 B9
Bethel 750 B7
Bethel• 2,329 B7
Biddeford 20,710 B9
Biddeford Pool 500 C9
Bingham 1,074 D5
Bingham• 1,071 D5
Birch Harbor 300 H7
Blaine-Mars Hill 1,921 H2
Blaine• 784 H2
Blanchard 78 D5
Blue Hill 850 F7
Blue Hill• 1,941 F7
Bolsters Mills 150 B7
Boothbay 200 D8
Boothbay• 2,648 D8
Boothbay Harbor 1,267 D8
Bowdoinham• 2,192 D7
Bowerbank• 72 E5
Bradford 150 F5
Bradford• 1,103 F5
Bradley• 1,136 F6
Brewer 9,021 F6
Bridgewater• 647 H3
Bridgton 1,639 B7
Bridgton• 2,195 B7
Brighton• 94 D5
Bristol 450 D8
Bristol• 2,326 D8
Brooklin• 785 F7
Brooks 900 E6
Brooksville• 760 F7
Brookton 175 H4
Brownfield 300 B8
Brownfield• 1,034 B8
Brownville 600 E5
Brownville• 1,506 E5
Brownville Junction 950 E5
Brunswick 10,990 C8
Brunswick• 14,683 C8
Bryant Pond 600 B7
Buckfield• 1,566 C7
Bucks Harbor 300 J6
Bucksport 2,853 F6
Bucksport• 2,989 F6
Burlington• 360 G5
Burnham• 961 E6
Buxton• 6,494 C8
Byron• 111 B6
Calais 3,963 J5
Cambridge• 490 E5
Camden 3,743 F7
Camden• 4,022 F7
Canaan• 1,636 D6
Canton• 951 C7
Cape Neddick 2,193 B9
Cape Porpoise 500 C9
Caratunk 98 C5
Cardville 223 F5
Caribou 9,415 G2
Carmel• 1,906 E6
Carrabassett Valley• 325 C5
Carroll• 185 G5
Carthage• 458 C6
Cary• 235 H4
Casco 400 B7
Casco• 3,018 B7
Castine• 1,161 F7
Centerville• 30 H6
Chapman• 422 G2
Charleston• 1,187 F5
Charlotte• 271 J5
Chebeague Island 900 C8
Chelsea• 2,497 D7
Cherryfield• 1,183 H6
Chester• 442 F5
Chesterville• 1,012 C6
China 2,918 E7
China• 3,713 E7
Chisholm 1,653 C7
Clifton• 607 G6
Clinton 1,305 D6
Clinton• 1,485 D6
Columbia• 437 H6
Columbia Falls• 552 H6
Cooper• 124 H6
Coopers Mills 200 E7
Corea 375 H7
Corinna• 2,196 E6
Cornish• 1,178 B8
Cornville• 1,008 D6
Costigan 200 F5
Cranberry Isles• 189 G7
Crawford• 89 H5
Crescent Lake 325 C7
Criehaven F8
Crouseville 450 G2
Crystal• 303 G4
Cumberland Center 2,015 C8
Cumberland Center• 1,890 C8
Cundys Harbor 150 D8
Cushing• 988 E7
Cutler 400 J6
Cutler• 779 J6
Damariscotta• 1,811 E7
Damariscotta-Newcastle 1,567 E7
Danforth 650 H4
Danforth• 710 H4
Deblois• 73 H6
Dedham• 1,229 F6
Deer Isle 600 F7
Deer Isle• 1,829 F7
Denmark• 855 B8
Dennysville• 355 J6
Derby 300 E5
Detroit• 751 E6
Dexter 3,118 E5
Dexter• 2,650 E5
Dixfield 1,725 C6
Dixfield• 1,300 C6
Dixmont• 1,007 E6
Dover-Foxcroft▲ 2,974 E5
Dover-Foxcroft• 3,077 E5
Dresden• 1,332 D7
Dry Mills 700 C8
Dryden 675 C6
Dyer Brook• 243 G3
Eagle Lake 675 F1
Eagle Lake• 942 F1
East Andover 250 B6
East Baldwin 175 B8
East Blue Hill 150 G7
East Boothbay 800 D8
East Corinth 525 F5
East Dixfield 250 C6
East Eddington 200 F6
East Hiram 198 B8
East Holden 600 F6
East Lebanon 950 B9
East Limington 200 B8
East Livermore 500 C7
East Machias 850 J6
East Machias• 1,218 J6
East Madison 400 D6
East Millinocket 2,361 F4
East Millinocket• 2,075 F4
East Parsonfield 400 B8
East Peru 200 C7
East Poland 200 C7
East Stoneham 300 B7
East Sullivan 496 G6
East Vassalboro 300 D7
East Waterboro 365 B8
East Wilton 650 C6
Easton• 1,291 H2
Eastport 1,965 K6
Eddington 250 F6
Eddington• 1,947 F6
Edgecomb• 993 D8
Edmunds 430 J6
Eliot• 5,329 B9
Ellsworth▲ 5,975 F6
Enfield 150 F5
Enfield• 1,476 F5
Etna• 977 E6
Eustis• 616 B5
Exeter• 937 E6
Fairbanks 400 C6
Fairfield 3,169 D6
Fairfield Center 975 D6
Fairfield• 2,794 D6
Falmouth 1,655 C8
Falmouth• 7,610 C8
Farmingdale 2,014 D7
Farmingdale• 2,070 D7
Farmington▲ 3,583 C6
Farmington• 4,197 C6
Farmington Falls 500 C6
Fayette• 855 C7
Five Islands 225 D8
Fort Fairfield 2,282 H2
Fort Fairfield• 1,729 H2
Fort Kent 2,375 F1
Fort Kent• 2,123 F1
Fort Kent Mills 200 F1
Foxcroft 2,974 E5
Frankfort• 1,020 F6
Franklin 350 G6
Franklin• 1,141 G6
Freedom• 593 E7
Freeport 1,906 C8
Freeport• 1,829 C8
Frenchboro• 44 G7
Frenchville 980 G1
Frenchville• 1,338 G1
Friendship 700 E7
Friendship• 1,099 E7
Fryeburg 1,644 A7
Fryeburg• 1,580 A7
Gardiner• 6,746 D7
Garland 300 E5
Garland• 1,064 E5
Georgetown 190 D8
Georgetown• 914 D8
Gilead• 204 B7
Glen Cove 250 E7
Glenburn• 3,198 F6
Goodwins Mills 340 B8
Goose Rocks Beach 200 C9
Gorham 4,052 C8
Gorham• 3,618 C8
Gouldsboro 498 H7
Gouldsboro• 1,986 H7
Grand Isle 600 G1
Grand Isle• 558 G1
Grand Lake Stream• 174 H5
Gray 525 C8
Gray• 5,904 C8
Great Pond• 59 G6
Greene• 3,661 C7
Greenville• 1,839 D5
Greenville 1,601 D5
Greenville Junction 650 D5
Guilford 1,235 E5
Guilford• 1,082 E5
Hallowell 2,534 D7
Hamlin• 204 H1
Hampden 3,538 F6
Hampden• 3,895 F6
Hampden Highlands 950 F6
Hancock• 1,757 G6
Hanover• 272 B7
Harmony 450 D6
Harmony• 838 D6
Harpswell• 5,012 D8
Harrington• 893 H6
Harrison• 1,951 B7
Hartford• 722 C7
Hartland 1,041 D6
Hartland• 1,038 D6
Haynesville• 243 G4
Hebron• 878 C7
Hermon• 3,755 F6
Highland Lake 600 C8
Hiram 175 B8
Hiram• 1,260 B8
Hodgdon• 1,257 H3
Hollis Center• 2,892 B8
Hope 175 E7
Hope• 1,017 E7
Houlton▲ 5,730 H3
Houlton• 5,627 H3
Howland 1,502 F5
Howland• 1,304 F5
Hudson• 1,048 F5
Hulls Cove 200 G7
Island Falls• 897 G3
Isle Au Haut• 57 F7
Islesboro 200 F7
Islesboro• 579 F7
Jackman 700 C4
Jackman• 920 C4
Jacksonville 200 J6
Jay 850 C7
Jay• 5,080 C7
Jefferson• 2,111 D7
Jonesboro• 585 J6
Jonesport 1,050 H6
Jonesport• 1,525 H6
Keegan 450 G1
Kenduskeag• 1,234 E6
Kennebunk 3,294 B9
Kennebunk• 4,206 B9
Kennebunk Beach 200 C9
Kennebunkport 1,685 C9
Kennebunkport• 1,100 C9
Kents Hill 300 D7
Kezar Falls 680 B8
Kingfield• 1,114 C6
Kingman 246 G4
Kingsbury• 13 D5
Kittery 5,465 B9
Kittery• 5,151 B9
Kittery Point 1,093 B9
Knox• 681 E6
Lagrange 250 F5
Lagrange• 509 F5
Lake View• 23 F5
Lamoine• 1,311 G7
Lee• 832 G5
Leeds• 1,669 C7
Levant• 1,627 F6
Lewiston 39,757 C7
Liberty 200 E7
Liberty• 790 E7
Lille 300 G1
Limerick• 1,688 B8
Limestone 1,334 H2
Limestone• 1,245 H2
Limington• 2,796 B8
Lincoln 3,524 G5
Lincoln• 3,399 G5
Lincoln Center 325 G5
Lincolnville 800 E7
Lincolnville• 1,809 E7
Lincolnville Center 200 E7
Linneus• 810 H3
Lisbon• 9,457 C7
Lisbon Falls 4,674 D7
Lisbon-Lisbon Center 1,865 C7
Litchfield• 2,650 D7
Little Deer Isle 475 F7
Little Falls-South Windham 1,715 C8
Littleton• 956 H3
Livermore 280 C7
Livermore• 1,950 C7
Livermore Falls 2,441 C7
Livermore Falls• 1,935 C7
Locke Mills 600 B7
Lovell 180 B7
Lovell• 888 B7
Lowell• 267 F5
Lubec 900 K6
Lubec• 1,853 K6
Ludlow• 430 G3
Machias▲ 1,277 J6
Machias• 1,773 J6
Machiasport 374 H6
Machiasport• 1,166 H6
Macwahoc• 114 G4
Madawaska 4,165 G1
Madawaska• 3,653 G1
Madison 2,788 D6
Madison• 2,956 D6
Madrid• 178 B6
Manchester• 2,099 D7
Mapleton• 1,853 G2
Mars Hill• 1,760 H2
Mars Hill-Blaine 1,717 H2
Masardis• 305 G3

(continued on following page)

Agriculture, Industry and Resources

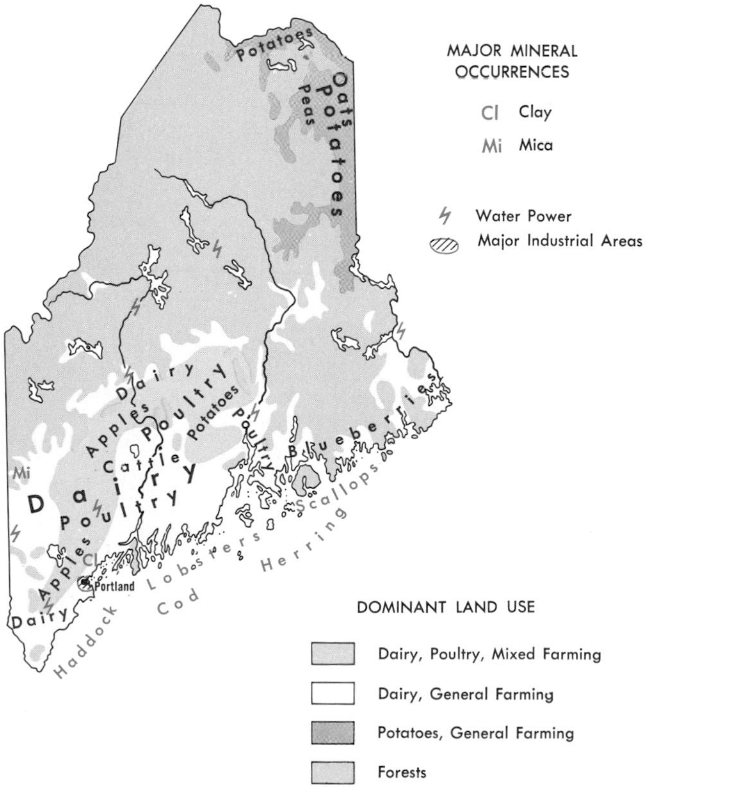
Potatoes
Peas
Oats
Potatoes
Dairy
Poultry
Potatoes
Apples
Poultry
Cattle
Dairy
Poultry
Blueberries
Scallops
Mi
Dairy
Poultry
Apples
Cl
Portland
Lobsters
Herring
Cod
Haddock
Dairy
MAJOR MINERAL OCCURRENCES
Cl Clay
Mi Mica
Water Power
Major Industrial Areas
DOMINANT LAND USE
Dairy, Poultry, Mixed Farming
Dairy, General Farming
Potatoes, General Farming
Forests

(continued)

Matinicus 66 ....F8
Mattawamkeag • 830....G5
Mechanic Falls 2,198 ....C7
Mechanic Falls • 2,388 ....C7
Meddybemps • 133....J5
Medford 194 ....F5
Medway • 1,922 ....G4
Mercer • 593 ....D6
Mexico 3,207 ....B6
Mexico • 2,302 ....B6
Milbridge • 1,305 ....H6
Milford 1,688 ....F6
Milford • 2,228....F6
Millinocket • 6,922....F4
Milo 2,255....F5
Milo • 2,129 ....F5
Minot 250 ....C7
Minot • 1,664 ....C7
Minturn 150....G7
Monhegan • 88 ....E8
Monmouth 500....D7
Monmouth • 3,353 ....C7
Monroe • 802....E6
Monson • 744....E5
Monticello • 872....H3
Montville • 877 ....E7
Moody 500 ....B9
Moose River • 233....C4
Morrill • 644 ....E7
Mount Desert 150....G7
Mount Desert • 1,899....G7
Mount Vernon • 1,362....D7
Naples • 2,860....B8
New Gloucester 400....C8
New Gloucester • 3,916....C8
New Harbor 850....E8
New Limerick • 524....G3
New Portland 300 ....C6
New Portland • 789 ....C6
New Sharon • 1,175 ....C6
New Sweden 175....G2
New Sweden • 715....G2
New Vineyard • 661....C6
Newburgh • 1,317....F6
Newcastle • 1,538 ....D7
Newcastle-Damariscotta 1,411....E7
Newfield 200....B8
Newfield • 1,042....B8
Newport 1,748 ....E6
Newport • 1,843 ....E6
Newry • 316....B6
Nobleboro • 1,455....D7
Norridgewock 1,318....D6
Norridgewock • 1,496 ....D6
North Anson 950 ....D6
North Belgrade 300 ....D7
North Berwick 1,436....B9
North Berwick • 1,568 ....B9
North Bridgton 300....B7
North Cutler 153....J6
North Fryeburg 250....B7
North Haven 400....F7
North Haven • 332 ....F7
North Jay 800 ....C6
North Limington 400 ....B8
North Livermore 250 ....C7
North Lubec 250 ....J6
North New Portland 500 ....C6
North Penobscot 403 ....F7
North Raymond 225 ....C8
North Turner 350....C7
North Vassalboro 950....D7
North Waldoboro 250 ....E7
North Waterboro 200....B8
North Waterford 390....B7
North Wayne 175....C7
North Whitefield 300 ....D7
North Windham 4,077 ....C8
North Yarmouth 500....C8
North Yarmouth • 2,429....C8
Northeast Harbor 800....G7
Northfield • 99....H6
Northport • 1,201 ....E7
Norway 2,653 ....B7
Norway • 3,023....B7
Oakfield • 846....G3
Oakland 3,387 ....D6
Oakland • 3,510....D6
Ocean Park 200 ....C9
Ogunquit 974....B9
Olamon 150....F5
Old Orchard Beach 6,023....C9
Old Orchard Beach • 7,789....C9
Old Town 8,317....F6
Oquossoc 150....B6
Orient • 157....H4
Orland 200 ....F6
Orland • 1,805....F6
Orono 9,891 ....F6
Orono • 9,789 ....F6
Orrington 250....F6
Orrington • 3,309....F6
Orrs Island 600....D8
Otisfield • 1,136....B7
Otter Creek 260 ....G7
Owls Head • 1,574 ....F7
Oxbow • 69 ....G3
Oxford 550....B7
Oxford • 1,284....B7
Palermo • 1,021....E7
Palmyra • 1,867....E6
Paris • 4,492....B7
Parkman • 790 ....D5
Passadumkeag • 428 ....F5
Patten 1,057....F4
Patten • 1,256....F4
Pejepscot 200....D8
Pemaquid 200....E8
Pembroke 300....J6
Pembroke • 852....J6
Penobscot 150 ....F7
Penobscot • 1,131 ....F7
Perham • 395....G2
Perry • 758....J6
Peru • 1,541 ....C6
Phillips • 1,148....C6
Phippsburg 1,527....D8
Phippsburg • 1,815....D8
Pine Point 650....C8
Pittsfield 3,117....E6
Pittsfield • 3,222....E6
Pittston • 2,444....D7
Plymouth • 1,152....E6
Poland 500 ....C7
Poland • 4,342....C7
Port Clyde 400....E8
Portage • 562....G2
Porter 225....B8
Porter • 1,301....B8
Portland▲ 64,358....C8
Pownal • 1,262....C8
Prentiss • 245 ....G5
Presque Isle 10,550....H2
Princeton • 973 ....H5
Prospect • 542....F6
Prospect Harbor 445 ....H7
Randolph • 1,949 ....D7
Rangeley 900....B6
Rangeley • 103 ....B6
Raymond 550 ....B8
Raymond • 3,311 ....B8
Readfield 300 ....D7
Readfield • 2,033....D7
Red Beach 210....J5
Richmond 1,578....D7
Richmond • 1,775....D7
Richmond Corner 200 ....D7
Ripley • 445....E5
Robbinston 200....J5
Robbinston • 495....J5
Robinsons 160 ....H3
Rockland▲ 7,972....E7
Rockport 875 ....E7
Rockport • 2,854 ....E7
Rockville 250 ....E7
Rockwood 265 ....D4
Rome • 758....D6
Roque Bluffs • 234....H6
Round Pond 400....E8
Roxbury • 437 ....B6
Rumford 6,256 ....B6
Rumford • 5,419....B6
Rumford Center 325....B7
Rumford Point 320....B6
Sabattus 1,234....C7
Sabattus • 3,696....C7
Saco 15,181....C8
Saint Agatha • 1,035 ....G1
Saint Albans • 1,400....E6
Saint David 915....G1
Saint Francis • 839 ....E1
Saint George 700....E7
Saint George • 1,948 ....E7
Saint John • 322....F1
Sandy Point 350....F7
Sanford 10,268....B9
Sanford • 10,296....B9
Sangerville • 1,398 ....E5
Scarborough 2,280....C8
Scarborough • 2,586....C8
Seal Cove 215....G7
Seal Harbor 500....G7
Searsmont 400 ....E7
Searsmont • 938....E7
Searsport 1,348 ....F7
Searsport • 1,151....F7
Sebago Lake 800 ....B8
Sebec • 554 ....E5
Seboeis • 40....F5
Sedgwick • 905....F7
Shapleigh • 1,911 ....B8
Shawmut 500 ....D6
Sheepscott 150....D7
Sheridan 300....F2
Sherman 1,021 ....G4
Sherman • 1,027 ....G4
Sherman Mills 600 ....G4
Sherman Station 650 ....F4
Shirley Mills 242....D5
Shirley Mills • 208....D5
Sidney • 2,593....D7
Sinclair • 264....G1
Skowhegan▲ 6,517....D6
Skowhegan • 6,990....D6
Smithfield • 865 ....D6
Smyrna Mills • 354....G3
Soldier Pond 500 ....F1
Solon • 916 ....D6
Somerville • 458....D7
Somesville (Mount Desert) 150....D7
Sorrento • 295....G7
South Berwick 2,120....B9
South Berwick • 5,877....B9
South Bridgton 373 ....B8
South Bristol • 825....D8
South Casco 750 ....B8
South China 225....D7
South Eliot 3,1,12....B9
South Harpswell 650 ....C8
South Hiram 350 ....B8
South Hope 200....E7
South La Grange 150 ....F5
South Lebanon 200 ....A9
South Lincoln 150....F5
South Monmouth 400 ....D7
South Orrington 400 ....F6
South Paris▲ 2,320....C7
South Penobscot 150....F7
South Portland 23,163....C8
South Sanford 3,929....B9
South Thomaston • 1,227....E7
South Waldoboro 300....E7
South Waterford 300 ....B7
South Windham (Little Falls-South Windham) C8
Southport 400 ....D8
Southport • 645....D8
Southwest Harbor 1,052....G7
Southwest Harbor • 1,952....G7
Springfield • 406 ....G5
Springvale 3,542....B9
Stacyville 155....F4
Stacyville • 480 ....F4
Standish 700....B8
Standish • 7,678....B8
Starks • 508 ....D6
Steep Falls 500 ....B8
Stetson • 847....E6
Steuben 190 ....H6
Steuben • 1,084 ....H6
Stillwater 700 ....F6
Stockholm • 286 ....G1
Stockton Springs 500....F7
Stockton Springs • 1,383....F7
Stonington • 1,252....F7
Stow • 283 ....A7
Stratton 600....B5
Strong • 1,217....C6
Sullivan • 1,118....G6
Sumner • 761 ....C7
Sunset 165....F7
Surry • 1,004 ....F7
Swans Island • 348 ....G7
Swanville • 1,130....E6
Sweden • 222 ....B7
Temple • 560....C6
Tenants Harbor 900 ....E8
Thomaston 2,348....E7
Thomaston • 2,445 ....E7
Thorndike • 702....E6
Topsfield • 235....H5
Topsham 4,657 ....D8
Topsham • 6,147....D8
Tremont 175....G7
Tremont • 1,324....G7
Trenton • 1,060....G7
Trevett 400 ....D8
Troy • 802....E6
Turner 400....C7
Turner • 4,315 ....C7
Union 300 ....E7
Union • 1,989 ....E7
Unity • 36....E6
Upper Frenchville 405....G1
Upton • 70....B6
Van Buren 3,282....G1
Van Buren • 2,759....G1
Vanceboro • 201 ....J4
Vassalboro • 3,679....D7
Veazie • 1,633....F6
Vienna • 417....D6
Vinalhaven • 1,072....F7
Waite • 119 ....H5
Waldo • 626....E7
Waldoboro 1,195 ....E7
Waldoboro • 1,420 ....E7
Walnut Hill 400 ....C8
Waltham • 276 ....G6
Warren 770....E7
Warren • 3,192 ....E7
Washburn 1,221....G2
Washburn • 1,880....G2
Washington • 1,185....E7
Waterboro 700....B8
Waterboro • 4,510....B8
Waterford • 1,299....B7
Waterville 17,173....D6
Wayne 175 ....D7
Wayne • 1,029....D7
Weeks Mills 235....E7
Weld • 430....C6
Wellington • 270 ....D5
Wells 950....B9
Wells • 7,778....B9
Wells Beach 600 ....B9
Wesley • 146....H6
West Baldwin 198....B8
West Bath • 1,716 ....D8
West Bethel 160....B7
West Brooksville 156 ....F7
West Buxton 185 ....B8
West Enfield 609....F5
West Farmington 700 ....C6
West Forks • 63....D5
West Franklin 350....G6
West Gouldsboro 225....G7
West Jonesport 400 ....H6
West Kennebunk 750....B9
West Lubec 275 ....J6
West Minot 400 ....C7
West Newfield 300....B8
West Paris • 1,514....B7
West Peru 700 ....C7
West Poland 250 ....C7
West Rockport 350 ....E7
West Scarborough 500....C8
West Tremont 250....G7
Westbrook 16,121 ....C8
Westfield • 589....G2
Weston • 207 ....H4
Whitefield 550 ....D7
Whitefield • 1,931....D7
Whiting • 407....J6
Whitneyville • 241 ....H6
Willimantic • 170 ....E5
Wilton 4,382....C6
Wilton • 2,453 ....C6
Windsor • 1,895....D7
Winn 250....G5
Winn • 479....G5
Winslow 5,903....D6
Winslow • 5,436....D6
Winter Harbor • 1,157....G7
Winterport 1,126....F6
Winterport • 1,274....F6
Winterville • 217 ....F2
Winthrop 3,264....C7
Winthrop • 2,819....C7
Wiscasset 975 ....D7
Wiscasset • 1,233 ....D7
Woodland • 1,287 ....H5
Woolwich • 2,570....D8
Wyman Dam 300....D5
Yarmouth 2,981....C8
Yarmouth • 3,338....C8
York 4,530....B9
York Beach 900 ....B9
York Harbor 2,555....B9
York • 9,818 ....B9

OTHER FEATURES

Abraham (mt.) C5
Acadia Nat'l Park G7
Allagash (lake)....D3
Allagash (riv.)....E2
Androscoggin (riv.)....C7
Aroostook (riv.) G2
Attean (pond)....C4
Baker (lake) D3
Baskahegan (lake) H5
Bear (riv.)....B6
Big (brook)....E2
Big (lake) H5
Big Black (riv.)....D2
Bigelow (bight) C9
Big Spencer (mt.)....E4
Black (pond)....D3
Blue (mt.)....C6
Blue Hill (bay)....G7
Bog (lake)....H6
Brassua (lake)....D4
Casco (bay)....C8
Cathance (lake) J6
Caucomgomoc (lake) D3
Center (pond)....E5
Chamberlain (lake)....E3
Chemquasabamticook (lake) ..D3
Chesuncook (lake) E3
Chiputneticook (lakes)....H4
Clayton (lake) D2
Clifford (lake)....H5
Cold Stream (pond)....G5
Crawford (lake)....H5
Cross (isl.) J6
Cross (lake)....G1
Cupsuptic (riv.)....B5
Dead (riv.)....C5
Deer (isl.) F7
Duck (isls.) G7
Eagle (lake) E3
Eagle (lake) F1
East Machias (riv.)....H6
East Musquash (lake) H5
Elizabeth (cape) C8
Ellis (pond) B6
Ellis (riv.) B6
Embden (pond)....D6
Endless (lake)....F5
Englishman (bay) J6
Eskutassis (pond)....G5
Fifth (lake) H5
Fish (riv.)....F2
Fish River (lake) F2
Flagstaff (lake) C5
Fourth (lake)....H5
Frenchman (bay) G7
Gardner (lake) J6
Georges (isls.) E8
Graham (lake)....G6
Grand (lake)....H4
Grand Falls (lake)....H5
Grand Lake Seboeis (lake)....F3
Grand Manan (chan.)....K6
Great Moose (lake) D6
Great Wass (isl.) J7
Green (isl.) F8
Harrington (lake)....E4
Haut (isl.)....G7
Indian (pond)....D4
Islesboro (isl.)....F7
Jo-Mary (lakes)....E4
Katahdin (mt.) F4
Kennebec (riv.) D7
Kezar (lake)....B7
Kezar (pond) B7
Kingsbury (pond) D5
Little Black (riv.)....E1
Little Madawaska (riv.) G2
Lobster (lake)....E4
Long (lake) B7
Long (lake)....E2
Long (lake) G1
Long (pond)....C4
Long (pond) D6
Long (pond)....E5
Long Falls (dam)....C5
Longfellow (mts.) B6
Loon (lake) D3
Loring A.F.B. 7,829....H2
Lower Roach (pond) E4
Lower Sysladobsis (lake)....G5
Machias (bay) J6
Machias (riv.) F2
Machias (riv.) H6
Machias Seal (isl.)....J7
Madagascal (pond)....G5
Marshall (isl.) G7
Matinicus Rock (isl.) F8
Mattamiscontis (lake)....F4
Mattawamkeag (lake) G4
Mattawamkeag (riv.)....G4
Meddybemps (lake)....J5
Metinic (isl.)....E8
Millinocket (lake)....F3
Millinocket (lake)....F4
Molunkus (lake)....G4
Monhegan (isl.)....E8
Moose (pond)....B7
Moose (riv.)....D4
Moosehead (lake)....D4
Mooseleuk (stream) F2
Mooselookmeguntic (lake) B6
Mopang (lake) H6
Mount Desert (isl.) G7
Mount Desert Rock (isl.) G8
Moxie (lake)....D5
Munsungan (lake)....E3
Muscongus (bay)....E8
Musquacook (lakes)....E2
Nahmakanta (lake)....E4
Nicatous (lake) G5
Nollesemic (lake)....F4
Old (stream) H6
Onawa (lake)....E5
Parlin (pond)....C4
Parmachenee (lake) B5
Passamaquoddy (bay)....J5
Passamaquoddy Ind. Res....J6
Pemadumcook (lake) E4
Penobscot (bay)....F7
Penobscot (lake)....C4
Penobscot (riv.) F5
Penobscot Ind. Res. F6
Pierce (pond)....C5
Piscataqua (riv.)....B9
Piscataquis (riv.)....E5
Pleasant (lake) E3
Pleasant (lake) G3
Pleasant (lake)....H5
Pleasant (riv.)....H6
Pocomoonshine (lake)....H5
Portage (lake)....F2
Presque Isle A.F.B. G2
Priestly (lake)....E2
Pushaw (lake) F6
Ragged (isl.)....F8
Ragged (lake)....E4
Rainbow (lake)....E4
Rangeley (lake)....B6
Richardson (lakes)....B6
Rocky (lake) J6
Round (pond) E2
Rowe (lake)....F2
Saco (riv.)....B8
Saint Croix (riv.)....J5
Saint Croix Island Nat'l Mon....J5
Saint Francis (riv.)....E1
Saint Froid (lake)....F2
Saint John (pond)....D3
Saint John (riv.)....G1
Salmon Falls (riv.)....B9
Sandy (riv.)....C6
Schoodic (lake) F5
Scraggly (lake)....F3
Scraggly (lake) H5
Seal (isl.)....F8
Sebago (lake)....B8
Sebasticook (lake)....E6
Seboeis (lake) F5
Seboeis (riv.)....F3
Seboomook (lake) D4
Shallow (lake) E3
Small (cape) D8
Sourdnahunk (lake)....F3
Spencer (pond)....D4
Spencer (stream)....C5
Spider (lake) E3
Squa Pan (lake)....G2
Square (lake) G1
Sunday (riv.)....B6
Swift (riv.)....B6
Sysladobsis, Lower (lake)....G5
Third (lake)....H5
Twin (lakes)....F4
Umbagog (lake) A6
Umcalcus (lake)....G3
Umsaskis (lake) E2
Union, West Branch (riv.)....G6
Vinalhaven (isl.) F7
Wassataquoik (stream) F4
Webb (lake) C6
Webster (brook)....E3
West Grand (lake)....H5
West Musquash (lake)....H5
West Quoddy (head)....K6
Wilson (ponds) E5
Winnecook (lake) E6
Wooden Ball (isl.)....F8
Wyman (lake) C5
Wytopitlock (lake)....G4

▲County seat.
• Population of town or township.

Topography

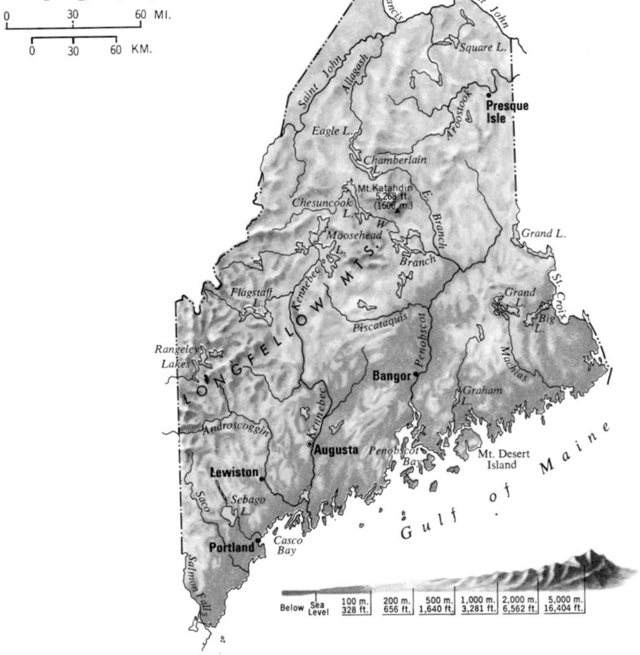

0
30
60 MI.
0
30
60 KM.
St. Francis
Saint John
Square L.
Saint John
Allagash
Aroostook
Presque Isle
Eagle L.
Chamberlain L.
Mt. Katahdin 5,268 ft. (1606 m.)
Chesuncook L.
E. Branch
W. Branch
Moosehead L.
Grand L.
LONGFELLOW MTS.
Flagstaff L.
Kennebec
Grand L.
St. Croix
Big L.
Piscataquis
Penobscot
Rangeley Lakes
Machias
Bangor
Graham L.
Androscoggin
Kennebec
Augusta
Penobscot Bay
Mt. Desert Island
Gulf of Maine
Lewiston
Saco
Sebago L.
Portland
Casco Bay
Salmon Falls
Below Sea Level
100 m. 328 ft.
200 m. 656 ft.
500 m. 1,640 ft.
1,000 m. 3,281 ft.
2,000 m. 6,562 ft.
5,000 m. 16,404 ft.

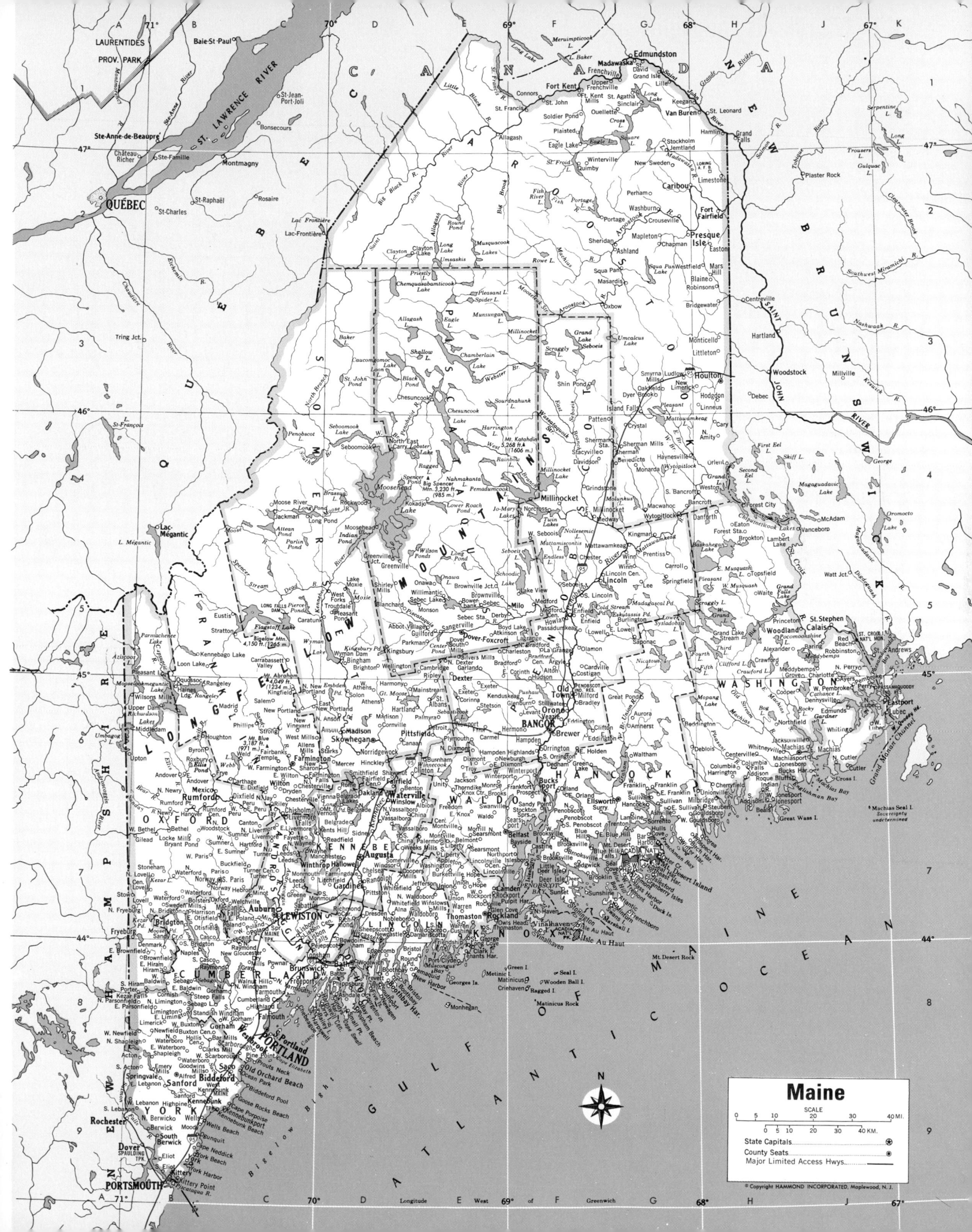

Maine

SCALE

| 0 | 5 | 10 | 20 | 30 | 40 MI. |

| 0 | 5 | 10 | 20 | 30 | 40 KM. |

State Capitals .... ⊛
County Seats .... ◉
Major Limited Access Hwys. .... ▬

© Copyright HAMMOND INCORPORATED, Maplewood, N.J.

(continued)

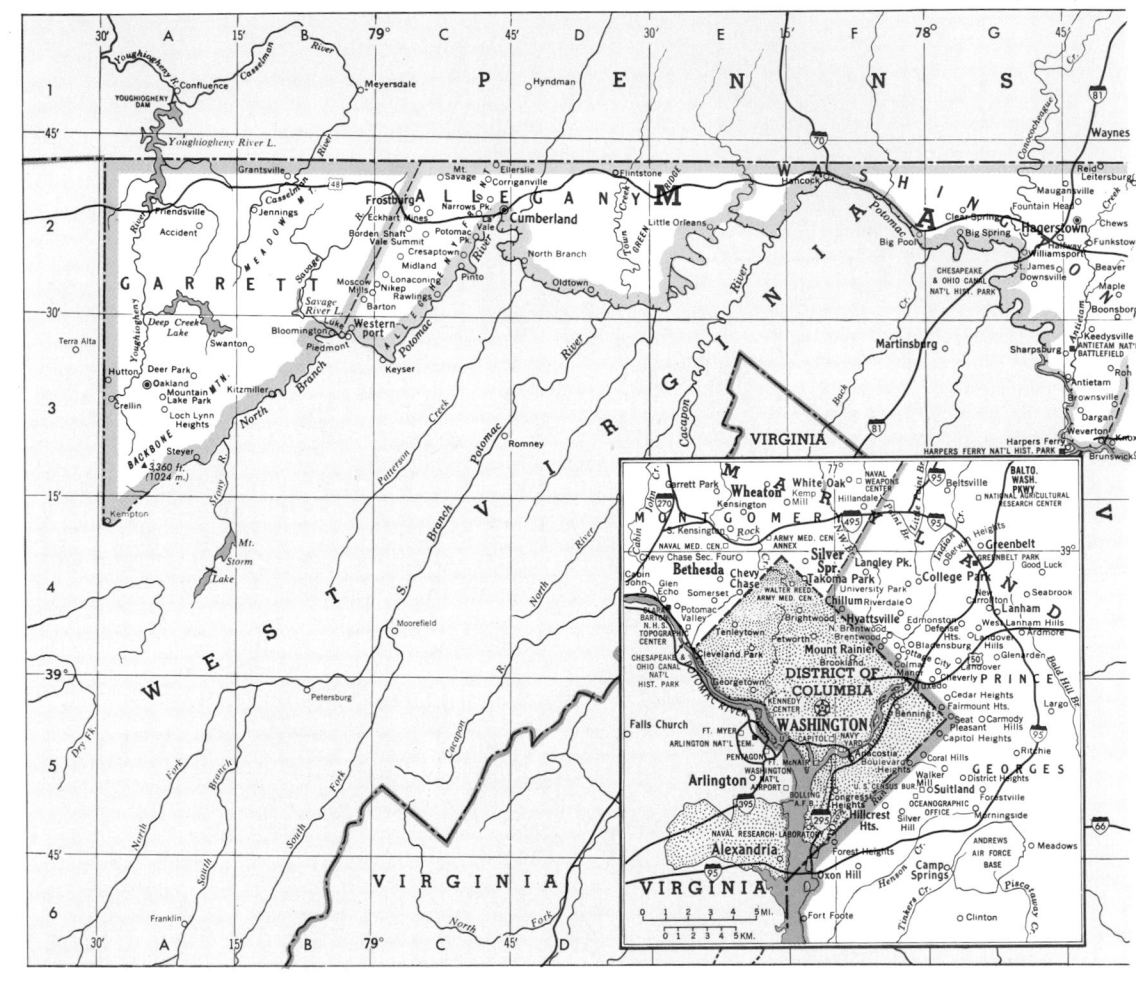

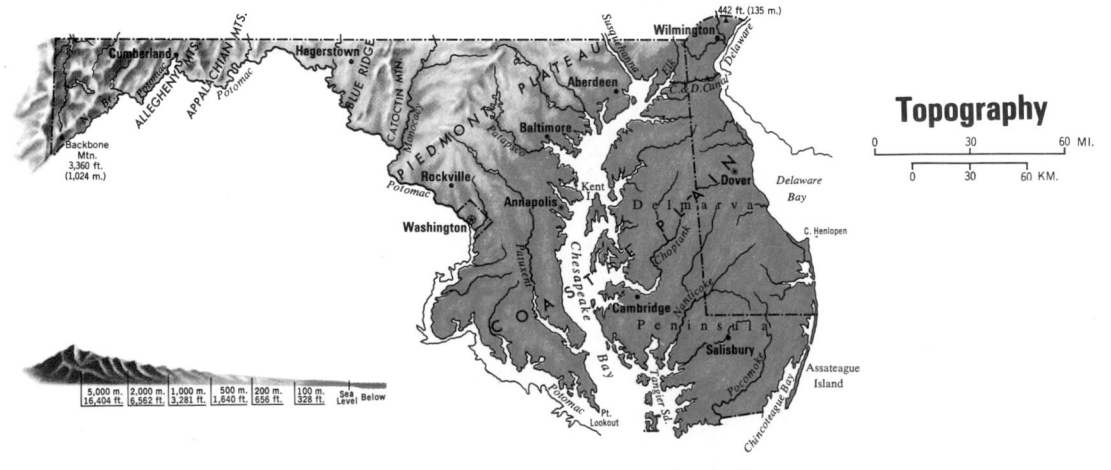

Topography

MARYLAND

AREA 10,460 sq. mi. (27,091 sq. km.)
POPULATION 4,798,622
CAPITAL Annapolis
LARGEST CITY Baltimore
HIGHEST POINT Backbone Mtn. 3,360 ft. (1024 m.)
SETTLED IN 1634
ADMITTED TO UNION April 28, 1788
POPULAR NAME Old Line State; Free State
STATE FLOWER Black-eyed Susan
STATE BIRD Baltimore Oriole

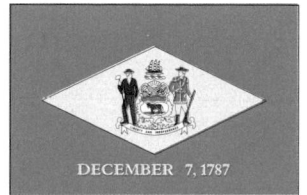

DECEMBER 7, 1787

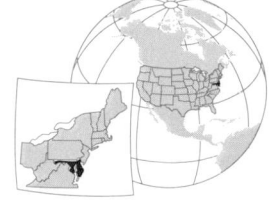

DELAWARE

AREA 2,044 sq. mi. (5,294 sq. km.)
POPULATION 668,696
CAPITAL Dover
LARGEST CITY Wilmington
HIGHEST POINT Ebright Road 442 ft. (135 m.)
SETTLED IN 1627
ADMITTED TO UNION December 7, 1787
POPULAR NAME First State; Diamond State
STATE FLOWER Peach Blossom
STATE BIRD Blue Hen Chicken

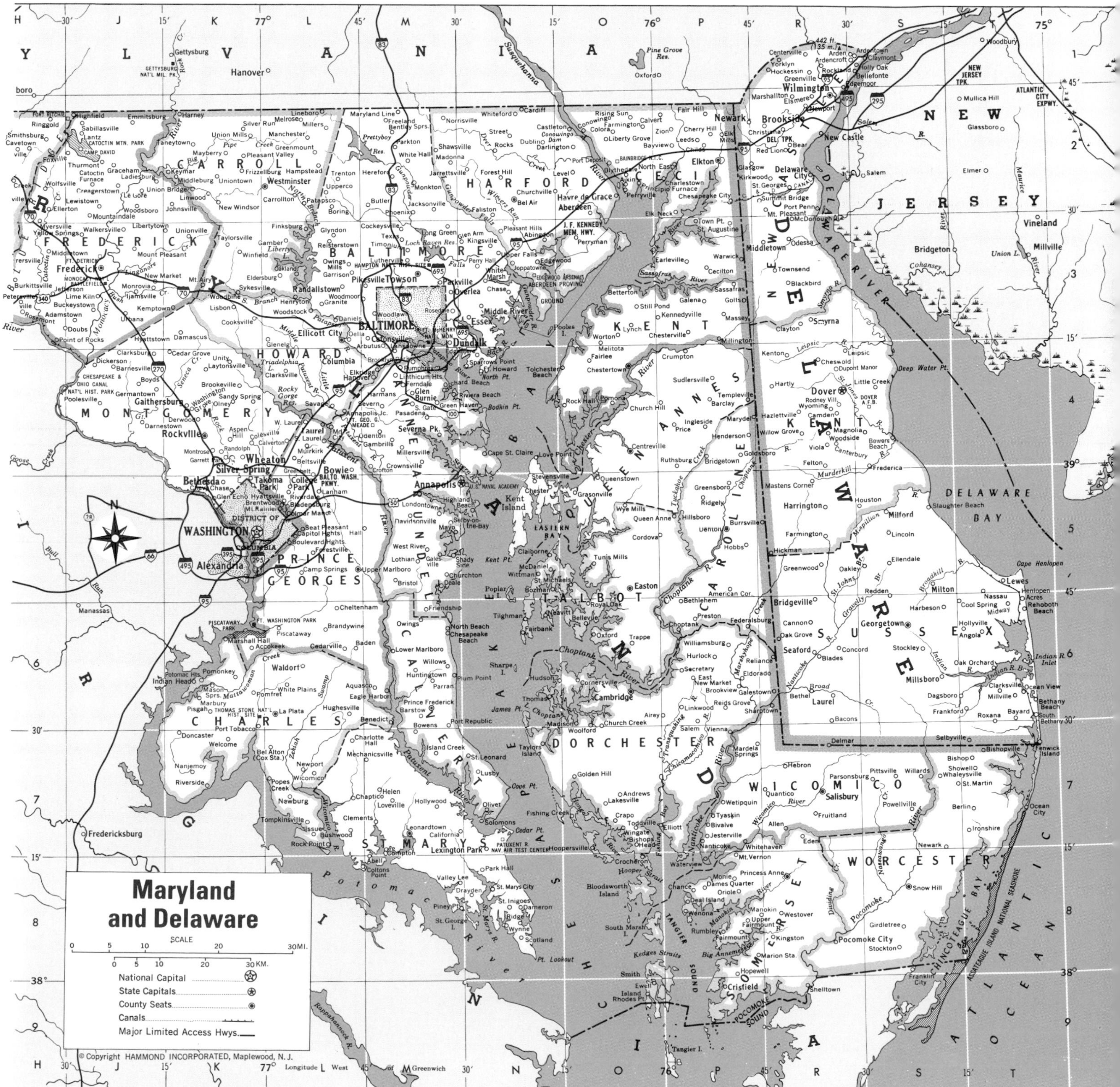

Maryland and Delaware

SCALE

National Capital .... ✪
State Capitals .... ✶
County Seats .... ⊙
Canals
Major Limited Access Hwys. ___

© Copyright HAMMOND INCORPORATED, Maplewood, N.J.

Agriculture, Industry and Resources

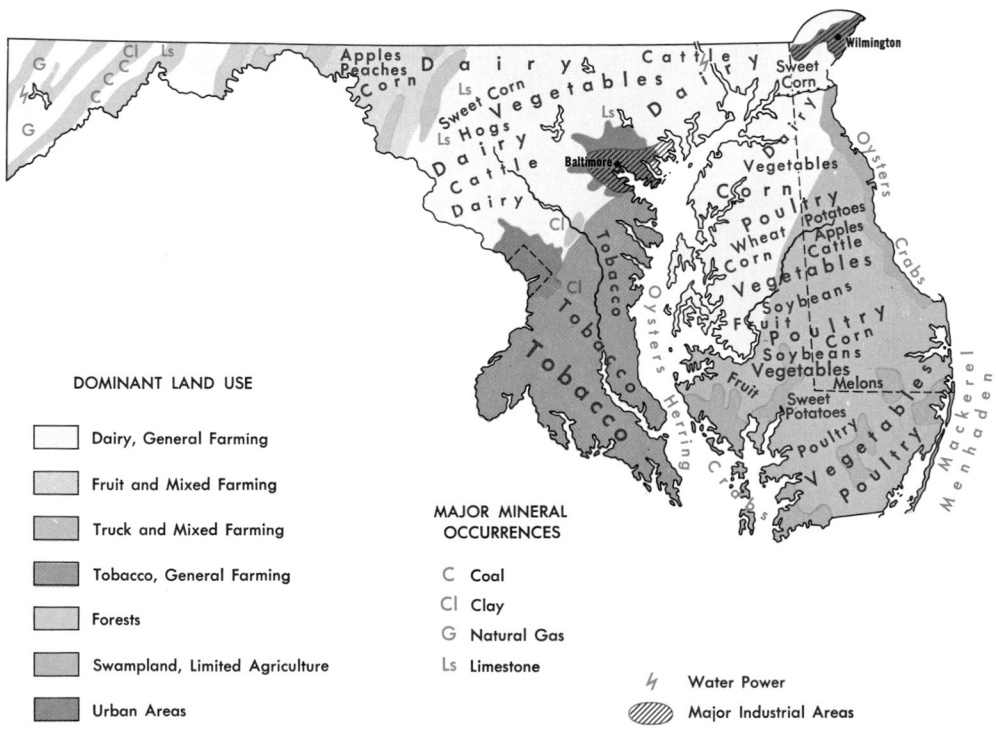

DOMINANT LAND USE

Dairy, General Farming

Fruit and Mixed Farming

Truck and Mixed Farming

Tobacco, General Farming

Forests

Swampland, Limited Agriculture

Urban Areas

MAJOR MINERAL OCCURRENCES

C Coal

Cl Clay

G Natural Gas

Ls Limestone

⚡ Water Power

▨ Major Industrial Areas

▲County seat.

MASSACHUSETTS

AREA 8,284 sq. mi. (21,456 sq. km.)
POPULATION 6,029,051
CAPITAL Boston
LARGEST CITY Boston
HIGHEST POINT Mt. Greylock 3,491 ft.
(1064 m.)
SETTLED IN 1620
ADMITTED TO UNION February 6, 1788
POPULAR NAME Bay State; Old Colony
STATE FLOWER Mayflower
STATE BIRD Chickadee

RHODE ISLAND

AREA 1,212 sq. mi. (3,139 sq. km.)
POPULATION 1,005,984
CAPITAL Providence
LARGEST CITY Providence
HIGHEST POINT Jerimoth Hill 812 ft.
(247 m.)
SETTLED IN 1636
ADMITTED TO UNION May 29, 1790
POPULAR NAME Little Rhody; Ocean State
STATE FLOWER Violet
STATE BIRD Rhode Island Red

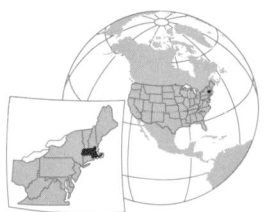

Agriculture, Industry and Resources

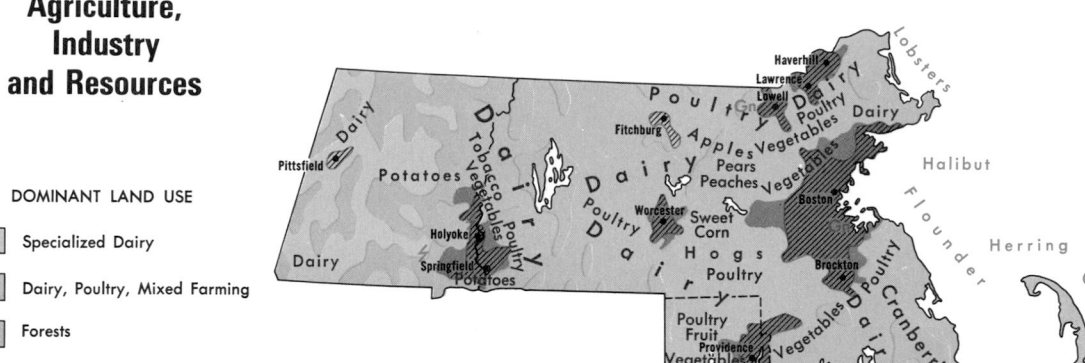

DOMINANT LAND USE

- Specialized Dairy
- Dairy, Poultry, Mixed Farming
- Forests
- Urban Areas

MAJOR MINERAL OCCURRENCES

Gn Granite

⚡ Water Power ▨ Major Industrial Areas

(continued on following page)

Pembroke • 14,544 .... L4	Raynham Center 3,709 ...... K5	Salem▲ 38,091 .... E5	Sherborn • 3,989 .... A8
Pepperell 2,350 .... H2	Raynham 9,867 .... K5	Salisbury 3,729 .... L1	Shirley 1,559 .... H2
Pepperell • 10,098 .... H2	Reading • 22,539 .... C5	Salisbury 6,882 .... L1	Shirley • 6,118 .... H2
Petersham • 1,131 .... F3	Readville C8	Salisbury Beach 950 .... L1	Shore Acres D4
Phillipston • 1,485 .... F2	Rehoboth • 8,656 .... D6	Sand Hills M4	Shrewsbury • 24,146 .... H3
Pigeon Cove M2	Revere 42,786 .... D6	Sandisfield 667 .... B4	Shutesbury • 1,561 .... E3
Pinehurst 6,614 .... B5	Richmond • 1,677 .... A3	Sandwich 2,998 .... N5	Somerset • 17,655 .... M6
Pittsfield 48,622 .... A3	Rochdale 1,105 .... G4	Sandwich • 15,489 .... N5	Somerville 76,210 .... C6
Plainfield • 571 .... C2	Rochester 3,921 .... L6	Saugus • 25,549 .... D6	South Acton 950 .... J3
Plainville • 6,871 .... J4	Rockland 16,123 .... L4	Saundersville 975 .... G4	South Amherst 5,053 .... E3
Pleasant Lake 525 .... O6	Rockport 5,448 .... M2	Savoy • 634 .... B2	South Ashburnham 1,110 .... F2
Plymouth▲ 7,258 .... M5	Rowe • 378 .... C2	Saxonville A7	South Barre 900 .... F3
Plymouth • 45,608 .... M5	Rowley 1,144 .... L2	Scituate 5,180 .... F8	South Braintree • D8
Plympton • 2,384 .... M6	Rowley • 4,452 .... L2	Scituate • 16,786 .... F8	South Carver 750 .... L6
Pocasset 2,756 .... M5	Roxbury C7	Seekonk • 13,046 .... J5	South Chatham 725 .... O6
Princeton • 3,189 .... G3	Royalston • 1,147 .... F2	Sharon 5,893 .... K4	South Dartmouth L6
Provincetown▲ 3,374 .... O4	Russell 1,594 .... C4	Sharon • 15,517 .... K4	South Deerfield 1,906 .... D3
Provincetown • 3,561 .... O4	Rutland 2,145 .... G3	Shawsheen Village K2	South Dennis 3,559 .... O6
Quincy 84,985 .... D7	Rutland • 4,936 .... G3	Sheffield • 2,910 .... A4	South Duxbury 3,017 .... M4
Randolph • 30,093 .... D8	Sagamore 2,589 .... M5	Shelburne Falls 1,996 .... D2	South Easton K4

South Egremont 700 .... A4	Southbridge 13,631 .... G4	Swansea Center 950 .... K5
South Grafton (Fisherville) ... H4	Southbridge • 17,816 .... G4	Taunton▲ 49,832 .... K5
South Groveland 950 .... L2	Southville 600 .... H3	Teaticket 1,856 .... M6
South Hadley Falls D4	Southwick • 7,667 .... C4	Templeton • 6,438 .... F2
South Hadley • 16,685 .... D4	Spencer 6,306 .... F3	Tewksbury 27,266 .... K2
South Hanover L4	Spencer • 11,645 .... F3	Thorndike 900 .... E4
South Harwich 875 .... O6	Springfield▲ 156,983 .... D4	Three Rivers 3,006 .... E4
South Lancaster 1,772 .... H3	Sterling • 6,481 .... G3	Tolland 289 .... B4
South Lee 600 .... A3	Stockbridge 2,408 .... A3	Topsfield 2,711 .... L2
South Lynnfield D5	Stockbridge • 2,328 .... A3	Topsfield • 5,754 .... L2
South Middleboro 600 .... L5	Stoneham • 22,203 .... C6	Townsend 1,164 .... H2
South Natick A7	Stoughton 26,777 .... K4	Townsend • 8,496 .... H2
South Orleans 800 .... O6	Stow • 5,328 .... H3	Townsend Harbor 600 .... G2
South Sudbury J3	Sturbridge 2,093 .... F4	Truro • 1,573 .... O5
South Walpole K4	Sturbridge • 7,775 .... F4	Turners Falls 4,731 .... D2
South Wellfleet 583 .... P5	Sudbury • 14,358 .... A6	Tyngsboro 5,683 .... J2
South Weymouth E8	Sunderland • 3,399 .... D3	Tyringham • 369 .... A4
South Yarmouth 10,358 .... O6	Sutton 6,824 .... G4	Upton-West Upton 2,347 ...... H4
Southampton • 4,478 .... D4	Swampscott 13,650 .... E6	Upton • H4
Southborough • 6,628 .... H3	Swansea 15,411 .... K5	Uxbridge • 10,415 .... H4

Boston and Vicinity

Vineyard Haven 1,762 .... M7
Waban B7
Wakefield 24,825 .... C5
Wales • 1,566 .... F4
Walpole 5,495 .... B8
Walpole • 20,212 .... B8
Waltham 57,878 .... B6
Ware 6,533 .... E3
Ware • 9,808 .... E3
Wareham 19,232 .... L5
Wareham • 18,457 .... L5
Wareham Center 2,607 .... L5
Warren 1,516 .... F4
Warren • 4,437 .... F4
Warwick 740 .... B3
Washington • 615 .... B3
Watertown 33,284 .... B6
Waverley B6
Wayland • 11,874 .... A7
Webster 11,849 .... G4

Webster • 16,196 .... G4
Wellesley • 26,615 .... B7
Wellesley Hills B7
Wellfleet • 2,493 .... O5
Wendell • 899 .... E2
Wenham • 4,212 .... L2
West Acton 975 .... H3
West Barnstable 1,508 .... N6
West Boxford 950 .... K2
West Boylston • 6,611 .... G3
West Bridgewater • 6,389 .... K4
West Brookfield 1,419 .... F4
West Brookfield • 3,532 .... F4
West Chatham 1,504 .... O6
West Chelmsford J2
West Concord 5,761 .... A6
West Dennis 2,307 .... O6
West Falmouth 1,752 .... M6
West Groton 950 .... H2
West Hanover L4

West Harwich 883 .... O6
West Mansfield 950 .... K5
West Medway J4
West Newbury • 3,421 .... L1
West Newton B7
West Springfield 27,537 .... D4
West Stockbridge • 1,483 .... A3
West Tisbury • 1,704 .... M7
West Townsend 950 .... H2
West Upton-Upton H4
West Wareham 2,059 .... L5
West Warren F4
West Yarmouth 5,409 .... N6
Westborough 3,917 .... H3
Westborough • 14,133 .... H3
Westfield • 38,372 .... D4
Westford • 16,392 .... J2
Westhampton • 1,327 .... C3
Westminster • 6,191 .... G2
Weston • 10,200 .... B6

Westport 13,852 .... K6
Westport • 13,763 .... K6
Westwood • 12,557 .... B8
Weymouth 54,063 .... D8
Whately • 1,375 .... D3
Whitinsville 5,639 .... H4
Whitman • 13,240 .... L4
Wilbraham 3,352 .... E4
Wilbraham • 12,635 .... E4
Williamsburg • 2,515 .... C3
Williamstown 4,791 .... B2
Williamstown • 8,220 .... B2
Wilmington • 17,654 .... C5
Winchendon 4,316 .... F2
Winchendon • 8,805 .... F2
Winchester • 20,267 .... C6
Windsor • 770 .... B2
Winthrop • 18,127 .... D6
Woburn 35,943 .... C6
Woods Hole 1,080 .... M6
Worcester▲ 169,759 .... H3
Worthington • 1,156 .... C3
Wrentham • 9,006 .... J4
Yarmouth Port 4,271 .... N6
Yarmouth • 21,174 .... O6

OTHER FEATURES

Adams Nat'l Hist. Site D7
Agawam (riv.) M5
Allerton (pt.) E7
Ann (cape) M2
Ashmere (lake) B3
Assabet (riv.) H3
Assawompset (pond) L5
Batchelor (brook) D3
Berkshire (hills) B4
Big (pond) B4
Bigelow (bight) M1
Blackstone (riv.) G3
Blue (hills) C8
Boston (bay) E6
Boston (harb.) D7
Boston Nat'l Hist. Park D6
Brewster (isls.) E7
Buel (lake) A4
Buzzards (bay) L7
Cambridge (res.) B6
Cape Cod (bay) N5
Cape Cod (canal) N5
Cape Cod Nat'l Seashore P5
Chappaquiddick (isl.) N7
Charles (riv.) C7
Chicopee (riv.) D4
Cobble Mountain (res.) C4
Cochituate (lake) A7
Cod (cape) O4
Concord (riv.) J2
Congamond (lakes) D4
Connecticut (riv.) D2
Cuttyhunk (isl.) L7
Deer (isl.) E7
Deerfield (riv.) C2
East (pt.) E6
East Chop (pt.) M7
Eastern (pt.) M2
Elizabeth (isls.) L7
Everett (mt.) A4
Falls (riv.) D2
Fort Devens 8,973 .... H2
Fresh (pond) C6
Gammon (pt.) N6

Gay Head (prom.) L7
Grace (mt.) E2
Great (pt.) O7
Green (riv.) B2
Greylock (mt.) B2
Gurnet (pt.) M4
Hingham (bay) E7
Holyoke (range) D3
Hoosac (mts.) B2
Hoosic (riv.) A1
Housatonic (riv.) A4
Ipswich (riv.) L2
John F. Kennedy
Nat'l Hist. Site C7
Knightville (res.) C3
Laurence G. Hanscom Field .. B6
Little (riv.) C4
Logan Int'l Airport D7
Long (isl.) E7
Long (isl.) O4
Long (pond) L5
Longfellow Nat'l Hist. Site .. C6
Lowell Nat'l Hist. Park J2
Maine (gulf) M2
Manhan (riv.) D4
Manomet (pt.) N5
Marblehead (neck) F6
Martha's Vineyard (isl.) M7
Massachusetts (bay) M4
Merrimack (riv.) K1
Mill (riv.) C3
Mill (riv.) D3
Millers (riv.) E2
Minute Man Nat'l Hist. Park .. B6
Mishaum (pt.) L6
Monomonac (lake) G2
Monomoy (isl.) O6
Monomoy (isl.) O6
Mount Hope (bay) K6
Muskeget (chan.) N7
Muskeget (isl.) N7
Mystic (lake) C6
Mystic (riv.) C6
Nahant (bay) E6
Nantucket (isl.) O8
Nantucket (sound) N6
Nashawena (isl.) L7
Nashua (riv.) H3
Naushon (isl.) L7
Neponset (riv.) C8
Nomans Land (isl.) L7
Nonamesset (isl.) M6
North (riv.) D2
North (riv.) L4
Onota (lake) A3
Otis (res.) B4
Otis A.F.B. M6
Pasque (isl.) L7
Plum (isl.) L2
Plymouth (bay) M5
Poge (cape) N7
Pontoosuc (lake) A3
Quabbin (res.) E3
Quaboag (riv.) F4
Quincy (bay) D7
Quinebaug (riv.) F4
Race (pt.) N4
Salem Maritime
Nat'l Hist. Site E5
Saugus Iron Works
Nat'l Hist. Site D6
Shawsheen (riv.) K2

Silver (lake) L4
South (riv.) D2
South Weymouth
Nav. Air Sta. E8
Springfield Armory
Nat'l Hist. Site D4
Squibnocket (pt.) M7
Stillwater (riv.) G3
Sudbury (res.) H3
Sudbury (riv.) A6
Swift (riv.) E4
Taconic (mts.) A3
Taunton (riv.) K5
Thompson (isl.) D7
Toby (mt.) E3
Tom (mt.) D3
Tuckernuck (isl.) N7
Vineyard (sound) M7
Wachusett (mt.) G3
Wachusett (res.) G3
Walden (pond) A6
Ware (riv.) E3
Watuppa (pond) K6
Webster (lake) G4
Wellfleet (harb.) O5
West (riv.) C3
Westfield (riv.) C3
Westover A.F.B. D4
Weweantic (riv.) L5
Whitman (riv.) C7
Winter I. Coast Guard Air Sta..E5

RHODE ISLAND

COUNTIES

Bristol 48,859 .... J6
Kent 161,135 .... H6
Newport 87,194 .... K6
Providence 596,270 .... H5
Washington 110,006 .... H7

CITIES and TOWNS

Anthony H6
Apponaug J6
Arctic J6
Arnold Mills J5
Ashaway 1,584 .... H7
Ashton J5
Barrington • 15,849 .... J6
Block Island • H8
Bradford 1,604 .... H7
Bristol▲ • 21,625 .... J6
Centerdale J5
Central Falls 17,637 .... J5
Charlestown 6,478 .... H7
Conimicut J6
Coventry (Washington)
31,083 .... H6
Coventry Center H6
Cranston 76,060 .... J5
East Greenwich • 11,865 .... J6
East Providence 50,380 .... J5
Esmond J5
Exeter • 5,461 .... H6
Georgiaville J5
Greenville 8,303 .... I5
Harrisville 1,654 .... H5
Hillsgrove J6
Hope Valley 1,446 .... H6

Hopkinton • 6,873 .... H7
Island Park J6
Jamestown 4,999 .... J6
Jamestown • 4,040 .... J6
Kingston 6,504 .... J7
La Fayette H6
Little Compton • 3,339 .... K6
Lonsdale J5
Manville H5
Middletown • 19,460 .... J6
Narragansett 14,985 .... J7
Narragansett • 12,088 .... J7
Natick H6
New Shoreham
(Block Island) • 836 .... H8
Newport▲ 28,227 .... J7
North Kingstown 23,786 .... J6
North Providence • 32,090 .... J5
North Tiverton K6
Norwood J6
Oakland Beach J6
Pascoag 5,011 .... H5
Pawtucket 72,644 .... J5
Peace Dale-Wakefield 7,134 .... J7
Pontiac J6
Portsmouth • 16,857 .... J6
Providence (cap.)▲ • 160,728 .... H5
Riverside J5
Rumford J5
Tiverton 7,259 .... K6
Tiverton • 14,312 .... K6
Valley Falls 11,175 .... J5
Wakefield-Peace Dale 7,134 .... J7
Warren • 11,385 .... J6
Warwick 85,427 .... J6
Watch Hill 300 .... G7
West Kingstown 950 .... H7
West Warwick 29,268 .... H6
Westerly 16,477 .... G7
Westerly • 21,605 .... G7
Woonsocket▲ 43,877 .... J4

OTHER FEATURES

Black Rock (pt.) H8
Block (isl.) H8
Block Island (sound) H8
Brenton (pt.) J7
Conanicut (isl.) J6
Dickens (pt.) H8
Durfee (hill) G5
Grace (pt.) H8
Jerimoth (hill) G5
Judith (pt.) J7
Mount Hope (bay) K6
Narragansett (bay) J6
Noyes (pt.) H7
Pawcatuck (riv.) G7
Prudence (isl.) J6
Rhode Island (isl.) J6
Rhode (sound) H8
Roger Williams Nat'l Mem. J5
Sakonnet (pt.) K7
Sakonnet (riv.) K7
Sandy (pt.) H8
Scituate (res.) H5
Touro Synagogue
Nat'l Hist. Site J7
Watch Hill (pt.) G7

▲County seat or Shire town
• Population of town or township

Topography

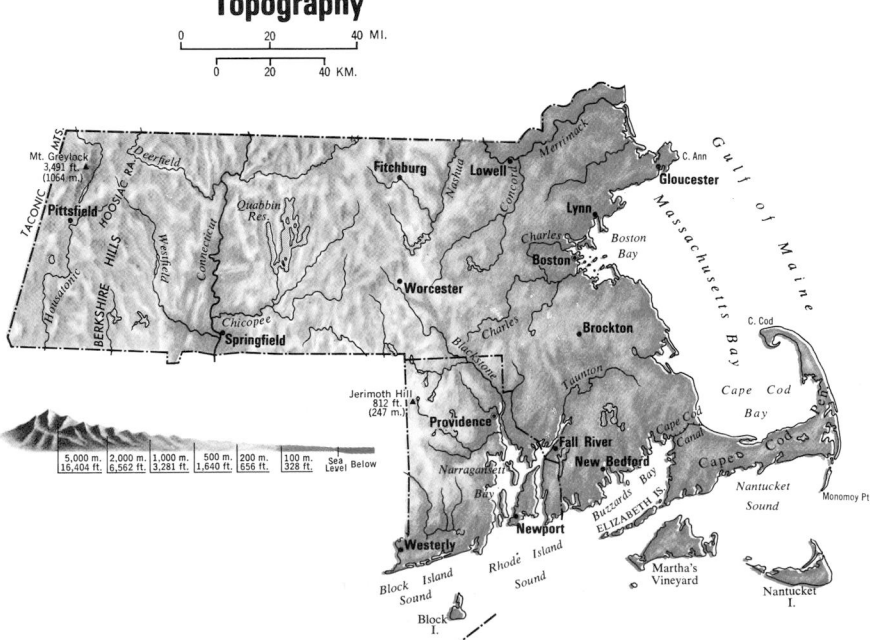

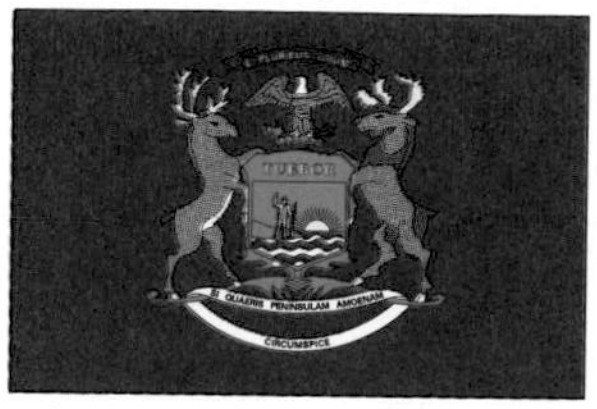

AREA 58,527 sq. mi. (151,585 sq. km.)
POPULATION 9,328,784
CAPITAL Lansing
LARGEST CITY Detroit
HIGHEST POINT Mt. Curwood 1,980 ft. (604 m.)
SETTLED IN 1650
ADMITTED TO UNION January 26, 1837
POPULAR NAME Wolverine State
STATE FLOWER Apple Blossom
STATE BIRD Robin

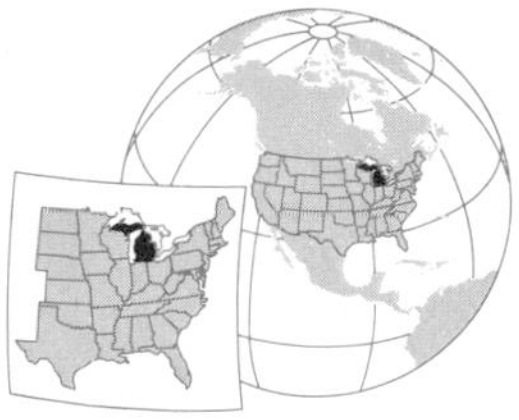

Topography

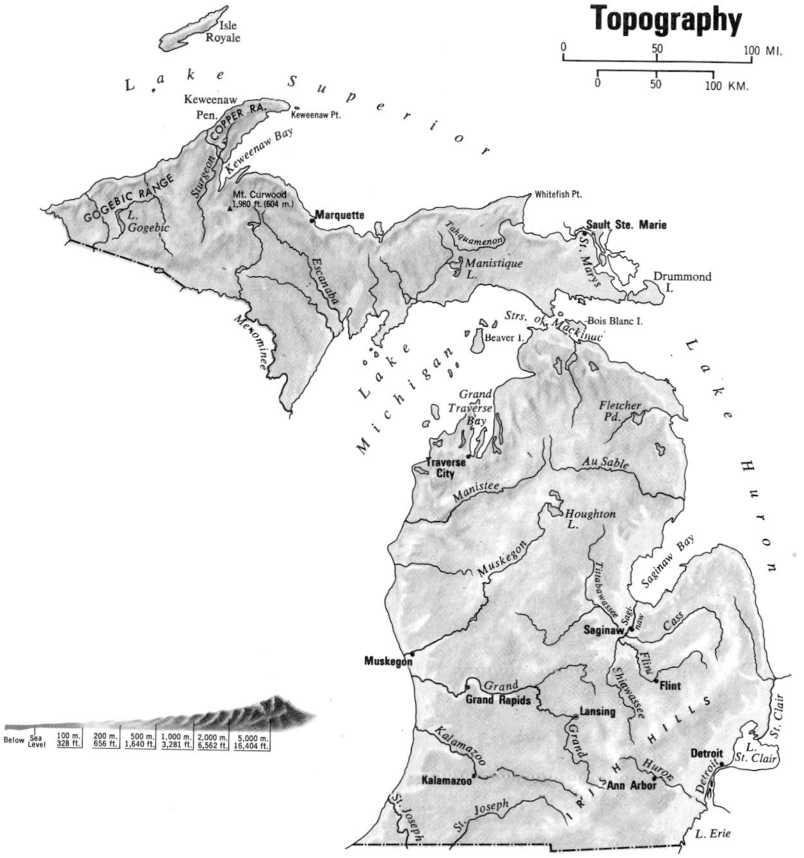

COUNTIES

Alcona 10,145 ..... F4
Alger 8,972 ..... C2
Allegan 90,509 ..... D6
Alpena 30,605 ..... F4
Antrim 18,185 ..... D3
Arenac 14,931 ..... F4
Baraga 7,954 ..... A2
Barry 50,057 ..... D6
Bay 111,723 ..... E5
Benzie 12,200 ..... C4
Berrien 161,378 ..... C7
Branch 41,502 ..... D7
Calhoun 135,982 ..... D6
Cass 49,477 ..... C7
Charlevoix 21,468 ..... D3
Cheboygan 21,398 ..... E3
Chippewa 34,604 ..... E2
Clare 24,952 ..... E5
Clinton 57,883 ..... E6
Crawford 12,260 ..... E4
Delta 37,780 ..... C2
Dickinson 26,831 ..... B2
Eaton 92,879 ..... E6
Emmet 25,040 ..... E3
Genesee 430,459 ..... F5
Gladwin 21,896 ..... E4
Gogebic 18,052 ..... F2
Grand Traverse 64,273 ..... D4
Gratiot 38,982 ..... E5
Hillsdale 43,431 ..... E7
Houghton 35,446 ..... G1
Huron 34,951 ..... F5
Ingham 281,912 ..... E6
Ionia 57,024 ..... D6
Iosco 30,209 ..... F4
Iron 13,175 ..... G2
Isabella 54,624 ..... E5
Jackson 149,756 ..... E6
Kalamazoo 223,411 ..... D6
Kalkaska 13,497 ..... D4
Kent 500,631 ..... D5
Keweenaw 1,701 ..... A1
Lake 8,583 ..... D5
Lapeer 74,768 ..... F5
Leelanau 16,527 ..... D4
Lenawee 91,476 ..... E7
Livingston 115,645 ..... F6
Luce 5,763 ..... D2
Mackinac 10,674 ..... D2
Macomb 717,400 ..... G6
Manistee 21,265 ..... C4
Marquette 70,887 ..... B2
Mason 25,537 ..... C4
Mecosta 37,308 ..... D5
Menominee 24,920 ..... B3
Midland 75,651 ..... E5
Missaukee 12,147 ..... D4
Monroe 133,600 ..... F7
Montcalm 53,059 ..... D5
Montmorency 8,936 ..... E3
Muskegon 158,983 ..... C5
Newaygo 38,202 ..... D5
Oakland 1,083,592 ..... F6
Oceana 22,454 ..... C5
Ogemaw 18,681 ..... E4
Ontonagon 8,854 ..... F1
Osceola 20,146 ..... D5
Oscoda 7,842 ..... E4
Otsego 17,957 ..... E3
Ottawa 187,768 ..... C6
Presque Isle 13,743 ..... F3
Roscommon 19,776 ..... E4
Saginaw 211,946 ..... E5
Saint Clair 138,802 ..... G6
Saint Joseph 56,083 ..... D7
Sanilac 39,928 ..... G5
Schoolcraft 8,302 ..... C2
Shiawassee 69,770 ..... E6
Tuscola 55,498 ..... F5
Van Buren 66,814 ..... C6
Washtenaw 282,937 ..... F6
Wayne 2,111,687 ..... F6
Wexford 26,360 ..... D4

CITIES and TOWNS

Addison 632 ..... E7
Adrian▲ 22,097 ..... F7
Akron 421 ..... F5
Alabaster 46 ..... F4
Alanson 677 ..... E3
Albion 10,066 ..... E6
Algonac 4,551 ..... G6
Allegan▲ 4,547 ..... D6
Allen 201 ..... E7
Allen Park 31,092 ..... B7
Alma 9,034 ..... E5
Almont 2,354 ..... F6
Alpena▲ 11,354 ..... F3
Alpha 219 ..... A2
Anchorville 3,202 ..... G6
Ann Arbor▲ 109,592 ..... F6
Applegate 297 ..... G5
Arcadia 780 ..... C4
Armada 1,548 ..... G6
Ashley 518 ..... E5
Athens 990 ..... D6
Atlanta▲ 475 ..... E3
Atlantic Mine 809 ..... G1
Au Gres 838 ..... F4
Au Sable 1,542 ..... F4
Auburn 1,855 ..... F5
Auburn Heights 7,500 ..... F6
Augusta 927 ..... D6
Averill 800 ..... E5
Bad Axe▲ 3,484 ..... G5
Baldwin▲ 821 ..... D5
Bancroft 599 ..... E6
Bangor 1,922 ..... C6
Baraga 1,231 ..... G1
Bark River 800 ..... B3
Baroda 657 ..... C7
Barryton 393 ..... D5
Barton Hills 320 ..... F6
Battle Creek 53,540 ..... D6
Bay City▲ 38,936 ..... F5
Bay Port 750 ..... F5
Beal City 345 ..... D5
Bear Lake 339 ..... C4
Beaverton 1,150 ..... E5
Beechwood 2,676 ..... C6
Belding 5,969 ..... D5
Bellaire▲ 1,104 ..... D4
Belleville 3,270 ..... F6
Bellevue 1,401 ..... E6
Benton Harbor 12,818 ..... C6
Benton Heights 5,465 ..... C6
Benzonia 449 ..... D4
Berkley 16,960 ..... B6
Berrien Springs 1,927 ..... C7
Bessemer▲ 2,272 ..... F2
Beulah▲ 421 ..... C4
Beverly Hills 10,610 ..... B6
Big Rapids▲ 12,603 ..... D5
Birch Run 992 ..... F5
Birmingham 19,997 ..... B6
Bitely 750 ..... D5
Blissfield 3,172 ..... F7
Bloomfield Hills 4,288 ..... B6
Bloomingdale 503 ..... C6
Boyne City 3,478 ..... E3
Boyne Falls 369 ..... E3
Breckenridge 1,301 ..... E5
Breedsville 213 ..... C6
Bridgeport 8,569 ..... F5
Bridgman 2,140 ..... C7
Brighton 5,686 ..... F6
Britton 694 ..... F6
Bronson 2,342 ..... D7
Brooklyn 1,027 ..... E6
Brown City 1,244 ..... G5
Buchanan 4,992 ..... C7
Buckley 402 ..... D4
Burlington 294 ..... D6
Burr Oak 882 ..... D7
Burt 1,169 ..... F5
Burton 27,617 ..... F6
Byron 573 ..... E6
Byron Center 900 ..... D6
Cadillac▲ 10,104 ..... D4
Caledonia 885 ..... D6
Calumet 818 ..... A1
Camden 482 ..... E7
Capac 1,583 ..... G5
Carleton 2,770 ..... F6
Carney 197 ..... B3
Caro▲ 4,054 ..... F5
Carrollton 6,521 ..... E5
Carson City 1,158 ..... E5
Carsonville 583 ..... G5
Caseville 857 ..... F5
Casnovia 376 ..... D5
Caspian 1,031 ..... G2
Cass City 2,276 ..... F5
Cassopolis▲ 1,822 ..... C7
Cedar Springs 2,600 ..... D5
Cement City 493 ..... E6
Center Line 9,026 ..... B6
Central Lake 954 ..... D3
Centreville▲ 1,516 ..... D7
Charlevoix▲ 3,116 ..... D3
Charlotte▲ 8,083 ..... E6
Chatham 268 ..... B2
Cheboygan▲ 4,999 ..... E3
Chelsea 3,772 ..... E6
Chesaning 2,567 ..... E5
Clare 3,021 ..... E5
Clarkston 1,005 ..... F6
Clarksville 360 ..... D6
Clawson 13,874 ..... B6
Clayton 384 ..... E7
Clifford 354 ..... F5
Climax 677 ..... D6
Clinton 2,475 ..... F6
Clio 2,629 ..... F5
Coldwater▲ 9,607 ..... D7
Coleman 1,237 ..... E5
Coloma 1,679 ..... C6
Colon 1,224 ..... D7
Columbiaville 934 ..... F5
Comstock• 11,162 ..... D6
Concord 944 ..... E6
Constantine 2,032 ..... D7
Coopersville 3,421 ..... C5
Copemish 222 ..... D4
Copper City 198 ..... A1
Corunna▲ 3,091 ..... E6
Croswell 2,174 ..... G5
Crystal 800 ..... E5
Crystal Falls▲ 1,922 ..... A2
Curtis 800 ..... D2
Custer 312 ..... C5
Cutierville 11,228 ..... D6
Daggett 260 ..... B3
Dansville 437 ..... E6
Davison 5,693 ..... F5
De Tour Village 407 ..... E3
De Witt 3,964 ..... E6
Dearborn 89,286 ..... B7
Dearborn Heights 60,838 ..... B7
Decatur 1,760 ..... C6
Deckerville 1,015 ..... G5
Deerfield 922 ..... F7
Detroit Beach 2,113 ..... F7
Detroit▲ 1,027,974 ..... B7
Dexter 1,497 ..... F6
Dimondale 1,247 ..... E6
Dollar Bay 950 ..... G1
Douglas 1,040 ..... C6
Dowagiac 6,409 ..... D6
Drayton Plains F6
Drummond Island• 746 ..... F3
Dryden 628 ..... F6
Dundee 2,664 ..... F7
Durand 4,283 ..... E6
Eagle River▲ 20 ..... A1
East Detroit 35,283 ..... B6
East Grand Rapids 10,807 ..... D6
East Jordan 2,240 ..... D3
East Kingsford A3
East Lansing 50,677 ..... E6
East Tawas 2,887 ..... F4
Eastlake 473 ..... C4
Eastwood 6,340 ..... D6
Eaton Rapids 4,695 ..... E6
Eau Claire 494 ..... C6
Ecorse 12,180 ..... B7
Edmore 1,126 ..... E5
Edwardsburg 1,142 ..... C7
Elberta 478 ..... C4
Elk Rapids 1,626 ..... D4
Elkton 958 ..... F5
Ellsworth 418 ..... D3
Elsie 957 ..... E5
Emmett 297 ..... G6
Empire 355 ..... C4
Erie 750 ..... F7
Escanaba▲ 13,659 ..... C3
Essexville 4,088 ..... F5
Estral Beach 430 ..... F7
Evart 1,744 ..... D5
Ewen 821 ..... F2
Fair Haven 1,505 ..... G6
Fair Plain 8,051 ..... C6
Fairgrove 592 ..... F5
Farmington 10,132 ..... F6
Farmington Hills 74,652 ..... F6
Farwell 851 ..... E5
Fennville 1,023 ..... C6
Fenton 8,444 ..... F6
Ferndale 25,084 ..... B6
Ferrysburg 2,919 ..... C5
Fife Lake 394 ..... D4
Flat Rock 7,290 ..... F6
Flint▲ 140,761 ..... F5
Flushing 8,542 ..... F5
Fountain 165 ..... C4
Fowler 912 ..... E5
Fowlerville 2,648 ..... F6
Frankenmuth 4,408 ..... F5
Frankfort 1,546 ..... C4
Franklin 2,626 ..... B6
Fraser 13,899 ..... B6
Freeland 1,421 ..... E5
Freeport 458 ..... D6
Fremont 3,875 ..... D5
Fruitport 1,090 ..... C5
Gaastra 376 ..... G2
Gagetown 337 ..... F5
Gaines 427 ..... F6
Galesburg 1,863 ..... D6
Galien 596 ..... C7
Garden 268 ..... C3
Garden City 31,846 ..... F6
Gaylord▲ 3,256 ..... E3
Gibraltar 4,297 ..... F6
Gladstone 4,565 ..... C3
Gladwin▲ 2,682 ..... E5
Gobles 769 ..... D6
Goodrich 916 ..... F6
Grand Blanc 7,760 ..... F6
Grand Haven▲ 11,951 ..... C5
Grand Ledge 7,579 ..... E6
Grand Rapids▲ 189,126 ..... D5
Grandville 15,624 ..... D6
Grant 764 ..... D5
Grass Lake 903 ..... E6
Grayling▲ 1,944 ..... E4
Greenville 8,101 ..... D5
Grosse Ile 9,781 ..... B7
Grosse Pointe 5,681 ..... B7
Grosse Pointe Farms 10,092 ..... B6
Grosse Pointe Park 12,857 ..... B7
Grosse Pointe Shores 2,955 ..... B6
Grosse Pointe Woods 17,715 ..... B6
Gulliver 962 ..... D2
Gwinn 2,370 ..... B2
Hamilton 950 ..... C6
Hamtramck 18,372 ..... B6
Hancock 4,547 ..... G1
Hanover 481 ..... E6
Harbor Beach 2,089 ..... G5
Harbor Springs 1,540 ..... D3
Harper Woods 14,903 ..... B6
Harrison▲ 1,835 ..... E4
Harrisville▲ 470 ..... F4
Hart▲ 1,942 ..... C5
Hartford 2,341 ..... C6
Haslett 10,230 ..... E6
Hastings▲ 6,549 ..... D6
Hazel Park 20,051 ..... B6
Hemlock 1,601 ..... E5
Hermansville 950 ..... B3
Hersey 354 ..... D5
Hesperia 846 ..... D5
Highland Park 20,121 ..... B6
Hillman 643 ..... F3
Hillsdale▲ 8,170 ..... E7
Holland 30,745 ..... C6
Holly 5,595 ..... F6
Holt 11,744 ..... E6
Homer 1,758 ..... E6
Honor 292 ..... D4
Hopkins 546 ..... D6
Houghton Lake 3,353 ..... E4
Houghton Lake Heights E4
Houghton▲ 7,498 ..... G1
Howard City 1,351 ..... D5
Howell▲ 8,184 ..... E6
Hubbardston 404 ..... E5
Hubbell 1,174 ..... A1
Hudson 2,580 ..... E7
Hudsonville 6,170 ..... D6
Huntington Woods 6,419 ..... B6
Ida 970 ..... F7
Imlay City 2,921 ..... F5
Indian River 950 ..... E3
Inkster 30,772 ..... B7
Interlochen 600 ..... D4
Ionia▲ 5,935 ..... D6
Iron Mountain▲ 8,525 ..... B3
Iron River 2,095 ..... G2
Ironwood 6,849 ..... F2
Ishpeming 7,200 ..... B2
Isle Royale National Park E1
Ithaca▲ 3,009 ..... E5
Jackson▲ 37,446 ..... E6
Jenison 17,882 ..... D6
Jonesville 2,283 ..... E6
Kalamazoo▲ 80,277 ..... D6
Kaleva 484 ..... C4
Kalkaska▲ 1,952 ..... D4
Keego Harbor 2,932 ..... F6
Kent City 899 ..... D5
Kentwood 37,826 ..... D6
Kinde 473 ..... G5
Kingsford 5,480 ..... A3
Kingsley 738 ..... D4
Kingston 439 ..... F5
L'Anse▲ 2,151 ..... G1
Laingsburg 1,148 ..... E6
Lake Ann 217 ..... D4
Lake City▲ 858 ..... D4
Lake George 950 ..... E5
Lake Linden 1,203 ..... A1
Lake Michigan Beach 1,694 ..... C6
Lake Odessa 2,256 ..... D6
Lake Orion 3,057 ..... F6
Lakeview 1,108 ..... D5
Lakewood Club 659 ..... C5

(continued on following page)

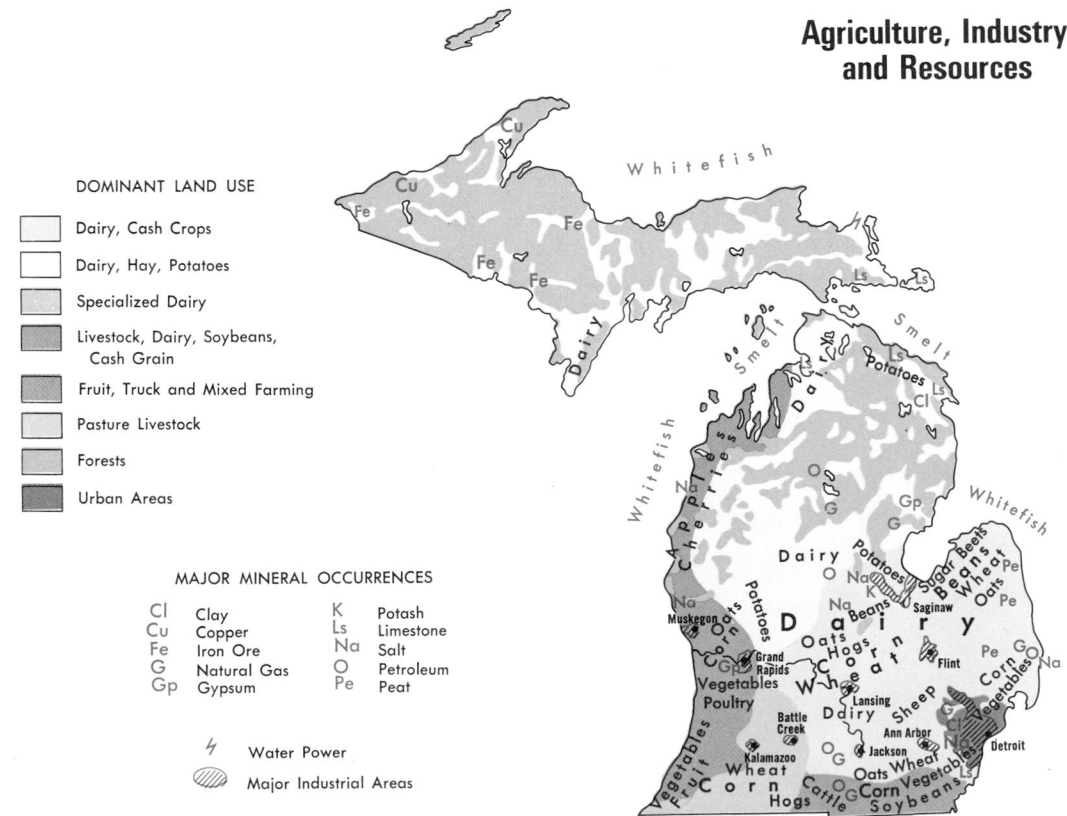

Agriculture, Industry and Resources

DOMINANT LAND USE

- Dairy, Cash Crops
- Dairy, Hay, Potatoes
- Specialized Dairy
- Livestock, Dairy, Soybeans, Cash Grain
- Fruit, Truck and Mixed Farming
- Pasture Livestock
- Forests
- Urban Areas

MAJOR MINERAL OCCURRENCES

- Cl Clay
- Cu Copper
- Fe Iron Ore
- G   Natural Gas
- Gp Gypsum
- K   Potash
- Ls Limestone
- Na Salt
- O   Petroleum
- Pe Peat

⚡ Water Power

▨ Major Industrial Areas

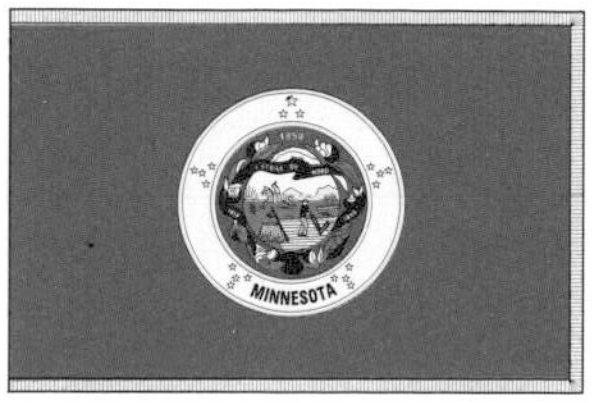
MINNESOTA

AREA 84,402 sq. mi. (218,601 sq. km.)
POPULATION 4,387,029
CAPITAL St. Paul
LARGEST CITY Minneapolis
HIGHEST POINT Eagle Mtn. 2,301 ft. (701 m.)
SETTLED IN 1805
ADMITTED TO UNION May 11, 1858
POPULAR NAME North Star State; Gopher State
STATE FLOWER Pink & White Lady's-Slipper
STATE BIRD Common Loon

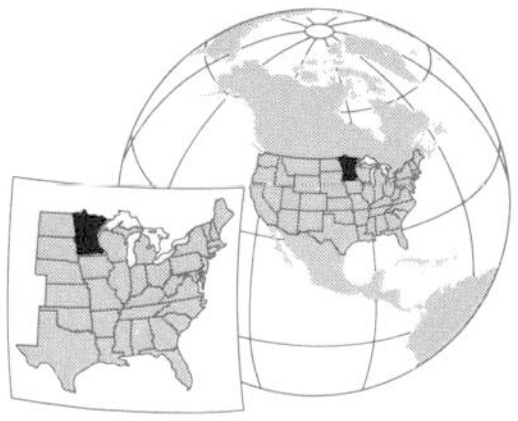

COUNTIES

Aitkin 12,425 E4
Anoka 243,641 E5
Becker 27,881 C4
Beltrami 34,384 C2
Benton 30,185 D5
Big Stone 6,285 B5
Blue Earth 54,044 D6
Brown 26,984 D6
Carlton 29,259 F4
Carver 47,915 E6
Cass 21,791 D4
Chippewa 13,228 C5
Chisago 30,521 F5
Clay 50,422 B4
Clearwater 8,309 C3
Cook 3,868 H3
Cottonwood 12,694 C6
Crow Wing 44,249 D4
Dakota 275,227 E6
Dodge 15,731 F7
Douglas 28,674 C5
Faribault 16,937 D7
Fillmore 20,777 F7
Freeborn 33,060 E7
Goodhue 40,690 F6
Grant 6,246 B5
Hennepin 1,032,431 E5
Houston 18,497 G7
Hubbard 14,939 D3
Isanti 25,921 E5
Itasca 40,863 E3
Jackson 11,677 C7
Kanabec 12,802 E5
Kandiyohi 38,761 C5
Kittson 5,767 B2
Koochiching 16,299 E2
Lac qui Parle 8,924 B6
Lake 10,415 G3
Lake of the Woods 4,076 D2
Le Sueur 23,239 E6
Lincoln 6,890 B6
Lyon 24,789 C6
Mahnomen 5,044 C3
Marshall 10,993 B2
Martin 22,914 D7
McLeod 32,030 D6
Meeker 20,846 D5
Mille Lacs 18,670 E5
Morrison 29,604 D4
Mower 37,385 F7
Murray 9,660 C6
Nicollet 28,076 D6
Nobles 20,098 C7
Norman 7,975 B3
Olmsted 106,470 F7
Otter Tail 50,714 C4
Pennington 13,306 B2
Pine 21,264 F4
Pipestone 10,491 B6
Polk 32,498 B3
Pope 10,745 C5
Ramsey 485,765 E5
Red Lake 4,525 B3
Redwood 17,254 C6
Renville 17,673 C6
Rice 49,183 E6
Rock 9,806 B7
Roseau 15,026 C2
Saint Louis 222,229 F3
Scott 57,846 E6
Sherburne 41,945 E5
Sibley 14,366 D6
Stearns 118,791 D5
Steele 30,729 E7
Stevens 10,634 B5
Swift 10,724 C5
Todd 23,363 D4
Traverse 4,463 B5
Wabasha 19,744 F6
Wadena 13,154 D4
Waseca 18,079 E6
Washington 145,896 F5
Watonwan 11,682 D7
Wilkin 7,516 B4
Winona 47,828 G6
Wright 68,710 D5
Yellow Medicine 11,684 B6

CITIES and TOWNS

Ada▲ 1,708 B3
Adams 756 F7
Adrian 1,141 C7
Afton 2,645 F6
Aitkin▲ 1,698 E4
Akeley 393 D3
Albany 1,548 D5
Albert Lea▲ 18,310 E7
Alberta 136 B5
Albertville 1,251 E5
Alborn 500 F4
Alden 623 E7
Aldrich 70 C4
Alexandria▲ 7,838 C5
Alpha 105 D7
Altura 349 G6
Alvarado 356 B2
Amboy 517 D7
Andover 15,216 E5
Annandale 2,054 D5
Anoka▲ 17,192 E5
Apple Valley 34,598 G6
Appleton 1,552 C5
Arco 104 B6
Argyle 636 B2
Arlington 1,886 D6
Arnold 2,891 F4
Ashby 469 C4
Askov 343 F4
Atwater 1,053 D5
Audubon 411 C4
Aurora 1,965 F3
Austin▲ 21,907 E7
Avoca 150 C7
Avon 970 D5
Babbitt 1,562 G3
Backus 240 D4
Badger 381 B2
Bagley▲ 1,388 C3
Balaton 737 C6
Barnesville 2,066 B4
Barnum 482 F4
Barrett 350 B5
Barry 40 B5
Battle Lake 698 C4
Baudette▲ 1,146 D2
Baxter 3,695 D4
Bayport 3,200 F5
Beardsley 297 B5
Beaver Bay 147 G3
Beaver Creek 249 B7
Becker 902 E5
Bejou 110 B3
Belgrade 700 C5
Belle Plaine 3,149 E6
Bellechester 110 F6
Bellingham 247 B5
Beltrami 137 B3
Belview 383 C6
Bemidji▲ 11,245 D3
Bena 147 D3
Benson▲ 3,235 C5
Bertha 507 C4
Bethel 394 E5
Big Falls 341 E2
Big Lake 3,113 E5
Bigelow 232 C7
Bigfork 384 E3
Bingham Lake 155 C7
Bird Island 1,326 D6
Biscay 113 D6
Biwabik 1,097 F3
Blackduck 718 D3
Blaine 38,975 G5
Blomkest 183 D6
Blooming Prairie 2,043 E7
Bloomington 86,335 G6
Blue Earth▲ 3,745 D7
Bluffton 187 C4
Bock 115 E5
Borup 119 B3
Bovey 662 E3
Bowlus 260 D5
Boy River 43 D3
Boyd 251 C6
Braham 1,139 E5
Brainerd▲ 12,353 D4
Branch 2,400 F5
Brandon 441 C5
Breckenridge▲ 3,708 B4
Breezy Point 432 D4
Brewster 532 C7
Bricelyn 426 E7
Brook Park 125 F5
Brooklyn Center 28,887 G5
Brooklyn Park 56,381 G5
Brooks 158 B3
Brookston 107 F4
Brooten 589 C5
Browerville 782 D4
Browns Valley 804 B5
Brownsdale 695 F7
Brownsville 415 G7
Brownton 781 D6
Bruno 89 F4
Buckman 201 D5
Buffalo Lake 734 D6
Buffalo▲ 6,856 E5
Buhl 915 F3
Burnsville 51,288 E6
Burtrum 172 D5
Butterfield 509 D7
Byron 2,441 F6
Caledonia▲ 2,846 G7
Callaway 212 C3
Calumet 382 E3
Cambridge▲ 5,094 E5
Campbell 233 B4
Canby 1,826 B6
Cannon Falls 3,232 F6
Canton 362 F7
Carlos 361 C5
Carlton▲ 923 F4
Carver 744 F6
Cass Lake 923 D3
Cedar Mills 80 D6
Center City▲ 451 F5
Centerville 1,633 E5
Ceylon 461 D7
Champlin 16,849 G5
Chandler 316 C7
Chanhassen 11,732 F6
Chaska▲ 11,339 F6
Chatfield 2,226 F7
Chickamaw Beach 132 D4
Chisago City 2,009 E5
Chisholm 5,290 E3
Chokio 521 B5
Circle Pines 4,704 G5
Clara City 1,307 C6
Claremont 530 E6
Clarissa 637 C4
Clarkfield 924 C6
Clarks Grove 675 E7
Clear Lake 315 E5
Clearbrook 560 C3
Clearwater 597 D5
Clements 191 D6
Cleveland 699 E6
Climax 264 B3
Clinton 574 B5
Clitherall 109 C4
Clontarf 172 C5
Cloquet 10,885 F4
Coates 186 E6
Cobden 62 D6
Cohasset E3
Cokato 2,180 D5
Cold Spring 2,459 D5
Coleraine 1,041 E3
Cologne 563 E6
Columbia Heights 18,910 G5
Comfrey 433 D6
Comstock 123 B4
Conger 143 E7
Cook 680 F3
Coon Rapids 52,978 G5
Corcoran 5,199 F5
Correll 60 B5
Cosmos 610 D6
Cottage Grove 22,935 F6
Cotton 982 F3
Cottonwood 924 C6
Courtland 412 D6
Cromwell 221 F4
Crookston▲ 8,119 B3
Crosby 2,073 D4
Crosslake 1,132 E4
Crystal 23,788 G5
Currie 303 C6
Cuyuna 172 E4
Cyrus 328 C5
Dakota 360 G7
Dalton 234 C4
Danube 562 C6
Danvers 98 C5
Darfur 128 D6
Darwin 252 D5
Dassel 1,082 D5
Dawson 1,626 B6
Day 4,443 E5
Dayton 4,070 E5
De Graff 149 C5
Deephaven 3,653 G5
Deer Creek 303 C4
Deer River 838 E3
Deerwood 524 E4
Delano 2,709 E5
Delavan 245 D7
Delhi 69 C6
Dellwood 887 F5
Denham 36 F4
Dennison 152 E6
Dent 177 C4
Detroit Lakes▲ 6,635 C4
Dexter 303 F7
Dilworth 2,562 B4
Dodge Center 1,954 F6
Donaldson 57 B2
Donnelly 221 B5
Doran 78 B4
Dover 416 F7
Dovray 60 C6
Duluth▲ 85,493 F4
Dumont 126 B5
Dundas 473 E6
Dundee 107 C7
Dunnell 187 D7
Eagan 47,409 G6
Eagle Bend 524 D4
Eagle Lake 1,703 E6
East Bethel 8,050 E5
East Grand Forks 8,658 B3
East Gull Lake 687 D4
Easton 229 E7
Echo 304 C6
Eden Prairie 39,311 G6
Eden Valley 732 D5
Edgerton 1,106 B7
Edina 46,070 G5
Effie 130 E3
Eitzen 221 G7
Elba 220 F6
Elbow Lake▲ 1,186 B5
Elgin 733 F6
Elizabeth 152 B4
Elk River▲ 11,143 E5
Elko 223 E6
Elkton 142 F7
Ellendale 549 E7
Ellsworth 580 C7
Elmdale 130 D5
Elmore 709 D7
Elrosa 205 C5
Ely 3,968 G3
Elysian 445 E6
Emily 613 E4
Emmons 439 E7
Erhard 181 B4
Erskine 422 B3
Esko 500 F4
Evan 83 D6
Evansville 566 C4
Eveleth 4,064 F3
Excelsior 2,367 E6
Eyota 1,448 F7
Fairfax 1,276 D6
Fairmont▲ 11,265 D7
Falcon Heights 5,380 G5
Faribault▲ 17,085 E6
Farmington 5,940 E6
Farwell 74 C5
Federal Dam 118 D3
Felton 211 B3
Fergus Falls▲ 12,362 B4
Fertile 853 B3
Fifty Lakes 299 D4
Finlayson 242 F4
Fisher 413 B3
Flensburg 213 D5
Floodwood 574 E4
Florence 53 B6
Florenton 635 F3
Foley▲ 1,854 D5
Forada 171 C5
Forest Lake 5,833 F5
Foreston 354 E5
Fort Ripley 92 D4
Fosston 1,529 C3
Fountain 327 F7
Foxhome 160 B4
Franklin 512 D6
Frazee 1,176 C4
Freeborn 301 E7
Freeport 556 D5
Fridley 28,335 G5
Frost 236 D7
Fulda 1,212 C7
Garfield 203 C5
Garrison 138 E4
Garvin 149 C6
Gary 200 B3
Gaylord▲ 1,935 D6
Geneva 444 E7
Genola 85 D5
Georgetown 107 B3
Ghent 316 C6
Gibbon 712 D6
Gilbert 1,934 F3
Gilman 192 E5
Glen 4,648 E4
Glencoe▲ 4,396 D6
Glenville 778 E7
Glenwood▲ 2,573 C5
Glyndon 862 B4
Golden Valley 20,971 G5
Gonvick 302 C3
Good Thunder 561 D6
Goodhue 533 F6
Goodridge 115 C2
Goodview 2,878 G6
Graceville 671 B5
Granada 374 D7
Grand Marais▲ 1,171 G2
Grand Meadow 967 F7
Grand Rapids▲ 7,976 E3
Granite Falls▲ 3,083 C6
Grasston 119 E5
Green Isle 239 E6
Greenbush 800 B2
Greenfield 1,450 F5
Greenwald 209 D5
Grey Eagle 353 D5
Grove City 547 D5
Grygla 220 C2
Gully 128 C3
Hackensack 245 D4
Hadley 94 C7
Hallock▲ 1,304 A2
Halma 73 B2
Halstad 611 B3
Ham Lake 8,924 E5
Hamburg 492 D6
Hamel F5
Hammond 205 F6
Hampton 363 E6
Hancock 723 C5
Hanley Falls 246 C6
Hanover 787 E5
Hanska 443 D6
Harding 76 E4
Hardwick 234 B7
Harmony 1,081 F7
Harris 843 F5
Hartland 270 E7
Hastings▲ 15,445 F6
Hatfield 66 B7
Hawley 1,655 B4
Hayfield 1,283 F7
Hayward 246 E7
Hazel Run 81 C6
Hector 1,145 D6
Heidelberg 73 E6
Henderson 746 E6
Hendricks 684 B6
Hendrum 309 B3
Henning 738 C4
Henriette 78 E5
Herman 485 B5
Hermantown 6,761 F4
Heron Lake 730 C7
Hewitt 269 C4
Hibbing 18,046 F3

(continued on following page)

Agriculture, Industry and Resources

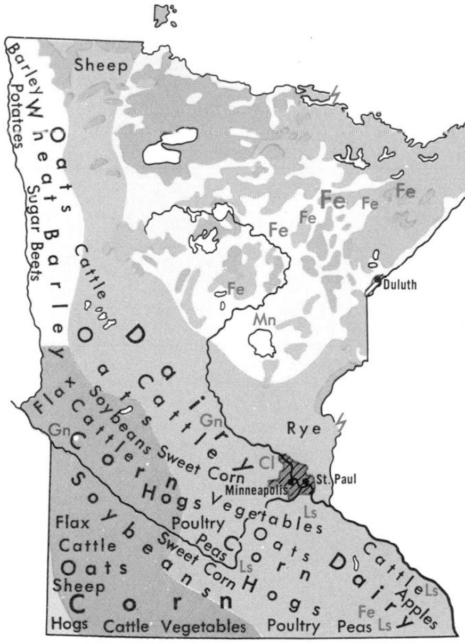
Sheep
Barley
Wheat
Potatoes
Oats
Sugar Beets
Cattle
Dairy
Fe
Mn
Duluth
Rye
Gn
Cl
Minneapolis
St. Paul
Ls
Flax
Soybeans
Sweet Corn
Corn
Hogs
Vegetables
Poultry
Peas
Apples

MAJOR MINERAL OCCURRENCES

Cl Clay
Fe Iron Ore
Gn Granite
Ls Limestone
Mn Manganese

Water Power
Major Industrial Areas

DOMINANT LAND USE

Wheat, General Farming
Dairy, Livestock
Dairy, Hay, Potatoes
Cattle Feed, Hogs
Livestock, Cash Grain
Forests
Swampland, Limited Agriculture
Urban Areas

Hill City 469 E4
Hillman 45 E4
Hills 607 B7
Hinckley 946 E4
Hitterdal 242 B4
Hoffman 576 C5
Hokah 687 G7
Holdingford 561 D5
Holland 216 B6
Hollandale 289 E7
Holloway 123 C5
Holt 88 B2
Hopkins 16,534 G5
Houston 1,013 G7
Howard Lake 1,343 D5
Hoyt Lakes 2,348 F3
Hugo 4,417 E5
Humboldt 74 A2
Hutchinson 11,523 D6
Ihlen 101 B7
Independence 2,822 F5
Indus E2
International Falls▲ 8,325 E2
Inver Grove Heights 22,477 E6
Iona 158 C7
Iron 133 F3
Ironton 553 D4
Isanti 1,228 E5
Island View 150 E2
Isle 566 E4
Ivanhoe▲ 751 B6
Jackson▲ 3,559 C7
Janesville 1,969 E6
Jasper 599 B7
Jeffers 443 C6
Jenkins 262 D4
Johnson 46 B5
Jordan 2,909 E6
Kandiyohi 506 D5
Karlstad 881 B2
Kasota 655 D6
Kasson 3,514 F6
Keewatin 1,118 E3
Kelliher 348 D3
Kellogg 423 G6
Kelly Lake 900 F3
Kennedy 337 B2
Kenneth 81 B7
Kensington 295 C5
Kent 131 B4
Kenyon 1,552 E6
Kerkhoven 732 C5
Kerrick 56 F4
Kettle River 190 E4
Kiester 606 E7
Kilkenny 167 E6
Kimball 690 D5
Kingston 131 D5
Kinney 257 F3
La Crescent 4,311 G7
La Prairie 438 E3
La Salle 98 D6
Lafayette 462 D6
Lake Benton 693 B6
Lake Bronson 272 B2
Lake City 4,391 F6
Lake Crystal 2,084 D6
Lake Elmo 5,903 F6
Lake Henry 90 D5
Lake Lillian 229 C6
Lake Park 638 B4
Lake Saint Croix Beach 1,078 F6
Lake Shore 693 D4
Lake Wilson 319 B7
Lakefield 1,679 C7
Lakeland 2,000 F6
Lakeville 24,854 E6
Lamberton 972 C6
Lancaster 342 B2
Lanesboro 858 G7
Laporte 101 D3
Lastrup 112 D4
Lauderdale 2,700 G5
Le Center▲ 2,006 E6
Le Roy 904 F7
Le Sueur 3,714 E6
Lengby 112 C3
Leonard 26 C3
Leonidas 70 F3
Lester Prairie 1,180 D6
Lewiston 1,298 G7
Lewisville 255 D7
Lexington 2,279 G5
Lilydale 506 G5
Lindstrom 2,461 F5
Lino Lakes 8,807 G5
Lismore 248 B7
Litchfield▲ 6,041 D5
Little Falls▲ 7,232 D5
Little Rock 714 D5
Littlefork 838 E2
Long Beach 204 C5
Long Lake 1,984 F5
Long Prairie▲ 2,786 D5
Longville 224 D4
Lonsdale 1,252 E6
Loretto 404 F5
Louisburg 42 B5
Lowry 233 C5
Lucan 235 C6
Luverne▲ 4,382 B7
Lyle 504 F7
Lynd 287 C6
Mabel 745 G7
Madelia 2,237 D6
Madison Lake 643 E6
Madison▲ 1,951 B5
Magnolia 155 B7
Mahnomen▲ 1,154 C3
Mahtomedi 5,569 F5
Manchester 69 E7
Manhattan Beach 61 E4
Mankato▲ 31,477 E6
Mantorville▲ 874 F6
Maple Grove 38,736 G5
Maple Lake 1,394 D5
Maple Plain 2,005 F5
Mapleton 1,526 E7
Mapleview 206 E7
Maplewood 30,954 G5
Marble 618 E3
Marietta 211 B5
Marine on Saint Croix 602 F5
Marshall▲ 12,023 C6
Mayer 471 E6
Maynard 419 C6
Mazeppa 722 F6
McGrath 62 E4
McGregor 376 E4
McIntosh 665 C3
McKinley 116 F3
Meadowlands 92 F3
Medford 733 E6
Medicine Lake 385 G5
Medina (Hamel) 3,096 F5
Meire Grove 124 C5
Melrose 2,561 D5
Menahga 1,076 C4
Mendota 164 G5
Mendota Heights 9,431 G6
Mentor 94 B3
Middle River 285 B2
Miesville 135 F6
Milaca▲ 2,182 E5
Milan 353 C5
Millerville 104 C4
Millville 163 F6
Milroy 297 C6
Miltona 181 C4
Minneapolis▲ 368,383 G5
Minneiska 127 G6
Minneota 1,417 C6
Minnesota City 258 G6
Minnesota Lake 681 E7
Minnetonka 48,370 G5
Minnetrista 3,439 F5
Mizpah 100 D3
Montevideo▲ 5,499 C6
Montgomery 2,399 E6
Monticello 4,941 E5
Montrose 1,008 E5
Moorhead▲ 32,295 B4
Moose Lake 1,206 F4
Mora▲ 2,905 E5
Morgan 965 D6
Morris▲ 5,613 C5
Morristown 784 E6
Morton 448 C6
Motley 441 D4
Mound 9,634 E6
Mounds View 12,541 G5
Mountain Iron 3,362 F3
Mountain Lake 1,906 D7
Murdock 282 C5
Myrtle 72 E7
Nashua 63 B4
Nashwauk 1,026 E3
Nassau 83 B5
Naytahwaush 378 C3
Nelson 177 C5
Nerstrand 210 E6
Nevis 375 D4
New Auburn 363 D6
New Brighton 22,207 G5
New Germany 353 E6
New Hope 21,853 G5
New London 971 C5
New Market 227 E6
New Munich 314 D5
New Prague 3,569 E6
New Richland 1,237 E7
New Trier 96 F6
New Ulm▲ 13,132 D6
New York Mills 940 C4
Newfolden 345 B2
Newport 3,720 F6
Nicollet 795 D6
Nielsville 100 B3
Nimrod 65 D4
Nisswa 1,391 D4
Norcross 86 B5
North Branch 1,867 F5
North Mankato 10,164 D6
North Oaks 3,386 G5
North Redwood 203 D6
North Saint Paul 12,376 G5
Northfield 14,684 E6
Northome 283 D3
Northrop 276 D7
Norwood 1,351 E6
Oak Park 3,486 E5
Oakdale 18,374 E5
Odessa 155 B5
Odin 102 D7
Ogema 164 C3
Ogilvie 510 E5
Okabena 223 C7
Oklee 441 C3
Olivia▲ 2,623 C6
Onamia 676 E4
Ormsby 159 D7
Oronoco 727 F6
Orr 265 F2
Ortonville▲ 2,205 B5
Osakis 1,256 C5
Oslo 362 A2
Osseo 2,704 G5
Ostrander 276 F7
Ottertail 313 C4
Owatonna▲ 19,386 E6
Palisade 144 E4
Park Rapids▲ 2,863 D4
Parkers Prairie 956 C4
Payne 2,275 F3
Paynesville 2,140 D5
Pease 178 E5
Pelican Lakes (Breezy Point) D4
Pelican Rapids 1,886 B4
Pemberton 228 E7
Pengilly 625 E3
Pennock 476 C5
Pequot Lakes 843 D4
Perham 2,075 C4
Perley 132 B3
Peterson 259 G7
Pierz 1,014 D5
Pillager 306 D4
Pine City▲ 2,613 F5
Pine Island 2,125 F6
Pine River 871 D4
Pipestone▲ 4,554 B7
Plainview 2,768 F6
Plato 355 D6
Pleasant Lake 79 D5
Plummer 277 B3
Plymouth 50,889 G5
Ponemah 704 D2
Porter 210 B6
Preston▲ 1,530 F7
Princeton 3,719 E5
Prinsburg 502 C6
Prior Lake 11,482 E6
Proctor 2,974 F4
Quamba 124 E5
Racine 288 F7
Ramsey 12,408 E5
Randall 571 D4
Randolph 331 E6
Ranier 199 E2
Ray 668 E2
Raymond 723 C5
Red Lake Falls▲ 1,481 B3
Red Wing▲ 15,134 F6
Redby 787 D3
Redwood Falls▲ 4,859 C6
Regal 51 D5
Remer 342 E3
Renville 1,315 C6
Revere 117 C6
Rice 610 D5
Richfield 35,710 G6
Richmond 965 D5
Richville 121 C4
Riverton 122 D4
Robbinsdale 14,396 G5
Rochester▲ 70,745 F6
Rock Creek 1,040 F5
Rockford 2,665 F5
Rockville 579 D5
Rogers 698 E5
Rollingstone 697 G6
Ronneby 58 E5
Roosevelt 180 C2
Roscoe 141 D5
Rose Creek 363 F7
Roseau▲ 2,396 C2
Rosemount 8,622 E6
Roseville 33,485 G5
Rothsay 443 B4
Round Lake 463 C7
Royalton 802 D5
Rush City 1,497 F5
Rushford 1,485 G7
Rushmore 381 C7
Russell 394 C6
Ruthton 328 B6
Rutledge 152 F4
Sabin 495 B4
Sacred Heart 603 C6
Saint Anthony 7,727 G5
Saint Anthony 81 D5
Saint Bonifacius 1,180 F5
Saint Charles 2,642 F7
Saint Clair 633 E6
Saint Cloud▲ 48,812 D5
Saint Francis 2,538 E5
Saint Hilaire 298 B2
Saint James▲ 4,364 D7
Saint Joseph 3,294 D5
Saint Leo 111 C6
Saint Louis Park 43,787 G5
Saint Martin 274 D5
Saint Michael 2,506 E5
Saint Paul (cap.)▲ 272,235 G6
Saint Paul Park 4,965 G6
Saint Peter▲ 9,421 E6
Saint Rosa 75 D5
Saint Stephen 607 D5
Saint Vincent 116 A2
Sanborn 459 C6
Sandstone 2,057 F4
Sargeant 78 F7
Sartell 5,393 D5
Sauk Centre 3,581 C5
Sauk Rapids 7,825 D5
Savage 9,906 G6
Scanlon 878 F4
Seaforth 87 C6
Sebeka 662 C4
Sedan 63 C5
Shafer 368 F5
Shakopee▲ 11,739 F6
Shelly 225 B3
Sherburn 1,105 D7
Shevlin 157 C3
Shoreview 24,587 G5
Shorewood 5,917 F5
Silver Bay 1,894 G3
Silver Lake 764 D6
Skyline 272 D6
Slayton▲ 2,147 C7
Sleepy Eye 3,694 D6
Sobieski 199 D5
Solway 74 C3
Soudan 900 F3
South Haven 193 D5
South International Falls 2,806 E2
South Saint Paul 20,197 G6
Spicer 1,020 C5
Spring Grove 1,153 G7
Spring Hill 77 D5
Spring Lake 6,532 E5
Spring Lake Park 6,477 E5
Spring Park 1,571 F5
Spring Valley 2,461 F7
Springfield 2,173 C6
Squaw Lake 139 D3
Stacy 1,081 E5
Staples 2,754 D4
Starbuck 1,143 C5
Steen 176 B7
Stephen 707 A2
Stewart 566 D6
Stewartville 4,520 F7
Stillwater▲ 13,882 F5
Stockton 529 G6
Storden 283 C6
Strandquist 98 B2
Strathcona 40 B2
Sturgeon Lake 230 F4
Sunburg 117 C5
Sunfish Lake 413 E6
Swanville 324 D5
Taconite 310 E3
Tamarack 53 E4
Taopi 83 F7
Taunton 175 B6
Taylors Falls 694 F5
Tenstrike 184 D3
Thief River Falls▲ 8,010 B2
Thomson 132 F4
Tintah 74 B5
Tonka Bay 1,472 F5
Tower 502 F3
Tracy 2,059 C6
Trail 67 C3
Trimont 745 D7
Trommald 80 D4
Trosky 120 B7
Truman 1,292 D7
Turtle River 62 D3
Twin Lakes 154 E7
Twin Valley 821 B3
Two Harbors▲ 3,651 G3
Tyler 1,257 B6
Ulen 547 B3
Underwood 284 C4
Upsala 371 D5
Urbank 73 C4
Utica 220 G7
Vadnais Heights 11,041 G5
Vergas 287 C4
Vermillion 510 F6
Verndale 560 C4
Vernon Center 339 D7
Vesta 302 C6
Victoria 2,354 F6
Viking 103 B2
Villard 247 C5
Vining 84 C4
Virginia 9,410 F3
Wabasha▲ 2,384 G6
Wabasso 684 C6
Waconia 3,498 E6
Wadena▲ 4,131 C4
Wahkon 197 E4
Waite Park 5,020 D5
Waldorf 243 E7
Walker▲ 950 D3
Walnut Grove 625 C6
Walters 86 E7
Waltham 170 F7
Wanamingo 847 F6
Wanda 103 C6
Warba 137 E3
Warren▲ 1,813 B2
Warroad 1,679 C2
Waseca▲ 8,385 E6
Watertown 2,408 E6
Waterville 1,771 E6
Watkins 849 D5
Watson 211 C5
Waubun 330 C3
Waverly 600 E5
Wayzata 3,806 G5
Welcome 790 D7
Wells 2,465 E7
Wendell 159 B4
West Concord 871 F6
West Saint Paul 19,248 G5
West Union 54 C5
Westbrook 853 C6
Westport 47 C5
Whalan 94 G7
Wheaton▲ 1,615 B5
White Bear Lake 24,704 G5
White Earth 319 C3
Wilder 83 C7
Willernie 584 G5
Williams 212 D2
Willmar▲ 17,531 C5
Willow River 284 F4
Wilmont 351 C7
Wilton 171 C3
Windom▲ 4,283 C7
Winger 167 B3
Winnebago 1,565 D7
Winona▲ 25,399 G6
Winsted 1,581 D6
Winthrop 1,279 D6
Winton 169 G3
Wolf Lake 35 C4
Wolverton 158 B4
Wood Lake 406 C6
Woodbury 20,075 F6
Woodstock 159 B7
Worthington▲ 9,977 C7
Wrenshall 296 F4
Wright 144 E4
Wykoff 493 F7
Wyoming 2,142 F5
Young America 1,354 E6
Zemple 63 E3
Zim 1,350 F3
Zumbro Falls 237 F6
Zumbrota 2,312 F6

OTHER FEATURES

Ash (riv.) F2
Bald Eagle (lake) G3
Basswood (lake) G2
Battle (riv.) D3
Baudette (riv.) D2
Bear (riv.) E3
Bemidji (lake) D3
Benton (lake) B6
Big Fork (riv.) E2
Big Sandy (lake) E4
Big Stone (lake) B5
Birch (lake) G3
Black (riv.) D2
Blue Earth (riv.) D7
Bois de Sioux (riv.) B4
Bowstring (lake) E3
Buffalo (riv.) B4
Burntside (lake) F3
Cass (lake) D3
Cedar (riv.) F7
Chippewa (riv.) C5
Christina (lake) C4
Clearwater (riv.) C3
Cloquet (riv.) F4
Cobb (riv.) E7
Cottonwood (riv.) C6
Crooked (creek) F4
Crooked (lake) G2
Crow (riv.) D5
Crow Wing (riv.) D4
Cuyuna (range) D4
Dead (lake) C4
Deer (lake) E3
Des Moines (riv.) C7
Eagle (mt.) G2
East Swan (riv.) F3
Elbow (lake) C3
Emily (lake) C5
Fond du Lac Ind. Res. F4
Grand Portage Ind. Res. G2
Grand Portage Nat'l Mon. G2
Green (lake) D5
Greenwood (lake) G3
Gull (lake) D4
Heron (lake) C7
Hill (riv.) C3
Independence (lake) F5
Isabella (lake) G3
Itasca (lake) C3
Kabetogama (lake) E2
Kananranzi (creek) C7
Kettle (riv.) F4
Knife (lake) G2
La Croix (lake) F2
Lac qui Parle (lake) C5
Lac qui Parle (riv.) B6
Lake of the Woods (lake) D1
Leaf (riv.) C4
Leech (lake) D3
Leech Lake Ind. Res. D3
Lida (lake) C4
Little Fork (riv.) E2
Little Rock (creek) C7
Long (lake) D4
Long (lake) F3
Long Prairie (riv.) D4
Lost (riv.) C3
Lower Red (lake) C3
Maple (lake) B3
Maple (riv.) E7
Marsh (lake) B5
Mary (lake) C5
Mesabi (range) E3
Middle (riv.) B2
Mille Lacs Ind. Res. E4
Mille Lacs (lake) E4
Miltona (lake) C4
Minneapolis-Saint Paul Airport G5
Minnesota (riv.) E6
Minnetonka (lake) F5
Minnewaska (lake) C5
Misquah (hills) F2
Mississippi (riv.) D4
Moose (riv.) C2
Mud (lake) C2
Mud (riv.) C2
Muskeg (bay) C2
Mustinka (riv.) B5
Nemadji (riv.) F4
Nett (lake) E2
Nett Lake Ind. Res. E2
North (lake) F1
Otter Tail (lake) C4
Otter Tail (riv.) B4
Partridge (riv.) G3
Pelican (lake) C4
Pelican (lake) D4
Pelican (riv.) F2
Pelican (riv.) B4
Pelican (riv.) F2
Pepin (lake) F6
Pigeon (riv.) G2
Pike (riv.) F3
Pipestone Nat'l Mon. B6
Pokegama (lake) E3
Pomme de Terre (riv.) C5
Poplar (riv.) C3
Prairie (riv.) E3
Rainy (lake) E2
Rainy (riv.) D2
Rapid (riv.) D2
Redeye (riv.) D4
Red Lake (riv.) B2
Red Lake Ind. Res. C2
Red River of the North (riv.) A2
Redeye (riv.) D4
Redwood (riv.) C6
Reno (lake) C5
Rice (lake) E4
Rock (riv.) B7
Root (riv.) G7
Roseau (riv.) B2
Rum (riv.) E5
Saganaga (lake) H2
Saint Croix (riv.) F5
Saint Louis (riv.) F4
Sand (creek) F5
Sand Hill (riv.) B3
Sarah (lake) F5
Schoolcraft C3
Shakopee (creek) C5
Shell (riv.) C4
Shetek (lake) C6
Sleepy Eye (creek) C6
Snake (riv.) A2
Snake (riv.) E4
South Fowl (lake) G1
Star (lake) C4
Sturgeon (riv.) F3
Superior (lake) G3
Swan (lake) D6
Tamarac (riv.) A2
Tamarack (riv.) D2
Thief (lake) C2
Thief (riv.) B2
Traverse (lake) B5
Trout (lake) F2
Two Rivers (riv.) A1
Upper Red (lake) D2
Vermilion (lake) F3
Vermilion (range) F3
Vermilion (riv.) F2
Voyageurs Nat'l Park F2
Wabatawangang (lake) D3
West Swan (riv.) F3
White Earth Ind. Res. C3
Whiteface (riv.) F3
Whitefish (lake) D4
White Iron (lake) G3
Wild Rice (lake) F4
Wild Rice (riv.) B3
Willow (riv.) E4
Winnibigoshish (lake) D3
Woods (lake) D1
Zumbro (riv.) F6

▲County seat

Topography

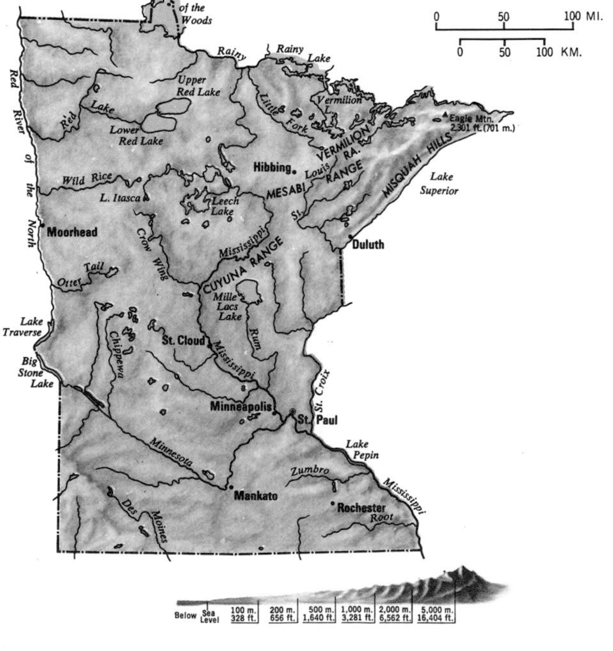

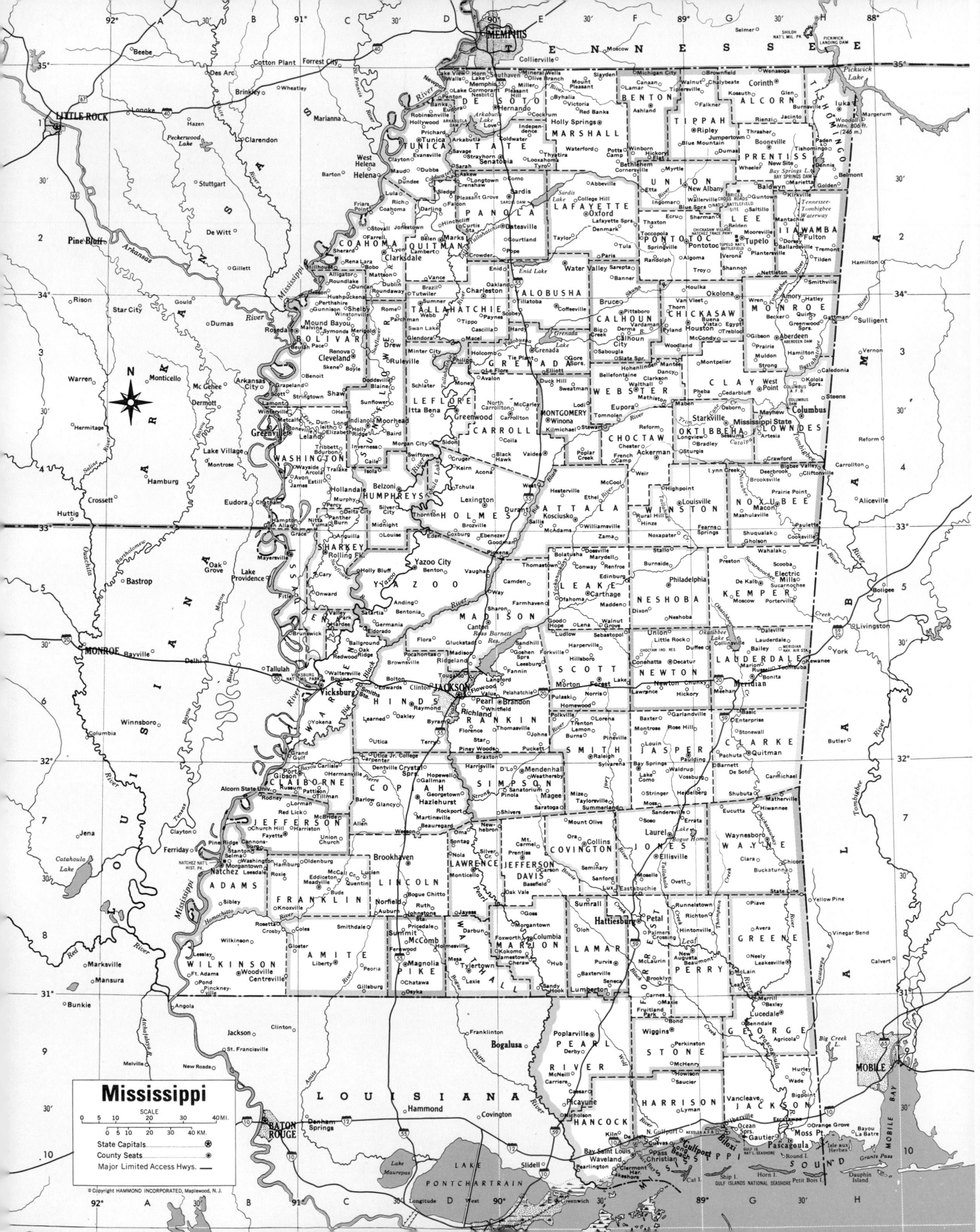

Mississippi

SCALE

0 5 10   20   30   40 MI.

0 5 10   20   30   40 KM.

State Capitals..................⊛
County Seats....................◉
Major Limited Access Hwys.____

© Copyright HAMMOND INCORPORATED, Maplewood, N.J.

COUNTIES

Adams 35,356 B8
Alcorn 31,722 G1
Amite 13,328 C8
Attala 18,481 E4
Benton 8,046 F1
Bolivar 41,875 C3
Calhoun 14,908 F3
Carroll 9,237 E4
Chickasaw 18,085 G3
Choctaw 9,071 F4
Claiborne 11,370 C7
Clarke 17,313 G6
Clay 21,120 G3
Coahoma 31,665 C2
Copiah 27,592 D7
Covington 16,527 E7
De Soto 53,930 E1
Forrest 68,314 F8
Franklin 8,377 C8
George 16,673 G9
Greene 10,220 G8
Grenada 21,555 E3
Hancock 31,760 E10
Harrison 165,365 F10
Hinds 254,441 D6
Holmes 21,604 D4
Humphreys 12,134 C4
Issaquena 1,909 B5
Itawamba 20,017 H2
Jackson 115,243 G9
Jasper 17,114 F6
Jefferson 8,653 B7
Jefferson Davis 14,051 E7
Jones 62,031 F7
Kemper 10,356 G5
Lafayette 31,826 E2
Lamar 30,424 E8
Lauderdale 75,555 G6
Lawrence 12,458 D7
Leake 18,436 E5
Lee 65,581 G2
Leflore 37,341 D3
Lincoln 30,278 D8
Lowndes 59,308 H4
Madison 53,794 D5
Marion 25,544 E8
Marshall 30,361 E1
Monroe 36,582 H3
Montgomery 12,388 E4
Neshoba 24,800 F5
Newton 20,291 F6
Noxubee 12,604 G4
Oktibbeha 38,375 G4
Panola 29,996 E2
Pearl River 38,714 E9
Perry 10,865 G8
Pike 36,882 D8
Pontotoc 22,237 F2
Prentiss 23,278 G1
Quitman 10,490 D2
Rankin 87,161 E6
Scott 24,137 E6
Sharkey 7,066 C5
Simpson 23,953 E7
Smith 14,798 E6
Stone 10,750 F9
Sunflower 32,867 C3
Tallahatchie 15,210 D3
Tate 21,432 E1
Tippah 19,523 G1
Tishomingo 17,683 H1
Tunica 8,164 D1
Union 22,085 F2
Walthall 14,352 D8
Warren 47,880 C6
Washington 67,935 C4
Wayne 19,517 G7
Webster 10,222 F3
Wilkinson 9,678 B8
Winston 19,433 F4
Yalobusha 12,033 E2
Yazoo 25,506 D5

CITIES and TOWNS

Abbeville 399 F2
Aberdeen▲ 6,837 H3
Ackerman▲ 1,573 F4
Acona 200 D4
Agricola 200 G9
Alcorn State University B7
Algoma 420 G2
Alligator 187 C2
Amory 7,093 H3
Anguilla 883 C5
Arcola 564 C4
Arkabutla 400 D1
Artesia 484 G4
Ashland▲ 490 F1
Askew 300 D1
Auburn 500 C8
Avalon 100 D3
Avera 150 G8
Avon 400 B4
Bailey 320 G6
Baird 150 C4
Baldwyn 3,204 G2
Ballardsville 105 H2
Banks 100 D1
Banner 120 F2
Bassfield 249 E8
Batesville▲ 6,403 E2
Baxterville 100 E8
Bay Saint Louis▲ 8,063 F10
Bay Springs▲ 1,729 F7
Beaumont 1,054 G8
Beauregard 206 D7
Becker 350 G3
Belden 241 G2
Belen 400 D2
Bellefontaine 400 F3
Belmont 1,554 H1
Belzoni▲ 2,536 C4
Benndale 500 G9
Benoit 641 C3
Benton 390 D5
Bentonia 518 D5
Bethlehem 210 F1
Beulah 460 B3
Bexley 130 G9
Big Creek 123 F3
Bigbee Valley 370 H4
Bigpoint 350 H9
Biloxi 46,319 G10
Blue Mountain 667 G1
Blue Springs 140 G2
Bobo 200 C2
Bogue Chitto 689 D8
Bolatusha 87 E5
Bolton 637 D6
Bond 350 F9
Bonita 300 G6
Booneville▲ 7,955 G1
Bourbon 200 C4
Boyle 651 C3
Brandon▲ 11,077 E6
Braxton 141 D6
Brazil 229 D2
Brookhaven▲ 10,243 C7
Brooklyn 450 F8
Brooksville 1,098 G4
Brownfield 125 G1
Brownsville 200 D6
Brozville 150 D4
Bruce 2,127 F3
Brunswick 90 C5
Buckatunna 500 G7
Bude 969 C8
Burns 949 E6
Burnsville 889 H1
Byhalia 955 E1
Byram 250 D6
Caesar 80 E9
Caledonia 821 H3
Calhoun City 1,838 F3
Camden 150 E5
Canaan 200 F1
Cannonsburg 240 B7
Canton▲ 10,062 D5
Carlisle 425 C7
Carpenter 200 C6
Carriere 900 E9
Carrollton▲ 221 E4
Carson 400 E7
Carthage▲ 3,819 E5
Cary 392 C5
Cascilla 230 D3
Cedarbluff 175 G3
Centreville 1,771 B8
Chalybeate 350 G1
Charleston▲ 2,328 D2
Chatawa 300 D8
Chatham 150 B4
Cheraw 100 E8
Chunky 292 G6
Church Hill 350 B7
Clara 275 G7
Clarksdale▲ 19,717 D2
Clarkson 100 F3
Clermont Harbor 550 F10
Cleveland▲ 15,384 C3
Cliftonville 280 H4
Clinton 21,847 D6
Coahoma 254 C2
Cockrum 150 E1
Coffeeville▲ 825 E3
Coldwater 1,502 E1
Coles 150 C8
College Hill 150 E2
Collins▲ 2,541 E7
Collinsville 1,364 G6
Columbia▲ 6,815 E8
Columbus▲ 23,799 H3
Como 1,387 E1
Conehatta 925 F6
Corinth▲ 11,820 G1
Courtland 329 E2
Coxburg 300 D5
Crawford 668 G4
Crenshaw 978 D2
Crosby 465 B8
Crowder 758 D2
Cruger 548 D4
Crystal Springs 5,643 D7
Cuevas 200 F10
Curtis Station 350 D2
D'Iberville 6,566 G10
D'Lo 421 E7
Daleville 210 G5
Dancy 116 F3
Darbun 100 D8
Darling 275 D2
De Kalb▲ 1,073 G5
De Lisle 450 F10
De Soto 150 G7
Decatur▲ 1,248 F6
Delta City 310 C4
Dennis 150 H1
Dentville 175 C7
Derby 298 F9
Derma 959 F3
Dixon 125 F5
Doddsville 149 C3
Dorsey 100 H2
Drew 2,349 C3
Dublin 100 C2
Duck Hill 586 E3
Duffee 175 G6
Dumas 407 G1
Duncan 416 C2
Dundee 600 D1
Dunleith 140 C4
Durant 2,838 E4
Eastabuchie 200 F8
Ebenezer 200 D5
Ecru 696 F2
Eden 88 D5
Edinburg 200 F5
Edwards 1,279 C6
Egypt 100 G3
Electric Mills 100 G5
Elizabeth 500 C4
Elliott 200 E3
Ellisville▲ 3,634 F7
Enid E2
Enterprise 477 G6
Errata 85 F7
Escatawpa 3,902 G10
Estill 100 C4
Ethel 454 F4
Eudora 200 D1
Eupora 2,145 F3
Falcon 167 D2
Falkner 232 G1
Fannin 250 E6
Farrell 300 C2
Fayette▲ 1,853 B7
Fernwood 500 D8
Fitler 175 B5
Flora 1,482 D5
Florence 1,831 D6
Flowood 2,860 D6
Forest▲ 5,060 F6
Forkville 185 E6
Foxworth 800 E8
French Camp 320 F4
Friars Point 1,334 C2
Fulton▲ 3,387 H2
Gallman D7
Garlandville 150 F6
Gattman 120 H3
Gautier 10,088 G10
Georgetown 332 D7
Glen 165 H1
Glen Allan 650 B4
Glendora 220 D3
Gloster 1,323 B8
Gluckstadt 150 D5
Golden 202 H2
Good Hope 125 E5
Goodman 1,256 E5
Gore Springs 125 E3
Goshen Springs 100 E6
Goss 100 E8
Grace 325 C5
Grapeland 200 B3
Greenville▲ 45,226 B4
Greenwood Springs 170 H3
Greenwood▲ 18,906 D4
Grenada▲ 10,864 E3
Gulfport▲ 40,775 F10
Gunnison 611 C3
Guntown 692 G2
Hamburg 150 B7
Hamilton 500 H3
Hampton 200 B4
Hardee 100 C5
Harperville 200 E6
Harriston 500 C7
Harrisville 500 D7
Hatley 529 H3
Hattiesburg▲ 41,882 F8
Hazlehurst▲ 4,221 D7
Heidelberg 981 F7
Helm 80 C4
Hermanville 750 C7
Hernando▲ 3,125 E1
Hickory 493 F6
Hickory Flat 535 F1
Hillsboro 800 E6
Hintonville 300 F8
Hiwannee 250 G7
Hohenlinden 96 F3
Hollandale 3,576 C4
Holly Bluff 700 C5
Holly Ridge 350 C4
Holly Springs▲ 7,261 E1
Hollywood 80 D1
Hopewell 250 D7
Horn Lake 9,069 D1
Houlka G2
Houston▲ 3,903 G3
Howison 300 F9
Hub 80 E8
Hurley 500 H9
Independence 150 E1
Indianola▲ 11,809 C4
Ingomar 150 F2
Inverness 1,174 C4
Isola 732 C4
Itta Bena 2,377 D4
Iuka▲ 3,122 H1
Jackson (cap.)▲ 196,637 D6
James 100 B4
Jayess 200 D8
Johns 90 E6
Jonestown 1,467 D2
Jumpertown 438 G1
Kewanee 250 H6
Kilmichael 826 E4
Kiln 1,262 F10
Kirkville 200 H2
Kokomo 250 E8
Kolola Springs 100 H3
Kosciusko▲ 6,986 E4
Kossuth 245 G1
Lafayette Springs 80 F2
Lake 369 F6
Lake Como 150 F7
Lake Cormorant 300 D1
Lake View 125 D1
Lakeshore 550 F10
Lamar 200 F1
Lambert 1,131 D2
Lamont 400 B3
Langford 100 E6
Lauderdale 600 G5
Laurel▲ 18,827 F7
Lawrence 250 F6
Le Flore 99 D3
Leaf 250 G8
Leakesville▲ 1,129 G8
Learned 111 C6
Leland 6,366 C4
Lemon 90 E6
Lena 175 E5
Lexington▲ 2,227 D4
Liberty▲ 624 C8
Long 15,804 C4
Long Beach 7,967 F10
Longtown 150 D1
Longview 800 G4
Looxahoma 200 E1
Lorena 90 F6
Lorman 350 B7
Louin 289 F6
Louise 343 C5
Louisville▲ 7,169 G4
Lucedale▲ 2,592 G9
Ludlow 350 E5
Lula 224 C2
Lumberton 2,121 E8
Lyman 1,117 F10
Lyon 446 D2
Maben 752 F3
Macon▲ 2,256 G4
Madden 450 F5
Madison 7,471 D6
Magee 3,607 E7
Magnolia▲ 2,245 D8
Malvina 100 C3
Mantachie 651 H2
Mantee 134 F3
Marietta 287 H2
Marion 1,359 G6
Marks▲ 1,758 D2
Marydell 99 F5
Mashulaville 227 G4
Matherville 150 G7
Mathiston 818 F3
Mattson 200 C2
Maxie 233 F9
Mayersville▲ 329 B5
Mayhew 150 G4
McAdams 350 E4
McCall Creek 250 C7
McCarley 250 E3
McComb 11,591 D8
McCondy 150 G3
McCool 169 F4
McHenry 660 F9
McLain 536 G8
McLaurin 100 F8
McNeill 800 E9
Meadville▲ 453 C8
Meehan 100 G6
Mendenhall▲ 2,463 E7
Meridian▲ 41,036 G6
Merigold 572 C3
Merrill 100 G9
Metcalfe 1,092 B4
Michigan City 350 F1
Midnight 500 C4
Mineral Wells 250 E1
Minter City 150 D3
Mississippi State G4
Mize 312 E7
Money 350 D3
Monticello▲ 1,755 D7
Montpelier 175 G3
Montrose 106 F6
Mooreville 200 G2
Moorhead 2,417 C4
Morgan City 139 D4
Morgantown 32,880 B7
Morgantown 325 E8
Morton 3,212 E6
Moselle 525 F8
Moss 17,837 F7
Moss Point 18,998 G10
Mound Bayou 2,222 C3
Mount Olive 914 E7
Mount Pleasant 250 E1
Murphy 100 C4
Myrtle 358 F1
Natchez▲ 19,460 B7
Neely 270 G8
Nesbit 366 D1
Neshoba 250 F5
Nettleton 2,462 G2
New Albany▲ 6,775 G2
New Augusta▲ 668 F8
New Houlka (Houlka) 558 G2
New Site 100 H1
Newhebron 470 D7
Newton 3,701 F6
Nicholson 400 E10
Nitta Yuma 150 C4
Nola 120 D7
North Carrollton 578 E3
North Gulfport 4,966 F10
Noxapater 441 F5
Oak Ridge 350 C6
Oak Vale E8
Oakland 553 E2
Oakley 133 D6
Ocean Springs 14,658 G10
Ofahoma 350 E5
Okolona▲ 3,267 G2
Olive Branch 3,567 E1
Oloh 93 E8
Oma 200 D7
Ora 15,676 E7
Orange Grove H10
Osyka 483 D8
Ovett 600 F8
Oxford▲ 9,984 F2
Pace 354 C3
Pachuta 268 G6
Paden 123 H1
Palmers Crossing 2,765 F8
Panther Burn 300 C4
Parchman 200 D3
Paris 253 F2
Pascagoula▲ 25,899 G10
Pass Christian 5,557 F10
Pattison 540 C7
Paulding▲ 630 F6
Paulette 230 H4
Paynes 100 D3
Pearl 19,588 D6
Pearlington 1,603 E10
Pelahatchie 1,553 E6
Penton 175 D1
Peoria 100 C8
Perkinston 950 F9
Petal 7,883 F8
Pheba 280 G3
Philadelphia▲ 6,758 F5
Philipp 975 D3
Piave 150 G8
Picayune 10,633 E9
Pickens 1,285 E5
Pine Ridge 175 B7
Pineville 80 F6
Piney Woods 450 D6
Pinola E7
Pittsboro▲ 277 F3
Plantersville 1,046 G2
Pleasant Grove 100 D2
Pleasant Hill 400 E1
Polkville 129 E6

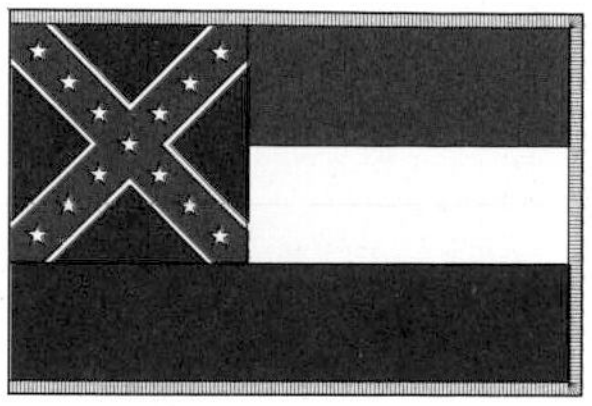

AREA 47,689 sq. mi. (123,515 sq. km.)
POPULATION 2,586,443
CAPITAL Jackson
LARGEST CITY Jackson
HIGHEST POINT Woodall Mtn. 806 ft. (246 m.)
SETTLED IN 1716
ADMITTED TO UNION December 10, 1817
POPULAR NAME Magnolia State
STATE FLOWER Magnolia
STATE BIRD Mockingbird

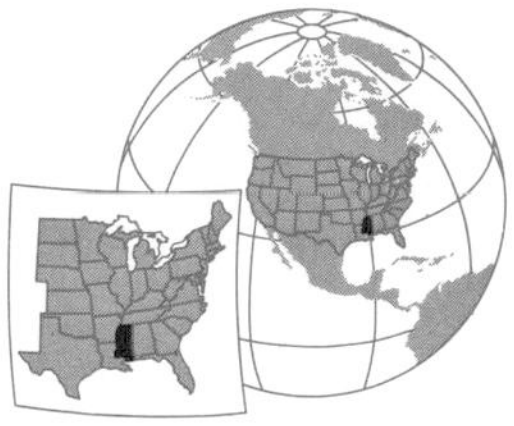

Topography

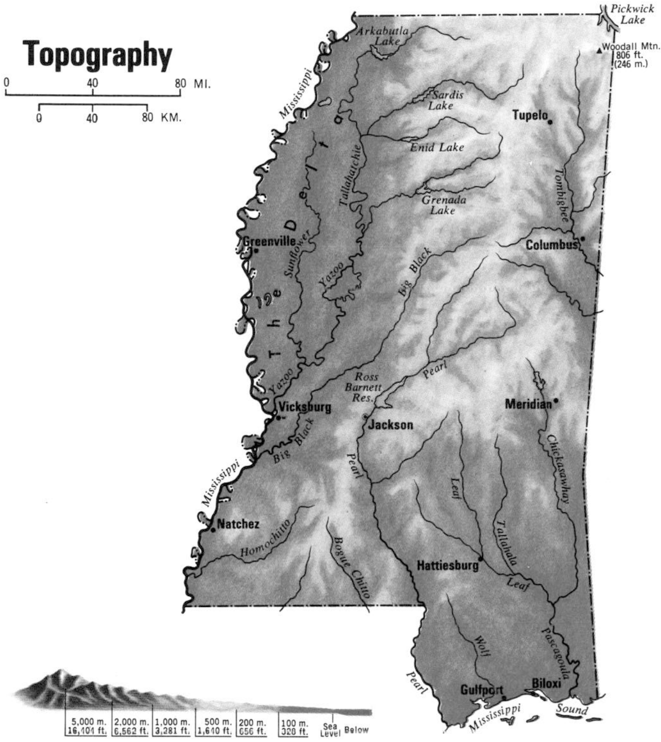

(continued on following page)

Mississippi-Missouri River System

MILES
0   100   200   300

Navigable Waterways
over 9 feet deep............
Major River Ports.............⊙

©Copyright HAMMOND INCORPORATED.

Agriculture, Industry and Resources

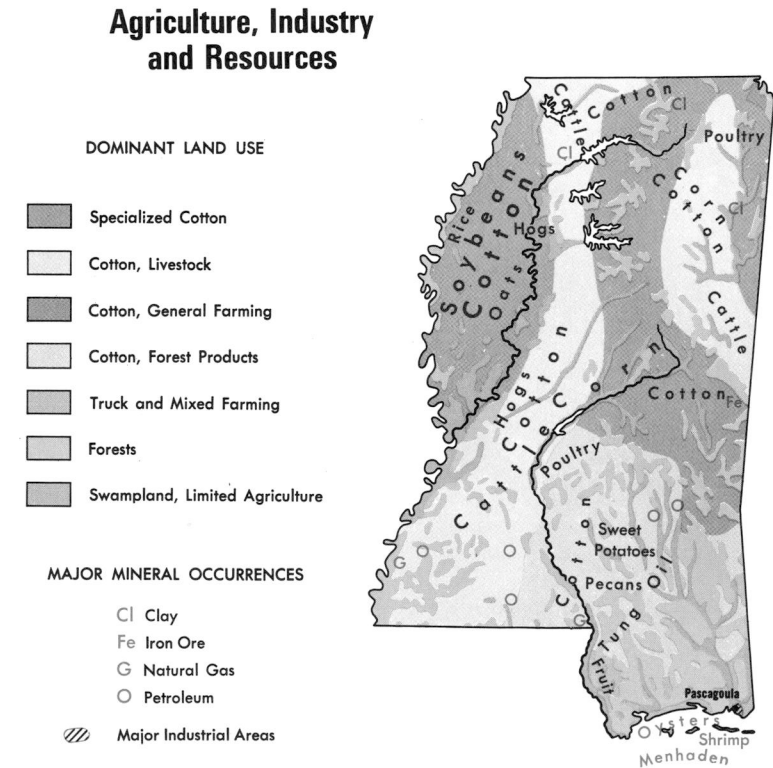

DOMINANT LAND USE

- Specialized Cotton
- Cotton, Livestock
- Cotton, General Farming
- Cotton, Forest Products
- Truck and Mixed Farming
- Forests
- Swampland, Limited Agriculture

MAJOR MINERAL OCCURRENCES

- Cl Clay
- Fe Iron Ore
- G Natural Gas
- O Petroleum
- ⁄⁄⁄ Major Industrial Areas

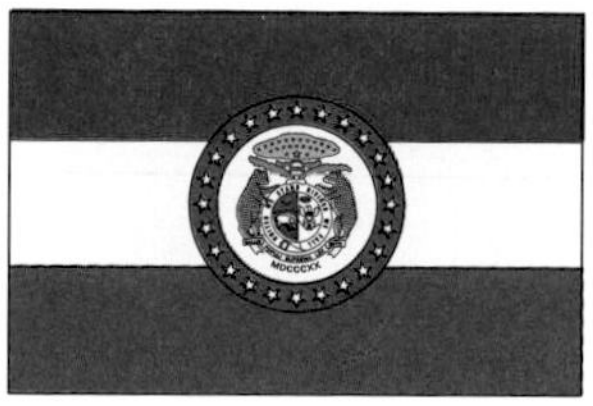

AREA 69,697 sq. mi. (180,515 sq. km.)
POPULATION 5,137,804
CAPITAL Jefferson City
LARGEST CITY St. Louis
HIGHEST POINT Taum Sauk Mtn. 1,772 ft. (540 m.)
SETTLED IN 1764
ADMITTED TO UNION August 10, 1821
POPULAR NAME Show Me State
STATE FLOWER Hawthorn
STATE BIRD Bluebird

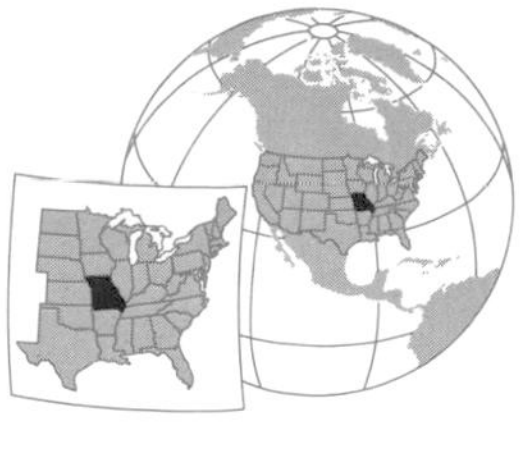

COUNTIES

Adair 24,577 ... G2
Andrew 14,632 ... C3
Atchison 7,457 ... B2
Audrain 23,599 ... J4
Barry 27,547 ... E9
Barton 11,312 ... D7
Bates 15,025 ... D6
Benton 13,859 ... F6
Bollinger 10,619 ... M8
Boone 112,379 ... H4
Buchanan 83,083 ... C3
Butler 38,765 ... M9
Caldwell 8,380 ... E3
Callaway 32,809 ... J5
Camden 27,495 ... G6
Cape Girardeau 61,633 ... N8
Carroll 10,748 ... F4
Carter 5,515 ... L9
Cass 63,808 ... D5
Cedar 12,093 ... E7
Chariton 9,202 ... F3
Christian 32,644 ... F9
Clark 7,547 ... J2
Clay 153,411 ... D4
Clinton 16,595 ... D3
Cole 63,579 ... H6
Cooper 14,835 ... G5
Crawford 19,173 ... K7
Dade 7,449 ... E8
Dallas 12,646 ... F7
Daviess 7,865 ... E3
De Kalb 8,222 ... D3
Dent 13,702 ... J7
Douglas 11,876 ... G9
Dunklin 33,112 ... M1
Franklin 80,603 ... K6
Gasconade 14,006 ... J6
Gentry 6,848 ... D2
Greene 207,949 ... F8
Grundy 10,536 ... E2
Harrison 8,469 ... E2
Henry 20,044 ... E6
Hickory 7,335 ... F7
Holt 6,034 ... B2
Howard 9,631 ... G4
Howell 31,447 ... J9
Iron 10,726 ... L7
Jackson 633,232 ... R5
Jasper 90,465 ... D8
Jefferson 171,380 ... L6
Johnson 42,514 ... E5
Knox 4,482 ... H2
Laclede 27,158 ... G7
Lafayette 31,107 ... E4
Lawrence 30,236 ... E8
Lewis 10,233 ... J2
Lincoln 28,892 ... L4
Linn 13,885 ... F3
Livingston 14,592 ... E3
Macon 15,345 ... G3
Madison 11,127 ... M8
Maries 7,976 ... J6
Marion 27,682 ... J3
McDonald 16,938 ... D9
Mercer 3,723 ... E2
Miller 20,700 ... H6
Mississippi 14,442 ... O9
Moniteau 12,298 ... G5
Monroe 9,104 ... H3
Montgomery 11,355 ... K5
Morgan 15,574 ... G6
New Madrid 20,928 ... N9
Newton 44,445 ... D9
Nodaway 21,709 ... C2
Oregon 9,470 ... K9
Osage 12,018 ... J6
Ozark 8,598 ... H9
Pemiscot 21,921 ... N1
Perry 16,648 ... N7
Pettis 35,437 ... F5
Phelps 35,248 ... J7
Pike 15,969 ... K4
Platte 57,867 ... C4
Polk 21,826 ... F7
Pulaski 41,307 ... H7
Putnam 5,079 ... F2
Ralls 8,476 ... J3
Randolph 24,370 ... G3
Ray 21,971 ... E4
Reynolds 6,661 ... L8
Ripley 12,303 ... L9
Saint Charles 144,107 ... M2
Saint Clair 8,622 ... E6
Saint Francois 42,600 ... M7
Saint Louis 974,180 ... O3
Saint Louis (city county) 452,801 ... P3
Sainte Genevieve 15,180 ... M7
Saline 23,523 ... F4
Schuyler 4,236 ... G2
Scotland 4,822 ... H2
Scott 39,376 ... N8
Shannon 7,613 ... K8
Shelby 6,942 ... H3
Stoddard 28,895 ... N9
Stone 19,078 ... F9
Sullivan 6,326 ... F2
Taney 25,561 ... F9
Texas 21,476 ... J8
Vernon 19,041 ... D7
Warren 19,534 ... K5
Washington 20,380 ... L7
Wayne 11,543 ... L8
Webster 23,753 ... G8
Worth 2,440 ... D2
Wright 16,758 ... H8

CITIES and TOWNS

Adrian 1,582 ... D6
Advance 1,139 ... N8
Affton 21,106 ... P4
Agency 642 ... C3
Alba 465 ... D8
Albany▲ 1,958 ... D2
Alexandria 341 ... K2
Alma 446 ... E4
Altamont 188 ... D3
Altenburg 307 ... O7
Alton▲ 692 ... K9
Amazonia 257 ... C3
Amoret 212 ... C6
Amsterdam 237 ... D6
Anderson 1,432 ... D9
Annapolis 363 ... L8
Anniston 288 ... O9
Appleton City 1,280 ... D6
Arbyrd 597 ... M10
Arcadia 609 ... L7
Archie 799 ... D5
Argyle 178 ... J6
Armstrong 310 ... G4
Arnold 18,828 ... M6
Asbury 220 ... C8
Ash Grove 1,128 ... E8
Ashland 1,252 ... H5
Atlanta 411 ... H3
Augusta 263 ... L5
Aurora 6,459 ... E9
Auxvasse 821 ... J4
Ava▲ 2,938 ... G9
Avondale 550 ... P5
Bakersfield 292 ... H9
Ballwin 21,816 ... N3
Baring 182 ... H2
Barnard 234 ... C2
Barnett 215 ... G6
Bates City 197 ... E5
Battlefield 1,526 ... F8
Bel-Nor 2,935 ... P2
Bel-Ridge 3,199 ... P2
Bell City 469 ... N8
Bella Villa 708 ... R4
Belle 1,218 ... J6
Bellefontaine 10,922 ... N2
Bellefontaine Neighbors 12,082 ... R2
Bellflower 413 ... K4
Belton 18,150 ... C5
Benton City 139 ... J4
Benton▲ 575 ... O8
Berger 247 ... K5
Berkeley 12,450 ... P2
Bernie 1,847 ... M9
Bertrand 692 ... O9
Bethany▲ 3,005 ... E2
Beverly 660 ... O4
Bevier 643 ... G3
Billings 989 ... F8
Birch Tree 599 ... K9
Birmingham 222 ... R5
Bismarck 1,579 ... L7
Black 6,128 ... L7
Black Jack 5,293 ... R1
Blackburn 308 ... F4
Blackwater 221 ... G5
Blairstown 185 ... E5
Bland 651 ... J6
Blodgett 202 ... O8
Bloomfield▲ 1,800 ... M9
Bloomsdale 353 ... M6
Blue Springs 40,153 ... R6
Bogard 228 ... E4
Bolckow 253 ... C2
Bolivar▲ 6,845 ... F7
Bonne Terre 3,871 ... L7
Boonville▲ 7,095 ... G5
Bosworth 334 ... F4
Bourbon 1,188 ... K6
Bowling Green▲ 2,976 ... K4
Brandsville 167 ... J9
Branson 3,706 ... F9
Brashear 318 ... H2
Braymer 886 ... E3
Breckenridge 418 ... E3
Breckenridge Hills 5,404 ... O2
Brentwood 8,150 ... P3
Bridgeton 17,779 ... O2
Bridgeton Terrace 334 ... O2
Bronaugh 211 ... C7
Brookfield 4,888 ... F3
Browning 331 ... F2
Brunswick 1,074 ... F4
Bucklin 616 ... G3
Buckner 2,873 ... R5
Buffalo▲ 2,414 ... F7
Bunceton 341 ... G5
Bunker 390 ... K8
Burlington Junction 634 ... B2
Butler▲ 4,099 ... D6
Butterfield 248 ... E9
Cabool 2,006 ... H8
Cainsville 387 ... E2
Cairo 282 ... H4
Caledonia 142 ... L7
Calhoun 450 ... E6
California▲ 3,465 ... H5
Callao 332 ... G3
Calverton Park 1,404 ... P2
Camden 238 ... D4
Camden Point 373 ... C4
Camdenton▲ 2,561 ... G6
Cameron 4,831 ... D3
Campbell 2,165 ... M9
Canalou 319 ... N9
Canton 2,623 ... J2
Cape Girardeau 34,438 ... O8
Cardwell 792 ... M10
Carl Junction 4,123 ... C8
Carrollton▲ 4,406 ... E4
Carterville 2,013 ... D8
Carthage▲ 10,747 ... D8
Caruth 7,389 ... N10
Caruthersville▲ 7,958 ... N10
Carytown 149 ... D8
Cassville▲ 2,371 ... E9
Cedar City 427 ... H5
Cedar Hill Lakes 227 ... L6
Center 552 ... J3
Centertown 356 ... H5
Centerview 214 ... E5
Centerville▲ 89 ... L8
Centralia 3,414 ... H4
Chaffee 3,059 ... N8
Chamois 449 ... J5
Charlack 1,388 ... P2
Charleston▲ 5,085 ... O9
Chesterfield 37,991 ... N2
Chilhowee 335 ... E5
Chillicothe▲ 8,804 ... E3
Chula 183 ... F3
Circle City 154 ... N9
Clarence 1,026 ... H3
Clark 257 ... H4
Clarksburg 358 ... G5
Clarksdale 287 ... D3
Clarkson Valley 2,508 ... N3
Clarksville 480 ... K4
Clarkton 1,113 ... M10
Claycomo 1,668 ... P5
Clayton▲ 13,874 ... P3
Clearmont 175 ... C1
Cleveland 506 ... C5
Clever 580 ... F8
Clinton▲ 8,703 ... E6
Cobalt City 254 ... M7
Cole Camp 1,054 ... F6
Collins 144 ... E7
Columbia▲ 69,101 ... H5
Commerce 173 ... O8
Conception Junction 236 ... C2
Concord 19,859 ... P4
Concordia 2,160 ... E5
Conway 629 ... G7
Cool Valley 1,407 ... P2
Cooter 451 ... N10
Corder 485 ... E4
Cottleville 2,936 ... M2
Country Club Village 1,234 ... C3
Cowgill 257 ... E3
Craig 346 ... B2
Crane 1,218 ... E9
Creighton 289 ... D6
Crestwood 11,234 ... O3
Creve Coeur 12,304 ... O2
Crocker 1,077 ... H7
Cross Timbers 168 ... F6
Crystal City 4,088 ... M6
Crystal Lake Park 506 ... O3
Cuba 2,537 ... K6
Curryville 261 ... K4
Dadeville 220 ... E8
De Kalb 222 ... C3
De Soto 5,993 ... L6
Dearborn 480 ... C3
Deepwater 441 ... E6
Dellwood 5,245 ... R2
Delta 450 ... N8
Des Arc 173 ... L8
Des Peres 8,395 ... O3
Desloge 4,150 ... M7
Dexter 7,559 ... N9
Diamond 775 ... D9
Diehlstadt 145 ... N9
Diggins 258 ... G8
Dixon 1,585 ... H6
Doniphan▲ 1,713 ... L9
Doolittle 599 ... J7
Downing 359 ... H2
Drexel 936 ... C6
Dudley 271 ... M9
Duenweg 940 ... D8
Duquesne 1,229 ... D8
Eagleville 275 ... D2
East Lynne 289 ... D5
East Prairie 3,416 ... O9
Easton 232 ... C3
Edgar Springs 215 ... J7
Edgerton 565 ... C3
Edina▲ 1,283 ... H2
Edmundson 1,111 ... O2
El Dorado Springs 3,830 ... E7
Eldon 4,419 ... G6
Ellington 994 ... L8
Ellisville 7,545 ... M3
Ellsinore 405 ... L9
Elmo 179 ... B1
Elsberry 1,898 ... L4
Elvins 1,391 ... L7
Eminence▲ 582 ... K8
Emma 194 ... F5
Eolia 389 ... L4
Essex 531 ... N9
Esther 1,071 ... M7
Eugene 141 ... H6
Eureka 4,683 ... M4
Everton 325 ... E8
Ewing 463 ... J2
Excelsior Springs 10,354 ... R4
Exeter 597 ... D9
Fair Grove 919 ... F8
Fair Play 442 ... E7
Fairfax 699 ... B2
Fairview 298 ... D9
Farber 418 ... J4
Farley 217 ... O4
Farmington▲ 11,598 ... M7
Fayette▲ 2,888 ... G4
Fenton 3,346 ... O4
Ferguson 22,286 ... P2
Ferrelview 338 ... O4
Festus 8,105 ... M6
Fillmore 256 ... C2
Fisk 422 ... M9
Flat 4,823 ... J7
Flat River 4,443 ... M7
Fleming 130 ... D4
Flemington 141 ... F7
Flinthill 219 ... L5
Florissant 51,206 ... P1
Foley 209 ... L4
Fordland 523 ... G8
Forest City 380 ... B3
Foristell 144 ... L5
Forsyth▲ 1,175 ... F9
Foster 161 ... D6
Frankford 396 ... K4
Franklin 181 ... G4
Fredericktown▲ 3,950 ... M7
Freeburg 446 ... J6
Freeman 480 ... C5
Freistatt 166 ... E8
Fremont 201 ... K9
Frohna 162 ... N7
Frontenac 3,374 ... O3
Fulton▲ 10,033 ... J5
Gainesville▲ 659 ... G9
Galena▲ 401 ... F9
Gallatin▲ 1,864 ... E3
Galt 296 ... F2
Garden City 1,225 ... D5
Gasconade 253 ... J5
Gerald 888 ... K6
Gideon 1,104 ... N10
Gilliam 212 ... F4
Gilman City 393 ... D2
Gladstone 26,243 ... P5
Glasgow 1,295 ... G4
Glenaire 597 ... R5
Glendale 5,945 ... P3
Glenwood 195 ... G1
Golden 794 ... E9
Golden City 900 ... D8
Goodman 1,094 ... C9
Gordonville 345 ... N8
Gower 1,249 ... C3
Graham 204 ... C2
Grain Valley 1,898 ... S6
Granby 1,945 ... D9
Grandin 233 ... L9
Grandview 24,967 ... P6
Grant City▲ 998 ... D2
Grantwood 904 ... O4
Gray Summit 2,505 ... L6
Green Castle 285 ... G2
Green City 671 ... F2
Green Ridge 452 ... F5
Greenfield▲ 1,416 ... E8
Greentop 425 ... H2
Greenville▲ 437 ... M8
Greenwood 1,505 ... R6
Hale 480 ... F3
Half Way 157 ... F7
Hallsville 917 ... H4
Halltown 161 ... E8
Hamilton 1,737 ... E3
Hanley Hills 2,325 ... P2
Hannibal 18,004 ... K3
Hardin 598 ... E4
Harrisburg 169 ... H4
Harrisonville▲ 7,683 ... D5
Hartville▲ 495 ... G8
Hawk Point 472 ... K5
Hayti 3,280 ... N10
Hayti Heights 893 ... N10
Haywood City 263 ... N9
Hazelwood 15,324 ... P2
Henrietta 412 ... E4
Herculaneum 2,263 ... M6
Hermann▲ 2,754 ... K5
Hermitage▲ 512 ... F7
Higbee 639 ... H4
Higginsville 4,693 ... E4
High Hill 204 ... K5

(continued on following page)

Agriculture, Industry and Resources

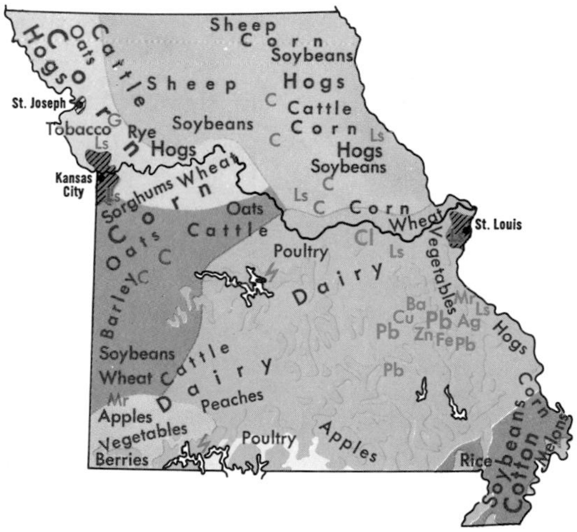

DOMINANT LAND USE

- Cattle Feed, Hogs
- Livestock, Cash Grain, Dairy
- Pasture Livestock
- Specialized Cotton
- General Farming, Dairy, Livestock, Poultry
- General Farming, Livestock, Truck Farming, Cotton
- Fruit and Mixed Farming
- Forests
- Urban Areas

MAJOR MINERAL OCCURRENCES

Ag	Silver	G	Natural Gas
Ba	Barite	Ls	Limestone
C	Coal	Mr	Marble
Cl	Clay	Pb	Lead
Cu	Copper	Zn	Zinc
Fe	Iron Ore		

Water Power — Major Industrial Areas

High Ridge 4,423 ....M6
Hillsboro▲ 1,625 ....L6
Hillsdale 1,948 ....R2
Holcomb 531 ....N10
Holden 2,389 ....E5
Holland 237 ....N10
Holliday 139 ....H3
Hollister 2,628 ....F9
Holt 311 ....D4
Holts Summit 2,292 ....H5
Homestown 230 ....N10
Hopkins 575 ....C1
Horine 1,043 ....M6
Hornersville 629 ....M10
Houston Lake 303 ....O5
Houston▲ 2,118 ....J8
Houstonia 283 ....F5
Howardville 440 ....N9
Hughesville 174 ....F5
Hume 287 ....C6
Hunnewell 219 ....J3
Huntleigh 392 ....O3
Huntsville▲ 1,567 ....H4
Hurdland 212 ....H2
Hurricane Deck 210 ....G6
Iberia 650 ....H6
Illmo 1,368 ....O8
Imperial 4,156 ....M6
Independence▲ 112,301 ....R5
Iron Gates 309 ....C8
Irondale 474 ....L7
Ironton▲ 1,539 ....L7
Jackson▲ 9,256 ....N8
Jameson 149 ....E2
Jamesport 570 ....E3
Jamestown 298 ....G5
Jasper 994 ....D8
Jefferson City (cap.)▲ 35,481 ....H5
Jennings 15,905 ....R2
Jerico Springs 247 ....E7
Jonesburg 630 ....J5
Joplin 40,961 ....C8
Junction City 326 ....M7
Kahoka▲ 2,195 ....J2
Kansas City 435,146 ....P5
Kearney 1,790 ....D4
Kelso 526 ....O8
Kennett▲ 10,941 ....M10
Keytesville▲ 564 ....G4
Kidder 241 ....D3
Kimberling City 1,590 ....F9
Kimmswick 135 ....M6
King City 986 ....D2
Kingston▲ 279 ....E3
Kingsville 279 ....D5
Kinloch 2,702 ....P2
Kirksville▲ 17,152 ....H2
Kirkwood 27,291 ....O3
Knob Noster 2,261 ....E5
Knox City 262 ....H2
Koshkonong 198 ....J9
La Belle 655 ....J2
La Grange 1,102 ....K2
La Monte 995 ....F5
La Plata 1,401 ....H2
Laclede 410 ....F3
Laddonia 581 ....J4
Ladue 8,847 ....P3
Lake Lotawana 2,141 ....R6
Lake Ozark 681 ....G6
Lake Saint Louis 7,400 ....L5
Lake Tapawingo 761 ....R6
Lake Waukomis 1,027 ....P5

Lake Winnebago 748 ....R6
Lakeshire 1,467 ....P4
Lamar Heights 176 ....D8
Lamar▲ 4,168 ....D8
Lanagan 501 ....C9
Lancaster▲ 785 ....H1
Laredo 205 ....E2
Lathrop 1,794 ....D3
Laurie 507 ....G6
Lawson 1,876 ....D4
Leadington 201 ....M7
Leadwood 1,247 ....L7
Leasburg 289 ....K6
Lebanon▲ 9,983 ....G7
Lee's Summit 46,418 ....R6
Leeton 632 ....R4
Lemay 18,005 ....P4
Levasy 279 ....S5
Lewis 142 ....E6
Lewis and Clark Village 131 ....C3
Lewistown 453 ....J2
Lexington▲ 4,860 ....E4
Liberal 684 ....D7
Liberty▲ 20,459 ....R5
Licking 1,328 ....J8
Lilbourn 1,378 ....N9
Lincoln 874 ....F6
Linn Creek 232 ....G6
Linn▲ 1,148 ....J5
Linneus▲ 364 ....F3
Lockwood 1,041 ....E8
Lohman 154 ....H5
Lone Jack 392 ....S6
Louisiana 3,967 ....K4
Lowry City 723 ....E6
Ludlow 147 ....E3
Luebbering 1,865 ....M8
Lutesville 865 ....N8
Mackenzie 148 ....P3
Macks Creek 272 ....G7
Macon▲ 5,571 ....H3
Madison 518 ....H4
Maitland 338 ....B2
Malden 5,123 ....M9
Malta Bend 289 ....F4
Manchester 6,542 ....O3
Mansfield 1,429 ....G8
Maplewood 9,962 ....P3
Marble Hill▲ 1,447 ....N8
Marceline 2,645 ....F3
Marionville 1,920 ....E8
Marlborough 1,949 ....P3
Marquand 278 ....M8
Marshall▲ 12,711 ....F4
Marshfield▲ 4,374 ....G8
Marston 689 ....N9
Marthasville 674 ....L5
Martinsburg 337 ....J4
Maryland Heights 25,407 ....O2
Maryville▲ 10,663 ....C2
Matthews 614 ....N9
Maysville▲ 1,176 ....D3
Mayview 279 ....E4
McFall 142 ....D2
Meadville 360 ....F3
Mehlville 27,557 ....P4
Memphis▲ 2,094 ....H2
Mendon 207 ....F3
Mercer 297 ....F2
Meta 249 ....H6
Mexico▲ 11,290 ....J4
Miami 507 ....G6
Middletown 217 ....J4
Milan▲ 1,767 ....F2
Mill Spring 252 ....L8

Miller 753 ....E8
Mindenmines 346 ....C8
Mine La Motte 125 ....M7
Miner 1,218 ....N9
Mineral Point 384 ....L7
Missouri City 348 ....R5
Moberly 12,839 ....G4
Mokane 186 ....J5
Moline Acres 2,710 ....R2
Monett 6,529 ....E9
Monroe City 2,701 ....J3
Montgomery City▲ 2,281 ....K5
Monticello▲ 106 ....J2
Montrose 440 ....E6
Morehouse 1,068 ....N9
Morley 683 ....N8
Morrison 160 ....J5
Morrisville 293 ....F8
Mosby 194 ....R4
Moscow Mills 924 ....K5
Mound City 1,273 ....B2
Moundville 140 ....C7
Mount Vernon▲ 3,726 ....E8
Mountain Grove 4,182 ....H8
Mountain View 2,036 ....J8
Murphy 9,342 ....O3
Napoleon 233 ....E4
Naylor 642 ....L9
Neelyville 381 ....M9
Nelson 181 ....F4
Neosho▲ 9,254 ....D9
Nevada▲ 8,597 ....D7
New Bloomfield 480 ....J5
New Cambria 232 ....G3
New Florence 801 ....K5
New Franklin 1,107 ....G4
New Hampton 320 ....D2
New Haven 1,757 ....K5
New London▲ 988 ....K3
New Madrid▲ 3,350 ....O9
New Melle 486 ....L5
Newburg 589 ....J7
Newtonia 204 ....D9
Niangua 459 ....G8
Nixa 4,707 ....F8
Noel 1,169 ....D9
Norborne 856 ....E4
Normandy 4,480 ....R2
North Kansas City 4,130 ....P5
Northmoor 441 ....O5
Northwoods 5,106 ....R2
Norwood 449 ....H8
Novelty 143 ....H2
Novinger 542 ....G2
O'Fallon 18,698 ....L5
Oak Grove 4,067 ....S6
Oak Grove 402 ....K6
Oak Ridge 202 ....N7
Oakland 1,593 ....P5
Oaks 130 ....P5
Oakview 351 ....P5
Oakwood 212 ....P5
Oakwood Manor 137 ....P5
Oakwood Park 213 ....P5
Odessa 3,695 ....E4
Old Monroe 242 ....L5
Olivette 7,573 ....O2
Olympian Village 752 ....M6
Oran 1,164 ....N8
Oregon▲ 935 ....B2
Oronogo 595 ....D8
Orrick 935 ....D4
Osage Beach 2,599 ....G6
Osborn 400 ....D3

Osceola▲ 755 ....E6
Otterville 507 ....F5
Overland 17,987 ....O2
Owensville 2,325 ....K6
Ozark▲ 4,243 ....F8
Pacific 4,350 ....L5
Pagedale 3,771 ....P2
Palmyra▲ 3,371 ....J3
Paris▲ 1,486 ....J4
Parkdale 270 ....F6
Parkville 2,402 ....O5
Parkway 277 ....L6
Parma 995 ....N9
Parnell 157 ....C2
Patton 414 ....M8
Pattonsburg 502 ....D2
Peculiar 1,777 ....D5
Perry 711 ....J4
Perryville▲ 6,933 ....N7
Pevely 2,831 ....M6
Phillipsburg 170 ....G7
Pickering 171 ....C2
Piedmont 2,166 ....L8
Pierce City 1,382 ....E8
Pilot Grove 714 ....G5
Pilot Knob 783 ....L7
Pine 5,092 ....K9
Pine Lawn 6,600 ....R2
Pineville▲ 580 ....D9
Platte City▲ 2,947 ....C4
Platte Woods 427 ....O5
Plattsburg▲ 2,248 ....D3
Pleasant Hill 3,827 ....D5
Pleasant Hope 360 ....F8
Pleasant Valley 2,731 ....R5
Polo 539 ....D3
Poplar Bluff▲ 16,996 ....L9
Portage Des Sioux 503 ....M5
Portageville 3,401 ....N10
Potosi▲ 2,683 ....L7
Prairie Home 215 ....G5
Princeton▲ 1,021 ....E2
Purcell 359 ....D8
Purdin 217 ....F3
Purdy 977 ....E9
Puxico 819 ....M9
Queen City 704 ....H2
Qulin 384 ....M9
Ravenwood 409 ....C2
Raymondville 425 ....J8
Raymore 5,592 ....D5
Raytown 30,601 ....P6
Rayville 170 ....E4
Reeds Spring 411 ....F9
Renick 195 ....H4
Republic 6,292 ....E8
Rhineland 157 ....J5
Rich Hill 1,317 ....D6
Richland 2,029 ....H7
Richmond Heights 10,448 ....P3
Richmond▲ 5,738 ....D4
Ridgeway 379 ....D2
Risco 434 ....N9
Rivermines 459 ....L7
Riverside 3,010 ....O5
Riverview 3,242 ....R2
Rocheport 255 ....H5
Rock Hill 5,217 ....P3
Rock Port▲ 1,438 ....B2
Rockaway Beach 275 ....F9
Rockville 193 ....D6
Rogersville 995 ....G8
Rolla▲ 14,090 ....J7
Rosebud 380 ....K6

Rosendale 186 ....C2
Rushville 306 ....B3
Russellville 869 ....H6
Saginaw 384 ....C8
Saint Ann 14,489 ....O2
Saint Charles▲ 54,555 ....N1
Saint Clair 3,917 ....K6
Saint Elizabeth 257 ....H6
Saint George 1,270 ....P4
Saint James 3,256 ....J6
Saint John 7,466 ....P2
Saint Joseph▲ 71,852 ....C3
Saint Louis▲ 396,685 ....R3
Saint Martins 717 ....H5
Saint Marys 461 ....M7
Saint Paul 1,192 ....L5
Saint Peters 45,779 ....M1
Saint Robert 1,730 ....H7
Saint Thomas 263 ....H6
Sainte Genevieve▲ 4,411 ....M6

Salem▲ 4,486 ....J7
Salisbury▲ 1,881 ....G4
Sappington 10,917 ....O4
Sarcoxie 1,330 ....D8
Savannah▲ 4,352 ....C3
Schell City 292 ....D6
Scott City 4,292 ....O8
Sedalia▲ 19,800 ....F5
Sedgewickville 138 ....N7
Seligman 593 ....D9
Senath 1,622 ....M10
Seneca 1,885 ....C9
Seymour 1,636 ....G8
Shelbina 2,172 ....H3
Shelbyville▲ 582 ....H3
Sheldon 464 ....D7
Sheridan 174 ....C1
Shrewsbury 6,416 ....P3
Sibley 367 ....S5
Sikeston 17,641 ....N9

Silex 197 ....K4
Skidmore 404 ....B2
Slater 2,186 ....G4
Smithton 532 ....F5
Smithville 2,525 ....D4
South West City 600 ....D9
Sparta 751 ....F8
Spanish Lake 20,322 ....R1
Spickard 326 ....F2
Springfield▲ 140,494 ....F8
Stanberry 1,310 ....C2
Stanley 2,395 ....N10
Steele 2,395 ....N10
Steelville▲ 1,465 ....K7
Stewartsville 732 ....C3
Stockton▲ 1,579 ....E7
Stotts City 235 ....E8
Stoutland 207 ....G7
Stover 964 ....G6
Strafford 1,166 ....F8
Sturgeon 838 ....H4

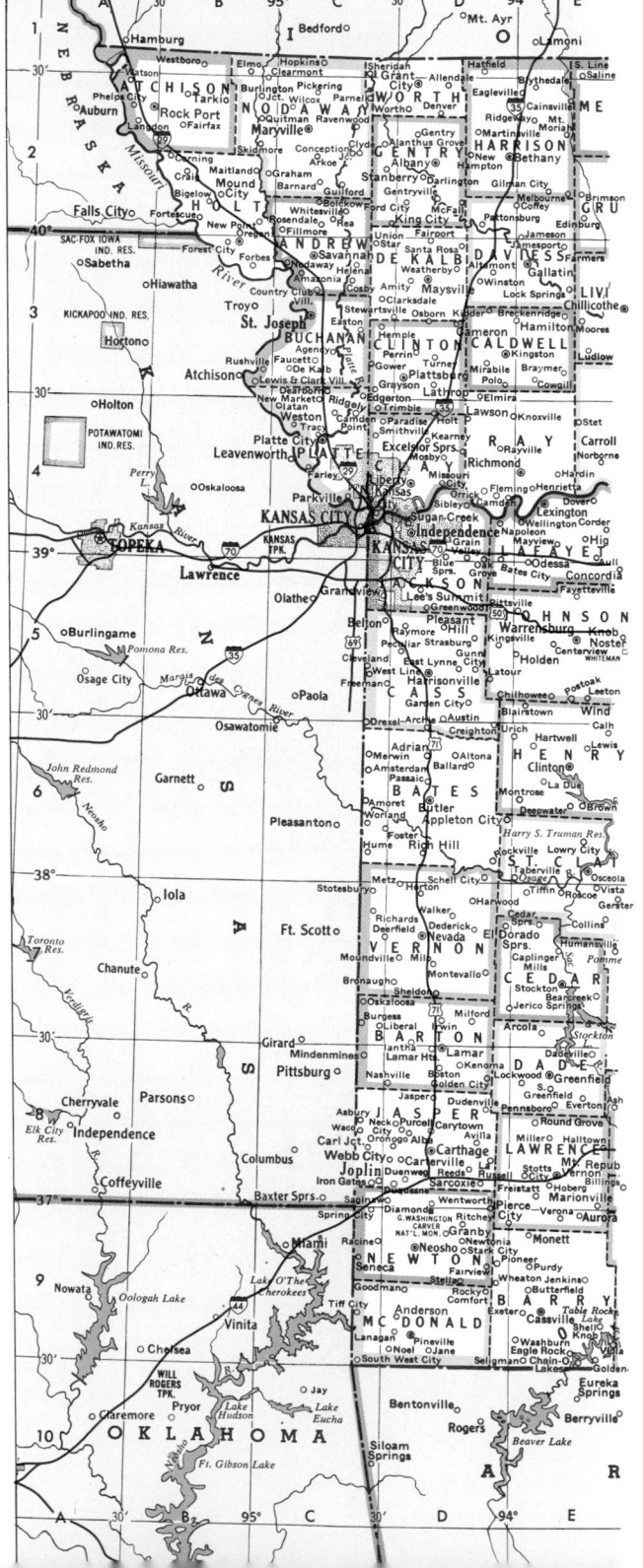

Topography

0   40   80 MI.
0   40   80 KM.

St. Joseph

Kansas City

Independence

Columbia

St. Charles

St. Louis

Jefferson City

OZARK

Lake of the Ozarks

PLATEAU

Springfield

Joplin

Stockton Lake

ST. FRANCOIS
Taum Sauk Mtn.
1,772 ft. (540 m.)
MTS.

Clearwater Lake

Cape Girardeau

L. Wappapello

Table Rock Lake

Bull Shoals Lake

5,000 m. 2,000 m. 1,000 m. 500 m. 200 m. 100 m. Sea Below
16,404 ft. 6,562 ft. 3,281 ft. 1,640 ft. 656 ft. 328 ft. Level

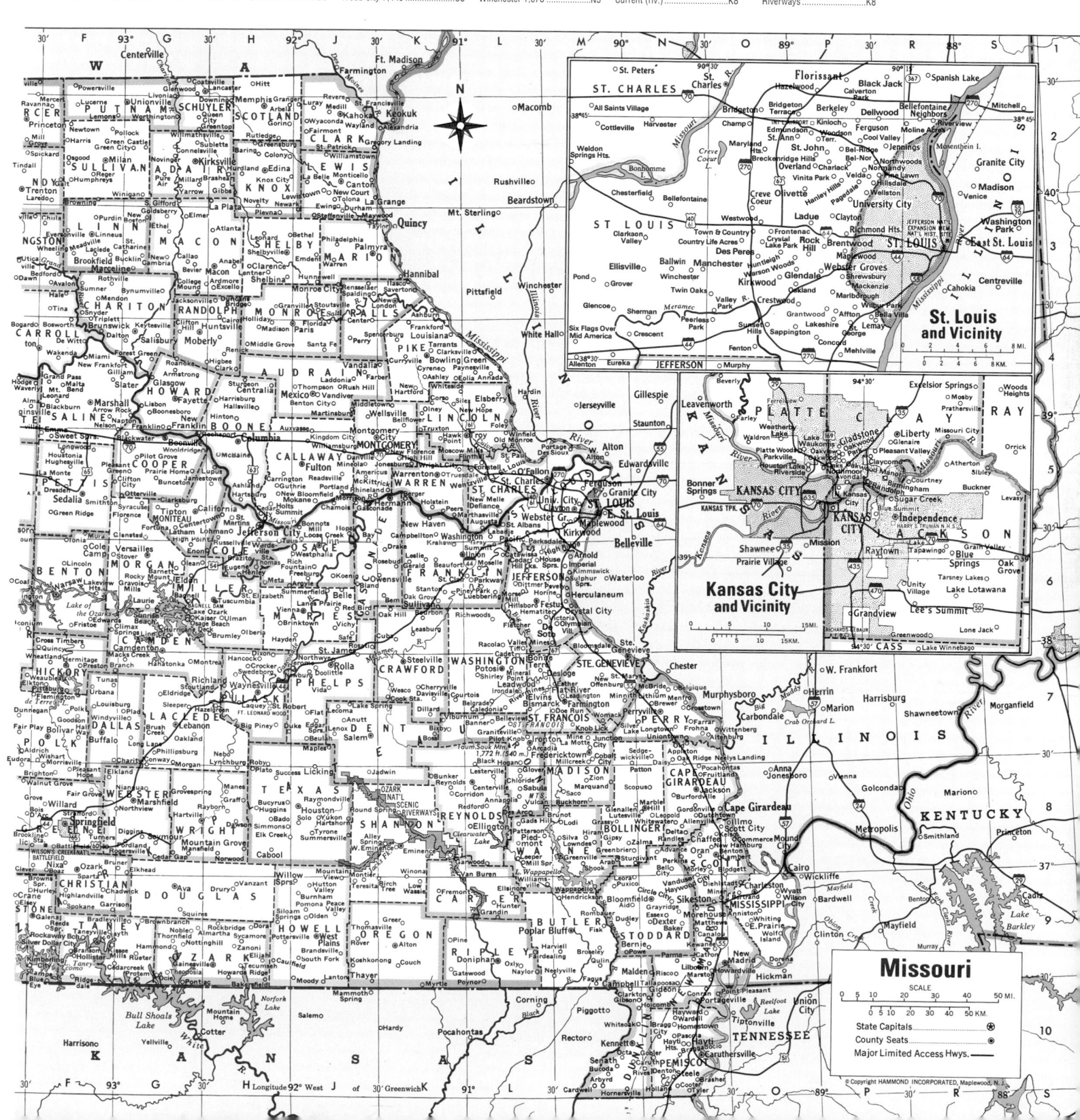

Agriculture, Industry and Resources

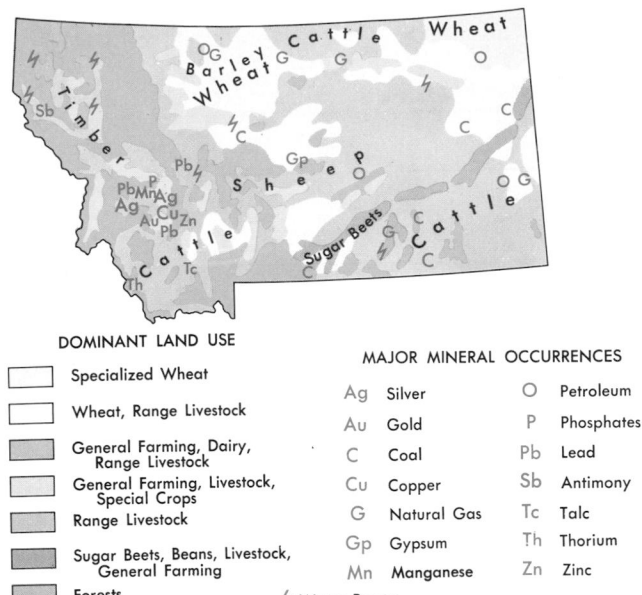

DOMINANT LAND USE

- Specialized Wheat
- Wheat, Range Livestock
- General Farming, Dairy, Range Livestock
- General Farming, Livestock, Special Crops
- Range Livestock
- Sugar Beets, Beans, Livestock, General Farming
- Forests

MAJOR MINERAL OCCURRENCES

Ag	Silver	O	Petroleum
Au	Gold	P	Phosphates
C	Coal	Pb	Lead
Cu	Copper	Sb	Antimony
G	Natural Gas	Tc	Talc
Gp	Gypsum	Th	Thorium
Mn	Manganese	Zn	Zinc

⚡ Water Power

COUNTIES

Beaverhead 8,424 ....C5
Big Horn 11,337 ....J5
Blaine 6,728 ....G2
Broadwater 3,318 ....E4
Carbon 8,080 ....G5
Carter 1,503 ....M5
Cascade 77,691 ....E3
Chouteau 5,452 ....F3
Custer 11,697 ....L4
Daniels 2,266 ....L2
Dawson 9,505 ....M3
Deer Lodge 10,278 ....C5
Fallon 3,103 ....M4
Fergus 12,083 ....G3
Flathead 59,218 ....B2
Gallatin 50,463 ....E5
Garfield 1,589 ....J3
Glacier 12,121 ....C2
Golden Valley 912 ....G4
Granite 2,548 ....C4
Hill 17,654 ....F2
Jefferson 7,939 ....D4
Judith Basin 2,282 ....F4
Lake 21,041 ....B3
Lewis and Clark 47,495 ....D3
Liberty 2,295 ....E2
Lincoln 17,481 ....A2
McCone 2,276 ....L3
Madison 5,989 ....D5
Meagher 1,819 ....F4
Mineral 3,315 ....B3
Missoula 78,687 ....C3
Musselshell 4,106 ....H4
Park 14,562 ....F5
Petroleum 519 ....H3
Phillips 5,163 ....J2
Pondera 6,433 ....D2
Powder River 2,090 ....L5
Powell 6,620 ....D4
Prairie 1,383 ....L4
Ravalli 25,010 ....B4
Richland 10,716 ....M3
Roosevelt 10,999 ....L2
Rosebud 10,505 ....K4
Sanders 8,669 ....A3
Sheridan 4,732 ....M2
Silver Bow 33,941 ....D5
Stillwater 6,536 ....G5
Sweet Grass 3,154 ....G5
Teton 6,271 ....D3
Toole 5,046 ....E2
Treasure 874 ....J4
Valley 8,239 ....K2
Wheatland 2,246 ....G4
Wibaux 1,191 ....M4
Yellowstone 113,419 ....H4

CITIES and TOWNS

Absarokee 1,067 ....G5
Acton 50 ....H5
Alberton 354 ....B3
Alder 120 ....D5
Alzada 52 ....M5
Amsterdam 130 ....E5
Anaconda-Deer Lodge County▲ C4
Angela 50 ....K4
Antelope 83 ....M2
Apgar 25 ....B2
Armington 75 ....E3
Ashland 484 ....K5
Augusta 497 ....D3
Avon 125 ....D4
Babb 150 ....C2
Bainville 165 ....M2
Baker▲ 1,818 ....M4
Ballantine 380 ....J5
Bannack 2 ....C5
Basin 350 ....D4
Bearcreek 37 ....G5
Becket 35 ....G4
Belfry 300 ....H5
Belgrade 3,411 ....E5
Belt 571 ....E3
Biddle 28 ....L5
Big Arm 250 ....B3
Big Sandy 740 ....F2
Big Sky 50 ....E5
Big Timber▲ 1,557 ....G5
Bigfork 1,080 ....C2
Billings▲ 81,151 ....H4
Birney 100 ....K5
Black Eagle 1,500 ....E3
Blackfoot 100 ....D2
Bloomfield 28 ....M3
Bonner-West Riverside 1,669 .C4
Boulder▲ 1,316 ....E4
Box Elder 300 ....F2
Boyd 32 ....G5
Bozeman▲ 22,660 ....E5
Brady 450 ....D2
Bridger 692 ....H5
Broadus▲ 572 ....L5
Broadview 133 ....H4
Brockton 365 ....M2
Brockway 55 ....L3
Browning 1,170 ....C2
Busby 409 ....J5
Butte-Silver Bow County▲ 33,336 ....D5
Bynum 49 ....D3
Camas Prairie 160 ....B3
Cameron 150 ....E5
Canyon Creek 100 ....D4
Canyon Ferry 60 ....E4
Cardwell 34 ....E5
Carter 70 ....E3
Cartersville 115 ....K4
Cascade 729 ....E3
Charlo 358 ....B3
Chester▲ 942 ....E2
Chinook▲ 1,512 ....G2
Choteau▲ 1,741 ....D3
Christina 60 ....G3
Circle▲ 805 ....L3
Clancy 550 ....E4
Clinton 250 ....C4
Clyde Park 282 ....F5
Coffee Creek 62 ....F3
Colstrip 3,035 ....K5
Columbia Falls 2,942 ....B2
Columbus▲ 1,573 ....G5
Condon 300 ....C3
Conner 420 ....B5
Conrad▲ 2,891 ....D2
Cooke City 120 ....G5
Coram 450 ....C2
Corvallis 500 ....C4
Craig 100 ....D3
Crane 163 ....M3
Creston 60 ....C2
Crow Agency 1,446 ....J5
Culbertson 796 ....M2
Custer 300 ....J4
Cut Bank▲ 3,329 ....D2
Dagmar 35 ....M2

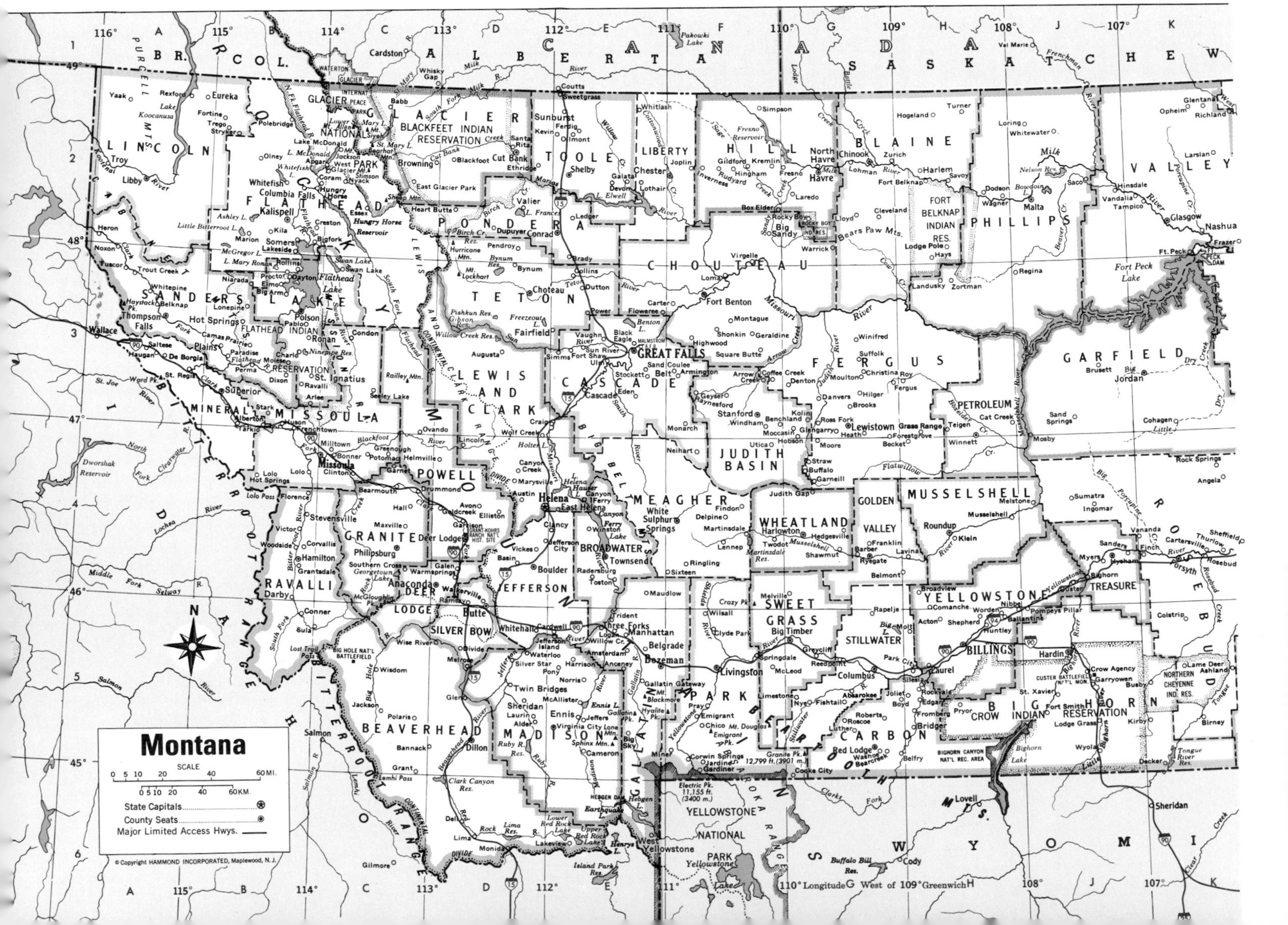

Montana

SCALE
0 5 10 20 40 60 MI.
0 5 10 20 40 60 KM.

State Capitals ⊛
County Seats ◉
Major Limited Access Hwys. ▬

Montana 263

Topography

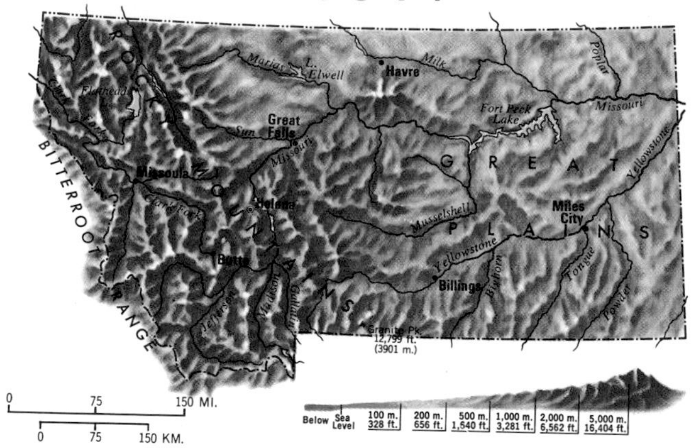
Havre
Marias
L. Elwell
Milk
Poplar
Flathead
Great Falls
Sun
Fort Peck Lake
Missouri
Missoula
Helena
Butte
Billings
Miles City
Musselshell
Yellowstone
Bighorn
Tongue
Powder
GREAT PLAINS
BITTERROOT RANGE
Granite Pk. 12,799 ft. (3901 m.)
0 75 150 MI.
0 75 150 KM.
Below Sea Level
100 m. 328 ft.
200 m. 656 ft.
500 m. 1,640 ft.
1,000 m. 3,281 ft.
2,000 m. 6,562 ft.
5,000 m. 16,404 ft.

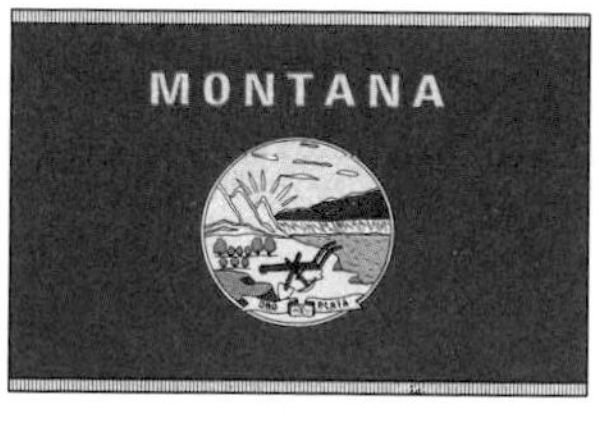
MONTANA

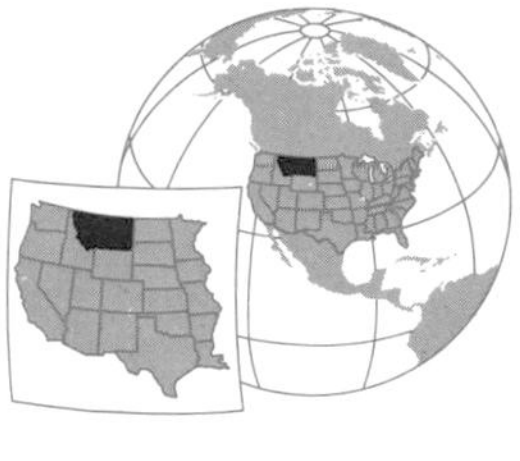

AREA 147,046 sq. mi. (380,849 sq. km.)
POPULATION 803,655
CAPITAL Helena
LARGEST CITY Billings
HIGHEST POINT Granite Pk. 12,799 ft. (3901 m.)
SETTLED IN 1809
ADMITTED TO UNION November 8, 1889
POPULAR NAME Treasure State; Big Sky Country
STATE FLOWER Bitterroot
STATE BIRD Western Meadowlark

Darby 625 ... B4
Dayton 140 ... B3
De Borgia 300 ... A3
Decker 150 ... K5
Deer Lodge▲ 3,378 ... D4
Dell 29 ... D6
Delpine 33 ... F4
Denton 350 ... G3
Dillon▲ 3,991 ... D5
Divide 275 ... D5
Dixon 550 ... B3
Dodson 137 ... H2
Drummond 264 ... D4
Dupuyer 105 ... D2
Dutton 392 ... E3
East Glacier Park 326 ... C2
East Helena 1,538 ... C4
Edgar 220 ... H5
Ekalaka▲ 439 ... M5
Elliston 250 ... D4
Elmo 250 ... B3
Emigrant 80 ... F5
Ennis 773 ... E5
Epsie 60 ... L5
Essex 48 ... C2
Eureka 1,043 ... B2
Fairfield 660 ... D3
Fairview 869 ... M3
Fallon 225 ... L4
Fishtail 46 ... G5
Flaxville 88 ... L2
Florence 700 ... B4
Floweree 48 ... E3
Forestgrove 100 ... H3
Forsyth▲ 2,178 ... K4
Fort Belknap 422 ... H2
Fort Benton▲ 1,660 ... F3
Fort Peck 325 ... K2
Fort Shaw 200 ... E3
Fort Smith 300 ... J5
Fortine 250 ... A2
Four Buttes 50 ... L2
Frazer 403 ... K2
Frenchtown 300 ... B3
Froid 195 ... M2
Fromberg 370 ... H5
Galata 100 ... E2
Galen 210 ... D4
Gallatin Gateway 600 ... E5
Gardiner 600 ... F5
Garneill 61 ... G4
Garrison 300 ... D4
Garryowen 200 ... J5
Geraldine 299 ... F3
Geyser 125 ... F3
Gildford 250 ... F2
Glasgow▲ 3,572 ... K2
Glen 4,802 ... D5
Glendive▲ 5,978 ... M3
Goldcreek 100 ... D4
Grant 25 ... C5
Grantsdale 500 ... B4
Grass Range 159 ... H3
Great Falls▲ 55,097 ... E3
Greenough 120 ... C4
Greycliff 37 ... G5
Hall 130 ... C4
Hamilton▲ 2,737 ... B4
Hardin▲ 2,940 ... J5
Harlem 882 ... H2
Harlowton▲ 1,049 ... F4
Harrison 94 ... E5
Hathaway 55 ... K4
Haugan 90 ... A3
Havre▲ 10,201 ... G2
Hays 333 ... H2
Heart Butte 499 ... C2
Helena (cap.)▲ 24,569 ... E4
Helmville 250 ... C4
Heron 79 ... A2
Highwood 150 ... F3
Hilger 38 ... G3
Hingham 181 ... F2
Hinsdale 260 ... K2
Hobson 226 ... G4
Hodges 50 ... M4
Hogeland 35 ... H2
Homestead 50 ... M2
Hot Springs 411 ... B3
Hungry Horse 700 ... C2
Huntley 250 ... H5
Huson 97 ... B3
Hysham▲ 361 ... J4
Ingomar 48 ... J4
Intake 60 ... M3
Inverness 150 ... F2
Jackson 210 ... C5
Jardine 30 ... F5
Jeffers 70 ... E5
Jefferson City 162 ... E4
Jefferson Island 25 ... E5
Joliet 522 ... G5
Joplin 300 ... F2
Jordan▲ 494 ... J3
Judith Gap 133 ... G4
Kalispell▲ 11,917 ... B2
Kevin 185 ... D2
Kila 350 ... B2
Kinsey 100 ... L4
Kirby 30 ... J5
Klein 250 ... H4
Kremlin 304 ... F2
Lakeside 663 ... B2
Lakeview 28 ... E6
Lambert 203 ... M3
Lame Deer 1,918 ... K5
Landusky 40 ... H3
Laurel 5,686 ... H5
Laurin 60 ... D5
Lavina 151 ... H4
Lewistown▲ 6,051 ... G3
Libby▲ 2,532 ... A2
Lima 265 ... D6
Lincoln 473 ... D4
Lindsay 50 ... L3
Livingston▲ 6,701 ... F5
Locate 55 ... L4
Lodge Grass 517 ... J5
Lodge Pole 292 ... H2
Logan 53 ... E5
Lohman 25 ... G2
Lolo 2,746 ... B4
Lolo Hot Springs 25 ... B4
Loma 200 ... F3
Lonepine 50 ... B3
Lothair 29 ... E2
Malta▲ 2,340 ... J2
Manhattan 1,034 ... E5
Marion 450 ... B2
Martinsdale 75 ... F4
Marysville 76 ... D4
Maxville 44 ... C4
McAllister 55 ... E5
McLeod 150 ... G5
Medicine Lake 357 ... M2
Melrose 350 ... D5
Melstone 166 ... H4
Melville 100 ... F4
Miles City▲ 8,461 ... L4
Mill Iron 66 ... M5
Milltown 300 ... C4
Missoula▲ 42,918 ... C4
Moccasin 57 ... F3
Molt 31 ... H5
Monarch 120 ... F3
Moore 211 ... G4
Musselshell 117 ... H4
Myers 120 ... J4
Nashua 375 ... K2
Neihart 53 ... F4
Nibbe 30 ... H4
Norris 55 ... E5
North Havre 1,230 ... G2
Noxon 800 ... A3
Nye 50 ... G5
Oilmont 50 ... E2
Olney 200 ... B2
Opheim 145 ... K2
Oswego 75 ... L2
Outlook 109 ... M2
Ovando 300 ... C3
Pablo 1,298 ... B3
Paradise 400 ... B3
Park City 800 ... H5
Peerless 110 ... L2
Pendroy 100 ... D2
Perma 50 ... B3
Philipsburg▲ 925 ... C4
Plains 992 ... B3
Plentywood▲ 2,136 ... M2
Plevna 140 ... M4
Polaris 53 ... C5
Polson▲ 3,283 ... B3
Pompeys Pillar 300 ... J5
Pony 130 ... E5
Poplar 881 ... L2
Potomac 80 ... C4
Power 159 ... E3
Pray 40 ... F5
Proctor 150 ... B3
Pryor 654 ... H5
Radersburg 104 ... E4
Ramsay 95 ... D4
Rapelje 50 ... G5
Ravalli 150 ... B3
Raymond 26 ... M2
Raynesford 35 ... F3
Red Lodge▲ 1,958 ... G5
Redstone 40 ... M2
Reedpoint 160 ... G5
Regina 83 ... J3
Reserve 80 ... M2
Rexford 132 ... A2
Richey 259 ... L3
Richland 48 ... K2
Ringling 102 ... F4
Roberts 312 ... G5
Rocky Boy 150 ... G2
Rollins 200 ... B3
Ronan 1,547 ... C3
Roscoe 40 ... G5
Rosebud 259 ... K4
Roundup▲ 1,808 ... H4
Roy 200 ... H3
Rudyard 450 ... F2
Ryegate▲ 260 ... G4
Saco 261 ... J2
Saint Ignatius 778 ... C3
Saint Regis 500 ... A3
Saint Xavier 200 ... J5
Saltese 90 ... A3
Sand Coulee 600 ... E3
Sanders 50 ... J4
Santa Rita 120 ... D2
Savage 300 ... M3
Scobey▲ 1,154 ... L2
Seeley Lake 900 ... C3
Shawmut 66 ... G4
Sheffield 49 ... K4
Shelby▲ 2,763 ... E2
Shepherd 200 ... H5
Sheridan 652 ... D5
Sidney▲ 5,217 ... M3
Silesia 90 ... H5
Silver Star 125 ... D5
Simms 200 ... E3
Simpson 70 ... F2
Somers 700 ... B2
Sonnette 42 ... L5
Springdale 45 ... F5
Square Butte 48 ... F3
Stanford▲ 529 ... F3
Stark 51 ... B3
Stevensville 1,221 ... C4
Stockett 500 ... E3
Stryker 96 ... B2
Suffolk 45 ... G3
Sula 200 ... B5
Sun River 300 ... E3
Sunburst 437 ... E2
Superior▲ 881 ... B3
Swan Lake 100 ... C3
Sweetgrass 250 ... F2
Terry▲ 659 ... L4
Thompson Falls▲ 1,319 ... A3
Three Forks 1,203 ... E5
Thurlow 84 ... K4
Toston 70 ... E4
Townsend▲ 1,635 ... E4
Trego 50 ... B2
Trident 50 ... E5
Trout Creek 300 ... A3
Troy 953 ... A2
Turner 150 ... H2
Twin Bridges 374 ... D5
Twodot 285 ... F4
Ulm 450 ... E3
Utica 30 ... F4
Valier 519 ... D2
Vananda 50 ... K4
Vandalia 35 ... J2
Vaughn 2,270 ... E3
Victor 700 ... B4
Vida 50 ... L3
Virgelle 28 ... F2
Virginia City▲ 142 ... E5
Volborg 125 ... L5
Wagner 32 ... H2
Walkerville 605 ... D4
Warmsprings 500 ... D4
Waterloo 102 ... D5
West Glacier 150 ... C2
West Yellowstone 913 ... E6
Westby 253 ... M2
White Sulphur Springs▲ 963 ... E4
Whitefish 4,368 ... B2
Whitehall 1,067 ... D5
Whitetail 150 ... L2
Whitewater 100 ... J2
Whitlash 50 ... E2
Wibaux▲ 628 ... M3
Wickes 60 ... D4
Willow Creek 150 ... E5
Wilsall 250 ... F5
Windham 63 ... F3
Winifred 150 ... G3
Winnett▲ 188 ... H4
Winston 120 ... E4
Wisdom 140 ... C5
Wise River 150 ... C5
Wolf Creek 500 ... D3
Wolf Point▲ 2,880 ... L2
Woodside 75 ... B4
Worden 600 ... H5
Wyola 350 ... J5
Zurich 60 ... G2

OTHER FEATURES

Absaroka (range) ... F5
Allen (mt.) ... C2
Arrow (creek) ... F3
Ashley (lake) ... B2
Battle (creek) ... G1
Bearhat (mt.) ... C2
Bears Paw (mts.) ... G2
Beartooth (mts.) ... G5
Beaver (creek) ... J2
Beaverhead (riv.) ... D5
Benton (lake) ... E3
Big (lake) ... G5
Big Belt (mts.) ... E4
Big Dry (creek) ... K3
Big Hole (riv.) ... C5
Big Hole Nat'l Battlefield ... C5
Bighorn (lake) ... H5
Bighorn (riv.) ... J5
Bighorn Canyon Nat'l Rec. Area ... H5
Big Muddy (riv.) ... M2
Big Porcupine (creek) ... J4
Birch (creek) ... D2
Birch Creek (res.) ... D2
Bitterroot (range) ... B4
Bitterroot (riv.) ... B4
Blackfeet Ind. Res. ... D2
Blackfoot (riv.) ... C4
Blackmore (mt.) ... F5
Bowdoin (lake) ... J2
Boxelder (creek) ... H3
Boxelder (creek) ... M5
Bynum (res.) ... D2
Cabinet (mts.) ... A2
Canyon Ferry (lake) ... E4
Clark Canyon (res.) ... D6
Clark Fork (riv.) ... A3
Clarks Fork, Yellowstone (riv.) ... G6
Cottonwood (creek) ... E2
Cow (creek) ... G2
Crazy peak) ... F4
Crow Ind. Res. ... H5
Cut Bank (creek) ... D2
Douglas (mt.) ... F5
Earthquake (lake) ... E6
Electric (peak) ... F6
Elwell (lake) ... E2
Emigrant (peak) ... F5
Ennis (lake) ... E5
Flathead (lake) ... C3
Flathead (riv.) ... B2
Flathead, North Fork (riv.) ... B2
Flathead, South Fork (riv.) ... C3
Flathead Ind. Res. ... B3
Flatwillow (creek) ... H4
Fort Belknap Ind. Res. ... H2
Fort Peck (lake) ... K3
Fort Union Trading Post Nat'l Hist. Site ... N2
Frances (lake) ... D2
Freezeout (lake) ... D3
Frenchman (riv.) ... J1
Fresno (res.) ... F2
Gallatin (peak) ... E5
Gallatin (riv.) ... E5
Georgetown (lake) ... C4
Gibson (res.) ... D3
Glacier Nat'l Park ... C2
Granite (peak) ... F5
Grant-Kohrs Ranch Nat'l Hist. Site ... D4
Hauser (lake) ... E4
Haystack (peak) ... A3
Hebgen (lake) ... E6
Helena (lake) ... F4
Holter (lake) ... D4
Hungry Horse (res.) ... C2
Hurricane (mt.) ... D2
Hyalite (peak) ... E5
Jackson (mt.) ... C2
Jefferson (riv.) ... D5
Judith (riv.) ... G3
Koocanusa (lake) ... A2
Kootenai (riv.) ... A2
Lemhi (pass) ... C6
Lewis and Clark (range) ... C3
Lima (res.) ... D6
Little Bighorn (riv.) ... J5
Little Bitterroot (lake) ... B2
Little Dry (creek) ... K3
Little Missouri (riv.) ... M5
Lockhart (mt.) ... D3
Lodge (creek) ... G1
Lolo (pass) ... B4
Lone (mt.) ... E5
Lost Trail (pass) ... B5
Lower Red Rock (lake) ... E6
Lower Saint Mary (lake) ... C2
Madison (riv.) ... E5
Malmstrom A.F.B. 5,938 ... E3
Marias (riv.) ... D2
Martinsdale (res.) ... F4
Mary Ronan (lake) ... B3
McDonald (lake) ... B2
McGloughlin (peak) ... C4
McGregor (lake) ... B3
Medicine (lake) ... M2
Milk (riv.) ... J2
Mission (range) ... C3
Missouri (riv.) ... L3
Musselshell (riv.) ... J3
Nelson (res.) ... J2
Ninepipe (res.) ... C3
Northern Cheyenne Indian Reservation ... K5
O'Fallon (creek) ... L4
Pishkun (res.) ... D3
Poplar (riv.) ... L2
Porcupine (creek) ... K2
Powder (riv.) ... L4
Purcell (mts.) ... A2
Railley (mt.) ... C3
Red Rock (lakes) ... E6
Red Rock (riv.) ... D6
Redwater (riv.) ... L3
Rock (creek) ... C4
Rocky (mts.) ... D4
Rocky Boy's Ind. Res. ... G2
Rosebud (creek) ... K4
Ruby (riv.) ... D5
Ruby River (res.) ... D5
Sage (creek) ... F2
Saint Mary (lake) ... C2
Saint Mary (riv.) ... C1
Sandy (creek) ... F2
Sheep (mt.) ... C2
Shields (riv.) ... F4
Siyeh (mt.) ... C2
Smith (riv.) ... E3
Sphinx (mt.) ... E5
Stillwater (riv.) ... G5
Stimson (mt.) ... C2
Sun (riv.) ... D3
Swan (lake) ... C3
Teton (riv.) ... E3
Tongue (riv.) ... K5
Upper Red Rock (lake) ... E6
Ward (peak) ... A3
Waterton-Glacier Int'l Peace Park ... C2
Whitefish (lake) ... B2
Willow (creek) ... E2
Willow Creek (res.) ... D3
Yellowstone (riv.) ... M3
Yellowstone National Park ... F6

▲County seat

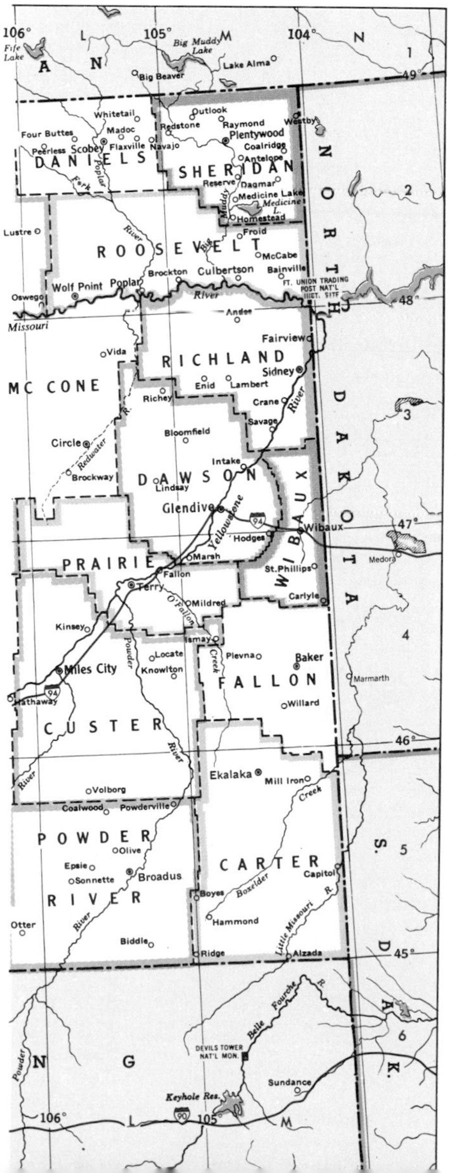
DANIELS
SHERIDAN
ROOSEVELT
RICHLAND
MC CONE
DAWSON
WIBAUX
PRAIRIE
FALLON
CUSTER
POWDER RIVER
CARTER
NORTH DAKOTA
Scobey
Plentywood
Wolf Point
Poplar
Culbertson
Sidney
Circle
Glendive
Wibaux
Terry
Miles City
Baker
Ekalaka
Broadus
Missouri
Yellowstone
Powder
River

COUNTIES

Adams 29,625 F4
Antelope 7,965 F2
Arthur 462 C3
Banner 852 A3
Blaine 675 E3
Boone 6,667 F3
Box Butte 13,130 A2
Boyd 2,835 F2
Brown 3,657 E2
Buffalo 37,447 E4
Burt 7,868 H3
Butler 8,601 G3
Cass 21,318 H4
Cedar 10,131 G2
Chase 4,381 C4
Cherry 6,307 C2
Cheyenne 9,494 A3
Clay 7,123 F4
Colfax 9,139 G3
Cuming 10,117 H3
Custer 12,270 E3
Dakota 16,742 H2
Dawes 9,021 A2
Dawson 19,940 E4
Deuel 2,237 B3
Dixon 6,143 H2
Dodge 34,500 H3
Douglas 416,444 H3
Dundy 2,582 C4
Fillmore 7,103 G4
Franklin 3,938 F4
Frontier 3,101 D4
Furnas 5,553 E4
Gage 22,794 H4
Garden 2,460 B3
Garfield 2,141 F3
Gosper 1,928 E4
Grant 769 C3
Greeley 3,006 F3
Hall 48,925 F4
Hamilton 8,862 F4
Harlan 3,810 E4
Hayes 1,222 C4
Hitchcock 3,750 C4
Holt 12,599 F2
Hooker 793 C3
Howard 6,055 F3
Jefferson 8,759 G4
Johnson 4,673 H4
Kearney 6,629 F4
Keith 8,584 C3
Keya Paha 1,029 E2
Kimball 4,108 A3
Knox 9,534 G2
Lancaster 213,641 H4
Lincoln 32,508 D4
Logan 878 D3
Loup 683 E3
Madison 32,655 G3
McPherson 546 C3
Merrick 8,042 F3
Morrill 5,423 A3
Nance 4,275 F3
Nemaha 7,980 J4
Nuckolls 5,786 F4
Otoe 14,252 H4
Pawnee 3,317 H4
Perkins 3,367 C4
Phelps 9,715 E4
Pierce 7,827 G2
Platte 29,820 G3
Polk 5,675 G3
Red Willow 11,705 D4
Richardson 9,937 J4
Rock 2,019 E2
Saline 12,715 G4
Sarpy 102,583 H3
Saunders 18,285 H3
Scotts Bluff 36,025 A3
Seward 15,450 G4
Sheridan 6,750 B2
Sherman 3,718 F3
Sioux 1,549 A2
Stanton 6,244 G3
Thayer 6,635 G4
Thomas 851 D3
Thurston 6,936 H2
Valley 5,169 E3
Washington 16,607 H3
Wayne 9,364 G2
Webster 4,279 F4
Wheeler 948 F3
York 14,428 G4

CITIES and TOWNS

Adams 472 H4
Ainsworth▲ 1,870 D2
Albion▲ 1,916 F3
Alda 540 F4
Alexandria 224 G4
Allen 331 H2
Alliance▲ 9,765 A2
Alma▲ 1,226 E4
Alvo 164 H4
Amherst 231 E4
Anselmo 189 E3
Ansley 555 E3
Arapahoe 1,001 E4
Arcadia 385 F3
Arlington 1,178 H3
Arnold 679 D3
Arthur▲ 128 C3
Ashland 2,136 H3
Ashton 251 F3
Atkinson 1,380 E2
Auburn▲ 3,443 J4
Aurora▲ 3,810 F4
Avoca 254 H4
Axtell 707 E4
Bancroft 494 H2
Bartlett▲ 131 F3
Bartley 339 D4
Bassett▲ 739 E2
Battle Creek 997 G3
Bayard 1,196 A3
Beatrice▲ 12,354 H4
Beaver City▲ 707 E4
Beaver Crossing 448 G4
Bee 209 H3
Beemer 672 H3
Belden 149 G2
Belgrade 157 G3
Bellevue 30,982 J3
Bellwood 395 G3
Benedict 230 G3
Benkelman▲ 1,193 C4
Bennet 544 H4
Bennington 866 H3
Bertrand 708 E4
Big Springs 495 B3
Bladen 280 F4
Blair▲ 6,860 H3
Bloomfield 1,181 G2
Blue Hill 810 F4
Blue Springs 431 H4
Boys Town 794 H3
Bradshaw 330 G4
Brady 331 D3
Brainard 326 G3
Brewster▲ 22 D3
Bridgeport▲ 1,581 A3
Broadwater 160 B3
Brock 143 H4
Broken Bow▲ 3,778 E3
Brownville 148 J4
Brule 411 C3
Bruning 332 G4
Bruno 141 G3
Brunswick 182 G2
Burwell▲ 1,278 E3
Butte▲ 452 F2
Cairo 733 F3
Callaway 539 D3
Cambridge 1,107 D4
Campbell 432 F4
Carleton 144 G4
Carroll 237 G2
Cedar Bluffs 591 H3
Cedar Creek 334 H3
Cedar Rapids 396 F3
Center▲ 112 G2
Central City▲ 2,868 F3
Ceresco 825 H3
Chadron▲ 5,588 B2
Chambers 341 F2
Chapman 292 F3
Chappell▲ 979 B3
Chester 351 G4
Clarks 379 G3
Clarkson 699 G3
Clatonia 296 H4
Clay Center▲ 825 F4
Clearwater 401 F2
Cody 177 C2
Coleridge 596 G2
Columbus▲ 19,480 G3
Concord 156 H2
Cook 333 H4
Cordova 147 G4
Cortland 393 H4
Cozad 3,823 E4
Craig 228 H3
Crawford 1,115 A2
Creighton 1,223 G2
Creston 220 G3
Crete 4,841 G4
Crofton 820 G2
Culbertson 795 C4
Curtis 791 D4
Dakota City▲ 1,470 H2
Dalton 282 B3
Dannebrog 324 F3
Davenport 383 G4
Davey 160 H4
David City▲ 2,522 G3
Dawson 157 J4
Daykin 188 G4
De Witt 598 G4
Decatur 641 H2
Denton 161 H4
Deshler 892 G4
Diller 298 H4
Dix 229 A3
Dodge 693 H3
Doniphan 736 F4
Dorchester 614 G4
Douglas 199 H4
Dunbar 171 J4
Duncan 387 G3
Dwight 227 G3
Eagle 1,047 H4
Edgar 600 F4
Edison 148 E4
Elba 196 F3
Elgin 731 F3
Elkhorn 1,398 H3
Elm Creek 852 E4
Elmwood 584 H4
Elsie 153 C4
Elwood▲ 679 E4
Emerson 791 H2
Endicott 163 G4
Eustis 452 D4
Ewing 449 F2
Exeter 661 G4
Fairbury▲ 4,335 G4
Fairfield 458 G4
Fairmont 708 G4
Falls City▲ 4,769 J4
Farnam 188 D4
Farwell 152 F3
Filley 157 H4
Firth 471 H4
Fordyce 190 G2
Fort Calhoun 648 J3
Franklin▲ 1,112 E4
Fremont▲ 23,680 H3
Friend 1,111 G4
Fullerton▲ 1,452 F3
Funk 198 E4
Garland 247 G4
Geneva▲ 2,310 G4
Genoa 1,082 G3
Gering▲ 7,946 A3
Gibbon 1,525 F4
Giltner 367 F4
Glenvil 304 F4
Goehner 192 G4
Gordon 1,803 B2
Gothenburg 3,232 D4
Grafton 167 G4
Grand Island▲ 39,386 F4
Grant▲ 1,239 C4
Greeley▲ 562 F3
Greenwood 531 H3
Gresham 253 G3
Gretna 2,249 H3
Guide Rock 290 F4
Gurley 198 B3
Hadar 291 G2
Haigler 225 C4
Hallam 309 H4
Hampton 432 G4
Hardy 206 G4
Harrisburg▲ 75 A3
Harrison▲ 291 A2
Hartington▲ 1,583 G2
Harvard 976 F4
Hastings 22,837 F4
Hay Springs 693 B2
Hayes Center▲ 259 C4
Hebron▲ 1,765 G4
Hemingford 953 A2
Henderson 999 G4
Henry 145 A2
Herman 186 H3
Hershey 579 D3
Hickman 1,081 H4
Hildreth 364 E4
Holbrook 233 D4
Holdrege▲ 5,671 E4
Holstein 207 F4
Homer 553 H2
Hooper 850 H3
Hordville 164 G3
Hoskins 307 G2
Howells 615 H3
Hubbard 199 H2
Humboldt 1,003 J4
Humphrey 741 G3
Hyannis▲ 210 C3
Imperial▲ 2,007 C4
Indianola 672 D4
Inglewood 286 H3
Inman 159 F2
Jackson 230 H2
Johnson 323 J4
Juniata 811 F4
Kearney▲ 24,396 E4
Kenesaw 818 F4
Kennard 371 H3
Kimball▲ 2,574 A3
La Vista 9,840 J3
Laurel 981 G2
Lawrence 323 F4
Leigh 447 G3
Lewellen 307 B3
Lexington▲ 6,601 E4
Lincoln (cap.)▲ 191,972 H4
Lindsay 321 G3
Litchfield 314 E3
Lodgepole 368 B3
Long Pine 396 E2
Loomis 376 E4
Louisville 998 H3
Loup City▲ 1,104 E3
Lyman 452 A3
Lynch 296 F2
Lyons 1,144 H3
Macy 836 H2
Madison▲ 2,135 G3
Madrid 288 C4
Malcolm 181 H4
Manley 170 H4
Marquette 211 G4
Mason City 160 E3
Max 285 C4
Maxwell 410 D3
Maywood 313 D4
McCook▲ 8,112 D4
McCool Junction 372 G4
Mead 513 H3
Meadow Grove 332 G2
Merna 377 E3
Merriman 151 C2
Milford 1,886 H4
Milligan 328 G4
Minatare 807 A3
Minden▲ 2,749 F4
Mitchell 1,743 A3
Monroe 309 G3
Morrill 974 A3
Mullen▲ 554 C2
Murdock 267 H4
Murray 418 J4
Nebraska City▲ 6,547 J4
Nehawka 260 H4
Neligh▲ 1,742 G2
Nelson▲ 627 F4
Nemaha 188 J4
Newcastle 271 H2
Newman Grove 787 G3
Newport 136 E2
Nickerson 291 H3
Niobrara 376 G2
Norfolk 21,476 G2
North Bend 1,249 H3
North Loup 361 F3
North Platte▲ 22,605 D3
O'Neill▲ 4,049 F2
Oakdale 362 F2
Oakland 1,279 H3
Oconto 147 E3
Odell 291 H4
Ogallala▲ 5,095 C3
Ohiowa 146 G4
Omaha▲ 335,795 J3
Orchard 439 F2
Ord▲ 2,481 F3
Orleans 490 E4
Osceola▲ 879 G3
Oshkosh▲ 986 B3
Osmond 774 G2
Otoe 196 H4
Overton 547 E4
Oxford 949 E4
Page 191 F2
Palisade 381 C4
Palmer 753 F3
Palmyra 545 H4
Panama 207 H4
Papillion▲ 10,372 J3
Pawnee City▲ 1,008 H4
Paxton 536 C3
Pender▲ 1,208 H2
Peru 1,110 J4
Petersburg 388 G3
Phillips 316 F4
Pickrell 201 H4
Pierce▲ 1,615 G2
Pilger 361 G2
Plainview 1,333 G2
Platte Center 387 G3
Plattsmouth▲ 6,412 J3
Pleasant Dale 253 G4
Pleasanton 372 E4
Plymouth 455 G4
Polk 345 G3
Ponca▲ 877 H2
Potter 388 A3
Prague 282 H3
Ralston 6,236 J3
Randolph 983 G2
Ravenna 1,317 F4
Raymond 167 H4
Red Cloud▲ 1,204 F4
Republican City 199 E4
Rising City 341 G3
Riverdale 208 E4
Riverton 162 F4
Rosalie 178 H2
Rose 247 E2
Roseland 254 F4
Rulo 191 J4
Rushville▲ 1,127 B2
Ruskin 187 G4
Saint Edward 822 G3
Saint Paul▲ 2,009 F3
Salem 160 J4
Santee 365 G2
Sargent 710 E3
Schuyler▲ 4,052 G3
Scotia 318 F3
Scottsbluff 13,711 A3
Scribner 950 H3
Seward▲ 5,634 H4
Shelby 690 G3
Shelton 954 F4
Shickley 360 G4
Shubert 237 J4
Sidney▲ 5,959 B3
Silver Creek 625 G3
Snyder 280 H3
South Sioux City 9,677 H2
Spalding 592 F3
Spencer 536 F2
Sprague 157 H4
Springfield 1,426 H3
Springview▲ 304 E2
Stamford 188 E4
Stanton▲ 1,549 G3
Staplehurst 281 G4
Stapleton▲ 299 D3
Stella 248 J4
Sterling 451 H4
Stockville▲ 32 D4
Stratton 427 C4
Stromsburg 1,241 G3
Stuart 650 E2
Sumner 210 E4
Superior 2,397 F4
Sutherland 1,032 C3
Sutton 1,353 G4
Swanton 145 H4
Syracuse 1,646 H4
Table Rock 308 H4
Talmage 246 H4
Taylor▲ 186 E3
Tecumseh▲ 1,702 H4
Tekamah▲ 1,852 H3
Terrytown 656 A3
Thedford▲ 243 D3
Tilden 895 G2

Agriculture, Industry and Resources

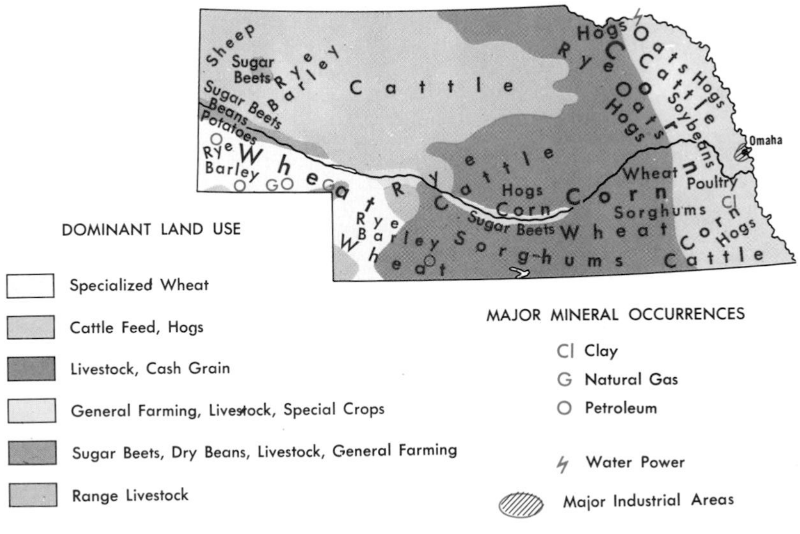

Sheep
Sugar Beets
Rye
Barley
Cattle
Sugar Beets
Beans
Potatoes
Rye
Barley
Wheat
Hogs
Corn
Sugar Beets
Sorghums
Oats
Soybeans
Poultry
Omaha
DOMINANT LAND USE
Specialized Wheat
Cattle Feed, Hogs
Livestock, Cash Grain
General Farming, Livestock, Special Crops
Sugar Beets, Dry Beans, Livestock, General Farming
Range Livestock
MAJOR MINERAL OCCURRENCES
Cl Clay
G Natural Gas
O Petroleum
Water Power
Major Industrial Areas

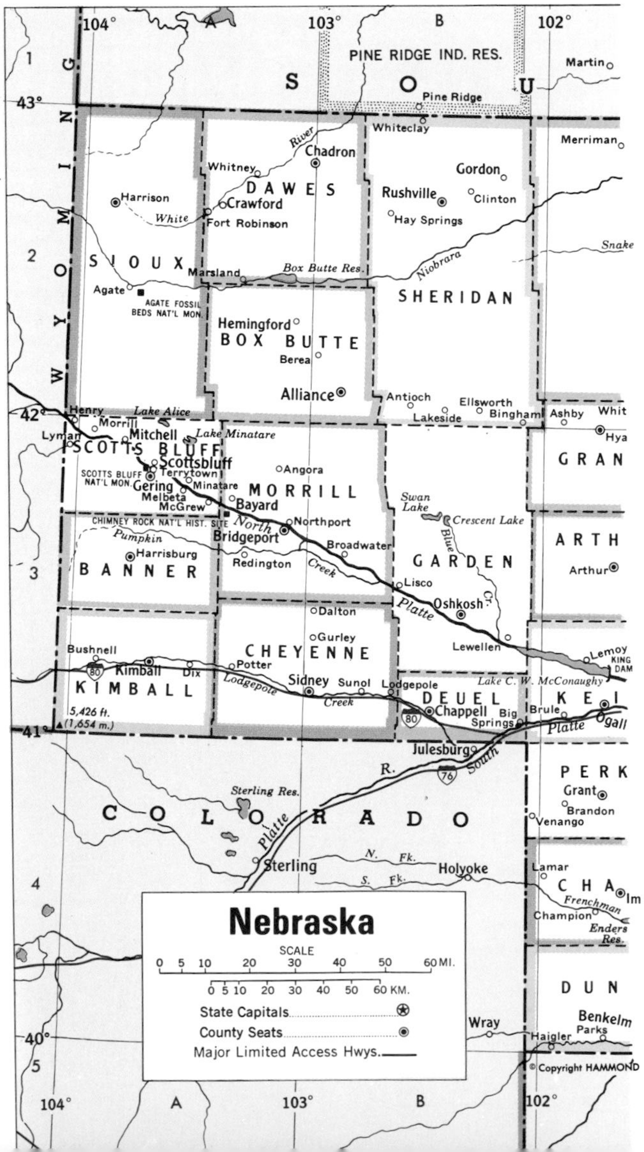

Nebraska
SCALE
0 5 10 20 30 40 50 60 MI.
0 5 10 20 30 40 50 60 KM.
State Capitals
County Seats
Major Limited Access Hwys.
PINE RIDGE IND. RES.
SIOUX
DAWES
SHERIDAN
BOX BUTTE
SCOTTS BLUFF
MORRILL
GARDEN
BANNER
CHEYENNE
KIMBALL
DEUEL
COLORADO
WYOMING
Chadron
Crawford
Harrison
Rushville
Gordon
Alliance
Hemingford
Scottsbluff
Gering
Bridgeport
Sidney
Kimball
Chappell
Oshkosh
Julesburg
Sterling
Holyoke
Wray
© Copyright HAMMOND

▲County seat

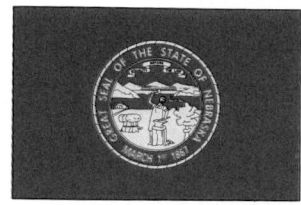

AREA 77,355 sq. mi. (200,349 sq. km.)
POPULATION 1,584,617
CAPITAL Lincoln
LARGEST CITY Omaha
HIGHEST POINT (Kimball Co.) 5,246 ft. (1654 m.)
SETTLED IN 1847
ADMITTED TO UNION March 1, 1867
POPULAR NAME Cornhusker State
STATE FLOWER Goldenrod
STATE BIRD Western Meadowlark

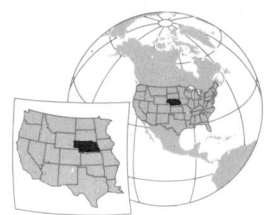

Topography

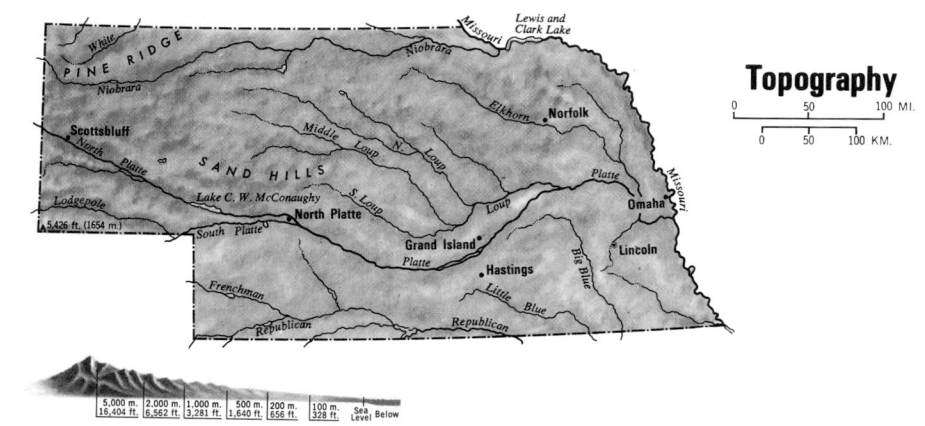

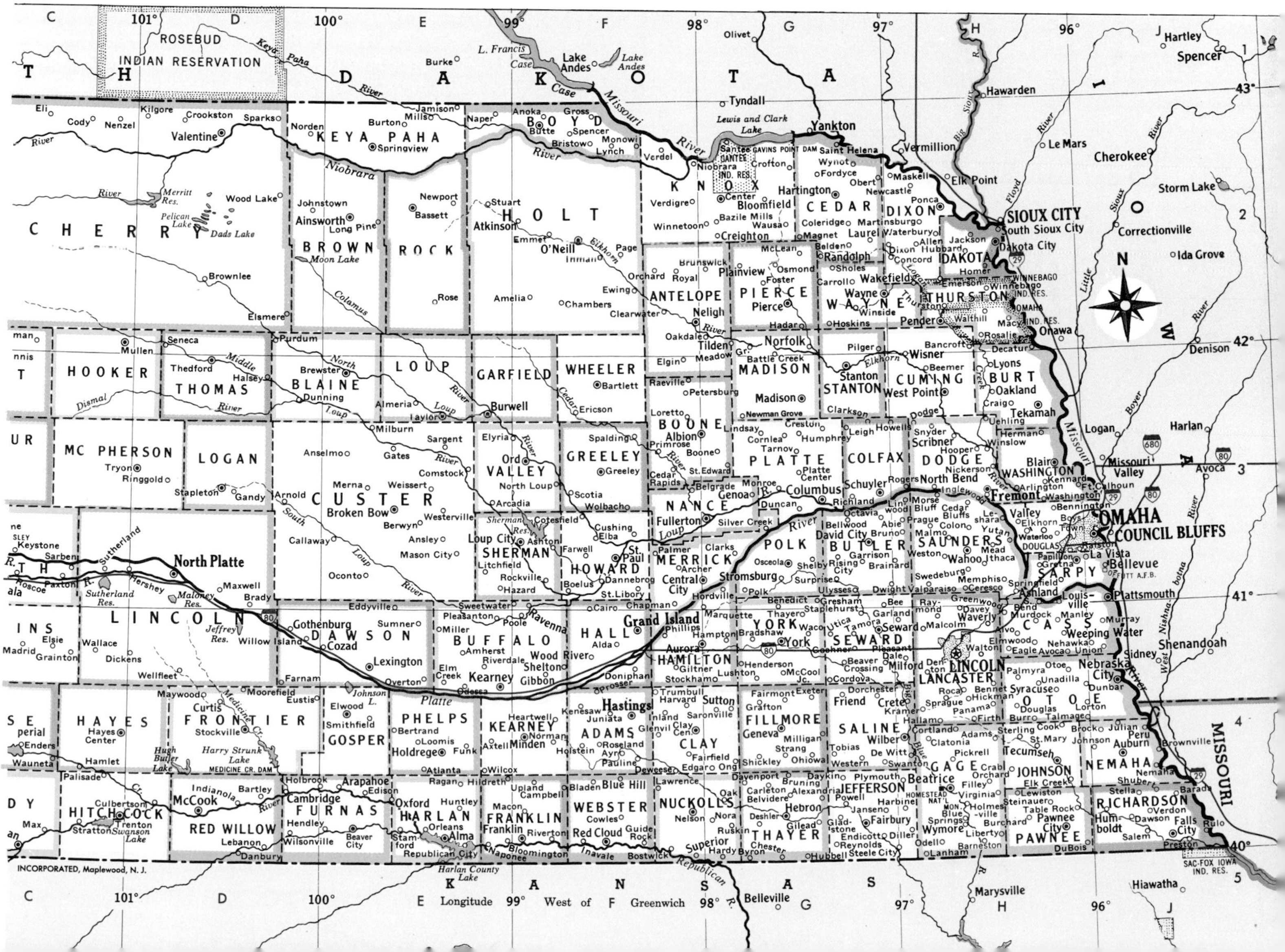

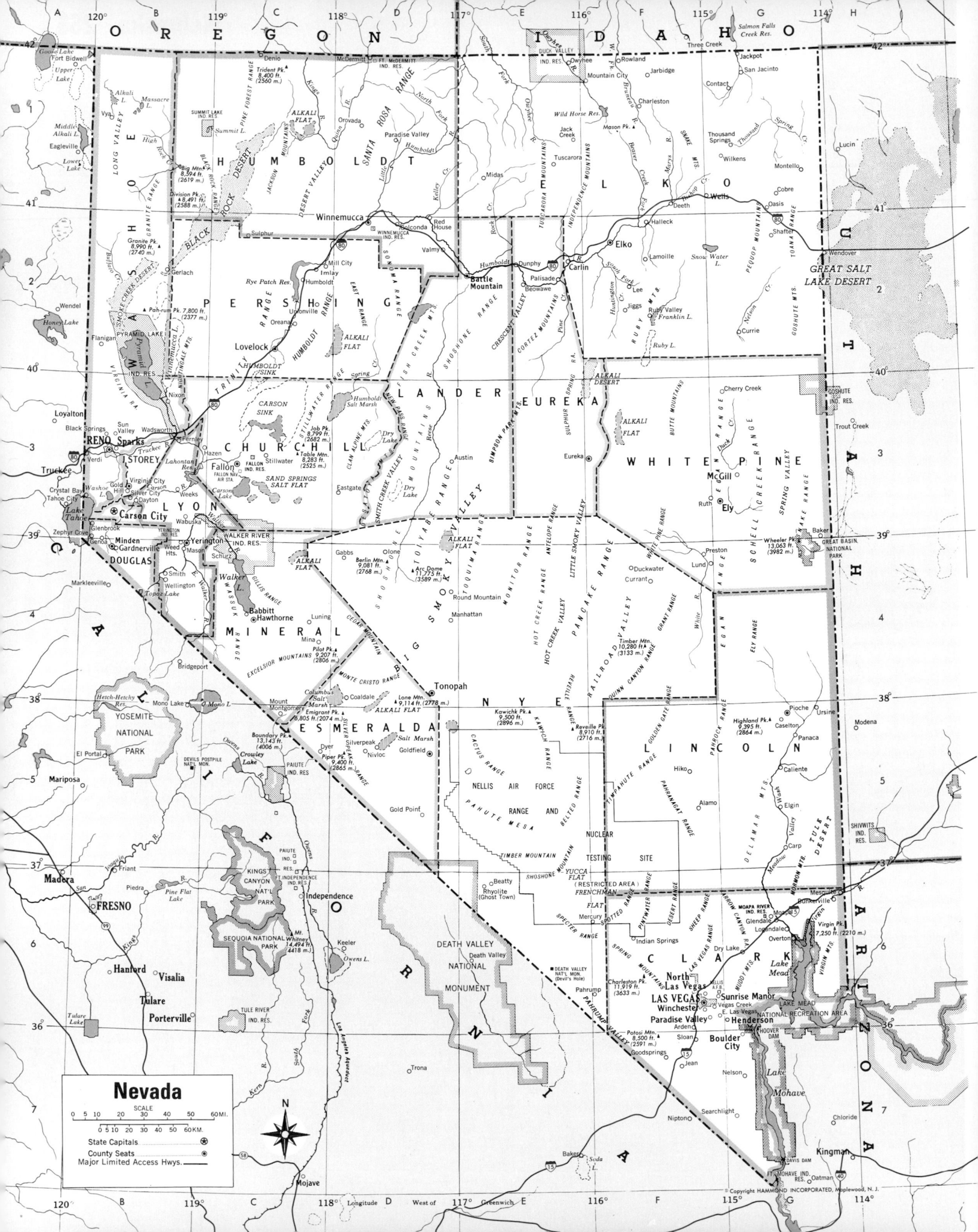

Nevada

SCALE

| 0 5 10 | 20 | 30 | 40 | 50 | 60 MI. |

| 0 5 10 | 20 | 30 | 40 | 50 | 60 KM. |

State Capitals ⊛
County Seats ◉
Major Limited Access Hwys. ▬

© Copyright HAMMOND INCORPORATED, Maplewood, N.J.

Nevada 267

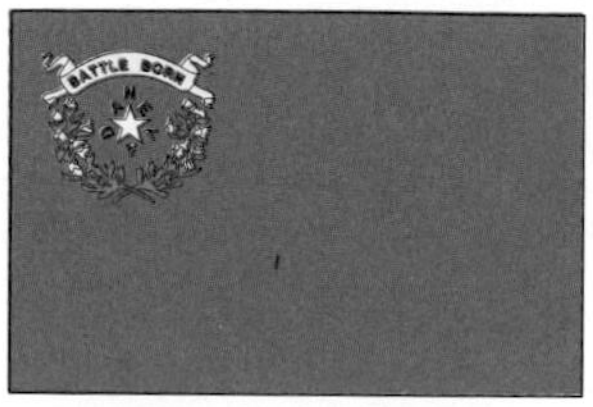
BATTLE BORN

AREA 110,561 sq. mi. (286,353 sq. km.)
POPULATION 1,206,152
CAPITAL Carson City
LARGEST CITY Las Vegas
HIGHEST POINT Boundary Pk. 13,143 ft. (4006 m.)
SETTLED IN 1850
ADMITTED TO UNION October 31, 1864
POPULAR NAME Silver State; Sagebrush State
STATE FLOWER Sagebrush
STATE BIRD Mountain Bluebird

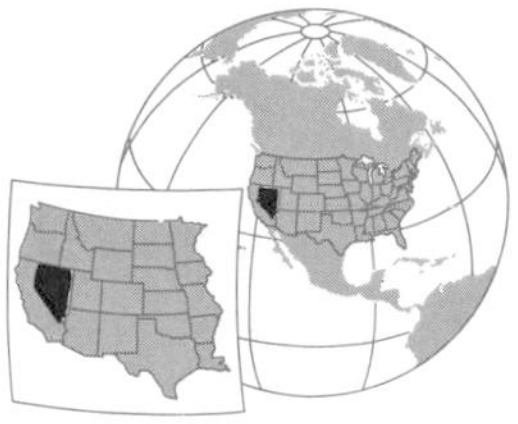

MAJOR MINERAL OCCURRENCES

Ag Silver
Au Gold
Ba Barite
Cu Copper
Gp Gypsum
Hg Mercury
Lt Lithium
Mg Magnesium
Mo Molybdenum
Na Salt
O Petroleum
Pb Lead
S Sulfur
W Tungsten
Zn Zinc
Water Power

DOMINANT LAND USE

General Farming, Dairy, Livestock
General Farming, Livestock, Special Crops
Range Livestock
Forests
Nonagricultural Land

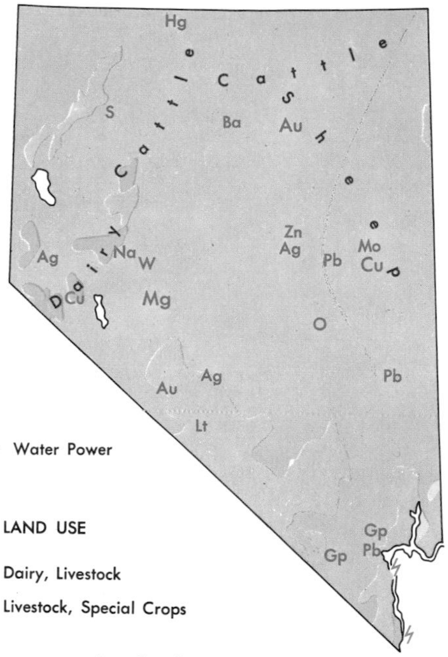
Hg
Cattle
S
Ba
Au
Sheep
Dairy Cattle
Zn
Ag
Mo
Cu
Pb
Na
W
Mg
O
Lt
Gp

Agriculture, Industry and Resources

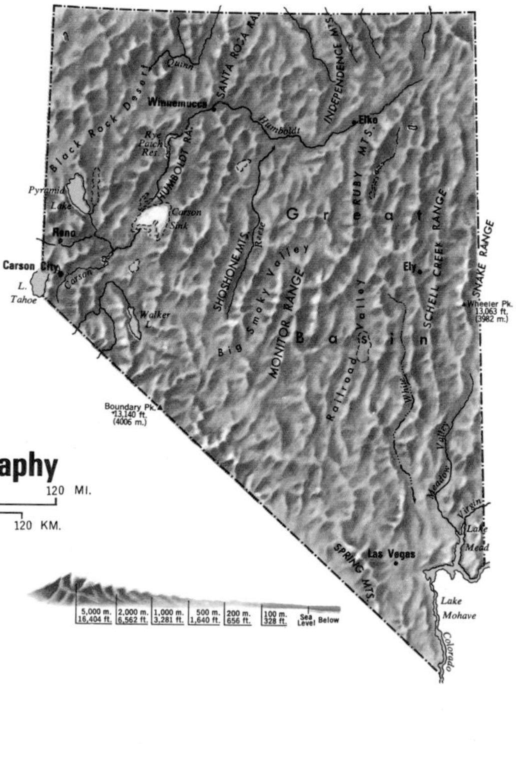
Black Rock Desert
SANTA ROSA RA.
INDEPENDENCE MTS.
Winnemucca
Humboldt
Elko
Rye Patch Res.
HUMBOLDT RA.
Pyramid Lake
Carson Sink
Reno
Carson City
L. Tahoe
Carson
Walker
RUBY MTS.
Great Basin
SHOSHONE MTS.
Big Smoky Valley
MONITOR RANGE
SCHELL CREEK RANGE
SNAKE RANGE
Ely
Wheeler Pk. 13,063 ft. (3982 m.)
Railroad Valley
Boundary Pk. 13,140 ft. (4006 m.)
SPRING MTS.
Las Vegas
Virgin
Lake Mead
Lake Mohave
Colorado
5,000 m. 16,404 ft.
2,000 m. 6,562 ft.
1,000 m. 3,281 ft.
500 m. 1,640 ft.
200 m. 656 ft.
100 m. 328 ft.
Sea Level
Below

Topography

0 60 120 MI.
0 60 120 KM.

COUNTIES

Carson City (city) 40,443 .... B3
Churchill 17,938 .... C3
Clark 741,459 .... F6
Douglas 27,637 .... B4
Elko 33,530 .... F1
Esmeralda 1,344 .... D5
Eureka 1,547 .... E3
Humboldt 12,844 .... C1
Lander 6,266 .... D3
Lincoln 3,775 .... F5
Lyon 20,001 .... B3
Mineral 6,475 .... C4
Nye 17,781 .... E4
Pershing 4,336 .... C2
Storey 2,526 .... B3
Washoe 254,667 .... B2
White Pine 9,264 .... F3

CITIES and TOWNS

Alamo 300 .... F5
Austin 300 .... E3
Babbitt C4
Baker 140 .... G3
Battle Mountain▲ 3,542 .... E2
Beatty 1,623 .... E6
Beowawe 77 .... E2
Black Springs 180 .... B3
Boulder City 12,567 .... G7
Bunkerville 300 .... G6
Caliente 1,111 .... G5
Carlin 2,220 .... E2
Carp 30 .... G5
Carson City (cap.) 40,443 .... B3
Caselton G5
Cherry Creek 80 .... G3
Coaldale 31 .... D4
Crystal Bay 6,225 .... A3
Currant 30 .... F4
Dayton 2,217 .... B3
Deeth 125 .... F1
Denio 35 .... C1
Duckwater 80 .... F4
Dunphy 25 .... E2
Dyer 56 .... C5
East Las Vegas 11,087 .... F6
Elko▲ 14,736 .... F2
Ely▲ 4,756 .... G3
Eureka▲ 300 .... E3
Fallon▲ 6,438 .... C3
Fernley 5,164 .... B3
Gabbs 667 .... D4
Gardnerville 2,177 .... B4
Genoa 254 .... B4
Gerlach 400 .... B2
Glenbrook 800 .... B3
Glendale 25 .... G6
Golconda 275 .... D2
Gold Hill 80 .... B3
Goldfield▲ 500 .... D5
Goodsprings 80 .... F7
Halleck 68 .... F2
Hawthorne▲ 4,162 .... C4
Hazen 76 .... C3
Henderson 64,942 .... G6
Hiko 210 .... F5
Imlay 250 .... C2
Indian Springs 1,164 .... F6
Jack Creek E1
Jackpot 400 .... G1
Jean 125 .... F7
Lamoille 100 .... F2
Las Vegas▲ 258,295 .... F6
Lee 125 .... F2
Logandale 410 .... G6
Lovelock▲ 2,069 .... C2
Lund 380 .... F4
Luning 90 .... C4
Manhattan 93 .... E4
Mason 200 .... B4
McDermitt 373 .... D1
McGill 1,258 .... G3
Mercury 900 .... E6
Mesquite 1,871 .... G6
Mina 450 .... C4
Minden▲ 1,441 .... B4
Moapa 3,444 .... G6
Montello 100 .... G1
Mountain City 100 .... F1
Nelson 75 .... G7
Nixon 400 .... B3
North Las Vegas 47,707 .... F6
Oreana 45 .... C2
Orovada 200 .... D1
Overton 1,111 .... G6
Owyhee 908 .... F1
Pahrump 7,424 .... E6
Panaca 650 .... G5
Paradise Valley 115 .... D1
Paradise Valley 84,818 .... F6
Pioche▲ 850 .... G5
Preston 50 .... G4
Reno▲ 133,850 .... B3
Round Mountain 400 .... E4
Ruby Valley 150 .... F2
Ruth 455 .... F3
Schurz 617 .... C4
Searchlight 500 .... F7
Silver City 150 .... B3
Silverpeak 100 .... D5
Sloan 30 .... F7
Smith 1,033 .... B4
Sparks 53,367 .... B3
Stillwater 150 .... C3
Sulphur C2
Sun Valley 11,391 .... B3
Sunrise Manor 95,362 .... F6
Thousand Springs G1
Tonopah▲ 3,616 .... D4
Ursine 45 .... G5
Valmy 200 .... D2
Vegas Creek G6
Verdi 100 .... B3
Virginia City▲ 750 .... B3
Wabuska 150 .... B3
Wadsworth 640 .... B3
Wellington 505 .... B4
Wells 1,256 .... G1
Winchester 23,365 .... F6
Winnemucca▲ 6,134 .... D2
Yerington▲ 2,367 .... B4
Zephyr Cove 1,434 .... A3

OTHER FEATURES

Alkali (lake) B1
Antelope (range) E3
Arc Dome (mt.) D4
Arrow Canyon (range) G6
Beaver Creek Fork, Humboldt (riv.) F1
Belted (range) E5
Berlin (mt.) D4
Big (mt.) B1
Big Smoky (valley) D4
Bishop (creek) F1
Black Rock (des.) B2
Black Rock (range) B1
Boundary (peak) C5
Buffalo (creek) B2
Butte (mts.) F3
Cactus (range) E5
Carson (lake) C3
Carson (riv.) B3
Carson (sink) C3
Cedar (mt.) D4
Charleston (peak) F6
Clan Alpine (mts.) D3
Columbus (salt marsh) C4
Cortez (mts.) E2
Crescent (valley) E2
Davis (dam) G7
Death Valley Nat'l Mon. E6
Delamar (mts.) G5
Desatoya (mts.) D3
Desert (range) F6
Desert (valley) C1
Devil's Hole (Death Valley Nat'l Mon.) E6
Division (peak) B1
Duck (creek) G3
Duck Valley Ind. Res. E1
East (range) D2
East Walker (riv.) B4
Egan (range) G4
Ely (range) G4
Emigrant (peak) C5
Excelsior (mts.) C4
Fallon Ind. Res. C3
Fallon Nav. Air Sta. C3
Fish Creek (mts.) D2
Fort McDermitt Ind. Res. D1
Fort Mohave Ind. Res. G7
Franklin (lake) F2
Frenchman Flat (basin) F6
Gillis (range) C4
Golden Gate (range) F5
Goshute (mts.) G2
Goshute Ind. Res. G3
Granite (peak) B2
Granite (range) B2
Grant (range) F4
Great Basin Nat'l Park G4
Great Salt Lake (des.) H2
High Rock (creek) B1
Highland (peak) G5
Hoover (dam) G7
Hot Creek (range) E4
Hot Creek (valley) E4
Humboldt (range) C2
Humboldt (riv.) E2
Humboldt (salt marsh) D3
Humboldt (sink) C2
Huntington (creek) F2
Independence (mts.) E1
Jackson (mts.) C1
Job (peak) C3
Kawich (range) E5
Kelley (creek) D1
Kings (riv.) C1
Lahontan (res.) B3
Lake Mead National Rec. Area G6
Las Vegas (range) F6
Little Humboldt (riv.) D1
Little Smoky (valley) E4
Lone (mt.) D4
Long (valley) B1
Marys (riv.) F1
Mason (peak) F1
Massacre (lake) B1
Mead (lake) G6
Meadow Valley Wash (riv.) G5
Moapa River Ind. Res. G6
Mohave (lake) G7
Monitor (range) E4
Monte Cristo (range) D4
Mormon (mts.) G5
Muddy (mts.) G6
Nellis A.F.B. 8,377 .... F6
Nellis Air Force Range and Nuclear Test Site E5
Nelson (creek) G2
New Pass (range) D3
Nightingale (mts.) B2
Owyhee (riv.) E1
Pahranagat (range) F5
Pahrock (range) F5
Pah-rum (peak) B2
Pahrump (valley) F6
Pahute (mesa) E5
Pancake (range) F4
Pequop (mts.) G2
Pilot (peak) C4
Pine (creek) E2
Pine Forest (range) C1
Pintwater (range) F6
Piper (peak) D5
Potosi (mt.) F7
Pyramid (lake) B2
Pyramid Lake Ind. Res. B2
Quinn (riv.) D1
Quinn Canyon (range) F4
Railroad (valley) F4
Reese (riv.) D3
Reveille (peak) E5
Reveille (range) E4
Ruby (lake) F2
Ruby (mts.) F2
Rye Patch (res.) C2
Sand Springs (salt flat) C3
Santa Rosa (range) D1
Schell Creek (range) G3
Sheep (range) F6
Shoshone (mt.) E6
Shoshone (mts.) D3
Shoshone (range) E2
Silver Peak (range) D5
Simpson Park (mts.) E3
Smith Creek (valley) D3
Smoke Creek (des.) B2
Snake (mts.) F1
Snake (range) G3
Snow Water (lake) G2
Sonoma (range) D2
Specter (range) E6
Spotted (range) F6
Spring (creek) D2
Spring (mts.) F6
Spring (valley) G3
Stillwater (range) C3
Sulphur Spring (range) E3
Summit (lake) C1
Summit Lake Ind. Res. B1
Table (mt.) C3
Tahoe (lake) B3
Thousand Spring (creek) G1
Timber (mt.) E5
Timber (mt.) F4
Timpahute (range) F5
Toana (range) G2
Toiyabe (range) D3
Topaz (lake) B4
Toquima (range) E4
Trident (peak) C1
Trinity (range) C2
Truckee (riv.) B3
Tule (des.) G5
Tuscarora (mts.) E1
Virgin (mts.) G6
Virgin (peak) G6
Virgin (riv.) G6
Virginia (range) B3
Walker (lake) C4
Walker (riv.) C3
Walker River Ind. Res. C3
Washoe (lake) B3
Wassuk (range) C4
Wheeler (peak) G4
White (riv.) F4
White Pine (range) F3
Wild Horse (res.) E1
Winnemucca (lake) B2
Winnemucca Ind. Res. D2
Yerington Ind. Res. B3
Yucca Flat (basin) E6

▲County seat

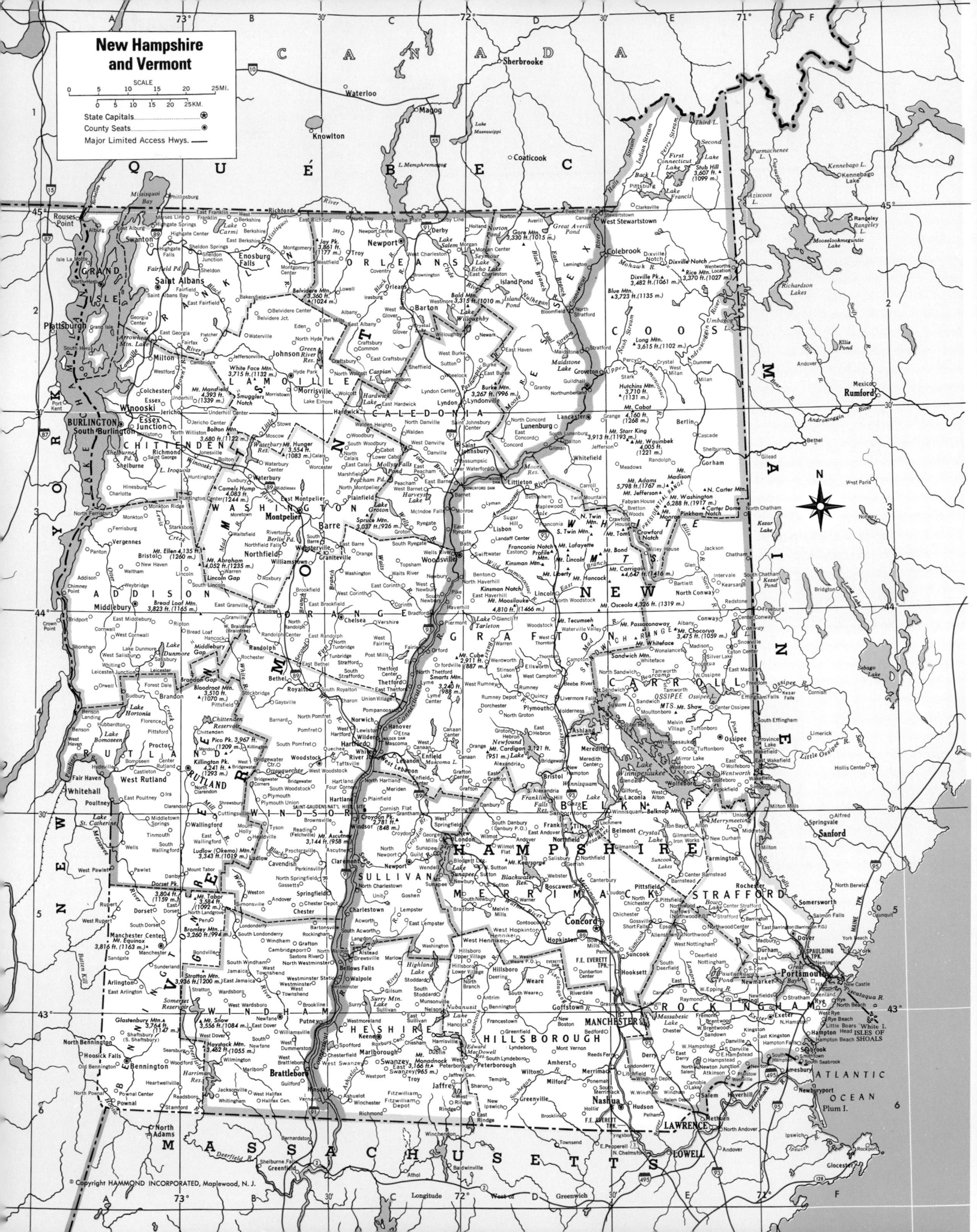

New Hampshire and Vermont

SCALE
0 5 10 15 20 25 MI.
0 5 10 15 20 25 KM.

State Capitals ⊛
County Seats ◎
Major Limited Access Hwys. ▬▬

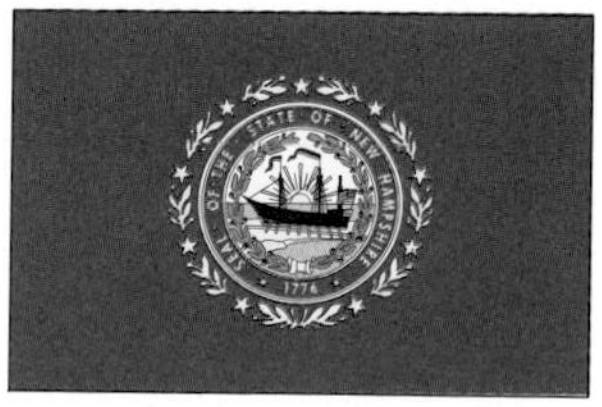

NEW HAMPSHIRE

AREA 9,279 sq. mi. (24,033 sq. km.)
POPULATION 1,113,915
CAPITAL Concord
LARGEST CITY Manchester
HIGHEST POINT Mt. Washington 6,288 ft. (1917 m.)
SETTLED IN 1623
ADMITTED TO UNION June 21, 1788
POPULAR NAME Granite State
STATE FLOWER Purple Lilac
STATE BIRD Purple Finch

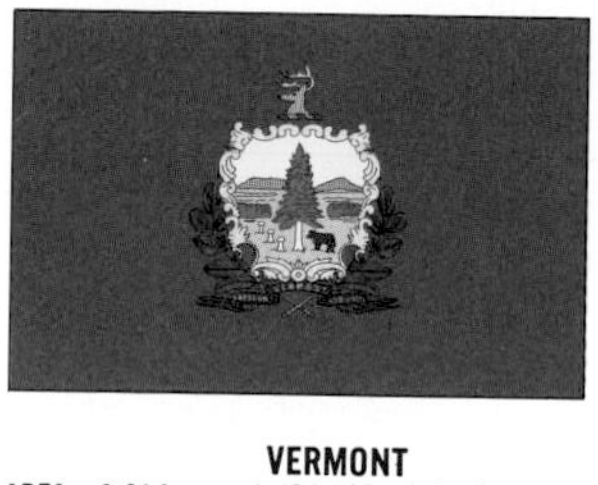

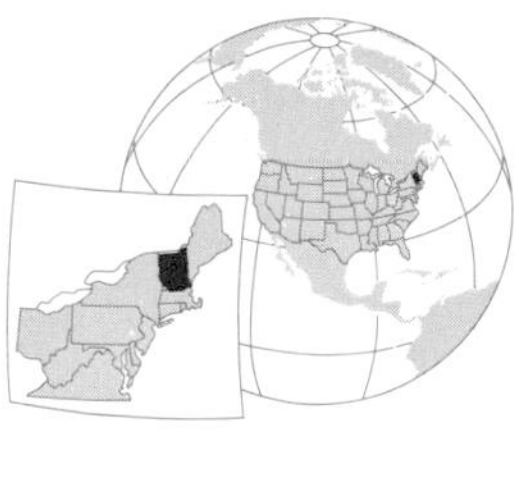

VERMONT

AREA 9,614 sq. mi. (24,900 sq. km.)
POPULATION 564,964
CAPITAL Montpelier
LARGEST CITY Burlington
HIGHEST POINT Mt. Mansfield 4,393 ft. (1339 m.)
SETTLED IN 1764
ADMITTED TO UNION March 4, 1791
POPULAR NAME Green Mountain State
STATE FLOWER Red Clover
STATE BIRD Hermit Thrush

Topography

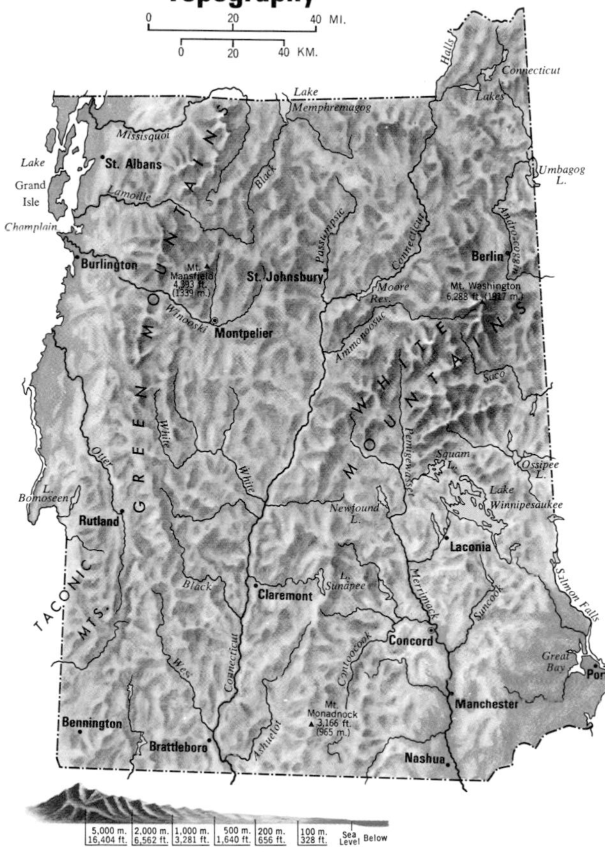

NEW HAMPSHIRE

COUNTIES

Belknap 49,216 .... D4
Carroll 35,410 .... E4
Cheshire 70,121 .... C6
Coos 34,828 .... E2
Grafton 74,929 .... D4
Hillsborough 336,073 .... D6
Merrimack 120,005 .... D5
Rockingham 245,845 .... E5
Strafford 104,233 .... E5
Sullivan 38,592 .... C5

CITIES and TOWNS

Acworth• 776 .... C5
Albany• 536 .... E4
Alexandria• 1,190 .... D4
Allenstown• 4,649 .... E5
Alstead• 1,721 .... C5
Alton Bay 500 .... E5
Alton• 3,286 .... E5
Amherst• 9,068 .... D6
Andover• 1,883 .... D5
Antrim 1,325 .... D5
Antrim• 2,360 .... D5
Ashland 1,915 .... D4
Ashland• 1,807 .... D4
Ashuelot 810 .... C6
Atkinson• 5,188 .... E6
Auburn• 4,085 .... E5
Barnstead• 3,100 .... E5
Barrington• 6,164 .... F5
Bartlett• 2,290 .... E3
Bath• 784 .... D3
Bedford• 12,563 .... D6
Beebe River 355 .... D4
Belmont• 5,796 .... E5
Bennington• 1,236 .... D5
Benton• 330 .... D3
Berlin 11,824 .... E3
Bethlehem• 2,033 .... D3
Boscawen• 3,586 .... D5
Bow Mills 802 .... D5
Bradford• 1,405 .... D5
Brentwood• 2,590 .... E6
Bretton Woods E3
Bridgewater• 796 .... D4
Bristol 1,483 .... D4
Bristol• 2,537 .... D4
Brookfield• 518 .... E4
Brookline• 2,410 .... D6
Campton• 2,377 .... D4
Canaan• 3,045 .... C4
Candia• 3,557 .... E5
Canobie Lake 500 .... E6
Canterbury• 1,687 .... D5
Carroll• 528 .... D3
Cascade 350 .... E3
Center Barnstead 400 .... E5
Center Conway 558 .... E4
Center Harbor• 996 .... E4
Center Ossipee• 800 .... E4
Center Tuftonboro 300 .... E4
Charlestown 1,173 .... C5
Charlestown• 4,630 .... C5
Chatham• 268 .... E3
Chester• 2,691 .... E6
Chesterfield• 3,112 .... C6
Chichester• 1,942 .... E5
Chocorua 575 .... E4
Claremont 13,902 .... C5
Clarksville• 232 .... E1
Colebrook 2,444 .... E2
Colebrook• 2,459 .... E2
Concord• (cap.) 36,006 .... D5
Contoocook 1,334 .... D5
Conway 1,604 .... E4
Conway• 7,940 .... E4
Cornish Flat 450 .... C4
Croydon• 627 .... C5
Dalton• 827 .... D3
Danbury• 881 .... D4
Danville• 2,534 .... E6
Deerfield• 3,124 .... E5
Deering• 1,707 .... D5
Derry 20,446 .... E6
Derry• 29,603 .... E6
Dorchester• 392 .... D4
Dover▲ 25,042 .... F5
Dublin• 1,474 .... C6
Dummer• 327 .... E2
Durham 9,236 .... F5
Durham• 11,818 .... F5
East Andover 500 .... D5
East Hampstead 900 .... E6
East Kingston• 1,352 .... F6
East Lempster 300 .... C5
East Sullivan 300 .... C6
East Swanzey 500 .... C6
East Wolfeboro 400 .... E4
Easton• 223 .... D3
Eaton (Eaton Center) 362 .... E4
Ellsworth• 74 .... D4
Enfield 1,560 .... C4
Enfield• 3,979 .... C4
Epping 1,384 .... E5
Epping• 5,162 .... E5
Epsom• 3,591 .... E5
Errol• 292 .... E2
Etna 550 .... C4
Exeter▲ 9,556 .... F6
Exeter• 12,481 .... F6
Farmington 3,567 .... E5
Farmington• 5,739 .... E5
Fitzwilliam• 2,011 .... C6
Fitzwilliam Depot 350 .... C6
Francestown• 1,217 .... D6
Franconia• 811 .... D3
Franklin 8,304 .... D5
Freedom• 935 .... E4
Fremont• 2,576 .... E6
Georges Mills 375 .... C5
Gerrish 500 .... D5
Gilford• 5,867 .... E4
Gilmanton• 2,609 .... E5
Gilmanton Iron Works 300 .... E5
Gilsum• 745 .... C5
Glen 600 .... E3
Goffstown• 14,621 .... D5
Gorham 1,910 .... E3
Gorham• 3,173 .... E3
Goshen• 742 .... C5
Grafton• 923 .... D4
Grantham• 1,247 .... C5
Grasmere 400 .... D5
Greenfield• 1,519 .... D6
Greenland• 2,768 .... F5
Greenville 1,135 .... D6
Greenville• 2,231 .... D6
Groton• 318 .... D4
Groveton 1,255 .... D2
Guild 500 .... C5
Hampstead• 6,732 .... E6
Hampton 7,989 .... F6
Hampton• 12,278 .... F6
Hampton Beach 975 .... F6
Hampton Falls• 1,503 .... F6
Hancock• 1,604 .... C6
Hanover 6,538 .... C4
Hanover• 9,212 .... C4
Harrisville• 981 .... C6
Haverhill• 4,164 .... C3
Hebron• 386 .... D4
Henniker 1,693 .... D5
Henniker• 4,151 .... D5
Hill• 814 .... D4
Hillsboro 1,826 .... D5
Hillsboro• 4,498 .... D5
Hinsdale 1,718 .... C6
Hinsdale• 3,936 .... C6
Holderness• 1,694 .... D4
Hollis• 5,705 .... D6
Hooksett 2,573 .... E5
Hooksett• 8,767 .... E5
Hopkinton• 4,806 .... D5
Hudson 7,626 .... E6
Hudson• 19,530 .... E6
Intervale 725 .... E3
Jackson• 678 .... E3
Jaffrey 2,558 .... C6
Jaffrey• 5,361 .... C6
Jaffrey Center 340 .... C6
Jefferson• 965 .... D3
Kearsarge 350 .... E3
Keene▲ 22,430 .... C6
Kingston• 5,591 .... E6
Laconia▲ 15,743 .... E4
Lancaster▲ 1,859 .... D3
Lancaster• 3,522 .... D3
Landaff• 350 .... D3
Langdon• 580 .... C5
Lebanon 12,183 .... C4
Lee• 3,729 .... F5
Lempster• 947 .... C5
Lincoln• 1,229 .... D3
Lisbon 1,246 .... D3
Lisbon• 1,664 .... D3
Litchfield• 5,516 .... E6
Littleton 4,633 .... D3
Littleton• 5,827 .... D3
Lochmere 300 .... D5
Londonderry• 19,781 .... E6
Loudon• 4,114 .... E5
Lyman• 388 .... D3
Lyme• 1,496 .... C4
Lyndeborough• 1,294 .... D6
Madbury• 1,404 .... F5
Madison• 1,704 .... E4
Manchester 99,567 .... E6
Marlborough 1,211 .... C6
Marlborough• 1,927 .... C6
Marlow• 650 .... C5
Melvin Village 450 .... E4
Meredith 1,654 .... D4
Meredith• 4,837 .... D4
Meriden 800 .... C4
Merrimack• 22,156 .... D6
Middleton• 1,183 .... E5
Milan• 1,295 .... E2
Milford 8,015 .... D6
Milford• 11,795 .... D6
Milton• 3,691 .... F5
Milton Mills 450 .... F4
Mirror Lake 350 .... E4
Monroe• 746 .... C3
Mont Vernon• 1,812 .... D6
Moultonboro• 2,956 .... E4
Nashua▲ 79,662 .... D6
Nelson• 535 .... C5
New Boston• 3,214 .... D6
New Castle• 840 .... F5
New Durham• 1,974 .... E5
New Hampton• 1,606 .... D4
New Ipswich• 4,014 .... D6
New London 3,180 .... D5
New London• 2,935 .... D5
Newbury• 1,347 .... C5
Newfields• 888 .... F5
Newington• 990 .... F5
Newmarket 4,917 .... F5
Newmarket• 7,157 .... F5
Newport▲ 3,772 .... C5
Newport• 6,110 .... C5
Newton Junction 450 .... E6
Newton• 3,473 .... E6
North Chichester 450 .... E5
North Conway 2,032 .... E3
North Hampton• 3,637 .... F6
North Haverhill 400 .... D3
North Stratford 600 .... D2
North Walpole 950 .... C5
North Weare 400 .... D5
North Woodstock 750 .... D3
Northfield-Tilton D5
Northfield• 4,263 .... D5
Northumberland• 2,492 .... D2
Northwood• 3,124 .... E5
Northwood Narrows 325 .... E5
Nottingham• 2,939 .... E5
Orange• 237 .... D4
Orford• 1,008 .... C4
Ossipee 3,309 .... E4
Pelham• 9,408 .... E6
Pembroke• 6,561 .... E5
Peterborough 2,685 .... D6
Peterborough• 5,239 .... D6
Piermont• 624 .... C4
Pike 433 .... C3
Pittsburg• 901 .... E1
Pittsfield 1,717 .... E5
Pittsfield• 3,701 .... E5
Plainfield• 2,056 .... C4
Plaistow• 7,316 .... E6
Plymouth 3,967 .... D4
Plymouth• 5,811 .... D4
Portsmouth 25,925 .... F5
Randolph• 371 .... E3
Raymond 2,516 .... E5
Raymond• 8,713 .... E5
Redstone 300 .... E3
Richmond• 877 .... C6
Rindge• 4,941 .... C6
Rochester 26,630 .... E5
Roxbury• 248 .... C6
Rumney• 1,446 .... D4
Rye• 4,612 .... F5
Rye Beach 600 .... F6
Rye North Beach 700 .... F5
Salem• 25,746 .... E6
Salem Depot 975 .... E6
Salisbury• 1,061 .... D5
Salmon Falls 950 .... F5
Sanbornton• 2,136 .... D5
Sanbornville 750 .... F4
Sandown• 4,060 .... E6
Sandwich• 1,066 .... E4
Seabrook• 6,503 .... F6
Sharon• 299 .... D6
Shelburne 437 .... E3
Shelburne• 318 .... E3
Silver Lake 350 .... E4
Somersworth 11,249 .... F5
South Deerfield 500 .... E5
South Hampton• 740 .... F6
South Lyndeboro 300 .... D6
South Merrimack 650 .... D6
South Seabrook 500 .... F6
South Weare 400 .... D5
Spofford 750 .... C6
Springfield• 788 .... C4
Stark• 518 .... E2
Stewartstown• 1,048 .... E2
Stoddard• 622 .... C5
Strafford• 2,965 .... E5
Stratford• 927 .... D2
Stratham• 4,955 .... F5
Sugar Hill• 464 .... D3
Sullivan• 706 .... C5
Sunapee• 2,559 .... C5
Suncook 5,214 .... C5
Surry• 667 .... C5
Sutton• 1,457 .... D5
Swanzey• 6,236 .... C6
Tamworth• 2,165 .... E4
Temple• 1,194 .... D6
Thornton• 1,505 .... D4
Tilton-Northfield 3,081 .... D5
Tilton• 3,240 .... D5
Troy 2,097 .... C6
Troy• 2,131 .... C6
Tuftonboro• 1,842 .... E4
Twin Mountain 500 .... D3
Unity• 1,341 .... C5
Wakefield• 3,057 .... F4
Walpole• 3,210 .... C5
Warner• 2,250 .... D5
Warren• 820 .... D4
Washington• 628 .... C5
Waterville Valley• 151 .... D4
Weare• 6,193 .... D5
Webster• 1,405 .... D5
Wentworth• 630 .... D4
Wentworths Location 53 .... E2
West Campton 400 .... D4
West Epping 400 .... E5
West Henniker 500 .... D5
West Lebanon C4
West Milan 350 .... E2
West Rye 350 .... F6
West Stewartstown 700 .... E2
West Swanzey 1,055 .... C6
Westmoreland• 1,596 .... C6
Westville 750 .... E6
Whitefield 1,041 .... D3
Whitefield• 1,909 .... D3
Wilmot Flat 450 .... D5
Wilmot• 935 .... D5
Wilton 1,165 .... D6
Wilton• 3,122 .... D6
Winchester• 1,735 .... C6
Windham• 9,000 .... E6
Winnisquam 500 .... E5
Wolfeboro 2,783 .... E4
Wolfeboro• 4,807 .... E4
Wolfeboro Falls 600 .... E4
Woodstock• 1,167 .... D4
Woodsville▲ 1,122 .... C3

OTHER FEATURES

Adams (mt.) E3
Ammonoosuc (riv.) D3
Androscoggin (riv.) E2
Ashuelot (riv.) C6
Back (lake) E1
Baker (riv.) D4
Bearcamp (riv.) E4
Beaver (brook) E6
Belknap (mt.) E5
Blackwater (res.) D5
Blue (mt.) E2
Bond (mt.) E3
Bow (lake) E5
Cabot (mt.) E2
Cannon (mt.) D3
Cardigan (mt.) D4
Carrigain (mt.) E3
Carter Dome (mt.) E3
Chocorua (mt.) E4
Cocheco (riv.) E5
Cold (riv.) C5
Comerford (dam) D3
Connecticut (riv.) B6
Contoocook (riv.) D6
Conway (lake) E4
Crawford Notch (pass) E3
Croydon (peak) C5
Croydon Branch, Sugar (riv.) C5
Crystal (lake) E5
Cube (mt.) D4
Dixville (peak) E2
Dixville Notch (pass) E2
Edward MacDowell (res.) D6
Ellis (riv.) E3
Everett (dam) D5
Exeter (riv.) E6
First Connecticut (lake) E1
Francis (lake) E1
Franconia Notch (pass) D3
Franklin Falls (res.) D4
Gale (riv.) D3
Great (bay) F5
Halls (stream) E1
Hancock (mt.) D3
Highland (lake) C5
Hutchins (mt.) E2
Indian (stream) E1
Jefferson (mt.) E3
Kearsarge (mt.) D5
Kinsman (mt.) D3
Kinsman Notch (pass) D3
Lafayette (mt.) D3
Lamprey (riv.) E5
Liberty (mt.) D3
Lincoln (mt.) D3
Long (mt.) E2
Mad (riv.) D4
Madison (mt.) E3
Mascoma (lake) C4
Massabesic (lake) E6
Merrimack (riv.) D5
Merrymeeting (lake) E5
Mohawk (riv.) E2
Monadnock (mt.) C6
Monroe (mt.) E3
Moore (dam) D3
Moore (res.) D3
Moosilauke (mt.) D3
Nash (stream) E2
Newfound (lake) D4
North Carter (mt.) E3
North Twin (mt.) D3
Nubanusit (lake) C5
Osceola (mt.) E3
Ossipee (lake) E4
Ossipee (mts.) E4
Ossipee (riv.) F4
Passaconaway (mt.) E4
Pawtuckaway (pond) E5
Pease A.F.B. F5
Pemigewasset (riv.) D4
Perry (stream) E1
Pine (riv.) E4
Pinkham Notch (pass) E3
Piscataqua (riv.) F5
Piscataquog (riv.) D5
Presidential (range) E3
Rice (mt.) E2
Saco (riv.) E3

Agriculture, Industry and Resources

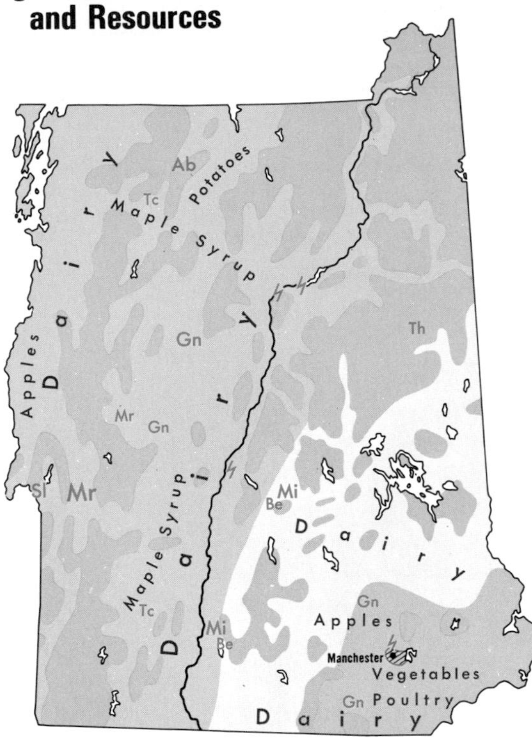

DOMINANT LAND USE

- Specialized Dairy
- Dairy, General Farming
- Dairy, Poultry, Mixed Farming
- Forests

- Water Power
- Major Industrial Areas

MAJOR MINERAL OCCURRENCES

Ab	Asbestos	Mr	Marble
Be	Beryl	Sl	Slate
Gn	Granite	Tc	Talc
Mi	Mica	Th	Thorium

Saint-Gaudens Nat'l Hist. Site B4
Salmon Falls (riv.) F5
Sandwich (mt.) E4
Sandwich (range) E4
Second (lake) E1
Shaw (mt.) E4
Shoals (isls.) F6
Smarts (mt.) C4
Souhegan (riv.) D6
South Twin (mt.) D3
Squam (lake) E4
Starr King (mt.) E3
Stub Hill (mt.) E1
Sugar (riv.) C5
Sunapee (lake) C5
Suncook (lakes) E5
Suncook (riv.) E5
Surry Mountain (lake) C5
Tarleton (lake) D4
Tecumseh (mt.) D4
Third (lake) E1
Tom (mt.) E3
Umbagog (lake) E2
Upper Ammonoosuc (riv.) E2
Warner (riv.) D5
Washington (mt.) E3
Waumbek (mt.) E3
Wentworth (lake) E4
White (isl.) F6
White (mts.) E3
Whiteface (mt.) E4
Wild Ammonoosuc (riv.) D3
Wilder (dam) C4
Winnipesaukee (lake) E4
Winnipesaukee (riv.) D5
Winnisquam (lake) D4

VERMONT

COUNTIES

Addison 32,953 A3
Bennington 35,845 A6
Caledonia 27,846 C2
Chittenden 131,761 A3
Essex 6,405 D2
Franklin 39,980 B2
Grand Isle 5,318 A2
Lamoille 19,735 B2
Orange 26,149 C3
Orleans 24,053 C2
Rutland 62,142 A4
Washington 54,928 B3
Windham 41,588 B5
Windsor 54,055 B4

CITIES and TOWNS

Addison 1,023 A2
Albany 180 C2
Albany• 782 C2
Alburg 436 A1
Alburg• 1,362 A2
Andover• 373 B5
Arlington 1,311 A4
Arlington• 2,299 A5
Ascutney 274 C5
Averill• 7 D2
Bakersfield• 977 B1
Barnard• 872 B4
Barnet• 1,415 C2
Barre 9,482 C2
Barre• 7,411 C3
Barton 908 C1
Barton• 2,967 C2
Bartonsville 300 B5
Beebe Plain 500 C2
Beecher Falls 950 D1
Bellows Falls 3,313 C4
Belvidere• 228 B2
Bennington▲ 9,532 A5
Bennington• 16,451 A6
Benson• 847 A4
Berkshire• 1,190 B2
Bethel 1,866 B3
Bethel• 1,715 B4
Bloomfield• 253 D1
Bolton• 971 B3
Bomoseen 700 A4
Bondville 500 B5
Bradford 672 C2
Bradford• 2,522 C3
Braintree• 1,174 B4
Brandon 1,902 A4
Brandon• 4,223 A3
Brattleboro 8,612 B5
Brattleboro• 12,241 B6
Bridgewater• 895 B3
Bridport• 1,137 A4
Bristol 1,801 A2
Bristol• 3,762 A3
Brookfield• 1,089 B3
Brookline• 403 B5
Brownington• 705 C2
Burke• 1,406 D2
Burlington▲ 39,127 A3
Cabot 220 C2
Cabot• 1,043 C3
Calais• 1,521 B3
Cambridge 292 B2
Cambridge• 2,667 B2
Canaan• 1,121 D1
Castleton• 4,278 A3
Cavendish• 1,323 B5
Center Rutland 465 A4
Charlotte• 3,148 A3
Chelsea• 1,166 C3
Chester-Chester Depot 1,057 B4
Chester• 2,832 B5
Chittenden• 1,102 B4
Clarendon• 2,835 A4
Colchester• 14,731 A1
Concord• 1,093 D2
Corinth• 1,244 C3
Cornwall• 1,101 A4
Coventry• 806 C2
Craftsbury• 994 C2
Cuttingsville 200 B4
Danby• 1,193 B4
Danville• 1,917 C2
Derby• 4,479 C2
Derby (Derby Center) 684 C1
Derby Line 855 C1
Dorset• 1,918 A4
Duxbury• 976 B3
East Albany 250 C2
East Arlington 600 A5
East Barre-Graniteville C3
East Berkshire 200 B2
East Charleston 300 D2
East Dorset• 550 A5
East Dover 275 B6
East Hardwick 200 C2
East Haven• 269 D2
East Jamaica 200 B5
East Middlebury 550 A3
East Montpelier• 2,239 B2
East Poultney 450 A4
East Ryegate 210 C3
East Wallingford 500 B5
Eden Mills 200 C2
Eden• 840 B1
Enosburg Falls 1,350 B1
Essex Junction 8,396 A2
Essex• 16,498 A1
Fair Haven 2,432 A3
Fair Haven• 2,887 A4
Fairfax• 2,486 B1
Fairfield• 1,680 B2
Fairlee• 883 C4
Ferrisburg• 2,317 A3
Fletcher• 941 B2
Florence 250 A4
Forest Dale 500 A3
Franklin• 1,068 B2
Georgia• 3,753 A2
Georgia Center 225 A2
Gilman 600 D2
Glover• 820 C2
Grafton• 602 B5
Granby• 85 D2
Grand Isle• 1,642 A1
Graniteville-East Barre 2,189 B2
Granville• 309 B3
Greensboro• 717 C1
Groton• 862 C2
Guildhall 270 D1
Guilford• 1,941 B6
Halifax• 588 B6
Hancock• 340 B4
Hardwick 2,964 C2
Hardwick• 2,613 C2
Hartford• 9,404 C3
Hartland• 2,988 C4
Hartland Four Corners 400 C4
Highgate• 3,020 B2
Highgate Center 350 B2
Highgate Falls 400 A2
Hinesburg• 3,780 A3
Holland• 423 D2
Hubbardton• 576 A4
Huntington• 1,609 B3
Hyde Park▲ 457 B2
Hyde Park• 2,344 B2
Hydeville 500 A4
Ira• 426 A4
Irasburg• 907 C2
Island Pond 1,222 D2
Isle La Motte• 408 A2
Jacksonville 244 B6
Jamaica• 754 B5
Jay• 381 C2
Jeffersonville 462 B2
Jericho 1,405 A2
Jericho• 4,302 A2
Johnson 1,470 B2
Johnson• 3,156 B2
Jonesville 300 B3
Killington 700 B4
Lake Elmore 250 B2
Leicester• 871 A4
Lemington• 102 D2
Lincoln• 974 B3
Londonderry• 1,506 B5
Lowell• 594 C2
Ludlow 1,123 B5
Ludlow• 2,302 B5
Lunenburg• 1,176 D3
Lyndon• 5,371 C2
Lyndon Center C2
Lyndonville 1,255 D2
Maidstone• 131 D2
Manchester▲ 561 A5
Manchester• 3,622 A5
Manchester Center 1,574 A5
Marlboro• 924 B6
Marshfield 257 C3
Marshfield• 1,331 C3
Mendon• 1,049 B4
Middlebury▲ 6,007 A3
Middlebury• 8,034 A3
Middlesex• 1,514 B3
Middletown Springs• 686 A5
Milton 1,578 A2
Milton• 8,404 A2
Monkton 1,482 A3
Montgomery• 823 B2
Montgomery Center 400 B2
Montpelier▲ (cap.) 8,247 B3
Moretown• 1,415 B3
Morgan• 497 D2
Morristown• 4,733 B2
Morrisville 1,984 B2
Morses Line 200 B2
Moscow 250 B3
Mount Holly• 1,093 B5
Mount Tabor• 214 B5
New Haven• 1,375 A3
Newark• 354 D2
Newbury 412 C3
Newbury• 1,985 C3
Newfane▲ 164 B6
Newfane• 1,555 B6
Newport▲ 4,434 C2
Newport Center 250 C2
North Bennington 1,520 A6
North Clarendon 750 B4
North Concord 263 D3
North Hartland 500 C4
North Hero• 502 A2
North Hyde Park 450 B2
North Pomfret 400 B4
North Pownal 700 A6
North Springfield 1,200 B5
North Thetford 350 C4
North Troy 723 C2
North Westminster 268 B5
North Williston 300 A3
Northfield 1,889 B3
Northfield• 5,610 B3
Northfield Falls 600 B3
Norton• 169 D2
Norwich• 3,093 C4
Old Bennington 279 A6
Orange• 915 C3
Orleans 806 C2
Orwell• 1,114 A4
Panton• 606 A3
Pawlet• 1,314 A5
Peacham• 627 C3
Perkinsville 148 B5
Peru• 324 B5
Pittsfield• 389 B4
Pittsford• 2,919 A4
Plainfield 1,302 C3
Plainfield• 1,249 C3
Plymouth• 440 B4
Pomfret• 874 B4
Post Mills 500 C4
Poultney 1,731 A4
Poultney• 3,498 A4
Pownal• 3,485 A6
Pownal Center 250 A6
Proctor• 1,979 A4
Proctorsville 481 B5
Putney• 2,352 B6
Quechee 900 C4
Randolph 4,764 B4
Randolph• 4,689 B4
Reading• 647 B5
Reading (Felchville) 614 B5
Readsboro• 762 B6
Richford 1,425 B2
Richford• 2,178 B2
Richmond• 3,729 A3
Ripton• 444 A4
Riverton 250 B3
Rochester• 1,181 B4
Rockingham• 5,484 B5
Roxbury• 575 B3
Royalton• 2,389 B4
Rupert• 654 A5
Rutland▲ 18,230 B4
Rutland• 3,781 B4
Ryegate• 1,058 C3
Saint Albans▲ 7,339 A2
Saint Albans• 4,606 A2
Saint Albans Bay 350 A2
Saint George• 705 A2
Saint Johnsbury▲ 6,424 D3
Saint Johnsbury• 7,608 D3
Saint Johnsbury Center 400 D3
Salisbury• 1,024 A4
Sandgate• 278 A5
Saxtons River 541 B5
Searsburg• 85 A6
Shaftsbury• 3,368 A6
Sharon• 1,211 C4
Sheffield• 541 C2
Shelburne• 5,871 A3
Sheldon• 1,748 B2
Sheldon Springs 300 A2
Shoreham• 1,115 A4
Shrewsbury• 1,107 B4
South Barre 1,314 B3
South Burlington 12,809 A3
South Hero• 1,404 A2
South Londonderry 500 B5
South Pomfret 250 B4
South Royalton 700 C4
South Ryegate 400 C3
South Shaftsbury 650 A6
South Strafford 260 C4
South Woodstock 360 B4
Springfield 4,207 B5
Springfield• 9,579 B5
Stamford• 773 A6
Starksboro• 1,511 A3
Stockbridge• 618 B4
Stowe 450 B3
Stowe• 3,433 B3
Strafford• 902 C4
Stratton• 121 B5
Sudbury• 516 A4
Sunderland• 872 A5
Sutton• 854 C2
Swanton 2,360 A2
Swanton• 5,636 A2
Taftsville 260 C4
Thetford• 2,438 C4
Tinmouth• 455 A5
Topsham• 944 C3
Townshend• 1,019 B5
Troy• 1,609 C2
Tunbridge• 1,154 C4
Underhill• 2,799 B2
Underhill Center 575 B2
Vergennes 2,578 A3
Vernon• 1,850 B6
Vershire• 560 C4
Waitsfield• 1,422 B3
Walden• 703 C3
Wallingford 1,148 B5
Wallingford• 2,184 B5
Waltham• 454 A3
Wardsboro• 654 B5
Warren• 1,172 B3
Washington• 937 C3
Waterbury 1,702 B3
Waterbury• 4,589 B3
Waterbury Center 900 B3
Waterville• 532 B2
Websterville 700 B3
Wells• 902 A5
Wells River 424 C3
West Brattleboro 3,135 B6
West Burke 353 C2
West Cornwall 350 A4
West Danville 225 C3
West Dover 550 B6
West Fairlee• 633 C4
West Glover C2
West Hartford 300 C4
West Haven• 273 A4
West Pawlet 300 A5
West Rupert 300 A5
West Rutland 2,246 A4
West Rutland• 2,448 A4
West Townshend 500 B5
West Woodstock 250 B4
Westfield• 422 C2
Westford• 1,740 A2
Westminster 399 C5
Westminster• 3,026 C5
Westminster West 400 B5
Westmore• 305 C2
Weston• 488 B5
Weybridge• 749 A3
Wheelock• 481 C2
White River Junction 2,521 C4
Whiting• 407 A4
Whitingham• 1,177 B6
Wilder 1,576 C4
Williamstown• 2,839 B3
Williston• 4,887 A3
Wilmington• 1,968 B6
Windham• 251 B5
Windsor 3,714 C5
Windsor• 4,084 C5
Winooski 6,649 A2
Wolcott• 1,229 C2
Woodbury• 766 C3
Woodford• 331 A6
Woodstock▲ 1,037 B4
Woodstock• 3,212 B4
Worcester• 906 B3

OTHER FEATURES

Abraham (mt.) B3
Arrowhead Mountain (lake) A2
Ascutney (mt.) C5
Bald (mt.) D2
Barton (riv.) C2
Batten Kill (riv.) A5
Belvidere (mt.) B2
Black (riv.) B5
Black (riv.) C2
Bloodroot (mt.) B4
Bolton (mt.) B3
Bomoseen (lake) A4
Brandon Gap (pass) B4
Bread Loaf (mt.) A3
Bromley (mt.) B5
Brown's (riv.) A2
Burke (mt.) D2
Camels Hump (mt.) B3
Carmi (lake) B2
Caspian (lake) C2
Champlain (lake) A2
Chittenden (res.) B4
Clyde (riv.) C2
Comerford (dam) D3
Connecticut (riv.) C4
Crystal (lake) C2
Dorset (peak) A5
Dunmore (lake) A4
Echo (lake) D2
Ellen (mt.) B3
Equinox (mt.) A5
Fairfield (pond) A2
Glastenbury (mt.) A6
Gore (mt.) D2
Green (mts.) B4
Green River (res.) B2
Groton (lake) C3
Hardwick (lake) C2
Harriman (res.) B6
Harveys (lake) C3
Haystack (mt.) B6
Hoosic (riv.) A6
Hortonia (lake) A4
Hunger (mt.) B3
Iroquois (lake) A3
Island (pond) D2
Jay (peak) B2
Joes (brook) C3
Killington (peak) B4
Lamoille (riv.) A2
Lewis (creek) A3
Lincoln Gap (pass) B3
Little (riv.) B3
Mad (riv.) B3
Maidstone (lake) D2
Mansfield (mt.) B2
Memphremagog (lake) C1
Mettawee (riv.) A5
Middlebury Gap (pass) B4
Mill (riv.) B4
Missisquoi (riv.) B2
Mollys Falls (pond) C3
Moore (dam) D3
Moore (res.) D3
Moose (riv.) D2
Norton (pond) D2
Nulhegan (riv.) D2
Ottauquechee (riv.) B4
Otter (creek) A3
Passumpsic (riv.) D2
Pico (peak) B4
Poultney (riv.) A4
Saint Catherine (lake) A5
Salem (lake) C2
Seymour (lake) D2
Shelburne (pond) A3
Smugglers Notch (pass) B2
Snow (mt.) B6
Somerset (res.) A5
Spruce (mt.) C3
Stratton (mt.) B5
Tabor (mt.) B5
Trout (riv.) B2
Waits (riv.) C3
Waterbury (res.) B3
Wells (riv.) C3
West (riv.) B5
White (riv.) C4
White Face (mt.) B2
Wilder (dam) C4
Willoughby (lake) D2
Winooski (riv.) B3

▲County seat.
•Population of town or township.

AREA 7,787 sq. mi. (20,168 sq. km.)
POPULATION 7,748,634
CAPITAL Trenton
LARGEST CITY Newark
HIGHEST POINT High Point 1,803 ft. (550 m.)
SETTLED IN 1617
ADMITTED TO UNION December 18, 1787
POPULAR NAME Garden State
STATE FLOWER Purple Violet
STATE BIRD Eastern Goldfinch

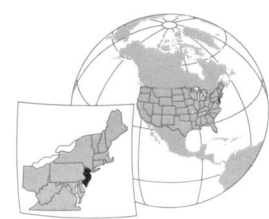

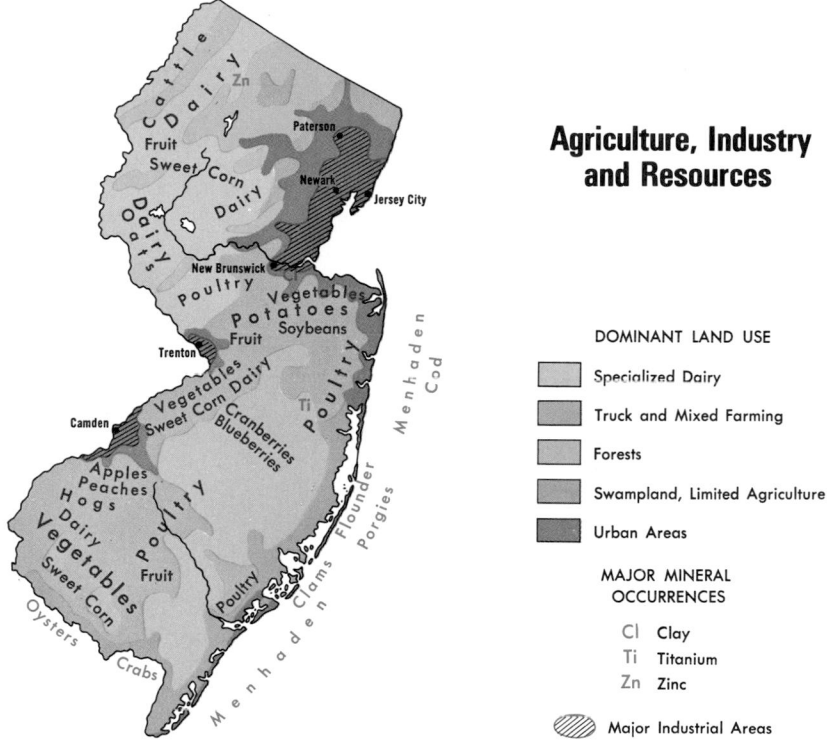

Agriculture, Industry and Resources

DOMINANT LAND USE

- Specialized Dairy
- Truck and Mixed Farming
- Forests
- Swampland, Limited Agriculture
- Urban Areas

MAJOR MINERAL OCCURRENCES

Cl Clay
Ti Titanium
Zn Zinc

Major Industrial Areas

The Urban Northeast

- Urbanized Areas
- • Places with more than 10,000 inhabitants
- • Places with 5,000-10,000 inhabitants
- • Places with 2,500-5,000 inhabitants

© Copyright HAMMOND INCORPORATED, Maplewood, N. J.

COUNTIES

Atlantic 224,327	D5
Bergen 825,380	E2
Burlington 395,066	D4
Camden 502,824	D4
Cape May 95,089	D5
Cumberland 138,053	C5
Essex 778,206	E2
Gloucester 230,082	C4
Hudson 553,099	E2
Hunterdon 107,776	D2
Mercer 325,824	D3
Middlesex 671,780	E3
Monmouth 553,124	E3
Morris 421,353	D2
Ocean 433,203	E4
Passaic 453,060	E1
Salem 65,294	C4
Somerset 240,279	D2
Sussex 130,943	D1
Union 493,819	E2
Warren 91,607	C2

CITIES and TOWNS

Aberdeen 17,235	E3
Absecon 7,298	D5
Allamuchy 600	D2
Allendale 5,900	B1
Allenhurst 759	F3
Allentown 1,828	D3
Allenwood	E3
Alloway 1,371	C4
Alpha 2,530	C2
Alpine 1,716	C1
Andover 700	D2
Annandale 1,074	D2
Asbury Park 16,799	F3
Ashland	B3
Atlantic City 37,986	E5
Atlantic Highlands 4,629	F3
Audubon 9,205	B3
Audubon Park 1,150	B3
Augusta 500	D1
Aura 500	C4
Avalon 1,809	D5
Avenel 15,504	E2
Avon By The Sea 2,165	E3
Barnegat 1,160	E4
Barnegat Light 675	E4
Barrington 6,774	B3
Basking Ridge	D2
Bay Head 1,226	E3
Beach Haven 1,175	E4
Beach Haven Crest 500	E4
Beach Haven Terrace 500	E4
Beachwood 9,324	E4
Bedminster • 2,469	D2
Belford	E3
Belle Mead	D3
Belleplain 500	D5
Belleville 34,213	B2
Bellmawr 12,603	B3
Belmar 5,877	E3
Belvidere▲ 2,669	C2
Bergenfield 24,458	C1
Berkeley Heights • 11,980	E2
Berlin 5,672	D4
Bernardsville 6,597	D2
Beverly 2,973	D3
Blackwood 5,120	C4
Blackwood Terrace	C4
Blairstown • 4,360	C2
Bloomfield 45,061	B2
Bloomingdale 7,530	E1
Bloomsbury 890	C2
Bogota 7,824	B2
Boonton 8,343	E2
Bordentown 4,341	D3
Bound Brook 9,487	D2
Bradley Beach 4,475	F3
Branchville 851	D1
Brant Beach 500	E4
Breton Woods	E3
Brick • 66,473	E3
Bridgeport 750	C4
Bridgeton▲ 18,942	C5
Bridgewater • 29,175	D2
Brielle 4,406	E3
Brigantine 11,354	E5
Brooklawn 1,805	B3
Brookside	D2
Browns Mills 11,429	D4
Budd Lake 7,272	D2
Buena 4,441	D4
Burlington 9,835	D3
Butler • 7,392	E2
Caldwell 7,549	B2
Califon 1,073	D2
Camden▲ 87,492	B3
Candlewood 6,750	E3
Cape May 4,668	D6
Cape May Court House▲ 4,426	D5

Cape May Point 248	D6
Carlstadt 5,510	B2
Carneys Point 7,686	C4
Carteret 19,025	E2
Cedar Brook 600	D4
Cedar Grove▲ 12,053	B2
Cedar Knolls	E2
Cedarville 900	C5
Cedarwood Park	E3
Chatham 8,007	E2
Chatsworth 700	D4
Cheesequake	E3
Cherry Hill • 69,319	B3
Chesilhurst 1,526	D4
Chester 1,214	D2
Chesterfield • 3,867	D3
Cinnaminson • 14,583	B3
Clark • 14,629	A3
Clarksboro	C4
Clarksburg 800	E3
Clayton 6,155	C4
Clementon 5,601	D4
Cliffside Park 20,393	C2
Cliffwood	E3
Clifton 71,742	B2
Clinton 2,054	D2
Closter 8,094	C1
Cold Spring 500	D6
Collingswood 15,289	B3
Cologne 800	D4
Colonia 18,238	E2
Colts Neck 950	E3
Columbia 600	C2
Columbus 800	D3
Convent Station	E2
Corbin City 412	D5
Cranberry Lake 500	D2
Cranbury 1,255	E3
Cranford • 22,624	E2
Cresskill 7,558	C1
Dayton 4,321	D3
Deal 1,179	F3
Deepwater 800	C4
Delanco • 3,316	D3
Delran • 14,811	B3
Demarest 4,800	C1
Dennisville 890	D5
Denville • 14,380	D2
Deptford • 23,473	B4
Dividing Creek 500	C5
Dorchester 500	D5
Dorothy 900	D5
Dover 15,115	D2
Dumont 17,187	C1
Dunellen 6,528	D2
East Brunswick • 43,548	E3
East Hanover • 9,926	E2
East Keansburg	E3
East Millstone 950	D3
East Newark 2,157	B2
East Orange 73,552	B2
East Rutherford 7,902	B2
Eatontown 13,800	E3
Edgewater 5,001	C2
Edgewater Park • 8,388	D3
Edison • 88,680	E2
Egg Harbor City 4,583	D4
Elberon	F3
Elizabeth▲ 110,002	B2
Elmer 1,571	C4
Elmwood Park 17,623	B2
Elwood 1,538	D4
Emerson 6,930	B1
Englewood 24,850	C2
Englewood Cliffs 5,634	C2
English Creek 500	D5
Englishtown 1,268	E3
Essex Fells 2,363	B2
Estell Manor 1,404	D5
Ewan 610	C4
Ewing 34,185	D3
Fair Haven 5,270	E3
Fair Lawn 30,548	B1
Fairfield • 7,615	A2
Fairton 1,359	C5
Fairview 10,733	C2
Fanwood 7,115	E2
Far Hills 657	D2
Farmingdale 1,462	E3
Fieldsboro 579	D3
Flagtown 800	D2
Flanders	D2
Flemington▲ 4,047	D2
Florence-Roebling 8,564	D3
Florham Park 8,521	E2
Folsom 2,181	D4
Fords 14,392	E2
Forked River 4,243	E4
Fort Lee 31,997	C2
Franklin 4,977	D1
Franklin Lakes 9,873	B1
Franklin Park • 31,358	D3
Franklinville	C4
Freehold▲ 10,742	E3
Frenchtown 1,528	C2
Garfield 26,727	B2

(continued on following page)

Garwood 4,227 ... E2
Gibbsboro 2,383 ... B4
Gibbstown 3,902 ... C4
Gilford Park 8,668 ... E4
Gillette ... E2
Glassboro 15,614 ... C4
Glasser ... D2
Glen Gardner 1,665 ... D2
Glen Ridge 7,076 ... B2
Glen Rock 10,883 ... B1
Glendora 5,201 ... B4
Glenwood 500 ... D1
Gloucester City 12,649 ... B3
Green Brook ... D2
Green Creek 600 ... D5
Green Pond 800 ... E1
Green Village 800 ... D2
Greenwich• 973 ... C5
Grenloch 700 ... C4
Greystone Park ... D2
Groveville ... D3
Guttenberg 8,268 ... C2
Hackensack▲ 37,049 ... B2
Hackettstown 8,120 ... D2
Haddon Heights 7,860 ... B3
Haddonfield 11,628 ... B3
Hainesport• 3,236 ... D4
Haledon 6,951 ... B1
Hamburg 2,566 ... D1
Hamilton Square-
Mercerville ... D3
Hammonton 12,208 ... D4
Hampton 1,515 ... D2
Harrington Park 4,623 ... C1
Harrison 13,425 ... B2
Hartford 650 ... D4
Harvey Cedars 362 ... E4
Hasbrouck Heights 11,488 ... B2
Haskell ... A1
Haworth 3,384 ... C1
Hawthorne 17,084 ... B2
Hazlet 23,013 ... E3
Helmetta 1,211 ... E3
Hewitt 950 ... E1
Hi-Nella 1,045 ... B4
High Bridge 3,886 ... D2
Highland Lakes 4,550 ... E1
Highland Park 13,279 ... D2
Highlands 4,849 ... F3
Hightstown 5,126 ... D3
Hillsdale 9,750 ... B1
Hillside• 21,044 ... B2
Ho Ho Kus 3,935 ... B1
Hoboken 33,397 ... C2
Holmdel• 8,447 ... E3
Hopatcong 15,586 ... D2
Hopewell 1,968 ... D3
Howell• 25,065 ... E3
Huntington ... C2
Interlaken 910 ... E3
Ironia ... D2
Irvington 59,774 ... B2
Iselin 16,141 ... E2
Island Heights 1,470 ... E4
Jackson• 25,644 ... E3
Jamesburg 5,294 ... E3
Jersey City▲ 228,537 ... B2
Johnsonburg 600 ... D2
Juliustown 500 ... D3
Keansburg 11,069 ... E3
Kearny 34,874 ... B2
Keasbey ... E2
Kendall Park 7,127 ... D3
Kenilworth 7,574 ... E2
Keyport 7,586 ... E3
Kingston 1,047 ... D3
Kinnelon 8,470 ... E2
Kirkwood 800 ... B4
Lafayette 900 ... D1
Lake Hiawatha ... E2
Lake Hopatcong ... D2
Lake Mohawk 8,930 ... D1
Lakehurst 3,078 ... E3
Lakewood 26,095 ... E3
Lambertville 3,927 ... D3
Landisville ... D4
Lanoka Harbor ... E4
Laurel Springs 2,341 ... B4
Laurence Harbor 6,361 ... E3
Lavallette 2,299 ... E4
Lawnside 2,841 ... B3
Lawrenceville 6,446 ... D3
Layton 700 ... D1
Lebanon 1,036 ... D2
Ledgewood ... D2
Leeds Point 500 ... E4
Leesburg 700 ... D5
Leonardo 3,788 ... E3
Leonia 8,365 ... C2
Liberty Corner ... D2
Lincoln Park 10,978 ... A1
Lincroft 6,193 ... E3
Linden 36,701 ... A3
Lindenwold 18,734 ... B4
Linwood 6,866 ... D5
Little Falls• 11,294 ... B2
Little Ferry 9,989 ... B2
Little Silver 5,721 ... F3
Livingston• 26,609 ... E2
Lodi 22,355 ... B2
Long Branch 28,658 ... F3
Long Valley 1,744 ... D2
Longport 1,224 ... D5
Lumberton 600 ... D4
Lyndhurst• 18,262 ... B2
Lyons ... D2
Madison 15,850 ... E2
Magnolia 4,861 ... B3
Mahwah• 12,127 ... E1
Malaga 950 ... C4
Manahawkin 1,594 ... E4
Manasquan 5,369 ... E3
Mantoloking 334 ... E3
Mantua• 9,193 ... C4
Manville 10,567 ... D2
Maple Shade• 19,211 ... B3
Maplewood• 21,756 ... E2
Marcella 540 ... E2
Margate City 8,431 ... E5
Marlboro• 17,560 ... E3
Marlton 10,228 ... D4
Marmora 650 ... D5
Martinsville ... D2
Matawan 9,270 ... E3
Mays Landing▲ 2,090 ... D5
Maywood 9,473 ... B2
McAfee 800 ... D1
McKee City 950 ... D5
Medford ... D4
Medford Lakes 4,462 ... D4
Mendham 4,890 ... D2
Menlo Park ... E2
Mercerville-Hamilton
Square 26,873 ... D3
Merchantville 4,095 ... B3
Metuchen 12,804 ... E2
Mickleton 950 ... C4
Middlesex 13,055 ... E2
Middletown• 62,298 ... E3
Midland Park 7,047 ... B1
Milford 1,273 ... C2
Millburn• 18,630 ... E2
Millington 975 ... D2
Millstone 450 ... D2
Milltown 6,968 ... E3
Millville 25,992 ... C5
Milmay 798 ... D5
Milton ... D1
Mine Hill• 3,325 ... D2
Minotola ... D4
Mizpah 900 ... D5
Monmouth Beach 3,303 ... F3
Monmouth Junction 1,570 ... D3
Monroe• 15,858 ... D1
Montague 750 ... D1
Montclair 37,729 ... B2
Montvale 6,946 ... B1
Montville• 14,290 ... E2
Moonachie 2,817 ... B2
Moorestown 13,695 ... B3
Morganville ... E3
Morris Plains 5,219 ... D2
Morristown▲ 16,189 ... D2
Mount Arlington 3,630 ... D2
Mount Ephraim 4,517 ... B3
Mount Freedom ... D2
Mount Holly 10,639 ... D4
Mount Hope ... D2
Mount Laurel• 17,614 ... D4
Mount Olive• 18,748 ... D2
Mount Royal 900 ... C4
Mountain Lakes 3,847 ... E2
Mountain View ... B2
Mountainside 6,657 ... E2
Mullica Hill 1,117 ... C4
Mystic Islands 7,400 ... E4
National Park 3,413 ... B3
Navesink ... E3
Neptune City 4,997 ... E3
Neshanic Station ... D3
Netcong 3,311 ... D2
New Brunswick▲ 41,711 ... E3
New Egypt 2,327 ... E3
New Gretna 800 ... E4
New Milford 15,990 ... B1
New Providence 11,439 ... E2
New Vernon ... D2
Newark▲ 275,221 ... B2
Newfield 1,592 ... D4
Newfoundland 900 ... D1
Newport 700 ... C5
Newton▲ 7,521 ... D1
Newtonville 950 ... D4
Nixon ... E2
North Ar'ˈ igton 13,790 ... B2
North Bergen• 48,414 ... B2
North Branch 610 ... D2
North Brunswick• 31,287 ... D3
North Caldwell 6,706 ... B2
North Cape May 3,574 ... C6
North Haledon 7,987 ... B1
North Plainfield 18,820 ... E2
North Wildwood 5,017 ... D6
Northfield 7,305 ... D5
Northvale 4,563 ... F1
Norwood 4,858 ... C1
Nutley 27,099 ... B2
Oak Ridge 750 ... E1
Oakhurst 4,130 ... E3
Oakland 11,997 ... B1
Oaklyn 4,430 ... B3
Ocean City 15,512 ... D5
Ocean Gate 2,078 ... E4
Ocean Grove 4,818 ... F3
Ocean View 950 ... D5
Oceanport 6,146 ... F3
Oceanville 600 ... D5
Ogdensburg 2,722 ... D1
Old Bridge 22,151 ... E3
Old Tappan 4,254 ... C1
Oradell 8,024 ... B1
Orange 29,925 ... B2
Osbornsville ... E3
Oxford 1,767 ... C2
Packanack Lake ... B1
Palermo 600 ... D5
Palisades Park 14,536 ... C2
Palmyra 7,056 ... B3
Paramus 25,067 ... B1
Park Ridge 8,102 ... B1
Parsippany-Troy Hills•
48,478 ... E2
Passaic 58,041 ... E2
Paterson▲ 140,891 ... B2
Paulsboro 6,577 ... C4
Peapack-Gladstone 2,111 ... D2
Pedricktown ... C4
Pemberton 1,367 ... D4
Pennington 2,537 ... D3
Penns Grove 5,228 ... C4
Pennsauken• 34,733 ... B3
Pennsville 12,218 ... C4
Pequannock• 12,844 ... B1
Perth Amboy 41,967 ... E2
Petersburg 750 ... D5
Phillipsburg 15,757 ... C2
Pine Beach 1,954 ... E4
Pine Brook ... E2
Pine Hill 9,854 ... D4
Piscataway• 42,223 ... D2
Pitman 9,365 ... C4
Plainfield 46,567 ... E2
Plainsboro ... D3
Pleasantville 16,027 ... D5
Point Pleasant 18,177 ... E3
Point Pleasant Beach 5,112 ... E3
Pomona 2,624 ... D5
Pompton Lakes 10,539 ... A1
Pompton Plains ... B1
Port Monmouth 3,558 ... E3
Port Morris 616 ... D2
Port Norris 1,701 ... C5
Port Reading 3,977 ... E2
Port Republic 992 ... D4
Princeton 12,016 ... D3
Princeton Junction 2,362 ... D3
Prospect Park 5,053 ... B1
Quinton 750 ... C4
Rahway 25,325 ... E2
Ralston 650 ... D2
Ramblewood 6,181 ... D4
Ramsey 13,228 ... B1
Randolph• 17,828 ... D2
Raritan 5,798 ... D2
Red Bank 10,636 ... E3
Richland 950 ... D5
Ridgefield 9,996 ... B2
Ridgefield Park 12,454 ... B2
Ridgewood 24,152 ... B1
Ringoes 682 ... D3
Ringwood 12,623 ... E1
Rio Grande 2,505 ... D5
River Edge 10,603 ... B1
River Vale• 9,410 ... B1
Riverdale 2,370 ... A1
Riverside• 7,974 ... B3
Riverton 2,775 ... B3
Robbinsville 650 ... D3
Rochelle Park• 5,587 ... B2
Rockaway 6,243 ... D2
Rockleigh 270 ... C1
Rocky Hill 693 ... D3
Roebling-Florence ... D3
Roosevelt 884 ... E3
Roseland 4,847 ... A2
Roselle 20,314 ... B2
Roselle Park 12,805 ... A2
Rosenhayn 1,053 ... C5
Roxbury• 18,878 ... D2
Rumson 6,701 ... F3
Runnemede 9,042 ... B3
Rutherford 17,790 ... B2
Saddle Brook• 13,296 ... B1
Saddle River 2,950 ... B1
Salem▲ 6,883 ... C4
Sayreville 34,986 ... E3
Scotch Plains• 21,160 ... E2
Sea Bright 1,693 ... F3
Sea Girt 2,099 ... E3
Sea Isle City 2,692 ... D5
Seabrook 1,457 ... C5
Seaside Heights 2,366 ... E4
Seaside Park 1,871 ... E4
Secaucus 14,061 ... B2
Sewaren 2,569 ... E2
Sewell ... C4
Shiloh 408 ... C5
Ship Bottom 1,352 ... E4
Shore Acres ... E3
Short Hills ... E2
Shrewsbury 3,096 ... E3
Sicklerville ... D4
Singac ... B2
Skillman ... D3
Smithburg 750 ... E3
Somerdale 5,440 ... B4
Somers Point 11,216 ... D5
Somerville▲ 11,632 ... D2
South Amboy 7,863 ... E3
South Belmar 1,482 ... E3
South Bound Brook 4,185 ... E2
South Brunswick• 17,127 ... E3
South Orange• 16,390 ... A2
South Plainfield 20,489 ... E2
South River 13,692 ... E3
South Seaville 600 ... D5
South Toms River 3,869 ... E4
Sparta• 13,333 ... D1
Spotswood 7,983 ... E3
Spring Lake 3,499 ... F3
Spring Lake Heights 5,341 ... E3
Springfield• 13,420 ... E2
Stanhope 3,393 ... D2
Stanton 700 ... D2
Stewartsville 950 ... C2
Stirling ... E2
Stockholm ... D1
Stockton 629 ... D3
Stone Harbor 1,025 ... D5
Stratford 7,614 ... B4
Strathmore 7,060 ... E3
Succasunna 10,931 ... D2
Summit 19,757 ... E2
Surf City 1,375 ... E4
Sussex 2,201 ... D1
Swedesboro 2,024 ... C4
Teaneck• 37,825 ... B2
Tenafly 13,326 ... C1
Teterboro 22 ... B2
Thorofare ... B4
Three Bridges 750 ... D2
Tinton Falls 12,361 ... E3
Titusville 900 ... D3
Toms River▲ 7,524 ... E4
Totowa 10,177 ... B1
Towaco ... E2
Townsends Inlet ... D5
Trenton (cap.)▲ 88,675 ... D3
Tuckerton 3,048 ... E4
Turnersville 3,843 ... C4
Union Beach 6,156 ... E3

Topography

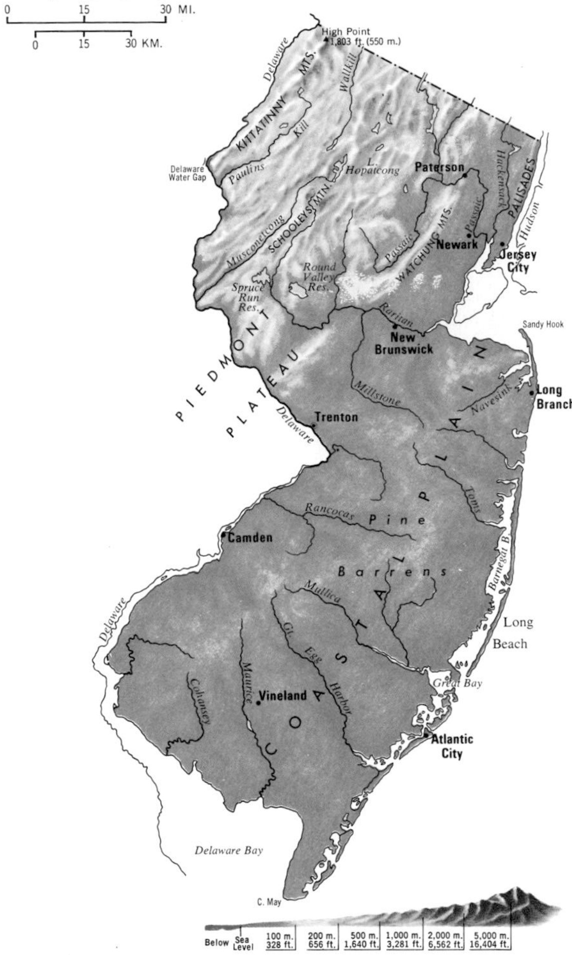

Union City 58,012 ... C2
Union• 50,024 ... A2
Upper Greenwood Lake 2,734 ... E1
Upper Saddle River 7,198 ... B1
Vauxhall ... A2
Ventnor City 11,005 ... E5
Vernon 800 ... E1
Verona 13,597 ... B2
Villas 8,136 ... D5
Vincentown 900 ... D4
Vineland 54,780 ... C5
Voorhees• 12,919 ... B3
Waldwick 9,757 ... B1
Wall• 18,952 ... E3
Wallington 10,828 ... B2
Wanamassa 4,530 ... E3
Wanaque 9,711 ... B1
Waretown 1,283 ... E4
Warren• 9,805 ... D2
Washington 6,474 ... D2
Watchung 5,110 ... E2
Waterford Works 950 ... D4
Wayne• 47,025 ... A1
Weehawken• 12,385 ... C2
Wenonah 2,331 ... C4
West Berlin ... D4
West Caldwell 10,422 ... A2
West Cape May 1,026 ... D6
West Creek 827 ... E4
West Deptford• 18,002 ... B3
West Long Branch 7,690 ... F3
West Milford 25,430 ... E1
West New York 38,125 ... C2
West Orange 39,103 ... A2
West Paterson 10,982 ... B2
West Trenton ... D3
West Wildwood 453 ... D6
Westfield 28,870 ... E2
Westmont 15,875 ... B3
Westville 4,573 ... B3
Westwood 10,446 ... B1
Wharton 5,405 ... D2
Whippany ... E2
White House Station 1,287 ... D2
White Meadow Lake 8,002 ... D2
Whitehouse 852 ... D2
Whitesboro 1,583 ... D5
Whitesville 600 ... E3
Whiting 750 ... E4
Wickatunk 950 ... E3
Wildwood 4,484 ... D6
Wildwood Crest 3,631 ... D6
Williamstown 10,891 ... D4
Willingboro• 36,291 ... D3
Winfield• 1,785 ... B2
Winslow 950 ... D4
Wood-Lynne 2,578 ... B3
Wood-Ridge 7,506 ... B2
Woodbine 2,678 ... D5
Woodbridge• 90,074 ... E2
Woodbury Heights 3,392 ... B4
Woodbury▲ 10,904 ... B4
Woodcliff Lake 5,303 ... B1
Woodport ... D2
Woodstown 3,154 ... C4
Wrightstown 3,843 ... D3
Wyckoff• 15,372 ... B1
Yardville 9,414 ... D3

OTHER FEATURES

Absecon (inlet) ... E5
Alloways (creek) ... C4
Arthur Kill (str.) ... B3
Atlantic Highlands (ridge) ... E3
Barnegat (bay) ... E4
Batsto (riv.) ... D4
Bayonne Military Ocean
Terminal ... B2
Beach Haven (inlet) ... E4
Beaver (brook) ... C2
Ben Davis (pt.) ... C5
Big Flat (brook) ... D1
Big Timber (creek) ... C4
Boonton (res.) ... E2
Brigantine (inlet) ... E5
Budd (lake) ... D2
Canistear (res.) ... E1
Cedar (creek) ... E4
Clinton (res.) ... E1
Cohansey (riv.) ... C5
Cooper (riv.) ... B3
Corson (inlet) ... D5
Crosswicks (creek) ... D3
Culvers (lake) ... D1
Delaware (bay) ... C5
Delaware (riv.) ... D3
Delaware Water Gap
Nat'l Rec. Area ... C1
Earle Naval Weapons Sta. ... E3
Echo (lake) ... E1
Edison Nat'l Hist. Site ... A2
Egg Island (pt.) ... C5
Fort Dix 10,205 ... D3
Fort Hancock ... F3
Fort Monmouth ... E3
Gateway Nat'l Rec. Area ... E2
Great (bay) ... E4
Great Egg Harbor (inlet) ... E5
Greenwood (lake) ... E1
Hackensack (riv.) ... C1
Hereford (inlet) ... D5
High Point (mt.) ... D1
Hopatcong (lake) ... D2
Hudson (riv.) ... C1
Island (beach) ... E4
Kill Van Kull (str.) ... B2
Kittatinny (mts.) ... D1
Lakehurst Naval Air-
Engineering Center ... E3
Lamington (riv.) ... D2
Landing (creek) ... D4
Little Egg (harb.) ... E4
Lockatong (creek) ... C3
Long (beach) ... E4
Long Beach (isl.) ... E4
Lower New York (bay) ... E2
Manasquan (riv.) ... E3
Manumuskin (riv.) ... D5
Maurice (riv.) ... C4
May (cape) ... C6
McGuire A.F.B. 7,580 ... D3
Metedeconk (riv.) ... E3
Mill (creek) ... E4
Millstone (riv.) ... D3
Mohawk (lake) ... D1
Morristown Nat'l Hist. Park ... D2
Mullica (riv.) ... D4
Musconetcong (riv.) ... C2
Navesink (riv.) ... E3
Newark (bay) ... B2
Oak Ridge (res.) ... D1
Oldmans (creek) ... C4
Oradell (res.) ... B1
Oswego (riv.) ... E4
Owassa (lake) ... D1
Palisades (cliffs) ... C1
Passaic (riv.) ... E2
Paulins Kill (riv.) ... D1
Pennsauken (creek) ... B3
Pequest (riv.) ... D2
Picatinny Arsenal ... D2
Pohatcong (creek) ... C2
Pompton (lake) ... B1
Raccoon (creek) ... C4
Ramapo (riv.) ... E1
Rancocas (creek) ... D3
Raritan (bay) ... E3
Raritan (riv.) ... D2
Ridgeway Branch, Toms (riv.) ... E3
Round Valley (res.) ... D2
Saddle (riv.) ... B1
Salem (riv.) ... C4
Sandy Hook (split) ... F3
Shoal Branch, Wading (riv.) ... D4
Spruce Run (res.) ... D2
Statue of Liberty Nat'l Mon. ... B2
Stony (brook) ... D3
Stow (creek) ... C5
Swartswood (lake) ... D1
Tappan (lake) ... C1
The Narrows (str.) ... E2
Toms (riv.) ... E3
Townsend (inlet) ... D5
Tuckahoe (riv.) ... D5
Union (lake) ... C5
Upper New York (bay) ... B2
Wading (riv.) ... D4
Wallkill (riv.) ... D1
Wanaque (res.) ... E1
Wawayanda (lake) ... E1

▲County Seat
•Population of town or township

New Jersey

SCALE
0 — 5 — 10 — 15 — 20 MI.
0 — 5 — 10 — 15 — 20 KM.

State Capitals .... ⊛
County Seats .... ⊙
Canals ....
Major Limited Access Hwys. ——

Longitude 75° West of Greenwich

Espanola 8,389 .... C3
Estancia▲ 792 .... D4
Eunice 2,676 .... F6
Fairacres 700 .... C6
Farmington 33,997 .... A2
Faywood 100 .... B6
Fence Lake 150 .... A4
Fierro 200 .... A6
Flora Vista 1,021 .... A2
Floyd 117 .... F4
Folsom 71 .... F2
Fort Bayard 400 .... A6
Fort Stanton 80 .... D5
Fort Sumner▲ 1,269 .... E4
Fort Wingate 800 .... A3
Fruitland 800 .... A2
Galisteo 125 .... D3
Gallina 420 .... C2
Gallup▲ 19,154 .... A3
Gamerco 800 .... A3
Garfield 600 .... B6
Garita 66 .... E3
Gila 350 .... A6
Glencoe 125 .... D5
Glenwood 220 .... A5
Glorieta 300 .... D3
Golden 100 .... C3
Grady 110 .... F4
Grants▲ 8,626 .... B3
Guadalupita 300 .... D2
Hachita 75 .... A7
Hagerman 961 .... E5
Hanover 300 .... A6
Hatch 1,136 .... B6
Hernandez 500 .... C2
High Rolls-Mountain Park 555 .... D5
Hillsboro 175 .... B6
Hobbs 29,115 .... F6
Holman 400 .... D2
Hondo 425 .... D5
Hope 101 .... E6
Hot Springs▲ (Truth or Consequences) 6,221 .... B5
House 85 .... F4
Humble City 65 .... F6
Hurley 1,534 .... A6
Ilfeld 68 .... D3
Isleta 1,703 .... C4
Jal 2,156 .... F6
Jarales 700 .... C4
Jemez Pueblo 1,301 .... C3
Jemez Springs 413 .... C3
Kenna 100 .... F5
Kirtland 3,552 .... A2
La Cueva 200 .... D3
La Jara 210 .... B2
La Luz 1,625 .... C6
La Madera 200 .... C2
La Mesa 900 .... C6
La Plata 150 .... A2
La Union 200 .... C7
Laguna 434 .... B3
Lajoya 97 .... C4
Lake Arthur 336 .... E5
Lamy 66 .... D3
Las Cruces▲ 62,126 .... C6
Las Vegas▲ 14,753 .... D3
Ledoux 300 .... D3
Lemitar 800 .... B4
Lincoln 100 .... D5
Lindrith 349 .... C2
Llano 325 .... D2
Loco Hills 375 .... F6
Logan 870 .... F3
Lordsburg▲ 2,951 .... A6
Los Alamos▲ 11,455 .... C3
Los Lunas▲ 6,013 .... C4
Los Ojos C2
Los Ranchos de Albuquerque 3,955 .... C3
Loving 1,243 .... E6
Lovington▲ 9,322 .... F6
Lumberton 175 .... C2
Luna 200 .... A5
Magdalena 861 .... B4
Malaga 300 .... E6
Manuelito 200 .... A3
Manzano 65 .... C4
Maxwell 247 .... E2
Mayhill 300 .... D6
McAlister 320 .... F4
McDonald 65 .... F5
McIntosh 325 .... D4
Meadow Vista 3,377 .... C7
Melrose 662 .... F4
Mentmore 315 .... A3
Mescalero 1,159 .... D5
Mesilla 1,975 .... C6
Mesilla Park C6
Mesquite 500 .... C6
Mexican Springs 242 .... A3
Miami 112 .... E2
Milan 1,911 .... B3
Mimbres 300 .... B6
Montezuma 250 .... D3
Monticello 125 .... B5
Monument 300 .... F6
Mora▲ D3
Moriarty 1,399 .... D4
Mosquero▲ 164 .... F3
Mountainair 926 .... C4
Mule Creek 62 .... A5
Nambe 1,246 .... D3
Nara Visa 250 .... F3
Navajo 1,985 .... A3
New Laguna 250 .... B4
Newcomb 388 .... A2
Newkirk 54 .... E3
Nogal 150 .... D5
Ocate 75 .... E2
Oil Center 236 .... F6
Ojo Caliente 600 .... D2
Ojo Feliz 133 .... E2
Ojo Sarco 380 .... D2
Organ 300 .... C6
Orogrande 80 .... D6
Otis 200 .... E6
Paguate 492 .... B3
Pecos 1,012 .... D3
Pena Blanca 300 .... C3
Penasco 648 .... D2
Peralta 3,182 .... C4
Petaca 84 .... C2
Picacho 100 .... D5
Pie Town 90 .... A4
Pinos Altos 250 .... A6
Placitas 1,611 .... C3
Pleasanton 70 .... A5
Pojoaque 1,037 .... C3
Ponderosa 300 .... C3
Portales▲ 10,690 .... F4
Prewitt 300 .... B3
Puerto de Luna 175 .... E4
Questa 1,707 .... D2
Radium Springs 150 .... B6
Rainsville 350 .... D2
Ramah 574 .... A3
Ranchos de Taos 1,779 .... D2
Raton▲ 7,372 .... E2

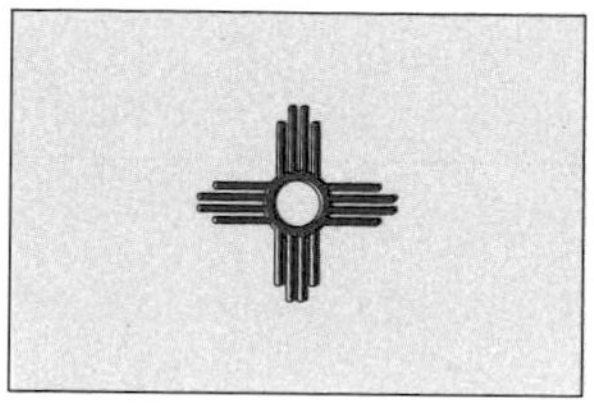

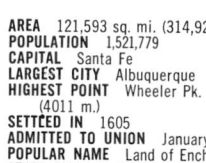

AREA 121,593 sq. mi. (314,926 sq. km.)
POPULATION 1,521,779
CAPITAL Santa Fe
LARGEST CITY Albuquerque
HIGHEST POINT Wheeler Pk. 13,161 ft. (4011 m.)
SETTLED IN 1605
ADMITTED TO UNION January 6, 1912
POPULAR NAME Land of Enchantment
STATE FLOWER Yucca
STATE BIRD Road Runner

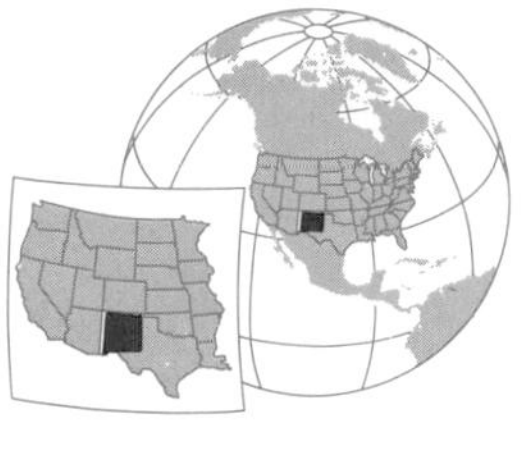

Red River 387 .... D2
Regina 80 .... B2
Rehoboth 200 .... A3
Reserve▲ 319 .... A5
Ribera 84 .... D3
Rincon 300 .... C6
Rio Rancho 32,505 .... C3
Rociada 140 .... D3
Rodarte 650 .... D2
Rodeo 200 .... A7
Roswell▲ 44,654 .... E5
Rowe 290 .... D3
Roy 362 .... E3
Ruidoso 4,600 .... D5
Ruidoso Downs 920 .... D5
Rutheron 95 .... C2
Salem 400 .... B6
San Acacia 286 .... B4
San Antonio 359 .... B5
San Cristobal 350 .... D2
San Felipe Pueblo 1,557 .... C3
San Fidel 150 .... B3
San Ildefonso 447 .... C3
San Jon 277 .... F3
San Jose 150 .... D3
San Juan Pueblo 4,107 .... C2
San Lorenzo 200 .... B6
San Mateo 200 .... B3
San Miguel 400 .... C6
San Patricio 300 .... D5
San Rafael 300 .... A3
San Ysidro 233 .... C3
Sandia Park 450 .... C3
Santa Cruz 2,504 .... D2
Santa Fe (cap.)▲ 55,859 .... C3
Santa Rita 600 .... B6
Santa Rosa▲ 2,263 .... E4
Santo Domingo Pueblo 2,866 .... C3
Sapello 600 .... D3
Seboyeta 125 .... B3
Sedan 60 .... F2
Sena 150 .... D3
Serafina 225 .... D3
Sherman 100 .... B6
Shiprock 7,687 .... A2
Silver City▲ 10,683 .... A6
Socorro▲ 8,159 .... C4
Soham 104 .... D3
Solano 114 .... E3
Springer 1,262 .... E2
Sunspot 78 .... D6
Taiban 120 .... F4
Tajique 145 .... C4
Taos Pueblo 1,187 .... D2
Taos▲ 4,065 .... D2
Tatum 768 .... F5
Tesuque 1,490 .... C3
Texico 966 .... F4
Thoreau 1,099 .... A3
Tierra Amarilla▲ 850 .... C2
Tijeras 340 .... C3
Tinnie 100 .... D5
Toadlena 200 .... A2
Tohatchi 661 .... A3
Tome 500 .... C4
Torreon 200 .... C4
Trampas 76 .... D2
Trementina 80 .... E3
Tres Piedras 200 .... D2
Truchas 275 .... D2
Trujillo 148 .... E3
Truth or Consequences▲ 6,221 .... B5
Tucumcari▲ 6,831 .... F3
Tularosa 2,615 .... C5
Tyrone 100 .... A6
University Park 4,520 .... C6
Ute Park 67 .... D2
Vadito 283 .... D2
Vado 325 .... C6
Valdez 300 .... D2
Valencia 3,917 .... C4
Vallecitos 450 .... C2
Vanadium 150 .... A6
Vaughn 633 .... D4
Velarde 950 .... C2
Vermejo Park 85 .... D2
Villanueva 500 .... D3
Virden 108 .... A6
Wagon Mound 319 .... E2
Waterflow 475 .... A2
Watrous 175 .... D3
White Horse Lake B3
White Rock 6,192 .... C3
White Sands Missile Range 2,616 .... C6
Willard 183 .... D4
Williamsburg 456 .... B5
Yeso 200 .... E4
Youngsville 125 .... C2
Zia Pueblo 637 .... C3
Zuni 5,551 .... A3

OTHER FEATURES

Abiquiu (res.) C2
Alamosa (riv.) B5
Animas (riv.) B1
Avalon (res.) E6
Aztec Ruins Nat'l Mon. A2
Baldy (peak) D3
Bandelier Nat'l Mon. C3
Big Burro (mts.) A6
Black (mt.) A6
Black (range) B5
Blanco (creek) F4
Bluewater (creek) B4
Bluewater (creek) D6
Bluewater (lake) A3
Boulder (lake) C2
Brazos (peak) C2
Burford (lake) C2
Caballo (res.) B6
Canadian (riv.) F3
Cannon A.F.B. 3,312 .... F4
Canyon Blanco (creek) B2
Capitan (mts.) D5
Capitan (peak) D5
Capulin Volcano Nat'l Mon. E2
Carlsbad Caverns Nat'l Park E6
Carrizo (creek) F2
Chaco (mesa) B3
Chaco (riv.) A2
Chaco Culture Nat'l Hist. Park B2
Chico Arroyo (creek) B3
Chivato (mesa) B3
Chupadera (mesa) C5
Chuska (mts.) A2
Cimarron (riv.) E2
Colorado, Arroyo (riv.) B4
Compañero, Arroyo (creek) B2
Conchas (lake) E3
Conchas (riv.) E3
Cookes (range) B6
Corrumpa (creek) F2
Costilla (peak) D2
Cuchillo Negro (creek) B5
Cuervo (creek) E3
Dark Canyon (creek) E6
Datil (mts.) B4
Dry Cimarron (riv.) F2
Eagle Nest (lake) D2
Elephant Butte (res.) B5
El Morro Nat'l Mon. A3
El Rito (riv.) C2
Fifteenmile Arroyo (creek) D4
Florida (mts.) B7
Fort Bliss Mil. Res. C6
Fort Union Nat'l Mon. E3
Gallinas (mts.) B4
Gallinas (riv.) E3
Gila (riv.) A6
Gila Cliff Dwellings Nat'l Mon. A5
Grouse (mt.) A5
Guadalupe (mts.) D6
Hatchet (mts.) A7
Holloman A.F.B. 5,891 .... C6
Hueco (mts.) D6
Jemez (riv.) C3
Jemez Canyon (res.) C3
Jicarilla Ind. Res. B2
Jornada del Muerto (valley) C5
Kirtland A.F.B. C3
Ladron (mts.) B4
La Plata (riv.) A1
Lake Avalon (res.) E6
Largo, Cañon (creek) B2
Las Animas (creek) B5
Llano Estacado (Staked) (plain) F5
Lucero (lake) C6
Macho, Arroyo del (creek) D5
Magdalena (mts.) B4
Manzano (mts.) C4
Manzano (peak) C4
McMillan (lake) E6
Mescalero (ridge) F6
Mescalero (valley) F5
Mescalero Apache Ind. Res. D5
Mimbres (mts.) B6
Mimbres (riv.) B6
Mogollon (mts.) A5
Mogollon Baldy (peak) A5
Montosa (mesa) E3
Mora (riv.) E3
Nacimiento (mts.) C3
Nacimiento (peak) C2
Navajo (res.) B2
Navajo Ind. Res. A2
North Truchas (peak) D3
Ocate (creek) E2
O'Keeffe Nat'l Hist. Site C2
Oscura (mts.) C5
Osha (peak) C4
Padilla (creek) D5
Pajarito (creek) A2
Pecos (riv.) E5
Pecos Nat'l Mon. D3
Peloncillo (mts.) A6
Perro (lake) D4
Pinos, Rio de los (riv.) B2
Pintada Arroyo (creek) E4
Playas (lake) A7
Potrillo (mts.) B7
Pueblo Ind. Res. B4
Pueblo Ind. Res. C4
Pueblo Ind. Res. D2
Pueblo Ind. Res. D3
Puerco (riv.) A3
Red Bluff (lake) E7
Revuelto (creek) F3
Rio Brazos (riv.) C2
Rio Chama (riv.) C2
Rio Felix (riv.) E5
Rio Grande (riv.) C5
Rio Hondo (riv.) E5
Rio Penasco (riv.) E6
Rio Puerco (riv.) C4
Rio Salado (riv.) B4
Rocky (mts.) C1
Sacramento (mts.) D6
Salinas Pueblo Missions Nat'l Mon. C4
Salt (creek) E5
Salt (lake) F4
San Agustin (plains) B5
San Andres (mts.) C6
San Antonio (peak) C2
Sandia (peak) C3
San Francisco (riv.) A5
Sangre de Cristo (mts.) D3
San Jose (riv.) B3
San Juan (riv.) B2
San Mateo (mts.) B5
Seven Rivers (riv.) E6
Ship Rock (peak) A2
Sierra Blanca (peak) C5
Staked (Llano Estacado) (plain) F5
Sumner (lake) E4
Taylor (mt.) B3
Tecolote (creek) D3
Tequesquite (creek) E2
Thompson (peak) D3
Tierra Blanca (creek) B6
Tramperos (creek) F2
Tularosa (valley) C6
Ute (creek) F3
Ute (peak) D2
Ute (res.) F3
Ute Mountain Ind. Res. A1
Vermejo (riv.) E2
Wheeler (peak) D2
White Sands (des.) C5
White Sands Missile Range C5
White Sands Nat'l Mon. C6
Whitewater Baldy (mt.) A5
Wingate Army Depot A3
Yeso (creek) E4
Zuni (mts.) A3
Zuni (riv.) A3
Zuni-Cibola Nat'l Hist. Park A3
Zuni Ind. Res. A3

▲County seat

Topography

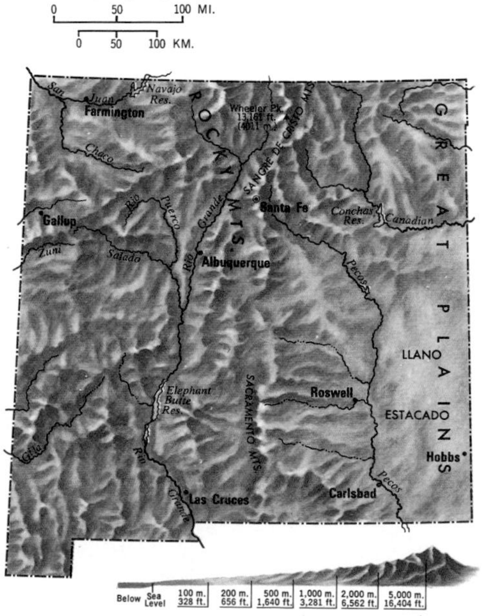
0 50 100 MI.
0 50 100 KM.
San Juan
Navajo Res.
Farmington
Wheeler Pk. 13,161 ft. (4011 m.)
ROCKY MTS.
SANGRE DE CRISTO MTS.
GREAT PLAINS
Chaco
Santa Fe
Conchas Res.
Canadian
Gallup
Zuni
Salado
Rio Puerco
Rio Grande
Albuquerque
Pecos
LLANO ESTACADO
SACRAMENTO MTS.
Elephant Butte Res.
Roswell
Hobbs
Gila
Las Cruces
Carlsbad
Below Sea Level 100 m. 328 ft. 200 m. 656 ft. 500 m. 1,640 ft. 1,000 m. 3,281 ft. 2,000 m. 6,562 ft. 5,000 m. 16,404 ft.

Agriculture, Industry and Resources

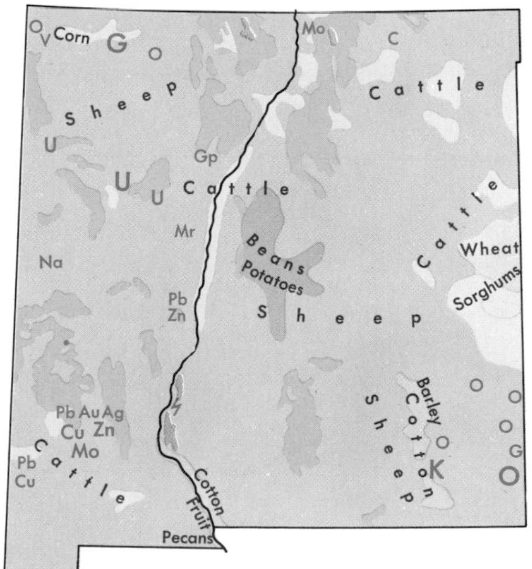
Corn
G
Mo
C
Sheep
Cattle
U
Gp
U
Cattle
Mr
Beans
Potatoes
Wheat
Sorghums
Na
Pb
Zn
Sheep
Barley
Cotton
Sheep
Pb Au Ag
Cu Zn
Mo
Pb
Cu
Cattle
Cotton
Fruit
Pecans
K
O
G

DOMINANT LAND USE

- Wheat, Grain Sorghums, Range Livestock
- General Farming, Livestock, Special Crops
- General Farming, Livestock, Cash Grain
- Dry Beans, General Farming
- Cotton, Forest Products
- Range Livestock
- Forests
- Nonagricultural Land

MAJOR MINERAL OCCURRENCES

Ag Silver
Au Gold
C Coal
Cu Copper
G Natural Gas
Gp Gypsum
K Potash
Mo Molybdenum
Mr Marble
Na Salt
O Petroleum
Pb Lead
U Uranium
V Vanadium
Zn Zinc
Water Power

New York

SCALE
0 5 10   20   30   40 MI.
0 5 10   20   30   40 KM.

State Capitals .... ⊛
County Seats .... ◉
Canals ....
Major Limited Access Hwys. ————

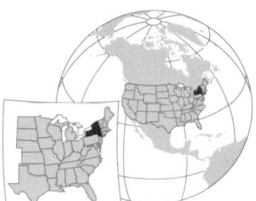

AREA 49,108 sq. mi. (127,190 sq. km.)
POPULATION 18,044,505
CAPITAL Albany
LARGEST CITY New York
HIGHEST POINT Mt. Marcy 5,344 ft.
(1629 m.)
SETTLED IN 1614
ADMITTED TO UNION July 26, 1788
POPULAR NAME Empire State
STATE FLOWER Rose
STATE BIRD Bluebird

Topography

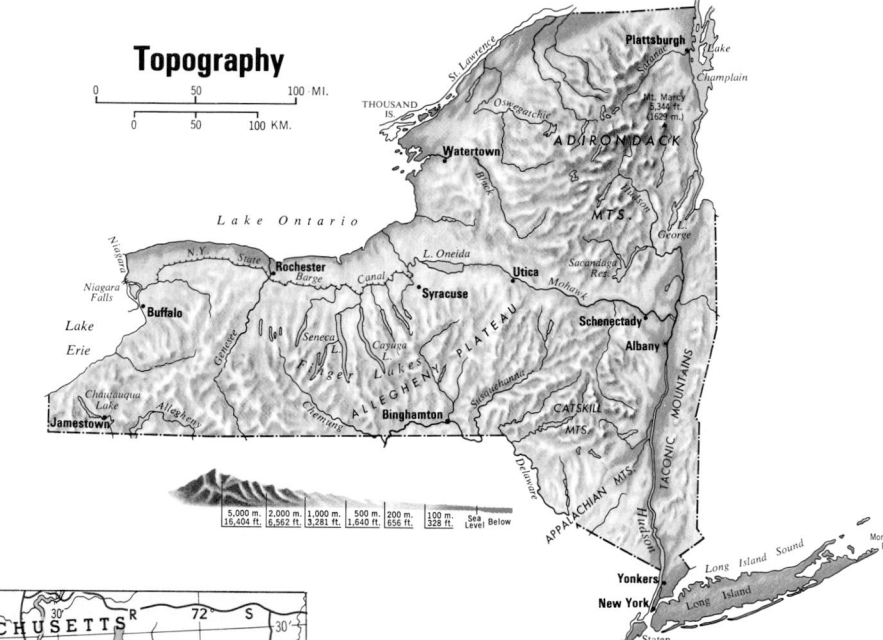

Dix Hills 25,849	O9		Gasport 1,336	C4
Dobbs Ferry 9,940	O6		Geneseo▲ 7,187	E5
Dolgeville 2,452	L4		Geneva 14,143	G5
Dover Plains 1,847	O7		Glasco 1,538	M6
Dryden 1,908	H6		Glen Cove 24,149	R6
Dundee 1,588	F5		Glens Falls 15,023	N4
Dunkirk 13,989	B5		Gloversville 16,656	M4
Earlville 883	J5		Golden's Bridge 1,589	N8
East Aurora 6,647	C5		Goshen▲ 5,255	M8
East Greenbush 3,784	N5		Gouverneur 4,604	K2
East Hampton 1,402	R9		Gowanda 2,901	B6
East Hills 6,746	R7		Granville 2,646	U4
East Meadow 36,909	R7		Great Neck 8,745	P6
East Moriches 4,021	P9		Greece 15,632	E4
East Northport 20,411	O9		Green Island 2,490	N5
East Rochester 6,932	F4		Greene 1,812	J6
East Rockaway 10,152	R7		Greenport 2,070	P8
East Syracuse 3,343	H4		Greenwich 1,961	O4
Eastchester 18,537	P6		Greenwood Lake 3,208	M8
Eden 3,088	C5		Groton 2,398	H5
Elba 703	D4		Hadley-Lake Luzerne 1,988	N4
Elbridge 1,099	H5		Hagaman 1,377	M5
Elizabethtown▲ 659	N2		Hamburg 10,442	C5
Ellenville 4,243	M7		Hamilton 3,790	J5
Elma 2,354	C5		Hammondsport 929	F6
Elmira Heights 4,359	G6		Hampton Bays 7,893	R9
Elmira▲ 33,724	G6		Hancock 1,330	K7
Elmont 28,612	P7		Hannibal 680	G4
Elmsford 3,938	O6		Harriman 2,288	M8
Elwood 10,916	O9		Harrison 23,308	P6
Endicott 13,531	H6		Harrisville 703	K2
Endwell 12,602	H6		Hartsdale 9,587	P6
Evans Mills 661	J2		Hastings On Hudson 8,000	O6
Fair Haven 895	G4		Hauppauge 19,750	O9
Fairport 5,943	F4		Haverstraw 9,438	M8
Fairview 4,811	N7		Hawthorne 4,764	O6
Falconer 2,653	B6		Hempstead 49,453	R7
Farmingdale 8,022	R7		Herkimer▲ 7,945	L4
Fayetteville 4,248	J5		Heuvelton 771	K1
Fernwood 3,640	N4		Hewlett 6,620	P7
Fishkill 1,957	N7		Hewlett Harbor 1,193	P7
Flanders-Riverside 5,400	P9		Hicksville 40,174	R7
Floral Park 15,947	P7		Highland 4,492	M7
Florida 2,497	M8		Highland Falls 3,937	M8
Fonda▲ 1,007	M5		Hillburn 892	M8
Forestville 738	B6		Hillcrest 6,447	K8
Fort Covington• 1,804	M1		Hilton 5,216	E4
Fort Edward 3,561	O4		Holcomb 790	F5
Fort Johnson 615	M5		Holland 1,288	C5
Fort Plain 2,416	L5		Holley 1,890	D4
Frankfort 2,693	K4		Homer 3,476	H5
Franklin Square 28,205	R7		Hoosick Falls 2,340	F5
Franklinville 1,739	D6		Hopewell Junction 1,786	N7
Fredonia 10,436	B6		Hornell 9,877	E6
Freeport 39,894	R7		Horseheads 6,802	D6
Frewsburg 1,817	B6		Friendship 1,740	D6
Friendship 1,423	D6		Hudson Falls▲ 7,651	O4
Fulton 12,929	H4		Hudson▲ 8,034	N6
Fultonville 748	M5		Huntington 18,243	R6
Garden City 21,686	R7		(continued on following page)	

Huntington Station 28,247 .....R6
Hurley 4,644 .....M7
Hyde Park 2,550 .....N6
Ilion 8,888 .....K5
Interlaken 680 .....G5
Inwood 7,767 .....P7
Irondequoit 52,322 .....E4
Irvington 6,348 .....O6
Island Park 4,860 .....R7
Islip 18,924 .....O9
Ithaca▲ 29,541 .....G6
Jamestown 34,681 .....B6
Jericho 13,141 .....R6
Johnson City 16,890 .....J6
Johnstown▲ 9,058 .....M4
Jordan 1,325 .....H4
Keeseville 1,854 .....O2
Kenmore 17,180 .....C5
Kerhonkson 1,629 .....M7
Keuka Park 1,153 .....F5
Kinderhook 1,293 .....N6
Kings Park 17,773 .....O9
Kings Point 4,843 .....P6
Kingston▲ 23,095 .....M7
Lackawanna 20,585 .....B5
Lake Carmel 8,489 .....N8
Lake Erie Beach 4,509 .....B5
Lake George▲ 933 .....N4
Lake Katrine 1,998 .....M7
Lake Luzerne-Hadley 2,042 .....N4
Lake Placid 2,485 .....N2
Lake Pleasant▲ 700 .....M4
Lake Success 2,484 .....P7
Lakewood 3,564 .....B6
Lancaster 11,940 .....C5
Lansing 3,281 .....H5
Larchmont 6,181 .....P7
Latham 10,131 .....N5
Lattingtown 1,859 .....R6
Lawrence 6,513 .....P7
Le Roy 4,974 .....E5
Levittown 53,286 .....R7
Lewiston 3,048 .....B4
Liberty 4,128 .....L7
Lima 2,165 .....E5
Lindenhurst 26,879 .....O9
Little Falls 5,829 .....L4
Little Valley▲ 1,188 .....C6
Liverpool 2,624 .....H4
Livingston Manor 1,482 .....L7
Livonia 1,434 .....E5
Lloyd Harbor 3,343 .....R6
Lockport▲ 24,426 .....C4
Locust Grove 9,670 .....R6
Long Beach 33,510 .....R7
Lowville▲ 3,632 .....J3
Lynbrook 19,208 .....P7
Lyndonville 953 .....D4
Lyons Falls 698 .....K3
Lyons▲ 4,280 .....F4
Macedon 1,400 .....F4
Machias 1,191 .....D6
Mahopac 7,755 .....N8
Malone▲ 6,777 .....M1
Malverne 9,054 .....R7
Mamaroneck 17,325 .....P7
Manchester 1,598 .....F5
Manhasset 7,718 .....P7
Manhattan (borough) M9
Manlius 4,764 .....J5
Manorville 6,198 .....P9
Marathon 1,107 .....J6
Marcellus 1,840 .....H5
Margaretville 639 .....L6
Marion 1,080 .....F4
Marlboro 2,200 .....M7
Massapequa 22,018 .....R7
Massapequa Park 18,044 .....R7
Massena 11,719 .....L1
Mastic Beach 10,293 .....P9
Mattituck 3,902 .....P9
Maybrook 2,802 .....M8
Mayfield 817 .....M4
Mayville▲ 1,636 .....A6
McGraw 1,074 .....H5
Mechanicville 5,249 .....N5
Medina 6,686 .....D4
Melrose Park 2,091 .....G5
Melville 12,586 .....S7
Menands 4,333 .....N5
Merrick 23,042 .....R7
Mexico 1,555 .....H4
Middle Hope 3,229 .....M7
Middleburgh 1,436 .....M5
Middleport 1,876 .....C4
Middletown 24,160 .....L8
Middleville 624 .....K4
Mill Neck 977 .....R6
Millbrook 1,339 .....N7
Millerton 884 .....O7
Milton 1,140 .....M7
Milton 2,063 .....N4
Mineola▲ 18,994 .....R7
Minetto 1,252 .....H4
Mineville-Witherbee 1,740 .....O2
Minoa 3,745 .....H4
Mohawk 2,986 .....L4
Monroe 6,672 .....M8
Monsey 13,986 .....J8
Montauk 3,001 .....S8
Montgomery 2,696 .....M7
Monticello▲ 6,597 .....L7
Montour Falls 1,845 .....G6
Moravia 1,559 .....H5
Morris 642 .....K5
Morrisonville 1,742 .....N1
Morrisville 2,732 .....J5
Mount Kisco 9,108 .....N8
Mount Morris 3,102 .....E5
Mount Vernon 67,153 .....O7
Nanuet 14,065 .....K8
Napanoch 1,068 .....M7
Naples 1,237 .....F5
Nassau 1,254 .....N5
New Berlin 1,220 .....K5
New City▲ 33,673 .....K8
New Hartford 2,111 .....K4
New Hyde Park 9,728 .....P7
New Paltz 5,463 .....M7
New Rochelle 67,265 .....P7
New Square 2,605 .....K8
New Windsor 8,898 .....N8
New York Mills 3,534 .....K4
New York▲ 7,322,564 .....M9
Newark 9,849 .....G4
Newark Valley 1,082 .....H6
Newburgh 26,454 .....M7
Newfane 3,001 .....C4
Newport 676 .....K4
Niagara Falls 61,840 .....C4
Nichols 573 .....H6
Niskayuna 4,942 .....N5
Norfolk 1,412 .....K1
North Boston 2,581 .....C5
North Collins 1,335 .....C5
North Hornell 822 .....E6
North Syracuse 7,363 .....H4
North Tarrytown 8,152 .....O6
North Tonawanda 34,989 .....C4
Northport 7,572 .....O9
Northville 1,180 .....M4
Norwich▲ 7,613 .....J5
Norwood 1,841 .....L1
Nunda 1,347 .....E5
Nyack 6,558 .....K8
Oakfield 1,818 .....D4
Oceanside 32,423 .....R7
Odessa 986 .....G6
Ogdensburg 13,521 .....K1
Olcott 1,432 .....C4
Old Forge 1,061 .....L3
Olean 16,946 .....D6
Oneida 10,850 .....J4
Oneonta 13,954 .....K6
Orangeburg 3,583 .....K8
Orchard Park 3,280 .....C5
Oriskany 1,450 .....K4
Oriskany Falls 795 .....J5
Ossining 22,582 .....N8
Oswego▲ 19,195 .....G4
Otego 1,068 .....K6
Otisville 1,078 .....L8
Ovid 660 .....G5
Owego▲ 4,442 .....H6
Oxford 1,738 .....J6
Oyster Bay 6,687 .....R6
Painted Post 1,950 .....F6
Palmyra 3,566 .....F4
Patchogue 11,060 .....P9
Pawling 1,974 .....N7
Pearl River 15,314 .....K8
Peconic 1,100 .....P8
Peekskill 19,536 .....N8
Pelham 6,413 .....O7
Pelham Manor 5,443 .....O7
Penn Yan▲ 5,248 .....F5
Perry 4,219 .....D5
Peru 1,565 .....N1
Phelps 1,978 .....F5
Philadelphia 1,478 .....J2
Philmont 1,623 .....N6
Phoenix 2,435 .....H4
Piermont 2,163 .....K8
Pine Bush 1,445 .....M7
Pine Plains 1,312 .....N7
Pine Valley 1,486 .....G6
Pittsford 1,488 .....E4
Plainview 26,207 .....R7
Plattsburgh▲ 21,255 .....O1
Pleasantville 6,592 .....N8
Port Byron 1,359 .....G4
Port Chester 24,728 .....P7
Port Dickinson 1,785 .....J6
Port Ewen 3,444 .....N7
Port Henry 1,263 .....O2
Port Jefferson 7,455 .....P9
Port Jervis 9,060 .....L8
Port Leyden 723 .....K3
Port Washington 15,387 .....R6
Portville 1,040 .....D6
Potsdam 10,251 .....K1
Poughkeepsie▲ 28,844 .....N7
Prattsburg• 1,657 .....F5
Pulaski 2,525 .....H3
Putnam Valley• 8,994 .....N8
Queens (borough) N9
Quogue 898 .....P9
Randolph 1,298 .....C6
Ransomville 1,542 .....C4
Ravena 3,547 .....N6
Red Hook 1,794 .....N7
Red Oaks Mill 4,906 .....N7
Rensselaer 8,255 .....N5
Rhinebeck 2,725 .....N7
Richfield Springs 1,565 .....K5
Richmond (borough) (Staten Island) M9
Richmondville 843 .....M5
Ripley 1,189 .....A6
Riverhead▲ 8,814 .....P9
Rochester▲ 231,636 .....E4
Rockville Centre 24,727 .....R7
Rome 44,350 .....J4
Ronkonkoma 20,391 .....O9
Roosevelt 15,030 .....R7
Rosendale 1,134 .....M7
Roslyn 1,965 .....R6
Rotterdam Junction 1,010 .....N5
Round Lake 765 .....N5
Rouses Point 2,377 .....O1
Rye 14,936 .....P6
Sackets Harbor 1,313 .....H3
Sag Harbor 2,134 .....R8
Saint James 12,703 .....O9
Saint Johnsville 1,825 .....L5
Salamanca 6,566 .....C6
Salem 958 .....O4
Sand Ridge 1,312 .....H4
Sands Point 2,477 .....P6
Sandy Creek 793 .....H3
Saranac Lake 5,377 .....M2
Saratoga Springs 25,001 .....N4
Saugerties 3,915 .....M6
Savannah• 1,905 .....G4
Savona 974 .....F6
Sayville 16,550 .....O9
Scarsdale 16,987 .....P6
Schaghticoke 794 .....N5
Schenectady▲ 65,566 .....M5
Schoharie▲ 1,045 .....M5
Schuylerville 1,364 .....N4
Scotia 7,359 .....N5
Scottsville 1,912 .....E4
Sea Cliff 5,054 .....R6
Seaford 15,597 .....R7
Seneca Falls 7,370 .....G5
Sherburne 1,531 .....K5
Sherman 694 .....A6
Sherrill 2,864 .....J4
Shortsville 1,485 .....F5
Sidney 4,720 .....K6
Silver Creek 2,927 .....B5
Silver Springs 852 .....E5
Sinclairville 708 .....B6
Skaneateles 2,724 .....H5
Sloan 3,830 .....C5
Sloatsburg 3,035 .....M8
Smithtown 25,638 .....O9
Sodus 1,904 .....G4
Sodus Point 1,190 .....G4
Solvay 6,717 .....H4
South Corning 1,025 .....F6
South Fallsburg 2,115 .....L7
South Glens Falls 3,506 .....N4
South Nyack 3,352 .....K8
Southampton 1,302 .....R9
Southold 5,192 .....P8
Southport 7,753 .....G6
Sparrow Bush 1,049 .....L8
Spencer 815 .....H6
Spencerport 3,606 .....E4
Spring Valley 21,802 .....K8
Springville 4,310 .....C5
Stamford 1,211 .....L6
Stannards 1,028 .....E6
Star Lake 1,092 .....K2
Staten Island (borough) M9
Stillwater 1,531 .....N5
Stony Brook 13,726 .....O9
Stony Point 10,587 .....M8
Stottville 1,369 .....N6
Suffern 11,055 .....J8
Sylvan Beach 1,119 .....J4
Syosset 18,967 .....R6
Syracuse▲ 163,860 .....H4
Tappan 6,867 .....K8
Tarrytown 10,739 .....O6
Theresa 889 .....J2
Thomaston 2,612 .....P7
Ticonderoga 2,770 .....N3
Tillson 1,688 .....M7
Tivoli 1,035 .....N6
Tonawanda 17,284 .....B4
Troy▲ 54,269 .....N5
Trumansburg 1,611 .....G5
Tuckahoe 6,302 .....O7
Tully 911 .....H5
Tupper Lake 4,087 .....M2
Tuxedo Park 706 .....M8
Unadilla 1,265 .....K6
Union Springs 1,142 .....G5
Uniondale 20,328 .....R7
Utica▲ 68,637 .....K4
Valatie 1,487 .....N6
Valley Cottage 9,007 .....K8
Valley Stream 33,946 .....P7
Vestal• 27,238 .....H6
Victor 2,308 .....F5
Victory Mills 571 .....N4
Viola 4,504 .....J8
Voorheesville 3,225 .....M5
Waddington 944 .....K1
Wading River 5,317 .....P9
Walden 5,836 .....M7
Wallkill 2,125 .....M7
Walton 3,326 .....K6
Wampsville▲ 501 .....J4
Wantagh 18,567 .....R7
Wappingers Falls 4,605 .....N7
Warrensburg 3,204 .....N3
Warsaw▲ 3,830 .....D5
Warwick 5,984 .....M8
Washingtonville 4,906 .....M8
Waterford 2,370 .....N5
Waterloo▲ 5,116 .....G5
Watertown▲ 29,429 .....J3
Waterville 1,664 .....K5
Watervliet 11,061 .....N5
Watkins Glen▲ 2,207 .....G6
Waverly 4,787 .....G7
Wayland 1,976 .....E5
Webster 5,464 .....F4
Weedsport 1,996 .....G4
Wellsburg 617 .....G6
Wellsville 5,241 .....E6
West Carthage 2,166 .....J3
West Elmira 5,218 .....G6
West Glens Falls 5,964 .....N4
West Hurley 2,252 .....M6
West Nyack 3,437 .....K8
West Point 8,024 .....M8
West Sayville 4,680 .....O9
West Seneca 47,866 .....C5
West Winfield 871 .....K5
Westbury 13,060 .....R7
Westfield 3,451 .....A6
Westhampton 2,129 .....P9
Westhampton Beach 1,571 .....P9
Westons Mills 1,837 .....D6
White Plains▲ 48,718 .....P6
Whitehall 3,071 .....O3
Whitesboro 4,195 .....K4
Whitney Point 1,054 .....J6
Willard 1,339 .....G5
Williamson 1,768 .....F4
Williamsville 5,583 .....C5
Williston Park 7,516 .....R7
Wilson 1,307 .....C4
Windsor 1,051 .....J6
Witherbee-Mineville 1,925 .....N2
Wolcott 1,544 .....G4
Woodmere 15,578 .....P7
Woodridge 783 .....L7
Woodstock 1,870 .....M6
Wurtsboro 1,048 .....L7
Wyandanch 8,950 .....N9
Yonkers 188,082 .....O6
Yorkshire 1,340 .....D5
Yorktown Heights 7,690 .....N8
Yorkville 2,972 .....K4
Youngstown 2,075 .....C4

OTHER FEATURES

Adirondack (mts.) M3
Algonquin (peak) M2
Allegany Ind. Res. C6
Allegheny (res.) C7
Allegheny (riv.) C6
Ashokan (res.) M7
Ausable (riv.) N2
Batten Kill (riv.) O4
Beaver (riv.) K3
Big Moose (lake) L3
Black (lake) J1
Black (riv.) K3
Block Island (sound) S8
Blue Mountain (lake) M3
Bonaparte (lake) K2
Brandreth (lake) L3
Brant (lake) N3
Brookhaven Nat'l Lab. P9
Butterfield (lakes) J2
Canandaigua (lake) F5
Canisteo (riv.) F6
Cannonsville (res.) K6
Catskill (lake) L6
Cattaraugus (creek) C6
Cattaraugus Ind. Res. C5
Cayuga (lake) G5
Champlain (lake) O1
Chateaugay, Upper (lake) M1
Chautauqua (lake) A6
Chazy (lake) N1
Chenango (riv.) J6
Cohocton (riv.) F6
Conesus (lake) E5
Conewango (creek) B6
Cranberry (lake) L2
Deer (riv.) J3
Deer (riv.) L1
Delaware (riv.) K7
East (riv.) N9
Erie (lake) A5
Fire Island Nat'l Seashore P9
Fishers (isl.) S8
Forked (lake) L3
Fort Drum 11,578 .....J2
Fort Niagara C4
Fort Stanwix Nat'l Mon. J4
Fulton Chain (lakes) K3
Galloo (isl.) H3
Gardiners (bay) R8
Gardiners (isl.) R8
Gateway Nat'l Rec. Area M9
Genesee (riv.) E5
George (lake) N4
Grand (isl.) B5
Grass (riv.) K1
Great Sacandaga (lake) M4
Great South (bay) O9
Great South (beach) O9
Greenwood (lake) M8
Grenadier (isl.) H2
Griffiss A.F.B. K4
Haystack (mt.) N2
Hemlock (lake) E5
Hinckley (res.) K4
Honeoye (lake) F5
Honnedaga (lake) L3
Hudson (riv.) N7
Hunter (mt.) M6
Indian (lake) M3
Jones (beach) R7
Keuka (lake) F5
Lila (lake) L2
Little Tupper (lake) L2
Long (isl.) P9
Long (lake) M2
Long Island (sound) P9
Lower Saranac (lake) M2
Manhattan (isl.) M9
Marcy (mt.) N2
Martin Van Buren Nat'l Hist. Site N6
Meacham (lake) M1
Mohawk (riv.) L5
Montauk (pt.) S8
Moose (riv.) K3
Neversink (res.) L7
New York State Barge (canal) C4
Niagara (riv.) B4
Oil Spring Ind. Res. D6
Oneida (lake) J4
Onondaga Ind. Res. H5
Ontario (lake) F3
Orient (pt.) R8
Oswegatchie (riv.) K2
Oswego (riv.) H4
Otisco (lake) H5
Otsego (lake) L5
Otselic (riv.) J5
Owasco (lake) G5
Peconic (bay) R9
Peninsula (pt.) H3
Pepacton (res.) L6
Piseco (lake) M4
Placid (lake) N2
Plattsburgh A.F.B. 5,483 .....N1
Pleasant (lake) M4
Plum (isl.) R8
Poosepatuck Ind. Res. P9
Raquette (lake) L3
Rondout (pt.) M7
Round (lake) L2
Sacandaga (lake) L3
Sackets (harb.) H3
Sagamore Hill Nat'l Hist. Site R6
Saint Lawrence (lake) K1
Saint Lawrence (riv.) J2
Saint Regis (riv.) L1
Saint Regis Ind. Res. M1
Salmon (res.) J3
Salmon (riv.) H3
Salmon (riv.) M1
Saranac (lakes) M2
Saranac (riv.) N1
Saratoga (lake) N4
Saratoga Nat'l Hist. Park N4
Schoharie (res.) M6
Schroon (lake) N3
Seneca (lake) G5
Seneca (riv.) G5
Shelter (isl.) R8
Shinnecock Ind. Res. R9
Silver (lake) N1
Skaneateles (lake) H5
Skylight (mt.) M2
Slide (mt.) L6
Staten (isl.) M9
Statue of Liberty Nat'l Mon. M9
Stony (isl.) H3
Stony (pt.) H3
Susquehanna (riv.) H6
Thousand (isls.) H2
Tioughnioga (riv.) H6
Titus (lake) M1
Tomhannock (res.) O5
Tonawanda Ind. Res. D4
Toronto (res.) L7
Tupper (lake) M2
Tuscarora Ind. Res. B4
Unadilla (riv.) K5
Upper Chateaugay (lake) M1
Valcour (isl.) N1
Wallkill (riv.) L8
Whiteface (mt.) N2
Whitney Point (lake) J6
Woodhull (lake) L3

▲County seat
•Population of town or township

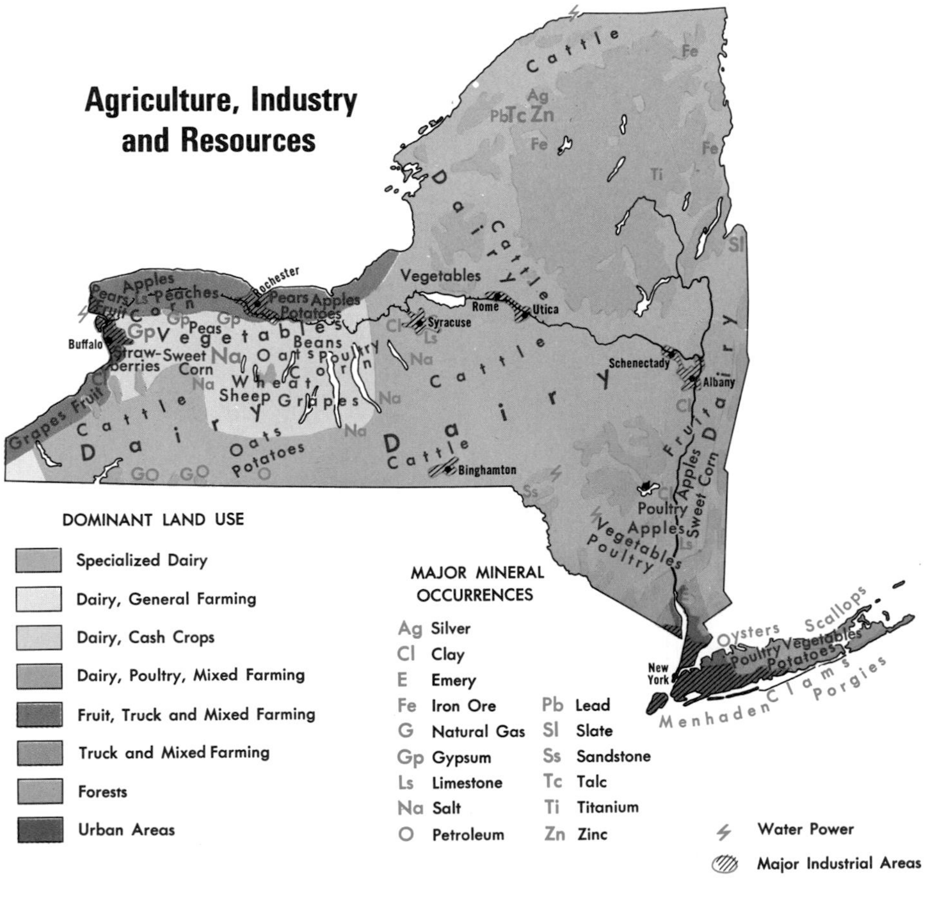
Agriculture, Industry and Resources
DOMINANT LAND USE
Specialized Dairy
Dairy, General Farming
Dairy, Cash Crops
Dairy, Poultry, Mixed Farming
Fruit, Truck and Mixed Farming
Truck and Mixed Farming
Forests
Urban Areas
MAJOR MINERAL OCCURRENCES
Ag Silver
Cl Clay
E Emery
Fe Iron Ore
G Natural Gas
Gp Gypsum
Ls Limestone
Na Salt
O Petroleum
Pb Lead
Sl Slate
Ss Sandstone
Tc Talc
Ti Titanium
Zn Zinc
Water Power
Major Industrial Areas
Cattle
Dairy
Vegetables
Apples
Peaches
Pears
Potatoes
Corn
Grapes
Fruit
Straw-berries
Sweet Corn
Beans
Oats
Poultry
Wheat
Sheep
Buffalo
Rochester
Syracuse
Rome
Utica
Schenectady
Albany
Binghamton
New York
Oysters
Scallops
Clams
Porgies
Menhaden

AREA 52,669 sq. mi. (136,413 sq. km.)
POPULATION 6,657,630
CAPITAL Raleigh
LARGEST CITY Charlotte
HIGHEST POINT Mt. Mitchell 6,684 ft. (2037 m.)
SETTLED IN 1650
ADMITTED TO UNION November 21, 1789
POPULAR NAME Tarheel State
STATE FLOWER Flowering Dogwood
STATE BIRD Cardinal

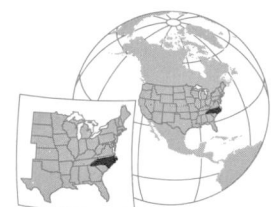

COUNTIES

Alamance 108,213	L3
Alexander 27,544	G3
Alleghany 9,590	G1
Anson 23,474	J4
Ashe 22,209	F2
Avery 14,867	F2
Beaufort 42,283	R4
Bertie 20,388	P2
Bladen 28,663	M5
Brunswick 50,985	N6
Buncombe 174,821	D3
Burke 75,744	F3
Cabarrus 98,935	H4
Caldwell 70,709	F3
Camden 5,904	S2
Carteret 52,556	R5
Caswell 20,693	L2
Catawba 118,412	G3
Chatham 38,759	L3
Cherokee 20,170	A4
Chowan 13,506	R2
Clay 7,155	B4
Cleveland 84,714	F4
Columbus 49,587	M6
Craven 81,613	P4
Cumberland 274,566	M4
Currituck 13,736	S2
Dare 22,746	T3
Davidson 126,677	J3
Davie 27,859	H3
Duplin 39,995	O5
Durham 181,835	M3
Edgecombe 56,558	O3
Forsyth 265,878	J2
Franklin 36,414	N2
Gaston 175,093	G4
Gates 9,305	R2
Graham 7,196	B4
Granville 38,345	M2
Greene 15,384	O3
Guilford 347,420	K3
Halifax 55,516	O2
Harnett 67,822	M4
Haywood 46,942	C3
Henderson 69,285	D4
Hertford 22,523	P2
Hoke 22,856	L4
Hyde 5,411	S3
Iredell 92,931	H3
Jackson 26,846	C4
Johnston 81,306	N4
Jones 9,414	P4
Lee 41,374	L4
Lenoir 57,274	O4
Lincoln 50,319	G3
Macon 23,499	B4
Madison 16,953	D3
Martin 25,078	P3
McDowell 35,681	E3
Mecklenburg 511,433	H4
Mitchell 14,433	E2
Montgomery 23,346	K4
Moore 59,013	L4
Nash 76,677	O2
New Hanover 120,284	O6
Northampton 20,798	P2
Onslow 149,838	P5
Orange 93,851	L2
Pamlico 11,372	R4
Pasquotank 31,298	S2
Pender 28,855	O5
Perquimans 10,447	S2
Person 30,180	M2
Pitt 107,924	P3
Polk 14,416	E4
Randolph 106,546	K3
Richmond 44,518	K4
Robeson 105,179	L5
Rockingham 86,064	K2
Rowan 110,605	H3
Rutherford 56,918	E4
Sampson 47,297	N4
Scotland 33,754	L5
Stanly 51,765	J4
Stokes 37,223	J2
Surry 61,704	H2
Swain 11,268	B3
Transylvania 25,520	D4
Tyrrell 3,856	S3
Union 84,211	H4
Vance 38,892	M2
Wake 423,380	M3
Warren 17,265	N2
Washington 13,997	R3
Watauga 36,952	F2
Wayne 104,666	N4
Wilkes 59,393	G2
Wilson 66,061	O3
Yadkin 30,488	H2
Yancey 15,419	E3

CITIES and TOWNS

Abbottsburg 425	M5
Aberdeen 2,700	L4
Acme	N6
Advance	J3
Ahoskie 4,391	P2
Alamance 258	K2
Alarka 900	C4
Albemarle▲ 14,939	J4
Alexander Mills 662	F4
Alliance 583	R4
Altamahaw 1,076	L2
Andrews 2,551	B4
Angier 2,235	M4
Ansonville 614	J4
Apex 4,968	M3
Arapahoe 404	R4
Archdale 6,913	K3
Arlington 795	H2
Ash 16,362	N6
Asheboro▲ 15,252	K3
Asheville▲ 61,607	D3
Askewville 201	R2
Atkinson 275	N5
Atlantic 1,938	S5
Atlantic Beach 941	R5
Aulander 1,209	P2
Aurora 654	R4
Autryville 166	M4
Avon 500	U4
Avondale	F4
Ayden 4,740	P4
Badin 1,481	J4
Bahama 280	M2
Bailey 553	N3
Bakersville▲ 332	E2
Balfour 1,118	E4
Banner Elk 933	F2
Bannertown 1,028	H1
Barco 325	T2
Barker Heights 1,137	D4
Bat Cave 450	E4
Bath 154	R4
Battleboro 447	O2
Bayboro▲ 733	R4
Bear Creek 500	L3
Beargrass 77	P3
Beaufort▲ 3,808	R5
Belhaven 2,269	R3
Bellarthur 350	O3
Belmont 8,434	H4
Belvidere 275	S2
Belville 66	N6
Belwood 631	F4
Benham 400	G2
Bennett 254	K3
Benson 2,810	N4
Bessemer City 4,698	G4
Beta 500	C4
Bethel 1,842	P3
Beulaville 933	O5
Biltmore Forest 1,327	E3
Biscoe 1,481	K4
Black Creek 615	O3
Black Mountain 5,418	E3
Bladenboro 1,821	M5
Blowing Rock 1,257	F2
Boardman 250	M6
Boger City 1,373	G4
Boiling Spring Lakes 1,650	N7
Boiling Springs 2,445	F4
Bolivia▲ 228	N6
Bolton 531	N6
Bonlee 300	L3
Boomer 250	G2
Boone▲ 12,915	F2
Boonville 1,009	H2
Brevard▲ 5,388	D4
Bridgeton 453	R4
Broadway 973	L4
Brookford 451	G3
Browns Summit 500	K2
Brunswick 302	M6
Bryson City▲ 1,145	C4
Buies 2,085	L5
Buies Creek 1,939	M4
Bullock 525	M2
Bunn 364	N3
Bunnlevel	M4
Burgaw▲ 1,807	N5
Burlington 39,498	K2
Burnsville▲ 1,482	E3
Butner 4,679	M2
Buxton 700	U4
Bynum 312	L3
Calabash 1,210	M7
Calypso 481	N4
Camden▲ 300	S2
Cameron 215	L4
Candler 950	D3
Candor 748	K4
Canton 3,790	D3
Cape Carteret 1,008	P5
Carolina Beach 3,630	O6
Carrboro 11,553	L3
Carthage▲ 976	K4
Cary 43,858	M3
Casar 328	F3
Cashiers 553	C4
Castalia 261	O2
Castle Hayne 1,182	O6
Caswell Beach 175	N7
Catawba 467	G3
Catharine Lake 500	O5
Cedar Falls 400	K3
Cedar Grove 250	L2
Cedar Island 310	S5
Cedar Mountain 250	D4
Centerville 115	N2
Cerro Gordo 227	M6
Chadbourn 2,005	M6
Chadwick Acres 15	P6
Chapel Hill 38,719	L3
Charlotte▲ 395,934	H4
Cherokee 975	C4
Cherry 4,756	R3
Cherryville 4,844	G4
China Grove 2,732	H3
Chinquapin 280	O5
Chocowinity 624	P4
Claremont 980	G3
Clarendon 300	M6
Clark 739	P4
Clarkton 664	M6
Clayton 4,756	N3
Clemmons 6,020	J2
Cleveland 696	H3
Cliffside 950	F4
Climax 475	K3
Clinton▲ 8,204	N5
Clyde 1,041	D3
Coats 1,493	M4
Cofield 407	R2
Coinjock 650	S2
Colerain 139	R2
Collettsville 275	F3
Columbia▲ 836	S3
Columbus▲ 812	E4
Comfort 325	O5
Como 71	P1
Concord▲ 27,347	H4
Conetoe 292	O3
Connellys Springs 500	F3
Conover 5,465	G3
Conway 759	P2
Cooleemee 971	H3
Cornelius 2,581	H4
Council	M6
Cove City 497	P4
Cramerton 2,371	G4
Creedmoor 1,504	M2
Creswell 361	S3
Crisp 85	O3
Crossnore 271	F2
Cruso 800	D4
Culberson	A4
Cullowhee 4,029	C4
Cumberland 400	M5
Currie 294	N6
Currituck▲ 700	T2
Dallas 3,012	G4
Dalton 400	J2
Danbury▲ 119	J2
Davidson 4,046	H4
Davis 612	R5
Delco 450	N6
Denton 1,292	J3
Dillsboro 95	C4
Dobson▲ 1,195	H2
Dortches 840	O2
Dover 451	P4
Drexel 1,746	F3
Dublin 246	M5
Dudley	N4
Dulah 350	M6
Dundarrach	L5
Dunn 8,336	M4
Durham▲ 136,611	M2
Dysartsville 950	F3
Eagle Springs 280	K4
Earl 230	F4
East Arcadia 468	N6
East Bend 619	H2
East Flat Rock 3,218	E4
East Laurinburg 302	L5
East Marion 1,851	F3
East Spencer 2,055	H3
Eden 15,238	K1
Edenton▲ 5,268	R2
Edward	R4
Efland 600	L2
Elizabeth City▲ 14,292	S2
Elizabethtown▲ 3,704	M5
Elk Park 486	E2
Elkin 3,790	H2
Ellenboro 514	F4
Ellerbe 1,132	K4
Elm City 1,624	O3
Elon College 4,394	L2
Emerald Isle 2,434	P5
Enfield 3,082	O2
Engelhard 500	T3
Enka 5,567	D3
Ernul 350	P4
Erwin 4,061	M4
Ether 425	K4
Etowah 1,997	D4
Eure 282	R2

(continued on following page)

Agriculture, Industry and Resources

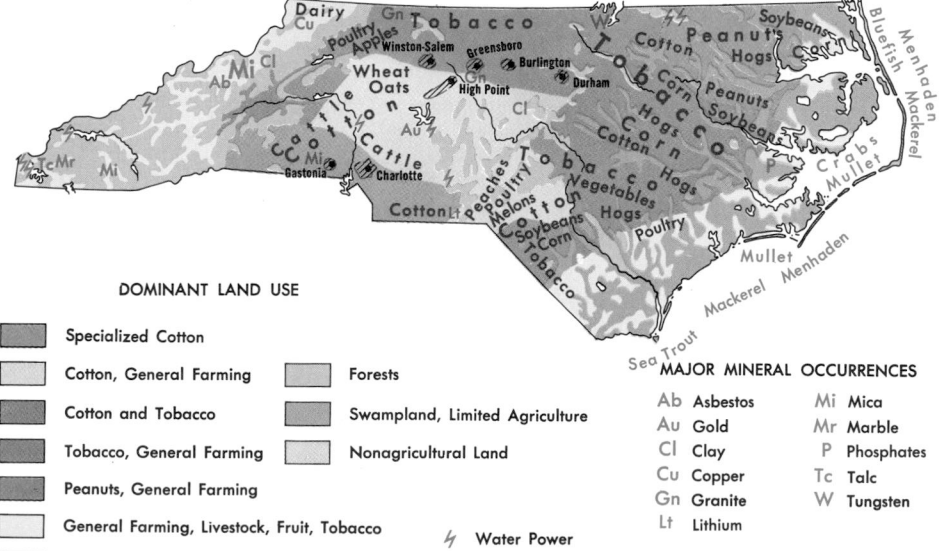

DOMINANT LAND USE

- Specialized Cotton
- Cotton, General Farming
- Cotton and Tobacco
- Tobacco, General Farming
- Peanuts, General Farming
- General Farming, Livestock, Fruit, Tobacco
- General Farming, Truck Farming, Tobacco, Livestock
- Forests
- Swampland, Limited Agriculture
- Nonagricultural Land

MAJOR MINERAL OCCURRENCES

Ab	Asbestos		Mi	Mica
Au	Gold		Mr	Marble
Cl	Clay		P	Phosphates
Cu	Copper		Tc	Talc
Gn	Granite		W	Tungsten
Lt	Lithium			

⚡ Water Power
▨ Major Industrial Areas

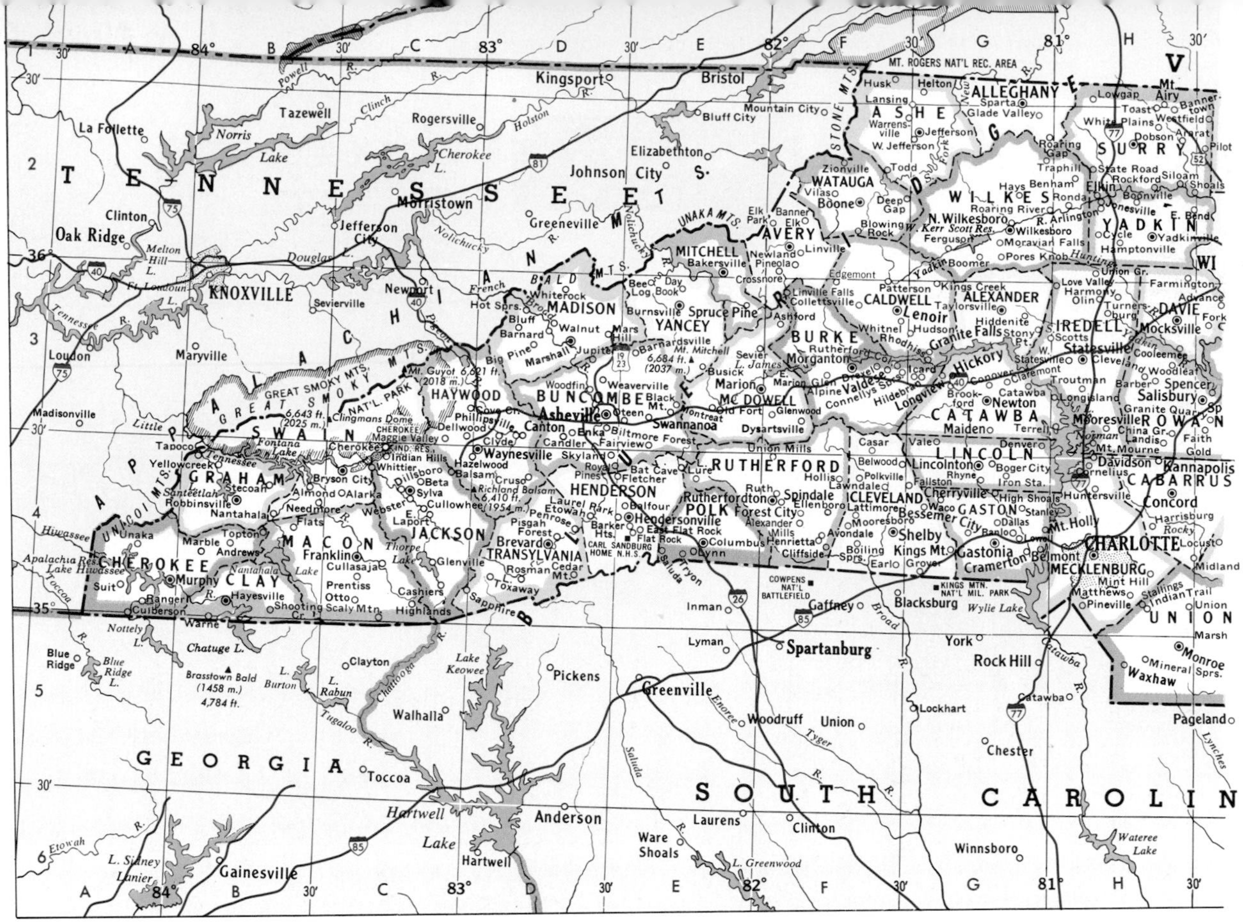

Topography

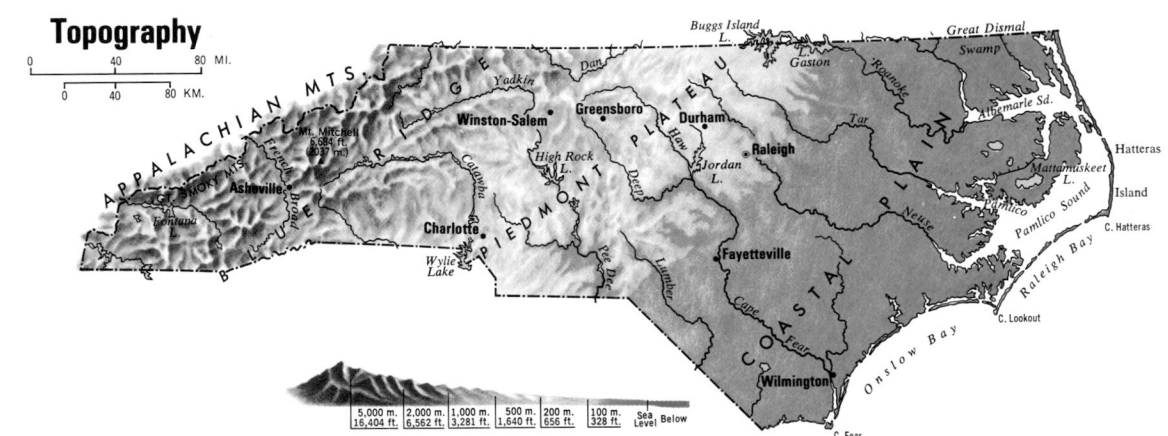

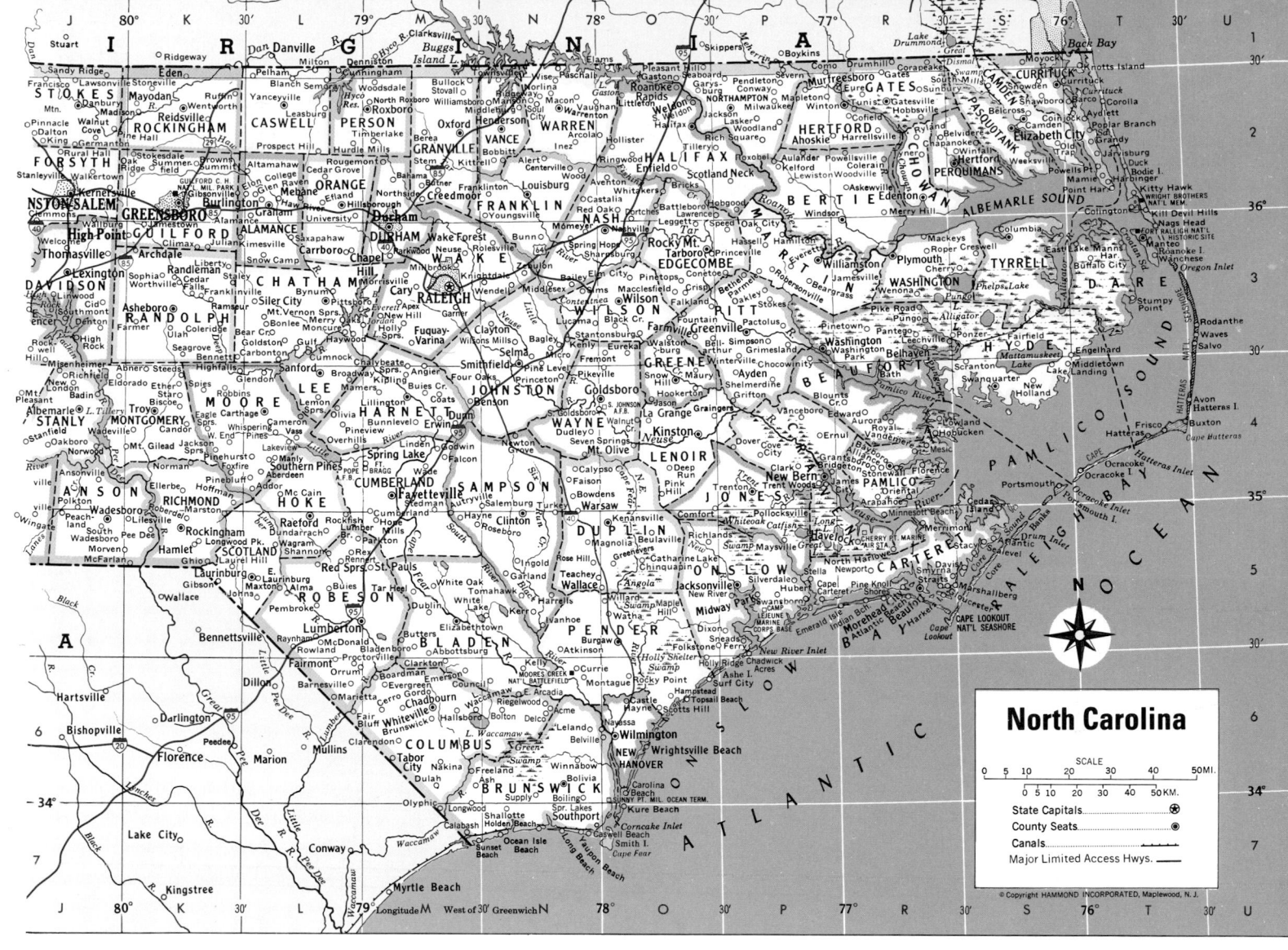

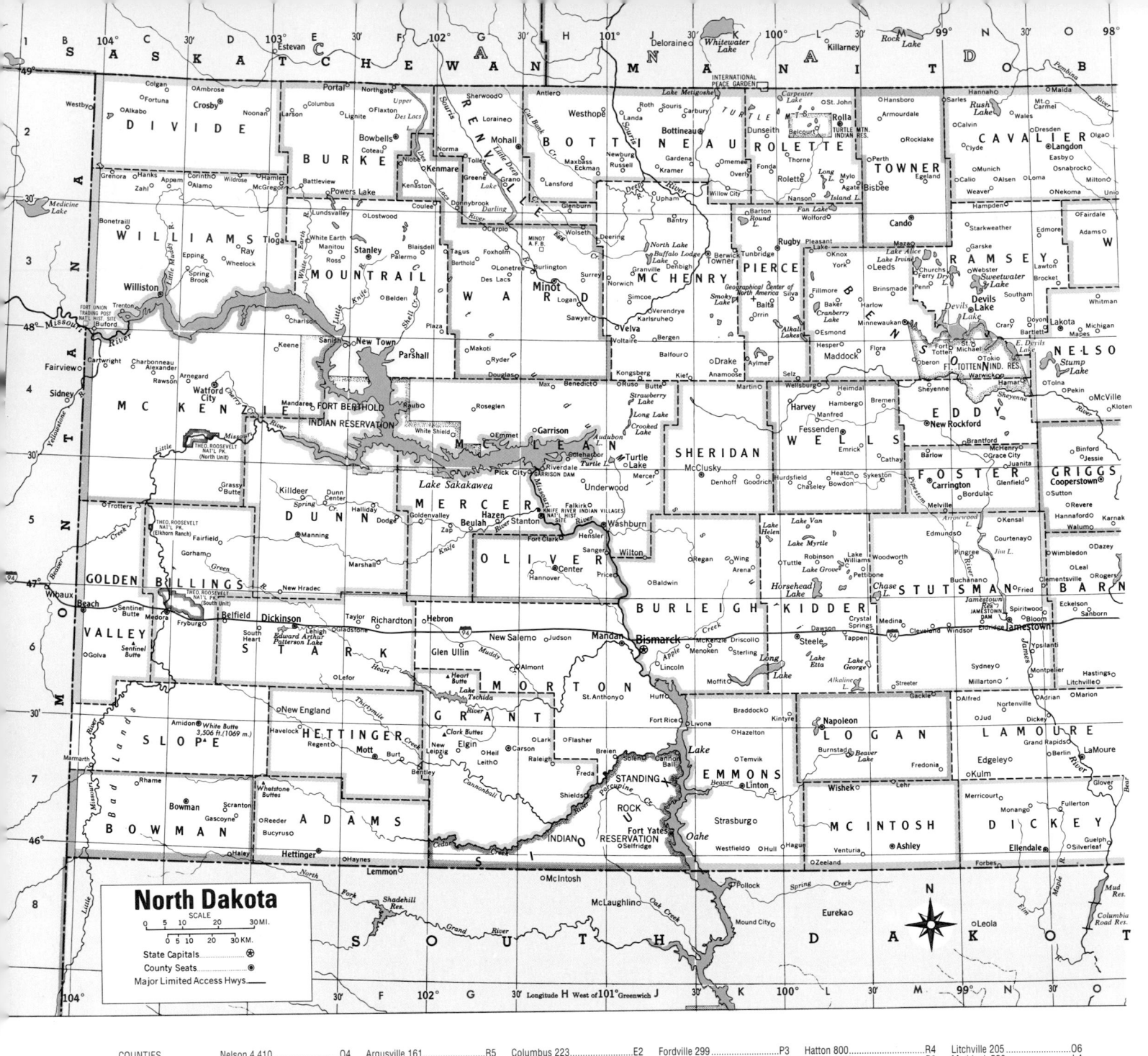

North Dakota

SCALE

0 5 10   20   30 MI.

0 5 10   20   30 KM.

State Capitals........................⊛

County Seats..........................◉

Major Limited Access Hwys._____

COUNTIES

Adams 3,174 ....F7
Barnes 12,545 ....O5
Benson 7,198 ....M3
Billings 1,108 ....D5
Bottineau 8,011 ....J2
Bowman 3,596 ....C7
Burke 3,002 ....E2
Burleigh 60,131 ....J6
Cass 102,874 ....R5
Cavalier 6,064 ....N2
Dickey 6,107 ....N7
Divide 2,899 ....C2
Dunn 4,005 ....E5
Eddy 2,951 ....N4
Emmons 4,830 ....K7
Foster 3,983 ....N5
Golden Valley 2,108 ......C5
Grand Forks 70,683 ......P3
Grant 3,549 ....G6
Griggs 3,303 ....O5
Hettinger 3,445 ....E7
Kidder 3,332 ....L6
LaMoure 5,383 ....N7
Logan 2,847 ....L7
McHenry 6,528 ....J3
McIntosh 4,021 ....L7
McKenzie 6,383 ....D4
McLean 10,457 ....G4
Mercer 9,808 ....G5
Morton 23,700 ....H6
Mountrail 7,021 ....E3

Nelson 4,410 ....O4
Oliver 2,381 ....H5
Pembina 9,238 ....P2
Pierce 5,052 ....K3
Ramsey 12,681 ....N3
Ransom 5,921 ....P7
Renville 3,160 ....G2
Richland 18,148 ....R7
Rolette 12,772 ....L2
Sargent 4,549 ....P7
Sheridan 2,148 ....K4
Sioux 3,761 ....H7
Slope 907 ....C7
Stark 22,832 ....E6
Steele 2,420 ....P4
Stutsman 22,241 ....M5
Towner 3,627 ....M2
Traill 8,752 ....R5
Walsh 13,840 ....P3
Ward 57,921 ....G3
Wells 5,864 ....L4
Williams 21,129 ....C3

CITIES and TOWNS

Abercrombie 252 ....S7
Adams 248 ....O3
Alexander 216 ....C4
Almont 117 ....H6
Alsen 113 ....N2
Amidon▲ 24 ....D7
Anamoose 277 ....K4
Aneta 314 ....P4

Argusville 161 ....R5
Arnegard 122 ....D4
Arthur 400 ....R5
Ashley▲ 1,052 ....M7
Beach▲ 1,205 ....C6
Belcourt 2,458 ....L2
Belfield 887 ....D6
Berthold 409 ....G3
Beulah 3,363 ....G5
Binford 233 ....O4
Bisbee 227 ....M2
Bottineau▲ 2,598 ....J2
Bowbells▲ 498 ....F2
Bowdon 196 ....L5
Bowman▲ 1,741 ....D7
Buffalo 204 ....R6
Burlington 995 ....H3
Butte 129 ....J4
Buxton 343 ....R4
Cando▲ 1,508 ....M3
Cannon Ball 702 ....J7
Carpio 178 ....G3
Carrington▲ 2,267 ....M5
Carson▲ 388 ....H7
Casselton 1,601 ....R6
Center▲ 826 ....H5
Christine 160 ....S6
Church's Ferry 118 ......M3
Cleveland 121 ....M6
Cogswell 184 ....P7
Coleharbor 88 ....H4

Columbus 223 ....E2
Cooperstown▲ 1,247 ....O5
Crary 145 ....N3
Crosby▲ 1,312 ....D2
Crystal 199 ....P2
Davenport 218 ....R6
Dazey 129 ....O5
Deering 99 ....J3
Des Lacs 216 ....G3
Devils Lake▲ 7,782 ......N3
Dickinson▲ 16,097 ......E6
Dodge 135 ....F5
Donnybrook 106 ....G2
Drake 361 ....K4
Drayton 961 ....R2
Dunn Center 128 ....E5
Dunseith 723 ....K2
Edgeley 680 ....N7
Edinburg 284 ....P3
Edmore 329 ....O3
Egeland 103 ....M2
Elgin 765 ....G7
Ellendale▲ 1,798 ....N7
Emerado 483 ....P3
Enderlin 997 ....R6
Esmond 196 ....L3
Fairmount 427 ....S7
Fessenden▲ 655 ....L4
Fingal 138 ....O6
Finley▲ 543 ....P4
Flasher 317 ....H7
Flaxton 121 ....F2

Fordville 299 ....P3
Forest River 148 ....P3
Forman▲ 586 ....P7
Fort Ransom 111 ....P6
Fort Totten 867 ....M4
Fort Yates▲ 183 ....J7
Frontier 218 ....S6
Fullerton 94 ....O7
Gackle 450 ....M6
Galesburg 161 ....O5
Garrison 1,530 ....H4
Gilby 262 ....R3
Gladstone 224 ....F6
Glen Ullin 927 ....G6
Glenburn 439 ....H2
Glenfield 118 ....N5
Goldenvalley 287 ....F5
Golva 101 ....C6
Goodrich 192 ....K5
Grace City 108 ....N4
Grafton▲ 4,840 ....R3
Grand Forks▲ 49,425 ..R3
Grandin 213 ....R5
Granville 236 ....J3
Great Bend 108 ....S7
Grenora 261 ....C2
Hague 109 ....L7
Halliday 288 ....F5
Hankinson 1,038 ....S7
Hannaford 204 ....O5
Harvey 2,263 ....L4
Harwood 590 ....S6

Hatton 800 ....R4
Havana 124 ....P8
Hazelton 240 ....K7
Hazen 2,818 ....G5
Hebron 888 ....G6
Hettinger▲ 1,574 ....E8
Hillsboro▲ 1,488 ....S5
Hoople 310 ....P2
Hope 281 ....P5
Horace 662 ....S6
Hunter 341 ....R5
Inkster 95 ....P3
Jamestown▲ 15,571 ....N6
Karlsruhe 143 ....J3
Kenmare 1,214 ....G2
Kensal 191 ....N5
Killdeer 722 ....E5
Kindred 569 ....R6
LaMoure▲ 970 ....O7
Lakota▲ 898 ....O3
Langdon▲ 2,241 ....O2
Lankin 152 ....P3
Lansford 249 ....H2
Larimore 1,464 ....P4
Leeds 542 ....M3
Lehr 191 ....M7
Leonard 310 ....R6
Lidgerwood 799 ....P7
Lignite 242 ....F2
Lincoln 1,132 ....J6
Linton▲ 1,410 ....K7
Lisbon▲ 2,177 ....P7

Litchville 205 ....O6
Maddock 559 ....L4
Makoti 145 ....G4
Mandan▲ 15,177 ....J6
Mandaree 367 ....E4
Manning▲ 75 ....E5
Manvel 333 ....R3
Mapleton 682 ....R6
Marion 169 ....O6
Marmarth 144 ....B7
Martin 117 ....K4
Max 301 ....H4
Maxbass 123 ....J2
Mayville 2,092 ....R4
McClusky▲ 492 ....K4
McVille 559 ....O4
Medina 387 ....M6
Medora▲ 101 ....C6
Mercer 104 ....J5
Michigan 413 ....O3
Milnor 671 ....P7
Milton 133 ....O2
Minnewaukan▲ 401 ....M3
Minot▲ 34,544 ....H3
Minto 560 ....R3
Mohall▲ 931 ....G2
Mooreton 193 ....S7
Mott▲ 1,019 ....F7
Mountain 134 ....P2
Munich 310 ....N2
Napoleon▲ 930 ....L7
Neche 434 ....P2
New England 663 ......E6

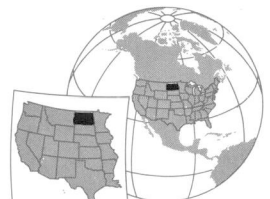

AREA 70,702 sq. mi. (183,118 sq. km.)
POPULATION 641,364
CAPITAL Bismarck
LARGEST CITY Fargo
HIGHEST POINT White Butte 3,506 ft.
(1069 m.)
SETTLED IN 1780
ADMITTED TO UNION November 2, 1889
POPULAR NAME Flickertail State; Sioux
State
STATE FLOWER Wild Prairie Rose
STATE BIRD Western Meadowlark

Topography

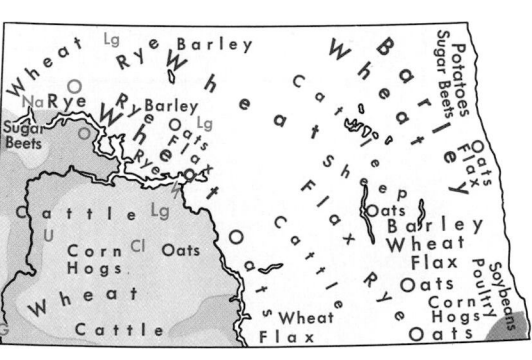

Topographic elevation scale:
5,000 m. / 16,404 ft. — 2,000 m. / 6,562 ft. — 1,000 m. / 3,281 ft. — 500 m. / 1,640 ft. — 200 m. / 656 ft. — 100 m. / 328 ft. — Sea Level — Below

Scale: 0 — 50 — 100 MI. / 0 — 50 — 100 KM.

Agriculture, Industry and Resources

DOMINANT LAND USE

- Specialized Wheat
- Wheat, General Farming
- Wheat, Range Livestock
- Livestock, Cash Grain
- Sugar Beets, Dry Beans, Livestock, General Farming
- Range Livestock
- ⚡ Water Power

MAJOR MINERAL OCCURRENCES

- Cl Clay
- G Natural Gas
- Lg Lignite
- Na Salt
- O Petroleum
- U Uranium

Copyright HAMMOND INCORPORATED, Maplewood, N.J.

Ohio

SCALE

0 5 10   20   30   40 MI.

0 5 10 20 30 40 KM.

State Capitals .... ⊛

County Seats .... ⊗

Major Limited Access Hwys. ───

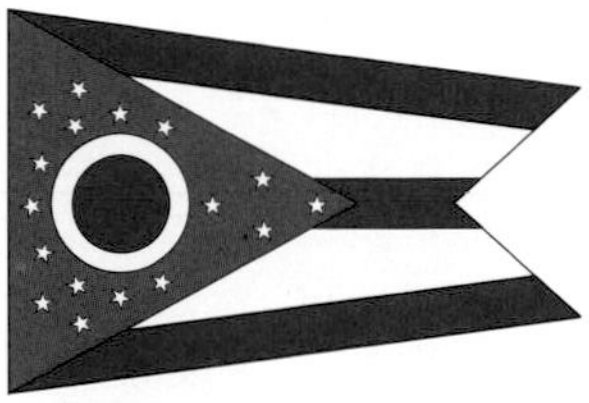

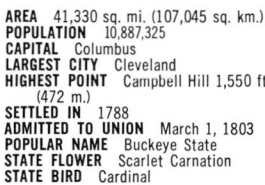

AREA 41,330 sq. mi. (107,045 sq. km.)
POPULATION 10,887,325
CAPITAL Columbus
LARGEST CITY Cleveland
HIGHEST POINT Campbell Hill 1,550 ft. (472 m.)
SETTLED IN 1788
ADMITTED TO UNION March 1, 1803
POPULAR NAME Buckeye State
STATE FLOWER Scarlet Carnation
STATE BIRD Cardinal

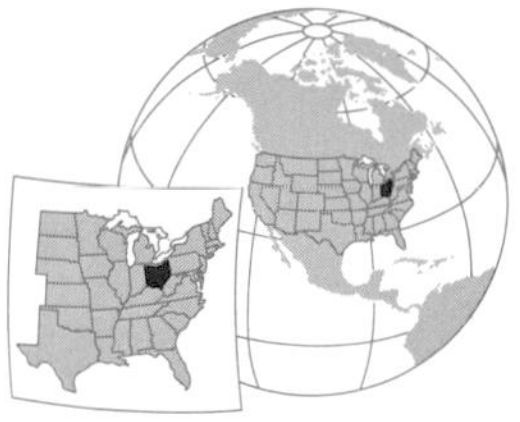

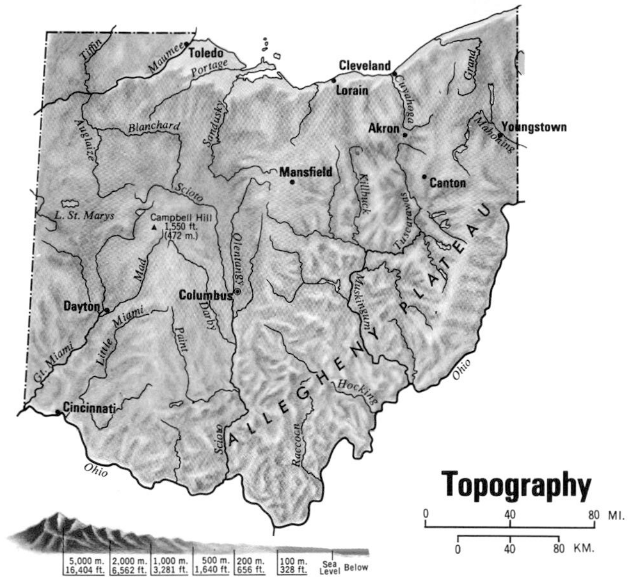
Toledo
Maumee
Tiffin
Portage
Cleveland
Lorain
Cuyahoga
Grand
Akron
Youngstown
Mahoning
Blanchard
Sandusky
Auglaize
Mansfield
Canton
Kilbuck
Tuscarawas
L. St. Marys
Campbell Hill
1,550 ft.
(472 m.)
Scioto
Olentangy
Columbus
Dayton
Mad
Darby
Miami
Little Miami
Gt. Miami
Paint
Muskingum
PLATEAU
ALLEGHENY
Hocking
Ohio
Cincinnati
Scioto
Raccoon
Ohio
0 40 80 MI.
0 40 80 KM.
5,000 m. 16,404 ft.
2,000 m. 6,562 ft.
1,000 m. 3,281 ft.
500 m. 1,640 ft.
200 m. 656 ft.
100 m. 328 ft.
Sea Level
Below

Topography

COUNTIES

Adams 25,371 D8
Allen 109,755 B4
Ashland 47,507 F4
Ashtabula 99,821 J2
Athens 59,549 F7
Auglaize 44,585 B4
Belmont 71,074 J5
Brown 34,966 C8
Butler 291,479 A7
Carroll 26,521 H4
Champaign 36,019 C5
Clark 147,548 C6
Clermont 150,187 B7
Clinton 35,415 C7
Columbiana 108,276 J4
Coshocton 35,427 G5
Crawford 47,870 E4
Cuyahoga 1,412,140 G3
Darke 53,619 A5
Defiance 39,350 A3
Delaware 66,929 D5
Erie 76,779 E3
Fairfield 103,461 E6
Fayette 27,466 D6
Franklin 961,437 E5
Fulton 38,498 B2
Gallia 30,954 F8
Geauga 81,129 H3
Greene 136,731 C6
Guernsey 39,024 H5
Hamilton 866,228 A7
Hancock 65,536 C3
Hardin 31,111 C4
Harrison 16,085 H5
Henry 29,108 B3
Highland 35,728 C7
Hocking 25,533 F6
Holmes 32,849 G4
Huron 56,240 E3
Jackson 30,230 E7
Jefferson 80,298 J5
Knox 47,473 F5
Lake 215,499 H2
Lawrence 61,834 E8
Licking 128,300 F5
Logan 42,310 C5
Lorain 271,126 F3
Lucas 462,361 C2
Madison 37,068 D6
Mahoning 264,806 J4
Marion 64,274 D4
Medina 122,354 G3
Meigs 22,987 F7
Mercer 39,443 A4
Miami 93,182 B5
Monroe 15,497 H6
Montgomery 573,809 B6
Morgan 14,194 G6
Morrow 27,749 E4
Muskingum 82,068 G5
Noble 11,336 G6
Ottawa 40,029 D2
Paulding 20,488 A3
Perry 31,557 F6
Pickaway 48,255 D6
Pike 24,249 D7
Portage 142,585 H3
Preble 40,113 A6
Putnam 33,819 B3
Richland 126,137 E4
Ross 69,330 D7
Sandusky 61,963 D3
Scioto 80,327 D8
Seneca 59,733 D3
Shelby 44,915 B5
Stark 367,585 H4
Summit 514,990 G3
Trumbull 227,813 J3
Tuscarawas 84,090 H5
Union 31,969 D5
Van Wert 30,464 A4
Vinton 11,098 E7
Warren 113,909 B7
Washington 62,254 H7
Wayne 101,461 G4
Williams 36,956 A2
Wood 113,269 C3
Wyandot 22,254 D4

CITIES and TOWNS

Aberdeen 1,329 C8
Ada 5,413 C4
Adamsville 151 G5
Addyston 1,198 B9
Adelphi 398 E7
Adena 842 J5
Akron▲ 223,019 G3
Albany 795 F7
Alexandria 468 E5
Alger 864 C4
Alliance 23,376 H4
Alvordton 298 A2
Amanda 729 E6
Amberley 3,108 C9
Amelia 1,837 D10
Amesville 250 F7
Amherst 10,332 F3
Amsterdam 669 J5
Andover 1,216 J2
Anna 1,164 B5
Ansonia 1,279 A5
Antioch 68 H6
Antwerp 1,677 A3
Apple Creek 860 G4
Aquilla 360 H2
Arcadia 546 D3
Arcanum 1,953 A6
Archbold 3,440 B2
Arlington 1,267 C4
Arlington Heights 1,084 C9
Ashland▲ 20,079 F4
Ashley 1,059 E5
Ashtabula 21,633 J2
Ashville 2,254 E6
Athalia 346 F8
Athens▲ 21,265 F7
Attica 944 E3
Aurora 9,192 H3
Austintown 32,371 J3
Avon 7,337 F3
Avon Lake 15,066 F2
Bailey Lakes 367 F4
Bainbridge 968 D7
Bairdstown 130 C3
Ballville 3,083 D3
Baltic 659 G5
Baltimore 2,971 E6
Barberton 27,623 G4
Barnesville 4,326 H6
Barnhill 313 H5
Barton 1,039 J5
Batavia▲ 1,700 B7
Batesville 95 H6
Bay View 739 E3
Bay Village 17,000 G9
Beach City 1,051 G4
Beachwood 10,677 J9
Beallsville 464 J6
Beaver 336 E7
Beavercreek 33,626 C6
Beaverdam 467 C4
Bedford 14,822 H9
Bedford Heights 12,131 J9
Bellaire 6,028 J5
Bellbrook 6,511 C6
Belle Center 796 C4
Belle Valley 267 G6
Bellefontaine▲ 12,142 C5
Bellevue 8,146 E3
Bellville 1,568 E4
Belmont 471 J5
Belmore 161 B3
Beloit 1,037 J4
Belpre 6,796 G7
Bentleyville 674 J9
Benton 351 G4
Benton Ridge 343 C4
Berea 19,051 G10
Bergholz 713 J4
Berkey 264 C2
Berlin 691 G4
Berlin Heights 756 F3
Bethel 2,407 B8
Bethesda 1,161 H5
Bettsville 752 D3
Beverly 1,444 G6
Bexley 13,088 E6
Blakeslee 128 A2
Blanchester 4,206 B7
Bloomdale 632 D3
Bloomingburg 769 D6
Bloomingdale 227 J5
Bloomville 949 D3
Blue Ash 11,860 C9
Bluffton 3,367 C4
Boardman 38,596 J3
Bolivar 914 G4
Boston Heights 733 J10
Botkins 1,340 B5
Bowerston 343 H5
Bowersville 225 C6
Bowling Green▲ 28,176 C3
Bradford 2,005 B5
Bradner 1,093 C3
Brady Lake 490 H3
Brecksville 11,818 H10
Bremen 1,386 F6
Brewster 2,307 G4
Brice 109 E6
Bridgeport 2,318 J5
Bridgetown 11,748 B9
Brilliant 1,672 J5
Brimfield 3,223 H3
Broadview Heights 12,219 H10
Brook Park 22,865 G9
Brookfield 1,396 J3
Brooklyn 11,706 H9
Brooklyn Heights 1,450 H9
Brookside 703 J5
Brookville 4,621 B6
Broughton 151 B3
Brunswick 28,230 G3
Bryan▲ 8,348 A3
Buchtel 640 F7
Buckeye Lake 2,986 F6
Buckland 239 B4
Bucyrus▲ 13,496 E4
Burbank 289 F4
Burgoon 224 D3
Burkettsville 268 A5
Burlington 3,003 F9
Burton 1,349 H3
Butler 968 F4
Butlerville 188 B7
Byesville 2,435 G6
Cadiz▲ 3,439 J5
Cairo 473 B4
Calcutta 1,212 J4
Caldwell▲ 1,786 G6
Caledonia 644 D4
Cambridge▲ 11,748 G5
Camden 2,210 A6
Campbell 10,038 J3
Canal Fulton 4,157 H4
Canal Winchester 2,617 E6
Canfield 5,409 J3
Canton▲ 84,161 H4
Cardington 1,770 E5
Carey 3,684 D4
Carlisle 4,872 B6
Carroll 558 E6
Carrollton▲ 3,042 J4
Casstown 246 B5
Castalia 915 E3
Castine 163 A6
Catawba 268 C6
Cecil 249 A3
Cedarville 3,210 C6
Celina▲ 9,650 A4
Centerburg 1,323 E5
Centerville 128 B6
Chagrin Falls 4,146 J9
Chardon▲ 4,446 H2
Chatfield 206 E4
Chauncey 980 F7
Cherry Fork 178 C8
Cherry Grove 4,972 C10
Chesapeake 1,073 E9
Cheshire 250 F8
Chester 309 G7
Chesterhill 395 G6
Chesterland 2,078 H2
Chesterville 286 E5
Cheviot 9,616 B9
Chickasaw 378 A5
Chillicothe▲ 21,923 E7
Chilo 130 B8
Christiansburg 599 C5
Cincinnati▲ 364,040 B9
Circleville▲ 11,666 D6
Clarington 406 J6
Clark 523 G5
Clarksburg 483 D7
Clarksville 485 C7
Clay Center 289 D2
Clayton 713 B6
Cleveland Heights 54,052 H9
Cleveland▲ 505,616 H9
Cleves 2,208 B9
Clinton 1,175 G4
Cloverdale 270 B3
Clyde 5,776 E3
Coal Grove 2,251 E9
Coalton 553 E7
Coldwater 4,335 A5
College Corner 379 A6
Columbiana 4,961 J4
Columbus (cap.)▲ 632,910 E6
Columbus Grove 2,231 B4
Commercial Point 405 D6
Conesville 420 G5
Congress 162 F4
Conneaut 13,241 J2
Continental 1,214 B3
Convoy 1,200 A4
Coolville 663 G7
Corning 703 F6
Cortland 5,666 J3
Corwin 225 B6
Coshocton▲ 12,193 G5
Cove 6,669 E8
Covedale 5,830 B10
Covington 2,603 B5
Craig Beach 1,402 H3
Crestline 4,934 E4
Creston 1,848 G3
Cridersville 1,885 B4
Crooksville 2,601 F6
Crown City 445 F8
Cumberland 318 G6
Custar 209 C3
Cuyahoga Falls 48,950 G3
Cuyahoga Heights 682 H9
Cygnet 560 C3
Dalton 1,377 G4
Danville 1,001 F5
Darbydale 825 D6
Darbyville 272 D6
Dayton▲ 182,044 B6
Deer Park 6,181 C9
Deersville 86 H5
Defiance▲ 16,768 B3
Degraff 1,331 C5
Delaware▲ 20,030 E5
Dellroy 314 H4
Delphos 7,093 B4
Delta 2,849 B2
Dennison 3,282 H5
Dent 6,416 B9
Deshler 1,876 C3
Devola 2,736 H7
Dexter City 161 G6
Dillonvale 857 J5
Dover 11,329 G4
Doylestown 2,668 G4
Dresden 1,581 G5
Dublin 16,366 D5
Dunkirk 869 C4
Dupont 279 B3
East Canton 1,742 H4
East Cleveland 33,096 H9
East Liverpool 13,654 J4
East Palestine 5,168 J4
East Sparta 771 H4
Eastlake 21,161 J8
Eaton Estates 1,586 G3
Eaton▲ 7,396 A6
Edgerton 1,896 A3
Edgewood 5,189 J2
Edison 488 E4
Edon 880 A2
Eldorado 549 A6
Elgin 71 A4
Elida 1,486 B4
Elmore 1,334 D3
Elmwood Place 2,937 B9
Elyria▲ 56,746 F3
Empire 364 J5
Englewood 11,432 B6
Euclid 54,875 J9
Evendale 3,175 C9
Fairborn 31,300 B6
Fairfax 2,029 C9
Fairfield 39,729 A7
Fairlawn 5,779 G3
Fairport Harbor 2,978 H2
Fairview Park 18,028 G9
Farmer 932 A3
Farmersville 950 A6
Fayette 1,248 B2
Fayetteville 393 C7
Felicity 856 B8
Findlay▲ 35,703 C3
Fletcher 545 B5
Florida 304 B3
Flushing 1,042 J5
Forest 1,594 C4
Forest Park 18,609 B9
Forestville 9,185 C10
Fort Jennings 436 B4
Fort Loramie 1,042 B5
Fort McKinley 9,740 B6
Fort Recovery 1,313 A5
Fort Shawnee 4,128 B4
Fostoria 14,983 D3
Frankfort 1,065 D7
Franklin 11,026 B6
Franklin Furnace 1,212 E8
Frazeysburg 1,165 F5
Fredericksburg 502 G4
Fredericktown 2,443 F5
Freeport 475 H5
Fremont▲ 17,648 D3
Fulton 325 E5
Fultonham 178 F6
Gahanna 27,791 E5
Galena 361 E5
Galion 11,859 E4
Gallipolis▲ 4,831 F8
Gambier 2,073 F5
Garfield Heights 31,739 J9
Garrettsville 2,014 H3
Gates Mills 2,508 J9
Geneva 6,597 J2
Geneva-on-the-Lake 1,626 H2
Genoa 2,262 D2
Georgetown▲ 3,627 C8
Germantown 4,916 B6
Gettysburg 539 A5
Gibsonburg 2,579 D3
Gilboa 208 C3
Girard 11,304 J3
Glandorf 829 B3
Glendale 2,445 C9
Glenford 208 F6
Glenmont 233 F4
Glenwillow 455 J10
Glouster 2,001 F6
Gnadenhutten 1,226 G5
Golf Manor 4,154 C9
Gordon 206 B6
Grafton 3,344 F3
Grand Rapids 955 C3
Grand River H2
Grandview 1,301 H7
Grandview Heights 7,010 D6
Granville 4,353 F5
Gratiot 195 F6
Gratis 998 A6
Green Camp 393 D4
Green Springs 1,446 E3
Greenfield 5,172 D7
Greenhills 4,393 B9
Greensburg 3,306 G4
Greentown 1,856 H4
Greenville▲ 12,863 A5
Greenwich 1,442 E3
Groesbeck 6,684 B9
Grove City 19,661 D6
Groveport 2,948 E6
Grover Hill 518 B3
Hamden 877 F7
Hamersville 586 C8
Hamilton▲ 61,368 A7
Hamler 623 B3
Hanging Rock 306 E8
Hanover 803 F5
Hanoverton 434 J4
Harbor View 122 C2
Harpster 233 D4
Harrisburg 340 D6
Harrison 7,518 A9
Harrisville 308 J5
Harrod 537 C4
Hartford 418 J3
Hartford 444 E5
Hartville 2,031 H4
Harveysburg 437 C7
Haskins 549 C3
Haviland 210 A3
Hayesville 457 F4
Heath 7,231 F5
Hebron 2,076 F6
Helena 267 D3
Hemlock 203 F6
Hicksville 3,664 A3
Higginsport 298 C8
Highland 275 C7
Highland Heights 6,249 J9
Hilliard 11,796 D5
Hillsboro▲ 6,235 C7
Hiram 1,330 H3
Holgate 1,290 B3
Holland 1,210 C2
Hollansburg 300 A5
Holloway 354 H5
Holmesville 419 G4
Hopedale 685 J5
Hoytville 301 C3
Hubbard 8,248 J3
Huber Heights 38,696 B6
Hudson 5,159 H3
Hunting Valley 799 J9
Huntsville 343 C5
Huron 7,030 E3
Independence 6,500 H9
Indian Hill 5,383 C9
Irondale 382 J4
Ironton▲ 12,751 E8
Ithaca 119 A6
Jackson Center 1,398 B5
Jackson▲ 6,144 E7
Jacksonville 544 F7
Jamestown 1,794 C6
Jefferson (West Jefferson) 3,331 D6
Jefferson▲ 2,952 J2
Jeffersonville 1,281 C6
Jenera 285 C4
Jeromesville 582 F4
Jerry City 517 C3
Jerusalem 144 H6
Jewett 778 H5
Johnstown 3,237 E5
Junction City 770 F6
Kalida 947 B4
Kelleys Island 172 E2
Kent 28,835 H3
Kenton▲ 8,356 C4
Kettering 60,569 B6
Kettlersville 194 B5
Killbuck 809 G5
Kimbolton 134 G5
Kingston 1,153 E7
Kingsville 1,243 J2
Kipton 283 F3
Kirby 155 D4
Kirkersville 563 E6
Kirtland 5,881 H2
Kirtland Hills 628 H2
La Rue 802 D4
Lafayette 449 C4
Lagrange 1,199 F3
Lakeline 210 J8
Lakemore 2,684 H3
Lakeview 1,056 C4
Lakewood 59,718 G9
Lancaster▲ 34,507 E6
Latty 205 A3
Laura 483 B6
Laurelville 605 E7
Lawrenceville 304 C6
Lebanon▲ 10,453 B7
Leesburg 1,063 D7
Leesville 156 H5
Leetonia 2,070 J4
Leipsic 2,203 C3
Lewisburg 1,584 A6
Lewisville 261 H6
Lexington 4,124 E4
Liberty Center 1,084 B3
Lima▲ 45,549 B4
Limaville 152 H4
Lincoln Heights 4,805 C9
Lindsey 529 D3
Linndale 159 G9
Lisbon▲ 3,037 J4
Lithopolis 563 E6
Lockbourne 173 E6
Lockington 214 B5
Lockland 4,357 C9
Lodi 3,042 F3
Logan▲ 6,725 F6
London▲ 7,807 C6
Lorain 71,245 F3
Lordstown 3,404 J3
Lore City 384 H6
Loudonville 2,915 F4
Louisville 8,087 H4
Loveland 9,990 D9
Lowell 617 H6
Lowellville 1,349 J3
Lower Salem 103 H6
Lucas 730 F4
Lucasville 1,575 E8
Luckey 848 D3
Ludlow Falls 300 B6
Lynchburg 1,212 C7
Lyndhurst 15,982 J9
Lyons 579 B2
Macedonia 7,509 J10
Mack 2,816 B9
Macksburg 218 G6
Madeira 9,141 C9
Madison 2,477 H2
Magnetic Springs 373 D5
Magnolia 937 H4
Maineville 359 C9
Malinta 294 B3

(continued on following page)

Agriculture, Industry and Resources

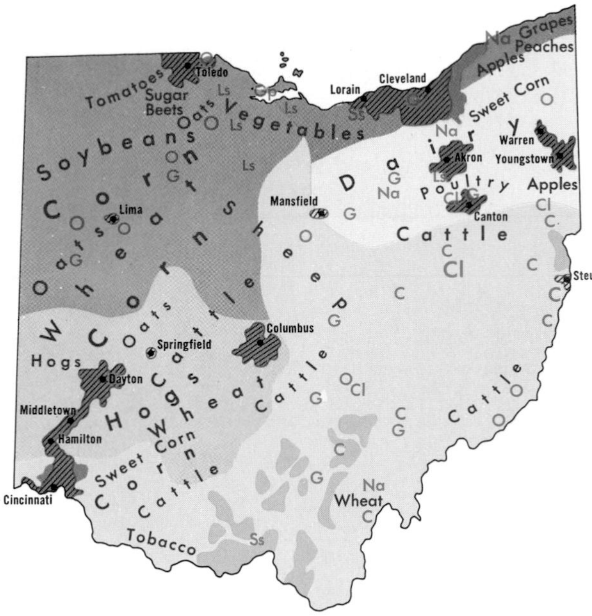

DOMINANT LAND USE

- Hogs, Soft Winter Wheat
- Livestock, Dairy, Soybeans, Cash Grain
- Dairy, General Farming
- General Farming, Livestock, Tobacco
- Fruit, Truck and Mixed Farming
- Forests
- Urban Areas

MAJOR MINERAL OCCURRENCES

- C Coal
- Cl Clay
- G Natural Gas
- Gp Gypsum
- Ls Limestone
- Na Salt
- O Petroleum
- Ss Sandstone
- Major Industrial Areas

Malta 802 ... G6
Malvern 1,112 ... H4
Manchester 2,223 ... C8
Mansfield▲ 50,627 ... F4
Mantua 1,178 ... H3
Maple Heights 27,089 ... H9
Marblehead 745 ... E2
Marengo 393 ... E5
Mariemont 3,118 ... C9
Marietta▲ 15,026 ... G7
Marion▲ 34,075 ... D4
Marseilles 130 ... D4
Marshall 758 ... C7
Marshallville 788 ... G4
Martin 7,990 ... D2
Martins Ferry 9,331 ... J5
Martinsburg 213 ... F5
Martinsville 476 ... C7
Marysville▲ 9,656 ... D5
Mason 11,452 ... B7
Massillon 31,007 ... H4
Masury 1,836 ... J3
Maumee 15,561 ... C2
Mayfield 3,462 ... J9
Mayfield Heights 19,847 ... J9
McArthur▲ 1,541 ... F7
McClure 781 ... C3
McComb 1,544 ... C3
McConnelsville▲ 1,804 ... G6
McDonald 3,526 ... J3
McGuffey 550 ... C4
Mechanicsburg 1,803 ... D5
Medina▲ 19,231 ... G3
Melrose 307 ... B3
Mendon 717 ... A4
Mentor 47,358 ... H2
Mentor-on-the-Lake 8,271 ... G2
Metamora 543 ... C2
Meyers Lake 493 ... H4
Miamisburg 17,834 ... B6
Middle Point 639 ... B4
Middleburg 14,702 ... C5
Middleburg Heights 16,218 ... G10
Middlefield 1,898 ... H3
Middleport 2,725 ... F7
Middletown 46,022 ... A6
Midland 319 ... C7
Midvale 575 ... H5
Mifflin 162 ... F4
Milan 1,464 ... E3
Milford 5,660 ... D9
Milford Center 651 ... D5
Millbury 1,081 ... D2
Milledgeville 120 ... C6
Miller 173 ... F8
Miller City 168 ... B3
Millersburg▲ 3,051 ... F4
Millersport 1,010 ... E6
Millville 755 ... A7
Milton Center 200 ... C3
Mineral 725 ... F7
Mineral City 884 ... H4
Minerva 4,318 ... H4
Minerva Park 1,463 ... E5
Mingo 4,297 ... C5
Mingo Junction 4,834 ... J5
Minster 2,650 ... B5
Mogadore 4,008 ... H3
Monroe 4,490 ... B7
Monroeville 1,381 ... E3
Montezuma 199 ... A4
Montgomery 9,753 ... C9
Montpelier 4,299 ... A2
Moraine 5,989 ... B6
Moreland Hills 3,354 ... J9
Morral 373 ... D4
Morristown 296 ... H5
Morrow 1,206 ... B7
Moscow 279 ... B8
Mount Blanchard 491 ... D4
Mount Carmel 4,462 ... C10
Mount Cory 245 ... C4
Mount Eaton 236 ... G4
Mount Gilead▲ 2,846 ... E4
Mount Healthy 7,580 ... B9
Mount Orab 1,929 ... C7
Mount Pleasant 498 ... J5
Mount Sterling 1,647 ... D6
Mount Vernon▲ 14,550 ... E5
Mount Victory 551 ... D4
Mowrystown 460 ... C7
Mulberry 2,856 ... B7
Munroe Falls 5,359 ... H3
Murray City 499 ... F6
Mutual 126 ... C5
Napoleon▲ 8,884 ... B3
Nashville 181 ... F4
Navarre 1,635 ... H4
Neffs 1,213 ... J5
Nellie 130 ... F5
Nelsonville 4,563 ... F7
Nevada 849 ... D4
Neville 226 ... B8
New Albany 1,621 ... E5
New Alexandria 257 ... J5
New Athens 370 ... H5
New Bloomington 282 ... D4
New Boston 2,717 ... E8
New Bremen 2,558 ... B5
New Carlisle 6,049 ... C6
New Concord 2,086 ... G6
New Holland 841 ... D6
New Knoxville 838 ... B5
New Lebanon 4,323 ... B6
New Lexington▲ 5,117 ... F6
New London 2,642 ... F3
New Madison 928 ... A6
New Miami 2,555 ... A7
New Middletown 1,912 ... J4
New Paris 1,801 ... A6
New Philadelphia▲ 15,698 ... G5
New Richmond 2,408 ... B8
New Riegel 298 ... D3
New Straitsville 865 ... F6
New Vienna 932 ... C7
New Washington 1,057 ... E4
New Waterford 1,278 ... J4
New Weston 148 ... A5
Newark▲ 44,389 ... F5
Newburgh Heights 2,310 ... H9
Newcomerstown 4,012 ... G5
Newton Falls 4,866 ... J3
Newtonsville 427 ... B7
Newtown 1,589 ... C10
Ney 331 ... B3
Niles 21,128 ... J3
North Baltimore 3,139 ... C3
North Bend 541 ... B9
North Canton 14,748 ... H4
North College Hill 11,002 ... B9
North Fairfield 504 ... E3
North Hampton 417 ... C5
North Kingsville 2,672 ... J2
North Lewisburg 1,160 ... C5
North Madison 8,699 ... H2
North Olmsted 34,204 ... G9
North Perry 824 ... H2
North Randall 977 ... H9
North Ridgeville 21,564 ... F3
North Robinson 216 ... E4
North Royalton 23,197 ... H10
North Star 246 ... A5
North Zanesville 2,121 ... G6
Northfield 3,624 ... J10
Northridge 5,939 ... B6
Northwood 5.506 ... D2
Norton 11,477 ... G3
Norwalk▲ 14,731 ... E3
Norwich 133 ... G6
Norwood 23,674 ... C9
Oak Harbor 2,637 ... D2
Oak Hill 1,831 ... E8
Oakwood 709 ... H9
Oakwood 886 ... B3
Oakwood 9,372 ... B6
Oberlin 8,191 ... F3
Obetz 3,167 ... E6
Ohio City 899 ... A4
Olmsted Falls 6,741 ... G9
Ontario 4,026 ... E4
Orange 2,810 ... J9
Orangeville 253 ... J3
Oregon 18,334 ... D2
Orient 273 ... D6
Orrville 7,712 ... G4
Orwell 1,258 ... J2
Osgood 255 ... A5
Ostrander 431 ... D5
Ottawa Hills 4,543 ... C2
Ottawa▲ 3,999 ... B3
Ottoville 842 ... B4
Otway 105 ... D8
Owensville 1,019 ... B7
Oxford 18,937 ... A6
Painesville▲ 15,699 ... H2
Palestine 197 ... A5
Pandora 1,009 ... C4
Parma 87,876 ... H9
Parma Heights 21,448 ... G9
Parral 255 ... G4
Pataskala 3,046 ... E5
Patterson 145 ... C4
Paulding▲ 2,605 ... A3
Payne 1,244 ... A3
Peebles 1,782 ... D8
Pemberville 1,279 ... C3
Peninsula 562 ... G3
Pepper Pike 6,185 ... J9
Perry 1,012 ... H2
Perrysburg 12,551 ... C2
Perrysville 691 ... F4
Phillipsburg 644 ... B6
Philo 810 ... G6
Pickerington 5,668 ... E6
Piketon 1,717 ... E7
Pioneer 1,287 ... A2
Piqua 20,612 ... B5
Pitsburg 425 ... A6
Plain City 2,278 ... D5
Plainfield 178 ... G5
Pleasant City 419 ... G6
Pleasant Hill 1,066 ... B5
Pleasant Plain 138 ... B7
Pleasantville 926 ... F6
Plymouth 1,942 ... E4
Poland 2,992 ... J3
Polk 355 ... F4
Pomeroy▲ 2,259 ... G7
Port Clinton▲ 7,106 ... E2
Port Jefferson 381 ... C5
Port Washington 513 ... G5
Port Wiliam 242 ... C6
Portage 469 ... C3
Portsmouth▲ 22,676 ... D8
Potsdam 250 ... B6
Powell 2 154 ... D5
Powhatan Point 1,807 ... J6
Proctorville 765 ... F9
Prospect 1,148 ... D5
Put-in-Bay 141 ... E2
Quaker City 560 ... H6
Quincy 697 ... C5
Racine 729 ... G8
Rarden 184 ... D8
Ravenna▲ 12,069 ... H3
Rawson 482 ... C4
Ray 490 ... E7
Rayland 566 ... J5
Reading 12,038 ... C9
Reminderville 2,163 ... J10
Republic 611 ... D3
Reynoldsburg 25,748 ... E6
Richfield 3,117 ... G3
Richmond (Grand River) ... H2
Richmond 624 ... J5
Richmond Heights 9,611 ... H9
Richwood 2,186 ... D5
Ridgeway 378 ... C4
Rio Grande 995 ... F8
Ripley 1,816 ... C8
Risingsun 659 ... C3
Rittman 6,147 ... G4
Riverlea 503 ... D5
Rochester 206 ... F3
Rock Creek 553 ... J2
Rockford 1,119 ... A4
Rocky Ridge 425 ... D2
Rocky River 20,410 ... G9
Rogers 247 ... J4
Rome 99 ... J2
Rosemount 1,926 ... D8
Roseville 1,847 ... F6
Ross 2,124 ... B9
Rossburg 250 ... A5
Rossford 5,861 ... C2
Roswell 257 ... H5
Rushsylvania 573 ... C5
Rushville 229 ... F6
Russells Point 1,504 ... C5
Russellville 459 ... C8
Russia 442 ... B5
Rutland 469 ... F7
Sabina 2,662 ... C7
Saint Bernard 5,344 ... B9
Saint Clairsville▲ 5,162 ... J5
Saint Henry 1,907 ... A5
Saint Louisville 372 ... F5
Saint Martin 141 ... C7
Saint Marys 8,441 ... B4
Saint Paris 1,842 ... C5
Salem 12,233 ... J4
Salineville 1,474 ... J4
Sandusky▲ 29,764 ... E3
Sarahsville 162 ... H6
Sardinia 792 ... C7
Savannah 363 ... F4
Scio 856 ... H5
Sciotodale 1,128 ... E8
Scott 339 ... A4
Seaman 1,013 ... C8
Sebring 4,848 ... H4
Senecaville 434 ... H6
Seven Hills 12,339 ... H9
Seven Mile 804 ... A7
Seville 1,810 ... G3
Shadyside 3,934 ... J6
Shaker Heights 30,831 ... H9
Sharon 13,153 ... G6
Sharonville 10,108 ... C9
Shawnee 742 ... F6
Shawnee Hills 423 ... D5
Sheffield 1,943 ... F3
Sheffield Lake 9,825 ... F3
Shelby 9,564 ... E4
Sherrodsville 284 ... H4
Sherwood 828 ... A3
Shiloh 778 ... E4
Shreve 1,584 ... F4
Sidney▲ 18,710 ... B5
Silver Lake 3,052 ... G3
Silverton 5,859 ... C9
Sinking Spring 189 ... D7
Smithfield 722 ... J5
Smithville 1,354 ... G4
Solon 18,548 ... J9
Somerset 1,390 ... F6
Somerville 279 ... A6
South Amherst 1,765 ... F3
South Bloomfield 900 ... D6
South Charleston 1,626 ... C6
South Euclid 23,866 ... H9
South Lebanon 2,696 ... B7
South Point 3,823 ... E9
South Russell 3,402 ... H3
South Salem 227 ... D7
South Solon 379 ... C6
South Vienna 550 ... C6
South Webster 806 ... E8
South Zanesville 1,969 ... F6
Sparta 201 ... E5
Spencer 726 ... F3
Spencerville 2,288 ... B4
Spring Valley 507 ... C6
Springboro 6,590 ... B6
Springdale 10,621 ... B9
Springfield▲ 70,487 ... C6
Steubenville▲ 22,125 ... J5
Stockport 462 ... G6
Stone Creek 181 ... G5
Stout 518 ... D8
Stoutsville 537 ... E6
Stow 27,702 ... H3
Strasburg 1,995 ... G4
Stratton 278 ... J4
Streetsboro 9,932 ... H3
Strongsville 35,308 ... G10
Struthers 12,284 ... J3
Stryker 1,468 ... B3
Sugar Grove 465 ... E6
Sugarcreek 2,062 ... G5
Summerfield 295 ... H6
Summitville 125 ... J4
Sunbury 2,046 ... E5
Swanton 3,557 ... C2
Sycamore 919 ... D4
Sylvania 17,301 ... C2
Syracuse 827 ... G7
Tallmadge 14,870 ... H3
Tarlton 315 ... E6
Taylorsville (Philo) ... G6
Terrace Park 2,133 ... D9
The Plains 2,644 ... F7
Thornville 758 ... F6
Thurston 539 ... E6
Tiffin▲ 18,604 ... D3
Tiltonsville 1,517 ... J5
Timberlake 833 ... J8
Tipp City 6,027 ... B6
Tiro 246 ... E4
Toledo▲ 332,943 ... D2
Tontogany 364 ... C3
Toronto 6,127 ... J5
Tremont City 493 ... C5
Trenton 6,189 ... B7
Trimble 441 ... F7
Trotwood 8,816 ... B6
Troy▲ 19,478 ... B5
Tuscarawas 826 ... H5
Twinsburg 9,606 ... J10
Uhrichsville 5,604 ... H5
Union 5,501 ... B6
Union City 1,984 ... A5
Uniontown 3,074 ... H4
Unionville 238 ... J2
Unionville Center 272 ... D5
Uniopolis 261 ... B4
University Heights 14,790 ... H9
Upper Arlington 34,128 ... D6
Upper Sandusky▲ 5,906 ... D4
Urbana▲ 11,353 ... C5
Urbancrest 862 ... D6
Utica 1,997 ... F5
Valley Hi 217 ... C5
Valley View 2,137 ... H9
Valley View 730 ... D6
Van Buren 337 ... C3
Van Wert▲ 10,891 ... A4
Vandalia 13,882 ... B6
Vanlue 373 ... C4
Venedocia 158 ... B4
Vermilion 11,127 ... F3
Verona 472 ... A6
Versailles 2,351 ... A5
Vienna 1,067 ... J3
Vinton 293 ... F8
Wadsworth 15,718 ... G3
Waite Hill 454 ... H2
Wakeman 948 ... F3
Walbridge 2,736 ... C2
Waldo 340 ... D5
Walton Hills 2,371 ... J10
Wapakoneta▲ 9,214 ... B4
Warren▲ 50,793 ... J3
Warrensville Heights 15,745 ... H9
Warsaw 699 ... G5
Washington Court House▲ 12,682 ... D6
Washingtonville 894 ... J4
Waterville 4,517 ... C3
Wauseon▲ 6,322 ... B2
Waverly▲ 4,477 ... D7
Wayne 803 ... C3
Waynesburg 1,068 ... H4
Waynesfield 831 ... C4
Waynesville 1,949 ... B6
Wellington 4,140 ... F3
Wellston 6,049 ... F7
Wellsville 4,532 ... J4
West Alexandria 1,460 ... A6
West Carrollton 14,403 ... B6
West Elkton 208 ... A6
West Farmington 542 ... J3
West Jefferson ... D6
West Lafayette 2,129 ... G5
West Leipsic 244 ... B3
West Liberty 1,613 ... C5
West Manchester 464 ... A6
West Mansfield 830 ... C5
West Millgrove 171 ... C3
West Milton 4,348 ... B6
West Portsmouth 3,551 ... D8
West Rushville 134 ... E6
West Salem 1,534 ... F4
West Union▲ 3,096 ... C8
West Unity 1,677 ... B2
Westerville 30,269 ... D5
Westfield Center 784 ... G3
Westlake 27,018 ... G9
Weston 1,716 ... C3
Wharton 378 ... D4
Wheelersburg 5,113 ... E8
Whitehall 20,572 ... E6
Whitehouse 2,528 ... C2
Wickliffe 14,558 ... J9
Wilberforce 2,639 ... C6
Wilkesville 151 ... F7
Willard 6,210 ... E3
Williamsburg 2,322 ... B7
Williamsport 851 ... D6
Willoughby 20,510 ... J8
Willoughby Hills 8,427 ... J9
Willowick 15,269 ... J8
Willshire 541 ... A4
Wilmington▲ 11,199 ... C7
Wilmot 261 ... G4
Wilson 136 ... H6
Winchester 978 ... C8
Windham 2,943 ... H3
Wintersville 4,102 ... J5
Withamsville 2,834 ... B7
Woodlawn 2,674 ... C9
Woodmere 834 ... J9
Woodsfield▲ 2,832 ... H6
Woodstock 296 ... C5
Woodville 1,953 ... D3
Wooster▲ 22,191 ... G4
Worthington 14,869 ... E5
Wren 190 ... A4
Wyoming 8,128 ... C9
Xenia▲ 24,664 ... C6
Yankee Lake 88 ... J3
Yellow Springs 3,973 ... C6
Yorkshire 126 ... B5
Yorkville 1,246 ... J5
Youngstown▲ 95,732 ... J3
Zaleski 294 ... F7
Zanesfield 183 ... C5
Zanesville▲ 26,778 ... G6
Zoar 177 ... H4

OTHER FEATURES

Atwood (lake) ... H4
Auglaize (riv.) ... B4
Berlin (lake) ... H4
Big Walnut (creek) ... E5
Black (riv.) ... F3
Black Fork, Mohican (riv.) ... F4
Blanchard (riv.) ... C4
Blennerhassett (isl.) ... G7
Buckeye (lake) ... F6
Campbell (hill) ... C5
Captina (creek) ... J6
Cedar (pt.) ... D2
Chagrin (riv.) ... J8
Clear Fork (res.) ... E4
Clear Fork, Mohican (riv.) ... F4
Clendening (lake) ... H5
Cuyahoga (riv.) ... H10
Cuyahoga Valley Nat'l Rec. Area ... H10
Darby (creek) ... D5
Deer (creek) ... D6
Deer Creek (lake) ... D6
Delaware (lake) ... E5
Dillon (lake) ... F5
Dover (lake) ... H4
Duck (creek) ... H6
Erie (lake) ... H1
Grand (riv.) ... H2
Great Miami (riv.) ... A7
Hocking (riv.) ... F7
Hoover (res.) ... E5
Huron (riv.) ... E3
Indian (lake) ... C5
James A. Garfield Nat'l Hist. Site ... G2
Kelleys (isl.) ... E2
Killbuck (creek) ... G4
Kokosing (riv.) ... E5
Leesville (lake) ... H5
Licking (riv.) ... F5
Little Beaver (creek) ... J4
Little Miami (riv.) ... B6
Little Miami, East Fork (riv.) ... C7
Little Muskingum (riv.) ... H6
Loramie (lake) ... B5
Mad (riv.) ... C6
Maumee (bay) ... D2
Maumee (riv.) ... A3
Middle Bass (isl.) ... E2
Mohican (riv.) ... F4
Mosquito Creek (lake) ... J3
Mound City Group Nat'l Mon. ... E7
Muskingum (riv.) ... G6
North Bass (isl.) ... E2
Ohio (riv.) ... B8
Ohio Brush (creek) ... D8
Olentangy (riv.) ... D4
Paint (creek) ... D7
Perry's Victory and Int'l Peace Mem. ... E2
Piedmont (lake) ... H5
Portage (riv.) ... D3
Pymatuning (res.) ... J2
Raccoon (creek) ... F8
Rattlesnake (creek) ... C7
Rickenbacker A.F.B. ... E6
Rocky (riv.) ... G9
Rocky Fork (lake) ... D7
Saint Joseph (riv.) ... A3
Saint Marys (lake) ... A4
Saint Marys (riv.) ... A4
Salt Fork (creek) ... H5
Sandusky (bay) ... E3
Sandusky (riv.) ... D3
Scioto (riv.) ... D8
Senecaville (lake) ... H6
Sevenmile (creek) ... A6
South Bass (isl.) ... E2
Stillwater (riv.) ... B5
Symmes (creek) ... F8
Tappan (lake) ... H5
Tiffin (riv.) ... B3
Tuscarawas (riv.) ... H5
Vermilion (riv.) ... F3
Wabash (riv.) ... A5
West Sister (isl.) ... D2
Whiteoak (creek) ... C7
William H. Taft Nat'l Hist. Site ... C10
Wills (creek) ... G5
Wills Creek (lake) ... G5
Wright-Patterson A.F.B. 8,579 ... B6
Yellow (creek) ... J4

▲County seat

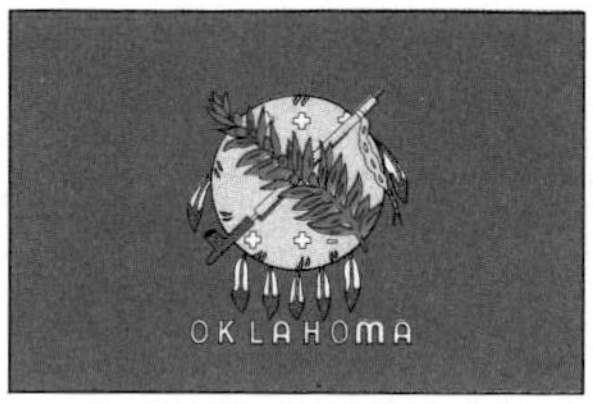

AREA 69,956 sq. mi. (181,186 sq. km.)
POPULATION 3,157,604
CAPITAL Oklahoma City
LARGEST CITY Oklahoma City
HIGHEST POINT Black Mesa 4,973 ft. (1516 m.)
SETTLED IN 1889
ADMITTED TO UNION November 16, 1907
POPULAR NAME Sooner State
STATE FLOWER Mistletoe
STATE BIRD Scissor-tailed Flycatcher

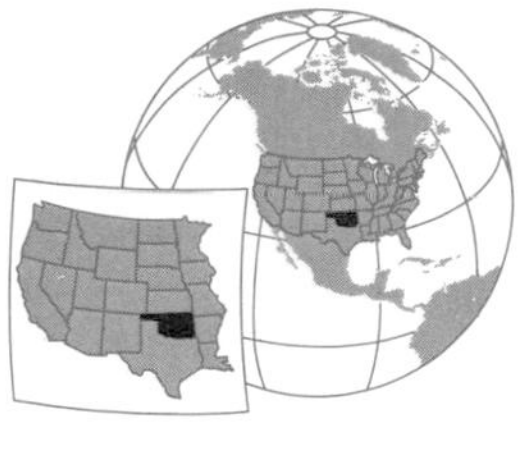

COUNTIES

Adair 18,421 S3
Alfalfa 6,416 K1
Atoka 12,778 O6
Beaver 6,023 E1
Beckham 18,812 G4
Blaine 11,470 K3
Bryan 32,089 O7
Caddo 29,550 K4
Canadian 74,409 K3
Carter 42,919 M6
Cherokee 34,049 R3
Choctaw 15,302 P6
Cimarron 3,301 A1
Cleveland 174,253 M4
Coal 5,780 O5
Comanche 111,486 K5
Cotton 6,651 K6
Craig 14,104 R1
Creek 60,915 O3
Custer 26,897 H3
Delaware 28,070 S2
Dewey 5,551 H2
Ellis 4,497 G2
Garfield 56,735 L2
Garvin 26,605 M5
Grady 41,747 L5
Grant 5,689 L1
Greer 6,559 G5
Harmon 3,793 G5
Harper 4,063 G1
Haskell 10,940 R4
Hughes 13,023 O4
Jackson 28,764 H5
Jefferson 7,010 L6
Johnston 10,032 N6
Kay 48,056 M1
Kingfisher 13,212 L3
Kiowa 11,347 J5
Latimer 10,333 R5
Le Flore 43,270 S5
Lincoln 29,216 N3
Logan 29,011 M3
Love 8,157 M7
Major 8,055 K2
Marshall 10,829 N6
Mayes 33,366 R2
McClain 22,795 L5
McCurtain 33,433 S6
McIntosh 16,779 P4
Murray 12,042 M6
Muskogee 68,078 R3
Noble 11,045 M2
Nowata 9,992 P1
Okfuskee 11,551 O3
Oklahoma 599,611 M3
Okmulgee 36,490 P3
Osage 41,645 O1
Ottawa 30,561 S1
Pawnee 15,575 N2
Payne 61,507 N2
Pittsburg 40,581 P5
Pontotoc 34,119 N5
Pottawatomie 58,760 N4
Pushmataha 10,997 R6
Roger Mills 4,147 G3
Rogers 55,170 P2
Seminole 25,412 N4
Sequoyah 33,828 S3
Stephens 42,299 L6
Texas 16,419 C1
Tillman 10,384 J6
Tulsa 503,341 P2
Wagoner 47,883 P3
Washington 48,066 P1
Washita 11,441 J4
Woods 9,103 J1
Woodward 18,976 H2

CITIES and TOWNS

Achille 491 O7
Ada▲ 15,820 N5
Adair 685 R2
Adams 150 D1
Adamson 150 P5
Addington 100 L6
Afton 915 S1
Agra 334 N3
Akins 250 S3
Albany 65 O7
Albert 100 K4
Albion 88 R5
Alderson 395 P5
Alex 639 L5
Altalta 70 J4
Aline 295 K1
Allen 972 O5
Altus▲ 21,910 H5
Alva▲ 5,495 J1
Amber 418 L4
Ames 268 K2
Amorita 56 K1
Anadarko▲ 6,586 K4
Antlers▲ 2,524 P6
Apache 1,591 K5
Apperson 30 N1
Aqua Park R3
Arapaho▲ 802 H3
Arcadia 320 M3
Ardmore▲ 23,079 M6
Arkoma 2,393 T4
Arnett▲ 547 G2
Asher 449 N5
Ashland 56 O5
Atoka▲ 3,298 O6
Atwood 225 O5
Avant 369 O2
Avard 37 J1
Avery 35 N3
Bache 100 P5
Bacone 786 R3
Baker 70 D1
Balko 100 E1
Barnsdall 1,316 O1
Baron 300 S3
Bartlesville▲ 34,256 O1
Battiest 250 S6
Bearden 142 O4
Beaver▲ 1,584 F1
Beggs 1,150 P3
Belzoni 50 R6
Bengal 300 R5
Bennington 251 P7
Bentley 75 O6
Berlin 50 G4
Bernice 330 S1
Bessie 248 H4
Bethany 20,075 L3
Bethel 2,505 S6
Bethel Acres 2,314 M4
Big Cabin 271 R1
Billings 555 M1
Binger 724 K4
Bison 103 L2
Bixby 9,502 P3
Blackburn 110 N2
Blackgum 150 S3
Blackwell 7,538 M1
Blair 922 H5
Blanchard 1,922 L4
Blanco 215 P5
Blocker 135 P4
Blue 175 O7
Bluejacket 247 R1
Boggy Depot 100 O6
Boise City▲ 1,509 B1
Bokchito 576 O6
Bokhoma 35 S7
Bokoshe 403 S4
Boley 908 O4
Boswell 643 P6
Bowlegs 398 N4
Bowring 115 O1
Boyd 10 E1
Boynton 391 P3
Braden 15 S4
Bradley 166 L5
Braggs 308 R3
Braman 251 M1
Bray 925 L5
Breckinridge 261 L2
Briartown 55 R4
Bridgeport 137 K3
Brinkman G4
Bristow 4,062 O3
Broken Arrow 58,043 P2
Broken Bow 3,961 S7
Bromide 162 N6
Brooksville 69 M4
Bryant 74 P4
Buffalo▲ 1,312 G1
Bunch 64 S3
Burbank 165 N1
Burlington 169 K1
Burneyville 150 M7
Burns Flat 1,027 H4
Butler 341 H3
Byars 263 N5
Byng 755 N5
Byron 57 K1
Cache 2,251 J5
Caddo 918 O6
Cairo 50 O5
Calera 1,536 O7
Calumet 560 K3
Calvin 251 O5
Camargo 185 H2
Cameron 327 T4
Canadian 261 P4
Canadian City L4
Caney 184 O6
Canton 632 J2
Canute 538 H4
Capron 38 J1
Cardin 165 S1
Carmen 459 J1
Carnegie 1,593 J4
Carney 558 N3
Carrier 171 K2
Carter 286 H4
Cartersville 79 S4
Cashion 430 L3
Castle 94 O4
Catoosa 2,954 P2
Cement 642 K5
Center 100 N5
Centrahoma 106 O5
Centralia R1
Chandler▲ 2,596 N3
Chattanooga 437 J6
Checotah 3,290 R4
Chelsea 1,620 P1
Cherokee▲ 1,787 K1
Chester 104 J2
Cheyenne▲ 948 G3
Chickasha▲ 14,988 L4
Chilocco 400 M1
Choctaw 8,545 M3
Chouteau 1,771 R2
Christie 375 S3
Cimarron 71 L3
Claremore▲ 13,280 R2
Clarita 72 O6
Clayton 636 R5
Clearview 47 O4
Clemscot 52 L6
Cleo Springs 359 K2
Cleora 45 S1
Cleveland 3,156 O2
Clinton 9,298 H3
Cloud Chief 12 J4
Cloudy 175 R6
Coalgate▲ 1,895 O5
Cogar 40 K4
Colbert 1,043 O7
Colcord 628 S2
Cold Springs 24 J5
Cole 355 L4
Coleman 200 O6
Collinsville 3,612 P2
Colony 163 J4
Comanche 1,695 L6
Commerce 2,426 R1
Concho 300 L3
Connerville 150 N6
Cooperton 15 J5
Copan 809 P1
Cordell▲ H4
Corinne 100 R6
Corn 548 J4
Cornish 164 L6
Council Hill 139 P3
Countyline 550 L6
Courtney 12 L7
Covington 590 L2
Coweta 6,159 P3
Cowlington 756 S4
Cox City 285 L5
Coyle 289 M3
Crawford 53 G3
Crescent 1,236 L3
Cromwell 268 N4
Crowder 339 P4
Cumberland 100 N6
Curtis 30 H2
Cushing 7,218 N3
Custer City 443 J3
Cyril 1,072 K5
Dacoma 182 J1
Daisy 250 P5
Dale 160 M4
Darwin 50 P6
Davenport 979 N3
Davidson 473 J6
Davis 2,543 M5
Deer Creek 124 L1
Del City 23,928 L4
Dela 434 P6
Delaware 544 P1
Delhi 41 G4
Depew 502 O3
Devol 165 J6
Dewar 921 P4
Dewey 3,326 P1
Dibble 181 L4
Dickson 942 M6
Dill City 622 H4
Disney 257 S2
Dougherty 138 M6
Douglas 55 L2
Douthat 30 S1
Dover 376 L3
Dow 300 P5
Driftwood K1
Drummond 408 L2
Drumright 2,799 N3
Duke (E. Duke) 360 G5
Duncan▲ 21,732 L5
Durant▲ 12,823 O6
Durham 30 G3
Dustin 429 O4
Eagle City 56 J3
Eagletown 650 S6
Eakly 277 K4
Earlsboro 535 N4
Edmond 52,315 M3
El Reno▲ 15,414 K3
Eldorado 573 G6
Elgin 975 K5
Elk City 10,428 G4
Elmer 132 H6
Elmore City 493 M5
Elmwood 300 F1
Empire City 219 L6
Enid▲ 45,309 L2
Enterprise 130 R4
Erick 1,083 G4
Eucha 210 S2
Eufaula▲ 2,652 P4
Fair Oaks 1,133 P2
Fairfax 1,749 N1
Fairland 916 S1
Fairmont 129 L2
Fairview▲ 2,936 J2
Fallis 49 M3
Fanshawe 331 S5
Fargo 299 G2
Farris 100 P6
Faxon 127 J6
Fay 140 J3
Featherston 75 P4
Felt 120 A1
Fillmore 60 N6
Finley 350 R6
Fittstown 500 N5
Fitzhugh 196 N5
Fleetwood 12 L7
Fletcher 1,002 K5
Foraker 25 O1
Forest Park 1,249 M3
Forgan 489 E1
Fort Cobb 663 K4
Fort Gibson 3,359 R3
Fort Supply 369 G1
Fort Towson 568 R7
Foss 148 H4
Foster 100 M5
Fox 400 M6
Foyil 86 R2
Francis 346 N5
Frederick▲ 5,221 H6
Freedom 264 H1
Gage 473 G2
Gans 218 S4
Garber 959 M2
Garvin 128 S7
Gate 159 F1
Geary 1,347 K3
Gene Autry 97 N6
Geronimo 990 K6
Gerty 95 O5
Glencoe 473 M2
Glenpool 6,688 P3
Glover 244 S6
Golden 300 S6
Goldsby 816 L4
Goltry 297 K1
Goodwater 240 S7
Goodwell 1,065 C1
Gore 690 R3
Gotebo 370 J4
Gould 237 G5
Gowen 75 R5
Gracemont 339 K4
Grady 85 L6
Graham 200 M6
Grainola 58 N1
Grand Lake Towne 58 S1
Grandfield 1,224 J6
Granite 1,844 H5
Grant R7
Gray Horse 60 N1
Grayson 66 P3
Greenfield 200 K3
Griggs 15 B1
Grove 4,020 S1
Guthrie▲ 10,518 M3
Guymon▲ 7,803 D1
Haileyville 918 P5
Hall Park 1,090 M4
Hallett 159 N2
Hammon 611 H3
Hanna 99 P4
Hanson 250 S4
Hardcn City 250 N5
Hardesty 228 D1
Hardy N1
Harjo 35 N4
Harmon 27 G2
Harrah 4,206 M4
Harris 192 S7
Hartshorne 2,120 R5
Haskell 2,143 P3
Hastings 164 K6
Haworth 293 S7
Haywood 175 P5
Headrick 183 H5
Healdton 2,872 M6
Heavener 2,601 S5
Helena 1,043 K1
Hendrix 108 O7
Hennepin 300 M5
Hennessey 1,902 L2
Henryetta 5,872 O4
Herd 18 O1
Hess 29 H6
Hester 25 H5
Hickory 77 N5
Hillsdale 96 K1
Hinton 1,233 K4
Hitchcock 139 K3
Hitchita 118 P3
Hobart▲ 4,305 J5
Hockerville 125 S1
Hodgen 150 S5
Hoffman 175 P4
Holdenville▲ 4,792 O4
Hollis▲ 2,584 G5
Hollister 59 J6
Homestead 35 K2
Hominy 2,342 O2
Honobia 80 R5
Hooker 1,551 D1
Hoot Owl 5 R2
Hopeton 42 J1
Howe 510 S5
Hoyt 160 R4
Hugo▲ 5,978 P7
Hulah 50 O1
Hulbert 499 R3
Humphreys 68 H5
Hunter 218 L1
Hydro 977 J3
Idabel▲ 6,957 S7
Indiahoma 337 J5

(continued on following page)

Agriculture, Industry and Resources

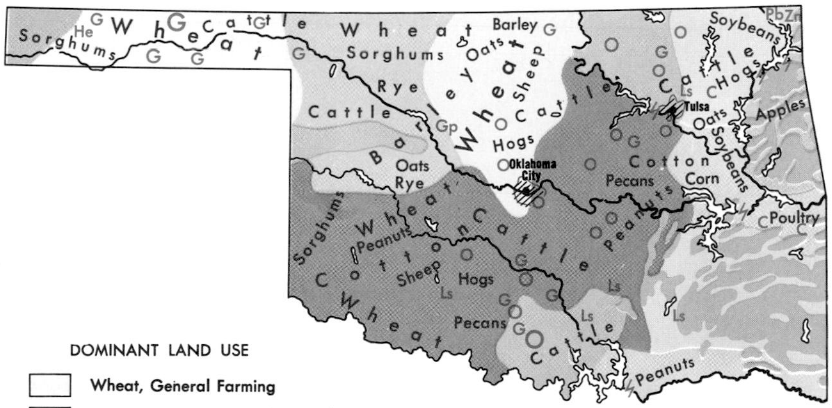

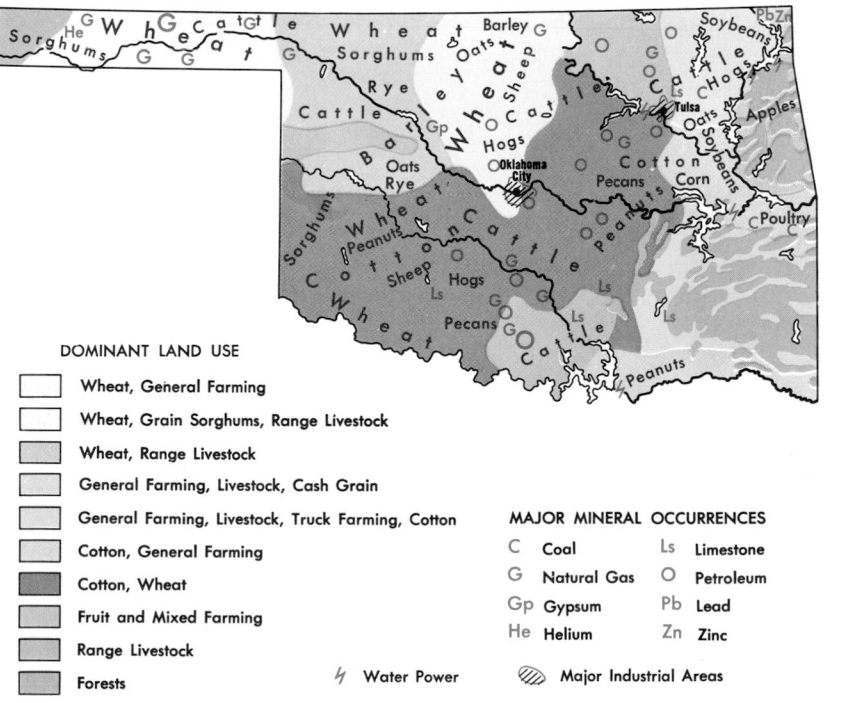

DOMINANT LAND USE

- Wheat, General Farming
- Wheat, Grain Sorghums, Range Livestock
- Wheat, Range Livestock
- General Farming, Livestock, Cash Grain
- General Farming, Livestock, Truck Farming, Cotton
- Cotton, General Farming
- Cotton, Wheat
- Fruit and Mixed Farming
- Range Livestock
- Forests

MAJOR MINERAL OCCURRENCES

- C Coal
- G Natural Gas
- Gp Gypsum
- He Helium
- Ls Limestone
- O Petroleum
- Pb Lead
- Zn Zinc

Water Power

Major Industrial Areas

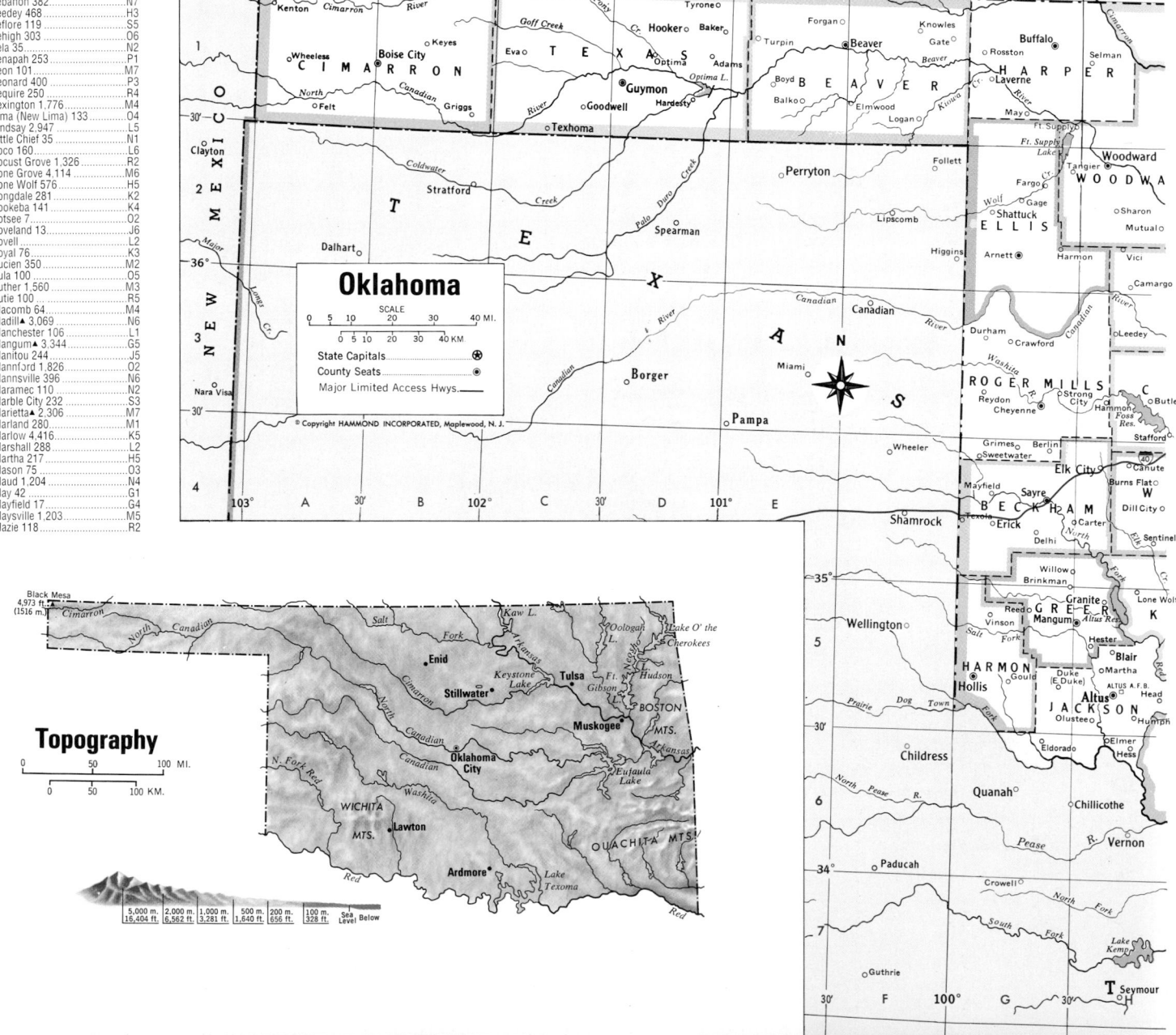

Oklahoma

SCALE
0 5 10   20   30   40 MI.
0 5 10   20   30   40 KM

⊛ State Capitals
⊙ County Seats
Major Limited Access Hwys.

© Copyright HAMMOND INCORPORATED, Maplewood, N.J.

Topography

0   50   100 MI.
0   50   100 KM.

Black Mesa 4,973 ft. (1516 m.)

5,000 m. | 2,000 m. | 1,000 m. | 500 m. | 200 m. | 100 m. | Sea Level | Below
16,404 ft. | 6,562 ft. | 3,281 ft. | 1,640 ft. | 656 ft. | 328 ft.

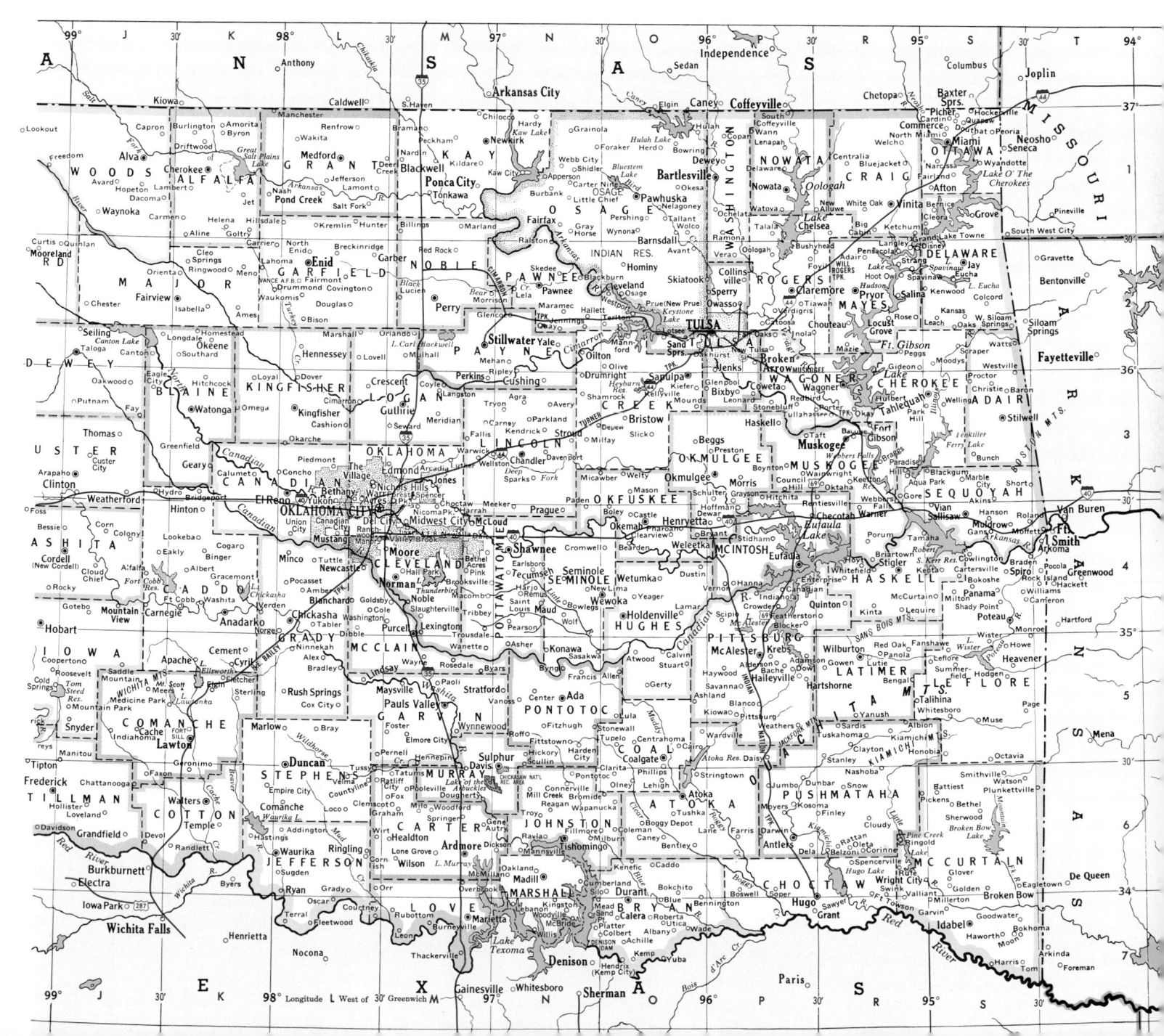

290 Oregon

COUNTIES

Baker 15,317	K3
Benton 70,811	D3
Clackamas 278,850	E2
Clatsop 33,301	D1
Columbia 37,557	D2
Coos 60,273	C4
Crook 14,111	G3
Curry 19,327	C5
Deschutes 74,958	F4
Douglas 94,649	D4
Gilliam 1,717	G2
Grant 7,853	J3
Harney 7,060	H4
Hood River 16,903	F2
Jackson 146,389	E5
Jefferson 13,676	F3
Josephine 62,649	D5
Klamath 57,702	F5
Lake 7,186	G5
Lane 282,912	D3
Lincoln 38,889	D3
Linn 91,227	E3
Malheur 26,038	K4
Marion 228,483	E3
Morrow 7,625	H2
Multnomah 583,887	E2
Polk 49,541	D3
Sherman 1,918	G2
Tillamook 21,570	D2
Umatilla 59,249	J2
Union 23,598	J2
Wallowa 6,911	K2
Wasco 21,683	F2
Washington 311,554	D2
Wheeler 1,396	G3
Yamhill 65,551	D2

CITIES and TOWNS

Adair Village 554	D3
Adams 223	J2
Adel 24	H5
Adrian 131	K4
Agate Beach 975	C3
Agness 150	C5
Airlie 40	D3
Albany▲ 29,462	D3
Algoma 77	F5
Alicel 30	J2
Allegany 300	D4
Alpine 80	D3
Alsea 125	D3
Altamont 18,591	F5
Alvadore 300	D3
Amity 1,175	D2
Andrews 10	J5
Antelope 34	G3
Antone 40	H3
Applegate 150	D5
Arago 200	C4
Arch Cape 100	C1
Arlington 425	G2
Arock 31	K5
Ash 80	D4
Ashland 16,234	E5
Ashwood 98	G3
Astoria▲ 10,069	D1
Athena 997	J2
Aumsville 1,650	D3
Aurora 567	B2
Austin 19	J3
Azalea 900	D5
Baker▲ 9,140	K3
Ballston 120	D2
Bancroft 40	D5
Bandon 2,215	C4
Banks 563	A1
Bar View 170	C2
Barlow 118	B2
Barton 100	B2
Barview 1,402	C4
Bates 56	J3
Bay City 1,027	D2
Beatty 350	F5
Beaver 350	D2
Beavercreek 708	B2
Beaverton 53,310	A2
Bellfountain 50	D3
Bend▲ 20,469	F3
Biggs 50	G2
Birkenfeld 38	D1
Blachly 80	D3
Blaine 38	D2
Blodgett 250	D3
Blue River 318	E3
Bly 800	F5
Boardman 1,387	H2
Bonanza 323	F5
Bonneville 80	E2
Boring 150	E2
Boyd 20	F2
Breitenbush 50	F3
Bridal Veil 20	B2
Bridge 200	D4
Bridgeport 60	K3
Brighton 150	C2
Brightwood 200	E2
Broadacres 80	A3
Broadbent 400	C4
Brogan 130	K3
Brookings 4,400	C5
Brooks 490	D3
Brothers 11	G4
Brownlee 50	L3
Brownsboro 150	E5
Brownsville 1,281	E3
Buena Vista 130	D3
Bunker Hill 1,242	C4
Burns Junction 14	K5
Burns▲ 2,913	H4
Butte Falls 252	E5
Butteville 20	A2
Buxton 450	D2
Camas Valley 750	D4
Camp Sherman 350	F3
Canary 23	D3
Canby 8,983	B2
Cannon Beach 1,221	C1
Canyon City▲ 648	J3
Canyonville 1,219	D5
Carlton 1,289	D2
Carpenterville 30	C5
Cascade Locks 930	E2
Cascade Summit 10	F4
Cascadia 250	E3
Cave Junction 1,126	D5
Cayuse 200	J2
Cecil 75	H2
Cedar Hills 9,294	A2
Cedar Mill 9,697	A2
Celilo 50	G2
Central Point 7,509	D5
Charleston 500	C4
Chemawa 400	A3
Chemult 800	F4
Chenoweth 3,246	F2
Cherry Grove 350	C2
Cherryville 75	E2
Cheshire 300	D3
Chiloquin 673	F5
Clackamas 2,578	B2
Clatskanie 1,629	D1
Cloverdale 260	D2
Coburg 763	E3
Colton 305	B3
Columbia City 1,003	E2
Condon▲ 635	G2
Coos Bay 15,076	C4
Coquille▲ 4,121	C4
Cornelius 6,148	A2
Corvallis▲ 44,757	D3
Cottage Grove 7,402	D4
Cove 507	K2
Cove Orchard 50	D2

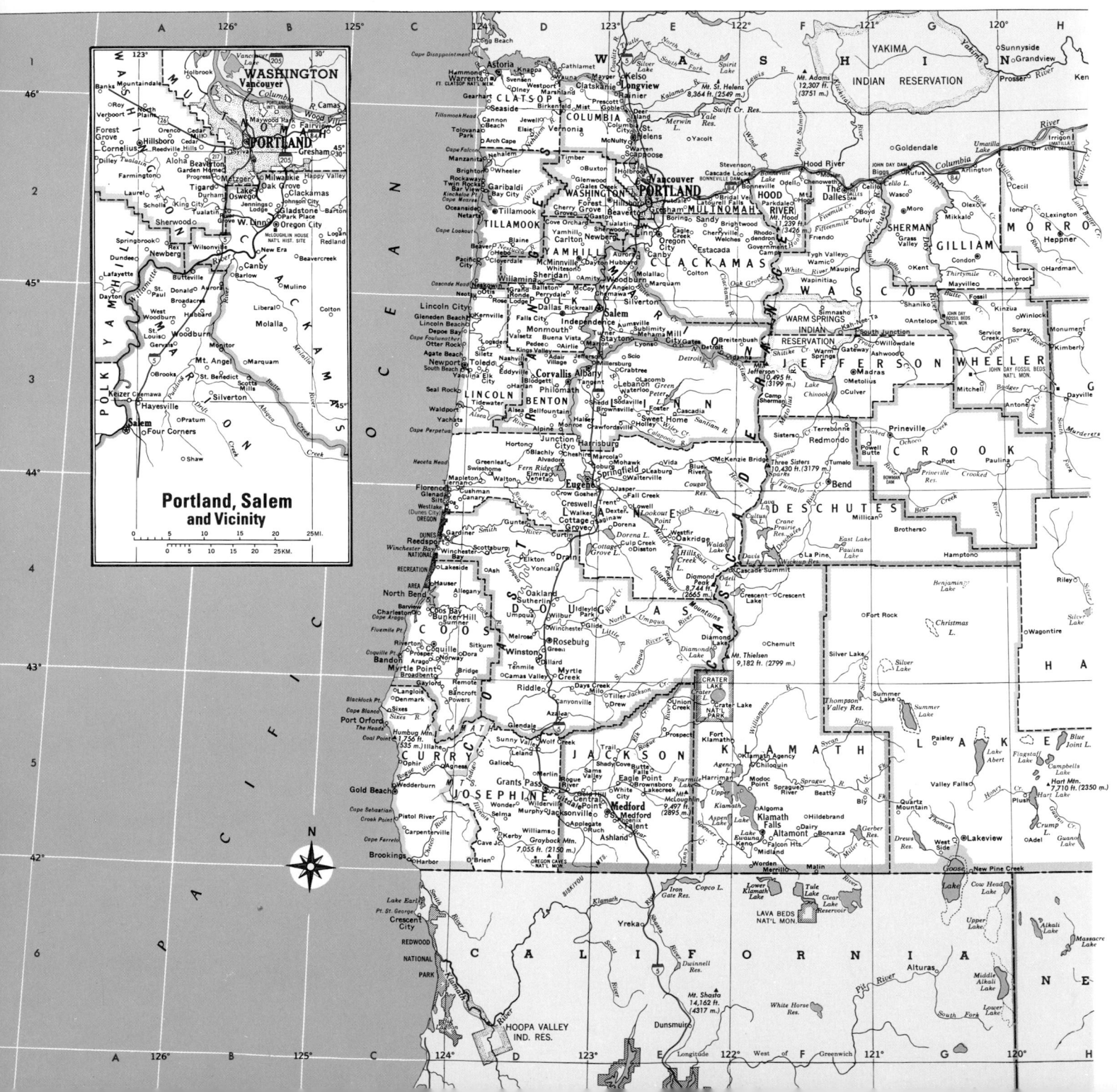

AREA 97,073 sq. mi. (251,419 sq. km.)
POPULATION 2,853,733
CAPITAL Salem
LARGEST CITY Portland
HIGHEST POINT Mt. Hood 11,239 ft. (3426 m.)
SETTLED IN 1810
ADMITTED TO UNION February 14, 1859
POPULAR NAME Beaver State
STATE FLOWER Oregon Grape
STATE BIRD Western Meadowlark

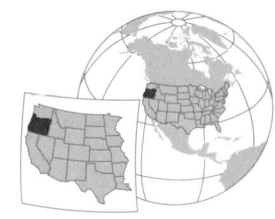

Topography

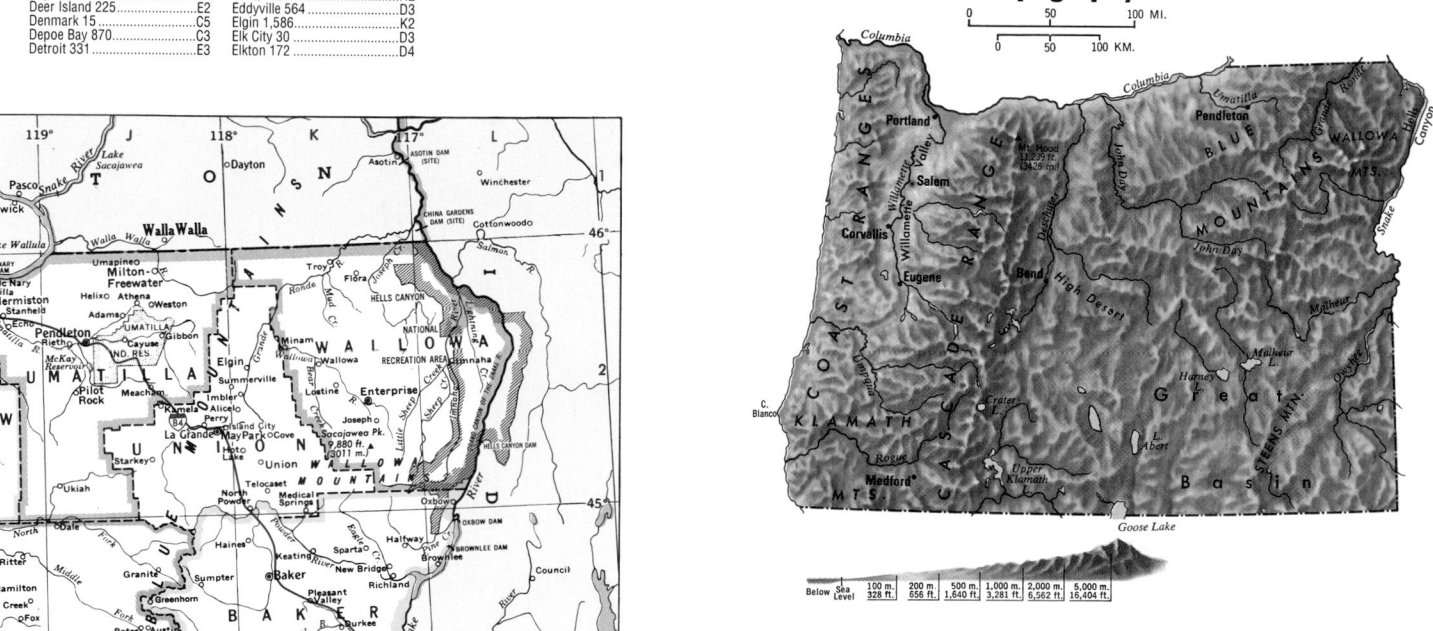

Below Sea Level	100 m. 328 ft.	200 m. 656 ft.	500 m. 1,640 ft.	1,000 m. 3,281 ft.	2,000 m. 6,562 ft.	5,000 m. 16,404 ft.

(continued on following page)

Oregon

SCALE
0 5 10 20 30 40 50 60 MI.
0 5 10 20 30 40 50 60 KM.

State Capitals ⊛
County Seats ◉
Major Limited Access Hwys. ▬

© Copyright HAMMOND INCORPORATED, Maplewood, N.J.

Agriculture, Industry and Resources

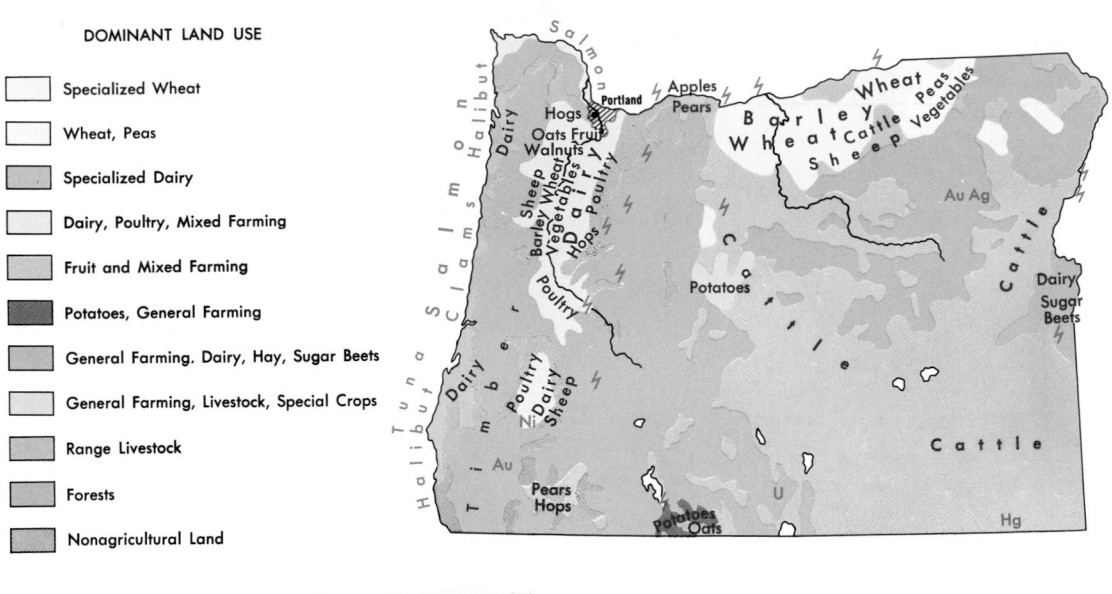

DOMINANT LAND USE

- Specialized Wheat
- Wheat, Peas
- Specialized Dairy
- Dairy, Poultry, Mixed Farming
- Fruit and Mixed Farming
- Potatoes, General Farming
- General Farming. Dairy, Hay, Sugar Beets
- General Farming, Livestock, Special Crops
- Range Livestock
- Forests
- Nonagricultural Land

MAJOR MINERAL OCCURRENCES

Ag Silver   Hg Mercury   ⚡ Water Power

Au Gold   Ni Nickel   ▨ Major Industrial Areas

U Uranium

DOMINANT LAND USE

- Specialized Dairy
- Dairy, General Farming
- Fruit and Mixed Farming
- Fruit, Truck and Mixed Farming
- General Farming, Livestock, Tobacco
- General Farming, Livestock, Fruit, Tobacco
- Forests
- Urban Areas

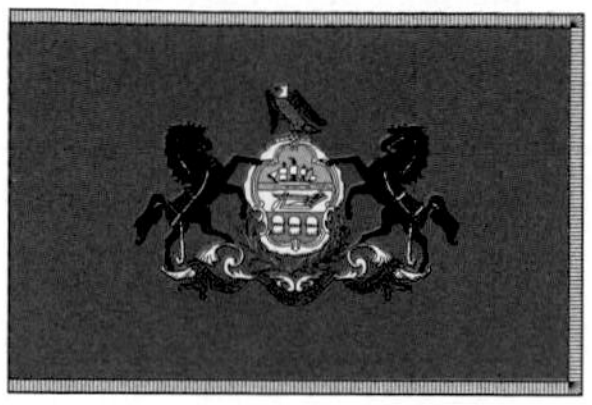

AREA 45,308 sq. mi. (117,348 sq. km.)
POPULATION 11,924,710
CAPITAL Harrisburg
LARGEST CITY Philadelphia
HIGHEST POINT Mt. Davis 3,213 ft. (979 m.)
SETTLED IN 1682
ADMITTED TO UNION December 12, 1787
POPULAR NAME Keystone State
STATE FLOWER Mountain Laurel
STATE BIRD Ruffed Grouse

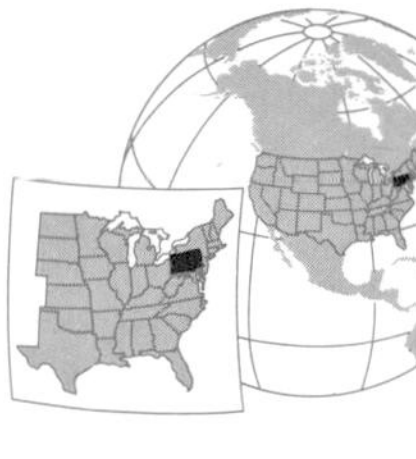

MAJOR MINERAL OCCURRENCES

C	Coal	G	Natural Gas	Sl	Slate
Cl	Clay	Ls	Limestone	Ss	Sandstone
Co	Cobalt	O	Petroleum	Zn	Zinc
Fe	Iron Ore				

Water Power
Major Industrial Areas

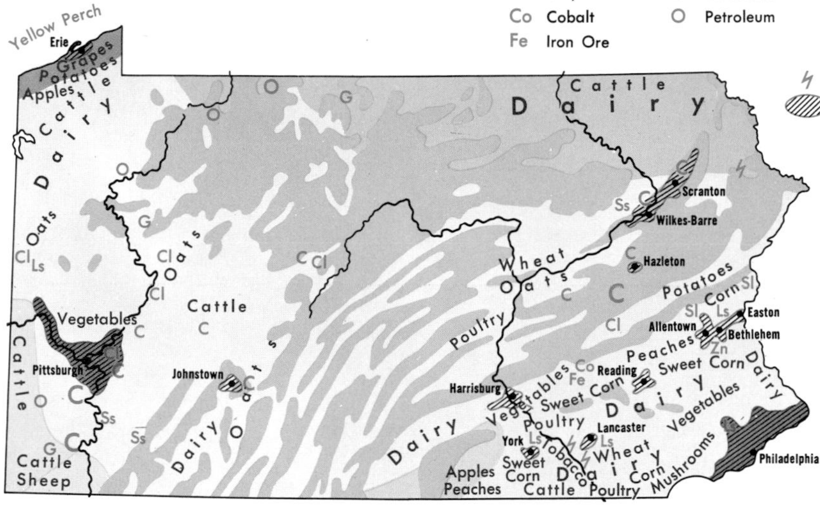

Agriculture, Industry and Resources

COUNTIES

Adams 78,274 ... H6
Allegheny 1,336,449 ... B5
Armstrong 73,478 ... D4
Beaver 186,093 ... B4
Bedford 47,919 ... E6
Berks 336,523 ... K5
Blair 130,542 ... F4
Bradford 60,967 ... J2
Bucks 541,174 ... M5
Butler 152,013 ... C4
Cambria 163,029 ... E4
Cameron 5,913 ... F3
Carbon 56,846 ... L4
Centre 123,786 ... G4
Chester 376,396 ... L6
Clarion 41,699 ... D3
Clearfield 78,097 ... F3
Clinton 37,182 ... G3
Columbia 63,202 ... K3
Crawford 86,169 ... B2
Cumberland 195,257 ... H5
Dauphin 237,813 ... J5
Delaware 547,651 ... M6
Elk 34,878 ... E3
Erie 275,572 ... B2
Fayette 145,351 ... C6
Forest 4,802 ... D2
Franklin 121,082 ... G6
Fulton 13,837 ... F6
Greene 39,550 ... B6
Huntingdon 44,164 ... F5
Indiana 89,994 ... D4
Jefferson 46,083 ... D3
Juniata 20,625 ... H4
Lackawanna 219,039 ... L3
Lancaster 422,822 ... K5
Lawrence 96,246 ... B4
Lebanon 113,744 ... K5
Lehigh 291,130 ... L4
Luzerne 328,149 ... L3
Lycoming 118,710 ... H3
McKean 50,635 ... E2
Mercer 121,003 ... B3
Mifflin 46,197 ... G4
Monroe 95,709 ... M3
Montgomery 678,111 ... M5
Montour 17,735 ... J3
Northampton 247,105 ... M4
Northumberland 96,771 ... J4
Perry 41,172 ... H5
Philadelphia (city county) 1,688,210 ... M6
Pike 27,966 ... M3
Potter 16,717 ... G2
Schuylkill 152,585 ... K4
Snyder 36,680 ... H4
Somerset 78,218 ... D6
Sullivan 6,104 ... J3
Susquehanna 40,380 ... L2
Tioga 41,126 ... H2
Union 36,176 ... H4
Venango 59,381 ... C3
Warren 45,050 ... D2
Washington 204,584 ... B5
Wayne 39,944 ... M2
Westmoreland 370,321 ... D5
Wyoming 28,076 ... K2
York 339,574 ... J6

CITIES and TOWNS

Abbottstown 539 ... J6
Abington• 58,836 ... M5
Adamstown 1,108 ... K5
Akron 3,869 ... K5
Albion 1,575 ... B2
Alburtis 1,415 ... L5
Aldan 4,549 ... M7
Alexandria 411 ... F4
Aliquippa 13,374 ... B4
Allentown▲ 105,090 ... L4
Allison Park 10,000 ... C4
Altoona 51,881 ... F4
Ambler 6,609 ... M5
Ambridge 8,133 ... B4
Annville 4,294 ... J5
Apollo 1,895 ... C4
Archbald 6,291 ... F6
Ardmore 12,646 ... M6
Arendtsville 693 ... H6
Arnold 6,113 ... C4
Ashland 3,859 ... K4
Ashley 3,291 ... E7
Aspinwall 2,880 ... C6
Atglen 825 ... K6
Athens 3,468 ... K2
Atlas 1,162 ... K4
Auburn 913 ... K4
Austin 569 ... F2
Avalon 5,784 ... B6
Avella 900 ... B5
Avis 1,506 ... H3
Avoca 2,897 ... F7
Avondale 954 ... L6
Avonmore 1,089 ... C4
Baden 5,074 ... B4
Bala-Cynwyd ... N6
Baldwin 21,923 ... B7
Bally 973 ... L5
Bangor 5,383 ... M4
Barnesboro 2,530 ... E4
Bath 2,358 ... M4
Beallsville 530 ... C5
Beaver Falls 10,687 ... B4
Beaver Meadows 985 ... L4
Beaver▲ 5,028 ... B4
Beaverdale 1,187 ... E5
Beavertown 853 ... H4
Bedford▲ 3,137 ... F5
Beech Creek 716 ... G3
Belle Vernon 1,213 ... C5
Bellefonte▲ 6,358 ... G4
Belleville 1,589 ... G4
Bellevue 9,126 ... B6
Bellwood 1,976 ... F4
Ben Avon 2,096 ... B6
Bendersville 560 ... H6
Bentleyville 2,673 ... B5
Benton 958 ... K3
Berlin 2,064 ... E6
Bernville 789 ... K5
Berrysburg 376 ... J4
Berwick 10,976 ... K3
Berwyn Devon 5,019 ... L5
Bessemer 1,196 ... B4
Bethel Park 33,823 ... B7
Bethlehem 71,428 ... M4
Big Run 699 ... E4
Biglerville 993 ... H6
Birdsboro 4,222 ... L5
Black Lick 1,100 ... D4
Blairsville 3,595 ... D5
Blakely 7,222 ... F6
Blawnox 1,626 ... C6
Bloomfield (New Bloomfield)▲ 1,092 ... H5
Blooming Valley 391 ... B2
Bloomsburg▲ 12,439 ... J3
Blossburg 1,571 ... H2
Boalsburg 2,206 ... G4
Bobtown 1,008 ... B6
Boiling Springs 1,978 ... H5
Bolivar 544 ... D5
Boothwyn 5,069 ... L7
Boswell 1,485 ... E5
Bowmanstown 888 ... L4
Boyertown 3,759 ... L5
Brackenridge 3,784 ... C4
Braddock 4,682 ... C7
Bradford 9,625 ... E2
Brentwood 10,823 ... B7
Briar Creek 616 ... K3
Brickerville 1,268 ... K5
Bridgeport 4,292 ... M5
Bridgeville 5,445 ... B5
Bridgewater 751 ... B4
Brisbin 369 ... F4
Bristol 10,405 ... N5
Bristol• 587,330 ... N5
Broad Top 331 ... F5
Brockway 2,207 ... E3
Brodheadsville 1,389 ... M4
Brookhaven 8,567 ... M7
Brookville▲ 4,184 ... D3
Broomall 10,930 ... M6
Brownstown 937 ... K5
Brownsville 3,164 ... C5
Bruin 646 ... C3
Bryn Athyn 1,081 ... M5
Bryn Mawr 3,271 ... M5
Burgettstown 1,634 ... A5
Burlington 479 ... J2
Burnham 2,197 ... H4
Burnside 350 ... E4
Butler▲ 15,714 ... C4
Cadogan• 459 ... C4
Cairnbrook 1,081 ... E5
California 5,748 ... C5
Callery 420 ... C4
Cambridge Springs 1,837 ... C2
Camp Hill 7,831 ... H5
Canonsburg 9,200 ... B5
Canton 1,966 ... J2
Carbondale 10,664 ... L2
Carlisle▲ 18,419 ... H5
Carmichaels 532 ... B6
Carnegie 9,278 ... B7
Carroll Valley 1,457 ... H6
Carrolltown 1,286 ... E4
Castle Shannon 9,135 ... B7
Catasauqua 6,662 ... M4
Catawissa 1,683 ... K4
Centerville 4,207 ... B6
Central City 1,246 ... E5
Centre Hall 1,203 ... G4
Chalfont 3,069 ... M5
Chambersburg▲ 16,647 ... G6
Charleroi 5,014 ... C5
Cheltenham• 35,509 ... M5
Cherry Tree 431 ... E4
Chester 41,856 ... L7
Chester Heights 2,273 ... L7
Chester Hill 945 ... F4
Cheswick 1,971 ... C6
Chicora 1,058 ... C4
Christiana 1,045 ... K6
Churchill 3,883 ... C7
Clairton 9,656 ... C7
Clarendon 650 ... D2
Clarion▲ 6,457 ... D3
Clark (Clarksville) 610 ... B3
Clarks Green 1,603 ... F6
Clarks Summit 5,433 ... F6
Claysburg 1,399 ... F5
Claysville 962 ... B5
Clearfield▲ 6,633 ... F3
Clifton Heights 7,111 ... M7
Clintonville 520 ... C3
Clymer 1,499 ... E4
Coalport 578 ... E4
Coatesville 11,038 ... L5
Cochranton 1,174 ... B2
Codorus (Jefferson) 685 ... J6
Cokeburg 724 ... B5
Collegeville 4,227 ... M5
Collingdale 9,175 ... N7
Columbia 10,701 ... K5
Colver 1,024 ... E4
Colwyn 2,613 ... N7
Confluence 873 ... D6
Conneaut Lake 699 ... B2
Conneautville 822 ... A2
Connellsville 9,229 ... C5
Connoquenessing 507 ... B4
Conshohocken 8,064 ... M5
Conway 2,424 ... B4
Conyngham 2,060 ... K3
Coopersburg 2,599 ... M5
Cooperstown 506 ... C2
Coplay 3,267 ... L4
Coraopolis 6,747 ... B4
Cornwall 3,231 ... K5
Corry 7,216 ... C2
Coudersport▲ 2,854 ... G2
Crabtree 900 ... D5
Crafton 7,188 ... B7
Cranesville 598 ... B2
Cresson 1,784 ... E5
Cressona 1,694 ... K4
Cross Roads 322 ... J6
Curwensville 2,924 ... E4
Dale 1,642 ... E5
Dallas 2,567 ... E7
Dallastown 3,974 ... J6
Dalton 1,369 ... L2
Danville▲ 5,165 ... J4
Darby 10,955 ... M7
Dauphin 845 ... J5
Dayton 572 ... D4
Delaware Water Gap 733 ... M4
Delmont 2,041 ... D5
Delta 761 ... K6
Denver 2,861 ... K5
Derry 2,950 ... D5
Dickson City 6,276 ... F7
Dillsburg 1,925 ... J5
Donora 5,928 ... C5
Dormont 9,772 ... B7
Dover 1,884 ... J6
Downingtown 7,749 ... L5
Doylestown▲ 8,575 ... M5
Dravosburg 2,377 ... C7
Drexel Hill 29,744 ... M6
Drifton 1,786 ... L3
DuBois 8,286 ... E3
Dublin 1,985 ... M5
Duboistown 1,201 ... H3
Dunbar 1,213 ... C6
Duncannon 1,450 ... H5
Duncansville 1,309 ... F5
Dunmore 15,403 ... F7
Dupont 2,984 ... F7
Duquesne 8,525 ... C7
Duryea 4,869 ... F7
Dushore 738 ... K2
East Bangor 1,006 ... M4
East Berlin 1,175 ... J6
East Berwick 2,128 ... K3
East Brady 1,047 ... C3
East Butler 725 ... C4
East Conemaugh 1,470 ... E5
East Faxon 3,951 ... J3
East Greenville 3,117 ... L5
East Lansdowne 2,691 ... M7
East Petersburg 4,197 ... K5
East Pittsburgh 2,160 ... C7
East Prospect 558 ... J6
East Stroudsburg 8,781 ... M4
East Washington 2,126 ... B5
Easton▲ 26,276 ... M4
Eau Claire 371 ... C3
Ebensburg▲ 3,872 ... E5
Economy 9,519 ... B4
Eddystone 2,446 ... M7
Edgewood 2,719 ... B7
Edgeworth 1,670 ... B4
Edinboro 7,736 ... B2
Edwardsville 5,399 ... E7
Elderton 371 ... D4
Eldred 869 ... F2
Elizabeth 1,610 ... C5
Elizabethtown 9,952 ... J5
Elizabethville 1,467 ... J4
Elkland 1,849 ... H1
Ellsworth 1,048 ... B5
Ellwood City 8,894 ... B4
Elverson 470 ... L5
Elysburg 1,890 ... K4
Emigsville 2,580 ... J5
Emlenton 834 ... C3
Emmaus 11,157 ... M4
Emporium▲ 2,513 ... F2
Emsworth 2,892 ... B6
Enola 5,961 ... J5
Enon Valley 355 ... B4
Ephrata 12,133 ... K5
Erie▲ 108,718 ... B1
Ernest 492 ... D4
Espy 1,430 ... K4
Etna 4,200 ... B6
Etters (Goldsboro) 477 ... J5
Evans City 2,054 ... B4
Everett 1,777 ... F5
Everson 939 ... C5
Exeter 5,691 ... F7
Export 981 ... C5
Factoryville 1,310 ... L2
Fairchance 1,918 ... C6
Fairfield 524 ... H6
Fairless Hills 9,026 ... N5
Falls Creek 1,087 ... E3
Farrell 6,841 ... A3
Fawn Grove 489 ... J6
Fayette City 713 ... C5
Fayetteville 3,033 ... G6
Felton 438 ... J6
Ferndale 2,020 ... E5
Finleyville 446 ... B5
Fleetwood 3,478 ... L5
Fleming (Unionville) 361 ... G4
Flemington 1,321 ... G3
Folcroft 7,506 ... M7
Folsom 8,173 ... M7
Ford City 3,413 ... D4
Ford Cliff 450 ... D4
Forest City 1,846 ... L2
Forest Hills 7,335 ... C7
Forty Fort 5,049 ... F7
Fountain Hill 4,637 ... L4
Fox Chapel 5,319 ... C6
Frackville 4,700 ... K4
Franklin▲ 7,329 ... C3
Franklintown 373 ... H5
Fredericksburg 1,269 ... B2
Fredericktown 1,052 ... C6
Fredonia 683 ... B3
Freeburg 640 ... H4
Freedom 1,897 ... B4
Freeland 3,909 ... L3
Freemansburg 1,946 ... M4
Freeport 1,983 ... C4
Galeton 1,370 ... G2
Gallitzin 2,003 ... E4
Gap 1,226 ... L6
Garden View 2,687 ... H3
Garrett 520 ... D6
Geistown 2,749 ... E5
Gettysburg▲ 7,025 ... H6
Gilberton 953 ... K4
Girard 2,879 ... B2
Girardville 1,889 ... K4
Glassport 5,582 ... C7
Glen Lyon 2,082 ... E7
Glen Rock 1,688 ... J6
Glenolden 7,260 ... M7
Glenside 8,704 ... M5
Grampian 395 ... E4
Gratz 696 ... J4
Great Bend 704 ... L2
Greencastle 3,600 ... G6
Greensburg▲ 16,318 ... D5
Greentree 4,905 ... B7
Greenville 6,734 ... B3
Grove City 8,240 ... B3
Halifax 911 ... J5
Hallstead 1,274 ... L2
Hamburg 3,987 ... L4
Hanover 14,399 ... J6
Harmony 1,054 ... B4
Harrisburg (cap.)▲ 52,376 ... H5
Harrisville 862 ... B3
Harveys Lake 2,746 ... E7
Hastings 1,431 ... E4
Hatboro 7,382 ... M5
Hatfield 2,650 ... M5
Haverford• 52,371 ... M6
Havertown ... M6
Hawley 1,244 ... M3
Hawthorn 528 ... D3
Hazleton 24,730 ... L4
Heidelberg 1,238 ... B7
Hellam (Hallam) 1,428 ... J6
Hellertown 5,662 ... M4
Herndon 422 ... J4
Hershey 11,860 ... J5
Highland Park 1,583 ... H4
Highspire 2,668 ... J5
Hollidaysburg▲ 5,624 ... F5
Homer City 1,809 ... D4
Homestead 4,179 ... B7
Honesdale▲ 4,972 ... M2
Honey Brook 1,184 ... L5
Hooversville 731 ... E5
Hop Bottom 345 ... L2
Hopwood 2,021 ... C6
Houston 1,445 ... B5
Houtzdale 1,204 ... F4
Howard 749 ... G3
Hughestown 1,734 ... F7
Hughesville 2,049 ... J3
Hummelstown 3,981 ... J5
Huntingdon▲ 6,843 ... G5
Hyde 1,643 ... F4
Hyde Park 542 ... D4
Hydetown 681 ... C2
Hyndman 1,019 ... E6
Imperial-Enlow 3,449 ... B5
Indian Lake 388 ... E5
Indiana▲ 15,174 ... D4
Industry 2,124 ... B4
Ingram 3,901 ... B7
Irvona 666 ... E4
Irwin 4,604 ... C5
Jacobus 1,370 ... J6
Jamestown 761 ... A3
Jeannette 11,221 ... C5
Jenkintown 4,574 ... M5
Jennerstown 635 ... D5
Jermyn 2,263 ... L2
Jerome 1,074 ... D5
Jersey Shore 4,353 ... H3
Jessup 4,605 ... F6
Jim Thorpe (Mauch Chunk)▲ 5,048 ... L4

(continued on following page)

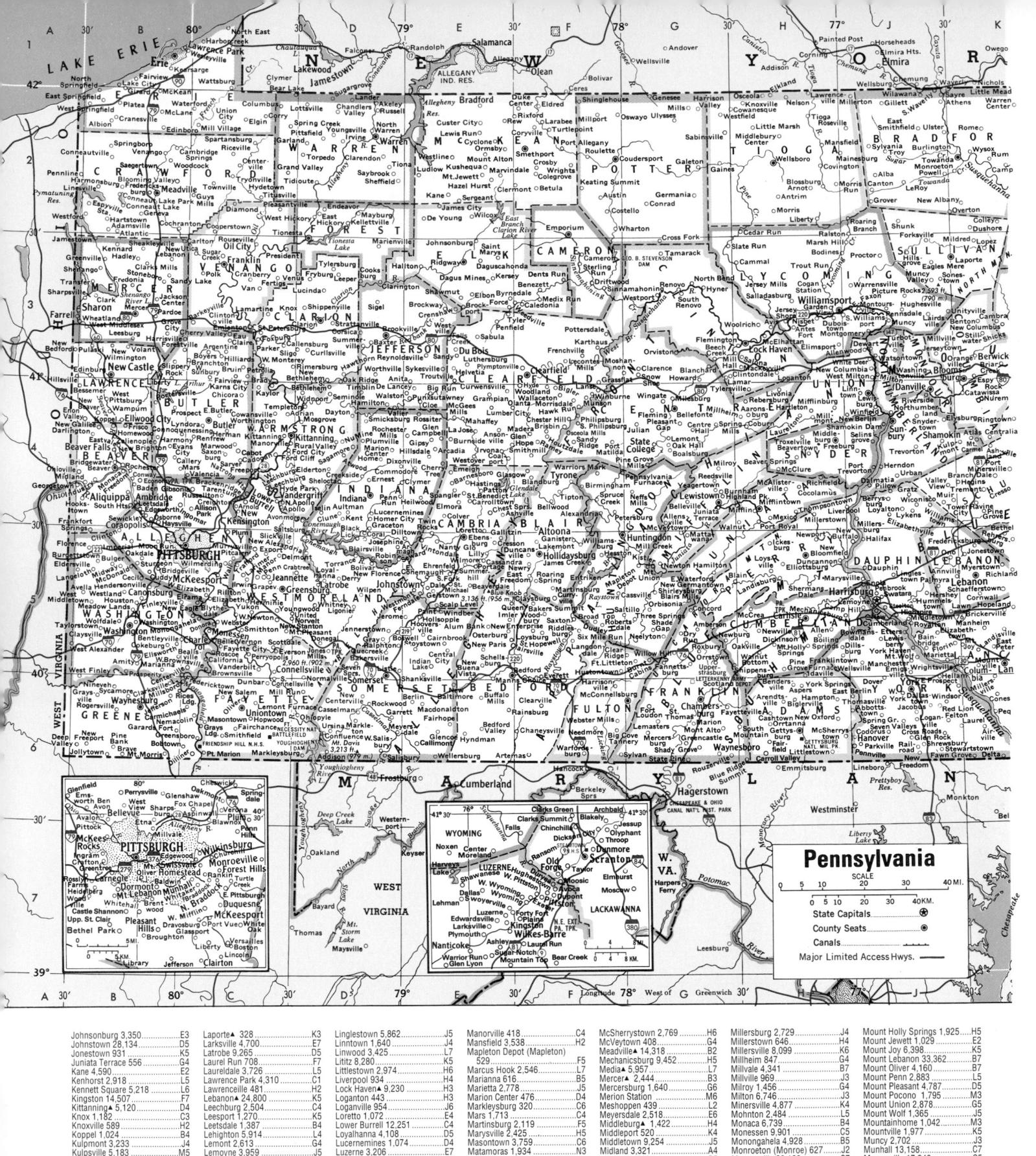

Pennsylvania

SCALE
5 10   20   30   40 MI.
0 5 10   20   30   40KM.

State Capitals............⊛
County Seats.............◉
Canals.....................
Major Limited Access Hwys.———

© Copyright HAMMOND INCORPORATED, Maplewood, N.J.

Petersburg 469	G4	
Philadelphia ▲ 1,585,577	N6	
Philipsburg 3,048	F4	
Phoenixville 15,066	L5	
Picture Rocks 660	J3	
Pillow 341	J4	
Pine Grove 2,118	K4	
Pine Grove Mills 1,129	G4	
Pitcairn 4,087	C5	
Pittsburgh ▲ 369,879	B7	
Pittston 9,389	F7	
Plains 4,694	F7	
Platea 467	B2	
Pleasant Gap 1,699	G4	
Pleasant Hills 8,884	B7	
Plum 25,609	C5	
Plumville 390	D4	
Plymouth 7,134	E7	
Plymptonville 1,074	E3	
Pocono Pines 824	M3	
Point Marion 1,344	C6	
Polk 1,267	C3	
Port Allegany 2,391	F2	
Port Carbon 2,134	K4	
Port Matilda 669	H4	
Port Royal 836	H4	
Port Vue 4,641	C7	
Portage 3,105	E5	
Portland 516	M4	
Pottstown 21,831	L5	
Pottsville ▲ 16,603	K4	
Prospect 1,122	B4	
Prospect Park 6,764	M7	
Punxsutawney 6,782	E4	
Quakertown 8,982	M5	
Quarryville 1,642	K6	
Ramey 536	F4	
Rankin 2,503	C7	
Reading ▲ 78,380	L5	
Reamstown 2,649	K5	
Red Hill 1,794	L5	
Red Lion 6,130	J6	
Reedsville 1,023	G4	
Renovo 1,526	G3	
Reynoldsville 2,818	D3	
Rices Landing 457	C6	
Richland 1,457	K5	
Richlandtown 1,195	M5	
Ridgway ▲ 4,793	E3	
Ridley Park 7,592	M7	
Riegelsville 912	M4	
Rimersburg 1,053	D3	
Ringtown 853	K4	
Riverside 1,991	J4	
Roaring Spring 2,615	F5	
Robesonia 1,944	K5	
Rochester 4,156	B4	
Rockledge 2,679	M5	
Rockwood 1,014	D6	
Rome 475	K2	
Roscoe 872	C5	
Rose Valley 982	L7	
Roseto 1,555	M4	
Rosslyn Farms 483	B7	
Rouseville 583	C3	
Rouzerville 1,188	G6	
Royalton 1,120	J5	
Royersford 4,458	L5	
Rural Valley 957	D4	
Russellton 1,691	C4	
Rutledge 843	M7	
Saegertown 1,066	B2	
Saint Clair 3,524	K4	
Saint Marys 5,511	E3	
Saint Michael-Sidman 1,189	E5	
Saint Petersburg 349	C3	
Salisbury 716	D6	
Saltillo 347	G5	
Saltsburg 990	C4	
Sandy 1,795	E3	
Sandy Lake 722	B3	
Saxonburg 1,345	C4	
Saxton 838	F5	
Sayre 5,791	K2	
Scalp Level 1,158	E5	

Schnecksville 1,780	L4	
Schuylkill Haven 5,610	K4	
Schwenksville 1,326	L5	
Scottdale 5,184	C5	
Scranton ▲ 81,805	F7	
Selinsgrove 5,384	J4	
Sellersville 4,479	M5	
Seven Valleys 483	J6	
Seward 522	D5	
Sewickley 4,134	B4	
Shamokin 9,184	J4	
Shamokin Dam 1,690	J4	
Sharon 17,493	B3	
Sharon Hill 5,771	N7	
Sharpsburg 3,781	C5	
Sharpsville 4,729	A3	
Sheffield 1,294	F2	
Shenandoah 6,221	K4	
Shickshinny 1,108	K4	
Shillington 5,062	K5	
Shinglehouse 1,243	F2	
Shippensburg 5,331	H5	
Shippenville 474	D3	
Shoemakersville 1,443	K4	
Shrewsbury 2,672	J6	
Sinking Spring 2,467	K5	
Skippack 2,042	M5	
Slatington 4,678	L4	
Slickville 1,178	C5	
Sligo 706	C3	
Slippery Rock 3,008	B3	
Smethport ▲ 1,734	F2	
Smithfield 1,000	C6	
Smithton 388	C5	
Snow Shoe 800	G3	
Snydertown 416	J4	
Somerset ▲ 6,454	D6	
Souderton 5,957	M5	
South Bethlehem 479	D4	
South Connellsville 2,204	C6	
South Fork 1,197	E5	
South Heights 647	B4	
South Philipsburg 438	F4	
South Renovo 579	G3	
South Waverly 1,040	J2	
South Williamsport 6,496	J3	
Spangler 2,068	E4	
Spartansburg 403	C2	
Spring City 3,433	L5	
Spring Grove 1,863	J6	
Springboro 557	B2	
Springdale 3,992	C6	
Springfield 24,160	M7	
State College 38,923	G4	
State Line 1,253	H6	
Steelton 5,152	J5	
Stewartstown 1,308	K6	
Stockertown 641	M4	
Stoneboro 1,091	B3	
Stowe 3,598	L5	
Stoystown 389	D5	
Strasburg 2,568	K6	
Strattanville 490	D3	
Strausstown 353	K5	
Stroudsburg 5,312	M4	
Sturgeon 1,312	B5	
Sugar Creek 5,532	C3	
Sugar Notch 1,044	E7	
Sugargrove 630	D1	
Summerhill 614	E5	
Summerville 675	D3	
Summit Hill 3,332	L4	
Sunbury ▲ 11,591	J4	
Susquehanna 1,994	L2	
Swarthmore 6,157	M7	
Swatara ▲ 18,796	J5	
Swissvale 10,637	C7	
Sykesville 1,387	E3	
Tamaqua 7,943	L4	
Tarentum 5,674	C4	
Tatamy 873	M4	
Taylor 6,941	F7	
Telford 4,238	M5	
Temple 1,491	L5	

Terre Hill 1,282	L5	
Thompsontown 582	H4	
Three Springs 422	G5	
Throop 4,070	F7	
Tidioute 791	D2	
Tioga 638	H2	
Tionesta ▲ 634	C2	
Tipton 1,194	F4	
Titusville 6,434	C2	
Topton 1,987	L5	
Toughkenamon 1,273	L6	
Towanda ▲ 3,242	J2	
Tower City 1,518	J4	
Townville 358	C2	
Trafford 3,345	C5	
Trainer 2,271	M7	
Tremont 1,814	K4	
Tresckow 1,033	K4	
Trevorton 2,058	J4	
Troy 1,262	J2	
Trumbauersville 894	M5	
Tullytown 2,339	N5	
Tunkhannock ▲ 2,251	J2	
Turbotville 675	J3	
Turtle Creek 6,556	C7	
Tyrone 5,743	F4	
Ulysses (Lewisville) 653	G2	
Union City 3,537	C2	
Uniontown ▲ 12,034	C6	
Upland 3,334	M7	
Upper Darby ▲ 84,054	M6	
Upper Saint Claire ▲ 19,023	B7	
Valencia 364	C4	
Valley View 1,749	J4	
Vanderbilt 545	C6	
Vandergrift 5,904	D4	
Vandling 660	M2	
Verona 3,360	C6	
Versailles 2,150	C7	
Villanova	M6	
Vintondale 582	E5	
Wall 853	C5	
Walnutport 2,055	L4	
Wampum 646	B4	
Warren ▲ 11,122	E2	
Warrior Run 656	E7	
Washington ▲ 15,864	B5	
Waterford 1,492	B2	
Watsontown 2,310	J3	
Wattsburg 486	C1	
Waymart 1,337	M2	
Wayne	M6	
Waynesboro 9,578	G6	
Waynesburg ▲ 4,270	B6	
Weatherly 2,640	L4	
Wellsboro ▲ 3,430	H2	
Wernersville 1,934	K5	
Wesleyville 3,655	C1	
West Brownsville 1,170	C5	
West Chester ▲ 18,041	L6	
West Elizabeth 634	C5	
West Grove 2,128	L6	
West Hazleton 4,136	L4	
West Kittanning 1,253	C4	
West Lawn 1,606	K5	
West Leechburg 1,359	C4	
West Middlesex 982	B3	
West Newton 3,152	C5	
West Pittsburg 1,133	B4	
West Pittston 5,590	F7	
West View 7,734	B6	
West Wyoming 3,117	F7	
West York 4,283	J6	
Westfield 1,119	H2	
Westmont 5,789	D5	
Westover 446	E4	
Wheatland 760	B3	
Whitaker 1,416	C7	
White Haven 1,132	L3	
White Oak 8,761	C7	
Whitehall 14,451	B7	
Wiconisco 1,321	J4	
Wilkes-Barre ▲ 47,523	F7	

Wilkinsburg 21,080	C7	
Williamsburg 1,456	F5	
Williamsport ▲ 31,933	H3	
Williamstown 1,509	J4	
Willow Grove 16,325	M5	
Wilmerding 2,421	C5	
Wilson 7,830	M4	
Windber 4,756	E5	
Windgap 2,651	M4	
Windsor 1,355	J6	
Wolfdale 2,906	B5	
Womelsdorf 2,270	K5	
Woodlyn 10,151	M7	
Worthington 713	C4	
Wrightsville 2,396	J5	
Wyalusing 686	K2	
Wyoming 3,255	E7	
Wyomissing 7,332	K5	
Yardley 2,288	N5	
Yeadon 11,980	N7	
Yeagertown 1,150	G4	
York Haven 758	J5	
York Springs 547	H6	
York ▲ 42,192	J6	
Youngsville 1,775	D2	
Youngwood 3,372	D5	
Zelienople 4,158	B4	

OTHER FEATURES

Allegheny (res.)	E2
Allegheny (riv.)	D2
Allegheny Front (mts.)	E5
Appalachian (mts.)	H4
Ararat (mt.)	M2
Arthur (lake)	C4
Beaver (riv.)	B4
Blue (mt.)	G5
Blue Knob (mt.)	E5
Casselman (riv.)	D6
Clarion (riv.)	D3
Conemaugh (riv.)	D5
Conemaugh River (lake)	D5
Conewango (creek)	D1
Davis (mt.)	D6
Delaware (riv.)	N3
Delaware Water Gap Nat'l Rec.	N3
Erie (lake)	B1
Fort Necessity Nat'l Battlefield	C6
George B. Stevenson (dam)	G3
Gettysburg Nat'l Mil. Park	H6
Glendale (lake)	F4
Juniata (riv.)	G5
Laurel Hill (mt.)	D5
Lehigh (riv.)	L3
Letterkenny Army Depot	G6
Licking (creek)	F6
Little Tinicum (isl.)	M7
Lycoming (creek)	H3
Monongahela (riv.)	C6
North (mt.)	K3
Ohio (riv.)	A4
Oil (creek)	C2
Pine (creek)	H2
Pine Grove (res.)	K6
Pocono (mts.)	M3
Pymatuning (res.)	A2
Redbank (creek)	E3
Schuylkill (riv.)	M5
Shenango River (lake)	B3
Sinnemahoning (creek)	F3
South (mt.)	H6
Steamtown Nat'l Hist. Site	F7
Susquehanna (riv.)	K6
Tioga (riv.)	H1
Tionesta Creek (lake)	D3
Towanda (creek)	J2
Tuscarora (mt.)	G5
Wallenpaupack (lake)	M3
Youghiogheny River (lake)	D6

▲County seat
• Population of town or township

New Beaver 1,736	B4	
New Berlin 892	J4	
New Bethlehem 1,151	D3	
New Bloomfield ▲	H5	
New Brighton 6,854	B4	
New Britain 2,174	M5	
New Castle ▲ 28,334	B3	
New Cumberland 7,665	J5	
New Eagle 2,172	B5	
New Florence 854	D5	
New Freedom 2,920	J6	
New Galilee 500	A4	
New Holland 4,484	K5	
New Hope 1,400	N5	
New Kensington 15,894	C4	
New Milford 953	L2	
New Oxford 1,617	H6	
New Philadelphia 1,283	K4	
New Salem (Delmont) 669	D5	
New Stanton 2,081	C5	
New Wilmington 2,706	B3	
Newport 1,568	H5	
Newtown 2,565	N5	
Newtown Square ▲ 11,775	L6	

Newville 1,349	H5	
Nicholson 857	L2	
Norristown ▲ 30,749	M5	
North Apollo 1,391	D4	
North Braddock 7,036	C7	
North Catasauqua 2,867	L4	
North East 4,617	C1	
North Wales 3,802	M5	
North Warren 1,232	D2	
Northampton 8,717	M4	
Northumberland 3,860	J4	
Norvelt 2,541	D5	
Norwood 6,162	M7	
Nuangola 701	E7	
Oakdale 1,752	B5	
Oakland 641	C6	
Oakmont 6,961	C6	
Ohioville 3,865	B4	
Oil City 11,949	C3	
Old Forge 8,834	F7	
Oliver 3,271	C6	
Olyphant 5,222	F7	
Orangeville 504	K3	
Orbisonia 447	G5	

Orwigsburg 2,780	K4	
Osborne 565	B4	
Osceola Mills 1,310	F4	
Oxford 3,769	K6	
Paint 1,091	E5	
Palmerton 5,394	L4	
Palmyra 6,910	J5	
Paoli 5,603	M5	
Paradise 1,107	K5	
Parker 853	C3	
Parkesburg 2,981	L6	
Parkside 2,369	M7	
Parkville 6,014	J6	
Patton 2,206	E4	
Pen Argyl 3,492	M4	
Penbrook 2,791	J5	
Penn 511	D5	
Penn Hills 51,430	C7	
Penn Wynne 5,807	M6	
Penndel 2,703	N5	
Pennsburg 2,460	M5	
Pennville 1,559	J6	
Perkasie 7,878	M5	
Perryopolis 1,833	C5	

Topography

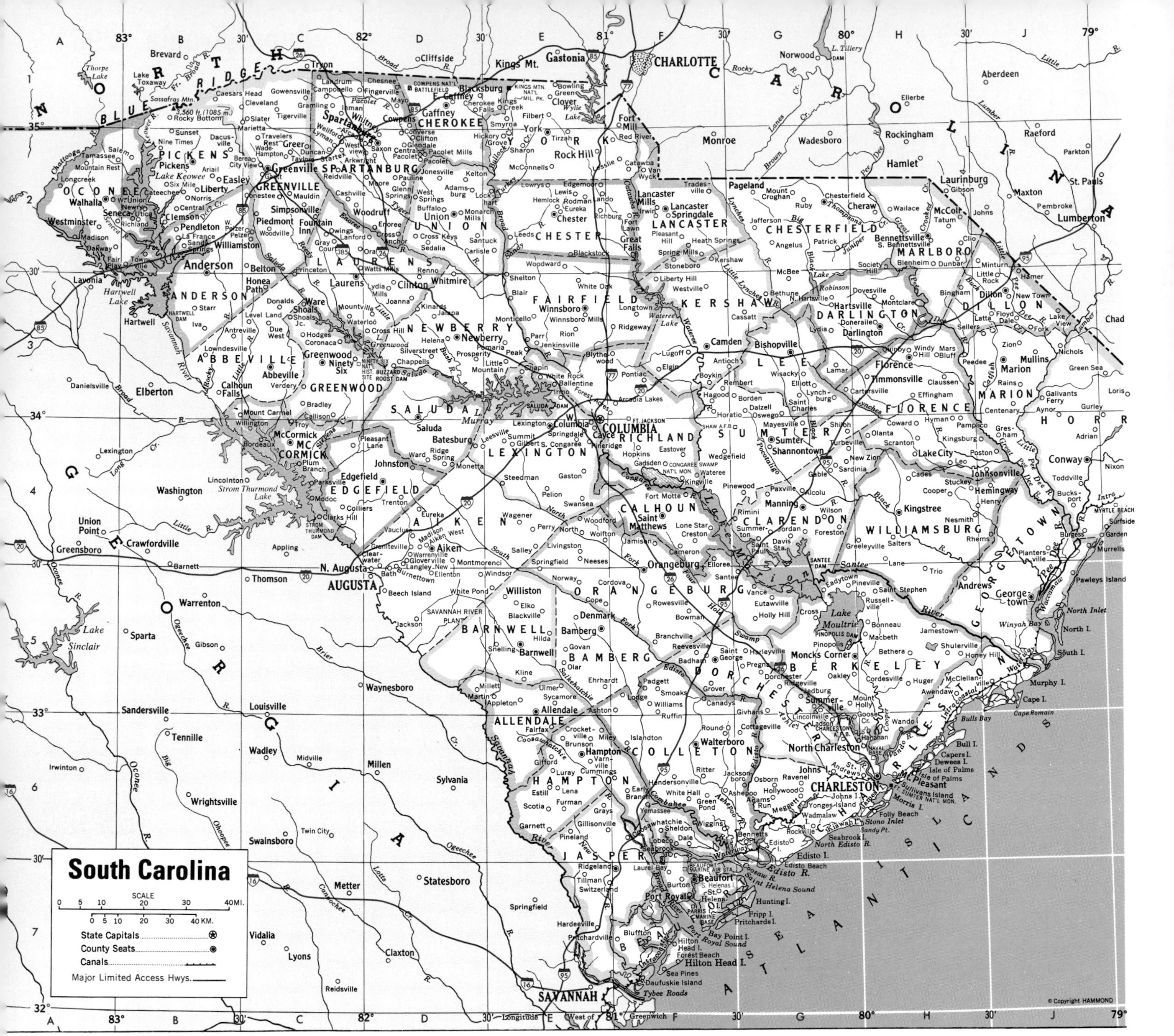

South Carolina

SCALE
0 5 10 20 30 40 MI.
0 5 10 20 30 40 KM.

State Capitals .... ⊛
County Seats .... ●
Canals ....
Major Limited Access Hwys. _____

Topography

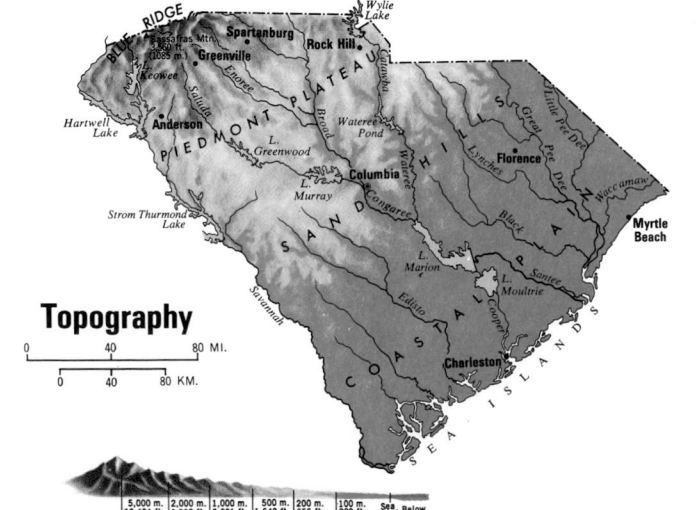

5,000 m. 2,000 m. 1,000 m. 500 m. 200 m. 100 m. Sea
16,404 ft. 6,562 ft. 3,281 ft. 1,640 ft. 656 ft. 328 ft. Level Below

COUNTIES

Abbeville 23,862 .... B3
Aiken 120,940 .... D4
Allendale 11,722 .... E6
Anderson 145,196 .... B2
Bamberg 16,902 .... E5
Barnwell 20,293 .... E5
Beaufort 86,425 .... F7
Berkeley 128,776 .... G5
Calhoun 12,753 .... F4
Charleston 295,039 .... H6
Cherokee 44,506 .... D1
Chester 32,170 .... E2
Chesterfield 38,577 .... F2
Clarendon 28,450 .... G4
Colleton 34,377 .... F6
Darlington 61,851 .... H3
Dillon 29,114 .... J3
Dorchester 83,060 .... G5
Edgefield 18,375 .... D4
Fairfield 22,295 .... E3
Florence 114,344 .... H4
Georgetown 46,302 .... J5
Greenville 320,167 .... C2
Greenwood 59,567 .... C3
Hampton 18,191 .... E6
Horry 144,053 .... J4
Jasper 15,487 .... E6
Kershaw 43,599 .... F3
Lancaster 54,516 .... F2
Laurens 58,092 .... D2
Lee 18,437 .... G3
Lexington 167,611 .... E4
Marion 33,899 .... J3
Marlboro 29,361 .... H2
McCormick 8,868 .... C4
Newberry 33,172 .... D3
Oconee 57,494 .... A2
Orangeburg 84,803 .... F5
Pickens 93,894 .... B2
Richland 285,720 .... F4
Saluda 16,357 .... D3
Spartanburg 226,800 .... D2
Sumter 102,637 .... G4
Union 30,337 .... D2
Williamsburg 36,815 .... H4
York 131,497 .... E2

CITIES and TOWNS

Abbeville▲ 5,778 .... C3
Adams Run 500 .... G6
Adamsburg 300 .... D2
Aiken West 3,083 .... D4
Aiken▲ 19,872 .... D4
Alcolu 600 .... G4
Allendale▲ 4,410 .... E5
Anderson 26,184 .... B2
Andrews 3,050 .... H5
Antioch 500 .... F3
Antreville 500 .... B3
Appleton 200 .... E5
Arcadia 899 .... C2
Arcadia Lakes 611 .... F3
Ariail 2,419 .... B2
Arkwright 2,623 .... C2
Atlantic Beach 446 .... K4
Awendaw 200 .... H5
Aynor 470 .... J3
Ballentine 550 .... E3
Bamberg▲ 3,843 .... E5
Barnwell▲ 5,255 .... E5
Batesburg 4,082 .... D4
Bath 2,242 .... D5
Beaufort▲ 9,576 .... F7
Beech Island 400 .... D5
Belton 4,646 .... C2
Bennettsville▲ 9,345 ...... H2
Berea 13,535 .... C2
Bethera 265 .... H5
Bethune 405 .... G3
Bingham 200 .... H3
Bishopville▲ 3,560 .... G3
Blacksburg 1,907 .... D1
Blackville 2,688 .... E5
Blenheim 191 .... H2
Bluffton 738 .... F7
Blythewood 164 .... E3
Bonneau 374 .... H5
Bowman 1,063 .... F5
Boykin 350 .... F4
Branchville 1,107 .... F5
Brunson 587 .... E6
Bucksport 1,022 .... J4
Buffalo 1,569 .... D2
Burgess 250 .... J4
Burnettown 493 .... D5
Burton 6,917 .... F7
Calhoun Falls 2,328 ...... B3
Camden▲ 6,696 .... F3
Cameron 504 .... F4
Campobello 465 .... C1
Canadys 130 .... F5
Carlisle 470 .... D2
Cashville 200 .... C2
Catawba 607 .... F2
Cateechee 225 .... B2
Cayce 11,163 .... E4
Centenary 700 .... J3
Central 2,438 .... B2
Central Pacolet 257 ...... D2
Chapin 282 .... D3
Chappells 45 .... D3
Charleston▲ 80,414 .... G6
Cheraw 5,505 .... H2
Cherokee Falls 250 .... D1
Chesnee 1,280 .... D1
Chester▲ 7,158 .... E2
Chesterfield▲ 1,373 ...... G2
City View 1,490 .... C2
Clarks Hill 300 .... C4
Claussen 500 .... H3
Clearwater 4,731 .... D5
Clemson 11,096 .... B2
Clifton 800 .... C2
Clio 882 .... H2
Clover 3,422 .... E1
Columbia (cap.)▲ 98,052 . F4

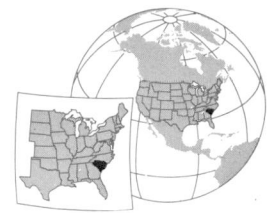

AREA 31,113 sq. mi. (80,583 sq. km.)
POPULATION 3,505,707
CAPITAL Columbia
LARGEST CITY Columbia
HIGHEST POINT Sassafras Mtn. 3,560 ft.
(1085 m.)
SETTLED IN 1670
ADMITTED TO UNION May 23, 1788
POPULAR NAME Palmetto State
STATE FLOWER Carolina (Yellow)
Jessamine
STATE BIRD Carolina Wren

INCORPORATED, Maplewood, N. J.

Agriculture, Industry and Resources

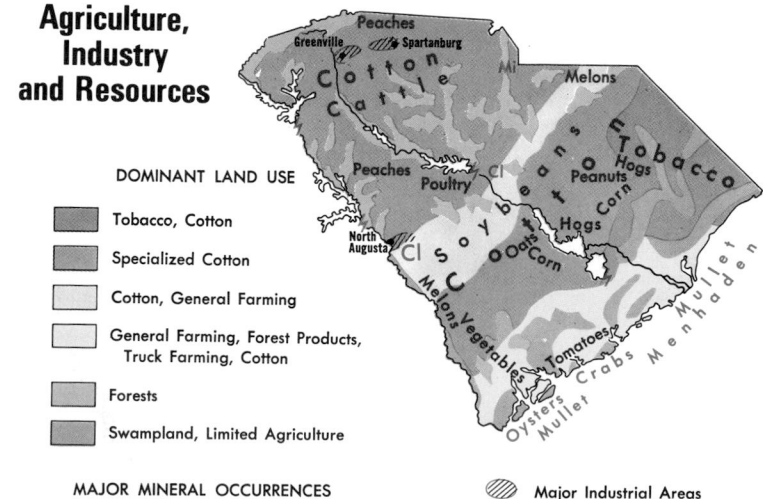

DOMINANT LAND USE

- Tobacco, Cotton
- Specialized Cotton
- Cotton, General Farming
- General Farming, Forest Products, Truck Farming, Cotton
- Forests
- Swampland, Limited Agriculture

MAJOR MINERAL OCCURRENCES

Cl Clay
Mi Mica

Major Industrial Areas
Water Power

COUNTIES

Aurora 3,135	M6
Beadle 18,253	N5
Bennett 3,206	F7
Bon Homme 7,089	O7
Brookings 25,207	R5
Brown 35,580	N2
Brule 5,485	L6
Buffalo 1,759	L5
Butte 7,914	B4
Campbell 1,965	J2
Charles Mix 9,131	M7
Clark 4,403	O4
Clay 13,186	R7
Codington 22,698	P4
Corson 4,195	G2
Custer 6,179	B6
Davison 17,503	N6
Day 6,978	O3
Deuel 4,522	R4
Dewey 5,523	G3
Douglas 3,746	N7
Edmunds 4,356	L3
Fall River 7,353	B7
Faulk 2,744	L3
Grant 8,372	R3
Gregory 5,359	L7
Haakon 2,624	F5
Hamlin 4,974	R5
Hand 4,272	L4
Hanson 2,994	N6
Harding 1,669	B2
Hughes 14,817	J3
Hutchinson 8,262	O7
Hyde 1,696	K4
Jackson 2,811	F6
Jerauld 2,425	M5
Jones 1,324	H6
Kingsbury 5,925	O5
Lake 10,550	P5
Lawrence 20,655	B5
Lincoln 15,427	R7
Lyman 3,638	J6
Marshall 4,844	O2
McCook 5,688	P6
McPherson 3,228	L2
Meade 21,878	D5
Mellette 2,137	H6
Miner 3,272	O5
Minnehaha 123,809	R6
Moody 6,507	R5
Pennington 81,343	C6
Perkins 3,932	D3
Potter 3,190	J3
Roberts 9,914	P2
Sanborn 2,833	N5
Shannon 9,902	D7
Spink 7,981	N4
Stanley 2,453	H5
Sully 1,589	J4
Todd 8,352	H7
Tripp 6,924	J7
Turner 8,576	P7
Union 10,189	R8
Walworth 6,087	J3
Yankton 19,252	P7
Ziebach 2,220	F4

CITIES and TOWNS

Aberdeen▲ 24,927	M3
Agar 82	J4
Akaska 52	J3
Albee 15	S3
Alcester 843	R7
Alexandria▲ 518	O6
Allen 300	F7
Alpena 251	N5
Altamont 48	R4
Amherst 75	O2
Andover 106	O3
Ardmore 16	B7
Arlington 908	R5
Armour▲ 854	N7
Artas 28	K2
Artesian 217	O6
Ashton 148	N3
Astoria 155	S4
Aurora 619	R5
Avon 576	N8
Badger 114	P5
Baltic 666	R6
Bancroft 30	O4
Barnard 65	N2
Batesland 124	E7
Bath 175	N3
Belle Fourche▲ 4,335	B4
Belvidere 63	G6
Beresford 1,849	R7
Big Stone City 669	S3
Bison 451	E2
Black Hawk 1,995	C5
Blunt 342	J4
Bonesteel 297	M7
Bowdle 589	K3
Box Elder 2,680	D5
Bradley 117	O3
Brandon 3,543	R6
Brandt 123	R4
Brentford 69	N3
Bridgewater 533	P6
Bristol 419	O3
Britton▲ 1,394	O2
Broadland 40	N4
Brookings▲ 16,270	R5
Bruce 235	R5
Buffalo Gap 173	C6
Buffalo▲ 488	B2
Bullhead 179	G2
Burbank 90	R8
Burke▲ 756	L7
Bushnell 81	R5
Butler 17	P5
Camp Crook 146	B2
Canistota 608	P6
Canning 40	L5
Canova 172	O6
Canton▲ 2,787	R7
Caputa 50	D5
Carter 7	J7
Carthage 221	O5
Castlewood 549	R4
Cavour 166	N5
Center 887	P6
Centerville 892	R7
Central City 185	B5
Chamberlain▲ 2,347	L6
Chancellor 276	R7
Chelsea 33	M3
Cherry Creek 500	F4
Chester 375	R6
Claire City 85	P2
Claremont 135	N2
Clark▲ 1,292	O4
Clear Lake▲ 1,247	R4
Colman 482	R6
Colome 309	K7
Colton 657	P6
Columbia 133	N2
Conde 203	N3
Corona 118	R3
Corsica 619	N7

(continued on following page)

AREA 77,116 sq. mi. (199,730 sq. km.)
POPULATION 699,999
CAPITAL Pierre
LARGEST CITY Sioux Falls
HIGHEST POINT Harney Pk. 7,242 ft.
  (2207 m.)
SETTLED IN 1856
ADMITTED TO UNION November 2, 1889
POPULAR NAME Coyote State; Sunshine
  State
STATE FLOWER Pasqueflower
STATE BIRD Ring-necked Pheasant

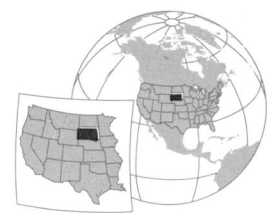

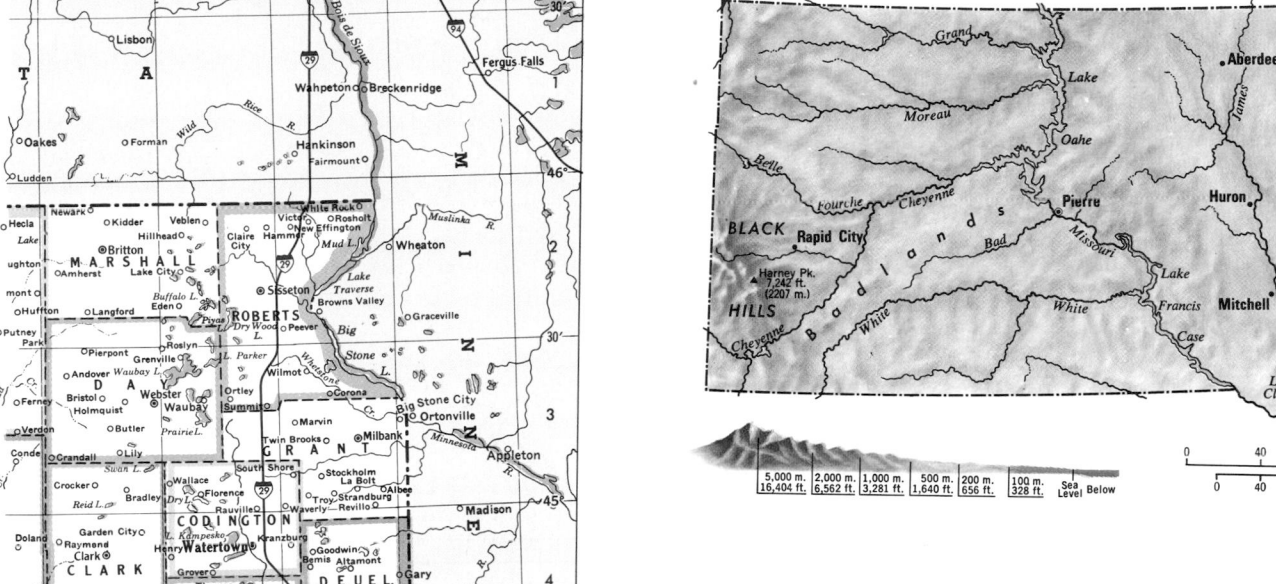

Topography

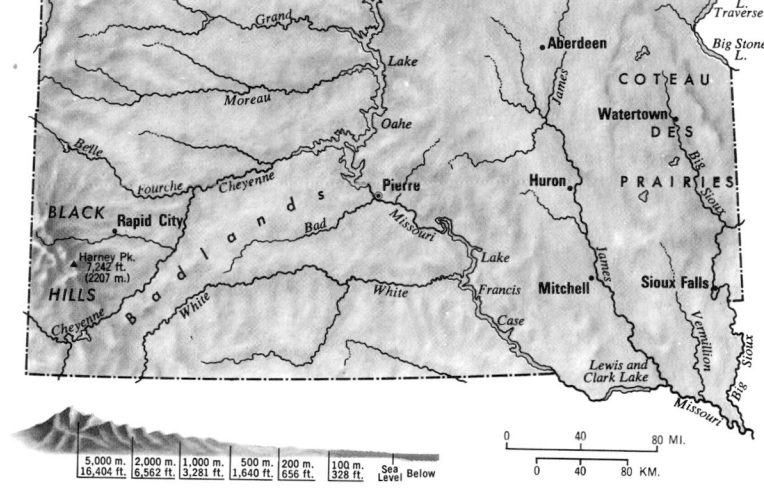

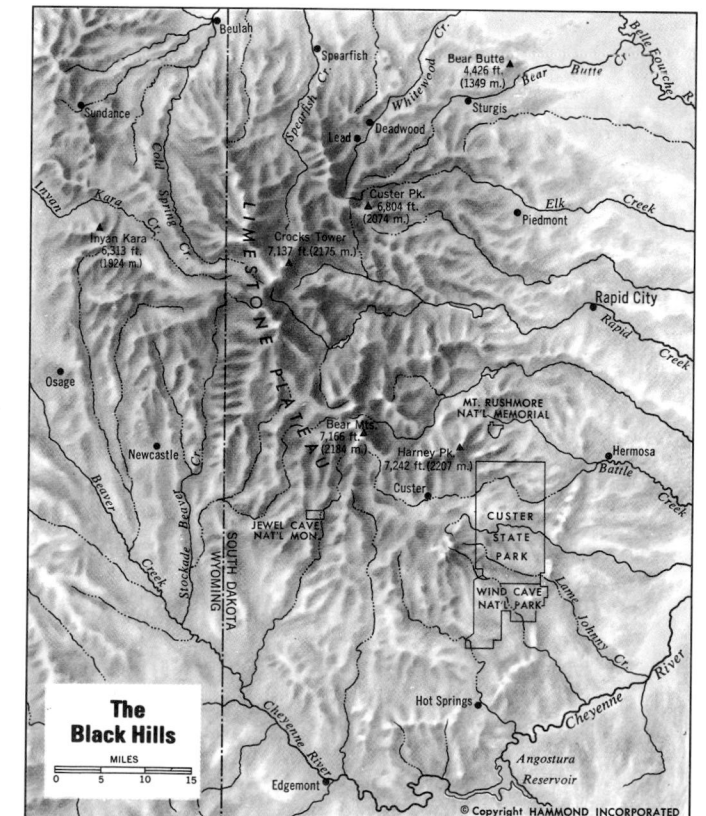

The Black Hills

MILES
0   5   10   15

© Copyright HAMMOND INCORPORATED

Agriculture, Industry and Resources

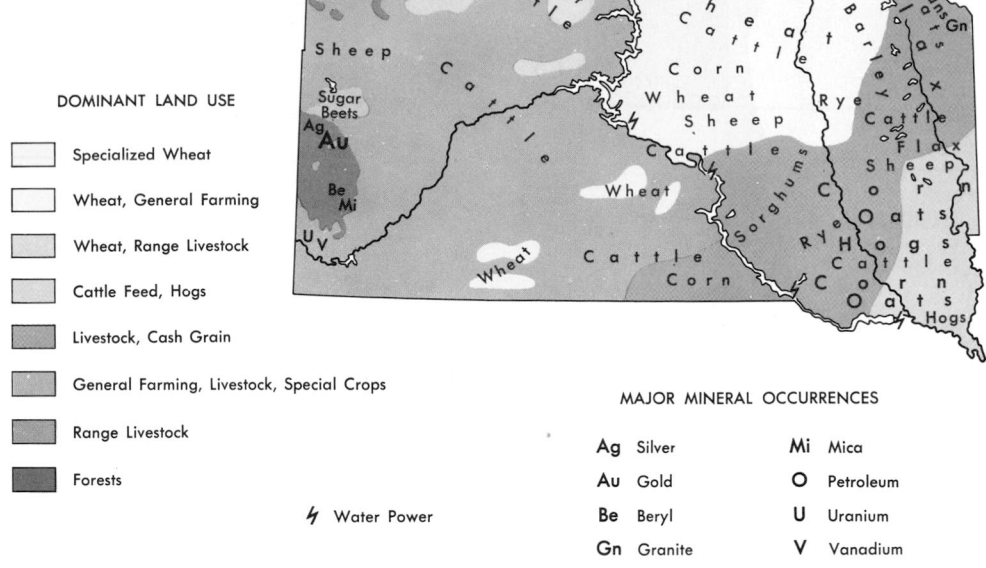

DOMINANT LAND USE

☐	Specialized Wheat
☐	Wheat, General Farming
☐	Wheat, Range Livestock
☐	Cattle Feed, Hogs
☐	Livestock, Cash Grain
☐	General Farming, Livestock, Special Crops
☐	Range Livestock
☐	Forests

⚡ Water Power

MAJOR MINERAL OCCURRENCES

Ag	Silver	Mi	Mica
Au	Gold	O	Petroleum
Be	Beryl	U	Uranium
Gn	Granite	V	Vanadium

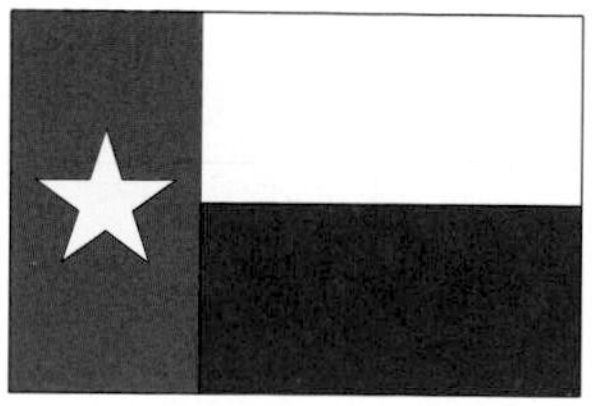

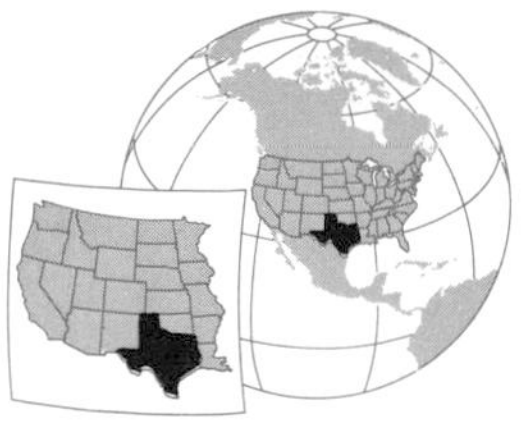

AREA 266,807 sq. mi. (691,030 sq. km.)
POPULATION 17,059,805
CAPITAL Austin
LARGEST CITY Houston
HIGHEST POINT Guadalupe Pk. 8,749 ft. (2667 m.)
SETTLED IN 1686
ADMITTED TO UNION December 29, 1845
POPULAR NAME Lone Star State
STATE FLOWER Bluebonnet
STATE BIRD Mockingbird

COUNTIES

- Anderson 48,024 J6
- Andrews 14,338 B5
- Angelina 69,884 K6
- Aransas 17,892 H10
- Archer 7,973 F4
- Armstrong 2,021 C3
- Atascosa 30,533 F9
- Austin 19,832 H8
- Bailey 7,064 B3
- Bandera 10,562 E8
- Bastrop 38,263 G7
- Baylor 4,385 E4
- Bee 25,135 G9
- Bell 191,088 G6
- Bexar 1,185,394 F8
- Blanco 5,972 F8
- Borden 799 C5
- Bosque 15,125 G6
- Bowie 81,665 K4
- Brazoria 191,707 J8
- Brazos 121,862 H7
- Brewster 8,681 A8
- Briscoe 1,971 C3
- Brooks 8,204 F11
- Brown 34,371 F6
- Burleson 13,625 H7
- Burnet 22,677 F7
- Caldwell 26,392 G8
- Calhoun 19,053 H9
- Callahan 11,859 E5
- Cameron 260,120 G11
- Camp 9,904 K5
- Carson 6,576 C2
- Cass 29,982 K4
- Castro 9,070 B3
- Chambers 20,088 K8
- Cherokee 41,049 J6
- Childress 5,953 D3
- Clay 10,024 F4
- Cochran 4,377 B4
- Coke 3,424 D6
- Coleman 9,710 E6
- Collin 264,036 H4
- Collingsworth 3,573 D3
- Colorado 18,383 H8
- Comal 51,832 F8
- Comanche 13,381 F5
- Concho 3,044 E6
- Cooke 30,777 G4
- Coryell 64,213 G6
- Cottle 2,247 D3
- Crane 4,652 B6
- Crockett 4,078 C7
- Crosby 7,304 C4
- Culberson 3,407 C11
- Dallam 5,461 B1
- Dallas 1,852,810 H5
- Dawson 14,349 C5
- De Witt 18,903 G9
- Deaf Smith 19,153 B3
- Delta 4,857 J4
- Denton 273,525 G4
- Dickens 2,571 D4
- Dimmit 10,433 E9
- Donley 3,696 D2
- Duval 12,918 F10
- Eastland 18,488 F5
- Ector 118,934 B6
- Edwards 2,266 D7
- El Paso 591,610 A10
- Ellis 85,167 H5
- Erath 27,991 F5
- Falls 17,712 H6
- Fannin 24,804 H4
- Fayette 20,095 H8
- Fisher 4,842 D5
- Floyd 8,497 C3
- Foard 1,794 E3
- Fort Bend 225,421 J8
- Franklin 7,802 J4
- Freestone 15,818 H6
- Frio 13,472 E9
- Gaines 14,123 B5
- Galveston 217,399 K8
- Garza 5,143 C4
- Gillespie 17,204 F7
- Glasscock 1,447 C6
- Goliad 5,980 G9
- Gonzales 17,205 G8
- Gray 23,967 D2
- Grayson 95,021 H4
- Gregg 104,948 K5
- Grimes 18,828 J7
- Guadalupe 64,873 G8
- Hale 34,671 C3
- Hall 3,905 D3
- Hamilton 7,733 F6
- Hansford 5,848 C1
- Hardeman 5,283 E3
- Hardin 41,320 K7
- Harris 2,818,199 J8
- Harrison 57,483 K5
- Hartley 3,634 B2
- Haskell 6,820 E4
- Hays 65,614 F7
- Hemphill 3,720 D2
- Henderson 58,543 J5
- Hidalgo 383,545 F11
- Hill 27,146 G5
- Hockley 24,199 B4
- Hood 28,981 G5
- Hopkins 28,833 J4
- Houston 21,375 J6
- Howard 32,343 C5
- Hudspeth 2,915 B10
- Hunt 64,343 H4
- Hutchinson 25,689 C2
- Irion 1,629 C6
- Jack 6,981 F4
- Jackson 13,039 H9
- Jasper 31,102 K7
- Jeff Davis 1,946 C11
- Jefferson 239,397 K8
- Jim Hogg 5,109 F11
- Jim Wells 37,679 F10
- Johnson 97,165 G5
- Jones 16,490 E5
- Karnes 12,455 G9
- Kaufman 52,220 H5
- Kendall 14,589 F8
- Kenedy 460 G11
- Kent 1,010 D4
- Kerr 36,304 E7
- Kimble 4,122 E7
- King 354 D4
- Kinney 3,119 D8
- Kleberg 30,274 G10
- Knox 4,837 E4
- La Salle 5,254 E9
- Lamar 43,949 J4
- Lamb 15,072 B3
- Lampasas 13,521 F6
- Lavaca 18,690 H8
- Lee 12,854 H7
- Leon 12,665 J6
- Liberty 52,726 K7
- Limestone 20,946 H6
- Lipscomb 3,143 D1
- Live Oak 9,556 F9
- Llano 11,631 F7
- Loving 107 A6
- Lubbock 222,636 C4
- Lynn 6,758 C4
- Madison 10,931 J6
- Marion 9,984 K5
- Martin 4,956 C5
- Mason 3,423 E7
- Matagorda 36,928 H9
- Maverick 36,378 D9
- McCulloch 8,778 E6
- McLennan 189,123 G6
- McMullen 817 F9
- Medina 27,312 E8
- Menard 2,252 E7
- Midland 106,611 B6
- Milam 22,946 H7
- Mills 4,531 F6
- Mitchell 8,016 D5
- Montague 17,274 G4
- Montgomery 182,201 J7
- Moore 17,865 C2
- Morris 13,200 K4
- Motley 1,532 D3
- Nacogdoches 54,753 K6
- Navarro 39,926 H5
- Newton 13,569 L7
- Nolan 16,594 D5
- Nueces 291,145 G10
- Ochiltree 9,128 D1
- Oldham 2,278 B2
- Orange 80,509 L7
- Palo Pinto 25,055 F5
- Panola 22,035 K5
- Parker 64,785 G5
- Parmer 9,863 B3
- Pecos 14,675 B7
- Polk 30,687 K7
- Potter 97,874 C2
- Presidio 6,637 C12
- Rains 6,715 J5
- Randall 89,673 C2
- Reagan 4,514 C6
- Real 2,412 E8
- Red River 14,317 J4
- Reeves 15,852 D11
- Refugio 7,976 G9
- Roberts 1,025 D2
- Robertson 15,511 H6
- Rockwall 25,604 H5
- Runnels 11,294 E6
- Rusk 43,735 K5
- Sabine 9,586 L6
- San Augustine 7,999 K6
- San Jacinto 16,372 J7
- San Patricio 58,749 G10
- San Saba 5,401 F6
- Schleicher 2,990 D7
- Scurry 18,634 D5
- Shackleford 3,915 E5
- Shelby 22,034 K6
- Sherman 2,858 C1
- Smith 151,309 J5
- Somervell 5,360 G5
- Starr 40,518 F11
- Stephens 9,010 F5
- Sterling 1,438 C6
- Stonewall 2,013 D4
- Sutton 4,135 D7
- Swisher 8,133 C3
- Tarrant 1,170,103 G5
- Taylor 119,655 E5
- Terrell 1,410 B7
- Terry 13,218 B4
- Throckmorton 1,880 E4
- Titus 24,009 K4
- Tom Green 98,458 D6
- Travis 576,407 G7
- Trinity 11,445 J6
- Tyler 16,646 K7
- Upshur 31,370 K5
- Upton 4,447 B6
- Uvalde 23,340 E8
- Val Verde 38,721 C8
- Van Zandt 37,944 J5
- Victoria 74,361 H9
- Walker 50,917 J7
- Waller 23,390 J8
- Ward 13,115 A6
- Washington 26,154 H7
- Webb 133,239 E10
- Wharton 39,955 H8
- Wheeler 5,879 D2
- Wichita 122,378 F3
- Wilbarger 15,121 E3
- Willacy 17,705 G11
- Williamson 139,551 G7
- Wilson 22,650 F8
- Winkler 8,626 A6
- Wise 34,679 G4
- Wood 29,380 J5
- Yoakum 8,786 B4
- Young 18,126 F4
- Zapata 9,279 E11
- Zavala 12,162 E9

CITIES and TOWNS

- Abernathy 2,720 B4
- Abilene▲ 106,654 E5
- Addison 8,783 G2
- Alamo 8,210 F11
- Alamo Heights 6,502 K10
- Albany▲ 1,962 E5
- Alice▲ 19,788 F10
- Allen 18,309 H1
- Alpine▲ 5,637 D12
- Alvarado 2,918 G5
- Alvin 19,220 J3
- Amarillo▲ 157,615 C2
- Anahuac▲ 1,993 K8
- Anderson▲ 500 J7
- Andrews▲ 10,678 B5
- Angleton▲ 17,140 J8
- Anson▲ 2,644 E5
- Anthony 3,328 A10
- Aransas Pass 7,180 G10
- Archer City▲ 1,748 F4
- Arlington 261,721 F2
- Aspermont▲ 1,214 D4
- Athens▲ 10,967 J5
- Atlanta 6,118 K4
- Austin (cap.)▲ 465,622 G7
- Azle 8,868 E2
- Bacliff 5,549 K2
- Baird▲ 1,658 E5
- Balch Springs 17,406 H2
- Balcones Heights 3,022 J10
- Ballinger▲ 3,975 E6
- Bandera▲ 877 F8
- Barrett 3,052 K1
- Bastrop▲ 4,044 G7
- Bay City▲ 18,170 H9
- Baytown 63,850 L2
- Beaumont▲ 114,323 K7
- Bedford 43,762 F2
- Beeville▲ 13,547 G9
- Bellaire 13,842 J2
- Bellmead 8,336 H6
- Bellville▲ 3,378 H8
- Belton▲ 12,476 G7
- Benavides 1,788 F10
- Benbrook 19,564 E2
- Benjamin▲ 225 E4
- Big Lake▲ 3,672 C6
- Big Spring▲ 23,093 C5
- Bishop 3,337 G10
- Bloomington 1,888 H9
- Blue Mound 2,133 E2
- Boerne▲ 4,274 J10
- Bonham▲ 6,686 H4
- Borger 15,675 C2
- Boston▲ 400 K4
- Bowie 4,990 G4
- Brackettville▲ 1,740 D8
- Brady▲ 5,946 E6
- Brazoria 2,717 J9
- Breckinridge▲ 5,665 F5
- Brenham▲ 11,952 H7
- Briar 3,899 E1
- Bridge City 8,034 L7
- Bridgeport 3,581 G4
- Brookshire 2,922 J8
- Brownfield▲ 9,560 B4
- Brownsville▲ 98,962 G12
- Brownwood▲ 18,387 F6
- Bryan▲ 55,002 H7
- Buda 1,795 G7
- Buna 2,127 L7
- Bunker Hill Village 3,391 J1
- Burkburnett 10,145 F3
- Burleson 16,113 F3
- Burnet▲ 3,423 F7
- Caldwell▲ 3,181 H7
- Cameron▲ 5,580 H7
- Canadian▲ 2,417 D2
- Canton▲ 2,949 J5
- Canutillo 4,442 A10
- Canyon▲ 11,365 C3
- Carrizo Springs▲ 5,745 E9
- Carrollton 82,169 G2
- Carthage▲ 6,496 K5
- Castle Hills 4,198 J10
- Castroville 2,159 J11
- Cedar Hill 19,976 G3
- Cedar Park 5,161 G7
- Center▲ 4,950 K6
- Centerville▲ 812 H6
- Channelview 25,564 K1
- Channing▲ 277 B2
- Childress▲ 5,055 D3
- Cisco 3,813 E5
- Clarendon▲ 2,067 C3
- Clarksville▲ 4,311 K4
- Claude▲ 1,199 C2
- Clear Lake Shores 1,096 K2
- Cleburne▲ 22,205 G5
- Cleveland 7,124 K7
- Clifton 3,195 G6
- Clute 8,910 J9
- Clyde 3,002 E5
- Cockrell Hill 3,746 G2
- Coldspring▲ 538 J7
- Coleman▲ 5,410 E6
- College Station▲ 52,456 H7
- Colleyville 12,724 F2
- Colorado City▲ 4,749 C5
- Columbus▲ 3,367 H8
- Comanche▲ 4,087 F6
- Commerce 6,825 J4
- Conroe▲ 27,610 J7
- Converse 8,887 K11
- Cooper▲ 2,153 J4
- Coppell 16,881 G2
- Copperas Cove 24,079 G6
- Corpus Christi▲ 257,453 G10
- Corsicana▲ 22,911 H5
- Cotulla▲ 3,694 E9
- Crane▲ 3,533 B6
- Crockett▲ 7,024 J6
- Crosby 1,811 J8
- Crosbyton▲ 2,026 C4
- Crowell▲ 1,230 E4
- Crowley 6,974 E3
- Crystal City▲ 8,263 E9
- Cuero▲ 6,700 G8
- Daingerfield▲ 2,572 K4
- Dalhart▲ 6,246 B1
- Dallas▲ 1,006,877 G2
- Dalworthington Gardens 1,758 F2
- Dayton 5,151 J7
- De Kalb 1,976 K4
- De Leon 2,190 F5
- De Soto 30,544 G3
- Decatur▲ 4,252 G4
- Deer Park 27,652 K2
- Del Rio▲ 30,705 D8
- Denison 21,505 H4
- Denton▲ 66,270 G4
- Denver City 5,145 B4
- Devine 3,928 E8
- Diboll 4,341 K6
- Dickens▲ 322 D4
- Dickinson 9,497 K3
- Dilley 2,632 E9
- Dimmitt▲ 4,408 B3
- Donna 12,652 F11
- Double Oak 1,664 F1

(continued on following page)

DOMINANT LAND USE

- Wheat, Grain Sorghums, Range Livestock
- Cotton, Wheat
- Specialized Cotton
- Cotton, General Farming
- Cotton, Forest Products
- Cotton, Range Livestock
- Rice, General Farming
- Peanuts, General Farming
- General Farming, Livestock, Cash Grain
- General Farming, Forest Products, Truck Farming, Cotton
- Fruit, Truck and Mixed Farming
- Range Livestock
- Forests
- Swampland, Limited Agriculture
- Nonagricultural Land
- Urban Areas

MAJOR MINERAL OCCURRENCES

- At Asphalt
- Cl Clay
- Fe Iron Ore
- G Natural Gas
- Gn Granite
- Gp Gypsum
- Gr Graphite
- He Helium
- Ls Limestone
- Na Salt
- O Petroleum
- S Sulfur
- Tc Talc
- U Uranium

- Water Power
- Major Industrial Areas

Agriculture, Industry and Resources

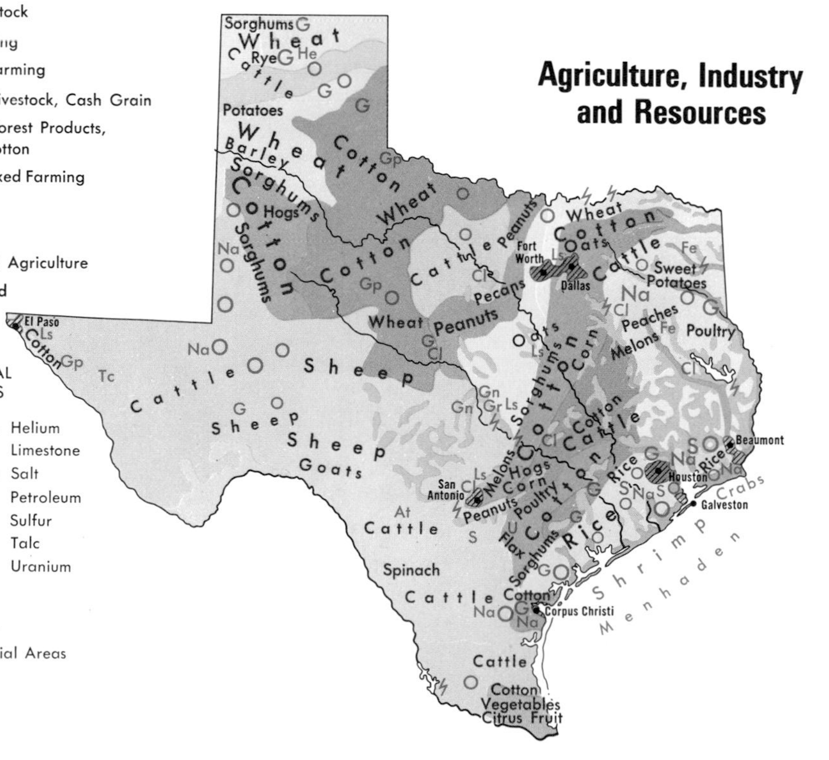

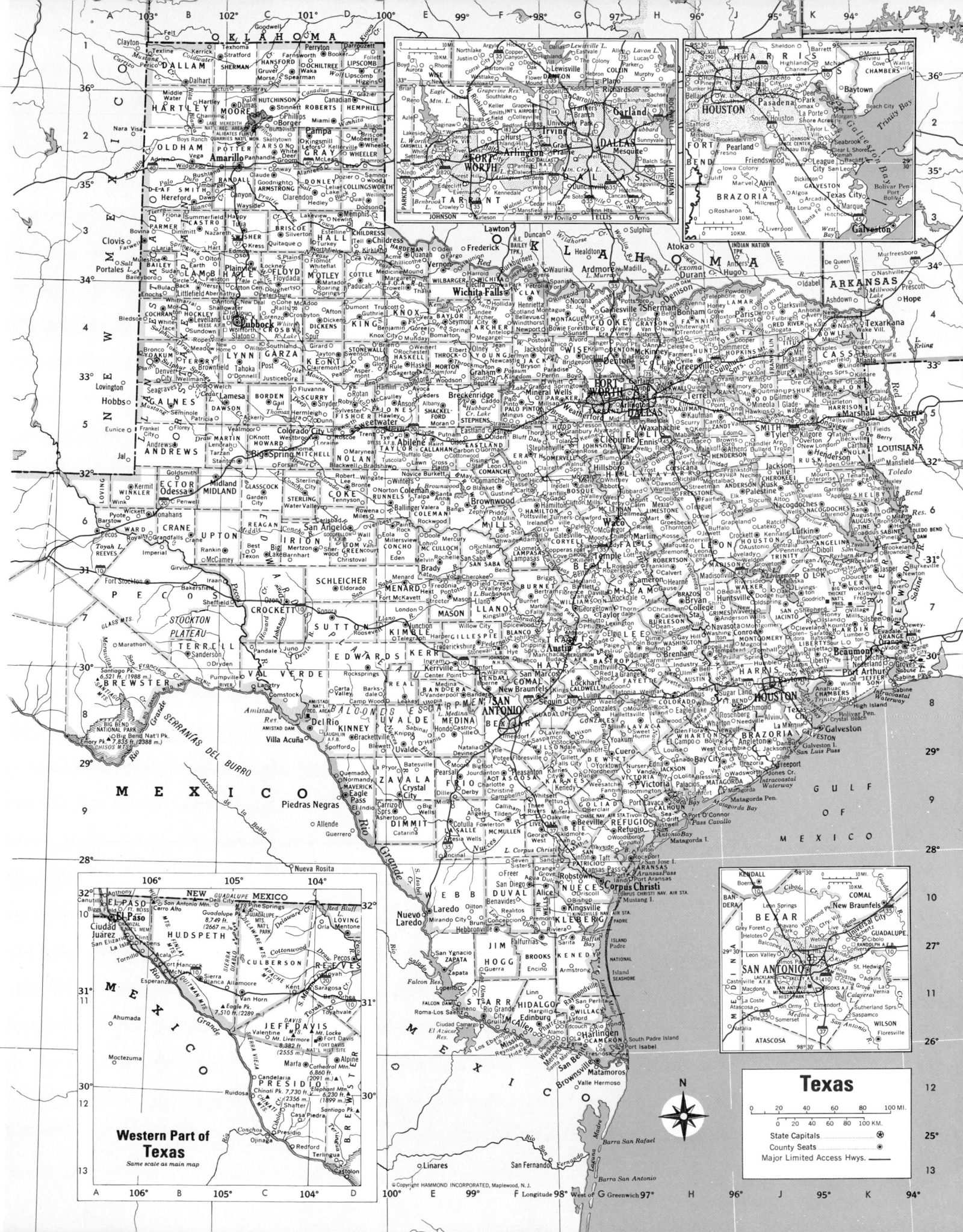

Texas

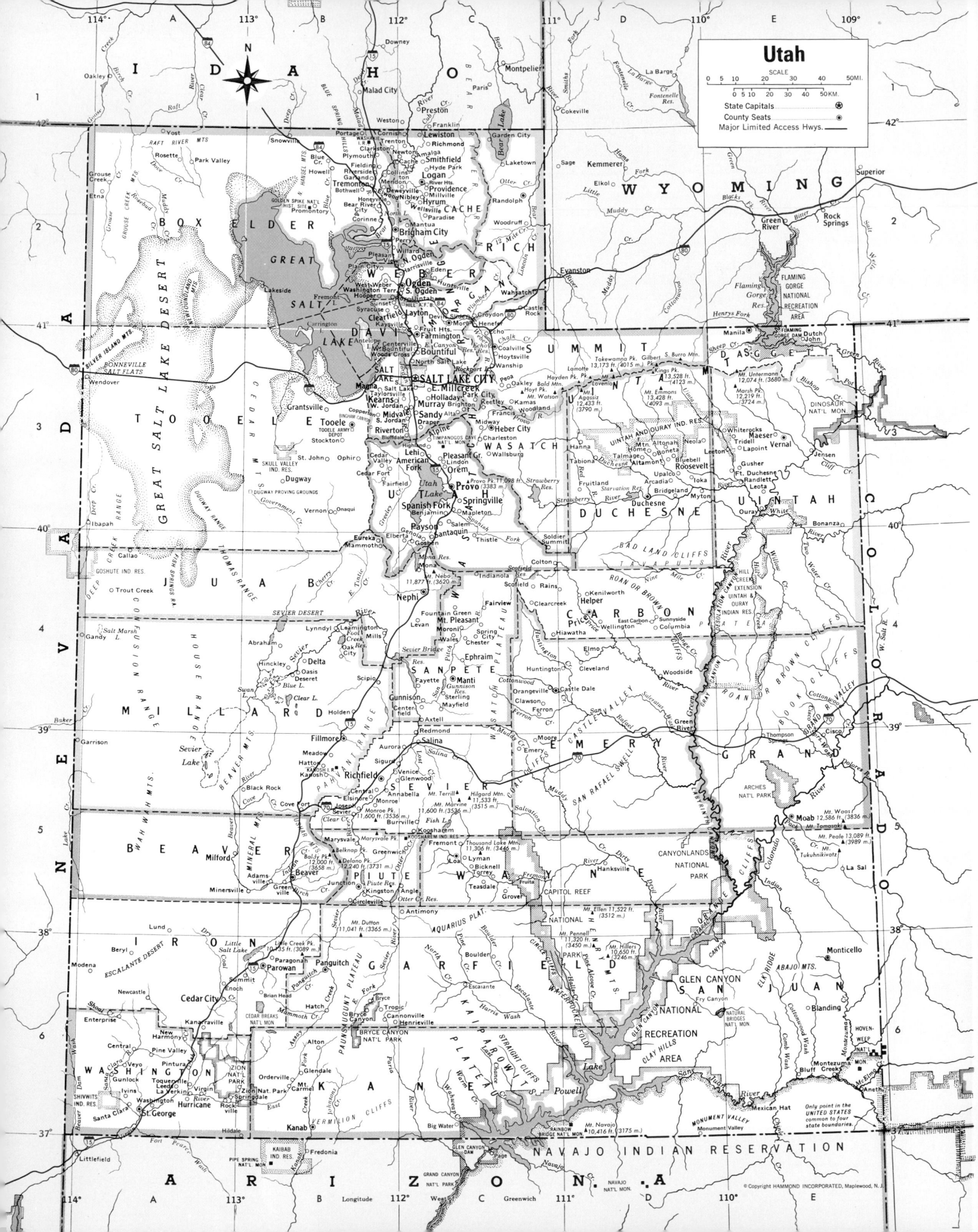

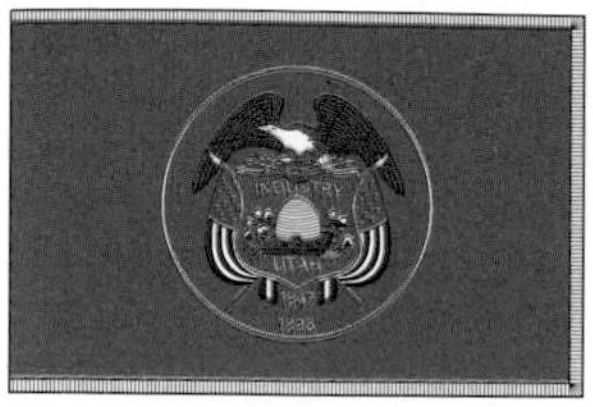

AREA 84,899 sq. mi. (219,888 sq. km.)
POPULATION 1,727,784
CAPITAL Salt Lake City
LARGEST CITY Salt Lake City
HIGHEST POINT Kings Pk. 13,528 ft. (4123 m.)
SETTLED IN 1847
ADMITTED TO UNION January 4, 1896
POPULAR NAME Beehive State
STATE FLOWER Sego Lily
STATE BIRD Sea Gull

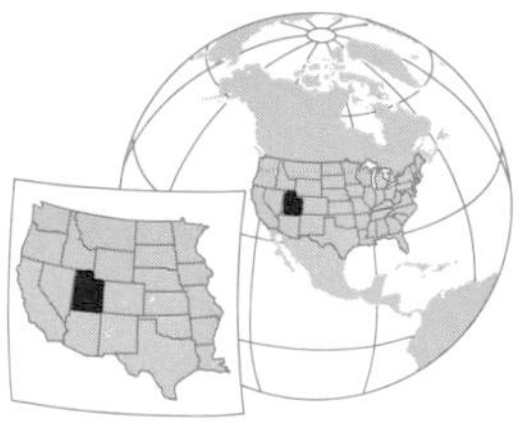

COUNTIES

Beaver 4,765 A5
Box Elder 36,485 A2
Cache 70,183 C2
Carbon 20,228 D4
Daggett 690 E3
Davis 187,941 B3
Duchesne 12,645 D3
Emery 10,332 D4
Garfield 3,980 C6
Grand 6,620 E5
Iron 20,789 A6
Juab 5,817 A4
Kane 5,169 B6
Millard 11,333 A4
Morgan 5,528 C2
Piute 1,277 B5
Rich 1,725 C2
Salt Lake 725,956 B3
San Juan 12,621 E6
Sanpete 16,259 C4
Sevier 15,431 C5
Summit 15,518 C5
Tooele 26,601 A3
Uintah 22,211 E3
Utah 263,590 C3
Wasatch 10,089 C3
Washington 48,560 A6
Wayne 2,177 C5
Weber 158,330 B2

CITIES and TOWNS

Alpine 3,492 C3
Alta 397 C3
Amalga 366 C2
American Fork 15,696 C3
Annabella 487 B5
Aurora 911 B5
Bear River City 700 B2
Beaver▲ 1,998 B5
Bicknell 327 C5
Big Water 326 C6
Blanding 3,162 E6
Bluffdale 2,152 B3
Bountiful 36,659 C3
Brigham City▲ 15,644 C2
Brighton 150 C3
Castle Dale▲ 1,704 D4
Castle Rock C2
Cedar City 13,443 A6
Cedar Fort 284 B3
Centerfield 766 C4
Centerville 11,500 C3
Charleston 336 C3
Circleville 417 B5
Clarkston 645 B2
Clearfield 21,435 B2
Cleveland 522 D4
Coalville▲ 1,065 C3
Corinne 639 B2
Delta 2,998 B4
Deweyville 318 B2
Draper 7,257 C3
Duchesne▲ 1,308 D3
Dugway 1,761 B3
East Carbon 1,270 D4
East Millcreek 21,184 C3
Elmo 267 D4
Elsinore 608 B5
Elwood 575 B2
Emery 300 C5
Enoch 1,947 A6
Enterprise 936 A6
Ephraim 3,363 C4
Escalante 818 C6
Eureka 562 B4
Fairview 960 C4
Farmington▲ 9,028 C4
Ferron 1,606 C4
Fielding 422 B2
Fillmore▲ 1,956 B5
Fort Duchesne 655 E3
Fountain Green 578 C4
Francis 381 C3
Fruit Heights 3,900 C2
Garden City 193 C2
Garland 1,637 B2
Genola 803 C4
Glendale 282 B6
Glenwood 437 C5
Goshen 578 C4
Grantsville 4,500 B3
Green River 866 D4
Gunnison 1,298 C4
Harrisville 3,004 C2
Heber City▲ 4,782 C3
Helper 2,148 D4
Henefer 554 C2
Highland 5,002 C3
Hildale 1,325 A6
Hinckley 658 B4
Holden 402 B4
Holladay 22,189 C3
Honeyville 1,112 B2
Hooper 3,468 B2
Howell 237 B2
Huntington 1,875 C4
Huntsville 561 C2
Hurricane 3,915 A6
Hyde Park 2,190 C2
Hyrum 4,829 C2
Ivins 1,630 A6
Joseph 198 B5
Junction▲ 132 B5
Kamas 1,061 C3
Kanab▲ 3,289 B6
Kanarraville 228 A6
Kanosh 386 B5
Kaysville 13,961 B2
Kearns 28,374 B3
Koosharem 266 C5
La Verkin 1,771 A6
Laketown 261 C2
Layton 41,784 C2
Leamington 253 B4
Leeds 254 A6
Lehi 8,475 C3
Levan 416 C4
Lewiston 1,532 C2
Lindon 3,818 C3
Loa▲ 444 C5
Logan▲ 32,762 C2
Lyman 198 C5
Maeser 2,598 E3
Magna 17,829 B3
Manila▲ 207 E3
Manti▲ 2,268 C4
Mantua 665 C2
Mapleton 3,572 C3
Marysvale 364 B5
Mayfield 438 C4
Meadow 250 B5
Mendon 684 B2
Mexican Hat 259 E6
Midvale 11,886 B3
Midway 1,554 A5
Milford 1,107 A5
Millville 1,202 C2
Minersville 608 A5
Moab▲ 3,971 E5
Mona 584 C4
Monroe 1,472 B5
Montezuma Creek 345 E6
Monticello▲ 1,806 E6
Morgan▲ 2,023 C2
Moroni 1,115 C4
Mount Pleasant 2,092 C4
Murray 31,282 C3
Myton 468 D3
Neola 511 D3
Nephi▲ 3,515 C4
Newton 659 C2
Nibley 1,167 C2
North Ogden 11,668 C2
North Salt Lake 6,474 C3
Oak City 587 B4
Oakley 522 C3
Ogden▲ 63,909 C2
Orangeville 1,459 C4
Orderville 422 B6
Orem 67,561 C3
Panguitch▲ 1,444 B6
Paradise 561 C2
Paragonah 307 B6
Park City 4,468 C3
Parowan▲ 1,873 B6
Payson 9,510 C3
Perry 1,211 C2
Plain City 2,722 B2
Pleasant Grove 13,476 C3
Pleasant View 3,603 B2
Plymouth 267 B2
Price▲ 8,712 D4
Providence 3,344 C2
Provo▲ 86,835 C3
Randlett 283 E3
Randolph▲ 488 C2
Redmond 648 C4
Richfield▲ 5,593 B5
Richmond 1,955 C2
River Heights 1,274 C2
Riverton 11,261 B3
Roosevelt 3,915 D3
Roy 24,603 C2
Saint George▲ 28,502 A6
Salem 2,284 C3
Salina 1,943 C5
Salt Lake City (cap.)▲ 159,936 C3
Sandy 75,058 C3
Santa Clara 2,322 A6
Santaquin 2,386 C4
Scipio 291 B4
Sigurd 385 B5
Smithfield 5,566 C2
South Jordan 12,220 B3
South Ogden 12,105 C2
South Salt Lake 10,129 C3
Spanish Fork 11,272 C3
Spring City 715 C4
Springdale 275 B6
Springville 13,950 C3
Stockton 426 B3
Sunnyside 339 D4
Sunset 5,128 B2
Syracuse 4,658 B2
Taylorsville-Bennion 52,351 B3
Tooele▲ 13,887 B3
Toquerville 488 A6
Tremonton 4,264 B2
Trenton 464 B2
Tropic 374 B6
Uintah 760 C2
Vernal▲ 6,644 E3
Wallsburg 252 C3
Washington 4,198 A6
Washington Terrace 8,189 B2
Wellington 1,632 D4
Wellsville 2,206 C2
Wendover 1,127 A3
West Bountiful 4,477 B3
West Jordan 42,892 B3
Whiterocks 312 E3
Willard 1,298 C2
Woods Cross 5,384 B3

OTHER FEATURES

Abajo (mts.) E6
Agassiz (mt.) D3
Antelope (isl.) B3
Aquarius (plat.) C5
Arches Nat'l Park E5
Assay (creek) B6
Bad Land (cliffs) D4
Baldy (peak) B5
Bear (lake) C2
Bear (riv.) B2
Beaver (mts.) A5
Beaver (riv.) A5
Beaver Dam Wash (creek) A6
Birch (creek) B5
Blue (creek) B2
Bonneville (salt flats) A3
Book (cliffs) E4
Bryce Canyon Nat'l Park B6
Canyonlands Nat'l Park D5
Capitol Reef Nat'l Park C5
Castle (valley) D4
Cedar (mts.) B3
Cedar Breaks Nat'l Mon. B6
Chalk (creek) C3
Chinle (creek) E6
Clear (lake) B4
Cliff (creek) E3
Coal (cliffs) C5
Colorado (riv.) E5
Confusion (range) A4
Cottonwood (creek) C4
Cub (creek) C1
Deep (creek) B1
Deep Creek (range) A4
Delano (peak) B5
Desolation (canyon) E4
Dinosaur Nat'l Mon. E3
Dirty Devil (riv.) D5
Dolores (riv.) E5
Dry Coal (creek) A6
Duchesne (riv.) D3
Dugway (range) A3
Dugway Proving Grounds B3
Dutton (mt.) B5
East Canyon (res.) C3
Echo (res.) C3
Elk (ridge) E6
Ellen (mt.) D5
Emmons (mt.) D3
Escalante (des.) A6
Escalante (riv.) C6
Fish (lake) C5
Fish Springs (range) A4
Flaming Gorge (res.) E3
Flaming Gorge Nat'l Rec. Area E2
Fool Creek (res.) B4
Fremont (isl.) B2
Fremont (riv.) C5
Glen Canyon Nat'l Rec. Area D6
Golden Spike Nat'l Hist. Site B2
Goshute Ind. Res. A4
Government (creek) B3
Gray (canyon) D4
Great Salt (lake) B2
Great Salt Lake (des.) A3
Greeley (creek) B3
Green (riv.) D4
Grouse (creek) A2
Grouse Creek (mts.) A2
Gunnison (res.) C4
Henry (mts.) D6
Hilgard (mt.) C5
Hill (creek) E4
Hill A.F.B. C2
Hill Creek Extension, Uintah and Ouray Ind. Res. E4
Hillers (mt.) D6
House (range) A4
Hovenweep Nat'l Mon. E6
Hoyt (peak) C3
Huntington (creek) C4
Indian (creek) B5
Jordan (riv.) C3
Kaiparowits (plat.) C6
Kanab (creek) B7
Kanosh Ind. Res. B5
Kings (peak) D3
Koosharem Ind. Res. C5
Little Creek (peak) B6
Little Salt (lake) A6
Malad (riv.) B1
Marsh (peak) E3
Marvine (mt.) C5
Mineral (mts.) B5
Mona (res.) C4
Monroe (peak) B5
Montezuma (creek) E6
Monument (valley) D6
Muddy (creek) C4
Natural Bridges Nat'l Mon. E6
Navajo (mt.) D6
Navajo Ind. Res. D7
Nebo (mt.) C4
Newfoundland (mts.) A2
Nine Mile (creek) D4
North (lake) B2
Orange (cliffs) D5
Otter (creek) C5
Otter Creek (res.) C5
Paria (riv.) B6
Paunsaugunt (plat.) B6
Pahvant (range) B5
Peale (mt.) E5
Pennell (mt.) D6
Piute (res.) B5
Plumber (creek) C2
Powell (lake) D6
Price (riv.) D4
Provo (peak) C3
Provo (riv.) C3
Raft River (mts.) A2
Rainbow Bridge Nat'l Mon. C6
Roan (cliffs) E4
Rockport (lake) C3
Salvation (creek) C5
San Juan (riv.) D6
San Pitch (riv.) C4
San Rafael (riv.) D4
San Rafael Swell (mts.) D5
Santa Clara (riv.) A6
Sevier (des.) B4
Sevier (lake) A5
Sevier (riv.) B4
Sevier Bridge (res.) C4
Shivwits Ind. Res. A6
Silver Island (mts.) A3
Skull Valley Ind. Res. B3
Spanish Fork (riv.) C3
Strait (cliffs) C6
Strawberry (res.) C3
Strawberry (riv.) D3
Swan (lake) B4
Tavaputs (plat.) D4
Thomas (range) A4
Thousand Lake (mt.) C5
Timpanogos Cave Nat'l Mon. C3
Tokewamna (peak) D3
Tooele Army Depot B3
Two Water (creek) E4
Uinta (mts.) D3
Uinta (riv.) D3
Uintah and Ouray Ind. Res. D3
Utah (lake) C3
Virgin (riv.) A6
Waas (mt.) E5
Wah Wah (mts.) A5
Wasatch (range) C3
Washakie Ind. Res. B2
Waterpocket Fold (cliffs) D6
Weber (riv.) C3
White (riv.) E3
Willow (creek) E4
Zion Nat'l Park A6

▲County seat

Agriculture, Industry and Resources

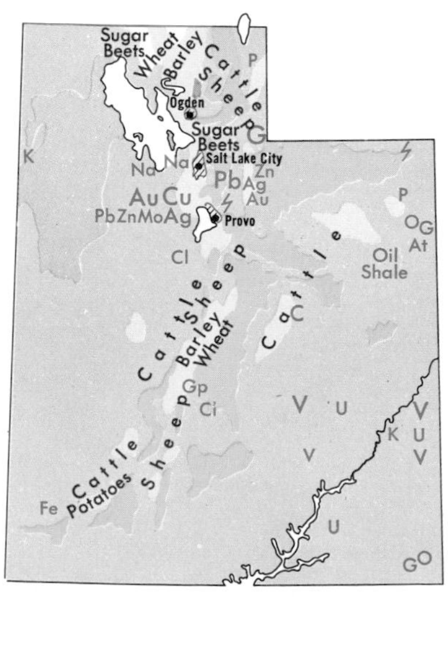
Sugar Beets
Wheat
Barley
Cattle
Sheep
Ogden
Salt Lake City
Provo
Oil Shale
Potatoes
DOMINANT LAND USE
Wheat, General Farming
General Farming, Livestock, Special Crops
Range Livestock
Forests
Nonagricultural Land
MAJOR MINERAL OCCURRENCES
Ag Silver
At Asphalt
Au Gold
C Coal
Cl Clay
Cu Copper
Fe Iron Ore
G Natural Gas
Gp Gypsum
K Potash
Mo Molybdenum
Na Salt
O Petroleum
P Phosphates
Pb Lead
U Uranium
V Vanadium
Zn Zinc
Water Power
Major Industrial Areas

Topography

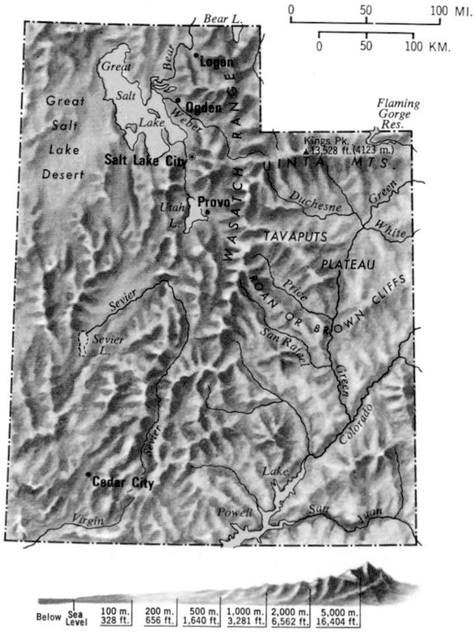
0 50 100 MI.
0 50 100 KM.
Bear L.
Great Salt Lake
Great Salt Lake Desert
Logan
Ogden
Salt Lake City
Provo
Utah L.
WASATCH RANGE
Flaming Gorge Res.
Kings Pk. 13,528 ft. (4123 m.)
UINTA MTS.
Duchesne
Green
White
TAVAPUTS PLATEAU
Price
ROAN OR BROWN CLIFFS
San Rafael
Sevier
Sevier L.
Colorado
Cedar City
Virgin
Lake Powell
San Juan
Below Sea Level
100 m. 328 ft.
200 m. 656 ft.
500 m. 1,640 ft.
1,000 m. 3,281 ft.
2,000 m. 6,562 ft.
5,000 m. 16,404 ft.

Topography

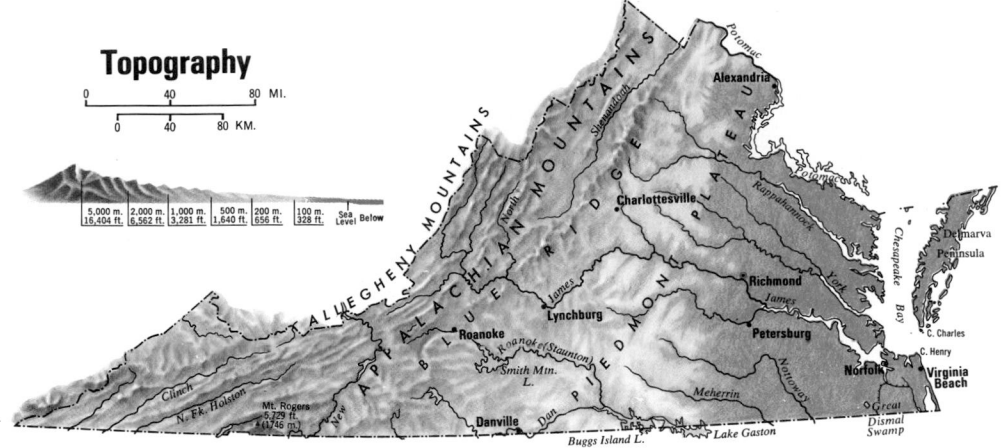

```
0    40   80 MI.
0    40   80 KM.
```

5,000 m. 2,000 m. 1,000 m. 500 m. 200 m. 100 m. Sea Level Below
16,404 ft. 6,562 ft. 3,281 ft. 1,640 ft. 656 ft. 328 ft.

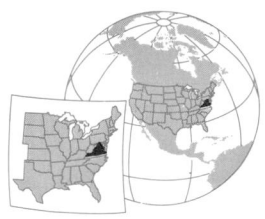

AREA 40,767 sq. mi. (105,587 sq. km.)
POPULATION 6,216,568
CAPITAL Richmond
LARGEST CITY Norfolk
HIGHEST POINT Mt. Rogers 5,729 ft. (1746 m.)
SETTLED IN 1607
ADMITTED TO UNION June 26, 1788
POPULAR NAME Old Dominion
STATE FLOWER Dogwood
STATE BIRD Cardinal

(continued on following page)

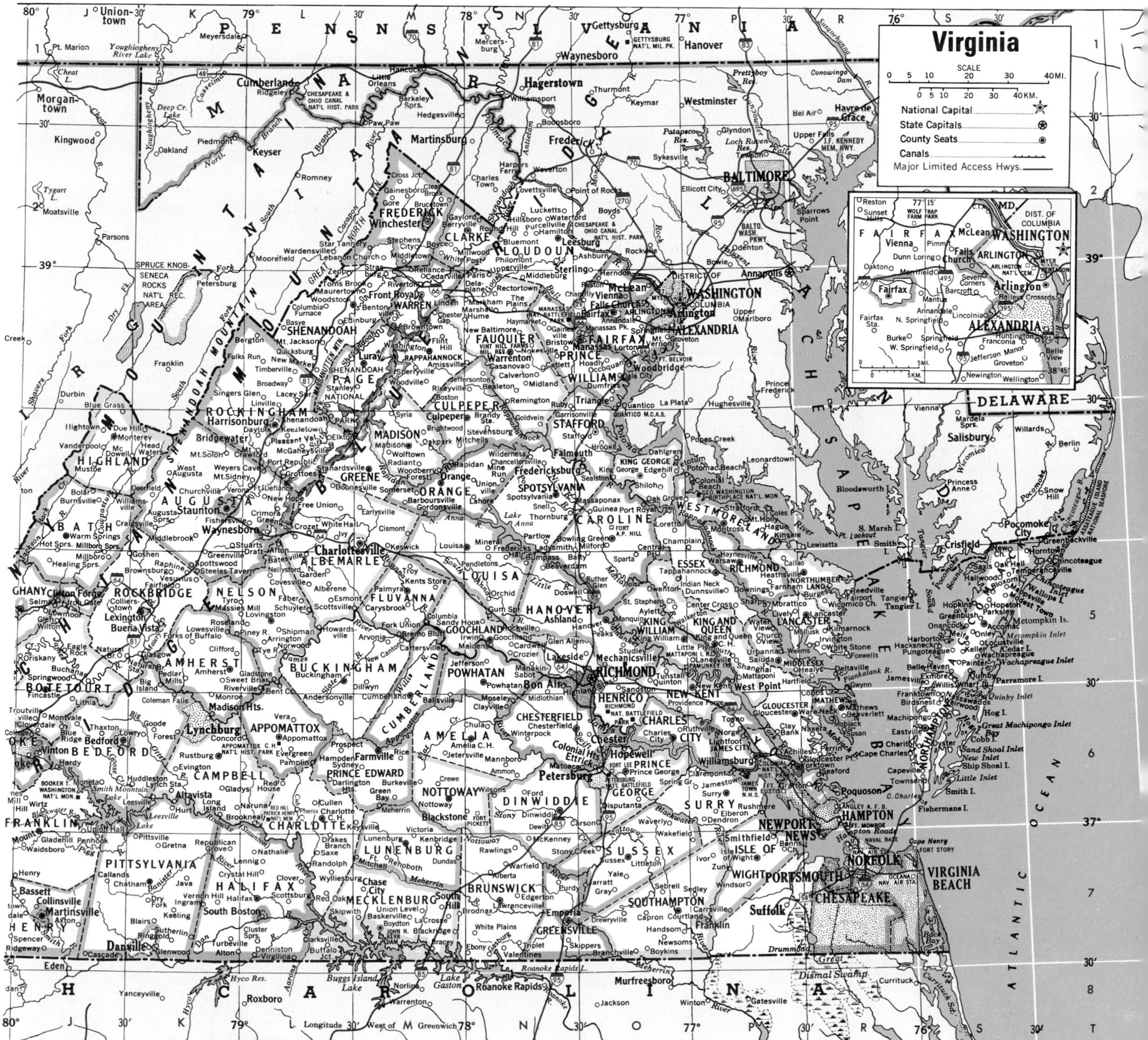

Agriculture, Industry and Resources

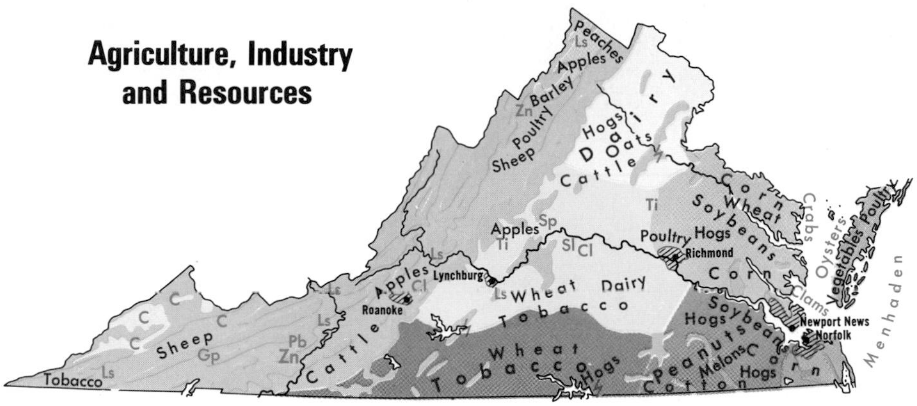
Peaches
Apples
Barley
Poultry
Zn
Sheep
Hogs
Dairy
Oats
Cattle
Ti
Corn
Wheat
Soybeans
Crabs
Oysters
Vegetables
Poultry
Apples
Sp
Sl
Cl
Ti
Poultry
Hogs
Richmond
Corn
Lynchburg
Apples
Cl
Ls
Wheat
Dairy
Roanoke
Tobacco
Clams
Menhaden
Hogs
Soybeans
Newport News
Norfolk
C
C
C
Sheep
Gp
Pb
Zn
Ls
Cattle
Wheat
Tobacco
Hogs
Peanuts
Melons
Cotton
Hogs
Corn
Tobacco
Ls

MAJOR MINERAL OCCURRENCES

C	Coal	Sl	Slate	ϟ	Water Power
Cl	Clay	Sp	Soapstone	(hatched)	Major Industrial Areas
Gp	Gypsum	Ti	Titanium		
Ls	Limestone	Zn	Zinc		
Pb	Lead				

DOMINANT LAND USE

- Dairy, General Farming
- General Farming, Livestock, Dairy
- General Farming, Livestock, Tobacco
- General Farming, Livestock, Fruit, Tobacco
- General Farming, Truck Farming, Tobacco, Livestock
- Tobacco, General Farming
- Peanuts, General Farming
- Fruit and Mixed Farming
- Truck and Mixed Farming
- Forests
- Swampland, Limited Agriculture

Haysi 222 .... D6
Healing Springs 175 .... J5
Heathsville▲ 300 .... P5
Henry 300 .... J7
Herndon 16,139 .... O3
Highland Springs 13,823 .... O5
Hillsville▲ 2,008 .... G7
Hiltons 300 .... D7
Hiwassee 250 .... G7
Hoadly 400 .... O3
Hollins College 12,295 .... H6
Honaker 950 .... D6
Hopewell (I.C.) 23,101 .... O6
Horntown 400 .... T5
Hot Springs 300 .... J4
Huddleston 200 .... K6
Hume 350 .... N3
Huntington 7,489 .... S3
Hurley 850 .... D6
Hurt 1,294 .... K6
Independence▲ 988 .... F7
Indian Valley 300 .... G7
Iron Gate 417 .... J5
Irvington 496 .... R5
Isle of Wight▲ 185 .... P7
Ivanhoe 900 .... G7
Ivor 324 .... P7
Ivy 900 .... L4
Jamestown 12 .... P6
Jamesville 500 .... S5
Jarratt 556 .... O7
Jefferson 25,782 .... N5
Jefferson Manor S3
Jeffersonton 300 .... N3
Jewell Ridge 600 .... E6
Jonesville▲ 927 .... B7
Keeling 680 .... K7
Keezletown 975 .... L4
Keller 235 .... S5
Kenbridge 1,264 .... M7
Kents Store 130 .... M5
Keokee 300 .... C7
Keswick 300 .... M4
Keysville 606 .... M6
Kilmarnock 1,109 .... R5
King George▲ 575 .... O4
King William▲ 100 .... O5
King and Queen Court House▲ 500 .... P5
Kinsale 250 .... P4
La Crosse 549 .... M7
Lacey Spring 140 .... L3
Ladysmith 360 .... N4
Lafayette-Elliston H6
Lake Barcroft 8,686 .... S3
Lakeside 12,081 .... N5
Lambsburg 800 .... G7
Lancaster▲ 110 .... R5
Laurel Fork 300 .... G7
Lawrenceville▲ 1,486 .... N7
Lebanon Church 300 .... L2
Lebanon▲ 3,206 .... D7
Leesburg▲ 16,202 .... N2
Lewisetta 125 .... R4
Lexington (I.C.)▲ 6,959 .... J5
Lincolnia 13,041 .... S3
Linden 320 .... M3
Linville 500 .... L3
Little Plymouth 195 .... P5
Lively 400 .... P5
Loretto 150 .... O4
Lorton 15,385 .... O3
Louisa▲ 1,088 .... M4
Lovettsville 749 .... N2
Lovingston▲ 600 .... L5
Lowesville 500 .... K5
Lowmoor 700 .... J5
Lucketts 500 .... N2
Lunenburg▲ 13 .... M7
Luray▲ 4,587 .... M3
Lynch Station 500 .... K6
Lynchburg (I.C.) 66,049 .... K6
Machipongo 400 .... S6
Madison Heights 11,700 .... K6
Madison▲ 267 .... M4
Manakin-Sabot 200 .... N5
Manassas (I.C.)▲ 27,957 .... O3
Manassas Park (I.C.) 6,734 .... O3
Mannboro 175 .... N6
Manquin 576 .... O5
Mantua 6,804 .... S3
Mappsville 700 .... T5
Marion▲ 6,630 .... E7
Markham 300 .... N3
Marshall 800 .... N3
Martinsville (I.C.)▲ 16,162 .... J7
Massies Mill 225 .... K5
Mathews▲ 500 .... R6
Matoaca 1,967 .... N6
Mattaponi 300 .... P5
Maurertown 158 .... L3
Max Meadows 782 .... G6
McClure 300 .... D6
McCoy 600 .... G6
McGaheysville 600 .... L4
McKenney 386 .... N7
McLean 38,168 .... S2
Meadows of Dan 150 .... H7
Meadowview-Emory 2,292 .... D7
Mechanicsburg 350 .... G6
Mechanicsville 22,027 .... O5
Meherrin 400 .... M6
Melfa 428 .... S5
Mendota 375 .... D7
Merrifield 8,399 .... S3
Middlebrook 125 .... K4
Middleburg 549 .... B3
Middletown 841 .... M2
Midland 600 .... N3
Midlothian 950 .... N6
Milford 650 .... O4
Millboro 400 .... J5
Millboro Springs 200 .... J4
Millwood 400 .... N2
Mine Run 450 .... N4
Mineral 471 .... N4
Mobjack 210 .... R6
Modest Town 225 .... T5
Mollusk 800 .... P5
Moneta 300 .... J6
Monroe 500 .... K6
Monterey▲ 222 .... K4
Montross▲ 359 .... P4
Montvale 900 .... J6
Morattico 225 .... I5
Moseley 210 .... N6
Mount Crawford 228 .... L4
Mount Holly 200 .... P4
Mount Jackson 1,583 .... L3
Mount Sidney 500 .... K4
Mount Solon 124 .... K4
Mount Vernon 27,485 .... O3
Mouth of Wilson 400 .... F7
Mustoe 150 .... K4
Narrows 2,082 .... G6
Naruna 175 .... L6
Nassawadox 564 .... S6
Nathalie 200 .... L7
Natural Bridge 200 .... J5
Natural Bridge Sta. 450 .... K5
Naxera 300 .... R6
Nellysford 290 .... L5
New Baltimore 125 .... N3
New Castle▲ 152 .... H5
New Church 427 .... S5
New Hope 200 .... L4
New Kent▲ 25 .... P5
New Market 1,435 .... L3
New River 500 .... G6
Newington 17,965 .... S3
Newport 600 .... H6
Newport News (I.C.) 170,045 .... P6
Newsoms 337 .... O7
Nickelsville 411 .... D7
Nokesville 520 .... N3
Nora 550 .... D6
Norfolk (I.C.) 261,229 .... R7
Norge 750 .... P6
North Garden 300 .... L5
North Pulaski 1,405 .... G6
North Springfield 8,996 .... S3
Norton (I.C.) 4,247 .... C7
Nottoway▲ 170 .... M6
Oak Hall 221 .... S5
Oakpark 150 .... M4
Oakton 24,610 .... R3
Oakwood 715 .... E6
Occoquan 361 .... O3
Onancock 1,434 .... S5
Onley 532 .... S5
Orange▲ 2,582 .... M4
Owenton 400 .... O5
Oyster 200 .... S6
Paint Bank 235 .... H5
Painter 259 .... S5
Palmyra▲ 250 .... M5
Pamplin 273 .... L6
Pardee 190 .... C6
Parksley 779 .... S5
Parrott 750 .... G6
Patrick Springs 800 .... H7
Peaks 500 .... D6
Pearisburg▲ 2,064 .... G6
Pembroke 1,064 .... G6
Penhook 500 .... J7
Pennington Gap 1,922 .... C7
Petersburg (I.C.) 38,386 .... N6
Phenix 260 .... L6
Philomont 265 .... N2
Pilot 360 .... H6
Pimmit 6,658 .... S2
Piney River 778 .... L5
Pittsville 600 .... K7
Pleasant Valley 150 .... L4
Pocahontas 513 .... F6
Poquoson 11,005 .... R6
Port Royal 204 .... O4
Portsmouth (I.C.) 103,907 .... R7
Potomac Beach 200 .... P4
Pound 995 .... C6
Pounding Mill 399 .... E6
Powhatan▲ 600 .... N5
Prince George▲ 150 .... O6
Prospect 275 .... L6
Providence Forge 500 .... P6
Pulaski▲ 9,985 .... G6
Pungoteague 500 .... S5
Purcellville 1,744 .... N2
Purdy 350 .... N7
Quantico 670 .... O3
Quicksburg 160 .... L3
Quinby 350 .... S5
Radford (I.C.) 15,940 .... G6
Radiant 250 .... M4
Randolph 150 .... L7
Raphine 500 .... K5
Rapiden 176 .... M4
Raven 2,640 .... E6
Rawlings 200 .... N7
Rectortown 225 .... N3
Red Ash 300 .... E6
Red House 150 .... L6
Red Oak 250 .... L7
Reedville 400 .... R5
Reliance 150 .... M3
Remington 460 .... N3
Republican Grove 125 .... K7
Reston 48,556 .... R2
Rice 194 .... M6
Rich Creek 746 .... G6
Richlands 4,456 .... E6
Richmond (cap.) (I.C.)▲ 203,056 .... O5
Ridgeway 752 .... J7
Riner 360 .... H6
Ringgold 150 .... K7
Ripplemead 600 .... G6
Riverton 500 .... M3
Rixeyville 150 .... M3
Roanoke (I.C.) 96,397 .... H6
Rockville 290 .... N5
Rocky Gap 200 .... F6
Rocky Mount▲ 4,098 .... J7
Rose Hill 12,675 .... B7
Rosedale 760 .... E7
Roseland 300 .... K5
Round Hill 514 .... N2
Rowe 150 .... D6
Ruby 188 .... N3
Rural Retreat 972 .... F7
Rushmere 1,064 .... P6
Rustburg▲ 650 .... K6
Ruther Glen 200 .... O5
Ruthville 300 .... P6
Saint Charles 206 .... B7
Saint Paul 1,007 .... D7
Saint Stephens Church 500 .... O5
Salem (I.C.)▲ 23,756 .... H6
Saltville 2,376 .... E7
Saluda▲ 150 .... P5
Sandy Hook 700 .... M5
Saxis 367 .... S5
Schuyler 250 .... L5
Scottsburg 152 .... L7
Scottsville 239 .... L5
Sealston 200 .... O4
Sebrell 160 .... O7
Sedley 523 .... P7
Selma 500 .... J5
Seven Corners 7,280 .... S3
Seven Mile Ford 425 .... E7
Shanghai 150 .... P5
Shawsville 1,260 .... H6
Shenandoah 2,213 .... L4
Shiloh 150 .... O4
Shipman 350 .... L5
Simpsons 150 .... H6
Singers Glen 155 .... K3
Skippers 150 .... O7
Skipwith 128 .... L7
Smithfield 4,686 .... P7
Snell 300 .... N4
Somerset 200 .... M4
South Boston (I.C.) 6,997 .... L7
South Hill 4,217 .... M7
Sparta 485 .... o4
Speedwell 650 .... F8
Spencer 500 .... J7
Sperryville 500 .... M3
Spotsylvania▲ 350 .... N4
Springfield 23,706 .... S3
Stafford▲ 750 .... O4
Stanardsville▲ 257 .... L4
Stanley 1,186 .... L3
Stanleytown 1,563 .... H7
Star Tannery 500 .... L2
Staunton (I.C.)▲ 24,461 .... K4
Steeles Tavern 200 .... K5
Stephens City 1,186 .... M2
Sterling 20,512 .... O2
Stevensburg 125 .... N4
Stonega 275 .... C7
Stony Creek 271 .... N7
Strasburg 3,762 .... M3
Stuart▲ 965 .... H7
Stuarts Draft 5,087 .... L4
Studley 500 .... O5
Suffolk (I.C.) 52,141 .... P7
Sugar Grove 1,027 .... E7
Surry▲ 192 .... P6
Susan 500 .... R6
Sussex▲ 75 .... O7
Sutherlin 180 .... K7
Sweet Briar 900 .... K5
Swords Creek 315 .... E6
Sylvatus 200 .... G7
Tacoma 150 .... C7
Tangier 659 .... R5
Tappahannock▲ 1,550 .... O5
Tazewell▲ 4,176 .... E6
Temperanceville 400 .... T5
Thaxton 450 .... J6
The Plains 219 .... N3
Thornburg 135 .... N4
Timberville 1,596 .... L3
Tiptop 175 .... F6
Toano 950 .... P6
Toms Brook 227 .... L3
Townsend 525 .... R6
Trammel 450 .... D6
Triangle 4,740 .... O3
Triplet 300 .... N7
Trout Dale 248 .... F7
Troutville 455 .... J6
Tyro 125 .... K5
Union Hall 125 .... J6
Unionville 500 .... N4
Upperville 250 .... N2
Urbanna 529 .... P5
Valentines 400 .... N7
Vansant 1,187 .... D6
Vera 150 .... L6
Vernon Hill 250 .... K7
Verona 3,479 .... K4
Vesta 350 .... H7
Vesuvius 500 .... K5
Victoria 1,830 .... M6
Vienna 14,852 .... R2
Vinton 7,665 .... J6
Virgilina 161 .... L7
Virginia Beach (I.C.) 393,069 .... S7
Wachapreague 291 .... S5
Wakefield 1,070 .... O7
Walkerton 985 .... O5
Warm Springs▲ 325 .... J4
Warrenton▲ 4,830 .... N3
Warsaw▲ 961 .... P5
Washington▲ 198 .... M3
Water View 265 .... P5
Waterford 350 .... N2
Waverly 2,223 .... O6
Waynesboro (I.C.) 18,549 .... K4
Weber City 1,377 .... C7
Weems 500 .... P5
Weirwood 300 .... S6
West Augusta 325 .... K4
West Point 2,938 .... P5
West Springfield 28,126 .... S3
Weyers Cave 300 .... L4
White Hall 250 .... L4
White Stone 372 .... R5
Whitetop 860 .... E7
Whitewood 350 .... E6
Wicomico Church 500 .... R5
Wilderness 200 .... N4
Williamsburg (I.C.)▲ 11,530 .... P6
Williamsville 145 .... J4
Willis 170 .... H7
Willis Wharf 360 .... S5
Winchester (I.C.)▲ 21,947 .... M2
Windsor 1,025 .... P7
Wirtz 500 .... J6
Wise▲ 3,193 .... C7
Wolftown 350 .... M4
Woodberry Forest 450 .... M4
Woodbridge 26,401 .... O3
Woodlawn 1,689 .... G7
Woodstock▲ 3,182 .... L3
Woodville 200 .... M3
Woodway 400 .... C7
Woolwine 150 .... H7
Wylliesburg 213 .... L7
Wytheville▲ 8,038 .... G7
Zuni 300 .... P7

OTHER FEATURES

Aarons (creek) L7
Allegheny (mts.) H5
Anna (lake) N4
Appalachian (mts.) J5
Appomattox (riv.) M6
Appomattox Court House Nat'l Hist. Park K6
Arlington Nat'l Cemetery T3
Assateague Island Nat'l Seashore T4
Back (bay) S7
Back (creek) J4
Banister (riv.) K7
Big Otter (riv.) K6
Blackwater (riv.) J6
Blackwater (riv.) O6
Blue Ridge (mts.) J6
Bluestone (lake) G5
Booker T. Washington Nat'l Mon. J6
Buggs Island (lake) L8
Bull Run (creek) N3
Cedar (isl.) S5
Central Intelligence Agency (C.I.A.) S2
Charles (cape) R6
Chesapeake (bay) R5
Chesapeake and Ohio Canal Nat'l Hist. Park O2
Chincoteague (bay) T4
Chincoteague (inlet) T5
Claytor (lake) G6
Clinch (riv.) C7
Cobb (isl.) S6
Colonial Nat'l Hist. Park P6
Cowpasture (riv.) J4
Craig (creek) H5
Cub (creek) L6
Cumberland (mt.) B7
Cumberland Gap Nat'l Hist. Park A7
Dan (riv.) K7
Drummond (lake) P7
Fishermans (isl.) S6
Flannagan (res.) C6
Flat (creek) M6
Fort A.P. Hill O4
Fort Belvoir 8,590 .... O3
Fort Eustis P6
Fort Lee 6,595 .... O6
Fort Monroe R6
Fort Myer T2
Fort Pickett N6
Fort Story S7
Gaston (lake) M8
George Washington Birthplace Nat'l Mon. P4
Goose (creek) J6
Goose (creek) N3
Great Machipongo (inlet) S6
Great North (mt.) L2
Hampton Roads (est.) R7
Henry (cape) R7
Hog (isl.) S6
Hog Island (bay) S6
Holston, North Fork (riv.) D7
Hyco (riv.) K8
Jackson (riv.) J4
James (riv.) O6
Jamestown Nat'l Hist. Site P6
John H. Kerr (dam) M7
Langley A.F.B. R6
Leesville (lake) K6
Levisa Fork (riv.) C5
Little (inlet) S6
Little (riv.) H7
Little (riv.) N5
Manassas Nat'l Battlefield Pk. N3
Massanutten (mt.) L3
Mattaponi (riv.) O5
Mattaponi Ind. Res. P5
Maury (riv.) K3
Meherrin (riv.) M7
Metompkin (inlet) T5
Metompkin (isl.) T5
Mobjack (bay) R6
Mount Rogers Nat'l Rec. Area F7
New (inlet) S6
New (riv.) F8
Ni (riv.) N4
North Anna (riv.) M4
Nottoway (riv.) O7
Oceana N.A.S. S7
Pamunkey (riv.) O5
Pamunkey Ind. Res. P5
Parramore (isl.) S5
Pentagon T3
Petersburg Nat'l Battlefield O6
Philpott (lake) H7
Piankatank (riv.) R5
Pigg (riv.) J7
Po (riv.) N4
Pocomoke (sound) S5
Potomac (riv.) O4
Powell (riv.) B7
Quantico Marine Corps Air Sta. O4
Quinby (inlet) S6
Rapidan (riv.) M4
Rappahannock (riv.) P4
Red Hill Patrick Henry Nat'l Mem. L6
Richmond Nat'l Battlefield Pk. O6
Rivanna (riv.) M5
Roanoke (riv.) N8
Rogers (mt.) E7
Russell Fork (riv.) C5
Sand Shoal (inlet) S6
Shenandoah (mt.) K3
Shenandoah (riv.) N2
Shenandoan Nat'l Park L3
Ship Shoal (isl.) S6
Slate (riv.) L5
Smith (isl.) S6
Smith (riv.) J7
Smith Mountain (lake) J6
South Anna (riv.) N5
South Holston (lake) E7
South Mayo (riv.) H7
Stony (creek) N6
Swift (creek) O6
Tangier (isl.) R5
Tangier (sound) S5
Tug Fork (riv.) D5
U.S. Naval Base R7
Vint Hill Farms Mil. Res. N3
Wachapreague (inlet) T6
Walker (creek) F6
Wallops (isl.) T5
Willis (riv.) M5
Wolf (creek) F6
Wolf Trap Farm Park S2
York (riv.) P6

I.C. Independent City
▲County seat

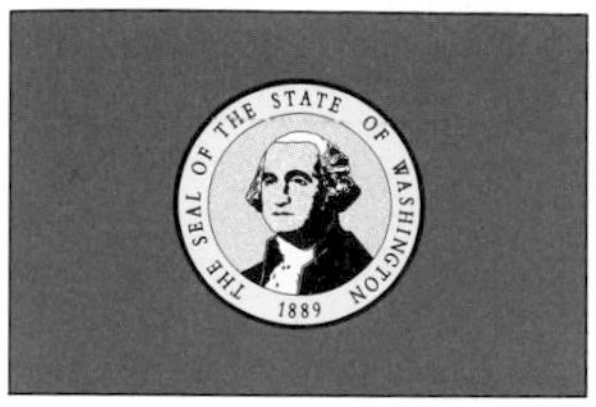

AREA 68,139 sq. mi. (176,480 sq. km.)
POPULATION 4,887,941
CAPITAL Olympia
LARGEST CITY Seattle
HIGHEST POINT Mt. Rainier 14,410 ft. (4392 m.)
SETTLED IN 1811
ADMITTED TO UNION November 11, 1889
POPULAR NAME Evergreen State
STATE FLOWER Western Rhododendron
STATE BIRD Willow Goldfinch

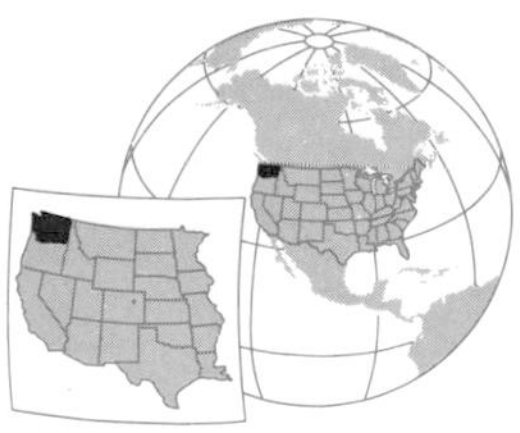

COUNTIES

Adams 13,603 ..... G3
Asotin 17,605 ..... H4
Benton 112,560 ..... F4
Chelan 52,250 ..... E3
Clallam 56,464 ..... B2
Clark 238,053 ..... C5
Columbia 4,024 ..... H4
Cowlitz 82,119 ..... C4
Douglas 26,205 ..... F3
Ferry 6,295 ..... G2
Franklin 37,473 ..... G4
Garfield 2,248 ..... H4
Grant 54,758 ..... F3
Grays Harbor 64,175 ..... B3
Island 60,195 ..... C2
Jefferson 20,146 ..... B3
King 1,507,319 ..... D3
Kitsap 189,731 ..... C3
Kittitas 26,725 ..... E3
Klickitat 16,616 ..... E5
Lewis 59,358 ..... C4
Lincoln 8,864 ..... G3
Mason 38,341 ..... B3
Okanogan 33,350 ..... F2
Pacific 18,882 ..... B4
Pend Oreille 8,915 ..... H2
Pierce 586,203 ..... C3
San Juan 10,035 ..... C2
Skagit 79,555 ..... D2
Skamania 8,289 ..... D5
Snohomish 465,642 ..... D2
Spokane 361,364 ..... H3
Stevens 30,948 ..... H2
Thurston 161,238 ..... C4
Wahkiakim 3,832 ..... B4
Walla Walla 48,439 ..... G4
Whatcom 127,780 ..... D2
Whitman 38,775 ..... H4
Yakima 188,823 ..... E4

CITIES and TOWNS

Aberdeen 16,565 ..... B3
Acme 500 ..... C2
Addy 180 ..... H2
Airway Heights 1,971 ..... H3
Albion 632 ..... H4
Alder 300 ..... C4
Algona 1,694 ..... C3
Allyn 850 ..... C3
Almira 310 ..... G3
Aloha 140 ..... A3
Amanda Park 495 ..... A3
Amboy 480 ..... C5
Anacortes 11,451 ..... C2
Appleton 120 ..... D5
Ardenvoir 150 ..... E3
Ariel 386 ..... C5
Arlington 4,037 ..... C2
Ashford 300 ..... C4
Asotin▲ 981 ..... H4
Auburn 33,102 ..... C3
Azwell 152 ..... F3
Bainbridge Island-Winslow (Winslow) A2
Baring 200 ..... D3
Battle Ground 3,758 ..... C5
Bay Center 187 ..... A4
Bay City 187 ..... B4
Beaux Arts Village 303 ..... B2
Beaver 450 ..... A2
Belfair 500 ..... C3
Bellevue 86,874 ..... B2
Bellingham▲ 52,179 ..... C2
Benton City 1,806 ..... F4
Beverly 200 ..... F4
Biglake 105 ..... C2
Bingen 645 ..... D5
Black Diamond 1,422 ..... D3
Blaine 2,489 ..... C2
Blanchard 125 ..... C2
Bonney Lake 7,494 ..... C3
Bothell 12,345 ..... B1
Bow 200 ..... C2
Boyds 125 ..... G2
Bremerton 38,142 ..... A2
Brewster 1,633 ..... F2
Bridgeport 1,498 ..... F3
Brier 5,633 ..... C3
Brinnon 500 ..... B3
Brownstown 200 ..... E4
Brush Prairie 2,650 ..... C5
Bryn Mawr-Skyway 12,514 ..... B2
Buckley 3,516 ..... C3
Bucoda 536 ..... C4
Buena 590 ..... E4
Burbank 1,745 ..... G4
Burien 25,089 ..... A2
Burley 300 ..... C3
Burlington 4,349 ..... C2
Burton 650 ..... C3
Camas 6,442 ..... C5
Carbonado 495 ..... D3
Carlsborg 500 ..... B2
Carlton 410 ..... F2
Carnation 1,243 ..... D3
Carson 500 ..... D5
Cashmere 2,544 ..... E3
Castle Rock 2,067 ..... B4
Cathlamet▲ 508 ..... B4
Cedar Falls 200 ..... D3
Central Park 2,669 ..... B3
Centralia 12,101 ..... C4
Chattaroy 250 ..... H3
Chehalis▲ 6,527 ..... C4
Chelan 2,060 ..... E3
Chelan Falls 250 ..... E3
Cheney 7,723 ..... H3
Chewelah 1,945 ..... H2
Chimacum 275 ..... C3
Chinook 928 ..... B4
Cinebar 200 ..... C4
Clallam Bay 600 ..... A2
Clarkston 6,753 ..... H4
Clayton 175 ..... H3
Cle Elum 1,778 ..... E3
Clearlake 750 ..... C2
Clearwater 194 ..... A3
Clinton 1,564 ..... C3
Clyde F4
Clyde Hill 2,972 ..... B2
Coalfield 500 ..... B2
Colbert 225 ..... H3
Colby 150 ..... A2
Colfax▲ 2,713 ..... H4
College Place 6,308 ..... G4
Colton 325 ..... H4
Columbia Heights 2,515 ..... C4
Colville▲ 4,360 ..... H2
Conconully 153 ..... F2
Concrete 735 ..... D2
Connell 2,005 ..... G4
Conway 150 ..... C2
Copalis Beach 600 ..... A3
Copalis Crossing 500 ..... B3
Cosmopolis 1,372 ..... B4
Coulee City 568 ..... F3
Coulee Dam 1,087 ..... G3
Coupeville▲ 1,377 ..... C2
Cowiche 150 ..... E4
Creston 230 ..... G3
Cumberland 250 ..... D3
Curlew 168 ..... G2
Cusick 195 ..... H2
Custer 300 ..... C2
Dallesport 600 ..... D5
Danville 215 ..... G2
Darrington 1,042 ..... D2
Davenport▲ 1,502 ..... G3
Dayton▲ 2,468 ..... H4
Deer Harbor 400 ..... B2
Deer Park 2,278 ..... H3
Deming 200 ..... C2
Des Moines 17,283 ..... B2
Dishman 9,671 ..... H3
Dixie 210 ..... G4
Doe Bay 150 ..... C2
Doty 245 ..... B4
Dryad 125 ..... B4
Dryden 500 ..... E3
Du Pont 592 ..... C3
Dungeness 675 ..... B2
Duvall 2,770 ..... D3
East Olympia 300 ..... B4
East Wenatchee 2,701 ..... E3
Easton 250 ..... D3
Eastsound 800 ..... B2
Eatonville 1,374 ..... C4
Edison 250 ..... C2
Edmonds 30,744 ..... C3
Edwall 150 ..... H3
Electric City 910 ..... F3
Ellensburg▲ 12,361 ..... E3
Elma 3,011 ..... B4
Elmer City 290 ..... G2
Eltopia 200 ..... G4
Endicott 320 ..... H4
Enetai 2,638 ..... A2
Entiat 449 ..... E3
Enumclaw 7,227 ..... D3
Ephrata▲ 5,349 ..... F3
Erlands Point 1,254 ..... A2
Ethel 180 ..... C4
Everett▲ 69,961 ..... C3
Everson 1,490 ..... C2
Fairfield 446 ..... H3
Fairview-Sumach 2,749 ..... E4
Fall City 1,582 ..... D3
Farmington 126 ..... H3
Ferndale 5,398 ..... C2
Fife 3,864 ..... C3
Finley 4,897 ..... F4
Fircrest 5,258 ..... C3
Fords Prairie 2,480 ..... B4
Forks 2,862 ..... A3
Four Lakes 500 ..... H3
Frances 144 ..... B4
Freeland 1,278 ..... C2
Freeman 150 ..... H3
Friday Harbor▲ 1,492 ..... B2
Fruitland 150 ..... G2
Fruitvale 4,125 ..... E4
Galvin 250 ..... B4
Garfield 544 ..... H3
Garrett 1,004 ..... G4
Geiger Heights H3
George 253 ..... F3
Gig Harbor 3,236 ..... C3
Glacier 150 ..... D2
Glenoma 500 ..... C4
Glenwood 626 ..... D4
Gold Bar 1,078 ..... D3
Goldendale▲ 3,319 ..... E5
Gorst 750 ..... C3
Grand Coulee 984 ..... G3
Grand Mound 1,394 ..... C4
Grandview 7,169 ..... F4
Granger 2,053 ..... E4
Granite Falls 1,060 ..... D2
Grapeview 250 ..... C3
Grayland 750 ..... A4
Grays River 350 ..... B4
Greenacres 4,626 ..... J3
Greenbank 600 ..... C2
Hadlock-Irondale 2,742 ..... C2
Hamilton 228 ..... D2
Hansville 250 ..... C3
Harper 300 ..... A2
Harrah 341 ..... E4
Harrington 449 ..... G3
Hartline 176 ..... F3
Hatton 71 ..... F4
Heisson 200 ..... C5
Hobart 500 ..... D3
Hoodsport 500 ..... B3
Hoquiam 8,972 ..... A3
Humptulips 275 ..... A3
Hunters 200 ..... G2
Hunts Point 513 ..... B2
Husum 200 ..... D5
Ilwaco 815 ..... A4
Inchelium 393 ..... G2
Index 139 ..... D3
Indianola 1,729 ..... A1
Ione 507 ..... H2
Issaquah 7,786 ..... C3
Joyce 375 ..... B2
Juanita 17,232 ..... B1
Kahlotus 167 ..... B4
Kalama 1,210 ..... C4
Kapowsin 500 ..... C4
Keller 195 ..... G2
Kelso▲ 11,820 ..... C4
Kenmore 8,917 ..... B1
Kennewick 42,155 ..... F4
Kent 37,960 ..... C3
Kettle Falls 1,272 ..... H2
Keyport 900 ..... A2
Kingston 1,270 ..... C3
Kiona 230 ..... F4
Kirkland 40,052 ..... B2
Kittitas 843 ..... E4
Klickitat 750 ..... D5
Krupp (Marlin) 53 ..... F3
La Center 451 ..... C5
La Conner 656 ..... C2
La Push 500 ..... A3
Lacey 19,279 ..... C3
Lacrosse 336 ..... H4
Lake Forest Park 4,031 ..... B1
Lake Stevens 3,380 ..... D3
Lakewood 58,412 ..... C2
Lamont 91 ..... H3
Langley 845 ..... C2
Latah 175 ..... H3
Laurel 972 ..... D5
Leavenworth 1,692 ..... E3
Lebam 275 ..... B4
Liberty Lake 2,015 ..... J3
Lind 472 ..... G4
Littlerock 850 ..... B4
Long Beach 1,236 ..... A4
Longbranch 640 ..... C3
Longview 31,499 ..... B4
Loomis 150 ..... F2
Loon Lake 500 ..... H2
Lummi Island 675 ..... C2
Lyle 580 ..... D5
Lyman 275 ..... D2
Lynden 5,709 ..... C2
Lynnwood 28,695 ..... C3
Mabton 1,482 ..... E4
Malaga 125 ..... E3
Malden 189 ..... H3
Malo 240 ..... G2
Malone 175 ..... B4
Malott 350 ..... F2
Manchester 4,031 ..... A2
Mansfield 311 ..... F3
Manson 220 ..... E3
Maple Falls 300 ..... D2
Maple Valley 1,211 ..... C3
Marblemount 300 ..... D2
Marcus 135 ..... H2
Marietta-Alderwood 2,766 ..... C2
Markham 117 ..... B4
Marlin F3
Marysville 10,328 ..... C2
Matlock 255 ..... D3
Mattawa 941 ..... F4
McCleary 1,235 ..... B3
McKenna 300 ..... C4
Mead H3
Medical Lake 3,664 ..... H3
Medina 2,981 ..... B2
Menlo 237 ..... B4
Mercer Island (city) 20,816 ..... B2
Mesa 252 ..... G4
Metaline 198 ..... H2
Metaline Falls 210 ..... H2
Mica 105 ..... H3
Milan 150 ..... H3
Millwood 1,559 ..... H3
Milton 4,995 ..... C3
Mineral 550 ..... C4
Moclips 500 ..... A3
Monitor 650 ..... E3
Monroe 4,278 ..... D3
Montesano▲ 3,064 ..... B4
Moses Lake 11,235 ..... F3
Mossyrock 452 ..... C4
Mount Vernon▲ 17,647 ..... C2
Mountlake Terrace 19,320 ..... B1
Moxee City 814 ..... E4
Mukilteo 7,007 ..... C3
Naches 596 ..... E4
Nahcotta 200 ..... A4
Napavine 745 ..... C4
Naselle 500 ..... B4
Navy Yard City 2,905 ..... A2
Neah Bay 916 ..... A2
Neilton 250 ..... B3
Nespelem 291 ..... G2
Newhalem 350 ..... D2
Newman Lake 102 ..... J3
Newport▲ 1,691 ..... H2
Nine Mile Falls 150 ..... H3
Nisqually 558 ..... C3
Nooksack 584 ..... C2
Nordland 706 ..... C2
Normandy Park 6,709 ..... A2
North Bend 2,578 ..... D3
North Bonneville 411 ..... C5
Northport 308 ..... H2
Oak Harbor 17,176 ..... C2
Oakesdale 346 ..... H3
Oakville 493 ..... B4

(continued on following page)

Agriculture, Industry and Resources

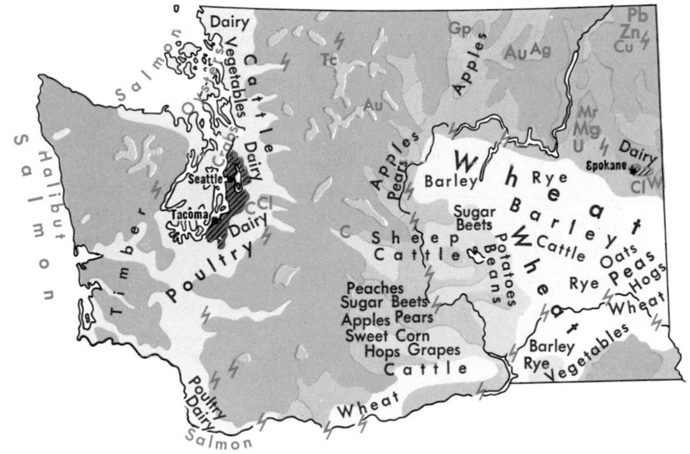

DOMINANT LAND USE

- Specialized Wheat
- Wheat, Peas
- Dairy, Poultry, Mixed Farming
- Fruit and Mixed Farming
- General Farming, Dairy, Range Livestock
- General Farming, Livestock, Special Crops
- Range Livestock
- Forests
- Urban Areas
- Nonagricultural Land

MAJOR MINERAL OCCURRENCES

Ag	Silver	Mr	Marble
Au	Gold	Pb	Lead
C	Coal	Tc	Talc
Cl	Clay	U	Uranium
Cu	Copper	W	Tungsten
Gp	Gypsum	Zn	Zinc
Mg	Magnesium		

Water Power
Major Industrial Areas

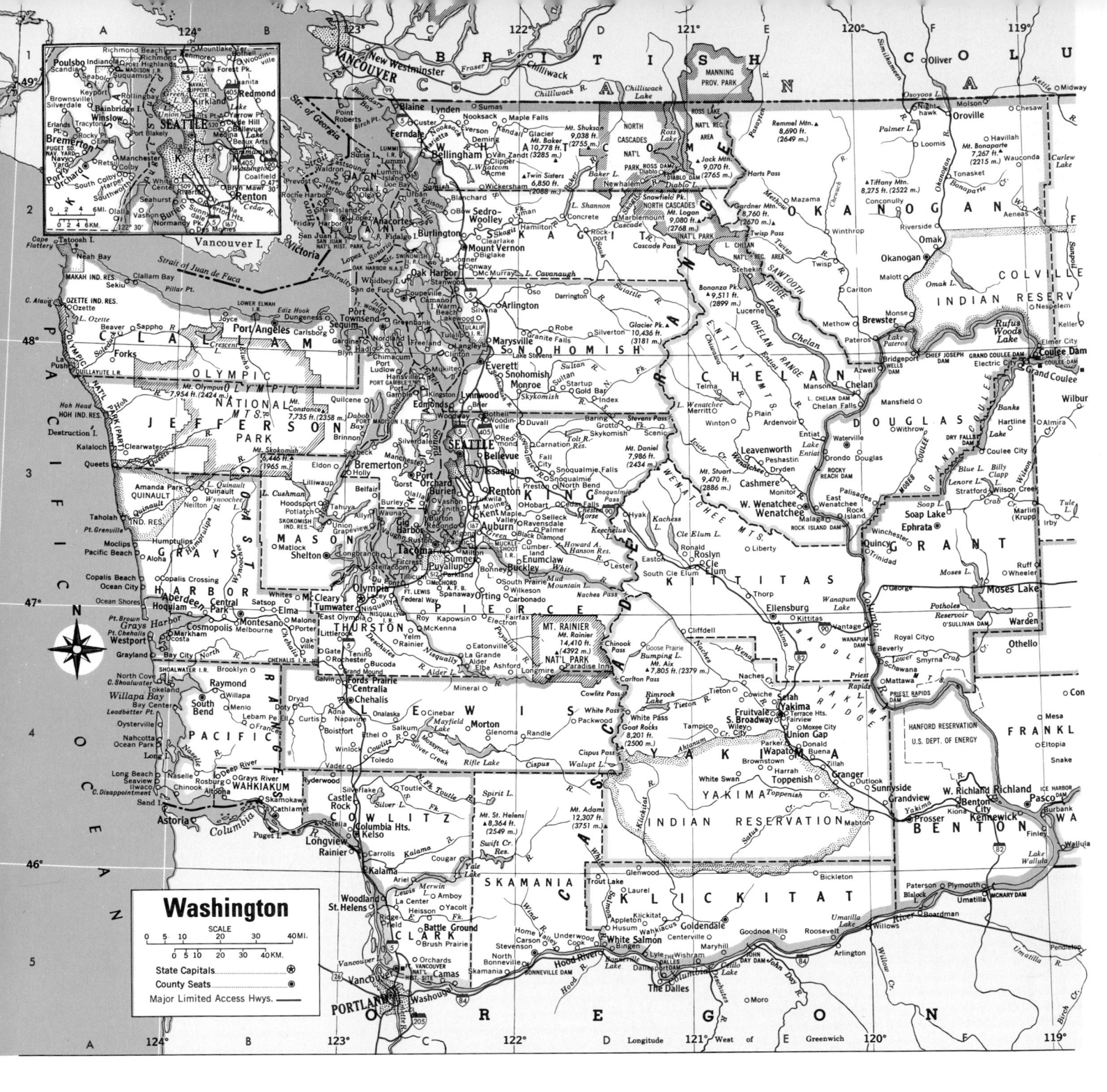

Washington

SCALE
0 5 10   20   30   40MI.
0 5 10 20   30   40KM.

State Capitals .... ⊛
County Seats .... ◉
Major Limited Access Hwys. ———

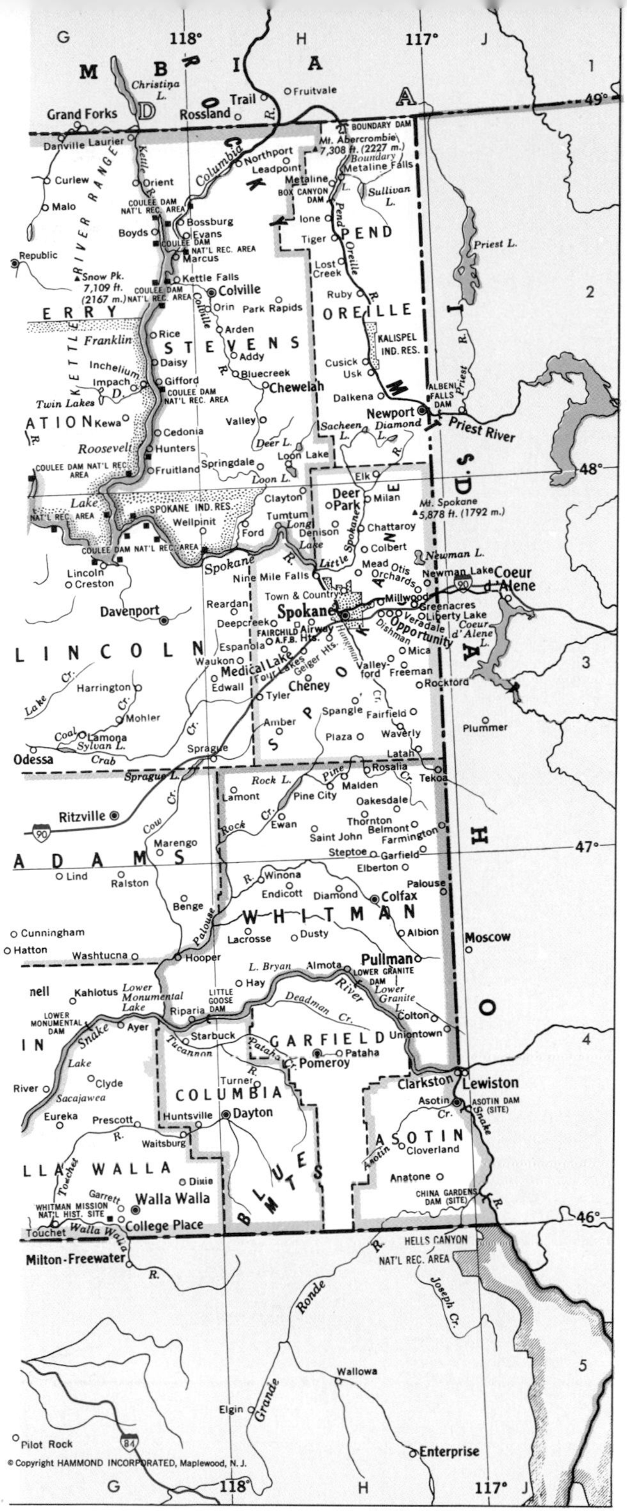

Map labels (main map, left)

G 118° H 117° J
1
MBIA D
Grand Forks · Christina L.
Danville Laurier · Rossland · Trail · Fruitvale
49°
Orient · Northport · BOUNDARY DAM · Mt. Abercrombie 7,308 ft. (2227 m.)
Curlew · Mt. Abercrombie · Boundary · Metaline Falls
Malo · Boyds · BOX CANYON DAM · Metaline · Ione
Republic · Bossburg · Evans · Marcus · Tiger · Sullivan L.
Snow Pk. 7,109 ft. (2167 m.) COULEE DAM NAT'L REC. AREA · Kettle Falls · Priest L.
2
ERRY · Colville · Orin · Park Rapids · Ruby
Franklin · Rice · Arden · Lost Creek
Daisy · Addy
STEVENS · Gifford · Chewelah · Cusick · Usk · KALISPEL IND. RES.
Inchelium · Bluecreek · ALBENI FALLS DAM
ATION · Impach · Valley · Newport · PRIEST RIVER
Kewa · Deer L. · Sacheen L. · Diamond
Roosevelt · Hunters · Springdale · Loon L. · Elk
Fruitland · Clayton · Milan
48°
COULEE DAM NAT'L REC. AREA · Deer Park · Mt. Spokane 5,878 ft. (1792 m.)
Lincoln · Creston · Wellpinit · SPOKANE IND. RES. · Ford · Chattaroy
Davenport · Reardan · Deepcreek · Spokane · Colbert · Newman L.
Coeur d'Alene
LINCOLN · Town & Country · Spokane · Greenacres · Liberty Lake
Harrington · Espanola · Medical Lake · FAIRCHILD A.F.B. · Geiger Hts. · Opportunity · Coeur d'Alene
Edwall · Cheney · Dishman · Mica
Mohler · Tyler · Valleyford · Freeman · Rockford
3
Amber · Spangle · Fairfield
Sprague · Plaza · Waverly · Plummer
Odessa · Crab · Sprague L. · Latah · Rosalia · Tekoa
Ritzville · Lamont · Malden · Oakesdale
ADAMS · Marengo · Rock L. · Pine City · Thornton · Belmont · Farmington
Lind · Ralston · Ewan · Saint John · Steptoe · Garfield · Elberton
Cunningham · Benge · Endicott · Diamond · Palouse
Hatton · Washtucna · Hooper · WHITMAN · Colfax · Albion
Lacrosse · Dusty · Moscow
nell · Kahlotus · L. Bryan · Almota · Pullman
LOWER MONUMENTAL DAM · LOWER GRANITE DAM
Lower Monumental Lake · Riparia · Hay · LITTLE GOOSE DAM · Lower Granite
River · Colton
4
IN · Starbuck · Pataha · GARFIELD · Uniontown
Ayer · Tucannon · Pomeroy
Turner · Clarkston · Lewiston
COLUMBIA · Asotin · ASOTIN DAM (SITE)
Eureka · Prescott · Huntsville · Dayton · Cr.
LLA · Waitsburg · WALLA · ASOTIN
WALLA · Dixie · Anatone
Garrett · CHINA GARDENS DAM (SITE)
Walla Walla · WHITMAN MISSION NAT'L HIST. SITE · College Place
Milton-Freewater · HELLS CANYON NAT'L REC. AREA
46°
BLUE MTS.
5
Wallowa
Pilot Rock · Elgin · Enterprise
© Copyright HAMMOND INCORPORATED, Maplewood, N.J.
G 118° H 117° J

Topography

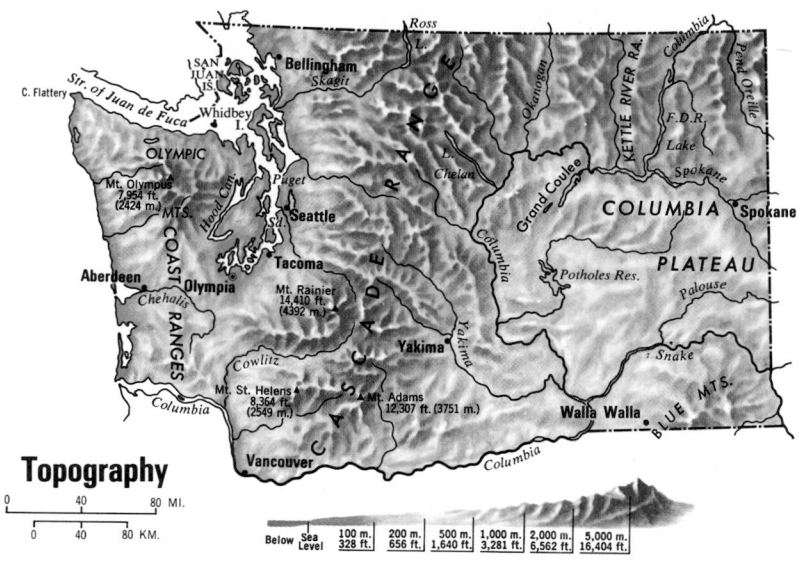

Ross · Bellingham · Skagit · Columbia · KETTLE RIVER RA.
SAN JUAN IS. · Whidbey I. · Okanogan · F.D.R. Lake · Pend Oreille
C. Flattery · Str. of Juan de Fuca · Puget · Chelan
OLYMPIC MTS. · Mt. Olympus 7,954 ft. (2424 m.) · Hood Canal · Seattle · Grand Coulee · COLUMBIA · Spokane
COAST RANGES · Tacoma · PLATEAU
Aberdeen · Olympia · Mt. Rainier 14,410 ft. (4392 m.) · Potholes Res. · Palouse
Chehalis · Yakima · Yakima · Snake
Cowlitz · Mt. St. Helens 8,364 ft. (2549 m.) · Mt. Adams 12,307 ft. (3751 m.) · Walla Walla · BLUE MTS.
CASCADE · Columbia · Vancouver

Topography

	Below Sea Level	100 m. 328 ft.	200 m. 656 ft.	500 m. 1,640 ft.	1,000 m. 3,281 ft.	2,000 m. 6,562 ft.	5,000 m. 16,404 ft.

Scale: 0 40 80 MI. / 0 40 80 KM.

Index — Cities and Towns

OTHER FEATURES

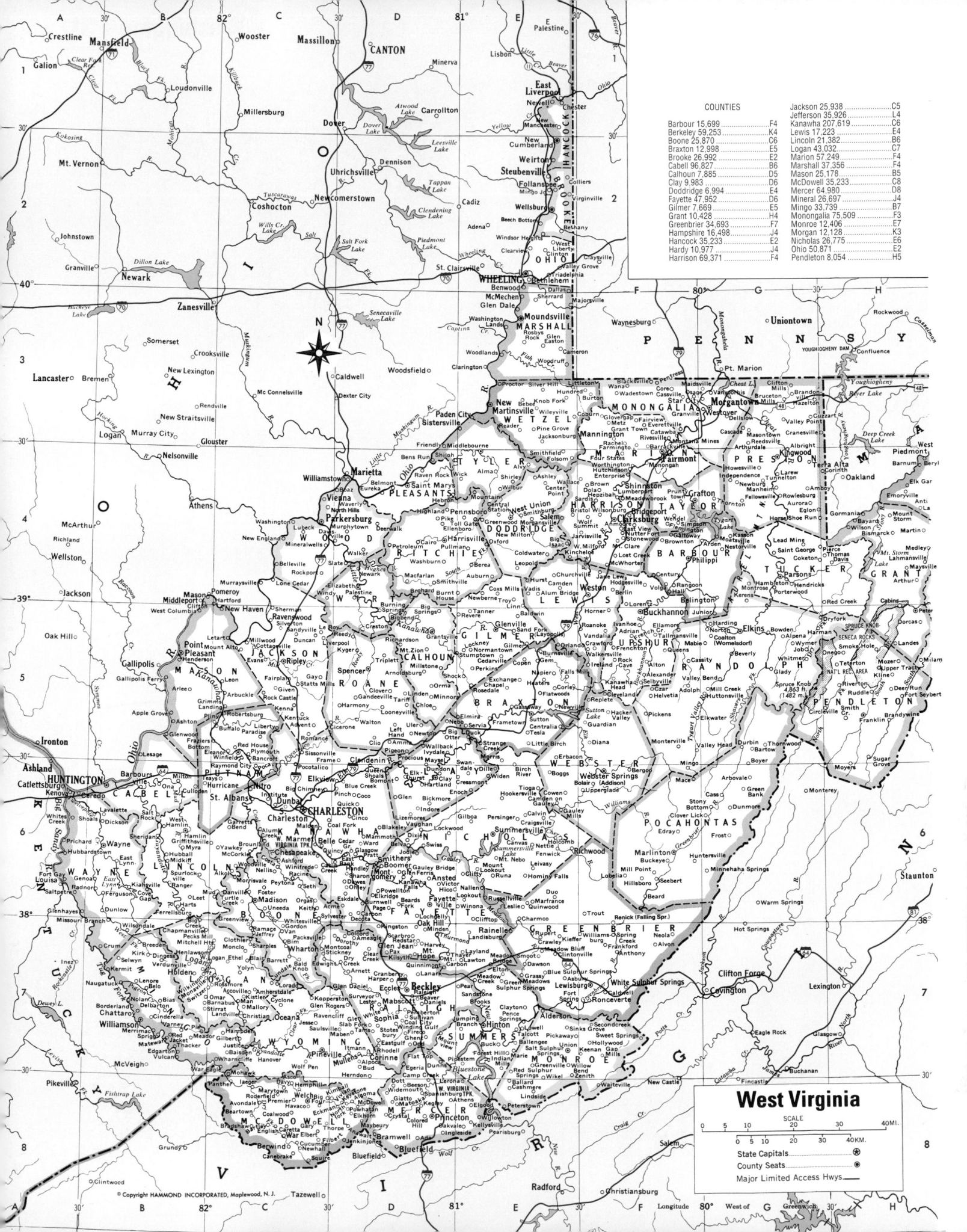

West Virginia

SCALE
0 5 10 20 30 40MI.
0 5 10 20 30 40KM.

State Capitals ⊛
County Seats ⊙
Major Limited Access Hwys. ▬

© Copyright HAMMOND INCORPORATED, Maplewood, N.J.

AREA 24,231 sq. mi. (62,758 sq. km.)
POPULATION 1,801,625
CAPITAL Charleston
LARGEST CITY Charleston
HIGHEST POINT Spruce Knob 4,863 ft.
  (1482 m.)
SETTLED IN 1774
ADMITTED TO UNION June 20, 1863
POPULAR NAME Mountain State
STATE FLOWER Big Rhododendron
STATE BIRD Cardinal

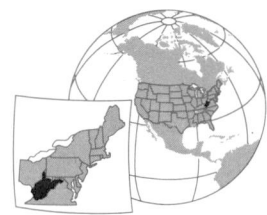

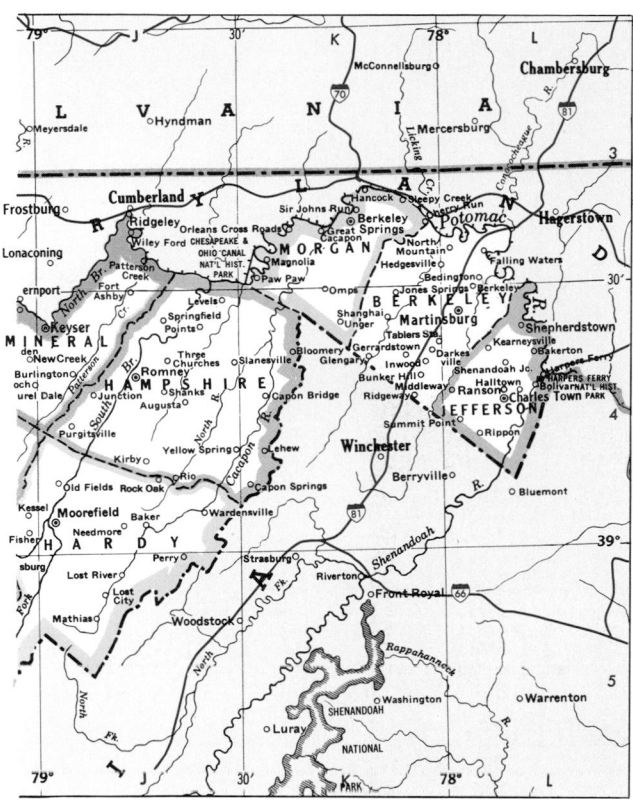

Topography

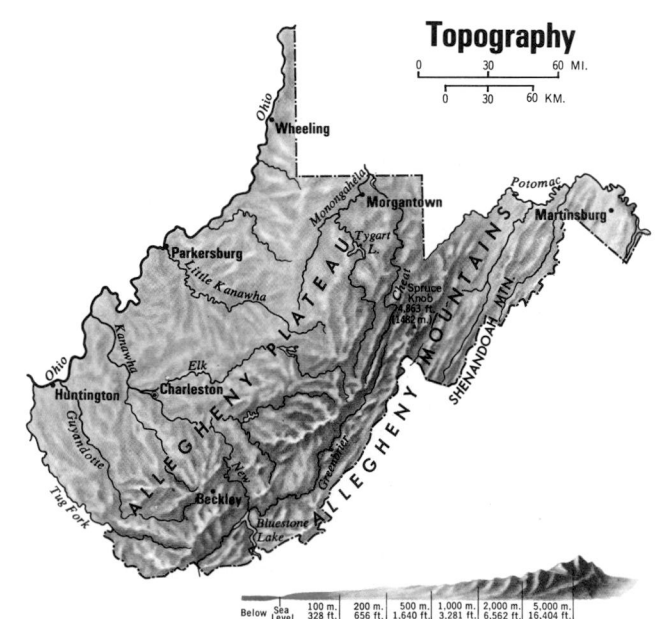

Below Sea Level	100 m. 328 ft.	200 m. 656 ft.	500 m. 1,640 ft.	1,000 m. 3,281 ft.	2,000 m. 6,562 ft.	5,000 m. 16,404 ft.

(continued on following page)

Agriculture, Industry and Resources

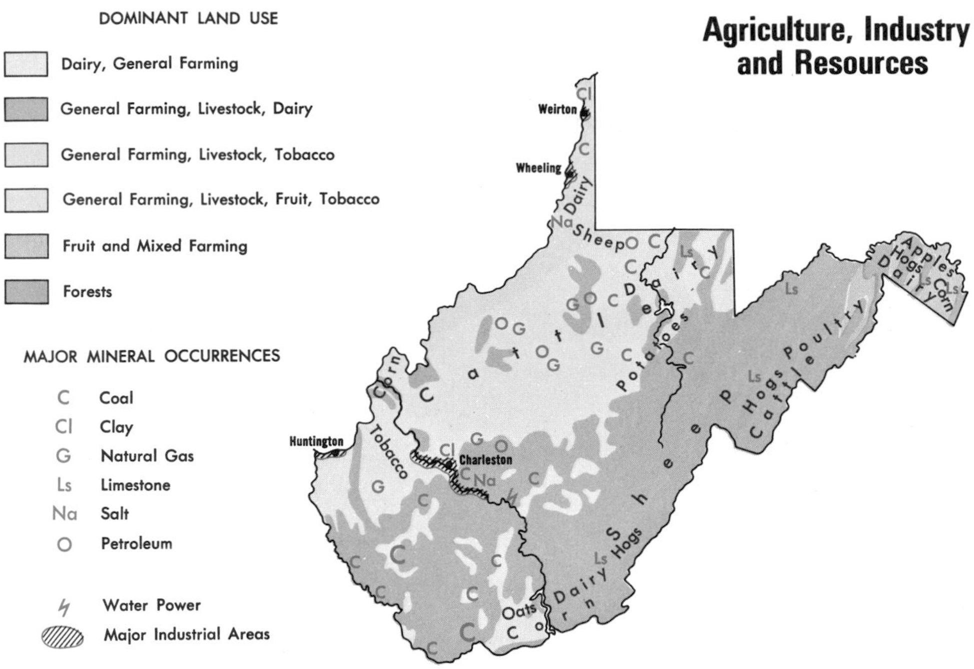
DOMINANT LAND USE
Dairy, General Farming
General Farming, Livestock, Dairy
General Farming, Livestock, Tobacco
General Farming, Livestock, Fruit, Tobacco
Fruit and Mixed Farming
Forests
MAJOR MINERAL OCCURRENCES
C Coal
Cl Clay
G Natural Gas
Ls Limestone
Na Salt
O Petroleum
Water Power
Major Industrial Areas
Weirton
Wheeling
Huntington
Charleston
Dairy
Sheep
Cattle
Potatoes
Tobacco
Corn
Hogs
Poultry
Apples
Oats

Harmony 600 D5
Harper 400 D7
Harpers Ferry 308 L4
Harrisville▲ 1,839 E4
Hartford 487 C4
Harts 2,332 B6
Harvey 300 D7
Havaco 350 C8
Heaters 440 E5
Hedgesville 227 K3
Helvetia 130 F5
Hemphill 700 C8
Henderson 549 B5
Hendricks 303 G4
Henlawson 900 B7
Hepzibah 600 F4
Herndon 500 D7
Hico 750 D6
Hillsboro 188 F6
Hinton▲ 3,433 E7
Hodgesville 200 F4
Holcomb 200 E6
Holden 1,246 B7
Hollywood 150 F7
Hominy Falls 175 E6
Hookersville 250 E6
Horse Shoe Run 500 G4
Howesville 600 G4
Hubball 145 B6
Hundred 386 E3
Huntington▲ 54,844 A6
Hurricane 4,461 C6
Hutchinson 285 F4
Huttonsville 211 G5
Iaeger 551 C8
Independence 200 G4
Indian Mills 150 E7
Indore 300 D6
Inwood 1,360 K4
Itmann 600 D7
Ivanhoe 200 F5
Ivydale 800 D5
Jacksonburg 400 E3
Jane Lew 439 F4
Jarvisville 250 F4
Jeffrey 900 C7
Jenkinjones 750 D8
Jesse 400 C7
Jodie 440 E6
Jumping Branch 700 E7
Junior 542 G5
Justice 600 C7
Kearneysville 250 L4
Kegley 900 D8
Keith 175 C6
Kellysville 165 E8
Kenna 150 C5
Kenova 3,748 A6
Kentuck 200 C5
Kermit 342 B7
Keyser▲ 5,870 J4
Keystone 627 D8
Kieffer 135 E7
Kilsyth 200 D7
Kimball 550 C8
Kingston 189 D7
Kingwood▲ 3,243 G4
Kirk 400 B7
Kistler 200 C7
Kopperston 700 C7
Lahmansville 200 H4
Lanark 559 D7
Landisburg 250 E7
Landville 400 C7
Lavalette 600 B6
Layland 500 E7
Layopolis (Sand Fork) E5
Leet 175 B6
Left Hand 700 D5
Leivasy 200 E6
Lenore 800 B7
Leon 145 C5
Lerona 550 D8
Lesage 600 B5
Leslie 350 E6
Lester 420 D7
Letart 350 C5
Levels 180 J4
Lewisburg▲ 3,598 E7
Liberty 150 C5
Lindside 225 E8
Linn 165 E4
Little Birch 400 E5
Littleton 198 F3
Lizemores 400 D6
Lochgelly 250 D6
Lockney 190 E5
Lockwood 300 D6
Logan▲ 2,206 B7
Lookout 200 E6
Lorado 400 C7
Lorentz 200 F4
Lost City 130 J5
Lost Creek 413 F4
Lost River 500 J5
Lowell 140 E7
Lubeck 1,579 C4
Lumberport 1,014 F4
Lundale 525 C7
Maben 450 D7
Mabie 550 F5
Mabscott 1,543 D7
Macfarlan 436 D4
Madison▲ 3,051 C6
Maidsville 500 F3
Malden 900 C6
Mallory 1,126 C7
Mammoth 563 D6
Man 914 C7
Mannington 2,184 F3
Marfrance 225 E6
Marlinton▲ 1,148 F6
Marmet 1,879 C6
Martinsburg▲ 14,073 K4
Mason 1,053 B4
Masontown 737 G3
Matewan 619 B7
Matoaka 366 D8
Maybeury 300 D8
Maysel 350 D5
Maysville 150 H4
McCorkle 300 C6
McDowell 500 D8
McMechen 2,130 E3
McWhorter 150 F4
Meador 225 B7
Meadow Bridge 325 E7
Meadow Creek 300 E7
Meadowbrook 500 F4
Merrimac 140 B7
Metz 150 F3
Middlebourne▲ 922 E3
Middleway 350 K4
Midkiff 650 B6
Mill Creek 685 G5
Mill Point 148 F6
Millstone 850 D5
Millwood 800 C5
Milton 2,242 B6
Minden 800 D7
Mineralwells 1,698 C4
Mingo 350 F5
Minnora 500 D5
Missouri Branch 250 A7
Mitchell Heights 265 B7
Moatsville 150 G4
Monaville 950 B7
Monclo 242 C7
Monongah 1,132 F4
Montana Mines 200 F3
Montcoal 150 D7
Monterville 250 F5
Montgomery 2,449 D6
Montrose 140 G4
Moorefield▲ 2,148 J4
Morgansville 164 E4
Morgantown▲ 25,879 F3
Morrisvale 450 C6
Moundsville▲ 10,753 E3
Mount Alto 200 C5
Mount Carbon 450 D7
Mount Clare 950 F4
Mount Gay 4,366 C7
Mount Hope 1,573 D7
Mount Lookout 500 E6
Mount Nebo 535 E6
Mount Storm 500 H4
Mount Zion 350 D5
Mountain 200 E4
Mud 143 C6
Mullens 2,006 D7
Murphytown 600 D4
Nallen 250 E6
Napier 158 E5
Naugatuck 500 B7
Nebo 200 D5
Nellis 600 C6
Neola 300 F7
Nettie 500 E6
New Cumberland▲ 1,363 E2
New England 335 C4
New Haven 1,632 C5
New Manchester 800 E1
New Martinsville▲ 6,705 E3
Newburg 378 G4
Newell 1,724 E1
Newhall 400 C8
Newton 390 D5
Newville 160 E5
Nitro 6,851 C6
Nolan 250 B7
North Hills 849 D4
Northfork 656 D8
Norton 400 G5
Nutter Fort 1,819 F4
Oak Hill 6,812 D6
Oakvale 165 D8
Oceana 1,791 C7
Odd 500 D7
Ohley 450 D6
Omar 900 C7
Ona 200 B6
Onego 400 H5
Orgas 500 C6
Orlando 700 E5
Orleans Cross Roads 150 K3
Orma D5
Osage 183 F3
Packsville 225 C7
Paden City 2,862 D3
Page 600 D6
Panther 450 C8
Parkersburg▲ 33,862 D4
Parsons▲ 1,453 G4
Patterson Creek 157 J3
Paw Paw 538 K3
Pax 167 D7
Pecks Mill 350 B7
Pemberton 300 D7
Pence Springs 300 E7
Pennsboro 1,282 E4
Pentress 250 F3
Petersburg▲ 2,360 H5
Peterstown 550 E8
Peytona 175 C6
Philippi▲ 3,132 G4
Pickaway 225 E7
Pickens 240 F5
Pie 250 B7
Piedmont 1,094 H4
Pinch 2,695 D6
Pine Grove 701 E3
Pineville▲ 865 C7
Pliny 900 B5
Poca 1,124 C6
Pocotalico 2,420 C6
Point Pleasant▲ 4,996 B5
Points 250 J4
Powellton 1,905 D6
Powhatan 400 D8
Pratt 640 D6
Premier 400 C8
Prichard 500 A6
Princeton▲ 7,043 D8
Procious 600 D5
Proctor 350 E3
Pruntytown 145 F4
Pullman 109 D4
Purgitsville 450 J4
Quick 400 D6
Quincy 150 C6
Quinwood 559 E6
Rachel 550 F3
Racine 725 C6
Radnor 300 A6
Rainelle 1,681 E7
Raleigh 900 D7
Ramage 350 C7
Ranger 300 B6
Ranson 2,890 L4
Ravencliff 350 C7
Ravenswood 4,189 C5
Raymond City 400 C6
Reader 950 E3
Red House 600 C5
Red Jacket 760 B7
Redstar 200 D7
Reedsville 482 G3
Reedy 271 D5
Renick F6
Replete 200 F5
Rhodell 221 D7
Richwood 2,808 F6
Ridgeley 779 J3
Ridgeway 200 K4
Rio 140 J4
Ripley▲ 3,023 C5
Rippon 500 L4
Rivesville 1,064 F3
Robertsburg 140 C5
Rock Cave 400 F5
Roderfield 900 C8
Romney▲ 1,966 J4
Ronceverte 1,754 F7
Rosedale 400 E5
Rossmore 200 C7
Rowlesburg 648 G4
Runa 150 E6
Rupert 1,104 E7
Russellville 280 E6
Saint Albans 11,194 C6
Saint George 150 F4
Saint Marys▲ 2,148 D4
Salem 2,063 E4
Salt Rock 350 B6
Sand Fork 196 E5
Sandstone 300 E7
Sandyville 500 C5
Saulsville 250 C7
Scarbo 800 D7
Selwyn 500 B7
Seth 950 C6
Shanghai 200 K4
Shanks 500 J4
Sharon 450 D6
Sharples 250 C7
Shenandoah Junction 600 L4
Shepherdstown 1,287 L4
Sheridan 160 B6
Sherrard 400 E3
Shinnston 2,543 F4
Shirley 275 E4
Shoals 150 B6
Shock 200 D5
Silverton 250 C5
Simpson 250 F4
Sinks Grove 156 F7
Sissonville 4,290 C5
Sistersville 1,797 D3
Slab Fork 210 D7
Slaneville 250 K4
Smithburg 130 E4
Smithers 1,162 D6
Smithfield 205 E4
Smithville 200 D4
Smoot 300 E7
Sophia 1,182 D7
South Charleston 13,645 C6
Spanishburg 550 D8
Spencer▲ 2,279 D5
Sprigg 225 B7
Springfield 250 J4
Spurlockville 250 B6
Squire 900 C8
Star City 1,251 F3
Statts Mills 400 C5
Stickney 150 D7
Stirrat 250 C7
Stonewood 1,996 F4
Stotesbury 199 D7
Strange Creek 175 E5
Sullivan 700 D7
Summersville▲ 2,906 E6
Summit Point 455 K4
Surveyor 300 D7
Sutton▲ 939 E5
Swiss 500 D6
Switzer 1,004 B7
Sylvester 191 C6
Talcott 800 E7
Tallmansville 140 F5
Tanner 375 E5
Teays 200 B6
Terra Alta 1,713 H4
Tesla 300 E5
Thacker 525 B7
Thomas 573 H4
Thornton 200 G4
Thorpe 600 D8
Three Churches 350 J4
Thurmond 39 D7
Tioga 825 E6
Triadelphia 835 E2
Troy 110 E4
Tunnelton 331 G4
Turtle Creek 566 C6
Uneeda 700 C6
Unger 300 K4
Union▲ 566 E7
Upper Tract 155 H5
Upperglade 750 F6
Vadis 130 E4
Valley Bend 950 F5
Valley Grove 569 E2
Valley Head 900 G5
Van 800 C7
Varney 750 B7
Vaughan 375 D6
Verdunville 950 B7
Victor 500 D6
Vienna 10,862 D4
Vivian 500 D8
Vulcan 130 B7
Wadestown 300 F3
Waiteville 230 F8
Walkersville 135 F5
Wallace 325 E4
Wallback 150 D5
Walton 550 D5
Wana 150 F3
War 1,081 C8
Ward 850 D6
Wardensville 140 K4
Washington 1,030 C4
Washington Lands 400 E3
Waverly 500 D4
Wayne▲ 1,128 B6
Webster Springs▲ 674 F6
Weirton 22,124 E2
Welch▲ 3,028 C8
Wellsburg▲ 3,385 E2
West Columbia 245 B5
West Hamlin 423 B6
West Liberty 1,434 E2
West Logan 524 C7
West Milford 519 F4
West Union▲ 830 E4
Weston▲ 4,994 F4
Westover 4,201 G3
Wharncliffe 900 C7
Wharton 450 C7
Wheeling▲ 34,882 E2
White Sulphur Springs 2,779 F7
Whites Creek 500 A6
Whitesville 486 C6
Whitmer 400 G5
Widen 230 E6
Wiley Ford 1,224 J3
Wileyville 175 E3
Wilkinson 975 B7
Williamsburg 350 F7
Williamson▲ 4,154 B7
Williamstown 2,774 C4
Wilsonburg 350 F4
Wilsondale 250 B7
Windsor Heights 800 E2
Winfield▲ 1,164 C5
Winifrede 750 C6
Winona 250 E6
Wolf Pen 175 C7
Wolf Summit 750 F4
Womelsdorf (Coalton) 277 G5
Woodlands 200 E3
Woodville 300 C6
Worthington 233 F4
Yawkey 985 C6
Yellow Spring 280 J4
Yolyn 400 C7

OTHER FEATURES

Big Sandy (riv.) A6
Bluestone (lake) E7
Buckhannon (riv.) F5
Cacapon (riv.) J4
Cheat (riv.) G3
Cherry (riv.) E6
Chesapeake and Ohio Canal Nat'l Hist. Park J3
Clear Fork, Guyandotte (riv.) C7
Coal (riv.) C6
Dry Fork (riv.) C8
Dry Fork (riv.) G5
East Lynn (lake) B6
Elk (riv.) D6
Fish (creek) E3
Gauley (riv.) D6
Greenbrier (riv.) F6
Guyandotte (riv.) B6
Harpers Ferry Nat'l Hist. Park L4
Hughes (riv.) D4
Kanawha (riv.) C5
Little Kanawha (riv.) D5
Meadow (riv.) E6
Mill (creek) C5
Monongahela (riv.) G3
Mount Storm (lake) H4
Mud (riv.) B6
New (riv.) E7
North (riv.) J4
Ohio (riv.) B5
Patterson (creek) J4
Pigeon (creek) B7
Pocatalico (riv.) C5
Pond Fork (riv.) C6
Potomac (riv.) L3
Potts (creek) F7
Reedy (creek) D5
Shavers Fork (riv.) G5
Shenandoah (riv.) K4
Spruce Knob (mt.) G5
Spruce Knob-Seneca Rocks Nat'l Rec. Area H5
Stony (riv.) H4
Summersville (lake) E6
Sutton (lake) F5
Tug Fork (riv.) B7
Twelvepole (creek) A6
Tygart (lake) G4
Tygart Valley (riv.) F5
West Fork (riv.) E5
Williams (riv.) F6

▲County seat

WISCONSIN
1848

AREA 56,153 sq. mi. (145,436 sq. km.)
POPULATION 4,906,745
CAPITAL Madison
LARGEST CITY Milwaukee
HIGHEST POINT Timms Hill 1,951 ft. (595 m.)
SETTLED IN 1670
ADMITTED TO UNION May 29, 1848
POPULAR NAME Badger State
STATE FLOWER Wood Violet
STATE BIRD Robin

COUNTIES

Adams 15,682 ....G7
Ashland 16,307 ....E3
Barron 40,750 ....C5
Bayfield 14,008 ....D3
Brown 194,594 ....L7
Buffalo 13,584 ....C7
Burnett 13,084 ....B4
Calumet 34,291 ....K7
Chippewa 52,360 ....D5
Clark 31,647 ....E6
Columbia 45,088 ....H9
Crawford 15,940 ....E9
Dane 367,085 ....H9
Dodge 76,559 ....J8
Door 25,690 ....M6
Douglas 41,758 ....C3
Dunn 35,909 ....D6
Eau Claire 85,183 ......D6
Florence 4,590 ....K4
Fond du Lac 90,083 ....K8
Forest 8,776 ....J4
Grant 49,264 ....E10
Green 30,339 ....G10
Green Lake 18,651 .....H8
Iowa 20,150 ....F9
Iron 6,153 ....F3
Jackson 16,588 ....F3
Jefferson 67,783 ....J9
Juneau 21,650 ....F8
Kenosha 128,181 ....K10
Kewaunee 18,878 ......L6
La Crosse 97,904 ......D8
Lafayette 16,076 ....F10
Langlade 19,505 ....H5
Lincoln 26,993 ....G5
Manitowoc 80,421 .....L7
Marathon 115,400 .....G6
Marinette 40,548 ......K5
Marquette 12,321 ......H8
Menominee 3,890 ......J5
Milwaukee 959,275 ....L9
Monroe 36,633 ....E8
Oconto 30,226 ....K6
Oneida 31,679 ....G4
Outagamie 140,510 ...K7
Ozaukee 72,831 ....L9
Pepin 7,107 ....C6
Pierce 32,765 ....B6
Polk 34,773 ....B5
Portage 61,405 ....G6
Price 15,600 ....F4
Racine 175,034 ....K10
Richland 17,521 ....F9
Rock 139,510 ....H10
Rusk 15,079 ....D5
Saint Croix 43,262 ....C5
Sauk 46,975 ....G9
Sawyer 14,181 ....D4
Shawano 37,157 ......J6
Sheboygan 103,877 ...L8
Taylor 18,901 ....E5
Trempealeau 25,263 ..D7
Vernon 25,617 ....E8
Vilas 17,707 ....G3
Walworth 75,000 .....J10
Washburn 13,772 .....C4
Washington 95,328 ...K9
Waukesha 304,715 ...K9
Waupaca 46,104 .....J6
Waushara 19,385 ....H7
Winnebago 140,320 ..J8
Wood 73,605 ....F7

CITIES and TOWNS

Abbotsford 1,916 ....F6
Abrams 300 ....L6
Adams 1,715 ....G8
Adell 510 ....L8
Afton 225 ....H10
Albany 1,140 ....G10
Albion 300 ....H10
Algoma 3,353 ....M6
Allenton 915 ....K9
Allouez 14,431 ....L7
Alma Center 416 ......E7
Alma▲ 790 ....C7
Almena 625 ....B5
Almond 455 ....G7
Alto 235 ....J8
Altoona 5,889 ....C6
Alvin 160 ....J4
Amberg 875 ....K5
Amery 2,657 ....B5
Amherst 792 ....H7
Amherst Junction 269 ..H7
Angelica 200 ....K6
Angelo 100 ....E3
Aniwa 249 ....H6
Antigo▲ 8,276 ....H5
Appleton▲ 65,695 ....J7
Arbor Vitae 900 ......G4
Arcadia 2,166 ....D7
Arena 525 ....G9

Argonne 600 ....G9
Argyle 798 ....G10
Arkansaw 400 ....B6
Arlington 440 ....H9
Armstrong Creek 615 ..K4
Arpin 312 ....G6
Ashippun 750 ....H1
Ashland▲ 8,695 ......E2
Ashwaubenon 16,376 ..K7
Athens 951 ....G5
Auburndale 665 ......F6
Augusta 1,510 ....D6
Auroraville 250 ......H7
Avoca 474 ....F9
Avon 120 ....H10
Babcock 250 ....F7
Bagley 306 ....D10
Baileys Harbor 250 ..M5
Baldwin 2,022 ....B6
Balsam Lake▲ 792 ..B5
Bancroft 355 ....G7
Bangor 1,076 ....E8
Baraboo▲ 9,203 ....G9
Barnes 225 ....D3
Barneveld 660 ....F10
Barron▲ 2,986 ......C5
Barronett 575 ....B4
Batavia 125 ....K8
Bay City 578 ....B6
Bayfield 686 ....E2
Bayside 4,789 ......M1
Bear Creek 418 ....J6
Beaver 100 ....K5
Beaver Dam 14,196 ..J9
Beetown 150 ....E10
Beldenville 175 ....A6
Belgium 928 ....L8
Bell Center 127 ....E9
Belleville 1,456 ....G10
Belmont 823 ....F10
Beloit 35,573 ......H10
Bennett 350 ....C3
Benton 898 ....F10
Berlin 5,371 ....H8
Bethel 210 ....F6
Bevent 200 ....H6
Big Bend 1,299 ...K2
Birchwood 443 ...C4
Birnamwood 603 ..I16
Biron 794 ....G7
Black Creek 1,152 ..K7
Black Earth 1,248 ..G9
Black River Falls▲ 3,490 ..F7
Blackwell 550 .....K4
Blair 1,126 ....D7
Blanchardville 802 ..G10
Bloom City 167 ....E8
Bloomer 3,085 ....D5
Bloomington 776 ..E10
Blue Mounds 446 ..G9
Blue River 438 ....E9
Boardman 100 ....A5
Boaz 131 ....E9
Bohners Lake 1,553 ..K10
Bonduel 1,210 ....K6
Boscobel 2,706 ...E9
Boulder Junction 780 ..G3
Bowler 279 ....J6
Boyceville 913 ....C5
Boyd 683 ....E6
Brackett 150 ......D6
Bradley 100 ....G4
Branch 300 ....L7
Brandon 872 ......J8
Brantwood 500 ...F4
Bridgeport 250 ...D9
Briggsville 250 ...H8
Brighton 100 ......K3
Brill 200 ....C4
Brillion 2,840 .....L7
Brodhead 3,165 ..G10
Brokaw 224 ....G5
Brooklyn 789 .....H10
Brooks 103 ....G8
Brothertown 100 ..K7
Brown Deer 12,236 ..L1
Brown's Lake 1,725 ..K3
Brownsville 415 ...J8
Browntown 256 ...G10
Bruce 844 ....D5
Brussels 500 ......L6
Buffalo 915 ....C7
Burlington 8,855 ..K10
Burnett 260 ....J9
Butler 2,079 ......K1
Butte Des Morts ..J7
Butternut 416 .....E3
Cable 227 ....D3
Cadott 1,328 ......D6
Caldwell 101 ......J2
Caledonia 100 ....L2
Cambria 768 ......H8
Cambridge 963 ...H9
Cameron 1,273 ...C5

Camp Douglas 512 ....F8
Camp Lake 2,291 ....K10
Campbellsport 1,732 ......K8
Canton 100 ....C5
Caroline 450 ....J6
Carter 100 ....J5
Cascade 620 ....K8
Casco 544 ....L6
Cashton 780 ....E8
Cassville 1,144 ....E10
Cataract 200 ....E7
Catawba 178 ....E4
Cazenovia 288 ....F8
Cecil 373 ....K6
Cedar Grove 1,521 .....L8
Cedarburg 9,895 ....L9
Centuria 790 ....A5
Chaseburg 365 ....D8
Chelsea 150 ....F5
Chenequa 601 ....J1
Chetek 1,953 ....C5
Chili 185 ....F6
Chilton▲ 3,240 ....K7
Chippewa Falls▲ 12,727 ..D6
City Point 110 ....F7
Clam Lake 140 ......E3
Clayton 450 ....B5
Clear Lake 932 ......B5
Clearwater Lake 200 ..H4
Cleveland 1,398 ....L8
Clinton 1,849 ......J10
Clintonville 4,351 ..J6
Clyman 370 ....J9
Cobb 440 ....F10
Cochrane 475 ......C7
Colby 1,532 ....F6
Coleman 839 ......L5
Colfax 1,110 ......C6
Coloma 383 ....H7
Columbus 4,093 ..H9
Combined Locks 2,190 ..K7
Commonwealth 240 ..K4
Como 1,353 ....K10
Comstock 160 .....C5
Concord 200 ......H1
Conover 480 ......H3
Conrath 92 ....E5
Coon Valley 817 ..E8
Cornell 1,541 ....D5
Cornucopia 250 ..D2
Couderay 92 .....D4
Crandon▲ 1,958 ..H4
Cream 120 ....C7
Crivitz 996 ......L5
Cross Plains 2,098 ..G9
Cuba City 2,024 ..F10
Cudahy 18,659 ...M2
Cumberland 2,163 ..C4
Curtiss 173 ....F6
Cushing 150 .....A4
Cylon 100 ....B5
Dale 410 ....J7
Dallas 452 ....C5
Dalton 300 ....H8
Danbury 350 .....B3
Dane 621 ....G9
Darien 1,158 .....J10
Darlington▲ 2,235 ..F10
De Forest 4,882 ..H9
De Pere 16,569 ...K7
De Soto 326 ......D9
Deer Park 237 ...B5
Deerfield 1,617 ..H9
Delafield 5,347 ..J1
Delavan 6,073 ...J10
Delavan Lake 2,177 ..J10
Dellwood 120 ....G7
Denmark 1,612 ...L7
Dexterville 100 ..F7
Diamond Bluff 100 ..A6
Dickeyville 862 ..E10
Dodge 185 ......D7
Dodgeville▲ 3,882 ..F10
Dorchester 697 ..F5
Dousman 1,277 ..J1
Downing 250 ....B5
Downsville 200 ..C6
Doylestown 316 ..H9
Draper 125 ......E4
Dresser 614 .....A5
Drummond 200 ..D3
Dunbar 106 .....K4
Durand▲ 2,003 ..C6
Dyckesville 300 ..L6
Eagle 1,182 .....J10
Eagle River▲ 1,374 ..H4
East Troy 2,664 ..J2
Eastman 369 ....D9
Easton 130 .....G8
Eau Claire▲ 56,856 ..D6
Eden 610 ....K8
Edgar 1,318 ....G6
Edgerton 4,254 ..H10
Egg Harbor 183 ..M5
Eland 247 ....H6
Elcho 500 ....H5

Elderon 175 ....H6
Eldorado 200 ....J8
Eleva 491 ....D6
Elk Mound 765 ....C6
Elkhart Lake 1,019 ....L8
Elkhorn▲ 5,337 ....J10
Ellison Bay 112 ......M5
Ellsworth▲ 2,705 ....A6
Elm Grove 6,261 .....K1
Elmwood 775 ....B6
Elmwood Park 534 ..M3
Elroy 1,533 ....F8
Elton 150 ....J5
Embarrass 461 ......J6
Emerald 128 ....B5
Endeavor 316 ....G8
Ephraim 261 ....M5
Ettrick 461 ....D7
Evansville 3,174 ....H10
Exeland 180 ....D4
Fair Water 310 .....J8
Fairchild 504 ....D6
Fall Creek 1,034 ...D6
Fall River 842 .....H9

Fence 200 ....K4
Fennimore 2,378 .....E9
Fenwood 214 ....F6
Ferryville 154 ....D9
Fifield 310 ....F4
Fish Creek 119 ....M5
Florence▲ 780 ....K4
Fond du Lac▲ 37,757 ..K8
Fontana 1,635 ....J10
Footville 764 ....H10
Forest Junction 140 ..K7
Forestville 470 ......L6
Fort Atkinson 10,227 ..J10
Fountain City 938 ...C7
Fox Lake 1,269 .....J8
Fox Point 7,238 ....M1
Foxboro 360 ....B2
Francis Creek 562 ..L7
Franklin 21,855 ....L2
Franksville 375 ....M3
Frederic 1,124 .....B4
Fredonia 1,558 ....L8
Fremont 632 ....J7
Friendship▲ 728 ...G8

Friesland 271 ....H8
Galesville 1,278 ....D7
Galloway 200 ....H6
Gays Mills 578 ....E9
Genesee 375 ....J2
Genesee Depot 350 ....J2
Genoa 266 ....D8
Genoa City 1,277 ......K11
Germantown 13,658 ...K1
Gibbsville 408 ....L8
Gillett 1,303 ....K6
Gilman 412 ....E5
Gilmanton 300 ......C7
Gleason 200 ....G5
Glen Flora 108 .....E4
Glen Haven 160 ...E10
Glenbeulah 386 ...L8
Glendale 14,088 ...M1
Glenwood City 1,026 ..B5
Glidden 940 ....E3
Goodman 875 .....K4
Gordon 600 ....C3
Gotham 250 ......F9
Grafton 9,340 .....L9

Grand Marsh 725 ....G8
Grand View 447 ....D3
Granton 379 ....E6
Grantsburg▲ 1,144 ....A4
Gratiot 207 ....F10
Green Bay▲ 96,466 ...K6
Green Lake▲ 1,064 ...H8
Green Valley 104 .....K6
Greendale 15,128 ....L2
Greenfield 33,403 ...L2
Greenleaf 300 ....L7
Greenville 900 ......J7
Greenwood 969 .....E6
Gresham 515 ....J6
Gurney 145 ....F3
Hager City 110 ......A6
Hales Corners 7,623 ..K2
Hallie D6
Hamburg 170 ....G5
Hammond 1,097 ...A6
Hancock 382 ....G7
Hartford 8,188 .....K9
Hartland 6,906 .....J1
Hatfield 500 ....E7

(continued on following page)

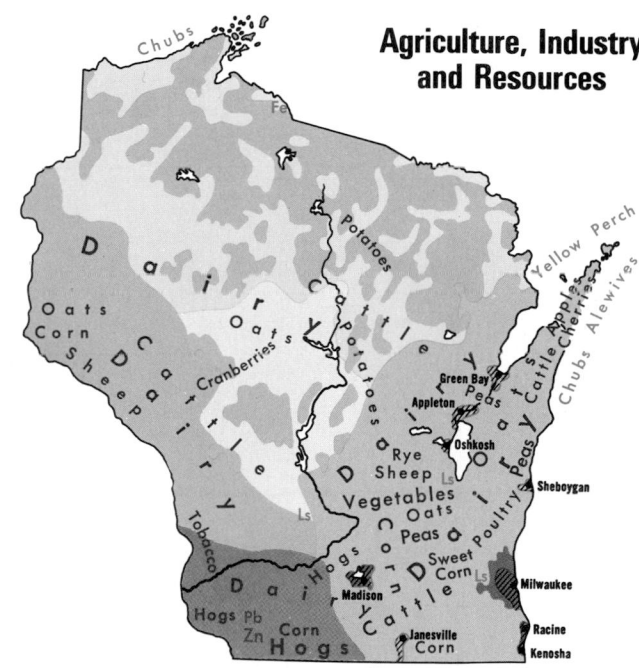

Agriculture, Industry and Resources

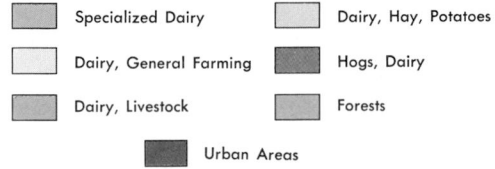

DOMINANT LAND USE

Specialized Dairy	Dairy, Hay, Potatoes
Dairy, General Farming	Hogs, Dairy
Dairy, Livestock	Forests
Urban Areas	

MAJOR MINERAL OCCURRENCES

Fe Iron Ore   Pb Lead

Ls Limestone   Zn Zinc

///// Major Industrial Areas

Hatley 295 .... H6
Haugen 305 .... C4
Hawkins 375 .... E4
Hawthorne 200 .... C3
Hayward▲ 1,897 .... D3
Hazel Green 1,171 .... F11
Hazelhurst 630 .... G4
Heafford Junction 110 .... G4
Hebron 450 .... J10
Helenville 300 .... J10
Hersey 125 .... B6
Hewitt 595 .... F6
High Bridge 525 .... E3
Highland 799 .... F9
Hilbert 1,211 .... K7
Hiles 350 .... J4
Hillsboro 1,288 .... F8
Hillsdale 160 .... C5
Hingham 250 .... K8
Hixton 345 .... E7
Holcombe 200 .... D5
Hollandale 256 .... G10
Holmen 3,220 .... D8
Holy Cross 150 .... L9
Honey Creek 300 .... J3
Horicon 3,873 .... J9
Hortonville 2,029 .... J7
Houlton 915 .... A5
Howard 9,874 .... K6
Howards Grove-Millersville 1,838 .... L8
Hubertus 600 .... K1
Hudson▲ 6,378 .... A6
Humbird 190 .... E6
Hurley▲ 1,782 .... F3
Hustisford 979 .... J9
Hustler 156 .... F8
Independence 1,041 .... D7
Ingram 91 .... E5
Iola 1,125 .... H6
Iron Belt 300 .... F3
Iron Ridge 887 .... K9
Iron River 878 .... D2
Ironton 200 .... F8
Ithaca 160 .... F9
Ixonia 525 .... H1
Jackson 2,486 .... K9
Jacksonport 150 .... M6
Janesville▲ 52,133 .... H10
Jefferson▲ 6,078 .... J10
Johnson Creek 1,259 .... J9
Juda 500 .... H10
Junction City 502 .... G6
Juneau▲ 2,157 .... J9
Kansasville 150 .... L3
Kaukauna 11,982 .... K7
Kekoskee 188 .... J8
Kellnersville 350 .... L7
Kempster 121 .... H5
Kendall 453 .... F8
Kennan 169 .... F5
Kenosha▲ 80,352 .... M3
Keshena▲ 685 .... J6
Kewaskum 2,515 .... K8
Kewaunee▲ 2,750 .... M7
Kiel 2,910 .... L8
Kieler 800 .... E10
Kimberly 5,406 .... K7
King H7
Kingston 346 .... H8
Knapp 419 .... B6
Knowlton 127 .... G6
Kohler 1,817 .... L8
Krakow 345 .... K6
La Crosse▲ 51,003 .... D8
La Farge 766 .... E8
La Pointe 300 .... E2
La Valle 446 .... F8
Lac La Belle 258 .... H1
Lac du Flambeau 1,423 .... G4
Ladysmith▲ 3,938 .... D5
Lake Church 175 .... L9
Lake Delton 1,470 .... G8
Lake Geneva 5,979 .... K10
Lake Mills 4,143 .... H9
Lake Nebagamon 900 .... C3
Lake Tomahawk 600 .... H4
Lake Wazeecha 2,278 .... G7
Lake Wissota 2,175 .... D6
Lakewood 425 .... K5
Lamartine 190 .... J8
Lancaster▲ 4,192 .... E10
Land O'Lakes 786 .... H3
Lannon 924 .... K1
Lebanon 250 .... H1
Lena 590 .... K6
Leopolis 200 .... J6
Lewis 200 .... B4
Lily 125 .... J5
Lima Center 175 .... J10
Limeridge 152 .... F9
Linden 429 .... F10
Little Chute 9,207 .... K7
Little Suamico 190 .... L6
Livingston 576 .... E10
Lodi 2,093 .... G9
Loganville 228 .... F9
Lohrville 368 .... H7
Lomira 1,542 .... J8
London 317 .... H9
Lone Rock 641 .... F9
Long Lake 150 .... J4
Loretta 200 .... E4
Lowell 300 .... J9
Loyal 1,244 .... E6
Lublin 129 .... E5
Luck 1,022 .... B4
Luxemburg 1,151 .... L6
Lyndon Station 474 .... F8
Lynn 117 .... F6
Lynxville 153 .... D9
Lyons 550 .... K10
Madison (cap.)▲ 191,262 .... H9
Maiden Rock 146 .... B6
Manawa 1,169 .... J7
Manchester 160 .... J8
Manitowoc▲ 32,520 .... L7
Maple 596 .... C2
Maplewood 200 .... M6
Marathon 1,606 .... G6
Marengo 130 .... E3
Maribel 372 .... L7
Marinette▲ 11,843 .... L5
Marion 1,242 .... J6
Markesan 1,496 .... J8
Marquette 182 .... H8
Marshall 2,329 .... H9
Marshfield 19,291 .... F6
Martell 200 .... B6
Mason 102 .... D3
Mattoon 431 .... J5
Mauston▲ 3,439 .... F8
Mayville 4,374 .... K9
Mazomanie 1,377 .... G9
McFarland 5,232 .... H10
McNaughton 450 .... H4
Medford▲ 4,283 .... F5
Mellen 935 .... E3
Melrose 551 .... E7
Melvina 115 .... E8
Menasha 14,711 .... J7
Menomonee Falls 26,840 .... K1
Menomonie▲ 13,547 .... C6
Mequon 18,885 .... L1
Mercer V3
Merrill▲ 9,860 .... G5
Merrillan 553 .... E7
Merrimac 392 .... G9
Merton 1,199 .... K1
Middle Inlet 200 .... K5
Middleton 13,289 .... G9
Mikana 200 .... C4
Milan 153 .... F6
Milladore 314 .... G6
Millston 110 .... E7
Milltown 786 .... J10
Milton 4,434 .... J10
Milwaukee▲ 628,088 .... M1
Mindoro 200 .... D7
Mineral Point 2,428 .... F10
Minocqua 950 .... G4
Minong 521 .... C3
Mishicot 1,296 .... L7
Mondovi 2,491 .... C6
Monico 250 .... H4
Monona 8,637 .... G10
Monroe▲ 10,241 .... G10
Montello▲ 1,329 .... H8
Monterey 150 .... J1
Montfort 676 .... E10
Monticello 1,140 .... G10
Montreal 838 .... F3
Morrisonville 375 .... G9
Mosinee 3,820 .... G6
Mount Calvary 558 .... K8
Mount Hope 173 .... D10
Mount Horeb 4,182 .... G10
Mount Sterling 217 .... D9
Mount Vernon 138 .... G10
Mountain 250 .... K5
Mukwonago 4,457 .... J2
Muscoda 1,287 .... F9
Muskego 16,813 .... K2
Nashotah 567 .... J1
Navarino 140 .... J6
Necedah 743 .... F7
Neenah 23,219 .... J7
Neillsville▲ 2,680 .... E6
Nekoosa 2,557 .... G7
Nelson 388 .... C7
Nelsonville 171 .... H7
Neopit 615 .... J6
Neosho 658 .... J9
Neshkoro 384 .... H8
New Amsterdam 120 .... C8
New Auburn 485 .... D5
New Berlin 33,592 .... K2
New Franken 150 .... L6
New Glarus 1,899 .... G10
New Holstein 3,342 .... K8
New Lisbon 1,491 .... F8
New London 6,658 .... J7
New Richmond 5,106 .... A5
Newald 375 .... J4
Newburg 875 .... K9
Niagara 1,999 .... K4
Nichols 254 .... K6
North Bay 246 .... M3
North Bend 200 .... D7
North Fond du Lac 4,292 .... J8
North Freedom 591 .... G9
North Hudson 3,101 .... A5
North Lake 400 .... J1
North Prairie 1,322 .... J2
North Shore 14,272 .... M1
Norwalk 564 .... E8
Oak Creek 19,513 .... M2
Oakdale 162 .... F8
Oakfield 1,003 .... J8
Oconomowoc 10,993 .... H1
Oconomowoc Lake 493 .... H1
Oconto Falls 2,584 .... K6
Oconto▲ 4,474 .... L6
Odanah 190 .... E2
Ogdensburg 220 .... J7
Ogema 238 .... E5
Okauchee 3,958 .... J1
Okee 250 .... H9
Oliver 265 .... B2
Omro 2,836 .... J8
Onalaska 11,284 .... D8
Oneida 808 .... K7
Ontario 407 .... E8
Oostburg 1,931 .... L8
Oregon 4,519 .... H10
Orfordville 1,219 .... H10
Osceola 2,075 .... A5
Oshkosh▲ 55,006 .... J8
Osseo 1,551 .... D6
Owen 895 .... F6
Oxford 499 .... H8
Packwaukee 271 .... G8
Paddock Lake 2,662 .... K10
Palmyra 1,539 .... H2
Pardeeville 1,630 .... H8
Park Falls 3,104 .... F4
Park Ridge 546 .... H6
Patch Grove 202 .... D10
Pearson 102 .... H5
Peeksville 250 .... E3
Pell Lake 2,018 .... K10
Pembine 500 .... L4
Pence 234 .... F3
Pensaukee 225 .... L6
Pepin 873 .... B7
Perrygo Place J10
Peshtigo 3,154 .... L5
Pewaukee 4,941 .... K1
Phelps 950 .... H3
Phillips▲ 1,592 .... E4
Phlox 150 .... J5
Pickerel 107 .... J5
Pickett 120 .... J8
Pigeon Falls 289 .... D7
Pine River 110 .... H7
Pittsville 838 .... F7
Plain 691 .... F9
Plainfield 839 .... G7
Plat 120 .... K1
Platteville 9,708 .... F10
Pleasant Prairie 11,961 .... L10
Plover 8,176 .... G7
Plum City 534 .... B6
Plymouth 6,769 .... L8
Polonia 200 .... H6
Poplar 516 .... C2
Port Edwards 1,848 .... G7
Port Washington▲ 9,338 .... L9
Port Wing 290 .... D2
Portage▲ 8,640 .... G8
Potosi 654 .... E10
Potter 252 .... K7
Pound 434 .... L5
Poy Sippi 425 .... J7
Poynette 1,662 .... G9
Prairie Farm 494 .... C5
Prairie du Chien▲ 5,659 .... D9
Prairie du Sac 2,380 .... G9
Prentice 571 .... F4
Prescott 3,243 .... A6
Presque Isle 251 .... G3
Princeton 1,458 .... H8
Pulaski 2,200 .... K6
Racine▲ 84,298 .... M3
Radisson 237 .... D4
Randolph 1,729 .... H8
Random Lake 1,439 .... K8
Raymond 300 .... L2
Readfield 200 .... J7
Readstown 420 .... E9
Red Cliff 250 .... E2
Redgranite 1,009 .... H7
Reedsburg 5,834 .... G8
Reedsville 1,182 .... L7
Reeseville 673 .... J9
Reserve 371 .... D4
Rewey 220 .... F10
Rhinelander▲ 7,427 .... H4
Rib Falls 145 .... G6
Rice Lake 7,998 .... F5
Richfield 247 .... K1
Richland Center▲ 5,018 .... F9
Ridgeland 246 .... B5
Ridgeway 577 .... F10
Rio 768 .... H9
Rio Creek 200 .... L6
Ripon 7,241 .... J8
River Falls 10,610 .... A6
River Hills 1,612 .... M1
Roberts 1,043 .... A6
Rochester 978 .... K3
Rock Falls 200 .... C6
Rock Springs 432 .... F8
Rockdale 235 .... J10
Rockfield 200 .... L1
Rockland 509 .... D8
Rome 200 .... H1
Rosendale 777 .... J8
Rosholt 512 .... H6
Rothschild 3,310 .... G6
Roxbury 260 .... G9
Royalton 200 .... J7
Rozellville 150 .... G6
Rubicon 261 .... K9
Rudolph 451 .... G7
Saint Cloud 494 .... K8
Saint Croix Falls 1,640 .... A5
Saint Francis 9,245 .... M2
Saint Joseph Ridge 450 .... D8
Saint Nazianz 693 .... L7
Sand Creek 225 .... C5
Sauk City 3,019 .... G9
Saukville 3,695 .... L9
Saxon 375 .... F3
Sayner 300 .... H4
Scandinavia 298 .... H7
Schofield 2,415 .... H6
School Hill 228 .... L8
Seneca 235 .... E9
Sextonville 225 .... F9
Seymour 1,557 .... K6
Sharon 1,250 .... J11
Shawano▲ 7,598 .... J6
Sheboygan▲ 49,676 .... L8
Sheboygan Falls 5,823 .... L8
Sheldon 268 .... D5
Shell Lake▲ 1,161 .... C4
Sherry 115 .... G6
Sherwood 837 .... K7
Shiocton 805 .... K7
Shopiere 350 .... H10
Shorewood 14,116 .... M1
Shorewood Hills 1,680 .... G9
Shullsburg 1,236 .... F10
Silver Lake 1,801 .... K10
Siren 863 .... B4
Sister Bay 675 .... M5
Slinger 2,340 .... K9
Soldiers Grove 564 .... E9
Solon Springs 575 .... C3
Somers 400 .... M3

Topography

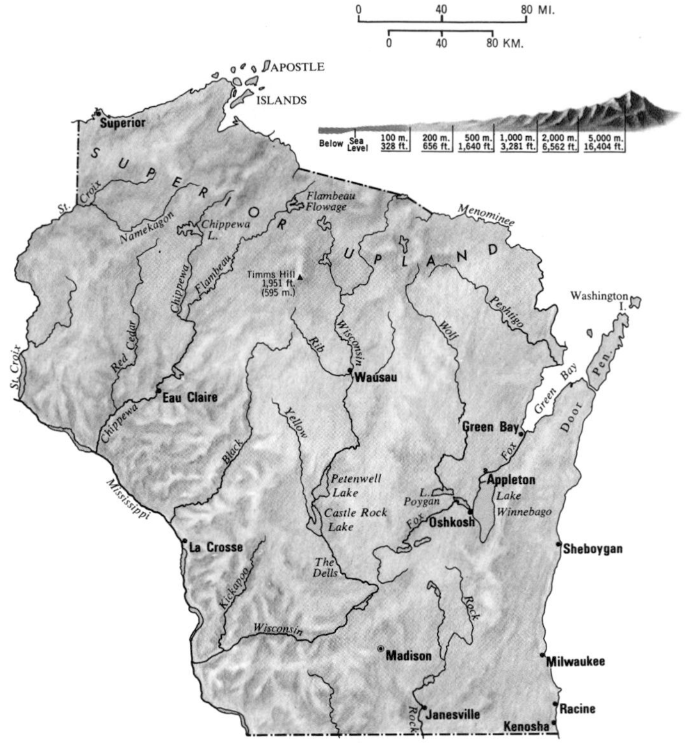

Somerset 1,065 .... A5
South Milwaukee 20,958 .... M2
South Range 149 .... B2
South Wayne 478 .... G10
Sparta▲ 7,788 .... E8
Spencer 1,757 .... F6
Spirit 400 .... F5
Spooner 2,464 .... B4
Spring Green 1,283 .... G9
Spring Valley 1,051 .... B6
Springbrook 150 .... C4
Stangelville 150 .... L7
Stanley 2,011 .... E6
Star Prairie 507 .... A5
Stetsonville 511 .... F5
Steuben 161 .... E9
Stevens Point▲ 23,006 .... G7
Stiles 300 .... L6
Stitzer 190 .... E10
Stockbridge 579 .... K7
Stoddard 775 .... D8
Stone Bank 390 .... J1
Stone Lake 210 .... C4
Stoughton 8,786 .... H10
Stratford 1,515 .... F6
Strum 949 .... D6
Sturgeon Bay▲ 9,176 .... M6
Sturtevant 3,803 .... M3
Suamico 900 .... K6
Sullivan 432 .... H1
Summit Lake 250 .... H5
Sun Prairie 15,333 .... H9
Superior▲ 27,134 .... C2
Superior Village 481 .... B2
Suring 626 .... K5
Sussex 5,039 .... K1
Symco 102 .... J6
Taycheedah 350 .... K8
Taylor 419 .... E7
Tennyson 378 .... E10
Theresa 771 .... K8
Thiensville 3,301 .... L1
Thorp 1,657 .... E6
Three Lakes 950 .... H4
Tichigan Lake 500 .... K2
Tigerton 815 .... H6
Tilleda 102 .... J6
Tisch Mills 315 .... L7
Tomah 7,570 .... F8
Tomahawk 3,328 .... G5
Tony 114 .... E5
Townsend 450 .... K5
Trego 280 .... C4
Trempealeau 1,039 .... C8
Troy Center 250 .... J2
Tunnel City 200 .... E7
Turtle Lake 817 .... B5
Tustin 101 .... J7
Twin Lakes 3,989 .... K11
Two Rivers 13,030 .... M7
Union Center 197 .... F8
Union Grove 3,669 .... L3
Unity 452 .... F6
Upson 115 .... F3
Valders 905 .... L7
Verona 5,374 .... G9
Vesper 598 .... F7
Viola 644 .... E8
Viroqua▲ 3,922 .... D8
Wabeno 800 .... J5
Waldo 442 .... L8
Wales 2,471 .... J1
Walworth 1,614 .... J10
Warrens 343 .... E7
Washburn▲ 2,285 .... D2
Washington Island 550 .... M5
Waterford 2,431 .... K3
Waterloo 2,712 .... J9
Watertown 19,142 .... J9
Waubeka 450 .... L9
Waukesha▲ 56,958 .... K1
Waumandee 115 .... C7
Waunakee 5,897 .... G9
Waupaca▲ 4,957 .... H7
Waupun 8,207 .... J8
Wausau▲ 37,060 .... G6
Wausaukee 656 .... K5
Wautoma▲ 1,784 .... H7
Wauwatosa 49,366 .... L1
Wauzeka 595 .... E9
Wayside 140 .... L7
Webster 623 .... B4
West Allis 63,221 .... L1
West Baraboo 1,021 .... G9
West Bend▲ 23,916 .... K9
West Milwaukee 3,973 .... L1
West Salem 3,611 .... D8
Westboro 750 .... F5
Westby 1,866 .... E8
Westfield 1,125 .... H8
Weston 8,775 .... G6
Weston 9,714 .... C6
Weyauwega 1,665 .... H7
Weyerhaeuser 283 .... D5
Wheeler 348 .... C5
White Lake 304 .... J5
Whitefish Bay 14,272 .... M1
Whitehall▲ 1,494 .... D7
Whitelaw 700 .... L7
Whitewater 12,636 .... J10
Whiting 1,838 .... H7
Wild Rose 676 .... H7
Williams Bay 2,108 .... J10
Wilson 163 .... B6
Wilton 478 .... F8
Winchester 300 .... G3
Wind Lake 3,748 .... K2
Wind Point 1,941 .... M2
Windsor 2,182 .... H9
Winnebago 1,433 .... J7
Winneconne 2,059 .... J7
Winter 383 .... E4
Wiota 125 .... G10
Wisconsin Dells 2,393 .... G8
Wisconsin Rapids▲ 18,245 .... G7
Withee 503 .... E6
Wittenberg 1,145 .... H6
Wonewoc 793 .... F8
Woodford 107 .... G10
Woodman 120 .... E9
Woodruff 850 .... G4
Woodville 942 .... B6
Wrightstown 1,262 .... K7
Wyeville 154 .... F7
Wyocena 620 .... H9
Yuba 77 .... F8

OTHER FEATURES

Apostle (isls.) F2
Apostle Islands Nat'l Lakeshore E1
Apple (riv.) A5
Bad River Ind. Res. E2
Bardon (lake) E2
Bear (isl.) E1
Beaver Dam (lake) J9
Beulah (lake) J2
Big Eau Pleine (res.) G6
Big Muskego (lake) L2
Big Rib (riv.) G5
Black (riv.) E7
Butternut (lake) J4
Castle Rock (lake) G8
Cat (isl.) E1
Chambers (isl.) M5
Chequamegon (bay) E2
Chetac (lake) D4
Chippewa (lake) D4
Chippewa (riv.) B7
Clam (lake) B4
Clam (riv.) A4
Dells, The (valley) G8
Denoon (lake) K2
Door (pen.) M6
Du Bay (lake) G6
Eagle (lake) H2
Eagle (lake) K3
Eau Claire (riv.) D6
Flambeau (riv.) E4
Flambeau Flowage (res.) F3
Fox (riv.) K2
Fox (riv.) K7
General Mitchell Field M2
Geneva (lake) K10
Golden (lake) H1
Green (bay) L6
Grindstone (lake) C4
Holcombe Flowage (res.) D5
Jump (riv.) E5
Kegonsa (lake) H10
Kickapoo (riv.) E9
Koshkonong (lake) H10
La Belle (lake) H1
Lac Court Oreilles Ind. Res. D4
Lac du Flambeau Ind. Res. G3
Long (lake) C4
Madeline (isl.) E2
Mendota (lake) H9
Menominee (riv.) L5
Menominee Ind. Res. J5
Metonga (lake) J4
Michigan (isl.) F2
Michigan (lake) M9
Mississippi (riv.) D10
Montreal (riv.) F2
Moose (lake) E3
Moose (lake) F3
Nagawicka (lake) J1
Namekagon (lake) D3
Namekagon (riv.) C3
North (lake) J1
Oak (isl.) E2
Oconomowoc (lake) H1
Oconto (riv.) K5
Okauchee (lake) J1
Outer (isl.) F1
Owen (lake) D3
Pecatonica (riv.) H11
Pelican (lake) H4
Pepin (lake) B7
Peshtigo (riv.) K5
Petenwell (lake) G7
Pewaukee (lake) K1
Phantom (lake) J2
Pine (lake) J1
Porte des Morts (str.) N5
Poygan (lake) J7
Puckaway (lake) H8
Red Cedar (riv.) C5
Red Cliff Ind. Res. E2
Rock (riv.) J9
Round (lake) F4
Round (lake) D3
Saint Croix (lake) A6
Saint Croix (riv.) A4
Saint Croix Flowage (res.) C3
Saint Louis (riv.) A2
Sand (isl.) D2
Shawano (lake) K6
Shell (lake) C4
Spider (lake) D3
Stockbridge Ind. Res. J6
Stockton (isl.) F2
Sugar (riv.) H10
Sugarbush Hill (mt.) J4
Superior (lake) F1
Thunder (lake) H4
Tichigan (lake) K2
Timms Hill (mt.) F5
Trempealeau (riv.) C7
Trout (lake) G3
Washington (isl.) M5
Willow (res.) F4
Wind (lake) K2
Winnebago (lake) K7
Wisconsin (riv.) E9
Wolf (riv.) J5
Yellow (lake) B4
Yellow (riv.) F7

▲County seat

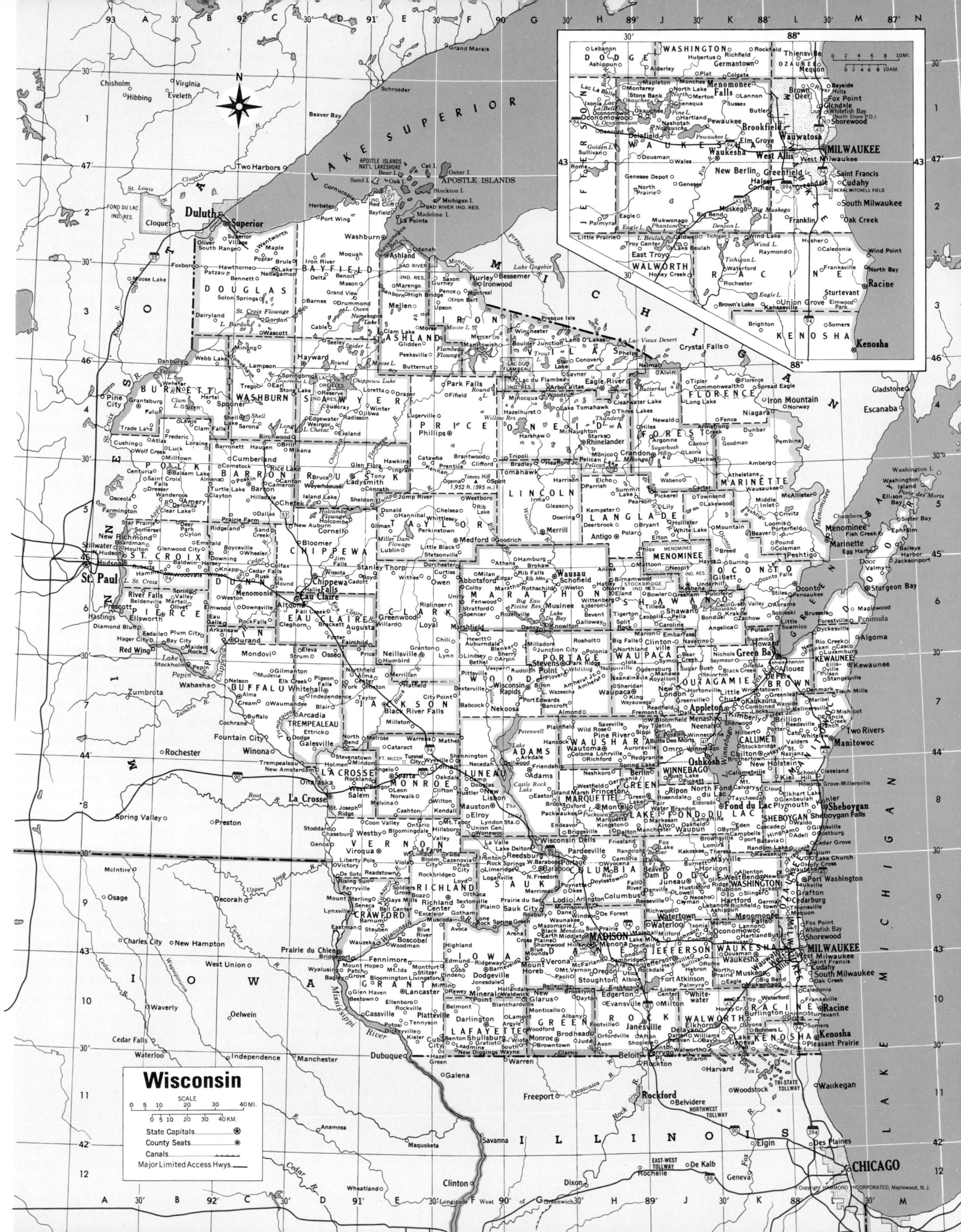

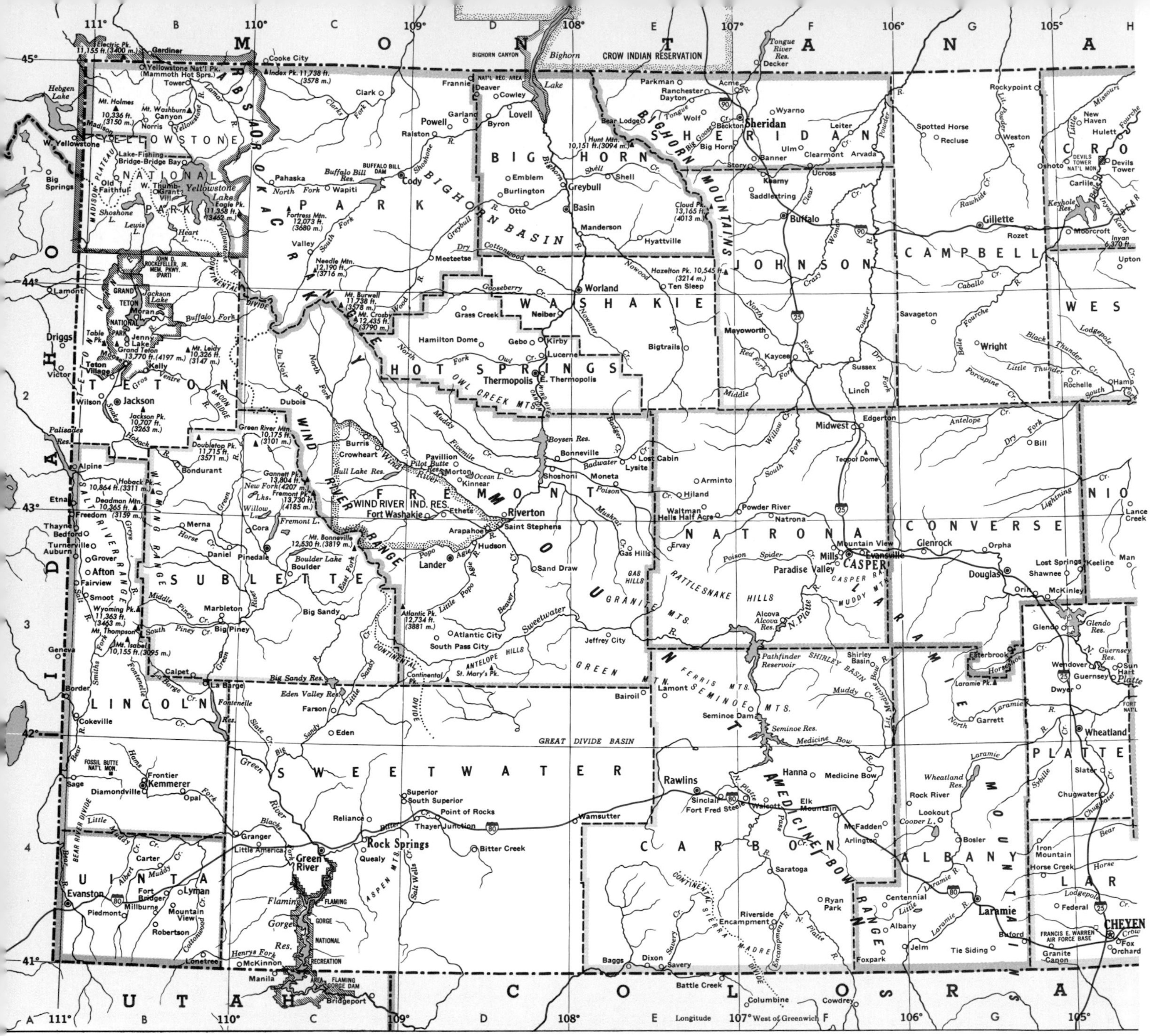

Agriculture, Industry and Resources

DOMINANT LAND USE

- Specialized Wheat
- Specialized Dairy
- General Farming, Livestock, Special Crops
- Sugar Beets, Dry Beans, Livestock, General Farming
- Range Livestock
- Forests
- Nonagricultural Land

MAJOR MINERAL OCCURRENCES

- C Coal
- Cl Clay
- Fe Iron Ore
- G Natural Gas
- O Petroleum
- P Phosphates
- So Soda Ash
- U Uranium
- V Vanadium
- Water Power

COUNTIES

Albany 30,797	G4
Big Horn 10,525	E1
Campbell 29,370	G1
Carbon 16,659	F4
Converse 11,128	G3
Crook 5,294	H1
Fremont 33,662	D2
Goshen 12,373	H4
Hot Springs 4,809	D2
Johnson 6,145	F1
Laramie 73,142	H4
Lincoln 12,625	B3
Natrona 61,226	F3
Niobrara 2,499	H2
Park 23,178	C1
Platte 8,145	H4
Sheridan 23,562	F1
Sublette 4,843	C3
Sweetwater 38,823	D4
Teton 11,172	B2
Uinta 18,705	B4
Washakie 8,388	E2
Weston 6,518	H2

CITIES and TOWNS

Acme 98	E1
Afton 1,394	B3
Albany 25	F4
Albin 120	H4

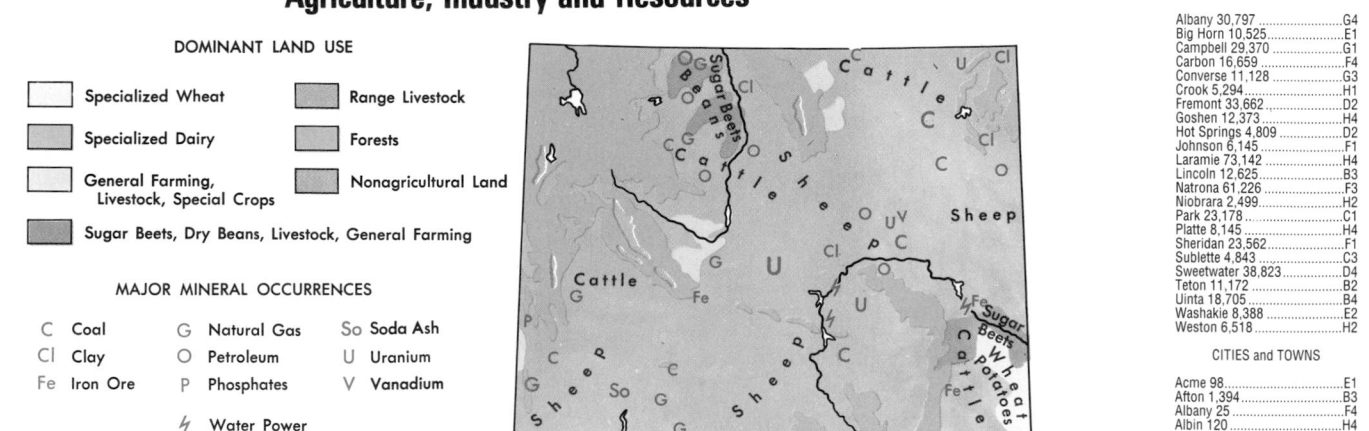

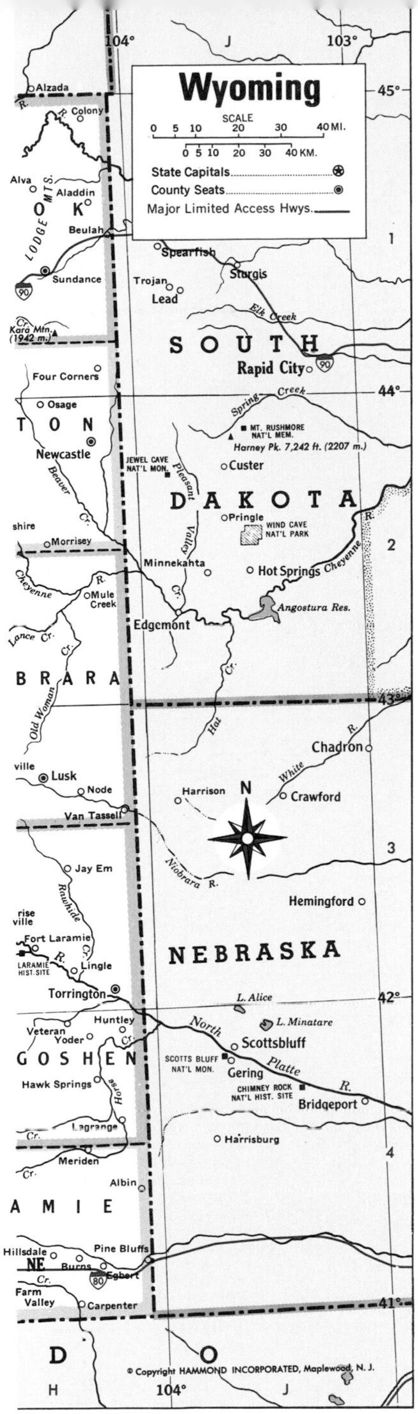

Wyoming
SCALE
0 5 10 20 30 40 MI.
0 5 10 20 30 40 KM.
State Capitals
County Seats
Major Limited Access Hwys.
104°
J
103°
45°
44°
43°
42°
41°
1
2
3
4
Alzada
Colony
Alva
Aladdin
Beulah
Sundance
LODGE MTS.
Spearfish
Sturgis
Trojan
Lead
Elk Creek
Kara Mtn. (1942 m.)
SOUTH
Rapid City
Four Corners
Osage
Spring Creek
MT. RUSHMORE NAT'L MEM.
Harney Pk. 7,242 ft. (2207 m.)
Newcastle
JEWEL CAVE NAT'L MON.
Custer
DAKOTA
Pringle
WIND CAVE NAT'L PARK
Morrisey
Minnekahta
Hot Springs
Cheyenne R.
Mule Creek
Angostura Res.
Edgemont
Lance Cr.
Hat Cr.
Chadron
Old Woman Cr.
Lusk
Node
White R.
Harrison
Crawford
Van Tassel
N
Jay Em
Niobrara R.
Rawhide Cr.
Hemingford
Fort Laramie
LARAMIE HIST. SITE
Lingle
NEBRASKA
Torrington
L. Alice
L. Minatare
Huntley
Veteran
Yoder
North Platte R.
Scottsbluff
GOSHEN
SCOTTS BLUFF NAT'L MON.
Gering
Hawk Springs
CHIMNEY ROCK NAT'L HIST. SITE
Bridgeport
Lagrange
Harrisburg
Meriden
Albin
AMIE
Hillsdale
Pine Bluffs
Burns
Egbert
Farm Valley
Carpenter
D
O
© Copyright HAMMOND INCORPORATED, Maplewood, N. J.
H
104°
J

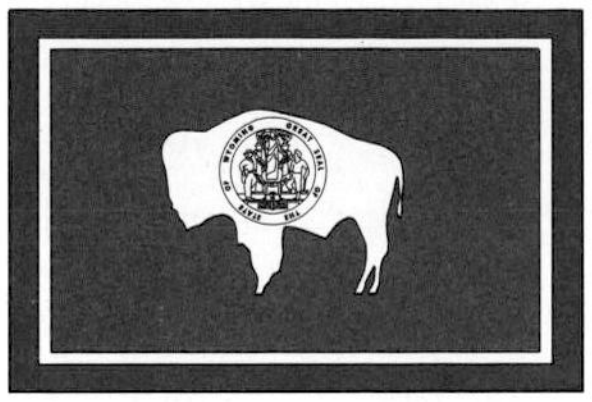

AREA 97,809 sq. mi. (253,325 sq. km.)
POPULATION 455,975
CAPITAL Cheyenne
LARGEST CITY Casper
HIGHEST POINT Gannett Pk. 13,804 ft. (4207 m.)
SETTLED IN 1834
ADMITTED TO UNION July 10, 1890
POPULAR NAME Equality State
STATE FLOWER Indian Paintbrush
STATE BIRD Meadowlark

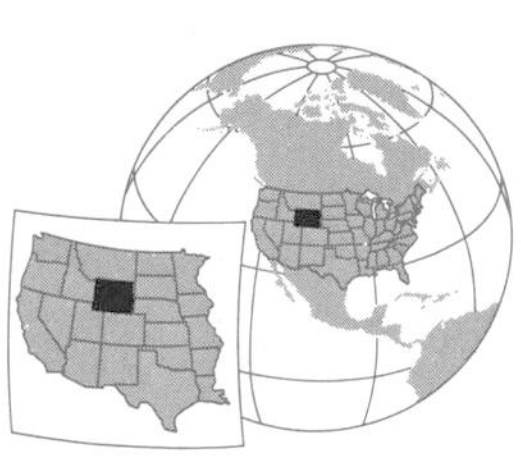

Topography

0 50 100 MI.
0 50 100 KM.

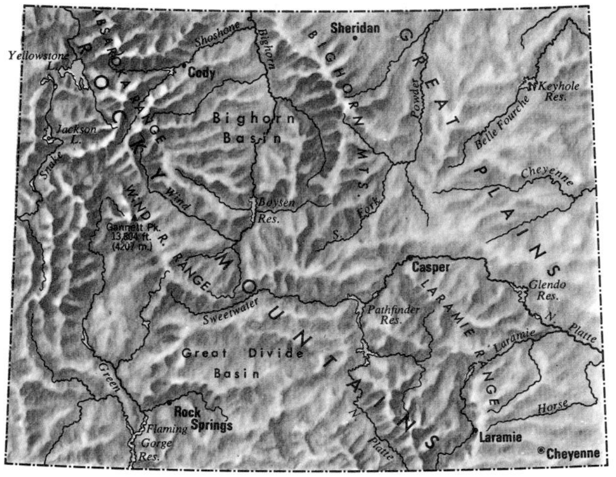

Yellowstone L.
Sheridan
Shoshone
Bighorn
Cody
BIGHORN MTS.
GREAT PLAINS
ABSAROKA RANGE
ROCKY
Powder
Keyhole Res.
Belle Fourche
Bighorn Basin
Jackson L.
Cheyenne
Snake
WIND R. RANGE
Wind
Boysen Res.
Gannett Pk. 13,804 ft. (4207 m.)
MOUNTAINS
Casper
LARAMIE
Glendo Res.
Pathfinder Res.
Sweetwater
Great Divide Basin
Laramie
N. Platte
RANGE
Green
Horse
Rock Springs
Flaming Gorge Res.
Platte
Laramie
Cheyenne

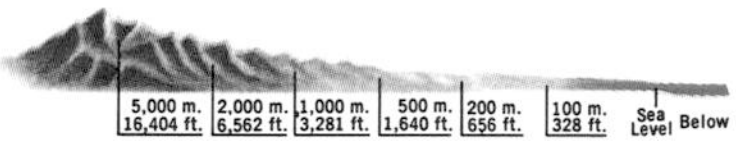

5,000 m. 16,404 ft.
2,000 m. 6,562 ft.
1,000 m. 3,281 ft.
500 m. 1,640 ft.
200 m. 656 ft.
100 m. 328 ft.
Sea Level
Below

Alcova 275 .... F3
Alpine 200 .... B2
Alva 50 .... H1
Arapahoe 393 .... D3
Arvada 30 .... F1
Atlantic City 25 .... D3
Auburn 360 .... A3
Baggs 272 .... E4
Bairoil 228 .... E3
Banner 40 .... F1
Basin▲ 1,180 .... E1
Beckton 110 .... E1
Bedford 350 .... A3
Beulah 184 .... H1
Big Horn 350 .... E1
Big Piney 454 .... B3
Bondurant 90 .... B2
Border 25 .... B3
Bosler 195 .... G4
Boulder 50 .... C3
Buffalo▲ 3,302 .... F1
Buford 36 .... G4
Burlington 184 .... D1
Burns 254 .... H4
Burris 30 .... C2
Byron 470 .... D1
Carpenter 75 .... H4
Carter 33 .... B4
Casper▲ 46,742 .... F3
Centennial 140 .... F4
Cheyenne (cap.)▲ 50,008 .... H4
Chugwater 192 .... H4
Clearmont 119 .... F1
Cody▲ 7,897 .... D1
Cokeville 493 .... B3
Colony 50 .... H1
Cowley 477 .... D1
Crowheart 200 .... C2
Daniel 130 .... B3
Dayton 565 .... E1
Deaver 199 .... D1
Devils Tower 28 .... H1
Diamondville 864 .... B4
Dixon 70 .... E4
Douglas▲ 5,076 .... G3
Dubois 895 .... C2
East Thermopolis 221 .... D2
Eden 198 .... C3
Edgerton 247 .... F2
Egbert 75 .... H4
Elk Mountain 174 .... F4
Encampment 611 .... F4
Ethete 1,059 .... D2
Etna 200 .... A2
Evanston▲ 10,903 .... B4
Evansville 1,403 .... F3
Fairview 150 .... B3
Farson 350 .... C3
Fort Bridger 300 .... B4
Fort Laramie 243 .... H3
Fort Washakie 1,334 .... C2
Fox Farm 2,850 .... H4
Foxpark 78 .... F4
Frannie 148 .... D1
Freedom 400 .... B3
Frontier 150 .... B4
Garland 57 .... D1
Gas Hills 150 .... E3
Gillotte▲ 17,635 .... G1
Glendo 195 .... G3
Glenrock 2,153 .... G3
Granger 126 .... C4
Granite Canon 80 .... G4
Grass Creek 152 .... D2
Green River▲ 12,711 .... C4
Greybull 1,789 .... E1
Grover 425 .... B3
Guernsey 1,155 .... H3
Hamilton Dome 80 .... D2
Hanna 1,076 .... F4
Hartville 78 .... H3
Hawk Springs 84 .... H4
Hillsdale 160 .... H4
Horse Creek 225 .... G4
Hudson 392 .... D3
Hulett 429 .... H1
Huntley 50 .... H4
Hyattville 110 .... E1
Iron Mountain 45 .... G4
Jackson▲ 4,472 .... B2
Jeffrey City 1,882 .... E3
Jelm 29 .... G4
Kaycee 256 .... F2
Kearny 49 .... F1
Kelly 100 .... B2
Kemmerer▲ 3,020 .... B4
Kinnear 145 .... D2
Kirby 59 .... D2
La Barge 493 .... B3
Lagrange 224 .... H4
Lamont 30 .... E3
Lance Creek 100 .... H2
Lander▲ 7,023 .... D3
Laramie▲ 26,687 .... G4
Leiter 46 .... F1
Linch 187 .... F2
Lingle 473 .... H3
Little America 175 .... C4
Lost Cabin 25 .... E2
Lovell 2,131 .... D1
Lucerne 240 .... D2
Lusk▲ 1,504 .... H3
Lyman 1,896 .... B4
Lysite 175 .... E2
Mammoth Hot Springs (Yellowstone Nat'l Park) 350 .... B1
Manderson 83 .... E1
Manville 97 .... H3
Marbleton 634 .... B3
Mayoworth F2
McFadden 47 .... F4
McKinnon 135 .... C4
Medicine Bow 389 .... F4
Meeteetse 368 .... D1
Meriden 55 .... H4
Midwest 495 .... F2
Millburne 54 .... B4
Mills 1,574 .... F3
Moorcroft 768 .... H1
Moose 150 .... B2
Moran 200 .... B2
Morrisey 28 .... H2
Morton 35 .... D2
Mountain View 1,345 .... B4
Mountain View 76 .... F3
Neiber D2
New Haven 35 .... H1
Newcastle▲ 3,003 .... H2
Old Faithful 75 .... B1
Opal 95 .... B4
Orchard Valley 3,327 .... H4
Osage 500 .... H2
Otto 50 .... D1
Pahaska 75 .... C1
Paradise Valley F3
Parkman 30 .... E1
Pavillion 126 .... D2
Piedmont 25 .... B4
Pine Bluffs 1,054 .... H4
Pinedale▲ 1,181 .... C3
Point of Rocks 425 .... D4
Powder River 70 .... F2
Powell 5,292 .... D1
Ralston 109 .... D1
Ranchester 676 .... E1
Rawlins▲ 9,380 .... E4
Recluse 225 .... G1
Reliance 325 .... C4
Riverside 85 .... F4
Riverton 9,202 .... D2
Robertson 142 .... B4
Rock River 190 .... G4
Rock Springs 19,050 .... C4
Rozet 30 .... G1
Saddlestring 100 .... F1
Sage 45 .... B4
Saint Stephens 80 .... D3
Sand Draw 40 .... D3
Saratoga 1,969 .... F4
Savageton 30 .... G2
Savery 29 .... E4
Shell 80 .... E1
Sheridan▲ 13,900 .... F1
Shirley Basin 400 .... F3
Shoshoni 497 .... D2
Sinclair 500 .... E4
Smoot 310 .... B3
South Superior 586 .... D4
Story 637 .... F1
Sundance▲ 1,139 .... H1
Sunrise 29 .... H3
Superior 273 .... D4
Sussex 25 .... F2
Ten Sleep 311 .... E1
Teton Village B2
Thayne 267 .... A3
Thermopolis▲ 3,247 .... D2
Torrington▲ 5,651 .... H3
Turnerville 65 .... A3
Ulm 25 .... F1
Upton 980 .... H1
Veteran 60 .... H4
Walcott 200 .... F4
Wamsutter 240 .... E4
Wapiti 130 .... C1
Wheatland▲ 3,271 .... H3
Wilson 480 .... B2
Worland▲ 5,742 .... E1
Wright 1,236 .... G2
Wyarno 101 .... F1
Yellowstone National Park 350 .... B1
Yoder 136 .... H4

OTHER FEATURES

Absaroka (range) C1
Antelope (creek) G2
Antelope (hills) D3
Aspen (mts.) C4
Atlantic (peak) D3
Bear (creek) H4
Bear (riv.) B4
Bear Lodge (mts.) H1
Bear River Divide (mts.) B4
Beaver (creek) D3
Beaver (creek) H2
Belle Fourche (riv.) H1
Big Goose (creek) E1
Bighorn (basin) D1
Bighorn (lake) D1
Bighorn (mts.) E1
Bighorn (riv.) D1
Bighorn Canyon Nat'l Rec. Area D1
Big Sandy (riv.) C3
Bitter (creek) C4
Blacks Fork, Green (riv.) C4
Black Thunder (creek) G2
Bonneville (mt.) C3
Boysen (res.) D2
Buffalo Bill (dam) C1
Buffalo Bill (res.) C1
Buffalo Fork, Snake (riv.) B2
Burwell (mt.) C2
Caballo (creek) G1
Casper (range) F3
Cheyenne (riv.) H2
Chugwater (creek) H4
Clarks Fork (riv.) C1
Clear (creek) F1
Cloud (peak) E1
Cottonwood (creek) B4
Crazy Woman (creek) F1
Crosby (mt.) C2
Crow (creek) H4
Deadman (mt.) B2
Devils Tower Nat'l Mon. H1
Doubletop (peak) B2
Dry (creek) C2
Dry Cottonwood (creek) D1
Eagle (peak) B1
Fivemile (creek) D2
Flaming Gorge (res.) C4
Flaming Gorge Nat'l Rec. Area C4
Fontenelle (creek) B3
Fontenelle (res.) B3
Fort Laramie Nat'l Hist. Site H3
Fortress (mt.) C1
Fossil Butte Nat'l Mon. B4
Francis E. Warren A.F.B. 3,832 .... G4
Fremont (lake) C3
Fremont (peak) C2
Gannett (peak) C2
Gas (hills) E3
Glendo (res.) H3
Gooseberry (creek) D1
Grand Teton (mt.) B2
Grand Teton Nat'l Park B2
Granite (mts.) E3
Great Divide (basin) E3
Green (mt.) E3
Green (riv.) C4
Green, East Fork (riv.) C3
Green River (mt.) C2
Greybull (riv.) D1
Greys (riv.) B3
Gros Ventre (riv.) B2
Guernsey (res.) H3
Hams Fork (riv.) B4
Hazelton (peak) E1
Henrys Fork, Green (riv.) C4
Hoback (peak) B2
Hoback (riv.) B2
Holmes (mt.) B1
Horse (creek) H4
Horseshoe (creek) G3
Hunt (mt.) E1
Index (peak) C1
Inyan Kara (creek) H1
Inyan Kara (mt.) H1
Isabel (mt.) B3
Jackson (lake) B2
Jackson (peak) B2
John D. Rockefeller, Jr., Mem. Pkwy. B1
Keyhole (res.) H1
Lamar (riv.) B1
Lance (creek) H2
Laramie (mts.) G3
Laramie (peak) G3
Laramie (riv.) G4
Leidy (mt.) B2
Lewis (lake) B1
Lightning (creek) G2
Little Missouri (riv.) H1
Little Muddy (creek) B4
Little Powder (riv.) G1
Little Sandy (creek) C3
Little Thunder (creek) G2
Lodgepole (creek) H2
Lodgepole (creek) H4
Madison (plat.) B1
Medicine Bow (range) F4
Medicine Bow (riv.) F3
Middle Piney (creek) B3
Muddy (creek) D2
Muskrat (creek) E2
Needle (mt.) C1
Niobrara (riv.) J3
North Laramie (riv.) G3
North Platte (riv.) H3
Nowater (creek) E2
Nowood (riv.) E1
Owl, North Fork (creek) D2
Owl Creek (mts.) D2
Palisades (res.) A2
Pass (creek) F4
Pathfinder (res.) F3
Poison (creek) E2
Poison Spider (creek) F3
Popo Agie (riv.) D3
Powder (riv.) F2
Rattlesnake (hills) E3
Rawhide (creek) G1
Rocky (mts.) C1
Salt (riv.) B3
Salt River (range) B3
Salt Wells (creek) D4
Seminoe (mts.) E3
Seminoe (res.) F3
Shell (creek) E1
Shirley (basin) F3
Shoshone (lake) B1
Shoshone (riv.) D1
Sierra Madre (mts.) E4
Slate (creek) C3
Smiths Fork (riv.) B3
Snake (riv.) B2
South Cheyenne (riv.) H2
South Piney (creek) B3
Sweetwater (riv.) D3
Sybille (creek) G4
Teapot Dome (mt.) F2
Teton (range) B2
Tongue (riv.) E1
Washburn (mt.) B1
Wheatland (res.) G4
Willow (creek) F2
Wind (riv.) C2
Wind River (canyon) D2
Wind River (range) C2
Wind River Ind. Res. C2
Wood (riv.) C2
Wyoming (peak) B3
Wyoming (range) B2
Yellowstone (lake) B1
Yellowstone (riv.) B1
Yellowstone Nat'l Park B1

▲County seat

Acquisitions of Territory

WASHINGTON

OREGON COUNTRY

OREGON 1846
Treaty with Great Britain

IDAHO

MONTANA

RED RIVER
Title Established 1818

NORTH DAKOTA

SOUTH DAKOTA

WYOMING

NEBRASKA

IOWA

MINNESOTA

WISCONSIN

MICHIGAN

NEW YORK

MAINE

VT. N.H.

MASS.

CONN. R.I.

NEVADA

UTAH

COLORADO

KANSAS

MISSOURI

ILLINOIS

INDIANA

OHIO

PENNSYLVANIA

NEW JERSEY

MEXICAN CESSION 1848

CALIFORNIA

ARIZONA

NEW MEXICO

GADSDEN PURCHASE 1853

OKLAHOMA

ARKANSAS

TEXAS
Annexed in 1845

KENTUCKY

UNITED STATES 1783

WEST VIRGINIA

VIRGINIA

MD.

DEL.

TENNESSEE

NORTH CAROLINA

SOUTH CAROLINA

MISSISSIPPI

ALABAMA

GEORGIA

LOUISIANA
Purchased from France 1803

FLORIDA 1819
Treaty with Spain

ALASKA
1867
Purchased from Russia

HAWAII
Annexed in 1898

The United States in 1783 comprised the thirteen original states and included lands acquired by conquest during the Revolution and by the Treaty of 1783.

Rank by Area

20 4 17 12 43 39
10 13 9 16 26 30 44
7 15 25 23 33 45 50
3 11 24 38 35 46 48
14 19 41 36 49 42
8 37 28
6 5 18 27 34 40
2 32 29 21
31 22
47
1

Rank by Area
MAP COLORS INDICATE RANKINGS IN GROUPS OF TEN

Rank by Population
1990
Rank by Population

18 44 47 48 38
29 42 50 45 20 16 8 2 41 13 43
39 35 26 36 30 6 14 5 27 46
24 32 15 23 34 12 19
37 28 33 17 10
3 21 22 11 25
49 40 4

YEAR OF ADMISSION TO THE UNION

State	Year
DELAWARE ☆	1787
PENNSYLVANIA ☆	
NEW JERSEY ☆	
GEORGIA ☆	1788
CONNECTICUT ☆	
MASSACHUSETTS ☆	
MARYLAND ☆	
SOUTH CAROLINA ☆	
NEW HAMPSHIRE ☆	
VIRGINIA ☆	
NEW YORK ☆	
NORTH CAROLINA ☆	1789
RHODE ISLAND ☆	1790
VERMONT ☆	1791
KENTUCKY ☆	1792
TENNESSEE ☆	1796
OHIO	1803
LOUISIANA	1812
INDIANA ☆	1816
MISSISSIPPI ☆	1817
ILLINOIS ☆	1818
ALABAMA ☆	1819
MAINE ☆	1820
MISSOURI ☆	1821

1959 ☆HAWAII ☆ALASKA

1912 ☆ARIZONA ☆NEW MEXICO

1907 ☆OKLAHOMA

☆NORTH DAKOTA
☆SOUTH DAKOTA

☆WEST VIRGINIA
☆MINNESOTA

☆CALIFORNIA
☆WISCONSIN
☆IOWA
☆FLORIDA
☆TEXAS

☆ARKANSAS
☆MICHIGAN

UTAH
WYOMING ☆ IDAHO ☆ MONTANA ☆WASHINGTON
COLORADO ☆
NEBRASKA
NEVADA ☆KANSAS ☆OREGON ☆

| 1896 | 1889 | 1876 | 1867 | 1864 | 1861 | 1858 | 1848 | 1845 | 1836 |
| | 1890 | | | 1863 | 1859 | | 1850 | 1846 | 1837 |

© Copyright
HAMMOND INCORPORATED

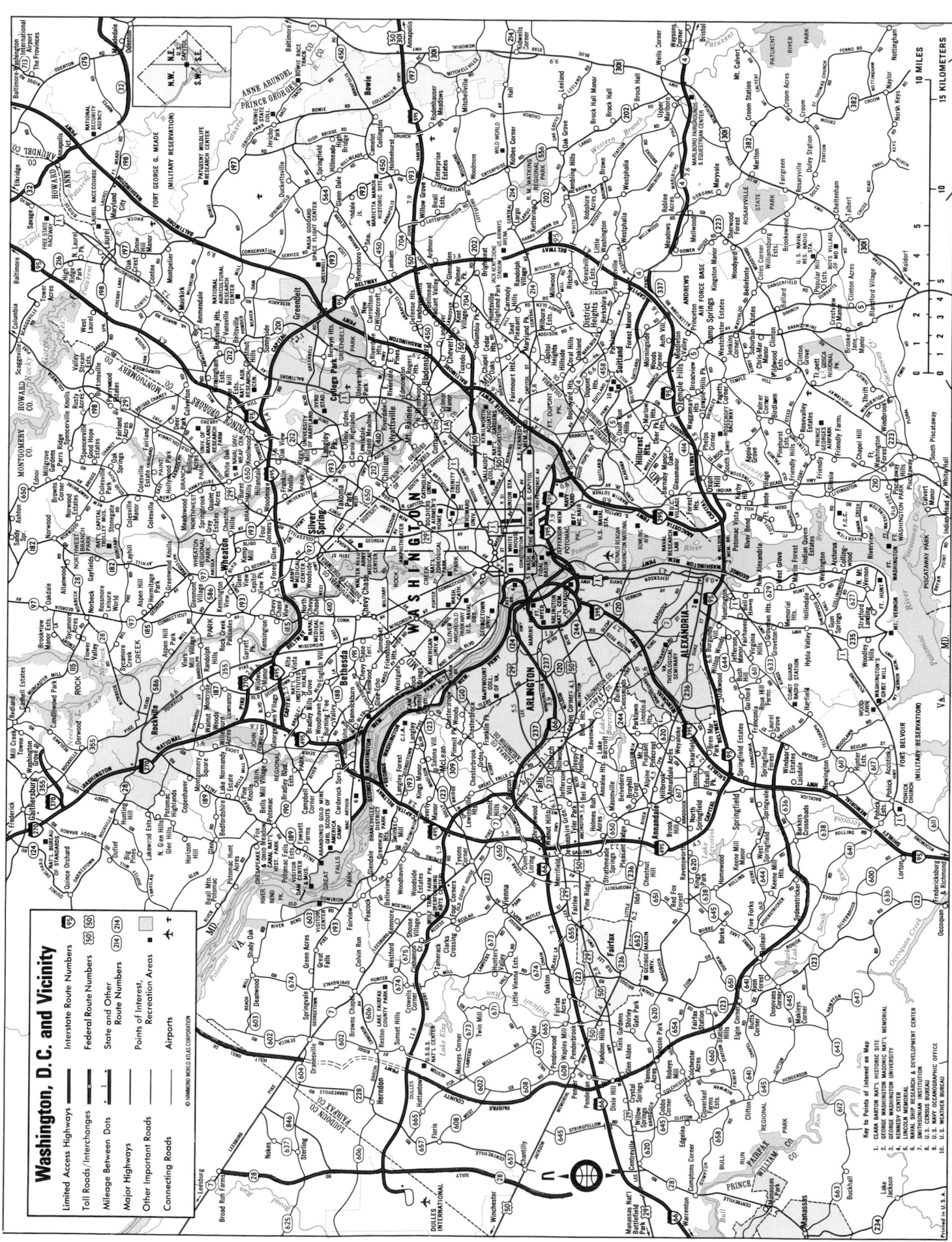

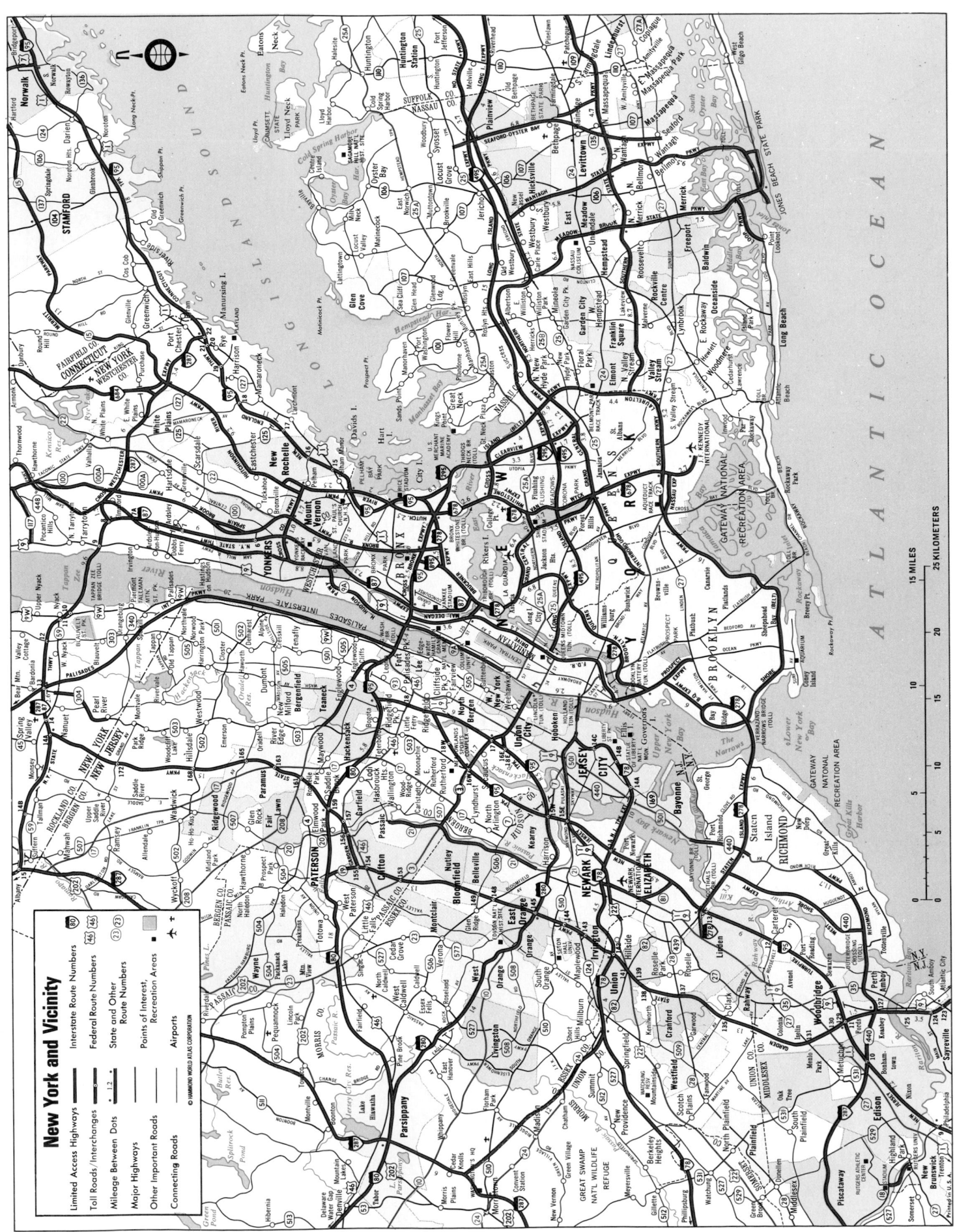

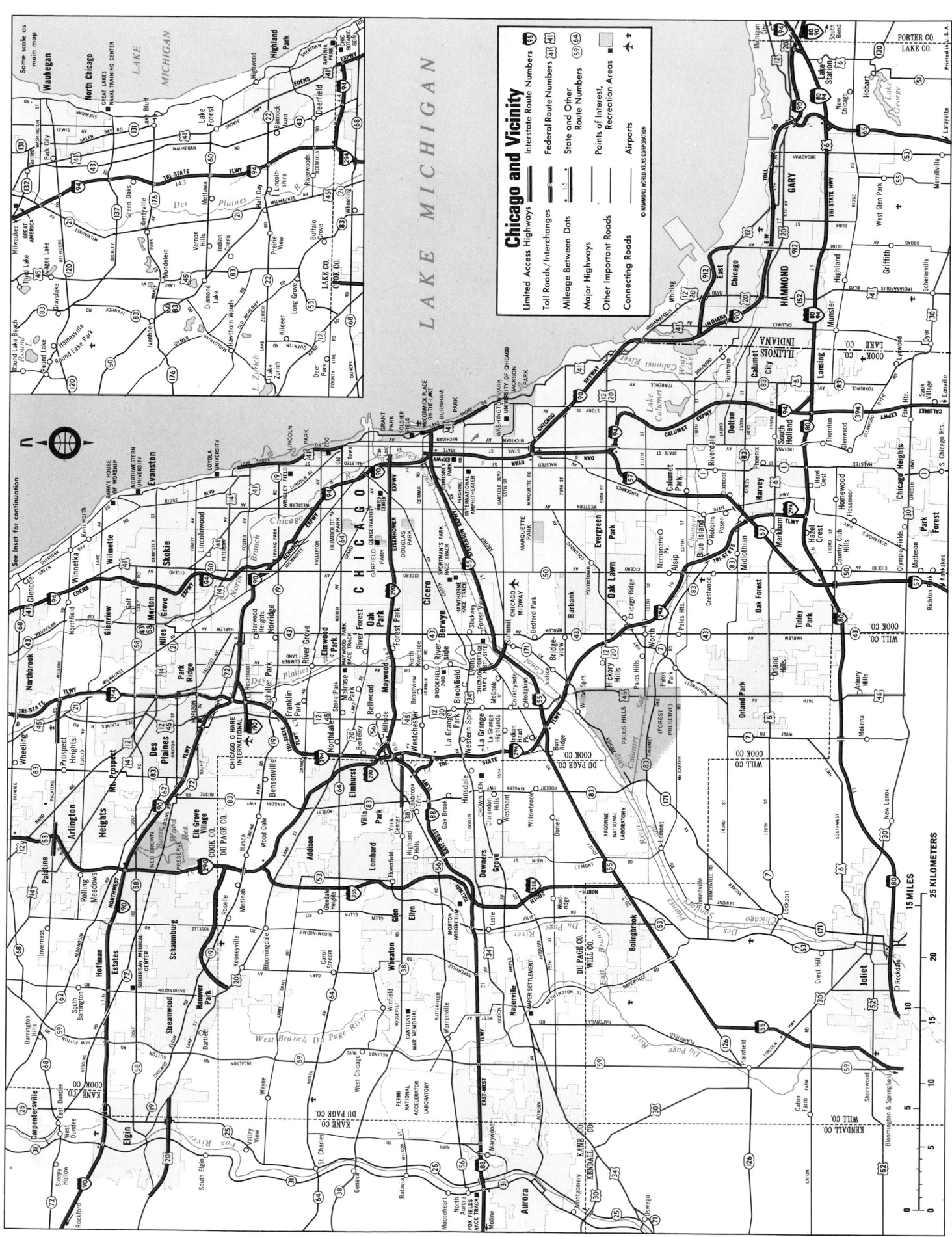

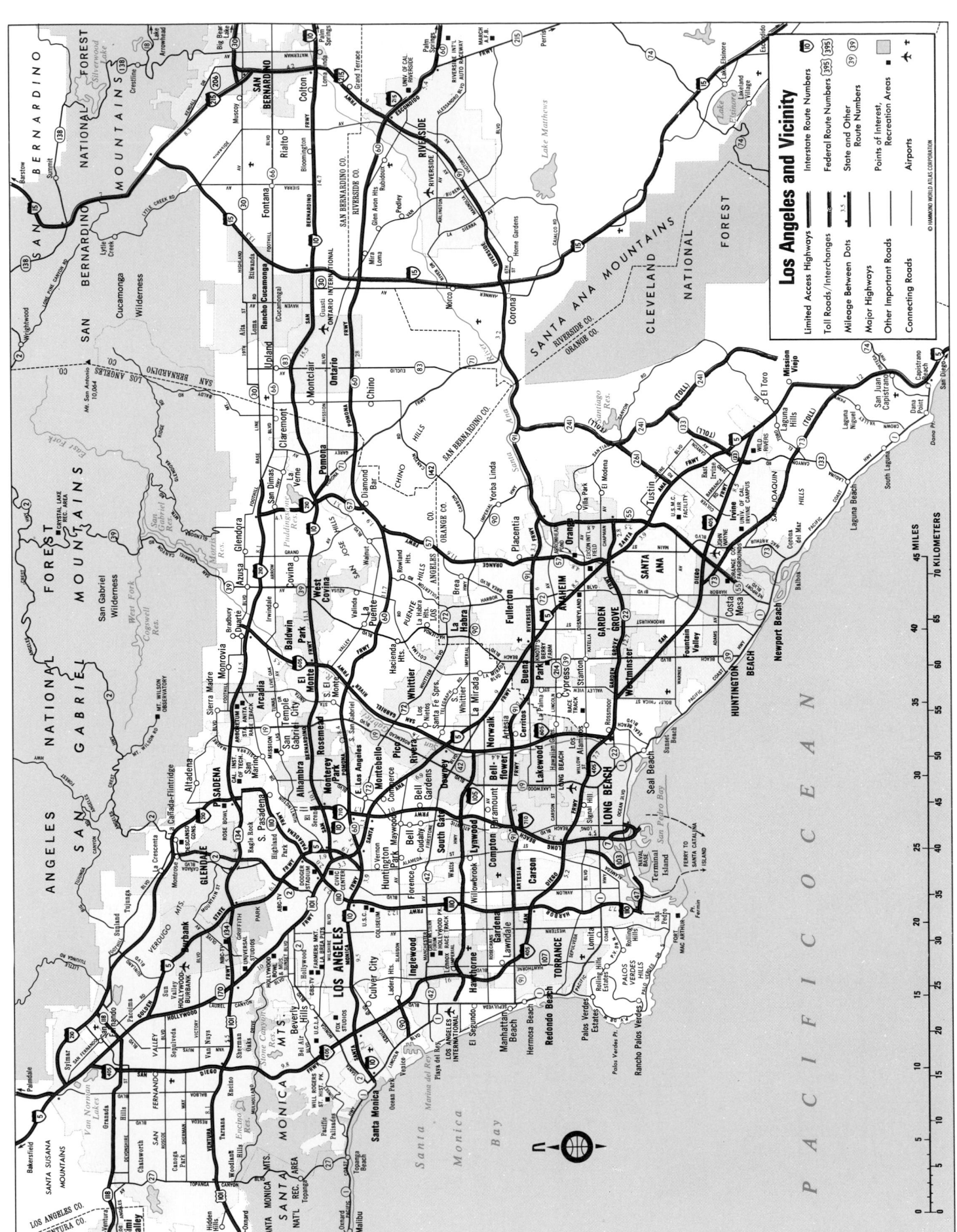

Los Angeles and Vicinity

Limited Access Highways
Toll Roads/Interchanges
Mileage Between Dots
Major Highways
Other Important Roads
Connecting Roads

Interstate Route Numbers
Federal Route Numbers
State and Other Route Numbers
Points of Interest, Recreation Areas
Airports

© HAMMOND WORLD ATLAS CORPORATION

GEOGRAPHICAL TERMS

A. = Arabic Burm. = Burmese Camb. = Cambodian Ch. = Chinese Czech. = Czechoslovakian Dan. = Danish Du. = Dutch Finn. = Finnish Fr. = French Ger. = German Ice. = Icelandic It. = Italian Jap. = Japanese Mong. = Mongol Nor. = Norwegian Per. = Persian Port. = Portuguese Russ. = Russian Sp. = Spanish Sw. = Swedish Turk. = Turkish

Å	Nor., Sw.	Stream
Aas	Dan., Nor.	Hills
Abajo	Sp.	Lower
Ada, Adasi	Turk.	Island
Altipiano	It.	Plateau
Altiplano	Sp.	Plateau
Alv, Alf, Elf	Sw.	River
Arrecife	Sp.	Reef
Asa	Nor., Sw.	Hill
Asaga	Turk.	Lower
Austral	Sp.	Southern
Baai	Du.	Bay
Bab	Arabic	Gate or Strait
Bahia	Sp.	Bay
Bahr	Arabic	Marsh, Lake, Sea, River
Baia	Port.	Bay
Baie	Fr.	Bay, Gulf
Baizo	Port.	Low
Bakke	Dan.	Hill
Bana	Jap.	Cape
Bañados	Sp.	Marshes
Band	Per.	Mt. Range
Bandao	Ch.	Peninsula
Bandar	Per.	Harbor
Barra	Sp.	Reef
Bel	Turk.	Pass
Belt	Ger.	Strait
Ben	Gaelic	Mountain
Bera	Du.	Mountain
Berg	Ger., Du.	Mountain
Bir	Arabic	Well
Boca	Sp.	Gulf, Inlet
Boğhaz	Turk.	Strait
Bolshoi, Bolshaya	Russ.	Big
Bolson	Sp.	Depression
Bong	Korean	Mountain
Boreal	Sp.	Northern
Breen	Nor.	Glacier
Bro	Dan., Nor., Sw.	Bridge
Bucht	Ger.	Bay
Bugt	Dan.	Bay
Bukhta	Russ.	Bay
Bukit	Malay	Hill, Mountain
Bukt	Nor., Sw.	Bay, Gulf
Burnu, Burun	Turk.	Cape, Point
By	Dan., Nor., Sw.	Town
Cabo	Port., Sp.	Cape
Campos	Port.	Plains
Canal	Port., Sp.	Channel
Cap, Capo	Fr., It.	Cape
Cataratas	Sp.	Falls
Catena	It.	Mt. Range
Catingas	Port.	Open Woodlands
Cayos	Sp.	Islands
Central, Centrale	Fr., It.	Middle
Cerrito, Cerro	Sp.	Hill
Cerros	Sp.	Hills, Mountains
Chai	Turk.	River
Chott	Arabic	Salt Lake
Ciénaga	Sp.	Swamp
Ciudad	Sp.	City
Col	Fr.	Pass
Cordillera	Sp.	Mt. Range, Mts.
Côte	Fr.	Coast
Csatoria	Magyar	Canal
Cuchilla	Sp.	Mt. Range
Curiche	Sp.	Swamp
Dağ, Daği	Turk.	Mountain, Peak
Dağlari	Turk.	Mt. Range
Dal	Nor., Sw.	Valley
Dar	Arabic	Land
Dar'ya	Russ.	River
Daryacheh	Per.	Marshy Lake
Dasht	Per.	Desert, Plain
Deniz, Denizi	Turk.	Sea, Lake
Desierto	Sp.	Desert
Détroit	Fr.	Strait
Djeziret	Arabic, Turk.	Island
Do	Korean	Island
Doi	Thai	Mountain
Eiland	Du.	Island
Elv	Dan., Nor.	River
Embalse	Sp.	Reservoir
Emi	Berber	Mountain
Erg	Arabic	Dune, Desert
Eski	Turk	Old
Est, Este	Fr., Port., Sp.	East
Estero	Sp.	Estuary, Creek
Estrecho, Estreito	Sp., Port.	Strait
Etang	Fr.	Pond, Lagoon, Lake
Feng	Ch.	Mountain
Fiume	It.	River
Fjäll	Sw.	Mountain
Fjeld, Fjell	Nor.	Hills, Mountain
Fjord	Dan., Nor., Sw.	Fiord
Fleuve	Fr.	River
Fljót	Ice.	Stream
Fluss	Ger.	River
Fors	Sw.	Waterfall
Fos, Foss	Dan., Nor.	Waterfall
Gamla	Nor.	Old
Gamle	Dan.	Old
Gata	Jap.	Lake
Gawa	Jap.	River
Gebel	Arabic	Mountain
Gebergte	Du.	Mt. Range
Gebirge	Ger.	Mt. Range
Gobi	Mongol	Desert
Goe	Jap.	Pass
Gol	Mongol, Turk.	Lake, Stream
Golf	Ger., Du.	Gulf
Golfe	Fr.	Gulf
Golfo	Sp., It., Port.	Gulf
Gölü	Turk.	Lake
Gora	Russ.	Mountain
Grand, Grande	Fr., Sp.	Big
Groot	Du.	Big
Gross	Ger.	Big
Grosso	It., Port.	Big
Guba	Russ.	Bay, Gulf
Gunto	Jap.	Archipelago
Gunung	Malay	Mountain
Hai	Ch.	Sea
Haixia	Ch.	Strait
Halbinsel	Ger.	Peninsula
Hamáda, Hammada	Arabic	Rocky Plateau
Hamn	Sw.	Harbor
Hamún	Per.	Marsh
Hanto	Jap.	Peninsula
Has, Hassi	Arabic	Well
Hav	Dan., Nor., Sw.	Sea, Ocean
Havet	Nor.	Bay
Havn	Dan., Nor.	Harbor
Havre	Fr.	Harbor
He	Ch.	River, Stream
Higashi, Higasi	Jap.	East
Hochebene	Ger.	Plateau
Hoek	Du.	Cape
Hoku	Jap.	North
Holm	Dan., Nor., Sw.	Island
Hory	Czech	Mountains
Hoved	Dan., Nor.	Cape, Promontory
Hu	Ch.	Lake
Huang	Ch.	Yellow
Huk	Dan., Nor., Sw.	Point
Hus, Huus	Dan., Nor., Sw.	House
Idehan	Arabic	Desert
Ile	Fr.	Island
Ilet	Fr.	Islet
Ilot	Fr.	Islet
Indre	Dan., Nor.	Inner
Inferieur, Inferiore	Fr., It.	Lower
Inner, Inre	Sw.	Inner
Insel	Ger.	Island
Irmak	Turk.	River
Isla	Sp.	Island
Isola	It.	Island
Jabal, Jebel	Arabic	Mountains
Järvi	Finn.	Lake
Jaure	Sw.	Lake
Jiang	Ch.	River, Stream
Jima	Jap.	Island
Joki	Finn.	River
Kaap	Du.	Cape
Kabir, Kebir	Arabic	Big
Kai	Jap.	Sea
Kaikyo	Jap.	Strait
Kami	Turk.	Upper
Kanaal	Du.	Canal
Kanal	Russ., Ger.	Canal, Channel
Kao	Thai	Mountain
Kap, Kapp	Nor., Sw., Ice.	Cape
Kaupunki	Finn.	Town
Kawa	Jap.	River
Khao	Thai	Mountain
Khrebet	Russ.	Mt. Range
Kita	Jap.	North
Klein	Du., Ger.	Small
Klint	Dan.	Promontory
Kô	Jap.	Lake
Ko	Thai	Island
Koh	Camb., Khmer	Island
Kop	Du.	Peak, Head
Köping	Sw.	Market, Borough
Körfez, Körfezi	Turk.	Gulf
Kosa	Russ.	Spit
Kosui	Jap.	Lake
Kraal	Du.	Native Village
Kuchuk	Turk.	Small
Kuh, Kuhha	Per.	Mt. Range, Mts.
Kul	Sinkiang Turki	Lake
Kum	Turk.	Desert
Kuro	Jap.	Black
Laag	Du.	Low
Lac	Fr.	Lake
Lago	Port., Sp., It.	Lake
Lagoa	Port.	Lagoon
Laguna	Sp.	Lagoon
Lagune	Fr.	Lagoon
Lahti	Finn.	Bay, Bight
Län	Sw.	County
Liedao	Ch.	Islands, Archipelago
Lilla	Sw.	Small
Lille	Dan., Nor.	Small
Ling	Ch.	Mountain
Llanos	Sp.	Plains
Mae Nam	Thai	River
Mali, Malaya	Russ.	Small
Man	Korean	Bay
Mar	Sp., Port.	Sea
Mare	It.	Sea
Medio	Sp.	Middle
Meer	Du.	Lake
Meer	Ger.	Sea
Mer	Fr.	Sea
Meridionale	It.	Southern
Meseta	Sp.	Plateau
Middelst, Midden	Du.	Middle
Minami	Jap.	Southern
Mis	Russ.	Cape
Misaki	Jap.	Cape
Mittel	Ger.	Middle
Mont	Fr.	Mountain
Montagne	Fr.	Mountain
Montaña	Sp.	Mountains
Monte	Sp., It., Port.	Mountain
More	Russ.	Sea
Mörön	Mong.	Stream
Morro	Port., Sp.	Mountain, Promontory
Morue	Fr.	Hill
Moyen	Fr.	Middle
Muang	Siamese	Town
Mui	Vietnamese	Cape, Point
Mys	Russ.	Cape
Nada	Jap.	Sea
Naka	Jap.	Middle
Nam	Burm., Lao.	River
Namakzar	Per.	Salt Waste
Nan	Jap.	South
Nes	Nor.	Cape, Point
Nevado	Sp.	Snow-covered Peak
Nieder	Ger.	Lower
Nishi, Nisi	Jap.	West
Nizhni, Nizhnyaya	Russ.	Lower
Njarga	Finn.	Peninsula, Promontory
Nong	Thai	Lake
Noord	Du.	North
Nord	Fr., Ger.	North
Norte	Sp., It., Port.	North
Nos	Russ.	Cape
Novi, Novaya	Russ.	New
Nur, Nuur	Ch., Mong.	Lake
Nuruu	Mong.	Mountains
Nusa	Malay	Island
Ny, Nya	Nor., Sw.	New
O	Jap.	Big
ö	Nor., Sw.	Island
Ober	Ger.	Upper
Occidental, Occidentale	Sp., It.	Western
Odde	Dan.	Point
Oeste	Port.	West
Ooster	Du.	Eastern
Opper, Over	Du.	Upper
Oriental	Sp., Fr.	Eastern
Orientale	It.	Eastern
Orta	Turk.	Middle
Ost	Ger.	East
Ostrov	Russ.	Island
Ouest	Fr.	West
öy	Nor.	Island
Ozero	Russ.	Lake
Pampa	Sp.	Plain
Pas	Fr.	Channel, Strait
Paso	Sp.	Pass
Passo	It., Port.	Pass
Peña	Sp.	Rock, Mountain
Pendi	Ch.	Basin
Penisola	It.	Peninsula
Pequeño	Sp.	Small
Pereval	Russ.	Pass
Peski	Russ.	Desert
Petit, Petite	Fr.	Small
Phu	Lao, Annamese	Mtn.
Pic	Fr.	Mountain
Piccolo	It.	Small
Pico	Port., Sp.	Mountain, Peak
Pik	Russ.	Mountain, Peak
Piton	Fr.	Mountain, Peak
Planalto	Port.	Plateau
Plato	Russ.	Plateau
Pointe	Fr.	Point
Poluostrov	Russ.	Peninsula
Ponta	Port.	Point
Presa	Sp.	Reservoir
Presqu'île	Fr.	Peninsula
Proliv	Russ.	Strait
Pulou, Pulo	Malay	Island
Punt	Du.	Point
Punta	Sp., It., Port.	Point
Qiryat	Hebrew	City, Settlement
Qum	Turk.	Desert
Qundao	Ch.	Islands
Rada	Sp.	Inlet
Rade	Fr.	Bay, Inlet
Ras	Arabic	Cape
Reka	Russ.	River
Retto	Jap.	Archipelago
Ria	Sp.	Estuary
Río	Sp.	River
Rivier, Rivière	Du., Fr.	River
Rud	Per.	River
Sai	Jap.	West
Saki	Jap.	Cape
Salar, Salina	Sp.	Salt Deposit
Salto	Sp., Port.	Falls
San	Jap., Korean	Hill
Sanmaek	Korean	Mt. Range
Schiereiland	Du.	Peninsula
Se	Camb., Khmer	River
See	Ger.	Sea, Lake
Selvas	Sp., Port.	Woods, Forest
Seno	Sp.	Bay, Gulf
Serra	Port.	Mts.
Serranía	Sp.	Mts.
Seto	Jap.	Strait
Settentrionale	It.	Northern
Severni, Severnaya	Russ.	North
Shamo	Ch.	Desert
Shan	Ch., Jap.	Hill, Mts.
Shankou	Ch.	Pass
Shatt	Arabic	River
Shima	Jap.	Island
Shimo	Jap.	Lower
Shin	Jap.	Land
Shiro	Jap.	White
Shoto	Jap.	Islands
Si	Ch.	West
Sierra	Sp.	Mt. Range, Mts.
Sjö	Nor., Sw.	Lake, Sea
Sok, Suk, Souk	Arabic	Market
Song	Annamese	River
Sopka	Russ.	Volcano
Spitze	Ger.	Mt. Peak
Sredni, Srednyaya	Russ.	Middle
Stad	Dan., Nor., Sw.	City
Stari, Staraya	Russ.	Old
Step	Russ.	Treeless Plain
Straat	Du.	Strait
Strasse	Ger.	Strait
Stretto	It.	Strait
Ström	Dan., Nor., Sw.	Sound
Stung	Camb., Khmer	River
Su	Turk.	River
Sud, Süd	Sp., Fr., Ger.	South
Suido	Jap.	Strait, Channel
Sul	Port.	South
Sund	Dan., Nor., Sw.	Sound
Sungei	Malay	River
Supérieur	Fr.	Upper
Superior, Superiore	Sp., It.	Upper
Sur	Sp.	South
Suyu	Turk.	River
Ta	Ch.	Big
Tafelland	Du.	Plateau
Tagh	Turk	Mt. Range
Take	Jap.	Peak, Ridge
Takht	Arabic	Lower
Tal	Ger.	Valley
Tanjung	Malay	Cape, Point
Tell	Arabic	Hill
Thale	Thai	Sea, Lake
Tind	Nor.	Peak
Tō	Jap.	East
To	Jap.	Island
Toge	Jap.	Pass
Trask	Finn.	Lake
Tugh	Somali	Dry River
Ujung	Malay	Point
Umi	Jap.	Bay
Unter	Ger.	Lower
Ura	Jap.	Inlet
Uul	Mong.	Mountain
Val	Fr.	Valley
Vatn	Nor.	Lake
Vecchio	It.	Old
Veld	Du.	Plain, Field
Velho	Port.	Old
Verkhni	Russ.	Upper
Vesi	Finn.	Lake
Viejo	Sp.	Old
Vik	Nor., Sw.	Bay
Vishni, Vishnyaya	Russ.	High
Vodokhranilishche	Russ.	Reservoir
Volcán	Sp.	Volcano
Vostochni, Vostochnaya	Russ.	East, Eastern
Wadi	Arabic	Dry River
Wald	Ger.	Forest
Wan	Jap.	Bay
Westersch	Du.	Western
Wüste	Ger.	Desert
Yama	Jap.	Mountain
Yug, Yuzhni, Yuzhnaya	Russ.	South, Southern
Zaki	Jap.	Cape
Zaliv	Russ.	Bay, Gulf
Zangbo	Tibetan	River, Stream
Zapadni, Zapadnaya	Russ.	Western
Zee	Du.	Sea
Zemlya	Russ.	Land
Zizhiqu	Ch.	Autonomous Region
Zuid	Du.	South

WORLD STATISTICS

Elements of the Solar System

	Mean Distance from Sun: in Miles	in Kilometers	Period of Revolution around Sun	Period of Rotation on Axis	Equatorial Diameter in Miles	in Kilometers	Surface Gravity (Earth = 1)	Mass (Earth = 1)	Mean Density (Water = 1)	Number of Satellites
Mercury	35,990,000	57,900,000	87.97 days	58.7 days	3,032	4,880	0.38	0.055	5.4	0
Venus	67,240,000	108,200,000	224.70 days	243.7 days†	7,521	12,104	0.91	0.815	5.2	0
Earth	93,000,000	149,700,000	365.26 days	23h 56m	7,926	12,755	1.00	1.00	5.5	1
Mars	141,610,000	227,900,000	686.98 days	24h 37m	4,221	6,794	0.38	0.107	3.9	2
Jupiter	483,675,000	778,400,000	11.86 years	9h 55m	88,846	142,984	2.36	317.8	1.3	16
Saturn	886,572,000	1,426,800,000	29.46 years	10h 30m	74,898	120,536	0.92	95.2	0.7	18
Uranus	1,783,957,000	2,871,000,000	84.01 years	17h 14m†	31,763	51,118	0.89	14.5	1.3	15
Neptune	2,795,114,000	4,498,300,000	164.79 years	16h 6m	30,778	49,532	1.13	17.1	1.6	8
Pluto	3,670,000,000	5,906,400,000	247.70 years	6.4 days†	1,413	2,274	0.07	0.002	2.1	1

† Retrograde motion

Source: NASA, National Space Science Data Center

Dimensions of the Earth

	Area in: Sq. Miles	Sq. Kilometers
Superficial area	196,939,000	510,072,000
Land surface	57,506,000	148,940,000
Water surface	139,433,000	361,132,000

	Distance in: Miles	Kilometers
Equatorial circumference	24,902	40,075
Polar circumference	24,860	40,007
Equatorial diameter	7,926.4	12,756.4
Polar diameter	7,899.8	12,713.6
Equatorial radius	3,963.2	6,378.2
Polar radius	3,949.9	6,356.8

Volume of the Earth	2.6×10^{11} cubic miles	10.84×10^{11} cubic kilometers
Mass or weight	6.6×10^{21} short tons	6.0×10^{21} metric tons
Maximum distance from Sun	94,600,000 miles	152,000,000 kilometers
Minimum distance from Sun	91,300,000 miles	147,000,000 kilometers

Oceans and Major Seas

	Area in: Sq. Miles	Sq. Kms.	Greatest Depth in: Feet	Meters
Pacific Ocean	63,855,000	166,241,000	36,198	11,033
Atlantic Ocean	31,744,000	82,217,000	28,374	8,648
Indian Ocean	28,417,000	73,600,000	25,344	7,725
Arctic Ocean	5,427,000	14,056,000	17,880	5,450
Caribbean Sea	970,000	2,512,300	24,720	7,535
Mediterranean Sea	969,000	2,509,700	16,896	5,150
South China Sea	895,000	2,318,000	15,000	4,600
Bering Sea	875,000	2,266,250	15,800	4,800
Gulf of Mexico	600,000	1,554,000	12,300	3,750
Sea of Okhotsk	590,000	1,528,100	11,070	3,370
East China Sea	482,000	1,248,400	9,500	2,900
Yellow Sea	480,000	1,243,200	350	107
Sea of Japan	389,000	1,007,500	12,280	3,740
Hudson Bay	317,500	822,300	846	258
North Sea	222,000	575,000	2,200	670
Black Sea	185,000	479,150	7,365	2,245
Red Sea	169,000	437,700	7,200	2,195
Baltic Sea	163,000	422,170	1,506	459

The Continents

	Area in: Sq. Miles	Sq. Kms.	Percent of World's Land
Asia	17,128,500	44,362,815	29.5
Africa	11,707,000	30,321,130	20.2
North America	9,363,000	24,250,170	16.2
South America	6,879,725	17,818,505	11.9
Antarctica	5,405,000	14,000,000	9.4
Europe	4,057,000	10,507,630	7.0
Australia	2,967,893	7,686,850	5.1

Major Ship Canals

	Length in: Miles	Kms.	Minimum Depth in: Feet	Meters
Volga-Baltic, Russia	225	362	–	–
Baltic-White Sea, Russia	140	225	16	5
Suez, Egypt	100.76	162	42	13
Albert, Belgium	80	129	16.5	5
Moscow-Volga, Russia	80	129	18	6
Volga-Don, Russia	62	100	–	–
Göta, Sweden	54	87	10	3
Kiel (Nord-Ostsee), Germany	53.2	86	38	12
Panama Canal, Panama	50.72	82	41.6	13
Houston Ship, U.S.A.	50	81	36	11

Largest Islands

	Area in: Sq. Miles	Sq. Kms.		Area in: Sq. Miles	Sq. Kms.		Area in: Sq. Miles	Sq. Kms.
Greenland	840,000	2,175,600	Hispaniola, Haiti & Dom. Rep.	29,399	76,143	Somerset, Canada	9,570	24,786
New Guinea	305,000	789,950	Banks, Canada	27,038	70,028	Sardinia, Italy	9,301	24,090
Borneo	286,000	740,740	Ceylon, Sri Lanka	25,332	65,610	Shikoku, Japan	6,860	17,767
Madagascar	226,656	587,040	Tasmania, Australia	24,600	63,710	New Caledonia, France	6,530	16,913
Baffin, Canada	195,928	507,454	Svalbard, Norway	23,957	62,049	Nordaustlandet, Norway	6,409	16,599
Sumatra, Indonesia	164,000	424,760	Devon, Canada	21,331	55,247	Samar, Philippines	5,050	13,080
Honshu, Japan	88,000	227,920	Novaya Zemlya (north isl.), Russia	18,600	48,200	Negros, Philippines	4,906	12,707
Great Britain	84,400	218,896	Marajó, Brazil	17,991	46,597	Palawan, Philippines	4,550	11,785
Victoria, Canada	83,896	217,290	Tierra del Fuego, Chile & Argentina	17,900	46,360	Panay, Philippines	4,446	11,515
Ellesmere, Canada	75,767	196,236	Alexander, Antarctica	16,700	43,250	Jamaica	4,232	10,961
Celebes, Indonesia	72,986	189,034	Axel Heiberg, Canada	16,671	43,178	Hawaii, United States	4,038	10,458
South I., New Zealand	58,393	151,238	Melville, Canada	16,274	42,150	Viti Levu, Fiji	4,010	10,386
Java, Indonesia	48,842	126,501	Southhampton, Canada	15,913	41,215	Cape Breton, Canada	3,981	10,311
North I., New Zealand	44,187	114,444	New Britain, Papua New Guinea	14,100	36,519	Mindoro, Philippines	3,759	9,736
Cuba	42,803	110,860	Taiwan, China	13,836	35,835	Kodiak, Alaska, U.S.A.	3,670	9,505
Newfoundland, Canada	42,031	108,860	Kyushu, Japan	13,770	35,664	Cyprus	3,572	9,251
Luzon, Philippines	40,420	104,688	Hainan, China	13,127	33,999	Puerto Rico, U.S.A.	3,435	8,897
Iceland	39,768	103,000	Prince of Wales, Canada	12,872	33,338	Corsica, France	3,352	8,682
Mindanao, Philippines	36,537	94,631	Spitsbergen, Norway	12,355	31,999	New Ireland, Papua New Guinea	3,340	8,651
Ireland	32,589	84,406	Vancouver, Canada	12,079	31,285	Crete, Greece	3,218	8,335
Hokkaido, Japan	30,436	75,066	Timor, Indonesia	11,527	29,855	Anticosti, Canada	3,066	7,941
Sakhalin, Russia	29,500	76,405	Sicily, Italy	9,926	25,708	Wrangel, Russia	2,819	7,301

Principal Mountains

	Height in : Feet	Meters		Height in : Feet	Meters		Height in : Feet	Meters
Everest, Nepal-China	29,028	8,848	Pissis, Argentina	22,241	6,779	Margherita, D.R. Congo-Uganda	16,795	5,119
K2 (Godwin Austen), Pakistan-China	28,250	8,611	Mercedario, Argentina	22,211	6,770	Kazbek, Georgia-Russia	16,558	5,047
Kanchenjunga, Nepal-India	28,208	8,598	Huascarán, Peru	22,205	6,768	Puncak Jaya, Indonesia	16,503	5,030
Lhotse, Nepal-China	27,923	8,511	Llullaillaco, Chile-Argentina	22,057	6,723	Blanc, France	15,771	4,807
Makalu, Nepal-China	27,789	8,470	Nevada Ancohuma, Bolivia	21,489	6,550	Klyuchevskaya Sopka, Russia	15,584	4,750
Dhaulagiri, Nepal	26,810	8,172	Chimborazo, Ecuador	20,561	6,267	Fairweather, Br. Col., Canada	15,300	4,663
Nanga Parbat, Pakistan	26,660	8,126	McKinley, Alaska	20,320	6,194	Dufourspitze, Italy-Switzerland	15,203	4,634
Annapurna, Nepal	26,504	8,078	Logan, Yukon, Canada	19,524	5,951	Ras Dashen, Ethiopia	15,157	4,620
Nanda Devi, India	25,645	7,817	Cotopaxi, Ecuador	19,347	5,897	Matterhorn, Switzerland	14,691	4,478
Rakaposhi, Pakistan	25,550	7,788	Kilimanjaro, Tanzania	19,340	5,895	Whitney, California, U.S.A.	14,494	4,418
Kongur Shan, China	25,325	7,719	El Misti, Peru	19,101	5,822	Elbert, Colorado, U.S.A.	14,433	4,399
Tirich Mir, Pakistan	25,230	7,690	Pico Cristóbal Colón, Colombia	18,947	5,775	Rainier, Washington, U.S.A.	14,410	4,392
Gongga Shan, China	24,790	7,556	Huila, Colombia	18,865	5,750	Shasta, California, U.S.A.	14,162	4,317
Ismail Samani Peak, Tajikistan	24,590	7,495	Citlaltépetl (Orizaba), Mexico	18,700	5,700	Pikes Peak, Colorado, U.S.A.	14,110	4,301
Pobeda Peak, Kyrgyzstan	24,406	7,439	Damavand, Iran	18,605	5,671	Finsteraarhorn, Switzerland	14,022	4,274
Chomo Lhari, Bhutan-China	23,997	7,314	El'brus, Russia	18,510	5,642	Mauna Kea, Hawaii, U.S.A.	13,796	4,205
Muztag, China	23,891	7,282	St. Elias, Alaska, U.S.A.-Yukon, Canada	18,008	5,489	Mauna Loa, Hawaii, U.S.A.	13,677	4,169
Cerro Aconcagua, Argentina	22,831	6,959	Dykhtau, Russia	17,070	5,203	Jungfrau, Switzerland	13,642	4,158
Ojos del Salado, Chile-Argentina	22,572	6,880	Kenya, Kenya	17,058	5,199	Grossglockner, Austria	12,457	3,797
Bonete, Chile-Argentina	22,546	6,872	Ararat, Turkey	16,946	5,165	Fuji, Japan	12,389	3,776
Tupungato, Chile-Argentina	22,310	6,800	Vinson Massif, Antarctica	16,864	5,140	Cook, New Zealand	12,349	3,764

Longest Rivers

	Length in : Miles	Kms.		Length in : Miles	Kms.		Length in : Miles	Kms.
Nile, Africa	4,145	6,671	Rio Grande, Mexico-U.S.A.	1,885	3,034	Kama, Russia	1,252	2,031
Amazon, S. America	4,007	6,448	Syrdar'ya-Naryn, Asia	1,859	2,992	Don, Russia	1,222	1,967
Mississippi-Missouri-Red Rock, U.S.A.	3,710	5,971	Indus, Asia	1,800	2,897	Red, U.S.A.	1,222	1,966
Chang Jiang (Yangtze), China	3,500	5,633	Danube, Europe	1,775	2,857	Columbia, U.S.A.-Canada	1,214	1,953
Ob'-Irtysh, Russia-Kazakhstan	3,362	5,411	Brahmaputra, Asia	1,700	2,736	Tigris, Asia	1,181	1,901
Yenisey-Angara, Russia	3,100	4,989	Tocantins, Brazil	1,677	2,699	Darling, Australia	1,160	1,867
Huang He (Yellow), China	2,950	4,747	Salween, Asia	1,675	2,696	Angara, Russia	1,135	1,827
Congo, Africa	2,780	4,474	Euphrates, Asia	1,650	2,655	Songhua Jiang (Sungari), Asia	1,130	1,819
Amur-Shilka-Onon, Asia	2,744	4,416	Xi Jiang, China	1,650	2,655	Pechora, Russia	1,124	1,809
Lena, Russia	2,734	4,400	Amudar'ya, Asia	1,616	2,601	Snake, U.S.A.	1,038	1,670
Mackenzie-Peace-Finlay, Canada	2,635	4,241	Nelson-Saskatchewan, Canada	1,600	2,575	Churchill, Canada	1,000	1,609
Paraná-La Plata, S. America	2,630	4,232	Orinoco, S. America	1,600	2,575	Pilcomayo, S. America	1,000	1,609
Mekong, Asia	2,610	4,200	Paraguay, S. America	1,584	2,549	Uruguay, S. America	994	1,600
Niger, Africa	2,580	4,152	Kolyma, Russia	1,562	2,514	Platte-N. Platte, U.S.A.	990	1,593
Missouri-Red Rock, U.S.A.	2,564	4,125	Ganges, Asia	1,550	2,494	Ohio, U.S.A.	981	1,578
Yenisey, Russia	2,500	4,028	Ural, Russia-Kazakhstan	1,509	2,428	Magdalena, Colombia	956	1,538
Mississippi, U.S.A.	2,348	3,778	Japurá, S. America	1,500	2,414	Pecos, U.S.A.	926	1,490
Murray-Darling, Australia	2,310	3,718	Arkansas, U.S.A.	1,450	2,334	Oka, Russia	918	1,477
Volga, Russia	2,290	3,685	Colorado, U.S.A.-Mexico	1,450	2,334	Canadian, U.S.A.	906	1,458
Madeira, S. America	2,013	3,240	Negro, S. America	1,400	2,253	Colorado, Texas, U.S.A.	894	1,439
Purus, S. America	1,995	3,211	Dnieper, Russia-Belarus-Ukraine	1,368	2,202	Dniester, Ukraine-Moldova	876	1,410
Yukon, Alaska-Canada	1,979	3,185	Orange, Africa	1,350	2,173	Fraser, Canada	850	1,369
Zambezi, Africa	1,950	3,138	Irrawaddy, Burma	1,325	2,132	Rhine, Europe	820	1,319
São Francisco, Brazil	1,930	3,106	Brazos, U.S.A.	1,309	2,107	Northern Dvina, Russia	809	1,302
St. Lawrence, Canada-U.S.A.	1,900	3,058	Ohio-Allegheny, U.S.A.	1,306	2,102	Ottawa, Canada	790	1,271

Principal Natural Lakes

	Area in: Sq. Miles	Sq. Kms.	Max. Depth in: Feet	Meters		Area in: Sq. Miles	Sq. Kms.	Max. Depth in: Feet	Meters
Caspian Sea, Asia	143,243	370,999	3,264	995	Lake Eyre, Australia*	3,500-0	9,065-0	–	–
Lake Superior, U.S.A.-Canada	31,820	82,414	1,329	405	Lake Titicaca, Peru-Bolivia	3,200	8,288	1,000	305
Lake Victoria, Africa	26,628	69,215	270	82	Lake Nicaragua, Nicaragua	3,100	8,029	230	70
Lake Huron, U.S.A.-Canada	23,010	59,596	748	228	Lake Athabasca, Canada	3,064	7,936	400	122
Lake Michigan, U.S.A.	22,400	58,016	923	281	Reindeer Lake, Canada*	2,568	6,651	–	–
Aral Sea, Kazakhstan-Uzbekistan	15,830	41,000	213	65	Lake Turkana (Rudolf), Africa	2,463	6,379	240	73
Lake Tanganyika, Africa	12,650	32,764	4,700	1,433	Issyk-Kul', Kyrgyzstan	2,425	6,281	2,303	702
Lake Baykal, Russia	12,162	31,500	5,316	1,620	Lake Torrens, Australia*	2,230	5,776	–	–
Great Bear Lake, Canada	12,096	31,328	1,356	413	Vänern, Sweden	2,156	5,584	328	100
Lake Nyasa (Malawi), Africa	11,555	29,928	2,320	707	Nettilling Lake, Canada*	2,140	5,543	–	–
Great Slave Lake, Canada	11,031	28,570	2,015	614	Lake Winnipegosis, Canada	2,075	5,374	38	12
Lake Erie, U.S.A.-Canada	9,940	25,745	210	64	Lake Mobutu Sese Seko (Albert), Africa	2,075	5,374	160	49
Lake Winnipeg, Canada	9,417	24,390	60	18	Lake Kariba, Zambia-Zimbabwe	2,050	5,310	295	90
Lake Ontario, U.S.A.-Canada	7,540	19,529	775	244	Lake Nipigon, Canada	1,872	4,848	540	165
Lake Balkhash, Kazakhstan	7,081	18,340	87	27	Lake Mweru, Dem. Rep. of the Congo-Zambia	1,800	4,662	60	18
Lake Ladoga, Russia	6,900	17,871	738	225	Lake Manitoba, Canada	1,799	4,659	12	4
Lake Maracaibo, Venezuela	5,120	13,261	100	31	Lake Taymyr, Russia	1,737	4,499	85	26
Lake Chad, Africa*	10,000–	25,900–			Lake Khanka, China-Russia	1,700	4,403	33	10
	4,000	10,360	25	8	Lake Kioga, Uganda	1,700	4,403	25	8
Lake Onega, Russia	3,761	9,741	377	115	Lake of the Woods, U.S.A.-Canada	1,679	4,349	70	21

* Figures subject to great seasonal variations.

TABLES OF AIRLINE DISTANCES

ALL DISTANCES IN STATUTE MILES

BETWEEN PRINCIPAL CITIES OF THE WORLD

FROM/TO	AZORES	BAGHDAD	BERLIN	BOMBAY	BUENOS AIRES	CALLAO	CAIRO	CAPE TOWN	CHICAGO	ISTANBUL	GUAM	HONOLULU	JUNEAU	LONDON	LOS ANGELES	MELBOURNE	MEXICO CITY	MONTREAL	NEW ORLEANS	NEW YORK	PANAMA	PARIS	RIO DE JANEIRO	SAN FRANCISCO	SANTIAGO	SEATTLE	SHANGHAI	SINGAPORE	TOKYO	WELLINGTON
AZORES	....	3906	2118	5930	5385	4825	3325	5670	3305	2880	8985	7421	4715	1562	5034	12190	4584	2548	3718	2604	3918	1617	4312	5114	5718	4720	7324	8338	7370	11475
BAGHDAD	3906	....	2040	2022	8215	8618	785	4923	6490	1085	6380	8445	6180	2568	7695	8150	8155	5814	7212	6066	7807	2385	7012	7521	8876	6848	4468	4443	5242	9782
BERLIN	2148	2040	....	3947	7411	6937	1823	5949	4458	1068	7158	7384	4638	575	5849	9992	6119	3776	5182	4026	5902	540	6246	5744	7842	5121	5323	6226	5623	11384
BOMBAY	5930	2022	3947	....	9380	10530	2698	5133	8144	3043	4831	8172	6992	4526	8810	6140	9818	7582	8952	7875	9832	4391	8438	8523	10127	7830	3219	2425	4247	7752
BUENOS AIRES	5385	8215	7411	9380	....	1982	7428	4332	5598	7638	10516	7653	7964	6919	6148	7336	4609	5619	4902	5295	3319	6891	1230	6487	731	6956	12295	9940	11601	6341
CALLAO	4825	8618	6937	10530	1982	....	7870	6195	3765	7666	9760	5993	5806	6376	4155	8196	2619	3954	2990	3633	1450	6455	2490	4500	1548	4964	10760	11700	9740	6696
CAIRO	3325	785	1823	2698	7428	7870	....	4476	6231	780	7175	8925	6352	2218	7675	8720	7807	5502	6862	5701	7230	2020	6242	7554	8100	6915	5290	5152	6005	10360
CAPE TOWN	5670	4923	5949	5133	4332	6195	4476	....	8551	5210	8918	11655	10382	5975	10165	6510	8620	7975	8390	7845	7090	5732	3850	10340	5080	10305	8179	6025	9234	7149
CHICAGO	3305	6490	4458	8144	5598	3765	6231	8551	....	5530	7510	4315	2310	4015	1741	9837	1690	750	827	727	2320	4219	5320	1875	5325	1753	7155	9475	6410	8465
ISTANBUL	2880	1085	1068	3043	7638	7666	780	5210	5530	....	7015	8200	5665	1540	6895	9189	7160	4825	6220	5060	6797	1390	6420	6770	8230	6124	5084	5440	5649	10790
GUAM	8985	6380	7158	4831	10516	9760	7175	8918	7510	7015	....	3896	5225	7605	6255	3497	7690	7840	7895	8115	9220	7675	11710	5952	9946	5785	1945	2990	1596	4206
HONOLULU	7421	8445	7384	8172	7653	5993	8925	11655	4315	8200	3896	....	2825	7320	2620	5581	3846	4992	4305	5051	5347	7525	8400	2407	6935	2707	5009	6874	3940	4676
JUNEAU	4715	6180	4638	6992	7964	5806	6352	10382	2310	5665	5225	2825	....	4496	1835	8162	3210	2647	2860	2874	4456	4700	7611	1530	7320	870	4968	7375	4117	7501
LONDON	1562	2568	575	4526	6919	6376	2218	5975	4015	1540	7605	7320	4496	....	5496	10590	5605	3370	4656	3500	5310	210	5747	5440	7275	4850	5841	6818	6050	11790
LOS ANGELES	5034	7695	5849	8810	6148	4155	7675	10165	1741	6895	6255	2620	1835	5496	....	8098	1445	2468	1695	2466	3025	5711	6360	345	5595	961	6598	8955	5600	6806
MELBOURNE	12190	8150	9992	6140	7336	8196	8720	6510	9837	9189	3497	5581	8162	10590	8098	....	8599	10553	9455	10541	9211	10500	8340	7970	7130	8330	4967	3768	5172	1655
MEXICO CITY	4584	8155	6119	9818	4609	2619	7807	8620	1690	7160	7690	3846	3210	5605	1445	8599	....	2247	940	2110	1532	5800	4810	1870	1422	2339	8120	10495	7190	7003
MONTREAL	2548	5814	3776	7582	5619	3954	5502	7975	750	4825	7840	4992	2647	3370	2468	10553	2247	....	1390	340	2545	3490	5110	2557	5461	2309	7141	9280	6546	9206
NEW ORLEANS	3718	7212	5182	8952	4902	2990	6862	8390	827	6220	7895	4305	2860	4656	1695	9455	940	1390	....	1161	1600	4846	4798	1960	4553	2137	7830	10255	6993	7950
NEW YORK	2604	6066	4026	7875	5295	3633	5701	7845	727	5060	8115	5051	2874	3500	2466	10541	2110	340	1161	....	2211	3600	4810	2606	5134	2440	7460	9617	6846	9067
PANAMA	3918	7807	5902	9832	3319	1450	7230	7090	2320	6797	9220	5347	4456	5310	3025	9211	1532	2545	1600	2211	....	5440	3311	3349	3000	3680	9430	11800	8560	7580
PARIS	1617	2385	540	4391	6891	6455	2020	5732	4219	1390	7675	7525	4700	210	5711	10500	5800	3490	4846	3600	5440	....	5710	5680	7300	5080	5855	6730	6132	11865
RIO DE JANEIRO	4312	7012	6246	8438	1230	2490	6242	3850	5320	6420	11710	8400	7611	5747	6360	8340	4810	5110	4798	4810	3311	5710	....	6655	1852	6945	11510	9875	11600	7510
SAN FRANCISCO	5114	7521	5744	8523	6487	4500	7554	10340	1875	6770	5952	2407	1530	5440	345	7970	1870	2557	1960	2606	3349	5680	6655	....	5960	692	6245	8440	5250	6800
SANTIAGO	5718	8876	7842	10127	731	1548	8100	5080	5325	8230	9946	6935	7320	7275	5595	7130	1422	5461	4553	5134	3000	7300	1852	5960	....	6466	11850	10270	10850	5925
SEATTLE	4720	6848	5121	7830	6956	4964	6915	10305	1753	6124	5785	2707	870	4850	961	8330	2339	2309	2137	2440	3680	5080	6945	692	6466	....	5780	8200	4863	7310
SHANGHAI	7324	4468	5323	3219	12295	10760	5290	8179	7155	5084	1945	5009	4968	5841	6598	4967	8120	7141	7830	7460	9430	5855	11510	6245	11850	5780	....	2395	1095	6080
SINGAPORE	8338	4443	6226	2425	9940	11700	5152	6025	9475	5440	2990	6874	7375	6818	8955	3768	10495	9280	10255	9617	11800	6730	9875	8440	10270	8200	2395	....	3350	5360
TOKYO	7370	5242	5623	4247	11601	9740	6005	9234	6410	5649	1596	3940	4117	6050	5600	5172	7190	6546	6993	6846	8560	6132	11600	5250	10850	4863	1095	3350	....	5730
WELLINGTON	11475	9782	11384	7752	6341	6696	10360	7149	8465	10790	4206	4676	7501	11790	6806	1655	7003	9206	7950	9067	7580	11865	7510	6800	5925	7310	6080	5360	5730	....

BETWEEN PRINCIPAL CITIES OF EUROPE

FROM/TO	AMSTERDAM	ATHENS	BAKU	BARCELONA	BELGRADE	BERLIN	BRUSSELS	BUCHAREST	BUDAPEST	COLOGNE	COPENHAGEN	ISTANBUL	DRESDEN	DUBLIN	FRANKFURT	HAMBURG	ST. PETERSBURG	LISBON	LONDON	LYON	MADRID	MARSEILLES	MILAN	MOSCOW	MUNICH	OSLO	PARIS	RIGA	ROME	SOFIA	STOCKHOLM	TOULOUSE	WARSAW	VIENNA	ZURICH
AMSTERDAM	....	1340	2218	770	875	365	105	1100	710	128	381	1360	385	468	228	232	1090	1140	220	458	912	627	517	1325	415	568	257	820	808	1073	695	625	673	580	375
ATHENS	1340	....	1395	1160	500	1112	1292	460	698	1200	1320	350	1022	1765	1113	1250	1535	1770	1476	1100	1463	1025	900	1388	925	1610	1300	1310	650	335	1495	1215	990	795	1000
BAKU	2218	1395	....	2427	1487	1867	2240	1220	1562	2127	1980	1070	1837	2490	2055	2020	1570	3050	2435	2238	2742	2238	2028	1175	1912	2118	2335	1590	1900	1360	1862	2425	1555	1700	2050
BARCELONA	770	1160	2427	....	998	925	658	1210	924	692	1085	1380	860	919	665	910	1740	610	707	327	316	211	450	1852	648	1330	518	1440	530	1072	1410	156	1150	830	513
BELGRADE	875	500	1487	998	....	618	850	295	205	750	840	502	530	1327	652	760	1165	1555	1040	752	1235	750	540	1160	475	1112	890	855	440	231	1005	930	510	300	590
BERLIN	365	1112	1867	925	618	....	401	798	425	300	225	1068	95	815	268	165	815	1410	575	601	1149	730	570	995	310	520	540	520	780	810	503	815	320	322	410
BRUSSELS	105	1292	2240	658	850	401	....	1110	700	110	475	1345	407	480	198	301	1175	998	202	352	807	521	435	1392	372	672	170	900	730	945	793	515	720	568	312
BUCHAREST	1100	460	1220	1210	295	798	1110	....	295	982	725	272	725	1560	890	950	1080	1842	1285	1025	1518	920	819	920	1152	1080	740	194	1080	1210	820	883	342	128	498
BUDAPEST	710	698	1562	924	205	425	700	295	....	590	629	650	345	1176	504	572	963	1515	900	680	1214	718	476	965	350	920	770	685	500	500	722	883	342	128	498
COLOGNE	128	1200	2127	692	750	300	110	982	590	....	400	1240	292	585	93	228	1090	1126	308	370	875	528	390	1285	282	635	250	805	675	945	722	875	602	460	259
COPENHAGEN	381	1320	1960	1085	840	225	475	920	629	400	....	1240	315	768	412	180	708	1520	590	760	1272	906	720	970	520	303	634	453	948	1010	330	962	415	538	595
ISTANBUL	1360	350	1070	1380	502	1068	1345	272	650	1240	1240	....	995	1830	1150	1222	1292	2005	1540	1238	1690	1205	1030	1180	975	1505	1390	1115	840	315	1340	1400	852	790	1090
DRESDEN	385	1022	1837	860	530	95	407	725	345	292	315	995	....	852	236	238	885	1380	592	540	1100	655	435	1210	227	620	523	585	630	730	598	762	325	235	342
DUBLIN	468	1765	2490	919	1327	815	480	1560	1176	585	768	1830	852	....	671	668	1440	1015	300	720	902	875	880	1728	855	786	480	1210	1175	1525	1010	761	1130	1040	768
FRANKFURT	228	1113	2055	665	652	268	198	890	504	93	412	1150	236	671	....	250	1075	1160	392	350	888	492	323	1240	193	675	295	780	698	860	730	560	550	370	193
HAMBURG	232	1250	2020	910	760	165	301	950	572	228	180	1222	238	668	250	....	880	1301	448	580	1098	730	570	1100	378	445	459	600	810	954	502	780	462	460	432
ST. PETERSBURG	1090	1535	1570	1740	1165	815	1175	1080	965	1090	708	1292	885	1440	1075	880	....	2235	1300	1420	1980	1540	1315	391	1100	670	1335	300	1440	1218	435	1635	640	975	1225
LISBON	1140	1770	3050	610	1555	1410	998	1842	1515	1126	1520	2005	1380	1015	1160	1301	2235	....	975	850	313	810	1030	3010	1208	1690	890	1940	1053	1848	1848	640	1700	1415	1058
LONDON	220	1476	2435	707	1040	575	202	1285	900	308	590	1540	592	300	392	448	1300	975	....	455	777	620	595	1540	526	720	210	1035	890	1235	885	550	890	762	480
LYON	458	1100	2238	327	752	601	352	1025	680	370	760	1238	540	720	350	580	1420	850	455	....	577	170	210	1560	352	1080	248	1122	462	928	1080	228	832	520	206
MADRID	912	1463	2742	316	1235	1149	807	1518	1214	875	1272	1690	1100	902	888	1098	1980	313	777	557	....	394	728	2120	910	1474	645	1670	840	1385	1598	344	1410	1110	765
MARSEILLES	627	1025	2238	211	750	730	521	1020	718	528	906	1205	655	875	492	730	1540	810	620	170	394	....	238	1642	445	1165	410	1238	372	895	1225	196	950	620	318
MILAN	517	900	2028	450	540	570	435	819	476	390	570	1315	530	1350	595	570	1350	1030	595	210	728	238	....	1408	215	1000	400	1010	295	715	1020	400	705	235	137
MOSCOW	1325	1388	1175	1852	1160	995	1392	920	965	1285	970	1180	1200	1728	1240	1100	391	3010	1540	1560	2120	1642	1408	....	1220	1030	1538	520	1462	1100	770	1770	710	1028	1350
MUNICH	415	925	1912	648	475	310	325	750	350	282	520	975	227	855	193	378	1100	1208	526	352	910	445	215	1220	....	1030	425	800	472	928	1385	425	500	222	158
OSLO	568	1610	2118	1330	1112	520	672	1245	920	635	303	1505	620	786	675	445	670	1690	720	1005	1474	1165	1000	1030	810	....	830	531	1242	1295	267	1140	653	835	869
PARIS	257	1300	2335	518	890	540	170	1152	770	250	634	1390	523	480	295	459	1335	890	210	248	645	410	400	1538	425	830	....	1050	690	1080	950	431	845	770	295
RIGA	820	1310	1590	1440	855	520	900	740	685	805	453	1115	585	1210	780	600	300	1940	1035	1122	1670	1238	1010	520	800	531	1050	....	1151	985	276	1335	350	685	930
ROME	808	650	1900	530	440	780	730	700	500	675	948	840	630	1175	698	810	1440	1053	890	462	840	372	295	1462	430	1242	690	1155	....	545	1220	569	810	470	421
SOFIA	1073	335	1360	1072	231	810	945	194	500	945	1010	315	730	1525	860	954	1218	1848	1235	928	1385	895	715	1100	928	1295	1080	985	545	....	1170	1080	662	500	780
STOCKHOLM	695	1495	1862	1410	1005	503	793	1080	722	722	330	1340	598	1010	730	502	435	1848	885	1080	1598	1225	1020	770	811	267	950	276	1220	1170	....	1281	500	770	908
TOULOUSE	625	1215	2425	156	930	815	515	1210	883	875	962	1400	762	761	560	780	1635	640	550	228	344	196	400	1770	570	1140	431	1335	569	1080	1281	....	1062	725	425
WARSAW	673	990	1555	1150	510	320	720	580	342	602	415	852	325	1130	550	462	640	1700	890	832	1410	950	705	710	500	653	845	350	810	662	500	1062	....	345	640
VIENNA	580	795	1700	830	300	322	568	520	128	460	538	790	235	1040	370	460	975	1415	762	520	1110	620	385	1028	222	835	770	685	470	500	770	725	345	....	365
ZURICH	375	1000	2050	513	590	410	312	855	498	259	595	1090	342	768	193	432	1225	1058	480	206	765	318	137	1350	158	869	295	930	421	780	908	425	640	365	....